THE ELGAR COMPANION TO PUBLIC CHOICE, SECOND EDITION

The Elgar Companion to Public Choice, Second Edition

Edited by

Michael Reksulak

Georgia Southern University, USA

Laura Razzolini

Virginia Commonwealth University, USA

William F. Shughart II

J. Fish Smith Professor in Public Choice, Utah State University, USA

Edward Elgar
Cheltenham, UK • Northampton, MA, USA

© Michael Reksulak, Laura Razzolini and William F. Shughart II 2013

All rights reserved. No part of this publication may be reproduced, stored in a retrieval system or transmitted in any form or by any means, electronic, mechanical or photocopying, recording, or otherwise without the prior permission of the publisher.

Published by
Edward Elgar Publishing Limited
The Lypiatts
15 Lansdown Road
Cheltenham
Glos GL50 2JA
UK

Edward Elgar Publishing, Inc.
William Pratt House
9 Dewey Court
Northampton
Massachusetts 01060
USA

A catalogue record for this book
is available from the British Library

Library of Congress Control Number: 2012938056

This book is available electronically in the ElgarOnline.com
Economics Subject Collection, E-ISBN 978 1 84980 603 9

ISBN 978 1 84980 285 7 (cased)

Typeset by Servis Filmsetting Ltd, Stockport, Cheshire
Printed and bound by MPG Books Group, UK

Contents

List of figures	ix
List of tables	x
List of contributors	xi
Preface to the second edition	xv
Preface to the first edition	xvii

PART I   THE CHOICE IN PUBLIC CHOICE

1	Individual choice and collective choice: an overview *Michael Reksulak, Laura Razzolini and William F. Shughart II*	3
2	Public choice: the origins and development of a research program *Charles K. Rowley*	12
3	Political science and public choice *Michael C. Munger*	39

PART II   THE FRAMEWORK OF GOVERNMENT

4	The origins of the state *Dennis C. Mueller*	57
5	Constitutional political economy *Alan Hamlin*	72
6	Autocrats and democrats *Armando Razo*	83

PART III   SYSTEMS OF COLLECTIVE DECISION-MAKING

7	Expressive voting *Geoffrey Brennan and Michael Brooks*	111
8	Direct democracy *John G. Matsusaka*	127
9	Legislatures *Nicole V. Crain and W. Mark Crain*	143
10	Parliaments *Fabio Padovano*	153
11	Federal systems *Randall G. Holcombe*	179
12	Tribal systems *Mwangi S. Kimenyi and Olumide Taiwo*	195

PART IV PUBLIC CHOICE ANALYSES OF THE TOOLS OF GOVERNMENT

13	The politics of elections and congressional oversight *Russell S. Sobel and Adam Pellillo*	217
14	Judges: why do they matter? *Robert K. Fleck and F. Andrew Hanssen*	233
15	Monetary policy *Rob Roy McGregor*	249
16	Fiscal policy *J. Stephen Ferris*	260
17	Regulatory policy *Amihai Glazer*	284
18	The public choice perspective on antitrust law *Fred S. McChesney and Katherine M. Larkin-Wong*	291

PART V PUBLIC CHOICE PERSPECTIVES ON THE RELATIONS BETWEEN GOVERNMENT AND THE GOVERNED

19	Rent seeking *Arye L. Hillman*	307
20	Campaign finance *Thomas Stratmann*	331
21	Public choice and the law *Paul H. Rubin and Joanna M. Shepherd*	345
22	Public choice and the modern welfare state *Roger D. Congleton, with Alberto Batinti, Feler Bose, Youngshin Kim and Rinaldo Pietrantonio*	362
23	Public choice and public education *Lawrence W. Kenny*	382
24	Public choice and religion *Robert B. Ekelund Jr and Robert D. Tollison*	400
25	Experimental public choice *Laura Razzolini*	415
26	Evolutionary public choice *Uwe Cantner and Michael Wohlgemuth*	427

PART VI PUBLIC CHOICE PERSPECTIVES ON THE RELATIONS BETWEEN INTERNATIONAL ACTORS

27	International organizations *Roland Vaubel*	451
28	The political economy of war and peace *Christopher J. Coyne and Adam Pellillo*	469

29	Collective action and (counter)terrorism *Daniel G. Arce M.*	494
References		507
Index		583

Figures

6.1	Derived typology of autocratic regimes	91
8.1	States with initiatives in 2010 (adoption year in parentheses)	133
8.2	Number of state-level initiatives	134
10.1	Biplot of parliamentary procedures to approve the financial bill, 12 EU countries (average for the 1980s, 1990s and 2000s)	171
10.2	Timing of the approval of laws	173
10.3	Fit between the empirical model and actual data	174
13.1	Number of disasters declared by President by year (re-election years shown as bars with diagonal lines)	228
16.1	Alternative cycles in the log of Canadian real GNP, 1870–2008	278
16.2	Alternative measures of fiscal intervention as a fraction of GDP: Canada, 1948–2008	280
22.1	Social insurance as a fraction of GDP, 1960–2000	363
22.2	Ratio of public to total health expenditure vs. life expectancy at 65	369
22.3	Health expenditure as share of GDP, average per subgroup of countries (in percent)	370
22.4	Distribution of citizen ideal safety net levels	377
27.1	Monitoring and influencing international organizations	452
27.2	Regulatory collusion and raising rivals' costs	455
29.1	Transnational counterterror collective action as PD^2	496
29.2	Colonel Blotto game	501

Tables

2.1	Plurality voting versus Condorcet voting	12
2.2	Condorcet paradox	13
4.1	The battle of the sexes	60
9.1	Legislative outcomes in the US House and Senate: 2007–08 (percentage)	145
9.2	Legislative outcomes in the New York Assembly and Senate: 2005–06 (percentage)	146
10.1	Main institutional characteristics of national parliaments in 2009	157
10.2	Estimates of equation 10.1	167
13.1	Congressional committee breakdown	218
23.1	Effect of state-wide or county-wide restrictions on the number of school districts in a state	385
23.2	Metropolitan population and number of school districts	386
23.3	Predicted percentage of 'Yes' votes on California's Proposition 38 in 'No Choice' and 'High Choice' metro areas (percentage)	391
27.1	Preferred levels of decision-making for the three most important issues in 10 EU member states (percentages based on responses)	453
27.2	EU-related opinions of the general public, 50 top Commission officials and 203 members of the European Parliament in nine EU member states (percentage)	454
27.3	EU-related opinions of the general public and top decision-makers among elected politicians, national civil servants and journalists (percentage)	454
27.4	A comparison of national referendums and parliamentary votes on issues of EU policy (percentage)	458
27.5	Relative net salaries at the European Commission and in the central governments of selected member states	463

Contributors

Daniel G. Arce M., Professor of Economics in the School of Economic, Political and Policy Sciences, University of Texas at Dallas, Richardson, Texas, USA.

Alberto Batinti, Postdoctoral Madison Fellow in Political Economy, Department of Economics, College of Business and Economics, West Virginia University, Morgantown, West Virginia, USA.

Feler Bose, Assistant Professor, Department of Economics, Alma College, Alma, MI, USA.

Geoffrey Brennan, Professor, School of Philosophy, Australian National University, Canberra, Australia; Department of Political Science, Duke University, Durham, North Carolina, USA; and Department of Philosophy, University of North Carolina at Chapel Hill, North Carolina, USA.

Michael Brooks, Associate Professor, School of Economics and Finance, University of Tasmania, Hobart, Australia.

Uwe Cantner, Professor of Economics, Chair for Microeconomics, Friedrich-Schiller-University Jena, Thüringen, Germany, and Professor of Economics, Department of Marketing and Management, I2M Group, University of Southern Denmark, Odense, Denmark.

Roger D. Congleton, BB&T Professor of Economics, Department of Economics, College of Business and Economics, West Virginia University, Morgantown, West Virginia, USA.

Christopher J. Coyne, F.A. Harper Professor of Economics at the Mercatus Center, Department of Economics, George Mason University, Fairfax, Virginia, USA.

Nicole V. Crain, Visiting Professor, Department of Economics, Lafayette College Easton, Pennsylvania, USA.

W. Mark Crain, William E. Simon Professor of Political Economy and Chair of Policy Studies, Lafayette College Easton, Pennsylvania, USA.

Robert B. Ekelund Jr, Eminent Scholar Emeritus, Auburn University, Auburn, Alabama, USA.

J. Stephen Ferris, Professor of Economics and Co-Director of the Centre for Monetary and Financial Economics, Carleton University, Ottawa, Canada.

Robert K. Fleck, Professor of Economics, John E. Walker Department of Economics, College of Business and Behavioral Science, Clemson University, Clemson, South Carolina, USA.

Amihai Glazer, Professor of Economics, Department of Economics, University of California, Irvine, California, USA.

Contributors

Alan Hamlin, Professor of Political Theory, School of Social Sciences, The University of Manchester, Manchester, UK.

F. Andrew Hanssen, Associate Professor of Economics, John E. Walker Department of Economics, College of Business and Behavioral Science, Clemson University, Clemson, South Carolina, USA.

Arye L. Hillman, William Gittes Chair, Professor of Economics, Department of Economics, Bar-Ilan University, Ramat Gan, Israel.

Randall G. Holcombe, DeVoe Moore Professor of Economics, Department of Economics, Florida State University, Florida, USA.

Lawrence W. Kenny, Professor of Economics, Department of Economics, University of Florida, Gainesville, Florida, USA.

Youngshin Kim, Korea Economic Research Institute, Seoul, South Korea.

Mwangi S. Kimenyi, Director, Africa Growth Initiative and Senior Fellow, Global Economy and Development, Brookings Institution, Washington, District of Columbia, USA.

Katherine M. Larkin-Wong, Northwestern University School of Law, Chicago, Illinois, USA.

John G. Matsusaka, Charles F. Sexton Chair in American Enterprise, Marshall School of Business, Gould School of Law, and Department of Political Science, University of Southern California, Los Angeles, California, USA.

Fred S. McChesney, de la Cruz-Mentschikoff Chair in Law and Economics, Professor of Law, University of Miami, Coral Gables, Florida, USA.

Rob Roy McGregor, Professor of Economics, Department of Economics, Belk College of Business, University of North Carolina at Charlotte, Charlotte, North Carolina, USA.

Dennis C. Mueller, Professor Emeritus, University of Vienna, Vienna, Austria.

Michael C. Munger, Professor of Political Science and Director, Joint UNC-Duke Philosophy, Politics, and Economics Program, Duke University, Durham, North Carolina, USA.

Fabio Padovano, Director, Condorcet Center for Political Economy, University of Rennes 1, Rennes, France and Associate Professor of Public Finance, University Rome Tre, Rome, Italy.

Adam Pellillo, Assistant Professor, International School of Economics, Tbilisi State University, Tbilisi, Georgia.

Rinaldo Pietrantonio, Visiting Assistant Professor, Department of Economics, College of Business and Economics, West Virginia University, Morgantown, West Virginia, USA.

Armando Razo, Associate Professor, Department of Political Science, Indiana University, Bloomington, Indiana, USA.

Laura Razzolini, Professor of Economics, Virginia Commonwealth University, Richmond, Virginia, USA.

Michael Reksulak, Associate Professor of Economics, College of Business Administration, Georgia Southern University, Statesboro, Georgia, USA.

Charles K. Rowley, General Director, The Locke Institute, Fairfax, Virginia, USA and Duncan Black Professor Emeritus of Economics, George Mason University, Fairfax, Virginia, USA.

Paul H. Rubin, Samuel Candler Dobbs Professor of Economics, Department of Economics, College of Arts and Sciences, Emory University, Atlanta, Georgia, USA.

Joanna M. Shepherd, Associate Professor of Law, Emory University School of Law, Atlanta, Georgia, USA.

William F. Shughart II, J. Fish Smith Professor in Public Choice, Jon M. Huntsman School of Business, Utah State University, Logan, Utah, USA.

Russell S. Sobel, Visiting Scholar, School of Business, Administration, The Citadel, Charleston, South Carolina, USA.

Thomas Stratmann, University Professor of Economics and Law at George Mason University, Department of Economics and The Center for the Study of Public Choice, Fairfax, Virginia, USA.

Olumide Taiwo, Africa Research Fellow, Global Economy and Development and Africa Growth Initiative, Brookings Institution, Washington, District of Columbia, USA.

Robert D. Tollison, J. Wilson Newman Professor, John E. Walker Department of Economics, Clemson University, Clemson, South Carolina, USA.

Roland Vaubel, Professor of Economics, Chair for Political Economy, Mannheim University, Baden-Württemberg, Germany.

Michael Wohlgemuth, Managing Researcher, Walter Eucken Institut, Freiburg im Breisgau, Baden-Württemberg, Germany.

Preface to the second edition

> I usually have a three-word description [of public choice] – it is 'politics without romance'. Politics is a romantic search for the good and the true and the beautiful. 'Public choice' came along and said, 'Why don't we model people more or less like everyday persons? Politicians and bureaucrats are no different from the rest of us. They will maximize their incentives just like everybody else.' By taking that very simple starting point, you get a completely different view of politics and its analysis.
>
> (James M. Buchanan on how to define 'public choice')[1]

When we were approached to commission contributions for a new edition of *The Elgar Companion to Public Choice* some two years ago, we envisioned it not to be simply a follow-up or extension to the original volume. In essence, we wanted it to serve as a complement, which would stand on its own and highlight additional facets of this field that lies at the intersection of the economic and political sciences.

Although the approach we took to topic selection and the solicitation of potential contributors was broad, the chapters in this volume continue to emphasize the application of public choice theory to the study of collective decision-making on Election Day, in committees, in legislatures and in many other non-market settings, where choices are made in the absence of explicit price and profit signals and where the agreement of a qualified majority is required before action can be taken. The readers of this new *Companion* will encounter a wealth of evidence concerning the ability of public choice models to explain and predict the behavior of *Homo economicus* in all walks of life and in many marketplaces, be they for public goods and services, votes, religions, revolutions or judicial rulings, to name just a few. To that end, we have included chapters on topics not covered in the first edition, such as antitrust law enforcement, tribal systems of governance, instrumental versus expressive motives for voting, the political economy of war and peace, and transnational terrorism. We have also broadened our coverage geographically by adding relatively more contributions from scholars based in Europe.

The editors of the first edition of the *Companion* have been heartened by the positive response it received when it was published more than a decade ago; we are hopeful that this second edition, too, will establish itself as a valuable reference tool and compendium of new ideas for students and scholars of public choice alike. In working with the authors of the various chapters included in this volume, we have been impressed, once more, by the vibrant nature and the continuing applicability and viability of the by now well-established public choice research program.

We are grateful to the outstanding and helpful support we received from the staff at Edward Elgar. As with the first edition, the publisher provided us with the necessary support to bring this undertaking to fruition while giving us a completely free hand regarding the content and direction of the various parts of the project. Thankfully, Edward Elgar was very understanding when unforeseen circumstances caused a delay or two regarding the delivery of certain chapters. We would also like to thank Joshua Blotter for his eagle-eyed error-checking of the reference section.

We are particularly indebted to the outstanding scholars who agreed to contribute to the first and the second editions of the *Companion*, most especially Randall Holcombe, who once again graciously came to the rescue when the promise made by another contributor fell through at the last minute. Given their prominence in the profession and the many time-intensive projects they are working on, we are aware of the high opportunity cost of their time. We, therefore, are even more appreciative of their commitment to this project.

Michael Reksulak
Laura Razzolini
William F. Shughart II

NOTE

1. 'Interview with James Buchanan, 1986 Nobel Prize Winner in Economics', available at: http://www.aims.ca/en/home/library/details.aspx/359 (accessed 20 January 2012).

Preface to the first edition

> A man who writes a book, thinks himself wiser or wittier than the rest of mankind; he supposes that he can instruct or amuse them, and the publick to whom he appeals, must, after all, be the judges of his pretensions.
>
> (Samuel Johnson)

This volume, which has been more than two years in the making and represents the collaborative effort of more than thirty scholars, is intended to encapsulate the field of public choice as it stands at the close of the twentieth century. While we are certainly not the first to attempt to do so, owing to the explosive growth of the literature over the past several decades, it has become nearly impossible to survey the theory and evidence of public choice comprehensively. Multiple perspectives by multiple authorities help to fill in the unavoidable gaps and to add the nuance necessary for a deeper understanding of what has been accomplished thus far and what questions remain unanswered.

This does not mean that we have not tried to be exhaustive. Far from it. Contributions to the *Companion* were solicited with an eye toward providing its readers with a thoroughgoing rehearsal of public choice principles. Undoubtedly, however, some topics have been overlooked and some of the relevant literature left uncited. For that we apologize. But we think that those who spend time with this volume will come away with a fuller appreciation of the power of the public choice model to illuminate the behavior of *Homo politicus*. It is our hope that students of public choice and scholars actively contributing to the field will find the *Companion* to be a valuable reference tool and will learn as much from reading as we did from writing and editing.

Many debts were accumulated in preparing this volume for publication. We are grateful to Edward Elgar for his confidence in our abilities to carry this project through to its conclusion, for the free hand given to our decisions about topical coverage and authorship, and for his patient willingness to await delivery of a manuscript acceptable to us. Once that point was at last reached, his staff supervised the production process with a high level of professional competency.

While each of the contributors to the volume deserves our thanks as well – they did most of the work, after all – a number of them merit special recognition. Lisa Anderson and Randall Holcombe came to the rescue when, at nearly the last minute, prior commitments with other contributors fell through. Mark Crain and Robert Tollison not only wrote their own chapters, but provided extremely useful comments and suggestions on several others as well.

Melissa Yeoh did yeoman's work tracking down obscure bibliographic details and corroborating classical allusions; we here thank her for her able research assistance. If not for Michael Reksulak's proofreading skills, there would have been many more errors in the final product. A timely and much appreciated summer grant from the Robert M. Hearin Support Foundation afforded the senior editor the opportunity to devote his full attention to finishing the project. While we are both grateful for all the help we received along the way, the two of us accept full responsibility for any remaining defects. We lay down our red pens, turn off our computers, and submit to the judgment of the market.

William F. Shughart II
Laura Razzolini

To Hsiao-Ting (Adeline), Claire ChinYan and Vivian TianAi – MR
To the memory of my father (1929–1991) and to my mother – LR
To Hilary, Willie and Frank – WFS

PART I

THE CHOICE IN PUBLIC CHOICE

1 Individual choice and collective choice: an overview
Michael Reksulak, Laura Razzolini and William F. Shughart II

At a time of this writing, a second World Congress of the Public Choice Societies is in the offing. The decision of the executive boards of the North American, European and Japanese societies to convene another joint meeting of their memberships in 2012 is one indicator of the flourishing of the public choice research program. An even more encouraging sign is the sheer volume of literature that, at the dawn of the 21st century, confronts anyone who dares to attempt to survey the field within the covers of a single scholarly book.

Fifty years after the publication of *The Calculus of Consent: Logical Foundations of Constitutional Democracy* (Buchanan and Tullock 1962), rational choice approaches to the analysis of human behavior in non-market settings where choices are made collectively have gained widespread acceptance in economics, political science and, to lesser extents, in sociology and psychology. Several generations of researchers have by now been trained to begin the study of how people choose, with the assumption that every individual pursues his or her own self-interests, broadly defined, within given institutional constraints, that the same motives guide human action in both private and public domains. It follows that public choices differ from private choices, not because people are motivated differently in the two settings but because the constraints on self-interested behavior are different. A person who casts a ballot for candidate A rather than B on Election Day is the same person who decides to buy apples instead of oranges at the grocery store.

One vote will not determine an election's outcome unless the votes of all others who turn out are split evenly between the two candidates. Given the (vanishingly) small chance of her vote being decisive, the voter has little or no incentive to become informed about the candidates and their policy positions – to choose 'wisely', to take account of the impact of her vote on the welfare of others, or even to vote at all. Even if her preferred candidate wins, she must share the benefits of that victory, in whatever form they may materialize, with everyone else on the winning side, while the costs of voting (registering, traveling to the polls, waiting in line and so on) fall squarely on her own shoulders. On the other hand, given her income and relative prices, choosing between apples and oranges in the grocery store confronts the decision-maker with immediate costs that only she will bear and with benefits that only she will capture. Hence, she will be a careful shopper, allocating her purchases of apples and oranges in a way that leaves her as well off as possible.

1 INDIVIDUAL CHOICE AND COLLECTIVE CHOICE

If one understands public choice in the words of James Buchanan as 'politics without romance', then one realizes that at the heart of this empirically based science is the question of how the incentives faced by the individual translate into collective action. The public choice model is grounded in 'methodological individualism', the idea that the individual person is the proper unit of analysis. Only individuals make choices; 'society', the 'government', or even small groups of people do not. In that sense, it is not enough merely to assume that an individual act is motivated by the goal of utility maximization in all walks of life, including the supermarket, on the football field or in the Oval Office. There has to be, in addition, a framework that permits one to analyze the different choices that result from this maximization process as determined by the distinct environmental or institutional constraints faced by the individual in those different settings.

Focusing on constraints rather than behavioral motivations does not mean modifying one's theory as circumstances require. That would be unscientific. It demands the hard work required to identify the specific institutional features of all kinds of markets, both private and public – for ordinary goods and services, for votes, for crime and punishment, for religion, for economic and social regulation and so on – that lead to different outcomes as self-interested, utility-maximizing individuals interact with one another. Only in that systematic manner can a naive 'public interest' theory be shown to be mistaken.

From the beginning, public choice scholars have wanted to go beyond the theory of individual decisions and their impact on collective choices, although theory always has been central to the development of the field. But in addition, emphasis has been placed on using the formal models to confront theory with empirical evidence. This approach has stood the test of time – hypotheses derived from models assuming that politicians, judges, bureaucrats and other actors pursue their private interests (for example, election or re-election to office) have been shown repeatedly to outperform models based on vague notions of 'justice', 'fairness' or 'society's welfare'.

If more proof were needed, then the subsequent 28 chapters provide exactly that. Spanning the universe of economics, political science and law, the contributors to this *Companion* make the case.

2 WHAT LIES AHEAD

2.1 Part I

The chapters of this second edition of *The Elgar Companion to Public Choice* are organized into six main parts. The first part describes the origins and subsequent growth of the field. Our introduction is followed by a tour de force overview of the founding works of public choice, contributed by Charles Rowley. It is highly informative to discover there the launching of a research program as memorialized in the words of contemporaneous book reviewers and commentators who seem, at times, uncertain how to treat this interdisciplinary insurgency. Duncan Black, Kenneth Arrow, Anthony Downs, William Riker, James Buchanan and Gordon Tullock, Mancur Olson, and William Niskanen not only come to life in that chapter, but Rowley also manages vividly to document the continuing influence these thinkers (the 'founding fathers') and their works have had on public choice. Most interestingly, he presents to us what some of them saw in each other's work at the time they were developing their ideas. What is unquestionable in Rowley's mind is the continuing impact of their path-breaking discoveries. As he concludes:

> The insights provided by the early public choice research program rank among the most important of all advances in economic science during the second half of the twentieth century, when measured in terms of their contribution to the wealth of nations and to the expansion of individual liberty.

The third chapter, by Michael Munger, supplies the reader with his perceptive charting of the overlaps and the conflicts between political science and public choice. Interposing *Homo economicus* and *Homo politicus*, his chapter discusses the various objections to the public choice assumptions of citizens as 'rational' and of the political world as being inhabited by self-interested individuals. He also sheds light on five significant research problems and compares and contrasts how they are approached by political scientists and public choice scholars (and, often, researchers who could wear both mantels) in ways that have cross-fertilized the two areas of study.

2.2 Part II

After having thus discussed the foundations of public choice, the *Companion* turns to an in-depth look at the fundamental frameworks of government. In this second part, the contributors emphasize theories of statehood, the emergence of constitutions and the various paths that may lead to democracy versus autocracy.

One of the most influential public choice scholars of our time, Dennis Mueller, reviews the origins of the state in Chapter 4. Not only does he assess numerous theoretical contributions to the field of public choice which add to our understanding of how states are formed, but Mueller also takes us back to the very beginnings of statehood in human history and presents an intriguing glimpse at the way in which theory can explain why the earliest saplings of states eventually took root. In doing so, he devotes attention to a lively modern debate about how democracy may have risen from the ashes of autocratic regimes. He juxtaposes two theories at the forefront of this important argument. On the one hand, a contribution by Acemoglu and Robinson (2006) predicts that switches towards democracy are more frequent in times of economic crisis. A powerful new hypothesis by Roger Congleton (2011), one of the contributors to this volume, amasses a large body of evidence to argue for a theory of the more gradual establishment of democracies.

The question of how the basic legal framework of any government is arrived at forms the basis of Alan Hamlin's chapter on constitutional political economy (CPE). While many public choice studies take the rules of the game as given and strive to explain the operation of 'in-period politics' following the creation of those overarching rules, CPE studies the question that goes to the very heart of how to organize the institutions of collective choice and what rules to adopt in the first place. Moreover, even if there is agreement regarding what activities of a polity should be 'regulated' in the broadest sense, questions emerge concerning the process by which such constraints should be agreed to in the formative stages of statehood. This chapter not only discusses the literature on the Rawlsian 'veil of ignorance' but also the core characteristics of CPE. It also distinguishes between the total and the marginal approach to the theory of political institutions. Combining this insight with a summary of instrumental versus expressive motives for voting, in Chapter 5 Hamlin provides an informative segue into the discussion of 'expressive voting' two chapters hence, by Geoffrey Brennan and Michael Brooks.

In the meantime, Armando Razo takes the reader on an exhaustive but not exhausting tour of the literature on autocracies and democracies. He places special emphasis on the emerging literature addressing the political economy of dictatorships. Perhaps most interestingly, Razo sheds light on the significant impact that the very different informational constraints facing democracies and autocracies determine how political authority can actually be exercised in the two distinct governmental environments.

2.3 Part III

The third part of the *Companion* introduces and discusses the various systems of collective decision-making invented by humans in the attempt to somehow close the wide gap between individual action and collective action.

There, we first turn to theories of voting behavior. As mentioned above, Geoffrey Brennan and Michael Brooks lay out the differences between the Downsian (1957) theory of instrumental voting, which fails to explain why hundreds of millions of people go to the polls in national elections (voting is irrational in that context, as adumbrated at the beginning of this introduction), and the more recent theory associated closely with the chapter's first-named author, that voting is 'expressive'. Brennan and Brooks also recognize the important role that 'identity' plays in expressive voting theories, and lay out reasons why they think it has been construed too narrowly in applying that theory. The authors make clear their view that voters and abstainers alike can be seen as acting rationally and that the challenge for researchers following their lead is to identify the proper utility functions that would be consistent with this conjecture.

There is clear connection between voting behavior and individual choices under the heading of 'direct democracy', exemplified in New England town meetings, by voter initiatives and referendums, and similar ballot propositions. A major contributor to that literature, John Matsusaka, provides in Chapter 8 a comprehensive overview of how public choice researchers have tackled the issues of structured forms of direct democracy. First, the theoretical foundations are explored in detail, with a focus on principal–agent problems, information asymmetries and bundling issues. Matsusaka supplies a wealth of empirical evidence to allow the reader to judge the veracity of the theoretical claims on this issue. Voter competencies, the roles of money, education, and pre-election information are only a few of the many issues addressed in his chapter.

When voters have cast their ballots in a representative democracy, political representation can take many forms. In Chapter 9 Nicole Crain and Mark Crain investigate how legislatures translate the 'voters' will' into political action. Particular emphasis is placed on the legislative committee system as fertile ground not only for incentive-driven political trades ('logrolling') but also for supplying data that are amenable to scientific analysis. Consequently, the relevant literature, especially the public choice literature, on committee-specific topics is voluminous and the authors summarize the main insights gleaned from that research. In the process, the chapter highlights the impact of institutional design on the incentives faced by legislators, including the use of committee assignments by party leaders to screen and reward rank-and-file members for supporting the leadership's policy agenda.

Picking up the theme and adopting an international comparative approach, Fabio Padovano reports on parliaments and parliamentary systems across the globe. After being introduced to the various ways in which parliaments can structure their work, readers are treated to an important application of public choice theory. Examining the budgetary approval process, Padovano gives an in-depth account of research into how different institutional environments impact this, most important, parliamentary output. Stylized facts as well as common pitfalls in this type of analysis are highlighted, thereby supplying scholars with fertile areas for future research into the operations of parliamentary bodies.

The next step, then, is to analyze the nature of federal systems of decision-making. Randall Holcombe starts off with Tiebout's (1956) 'vote with their feet' metaphor and introduces the origins of federal systems. His first emphasis is on the relationship among governments in such settings. The interplay and delegation of authority among local, regional and federal levels and how this influences the internalization of externalities and spending patterns represent one part of the analysis in this chapter. Another sheds light on questions of efficiency and whether or not federalism is a potent tool for checking the growth of government. Holcombe also asks whether consent or coercion is the hallmark of federal systems. This is a fundamental issue in the 21st century, given the recent struggles of the evolving model of federalism in the European Union.

An intriguing perspective on the topic of how to organize government is provided by Mwangi Kimenyi and Olumide Taiwo, in Chapter 12, who present a novel and one of the first modern analyses of tribal systems of collective decision-making. While admittedly historical in nature and focusing on sub-Saharan Africa, this review of how tribal cultures solved collective action problems provides valuable insights into current discussions regarding transitions toward modern nation-states. The chapter reviews the literature on which institutions make it more likely for such transitions to succeed and what, if any, impact the prior tribal organization has on 'post-tribal' societal structures. The chapter's main contribution is to show that the institutions for governing tribes were far from inefficient, as many commentators have concluded, but can instead be explained as innovative adaptations to the circumstances of time and place. Kimenyi and Taiwo thus point public choice scholars to new, fertile fields in which their theories and methods can be applied and to which they can contribute to development-friendly public policies that take account of indigenous – and vibrant – political institutions.

2.4 Part IV

As important as the question of the manner in which collective decisions are taken is the inquiry into how such decisions ultimately are implemented. The six chapters in Part IV survey, as comprehensively as possible, the public-choice perspective on institutions of government.

In light of the give-and-take, and checks-and-balances nature of the executive and legislative branches of government, public choice theory has much to say about congressional oversight of governmental action. Russell Sobel and Adam Pellillo analyze the impact of congressional influence on decision-makers in public sector agencies. Furthermore, their chapter sheds light on our understanding of how the timing of elections also may shape decisions by public officials who are appointed to office.

The so-called third branch of government is the judiciary. As the public has become more and more aware of how judicial elections are no different from political elections, the 'public interest' theory of judicial decision-making has fallen into disrepute. Public choice has been and is at the forefront in explaining judicial decision-making in the context of the incentives and institutional constraints faced by individual judges. Robert Fleck and Andrew Hanssen provide an in-depth look at how 'judicial independence' works in practice and what the implications of the institutional environment judges face are for judicial decision making. Not surprisingly, judges seem to be influenced by their own individual self-interests, such as the prospect of being promoted to a higher court. The results of Fleck and Hanssen's summary of the evidence situates the third branch squarely within the public choice model rather than – as often is rather romantically assumed – 'above' the executive and legislative branches of government.

Another aspect of policy that is often mistakenly, it turns out, assumed to be far removed from the 'rough and tumble' of everyday politics is monetary policy. Chapter 15 convincingly presents evidence of electoral and partisan influences on decisions in that policy arena. Tying the discussion to previous chapters, Rob Roy McGregor takes a look at central banks as bureaucracies and how the committee nature of central bank governance impacts, indeed compromises, its decision-making processes. The recent upheavals in financial markets and the drastic measures taken by many central banks, often in unison, will provide numerous research opportunities for public choice scholars, when more information is released on how those decisions were taken.

Stephen Ferris's chapter complements McGregor's discussion of monetary policy. Ferris's analysis of fiscal policy-making incorporates public choice reasoning into a macroeconomic framework of short-run tax and spending decisions; it also considers the factors that underpin the long-run growth of government. Such an approach allows for the discussion of how political processes and institutional settings lead to feedback effects on the larger economy. It also permits traders to consider how fiscal policy actions may diverge from the predictions implied by commonly utilized models of the macroeconomy.

One of the most effective tools of the executive branch of government, regulatory policy, is the subject of Chapter 17. Special-interest group explanations of regulatory activity have been a staple of public choice scholarship and Amihai Glazer outlines the main contributions of the public choice literature to the topic. The interest groups in question encompass business owners, workers, and other beneficiaries of regulatory intervention as well as the bureaucrats who administer them. One of the perplexing questions involved in the analysis of regulatory activities is the endogeneity problem. Also, no general model has yet been proposed to explain deregulation in various settings. Glazer provides a guide to how public choice scholars have been and are approaching such topics.

A special case in terms of how the executive and the judiciary regulate industries is the formulation and application of the antitrust law, the ostensible purpose of which is to protect consumers from the creation and exercise of monopoly power. The public agencies at the state and federal levels exercise considerable discretion in carrying out their law enforcement mandates. Fred McChesney, with a unique background in law and economics, in collaboration with Katherine Larkin-Wong, provides a unified public choice perspective on how this 'poor stepson in the house of public choice' has become an important part of how public choice researchers study government in action. Laying out the origins of antitrust, the authors then ask the provocative question as to whether antitrust law enforcement has improved consumer welfare. The answer, it seems, is no, which leaves McChesney and Larkin-Wong the task of explaining the persistence of antitrust activities. This is a rich field for exactly the kind of clear-eyed analysis of public officials and public institutions for which public choice has become known.

2.5 Part V

When governmental infrastructure is set up and the tools of government are defined, a natural question is how the governed and government interact. This part of the *Companion* reviews the public choice literature on rent-seeking, campaign finance, welfare programs, public education and religion. Moreover, a growing number of public choice researchers studying such issues have taken advantage of the methods of experimental economics; the results of these efforts are presented here as well.

There is hardly any topic more prominent in the public choice literature than rent-seeking, going back all the way to Gordon Tullock's seminal 1967 paper. Arye Hillman manages to condense the voluminous contributions to that literature into a comprehensible chapter. Hillman summarizes the many rent-seeking models as well as the theories and empirical methods later used to study them. Moreover, the chapter contributes to our understanding of the conditions under which rent-seeking is likely to be prevalent and most socially costly. Readers will likely be interested in the various applications of the model that Hillman identifies, in settings such as inside the government, inside academia and inside firms, to mention some.

The next chapter, by Thomas Stratmann on campaign finance, highlights how instrumental favor seeking may be to the political system at large. Money plays an increasingly important (inflation-adjusted) role in the financing of political campaigns. Recent Supreme Court rulings make it likely that this trend will only become more pronounced. Consequently, analyzing the connections between campaign contributions and electoral outcomes, legislation and the survival of firms and industries, will be ever more prominent in the economic analysis of political markets.

Facing constraints imposed on the legal profession by various levels of government and by the American tradition of tort law, seeking rents is an important part of what lawyers do and what judges referee. Paul Rubin and Joanna Shepherd lay out the ways in which the law of torts conforms with public choice theory and, in doing so, they extend the application of public choice reasoning to judicial decision-making outlined earlier by Fleck and Hanssen.

In the following two chapters, Roger Congleton and Lawrence Kenny discuss the demand for public goods on the part of the governed. Chapter 22 addresses the political economy of various social welfare programs and how their creation and growth have been explained by public choice research. The analytical similarities to the provision of public education, summarized in Chapter 23, are striking, especially when one takes into account the controversial debate on how these goods can optimally be provided by private firms rather than by governmental organizations. The extent to which market forces should be allowed to operate unencumbered is a seemingly never-ending fascination of the actors in the political marketplace for ideas.

A different area for transactions is the subject of the chapter by Robert Ekelund and Robert Tollison, who present an analysis of religion from a public choice perspective. Tracing the roots of that issue space all the way back to Adam Smith (1776 [2005]), the authors demonstrate convincingly that this good ('salvation') is amenable to a public choice approach that takes account of special-interest groups, rent-seeking and the sale and pricing of religious goods, such as the forgiveness of sin and entry into Heaven. In order to facilitate price discrimination among believers, the Medieval Catholic Church took advantage of vertical integration, making it the first multinational corporation, to extract rents from the faithful, but ultimately invited entry by Protestant denominations that cut out the 'middleman' priesthood standing between believers and an eternal afterlife.

The remaining chapters in this section concentrate on various methods that are employed by public choice researchers to test their theories. Laura Razzolini surveys how laboratory experiments have informed public choice theory. Uwe Cantner and Michael Wohlgemuth suggest that there may be – surprisingly, perhaps – some areas in which public choice analysis could benefit from the insights developed in the newer field of evolutionary economics.

2.6 Part VI

The final part of the *Companion* encompasses three entries that take the next step and ask how relations between the governed and governing organizations as well as between states and non-state actors can be extended to an international setting.

Roland Vaubel puts the spotlight on the class of 'international bureaucrats' in order to explain the functioning of international organizations. His chapter also highlights the difficulties involved in ensuring accountability when voters are far removed from the eventual decision-makers in a transnational setting, whether those are elected representatives, such as the members of the European Parliament, or appointed 'eurocrats'. Large transcontinental, transatlantic or global economic, monetary and judicial institutions are subjects of the analysis in this chapter.

Public choice has a lot to say about how individuals and groups may interact when no agreement can be reached. Christopher Coyne and Adam Pellillo highlight the logic of war and political violence, but also supply paths toward more peaceful solutions to cross-border conflicts. Violent solutions to economic and political grievances are quite likely in case of internal, regional or transnational terrorism, which Daniel Arce studies. Apart from a look at the motivations and incentives faced by those who engage in terrorism, public choice theory is utilized to inform our understanding of how the responses by nation-states to terrorist acts are shaped.

3 THE NEXT STEPS FOR PUBLIC CHOICE

After the first decade of the new millennium, there is no shortage of topics that are fertile fields for investigation by public choice scholars. With corporations having been assigned characteristics of 'persons' in the political process, with greater international integration, and given that non-state actors and organizations – in a sense 'super interest groups' – are appearing forcefully on the scene, public choice researchers are poised to keep enriching the discussion.

The question is whether individual choices will be more constrained or less so in impacting collective decision-making under these scenarios. One the one hand, accountability may be reduced on a wider scale. On the other hand, new technologies may permit us to overcome many of the impediments to non-governmental collective action that Olson (1965) identified. The cost of organizing, even the cost of achieving, consensus in large groups may soon become so small as to be negligible in the larger context of collective choice. In that case, much of what we assume to be stylized facts about how individual choices are translated into collective ones may have to be rethought and remodeled.

The methods, approaches and ideas represented in this second edition of the *Companion* are geared towards giving established scholars as well as new students of public choice an overview of what we know and what we do not now know. This volume, it is to be hoped, is a valuable resource for scholars, but also one to be evaluated critically as new developments in how societies are structured materialize in the future.

Great leaps have been made in the past 50 years in the field of public choice, interspersed with many small and sometimes arduous steps toward the next level of understanding. There is no doubt in our minds, that more leaps and bounds will follow.

2 Public choice: the origins and development of a research program
Charles K. Rowley[1]

1 INTRODUCTION

Public choice is a relatively new discipline located at the interface between economics and political science. Its modern founding was the achievement of Duncan Black (1948a, 1948b, 1948c) whose articles are widely viewed as the seminal contributions that launched scholarship in the application of economic analysis into the traditional domain of political science. Yet, its true founding goes back almost two centuries in time, to the late eighteenth-century contributions of two French *encyclopedistes*, the Compte de Borda and the Marquis de Condorcet. The two French noblemen shared a conviction that social sciences were amenable to mathematical rigor, and made significant contributions to the theory of voting. These contributions form the foundations on which much of modern public choice has been built.

In his pioneering work on elections, Condorcet sought to 'inquire by mere reasoning, what degree of confidence the judgment of assemblies deserves' (1785, p. iv). In modern jargon, he posed what is now known as the jury problem or the vote problem. The starting point, well-known to the *encyclopedistes*, is that majority voting is unambiguously the best voting rule only when two candidates are on stage. How might this rule be extended to three or more candidates? The naive but widely held answer is plurality voting, where each voter casts a vote for one candidate and the candidate with most votes is elected.

Condorcet raised doubts as to the general acceptability of the plurality vote rule. Suppose that 60 voters have opinions about three candidates A, B and C as shown in Table 2.1. In the illustration, candidate A wins by plurality. Yet, if A is opposed only by B he loses (25 to 35) and if A is opposed only by C he loses again (23 to 37). Thus the plurality rule does not convey accurately the opinion of the majority.

Using identical premises, in 1781 Borda had initiated the discussion of voting rules by questioning the effectiveness of the simple majority vote rule and by proposing the method of marks as a more appropriate rule. In this method, each candidate receives 2 points from a voter who places him first, 1 point from a voter who places him second and 0 points from a voter who places him third. Hence, by reference to Table 2.1, C is elected

Table 2.1 Plurality voting versus Condorcet voting

	23	19	16	2
Top	A	B	C	C
	C	C	B	A
Bottom	B	A	A	B

Table 2.2   Condorcet paradox

23	17	2	10	8
A	B	B	C	C
B	C	A	A	B
C	A	C	B	A

with a score of 78 points. Condorcet, however, in following up on the insight of Borda, sought a different solution.

Condorcet posited a simple binomial model of voter error. In every binary comparison, each voter has a probability $1/2 < p < 1$ of ordering the candidates correctly. Thus the relevant data are contained in the 'majority tournament' that results from taking all pairwise votes: B beats A 35 to 25; C beats A 37 to 23; C beats B 41 to 19. Condorcet (1785, p. 125) proposed that candidates should be ranked according to 'the most probable combination of opinions'. In modern terminology, this is a maximum likelihood criterion.

In the above example, the most probable combination is given by the ranking CBA, since this agrees with the greatest total number of votes. Condorcet's ranking criterion implies that an alternative obtaining a majority over every other alternative must be ranked first. Such an alternative, if one exists, is now known as a 'Condorcet winner'. However, as Condorcet established, some configurations of opinions may not produce such a winner because the majority tournament contains a cycle. Such an occurrence is now known as Condorcet's paradox and is illustrated in Table 2.2.

In this illustration, A beats B, 33 to 27; B beats C, 42 to 18; C beats A, 35 to 25. In such circumstances, pairwise voting results in intransitivity. According to Condorcet's maximum likelihood criterion, the cycle should be broken at its weakest point, namely A over B, which yields the ranking of B over C over A. Therefore, in this case, B would be declared the winner.

Condorcet's *Essai* contains other useful insights that now play an important role in public choice. Perhaps the most important is the issue of strategic manipulation, which is hinted at in several places, although it is never systematically explored (Moulin and Young 1987). For example, on page clxxix of the *Discours Preliminaire*, Condorcet criticizes Borda's method of marks as being vulnerable to a *cabale*. When confronted with this criticism, Borda was merely moved to comment: 'My scheme is only intended for honorable men' (Rowley 1987). It has since been established by modern game theory that any configuration of individual opinions that guarantees the existence of a Condorcet winner also defines a strategy proof voting rule. This remains an important argument in favor of Condorcet consistent rules designed to elect the Condorcet winner whenever it exists (Moulin 1983).

Because the publications by Condorcet and Borda were not widely circulated in the late eighteenth century, because they were somewhat densely written and because they were written in French, their ideas disappeared for some 150 years until they were rediscovered and proselytized by Duncan Black in 1958. Since then, the ideas have strongly influenced public choice theorists and have played a central role in many of the discipline's recent developments.

2 THE INSIGHTS OF DUNCAN BLACK

Ideas that are lost do not constitute any part of the litany of science. Duncan Black essentially rediscovered ideas that had been advanced earlier by the two eighteenth-century French noblemen only to be lost, then to be rediscovered late in the nineteenth century (1884) by Charles Dodgson (Lewis Carroll), then to be lost again. Since Black's discovery has not been lost, he must be viewed as the true founder of public choice (Rowley 1991). The work of Borda, Condorcet, and Dodgson is known today only because Black researched their writings and made them available to his own generation of scholars (Grofman 1987).

Duncan Black's vision as a young economist was that of developing a pure science of politics that would place political science on the same kind of theoretical footing as economics. All of his work was underpinned by the deceptively simple insight of modeling political phenomena 'in terms of the preferences of a given set of individuals in relation to a given set of motions, the same motions appearing on the preference schedule of each individual' (Black 1972, p. 3).

In this search, Black rediscovered Condorcet's paradox of cyclical majorities (Black 1948a, pp. 32–3) and thereby opened up an extremely fruitful avenue of public choice research. It is important to acknowledge Black's achievement because recognition for the rediscovery of the Condorcet paradox is frequently and incorrectly given to Kenneth Arrow. Black (1948a, 1948b, 1948c) raised a number of important questions and offered some preliminary answers related to this paradox (Grofman 1981). A first question asks whether the paradox is inevitable; a second asks how frequently the paradox can be expected to occur; a third asks how easy it is to detect a paradox from the available evidence on majority rule outcomes; and a fourth asks how large will a cycle be.

Black's answer to the first question is that the paradox is not inevitable. Embedded in this answer is the famous median voter theorem that will be outlined and evaluated later in this section. In answering the second question, Black focuses attention on the special case of three voters and three alternatives for what is now known as the 'impartial culture', that is, a committee in which all strong preference orderings are equally likely.

Black recognizes the wider significance of this question. He suggests that the likelihood of the paradox of cyclical majorities occurring increases rapidly as the number of motions under consideration and the number of committee members increased (Black 1958, p. 51). In this judgment he has been proven correct by subsequent analysis (Grofman 1981, p. 15).

In answering the third question, how easy it is to detect a paradox, Black provides two useful results. The first is that under standard amendment procedures, given sincere voting, a voting paradox will always be revealed if there are as many rounds of voting as there are alternatives less one. The second result is the theorem that the voting paradox is always revealed if data are available on all paired comparisons. This is a powerful result since Black also shows that if a majority winner exists no voter has an incentive to vote insincerely in such a complete balloting.

The fourth question, querying how many alternatives are likely to be located in a *top cycle*, is not directly addressed by Black. However, he does provide a number of insights on interrelationships between cycles. For example, he notes that if two intersecting cycles have one motion in common, it must be possible to form a cycle that includes all of the motions in both cycles (Black 1958, p. 48). He also examines the case of three non-intersecting cycles (where every motion in the first defeats every motion in the second, and where every motion in the second defeats every motion in the third). He demonstrates, in such circumstances, that every motion in the third may still defeat every motion in the first (Black 1958, p. 50). As subsequent analysis has confirmed, winning cycles are likely to include all alternatives (McKelvey 1976).

Black's answer to the first question, concerning the inevitability of the paradox of the voting cycle, has been left to the end because it is his most important legacy to public choice. His insight came in February 1942, while 'fire-watching' in case of air raids, late at night in the magnificent green drawing room of Warwick Castle (Black 1972, p. 4). While playing with diagrams that represented motions as points on a line and with preferences represented as single-peaked utility functions, Black saw 'in a shock of recognition' (ibid.) the property of the median optimum, or what we now refer to as the median voter theorem.

The idea of single-peakedness can be defined in a number of different ways. A set of preference schedules is said to be single-peaked if there occurs an ordering of the alternative motions such that the preference schedules of all committee members can be graphed as single-peaked curves (that is, as curves that change direction at most once, up or down).

Where this condition holds, Black establishes that a unique alternative exists capable of attracting a simple majority in pair-wise competition against all other alternatives. This majority winner is the alternative most preferred by the median voter. Hence, for single-peaked preferences defined over a single issue dimension, Black establishes that there is a stable majority choice at the median of the voter distribution. Furthermore, under this condition, majority rule gives rise to a transitive ordering of alternatives. As we now know (Black 1958), where the median voter theorem holds, majority rule always selects a Condorcet winner.

Black is to be viewed as the founding father of modern public choice. His seminal contributions to the subject were brought together in his now-famous 1958 book (Black 1958). It is useful therefore to reflect on the key early reviews of this book as a means of determining Black's initial impact on economists, political scientists and philosophers.

Anthony Downs (1959) provides an interesting review of Black (1958) from the perspective of economics. His commentary is noteworthy both because he himself had already made an important contribution to public choice (Downs 1957) and because he had not cited Black's works at all in that contribution. Understandably, given his own book, Downs criticizes Black for failing to present a complete theory of either committees or elections 'because he does not deal with big enough problems' (Downs 1959, p. 212). Ironically, he criticizes Black for failing to discuss Arrow's impossibility theorem – a failure that was grounded in Black's belief that Arrow (1950) had purloined his own ideas on vote cycling. Downs (1959, p. 212), perhaps correctly, concludes with a mixed judgment: 'Black has furnished the bedroom of political theory before the house has been designed, and the elegant furniture looks lonely standing there by itself. However, it is well-built and the tools he used to make it may prove useful when the house is constructed.'

Reviewing Black's book in 1965, once again from the perspective of economics, John Harsanyi (1965) writes with the advantage of new developments in the field of spatial voting theory. He confirms Black's status as the founder of a rigorous analytical treatment of committees, and he acknowledges Black's influence on Arrow's 1951 book. He notes that Black's work must be – and indeed, partly already had been – supplemented by further analysis of voting in the absence of single-peaked preference functions, and of voting contrary to one's real preferences, as well as by analytical models of political bargaining, and by models allowing for risk, uncertainty and bounded rationality.

Reviewing Black's book in 1959, from the perspective of political science, Fred Kort confirms the initial fear within that profession that Black's work would be unfathomably mathematical. However, he finds just the opposite and encourages his fellow political scientists to engage with the book:

> The insights which the author provides should persuade those who are skeptical about mathematical approaches to social phenomena that such attempts are not merely fashionable endeavors, but that they serve the purpose of discovering or comprehending relationships that cannot be fully explored by exclusive reliance on qualitative interpretation.
> (Kort 1959, p. 327)

Writing much more defensively from the perspective of political science, Freeman Holmer (1959) criticizes Black for his focus on mathematical accuracy in reflecting voters' behavior. In his judgment, Black's contribution is sterile because it does not address the practical problem of how to assure that electors have the information that they should have before making a choice: 'The theory of elections should not be left to the quantitative mercies of the mathematicians and economists. The insights of other disciplines can contribute qualitatively toward understanding and improving our election process' (Holmer 1959, p. 588).

Finally, writing from the perspective of philosophy, William Mays (1961) acknowledges that Black's work represents a valuable contribution to be balanced against 'the purely dialectical methods so long in use in political philosophy' (Mays 1961, p. 249). However, ultimately he is not convinced that the contribution is successful. 'If anything, economic science needs redirecting towards political studies' (ibid.).

So there we have it. Black's ideas were welcomed by economists well before they gained traction in political science. They have yet to penetrate significantly into political philosophy. Yet the discipline that Black founded – public choice – now plays a major role in all three fields of scholarly endeavor.

3 THE INSIGHTS OF KENNETH J. ARROW

Arrow's 1950 article, followed by his 1951 book, *Social Choice and Individual Values*, exerted a significant impact on the evolution of public choice, even though their primary concern was normative rather than positive in nature, focusing as they did on the desirable characteristics of alternative mechanisms of social choice. The primary public choice impact stems from Arrow's (erroneously attributed) rediscovery of Condorcet's paradox of cyclical fluctuations.

Under the doctoral supervision of Harold Hotelling, Arrow (1950, 1951) responded to the apparent collapse during the 1930s of Benthamite utilitarianism, as economists systematically retreated from the notion that utility is measurable on a cardinal scale and comparable across individuals. If the weak Pareto principle is all that remains of the once mighty utilitarian doctrine, what are the normative implications for the available mechanisms for effecting social choices? In his famous impossibility theorem, Arrow proved that any social welfare function involving at least three individuals choosing over at least three alternatives must violate at least one of six reasonable axioms of social choice, namely rationality, unbounded domain, the Pareto principle, non-dictatorship, non-imposition and independence of irrelevant alternatives.

Most important, from the perspective of public choice, was Arrow's proof that a social welfare function based on majority rule has the unsatisfactory property of being potentially intransitive when at least three individuals vote over at least three alternatives, even when the preferences of each person are strictly transitive. Arrow does not infer that majority rule will always produce cycles in such circumstances. Given the assumption of an unbounded domain, it suffices for him to demonstrate that certain configurations of individual preferences will result in the Condorcet paradox.

Although this insight is not original to Arrow (see Black with Newing 1951 and Coase 1981 for incontrovertible evidence that Black preceded Arrow in this respect), nevertheless, it is Arrow who has gained recognition for it. Although Arrow purposely avoided public choice even when it became better known, he must be considered as one of the founders of the discipline. Undoubtedly, Arrow's emphasis on the instability of majority rule contrasts sharply with Black's emphasis on the stability of the median voter outcome. Since these two impulses still course strongly through much of public choice analyses of the vote motive, it is convenient, if not strictly accurate, to distinguish them by reference to the two scholars.

As with Black, so with Arrow, it is useful to comb the early reviews of his 1951 book for indications of scholarly reaction. I commence with the 1952 book review by William Baumol since he later made significant contributions to public choice itself.

Baumol (1952, p.110) is not at all disturbed by Arrow's impossibility theorem, noting that 'the ideal of the democratic state requires a process of compromise whereby the diverse desires of the citizens can be prevented from forcing government into indecision and inaction'. He acknowledges the strength of Arrow's use of symbolic logic in proving that the class of acceptable social choice functions must be the null class; but he basically does not care about this insight. For Baumol, lower acceptability standards are simply required and, indeed, are generally endorsed in democratic systems. Occasional, carefully screened departures from transitivity 'may not be too serious' (ibid., p.110). Baumol is a pragmatist, not a perfectionist.

Martin Bronfenbrenner, writing in 1952, is less enthused even than Baumol by the significance of Arrow's book. Nor is he overly impressed by the symbolic logic utilized to derive results that appear intuitively obvious:

> When mathematical siege guns are turned on matters previously reserved primarily for verbal discussion, the nonmathematical reader is inclined to inspect the results with an eye biased by his inferiority feelings. What is there here, after all, that we could not have guessed before? *Parturiunt montes, nascitur ridiculusmus.* And so it will presumably be in this case.
> (Bronfenbrenner 1952, p.135)

T.M. Brown, writing in 1952, sees much more merit in the text and links the book to what later would become a key issue in constitutional political economy. He clearly recognizes the threat to individual freedom of choice implicit in Arrow's impossibility theorem:

> Dr. Arrow shows that, if no prior assumptions are made about the nature of individual orderings, neither the vote nor the market mechanism will produce a rational social choice. In fact the mathematical analysis shows that, when interpersonal comparisons of utility are excluded and a wide range of individual orderings is assumed, social welfare functions which conserve properties defining collective rationality cannot grant sovereignty to citizens; they must be imposed or dictatorial.
>
> (Brown 1952, p. 402)

As James Buchanan and Gordon Tullock would later suggest (Buchanan and Tullock 1962) and as Arrow explicitly recognizes, some consensus on values is essential for any lasting 'constitution', however devised. Arrow himself showed little inclination to believe in such consensus. He has remained a would-be 'dictatorial' economic planner throughout his subsequent career.

In an extremely profound 1953 book review, written from the perspective of sociology, Leo Goodman seizes on the central importance of vote intransitivity for the US political process. Conducting an experiment of the paradox of voting in a small community, immediately prior to the 1952 presidential election, Goodman discovered that in pairwise questionnaire comparisons a majority of the community preferred Adlai Stevenson to Dwight ('Ike') Eisenhower, that a majority preferred Eisenhower to Robert Taft, and yet that a majority also preferred Taft to Stevenson. Thus, four years prior to Anthony Downs's 1957 book, a sociologist had already explored the paradox of voting within the context of a national election.

4   THE INSIGHTS OF ANTHONY DOWNS

Both Black and Arrow analyze the majority vote mechanism in abstract terms, deliberately seeking generality at the cost of sacrificing institutional detail. Although their contributions, especially those of Arrow, sparked an almost obsessive interest among students of social choice, perhaps because of their abstractness, they failed to make much initial inroad into political economy and political science.

In 1957, Anthony Downs filled this institutional vacuum with a book entitled *An Economic Theory of Democracy* that would become a fulcrum for public choice analysis. Downs was a student of Kenneth Arrow, whose work on social choice theory clearly motivated his own scholarly work. Surprisingly, Downs displayed no knowledge of Black's contributions despite Arrow's evident acquaintance with them. Ironically, despite the fact that most public choice scholars identify Downs with the median voter theorem, the theorem is referred to nowhere in the book.

Downs instead adapts the spatial economic model of Harold Hotelling (1929) to demonstrate that competition between two political parties under conditions of parliamentary democracy often results in both parties converging in policy issue space to adopt identical platforms reflecting the preferences of a majority of the electorate. Since

Downs depicts normally distributed voter preference distributions, there is no means in his analysis of distinguishing between the mean, the median and the mode as the relevant point of party convergence.

The real contribution of Downs is not the median voter theorem (unequivocally the insight of Black) but rather the introduction of the rational choice approach to the study of political science. Pitting himself against the well-entrenched tradition of behavioral analysis among political scientists, Downs lays the foundations for a major research program that will apply rational choice theory to every aspect of the political marketplace.

By rational action, Downs means action that is efficiently designed to achieve the consciously selected political and/or economic ends of every actor in the political marketplace. From this perspective he develops an economic theory of democracy designed to understand and to predict political behavior within an environment of two-party representative democracy and, moreover, explains why a two-parties system can be expected to be the norm in a polity choosing by majority rule.

From the self-interest axiom springs Downs's view of what motivates the political actions of party members. They act 'solely in order to attain the income, prestige, and power which comes from being in office' (Downs 1957, p. 28). Politicians, in this model, never seek office as a means of promoting particular policies. Their only goal is to reap the rewards of holding office. The fundamental hypothesis of Downs's model is that 'parties formulate policies in order to win elections, rather than win elections to formulate policies' (ibid.). Thus, the application of the self-interest axiom leads Downs to the hypothesis of vote-maximizing politicians.

Downs also applies the self-interest axiom to voter behavior, hypothesizing that each citizen casts his vote for the party that he expects to provide him with the most benefits net of costs. As Downs recognizes, the concept of rational voting is deceptively complex, ambiguous and, hence, deserving of close scrutiny. The benefits that voters consider in making their decisions are streams of utility (referred to as utility income) derived from government activity.

Not all utility income is relevant to the vote decision, since utility income includes benefits that the recipient does not realize he will receive and also benefits of which he is aware without knowing their exact source. However, only the benefits of which rational voters are conscious at the time of the election can influence their voting decisions.

The unit of time over which voters evaluate utility-income flows is the election period, defined as the time elapsing between scheduled elections. Two or more such election periods enter into the calculus of the rational voter, namely, one period ending at the time of the election and the other following that election. Both periods are relevant to his determination of the expected party differential in utility income, the measure determining the party that will secure his vote.

In casting his vote, the voter is helping to select the government that will govern him during the coming inter-election period. His rational decision must reflect the expected future performances of the competing parties. Yet, he knows that political parties are neither obligated to honor nor always capable of carrying out their platform commitments.

In such circumstances, the most recent election period experience of the party in power is the best possible guide to its future behavior, assuming that its policies have some continuity. This performance must be weighed against the performance the opposition would have produced had it been in power. Downs asserts that it is rational for the voter to ground his voting decision primarily on current events, while applying two future-orienting modifiers to his current party differential.

The first modifier is the trend factor, an adjustment made by each citizen to his current-party differential to account for relevant trends in the behavior of the government during the current election period. The second modifier is the tie-breaker adjustment utilized only when the voter cannot distinguish between the parties. In such circumstances, voters cast their votes by comparing the performance of the incumbent government with that of its immediate predecessor. Voters who still cannot distinguish between the competing parties rationally abstain from voting.

Because Downs was not aware of the median voter theorem, his discussion of the basic logic of government decision-making is less precise than it might have been. In general, he suggests that vote-maximizing incumbents will follow the majority principle, subjecting each decision to a hypothetical poll and always choosing the alternative that the majority of voters prefers. He recognizes that such a strategy will not guarantee victory in every election.

The opposition party might defeat a majority-pleasing government by pursuing one of three possible strategies. The first such strategy is adoption of a program identical in every detail with that of the incumbent. Such a strategy forces the electorate to decide their votes by comparing the performance of the incumbent with those of previous governments. Only rarely would such a strategy be effective.

The second such strategy is that of opposing the incumbent by supporting minority positions on carefully selected issues, building a coalition of minorities into a majority vote for the next election. Such a strategy can succeed only where the preferences of those in the minority are more intensely held than the preferences of those in the majority, that is, where consensus is weak. In the case of passionate majorities, a sufficiently large-coalition of minorities will not emerge.

The third such strategy is available to an opposition once again only when there is a lack of consensus in the electorate. In this case, the lack of consensus takes the form of the Condorcet paradox of cyclical majorities. In such circumstances, any alternative that the government chooses can be defeated in an election paired with some other alternative. As long as the government must choose first, and must remain committed to this choice, a prescient opposition can always defeat it.

Downs correctly recognizes that his model appears to disintegrate at this point because of the false assumption of certainty. In reality, political parties do not fully know what voters prefer and voters do not fully know the consequences of governmental actions. If uncertainty is introduced into the model, the incumbents are saved from almost inevitable defeat at each succeeding election, but appear also to be freed from the grip of the majority principle. Therefore, Downs devotes a major part of his book to the effects of uncertainty on the behavior of political markets.

According to Downs, uncertainty divides voters into groups endowed with varying degrees of confidence in their voting decisions. Those who feel least well informed are vulnerable to persuasion by voters who are well informed and who provide correct but biased information favorable to their own causes. Interest groups that want government to adopt policies favorable to themselves pose as representatives of the popular will, simultaneously creating public opinion supportive of their views and convincing government that such public opinion exists. Political parties, once they have formed their policies, endeavor to extend electoral support for those policies. Uncertainty thus forces rational governments to regard some voters as more important than others. By so doing, it modifies the equality of influence that universal suffrage was designed to ensure.

Uncertainty limits the ability of the voter to relate every act of the government to his own view of good policy. The rational voter, in such circumstances, may lower his information costs by identifying party ideologies as a substitute for detailed policy platforms. Each political party in turn will develop an ideology consistent with its policy actions as a shortcut to gaining votes. According to Downs, all parties are forced by competition to be relatively honest and responsible in regard both to policies and ideologies.

From this economic perspective, Downs utilizes the theory of spatial competition invented by Harold Hotelling (1929), as refined by Arthur Smithies (1941), to elaborate a theory of political party competition under conditions of representative democracy. His version of Hotelling's spatial market consists of a linear scale running from zero to 100 in the usual left-right fashion. He assumes that all voters would agree on the ordering of both parties across this single dimensional left-right space, essentially by reference to the projected ideologies of the parties.

Downs further assumes that every voter's preferences are single-peaked over this left-right issue space, implying that each voter always prefers a position closer to his ideal point over one that is further away and that he always votes for the political party that is closer to his ideal point. If these conditions hold, and if all voters always vote, the two parties will converge to the center of the voter preference distribution in order to maximize their respective vote shares. However, if voters located at the two extremes of left-right space become alienated as the political parties move towards the center their threats to abstain may halt this process of convergence well short of the center of the distribution. In such circumstances the ideologies of the two parties may differ sharply and political consensus may not emerge.

If the condition of single-peaked preferences does not hold, and the distribution of voters across left-right issue space is bimodal, with modes located near each extreme, parties will locate themselves in proximity to their respective modes. The victorious party will implement policies radically opposed by the opposition. In such circumstances, Downs predicts that government policy will be unstable and that democracy may induce chaos, leading perhaps to its replacement by some form of autocracy.

Downs focuses particular attention on the causes and effects of rational voter abstention, recognizing that many citizens who are eligible to vote in democratic elections fail to do so. Downs assumed that a citizen's reward for voting is the value of his vote, that is, his party differential discounted to allow for the influence of other voters on the election's outcome. On this basis, he demonstrates that when voting is without cost every citizen who prefers one party over the other votes and every citizen who is indifferent between the parties abstains.

In reality, voting is always costly, because every human action takes time. The cost of voting may outweigh the returns, even for citizens who prefer one party to the other. Indeed, because the expected return to voting is often miniscule, even low voting costs may result in rational abstentions for citizens who view voting in elections solely from an instrumental perspective.

The importance of rational abstentions depends on its impact on political power. This impact in turn stems from two potential biases. The first potential impact arises from the distribution of the ability to bear the costs of voting. If the cost of voting consists primarily of poll taxes, loss of earnings and transportation costs, upper-income citizens obtain a political advantage since the ability to bear such costs typically varies inversely with income. If the cost of voting primarily is the loss of leisure, no income-correlated disparity exists.

The second potential impact arises from biases in the distribution of high returns. The total return each citizen receives from voting depends on (1) the benefits he obtains from democracy, (2) how much he wants a particular party to win, (3) how close he thinks the election will be and (4) how many other citizens he thinks will vote. Since the expected return predictably is larger for the high-income than for the low-income citizen, the former has a stronger incentive to become politically informed. He also has a greater incentive to vote on the basis of expected benefits.

Once again, it is informative to examine early reviews of Downs's book in order to assess the immediate impact of his contribution. Let us start with the 1959 book review in the *Journal of Political Economy* by Martin Diamond, which addresses Downs's contribution from the perspective of economics. Diamond, quoting Downs (1957, p. 28), grasps the essential message with acuity:

> 'The fundamental hypothesis of our model [is]: parties formulate policies in order to win elections rather than win elections in order to formulate policies.' That is by virtue of the 'self-interest axiom,' the model [assumes that] politicians' 'only goal is to reap the rewards of holding office per se,' and these are 'income, prestige and power'.

Again quoting Downs (1957, p. 21), Diamond (1959, p. 209) then comments:

> An equally fundamental hypothesis is that all model voters act in politics only to maximize their private goals, which seem to be primarily the enjoyment of material benefits. Manipulating these two notions imaginatively and rigorously, Downs grinds out the consequences. The consequence apparently most startling to him is that, despite these two assumptions that wholly private motives animate political behavior, his model of government is capable of 'performing the social functions of government'. As a result, much of the book is given to suggesting that the 'invisible hand' applies substantially in politics as well as in economics.

Well, this *was* 1959, and Diamond was far from comfortable with this approach, certainly not with the concept of the invisible hand, with respect either to private markets or to politics. Markets typically fail, he argues, following the conventional wisdom of the times. Politicians frequently are nobler creatures motivated by higher values than self. How might Abraham Lincoln be evaluated in terms of the self-interest calculus? Where are the notions of political equality and widespread distribution of benefits in the Downsian model? Downs makes his model work, Diamond urges, by focusing attention on the lowest common human denominator. Diamond concludes by stating that 'I cannot concede the value of the method' (ibid., p. 211).

Now one might think that political scientists would respond with naked rage at such an economic violation of their territory. And one would, to a significant extent, be wrong, as the 1958 book review by Roland Pennock, published in the *American Political Science Review*, clearly demonstrates. Tolerance, indeed, is not the correct word for this review, but rather adulation of Downs for reclaiming political theory from its putative coffin: 'this reviewer ventures to predict that Downs's volume will give a substantial fillip to democratic theory, especially in the application of game theory to democracy' (Pennock 1958, p. 539).

Pennock suggests that many of Downs's conclusions, especially with regard to the party system, fall into the category of the commonplace. But more important than the conclusions is the method. In this latter respect, the book is both stimulating and enlightening and should do, precisely what good theory ought to do, namely, give guidance to empirical research. How interesting that a political scientist grasped, whereas an economist did not, the logic of scientific discovery.

Lest the reader be concerned that a fluke brought Roland Pennock to the plate, let me draw attention to a second political science review of Downs's book, also in 1958, by Charles Farris in the *Journal of Politics*. Once again, a political scientist embraces Downs for his contribution:

> Downs'[s] theory of democracy . . . is an able exposition of a 'middle range' axiomatic or systematic theory. Many of the theory's logically generated hypotheses are in testable form, and many have already been verified by empirical research. . . . It is impossible to judge in detail the validity of Downs'[s] model. The odds are that, in some respects, it is probably deficient, but the specification of these respects must depend on their demonstrated inconsistency with the findings of research. At this stage in the development of political science, what is striking about Downs'[s] model are these things: that he produced it at all, and that a political scientist did not produce it.
>
> (Farris 1958, p. 573)

5 THE INSIGHTS OF WILLIAM H. RIKER

William Riker is the sole political scientist included in my list of founding fathers of public choice. He played an enormously important role, both with respect to his own seminal contributions, and in providing the intellectual leadership that brought a significant number of superb second- and third-generation political scientists into the public choice research program. Names such as Arthur Goldberg, Richard Niemi, John Mueller, Peter Ordeshook, Kenneth Shepsle, Richard Fenno, Jerry Kramer, Peter Aranson, Morris Fiorina, Richard McKelvey, and David Rohde, all came through Bill Riker's Rochester program, and made powerful contributions to public choice (Aldrich 2004).

Riker graduated from DePauw University in 1942, but deferred his entry into graduate studies in order to serve the war program as a time-and-motion analyst at the Radio Corporation of America. He studied for a conventional doctorate in political science at Harvard University between 1944 and 1948. In 1948, he accepted a junior position at Lawrence College (now Lawrence University) rising to the rank of full professor before he left, in 1962, for the University of Rochester, where he stayed for the remainder of his life.

Riker first acquired an interest in what would become known as public choice in 1954, after reading a paper on political power by two mathematical economists, Lloyd Shapley and Martin Shubik (Shapley and Shubik 1954). The power index offered a mathematical formula expressing the power of a legislator in terms of his ability to turn a losing coalition into a winning coalition. This triggered what would become Riker's long-standing interest in coalition theory, as well as signaling an analytical direction for his future research program. Riker quickly mastered the public choice scholarship of Duncan Black, Kenneth Arrow, and Anthony Downs as well as the game theory of John von Neumann and Oskar Morgenstern (1944).

In a sequence of three papers, Riker (1957, 1958a, 1958b) engaged in experiments in coalition formation, using a game-theory structure, without applying game theory in its formal sense. The papers combined theoretical analysis with empirical testing, and immediately set Riker aside from mainstream descriptive and behavioral political science as practiced at that time. As a result, he was selected as a fellow at the Center for Advanced Study in the Behavioral Sciences at Stanford University for the academic year 1960–61, with a clearly articulated vision of his future research program:

> I visualize the growth in political science of a body of theory somewhat similar to the neo-classical theory of value in economics. It seems to be that a number of propositions from the mathematical theory of games can perhaps be woven into a theory of politics. Hence, my main interest at present is attempting to use game theory for the construction of political theory.
> (Riker 1959, letter of application to CASBS, cited in Bueno de Mesquita and Shepsle 2001)

During his year at the Center, Riker fulfilled this promise, completing his seminal book, *The Theory of Political Coalitions* (Riker 1962a). In this book, Riker challenges, head on, the political model advanced by Anthony Downs (Downs 1957).

As readers will recall, the Downsian model indicates that, within the context of uni-dimensional issue space, in winner-take-all elections, politicians typically adopt centrist policy positions designed to maximize their vote shares. According to Downs, politicians care only about winning public office. They do not concern themselves with the policy or private goods concessions that they must make in order to win an election.

Riker rejects this prognosis, developing an alternative size principle for the case of n-person, zero-sum political games (Aldrich 2004, p. 322). Riker argues that maximizing votes is costly. Voters are attracted to a candidate on the basis of promises about private benefits. Candidates hold policy preferences of their own. Therefore, Riker suggests, rational politicians seek to attract just enough votes to win an election, and no more. Attempts to secure voters in excess of the minimal winning size occur only because of uncertainty about voter preferences or voter loyalty. By forming minimal winning coalitions, politicians make as few concessions as possible, while retaining sufficient support to maintain governmental authority and to pass legislation (Bueno de Mesquita and Shepsle 2001).

At this stage, Riker views political contests as zero-sum games. Later, he would relax this assumption to allow for positive-sum contests. The most important contribution of this book, however, was its impact on political science, opening up a long-lasting research program in empirically based rational choice analysis and, most especially, in the analysis of governing coalitions in multi-party parliaments.

From an empirical viewpoint, Riker's minimal winning coalition hypothesis has not dominated the Downsian alternative. Within the Western European political marketplace during the postwar era, around one-third of all the governing coalitions formed have been minimal-winning. Two-thirds of such coalitions have been either surplus majority or minority in nature (Hindmoor 2006). However, the book is truly notable for the new direction that it offered to political science research, literally dragging it out of its descriptive, polemical and behaviorist modes.

Once again, it is instructive to evaluate the immediate impact of Riker's 1962 book from the perspective of early book reviews, starting with Richard Fagen's 1963 contribution to the *American Political Science Review*. Fagen is not ill-disposed towards the venture, though he clearly is not convinced that it will prove ultimately to be successful: 'despite strong reservations about some of the parts, I found the total thought structure most impressive. It is bold and, in most instances, coherent. Whether it will also be useful in studying politics depends in large part – as Riker emphasizes – on its attractiveness to others' (Fagen 1963, p. 446).

Fagen admits that the political science profession is not well equipped technically to rise up to Riker's intellectual challenge. 'Those who would accept the challenge had better come prepared with a well sharpened kit of tools.' He ends his review on a note of optimism: 'One mark of the success of this book will be the number of controversies and derivative efforts that it engenders. It is to me a hopeful sign that such a book has appeared; even more encouraging would be a report that *The Theory* is being widely read by the political science community' (ibid., p. 447).

James Robinson writes a rave review of the book in 1963 for the *Journal of Conflict Resolution*: 'So rich a book deserves a summary before commentary' (Robinson 1963, p. 763). He supports Riker in his expressed desire that political scientists heed his example and recognize the advantages that the rational choice approach has for their discipline. He compares Riker's book favorably with the early work on game theory by Thomas Schelling (1960). He urges Riker to pursue actively the agenda outlined in his book and not to leave it to be fleshed out by others. In Robinson's judgment, the book is a harbinger of what is yet to come.

Robinson was correct in his prognosis about the likely future impact of Riker's contributions to political science. Sadly, no economist even deigned to review the book.

6 THE INSIGHTS OF JAMES M. BUCHANAN AND GORDON TULLOCK

Five years after Downs's (1957) masterpiece, there followed the most far-reaching and the only philosophical founding contribution, namely *The Calculus of Consent* by James M. Buchanan and Gordon Tullock (1962). Neither author was trained formally in philosophy or in political science. Yet, this book explicitly moved the analysis to the interface between economics, philosophy and political science, applying the tools of economics and economic philosophy to a detailed and far-ranging evaluation of political institutions in an attempt to delineate the logical foundations of constitutional democracy.

Buchanan and Tullock reject the emphasis placed by Downs on the group behavior of political parties in favor of a model of collective decision-making that is more closely analogous to the theory of private choice. Collective action is viewed as the action of individuals when they choose to accomplish goals collectively rather than individually. Government is viewed as a set of processes that allows collective action to take place. From this perspective of methodological individualism, the rule of unanimity is advanced as a weak ethical criterion for the 'good' in evaluating both new constitutions and initiatives for constitutional change. Buchanan and Tullock embed their analysis firmly within the framework of rational choice, acknowledging albeit that *Homo economicus* may not always be as narrowly self-seeking as neoclassical economics frequently assumes. They further acknowledge that in the effecting of collective choices, the individual has no way of knowing the final outcome at the time that he makes his own contribution to the communal decision. For this reason, individuals lose that full sense of personal responsibility inherent in the making of private choices.

The rational self-seeking individual will contemplate collective action only when such action increases his expected utility. In an environment devoid of any kind of Pareto-relevant externality, the state would have no utilitarian support. Buchanan and Tullock therefore rationalize the existence of collective action as a means for individuals to combine in order to reduce the burden of external costs imposed upon them by purely private or voluntary actions. In contemplating such collective action, the rational individual is concerned to minimize his relevant expected costs, defined as the sum of his expected residual external costs and of his expected costs of decision-making within a collective framework. It is important to understand that the economic theory of constitutions is built almost entirely on the basis of presumed individual speculation.

In deciding whether any particular activity belongs within the realm of collective rather than private choice, the rational individual will take account of the expected cost of voluntary cooperative arrangements. If such costs are zero, all Pareto-relevant externalities will be eliminated by voluntary private behavior (here we note an early application of the 1960 Coase theorem, itself developed during the late 1950s at the University of Virginia).

If the environment is one of positive transaction costs, however, the choice between non-cooperative private behavior, cooperative private behavior and collective political action will rest on the relative expected costs of these two alternatives. The existence of Pareto-relevant external effects from private behavior is neither a necessary nor a sufficient condition for an individual to entrust that activity to the realm of collective choice. In this regard, Buchanan and Tullock, *for the first time in formal economic analysis*, call specific attention to the fact that the collective organization of activities will also impose net expected external costs upon some individuals unless the collectivity itself is constrained to make decisions through a rule of unanimity, where every individual exercises the veto power.

Thus, the expected costs that collective choices impose on the individual depend on the decision-making rules chosen to govern such choices. In such circumstances, each individual will compare the expected costs of private choice with the expected costs of the most efficient form of collective action, when making his decision whether or not to submit to the latter.

From this perspective, Buchanan and Tullock design a generalized economic theory of constitutions specifically to analyze the problem of individual choice among alternative collective decision-making rules. This economic theory, now widely recognized as the most important and enduring insight of *The Calculus of Consent*, combines the two concepts of expected external costs and expected decision costs to formulate the expected total costs of collective action as a function of variations in the size of the minority or majority vote required to implement such actions. Because the authors demonstrate that simple majority rule is only one of any number of possible choices, the book stirred up a lot of resentment, both in economics and in political science.

The key insights of this contribution are that, for any random individual, the expected external costs of collective action will decline monotonically as the proportion of the total vote required for collective action increases, and will reach zero at unanimity, whereas the expected decision-making costs will start at near-zero when the individual is exclusively in charge (the assumption is that Hamlets are extremely rare) but will rise to infinity before unanimity is achieved. In consequence, the combined expected costs of collective action will tend to fall monotonically as the proportion of the total vote rises from very low levels, will reach a minimum at some vote proportion – which may be less than or more than a simple majority – and will rise exponentially as a required supra-majority increases towards unanimity. The rational individual will select the vote rule that reflects the minimum expected costs of collective action, if those costs lie below those of the entirely private alternative.

As Buchanan and Tullock emphasize, the calculus of individual consent does not require that all potential collective action will be organized through the operation of the same decision-making rule. In their view, two categories of potential collective action will emerge, even at this conceptual stage. In the first category are located those potential collective actions that are characteristically undertaken by government, as it is. In such instances, the random individual will select a relatively low vote proportion for collective action, though even this may be in excess of a simple majority.

In the second category are located those potential collective actions that modify the structure of established individual rights and property rights. The rational individual will foresee that collective action in this area potentially may inflict him with very severe (external) costs. In such instances, the rational individual at best will require a much more inclusive rule as the basis for consenting to collective actions. In the limit, the calculus of individual consent will break down entirely, and the individual will decline to enter into political society but will choose instead to protect this category of rights by private actions, by voluntary cooperation, or both.

Throughout this analysis, Buchanan and Tullock center attention on the calculus of a single individual as he confronts the constitutional choice concerning rules of decision-making. What we should now perceive as a significant weakness in their book is the limited attention that Buchanan and Tullock devote to dealing with the way in which individuals reach agreement concerning the rules that govern various forms of collective action. Since individuals are presumed to be heterogeneous, and to be aware of their own relative positions in society, at the moment of constitutional choice, they are also aware that decision-making rules short of unanimity will impose different expected external costs upon each of them.

For the most part, Buchanan and Tullock evade this issue, commenting that '[W]e prefer to put this issue aside and to assume, without elaboration, that at this ultimate stage, which we shall call the constitutional, the rule of unanimity holds' (Buchanan and Tullock 1962, p. 77). In fact, they did not completely put the issue aside. They relied upon the extended time horizon of the individual in making his constitutional choices to explain his greater willingness to consent to rules that potentially are harmful to his shorter-term interests.

Constitutional rules, by their nature, are expected to be long-lived, since constitutional change is usually subject to highly inclusive rules of decision-making. The rational individual, confronted with constitutional choice, is inevitably uncertain of his particular interest at some unspecified future time. In such circumstances, he will selfishly tend to choose rules of collective decision-making that maximize the utility of some random individual. Such far-sightedness in constitutional decision-making differs sharply from the more myopic, sectional-based approach of the individual in the ordinary business of politics.

Buchanan and Tullock recognize that uncertainty alone will not necessarily guarantee unanimity in the prior judgment of individuals as to the rules of collective decision-making that will minimize the expected costs of collective action. Nevertheless, they argue, albeit without a fully convincing logic, that any initial conflict of opinion over rules should be amenable to reasoned compromise during the constitutional debate.

Buchanan and Tullock liken the resolution of such conflicts to the discussion that might take place between potential participants as to the appropriate rules under which a game – let us say poker – shall be played. Since no player can anticipate which specific rules might benefit him during a particular play of the game, before the cards are dealt, he will not find it difficult to concur with others in devising a set of rules that will constitute the most interesting game for the average or representative player. The limit of this logic is that the rules will be established by players who already have a fairly good idea of their existing hands, even if they cannot know with certainty how those hands will change over an uncertain future.

Buchanan and Tullock recognize that the process of constitutional decision-making set out in their book has little relevance for any society that is deeply divided by reference to social class, race, religion, or ethnicity. Unanimity over a collective decision-making rule is especially unlikely when one or more such coalition is perceived to hold an especially advantageous position. Needless to say, this implies that *The Calculus of Consent* could not have been written in its existing form, at least with relevance for the United States, had the co-authors joined forces in the late 1960s rather than in the late 1950s.

In any event, the analysis of Buchanan and Tullock provides a number of important insights into constitutional political economy. First, it is rational to have a constitution, in the sense that there is more than one rule (simple majority rule) for collective decision-making. Second, there is no necessary justification for majority rule as the basis for collective decision-making. At best, majority rule should be viewed as one among many practical expedients made necessary by the costs of securing widespread agreement on political issues when individual interests diverge.

Third, it is rational to have a constitution that requires a more inclusive rule of collective decision-making with respect to incursion on individual rights and property rights than with respect to less fundamental issues. Fourth, the more inclusive the decision-making rule, the more willing individuals will be to entrust decision-making to collective choice. The range of collective decision-making, thus, is not independent of the rules that govern such activities in societies that respect the primacy of individual choice.

Finally, the analysis of Buchanan and Tullock suggests that the overall costs of collective decision-making are lower, with respect to any constitutional rule, in communities characterized by a more, than by a less, homogeneous population. From this perspective alone, from the perspective of expected decision-making costs, a more homogeneous community would adopt a more inclusive rule for collective choice. However, the homogeneity characteristic also affects expected external costs which are predictably lower the more homogeneous the society. On balance, Buchanan and Tullock, predict that the more homogeneous a society, the less inclusive will be the rules of collective choice, and the more extensive will be the range of actions encompassed within the collective sphere.

Buchanan and Tullock deploy the rational choice model to offer a number of important insights into the logic of constitutional design. A comprehensive review of these applications is beyond the scope of this essay. However, their evaluation of the rule of simple majority voting is illustrative of the general approach.

Buchanan and Tullock ground their discussion of the simple majority-vote rule on the generalized assumption that individuals vary in the intensity of their preferences for or against specific collective actions. In such circumstances, the rule of simple majority, applied to a single issue of collective choice, may provide minor gains in utility for a majority at the cost of imposing major losses in utility upon a minority (abstracting from the issue of the problem of measuring utility across individuals). Rational individuals will recognize this danger when engaging in constitutional decision-making and will protect themselves from its most serious consequences by providing institutional opportunities for logrolling (or the trading of votes).

An institutional environment in which logrolling cannot occur is the standard referendum on a single issue determined by a simple majority vote conducted by secret ballot. The rational individual, concerned about the potential tyranny of the majority, will therefore be extremely wary about endorsing decision-making by referendums as the basis for determining collective choices.

Buchanan and Tullock note that logrolling opportunities are prevalent in many of the political institutions of the Western democracies. Explicit logrolling is a common feature of all representative assemblies where exchanges of votes are easy to arrange and to observe. Such exchanges of votes significantly affect the political process. Implicit logrolling dominates the electoral process since the leaders of the political parties formulate complex mixtures of policies into electoral platforms designed to attract voters' support by appealing to intensely held preferences.

Buchanan and Tullock suggest that both explicit and implicit logrolling tend to improve the efficiency of the political process, even though these practices are widely criticized on ethical grounds. They demonstrate, however, that even when logrolling is possible, simple majority rule is likely to produce undesirable collective decisions, for example by over-investing in the public sector. But, they further demonstrate that a system in which the open buying and selling of political votes is encouraged tends to improve the efficiency of simple majority rule as evaluated in terms of the Pareto criterion.

Recognition of the fact that preference intensities over policy alternatives differ among the electorate may encourage the rational individual to favor the bicameral over the unicameral legislature as a basis for constitutional design. A properly designed bicameral legislature, offering different bases of representation, will discriminate automatically between legislation potentially affecting intense minorities and legislation on which the intensity of desires is more or less equal. This will significantly improve the efficiency of the political process.

A further improvement in political market efficiency occurs when the constitution provides a president or other player with veto power, effectively establishing a third house of the legislature. This third house represents the entire body of voters in one grand constituency, raising the minimum size of the logrolling coalitions and further protecting the individual voter from the excesses of rule of simple majority voting.

In this manner, Buchanan and Tullock outline the sort of calculus that the individual undertakes when he considers the question: can the pursuit of individual self-interest be turned to good account in politics as well as in economics? They are able to show that, even under the behavioral assumption of extreme self-interest, something akin to the constitutional democracy conceived of by the American Founding Fathers tends to emerge from the rational individual calculus. They conclude their epic on an extremely optimistic note, a note perhaps, that some 50 years on, they might no longer feel able to hold:

> With the philosophers of the Enlightenment we share the faith that man can rationally organize his own society, that existing organization can always be perfected, and that nothing in the social order should remain exempt from rational, critical, and intelligent discussion. Man's reason is the slave to his passions and recognizing this about himself, man can organize his own association with his fellows in such a manner that the mutual benefits from social interdependence can be effectively maximized.
> (Buchanan and Tullock 1962, p. 306)

Economists displayed considerably more interest in *The Calculus of Consent* than in the earlier texts cited in this essay. Even in this case, as we shall see, the primary interest came from scholars now embarked on public choice analysis. Let us start, however, with the 1963 book review in the *Economic Journal* by James Meade, by far the most distinguished scholar – and certainly no advocate of public choice – to evaluate the book during its infancy. Meade (1963, p. 101) is clearly intrigued by the new direction established by the authors of *The Calculus*:

> In discussing external economies and diseconomies economists have been much to ready to call in the State as a *deus ex machina* to remove the imperfections of the *laissez-faire* market without examining the implications of this view for the political, as contrasted with the economic behaviour of the individual citizen. Is it sensible to assume that citizens will act selfishly in the market-place but will nevertheless by a democratic process produce a Government which will intervene to secure the general good? Do we not in fact see democratic political mechanisms used to promote the interests of particular groups of citizens?

And, he adds, 'The book should prove at least a strong and stimulating gad-fly to goad others to join in the effort to build a political economy in which economic motives in political action are made as essentially a part of the whole as are economic motives in the market' (ibid., p. 103).

This is not to say that Meade is without criticism. He notes the emphasis by Buchanan and Tullock on efficiency motivations to strike bargains. Yet, political-economic decisions inevitably concern issues of wealth distribution, where bargains are much more costly to achieve. Furthermore, the book focuses attention on collective actions over small ongoing events. By avoiding major discrete events, such as whether or not a country should enter into the European Union, the authors skate over more difficult problems that may confront any constitutional calculus.

Writing in 1964 for the *Journal of Political Economy*, from the perspective of public choice, Anthony Downs (1964, pp. 87–8) provides enthusiastic support for the book:

> *The Calculus of Consent* is a brilliant and significant contribution to the literature concerning the analysis of political processes with the methods of economics . . . While economists refine the theoretical conditions for perfect competition down to the last gnat's eyebrow, the gigantic problems of economic choice and allocation within our political institutions are left largely to political scientists and to a few economists working on defense-oriented problems. But government action involves many of the same decision-making processes that economists are so much better tooled to analyze than political scientists. Buchanan and Tullock are pioneers in using these tools to analyze the critical problems of political decision-making.

Writing in 1962 for the *American Economic Review*, a young left-leaning Mancur Olson (1962, p. 1217) welcomes the book as 'a stimulating addition to this new literature' while commenting on its 'eccentric ideological quality that . . . unfortunately narrows their appeal and perhaps obscures the objective importance of some of their theories. In scholarship it is not perhaps necessity, but prejudice that is the mother of invention'.

Olson naturally criticizes Buchanan and Tullock for ignoring the logic of collective action when discussing the circumstances under which voluntary organizations may replace government interventions. He concludes with modest praise for the book: 'While the authors' practical conclusions are not always novel, their theoretical contributions are distinctly original. Because of these interesting theoretical constructions, their book deserves the careful attention and criticism of economists and social scientists generally' (Olson 1962, p. 1218).

With infinitely more charity than he received from economists, William Riker also reviewed *The Calculus of Consent* in 1962 for the *Midwest Journal of Political Science*. His evaluation is highly favorable:

> It is an honor and delight to review this book, which is an important addition to a small shelf of recent books that are remaking the field of political theory . . . There is a fourth school, to which the book here reviewed belongs, which offers some hope of a really successful reorientation of political theory . . . [T]hey seem to be capable not only of reformulating traditional problems in a more sophisticated way but also of dealing with problems beyond the ken of even the great theorists of the past . . .
>
> (Riker 1962b, pp. 408–9)

As readers will note, enthusiasm for this founding book runs deeper and wider than is evident in the reviews of the other founders' contributions. This judgment caught the attention of the Nobel Committee when it awarded the 1986 Nobel Prize in Economic Sciences to James M. Buchanan. Unfortunately, the Nobel Committee failed to recognize the fundamental contributions to *The Calculus of Consent* made by Gordon Tullock, thus depriving one of the true polymath geniuses of the second half of the twentieth century of his just desserts.

7 THE INSIGHTS OF MANCUR OLSON

Prior to 1965, public choice had been developed with a primary emphasis on the vote motive. It is true that Downs (1957) and Buchanan and Tullock (1962) both acknowledge the relevance of pressure group activities in the political process. Neither of them accord to interest groups the central role that they evidently play in the determination of political outcomes in the Western democracies. In his important 1965 book, *The Logic of Collective Action*, Mancur Olson fills this lacuna in the public choice literature with his rigorous application of the rational choice approach to the analysis of interest groups.

Prior to Olson's book, economists, sociologists and political scientists had taken for granted the notion that groups of individuals with common interests usually attempted, often successfully, to further those interests by the application of political pressure. This notion played a central conceptual role in early American theories of labor unions, in the 'group theory' of the pluralists in political science, in John Kenneth Galbraith's concept of 'countervailing power' and in the Marxian theory of class conflict. This theory of interest group behavior essentially transferred the logic of the theory of individual behavior to that of groups.

In *The Logic of Collective Action*, Olson provides a dramatically different view of collective action. If individuals in some group share a common interest, furtherance of that common interest automatically benefits each individual in that group whether or not he bears any of the costs of collective action to further that interest. Thus the existence of a common interest need not provide any incentive for individual action in the common interest, especially when any one member's efforts are highly unlikely to make the difference between group success and group failure.

From an analytical viewpoint, Olson demonstrates that the benefits of collective action take the form of public goods, in the sense that individual members of the group cannot easily be excluded from any benefits that ultimately accrue. Economists recognize that voluntary and spontaneous market mechanisms either do not arise or seriously under-provide public goods, as a consequence of the free-rider problem. This under-provision of markets is paralleled exactly by the under-provision of pressure in the case of large groups attempting to pursue a common interest.

Since many groups with common interests do not have the power to tax their memberships, Olson's theory predicts that many groups that would benefit from collective action will fail to organize effectively in pursuit of their common interests. This prediction is supported by evidence. There is no major country in which organizations of consumers effectively support consumer interests. There is no major country in which groups of unemployed workers are effectively organized for collective action. Neither are taxpayers nor are most of the poor typically organized to act in their respective common interests.

Although the logic of collective action indicates that some groups can never act collectively (they are 'latent groups' in Olson's terminology), Olson suggests that other groups, with the assistance of ingenious leadership, may be able to overcome the difficulties of collective action. He posits three conditions, any of which is ultimately sufficient to make collective action possible, namely (1) that the relevant group is small in size, (2) that the group has access to selective incentives or (3) that the group can coerce the supply of pressure.

Suppose that a group is composed of a small number of members each with identical preferences in favor of some common interest. An example of such a group would be an industry made up of two large firms that would gain equally from the provision of a government subsidy or a tax loophole. Since the lobbying activity of each firm, if successful, will exert a significant impact on profits, strategic bargaining between them predictably will result in a group-optimal outcome. As the number of firms in the industry increases, however, the incentive to act collectively erodes.

Even in an industry composed of many firms effective lobbying may occur where one firm has a differentially high absolute demand for collective action. In such circumstances, such a firm may engage in collective action, notwithstanding the inability of other firms to provide pressure of their own (or to be excluded from the collective benefits). This leads to the paradoxical exploitation of the great by the small. Olson illustrates the existence of this phenomenon in a variety of military alliances, in international organizations and in metropolitan areas in which collective goods are provided across an entire metropolis by independent municipalities of greatly different size.

If large groups are to organize themselves effectively to supply pressure, Olson argues that they must engage in the provision of selective incentives to their members. These selective incentives are functionally equivalent to the taxes that enable governments to supply public goods, except that interest group members, unlike taxpayers, cannot be coerced into accepting selective benefits.

Selective benefits either punish or reward individuals depending on whether or not they have borne a share of the costs of collective action. One example of this device is the provision of life insurance and medical policies to paid-up members of the American Association of Retired Persons at rates that would not be available to individual consumers. Another example is the mechanism whereby farm associations in the United States obtain most of their membership by deducting the dues owed by farm organizations from the patronage dividends or rebates of farm cooperatives and insurance companies associated with those organizations.

Large groups that fail to provide selective benefits may nevertheless overcome the free-rider problem associated with collective action where they are able to devise mechanisms for coercing the supply of pressure. An obvious device of this kind is the combination of the closed shop and the picket-line utilized by some trade unions to make union membership a condition of employment and to control the supply of union labor during strikes. Another conspicuous example is the statutory requirement extracted by state bar associations in the United States that only paid-up members of the Bar are allowed to engage in the practice of law.

Olson's application of the rational choice approach to the analysis of collective action offers disturbing insights into the political process. Since access to collective action is uneven, the application of pressure by groups in pursuit of common membership goals will be uneven across society. Legislatures that respond systematically to such uneven pressures (by taking advantage of rational ignorance among the electorate or by utilizing the campaign contributions to manipulate voters' preferences) may be able systematically to evade the centripetal pressures of two-party spatial politics while effectively providing tenure to incumbent representatives.

Olson's landmark contribution received a significant volume of early social science book reviews, once again while the economics profession stood silently in the wing. The two principal sources of interest were political science and sociology.

Political scientists reacted, for the most part, warily and with more than a modicum of skepticism. Writing for *Political Science Quarterly* in 1967, Earl Latham (1967, p. 148) expresses grave doubts about the rational choice approach:

There is a wonderful actor in the book, a favorite of Olson's and of workers with game theory – the Rational Man – whose goal is the maximizing of the expected value of some utility function within a set of pre-determined conditions. When he is in a small group, he works hard as though he were alone, if he thinks that he has something personal to gain. When he is a member of an intermediate group, he contributes to the production of collective goods only because everyone else is watching him. When he is a member of a large group, he shirks his contribution to the production of collective goods unless someone pushes him around or he figures that there is something special in it for him ... Surely this is an incomplete psychology even for economic analysis.

John Lewis, writing in 1967 for *The Annals of the American Academy of Political and Social Sciences*, is even less supportive:

there are difficulties with his theory, presented as a general theory of groups. He briefly deals with 'certain small groups', but concentrates on large ones; giving little attention to the multitude of groups between, he does not demonstrate that group-qualities are directly proportionate to size. He alludes to federations of groups, but – oddly – treats them as exceptional. His model fails to account for the social roles of ideological and 'reference' groups. His summaries of contemporary group theory, as developed by Truman and others, are remarkably oversimplified.
(Lewis 1967, pp. 210–11)

The reaction from sociology was a mixture of shock and awe. Robert Golembiewski, writing in 1966 for the *American Sociological Review*, expressed the shock: 'Mancur Olson's analytical strategy is to use the rich materials of formal economic analysis to illumine a problem-area as wide as man-in-society. However, the strategy often tethers his argument painfully short' (Golembiewski 1966, p. 117). And 'what exists by logical construction is also uncomfortably-often treated as if its reality class was thereby established' (ibid., p. 118).

Marion Levy, writing in 1966 for the *American Journal of Sociology*, expresses the awe:

Read, sociologists! Mancur Olson's little book may prove subversive of the status quo of much *soi-disant* theory in sociology, anthropology, and the fresh behavioral science developments of political science. His analysis has far-reaching implications for our very best intentioned positions on democracy, small groups, stratification, and many positions that will shortly be the rage among us on education, poverty programs, and other of our applied responsibilities. Beyond his substantive contributions – if that exists – Olson's troublesome little book requires that we put up or shut up about science.
(Levy 1966, p. 218)

In the event, Robert Golombieski was proved categorically wrong and Marion Levy categorically correct about the scientific relevance of *The Logic of Collective Action*. Economists were proved neither right nor wrong, since they enunciated no opinion at all, at least in 1966 and 1967.

8 THE INSIGHTS OF WILLIAM A. NISKANEN

Prior to 1965, when Gordon Tullock published *The Politics of Bureaucracy*, the intellectual climate in all Western countries was extremely favorable to bureaucracy. Bureaucrats were widely perceived to serve as impartial, almost omniscient, servants of the public good. As such, they were accorded respect, if not deference, by a large majority of social scientists, including economists. That such a perception no longer holds, is due in no small part to the rational choice contributions of Gordon Tullock (1965b), Anthony Downs (1967) and William Niskanen (1971), whose particular book, *Bureaucracy and Representative Government*, I here single out as the founding contribution of the public choice approach.

Following Niskanen's 1971 definition, bureaus are organizations endowed with the following characteristics: (1) the owners and employees of these organizations do not appropriate any part of the difference between revenues and costs as personal income; (2) some part of the recurring revenues of the organization derives from other than the sale of output at a per unit rate. In this sense, bureaus are non-profit organizations that are financed, at least in part, by a periodic publicly financed appropriation or grant.

This classification includes most educational institutions, some hospitals, and many forms of social, charitable, and religious organizations as well as all government departments and independent agencies. It is, however, to government departments and independent agencies that the public choice analysis here strictly applies, and to the understanding of which Niskanen made his seminal 1971 contribution.

'Work expands so as to fill the time available for its completion' (Parkinson 1957). With those fateful words C. Northcote Parkinson launched the modern theory of bureaucracy and challenged at its roots the earlier Weberian theory (Weber 1947). Parkinson's law that staff increases in any government bureau at a fixed rate per annum irrespective of any variation in the amount of work (if any) to be done, coincided with a rising undercurrent of popular criticism of bureaucrats on grounds of laziness and insensitivity to citizens' preferences. Parkinson's writings also attracted the attention of a young Gordon Tullock as he made his way to the University of Virginia in 1958.

In 1965, Tullock's book (1965b) appeared as the first fruit of the rational choice approach to bureaucracy, with the utility-maximizing model applied for the first time to *Homo bureaucraticus*. However, Tullock's contribution is restricted to analyzing the internal procedures of a bureau, rather than to placing the government bureau within the wider marketplace of politics. For this reason, I do not consider it to be *the* founding contribution.

In 1967, Anthony Downs followed suit with another epic contribution, *Inside Bureaucracy*. As the title indicates, Downs follows up on Tullock's (1965b) initiative, by providing a more focused utility-maximizing model that explores the inner workings of government bureaus from a rational choice perspective. Once again, Downs centers attention on the internal organization of bureaucracy, while ignoring the external environment against which senior bureaucrats make decisions.

All of this changed in 1971 with the publication of William Niskanen's *Bureaucracy and Representative Government*. Niskanen was uniquely well qualified to write the book, having served as Director of Economics at the Ford Motor Company, as a Defense Analyst at the Rand Corporation, as the Director of Special Studies in the Office of the Secretary of Defense, and as the Director of the Program Analysis Division at the Institute of Defense Analysis as well as Professor of Economics at the universities of California at Berkeley and at Los Angeles.

Because government bureaucrats cannot legally appropriate any part of the difference between revenues and costs as personal income, Niskanen hypothesizes that self-seeking senior bureaucrats – whose utility functions include power, money income, job security, perquisites of office and patronage – will pursue large and growing budgets as a means of accessing some appropriate mix of those personal utilities.

Niskanen simplifies the model to one in which senior bureaucrats maximize the sizes of their budgets. They do so subject to the constraint that the bureau must be able to supply the total output expected by its sponsoring legislative committee, that is, that the total budget must be equal to, or greater than, the minimum expected cost of supplying this level of output. Each bureau is viewed as being in a bilateral monopoly relationship with its respective legislative oversight/appropriations committee. Because of asymmetrical information, in favor of the bureau, the bureau is presumed to behave in an equivalent manner to a price discriminating monopolist, whereas the legislative committee is presumed to be unable or unwilling to exploit any monopsony power.

The basic model is thus a one-period model of a pure, single-service bureau which is a competitive purchaser of factor inputs. The total potential budget available to the bureau during the budget period is represented by the following budget-output function:

$$B = aQ - bQ^2, 0 \leq Q < a/2b \tag{2.1}$$

The maximum total cost during the budget period, given the competitive purchase of factor inputs, is represented by the following cost-output function:

$$TC = cQ + dQ^2, 0 \leq Q \tag{2.2}$$

The constraint that the budget must be equal to or greater than the minimum total cost is represented as follows:

$$B \geq TC \tag{2.3}$$

The equilibrium level of the expected output of services at the approved budget level differs according to whether the budget constraint is or is not binding. In the case where the budget constraint is non-binding – Niskanen calls this the case of the *demand-constrained bureau* – the senior bureaucrats simply maximize budget size B by setting the first derivative of (1) equal to zero. This yields the upper-level outcome where $Q = a/2b$.

In the case where the budget constraint is binding – Niskanen calls this the case of the *'budget-constrained bureau'* – the senior bureaucrats solve for the equality of (1) and (2). This yields the lower level outcome where $Q = (a - c)/(b + d)$.

In both cases, even assuming that the budget-output function itself is not bloated by political considerations, the output of the bureau exceeds the social optimum (in the specific case of Niskanen's quadratic functions, it is double the optimum). In the case of the *demand-constrained* outcome, the bureau is also technically inefficient since it supplies its output at above minimum total cost. However, in the case of the *budget-constrained* outcome, there is no 'fat' in the bureau. It produces an excessive output, but at minimum total cost.

Niskanen focuses attention also on the nature of the review process applied to government bureaus under conditions of representative democracy. He underlines the relative power of legislative committees in the Congress of the United States. He further argues that the committees overseeing the provision of each service will be dominated by representatives of the group with the highest relative demand for it. The reason for this is that advocacy is concentrated and opposition is diluted. The review committees thus recommend programs that maximize their perception of the net benefits accruing to the median voter in the geographic region they represent, subject to approval by the entire legislature. In this manner the budget-output functions confronting government bureaus tend to be high-demand, by reference to the preferences of the median voter writ large.

By developing a comprehensive theory of bureaucracy and representative government, Niskanan (1971) opens up a fruitful positive research program in public choice. Ongoing research would challenge some of the central precepts of Niskanen's original model. Indeed, Niskanen, (1994, 2001) fully recognizes the relevance of the discretionary budget-maximization model. Nevertheless, its discussion has never since reverted to the pre-rational choice approaches of political science and sociology or to the philosopher-king approach of economists.

By 1971, the public choice research program was well into its stride. So I shall select just two book reviews of Niskanen's founding contribution by prominent scholars of the field. The first is by Gordon Tullock, writing in 1972 for *Public Choice*. Tullock is enthusiastic about the book: 'I would anticipate that most readers of *Public Choice* will also become partisans of the book after reading it . . . With any luck, this book will set off a burst of empirical testing. It is my opinion that most of the hypotheses offered will turn out to be true' (Tullock 1972, pp. 119, 124).

William Mitchell, writing in 1974 for the *American Political Science Review*, is enormously impressed:

> *Bureaucracy and Representative Government*, by William A. Niskanen, Jr., is one of the more impressive books I have read in recent years. There can be no question that it is the most significant work yet produced by an economist on the role of bureaucracy in the determination of the supply of public goods and services. I fully expect the book to attain the status of a classic in the study of bureaucracy and, more generally, public choice.
>
> (Mitchell 1974, p. 1775)

Although Mitchell rightly expresses reservations about the political feasibility of implementing some of Niskanen's proposed reforms of the central bureaucratic process, he applauds Niskanen's willingness to speak truth to power:

> One does not always expect 'wisdom' in more or less technical expositions, but somehow Niskanen provides readers and especially classroom teachers with some highly quotable observations. Two that appeal to me . . . are the claim that 'the most dangerous of all politicians is one who is indifferent to his own reelection or the future of his party' and the play on Adam Smith – 'There is an "invisible hand" in government but it is a helping hand for some, a barely acceptable appendage to many, and a mailed fist for others'.
>
> (Mitchell 1974, p. 1777)

Both Tullock and Mitchell were correct in their judgment that Niskanen's book would become a classic.

9 CONCLUSIONS

The seven contributions evaluated in this chapter together comprise the founding content of the public choice research program. Because the European public choice program (Duncan Black's Britain excluded) lagged significantly behind that in the United States, six of the seven contributions are from the United States. By rejecting both the philosopher-king approach of economic science and the behavioral approach of political science, in favor of the rational choice approach, the Founding Fathers revolutionized our understanding of the political process.

When one reads a classic text, one should always be careful to evaluate it, not just in terms of the fruits of subsequent research, but also within the context of its own time. Texts become known as classics because they decisively change scholarly thinking. To ignore that contribution, while squirreling around for analytical faults, is to pursue a bureaucratic rather than an entrepreneurial approach to the evolution of science.

One important consequence of these seven contributions has been a dampening of the enthusiasm with which social scientists proffer policy advice to governments. A second important consequence has been the dampening of enthusiasm for active government even among scholars who still nurse strongly adverse suspicions concerning the behavior of private markets.

The Founding Fathers of public choice, in some cases by design, and in other cases by accident, effectively leveled the playing field in the debate over the relative merits of governments and private markets. This playing field, by the mid-1950s, had become undeniably prejudiced in favor of an allegedly omniscient and impartial government.

In balancing this playing field, the Founding Fathers of public choice played an indispensable role in stimulating the Western democracies to abandon their mid-twentieth-century flirtation with socialism, thereby paving the way for a resurgence of market processes. The insights provided by the early public choice research program rank among the most important of all advances in economic science during the second half of the twentieth century, when measured in terms of their contribution to the wealth of nations and to the expansion of individual liberty.

NOTE

1. This chapter is a significantly revised version of an essay written by Charles K. Rowley entitled 'Public choice from the perspective of the history of thought', published in Volume I of *The Encyclopedia of Public Choice*, edited by Charles K. Rowley and Friedrich Schneider, Kluwer Academic Publishers 2004, pp. 201–13. Permission from Springer to use the original essay as the basis for this updated version is gratefully acknowledged.

3 Political science and public choice
Michael C. Munger[1]

Political science is the study of power, cooperation, and the uses (legitimate or otherwise) of force. Public choice is the application of a general model of rational individual choice and action to a variety of problems of groups choosing in non-market settings.

The two approaches overlap substantially in areas where (almost) everyone in a group agrees that it is desirable to capture the gains from exchange and cooperation for every individual. In this situation, public choice is squarely in the tradition of thinkers such as Aristotle, Hobbes, Montesquieu, Madison, and in some ways even Rousseau, all of whom saw institutions as means of capturing benefits for every individual.

But in other realms political science and public choice have sharply conflicting predictions. Some political philosophers founded their theorizing on an organic conception of the society, a 'state' or 'general will' with its own goals and to which the individual owes core obligations. Public choice lies on different foundations.[2] The central disagreement in premises can be stated in terms of two enlightenment philosophers, Locke and Rousseau. Locke saw private property as the basis of autonomy, and conceived of that autonomy as the first step toward justifying society (Locke [1689/1764] 2010). That is, society exists because it benefits the individual.

Rousseau saw society as the core theoretical concept, and then conceived both personal autonomy and property as derivative and contingent (Rousseau [1762] 2010). In this second view, individual claims to rights such as property or free speech must be founded on some demonstrable collective benefit. That is, individuals are given liberties and personal autonomy because they benefit the society.

The origins and key features of the Public Choice school have been described by Charles Rowley, in the previous chapter of the present volume, and so need not be repeated here. I will focus instead on the connections and contradictions between political science and public choice. As I noted above, the main overlaps occur in the study of constitutions; the major tensions appear between public choice theorists and normative political theorists, and between public choice theorists and behaviorists who take sociological or psychological approaches to understanding group choices in non-market settings.

In this chapter, I examine both of these overlaps, and their areas of disagreement. First, though, it is useful to give a very brief background on the main schools in political science.

1 POLITICAL SCIENCE

There are at least four different schools or approaches to the problem of understanding and predicting group choices in political science. They can be listed as follows, in something like chronological order of their greatest impacts:

- Political philosophy – Normative theory, with sub-branches such as classical, continental, and modern. In many ways the oldest branch of political science, and still an important part of many academic departments.
- Functional and institutional theory – A mix of positive and normative theory, ranging from purely working accounts of how government is constructed to accounts of institutional survival and performance. A key part of many undergraduate curricula in American politics and policy.
- Behaviorism – Originated at the University of Chicago and the University of Michigan in the 1950s. The perspective was revolutionary because, in an emphasis borrowed from sociology in Europe and the United States, behaviorists focused on measuring and then testing for associations using statistical techniques such as correlation or multiple regression. Behaviorism's epistemological foundation was frankly inductive, though theories of cognition, attitudes, and persuasion were imported from psychology starting in the early 1960s. The revolution caused turmoil in a number of major departments, because of the antagonism between traditionally trained political scientists and the new behaviorist 'revolutionaries,' who insisted that measurement and analysis of data were required features of any legitimate research program.
- Rational choice – In political science, originated at the University of Rochester, in the mid-1960s. Like behaviorism, rational choice theory self-consciously conceived of itself as revolutionary, an improvement over other approaches, including behaviorism. Rational choice theorists borrowed both premises and tools from economics, but quickly created models that, though recognizable to economists, were quite different in terms of both their subject matter and what they sought to explain. The core precept of rational choice theory is purposeful or goal-oriented behavior, subject to constraints. Further, though empirical testing has sometimes been held to be important, the central epistemological precepts of rational choice theory are deductive. That is, implications are derived from a set of mathematical propositions. More recently, rational choice models in political science have focused more on game theory rather than constrained optimization theory, with extensions beyond the standard 'Nash Equilibrium' solution concept becoming more common.

Of these four approaches, public choice shares important elements with rational choice and institutionalism. There is very little public choice behaviorism, though recent work in experimental and behavioral rational choice at the Workshop for Political Theory and Policy Analysis at the University of Indiana would clearly fit in that area.

As was noted above, I am restricting myself to the two areas where the overlap, or tension, between mainstream political science and public choice are greatest. The first is the study of constitutions; the second is the approach to understanding the motivations and actions of people in 'political' rather than 'market' contexts.

2 PUBLIC CHOICE AND CONSTITUTIONS

The Greek word that is usually translated into the English word 'constitution' is *politaea*. But the literal translation is not accurate. The meaning of *politaea* would better be expressed as 'the definition, obligations, and rights of a citizen in a community, or *polis*.' Some translators, in trying to capture the sense of the word, have claimed that the *politaea* is to *polis* as the soul is to a person, the fundamental spark that both organizes and animates the body.

As an illustration of the problem of defining *politaea*, even in Greek, Aristotle asks a useful question. When would we say that a nation or constitution is the same, at different points in time, and when would it be changed?

> [S]hall we say that while the race of inhabitants, as well as their place of abode, remain the same, the city is also the same, although the citizens are always dying and being born, as we call rivers and fountains the same, although the water is always flowing away and coming again? Or shall we say that the generations of men, like the rivers, are the same, but that the state changes? For, since the state is a partnership, and is a partnership of citizens in a constitution, when the form of government changes, and becomes different, then it may be supposed that the state is no longer the same... And if this is true it is evident that the *sameness of the state consists chiefly in the sameness of the constitution* [politaea], and it may be called or not called by the same name, whether the inhabitants are the same or entirely different.
> (Aristotle [n.d.] 2005, p. 38, emphasis added)

This passage is important because it takes an explicitly institutional perspective: human beings are more or less the same, and apparent differences across nations have mostly to do with rules and norms. More accurately, humans are like the river, which though constantly changing in small ways is the 'same' river from one day to the next, because it follows the same channel.

What this means is that institutions determine outcomes. A group of humans may behave very differently depending on the institutional setting in which they find themselves. But different groups of people in the same institutional setting will by and large act in the same ways. This claim may not be strictly true, since cultural or other group-specific differences may be important. But this is the essential public choice claim: *human beings can be assumed to have similar natures, and can be assumed to make the same sorts of motivated choices; differences in choices or actions can then be explained by the constraints and incentives created by the institutions around them.* For the public choice theorist, then, the distinction between 'private' and 'public' actions has only to do with the differences in context and incentives. Differences do not rest on any claim that people are self-interested at the grocery store and public-interested in the voting booth.

The first two identifiably 'public choice' works on constitutions were by James M. Buchanan. The first article was by Buchanan (1959) on his own. Near the end of it, Buchanan (ibid., p. 134) makes this claim:

> In developing the argument of this essay, I have assumed that the social group is composed of reasonable men, capable of recognizing what they want, of acting on this recognition, and of being convinced of their own advantage after reasonable discussion. Governmental action, at the important margins of decision, is assumed to arise when such individuals agree that certain tasks should be collectively performed. To this extent, my argument rests on some implicit

acceptance of a contract theory of the state. Since it is carried out only after general agreement, collective action is essentially voluntary action. State or governmental coercion enters only insofar as individuals, through collectively imposed rules[.] prevent themselves from acting as they would act in the absence of such rules.

This contractarian view connects with much of the literature in political science, ranging from Hobbes to Rousseau to Rawls. The claim is that reasonable people should be able to negotiate an agreement for their mutual benefit, an agreement that satisfies the strong form of the Pareto criterion. Later in the paper, he admits that the approach must have an 'as if' element, since in fact true unanimity is unlikely, precisely because some people are not reasonable at all. It is interesting to contemplate the connections this suggestion has with later work in political philosophy, particularly that of John Rawls (1971) and his legion of disciples.

The second, and better known, work was the book Buchanan co-authored with Gordon Tullock and published in 1962, *The Calculus of Consent*. In the 'Introduction,' Buchanan and Tullock make this claim:

> Any theory of collective choice must attempt to explain or to describe the means through which conflicting interests are reconciled. In a genuine sense, economic theory is also a theory of collective choice, and, as such, provides us with an explanation of how separate individual interests are reconciled through the mechanism of trade or exchange. Indeed, when individual interests are assumed to be identical, the main body of economic theory vanishes. If all men were equal in interest and in endowment, natural or artificial, there would be no organized economic activity to explain. Each man would be a Crusoe. Economic theory thus explains why men co-operate through trade: *They do so because they are different.*
>
> Political theorists, by contrast, do not seem to have considered fully the implications of individual differences for a theory of political decisions. Normally, the choice-making process has been conceived of as the means of arriving at some version of 'truth,' some rationalist absolute which remains to be discovered through reason or revelation, and which, once discovered, will attract all men to its support. *The conceptions of rationalist democracy have been based on the assumption that individual conflicts of interest will, and should, vanish once the electorate becomes fully informed.*
>
> (1962, p. 3; emphases added)

While much more could be said about the conceptions of constitutions in political science and public choice, this last paragraph from Buchanan and Tullock (1962) above goes a long way toward highlighting the similarities and differences. Constitutions are central in both political science and public choice. But in political science, for at least some scholars, constitutions are the embodiment of core truths, of resolutions of key questions of distribution and normative values. These values are then transmitted to the preferences and beliefs of the citizens, becoming a central part of their political consciousness. The 'truths' of the values in the constitution are organic, and transcendent, reflecting a universal conception of the just society.

The public choice approach reverses, at least conceptually, the direction of causation. In this view, citizens have a wide variety of different preferences and goals. They come to the constitutional bargain fully formed, and capable of making intelligent and reasonable choices on their own behalf. The function of the constitution, in this view, is to secure the gains from exchange that result from diversity and difference. The constitution is a contract that rewards cooperation and punishes defection. The prior unanimous consent of citizens, and not the 'truth' of values it contains, is what gives the constitution its moral force.

Of course, each of these conceptions is an indefensible caricature, made for the sake of contrast in this chapter. Even the most doctrinaire defender of organic justice would prefer to obtain unanimous consent to the social contract. And even the most positivistic public choice scholar recognizes the importance of the constitution as the repository of symbolic statements about values. Still, the difference is real and significant.[3]

3 *HOMO ECONOMICUS* AND *HOMO POLITICUS*

> Is it self-interest or public interest that predominates in public life? Does political man try primarily to fulfill personal desires and needs, or does he act with the intent to further what he believes to be best for society as a whole?
>
> (Lewin 1991, p. 1)

Public choice is a branch of rational choice theory, at least within political science. The definition of 'rational,' for present purposes, is this: exhibiting and acting on preferences that are instrumental, complete, and transitive. So people are instrumental in the sense that they are goal-oriented and seek certain objectives, though of course these objectives might involve the welfare of others. Preferences are complete in the sense that given any pair of alternatives A and B the chooser can state (and be subjectively correct) that A is better, B is better, or that they are equally well-liked. And preferences are transitive in the sense that if A is preferred to B, and B is preferred to C, then it cannot be true that C is preferred to A.

The question posed by Lewin (1991) is one that often is posed by political scientists who encounter public choice. There are at least two senses in which the critique of rational choice theory in public choice might be intended.

1. People act on different preferences in political life than in their lives as consumers. It makes sense to think people are 'rational' when they go to buy apples, but not when they vote for president. *Homo economicus* and *Homo politicus* are different people, because *Homo economicus* is selfish and *Homo politicus* is concerned for the whole society.
2. People may have only one set of fundamental preferences, but the institutional context for political choice is so different that models of economic choice are simply inapplicable. There is limited information about alternatives, alternatives are 'bundled' in ways that make individual selection cumbersome, and voters have only tiny effects on likely outcomes. Further, there is little feedback, or accurate information about the value of different choices. In private markets, profits provide a test of whether certain ideas are viable. But in politics there is no analogous feedback information. Therefore choices in politics are better explained by heuristics, schema, or crude ideologies without much cognitive integration.

It is important to note that these are fundamentally different objections. The first, that we bring different preferences, in effect making us different people in the voting booth and the grocery store, is decisive if it is correct. That objection is not consistent with the public choice approach; either the objection or the approach is incorrect, or at least not entirely correct.

We might elaborate the first objection a bit, to be fair to its proponents. The core of the claim is not necessarily that citizens do in fact natively have different private and public preferences, but rather that they should. Most importantly, *it is the job of the state to ensure that they do*. As Gunnell (2006) points out, the founding documents of the American Political Science Association (APSA 1903) were self-consciously 'Progressive.'

As John Dewey (1920, p. 194) put it, in *Reconstruction in Philosophy*:

> [T]he state has the responsibility for creating institutions under which individuals can effectively realize the potentialities that are theirs . . . [While] social arrangements, laws, institutions are made for man . . . [these arrangements] are not means for obtaining something for individuals, not even happiness. They are means of *creating* [emphasis in original] individuals. . . . Individuality in a social and moral sense is something to be wrought out.

For Progressives, citizens are naive and powerless, incapable of making good decisions for themselves. And elites and market actors are disproportionately powerful and conniving, capable of manipulating not just outcomes but also the information that citizens receive. The source of countervailing power is the state, whose twin tasks are to educate citizens and regulate markets. It would appear that voters would lack the ability to make good choices in the voting booth, just as they lack the ability to make good choices in the grocery store or on the used car lot. But Progressives are optimistic that voters will use different, more informed and more socially oriented preferences in their political lives.

Woodrow Wilson was perhaps the most famous advocate of this view. What is necessary is that the state wrest control from helpless and poorly informed private individuals, and begin to do what is right for the society. He called this 'socialism', though this conception is quite different from Marx's conception of socialism as state ownership of the means of production. Here is Wilson's description:

> Roundly described, socialism is a proposition that every community, by means of whatever forms of organization may be most effective for the purpose, see to it for itself that each one of its members finds the employment for which he is best suited and is rewarded according to his diligence and merit, all proper surroundings of moral influence being secured to him by the public authority. 'State socialism' is willing to act though state authority as it is at present organized. It proposes that all idea of a limitation of public authority by individual rights be put out of view, and that the State consider itself bound to stop only at what is unwise or futile in its universal superintendence alike of individual and of public interests. The thesis of the state socialist is, that no line can be drawn between private and public affairs which the State may not cross at will; that omnipotence of legislation is the first postulate of all just political theory.
>
> . . . Many affairs of life which were once easily to be handled by individuals have now become so entangled amongst the complexities of international trade relations, so confused by the multiplicity of news-voices, or so hoisted into the winds of speculation that only powerful combinations of wealth and influence can compass them. Corporations grow on every hand, and on every hand not only swallow and overawe individuals but also compete with governments. The contest is no longer between government and individuals; it is now between government and dangerous combinations and individuals. Here is a monstrously changed aspect of the social world. In face of such circumstances, must not government lay aside all timid scruple and boldly make itself an agency for social reform as well as for political control?
>
> (Wilson 2005, pp. 78–9)

Public choice might be accurately described as 'anti-Progressive.' The reason is not that progressive political scientists and public choice scholars have differing goals; in fact, the goals of both groups largely are parallel. The disagreement is a scientific one, about means. Public choice scholars question whether in fact individuals are quite so helpless. And most centrally, public choice questions whether humans who in every other walk of life are greedy and grasping can actually undergo the moral transubstantiation assumed by Progressive political scientists. Public choice theorists would never deny that market actors are greedy, of course. They would simply add that politicians are greedy, too, because both market actors and politicians are human.

The second objection, that citizens are not 'rational,' is very different. The political scientists who have made this objection, including Stokes (1963), Converse (1964), Conover and Feldman (1981), and Green and Shapiro (1996), have significant empirical evidence on their side. But here a distinction must be made: the political science objection to 'rational choice' theory is in fact a strong argument for public choice theory!

The reason is that students of 'non-market' decisions, including Mises (1944), Downs (1957), Buchanan and Tullock (1962), Olson (1965), Niskanen (1971), and others actually make the same critique, almost word for word. The point is that at its base this is not a critique of public choice theory at all, but a confirmation of the core public choice precept: non-market collective decisions suffer from a variety of 'failures' analogous to so-called 'market failures'. Among these are the weak incentives to acquire information, the perverse incentives to distort vote choice, the collective action problem in group organizations, and the information asymmetry and principal–agent difficulties in bureaucratic organizations. In short, if by 'rational' one means fully informed and motivated to achieve maximum results, then public choice theorists have long argued that political actors lack both information and incentives.

Remember, the public choice critique of government action is not that people in government are bad, or that voters are inherently and irreducibly ignorant. Public choice holds that people in government are essentially like everyone else. The problems with government arise as a (perhaps unavoidable) result of the incentive problems created by the organizational form itself. Voters are not fully informed, but rather are rationally ignorant, because information is a public good and single votes do not matter much in determining election results. Government officials are not necessarily lazy and corrupt, but rather are responding rationally to the incentives of the bureaucratic form of organization.

It is important to be clear about the disagreement, because it is often misunderstood, perhaps willfully. First, some political scientists assert that instrumental, egoistic self-interest is simply not a useful model of political and social action. This criticism requires an empirical resolution, based on whether in fact the predictions of the public choice model are accurate and useful. Second, a number of other political scientists have pointed out that citizens have different levels of information, different incentives for cooperation, and different incentives for accurate revelation of preferences in social or political settings, compared with market settings. This second critique, far from being a threat to the public choice approach, is in fact at the very heart of that approach.

For example, Anthony Downs (1957) argued that rational citizens would have little accurate information about candidates, have limited incentives to vote, and would rely on ideological heuristics and shortcuts to guide their political choices. To be clear, all

46   *The Elgar companion to public choice*

of these predictions were derived from the assumption that voters were rationally self-interested. Since this is precisely what rationality would imply, it is hard to see why Stokes, Converse, Conover, and others (all of whom published long after Downs wrote his book) see limited incentives to vote, inaccurate information about candidates, and the use of crude ideological cues as proof that political choices are somehow irrational.

For this reason, it is the first objection, that political choices should be modeled as having different motivations from private choices, that alone constitutes a valid challenge to public choice theory. And it has long been recognized that this is a valid challenge. Consider the argument made by Buchanan ([1979] 1999, p. 49):

> Most of the scholars who have been instrumental in developing public choice theory have themselves been trained initially as economists. There has been, therefore, a tendency for these scholars to bring with them models that have been found useful within economic theory, models that have been used to develop empirically testable and empirically corroborated hypotheses. These models embody the presumption that persons seek to maximize their own utilities, and that their own narrowly defined economic well-being is an important component of these utilities. At this point, however, I do not want to enter into either a defense or an attack on the usefulness of *Homo economicus*, either in economics or in any theory of politics. I would say only, as I have many times before, that the burden of proof rests with those who suggest wholly different models of man apply in the political and economic realms of behavior.

'Burden of proof' may be too strong a claim, as Buchanan himself notes in the next paragraph. But it is an important point of empirical and methodological contention, and the key difference between rational/public choice theory and most of the rest of political science.

To conclude this section, it is useful to summarize the argument, because it has been rather complex. First, public choice theory differs with at least some scholars in political science over the idea, central to public choice, that the same person who enters the grocery store enters the voting booth, or visits the offices of a politician or a bureaucrat. Second, public choice theory actually accepts the 'critique' often offered by other political scientists that citizens making political choices have imperfect information and perverse incentives to report their preferences accurately. Third, the disagreement between political scientists and public choice theorists then comes down to an empirical claim that the public choice approach produces accurate and useful predictions about the behavior of citizens in the context of non-market decisions.

The following section briefly contrasts some work in public choice with political science research on five different central topics. Whether the predictions of public choice are in fact 'accurate and useful' is left to the reader to decide.

4   FIVE TOPICS: POLITICAL SCIENCE AND PUBLIC CHOICE

I have tried to establish that 'rational choice theory' in political science and 'public choice theory' are distinct, or at least are not identical. Part of the reason is that public choice is also an important school of thought in economics, and to a lesser extent in sociology, following the work of former Public Choice Society president James Coleman.[4] And even within political science's rational choice theory, public choice is distinct because it makes three key assumptions: (1) methodological individualism; (2) citizens are no smarter or more public spirited than consumers; (3) politicians are no more principled than corporate chief executive officers (CEOs).

With this introduction, I will state and discuss briefly each of five significant research problems that have been taken up by political scientists and by public choice researchers, and highlight similarities and differences in approach in results. Here are the five problems:

1. The information problem.
2. The democratic coherence problem.
3. The constitutional problem of scope.
4. The collective action problem.
5. The rent-seeking problem.

4.1 The Information Problem

Though various authors have made contributions to the knowledge problem, Hayek (1945, p. 519, original emphasis) gives the clearest statement.

> What is the problem we wish to solve when we try to construct a rational economic order? On certain familiar assumptions the answer is simple enough. *If* we possess all the relevant information, *if* we can start out from a given system of preferences, and *if* we command complete knowledge of available means, the problem which remains is purely one of logic. That is, the answer to the question of what is the best use of the available means is implicit in our assumptions. The conditions which the solution of this optimum problem must satisfy have been fully worked out and can be stated best in mathematical form: put at their briefest, they are that the marginal rates of substitution between any two commodities or factors must be the same in all their different uses.

Political science has tended to overemphasize one aspect of this problem, the asymmetry of information between buyer and seller, at the expense of an understanding of the role of markets in producing information. Political scientists have tended to accept rather uncritically the 'market failure' formulation that an asymmetry of information can, and in fact must, be solved by government intervention. Consequently, in domains that include cost–benefit analysis, drug regulation, and consumer protection, political scientists have argued by and large that state action is necessary.

Public choice theorists, particularly those who take an Austrian view, would question this conclusion. Most economists would now concede that the 'socialist calculation debate' (Farrant 1996) between Hayek and Lange (among others) was won by Hayek. There is simply no way to generate information about scarcity of resources and 'highest valued use' without relying on market processes to generate information in the forms of prices and profit, and diverse private ownership to take advantage of the particular knowledge of time and place. For some reason, however, this concession about markets has not filtered through to problems of cost–benefit analysis or recommending (and implementing) Pigouvian taxes and subsidies to internalize externalities.

But public choice theorists would say that the same logic applies. As O'Driscoll (1980, p. 359) points out, those who advocate cost–benefit analysis are 'actually grappling with the calculation problem'. That is, the problem of the socialist calculation debate for markets is precisely the same problem that hampers government solutions to the externality problem or the private information problem in consumer protection. As Stringham (2001) argues at some length, the problem of trying to estimate values without prices is not just a hard problem, it is impossible.

Coase (1960) and Niskanen (1971) are quite explicit about the nature of the problem. For Coase, private bargaining elicits information about willingness to pay or willingness to avoid externalities and nuisances. Private bargaining fosters incentives for honest revelation, at least at the limits of the bargaining space. But bureaucratic agencies that solicit information about 'values' for externalities will always get inaccurate information, because of the incentives for manipulation of the information revealed.

Niskanen points out, in a classic of the public choice literature, that the information possessed by bureaucratic agencies remains private, inaccessible to the 'oversight committees' of Congress. Since, as Mises (1944) argued, bureaucratic agencies specialize in precisely those services for which a fee-for-service arrangement is impractical, the information problem will be especially severe. This has been a very important area for public choice theorists, and an important contribution of public choice has been to raise questions about the uncritical acceptance of the market failure framework.

4.2 The Democratic Coherence Problem

It appears that the problem of democratic coherence has been discovered and forgotten as many as four times. Because of public choice theory, it will not be forgotten again. The basic result is that if there are three choices, three choosers, and disagreement, then there is a possibility of a cycle, meaning that majority rule is not capable of generating a determinate choice. This result is often called 'Condorcet's Paradox', arising from the fact that though each of the individual choosers has a transitive preference ordering the group has an intransitive ordering, and is therefore unable to make a determinate decision except through chance or agenda control.

In a remarkable piece of scholarship, Iain McLean of Nuffeld College argues that:

> the theory has in fact been discovered four times and lost three times. Ramon Lull (c1235–1315) proposed a Condorcet method (should we now call it a Lull method?) of pairwise comparisons; Nicolas of Cusa (1401–1464), also called Nicolas Cusanus, proposed a Borda (Cusanus?) method. Both writers discuss the problem of manipulation, Cusanus extensively.
> (McLean 1990, p. 99)

McLean makes an interesting argument. Political scientists who trace the beginning of democracy to Ancient Greece are wrong, he claims, though the Greeks were indeed concerned with politics. But most choices made by Greeks, at least for selecting officials, were made by lot or by simple voting procedures, since votes on propositions in the Athenian assembly were always, by constitution of the assembly, binary, or 'up or down'. They seemed uninterested in what we now think of as 'social choice', or the problem of devising fair voting rules for complex collective decisions.

Nonetheless, the problem of choosing among three or more alternatives was well established by the Middle Ages, and McLean found evidence that people worried about the problem in a variety of medieval contexts, including choosing Holy Roman Emperors, Popes, and Doges of Venice, among others. Orders of monks and nuns had to 'constitute' themselves as groups by choosing decision rules, and a study of their writings reveals a clear understanding of the problem of indeterminacy.

These insights were utterly lost, however, until they were independently derived anew by the Marquis de Condorcet, whose insights were lost in turn until they were rediscovered by one of the founders of the public choice school, Duncan Black. In fact, Black (1958), in addition to producing one of the core founding documents in public choice, played an important part in setting off the rational choice revolution in political science. Another founder of public choice, William Riker later wrote *Liberalism Against Populism* (Riker 1982), uniting the positive and normative theories of collective choice.

Riker argued, as Buchanan had also claimed, that the idea that voting could uncover determinate truths should be considered suspect. But much of the work in political science has taken exactly that suspect perspective. That is, political scientists have tended to think of voting problems as epistemological, of discovering a truth that is real but hidden, rather than the rather more difficult problem that is the focus of public choice: what if there is no core, no central tendency in the decision problem? That would mean that majority rule is being used to solve a problem with no solution, or rather with infinitely many solutions, because cycles imply not that there are too few majorities but rather too many.

In this sense, Ramon Lull's first effort at describing the problem, written in Mallorca between 1273 and 1275, might better be called 'political science.' It was actually called, 'The Art of Finding the Truth' (quoted in McLean 1990). What that meant was that there must be a hidden truth, in the form of the best candidate or the right policy, waiting to be discovered or revealed through the selection of the proper rule or procedure. In public choice, because of Condorcet's paradox, generalized by Arrow's impossibility theorem (Arrow 1951), it is now believed that the entire approach that Riker called 'populism' may be fatally flawed.

The reason is that voting processes may not be reducible to epistemology, because we cannot assume that the 'best policy' or 'best candidate' actually exists, hidden from view but recognizable once the right choice is revealed by the right procedure. Instead, if there are three choices, and three choosers who disagree with one another, then there may be two larger problems, problems that raise serious questions about the very existence of democracies that rely on majority rule.

The first problem is manipulation. Any decision rule other than unanimity can be manipulated by someone who can influence the agenda or strategically misrepresent his or her preferences. This may mean that the outcome is imposed by the agenda controller as a kind of dictator, if people do not vote strategically. Or the outcome can be arbitrary and false, if people do vote strategically by fibbing about what they want as a way of avoiding what they hate. Either way, it is hard to call such results 'democratic', in the way that normative political theorists want to use the term.[5]

The second problem is instability. Even if the first problem can be solved in some way that seems fair, the fact is that a majority is opposed to every alternative. It is that simple: regardless of the voting procedure, a majority is opposed to every alternative. Consequently, in times of disagreement over fundamental issues it is not clear that the nation can survive the internal pressures for revolution. And if there is a revolt, and a different alternative is imposed somehow, then a majority may oppose that new government as well. Even without a revolt, the debate over institutions of choice will 'inherit' the underlying instability of preferences, as Riker (1980) points out so forcefully. The problem may not be that the government is unresponsive to what 'the people' want; instead, the problem may be that the people do not know what they want, because democracy is fundamentally incoherent.

4.3 The Problem of Constitutional Scope

> What should government be allowed to do? What is the appropriate sphere of political action? How large a share of national product should be available for political disposition? What sort of political decision-structures should be adopted at the constitutional stage? Under what conditions and to what extent should individuals be franchised?
>
> (Buchanan [1979] 1984, p. 15)

When I teach a class, I try to illustrate what I call 'Buchanan's paradox'. It is not formally a paradox, but rather a variation on Juvenal's satirical question about hiring a man to guard one's wife, *'Quis custodiet ipsos custodes?'* (Who will watch the watchman?)

The question is this: how can the domain of majority rule be constrained? How can majority rule be used to restrict what a majority can decide? The answer is that it cannot, in practical terms. The only way a majority can be constrained in a democracy is by non-democratic means, which is the source of the paradox.

The illustration I use in class is *Roe* v. *Wade* (1973), the landmark decision on abortion. I ask, 'How many of you students favor democracy?' All raise their hands, of course. Then I say, 'How many of you think *Roe* v. *Wade* should be overturned?' One or two souls raise a hand. Then I ask, 'What would happen if *Roe* v. *Wade* were overturned? *Democracy would break out!'*

All *Roe* v. *Wade*, and for that matter the First Amendment and other rules, do is to thwart the will of the majority. But if these were laws instead of court decisions or constitutional provisions then, by definition, they could not stand against a majority. Only because the protections are insulated from majority rule can they constrain the majority.

Political science and public choice have a general and deep disagreement over the nature of law, and voice. Political scientists often think of the legislature as the organ that gives voice to the will of the people. Public choice theorists, following Buchanan, are much more likely to think of the Constitution (in the United States, at least) as the 'will of the people', with the Congress open to the blandishments of interest groups and the influence of agenda control.

There is an interesting comparison between these two points of view. Many political scientists would be happy with the 'protections' of speech and religion offered by the French 'Declaration of the Rights of Man,' in Rights 10 and 11:

> 10. No one is to be disquieted because of his opinions, even religious, *provided their manifestation does not disturb the public order established by law*.
> 11. Free communication of ideas and opinions is one of the most precious of the rights of man. Consequently every citizen may speak, write, and print freely *subject to responsibility for the abuse of such liberty in the cases determined by law*.
>
> (Emphases added)

Contrast these with the First Amendment to the US Constitution:

1. *Congress shall make no law* respecting an establishment of religion, or prohibiting the free exercise thereof; or abridging the freedom of speech, or of the press; or the right of the people peaceably to assemble, and to petition the government for a redress of grievances.

(Emphases added)

The difference is stark. The French Declaration of the Rights of Man is designed to protect individuals from each other, and to instantiate the will of the majority in the 'law'. The law cannot possibly be an unjust restriction on liberty. In the US system, by contrast, it is Congress and the law itself that is the most likely danger. Much of political science is devoted to the study of means of enabling the majority; much of public choice is devoted to the study of how to disable the majority, and to protect the individual.

Many political scientists believe, with Woodrow Wilson and the Progressives, that the Constitution is a 'living document', one whose interpretation and core meanings should be interpreted loosely and in keeping with changing times. This view reflects an essential optimism about the motives and goals of political actors, in contrast with the goals of market participants, who are assumed to be greedy and selfish.

The public choice claim is different: constitutional scope must be strictly limited, and rules are permanent unless there is something like unanimous agreement on changing them. There is a difference between writing down the rules and then playing by those rules. Most citizens, in this view, might well fully support the rules when the constitution is being formulated, and then eagerly look for loopholes in those rules once the constitution is ratified. For this reason, the founders of the journal *Constitutional Political Economy*, one of whom was James Buchanan, selected as their logo a drawing of Odysseus bound to the mast.

4.4 The Collective Action Problem

Mancur Olson's landmark book (Olson 1965) has had an enormous impact in political science. But Olson himself was trained as an economist, and was a President of the Public Choice Society, 1972–74. Not surprisingly, perhaps, the study of collective action problems is one area where political science and public choice overlap a great deal, and where there has been considerable agreement on a variety of issues.

The two most studied collective action problems are interest group politics and turnout models in voting. The idea of 'interest groups' was fundamentally changed by Olson's work, because he pointed out that some groups formed successfully, but that others remained 'latent,' or unorganized and impotent, in spite of their potential for dominance. Olson's basic insight was this:

> An individual in a latent group . . . cannot make a noticeable contribution to any group effort, and since no one in the group will react if he makes no contribution, he has no incentive to contribute. Accordingly, large or 'latent' groups have no incentive to act to obtain a collective good because, however valuable the collective good might be to the group . . . , it does not offer the individual any incentive . . . to bear in any . . . way any of the costs of the necessary collective action.
>
> Only a separate and 'selective' incentive will stimulate a rational individual in a latent group to act in a group-oriented way. In such circumstances group action can be obtained only through an incentive that operates, not indiscriminately, like the collective good, upon the

group as a whole, but rather selectively toward the individuals in the group. The incentive must be 'selective' so that those who do not join the organization working for the group's interest, or in other ways contribute to the attainment of the group's interest, can be treated differently from those who do.

(Olson 1965, pp. 50–1)

Olson himself recognized the importance of the application of this reasoning to voting and turnout. And many political science articles have built on this insight, some of them writing from a public choice perspective and some writing from a psychological or sociological point of view.

It is important to point out, however, that Olson never claimed that it was impossible for large groups to form, but rather that it was more difficult and required some organizing principle or selective incentive. There are two works by John Aldrich (1993, 1995) that summarize the marriage of Olson's public choice approach and a political science-institutional approach. Aldrich (1993) reviews the contributions of the rational choice work on turnout extensively and critically, and points out areas of success and failure. Aldrich (1995) retells American political history from a 'collective action problem' perspective, pointing out that parties have played a role in solving the collective action problem nearly 150 years before public choice theorists got around to naming it.

4.5 Rent-seeking

If there is one area that is central to public choice theory, but almost absent from political science, even in its rational choice manifestations, it is the study of rent-seeking. The original work on rent-seeking was done by Tullock (1967). That work was extended (and named!) by Anne Krueger (1974). Later work by Charles Rowley et al. (1988), Robert Tollison (1982) and a diverse collection of other public choice scholars have worked on this subject. And yet it is nearly unknown in political science. Why?

The technical definition of *rent* is any return to investment, or effort, that exceeds the opportunity cost rate of return. So, Albert Pujols of the Anaheim Angels baseball team earns a huge rent, or salary premium, because of his scarce talents as a baseball player. He could earn a living as a banker, or a waiter, or something else. But it is unlikely that he could earn anything close to the $25 million per year he makes as a baseball player. Those rents encourage competition. And in most economic situations, that competition for profits produces benefits. But in politics, competition for those rents is often destructive.

The greater the rent, the greater the costs people are willing to incur to win it. When government hands out what appears to be free money, people are going to scramble to get some of it. But they are incurring costs as long as their costly activities improve their chances of winning the 'free' money. Robert Tollison defines *rent-seeking* this way: 'Rent seeking is the expenditure of scarce resources to capture an artificially created transfer' (Tollison 1982, p. 578).

Public choice theorists have argued that many federal and state give-away programs encourage wasteful rent-seeking. Political scientists have not been so sure. Who is right, as with so many of the topics discussed here, is really an empirical question. But it is important to point out that the public choice critique of government programs based on rent-seeking is not that government cannot give away money. Rather, rent-seeking theory argues that it is nearly impossible to give away money without wasting an amount equal or greater than the amount being given away, as long as the criteria for awarding the funds are competitive.

5 CONCLUSION

This chapter has explored the boundaries, overlaps, and antagonisms between two related but distinct fields, political science and public choice. In some ways, the public choice school is well established in political science, with most of the top departments well represented at the annual meetings and in the journal *Public Choice*.

In other ways, however, public choice has failed to be fully integrated into mainstream political science. There are two likely explanations for this. First, public choice is seen (rightly) as being closely related to economics, rather than being 'real' political science. Some public choice scholars are seen as interlopers, because the citations and jargon in their research may be unfamiliar to mainstream political scientists – and even to many economists!

The second reason is that much political science research is an extension of the Progressive project, the application of reason to the problem of improving government and finding collective solutions to problems. Public choice theorists, on the other hand, are very skeptical of Progressivism, both as an approach to social science and as a normative program.

NOTES

1. I acknowledge the helpful comments of Peter Boettke and David Schmidtz, though all remaining errors are mine.
2. An important source for the 'ur-texts' of public choice and political science is Mitchell (1988). See also Dow and Munger (1990) for an investigation of the impact of public choice on political science course syllabi.
3. Much of my discussion here results from many conversations on the topic with Geoffrey Brennan, and his 2008 paper, 'Homo Politicus and Homo Economicus: An Introduction.' (Brennan 2008a). For the importance of rhetoric and issues in the ratification debates for the US Constitution, see Riker (1990). The discussion of the importance of constitutions, and the parallels and differences between political science and public choice, is presented more extensively in Hinich and Munger (forthcoming).
4. For more on the contributions of James Coleman to public choice in sociology, see Sorensen and Spillerman (1993).
5. The literature on 'manipulation' is enormous in political science. One of the first general treatments was Riker (1962a). Specific mathematical results, general in their own way and published in economics, include Gibbard (1973) and Satterthwaite (1975). A still more general treatment is Duggan and Schwartz (2000).

PART II

THE FRAMEWORK OF GOVERNMENT

4 The origins of the state
Dennis C. Mueller

The plural form of the word *origin* used in the title of this chapter connotes the fact that all states did not come into existence in exactly the same way, and the important difference in the literature is between theoretical accounts of the origin of hypothetical states, which go back as far as Thomas Hobbes ([1651] 1939) and the other contractarians, and positive analyses of how actual states have arisen. Because the chapter stresses the contributions of public choice to this question, more emphasis is given to the theoretical literature, both philosophical and political, than one might find in an essay written by an historian or political anthropologist. Some discussion of contributions from these scientific disciplines also is included, however.

When discussing *the origins of the state* it is also important to identify the *kind* of state one has in mind. The bulk of the public choice literature focuses naturally enough on *democratic* states, since it is concerned with the public – citizens – making choices. Historically, the vast majority of states have been dictatorships, however, and even today roughly half of the world's population continues to live under dictatorships of one form or another. Thus, both democratic and dictatorial states are discussed.

The chapter is *descriptive* in two senses. It describes the contributions to the literature on the origins of the state, and it describes in broad brush the actual origins of some of the earliest and most important states. Although the author, as most likely the reader, prefers to live in a democracy than a dictatorship, the chapter does not stress the normative issues surrounding the different forms of government, nor does it offer any policy prescriptions.

We proceed as follows. Section 1 reviews some of the theoretical literature on the origins of the state. Two streams are identified, one emphasizing the role of the state in providing public goods and creating wealth, the other its role in redistributing wealth. Because so much of the public choice literature has concentrated on the study of democratic institutions, they receive separate treatment in Section 2. In Section 3 we address the question of whether democracy emerges as part of a long, slow process of evolution or suddenly following revolutions and wars. The fourth section examines the origins and characteristics of some actual states. Space allows us to describe only a few examples, and so the discussion can in no way be deemed as a test of the theories discussed in the first section. But the histories shed some light on the relevance of the different theories. Conclusions are drawn in the final section.

1 FROM ANARCHY TO STATE

1.1 The State as the Outcome of a Social Contract

Thomas Hobbes ([1651] 1939) famously described life in anarchy as 'a war of all against all', which produced lives that are 'solitary, poore, nasty, brutish and short'. To escape this dreadful situation, individuals banded together to write a social contract that ceded power to a single individual – the monarch. The monarch enjoyed a monopoly on violence and thus was able to end the war of all against all. The ensuing peace allowed individuals to accumulate wealth and enjoy more tranquil and longer lives. Thus, Hobbes can be viewed as presenting both an account of the origin of the state, and a defense of a monarchical (dictatorial) state. In modern terms, Hobbes's social contract also created a state, which provided a public good for its citizens – the peace and prosperity due to the elimination of anarchy.

Where Thomas Hobbes used the metaphor of a social contract to justify the institution of constitutional monarchy, John Locke ([1690] 1939) used it to undermine the notion that kings ruled by divine right. He was able to reach this conclusion, because his description of the state of nature was quite different from that of Hobbes.

> To understand political power aright, and derive it from its original, we must consider what state all men are naturally in, and that is a state of perfect freedom to order their actions and dispose of their possessions and persons as they see fit, within the bounds of the law of nature, without asking leave, or depending on the will of any other man.
> A state also of equality, wherein all the power and jurisdiction is reciprocal, no one having more than another; there being nothing more evident than that creatures of the same species and rank, promiscuously born to all the same advantages of nature, and the use of the same faculties, should also be equal one amongst another without subordination or subjection.
> (Locke [1690] 1939, I, §4, p. 404)

In Locke's state of nature an extreme form of equality existed across all individuals. Starting from such a state of equality, it would be difficult to argue that one individual should be master over all others. Hobbes's defense of monarchy relied on the extreme violence present in the state of nature. Locke's state of nature was quite different, however.

> Though this be a state of liberty, yet it is not a state of licence ... The state of nature has a law of nature to govern it, which obliges everyone; and reason, which is that law, teaches all mankind who will but consult it, that, being all equal and independent, no one might harm another in his life, health, liberty, or possessions.
> (Locke [1690] 1939, p. 405)

With everyone in the state of nature obeying laws of nature that forbid harming the 'life, health, liberty, or possessions' of others, a justification for abandoning the state of nature is less obvious in Locke than in Hobbes. Locke finesses this difficulty in the following way.

> Men being ... by nature all free, equal, and independent, no one can be put out of this estate, and subject to the political power of another, without his own consent, which is done by agreeing with other men to join and unite into a community for their comfortable, safe, and peaceable living one amongst another, in a secure enjoyment of their properties, and a greater security against any that are not of it. This any number of men may do, because it injures not the freedom of the rest; they are left as they were in the liberty of the state of nature. When any number of men have so consented to make one community or government, they are thereby presently incorporated, and make one body politic, wherein the majority have the right to act and conclude the rest.
> (Locke [1690] 1939, VIII, §95, p. 441)

Despite starting from a quite different description of the state of nature, Locke winds up seeing a unanimous agreement to leave it for similar reasons as Hobbes – to obtain 'comfortable, safe, and peaceable living'. Thus, both Hobbes and Locke can be seen as describing the state as a provider of certain public goods.

1.2 The State as Outcome of a Constitutional Contract

Buchanan and Tullock (1962) also see the state emerging from a unanimous contractual agreement, but unlike the implicit social contract of Hobbes and Locke, theirs is a *written* contract – a constitution. Their state is more akin to that of Locke than of Hobbes for it is to be democratic and provide all sorts of public goods, not just police protection. Since everyone benefits from the creation of the state, and its *raison d'être* is the provision of public goods, unanimity should be possible not only with respect to the constitutional contract, which creates the state, but also over the types and quantities of public goods supplied after the state is formed. Through this reasoning, Buchanan and Tullock joined Knut Wicksell ([1896] 1967) as champions of the use of the unanimity rule for making collective decisions.

The seemingly obvious attraction of the unanimity rule for making public goods decisions – moves from which all of the community benefit – raises the question of why so few democratic bodies use the unanimity rule. To explain this phenomenon, Buchanan and Tullock introduced the concept of *decision-making costs* – the time required to reach a collective decision under a given voting rule. As the majority required to reach a decision increases, more and more time is needed to obtain the required majority.

Were decision-making costs the only costs associated with voting, the optimal voting rule would be dictatorship – as one person can make a decision faster than two or three. A dictator is likely to favor him or herself over others, however, thus imposing an *external cost* on the rest of the community. The optimal voting rule minimizes the sum of these external costs of collective decisions and decision-making costs.[1]

When deriving the optimal voting rule, Buchanan and Tullock assumed that individuals were uncertain about the future – on a given issue they did not know whether they would be on the winning or losing side. At the constitutional stage, this uncertainty leads citizens to choose unanimously a required majority for making future decisions that is less than unanimity. The use of uncertainty by Buchanan and Tullock to describe the choice of a constitution resembles Rawls's (1971) use of uncertainty to describe how unanimity is reached over a social contract. The constitution of Buchanan and Tullock is a kind of Rawlsian social contract.

1.3 The Constitution as a Convention

Several writers have criticized the depiction of a constitution as a kind of social contract, arguing instead that it resembles more a set of *conventions* that coordinate individual actions on certain equilibriums for the various social dilemmas a community faces.[2] An often used example is the convention of driving on either the left or right side of a road. Either side will do, but it is essential that everyone coordinate on the same option. A convention facilitates such coordination.

Table 4.1 The battle of the sexes

		Jane Movies		Jane Basketball	
Dick	Movies	2	3	1	0
	Basketball	1	0	3	2

The idea of a constitution as a set of conventions is inspired by a game-theoretic approach to collective decision-making. A good example of the benefits from adopting a convention is illustrated by the battle of sexes game – a somewhat sexist depiction of a social dilemma by today's standards. Dick prefers going to a basketball game to going to the movies, while Jane would rather go to the movies. Both are happier going somewhere together than going their separate ways, however. The payoffs are depicted in Table 4.1 with Dick's payoff given first.

It is obvious that they should either go to the movies or to the basketball game together, but how to decide? One convention would be to flip a coin each time such a choice comes up. In the long run both Dick and Jane would get the same average payoffs of 2.5. Another convention producing the same outcome would be to take turns each week selecting the form of entertainment. Rational people should be able to hit on one of these sorts of conventions.

An example of a constitutional arrangement that looks like such a coordination device might be a rule in a community with two ethnic groups that the president always comes from one group, the vice president from the other, and every four years a new president is selected who is not a member of the outgoing president's group.

The country that perhaps best fits the constitution as a convention metaphor is Great Britain. It has no written constitution. Its political institutions have evolved slowly with authority gradually shifting from the king to Parliament, and from the House of Lords to the House of Commons. The convention of holding an election at least every five years is just that – a convention, and one which has, on occasion, as most recently during World War II, been violated.

The notion that the US Constitution is not a contract but rather a set of coordination devices is a bit harder to press. The Constitution is written down and it was signed by its writers. Many of its provisions are quite precise. As Winston Churchill did, Franklin Roosevelt would not have found it as easy to set aside the presidential election of 1944, because the world was at war.

1.4 The State as a Stationary Bandit

Mancur Olson (1993) put forward a theory of the origin of the state that involves neither contracts nor coordination around certain equilibrium strategies. Olson's initial conditions resemble those depicted in Akira Kurosawa's classic *Seven Samurai*, although Olson claims to be describing China and not Japan. Small villages of farmers are preyed upon by roving bandits who periodically steal most of their crops and livestock. The villagers have little incentive to invest and work hard to produce surpluses, since the surpluses will be taken away when the bandits arrive. Banditry is, therefore, not very lucrative, as there is little agriculture surplus to steal when the bandits make their raids. In Olson's version of the story, the villagers are not saved by seven samurai who fight off the bandits, but by a bandit who decides to settle down in the village and protect it from other bandits. For this, of course, he expects to be well paid. Both the now stationary bandit and the villagers are better off under the new arrangement. Indeed, the stationary bandit has an incentive to provide public goods like dams and bridges, if they increase the yield from agriculture, since he shares in the villagers' good fortune.

In Hobbes's state of anarchy, each individual is at war with all other individuals, and thus they all voluntarily choose to join a contract and select a person to rule over them and provide order. Olson also describes a sort of anarchy in which groups of bandits are at war with groups of farmers. Olson's description comes closer to what we know about human societies that function without formal political institutions. Within a given tribe individuals are not at war with one another. They cooperate in hunting and warfare and punish those who fail to cooperate.[3] Most fighting takes place *between* tribes, not within them. Olson's state arises not because a group of individuals chooses a leader to protect them, but because an outsider imposes his leadership on the group.[4] No contract, explicit or implicit, is involved. The end result is similar in both scenarios, however. A group of people lives at peace protected by a dictator. The protection provided by the dictator is a form of public good, which improves the welfare of the governed. In Olson's telling of the story, the dictator provides additional public goods so long as they lead to greater agricultural surpluses in which he can share.

2 THE ORIGINS OF DEMOCRATIC STATES

Public choice arose as an attempt to apply the tools of economics to the study of politics. As the original contributors were based largely in the United States and the United Kingdom, it was natural for them to concentrate on explaining how *democratic* states function. Only after the discipline was fairly well established did public choice scholars turn their attention to the study of dictatorship. Given this concentration on democracy in the public choice literature, a closer look at the origins of *democratic* states is warranted.

Much of the literature on this topic falls in the area of political science and can be traced back to the classic contribution of Seymour M. Lipset (1959). Starting from the observation that democracy is most frequently observed in high-income countries, Lipset advanced the argument that democracy was an outgrowth of the process of *modernization* – modernization being the shift of economic activity from farming to manufacturing, the shift of population from rural to urban areas, and rising incomes and education levels. Several subsequent contributions to this topic have added possible determinants of the adoption of democratic institutions to this list.[5]

Acemoglu and Robinson (2006) criticize this literature for lacking a theoretical foundation. They claim that all of the empirical regularities that have been observed are mere correlations and do not constitute or necessarily reveal underlying causal relationships. They offer a theoretical structure for explaining shifts from democracy to dictatorship, from dictatorship to democracy, oscillations between the two, and stable democracies or dictatorships. Their theories rest on the premise that politics revolves around questions of income distribution. Political change or its absence is a consequence of successful or unsuccessful attempts to alter the distribution of income.

In the simplest version of their theory there are only two groups in a society – a relatively small, rich elite and a much larger class of poor people. If we assume that the starting point is a dictatorship run by the rich elite for its benefit, then the first issue is to determine the conditions under which this country will shift from dictatorship to democracy. When will this shift be permanent? Suppose first that income is distributed relatively evenly in the society – the rich are not much wealthier than the poor. In this situation, there is little incentive for the poor to mount a revolution to overthrow the regime and redistribute wealth, because there is little to redistribute and revolutions are costly.

As income asymmetry increases the gains to the poor from a revolution and at some point outweigh the costs of a revolution. At this point one of two outcomes is likely – the poor revolt successfully or unsuccessfully, or the rich avert a revolution by introducing democratic institutions, which allow the poor to redistribute some of the elite's wealth to themselves. A third possibility would be for the elite to retain dictatorial power and simply voluntarily redistribute enough to avoid a revolt. Acemoglu and Robinson argue, however, that such a maneuver may not be acceptable to the poor, because they know that the rich elite could always reverse the redistribution at some time in the future when the threat of revolution subsides. Introducing democratic institutions represents a *credible commitment* by the rich to lasting redistribution, since political institutions are costly to change.

With an extremely large disparity of wealth, the costs to the rich from introducing democracy may be so large that they choose to repress the poor and thwart any attempts at revolution. Thus, whether and when a country adopts democratic institutions depends on two factors – the inequality of the income distribution and the costs to the rich of repression. Acemoglu and Robinson give Singapore as an example of a country where income inequality is so low that a revolution by the poor is unattractive and a dictatorship by the relatively rich survives. Great Britain is cited as a case of somewhat greater inequality, but high costs of repression, so that democracy appears and survives in it. With significant income inequality and low costs of repression, a repressive dictatorship is expected to survive – exemplified by South Africa until 1994, when the dictatorship of the whites granted suffrage to the large black population in the country. Between Britain and South Africa in terms of income inequality and costs of repression falls Argentina, which oscillated between dictatorship and democracy over much of the twentieth century.

Acemoglu and Robinson extend this simple model in several dimensions – too many to cover here. To mention only one, they introduce in Chapter 8 a third class, a middle class. If the middle class as well as the poor are exploited by the elite, the gains from revolution increase and a shift to democracy becomes more likely. The model of politics that Acemoglu and Robinson employ assumes a single dimensional policy issue space, the amount of redistribution being the only issue to decide. The median voter is thus assumed to be decisive in a majoritarian democracy. If the median voter is a member of the middle class, she will demand less redistribution than if she were in the poor class and this may stabilize democratic institutions, once established, by reducing the gains to the elite from mounting a coup and subverting democracy.

Like all relatively simple theories put forward to explain complex phenomena, that of Acemoglu and Robinson abstracts from many of the factors that others have deemed important in explaining democratization. They make much of the beauty of Occam's razor. Nevertheless, by laying out a solid framework for studying both dictatorship and democracy, they have brought this important topic squarely into the domain of public choice and rational actor models, but not, it should be remarked, by acknowledging the contributions of their intellectual predecessors.

The most ambitious empirical attempt to identify the determinants of dictatorship and democracy is by Przeworski et al. (2000). Using data for a large sample of countries over the period 1950–90, they test several hypotheses about why countries shift from dictatorship to democracy, and from democracy to dictatorship. They reject the modernization hypothesis predicting that rising national income leads to shifts from dictatorship to democracy. High levels of income do seem to prevent countries, which have become democracies, from slipping back into dictatorship. This latter finding explains why stable democracy is associated with high incomes. Their limited data on income inequality nevertheless failed to reveal a strong relationship between inequality and shifts to or away from democracy.

3 THE RISE OF DEMOCRACY: BIG BANG REVOLUTION OR GRADUAL EVOLUTION?

Democracy often appears to arise suddenly after some cataclysmic event like defeat in a war. Thus, democracy first appears in Japan at the end of World War II, and reappears in Italy and Germany after the same event. In the model of Acemoglu and Robinson, shifts from democracy to dictatorship or from dictatorship to democracy are expected to be more frequent during an economic crisis, since the costs of a revolution or coup are lower.[6] Democracy emerged in Europe over the nineteenth century in part as a response of the reigning elites to the revolutions of 1848 and other uprisings, and in some cases to avoid the threat of revolution.

Roger Congleton (2011), on the other hand, sees a much more gradual shift to democracy over the previous several centuries as kings slowly ceded more and more power to elected assemblies – evolution and not revolution.[7] Great Britain, perhaps, best exemplifies this gradual process, with the first transfer of power away from the king occurring with the signing of the Magna Carta in 1215, a constitutional contract of sorts. In Congleton's interpretation of history the Glorious Revolution at the end of the seventeenth century is not so much a revolution as another step in the evolutionary shift from the dictatorship of the king to representative government.[8]

Whether one sees revolutions as seismic changes at certain junctures of history, or evolution and gradual change lies partly in the eye of the beholder. Both North and Weingast (1989) and Steven Pincus (2009), for example, see the Glorious Revolution as a much more significant event in British history than does Congleton. For some the American Revolution and the Constitution that followed it was a momentous event in the rise of democracy.[9] For Congleton, the US Constitution largely created institutions at the federal level that already existed in the colonies. As so often is the case, truth probably lies somewhere between these polar views. One's view on this issue also depends on where one looks for empirical verification. The collapse of communism in East Europe and the Soviet Union created several democracies with one 'big bang'. Shifts to democracy in Latin America have often occurred following revolutions or defeats in war and are heavily cited by Acemoglu and Robinson in support of their thesis. Europe, and particularly Britain and Sweden, come closer to Congleton's interpretation of history.

4 EXAMPLES OF NEW STATES

In this section, I briefly describe the origins of some actual states. The objective is not to *test* the various theories described in the previous sections, but to illustrate some of the salient features of the origins of states. The choice of examples is highly selective, and draws on my book *Reason, Religion, and Democracy* (Mueller 2009). Those wishing more examples and fuller treatment should consult the source upon which I relied heavily, S.E. Finer's (1997) masterful, three-volume treatise.

4.1 Sumer

In the sixth millennium, BCE, a stocky, round-headed people lived in the highlands above the Fertile Crescent. When the crops of these 'Sumerians' depleted the soil in one area, they moved to a different one. In the fifth or fourth millennium, they migrated into Mesopotamia, 'the land between the two rivers' (the Tigris and Euphrates). Occasional flooding deposited silt on the plains between the rivers, replenished the soil, and eliminated the necessity of migrating in search of more fertile locations. So the Sumerians settled in Mesopotamia.

Mesopotamia had too much water when the floods came, and too little during the dry season – perfect conditions for irrigation farming, and the Sumerians developed an elaborate solution, the first of its kind in the world. An irrigation system is a form of public good, but it could be provided only by coordinating the community's efforts and resources. It is a primary candidate for being *the* public good, which led to the creation of the Sumerian city-state.

Political anthropologists differ as to how this innovation came about. One group envisages an egalitarian, partially democratic tribal system collectively agreeing to introduce irrigation techniques. This interpretation nicely fits the kind of democratic leap from anarchy found in the contractarian literature. The second interpretation assumes a hierarchically structured society with a priest class in control of cereal production. Among its priestly functions was the study of the stars (the Sumerians invented the signs of the zodiac). The priests used their knowledge of the stars to interpret and predict events on earth. The ideas underlying the introduction of irrigation would most likely have arisen among this professional class of heaven-gazers, and they commanded that the innovation be implemented, supervised its introduction, and claimed the agricultural surplus it generated. Any champion of democracy, contractarian or otherwise, would hope that the first interpretation of the origin of the Sumerian state is the correct one.

Unfortunately, Finer claims that 'It is not supported by the slightest shred of evidence,' and makes a very convincing case for the second interpretation.[10]

In the Sumerian city-states, bureaucracy was highly developed and controlled nearly every aspect of economic and social life. The entire society shared a set of morals, beliefs, and expectations that were determined by its religion, as interpreted by the priests. The state was an absolute monarchy with religion for an ideology. The king was god's representative on earth, and immediately beneath him were the priests. Together they ran the state with the help of the large bureaucracy and a small number of scribes. The role of the masses was to serve god, which in effect meant to serve the king, whose power was absolute.

The Sumerians introduced an impressive array of innovations – an elaborate writing system, irrigation, the plow, wheeled carts, draft animals, brass and copper smelting, the potter's wheel, the sail boat, astronomy and, arguably the most important of all, the state. Prior to the Sumerians, there are no known peoples who organized their lives using hierarchical structures, which today can be readily recognized as constituting a nation-state.[11] The quality of the last invention is attested to by the longevity of the Sumerian city-state – anywhere from 800 to 1500 years depending on choice of starting and ending points (Finer 1997, pp. 99, 127–8). Finer (1997, p. 29) attributes longevity in a state to a congruence between a society's belief system and its social and political structure. In the Sumerian city-state, this congruence was as close as possible. 'In no other antique society did religion occupy such a prominent position ... the religious ideas promoted by the Sumerians played an extraordinary part in the public and private life of the Mesopotamians, modelling their institutions, colouring their works of art and literature, pervading every form of activity' (Roux 1980, p. 91, as quoted in Finer 1997, p. 115). Moreover, the Sumerian city-state's disappearance came about not because of some internal breakdown, but because of the development of superior military power by neighboring states. The salient characteristics of the Sumerian city-state can be found in Egypt, Persia, and the other major nations of the ancient world – monarchy, absolutism, a primary role for religion.

Thus, in this first of all states, we find evidence of the provision of an important public good at its founding, but also of the importance of distributional issues and the dominance of the mass of society by a small, educated elite.

4.2 China

The Chinese state was formed in much the same way as the Sumerian state – by tribes migrating into a river valley, in this case that of the Yellow River. Although legends tell of great kings in China before the Shang kingdom (1766–1122; all dates in this section are BCE), it was this one that invented writing and, thus, the history of the Chinese state begins with it. Cities also appeared during the Shang kingdom as did other inventions seen in the Sumerian city-state, such as bronze casting and the chariot.

Whether China was ever overrun by roving bandits to the extent suggested by Olson's essay is difficult to say. But periods of warfare among its various kings and warlords were frequent in its early history. During one such period, the scholar Confucius (551–479) wrote several texts proffering advice as to how to end these conflicts. His main message was that the warring states had to reclaim or rediscover the wisdom of an earlier, idolized era. Confucius saw mankind divided into 'superior' and 'mean' men, with superior men following what was essentially the 'golden rule' and cooperating with other men (Finer 1997, pp. 458–9). Men achieve their humanity through education. The family is the supreme institution of society with a son owing respect to his father; a wife to her husband; a younger brother to his older brother; and so on. Good government arises from having good rulers, not good laws.

A second reaction to recurring anarchy in China was *legalism*. Legalism was entirely antithetical to Confucianism. It derived no wisdom from the past and ridiculed filial duties. Legalists were

> forward-looking, practical and ruthless . . . [They] viewed the mass of humanity as irrevocably stupid and base and susceptible only to the carrot and the stick. Theirs is a philosophy of power vested in an absolute monarch who rules by severe punishments, through iron codes of law which apply to high and low alike, without any exceptions save the ruler himself, since he alone makes the law and therefore only he is dispensed from it.
>
> (Finer 1997, pp. 466–7)

The legalists' advice was put into practice during the Ch'in state (361–206) from which China derives its name. Of more interest is the Han Empire, which followed it and lasted more than four centuries, because 'the Han Empire . . . set the pattern for all future Chinese government up to and including the present day' (Finer 1997, p. 524). It established a large bureaucracy to administer a highly centralized state. Reflecting the influence of Confucianism, this bureaucracy was filled with educated scholars. However, the empire also had a rigid and harsh legal code that reflected the influence of legalism and functioned as a two-stratum state. At the top were educated bureaucrats, a kind of aristocracy of the intelligentsia, and at the bottom illiterate masses deferring to those of rank and obeying the legal code. Each person knew her position in society, to whom she owed obedience, and who owed obedience to her. Thus, in its social and political structure the Chinese state, of which the Han Empire was the embodiment, can be classified as an 'organic state' in which individuals qua individuals do not appear. In the Chinese state, 'the prevalent belief systems, and the social structure all came to support one another as never since the high days of Mesopotamian and Egyptian government and emphatically as never in the West' (Finer 1997, p. 442). This mutual reinforcement of ideology and social and political structures explains the great longevity of the Chinese state, but also the total lack of democracy during its long history.

China, throughout its history, resembled Sumer in having a large, uneducated population ruled by a relatively small educated elite. It differed primarily in the absence of religion as an ideology inducing loyalty to the ruler and the state. Confucianism and to some extent legalism filled this void. The primary public good provided by the Chinese state to its subjects was social order – protection from the wars and strife that characterized earlier ages.

4.3 Ancient Greece

As with other ancient civilizations, Greek society was formed by migrating bands that probably arrived in the Balkan Peninsula around 2000 BCE.[12] The area occupied by the Greeks consisted of many islands, and even the mainland was broken into pockets of inhabitable, arable land by its mountains, water, and rocky terrain. Thus, the physical characteristics of the area occupied by the Greeks favored the development of small, isolated, fairly autonomous communities. These geographic differences help explain why some city-states like Athens became democracies and others like Sparta remained autocracies. The dry, hilly, rocky terrain around Athens favored growing olives. Yields from olive trees vary greatly depending on labor inputs. Thus, there were high payoffs in Athens to providing farmers with strong incentives for putting effort into tending olive trees. Such efforts could be forthcoming only if individual farmers had rights to specific pieces of property and the products of their efforts. Moreover, because of the labor intensity of olive production and the dispersal of olive groves, it was difficult for the aristocratic elite to monitor the efforts of olive growers and skim off any economic surplus. Since the mass of citizens was needed to fight in time of war, the aristocracy also gained by granting voting rights to the rest of the society in exchange for their service in the army and navy. Thus, property rights and the suffrage of citizen-farmers emerged in Athens in part because of the physical characteristics of the land and the type of economic activity that they fostered (see Fleck and Hanssen 2006 and Tridimas 2010).

The appearance of democracy in Ancient Athens might appear to contradict the Acemoglu and Robinson thesis that democracy will not emerge when there is a relatively equal distribution of income and the costs of revolution are high. Its emergence can be explained by adding the public good benefits to both the aristocracy and the remaining population from enlisting everyone into the defense of the state. The costs of revolution also do not appear to have been particularly great. Some blood was shed during the transition to democracy, but not much in comparison to later 'revolutions'.[13]

In contrast to the area around Athens, the fertile plains surrounding Sparta lent themselves to large grain farms worked by disenfranchised serfs whose efforts could easily be monitored. Sparta thus remained an oligarchy run by rich owners of large estates, whereas Athens resembled more closely a community of yeomen farmers. The more egalitarian distribution of income that emerged in Athens because of its terrain and mode of agricultural production is consistent with Boix's (2003) thesis that democracy emerges only in communities with fairly egalitarian distributions of wealth.

One cannot help but be in awe of the Greeks' many contributions to architecture, astronomy, mathematics, philosophy, science, sculpture, the arts in general, and theater. All of these came about because for the first time in human history man's mind was freed from superstition to follow whatever path it chose. Of all the Greek gifts to mankind, perhaps the most important was the demonstration of the human potential for rational thought, the power of *reason*. It was because the Greeks were able to engage in rational thought and discourse that they became the first democratic state.

The first major step toward democracy in Greece was Solon's freeing of the serfs in 594. This action turned Attica into a land of small landholders, and set the stage for the development of democracy. Once they became landowners, the citizens of Athens had something to guard against foreign invasion. Each citizen knew that the defense of Athens and his property depended on his willingness to defend it, and thus a link between citizenship and serving in the military developed with Solon's reforms. One other of Solon's contributions was to create a council of 400 to prepare business for the popular assembly, a reform that Hornblower (1992, pp. 4–5) identifies as the first political innovation in European history.

The Athenian city-state of the fifth century is not only the first example of a true democracy, but it is the first and to this day one of the few examples of a set of political institutions consciously designed and created to achieve a democratic objective. During the seventh and sixth centuries, Athens was ruled in turn by various tyrants and aristocratic oligarchies. As wealth accumulated, different factions formed among the aristocracy based on tribal lineage, geographic location, or occupation. These factions engaged in the kinds of distributional struggles that James Madison ([1788] 1961) described so well in *Federalist 10*. Today we would call these factions *rent-seeking coalitions*. Toward the end of the sixth century, Cleisthenes – himself an aristocrat – put an end to the divisive rent seeking 'by inventing a preposterous paper-constitution which in fact worked perfectly' (Kitto 1957, p. 106).

The genius in Cleisthenes' design was to break up the existing coalitions into 10 divisions (*phylae*) that cut across the previous ethnic, economic, and geographic lines. In turn, each *phyle* was broken into smaller units called *deme*. Thus, Cleisthenes' constitution introduced a decentralized structure, which gave each citizen a strong incentive to participate in the democratic process. Moreover, because membership in a *phyle* cut across ethnic, class, economic, and geographic lines, each citizen's welfare was tied to that of the greater community rather than to a narrowly defined faction or interest group. 'A new Kleisthenic tribe was not a bunch of docile voters in the pocket of a great family; instead, it was a chimera, made up of bits from the three regional parts of Attica, and so much harder to bribe or coerce. Its members trained as soldiers together, they might act together as a pressure group in the law courts, and they served together as "tribe in *prytany*" for an annual month of presidency over the assembly' (Hornblower 1992, p. 9). Thus, Cleisthenes' constitution changed individual incentives away from zero-sum redistributions of wealth to positive sum improvements in the general welfare (Pagden 2008, pp. 17–18).

Under Cleisthenes' constitution, the assembly of citizens was the main decision-making body, with the council playing an agenda-setting role. The council at that time had 500 members selected by lot, 50 from each of the 10 *phylae* into which the polity was divided. The Council of Five Hundred was the key to Cleisthenes' reforms. It:

> was a way of involving all of Attica in decision-making, not just the city population which found it easiest to attend political meetings. The words for the regional equality thus produced was [sic] *isegoria* or 'equality of speaking' (in the council, that is). That word, and perhaps *demokratia* (quite literally, 'people-power'), are the only slogans we can associate with Kleithenes himself.
>
> (Hornblower 1992, p. 8)

Athens was an important development in the evolution of the state, because it was the first truly democratic one. It also illustrated that good institutions could be created by *design*. Finer (1997, pp. 367–8) summarized its accomplishments as follows: 'This [the Greek] polity is extraordinary. It was a miracle of ingenuity and design, one of the most successful, perhaps the most successful, of political artefacts in the history of government.' It is difficult not to share his judgment.

In Ancient Athens we find the provision of public goods to be an important explanation for the existence of the state and its democratic nature. The primary public goods provided were protection against invaders and security of property rights that led to prosperity through trade and commerce in times of peace. Distributional issues were again important, and support for the theses of Boix (2003) and Acemoglu and Robinson (2006) is also evidenced by the willingness of the aristocracy to cede power to the rest of the citizens and establish a democracy.

4.4 The United States

With the appearance of the Greek city state, the two polar forms of government – dictatorship and democracy – were established. Pagden (2008) characterizes world history from the conflict between the Greeks and the Persians in fifth century BCE onward as a clash between the despotic East and the enlightened West. Examples of democratic states in the East – defined as roughly the area from the Eastern shores of the Mediterranean to the western Pacific – are certainly difficult to identify until the installation of democratic institutions in Japan, with the helping hand of the occupying Americans, after World War II.[14] With the decline of the city-state in Greece, however, democracy also disappeared in the West. The 'Republic' of Rome from 509 to 82 BCE was more of an oligarchy controlled by the aristocracy than a republican form of government as we think of it today. In 82 BCE General Sulla effectively established a dictatorship, which lasted until the collapse of the Empire. Democracy, as we think of it today, only began to reappear in the West during the Renaissance with the establishment of the city-states in Italy. For our last example, therefore, we shall fast forward to the end of the eighteenth century and the founding of the American Republic.

Finer (1997, pp. 1501–16) identifies six major inventions in the US Constitution and constitutional process: a constitutional convention, a written constitution, a bill of rights, the separation of powers, judicial review, and federalism. All had been thought of before, however, and in some cases had even been implemented. The Levelers, for example, had proposed a written constitution for England as early as 1647 (Wootton 1990). American colonies were often formed by compacts signed before the colonists left Europe, like the famous Mayflower Compact. The idea of a separation of powers appears in both Locke and Montesquieu, and the Iroquois Indians of Northeast America were organized as a federation long before the convention met in Philadelphia. Yet, no country had ever implemented these institutions on the scale that the United States did and shown that they could work as well as they have.

Henry Steele Commager (1978) claimed that Europe created the Enlightenment but did not succeed in implementing its ideas, whereas the United States did so. To the extent that replacing monarchy with democracy was an important part of the Enlightenment agenda, this certainly was the case. European monarchies did implement many reforms in the eighteenth century, however, although often in a piecemeal fashion. The US Constitution, with its Bill of Rights, succeeded with one fell swoop in creating a republican form of government with a constrained executive, religious tolerance, free speech, and other liberties that the Enlightenment's *philosophes* sought (Finer 1997, p. 1487). In this respect, the American Revolution and US Constitution did transplant and implement the *program* of the Enlightenment – with one very important exception. The abolition of slavery was also a central component of Enlightenment thought. The US Constitution not only failed to guarantee this particular freedom, it actually guaranteed the perpetuation of this 'peculiar institution'. This failure, coupled with the ambiguous status of a state's right to secede from the Union, led to a bloody Civil War less than a century after the Union was formed, a fact that cannot be overlooked when assessing the success of America's constitutional experiment.

Nevertheless, with the founding of the American Republic, full-fledged democracy, although quite different in form from that introduced by the Greeks, returned to the West. Distributional issues might be invoked as a cause of the American Revolution, as the colonists were certainly unhappy with the restrictions on their trade imposed by England and the taxes that they paid to it. But the kind of 'class struggle' between a rich elite and the mass of poor people that figures in the theory of Acemoglu and Robinson (2006) is difficult to identify in the American case. The emergence of democracy, particularly in New England, *prior* to the Revolution does fit the theories of Boix (2003) and Acemoglu and Robinson (2006) rather nicely, however. The terrain and harsh New England climate favored small, labor-intensive farms as did the terrain in Ancient Athens. The large plantations manned by slave labor in the South resemble more closely the agriculture of Sparta and Rome. Given that democratic institutions were already well established in the colonies at the time of the Revolution, it is difficult to imagine Enlightenment thinkers like Madison and Jefferson opting for a New World monarchy, although some of the founding fathers, such as Alexander Hamilton, did favor an American version of monarchy.

5   CONCLUSIONS

Contractarian accounts of the origin of the state as in Buchanan and Tullock (1962) must be regarded as *normative* theories. The state *ought* to come into existence to advance the collective interests of the people who will become its citizens. The state should benefit all citizens and they will unanimously agree on its creation.

This view of the origin of the state contrasts dramatically with what we might call *positive* theories of how states actually came into existence. Here the emphasis is on redistribution as in Acemoglu and Robinson (2006), or on *bargaining* over distributional questions as in Stefan Voigt (1999).

Both the provision of public goods *and* distributional conflict have figured prominently in the founding of many states. An elaborate irrigation system allowed the Sumer city-states to prosper. An educated elite, however, used religious dogma to skim off much of the economic surplus created by this public good. In Athens, the aristocracy chose to share the economic surplus generated by agriculture and trade by giving each citizen a stake in the prosperity of the state, which induced them to participate as citizens and soldiers in its defense. Cleisthenes' constitution, designed to shift political activity from zero-sum rent-seeking to the provision of public goods, stands out as an example of the possibility for rational actors to *design* political institutions to advance the general welfare.

The United States might be regarded as yet another example of a community's capacity to shape its destiny through the design of political institutions. These institutions were forged at a constitutional convention of the type envisaged by the contractarians, although all citizens did not take part, and unanimity was not attained. The US Constitution also appears to have been the 'model' underlying the theory of constitutions put forward by Buchanan and Tullock (1962). But even in the case of the United States, the claim has been made that distributional considerations were paramount in the design of its institutions. Bondholders did not want the colonies to default on their interest obligations, and slaveholders wanted to protect their property rights.[15] The same dichotomy exists today regarding what states actually do, with some seeing them as institutions to advance the general welfare by supplying public goods and others as institutions for playing zero-sum games of redistribution.[16] Once again, the truth probably lies in between with respect to both what states do, and how they come into existence.

Ancient Athens and the United States might also be cited as examples in which revolutions produced democracy. In both cases, however, the revolutions were rather tame in comparison, say, to the French and Russian revolutions. The latter two underscore the importance of weighing the costs of revolution, when contemplating the overthrow of a dictatorship. In addition to the costs of the revolution itself in terms of human sacrifice, there is the danger that the revolution, however noble its original aims, results in a dictatorship that is even worse than the one it replaces.

NOTES

1. See Buchanan and Tullock (1962, pp. 63–91) and Mueller (2003, pp. 74–8).
2. See Hardin (1989), Ordeshook (1992), Binmore (1994), and Voigt (1999).
3. See Rubin (2002, ch. 2) and the references therein.
4. The bandits and warlords who dominated early Chinese history appear exclusively to have been males.
5. See discussions in Przeworski (1991) and Shin (1994).
6. See, for discussion and evidence, Acemoglu and Robinson (2006, pp. 65–8).
7. See, also, Barzel (2001).
8. In this, Congleton is traveling in good company. Edmund Burke ([1790] 1960) was much of the same opinion.
9. See, for example, Henry Steele Commager (1978).
10. See Finer (1997, pp. 111–12) and the references therein. Haas (1982) also contains an interesting discussion of the debate, describing it as one between liberals (conservative anthropologists) and Marxists.
11. This statement must be qualified by the observation that the Sumerians invented writing, and so we have no written records of the organizational structures of earlier communities.
12. All future dates referring to Greece in this chapter are BCE.
13. See, again, Tridimas (2010) and the references therein.
14. Australia and New Zealand, although perhaps geographically part of the East, must be considered part of the West due to the dominant influence of immigrants from Europe in establishing their forms of government.
15. The most famous assertion of the argument is Beard ([1913] 1968). See, also, McGuire (1988).
16. Both Paul Samuelson and Richard Musgrave were tireless champions of the state throughout their lives, for example, Samuelson (1954) and Musgrave (1959). William Riker (1962a) regarded all politics as a zero-sum game. Aranson and Ordeshook (1981) and Meltzer and Richard (1981) depict all state activity as redistribution.

5 Constitutional political economy
Alan Hamlin

1 INTRODUCTION

The phrase 'constitutional political economy' has, no doubt, appeared in the literature in a variety of contexts over many years, but for our purposes the key uses of the phrase as the label for a distinctive research program developed from the use of 'constitutional economics' over the period following the publication of *The Calculus of Consent* (Buchanan and Tullock 1962) and became firmly established in the sub-title of *The Reason of Rules* (Brennan and Buchanan 1985), and as the name of the journal launched in 1990.[1]

The most obvious distinction that identifies constitutional political economy (hereafter, CPE) from political economy more generally defined is that between the analysis of constitutional rules and the analysis of policy formulation and behavior under those rules. CPE is dedicated to the analysis of constitutional and institutional rules, where this includes both the study of the operating characteristics of alternative rules or sets of rules and the questions arising from the design and reform of constitutional rules. Of course, this distinction should not be taken to imply that the constitutional perspective can be fully separated from the study of behavior under constitutional rules. The implications of any set of particular rules for expected behavior will be a major factor to be accounted for in any discussion of the design and evaluation of rules. Nevertheless, the shift of focus from behavior-under-rules to the design of rules is a key element of CPE.

But it is by no means the only key element, and nor is it the case that CPE is necessarily best viewed as a constant and unchanging approach over time or across practitioners. This chapter attempts to provide a rather more detailed statement of the essential core of CPE and to discuss two debates within CPE that both illustrate the intellectual diversity of CPE and reflect some of the deeper differences in relation to fundamental issues in political economy.

2 CPE – THE CORE

At the most basic level we might identify three distinctive features which, taken together, define the core structure of CPE: we might label them constitutionalism, individualism, and contractualism. I briefly discuss each in turn.[2]

Constitutionalism captures the complex of ideas associated with the thought that the authority of a government is both derived from the governed and limited by a constitution, so that the various acts of government and, in particular, the act of law-making, are seen as governed and regulated by a higher, constitutional law. Any constitutionalist must place special weight on the distinction between the constitution which governs and regulates politics, and politics which operates within constitutional rules. Of course, this rough formulation of constitutionalism raises more questions than it answers; most obviously, what is the source of the constitution and its legitimating force? Answers to such further questions may come in a variety of forms and still be consistent with a commitment to constitutionalism. The variety of constitutionalism that underpins CPE might be termed democratic constitutionalism, in that it builds on both individualist and contractarian ideas (to be discussed below) to provide descriptive as well as normative content for the basic constitutionalist position.

Whatever the details, the constitutionalist position of CPE distinguishes it quite sharply from the pre-existing economic orthodoxy, which focused analytic attention almost entirely at the level of policies, rather than the political institutions and constitutions within which those policies are generated. In this respect, CPE derives from a clear critique of the approach adopted by traditional welfare economics, so that while it is now commonplace to describe CPE (or public choice analysis more generally) as the application of economics to politics, it is important to recall that public choice and CPE owe their origins as much to a critique of economics as they do to an expansion of the range of application of economic analysis.

Individualism is the aspect of CPE that draws most directly on the economic approach, although even here it is used to develop a rather different normative stance. It is important first to stress the distinction between methodological individualism and normative individualism. Although CPE is committed to both, they are quite distinct. In the methodological context, the emphasis on individualism simply insists that the ultimate explanation of social phenomena must relate to individuals. Methodological individualism, in the relevantly mild form, does not deny that non-individual entities play salient roles in social life; it merely insists that a full explanation of that salience must ultimately refer to the individuals who constitute those entities. It may be convenient to speak of a government acting in a certain way, or of a collective, such as a trade union or non-governmental organization (NGO), deciding on some matter, but when we speak in this way we are merely employing a shorthand for a deeper analysis in which individuals playing particular roles within the government, trade union or NGO interact to produce the observed behavior.[3]

There may seem to be a tension between this individualist position and a simple reading of constitutionalism, which appears to grant independent explanatory and normative power to the constitution, even though it certainly is not an individual. But this tension is no more than apparent within the CPE approach, since the deeper analysis of the constitution provided within CPE grounds it by reference to individuals, both in terms of explanation and in terms of normative authority. Before turning to the normative aspect, we might dwell a little longer on the descriptive or explanatory aspect of the relationship between individuals and political institutions and constitutions.

Constitutional political economy takes as one of its inputs a mild form of methodological individualism, and produces as one of its outputs a focus on political institutions and constitutions. That is, it generates a variety of institutionalism from an individualistic starting point. This may seem paradoxical to some, but there is no paradox here. The constitutionalist element of CPE points to the distinction between rules and actions under the rules.[4] So, in any political situation at any moment in time, the rules act to constrain, regulate or otherwise inform human action. Given the rules, individuals will act in accordance with their motivations (whatever they might be), so that the outcome of their various actions (which may include some breaking of the rules) will be seen as the equilibrium under the particular set of rules of the game. On the face of it this seems to combine the forces of agency and structure, granting structural rules an autonomous role in determining social outcomes. But this depends on the further analysis of the source of the rules, and CPE analysis identifies that source with prior individual behavior, either directly in terms of the explicit design of rules via some sort of constitutional decision making, or indirectly through some more evolutionary process (see, for example, Wärneryd 1990). In this way, rules and constitutions are seen as the embodiment of prior choices and behavior by individuals, so that while rules have an impersonal proximate influence on political outcomes, this is ultimately revealed to be an indirect form of individual agency rather than any acceptance of structural autonomy.[5]

We may now turn to normative individualism. The essential idea here is that all values are personal in the sense that for something to be of value it must be of value to someone. While this position rules out values that are fully independent of individual values, it certainly does not commit to any narrow notion of individual self-interest, or economic preferences, as being the only value to be recognized. An individual may hold any set of values, however own-regarding, altruistic, other-regarding or social they may be, and, to the extent that they are held by individuals, these values will be recognized by the normative individualist. All that is ruled out is the ascription of value where no individual values have been expressed; in this sense, normative individualism might be thought of as a form of global anti-paternalism.

But individualism of this rather general sort does not provide a sufficient account of the normative commitments of CPE; it is only in combination with a form of contractarianism that normative individualism is given the specific content that is characteristic of CPE and which contrasts with the more utilitarian or social-welfare orientation of traditional welfare economics, which is clearly also within the normative individualism camp.

The individualist/contractarian position is one in which the agreement of relevant individuals is taken as the key to identifying opportunities for increases in overall social value. Individuals typically will pursue a range of values so that their agreement to any particular proposal will normally involve an internal trade-off over different values, and the nature of such individual trade-offs may differ from individual to individual. But the central idea of the contractarianism associated with the CPE tradition is that only the individual is in a position to make appropriate trade-offs, and agreement is, in principle, the only reliable indicator of all-things-considered or net value to the individual.

This, then, is the source of two further key elements of the CPE approach – the idea of politics as exchange, and the normative status of a collective choice rule of unanimity.[6] The idea of politics as exchange sits in contrast to the idea of politics as choice: politics as exchange sees politics (at both the constitutional and in-period levels) as essentially concerned with interactions between individuals in search of mutual benefit, while politics as choice sees it as the making of choices by independently acting authoritative bodies (whether those bodies are individuals, as in the case of a citizen choosing how to vote, or collectives such as a government choosing a policy). While the distinction between exchange and choice is somewhat subtle (since choices and exchanges will often go together) the difference in perspective is significant. And once the idea of exchange is given center stage, it is clear that voluntary exchange requires unanimity among the parties to the exchange, and that this unanimity is the hallmark of value-enhancing exchange.

Contrast the CPE focus on individual values, exchange and unanimity with the focus of traditional welfare economics focus on individual utility, social welfare and Pareto optimality. Even if the traditional welfare economist is a normative individualist, so that the only arguments in the social welfare function are individual values, by constructing a metric of social welfare there tends to be a focus on aggregate choice rather than exchange; and while Pareto optimality and unanimity will be closely related in ideal circumstances, their different perspectives will come apart in more practical situations.

The final points to be stressed in this brief review of the basics of the CPE approach relate to the role of rationality and the idea of the 'veil of insignificance' (Kliemt 1986). Given the basic commitment to individualism some specification of individual motivation is clearly required to make CPE operational, and this takes the form of the assumption of individual rationality in the classic sense that an individual is rational to the extent that she acts maximally to satisfy her desires given her information and beliefs. There are two fundamental points to emphasize here. The first is the idea of motivational symmetry involving a single integrated model of individual behavior across all economic, social and political domains. Constitutional political economy, and public choice theory more broadly, insists that it is inappropriate to assume that the basic motivation of individuals shifts significantly as the individual moves from narrowly economic contexts to public or political contexts; or that some dramatic and systematic change in motivation applies to individuals who operate in political rather than economic arenas (see, for example, Brennan and Buchanan 1985, pp. 46–51). The idea of motivational symmetry should not be taken to imply that individuals actually behave identically in all settings, but rather that differences in behavior are to be explained by reference to specific aspects of the relevant institutional settings, rather than by stipulating a fundamental shift in the internal motivations of the individual. In other words, if political behavior is to differ from economic behavior, this must arise as a matter of analysis and argument rather than by simply asserting that the relevant individuals are motivated differently.

But this insistence on motivational symmetry still leaves open the question of how to specify individual motivation, and here it is clear that in the early CPE literature the specification of choice was that of a relatively narrow specification of self-interested rationality familiar from the model of *Homo economicus*. I would suggest two main reasons for this approach: first, and most obviously, a major part of the thrust of early public choice and CPE analysis was to offer a broadly positive analysis of behavior within political institutions that sat on all fours with the standard economic analysis of behavior within market institutions. Adopting the standard economic view of preferences and the utility maximizing conception of individual rationality provided both access to a wide range of techniques and results developed in the economics and game-theoretic literatures and direct comparability as between the political and economic domains.

Alongside this argument for adopting the *Homo economicus* specification, there was also an attempt at a direct methodological justification (ibid., pp. 51–4). There were two strands to this argument: first, that it was important to show that political cooperation could develop even where individual interests often were in conflict; and, second, that it was important to show that political institutions could be robust against individuals who were not assumed automatically to be compliant.[7] While these points are well taken, it is by no means clear that they imply that the *Homo economicus* specification is to be preferred to all others, since it is certainly possible to model individual motivations in such a way as to ensure an appropriate degree of inter-individual conflict and eliminate automatic compliance without adopting a narrowly self-interested conception of rationality.

As we will see, there have been significant attempts to broaden the understanding of individual motivation within the CPE approach, but it should be stressed that these attempts still operate within the general framework of individual rationality, and still take seriously the value of motivational symmetry between economic and political domains.

Given an assumption of individual rationality (whatever the detailed content of that assumption may be) and motivational symmetry, how does the distinction between in-period politics and constitutional politics operate to provide normative support for constitutional rather than policy choice? In one sense this is clearly the central issue for CPE. If individuals act rationally (perhaps self-interestedly) in their day-to-day political activities, surely the idea of motivational symmetry implies that they will act equally rationally (and equally self-interestedly) in making constitutional choices. And if this is so, how can we believe that the constitution generated from such behavior carries any significant normative weight in justifying, rather than merely explaining, the political structures and processes with constitutional credentials?[8]

The basic CPE line of argument here revolves around the claim that there is sufficient difference between constitutional choices and day-to-day politics to provide relevantly normative support for the constitutional over the merely political. And the relevant difference provides a 'veil of insignificance' which acts in a manner similar to that associated with the Rawlsian 'veil of ignorance' (Rawls 1971, section 24). Essentially, when facing a constitutional choice, for example, the choice between alternative voting rules, the individual is placed in a setting wherein she cannot accurately distinguish the impact of the alternatives under consideration on her own interests, despite the fact that she may be able to identify the alternatives as having very different general properties. This is simply because in considering a constitutional rule, the individual must expect it to operate over many particular cases, and over an extended period of time. Given that the individual does not know which cases will fall under the rule, or how those cases may impinge on her interests, it will be virtually impossible to choose the rule that best serves her interests. The argument then continues by suggesting that, in these circumstances, the individual will rationally view the constitutional choice at hand from the perspective of the general properties of the alternative rules on offer, and so reach a decision that is largely independent of personal interests and more dependent on judgments regarding the ability of the rules under consideration to serve the interests of citizens in general, whatever their particular interests might be.

Now, of course, the 'veil of insignificance' is not argued to transform self-interested political choice fully into disinterested constitutional choice; but it is argued to work in that direction. And this is important both in generating a normative presumption in favor of constitutionalism, and in providing a reason to expect a greater degree of agreement in the realm of constitutional choice than in the realm of day-to-day politics.

In considering the argument for the 'veil of insignificance' we might note several critical points. First, do we accept that the nature of constitutional rules implies that it will be difficult for any individual to identify those that can be expected to serve their personal interests? And, second, even if we accept this point, do we agree that this will imply that constitutional choices will be more disinterested and focus on more general benefits to citizens at large? I will consider these points in turn.

On the first issue, it is not too difficult to think of potential counterexamples. For instance, if an individual knows her own general economic and social position (in relation to, for example, education, religion and wealth) it may not be too difficult to work out that some potential constitutional arrangements will serve individuals of that general type even if they do so at the expense of individuals of other types. Equally, if an individual feels himself or herself relatively advantaged by the status quo political arrangements, that individual will have a clear incentive to support constitutional arrangements that limit the pace or extent of political change. In this way, it seems that the 'veil of insignificance' is too transparent to do the work required of it. But this is, perhaps, too hasty a conclusion. Notice that these claimed counterexamples are actually examples that work within the ambit of the CPE argument, by shifting the focus of attention from the specific personal interests of the individual to the more general interests of a class or type of individual with which the individual identifies (the educated, the religious, the advantaged, or whatever). One might add that any individual may be expected to identify with a number of groups, classes or types and, to the extent that the generalized interests of these groups differ, this will add further force to the claim that the individual's view of his or her interests will be attenuated. On these grounds, it seems reasonable to conclude that the CPE argument that the veil of insignificance tends to reduce the focus on personal interests and shifts the focus to the interests of broader groups succeeds, at least to some extent; there will be limitations in terms of the nature of the groups that are identified behind the veil.

Turning to the second issue, can we accept that this movement to a position behind the veil implies more disinterested constitutional choices that approximate the underlying normative contractarian ideal? Compare the discussion of the veil of insignificance with the classic public choice discussion of the paradox of voting (see, for example, Aldrich 1993). In the case of the paradox of voting the standard argument is that the insignificance of the individual voter in the context of a large-scale majoritarian election will effectively undermine the incentive to participate, and also undermine the incentive to become informed on the issue at hand. In this way, the standard discussion suggests that insignificance leads to rational ignorance and low voter turnout. Contrast this with the argument at the constitutional level, where insignificance is argued to produce disinterested and normatively salient participation. How can we reconcile these two lines of argument? Importantly, the details of the insignificance are rather different in the two cases; in the standard voting case the problem is the normal public good problem caused by large numbers of voters and the resultant very low probability of any individual vote being decisive. There is no assumption that it is difficult for any individual to take a view on which of the policy options is actually in their interests; it is just that the act of voting is disengaged from the calculus of interest by the mechanics of the voting process. In the constitutional case, this large numbers problem will, presumably, also arise; but the aspect of insignificance that is novel and additional is the distinction between a specific policy and a general rule. And it is this novel dimension of insignificance that is doing the work. But this work must be done in the context of the more standard form of insignificance.

Owing to the interaction between these two forms of insignificance, we might conclude that there are two forces at work: one pulling in the direction of rational ignorance and disengagement, the other in the direction of relatively disinterested engagement. The overall effect of these two forces is difficult to judge in principle, but the point here is that there may be no need to make a sweeping judgment; it depends on exactly what comparison is being made. If we take the ideal case of purely private decision-making as our basis for comparison, and stipulate that in such cases there is no veil of ignorance of either type, then it is reasonably clear that the basic voting case provides the most problematic comparison, while the constitutional case provides an intermediate instance in which some aspects of the disengagement associated with voting may be moderated. In this way, if the relevant comparison is between everyday politics and constitutional politics, it seems reasonable to argue, as the CPE tradition does, that the constitutional setting will provide at least some greater cause for optimism in relation to engagement. But this is a rather tentative conclusion, and one which raises the issue of the exact nature of the engagement, as we shall see.

I have suggested that the core of CPE is built around commitments to forms of constitutionalism, individualism and contractarianism which provide the base on which CPE constructs a distinctive position associated with the view of politics as exchange, the normative status of the idea of unanimity, the importance of the assumption of motivational symmetry, an interpretation of individual rationality, and the role of the veil of insignificance in generating a normatively salient distinction between the consideration of constitutional rules and simple policies. In the remainder of this chapter I turn to consider some of the variety within CPE, both in terms of its development over time and in terms of alternative positions taken.

There can be little doubt that the origins of CPE are deeply influenced by American traditions and contexts, and one of the notable developments in CPE relates to its geographic spread and the need for a theory to accommodate the wider understanding of constitutionalism required in this more varied setting. A similar point may be made in relation to history rather than geography. Constitutional political economy began with a focus on modern, developed democracies, but has broadened its scope to be at least somewhat concerned with the use of the analytic approach associated with CPE to issues from earlier periods.[9] But here I want to focus not on the geographic and historical extensions to the application of CPE, but rather on some of the more significant theoretical issues within CPE.

3 CPE – MARGINAL AND TOTAL APPROACHES

Brennan and Eusepi (2011) argue that there is a distinction to be made between two understandings of the CPE project, even when understood in terms of the work of James Buchanan. This distinction, is between the CPE of *The Calculus of Consent* and the CPE of *The Limits of Liberty*, and may be summarized in terms of the distinction between marginal and total approaches to the theory of political institutions introduced in *The Calculus of Consent* (Buchanan and Tullock 1962, pp. 318–19). The marginal approach starts from a given set of political arrangements – a given constitution – and considers only minor or modest changes in those institutions, so that it is clearly intended as an analysis of constitutional reform rather than wholesale constitutional design. Indeed, since the process of constitutional reform is normally itself governed by elements of the prevailing constitution, one can see the marginal approach to constitutional reform as an analysis that operates within a specified constitutional process and so is governed by rules already in place. By contrast, the total approach asks a much broader question as to the origins of a constitution and the de novo design and justification of the full set of constitutional arrangements. Buchanan, writing in *The Calculus of Consent*, explicitly places CPE in the marginal camp, while the Buchanan of *The Limits of Liberty* places CPE in the total camp.

As Brennan and Eusepi point out, the distinction is important not just for CPE's range of application but also for the nature of the normative argument presented within CPE. On the marginal view, justification is based at least in part on the pre-existing order. In simple terms, the relevant constitutional reform is legitimized by the very constitution that is being reformed, and so there is no need to generate either political institutions or normative arguments from the ground up, as it were. In this way, the process of constitutional reform is rather closer to the process of policy choice or law-making than might have been thought by reference to the strength of CPE's distinction between these activities, in that constitutional reform itself, like policy-making and law-making, is largely governed by, and justified by, the overarching constitution. But what justifies the overarching constitution? That is the fundamental normative question facing the total approach.

An alternative way of making this point is also explored by Brennan and Eusepi. If CPE is understood in terms of the analysis of the emergence and justification of rules, much of the work has been on the demand side, concerned with showing why and how individuals will benefit from general rules even where those rules constrain them. But CPE must also be concerned with the basic supply of rules; that is, the deep questions of the feasibility of rules, and the extent that this question can be addressed within the CPE framework.

There can be little doubt that CPE has contributed significantly to the debate of the feasibility of rules, but there can certainly be disagreement over the current state of that debate. We can identify a position in which the rationally constructivist account of the formation of rules is limited essentially to social situations which may be described as coordination games (see, for example, Hardin 2003), the key characteristic being that rules in such games are both agreeable *ex ante* and self-enforcing *ex post*, in the sense that individuals have strong incentives both to put the rule in place and to obey the rule once it is in place. But CPE sets itself a more ambitious task than the constitutional government of coordination games. Indeed, the standard game form at the heart of the CPE depiction of politics is the multi-person prisoners' dilemma game, rather than the coordination game, and here, while there is reason to suppose that a rule may be agreeable *ex ante*, there is no clear analysis supporting the view that such a rule would be obeyed once in place.[10]

Of course, there are many ways in which the prisoners' dilemma may be modified to escape the problem of enforcement, perhaps the most obvious being the indefinite repetition of the game which will allow a strategy of cooperation to emerge as a potential equilibrium, but the essential feature of all of these modifications is that they transform the underlying prisoners' dilemma game into a form of coordination game so that the desired equilibrium becomes self-enforcing.

This brief discussion of the prisoners' dilemma case indicates both the fundamental difficulty of overcoming the essential problem of enforcement, and the fact that the restriction to cooperation games may not be quite as restrictive as might first have appeared. But the most basic target of Buchanan's *The Limits of Liberty*, as indicated by its subtitle, *Between Anarchy and Leviathan*, is to argue for the feasibility of a constitutional order that involves a degree of enforced order while avoiding the full rigors of Hobbes's all-powerful Leviathan; and to argue that such a constitutional settlement is accessible to rational individuals.

This line of discussion points to the connection between CPE and one of the deepest questions in political philosophy. Since the CPE approach makes clear use of the idea of rationality in posing this question, it is appropriate that I now turn to a debate on the interpretation of rationality.

4 CPE – THE INSTRUMENTAL AND THE EXPRESSIVE

As already noted, the early CPE literature, and the continuing mainstream contributions to it adopt the *Homo economicus* assumption of relatively narrow self-interest as its substantive theory of rationality, and it is this understanding of rationality that informs the debate, summarized above, on the feasibility of rules and the possibility of enforcement. But more recently there has emerged a revisionist view of the appropriate treatment of individual motivation within CPE and public choice theory more generally, and one key part of this revisionist view is the idea of expressive rationality.[11]

The basic idea of expressive political behavior arose in the context of the paradox of voting, briefly discussed above. Once it is accepted that the purely instrumentally rational individual – that is an individual who is motivated entirely by reference to the anticipated effects that his or her action will have on final outcomes – will face no incentive to participate in an election in which her vote has a vanishingly small probability of being decisive. Hence, the question of how it can be rational to vote arises. And the obvious thought is that there must be some perceived value to the act of voting itself that does not depend on the outcome of the election. Such a value is expressive in the sense that simply registering one's preferences via the vote is sufficient to generate it. Once this thought is in place, it is natural to extend the application of the expressive idea beyond the realm of voting in large scale elections and recognize that a wide variety of political behavior may be associated with expressive (as well as instrumental) benefits and costs.

Recognizing the potential relevance of expressive considerations raises a number of issues. The first relates to the basic idea of motivational symmetry discussed above. Care must be taken to see that there is no breach of motivational symmetry. Individuals are argued to have both expressive and instrumental interests and values, and this basic motivational structure is invariant. Nevertheless, different circumstances and, in particular, different institutional settings will tend to render different aspects of the basic motivational structure salient, and so behavior may differ quite markedly as between different settings. This point then relates directly to the issue of the veil of insignificance in its constitutional setting. Recall that the theme of the veil of insignificance argument is that under the circumstances of the design or reform of constitutional rules, individuals will be unable to see their own (instrumental) interests, and that this may allow them to adopt a more general interest in selecting a rule that serves a wider interest. The idea of expressive values provides an intermediate step in this argument – as in the argument on the paradox of voting – by indicating that the rational individual in these circumstances will recognize that his or her instrumental interests are disengaged by the idea of insignificance, but that this does not necessarily lessen their expressive interest.

The idea of expressive interests also provides a potential connection to the positive analysis of normative motivations. It is an unfortunate feature of the standard *Homo economicus* model of motivation that it denies the possibility that any individual is motivated, however weakly, by directly normative concerns while at the same time holding that there is a relevant overarching normative criterion. In the traditional Paretian welfare economics literature, for example, while society is modeled as valuing Pareto optimality, no individual values it, in the sense that no individual is motivated, however weakly or conditionally, by a concern for Pareto optimality. By broadening the scope of individual motivations to include expressive as well as instrumental considerations, we gain the possibility of introducing both normative motivations and of furthering an analysis of the circumstances in which they may be more or less salient.

The concept of motivational heterogeneity that goes with the introduction of expressive motivations and the recognition that individuals will differ in their expressive concerns and dispositions also opens up the analysis of a further class of institutional arrangements. To the extent that CPE adopts the *Homo economicus* assumption it limits itself to the study of the class of institutional arrangements that operate by the use of incentives – both rewards and punishments. But as soon as we recognize a wider range of motivations, and the interpersonal heterogeneity of motivations, we open up institutional arrangements that rely not on incentives, but on selection or other social mechanisms that are difficult to render in the language of narrowly self-interested rational individuals (see Brennan and Hamlin 2000; Besley 2005, 2006).

Finally, we may attempt to make explicit the link between the expressive rationality idea and the fundamental problem of enforcement and political obligation introduced in the previous section. As we saw there, the challenge is to find a basis for a political constitution that lies between anarchy and Leviathan and which is accessible to rational individuals. Clearly the difficulty of this challenge depends crucially on the interpretation of rationality, and the introduction of the idea of expressive considerations within the field of rationality provides at least the possibility of addressing the challenge in new and interesting ways.

5 FINAL COMMENTS

In this brief chapter, I have attempted both to sketch the general or core nature of CPE as a research program – and to identify two of the deeper, more philosophical, debates within CPE. There is, of course, much that I have not covered. I have deliberately not attempted to identify the various contributions made within the CPE literature to our understanding of political institutions, such as federalism, the separation of powers, bicameralism, alternative voting methods, and so on, or to our understanding of the process of constitutional reform as it applies in developed, developing and transitional societies.

In many ways these contributions are the bread and butter of CPE, but I have taken the more abstract, more theoretical approach of trying to characterize (caricature, perhaps) CPE as a whole and to stress that while it is often seen as a rather narrowly economistic approach to the analysis of political institutions and constitutions, it also serves to connect aspects of the economic approach to some of the fundamental issues in both political philosophy and political psychology. While CPE does not hold all the answers to the issues involved in specifying the political motivations of individuals, or of analyzing the operating characteristics of alternative constitutional arrangements, or of providing a fully convincing account of the normative status of particular examples of them, it does at least offer a relatively flexible framework in which these questions can be explored.

NOTES

1. For an influential early use of 'constitutional economics', see McKenzie (1984). The first issue of the journal *Constitutional Political Economy* included Buchanan's (1990) 'The domain of constitutional economics'. More recent essays offering overviews are 'Constitutional political economy' (Voigt 2004), 'Constitutional economics I' (Farina 2005) and 'Constitutional economics II' (Van den Hauwe 2005).
2. For related discussion of these elements, see Brennan and Hamlin (1995).
3. Formally, methodological individualism of the sort identified here does not require that all collective or social phenomena are capable of being reduced to the individual level, but only that collective or social phenomena supervene on the individual level. See, for example, Currie (1984) and List and Pettit (2006).
4. This aspect of CPE is explored at length in Brennan and Buchanan (1985).
5. The balance between agency and the autonomy of constitutional rules, or between constructivist and non-constructivist accounts of constitutions, is one of the key distinguishing features between CPE in the tradition of Buchanan and more Hayekian accounts of social order. See, for example, Hayek (1960), Buchanan (1975) and Vanberg (1994).
6. See, for example, Buchanan (1975, pp. 50–5) and the Wicksellian references provided therein, along with chapter 2 of Brennan and Buchanan (1985).
7. These arguments, as with much in the CPE tradition, reflect a broadly Madisonian perspective (Hamilton et al. [1787–88] 2008).
8. This line of criticism, suggesting that the normative ambitions of CPE are undermined even if its positive ambitions are met, is developed in Hardin (1990, pp. 35ff) and Christiano (2004). See also Brennan and Hamlin (2009).
9. Restricting references to the recent contents of the journal *Constitutional Political Economy* provides examples of application to Taiwan, Greece, Kenya, Spain, the former Soviet Republics, and to the Hanseatic League, post-1806 Prussia, medieval England and Ancient Athens.
10. A further issue relates to the role of the status quo in both constitutional and political choice and the potential status quo bias; see Brennan and Hamlin (2004), Buchanan (2004).
11. On expressive rationality, see Brennan and Lomasky (1993), Schuessler (2000b), Hillman (2010), and Hamlin and Jennings (2011). On the implications for CPE, see Brennan and Hamlin (2000, 2002, 2008).

6 Autocrats and democrats
Armando Razo

1 INTRODUCTION

Although autocracies are not as common as they once were (Huntington 1991), their study remains a timely topic for several reasons.[1] First, there is ample scholarly concern about the poor quality of newly emerging democracies exhibiting various authoritarian tendencies (Hite and Cesarini 2004). Second, the decisions of some modern autocracies, such as China, North Korea, and Iran, among others, can have major economic and political repercussions at a regional or global scale. A systematic approach to the study of autocratic government is therefore essential for a contemporary understanding of the politics of developing democracies and key international players.

Interestingly, the study of autocracies or dictatorships is a relatively new endeavor within the public choice tradition. Indeed, a peculiar feature of the public choice literature has long been its fascination with the study of democratic institutions. Conversely, the broader literature on political development and dictatorships within political science largely has ignored the conceptual contributions of public choice scholars. As a matter of fact, seminal contributions to the political economy of dictatorship first originated in economics and only, until very recently, have they resonated and helped shape an emerging choice-theoretic literature in political science.

Notably, a founder of public choice, Gordon Tullock, has written about both democracies and autocracies. However, for a long time, studies of democracies and autocracies proceeded along divergent lines for at least two reasons. First, political regimes fits squarely into the discipline of political science, and hence, have received more attention there than in economics. Moreover, despite some pioneering efforts by public choice scholars, interdisciplinary approaches have been minimal. Second, public choice and related literatures in social choice theory, voting theory, and political institutions, have focused almost exclusively on deriving their results in democratic contexts. In consequence, the study of autocracies long lacked a solid analytical foundation.

Within the last decade, however, a new analytical literature on the political economy of dictatorships has emerged, which promises to build more bridges between economics and political science. In fact, a notable property of this literature is the greater participation from political scientists. Beyond interdisciplinarity, this new scholarship also blends the typical emphasis of political scientists on institutions and political organization with economic approaches that focus on methodological individualism and strategic behaviors.

As this is a literature literally in the making, it will be helpful to first present an overview of separate economic and political science approaches to the study of autocracies. This is done in section 2, which also serves to introduce the seminal contributions of Gordon Tullock (1987) and Ronald Wintrobe (1998), who studied autocracies in terms of a political survival problem.

Two subsequent sections review the latest work on the political economy of dictatorships. To present them, I make use of Diermeier and Krehbiel's (2003) useful distinction between 'theories of institutions' and 'institutional theories' in that order.[2] Section 3, 'Theories of autocratic institutions' thus summarizes contributions to the literature that analyze autocrats' decisions to establish democratic institutions (especially legislatures) as a commitment device to redistribute wealth to supporters. However, not all autocrats are able to make such choices, so we also need to ask what types of exogenous institutional constraints may distinguish autocrats from democrats, and how these constraints affect autocratic behavior. These questions are addressed in Section 4 ('Institutional theories of autocracies'), which presents two frameworks for understanding the impact of exogenous institutions. One of these frameworks is 'selectorate theory', which is not necessarily restricted to the study of autocracies (Bueno de Mesquita et al. 2000, 2003). The second is a relational theory of private policies and networks of overlapping protection (Razo 2008). Section 5 adopts a comparative perspective to inquire how autocrats differ from democrats. I claim that the key difference lies in the underlying political context. Although autocrats and democrats can both be modeled as self-interested actors, autocrats operate in less structured and less informative political environments than democrats, a situation that greatly complicates the exercise of authority. Section 6 concludes.

2 DISCIPLINARY PERSPECTIVES ON AUTOCRACY

Unlike democratic theory, which has benefitted greatly from the economic approaches of public choice and positive political theory, the study of autocracies has remained mostly a political science endeavor. This relative lack of scholarly cross-fertilization in the study of autocracies is somewhat ironic given that Tullock (1987, p. ix) himself has written that his primary motivation for engaging in a scientific analysis of politics (that is, the genesis of public choice) was to understand non-democratic regimes, specifically the case of China.

To understand autocracies, this section therefore starts in section 2.1 with a brief overview of traditional political science approaches to the study of dictatorships. Section 2.2 reviews economic contributions. Section 2.3 examines how public choice studies of dictatorships differ from more traditional economics and political science approaches.

2.1 Political Science Theories

The study of autocrats is as old as the study of government, dating back to Ancient Greece where political philosophers debated the problem of tyranny with respect to other political systems (Boesche 1996). Although an extensive review is not feasible for this chapter, one can nonetheless identify three major conceptual themes related to (1) the number of rulers; (2) dictators' motivations and individual characters; and (3) the nature of autocratic authority in relationship to subjects or citizens. This last theme, in turn, has inspired a newer literature on autocratic survival and democratization.

2.1.1 Number of rulers

The first theme relates to the issue of rule by the few or by the many. Ancient political philosophers did not agree on this point, but nonetheless showed a preference for a smaller number of rulers. Plato, for instance, not only highlighted the importance of enlightened (philosopher-king) leaders, but pointed out that the best governments were aristocratic rather than democratic (Plato [n.d.] 1945, p. 267). In his analysis of constitutions, Aristotle is critical of tyranny, but nonetheless admits the possibility that a few men can govern well when guided 'by the common interest'. However, he is clear about the undesirability of democracy, not just because of its many numbers but their presumed individual self-interest.

Contemporary democratic theory is more sanguine about the desirability of governance by the many due mostly to normative arguments for the benefits of broad political enfranchisement. Although there are various definitions of democracy, Dahl (1996) has been influential in focusing attention on the degree of inclusion and contestability, both of which reach an ideal state in polyarchy, a setting where many groups compete.[3]

2.1.2 Motivations and individual characters

In addition to numbers, ancient philosophers also placed much stress on leaders' motivations and personal characters, which identifies a second strand in the literature on autocracies. Both Plato and Aristotle supported the idea of just and wise men who would bring about better outcomes for their societies as opposed to the despotic behavior of ruthless individuals. That call resonates even today, especially in the face of dire internal or external threats to stability, when it is still commonly argued that societies need powerful and visionary leaders (Gray and McPherson 2001). As Wintrobe (1998, p. 6) notes, when democracy is thought incapable of solving major social problems, it is customary to suggest an autocratic solution and, in particular, to support elevating to power a well-informed and publicly oriented leader.

The distinction between tyrants and perfect monarchs or autocrats, however, is not readily established since their behavior is contingent on having virtuous qualities that may take time to observe. Political and historical studies that are able to make such assessment traditionally have emphasized the personal psychologies of autocrats (and sometimes the social psychology of the general population) as important determinants of autocratic behavior. In the context of developing countries, a childhood in poverty, lack of moral scruples, and egotistical tendencies, among other factors, bring to power particularly inept and corrupt leaders (Chehabi and Linz 1998, p. 13). Even more mature democracies or otherwise stable political regimes are affected by individual psychology. Recognizing that structural factors, such as economic collapse, enabled the rise of despotic governments, Lee (2000, p. 119) notes, for instance, that Benito Mussolini's behavior was the outcome of deep individual and social psychological needs for a cult of personality. Adolf Hitler's ineptitude is also attributed to his particular dislike of various administrative procedures, his brute will, and evil orientation (ibid., p. 234). In the former Soviet Union, Lee (ibid., p. 89) attributes Josef Stalin's terror tactics to his perpetual insecurity, along with physical and mental deterioration in old age. Stalin's fears were not restricted to the threat of being removed, but also were caused by a deep desire to impress others. As Todd (2002) describes it, Stalin suffered not only from an inferiority complex of perceived low intellectual status, but also from pure madness, partly as a result of personal tragedy after the suicide of his second wife.

2.1.3 Political authority and autocratic survival
A third, and dominant, theme in the study of autocracies has to do with the sociological concern, espoused by Max Weber (1947), of understanding the nature of political authority across various societies. In particular, this theme has focused on state–society relations and various types of legitimacy that reflect a historical progression towards modernity from charisma and tradition to bureaucracy (or rational-legal authority).

This modernizing and sociological focus continues to inform current disciplinary approaches to the study of autocracies (Brooker 2009). A leading figure in this literature in Juan J. Linz, who, in a pioneering 1975 article, first differentiated various types of autocracies systematically. Linz goes beyond the contemporary interest in understanding the atrocities of non-democratic regimes by proposing a major distinction between totalitarianism and authoritarianism. Building on the work of Friedrich and Brzezinski (1965), Linz identifies totalitarian regimes as possessing a set of organizational capabilities that enable their desire to control all aspects of society. These capabilities are summarized in terms of a monistic center of power, an official ideology, and massive mobilization through a single party (Linz 2000, p. 70). Simply put, totalitarian regimes are guided, not necessarily by an autocrat, but by a comprehensive ideology that constrains the behavior both of autocrats and society at large. In addition, totalitarian regimes possess superior organizational capacities, quintessentially represented by legitimizing a single political party, reinforced by creating various specialized organizations, such as secret police forces and a mass media, underpinned by a propaganda apparatus.

In contrast to totalitarian regimes, authoritarian regimes are relatively more disorganized in that they lack the capabilities (as well as the willingness) to fully control society. Whereas there is some element of organization inherent in the existence of stable rules for political interaction, which allows limited pluralism and some ability to mobilize the population, authoritarian regimes are particularly distinguished from totalitarian regimes by their lack of ideology. Instead of a coherent set of beliefs, authoritarian regimes are posited to have mentalities, which may reflect some notion of desired objectives, but not a well-defined and constraining vision (Linz 2000, pp. 12–64). Linz acknowledges the difficulty of identifying ideologies, but at the same time argues that one item of particular distinction vis-à-vis ideologies is that mentalities are more driven by emotions.

Although contemplated in his earlier work, but not fully formed until a 1998 collected volume, Linz and collaborators propose a distinctive third type of autocratic regimes, called *sultanistic* regimes, borrowing a term from Weber used to identify certain patterns of authority in the Middle East (Chehabi and Linz 1998, pp. 4–7). These autocratic regimes most closely correspond to Weber's ideal type of charismatic legitimacy, as they are essentially personalist regimes. In contrast to both authoritarian and totalitarian regimes, personalist regimes have even fewer organizational capabilities, and no systematic policy directives – not even a mentality.[4] Sultanistic regimes essentially describe personal rule as opposed to the collective authority of limited pluralism in authoritarianism or the ideological interests of an official single party under a totalitarian regime.

Interestingly, the study of autocratic regimes has not advanced much beyond the sociological framework developed in Linz's 1975 essay. As Linz (2000, p. 11) notes in subsequent reflections after more than two decades, 'the work in the last twenty-five years has been mostly excellent historical monographs and descriptive country studies'. It is also notable that Linz is apparently unaware of potential public choice contributions to the analysis, such as Tullock (1987), Olson (1993), and Wintrobe (1998).

One reason for the delayed development of this political sociology literature lies with its limited ability to engage in systematic empirical studies due to lack of adequate operational definitions and indicators. For instance, one problem with a distinction among sultanistic, authoritarian, and totalitarian regimes – in increasing order of modernization – is that these categories are not mutually exclusive. In the definitive work on sultanistic regimes, Chehabi and Linz (1998, p. 9) admit, for example, that: 'Yet even in the regimes we call sultanistic, elements of a legal-rational order or of a legitimizing ideology are not totally absent.'

2.1.4 Democratization and autocratic survival

Embedded in the literature on democratization is the last major contribution towards the conceptualization of autocratic regimes as espoused by Geddes (1999). Linz (2000, p. 173–5) has admitted the difficulty of classifying various types of authoritarian regimes. This difficulty causes much confusion when confronted with non-informative labels, such as post-totalitarianism or ambiguous labels, such as totalitarian authoritarianism (ibid., pp. 245–61).[5] Still informed by legitimacy concerns, but addressing the strategic problem of survival, Geddes has proposed a refined typology of autocratic regimes, which serves, in effect, as a way of categorizing authoritarian and sultanistic regimes (given the rarity of the totalitarian type). Geddes distinguishes among three major types: military regimes, single-party regimes, and personalist regimes, but also allows various hybrid mixtures. The relevance of this classification lies in the corresponding ability of autocrats to keep themselves in power. For example, the nature of political authority in personalist regimes makes them more vulnerable to challenges or to a sudden decrease in resources.[6]

More recently, the study of autocracies has again become relevant, although still subsidiary to the broader literature on democratization. Several related concerns explain this development. On the one hand, there are broad worries about and indeed disillusionment with the political and economic outcomes of new democracies. To a certain extent, scholars and practitioners appear to have come to pragmatic terms with the reality of multiple competing regime criteria (Collier and Levitsky 1997). The focus then moved on to assess the quality of democracies (O'Donnell 1999; O'Donnell et al. 2004). The 'quality' of democracies lends itself to a more substantive conception of democracy, a subjective exercise that generates much debate, but this is not a strictly outcome-oriented concern. Scholars have also noted or 'discovered' so-called embedded authoritarian tendencies in new democracies; that is, that many democracies in developing countries have institutions with autocratic tendencies, which is a topic of much active research.[7] On a related note, a leading indicator (POLITY) admits the possibility that a particular political system may have both democratic and autocratic characteristics (Marshall and Jaggers 2000). A related literature also has emerged around the notion of hybrid regimes, which are sometimes labeled as semi-democratic or semi-authoritarian (Brooker 2009, ch. 8). Research on autocracies in political science thus suffers from much conceptual confusion and a strong emphasis on democratic assessments rather than general examinations of autocratic behavior.

2.2 Economic Approaches

There are at least two distinct strands of autocratic studies in economics with a common conceptual foundation that recognize autocrats as self-interested leaders, who then make constrained rational choices given individual preferences. One economic approach, as identified in the literature on institutions and growth, examines autocracies in an indirect manner – in comparison to democratic institutions. A second strand, and the one more closely associated with the public choice tradition, explores directly the motivations that determine autocratic behavior.

2.2.1 New institutional economics

Although public choice, by definition, incorporated a systematic interest in political factors, it has not been the only economic approach to pay attention to politics. Economic historians and political economists independently have studied the political determinants of economic growth. The major theoretical claim that emanates from this literature is that economic development requires adequate institutions that protect property rights and that reduce the costs of economic exchange (North 1981, 1990). In particular, the historical record indicates that institutions of limited government have been key in the development of contemporary advanced economies (North and Weingast 1989).

The literature on institutions and growth has been very influential in both academic and policy-making circles. Indeed, the conventional wisdom that has emerged points to the superiority of democratic institutions in providing the right incentives for pro-growth economic activity. Institutions of limited government are especially important to restrain the potential governmental opportunism that arises with excessive authority. Institutions enable leaders to make credible commitments by effectively tying their hands (Root 1989). There is now an extensive empirical literature that has examined such propositions in both cross-country and longitudinal studies (Aron 2000).

For the most part, there is ample support for the general claim that growth requires so-called good institutions. Specific support for the advantages of democracy remains ambiguous, however. On the one hand, some studies point to the importance of some democratic constraints (Henisz 2000). But Przeworski and Limongi (1993) also note that theoretical arguments can be made for the relative advantages and disadvantages of *both* autocracies and democracies under various situations. In the most comprehensive study of its kind, Przeworski et al. (2000) clearly state that regime type has no impact on long-term economic performance. Notwithstanding these negative results, the notion of credible commitments enforced by limited government still has much currency among scholars and policy-makers (World Bank 2001a). On the other hand, economists disagree on the question of economic development under autocracies. Barro (1997, pp. 50–51), for instance, does not preclude such regimes' ability to foster growth. Olson notes that it is possible for autocracies to promote economic growth in his theory of stationary banditry (Olson 1993, 2000). Stationary bandits are posited to have the incentives to invest in public goods (the only possible technology in his growth theory) when they have long-term horizons and encompassing interests in their economy.[8]

2.2.2 Dictators as rational actors

To the best of my knowledge, Tullock (1987) represents the first attempt by a public choice scholar – indeed, one of the founders of the field – to study autocracies from an economic perspective.[9] Tullock makes at least three distinct contributions to the study of autocrats. First, regarding motivations, he notes that dictators are not particularly ideological; hence, his analysis does not highlight any particular autocratic policies, all of which are seen literally as instruments for survival. Autocratic behavior can be understood mainly in terms of an autocrat's need to satisfy the demands of his supporters, as is also the case in democracies. However, in democracies, the key supporters are a majority of the voting population. In contrast, Tullock notes that under autocracy, 'the people who must be pleased are a much smaller group' (ibid., p. 12).

Second, he addresses two distinct problems of autocrats. As a precursor of a common theme in this literature, Tullock notes that autocrats must continually take actions to maintain themselves in power. Unlike later studies, Tullock does not directly address this problem from the dictator's perspective when it comes to formalizing the logic of autocratic survival. To be sure, Tullock has an extensive discussion of various mechanisms to subvert rebellions, but it is the latter that are formalized. Tullock's main emphasis therefore lies with the incentives of potential challengers (or, more precisely, their potential supporters), in effect, focusing on the collective action problems that affect the autocrat's opposition.[10]

Tullock also notes that autocrats continually deal with the problem of succession. Succession is related to the autocrat's incentives to signal the regime's longevity for economic purposes (Olson 1993, 2000). However, Tullock adds a different spin to the problem of succession by examining strategic considerations that affect the autocrat's current ability to stay in power. Simply put, naming a successor can give that person incentive to dispose of the incumbent in short order of the incumbent. Why wait when the eventual transfer of power already has been made public?

Tullock identifies various solutions to the succession problem, which also help to identify distinct types of autocracies. In particular, Tullock makes a distinction between hereditary and non-hereditary monarchies. The former have institutionalized (or at least widely accepted) mechanisms for succession.[11] The latter are precisely those settings in which the timing of announcements of succession is critical for sitting autocrats. Inadequate solutions to the succession problem, in turn, have unintended effects for the political stability of non-hereditary regimes.

Tullock's insights on the strategic use of power to thwart rebellions, however, did not appear to have had a major impact on the public choice literature – insofar as they did not spur new contributions that studied autocracies in more detail. It took more than ten years before the publication in 1998 of *The Political Economy of Dictatorship* by Ronald Wintrobe, which provides the first systematic preference-based analysis of autocratic behavior. I summarize below four major contributions from Wintrobe's original analysis.

First, Wintrobe proposes that dictators can have two distinct motivations: power (π) and personal consumption (C). Power is distinguished from consumption in that it identifies non-monetary payoffs that simply are related to the autocrat's desire to control or otherwise impose his will on society. Preferences are therefore defined by a utility function $U(\pi,C)$ with two distinct arguments. However they obtain resources, dictators can choose to spend them on their own consumption or apply them to two instruments that can help them maintain power.

Wintrobe does not specify a functional form, but one could easily imagine a parametric approach that accounts for the relative weights afforded to either power or consumption (as made explicit in his initial contrast between 'totalitarian' and 'tinpot' dictatorships). Idiosyncratic factors would therefore come into play through the curvature of $U(\cdot)$.

Note also that this utility function, $U(\pi,C)$, is not conceptually different from that of democrats. However, the setting is different, and so is the set of policy instruments. Uncertainty forces the dictator to be aware of his continual need to survive. Hence, dictators maximize their utilities under different constraints than one would find in democratic settings. In Wintrobe's framework, utility is maximized indirectly by positing a power function $\pi(R, L)$, which is contingent on two major factors or survival instruments: (1) the ability to repress, R, which itself is a function of various political factors, especially the existence of effective political organizations to control the population; and (2) L, a loyalty (supply) function which depends on the 'price' of loyalty as well as the dictator's ability to deliver direct benefits to his supporters.

Second, Wintrobe notes that repression and loyalty have associated costs (or corresponding prices P_R and P_L). Repression is more or less costly depending on whether the regime possesses a political organization that makes repression relatively cheap. As Wintrobe puts it, the benefits of repression are determined mostly by political factors. The rate of return to buying loyalty, most often in the form of direct income transfers or other economic advantages, depends on the underlying economic system. The ability of a regime to foster the development of political and economic resources will therefore constrain the choice of (induced) power and consumption chosen by a particular dictator.

Third, an important insight from the general model of autocratic behavior is that the costs of repression and loyalty are endogenous in dictatorships. In particular, autocrats can use their power to generate resources, which can then be spent directly on consumption or accumulating further power via a derived money-to-power relation, $\pi(B - C)$. This choice results in a budget constraint that co-defines equilibrium levels of power and resources, $B(\pi) = P_\pi \pi(B - C) + C$. The money-to-power relation as well as the monetary price of power, P_π, will be affected by underlying political and economic technologies.

Finally, Wintrobe's framework serves to derive a typology of nondemocratic regimes as solutions to this general problem of maximizing $U(\pi, C)$ subject to the budget constraint, $B(\pi)$. As is standard in these types of optimization problems, the optimal choices of C and $\pi(R, L)$ will be determined by a condition in which the marginal rate of substitution between R and L equals their relative marginal costs. Four distinct configurations are derived from this general problem, which are illustrated in Figure 6.1 along with the corresponding real-world autocratic regimes. Totalitarian regimes, for instance, are defined as equilibrium configurations with high levels of both repression and loyalty.

Furthermore, because the dictator's budget constraint is determined endogenously, Wintrobe's framework enables an enhanced understanding of autocratic behavior when subject to various exogenous shocks.[12] Since the four types illustrated in Figure 6.1 correspond to distinct political and economic constraints, it follows that economic sanctions should not be expected to elicit the same response from every autocratic regime. For instance, it seems reasonable to predict that economic windfalls such as foreign aid will

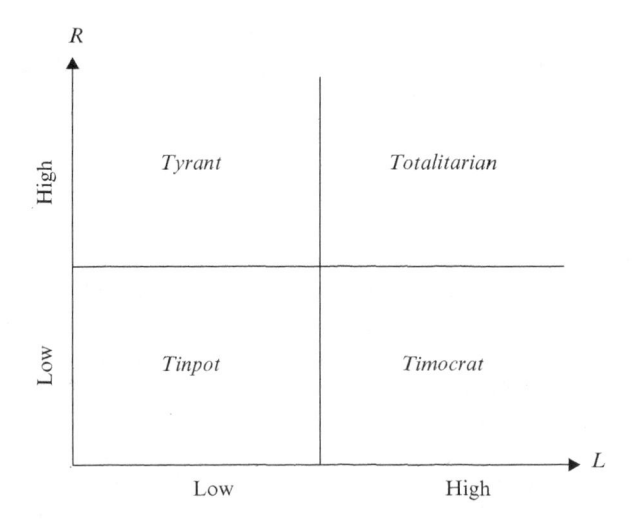

```
              R
              ▲
              |
High    Tyrant    |   Totalitarian
              |
     —————————+—————————
              |
Low     Tinpot    |   Timocrat
              |
              +————————————▶ L
         Low       High
```

Source: Adapted from Wintrobe (1998, p. 81).

Figure 6.1 Derived typology of autocratic regimes

reduce a dictator's optimal level of repression as the relative price of loyalty decreases (assuming that the autocrat can claim credit for the windfall). Indeed, a tinpot dictator, who is motivated by consumption alone, may want to substitute more loyalty for less repression. A totalitarian dictator, however, sees the increase in loyalty as an opportunity to get even more power, which induces even more repression. In general, the utility of Wintrobe's (1998) framework is to alert policy-makers to the importance of understanding the equilibrium effects of exogenous shocks, the comparative statics of which are contingent upon existing optimal combinations of R and L (or corresponding type of dictator).

3 THEORIES OF AUTOCRATIC INSTITUTIONS

Although not strictly a dynamic framework, Wintrobe's model of autocratic behavior lends itself to a variety of dynamic and institutional questions reflecting a *wider* range of options available to dictators beyond particular levels of R and L.[13] Wintrobe (1998) stresses that the dictator's dilemma is a perennial problem (for any given incumbent). Indeed, because it is a lack of credibility that induces insecurity, Wintrobe emphasizes that a process of institutionalization is critical to make policies more credible and effective in the long run (p. 30).

A general solution to credibility problems is simply to provide institutions that restrain the dictator's potentially opportunistic behavior.[14] In the limit, democratization – to the extent that a more constrained environment does indeed contribute to credibility – could, in principle, be a way out of the dictator's dilemma.[15] In Acemoglu and Robinson (2006), for instance, autocratic governments are willing to democratize in order to make credible commitments to the majority of poor citizens. They do so because, in equilibrium, they are not entirely left out of the system after a democratic transition. Whether an autocrat would ever consider the extreme democratization approach depends on his or her prospects of retaining or returning to power in a more competitive environment. Under general conditions, it seems more reasonable to assume that democratization is almost always undesirable for autocrats who would then forgo any ability to impose their will (the pure power embedded in π) or to consume more.[16]

If not democratization, what else can dictators do to lengthen their tenures?[17] The general answer is that autocrats, even if unresponsive to the general population, must still appeal to key constituencies. It is now widely recognized, especially in political economy studies of dictatorships, that all regimes require some measure of political support to survive (Bueno de Mesquita et al. 2003). Stopping well short of democratization, it seems likely – and necessary – that autocrats will consider institutional choices that would constrain them somehow vis-à-vis their core supporters.[18]

As was the case in political science with Linz's totalitarian-authoritarian framework, rational choice approaches to the study of autocracies did not immediately generate an active research community. At least one decade goes by between the work of Tullock (1987) and Wintrobe (1998). Even after Wintrobe's seminal contribution, almost another decade goes by before one starts seeing related efforts. As late as 2008, Myerson notes that strategic models of autocracies are virtually nonexistent.

3.1 Institutional Design

Autocrats may have variable opportunities to induce institutional changes for several reasons. First, autocrats may simply lack required institutions or political structures to enable the regular exercise of governmental authority. Indeed, as Przeworski et al. (2000) have noted, having any viable and durable institutions – especially good ones – requires resources that poor countries do not possess. Especially in the impoverished nations where autocrats are more likely to rule, an aspiring or recently installed autocrat necessarily must contemplate some institutional choices, if only for carrying out basic tasks. A second, and theoretically more important, reason is that dictators, by definition, have the prerogative of altering institutions. Even if some institutions already are in place, and they do not have to be created from scratch, existing constraints generally do not prevent an autocrat from instituting further changes.[19]

Gandhi and Przeworski (2007) represent one of the first efforts at proposing political institutions as potential solutions to the dictator's dilemma. Their work is motivated by the empirical record of dictators' variable successes in surviving over extended periods of time. They first qualify this problem by noting that it stems from two distinct sources. Dictators fear not only their close associates, but they also face threats from the population at large. Gandhi and Przeworski note that close associates can be dealt with informally, and so they focus their attention on institutional solutions for confronting external threats.

Whereas Gandhi and Przeworski also recognize the necessity of deterring rebellions, their analysis is restricted to instruments of co-optation. They argue that the threat posed by core supporters can be mitigated with direct transfers to them in the form of spoils. As they put it, these decisions 'concern transfer of particular goods to specific individuals or groups' (2007, p. 1282). In contrast, policy concessions cannot be disbursed so easily.

To induce other groups to cooperate, dictators must take the additional step of creating a forum in which groups with disparate interests can be brought together. These steps take the form of creating nominally democratic institutions, such as legislatures, whose main purpose is to enable distribution of benefits to large groups rather than to provide a forum for overall political representation.[20]

In subsequent work, Gandhi (2008) elaborates on the notion of policy concessions through institutional co-optation with a more elaborate theory of political cooperation. As has already been established, autocrats need compliance as well as cooperation. To induce the latter, other actors must be given incentives tied to the distribution of rents. As with Wintrobe (1998), the autocrat seeks to survive by buying loyalty. However, loyalty is not free. In addition to direct costs, Gandhi argues that the nature of autocracy introduces various political transaction costs that affect bargaining and the negotiation of agreements between the dictator and his potential supporters. In order to minimize those transaction costs, the autocrat must make it easier for other actors by entering into long-term political exchanges.

However, the decision to choose a nominally democratic institution depends on the credibility of the potential threats to the autocrat's regime. Gandhi formalizes this notion by adopting a uni-dimensional policy bargaining model where the autocrat proposes a policy $x \in [0,1]$. Policy concessions are modeled as policy choices, x, which deviate from the autocrat's ideal point, x_D.[21] There are two situations in which the opposition accepts the dictator's policy proposals. A nominally democratic institution is adopted only when the autocrat faces strong opposition, in which case he needs to offer more concessions, which also requires a greater ability to monitor and punish opportunistic behavior. If the opposition is weak, then the outcome is one of cooperation where the autocrat still proposes some concessions, although not as comprehensively as in the first case. The model also admits a third equilibrium outcome in which the autocrat's policy is rejected. This case entails the potential for overthrowing the dictator, albeit with low probability.

Although they share theoretical insights, the previous two works arrive at institutional solutions via two distinct chains of reasoning. Gandhi and Przeworski (2007, p. 1282) make a clear distinction between two threats: 'co-opting by distributing spoils and co-opting by making policy concessions entail different institutional mechanisms'. Moreover, the actual nature of benefits differs along with the corresponding institutional delivery. Rents appear to be the best means of mollifying some groups of supporters, especially when those groups are not decisive in ensuring the dictator's survival. Gandhi and Przeworski's main reason for choosing loyalty or repression therefore can be attributed to the heterogeneity of actual and potential opponents, especially when the dictator's regime faces credible threats from the general population. In contrast, Gandhi's formal model implies that choices hinge on the overall threat of rebellion. Her bargaining model considers only one aggregated opposition group (with a corresponding ideal policy point). In that model, it is not the distinction between close and distant threats that matters, but rather the overall threat of rebellion by all political opponents. In principle, the theory in Gandhi and Przeworski (2007) admits possible cases where the only viable threat is posed by close supporters, in which case there is no need for nominally democratic institutions. However, Gandhi's (2008) model admits the possibility that if these core supporters are well organized, they could pose enough of a threat to induce the autocrat to rely on co-optation based on policy concessions rather than just spoils.

Overall, both lines of work point to the strength of political opponents as a major determinant of not just policy concessions but institutional concessions as well. Several works follow this line of thought in a more dynamic framework. More closely related to the behavior of autocrats, Myerson (2008) examines the broader question of how autocrats can make credible commitments to supporters, which he identifies as a 'central moral-hazard problem in politics' (p. 125). The basic logic in his approach is the underlying need of leaders to recruit and maintain supporters. Without independent and reliable enforcement, which would be the case in autocracies, it is difficult for leaders to keep their promises. As a solution to the leader's problem, Myerson proposes courts and similar institutional reforms, as well as fine-tuning social relations between the autocrat and individual supporters. These so-called personal constitutions can help create trust between the leader and supporters by establishing norms that act as constitutional checks because they also provide incentives for supporters credibly to threaten to bring down the government. A key feature of this theory is the ability of supporters to coordinate their actions to mitigate opportunism.[22]

Along the same lines, Acemoglu and Robinson (2006) argue that dictators may democratize in order to avoid rebellions by making credible commitments to political opponents. In their framework, Acemoglu and Robinson also admit the possibility of partial non-democracy where political rights are extended to more people but not the whole population. Although these two works do not specify the actual institutional choice to be made, they share with Gandhi and Przeworski (2007) the idea that formal political institutions, sometimes apparently democratic, can enable long-term cooperation between an autocratic leader and his or her supporters.

3.2 Credibility of Power-sharing Institutions

A potential problem with autocratic institutional solutions is not their plausibility as credible commitments, but whether the institutions themselves are deemed viable or credible. As Boix and Svolik (2010) note, institutional solutions are not meant only to create channels for delivering benefits, but also have political dimensions as power-sharing arrangements. In other words, even if autocrats create a legislature solely for instrumental purposes – to forge profitable agreements with other actors, a major political consequence is that such choices constrain the autocrat's authority. Why would autocrats constrain their own powers?

To answer that question, Boix and Svolik formulate a game-theoretic model with a similar orientation to Myerson's model of autocratic commitments; namely, that informational asymmetries between a leader and his allies create a moral hazard problem, notwithstanding the gains from political exchange. Boix and Svolik further assume that allies themselves lack common knowledge about the leader's strength. Therefore, the set of allies or 'notables' that constitute the leader's recruited base of support faces a collective action problem in coordinating their efforts to punish the leader if he were to renege on his commitments (by lying as to the actual total benefits to be shared).

Boix and Svolik assume that allies receive private signals about the leader's strength, informed by the approach of global games (Carlsson and Van Damme 1993). As is assumed in these models, actors have common knowledge about all other aspects of the game. Although imperfect, these private signals can enable allies (implicitly) to coordinate their actions by following a simple strategy that depends only on whether the signal exceeds some threshold – not on others' expected behavior. Provided that all allies adopt this strategy, an equilibrium can emerge in which rebellion occurs with positive probability. The relevance of political institutions lies with their enhanced ability to reduce the frequency of unnecessary rebellions. In so doing, the probability of longer tenures for autocrats increases as well. To the extent that the autocrat and his allies want durable power-sharing schemes, then it is rational for both to establish legislatures and political parties to institutionalize their power-sharing agreement.

In the Boix–Svolik framework, survival is a by-product of the interaction between a leader and his allies, both of whom lack credibility. Both actors are motivated by a power-sharing scheme that provides them with direct benefits. However, the autocrat's promised benefits are not credible due to potential opportunism that cannot be punished by an independent third party. The allies themselves cannot credibly threaten a rebellion due to informational asymmetries that impede collective action. Rather than trying to survive by establishing a legislature, an autocrat is trying to make a credible commitment by helping solve his allies' collective action problem, enabling them credibly to threaten to remove him – albeit not too frequently.

3.3 Autocratic Survival Revisited

The problem of autocratic survival has also received much attention in the literature on sanctions against autocratic governments. An extensive review of this literature is beyond the scope of this chapter, but a brief discussion regarding the related issue of endogenous autocratic institutions is relevant here. Drawing on the more sociological orientation of political studies of dictatorships, there is a line of work that has examined the variable ability of dictators to survive not direct political opposition, but indirect challenges arising from the negative economic impact of externally imposed sanctions. The key point of departure for this literature is Geddes's aforementioned typology of autocratic regimes. One application of that contribution to the literature involves both the underlying capacities as well as nature of political authority of regimes as potential determinants of their ability to survive a sanction. For instance, the superior administrative capacity of military regimes, combined with their stronger corporate loyalty, makes them less vulnerable to economic sanctions than more personalist autocratic regimes that rely solely on the distribution of spoils. Escribà-Folch and Wright (2010) examine the impact of economic sanctions against autocracies for the period 1960–97. Among their other findings, military and single-party regimes are relatively immune to externally imposed economic sanctions. In contrast, the most vulnerable targets are personalist regimes.[23]

The implication of these results is that autocratic survival benefits from having more 'democratic' political structures and more institutional means of securing support from potential opponents. To the extent that dictators foresee sanctions, this literature indicates that they ought to be creating these types of institutions instead of relying solely on the instrumental support that is contingent on special privileges.[24]

3.4 Organizational Design

The work reviewed in this section thus far shares an implicit assumption that autocrats can engage in relatively unconstrained institutional design. That is to say that if autocrats perceive the need for a legislature, they can effectively create one. Missing from this line of reasoning is a better understanding of existing constraints on potential institutional choices; that is, whether autocrats actually make such choices in an institutional vacuum. For instance, if formal (and nominally democratic) institutions enhance the credibility of autocrats, why is it that all autocrats do not make that choice? In fact, when the choice has already been made – that is when legislatures already exist – why do new autocrats often try to suppress or destroy them?[25]

An organizational perspective adds a distinctive dimension to the range of options that autocrats can pursue to remain in power. Indeed, the study of political organizations has been a central feature of traditional studies of dictatorships in political science (see section 2.1). However, the traditional focus has been descriptive, aimed at differentiating rather than explaining different organizational configurations.

In a recent assessment of autocratic organizations from an analytical perspective, Haber (2006) has suggested that autocrats rely heavily on explicit organizational strategies to stay in power. In addition to the aforementioned need to repress and buy loyalty in Wintrobe's framework, Haber advances a distinctive 'logic of organizational proliferation' that gives autocrats incentives to alter the landscape of active political organizations. One particular dimension, among others, is the number of organizations that are allowed to operate in autocratic settings. From the perspective of survival, one would think that restricting the number of organized interests would invariably be a superior strategy for autocrats. As with Gandhi (2008), such a move would lower the political transaction costs necessary to enable cooperation with the regime. Also, the ability of societies to engage in collective action, especially in autocratic settings, often signals a credible threat of coups or revolutions (Acemoglu and Robinson 2006; Tullock 1987). However, Haber notes that sometimes it may be desirable to increase rather than to decrease the number of political organizations.

An organizational perspective can also illuminate the actual delivery of private and public policies in autocratic settings. Although not restricted to autocrats, the selectorate theory of Bueno de Mesquita and collaborators (2000, 2003) notes that regimes offer a mix of private and public policies. Private policies are restricted to core supporters whereas public policies have a wider reach that can benefit the population at large. This theory neither specifies how private or public policies are delivered nor how they affect directly general preferences over time. For instance, does enhanced access to education lead to a better informed citizenry that may demand not just more policies but a regime change?

An organizational logic provides a theoretical argument for a delivery mode that promotes the dictator's survival, but does not translate into greater or more viable demands for political freedoms. Put another way, whereas a logic of co-optation (or buying loyalty in Wintrobe's framework) is always applicable, the alternative is not restricted to repression or terror. A less direct, but not necessarily less effective approach may instead focus on controlling people by organizing how they interact with one another. In terms of private policies, Haber (2006) argues, based on insights from previous work (Haber et al. 2003), that autocrats have incentives to engage in a process of vertical political integration with key supporters, often behind the veil of public institutions. However, integration does not fully solve the credible commitment problem insofar as it requires a supporting organization to keep participants in check along the lines suggested in Boix and Svolik (2010).[26] Public policies aimed at broader segments of the population are not distributed indiscriminately either. However, with a larger number of recipients, autocrats may find it beneficial to pursue corporatist parties as well as to rely on informal – but no less systematic – clientelistic arrangements. All in all, autocrats deal with a variety of political actors, so the portfolio of organizational choices may include myriad formal political and informal organizations to serve different purposes. Political opponents can be controlled through organizational proliferation. Delivery of private services can be channeled through an exclusive organization. In turn, delivery of public policies can be controlled through official, centralized organizations.

We still lack a theoretical framework to fully understand this more general problem, so as to get a better appreciation of relevant trade-offs between institutional and organizational design. Sometimes autocrats are unable to manipulate existing political institutions – at least in the short run. In that situation, the only viable instrument beyond immediate policies, such as repression and private rewards for loyalty, is to alter the overall political organization of their country. On occasion, however, autocrats may be able to pursue both institutional and organizational approaches. One way to summarize the available political instruments for survival would be to differentiate more sharply among direct policy choices, such as repression and loyalty, institutional design to enable long-term cooperation or control, and separate attempts to alter the way in which other actors organize themselves for various purposes, which may include – but are not restricted to – overthrowing the regime.

4 INSTITUTIONAL THEORIES OF AUTOCRACY

Although autocrats are more able than democrats to alter their political environment, this greater flexibility does not always translate into the institutional choices described in the previous section. There are both practical and theoretical reasons for the limitations of such strategies. As a practical matter, the evidence shows that autocrats often inherit structures that may be more difficult to reform than posited by theories of autocratic institutions. Theoretically, the establishment of new institutions introduces higher-order credibility problems that are not immediately resolved. Not only is setting up institutions a costly endeavor, but it also takes much time to establish their viability and associated reliability.

Clearly, some autocrats will have the ability to engage in institutional design, but a more frequent situation would have them operate in somewhat constrained environments. Therefore, it remains a valid question as to how exogenous institutions affect the behavior of autocrats. Two related lines of work are discussed here to address this issue. One is selectorate theory, which provides a general framework for understanding political survival (Bueno de Mesquita et al 2000, 2003). The second is a theory of selective commitments when public enforcement mechanisms are unavailable (Razo 2008).

4.1 Selectorate Theory

Selectorate theory establishes relevant constraints on autocratic behavior in terms of two institutions, the size of the selectorate S and the size of the winning coalition W. The use of this terminology reflects the political identity and purpose of corresponding groups in society. The selectorate is specified by 'an institutionally granted right or norm' to select its leader (Bueno de Mesquita et al. 2000, p. 60). The winning coalition $W \in S$ is the subset of the selectorate that is crucial in maintaining the leader in power. The selectorate and winning coalitions are considered to be of institutional origin because of underlying political constraints that affect the ability of citizens to be members of one or both groups. An implication of these constraints is that those who do not belong to the selectorate are effectively disenfranchised.

The relevance of selectorate theory for the study of autocrats lies in the demands of the winning coalition and its size relative to the selectorate. To stay in power, leaders must be responsive to their supporters. Their responsiveness translates into two distinct types of policies: private policies distributed exclusively to the winning coalition and public policies that can benefit the general population. Because of the need to distribute different types of benefits, 'leaders face two problems: one of distribution and one of credible commitment' (ibid., p. 64). The credibility problem is well understood to apply to all autocrats. The distribution problem, in turn, entails a division of resources into private or public policies.

The two problems come together in the trade-off between the potential use of resources for public policies rather than the private policies required by the winning coalition. The logic of political survival requires leaders to be particularly attentive to their winning coalitions. Credibility is affected by the ratio W/S. The basic argument is that leaders must keep the members of W sufficiently happy that they do not pledge their support to a potential challenger. Given the exclusive benefits associated with W it matters how likely it is that current members may belong to future winning coalitions. The probability of this event becoming more likely is determined by the relative size of the selectorate, which by definition is the relevant subset of the population that ratifies the selection of a new leader. When the ratio W/S is trifling, the winning coalition is more dependent on the current leader, who can then appropriate more resources for himself.

The size of the selectorate varies greatly across autocracies, but the size of the winning coalition invariably is small, in which case theory predicts a predominance of private policies. Not only do these private policies not benefit most of the population, but the evidence also shows that they are often associated with bad government.

It bears noting that S and W are not direct measures of formal political institutions, but rather derived quantities. Notwithstanding this indirect conceptual definition, and the difficulty of gathering good indicators, Clark et al. (2009, pp. 335–6) note that selectorate theory does a good job of mapping onto well-known types of autocratic as well as democratic regimes. Empirical tests are supportive of the theoretical argument (Bueno de Mesquita el al. 2001).

4.2 Relational Perspective on the Political Economy of Dictatorships

A major problem affecting autocrats is that their lack of credibility is also an impediment to promoting economic development. Assuming that autocrats require the cooperation of private actors to invest in economic activities, the literature on institutions and growth suggests that inadequate political foundations (that is, the absence of institutions limiting the public sector's authority) impede such cooperation. Indeed, the historical record indicates that most autocracies are unable to grow, perhaps because they are unable to make credible commitments. However, the evidence also shows the possibility of extraordinary economic performance led by autocrats. Indeed, Przeworski et al. (2000) show that autocratic regimes virtually dominate the list of the globe's fastest growing economies in the postwar period. Well-known examples of such regimes include the so-called Southeast Asian tigers and contemporary China, but the link between growth and autocracy is not limited to the Far East.

Growth under autocratic government poses a theoretical puzzle: if not limited government, what underlies the credibility of economic policies in such countries? Clearly, there is room for external enforcement mechanisms, especially when courting foreign investors. The latter may sometimes appeal to their home governments for protection, or otherwise, assuming capital mobility, move their resources elsewhere. Generally, autocrats can develop reputations for good behavior and credible promises. However, these two mechanisms cannot tell the whole story because successful cases of growth under authoritarianism have also relied heavily on domestic investors who lacked external enforcement capabilities or mobility. Moreover, reputation cannot be obtained overnight. Reputation is, in fact, a by-product of credibility rather than a solution to credibility problems, at least with respect to domestic investors during early phases of development.

Two general solutions have been proposed to explain this puzzle, but they remain incomplete accounts. On the one hand, developmental scholars point to the existence of benevolent governments or developmental states who are led by rulers motivated to enhance the welfare of their societies (Evans 1989, 1995). Along similar lines, there are arguments that emphasize the importance of visionary leaders who know what decisive actions need to be taken (Gray and McPherson 2001). From a public choice perspective, the existence of benevolent government seems dubious without further explanation about underlying incentives to satisfy the needs of the general population. Empirically, it is difficult to identify benevolence at the time that rulers assume power, so such assessments invariably are retrospective. As with reputations, one can identify benevolent autocrats only after they have proven themselves, which also means that they were somehow able to solve their initial credibility problems, a task that remains unexplained in related literatures.

A second, and more widely accepted explanation, is that autocrats can become stationary bandits (Olson 1993, 2000). The theoretical argument presupposes that economic output is a positive function of public goods. The question of economic development is no longer one of credible commitments, but rather an examination of the incentives that would lead autocrats to promote investments in public goods (presumably in a credible manner). Olson identifies two critical conditions: (1) dictators must have long-term horizons; and (2) encompassing interests. Basically, autocrats internalize the external effects of predation, which limit output and hence revenue, by recognizing that they can get more revenue in the long run by forgoing some current benefits, otherwise expropriated predatorily, in return for sharing in expected future benefits.

Although intuitive, the theory of stationary banditry suffers from one or more problems that limit its applicability. First, it remains unclear how dictators are able to have long-term horizons without first having promoted economic performance to secure their survival in the first place. Second, even if stable institutions are in place to signal the longevity of an autocratic regime, there is no clear empirical referent for the concept of encompassing interests. In a formal version of this theory, these interests are modeled in a democratic rather than autocratic context (McGuire and Olson 1996). The question remains: who, beyond the autocrat, comprise the set of encompassing interests and how are these interests organized?

To address the theoretical puzzle of growth under authoritarianism, Razo (2008) first suggests the need for a general understanding of systematic policy-making differences between democracies and autocracies. Differentiating democratic and autocratic regimes has proven to be a somewhat elusive enterprise given the plethora of conceptual frameworks and operational definitions (Munck and Verkuilen 2002).[27] Building upon the work of Linz on authoritarian regimes, Razo proposes two major institutional dimensions that matter for policy purposes. First, there is the degree of policy discretion afforded to executive authorities. Second, there is the degree of public enforcement institutions.

In a comparative institutional perspective, it is reasonable to assume that autocrats have greater policy discretion than democrats. This discretion may extend to the realm of institutional design, but even when that is infeasible, autocrats have a comparative advantage in disbursing special privileges to selected actors. For this reason, policy-making in autocracies will be driven by attention to private policies with specific beneficiaries.[28] A private policy is private because of its limited scope, which confers narrowly targeted rather than broader public benefits. However, the actual institutional setting in which that bias takes place can be either formal or informal. Formally, requests for private policies can be managed through legislatures or bureaucracies. Often, however, they will come about through informal agreements and direct contacts with the autocrat. Although autocrats may sometimes offer policies of general public benefit, there is no such demand from all members of society. Disenfranchised individuals and groups certainly can demand more public goods for themselves. However, the beneficiaries of pre-existing special privileges, which are likely to be the autocrat's key supporters, would oppose such broad-based redistribution because it would reduce their own wealth. Moreover, autocratic promises to provide public goods may not always be believable, especially if they enable challengers to mount credible threats by stealing core supporters with the promise of delivering even larger private benefits to them (as selectorate theory would predict).

The procurement and awarding of special privileges must be attractive both to the autocrat and the favored recipients. Therefore, one implication of an autocrat's incentive to deliver selective benefits to key constituents is that private policies must generate rents. Because rents imply returns in excess of what actors would earn in competitive markets, it follows that economic activity in autocracies necessarily will focus on rent-seeking. Rent-seeking also occurs in democracies (Tullock 1967; Krueger 1974; Kitschelt and Wilkinson 2007). However, the historical record supports the claim that rents are essential in the autocratic case: early – and sometimes later – phases of sustained economic growth under autocracies is based on the predominance of large industrial groups and restricted competition.

Even if highly lucrative, potential rents address only the participation constraints of relevant actors. Given the existence of an autocrat, the credibility of private policies still remains a thorny issue. This is where the second institutional dimension of public enforcement is relevant. Autocrats, by definition, cannot guarantee their promises on the basis of public enforcement mechanisms. Setting up such a mechanism would not be credible initially either.[29] Therefore, for a systemic reliance on private policies to be successful for economic and even survival purposes, economic agents themselves must seek their own private protection. This is so even in cases where the autocrat has already made a commitment to a few actors because reputations are specialized. In autocracies, special privileges – just as they are awarded individually – can be altered individually, perhaps to give them to someone else. Autocracies therefore impede the development of general reputations that can act as reliable public signals to forecast the autocrat's interactions with any particular agent or group.

The logic of private protection induced by the predominance of private policies is essentially a decentralized process. The main reason is that an autocrat's attempt to propose 'independent' third-party enforcement is not credible given potential collusion between the autocrat and that third party. The ability of individual actors to obtain reliable private enforcement will then generally determine their prospects of securing their own private policies and property rights. Put another way, not all private policies generated in autocracies will be honored. Moreover, to the extent that economic actors can foresee their inability to secure third-party enforcement, private policies may not even be credible to begin with, so investors will refrain from cooperating at all with the autocrats.

In principle, it is plausible for recipients of special privileges to organize themselves to retaliate collectively against any act of autocratic predation. However, this ability requires a pre-existing capacity for collective action, which is not always available in the real world. Moreover, even if such capacity exists, it can be undermined by the prospect of still greater rents in a collusive agreement with the autocrat. In other words, the autocrat can induce free-riding in exchange for even more special privileges to prevent collective retaliation as a ready deterrent for predatory behavior.

Under what conditions can autocrats then promote their economies based on the theorized predominance of private policies? The answer lies partly with the distribution of power in autocracies. As a minimal requirement, the distribution cannot be lopsided in favor of the autocrat such that actors cannot find any reliable private enforcers. These private enforcers must be given incentives to punish predatory behavior. Therefore, some of the rents must now be shared with a third set of actors. Policy discretion already implied the need for private policies based on economic concentration. The addition of another party to share rents, due to lack of public enforcement, only serves to increase autocrats' incentives to promote even more concentrated markets to generate higher rents.

The size of this potential pool of enforcers is also critically important given the decentralized nature of private protection. If the pool is smaller than the number of recipients of private benefits, economic actors are more likely to recruit third-party enforcers even when their primary motivation is to protect a specific private policy. Overall, the procurement of private protection generates a network structure of overlapping private protection. It is this emergent structure which, with sufficient connectivity, creates the incentives for autocrats to make credible commitments.

Two relational mechanisms can potentially enable this network structure to discipline autocratic behavior.[30] First, there is the prospect of collective retaliation because the network structure defines, in effect, the encompassing or vested interests of relevant actors in society. Pooling resources from various private enforcers makes for a more formidable threat against predation. Second, and most importantly, such collective retaliation must be activated by the propagation of predation risk, which is endogenous and depends on third parties' willingness and ability to defend economic actors. If a third party does not enforce a particular private deal, expected rents for connected enforcers decrease as a dictator continues to prey on related (and potentially vulnerable) firms. A more connected network therefore increases fear and thus the incentives of third parties to defend their interests.

An explicitly network-analytic perspective illuminates the strategic considerations that underlie the credibility of private policies, which, by definition, have a relational character. It is important to note that the risk of predation can be propagated through other channels and other relations among economic and political actors. The theory in Razo (2008) examines only a minimal set of conditions that can induce generalized credible commitments to multiple private policies. Also, despite the emergence of networks of private protection, this is not necessarily a case of endogenous institutional or organizational change. For one, autocrats cannot control all social relations. Secondly, private protection does not strictly require the use of formal political institutions.

It has already been noted that the existing institutional framework of autocracies provides the impetus for private policies and the search for private protection. The latter may not always be successful. However, the procurement of private protection reveals another role for existing political institutions. These institutions not only identify the autocrat but other important political actors. Hence, formal institutions can reduce the search costs of procuring private protection. Moreover, existing formal institutions can also be used as a way to impose barriers to entry by future generations (and hence preserve the rents provided by current private policies).

Finally, the theory of overlapping protection serves both to qualify as well as to support the theory of stationary banditry. First, regarding the nature of policies, Razo (2008) departs from Olson (1993, 2000) in arguing that economic activity largely is based on private rather than public policies. It is not that public policies lack more desirable welfare properties, but simply that the institutional environment of autocracies impedes their credibility and, moreover, private policies require huge rents to induce participation. Hence, other things equal, we should expect policies benefitting the public at large to be less frequent in autocracies than in democracies.

Second, a network theory of private protection illuminates the nature and organization of encompassing interests in the theory of stationary banditry. In fact, network analysis can serve to map out those interests, especially when they are not already embedded in some type of formal organization, as would be the case with pre-existing political parties. The theory makes it clear, however, that the encompassing interests are not strictly organizational actors, but individuals who benefit directly from sharing rents generated by special privileges.

At the margin, even if constrained by incipient formal political institutions, an astute autocrat may recognize the importance of political organization and, hence, the possibility of trying to alter the ability of others to challenge him. However, an organizational perspective also reveals that it is not just formal institutions that matter but informal constraints as well (such as those enabled by a network of overlapping private protection). In general, relations among recipients of special privileges and their private protectors cannot completely be controlled by an autocrat. Therefore, the ability of autocrats to make credible commitments will then be relatively infrequent, which is consistent with the empirical evidence, and the mostly poor economic performances of autocracies.

5 HOW ARE AUTOCRATS DIFFERENT FROM DEMOCRATS?

5.1 Autocratic Dilemmas and the Irony of Excessive Power

In comparative perspective, autocrats appear to consume more perks of office than democrats. Even if these perks are not immediately available upon assuming office, autocrats can nonetheless make decisions to create and continually increase them. The main reason, which is not controversial, is that autocrats enjoy excessive power vis-à-vis their democratic counterparts. However, there is an inherent irony that comes with more political authority; namely, that more nominal political power does not readily translate into a greater ability to exercise that power for whatever purpose motivates the autocrat. A paradox that confronts autocrats is that more power is often less power primarily because of the inherent uncertainty that defines the dictator's (security) dilemma (Wintrobe 1998).

Underlying the dictator's security dilemma is the inability for autocrats credibly to commit to anyone in society, a situation known as the fundamental dilemma of government or *credibility dilemma* (Weingast 1995). For repression and loyalty to work, it must be the case that other actors believe such instruments to be credible punishments and rewards. Even if dictators are able to manage their own security dilemmas, all other actions (especially administrative and procedural ones) are questionable. The reason for a separate discussion of credibility stems from the fact that security and credibility dilemmas, although clearly related, are not logically equivalent. For instance, a credible autocrat – recognized as such by the possible existence of institutionalized power-sharing mechanisms – is not necessarily a secure autocrat. Indeed, as both Boix and Svolik (2010) and Razo (2008) argue, credibility ultimately requires vulnerability, thus suggesting a trade-off between instruments that aim to solve one dilemma or the other.

Finally, the theorized predominance of private policies also reveals the greater complexity that comes with the exercise of autocratic government.[31] Greater discretion imposes a heavier workload on autocrats, who are expected to provide special privileges for a variety of actors. The demand for these privileges is expected to be greater in autocracies than in democracies. Moreover, satisfying demands at one point in time does not mean placating future demands by former recipients or potentially new ones.

I refer to the above situation as an autocrat's *governability dilemma*.[32] In an attempt to survive and become credible, autocrats must also be responsive to more demands. Clearly, limited time and resources will provide incentives for autocrats to minimize their workloads. For instance, they can limit the number of recipients of special privileges. However, this is not an entirely endogenous choice given that the *security dilemma* implies that such number may also be determined by actions and information that are hidden from the autocrat. More formally, autocrats can create institutions or organizations that manage demands for private policies more effectively. Such formalization is feasible, however, only if the autocrat has already solved the credibility problems associated with such strategies.

Another obvious solution is for the autocrat to establish a modern bureaucracy. Indeed, a high-quality bureaucracy underlies many explanations about the success of East Asian autocracies in the postwar period. These so-called developmental states combine state capacity with good bureaucracies to make optimal decisions regarding growth-enhancing policies (Wade 1990). One problem with this explanation, as a general solution to the governability problem, is that bureaucratization and delegation are both strategic choices. Not all governments, especially autocratic ones, have incentive to create an efficient cadre of civil servants (Geddes 1994; Kang 2002). Even if a bureaucracy is proposed, bureaucrats would have two potential worries: that the autocrat may terminate their employment at will and, secondly, that the autocrat may reserve some independent authority to alter decisions previously delegated to bureaucrats.[33]

In sum, reconciling all three dilemmas in a way that guarantees survival, credibility, and a manageable workload is not an easy feat. We do not yet have a theoretical framework that allows us to derive optimal policy instruments for coping with all three dilemmas. However, as noted above, there are several reasons to suspect that autocrats cannot always deal with this broader problem. We should not be surprised that most autocrats fail, perhaps because they are forced to respond immediately to only one of them, especially the security dilemma – just to survive.

5.2 Informative and Structured Political Environments

An important distinction between autocracies and democracies is that the former lack adequate political structures to deal with all relevant tasks of government. Consider the problem of selecting a leader. As noted above, autocracies are notoriously vulnerable to the problem of succession. With the exception of hereditary monarchies, the rules governing succession may not be generally understood by all relevant parties. In contrast, a democracy enables the ready identification of candidates as well as electoral rules that determine who assumes political office.[34]

It is precisely this lack of structure, or what Shepsle (2006) calls *unstructured institutions*, that increases demands for private policies whose management and credibility further exacerbate an autocrat's governability dilemma.[35] Too little structure effectively not just enlarges choice sets for given domains, but also does so in multiple dimensions. In terms of the discussion above, not only are dictators able to offer *both* private and public policies, but they can also engage in a variety of repressive and loyalty strategies that, in turn, can be solved through a variety of institutional and organizational design choices.

A second relevant dimension is the provision of adequate information to fulfill government tasks. Revisiting the selection of leaders, selectorates may lack information about the individual preferences of 'candidates' (or their corresponding types – predispositions to be either benevolent or predatory). Eliciting that information is difficult in autocratic settings. Any signals that candidates provide are not likely to be informative because the common outcome is a pooling equilibrium where potential leaders make promises of good behavior. In contrast, elections in democracies provide for a more informative environment, even if most voters rationally will ignore it.[36]

In the end, recognizing informational and structural differences across autocracies and democracies also serves to qualify the differential approach to the study of those regimes. Empirical studies of autocrats, for instance, tend to emphasize the importance of particular leaders, thus impeding generalizable findings. In contrast, democratic theory allows for more impersonal and systemic analyses where the identity of leaders – while relevant in terms of individual preferences and policy decisions – is not as important due to the institutionalized constraints on public offices. A focus on idiosyncratic factors in autocracies is not entirely misguided, however, in extreme cases where the political environment does not provide any useful information or reliable procedures.

6 CONCLUSION

This chapter reviewed recent developments in economic approaches to the study of autocracies. Although the literature reviewed herein is still in its infancy, several general findings can be judged to have enhanced our understanding of autocratic behavior. First, endogenous institutional approaches provide a reasonable explanation for the prevalence of nominally democratic institutions, such as legislatures, in autocratic settings. The main theoretical argument is that such institutions serve primarily the autocrat's purpose of credibly engaging other political actors whose support is required to survive. Second, there is widespread consensus that autocrats rely on a mix of public and, especially, private benefits to secure political support. As Wintrobe has noted, autocrats rely on political exchange not unlike the interactions between democrats and their corresponding fellow citizens. Furthermore, the study of private policies serves to illuminate the nature of economic activity in successful autocracies. Contrary to previous theory and policy advice, autocrats can offer credible private policies only by providing lucrative privileges that, in turn, require highly concentrated markets populated by governmentally granted private monopolies or by state-owned enterprises.

From a comparative perspective, this chapter also offers three organizing principles to better appreciate differences between autocrats and democrats (and their corresponding political contexts). First, the identification of three autocratic dilemmas (security, credibility, and governability) serves to qualify further the more severe constraints that autocrats face in their daily exercise of governmental power. Second, the distinction between endogenous and exogenous institutions serves to differentiate the set of instruments actually available to autocrats. Those instruments were distinguished in terms of specific policies (or benefits), institutional choices, and organizational choices. One key difference between autocrats and democrats is that greater power enlarges the former's set of feasible instruments. However, having more choices is a double-edged sword because of the associated dilemmas of autocratic government. Finally, a distinction was made between environments that are more or less structured, and correspondingly more or less informative, as a better depiction of major institutional differences between democratic and autocratic regimes.

NOTES

1. Henceforth, I make a binary distinction between autocracies (or dictatorships) and democracies to identify the corresponding regimes associated with the editors' title for this review chapter. Making such a binary distinction is a topic of considerable debate in political science and is used here simply as a heuristic to avoid a lengthy discussion about the relative advantages or disadvantages of a more gradated approach to comparative regime analysis (Collier and Adcock 1999). Also, although the term dictatorship was originally invented for interim or 'crisis governments,' it is now widely used as a generic label for non-democratic regimes (Linz 2000, p. 61).
2. The former admit the possibility of some endogenous institutional choice, whereas the latter correspond to typical examinations of behavior under exogenous constraints.
3. See Shapiro (2003) for a more recent assessment of democratic theory.
4. Although depending on the context, and especially the need to secure external resources, sultanistic regimes may exhibit some apparently systematic policies, which are denoted as *distorted capitalism* (Chehabi and Linz 1998, pp. 21–3).
5. A related problem occurs in the literature on bureaucratic-authoritarian regimes, the definition of which applies only to a few, if not just one, case (Collier 1979a, 1979b; O'Donnell 1973).
6. This line of reasoning is central to a large literature on the impacts of sanctions on the stability of autocratic regimes wherein this classification has been easier to operationalize than the three-way classification proposed by Linz and collaborators (Escribà-Folch 2009; Escribà-Folch and Wright 2010).
7. A parallel literature has also emerged in an attempt to derive better operational definitions of regime types. There is, however, no consensus on the best dataset to identify regime differences. This is the result of both philosophical differences as well as methodological measurement problems. See Munck and Verkuilen (2002) for a relevant discussion.
8. This theory is revisited in section 4 on institutional theories of autocracy. A formalized version, and comparative analysis of democracy and autocracy, can be found in McGuire and Olson (1996).
9. It could be argued that this literature owes a great intellectual debt to the work of Machiavelli. However, a particularly important omission in *The Prince* is the lack of concern about credible commitments (Machiavelli [1515] 1984, pp. 58–60), which ignores crucial strategic considerations addressed by both Tullock (1987) and Wintrobe (1998). Tullock (1987, p. 26) also argues that Machiavelli ignores the problem of offering a reliable reward system that does not sound false alarms.
10. In this respect, Tullock's modeling approach builds upon earlier work of his on revolutions as well as Olson's logic of collective action, which helped spark a related, but distinct, literature on the economic analysis of rebellions and revolutions (Lichbach 1995; Olson 1965; Tullock 1971b).
11. Tullock also elaborates on alternative mechanisms, such as that used in the Vatican where a council elects a new leader after the incumbent Pope's death.
12. See Wintrobe (2001) for a summary of the policy implications of foreign aid and international sanctions.
13. Wintrobe himself examines a variety of institutional arrangements that were designed deliberately to help solve the dictator's dilemma in particular settings. His comparative statics also examine how potential institutional or exogenous changes alter equilibrium behavior. Although he does explicitly address institutional dynamics within his formal model, some key variables, such as the price of buying loyalty, can be endogenous. Readers are referred to the 1998 book for richer details.
14. This is, indeed, an old prescription. As Aristotle himself put it: 'The more restricted the functions of kings, the longer their power will last unimpaired; for then they are more moderate and not so despotic in their ways; and they are less envied by their subjects' (Aristotle [n.d.] 1996).
15. This is, in fact, the prescription that emanates from the literature on institutions and growth, namely, that political institutions of limited government provide the political foundations for economic growth.
16. The broader literature on democratization does indeed admit this possibility, although the number of willing abdications through elite-managed transitions is relatively small. See O'Donnell et al. (1986).
17. Even before physical factors, such as old age, come into play.
18. In the literature on the political foundations of growth, which has examined autocratic contexts explicitly, these required choices are depicted in terms of the need to tie the ruler's hands (Root 1989). As Buchanan (1987) notes, that literature draws inspiration from a public choice literature on constitutional econom-

ics, which focuses on explaining the choice of rules. See Brennan and Buchanan (1985), Voigt (1997), and Mueller (2008) to learn more about constitutional analysis from a public choice perspective.
19. A possible exception may be a totalitarian regime where it is presumed that ideology and an official single party place severe constraints on leaders. However, these regimes are relatively rare and, as noted in section 2, whether such constraints are binding is debatable (Cassinelli 1960).
20. Whether participants in these forums are indeed representative of the broader population is an open question. Legislatures would appear to be most useful when organized interests already exist, the representatives of which can be assembled under the umbrella of a formal political institution.
21. Rents are assumed to be positively related to policy concessions, so more concessions increase the potential of special privileges as well.
22. This is essentially the same argument of Weingast (1997), to the effect that constitutions can serve as focal points for coordinating collective action against abuse of authority. However, as Hardin (1997) cautiously notes, solving societal coordinational problems is not a trivial task.
23. For interested readers, this chapter also provides an extensive review of the literature on sanctions. Foreign policy issues regarding the desirability of various types of sanctions are also discussed in Wintrobe (2001). Wintrobe adds a more strategic perspective that admits the potential destabilizing effect of economic sanctions. Depending on the type of dictatorship, greater vulnerability need not imply compliance (for example, less repression) as dictators fight for survival under adverse conditions.
24. Along these lines, although for a different question regarding commitments to domestic actors, Wright (2008) notes that binding legislatures are desirable institutional instruments for inducing domestic investment. Legislatures can also be valuable for distributing spoils when domestic investors are not needed.
25. A decision to maintain existing institutions can be more easily explained by the theoretical argument that such institutions enhance the dictator's ability to interact with core supporters. It still seems necessary, however, to have a more general theory of institutional change in autocratic settings to also consider the option *not* to alter institutions.
26. This is a similar logic as in Gandhi and Przeworski (2007) and Gandhi (2008), but the instrument need not nominally be a democratic institution.
27. In particular, there remain important philosophical debates about whether the difference between democracies and autocracies is simply a matter of degree (along relevant dimensions) or the identification of two qualitatively distinct ontological regime types (Collier and Adcock 1999). Resolving these contentious issues is beyond the scope of this chapter but is worth noting these debates to qualify any approach that posits systematic institutional differences across regimes.
28. I use the term policy here in a broad sense as a variable of the government's choosing that constrains societal behavior. Since private policies are not available to the general population, they constitute a societal constraint on the allocation of (exclusive) benefits.
29. Wright (2008) proposes that dictators may pursue more institutional venues to secure support for a variety of purposes. When they need domestic investors, autocrats propose legislatures to enhance policy credibility. When domestic investors are not needed, legislatures serve to divide and conquer. Again, the idea here is that creating institutions is indeed a feasible choice. The distinction between binding and nonbinding legislatures is more difficult to make, especially when the latter already exist, in which case it is not created but ignored.
30. See Razo (2008, ch. 2) and Razo (2010) for formalizations of this argument.
31. Complexity is defined here in terms of the number of private policies that must credibly be enforced. As argued in Razo (2008), autocrats cannot make general commitments that guarantee all such private policies at once.
32. Although related to the political transaction costs described in Gandhi (2008), the governability dilemma is distinct in that it recognizes that each particular agreement is subject to transaction costs – thus the need for individual private enforcement – but there is also an endogenous additional cost of government that comes with greater discretion to offer private policies in the first place.
33. Bureaucracies also raise a wide range of issues about political control of agents. Even if delegation is rightly perceived as a solution to the governability dilemma, autocrats need to undertake additional efforts in monitoring their behavior. In other words, the governability dilemma is substituted for a principal–agent problem, which may not be any easier to solve. Both Olson (2000, ch. 7) and Wintrobe (1998, ch. 9–10) explain how the former Soviet Union attempted to mitigate these problems by using various competitive institutional designs that promised to elicit expected effort from bureaucrats.
34. Of course, not all public officials are elected in democracies, including the heads of administrative agencies, who in many cases are appointed by the chief executive of national or sub-national government. However, appointments are nonetheless indirectly related to elections insofar as citizens elect leaders who then bargain over appointments.
35. To be sure, Shepsle (2006) does not a draw a distinction between autocracies and democracies directly in terms of corresponding unstructured or structured situations. However, the conceptual jump is warranted

because unstructured situations resemble the 'state of nature', which is used by Tullock (1987, p. 28) to describe the context in which dictators operate.
36. The quantity of information need not be correlated with quality, however, as the free flow of information can contain a lot of noise. Nevertheless, it is more likely that a candidate's true type will be revealed publicly by an opponent.

PART III

SYSTEMS OF COLLECTIVE DECISION-MAKING

7 Expressive voting
Geoffrey Brennan and Michael Brooks

1 INTRODUCTION

There is now a considerable literature operating (one way or another) under the rubrics of 'expressive voting' and expressive political activity more generally. Some of the relevant ideas are to be found in early contributions by mainstream public choice scholars – such as Buchanan (1954b), Downs (1957) and Tullock (1971a) – but the contributions that make the expressive idea a centerpiece of the 'rational actor' approach to political behavior are of more recent origin. Notable examples include Goodin and Roberts (1975), Brennan and Buchanan (1984), Kliemt (1986), Brennan and Lomasky (1993), Schuessler (2000a, 2000b) and Brennan and Hamlin (1998); for more recent attempts, see Brennan (2008b), Hamlin and Jennings (2009) and Hillman (2010).

Hamlin and Jennings (2009, henceforth H&J) provide a general survey of this strand of work and seek to develop appropriate conceptual foundations for the category of 'expressive conduct'. We are in broad agreement with their approach and many of their conclusions. In particular, we think, like them:

1. That Hillman's focus on the relation between expressive behavior and identity draws the characterization of expressive behavior rather too narrowly – though, like H&J, we think identity is certainly *one* of the more important things that political actors might 'express' (and may be the most significant in some cases of interest).
2. That it is in some ways regrettable
   (a) that the literature on expressive activity has focused so intensely on voting, and
   (b) that expressive voting theory has been framed in explicit contrast to, and as a critique of, 'public choice' orthodoxy.
3. That there has been a lack of clarity in much of this literature as to what precisely expressive voting theory is a theory *of*. H&J draw a distinction between the decision of *whether* to vote (the macro element of which is aggregate turnout) and the question of *how* to vote (if one does) – including the kinds of considerations that are likely to weigh in voters' minds and (hence?) are likely to be mobilized by candidates in their attempts to garner support. H&J think, as we do, that the expressive voting account is primarily directed at the latter question – the 'how' question, as we shall put it – but the distinction itself begs questions about whether 'how' and 'whether' issues are related, and if so, in what sense.

In what follows, we take up each of these themes. We begin, however, with some remarks about a more abstract question concerning the perceived purpose of the whole exercise – specifically, whether the immediate ambition of any 'theory of voting behavior' is primarily empirical or theoretical. This will occupy us briefly in section 2. In section 3, we consider the 'theory of what?' issue. In section 4, we examine the implicit contrast between expressive and instrumental theories of voting in terms of how that contrast is framed – and specifically whether it is framed as a categorical distinction or as a spectrum of possibilities. We then turn in section 5 to the issue of 'identity' and what role identity should be seen as playing in the expressive voting account. We turn in section 6 to some challenges that we see expressive theory facing in terms of integration with the sort of general approach that public choice theory involves. Section 7 offers some brief conclusions.

2 THE 'LOGIC' VERSUS THE 'SCIENCE' OF ELECTORAL BEHAVIOR

In an interesting, and we think important, methodological paper, Buchanan ([1969] 2000) draws a threefold distinction between the 'logic of economic choice', the 'abstract science of economic behavior' and the 'predictive science of economic behavior'. In that formulation, the *logic* of choice can be distinguished from the *science* in terms of a distinction between the structure and the content of the agents' utility functions. The logic of choice can proceed by specifying the content of the utility function in terms of abstract Xs and Ys: the sign of the substitution effect can be determined and demand curves constructed, without any specification of what the Xs and Ys actually represent. To move from this exercise in logic to a predictive science requires a specification of what the Xs and Ys are in terms of observable and measurable magnitudes – and possibly of the sensitivity of the levels of X and Y to changes in their prices. The logic of choice can, in other words, proceed entirely in terms of hypothetical alternatives; the science of choice demands that those alternatives be grounded in the observable. Both structure and content claims concerning utility functions can be disputed – but the structure claims can be refuted only once the content claims are confirmed. That is, under any given assignment of meaning to the Xs and Ys, any refutation of predictions concerning behavior based on that assignment can be finessed by the claim that the assignment rather than the logic is wrong. In that sense, the logic of choice lies closer to the Lakatosian core of the rational choice approach than does the predictive science of choice.

Although Buchanan's discussion is explicitly framed in terms of *economic* choice, there is no reason at all why the argument should not be seen as fully applicable to the logic and predictive science of 'electoral choice'. Indeed, one might argue that one of the main examples of the power of the 'pure logic of choice' lies precisely in the contrast between electoral choice and choice in market settings. On the expressive account, the pure logic of choice is sufficient to show that electoral and market 'choices' are different in an interesting way. But, of course, this difference is a logical one and not necessarily a predictive one. And this fact raises a question of the status of purely logical considerations.

Suppose specifically that it were discovered that, whatever the logical niceties, the expressive account of voting ends up with much the same predictions about voting *behavior* as does the instrumental account. This is an empirical claim that, for example, Wickstrom has made on Brennan (2008c) in a commentary at a conference (without, it needs to be said, much in the way of empirical evidence). But what is relevant for our purposes is not so much the empirical claim but the conclusion he draws from it – namely, that *in the absence of empirical predictions* the expressive account is of no ultimate interest. We do not agree. Few economists have been content to settle for mere 'goodness of fit' as the sole test for their theories, entirely independent of the theory's internal logical coherence. For most of us, it makes a difference whether a conclusion follows from basic axioms by virtue of a priori logic or just happens, entirely contingently, to be the case.

At the risk of being tedious, it is we think worth repeating a point made by Brennan and Lomasky (1993, p. 21):

> Consider the argument – all swans are white; this creature is white; therefore [it] is a swan. To recognize that this argument is logically flawed is not to deny that the creature may after all, be a swan. It is rather to recognize that the argument as such provides no reason for thinking so.

If it turned out that many voters do vote in the manner that conventional public choice theory has claimed – that is, in accordance with what economists would normally interpret as narrow individual self-interest – there would remain two possible explanations for this fact: that the expressive account is flawed; or that (as expressive theorists would put it) expressive preferences and instrumental preferences happen to be highly correlated. Perhaps some radical behaviorists would say that the question of which dominates really does not matter – that in any such case, the expressive/instrumental distinction would turn out to be a distinction without a difference. But we do not think that any properly self-styled rational choice theorist would or could agree with this claim. Getting the logic of the argument right is, for any rational choice exponent, important in itself. Whether there is a significant payoff in terms of distinctive predictions is a downstream matter: the empirical chips will, after all, fall where they may!

To say this is not, however, to deny that there will be *some* pressure on any theory in the rational choice family to show that there are likely to be *some* empirical chips to fall, and to indicate what these might be. Hence, expressive theory has seen part of its task to involve providing plausible examples of how the logic might play out empirically (for example, Brennan and Lomasky 1993; Brennan and Hamlin 1998). That said, it is worth emphasizing that rejection of those examples does not falsify the logical claims. The 'expressive account' of voting is first and foremost located within the logic of choice: any rejection of it will require what seem to us to be rather strong general psychological claims – either that expressive benefits/costs do not exist; or that they are uniformly connected so closely to instrumental benefits that no distinction between instrumental and expressive concerns makes much sense.

3   THE CENTRAL CLAIM AND THE 'HOW' QUESTION

The point of departure for the expressive account of voting is the observation of a dis-analogy between individual choice in markets and individual voting at the ballot box. This dis-analogy is often rendered as a knife-edge distinction; but it is better thought of as a comparative matter, for reasons that we shall take up in the next section. Here, we seek merely to state where the dis-analogy lies.

The general point can be indicated by reference to an individual's rational calculus in voting on what is, for her, an issue of conscience. Consider voter J. Suppose that there is a candidate A who, if elected, will implement a policy that J judges is *the* right policy: J's conscience demands that she vote for it. However, the policy in question, though the morally right one, has a somewhat unfortunate feature for J: namely, it requires J to pay $5,000 per year in additional taxes. *Question*: how much will voting for A cost J? If you think the answer is $5,000 per annum, then you have committed the fallacy that expressive voters identify with much mainstream public choice theory: you have treated J's voting action as if it were decisive over the options. The correct answer, according to the expressive voting account, is $5,000 *times the probability that J will break (or make) a tie among all other voters* (h henceforth). In a normal democratic election, h is very small.[1] So the cost to J of voting according to her conscience may well be a matter of a few dollars – perhaps only a few cents.

Contrast that case with another, occurring in the marketplace, where for J to act in accordance with her conscience will involve her making a contribution of $5,000 to the relevant cause. In that case, J will be decisive over outcomes; and acting conscientiously will indeed cost her $5,000. In other words, at the ballot box, acting as conscience requires will cost J a tiny fraction of what acting conscientiously will cost her in the marketplace. Economists hold to a general belief that any such difference in costs is likely to make a difference in behavior. Actually, economists believe that behavioral responses would emerge even if the change in costs were a mere 50 percent – or even 20 percent. So when the difference is a factor of thousands, the behavioral difference is likely to be very large. The specific prediction is that J is more likely to behave 'morally' at the ballot box than in the marketplace.

But this moralized example should not be treated as canonical: the comparison between ballot-box and market is not restricted to cases involving morality. For example, in another case, there is a policy, offered by candidate A, which promises to increase J's income by $5,000. What is the benefit to J of voting for that policy? Again, $5,000 *times the probability that J will break (or make) a tie among all other voters* is a remarkably small amount. On the other hand, if J accepts the offer of $5,000 per annum in a marketplace transaction she will receive the full benefit of $5,000. The general point is that, if there are any considerations at all that dispose a voter to vote for one option rather than another for its own sake, the net benefits the voter will accrue from having that other option in place will play a relatively second-order role – relative specifically to the role such 'net-expected-personal-benefit' considerations would play in a market setting.

It is worth noting an implication concerning two different methods of 'buying votes' – one via policy offerings; the other via direct bribes. Suppose a political candidate A offers you $5,000 to cast your vote for him (and suppose the contract is enforceable): the 'logic of choice' shows that this would not be equivalent to A's offering a policy that will give you $5,000 if he gets elected. The former offer means that your voting for A will yield you $5,000: the latter offer means that your voting for A will increase your expected income by $5,000 *times h*. The incentive you have to change your voting behavior is very much smaller – *very* much smaller – under the latter arrangement than under the former. 'Buying votes' via policy offerings is not equivalent to 'buying votes' via direct bribery: that much is, on the expressive view, just an analytic fact!

The upshot of this is that among the various reasons J has to vote for A, increasing J's income via increasing the probability of A's victory is not likely to figure as a relatively major one. If J has any *other* reasons to vote one way rather than another, then those other reasons do not have to be very weighty to outweigh J's material interest in contributing to *A*'s being elected. Of course, for any voter whose sole concern is the maximization of his material income, there would by definition be no 'other reasons'. She will, by hypothesis, never be called on to sacrifice anything for her conscience: she does not have one! And she will always be disposed, if she votes at all, to vote for the party that offers her more in financial terms, because that is the only basis on which she can discriminate between parties. In that sense, the expressive argument depends on a rejection of a polar model of agent motivation involving exclusive income-maximization. And to the extent that mainstream public choice is committed to the polar income-maximization motivational model, the expressive account of voting behavior has no ground on which to get purchase.

But it should be emphasized that the expressive account of political behavior is not just a claim that individuals are somewhat altruistic, or somewhat moral, or in some other way more complicated motivationally, than simple models of *Homo economicus* allow. The claim is rather that, within this more complex (and surely more plausible) motivational structure, behavior at the ballot box and behavior in the marketplace are likely to diverge. But note, this *behavioral* divergence does not require any divergence in the underlying *motivations* operating in the two settings. There is no requirement to adopt 'wholly different models of man in the political and economic realms'[2] in generating very different models of behavior. Behavior differs because the relative reward from behaving contrary to one's interest goes down spectacularly as one moves from the market to the electoral arena. Considerations of self-interest that are paramount in the marketplace are second-order at the ballot box. And analogously, 'expressive' considerations that may be central in electoral politics are likely to be second-order in the marketplace.

The kind of psychology that is presupposed here may well run contrary to disciplinary habits both for economists and for philosophers – the former because they are disposed to think of all action in terms of furthering the actor's material interest; and the latter because they are disposed to argue as if moral considerations were behaviorally decisive. So consider a more or less ordinary character who is a utilitarian in moral stance, but biased somewhat in favor of his own interests in the arena of ordinary action. If he were a *perfect* utilitarian then he would operate in the market, as in the ballot-box,[3] in accordance with his utilitarian principles. No behavioral difference would emerge. But suppose he is the kind of mixed motive character stipulated. Then the terms of trade between own utility and total utility would shift according to context – own interest would be much less significant at the ballot-box than in the marketplace and we would expect that this fact would be reflected in behavior. He would predictably vote for the public interest; but act in the market for his private interest.

Consider the case of an Australian who visits the United States on a regular basis and so is exposed to a certain amount of media coverage of US politics. More or less spontaneously, this Australian will develop attitudes towards candidates and the policies they say they stand for. He may well follow the presidential primaries with some interest. He will consider certain candidates good and certain others better and some (especially perhaps vice-presidential ones) totally preposterous! He does this despite not being entitled to vote, or indeed without having any special reason[4] to acquire the attitudes in question: they accumulate willy-nilly. If called upon to say what he thinks, he will express those attitudes more or less honestly. But of course if he believes that such attitudes will prove disagreeable to his audience and if he does not wish to be disagreeable, he may moderate what he says. Unlike the attitudes themselves, which are more or less spontaneous, his expressions do not usually emerge willy-nilly; he has direct control over them.[5]

If this is true of the non-enfranchised Australian, it is no less true of the typical US citizen. If the citizen chooses to vote, it seems entirely natural that he would give expression to his attitudes without demur: there is little reason for him to do otherwise. If the stakes for him were say 12,500 times higher, he might do otherwise: he might then adjust his action according to where his particular interests lay. But it would seem entirely arbitrary (and indeed somewhat bizarre) to insist that his underlying attitudes to all public issues will happen to track his interests in the close way that would maintain consistency between market and electoral behavior.

This is the central message of the 'expressive' account. It is first and foremost a 'how' message. And its message is primarily negative – *there simply is no a priori reason to think that voters' attitudes will track their material interests*. And since it is voter attitudes that drive voting behavior, there is no reason to think that citizens' voting *behavior* in the aggregate will track their material interests either.

It perhaps goes without saying that the account has implications not just for *voter* behavior. The demand-side of politics will have implications for how the supply-side works as well. Politicians who seek votes will rationally appeal to the considerations that weigh in voter decisions. Accordingly, significant attitudes to charged issues – such as abortion, gay marriage, euthanasia, illegal immigrants, terrorists, crime more generally, poverty, taxation levels, global climate change, or (for the utilitarians, if any) global well-being – will be mobilized by vote-seeking politicians motivated to locate themselves in policy space so as to maximize their electoral appeal.

4 CATEGORY VERSUS COMPARISON

Much conceptual analysis proceeds by the drawing of distinctions – between rational and irrational behavior, say; or between self-interested and other-interested motivations. Such distinctions typically are constructed by creating categories – and isolating the features that determine whether a particular instance falls into one category rather than another. But sometimes, creating these categories involves drawing a dividing line somewhere along an identifiable spectrum; exactly where the line is to be drawn is itself somewhat arbitrary.

Often, knife-edge distinctions encourage rather silly debates in which protagonists seek to discredit the opposing side by showing that evidence does not fit the opposite polar extreme. We think that this has been the case in the case of expressive theory. So, for example, it is not a rejection of the expressive account that material interests play *some* role in explaining voting behavior, or that most voters think their voting exercises *some* influence on political outcomes. The expressive account is not committed to the view that it is 'irrational' to think that one's vote plays some role in the success of one's favored candidate – though it would presumably be irrational to believe that one's vote does indeed determine who will win.

Mackie (2008), for example, mounts what he sees as a major critique of expressive voting theory by appeal to the putative fact that sending a 'get well' card or cheering at a football match – analogies that are familiar in expressive theory – do not rule out an instrumental element. As Mackie puts it: 'Sending a get-well card can (imperceptibly) advance a friend's recovery' (p. 26) and

> [S]pectators of a live game do believe that their cheering and booing, although neither individually pivotal towards victory nor perceptible towards advance, influences the team's performance. Home advantage is an established phenomenon in sports science, although evidence is inconclusive that crowd support furthers it. A survey of English football fans, however, shows that they believe that crowd support is the most likely cause of home advantage. Moreover, 93% endorse the statement that 'the more supportive the crowd, the better its team will play,' and 80% endorse the statement that 'a quiet home crowd will discourage the home players' (Wolfson, Wakelin, and Lewis 2005). Such evidence, along with simple introspection, suggests that it is false that members of the audience do not intend to influence the outcome.
>
> (p. 24)

But Mackie goes on to assert that the cheering analogy itself is mistaken and that the right way to think about voting is in terms of 'playing the game' rather than cheering. In a sense, however, this latter distinction makes the expressive point. If there is a difference between playing and cheering, it does not, on Mackie's own argument, lie in the fact that players believe that their efforts increase the probability of winning, whereas cheerers hold no such beliefs. Presumably, the difference between players and cheerers is quantitative: the individual player exercises *more* influence on the outcome of the game than does the individual cheerer. It might make sense for a criminal book-maker to bribe a player to 'throw the game' (as has been alleged of the 2010 England/Pakistani cricket season). It would make much less sense for the book-maker to bribe English fans not to cheer (or to stay at home and watch the game on television).

It is a mistake, we think, to become preoccupied with analogies. There is nothing foundational to the expressive account of voting about a putative analogy between voting and cheering – still less with cheering specifically at sporting events. After all, people cheer (and possibly boo) at musical and theatrical performances too – even where, unlike the sporting or electoral contest, there is no direct competition between rival performances or rival works. People spend time being respondents to political opinion polls, where there is no formal connection to ensuring an electoral result. The point about any appeal to such examples of expressive behavior is just to establish that people do 'express their attitudes' in lots of contexts where the expression of the attitude is different from bringing about the outcome with respect to which the attitude is expressed. Actions, so the aphorism has it, speak louder than words: if so, there is a relevant distinction between actions and words – and the spectrum that that distinction embodies relates to the consequences of different behaviors. Drawing lines along that spectrum and allocating various behaviors to one side or the other of a notional divide can be unhelpful. The logic of choice insists that there is a relevant distinction between voting and expressing an opinion in response to a survey questionnaire. This is the same kind of distinction that operates between voting and market behavior. There should be no confusion involved in locating various points along the relevant spectrum and trying to assess where, relative to certain salient alternatives, the voting case lies. As Paul Samuelson (1955, p. 356) remarks in a different context, to argue that something 'is not located at the South Pole does not logically place it at the North Pole'! A setting in which the chooser is decisive over options lies at one pole; the setting in which the chooser exercises absolutely no effect at all on which option emerges lies at the other pole. The expressive claim is that voting lies between these extremes – and in large-scale democratic elections, rather closer to the latter pole than the former. In that sense, the distinction between market and electoral behavior is of a comparative kind; and once that point is understood, Mackie's observations seem somewhat beside the point.

5 IDENTITY, IDENTIFICATION AND THE 'WHETHER' QUESTION

> Individuals do not necessarily participate in collective action in order to produce outcomes but instead often do so in order to express who they are by attaching themselves to such outcomes.
> (Schuessler 2000b, p. 5)

The first thing to say about this quotation is that it reveals that self-proclaimed 'expressive' theorists can be no less guilty of 'categorization' than their critics. It would be no rejection of the idea that voters seek to 'attach' themselves to particular outcomes to allow for the possibility that they also think of themselves as 'producing' those outcomes in the sense of contributing to their victory. Presumably, lots of those voters who identify most strongly with particular candidates/parties/policies think of themselves as contributing to the success of the object of their identification.

The second thing to note about the quotation is Schuessler's assumptions concerning the *content* of expressiveness. Specifically, there is a distinction between voters' expressing *something* (say their attitudes concerning political issues of the day) and their expressing more specifically 'who they are'. Schuessler's formulation makes it seem as if the contrast is between the aim of producing outcomes and the aim of 'expressing who one is' – as if 'expressing who one is' just is the embodiment of expressive activity. In a similar spirit, Hillman (2010) defines expressive activity precisely *as* activity that asserts/confirms the actor's identity: 'Expressive behavior is the self-interested quest for utility through acts and declarations *that confirm a person's identity*' (Hillman 2010, p. 403; emphasis added). There is perhaps a trivial sense in which any action and any utterance reveals something of the nature of the actor/utterer: we might say that such action/utterance 'contributes to' the agent's identity. But it seems highly restrictive to characterize all expressions, of whatever content and purpose, as expressions specifically of 'who one is'. When *K* writes a letter to the editor of the local paper complaining about some feature of the modern world, she is first and foremost expressing that *complaint*. Equally, when *K* votes, she expresses her political opinion within the limited terms that the vote affords: it is an additional question whether the content of that expression is properly described as 'her identity'.

Mackie (2008) complains that the use of the term 'expressive' to describe the nature of the benefits that the voter derives from registering her opinion is misleading: he thinks the use of 'expressive' encourages an interpretation of voting as emotional, or self-indulgent, or in some sense orthogonal to the issues that are in play in the election. And the interpretation that Schuessler and Hillman each place on the expressive account seems to provide some fuel for Mackie's anxieties. In our formulation, the basic categories in the expressive account are: attitudes; expressions of those attitudes; and interests (as the alternative against which attitudes are to be set). Within those basic categories, 'how' questions are concerned with the difference between the content of attitudes and interests, presuming that the attitudes are expressed. 'Whether' questions, by contrast, are concerned with the distinction between *having* an attitude and *expressing* that attitude by voting (or by some other action). Claims about 'identity' in Schuessler and Hillman are claims about the specific content of the relevant attitudes. We see identity as a plausible contender for that role in at least some cases – but that is certainly not implied by the logic of expressive reasoning or in some other way the sole possibility.

Schuessler's use of the identity idea involves a desire to identify with *other voters*; and the arithmetic of his particular model depends on trading off the desire to identify with the (more popular) 'winning team' against the desire not to be excessively 'lost in the crowd'. His chief empirical predictions relate therefore to the sizes of majorities. In Hillman's (2010) treatment, the chief concern seems to be with the voter's (rational) desire to identify with attributes that the voter regards as honorable or otherwise applaudable (in particular, peaceableness and/or generous-spiritedness which can undermine rational responses to external threats). A related, though different, thought is that individuals often identify with ethnic, religious or other salient groups, and that the cost to them of expressing such identity at the ballot box, in cases where there is a conflict between action that identifies with that group and self-interest, is low. This thought is sometimes associated with the further conjecture that individuals' political values are typically formed in association with those with whom they have most (politically relevant) contact – so perhaps with other members of one's class or occupation or profession.[6] In this way, something of a broad 'economic interest' story about democratic politics becomes plausible, without any appeal to revealed preference logic. That account depends, however, on the claim that it is basically economic class categories that dominate in the determination of politically relevant divisions in the polity – and this may be less true of some polities than others. Hamlin and Jennings's (2007) treatment of the group conflict case, for example, is based on an expressive account of political behavior – specifically, on the tendency of groups to lend political support to leaders whose identities are crafted explicitly in opposition to the 'other' and whose postures are rather more bellicose than would be in the interests of all sides.

The central feature of 'identity' models of this kind is that membership in salient groups is what drives expressive behavior. That feature is to be distinguished from the idea that what voters seek is some measure of 'identification' with the political options available. A voter, J, may identify more closely with party A than with party B – without being especially closely identified with either. In voting for A she need not see herself as establishing her political identity or indeed as acting in accord with the interests or values of some other group with which she 'identifies'.

Nevertheless, the idea of 'identification' plays an important role in the expressive theory of voting in the weaker sense that if the political options are such that she cannot identify with any of them, then the expressive account suggests that she will not express a preference either way. The contrast here is with the instrumental account of voting, because under the instrumental account, the presumption is that a voter is more likely to vote as his 'ideal point' moves further from the given party positions. General concavity of the utility function gives this result.[7] In the instrumental account, there seems to be no decision-theoretic foundation for the concept of 'abstention by alienation': all abstention must be driven by indifference. But in the expressive account, abstention by alienation seems entirely natural: *J* will vote for the option that most closely matches her attitudes, but if none of the options available matches her attitudes closely enough, she will have no reason to express her support for any of them. The general prediction is that voters whose 'ideal points' are furthest from the available options are *ceteris paribus* less likely to vote (the 'alienation' hypothesis). This hypothesis has been subject to some empirical investigation – by Greene and Nelson (2002), Drinkwater and Jennings (2007) and Calcagno and Westley (2008) – with inconclusive results. That is, Greene and Nelson find no such effect, whereas the two more recent studies (both of them arguably more satisfactory on methodological grounds) offer support for the Brennan and Hamlin hypothesis.

This brings us back to 'whether' questions. It is, we think, a feature of the approach to voting behavior that comes out of basically instrumental models of human action (appropriate to market settings) that the question of why individuals vote should have seemed such a puzzle or occupied such a large part of the literature. If one thinks of voting as a means to further one's interests (to 'better one's condition' as Adam Smith might have put it) then the fact of voter inconsequentiality is an awkward pill to swallow. An unrelieved wealth-maximizer would, as already noted, derive very low expected benefits from voting and even in cases where the cost of voting also is low may well find the 'investment' not worth the effort. But there is, we think, no great puzzle that large numbers of people vote in large-scale political elections, that turnout is in many countries higher in national elections than in local (where the number of voters is much smaller and hence the probability of decisiveness considerably higher), or that turnout is higher among more educated and affluent people (whose opportunity cost of voting is presumably higher). We do not think these facts represent puzzles because we think that, if people have attitudes (even if only casually formed ones) and can express them at not too great a cost, they are likely to do so. The step from *possessing* attitudes to *expressing* those attitudes seems to us a small one – except where the cost of expression is high. Of course, this is not to deny that changes in the 'cost of expression' (for example, associated with bad weather, or the provision of independent attractions at the polls like bake sales) are likely to affect turnout in the predictable way. And it seems entirely consistent with the expressive picture that turnout will tend to be higher when the election is believed to be closer, just as attendance at sporting events tends to be larger for games that are expected to be more competitive, or that turnout among the better educated and/or better informed politically will tend to be higher for this group on account of the observation that the attitudes accumulated willy-nilly at well-to-do dinner parties are more likely to be about politics than say football.

On the other hand, it is not so clear that the expressive account of voting is as hospitable to 'co-location' equilibria (the famous median voter result) as is the standard instrumental account. If voters are likely to abstain for reasons of alienation (which as earlier noted does not sit easily with an account of voting behavior in which instrumental considerations predominate) then moving away from the median may well gain more votes than it loses. The cost to a party of 'losing its identity' – as it seems likely to do if it becomes indistinguishable from the opposition – is that it loses the basis on which voters might identify with it. If a party does not 'stand for' anything detectable by voters then it is difficult to see how voters could express anything by voting for that party. It seems to be a well-established empirical result, for example, that the ideological positions that parties adopt tend to be somewhat more extreme than the ideological positions of their electoral support. There may well be other explanations for this phenomenon; but one possible explanation is that parties need to be seen to stand for something in order for party support to be able to function expressively – or better put, that ideological distinctiveness increases expressive attractiveness.

In our view, the full implications of the expressive account of voting for questions of turnout and related matters of party location have yet to be fully worked out. As emphasized earlier, the expressive story is directed primarily at explaining the considerations that weigh in voters' decision-making calculus – and not at explaining turnout rates as such. Still, it is implausible to suggest that the 'whether' and 'how' questions are totally independent: the decision to vote is a decision to vote for one option rather than another. The fact that turnout levels are as high as they are is a challenge to the instrumental account of voting; but it should not be seen as a challenge to the rationality of voters (or for that matter, the rationality of abstainers!). Rational choice theory presumes that individuals are rational and then proceeds to understand their behavior in the light of that assumption: in that sense, debates as to whether it is voters or abstainers that are basically 'irrational' seem to us to be entirely against the spirit of rational choice theory. The obvious response within rational choice theory is that in general *both* voters and abstainers are rational – and then seek to give an account of citizen utility functions that would be consistent with that presumption. On the account favored here, abstainers abstain either because:

(a) They have no relevant attitudes that voting would express; or
(b) They have no desire to express their attitudes (or the strength of any such desire is not sufficient to overcome the costs associated with voting).

Aspect (a) would reflect either voters' indifference between options or their alienation from the options available – and our conjecture is that these factors are the more important element in explaining abstention. Aspect (b) would suggest that different individuals have different levels of desire to express whatever attitudes that person has. (Laband et al. 2009, for example, provide some empirical support for the hypothesis that people with tastes for expressive activity in other domains – display of support for a college football team, in their case – are more likely to vote.)

6   EXPRESSIVENESS VERSUS SIGNALING

There is one species of behavior already familiar in the economics literature that may seem to bear some relation to expressive behavior, but which we think is quite distinct. We refer to 'signaling'. Signaling has some relevance in political analysis, though at the level of candidate rather than that of voter behavior (see, for example, Besley 2006). In any event, it may be useful to say a little here about why, and in what ways, expressive behavior as we understand it does not fit the signaling category.

Wearing a T-shirt with 'Save the Whales' emblazoned on the front serves (at least) two obvious ends: shading the wearer's torso from the sun and declaring the wearer's attitudes/values concerning the 'great leviathan from the deep' (that is, not Hobbes's 'leviathan'!). But the wearer might choose this particular T-shirt (also) as a means to secure public sympathy or to attract a potential mate (serving the same role as commonly ascribed to peacock's feathers) or to impress a potential employer. This signaling role has been the object of analytic attention in various settings: Spence (1973, 2002) is the classic reference for the economic applications; Grafen (1990) provides a notable biological application.

In the standard economic case of signaling, a rational agent A makes a 'statement' X (or more generally undertakes some action) in order to reveal something about a hidden characteristic Y to some second party B: X is believed by B to be correlated with Y and it is advantageous to A that B believe that A has characteristic Y. A may send a get-well card to his aunt in order to persuade his employer B that A is a responsible and dutiful person, well-qualified for promotion within the firm. Note several features of the signaling case that seem not to apply in the kind of expressive activity setting we have been discussing so far. First, the agent's motivation in the signaling case is instrumental in two senses: it is motivated by the desire to produce a specific attitude in B or by A's desire to convince his aunt to remember him in her will. Second, in the signaling version of the get-well card case, the expressive act specifies an audience (the recipient of the card, A's aunt) that differs from the audience actually intended (A's employer): in the expressive theory version, the addressee of the expression just is the intended audience. Notice too that in the signaling case, the signal may or may not be 'truthful': A may or may not be responsible and dutiful (may or may not have the characteristic being 'signaled' to B). In the expressive theory account, the individual expresses her true attitude. Finally, it is critical in the whole signaling set-up that B is uncertain about whether or not the attribute the attitude 'expressed' by A is actually possessed by A. In the 'expressive' case we have discussed so far, the attitude possessed by the expressor may be fully known to the expressee.

The signaling model is relevant to the behavior of electoral candidates who may well be seeking to signal their (intrinsic) concern for various groups of voters to those voters, or their admirable moral qualities, or their competence (indeed total mastery) of issues relevant to holding office. Candidate X will have reason to signal those features if she believes that voters will come to believe that X possesses the relevant characteristics (L, M, N, and so on) and that such a perception will make X more attractive to voters. And she will have reason to signal those features whether she possesses them or not.

But when voters express their attitudes by voting, they need not be making their expression with an eye to any effects on third parties. Perhaps some voters go to the polls to signal their dutifulness and sense of civic responsibility – and perhaps some express their (carefully shaped) political opinions with an eye to the opinions and attitudes of their fellows (perhaps for esteem-related reasons[8] or perhaps with more material benefits in mind). It would be foolish to rule out such possibilities. But they clearly need not be in play in 'expressive voting' – whereas they are of the essence in any account of voting in which signaling plays a major role in explaining voting behavior. Again, if signaling were in play, it seems more applicable at the level of turnout – and less applicable to how people vote since that is usually (under the secret ballot) protected information.

7 MINDING ONE'S Ps AND Qs IN THE EXPRESSIVE DOMAIN

Public choice theory arose to a significant extent (at least in its 'Virginia' variant) out of public economics; and the normative questions it addressed were framed in terms of the public economics/welfare economics paradigm. As Buchanan ([1979] 1999, p. 46) puts it: 'I have often said that public choice offers a "theory of government failure" that is fully comparable to the "theory of market failure" that emerged from the theoretical welfare economics of the 1930s and 1940s.'

It therefore must have seemed natural to frame the normative questions in the same terms as the theoretical welfare economics had done, focusing attention on the level of supply of public goods. If public goods are routinely *under*-supplied in markets, will they be optimally supplied under democratic political arrangements? Or over-supplied? And at what prices? In engaging such questions, broadly Marshallian categories of quantity and price tended to be imported more or less without question into the analysis of political processes. In a way, Lindahl's (1919) bargaining model of the budget and Bowen's (1943) famous 'interpretation of voting' operated in much the same spirit – exploiting analogies with more familiar market settings and with the same normative focus.

The expressive story does not propose any radical change in normative focus, but it does rather question how directly the proper tools for *political analysis* translate into terms that are readily interpretable within that normative frame. For once we move into the expressive domain, the very conceptualization of political processes in terms of quantities and prices becomes problematic. In the case of oranges (or for that matter miles of road), there is a natural measure of quantity and hence a natural basis from which to calculate price. But with 'expressiveness', what is the metric? What is it that makes a statement or a policy a more intense expression of something than another statement or policy might be? It is tempting to think of the level of expenditure as just such a metric – and the opportunity cost therefore of any expression measured in terms of spending on some other 'expression' forgone. Mitchell and Munger (1991, p. 528) make a remark in this spirit: 'more expenditure without more taxation always yields a vote increase'.

But as the modern tea-party phenomenon suggests, that is not always so. It can sometimes be politically profitable to offer the constituents 'nothing but blood, sweat and tears'[9] or to insist that citizens shouldn't be asking about what their country can do for them, but rather what they can do for their country.[10]

The perspective that is encouraged by an expressive account of electoral processes involves seeing policies as instruments of rhetoric rather than as the direct object of electoral preference. And to the extent that this is so, any price/quantity analytics needs first to be expressed in terms of rhetorical strength. It is probably unhelpful in this connection to think in terms of units of rhetorical strength and the 'price' of such a unit in terms of its opportunity cost (or indeed, how the rhetorical defense of any public activity serves to drive out rhetorical defense of other public activities – if indeed it does). Admittedly, government activity operates within a set of specific constraints, of which time taken to enact bills and broad budgetary limits are two. Governments have to manage an optimization exercise. But on the expressive account, the ultimate optimization exercise is predominantly rhetorical – and the critical question is how various expenditures and regulatory changes and announcements of intention map into the rhetorical domain. It is not entirely clear how much assistance the analytic apparatus of economics can be in any such exercise.

When we say 'not entirely clear', that is exactly what we mean. We do not intend to convey the thought that the application of economic thinking to this exercise is impossible or necessarily unhelpful or misleading. We do mean to convey, however, the anxiety that the application exercise is more complex and considerably less direct than much public choice analysis has implied.

8 CONCLUSIONS

In this chapter we have sought to offer some ideas about the expressive account of voting and in particular to establish its location within a broader 'rational choice logic' of democratic electoral processes. As we see it, the expressive voting story is an application of the logic of choice – and indeed we think it represents an exemplary illustration of the power of that logic in social analysis. In other words, we think that the expressive account is correct *as a purely logical matter*. And we think that such 'logical matters' have status in economic thinking, somewhat independent of any empirical implications. In fact, to make specific claims about such empirical implications requires speculations about the nature of expressive considerations[11] that are ultimately just . . . speculations.[12]

The prime focus of the expressive account of voting is, we argue, concerned with 'how' questions – questions, that is, about the kinds of considerations that weigh in voters' deliberations and specifically why narrow self-interest is likely to play a smaller role in electoral decision-making than it does in (somewhat) analogous market settings. For many moral philosophers, who are inclined to see self-interest as the primary source of ethical failure,[13] the 'veil of insignificance' that characterizes behavior at the ballot-box is presumptively a 'good thing'.[14] We ourselves are inclined to emphasize the normative *ambiguity* of expressive behavior. But of course, no general conclusions about the normative implications of expressive behavior can be drawn without assumptions concerning the nature of the considerations that weigh in them.

To identify the expressive voting account as a matter of a priori logic perhaps encourages commentators to see it as a claim about whether particular actions or beliefs are rational or irrational – whether, say, voters are irrational to vote according to self-interest, to vote at all, to allow self-interest any role at all in their deliberations, or to see themselves as 'helping to bring about an outcome'. That kind of interpretation is we think a mistake; it mis-characterizes the nature of the claim that expressive theory makes. The claim that self-interest might play some explanatory role in voting behavior, or that voters might declare themselves to be 'helping their favored candidate to win' does not constitute a refutation of expressive voting theory. The logical claims of expressive voting theory are not about specific actions in isolation – they are grounded in a comparison between voting and choosing in the marketplace.

One important theme in some of the literature that self-identifies as expressive (Schuessler 2000a, 2000b and Hillman 2010, specifically) is the connection between expressive activity and identity. We think that there are some connections here worth exploration but that this strand of the literature draws expressive activity too narrowly. There is a tendency here to confuse 'expression' with 'self-expression', to confuse the self as the expressive *subject* (a necessary fact) with the self as the expressive *object* (an entirely contingent matter), or both. Conceivably, some voters will be such that how they vote will be a matter of deep political identity; for others, not. If you conduct an opinion poll on whether Brahms or Wagner is the better composer,[15] all actual respondents will express an opinion – but there is no presumption that most (or indeed any) need feel the issue to be a matter of their identity or an expression of their deepest selves. Presumably those who feel very strongly will be more disposed to *be* respondents; but among respondents will also be included the naturally opinionated, and those who enjoy expressing their opinions even when not fiercely (or informatively) held. The same applies to voting in democratic elections.

We do though think that voters are more likely to express their opinions under some conditions than others – and specifically when they can 'identify' with one or other of the candidates/parties/options. In that sense, 'identification' does play a role in the expressive account – but not we think so in the strong and rather special sense implied by 'identity' theorists.

In the competition for votes, candidates will attempt to locate themselves in such a way that more voters will 'identify' with them. Such identification means both a stronger pro-attitude towards the candidate by the voter; and a stronger disposition to express that attitude at the polls. But what is the space within which such identification takes place? What are the attributes the candidate has to exhibit – including the candidate's own policy preferences – that make it more likely that various voters will 'cheer' for her. In the candidate's calculus, what are the constraints on the various appeals she can make? What, in other words, is the opportunity cost of an appeal to group A or group B? In the case where the appeal takes the form of a particular expenditure that group A is believed to approve of, then budgetary constraints presumably will be relevant. But we (economists) need to take care that habits of thinking, drawn from familiar market choice settings, do not obtrude as a matter of course. It is just not obvious how the expressive domain is composed – or what 'optimization' within it might mean for the calculus of a vote-maximizing candidate. Saying 'not obvious' here is, as we see it, a plea for more work in the area, not a judgment that the quest is hopeless.

NOTES

1. No one in the debate, we think, contests that claim. To the extent that there is a debate, it is more about the relevance of h than its magnitude. For example, Goldman (1999), Mackie (2008) and Tuck (2008) all think that pivotality is relatively unimportant – though pivotality plays a critical role in Tuck's formulation of what is relevant to determining voter responsibility for electoral outcomes. There are, nevertheless, questions about how best to formulate the determination of h; and problems with the soundness of the most common method. The standard method involves treating the actual share of the vote for A (v_A) as a measure of the *ex ante* probability that any randomly selected voter (from the n actual voters) will vote for A; and then treat the election as a sequence of n individual drawings, each of which vote for A with probability v_A. This method yields maximal values of h for the United States of 1/12,500. But the procedure means that A will win with virtual certainty if v_A exceeds 50 percent by even the tiniest margin (given that n is large). It therefore seems inappropriate to treat the *ex ante* probability of a randomly selected voter voting for A as a single number: it should be drawn from an appropriate probability distribution. Perhaps indeed, v_A should be derived from the *ex ante* probabilities of various candidates winning. More generally, it seems dubious to treat each voter as an independent trial with identical probabilities of voting for A. What the implications of such refinements would be for the value of h are unclear. Nevertheless, it does seem entirely safe to conclude that in a large-scale election of the kind characteristic of western national democracies, h will be *very* much less than 1.

2. Something of which Buchanan ([1979] 1999) – and for that matter Kelman (1988) in a blistering attack on public choice methods – is properly skeptical.
3. Assuming that the 'perfect' utilitarian actually votes. Whether he should/will do so is a matter of some contention and motivates some of the contribution from philosophers about the role and significance of breaking/making a tie. See Goldman (1999) and Tuck (2008), for example.
4. When we say 'special reason' here, we mean a reason apart from being an observer of his environment and perhaps a more or less normal participant in social life (dinner parties, wine-tastings, golf foursomes, and so on, where conversation and the sharing of attitudes occurs); these features of ordinary life give him reason enough. Indeed, to form no attitudes at all towards such aspects of his environment would seem to require a certain resolute, slightly obstinate, detachment.
5. Cases where the expression, as well as the underlying attitudes, are more or less spontaneous – as in the case where one hits one's thumb with a hammer or is overtaken by a sense of outrage that simply cannot be contained – are the exception. Such cases do not seem to play any special role in an account of expressive behavior and there does not seem any reason to afford them special attention in the context of 'expressive theory'. A particular case where expressions are used for material benefit is studied in the 'signaling' literature which we take up briefly in section 7 below.
6. We associate this view with the work of Iversen and Soskice, in various collaborations, and most explicitly in Abrams et al. (forthcoming).
7. See Brennan and Hamlin (1998) for a detailed discussion of this point.
8. For an account of esteem-related activities, see Brennan and Pettit (2004). More generally, electoral participation is, in certain circles, a norm-governed activity, and norms tend to be lent support by the effects of esteem and disesteem (for violations).
9. More accurately, 'blood, toil, tears and sweat' – Winston Churchill, in an address to the House of Commons, 13 May 1940.
10. John F. Kennedy's 1961 Inaugural Address. It is perhaps worth noting that Churchill and Kennedy made these remarks *after* the relevant electoral process itself.
11. For the 'nature of expressive considerations', one might read the 'content of expressive preferences' – but that is to presume that the conceptualization of 'considerations' *as* 'preferences' is ultimately proper. We have some doubts, expressed mainly in section 8.
12. They are of course speculations that can be tested – by appeal to what voters actually do in elections. But rejection of any particular such speculation does not imply a rejection of the underlying logic.
13. John Rawls is in some ways a typical example – though an economistic philosopher in many ways. The 'veil of ignorance' construction is precisely designed to wash the 'self' out of 'interests'.
14. For more details on the 'veil of insignificance', see the contribution to this volume by Alan Hamlin.
15. A hot issue in certain circles in the nineteenth century.

8 Direct democracy
John G. Matsusaka

Direct democracy is a process by which citizens make laws or public policies without involving their elected representatives. The idea of participatory law-making is well known from classical Greece, the Swiss *Landsgemeinde* in the Middle Ages, and American colonial town meetings, and the idea of villages and other small communities assembling to resolve public issues is a feature of societies from the distant past to the present. Many modern states have grown too large for all citizens to deliberate face to face, however, so direct democracy nowadays takes more structured forms; citizens go to the polls to register their views for or against a particular law or a proposed constitutional amendment. While town meetings continue to be used in small polities, the more structured forms of direct democracy – initiatives, referendums, and other ballot propositions – are now the most visible and important means of democratic governance, and are the focus of this chapter.[1]

1 TERMS

While the main forms of modern direct democracy all involve voters registering their opinions on a specific law or constitutional amendment, the different forms vary in two important ways: in who has proposal power, and in whether the voters are deciding to approve a new law or to repeal an existing one. Citizens may be allowed to propose a law or propose repealing an existing one through a petition process that requires a minimum number of signatures to qualify the proposal for the ballot. Alternatively, the government itself may be the proposer.

The terminology of direct democracy is not entirely standardized, and sometimes a term carries different meanings in different contexts. For the purposes of this chapter, I employ the following terminology that represents the most common usage.

An *initiative* is a new law proposed by citizen petition. Jurisdictions vary in what kinds of laws may be proposed. Some allow amendments to constitutions or other core documents such as city charters, while others allow only statutes, ordinances, and so forth to be put to popular vote. The initiative is the most potent form of direct democracy, the most visible in practice, and the subject of most research.

A *referendum* is a vote on existing law. The election may be called by citizen petition (sometimes called a 'popular' referendum) or it may be required by the constitution or other governing document (sometimes called a 'legislative referendum' or 'legislative' proposition). On legislative propositions, for example, many American states require voter approval for constitutional amendments and bond issues proposed by the legislature or governor. Sitting governments may also hold elections of an advisory nature, such as national votes on matters concerning European integration (sometimes called 'plebiscites'). 'Referendum' is perhaps the most elastic term in the dictionary of direct

128 *The Elgar companion to public choice*

democracy, as it is sometimes used to refer to any proposal on the ballot, that is, it is sometimes used as a synonym for a ballot proposition. The standard (but not universal) practice in the literature has become to use the plural form 'referendums' rather than 'referenda', following the *Oxford English Dictionary*.

The actual law that is to be decided by popular vote, as opposed to the process itself, is called a 'proposition', 'measure', 'ballot question', and so forth. There is enormous variation in the details of how the processes work, some of them material, but few are discussed in this chapter. For example, approval might require a majority or a supermajority; approval might require a favorable vote in one election or multiple elections; some subjects may be allowed and others prohibited; popularly approved laws might be amendable by the government under some conditions or not at all; and so on.

2 FOR BETTER OR WORSE?

From a public choice perspective, a central issue concerning direct democracy is how it affects the performance of public decision-making and, in particular, whether it leads to better or worse outcomes in some normative sense. Buchanan and Tullock (1962) and other foundational works in public choice were aware of direct democracy, and made some attempts to sketch out its benefits and costs, but for the most part these scholars seem to have considered direct democracy impractical for modern states, and the inquiries were not pursued in depth. Those early analyses focused on trade-offs between internal decision-making costs (essentially transaction costs involved in discussion, negotiation, and bargaining) and external costs (anticipated costs due to majority decisions that harm the minority).

Legal scholars have been the most active in attempting normative evaluations of direct democracy, usually reaching a negative conclusion. A recurrent weakness of much of that work, as well as much work that has a public policy motivation, is framing the question as a choice between direct democracy and representative democracy, that is, asking if it is better for citizens to make decisions directly or through their elected representatives. A limitation of this framework is that replacement of representative institutions by direct democracy is not feasible or proposed as an option. The important forms of direct democracy that are being considered – ballot propositions – are always and everywhere grafted onto existing representative institutions. Thus, the relevant choice is actually between representative democracy, on the one hand, and representative democracy with an overlay of ballot propositions on the other. As will be seen, it is important to frame the choices correctly to understand the role and consequences of direct democracy.

3 THEORY

The theoretical literature has identified several roles played by direct democracy when grafted onto a representative political system, and made significant progress in understanding the strengths and weaknesses of ballot propositions in that context:

3.1 Agency Problems

Perhaps the central theme running through the theoretical literature is principal–agent problems between the voters and their elected representatives. Owing to free-rider problems among voters and asymmetric information, it is difficult for citizens to monitor and control their representatives. Seen from this perspective, a key purpose of initiatives and referendums is to give voters an opportunity to override their representatives when the representatives fail to act in the voters' interests. This purpose was the main motivation for reform groups who brought the initiative and referendum to the United States around the turn of the twentieth century, and remains the main attraction for supporters of direct democracy.

The theoretical analysis of agency problems in the direct democracy context was initiated by Romer and Rosenthal's (1979) analysis of referendums. They introduced the idea of agenda control, a modeling approach in which the outcome of political process depends on who has the power to make a proposal. The agenda control idea was first incorporated into a model of direct democracy by Gerber (1996), and extended to the important case of incomplete information by Matsusaka and McCarty (2001). A typical model in this literature is a spatial game in which the legislature moves first and establishes a status quo policy, then an outsider (a citizen, an interest group) has the option of incurring costs to challenge the status quo (propose an initiative or referendum), and if the challenge occurs, the citizens (median voter) make the final choice between the status quo and the challenger proposal.

This line of theory has established and clarified several ideas. It shows concretely how initiatives and referendums can ameliorate agency problems. Most obviously, if the legislature chooses a policy too distant from what the voters desire, the policy may be overridden by the voters. Less obviously, initiatives and referendums can influence legislative behavior simply by providing a threat. If the legislature dislikes being overridden, it may choose policies more appealing to the voters in order to deter the outsiders from challenging the status quo. One implication of this analysis is that initiatives and referendums may influence policy choices even if a proposition never appears on the ballot. This implication turns out to be important for empirical work in the area. The analysis also highlights the centrality to policy choices of petition and other costs required to qualify a measure for the ballot. The qualification cost establishes the cutoff point for a group to initiate a challenge, and therefore theory suggests that the legislature will tailor its policy choices more closely to voter preferences as qualification costs fall.

From a normative point of view, the basic complete-information model implies that voters are always better off in a world with direct democracy combined with representative democracy than in a world with representative democracy only.[2] This is because the effect of direct democracy is always to push policy closer to the voters' ideal point – either by overriding the government or by the government adjusting its policy choice to deter challenges. The initiative and referendum can never make policy more extreme than when the legislature has a monopoly because voters will not approve a proposal more extreme than the status quo, and the government will never respond to the threat of an initiative or referendum from an extreme group because it knows with certainty that the threatened proposal will be rejected if it goes to the voters.

However, this conclusion is too stark. Another implication of the complete information model that highlights its limitations is that it predicts no initiatives or referendums in equilibrium – the government is always better off tailoring its policy to deter a challenge rather than being overridden, so no group ever finds it optimal to propose an initiative or referendum. The fact that we do see ballot propositions in practice points out the significant limitation of the complete-information model.

3.2 Information Problems

A second theoretical theme is asymmetric information, in particular, the idea that politicians have incomplete information about the preferences of their constituents (the principal–agent problem discussed above is based in part on the idea that voters have incomplete information about the behavior of politicians). Introducing the former kind of information asymmetry leads to a number of additional insights about direct democracy.

Matsusaka and McCarty (2001) extend the model of Romer and Rosenthal (1979) and Gerber (1996) by introducing uncertainty about voter preferences. This changes the government's strategy because it means that the government cannot perfectly anticipate which initiative and referendum threats will be successful and which will fail. As a result, and in contrast to the complete information case, the government may respond to a threat from an extreme group by making its own policy choice more extreme, rather than run the risk that the group might happen to represent majority opinion. In this context, availability of the initiative and referendum can make the voters worse off by pushing the legislature to adopt more extreme policies than it would otherwise. (See Gerber and Lupia 1995 for a model with a similar conclusion, but adopting a different mechanism.)

A model with asymmetric information also allows initiatives and referendums to occur in equilibrium and thus generates a theory of initiative use. Matsusaka and McCarty develop this theory and provide some evidence showing that initiatives are more likely to be used when there is more information asymmetry, consistent with their prediction.

Information asymmetry is also important for the information aggregation properties of votes on ballot propositions. It has been recognized at least since Condorcet's jury theorem that one benefit of elections comes from pooling widely dispersed information to yield an informationally efficient collective decision, essentially allowing the law of large numbers to reveal the 'true' payoff from a proposed law (see Lupia 2001 for a simple exposition). Significant progress has been made in identifying conditions under which elections can and cannot effectively aggregate information, with the main insight being that information aggregation works well when voter preferences over the final outcome are highly correlated (what might be thought of as public good decisions) than when preferences are uncorrelated or negatively correlated (what might be thought of as distributional decisions); see Battacharya (2008). Most of this research has studied information aggregation in elections in general, and has not considered the specific institutional features of direct democracy. The only evidence related to this of which I am aware is Matsusaka (1992), who finds that initiatives are more common on issues where information aggregation is unlikely to work (distributional issues) than on issues where aggregation is effective, suggesting that ballot propositions are not being used primarily to aggregate information efficiently.

Another strand of literature focuses on the expertise of or information available to elected officials (Maskin and Tirole 2004; Kessler 2005). These models augment the basic theory by observing that the consequences of alternative policies are not known with certainty, and that elected officials *choose* how well to be informed about the issues they consider. A negative consequence of direct democracy is that it dulls the incentives of officials to acquire information when they anticipate that their decisions may be overridden by voters. Direct democracy, via this channel, can lead to worse outcomes by degrading the effectiveness of representative institutions.

3.3 Bundling

A third theme that has received some attention is the ability of direct democracy to 'unbundle' issues. Candidates for office typically take positions on numerous issues, and voters are forced in effect to choose between a small number (often two) of competing bundles. Because voters are unable to select candidates on an issue-by-issue basis but rather have to choose between bundles of policies, candidates might not reflect voter preferences on every issue.

Besley and Coate (2008) provide models showing how the bundling of issues in candidates can prevent congruence between representative and voter interests. Non-congruence can occur (i) when there is a single issue that dominates an election, in which case minor issues might not be congruent; (ii) when there are single-issue voters who hold minority views; and (iii) when an interest group provides campaign support to candidates who will support its non-majority view on a particular issue. In these contexts, making initiatives available can improve congruence by allowing voters to override their representatives on non-congruent dimensions and by giving candidates an incentive to converge on the non-congruent dimensions. Conversely, when the representative system delivers convergence, introduction of initiatives can lead to a non-congruent outcome.

Matsusaka (2008) identifies a second channel through which initiatives can address bundling problems. Because a voter can cast only a single vote, elections are a crude tool for signaling voter preferences. A successful candidate who took positions on multiple issues in the course of his campaign cannot be sure exactly why the voters elected him. The inability of voters to send a sharp message to elected officials makes voting an ineffective disciplinary or communication tool. By taking some issues out of the hands of elected officials, initiatives and referendums allow voters to send stronger signals in candidate elections. Matsusaka reports some evidence that voters do link their votes more closely to specific issues in initiative states than noninitiative states. To the extent that elections can be more closely tied to past performance and expectations of future performance, the functioning of representative democracy will be improved.

3.4 Overall Assessment

The theoretical literature has made significant progress in capturing some of the more important forces at work within the realm of direct democracy. A general message that emerges is that the effects of direct democracy are likely to be fairly contextual. For example, spatial models, like that of Matsusaka and McCarty (2001), predict that direct democracy moves policy toward voter preferences when preference uncertainty is small, but can lead to more extreme policies when preference uncertainty is large. Unlike much of the earlier literature in law and policy journals that tended to make strong normative claims about direct democracy (mostly negative) based on a priori arguments and little evidence, the recent theoretical literature indicates that the consequences of direct democracy depend on how, when, and where it is applied in practice, and, moreover, that it can both enhance and impair democratic governance, depending on the particulars of the situation. The conditionality of recent theoretical conclusions highlights the importance of empirical research for understanding and assessing the effects of direct democracy.

4 EMPIRICAL RESEARCH

Most research on direct democracy is empirical in nature, and revolves around a central set of questions. While these questions have been prominent in debates surrounding direct democracy for more than a century, in the last two decades researchers have made significant progress in answering some of the key ones.

4.1 Basic Facts for the United States

Most empirical research on direct democracy uses data from the United States and, to a lesser degree, Switzerland. Because so much of what we know about direct democracy is based on studies from the United States, it is useful to have a background sketch of direct democracy in the United States. Figure 8.1 identifies the American states that currently provide for the initiative at the state level, and the date of adoption. A list of states allowing popular referendums would look similar, with the difference being that Florida, Illinois, and Mississippi do not have the referendum, while Kentucky, Maryland, and New Mexico do. The first state to adopt the initiative and referendum was South Dakota in 1898. A burst of adoption activity followed over the next two decades mostly associated with the Progressive movement, so that by 1918, 19 states had adopted the initiative. As Figure 8.1 shows, the initiative is most popular west of the Mississippi River, but it is not exclusively a California or western phenomenon, appearing in all regions of the country, from Maine and Massachusetts in the northeast to Arkansas, Florida, Mississippi in the south, and to Michigan and Ohio in the central region.

The process of submitting legislative actions to the voters is even older and more common. Massachusetts held an election in 1780 to approve its new constitution. Rhode Island made popular approval mandatory for constitutional changes in 1842. Popular votes on constitutional changes were the norm by the late nineteenth century, and today, only one state (Delaware) does not require constitutional amendments to be put before the voters. In the mid-nineteenth century, a series of state and local governments defaulted on public bonds that were used to finance banks and public works, such as railroads, turnpikes, and canals; in response, many states adopted provisions restricting the issuance of public debt and currently 21 states require a popular vote before state bonds can be issued (Kiewiet and Szakaly 1996).

The initiative appeared in American cities at about the same time it appeared at the state level. California counties gained initiative rights in 1893, and the cities of San Francisco and Vallejo adopted the initiative in 1898. By 1910, all or substantially all

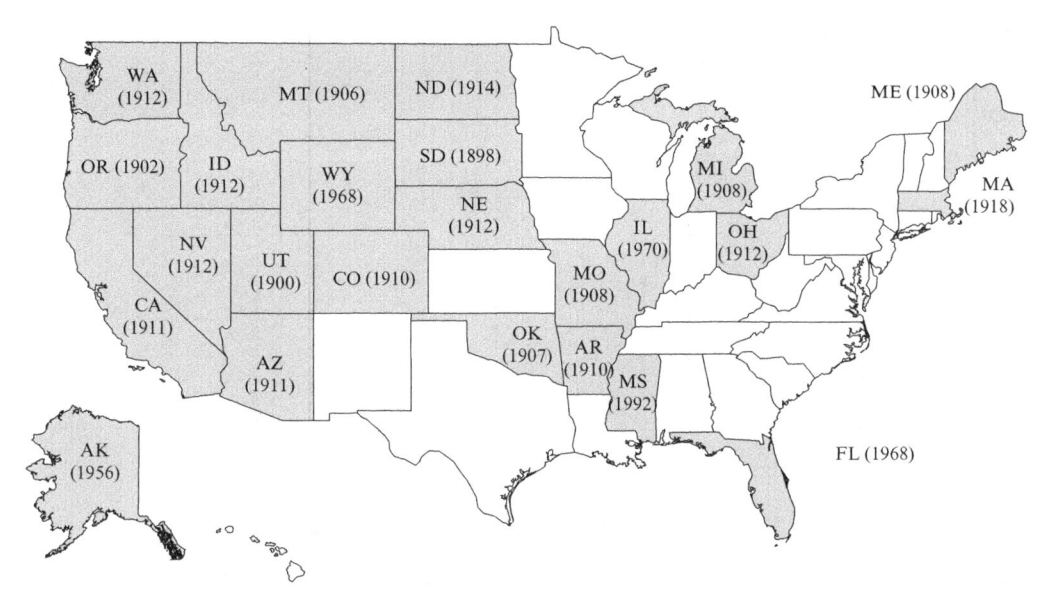

Figure 8.1   States with initiatives in 2010 (adoption year in parentheses)

municipalities in 10 states had been granted initiative rights, and it was available in individual cities in at least nine other states. The best estimate on current availability is that 80 percent of all cities in the country now have the initiative (Matsusaka 2009).

One remarkable development has been the explosion of citizen-initiated measures beginning in the late 1970s, sparked by California's tax-cutting Proposition 13 in 1978. Figure 8.2 shows the total number of initiatives by decade. The number of initiatives increased each decade from the 1960s through the 1980s, and then jumped to an historical high in the 1990s. Initiative use in the first decade of the twenty-first century continued at near the record level of the 1990s. In the years immediately after the passage of Proposition 13, some commentators speculated that the nation was undergoing a passing infatuation with direct law-making, but now it seems more likely that the United States has made a permanent shift toward more direct law-making (Matsusaka 2005a).

4.2   Policy Consequences

A central question in the scholarly literature and in practice is whether direct democracy enhances or impairs democratic performance. As we have seen above, theory suggests that there is not a simple answer to that question, and the answer is likely to vary according to the circumstances. A good place to begin a review of the empirical evidence is with a simpler question: does direct democracy make a difference for policy outcomes at all?

The answer to whether and how direct democracy impacts the policy formation process might at first glance seem obvious. One only has to read the headlines on Election Day to see that voters regularly approve ballot propositions. However, the fact that ballot propositions are approved does not establish that they actually change policy.

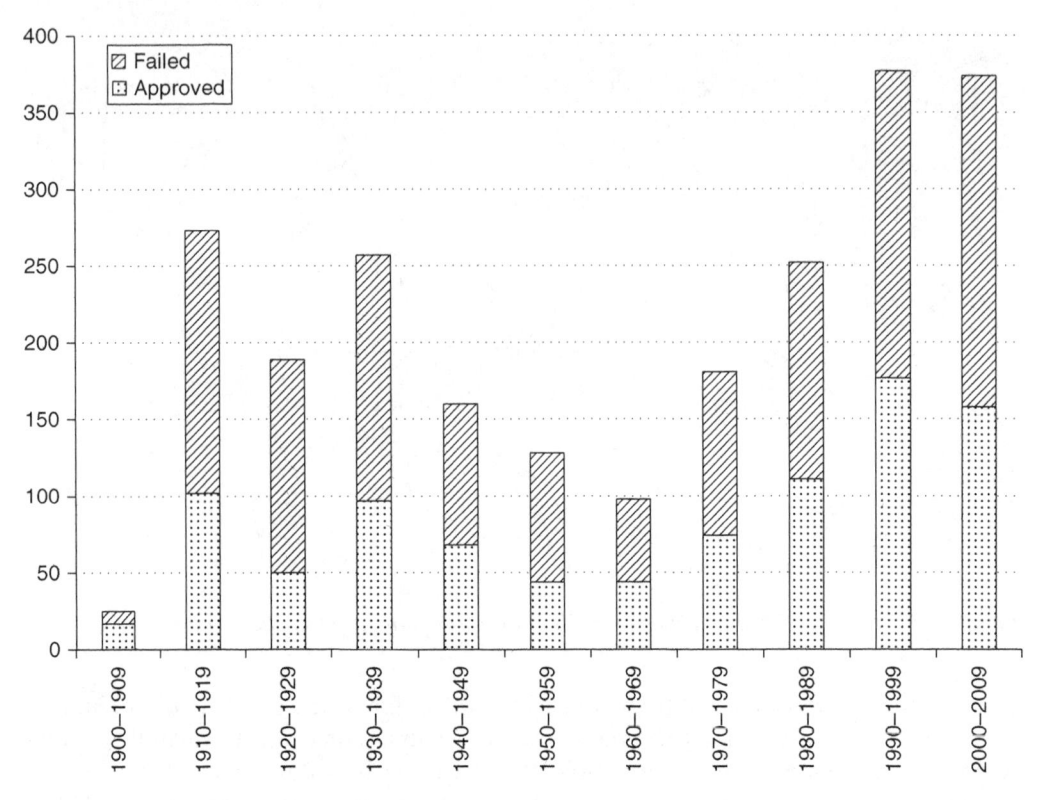

Figure 8.2 Number of state-level initiatives

It could be that the laws approved by voters would have been approved by legislatures if not for the ballot proposition. For example, while several states have approved bans on same-sex marriages through initiatives, other states have approved similar bans through the legislative process. A second reason we cannot infer their impact from the headlines is that direct democracy may influence policy choices even without measures appearing on the ballot, through the threat effect discussed above. It is theoretically possible for the presence of direct democracy to bring about material changes in policy without any measures appearing on the ballot. Yet another limitation of drawing conclusions from election returns is that a proposition might be approved by the voters but then nullified by a court or by a refusal of executive branch to enforce it, a possibility explored at length in Gerber et al. (2001).

To address these inference problems, most research on the policy effects of direct democracy employs a regression (or variant of a regression) of the form:

$$y_{it} = a_0 + a_1 D_{it} + a_2 X_{it} + e_{it}, \tag{8.1}$$

where y_{it} is a policy outcome (for example, government spending, or an indicator for a ban on same-sex marriage) in state (or city) i in year t, D_{it} is an indicator equal to 1 if the state allows direct democracy, X_{it} is a vector of control variables, e_{it} is an error term, and

a_0, a_1, and a_2 are parameters to be estimated. The parameter a_1 is intended to capture the effect of direct democracy on policy.

A virtue of equation (8.1) is that the coefficient a_1 in principle captures both the direct and indirect (threat) effect of direct democracy. The net effect of direct democracy on policy – whether as the result of an actual measure appearing on the ballot or the legislature altering its behavior to avoid a threat – will appear as a difference in the final outcome between initiative and noninitiative states. Furthermore, if y_{it} is a measure of actual policy outcomes (such as actual spending levels), equation (8.1) also avoids some of the difficulties stemming from implementation – if a measure is struck down by a court, we will not see a difference in policy outcomes between initiative and noninitiative states.

Regression (8.1) has been used to demonstrate that direct democracy has an impact on policy formation across a wide range of issues. The best documented outcomes are fiscal policies. Numerous studies beginning with Matsusaka (1995) find that initiative states tax and spend less than noninitiative states, at least from about the middle of the twentieth century. The effects are not huge: estimated per capita reductions in spending and taxes run in the range of 5 percent to 10 percent. Initiative states also appear to decentralize spending more than noninitiative states, that is, a smaller fraction of spending occurs at the state than at the local level, and initiative states appear to rely less on broad-based taxes and more on user fees and charges for services. Many of these patterns appear in Swiss data as well (Feld and Matsusaka 2003; Feld et al. 2008) and to some extent in cross-country data (Blume et al. 2009). Education is one of the largest categories of spending for state and local governments. Berry (2009) finds that initiative states spend less on education than non-initiative states, all else equal.

Significant differences between direct democracy and representative-only states have also been documented for social issues. In these studies, the policy outcome is often dichotomous (for example, 1 = ban on same-sex marriage, 0 = no ban), so a qualitative response version of (8.1) is employed, typically a logit or probit specification. Studies in this vein generally find that direct democracy is associated with more conservative social policies (Matsusaka 2007). For example, initiative states are more likely than non-initiative states to restrict access to abortion (Gerber 1999), permit the death penalty (ibid.), and ban same-sex marriage (Lupia et al. 2010).

Other research investigates the connection between direct democracy and government performance. Matsusaka (2009) reports that cities with the initiative tend to have fewer public employees and to pay them less than cities without the initiative. One of the most pronounced patterns, documented in several studies, is that initiative states are much more likely than non-initiative states to impose term limits on legislators. Indeed, having the initiative process available is almost a necessary and sufficient condition for term limits. However, evidence is much weaker for the notion that initiative states are more likely than non-initiative states to adopt other political reforms – campaign finance regulations, open primaries, and non-partisan redistricting (Bowler and Donovan 2004; Matsusaka 2006). In terms of administrative performance, Dalton (2008) reports mixed evidence that initiative states score lower than non-initiative states on an index of administrative capacity constructed by Syracuse University's Maxwell School.

While this literature is large and many of its findings seem to be fairly robust, the research methods have some nontrivial limitations. One is that the dummy variable approach in (8.1) assumes that initiative effects are uniform across jurisdictions. Theory suggests, on the other hand, that the effects of initiatives are likely to vary depending on the institutional features of the process. One important consideration is the ease of using the process. If the cost is low for a group to place an initiative on the ballot, its threat to do so is more credible, and the initiative should have a greater impact on policy. A simple approach to this issue is to allow interaction terms with the initiative dummy variable in (8.1). Matsusaka (1995) is an early attempt along these lines, which finds that the anti-spending effect of the initiative becomes stronger as signature requirements become less burdensome. Feld and Matsusaka (2003) report similar findings for Swiss cantons. However, signature requirements are only one dimension along which the rules implementing direct democracy vary. From a policy perspective it would be useful to identify the institutional features that are the most important, but typical samples do have enough degrees of freedom and the institutional characteristics tend to cluster, making it difficult to disentangle the various effects.

Another approach is to construct indexes that combine multiple institutional features. Bowler and Donovan (2004) is a pioneering effort in this direction that constructs two indexes – called 'qualification difficulty' and 'legislative insulation' – and shows that they are correlated with initiative effectiveness. Another index is proposed in Frey and Stutzer (2000). Existing indexes are ad hoc: different institutional features are simply assigned a score of 1 or 0 depending on whether the feature is present or absent, and the scores are summed to compute a total value. This approach makes two strong assumptions: the effects of the institutional features are (i) additive and (ii) have identical effects on policy. Both assumptions are surely false, but they could be close enough approximations to serve their purposes. A final limitation of indexes is that they obscure the precise features that drive the results, providing little guidance for policy-makers or reformers who are interested in improving the processes.

A related limitation of (8.1) is that it presumes that direct democracy pushes policy in the same direction in every state. For example, it presumes that initiatives either reduce spending in every state or increase spending in every state. This assumption is not supported by existing spatial models, which imply that the direction of effects depends on the relative positions of the legislature and of the median voter. For example, in the simplest models, if the legislature is to the left of the median voter, the initiative is predicted to push policy to the right, while if the legislature is to the right of the median voter, the initiative is predicted to push policy to the left. The coefficient a_1 in equation (8.1) should be interpreted as the *average* effect of direct democracy, and the fact that so many studies report coefficients significantly different from zero suggests that certain spatial configurations of legislators and voters are more common in the data studied. In particular, the evidence suggests that legislatures tend to be to the left of voters on most issues studied. Matsusaka (2004, ch. 7) explains why this configuration might be common in the post-1950 period that is most often examined. Underscoring the point that the directional effects of a_1 are not immutable but are likely to be context-specific, Matsusaka (2000a) finds that the spending and tax effects reverse sign (that is, initiative states spend and tax more than noninitiative states) in the early twentieth century, a period when legislatures were likely to have been more conservative than the median voter due to gerrymandering that favored rural interests.

Perhaps the most serious issue with (8.1) concerns whether a_1 can be interpreted as a causal effect. While there is significant variation in direct democracy processes across space (states, cities, cantons), there is little variation across time in most studies. As a result, the parameter a_1 for the most part is estimated based on the cross-sectional variation. The danger is that there could be an unmeasured factor correlated with initiative status that also drives policy choices.[3] A natural candidate for an omitted variable is voter ideology or culture: it could be that direct democracy states happen to be more conservative politically and that their conservativism is what drives their policy choices, not the initiative process per se. This particular source of spurious correlation can probably be ruled out: Matsusaka (2004) reports a large number of different public opinion measures, none of which show an important difference in political ideology between initiative and non-initiative states. Other known demographic differences, such as income, usually are controlled for in the regressions. I am not aware of any other candidates that have been proposed as possible omitted variables that create a spurious correlation, so the current state of knowledge seems to be that the obvious candidates can be rejected. As such, it seems appropriate at least provisionally to accept the existing estimates of a_1 as causal effects until other candidates for spurious correlation have been proposed.

4.3 For the Many or the Few?

A central claim by proponents of direct democracy is that initiatives allow voters to reestablish majority rule in the event that legislators become captured by special interests and therefore are unresponsive to public opinion. Despite the centrality of this argument – the idea of direct democracy loses much of its appeal if it is not effective in making policy more responsive to citizen interests – attempts to evaluate the argument rigorously have begun to appear only recently.

At first glance, it might seem that direct democracy brings about majoritarian outcomes by definition since a majority of voters is required to approve a ballot proposition. But there are several reasons why direct democracy might actually lead to policies that favor the few ('special interests') rather than the many. First, some pundits believe that citizens can be deceived by campaign advertising to vote against their interests, and may inadvertently approve policies that harm the majority. While a popular view among some journalists and politicians, its logical foundations have not yet been worked out by scholars. Second, some groups might be better at activating their members and getting them to vote than other groups. A longstanding theme in political economy (Olson 1965; Stigler 1971; Peltzman 1976) is that small groups are more effective politically than large groups because they are better at solving free-rider problems associated with active participation. According to this view, ballot propositions may garner a majority of votes from citizens turning out on Election Day, but the participants might be unrepresentative of the majority of the population.[4] Finally, and less often recognized, direct democracy has indirect effects, as discussed above, and theory suggests that the threat it poses to legislative decisions can lead elected representatives to adopt more extreme policies. In short, even though the majority rules on ballot propositions, it is possible in principle for availability of the initiative to enhance the power of special interests and bring about policies contrary to the interests of the majority.

Which of these effects – pro-majority or pro-interest group – dominates in practice is an empirical question, and in principle it is a straightforward one. Answering the question requires comparing policy outcomes with the preferences of voters and determining whether the majority prevails more or less often when direct democracy is available. However, the research task is complicated considerably by the limitations of public opinion polls. Perhaps the most extensive attempt to determine whether policy choices favor the many or the few is Matsusaka (2004), which studies fiscal policies. That study supplies evidence that the initiative process pushes state policy in a fiscally conservative direction – toward lower taxes and spending, toward decentralization of spending from state to local governments, and away from broad-based taxes to selective taxes and user fees – and shows (using a variety of survey data) that a majority of citizens expresses support for moving fiscal policies in these directions. My approach in that study is to assemble a variety of disparate sources of empirical evidence and to argue that there is only one reasonable way to fit the pieces of the puzzle together; but the evidence for a pro-majority effect is essentially indirect.

Another line of research attempts to determine whether direct democracy increases majority representation by estimating regressions of the form:

$$y_{it} = b_0 + b_1 D_{it} + b_2 O_{it} + b_3 D_{it} O_{it} + b_4 X_{it} + e_{it}, \qquad (8.2)$$

where the variables and subscripts are the same as in equation (8.1) above, except that O_{it} represents a measure of public opinion in state i in year t. Public opinion might be a direct measure of opinion about policy (for example, Gerber 1999 studies the death penalty and uses state-by-state survey data from the National Election Study) but more often it is a general measure of a state's 'ideology' (such as the measure in Erikson et al. 1993). In this line of research, the focus is on the coefficient b_3, and it is argued that $b_3 > 0$ implies that direct democracy states are more responsive to public opinion than non-direct democracy states (for example, Lascher et al. 1996; Camobreco 1998).

The argument is incorrect, however. While a value of $b_3 > 0$ does indicate a correlation between public policy and public opinion at the margin, it does not imply that initiative states choose policies closer to voters' opinion. This point initially was observed by Erikson et al. (1993) and developed in the direct democracy context by Matsusaka (2001). Intuitively, it is possible that direct democracy states as a group choose policies farther from the median voter's ideal point than legislature-only states, but show more responsiveness at the margin to changes in opinion (or conversely). As demonstrated in Matsusaka (ibid.), there are simple examples in which initiative states have chosen more congruent policies than non-initiative states with $b_3 > 0$, $b_3 < 0$, or $b_3 = 0$, depending on the context.

Matsusaka (2010) proposes a direct approach to measuring congruence. I focus on a set of issues with dichotomous policy outcomes (for example, permit or do not permit the death penalty) and for which state-by-state measures of public opinion are available. With such data, each state can be classified as either 'congruent' (choosing the policy outcome favored by the majority of voters = median outcome) or 'non-congruent' (choosing the policy favored by the minority). Studying 10 issues in 50 states, I find that overall congruence is only 59 percent, but that initiative states are 18 to 19 percent more likely to be congruent. This is the most direct evidence to date, and suggests that the majoritarian effect of the initiative outweighs whatever advantages it might offer to special interests.[5]

While the idea that the majority rules is central to democracy, another important democratic value is that the majority does not use its power to deny the basic rights of or to 'tyrannize' the minority. One fear about direct democracy is that by empowering the majority (as the evidence suggests that it does), it may threaten the rights of minorities. So far, research has focused on the rights of racial, ethnic, and sexual-orientation minorities. Too much of the literature on these issues employs unconvincing research designs and draws conclusions that are not merited by the evidence. Hajnal et al. (2002) is one of the notable exceptions. That study documents that ethnic and racial minority voters are only 1 percent less likely than white voters to be on the winning side of a ballot proposition vote. This finding suggests that although minority voters may lose on some issues, they are not likely to be hurt overall by the process any more than other voters. Consistent with this interpretation, opinion surveys show that minority voters are strong supporters of the initiative process, as are white voters (Matsusaka 2004).

4.4 The Role of Money

Related to the issue of interest group influence is the role of money in ballot proposition campaigns. As with elections in general, many observers are uncomfortable with the amount of money spent on ballot proposition campaigns, and are concerned that wealthy groups might be able to 'buy' favorable legislation.

The evidence on the impact of money is mixed. The first careful study, Lowenstein (1982), established one of the stylized facts in the literature, namely, that money is effective in opposing a ballot measure, but much less effective in supporting it. That is, rich groups can defeat a measure they do not like, but cannot buy favorable legislation. This basic pattern was confirmed in subsequent studies, such as Gerber (1999). However, most estimates of the relation between money and votes are vulnerable to the problem that afflicts the literature on campaign spending in general; endogeneity of the amount of money spent. For example, if supporters tend to spend more money when their proposition is in danger of failing, it would induce a negative relation between spending and votes. Recent studies have tried to address the endogeneity problem. Stratmann (2005a, 2006a) uses advertising spending at the metropolitan level and controls for a variety of fixed effects, and de Figueiredo et al. (2009) employ instrumental variables. These studies find that campaign spending matters, but contrary to the conventional wisdom, do not find a difference between supporter and opponent spending.

4.5 Voter Competence

Voter competence is another central concern for direct democracy. When voters make laws directly, it is important that they are able to choose wisely. Unfortunately, a large literature in political science demonstrates that many voters are uninformed about politics – they cannot identify their representatives and cannot answer basic questions about government. While this evidence is the basis for criticisms of direct democracy, it would seem to undercut the idea of representative democracy as much if not more so; a ballot proposition asks voters to decide a single issue, while a candidate election asks voters to decide on a bundle corresponding to all of the issues that the candidates might be called on to decide if elected.

However, recent research shows that voters might not need detailed, substantive knowledge about the issues before them in order to cast informed votes. If voters have access to information cues or, more simply, endorsements, they may be able to vote their interests without acquiring detailed substantive knowledge about ballot propositions. For example, an environmentalist may be able to vote his interests on a 'Forest Preservation Measure' without reading the text of the measure and independently forming an opinion on whether the measure preserves forests or is in fact a disguised attempt to allow timber companies to cut more trees, by observing the position of the Sierra Club and other environmental organizations on the issue. From this perspective, a 'competent' vote is a vote that reflects the person's interests and does not require substantive knowledge of the proposition.

While the idea that voters might be able to use information cues or endorsements to vote competently (in the preceding sense) is intuitive in principle, whether it works in practice is an empirical question. The most remarkable demonstration that endorsements can allow ordinary citizens to vote as if they were substantively informed is Lupia (1994). Lupia studies votes on five insurance regulation measures on the ballot in California in 1988. Those measures were highly technical in nature, and the differences between some of them were subtle. They were sponsored by an array of interest groups, including consumer activists, insurance companies, and trial lawyers. Lupia reports that voters who had access to simple information cues, such as the positions of Ralph Nader and the insurance industry but were uninformed about the substance of the measures, were able to replicate the voting pattern of voters who knew the details of the propositions.

Lupia's study establishes that voters are able to make competent decisions even on highly technical issues if they have enough cues. Subsequent research has attempted to identify the conditions under which cues are likely to be available. As shown in the pathbreaking analysis of Crawford and Sobel (1982), informative communication is likely to be difficult when the information sender and receiver have divergent interests even when communication is costless. Lupia and McCubbins (1998) extend this analysis specifically to the case of communication in elections and identify conditions that must hold for informative communication to take place. On the empirical side, Bowler and Donovan (1998) provide a variety of evidence that voters are influenced by endorsements, and are often able to register their interests. A number of studies summarized in Kahn and Matsusaka (1997) show that aggregate votes tend to reflect the underlying interests of the electorate, suggesting that voters are able to use cues effectively. For example, Kahn and Matsusaka find that those who stand to lose economically if a proposition is approved are significantly more likely to vote against it.

4.6 Education, Information, and Happiness

A recent strand of research investigates how direct democracy affects the knowledge and attitudes of citizens. Some supporters of direct democracy hope that by involving citizens more intimately in law-making, ballot propositions will cause citizens to be more informed, feel more efficacious, and otherwise be more satisfied with their government. Early research in this area reported a correlation between direct democracy and several behaviors that are considered to be civic virtues: when direct democracy is used, citizens appear to be more likely to vote, more informed about politics, express a greater sense of efficacy, trust government more, and report being more 'happy' (Smith 2002; Smith and Tolbert 2004; Frey and Stutzer 2000).

More recent research raises some questions about the robustness of the early findings. Spurious correlation is a risk in many of the studies. Turnout might be higher and citizens might be more informed in initiative states because citizens in those states are traditionally politically active, not because of initiatives – indeed, it could be the political activism of the citizenry that leads to adoption and use of direct democracy. The marginal statistical significance in some of the earlier studies also raises questions about robustness. Taken as a whole, the recent research employing more sophisticated empirical techniques casts doubt on the idea that there are important educative effects of direct democracy.[6]

4.7 Direct Democracy and Other Political Actors

Direct democracy is only one feature of the governance structure in any state or city. There is also a legislature, a chief executive, courts, administrative agencies, bureaucrats, and a constellation of interest groups. While much research has investigated the connection between direct democracy and the legislature, the connection with other parts of the governance structure is less well explored.

Courts can play an important role in direct democracy by removing issues from the ballot before an election, or striking down any approved measure. Manweller (2004) and Miller (2009) provide an overview of the amount of intervention into direct democracy by courts in American states over time, and frame many of the issues. Some research focuses on the 'single-subject rule', a legal requirement of some practical importance in many states that ballot propositions must confine themselves to one issue only. Lowenstein (1983) initiated the systematic study of this rule, noting that its theoretical underpinnings are weak, and suggesting that judges would be forced to use their subjective partisan inclinations to make decisions concerning the rule. Matsusaka and Hasen (2010) and Gilbert (2009) show that single-subject rulings indeed are often driven by the partisan leanings of the judges, with over 40 percent of judicial behavior attributable to their partisan inclinations in states with aggressive enforcement.

On the executive branch, Matsusaka (2008) provides a model showing how direct democracy can enhance or reduce the power of the executive branch, depending on the configuration of preferences of various actors. Ballot propositions are not subject to executive veto, which undercuts the executive's powers (when he or she has the veto power), but the executive's ability to drive the agenda can be enhanced by ballot propositions. In terms of administration, Dalton (2008) reports that non-initiative states adopt 'better' practices than initiative states, according to ratings by public administration scholars. Matsusaka (2009) shows that in cities, direct democracy serves to counteract the power of public employee unions; cities that allow initiatives tend to pay lower wages to municipal workers and have smaller public sector work forces. On the subject of interest groups, Boehmke (2005) provides an extensive analysis of the connection between initiatives and interest groups, and finds that initiative states have more interest groups, and in particular, more citizen groups and economic groups.

4.8 Conducting Research on Direct Democracy

Several reliable data sources are available concerning direct democracy. Information describing the institutional details of American states can be found in the appendixes of Gerber (1999) and Matsusaka (2004). Initiative status in a sample of over 1,500 American cities is in the Legal Landscape Database, available at www.iandrinstitute. org (city data from ICMA – the International City/County Management Association, sometimes used in research, are not reliable as far as the institutions of direct democracy are concerned, and should be avoided). Institutional information on initiatives and referendums in Swiss cantons is available in Trechsel and Serdült (1999), with much of the information summarized in English in Feld and Matsusaka (2003). The Initiative and Referendum Institute's Historical Database, available at www.iandrinstitute.org, is a comprehensive listing of initiatives in the American states. Partial lists of initiatives and other ballot propositions going back two or more decades are available at www.ncsl. org. A variety of other information on American states is collected in Waters (2003), although some of that information is now becoming dated.

NOTES

1. In order to keep the number of references manageable, I have not cited every relevant book or paper on this topic. For more comprehensive references, see the surveys by Lupia and Matsusaka (2004), Matsusaka (2005b) and Garrett (2010).
2. More precisely, in a complete information world direct democracy always makes the median voter better off. If voters are heterogeneous, direct democracy has distributional implications – it helps some individuals and hurts others – and any normative conclusions depend on a theory of how to trade off benefits to one group against costs to others.
3. Endogeneity is a perennial concern in research on institutions – institutions might be adopted specifically in order to bring about policy outcomes – but it is unlikely that there is an unmeasured factor that is driving initiative availability and policy choices because most states and cities with direct democracy adopted the process decades before the period studied.
4. Kenny (Chapter 23 in this volume) argues that the median voter in a special school bond election is more supportive of public education than is the median voter in a general election.
5. Lax and Phillips (2010) employ similar methods to study congruence on a larger number of issues than Matsusaka (2010), but use imputed public opinion rather than direct measures of it. They find low overall congruence as well, but do not find a positive connection between congruence and direct democracy. It is hard to know how to interpret their finding because their regressions with direct democracy as an explanatory variable also include a variable for term limits. Having term limits, as noted above, is an almost perfect predictor of having the initiative process, so it seems possible that the term limits effect they find (increasing congruence) is actually capturing an initiative effect.
6. For example, see Schlozman and Yohai (2008), Dyck (2009), and Dyck and Lascher (2009) on efficacy and trust; Childers and Binder (2010) on turnout; and Blume et al. (2009) and Dorn et al. (2008) on happiness.

9 Legislatures
Nicole V. Crain and W. Mark Crain

1 PURPOSE AND SCOPE

Legislatures are a pillar of representative democracy. Everyone past grade school knows roughly what a legislature is: an assembly whose members are elected to represent citizens' interests in government decision-making. And every school child in America learns that the legislature constitutes one of the three branches of the federal government. Likewise all 50 American state governments have a legislature. Globally, we cannot identify a democratic nation without a legislature.[1] A legislature appears to be a minimal institutional requirement for a modern democratic nation, and probably a requirement for all but the smallest polities where direct democracy or a single elected official is sufficient.

The purpose of this chapter is to illuminate features of legislatures that are not commonly emphasized in standard civics texts or in college-level political science courses. Such conventional treatments, in our view, are distressingly inadequate on a number of levels. For example, at best they offer only weak explanations for why public policies routinely deviate from those preferred by a majority of citizens. More than 70 percent of the respondents to most major opinion polls express disapproval when asked to evaluate the US Congress's performance.[2]

We describe several alternative models of legislatures that stress organizational rules and processes. In particular we focus on the role of institutions in affecting incentives and their implications for democratic performance. Our goal is to stimulate thinking about why outcomes of the legislative process reflect – or not – the preferences of the citizens electing legislators to represent them. The models offer frameworks for analyzing what works, what does not, and how the selection of institutional rules might improve the performance of representative democracy.

The powers of a legislature derive from the authority delineated in a constitution, and legislative decisions thus are enforceable by the power of the relevant state or federal government. In the United States, federal and state constitutions supply the institutional skeletons around which the various legislative bodies are formed. For example, constitutions include structural specifications, such as a unicameral chamber or bicameral chambers, eligibility for service, term lengths, expiration dates, term limits, and bases of representation for the chamber(s). Within a general constitutional structure, legislatures are largely self-organizing. Legislators typically use majoritarian principles to select most of the rules and procedures within which the legislative process operates and actions are taken.[3]

1.1 The Pre- and Post-constitutional Framework

The seminal work by Buchanan and Tullock (*The Calculus of Consent*, 1962), introduced a useful analytical device dividing the political process into pre- and post-constitutional stages of decision-making. This methodology serves a number of purposes, including performance evaluation, and suggests a different set of tools for analyzing the selection of constitutional rules versus studying outcomes once the game is afoot. It should be emphasized, however, that 'constitutional' in this context includes the procedural rules, and not solely those rules that are explicitly spelled out in the constitution. Rules of operation that follow customary norms and practices but are not reduced to writing in the constitution still can be classified as 'pre-constitutional,' the main difference being that these lack the durability of formal constitutional language.

For example, suppose a legislature creates 10 standing committees and adopts a rule that all bills must be submitted to and approved by a committee before being considered for a floor vote by the entire legislature. These are pre-constitutional choices that determine how subsequent legislative outcomes will be decided. After the procedural rules and processes are agreed upon and bills are being introduced, the post-constitutional phase begins. The fate of bills is determined within a given set of constitutional rules. This framework is useful on a number of levels, and it represents a fundamental contribution of the public choice tradition to the analysis of legislatures. It highlights the distinction between analyzing the legislative process as opposed to analyzing the outcomes of that process.

The theories of legislative organization described in this chapter focus on the pre-constitutional stage. In that context we address the self-organizing procedural rules selected by a majority vote of the legislators. Finally, we stress that the chapter deals with legislatures in the United States.

2 WHAT LEGISLATURES DO: SOME SUMMARY INDICATORS

Richard Fenno, in a classic 1973 work on legislatures, reduces the motivation of legislators to three elements: 're-election, influence within the House, and good public policy'. These three motives serve the purposes of our exposition very well, and cover most of the bases except perhaps the desire for approbation, fame, pay and perks, and more crass motives, such as post-election remuneration, influence peddling, and bribes. How do legislators achieve these goals? Legislators participate in the actions required to enact legislation, to block the enactment of legislation, and to repeal previously enacted legislation.

How laws are made, blocked, or repealed is determined by the procedural rules, and the basics of the legislative process are relatively easy to outline.[4] In US federal and state legislatures, legislative proposals encounter four key milestones: committee consideration in the first chamber, floor consideration in the first chamber, committee consideration in the second chamber, and floor consideration in the second chamber. In some cases, legislation encounters a fifth milestone: consideration by a 'conference committee,' which is a joint committee consisting of members from the two chambers, to reconcile major differences in the respective versions passed in the two chambers. After conference committee approval, the legislation would be returned for floor consideration in the two chambers separately.[5]

Table 9.1   Legislative outcomes in the US House and Senate: 2007–08 (percentage)

	Bills introduced, US House (N = 7,334)		Bills introduced, US Senate (N = 3,741)	
	Majority party author	Minority party author	Majority party author	Minority party author
Approval rate in committee, initial chamber	17.5	8.6	16.0	14.0
Approval rate in floor vote, initial chamber	15.3	8.0	4.3	4.1
Approval rate in committee, second chamber	6.5	4.4	2.7	2.8
Approved rate in floor vote, second chamber	5.1	2.9	2.7	2.7

2.1   Summary Statistics on Federal and State Legislation

Table 9.1 provides data that suggest the relative importance of the four major legislative milestones for the US House and Senate during the 2007–08 legislative session.[6]

For example, 7,334 bills were introduced by US House members in the 2007–08 biennium. Of these bills that had majority party authors (Democrats in that biennium), 17.5 percent were approved in House committees, 15.3 percent were approved on the House floor, 6.5 percent were approved in Senate committee, and 5.1 percent were approved on the Senate floor. The approval rates for minority party authors (Republicans in the 2007–08 biennium) were about half those rates at almost every legislative stage as shown in the third column of Table 9.1.

The approval rates for the 3,741 bills authored by US Senators were similarly low at all stages of the process. For example, 16 percent of US Senate bills authored by members of the majority party were approved in Senate committee, 4.3 percent were approved on the Senate floor, 2.7 percent were approved in House committee and 2.7 percent were approved on the House floor.

One difference stands out in Table 9.1 between legislative outcomes in the US Senate and the US House. Success rates for members of the majority party and minority party were roughly equal among US Senators, whereas success rates for minority party members are roughly half that for majority party members in the US House.

As a benchmark for comparing the fate of legislation at the federal and state levels, Table 9.2 presents data for the New York state legislature.

Of the 11,146 bills introduced into the New York Assembly, majority party members had a 36.3 percent approval rate at the committee stage, a 19.1 percent approval rate on the Assembly floor, a 7.3 percent approval rate in Senate committees, and a 6.7 percent approval rate on the Senate floor. Minority party Assembly members experience a

Table 9.2   Legislative outcomes in the New York Assembly and Senate: 2005–06 (percentage)

	Bills introduced, NY Assembly (N = 11,146)		Bills introduced, NY Senate (N = 8,105)	
	Majority party author	Minority party author	Majority party author	Minority party author
Approval rate in committee, initial chamber	36.3	9.5	54.5	5.9
Approval rate in floor vote, initial chamber	19.1	2.0	34.2	1.9
Approval rate in committee, second chamber	7.3	1.4	16.4	0.9
Approved rate in floor vote, second chamber	6.7	1.4	16.3	0.9

much lower approval rate. For example, minority party-authored bills in the New York Assembly had only a 9.5 percent approval rate in committee – and a paltry 1.4 percent approval rate on the Senate chamber floor.

In the New York State Senate, bills introduced by majority party senators had a 54.5 percent approval rate in Senate committees, dropping to a 16.3 percent approval rate in the second chamber's floor votes. Members of the minority party in the New York State Senate had a 5.9 percent approval rate in Senate committee and a scant 0.9 percent success rate on the New York Assembly floor.

The outcomes shown in Table 9.1 for the US Congress and in Table 9.2 for the New York legislature offer a reasonable depiction of two empirical facts that dominate US legislative processes. The first is that most legislation fails to move beyond the initial committee stage. The second is that party affiliation often matters in moving legislation successfully through the process.[7] Models of legislative organization ignore these two facts at their peril. These empirical regularities are quite relevant and help to form a unifying framework for understanding US legislatures.

3   THEORIES OF LEGISLATIVE ORGANIZATION

3.1   Crossing Disciplinary Boundaries: Legislative Process as an Exchange

Models of legislative organization have evolved in a sequence that roughly mirrors the evolution of models of the firm and that of the organization of industry. Beginning in the mid-twentieth century, models such as those developed in Downs (1957), Tullock (1959), and Buchanan and Tullock (1962) emphasized 'vote-trading'.[8] The quid pro quo whereby a legislator votes for a colleague's bill in exchange for that colleague's vote on her bill bears a close likeness to a market transaction. Subsequent work by Mayhew

(1966) and Ferejohn (1974) provided at least anecdotal evidence of vote-trading and logrolling at the US federal level.

The analogy between market exchanges familiar to economists and legislative exchanges familiar to political scientists provided a potent intellectual blend, perhaps the most fertile application of cross-disciplinary thinking ever experienced in the social sciences. In one sense, however, it was a diversion in terms of modeling legislatures realistically. This is because it focused so much attention on floor voting and logrolling patterns among legislators. This focus began to change with the industrial organization literature's growing awareness of the pivotal role of transaction costs and mechanisms for enforcing contractual agreements. As in the theory of the firm – where recognition that transaction costs were fundamental to the existence of firms, their sizes, and scopes – theories of legislatures began to see that vote-trading lacked costless enforcement mechanisms.

Without enforcement mechanisms, market transactions operate quite unsatisfactorily and so it is likewise for legislative transactions. What precludes a legislator from reneging on a deal, one that is at best loosely bound by an implicit vote-trading contract? Reputational capital is one possible road out of this enforcement dilemma, but because legislative careers are finite and uncertain, even well-intentioned legislators may not be around to deliver their promissory votes. The realization that legislative transactions, like market transactions, are costly to enforce, refocused the study of legislatures towards institutional mechanisms that would serve that function.[9] What this meant was that committees and the committee system emerged as the key to understanding legislatures. This was a giant leap forward, moving the theoretical analysis of legislatures much closer to reality.

3.2 The Committee System as a Mechanism to Facilitate Re-election

The second wave that followed in modeling legislative organization with its emphasis on transaction costs and committees owes an intellectual debt to the work of Kenneth Shepsle. His book *The Giant Jigsaw Puzzle* (1978) ushered in another noteworthy era of lateral, cross-disciplinary thinking: how and why members of legislatures get sorted into legislative committees. Here, scholars familiar with standard fare economic concepts such as revealed preference, self-interest, the specialization and division of labor, and comparative advantage reveled in the low-hanging fruit. This wave began to view the 'committee system' (and other legislative rules and institutions) through a novel lens: as mechanisms to reduce transaction costs, enforce implicit legislator contracts, and otherwise promote the durability of legislative agreements. As in market transactions, the value created by legislative transactions is integrally related to how long a law is expected to remain in force.

This new institutional perspective on legislative organization is intuitive and powerful. It captured the imagination of social scientists from all corners, attracted a multitude of fans and critics, and generated an outpouring of research that produced a voluminous literature.[10] A stylized version begins with the assumption that legislators are rational actors seeking re-election. Political parties are mostly sideshow actors with little influence, not an uncommon view among academics about US legislatures in the 1970s and 1980s. Atomistic, re-election seeking legislators develop an organizational structure for their institution that facilitates this goal, and the committee system is designed to cater to constituency-induced demands on legislators. Committees have specialized policy jurisdictions – agriculture, armed services, banking, financial services, and so forth – that provide for specialization and division of legislative labor. Legislators submit their assignment requests and self-select onto committees whose jurisdictions most closely match the interests of their constituencies (Shepsle 1978). For example, a US Representative elected from Manhattan gravitates to the Committee on Financial Services; a representative elected from the Kansas Corn Belt gravitates to the Committee on Agriculture. Legislative life is good, and everyone benefits by specializing in the policy domains that align with their constituents' interests.

For this system of committee-specific specialization to function as intended, another structural arch is required, and this is sometimes labeled a norm of universalism or deference. The principle is simple: 'I'll defer to your preferences on policies under your jurisdiction, if you'll defer to my preferences on policies under my jurisdiction.' The norm of deference creates value for legislators because even if the exchanged vote is not first-best for a legislator, that bill would be less relevant to her constituents than bills for which she traded her vote. Representative Madoff, representing Manhattan, votes 'aye' on the agricultural subsidies bill in exchange for Representative Jones's 'nay' vote on the financial services reform bill. Even if Rep. Madoff's constituents pay a little more for their food, this additional cost is less than what they gain from blocking the financial reform bill. Symmetrically, the gains to farmers in Rep. Jones's district from the farm subsidies exceed the costs to them of blocking financial reform.

This organizational framework that was built on the rock of the committee system casts a dark shadow on the process of representative democracy. This shadow is an implication that policies enacted might not reflect the preferences of the legislature as a whole (much less the preferences of citizens). As legislators gravitate toward those committees with constituent-specific specialties, the composition of committees will be skewed samples, as opposed to random samples of the membership of the entire legislative chamber. This is known as the 'preference-outlier' implication. The Committee on Agriculture will become populated not only by Rep. Jones from the Corn Belt, but also members from Nebraska, California's Central Valley, South Florida, and so forth. Generalizing, and recalling the norm of deference, this implies that policies will emerge from the committee system that are more extreme (that is, 'outliers') in comparison to the preference of the median legislator.

The veracity of the committee preference outlier phenomenon was first tested by Krehbiel (1990). Using a creative, straightforward empirical procedure, Krehbiel analyzed the average voting scores (ratings of Americans for Democratic Action) for the members of each standing committee in the US House as a way of gauging policy preferences. He then compared these committee averages to the average for all US House members. If committees are populated by preference outliers, then committee scores should differ from the overall House score. Krehbiel's findings were surprising. The evidence indicated that committee member preferences rarely deviated from the House as a whole. (The Committee on Agriculture seemed to be the exceptional committee populated by preference outliers.) The mismatch between theory and evidence delivered a Popperian blow to the prevailing wisdom. Krehbiel's 1990 paper was not the final empirical word on this subject, of course, and subsequent researchers offered varying degrees of support for the preference outlier hypothesis.[11] It nevertheless threw cold water in the faces of those who accepted the conventional wisdom that encouraged and enlivened efforts for the next wave of models of legislative organization.

3.3 Legislative Committees as Agenda-setters and Gatekeepers

Two major developments in the modeling of legislatures – agenda-setting and gatekeeping – were emerging in chronological tandem with the work represented by Shepsle (1978, 1979) and Weingast and Marshall (1988). The formal modeling of agenda-setting and gatekeeping similarly placed the function of committees at the apex of the legislative process in novel ways. The seminal paper by Romer and Rosenthal (1978) yielded one of the most widely applied models in political science. In what is sometimes labeled the 'setter model', the committee serves as the agenda setter, in the first stage of a two-stage decision-making process. In the second stage the committee's proposal is offered to the legislature for a floor vote on a take-it-or-leave-it basis (that is, the committee's proposal is considered by the entire legislature without the possibility of amendments or changes). With this agenda-setting power, Romer and Rosenthal show that the committee is able to achieve policy outcomes that differ significantly from the median legislator's ideal policy preference. In this framework the committee system, once again, produces policy outcomes that deviate from those that would prevail under a system that relies on a simple majority vote of all legislators.

The concept of legislative committees as gatekeepers was formally introduced in Denzau and Mackay (1983). The gatekeeping function is analogous to giving a committee veto power over legislative proposals; committees possess the power to prohibit a legislative proposal from being considered by the full legislative body. As in the Romer–Rosenthal two-stage process, the Denzau–Mackay committee decides in the first stage the proposals that will be allowed to be voted upon by the entire chamber (the second stage). The committee refuses to 'open the gate' for any proposal that is likely to make the committee's members worse off relative to policies that currently are in place. This means that some policy proposals that would be supported by a legislative majority are thwarted. Committee gatekeeping allows the status quo to prevail even when alternative policies exist that would be supported by a majority of legislators.[12]

3.4 Legislative Committees as Mechanisms to Promote Investments in Specialized Knowledge and Expertise

The several models of legislative organization that are summarized above leave a fundamental issue unsettled. The rules and procedures of the committee system are determined endogenously by a majority vote of the legislators. Why, then, would a majority consent to establish an organizational system that allows (and perhaps promotes) outcomes that would not be supported by a majority? One plausible answer is linked directly to constituent-specific specialization and the norm of deference; the electoral advantages are sufficiently large that incumbents forgo the potential for superior policy outcomes.

A second plausible explanation is far more sanguine and uplifting from a 'good government' point of view. The committee system and other institutional mechanisms persist in a majoritarian environment because these encourage investments in knowledge that is highly specialized. Public policy topics are often complex, requiring years of study and experience to develop the expertise necessary to make good decisions. Committee specialization, coupled with a seniority system whereby longevity of service on a committee (usually) determines a member's level of authority, is a way of organizing the legislature such that members are rewarded for accumulating expertise and mastering complex committee-specific policy areas. This 'legislative organizer' approach is developed in the work by Gilligan and Krehbiel (1987, 1989) and Krehbiel (1991). Baron (2000) offers a different, screening model of the information-generating role of committees. In contrast to the vote-trading norm of deference framework, yielding to the preferences of committee members takes advantage of investments in accumulating highly specialized policy information. Effective legislatures need policy specialists because many public policies are arcane. Informational asymmetries mean that members of a committee know more about the policy topic than non-committee members. Deference to committee members' expertise is therefore an efficiency enhancing phenomenon that improves decision-making, and promotes better governance. This contrasts starkly with the agenda-setting, gatekeeping, and distributive politics frameworks.[13]

3.5 Legislative Committees as Mechanisms for Party Discipline and Control

A final perspective on legislative organization views the committee system as a mechanism for maintaining party discipline and control. This perspective is an application to legislative organization of the economic models developed by Hirschman (1970), Akerlof (1983), and Spence (1973). It differs considerably in focus from the models discussed earlier, especially models in the Shepsle–Weingast–Marshall tradition that explicitly minimized the role of political parties. Here, the committee system is a mechanism employed by the parties to accomplish policy agendas.

The application of screening or filtering theory is straightforward. From the party leadership's perspective, assigning a party member to a committee is a long-term investment made with considerable uncertainty about how that member will vote on policy proposals in future years. This committee assignment decision is analogous to a firm's hiring decision when a worker's productivity will not be known for several years. An apt analogy is professional baseball. When major league teams hire players, they typically assign them first to a farm (minor league) team so as to develop their playing skills and to gauge and monitor their productivities and performances. Party leaders typically assign newly elected legislators to the less important committees, something like baseball's farm system. The leadership may then observe the member's voting record and assess the degree to which the member's performance conforms to the agenda of the party leadership. The committee system, with its varying layers of committee importance, thus becomes a filtering mechanism that encourages party loyalty and precludes less conforming members from serving on committees to which the most important legislation is referred.[14]

In this model, the committee system encourages members to signal their loyalty to the leadership through their voting records (Crain 1990). This is because committee seats are scarce relative to the number of members competing for assignments to them, especially so for those with important budget-making responsibilities, such as the Senate Finance Committee and the committees on Ways and Means and Appropriations in the US

House. Such competition for scarce committee seats creates the potential for bias; junior members seeking to move onto more powerful committees may overinvest in voting for the leadership's agenda.[15] For example, it creates an incentive for a member to ignore the best interests of her constituency if doing so gives her a leg-up in receiving a plum committee assignment in the future.

Coker and Crain (1994) present some empirical evidence that supports the committee filtering hypothesis. They create floor voting indices that measure the frequency with which each US House member voted in accordance with his or her party's leaders. These metrics are then averaged (separately for both parties) for the members assigned to each House standing committee. The findings generally indicate a positive and significant relationship between voting in conformity with the leadership and the importance of the committee to which legislators are awarded seats. However, the hypothesis of voting bias – voting too frequently with the leadership coming at the expense of voting for constituents – has not been tested empirically.

4 CONCLUDING COMMENTS

Dow and Munger (1990) made a somewhat discouraging observation about the influence of economics-based models in political science, noting that these models have not been well integrated into standard political science courses, despite a successful track record of publications in political science journals. This certainly holds for the focus of this chapter, legislatures. The models of legislative organization that have evolved in tandem with developments in the theory of the firm and industrial organization provide compelling insights. These insights have narrowed the gap between theory and practice by elevating the understanding of the committee system as the most important element in US legislatures. Virtually all important legislative outcomes there happen either in committees or because of the committee system.

In their essay, 'The unfinished business of public choice,' Shughart and Tollison (2005) emphasize that a key question on the public choice research agenda is how to model political institutions and processes that emerge in settings where the rules are written by players themselves. The US Constitution and those of the American states are silent about the institution of the committee system. Instead, this vital institution is indeed a creation of legislators actively engaged in the process who have vested interests. While we have described the argument behind the efficiency enhancing properties of the committee system, our goal has been to stimulate thinking about why outcomes of the legislative process may not reflect the preferences of the citizens that legislatures purportedly are elected to represent. Several models of the committee system described offer strong arguments for why and how this can happen.

NOTES

1. We can, however, identify many non-democratic regimes around the globe that also have legislative branches, but such assemblies often are mere 'window-dressing' or serve as conduits for distributing patronage to the regime's supporters. See Razo (Chapter 6 in this volume).

2. In the fall of 2010, six major polling organizations all reported that between 70 percent and 75 percent of respondents 'disapproved' when asked about the job rating of Congress. http://www.pollingreport.com/CongJob.htm, last accessed 15 November 2011.
3. In the US House of Representatives, for example, a resolution typically is passed by a majority vote at the start of each session that adopts the rules under which that chamber shall operate. Such resolutions usually begin by confirming the rules from the prior Congress and then listing any exceptions to or changes in them. In other words, at least for the US Congress, rather than starting each session *de novo*, change in the procedural rules is incremental.
4. Legislation, the output of legislatures, usefully is categorized into statutory laws and fiscal policies. These two outputs are produced using similar, but slightly different processes, and we discuss in a later section several relevant differences that are worth emphasis.
5. There is also a 'last milestone' – the presidential veto. The president can send an unsigned bill back to Congress within a 10-day period while Congress is in session or simply refuse to sign it ('pocket veto') when Congress is adjourned. It takes two-thirds majorities of the members present in both chambers of Congress to override a presidential veto.
6. These are the most recently available data for a complete congressional biennium.
7. The extent to which committees and party affiliation matter varies from state to state, but the general pattern is pervasive. A major exception is Colorado, where committees rarely reject bills. Note, however, that far fewer bills are introduced in Colorado's state legislature than in, say, that of New York: 353 in the Colorado House and 249 in the Colorado Senate for the 2005–06 biennium.
8. In his review of this literature, Stratmann (1995) traces the reference to logrolling back to Bentley (1907).
9. Holcombe and Parker (1991) adopt a property rights perspective to explain how committees lower transaction costs. Laband (1988) also focuses on mechanisms that reduce transaction costs in legislative production.
10. See, for example, Benson (1983), Coker and Crain (1994), Laband (1988), and Smith (1982).
11. See the reviews and subsequent analyses in Benson (1983), Groseclose (1994) and Krehbiel (2004).
12. Thomas and Grofman (1992) examine empirically factors that determine outcomes in the US House at the committee level, revealing the importance of being a committee 'insider'.
13. Epstein (1997) provides a relevant attempt to reconcile the information asymmetry and gatekeeping perspectives.
14. See Kanthak (2004) and Parker and Parker (1998).
15. The analogy in labor markets is the overinvestment in education when educational achievement is used by potential employers as a signal of future productivity.

10 Parliaments
Fabio Padovano[1]

1 INTRODUCTION

This chapter analyzes national parliaments from an international comparative perspective. Scholars thus far have focused their attention mainly on the organization and functioning of single legislatures, chiefly the US Congress (see Mueller 2003 for a review), a few other countries (for example, the French Fifth Republic in Tsebelis and Money 1997) or the European Parliament (Steunenerg 1994; Crombez 2000). Comparative analyses of the determinants of the different institutional features that characterize legislative assemblies have been limited to the 'natural laboratory' of the US state legislatures (McCormick and Tollison 1981; Crain and Tollison 1990; McCormick and Turner 2000). Here we will try to expand this research program to parliaments across the world. Thus, rather than aiming at providing a complete review of the vast literature on the legislative branch of government – which would include contributions from political science, constitutional law, industrial organization, constitutional economics and public choice, as well as from other disciplines – we focus on selected topics that we deem either especially relevant or where new research is producing interesting results, namely: the organizations of national parliaments throughout the world; the determinants of their institutional differences; the mechanisms by which various parliaments take decisions; the presence of cycles in the production of laws; and the origins of the main models of democratic parliaments.

2 DEFINITIONS AND CATEGORIZATIONS

In the modern meaning of the word, a parliament is defined as the body of people (in an institutional sense: a *legislature*) who meet to discuss matters of state and to enact laws implementing the parliamentary majority's position on those matters. The modern term derives from the French *parlement*, the action of speaking (*parler*); it eventually came to indicate the location of the meeting where these discussions took place.

Constitutional lawyers and political scientists (Cheibub 2002, 2007; Ginsburg and Elkins 2010) traditionally have categorized parliaments into two alternative systems of government, parliamentary and presidential (or congressional). The fact that the legislature operates within one of these systems affects its importance and functions. Parliamentary systems, on the one hand, are characterized by no clear-cut separation of powers between the executive and legislative branches, which leads to a different set of checks and balances compared to those found in presidential systems (Persson et al. 1997). In parliamentary systems the legislature plays a central role, expressed by the confidence that the legislative branch has in the executive branch to exercise its constitutional functions. If members of the parliament lose faith in the government (in some countries, such as Italy and the United Kingdom, also in single ministers) they can call a vote of no confidence and force the government (or the minister) to resign. Schofield (1997) notes that this can be particularly dangerous to a government when the distribution of seats is relatively even, in which case a new election is often called shortly thereafter. On the other hand, in case of general discontent with the head of government, he can be replaced very smoothly (Laver and Shepsle 1996; Diermeier and Merlo 2000). Supporters of parliamentarianism (Linz 1994) argue that, because this system requires the prime minister to have strong support from political parties in the legislature, it will be more effective in translating policy into legislation. Conversely, others criticize presidential systems, because their winner-take-all logic creates the potential for antidemocratic populism and for institutional conflict between the executive and legislative branches (Ginsburg and Elkins 2010).

The presidential system, on the other hand, often modeled on US political institutions, operates under a stricter separation of powers. Congress usually exercises law-making functions, to which the president has powers of proposal as well as of a (restricted) veto. The executive is not a part of, nor is appointed by, the parliamentary or legislative body; rather he is elected indirectly by voters. Typically, congresses do not select or dismiss heads of governments, and governments cannot request an early dissolution, as may be the case for parliamentary systems. The absence of the principle of the vote of no confidence tends to result in weak party discipline (Baron 1993). These institutional features make the governments of presidential systems more stable than those of parliamentary ones; yet the replacement of a very unpopular president is inherently more difficult (Diermeier et al. 2002).

An interesting, public-choice driven critique of legislatures in presidential systems is that they are allegedly more prone to rent-seeking than those in parliamentary ones. Moe and Caldwell (1994) argue that legislators in presidential systems turn out to be the representatives of special interests because they do not represent the national interest. The president, conversely, has a more encompassing and less redistributive objective function, being elected from the whole nation as a single constituency. The legislature will thus be more likely to be captured than the presidency, and the public interest will suffer. Incidentally, this is precisely the viewpoint taken by the special interest group theory of government (McCormick and Tollison 1981; Crain and Tollison 1990). Shugart (1999) maintains, however, that the reason why legislators in presidential systems seem to focus on localized interests is not the result of presidentialism *per se*, but follows from the combination of weak party discipline and plurality-based legislative districts.[2] Furthermore, parliamentary systems hardly are immune from localism and rent-seeking. Pure systems of proportional representation seem to empower small fringe parties to be crucial in producing governing coalitions (witness the case of the left-wing Italian governments led by Romano Prodi, who belonged to a small centrist party of the coalitional government). In contrast, the separation of powers, a core feature of presidentialism, increases the cost of legislation to interest groups (Macey 1988).

But parliamentary and presidential systems are not the only institutional frameworks wherein legislatures operate, at least in democracies. Some countries have developed a hybrid model, called the semi-presidential system, which combines a powerful president with an executive responsible to parliament. Some countries that experienced a series of unstable and paralyzed executives, such as France during the Fourth Republic, replaced the pre-existing parliamentary system that endowed the legislative branch with excessive political power with a variant of the semi-presidential system. At the opposite end, countries such as those in Eastern Europe, which emerged from experiences of dictatorship, adopted this model in the early 1990s rather than opting for a pure presidential system (Elgie 1999). The general claim is that the presidential system too closely resembled a dictatorial regime, with the strong powers allotted to the executive, which its proponents wanted to check with two-sided accountability, both to voters and to the parliament. Recent political economy research, however, suggests that it is weak parliamentary systems that face greater risks of decaying into dictatorial regimes rather than strong presidential ones (Acemoglu and Robinson 2001, 2006; Acemoglu 2006). Such a conclusion is disputed, as there is empirical support for the proposition that parliamentary systems underpin democratic survival (Cheibub and Limongi 2002; Boix and Adsera 2008). The logic of the argument is that presidential (and semi-presidential) systems tend to produce executives who lack the support of a majority of voters and to government gridlock, which in turn can encourage actors to take extra-constitutional steps to gain power, leading to political instability and eventually to the death of democracy.

A more recent, public-choice inspired categorization of parliamentary types distinguishes between the Westminster and the Consensus parliaments (Lijphart 1999). The reason for preferring this demarcation rather than the parliamentarism–presidentialism divide is that it focuses on how parliaments actually work and take decisions, rather than on the institutional framework that surrounds them. The Westminster system is usually found in anglophone Commonwealth countries, although it is neither universal within nor exclusive to them. These parliaments tend to have a more adversarial style of debate and plenary sessions are more important than legislative committees. Some parliaments in this model are elected using a plurality voting system (first-past-the-post), such as those of the United Kingdom, Canada and India, while others use proportional representation, as is the case in Ireland and New Zealand. Even when proportional representation systems are used, voting tends to allow individuals to cast their ballots for named candidates rather than a party list. The Westminster model does, however, allow for a greater separation of powers than the consensus one, since the governing party will often not have a majority in the upper house.

The consensus model of parliament, predominant in Western Europe (for example, Italy, Spain and Germany) tends to have a more concordant debating system, and usually has semi-cyclical debating chambers. Consensus systems are often associated with proportional representation (PR) and have greater tendencies to use party list systems than the Westminster model of legislatures. The history of electoral reforms in Italy sheds light on the strength of the link between consensus style parliaments and proportional representation. From its creation in 1948 until 1994, the Italian parliament had been elected through a PR system, when a popular referendum forced a switch to a mixed plurality system. In 2005, however, the struggles between political parties led to the reintroduction of PR with a party list, and the system is still in place. In consensual systems committees tend to be more important than the plenary chamber, and there is a greater tendency to adopt neo-corporatist forms of governance, which in fact deprives the parliament of its legislative powers (Galli and Padovano 2003). Some Western European parliaments (for example, the Netherlands, Sweden and Switzerland) implement the so-called principle of dualism as a way of separating legislative and executive powers (Bergman 2004). In that system, members of parliament must resign their legislative seats upon being appointed (or elected) as a minister. However, ministers in those countries normally participate actively in parliamentary debates – the main difference being their inability to vote. Switzerland is considered to be one the purest examples of a consensus system.

3 PARLIAMENTS ACROSS THE WORLD

But how are national parliaments actually organized? Why are some of them bicameral or unicameral, why are some large and some small? What is the origin and the role of the parliamentary committees? Public choice and positive constitutional economics scholars have focused their attention only recently on the differences among the institutional features of parliaments across the world. This is an area where theory seems to be ahead of comparative empirical analysis, partly because only lately have some scholars started to assemble consistent and comparable databases on the characteristics of national parliaments (for example, Ferree and Singh 1999). These databases have subsequently been included in the 2010 release of the Database of Political Institutions. Here we will exploit this information to first illustrate the major institutional features of parliaments and then to review their main theoretical explanations.

3.1 Main Institutional Features of National Parliaments

Table 10.1 summarizes the main characteristics of national parliaments collected according to standardized criteria. The data there are our selection drawn from the Database of Political Institutions (DPI) and refer to countries – whatever their level of democracy – having legislative assemblies in place as of year 2009.[3]

The variable *Total seats* indicates the total number of seats in the whole legislature if it is unicameral, or in the lower house when the country has an effective bicameral legislature. The DPI considers a legislature to be effectively bicameral if the members of both houses are elected, even if different electoral procedures apply to them; hence, countries where the upper house is composed of appointees, tribal chiefs, dignitaries, members of professional organizations or of individuals who are members of the lower house at the same time are considered to have a unicameral legislature.

The sizes of legislatures exhibit a very high variance, ranging from a minimum of 15 (Grenada) to a maximum number of nearly 3,000 representatives (People's Republic of China), with a mean value of 213 and a standard deviation of 266. Predictably, the rough index of representativeness that we propose (the size of the population divided by the number of seats) also shows a similar, although slightly smaller variability: from 2.45 (Maldives) to 2,080 (India), with a mean of 105.75 and a standard deviation of 186.77. Contrary to what might be expected, effective bicameral legislatures are the exception rather than the rule; only 56 countries out of 166 (that is, one-third) convene parliaments with elected lower and upper houses. Where a parliament is bicameral, the ratio of the size of the upper chamber to the total legislature (a crucial feature according to the special interest group theory of government) is reported. Germany and the Philippines are the countries where the two legislative chambers are most unequal in

Table 10.1 Main institutional characteristics of national parliaments in 2009

n.	Country	Total seats	Index of representativeness	N. of elected chambers	Ratio of upper chamber to whole parliament	Legislative democracy	Population (000s)	OECD member country
1	Afghanistan	249	128.07	2	0.299	4	31,889.920	No
2	Albania	140	25.72	1		7	3,600.523	No
3	Algeria	389	85.7654	2	0.27	7	33,362.740	No
4	Angola	220	55.74362	1		6	12,263.600	No
5	Argentina	256	156.4407	2	0.22	7	40,048.820	No
6	Armenia	131	22.68435	1		7	2,971.650	No
7	Australia	151	137.4147	2	0.34	7	20,749.630	Yes
8	Austria	183	44.80756	2	0.25	7	8,199.783	Yes
9	Azerbaijan	125	64.96198	1		7	8,120.247	No
10	Bahamas	41	7.455	2	0.29	7	305.655	No
11	Bahrain	40	17.71433	2	0.5	6	708.573	No
12	Bangladesh	296	513.6279	1		7	152,033.900	No
13	Barbados	30	9.411967	2	0.41	7	282.359	No
14	Belarus	110	88.40657	2	0.37	7	9,724.723	No
15	Belgium	150	69.28151	2	0.21	7	10,392.230	Yes
16	Belize	31	9.503548	1		6	294.610	No
17	Benin	93	89.01245	1		7	8,278.158	No
18	Bhutan	47	14.32666	1		6	673.353	No
19	Bolivia	130	72.5072	2	0.17	7	9,425.936	No
20	Bosnia-Herzegovina	42	108.3857	1		7	4,552.198	No
21	Botswana	57	33.56881	1		6	1,913.422	No
22	Brazil	513	378.0089	2	0.14	7	193,918.600	No
23	Bulgaria	240	30.51191	1		7	7,322.858	No
24	Burkina Faso	101	146.5067	1		7	14,797.170	No
25	Burundi	115	72.96091	2	0.29	7	8,390.505	No
26	Cambodia	123	113.7878	1		6	13,995.900	No
27	Cameroon	163	110.7999	1		6	18,060.380	No
28	Canada	307	107.2833	2	0.25	7	32,935.960	Yes
29	Cape Verde Is.	72	5.894375	1		7	424.395	No
30	Central African Rep.	104	42.09025	1		7	4,377.386	No
31	Chad	154	64.1926	1		7	9,885.661	No
32	Chile	120	135.8654	2	0.24	7	16,303.850	Yes
33	Colombia	166	267.347	2	0.38	7	44,379.600	No
34	Comoro Islands	33	21.55809	1		7	711.417	No
35	Congo	135	28.16542	2	0.33	7	3,802.332	No
36	Costa Rica	57	72.58551	1		7	4,137.374	No
37	Cote d'Ivoire	223	88.55134	1		7	19,746.950	No
38	Croatia	145	30.98836	1		7	4,493.312	No
39	Cuba	614	18.55707	1		4	11,394.040	No

158 *The Elgar companion to public choice*

Table 10.1 (continued)

n.	Country	Total seats	Index of representativeness	N. of elected chambers	Ratio of upper chamber to whole parliament	Legislative democracy	Population (000s)	OECD member country
40	Cyprus	56	14.07959	1		7	788.457	No
41	Czech Republic	200	51.14372	2	0.29	7	10,228.740	Yes
42	Denmark	170	32.16541	1		7	5,468.120	Yes
43	Djibouti	65	7.636523	1		5	496.374	No
44	Dominican Republic	178	52.61696	2	0.15	7	9,365.818	No
45	Ecuador	97	145.7212	1		7	14,134.960	No
46	Egypt	432	185.9607	1		6	80,335.040	No
47	El Salvador	84	82.71515	1		7	6,948.073	No
48	Equatorial Guinea	100	5.99763	1		6	599.763	No
49	Eritrea	150	35.71784	1		2	5,357.676	No
50	Estonia	101	13.02883	1		7	1,315.912	Yes
51	Ethiopia	549	145.6026	2	0.18	7	79,935.800	No
52	Finland	200	26.1923	1		7	5,238.460	Yes
53	France	580	109.7961	2	0.36	7	63,681.740	Yes
54	Gabon	122	11.93812	1		7	1,456.451	No
55	Gambia	48	35.17415	1		6	1,688.359	No
56	Georgia	150	30.97335	1		6	4,646.003	No
57	Germany	614	134.2036	2	0.09	7	82,401.000	Yes
58	Ghana	229	100.1367	1		7	22,931.300	No
59	Greece	300	35.68763	1		7	10,706.290	Yes
60	Grenada	15	6.000333	2	0.46	7	90.005	No
61	Guatemala	158	80.55766	1		7	12,728.110	No
62	Guinea-Bissau	100	14.7278	1		7	1,472.780	No
63	Guyana	65	11.83223	1		7	769.095	No
64	Haiti	99	87.98813	2	0.25	7	8,710.825	No
65	Honduras	128	58.4669	1		7	7,483.763	No
66	Hungary	386	25.79303	1		7	9,956.108	Yes
67	Iceland	63	4.792556	1		7	301.931	Yes
68	India	543	2080.785	2	0.31	7	1,129,866.000	No
69	Indonesia	548	428.2737	1		7	234,694.000	No
70	Iran	290	225.5087	1		5	65,397.520	No
71	Iraq	275	99.99868	1		7	27,499.640	No
72	Ireland	166	24.75353	2	0.27	7	4,109.086	Yes
73	Israel	120	58.25052	1		7	6,990.062	Yes
74	Italy	630	92.29799	2	0.34	7	58,147.730	Yes
75	Jamaica	60	46.37035	2	0.26	7	2,782.221	No
76	Japan	480	265.4864	2	0.33	7	127,433.500	Yes
77	Jordan	110	55.02903	1		6	6,053.193	No
78	Kazakhstan	98	155.9687	2	0.31	5	15,284.930	No

Table 10.1 (continued)

n.	Country	Total seats	Index of representa- tiveness	N. of elected chamb- ers	Ratio of upper chamber to whole parliament	Legislative democracy	Population (000s)	OECD member country
79	Kenya	207	178.3272	1		7	36,913.720	No
80	Korea (South)	299	161.3717	1		7	48,250.150	Yes
81	Kuwait	50	50.11118	1		5	2,505.559	No
82	Kyrgyzstan	90	58.71277	1		6	5,284.149	No
83	Laos	113	57.7168	1		5.5	6,521.998	No
84	Latvia	100	22.5981	1		7	2,259.810	No
85	Lebanon	131	29.96566	1		7	3,925.502	No
86	Lesotho	119	17.85934	2	0.22	7	2,125.262	No
87	Liberia	64	49.93642	2	0.32	7	3,195.931	No
88	Lithuania	141	25.35772	1		7	3,575.439	No
89	Luxembourg	60	8.0037	1		7	480.222	Yes
90	Macedonia	120	17.13263	1		7	2,055.915	No
91	Madagascar	126	154.3557	2	0.38	7	19,448.820	No
92	Malawi	187	72.74428	1		7	13,603.180	No
93	Malaysia	222	111.8705	2	0.24	7	24,835.240	No
94	Maldives	149	2.44945	1		4	364.968	No
95	Mali	147	81.60137	1		7	11,995.400	No
96	Malta	69	5.824348	1		7	401.880	No
97	Mauritania	95	31.38371	2	0.37	1	2,981.452	No
98	Mauritius	73	17.31368	1		7	1,263.899	No
99	Mexico	500	217.4018	2	0.2	7	108,700.900	Yes
100	Moldova	101	42.85956	1		7	4,328.816	No
101	Mongolia	76	38.83929	1		7	2,951.786	No
102	Morocco	325	104.0809	2	0.45	7	33,826.300	No
103	Mozambique	250	83.62234	1		7	20,905.590	No
104	Namibia	72	28.7365	2	0.27	6	2,069.028	No
105	Nepal	601	46.30265	1		7	27,827.890	No
106	Netherlands	156	106.2219	2	0.33	7	16,570.610	Yes
107	New Zealand	122	33.87165	1		7	4,132.341	Yes
108	Nicaragua	90	63.11342	1		7	5,680.208	No
109	Niger	113	125.7939	1		7	14,214.710	No
110	Nigeria	359	399.1981	2	0.23	7	143,312.100	No
111	Norway	169	27.38418	1		7	4,627.926	Yes
112	Oman	84	38.17745	2	0.46	4	3,206.906	No
113	Pakistan	336	503.9897	2	0.23	7	169,340.500	No
114	Panama	78	41.77345	1		7	3,258.329	No
115	Papua New Guinea	110	52.78215	1		7	5,806.036	No
116	Paraguay	80	83.36358	2	0.36	7	6,669.086	No
117	Peru	120	240.0775	1		7	28,809.300	No
118	Philippines	275	342.3908	2	0.09	7	94,157.470	No
119	Poland	460	83.73531	2	0.18	7	38,518.240	Yes

Table 10.1 (continued)

n.	Country	Total seats	Index of representativeness	N. of elected chambers	Ratio of upper chamber to whole parliament	Legislative democracy	Population (000s)	OECD member country
120	Portugal	230	46.2732	1		7	10,642.840	Yes
121	PRC	2967	445.518	1		3	1,321,852.000	No
122	Qatar	35	23.28277	1		1	814.897	No
123	Romania	334	66.69478	2	0.29	7	22,276.060	No
124	Russia	450	314.1728	2	0.28	7	141,377.800	No
125	Rwanda	53	186.9341	2	0.25	6	9,907.509	No
126	Samoa	49	4.372755	1		7	214.265	No
127	Saudi Arabia	150	183.9102	1		2	27,586.530	No
128	Senegal	150	86.54621	1		7	12,981.930	No
129	Sierra Leone	112	54.93178	1		7	6,152.359	No
130	Singapore	86	52.94197	1		6	4,553.009	No
131	Slovakia	150	36.31668	1		7	5,447.502	Yes
132	Slovenia	88	22.83233	2	0.31	7	2,009.245	Yes
133	Solomon Islands	43	13.18484	1		7	566.948	No
134	South Africa	400	120.9178	2	0.18	7	48,367.130	No
135	Spain	350	115.5663	2	0.37	7	40,448.190	Yes
136	Sri Lanka	225	93.00584	1		7	20,926.320	No
137	St Lucia	17	9.345588	2	0.4	7	158.875	No
138	Sudan	450	87.50968	1		2	39,379.360	No
139	Suriname	51	9.231059	1		7	470.784	No
140	Swaziland	65	17.43178	2	0.32	4	1,133.066	No
141	Sweden	349	25.87704	1		7	9,031.088	Yes
142	Switzerland	200	37.77331	2	0.19	7	7,554.661	Yes
143	Syria	250	77.25899	1		7	19,314.750	No
144	Taiwan	113	202.0226	1		7	22,828.560	No
145	Tajikistan	63	112.327	1		6	7,076.598	No
146	Tanzania	310	127.0459	1		6	39,384.220	No
147	Thailand	480	135.5586	1		7	65,068.150	No
148	Timor-Leste	21	70.38986	1		5.5	1,086.174	No
149	Togo	81	30.06856	1		7	5,701.579	No
150	Trinidad-Tobago	41	54.39794	1		7	1,232.811	No
151	Tunisia	189	136.1891	1		6	10,281.210	No
152	Turkey	549	38.19386	1		7	74,767.840	Yes
153	Turkmenistan	125	48.81066	1		5	4,774.232	No
154	Uganda	620	102.8886	1		6	30,262.610	No
155	Ukraine	450	111.1003	1		7	46,299.860	No
156	United Arab Emirates	40	94.22673	1		1	4,444.011	No
157	United Kingdom	645	692.5968	1		7	60,776.240	Yes

Table 10.1 (continued)

n.	Country	Total seats	Index of representativeness	N. of elected chambers	Ratio of upper chamber to whole parliament	Legislative democracy	Population (000s)	OECD member country
158	United States	435	34.95563	2	0.19	7	301,279.600	Yes
159	Uruguay	99	225.6606	2	0.23	7	3,460.607	No
160	Uzbekistan	120	4.083538	1		7	27,079.270	No
161	Vanuatu	52	155.8295	1		7	212.344	No
162	Venezuela	167	173.2975	1		7	26,023.530	No
163	Vietnam	492	73.85558	1		4	85,262.360	No
164	Yemen	301	189.3829	1		6	22,230.530	No
165	Zaire	340	75.50952	1		7	64,390.200	No
166	Zambia	152	128.072	1		7	11,477.450	No
	Mean	213.41	105.7479		0.28	6.47	39,362.110	
	Median	140	63.11342		0.29	7	8,710.830	
	Minimun	15	2.44945		0.09	1	90	
	Maximum	2967	2080.785		0.5	7	1,321,852.000	
	Standard deviation	266.32	186.7773		0.09	1.23	138,733.700	

size – the number of seats in the upper house being 9 percent of the whole parliament. At the other extreme is Bahrain, where the two houses of parliament have the same number of seats.

It must be noted that parliaments are by no means an exclusive feature of democratic countries: almost all countries in the world, even those that are openly or de facto non-democratic, do in fact have parliaments of some sort. This raises the question – still not adequately addressed in the theoretical literature – of whether the parliaments of non-democratic countries have unique features (especially in the way they are organized) that distinguish them from actually democratic legislatures. To control for the effect of democracy on the existence and composition of a nation's legislative branch, we report also the value of the LIEC, the Legislative Index of Electoral Competition (hereafter called *legislative democracy*) of Ferree and Singh (1999). This index takes the value of 1 if there is no legislature, 2 if the legislature is not elected, 3 if it elected but there is only one candidate for office, 4 if there is only one party with multiple candidates, 5 if multiple parties are legal but only one wins the seats, 6 if multiple parties win seats but the largest one obtained more than 75 percent of the seats and 7 if the largest party obtained less than 75 percent of the seats. One hundred and twenty-seven countries out of 167 in our sample have a value of 7 in 2009. The last two columns report the country's population and whether it belongs to the Organisation for Economic Co-operation and Development (OECD) or not – as a further check of the relationship between democracy and economic development. All OECD countries feature a level 7 of legislative democracy.

3.2 Bicameralism

A large part of Buchanan and Tullock's fundamental book *The Calculus of Consent* (1962) is devoted to the analysis of unicameral and multicameral legislatures. They placed great emphasis on bicameralism as a way to ensure super-majoritarian support for legislation. Their analysis aimed at providing a rigorous model to support Madison's, as well as Buchanan's and Tullock's, preference for multiple bases of representation. They argued that bicameralism functions somewhat like a supermajority rule because it raises the difficulty of passing new legislation; at the same time, however, bicameralism does not have the drawback of raising the decision making costs of approving news laws, because the size of each deliberative body is smaller than that of a comparable unicameral legislature. Furthermore, Buchanan and Tullock (1962) argue that bicameralism may reduce the agenda-setter's power, since the requirement of obtaining the approval of the second chamber diminishes the importance of the order with which bills are proposed and approved. Many years later, Cooter (2000) reinforced Buchanan and Tullock's conclusion when he suggested that bicameralism encourages bargaining among houses and leads to more consensual legislation. This point seems well taken, as most of the parliaments that Lijphart (1999) classifies as of the Westminster type feature *de facto* a unicameral legislature, while the majority of consensus type parliaments is bicameral.

More chambers and more complicated legislative processes generally have been viewed as ways of minimizing the chances of approving rent-seeking legislation (Eskridge 1988; Macey 1988; Ginsburg and Elkins 2010). Levmore (1992) makes the additional point that strong Condorcet winners, which would win under majority rule in both houses, might not prevail in a single house with a super-majority rule, inasmuch as small minorities therein could block new legislation. Bicameralism should thus allow more general public-spirited legislation to pass and, at the same time, should carry the incentive to expose and reject legislation that embodies wasteful rent-seeking and corruption. Such a view can be excessively optimistic, however, insofar as bicameralism also provides more veto points than unicameralism with a super-majority rule. Tsebelis (2002) demonstrates that this is often the case. If bicameralism makes passage of new legislation more difficult, *some* public spirited legislation may not go through because of the possibility of defeat by well-situated interest groups. While a super-majority rule allows, say, a one-third minority to block legislation, bicameral legislatures have more individuals in key positions that can be captured by special interests. Bicameral legislatures have not one but two agenda-setters who must be convinced to support a bill, and possibly two sets of committee chairs that can prevent legislation from floor consideration. Conference committees are intended to resolve inter-chamber discrepancies. That institution might also empower a very small but well-positioned minority to block legislation (Tsebelis 2002). This veto players' analysis may generate a status quo bias, consistent with some of the literature on presidential systems discussed in the previous section.

McCormick and Tollison (1981) started the analysis of the impact of the disparity of chamber sizes on the production of new legislation. Their discussion is grounded in a special interest group theory of government. Assuming that a majority of votes in both houses is required to pass a bill and that the marginal decision-making costs are increasing, the 'price' that a lobbyist has to pay to 'buy' an additional vote/representative in the larger chamber exceeds the savings of buying one vote/representative less in the smaller chamber. Hence the total costs for special interest groups of having a law approved increase as the relative sizes of the two chambers become less equal. In other words, *ceteris paribus*, it should be more expensive for interest groups to buy votes in the legislatures of the Philippines and Germany than in Bahrain. McCormick and Tollison (1981) indeed find some support for this hypothesis in the peculiar 'laboratory' for comparative institutional analysis represented by the US states legislatures. More empirical analysis at the level of national legislatures is thus warranted; yet, comparable data on the legislative outputs of national assemblies, together with the larger battery of control variables that an international sample requires, have so far prevented this analysis from being undertaken.

3.3 Committees

The *raison d'être* of [or 'underlying'] the committee structure of parliaments, especially that of the US Congress, is probably the institutional feature that has received the greatest interest by scholars of public choice and political science. Such interest began when the early literature on logrolling regarded committees as a way to minimize the costs of legislative deals (Mueller 1967). But it was the work of Weingast and Marshall (1988) that set the framework for modern analysis of parliamentary committees, giving birth to the so-called 'congressional dominance model'. They argue that the purpose of parliamentary committees is to make sure that legislative deals do not unravel and that bureaucracies in fact apply legislation with as little slack as possible in their principal–agent relationship with elected politicians. In many parliaments, committees have the power both to propose legislation and to monitor those entrusted with its implementation (although the actual specification of especially the latter function changes significantly across parliaments). This creates an incentive to fill these committees with legislators who have a strong interest in the promotion (and the blockage) of legislation assigned to each committee.

Furthermore, when committees are endowed with the 'power of the purse', as they are in the US Congress, they can use their budgetary authority (as well as senators' constitutional powers to confirm or not the president's nominations of executive branch bureau heads) to discipline the agencies that report to them. Because members of the committees have strong interests in the way legislation is implemented, free-riding problems in gathering information and monitoring the bureaucratic agencies are mitigated. Committee members can also rely on their constituents and special interest groups to do the monitoring for them. But even when the power of the purse entrusted to committees is limited or non-existant, parliaments can effectively control bureaucracies through their power to set the administrative procedures under which the agencies must operate (McCubbins et al. 1987, 1989). By requiring that an agency hold public hearings on a proposed policy change before implementing it, parliament ensures that the interest groups with vested stakes in policy outcomes have a venue to express their positions before final decisions are taken. The empirical support favoring the many variants of the congressional dominance model is considerable, especially insofar as the role of parliamentary committees is concerned; yet the large majority of these studies refer only to the US Congress (Mueller 2003). Napolitano and Abrescia (2010) provide some further, albeit anecdotal, evidence supporting this model drawn from international case studies.

3.4 Size

The special interest group theory of government lays the groundwork for the analysis of the effects of the sizes of parliaments on legislative output. Building on Stigler (1979), and reasoning within the institutional framework of US state legislatures as the background model, McCormick and Tollison (1981) argue that the total size of legislatures has an ambiguous effect on legislative productivity. On the one hand, by reducing the average number of constituents per member, larger legislatures should lower voters' costs of monitoring their elected representatives. On the other hand, because each member of a large legislature can be expected to have less influence on the overall legislative process, such monitoring will pay fewer benefits. Thus large legislatures effectively reduce the average value of each legislator's vote, which in turn lowers the price at which special interest groups can buy influence. The logic of collective action somewhat tempers the value of this argument, by suggesting that in large legislatures it will be more difficult for a majority of members to muster the necessary coordination to approve legislation. This model has implications in the domain of campaign finance. Insofar as the value of a seat is smaller as the size of the legislature becomes large, fewer resources should be invested in campaigns for legislative seats, all other things being equal.

The complexity and ambiguity of the predictions make it difficult to obtain clear-cut results in empirical analysis. The evidence reported by McCormick and Tollison (1981) in their sample of the US states is mixed at best, and the situation does not improve in international samples. Fiorino and Ricciuti (2007) analyze the effect of different legislature sizes on per capita expenditures in selected regions of Italy. They argue that legislature size has an ambiguous impact on government spending a priori because of the counter-balancing effects of logrolling and transaction costs. The net outcome is therefore empirical; Fiorino and Ricciuti (2007) find a large and significantly positive effect of the number of legislators on public spending, on the order of 1.2. The authors' estimate suggests that, on average, increasing the size of the legislature by 10 percent raises regional government spending by 12 percent.

4 EMPIRICAL ANALYSIS

In this section, we test some of the theories of the determinants of the institutional features of parliaments reviewed in section 3. To this end, we use the cross-country sample of the characteristics reported in Table 10.1, as well as other information made available by the 2010 release of the Database of Political Institutions. Specifically, the theories reviewed so far and data availability prompt us to offer answers to the following three questions:

1. What are the determinants of the total sizes of parliaments?
2. What are the determinants of the relative sizes of the two chambers in bicameral legislatures?
3. Why do some countries have a bicameral legislature and others a unicameral one?

The empirical analysis can be summarized by the following simple empirical model:

$$\mathbf{PF}_i - \varepsilon_i = f(\mathbf{IF}_i + \mathbf{EF}_i + POP_i), \tag{10.1}$$

where **PF** (Parliamentary Features) is a vector of three dependent variables: (1) TOTALSEATS, the number of seats of the whole Parliament in case of unicameral legislatures or of the lower house in case of bicameral ones; (2) SSH, the ratio of the seats in the upper house (or Senate) to the total seats of the whole Parliament; and (3) DOUBLE, a dummy variable that takes the value of 1 if the legislature is bicameral, and 0 otherwise. While the first and third questions are asked of the full sample of 166 countries, indexed by i, the second one is analyzed in the subsample of the 56 countries with bicameral legislatures. The variable ε_i is a disturbance term from an OLS regression in the first two models, and of a logistic regression in the third. Since theory does not suggest particular functional forms, and in some cases does not even specify all potentially influencing factors, we have opted for the simplest estimator.

IF is a vector of Institutional Features including: SYSTEM, a multivariate qualitative variable that takes the value of 2 for parliamentary systems, 1 for assembly-elected presidents and 0 for presidential systems; MILITARY and DEFMIN, two dummies that take the value of 1 if, respectively, the chief executive or the defense minister are military officers. This variable is introduced to check whether the country is in fact a democracy. FRAUD is another control for advanced democracy, and takes the value of 0 if, according to DPI, elections are free from extra-constitutional irregularities. LIEC, another control for the country's degree of democracy, is the index of electoral competitiveness already explained in section 3.1; MDMH is the weighted average of the number of representatives elected by each constituency size; PLURALITY takes the value of 1 in countries where legislators are elected using a winner-take all/first-past-the-post rule; similarly, PR stands for proportional representation. TRESH records the minimum popular vote share that a party must obtain in order to win at least one seat in a PR system – when there are no thresholds, the variable takes the value of 0. TENSYS measures the number of years over which the country has been considered to be a liberal competitive democracy, that is, assigned a value of 7 in the LIEC scale. CHECKS measures the effectiveness of checks and balances in the country's institutional setting.

To make the interpretation of the variable more intuitive than in its original DPI format, CHECKS equals 0 in countries scoring 6 or lower on the LIEC scale, but 1 is added to that scale in the following cases: in presidential systems, if the party of the president does not control both chambers, and for all parties within the governing coalition whose ideological orientation are closer to that of the opposition; in parliamentary systems, the value of CHECKS is increased by 1 for every party in the governing majority whose support is essential for the government to stand, and for every party in the government coalition whose ideological orientation is closer to that of the opposition. In short, CHECKS measures the extent to which the executive and the legislative effectively control each other, in the sense of Persson et al. (1997).

Finally, the degree of government decentralization of the country can also affect the characteristics of the parliament. To verify that conjecture, we have considered whether municipal governments (dummy MUNI), or state/provincial governments (dummy STATE) are elected locally; we have also examined whether the states/provinces have authority over taxing, spending or legislating (dummy AUTHOR, which takes the value of 1 if any of these categories are in fact true). All of the PF and IF variables refer to the year 2009 and are taken from DPI.

EF is a vector of economic features that could affect the structure of the legislature, namely: KG, the size of the public sector over GDP, to check whether governments with stronger grips and greater stakes in the private economy also have larger legislatures; OPENK, measuring the country's degree of globalization (in fact, the sum of exports and imports over GDP), is introduced with an opposite rationale to that of including KG; Y is the country's per capita GDP relative to that of the United States in purchasing power parity, to verify whether richer countries also have larger and more complex legislatures. Finally, the covariate POP, the size of the country's population in thousands in the year 2007, controls for the degree of representativeness of the parliament. This control variable is always found in this type of analysis since the work of Barro (1973). All of these series are drawn from the Penn World Tables Mark 6.2.

Not all variables are appropriate for the three regressors, nor did all of them turn out to carry any significant explanatory power; hence the expected relationships of those that proved to be relevant are identified in the discussion of the regression results. Table 10.2 reports them.

Beginning with the models explaining the variance of the full sample of TOTALSEATS, we observe that parliamentary systems tend to have larger legislatures than presidential systems, a result that is compatible with the central role parliaments play in those systems; on the other hand, this result is not consistent with Moe and Caldwell's (1994) view that representatives in presidential systems are more parochial in terms of their distance from national interests and thus are more prone to enact legislation that delivers narrow benefits, but the costs of which are spread diffusely over the taxpayers in general. If anything, the finding that legislatures tend to have more seats in parliamentary systems, holding population constant, suggests that electoral districts also tend to be smaller in terms of number of voters in such systems; hence, by the same logic of Moe and Caldwell (1994) we expect to find more pork barrel legislation in parliamentary systems than in presidential ones.

Controls for the degree of democracy, such as MILITARY and LIEC, suggest that, where parliaments operate in institutional frameworks that are *de facto* less democratic, the legislature tends to be larger. Two possible explanations come to the fore: one is that the executive uses the legislature as a means of maximizing control over the military's top brass and the regime's key supporters, by uniting them all in the legislative branch. Alternatively, in truly dictatorial regimes, a parliamentary seat (with its salary, perks and status) can be seen as recognition and reward for the crucial supporters of the dictator, who distributes the seats to maximize support (Wintrobe 1998).

The average number of representatives elected per constituency, MDMH, has a predictably positive impact on the size of the legislature, just as in the adoption of PLURALITY electoral systems. The presence of an effective system of (horizontal) checks and balances is instead correlated with a smaller number of parliamentary seats. This result is expected; it shows that when checks and balances are stronger, the other government branches (here, chiefly, the executive) are better able to limit the expansion of the legislative branch, here also in 'physical' terms. In addition, more effective checks and balances between government branches reduce the need for electoral control of elected officials, which allows for larger districts (that is, more voters per representative).

Table 10.2   Estimates of equation 10.1

	TOTAL SEATS		SSH		DOUBLE	
	Whole sample	LIEC = 7 countries	Whole sample	LIEC = 7 countries	Whole sample	LIEC = 7 countries
SYSTEM	39.35***	40.51***	0.033*	0.033*	−0.77	−3.04*
	(15.5)	(15.86)	(0.02)	(0.018)	(0.58)	(1.84)
MILITARY	53.06				1.87	5.29**
	(44.6)				(1.25)	(2.99)
LIEC	126.5**		−0.152***		−4.37	
	(70.37)		(0.06)		(4.13)	
MDMH	1.03***	1.18***			−0.06*	−0.15
	(0.47)	(0.48)			(0.03)	(0.11)
PLURALITY	62.79	56.43**	−0.034	−0.06	1.26***	5.81*
	(28.71)	(30.33)	(0.04)	(0.04)	(1.12)	(3.52)
CHECKS	−32.27***	−22.46**	−0.005	0.005		2.78
	(10.07)	(11.15)	(0.006)	(0.006)		(1.85)
MUNI	39.00**	29.61	−0.05***	−0.05**		
	(18.61)	(20.81)	(0.02)	(0.02)		
AUTHOR					2.21**	3.67*
					(1.1)	(2.23)
KC	1.4**	1.95***				
	(0.71)	(0.83)				
OPENK	−0.74***	−1.18***				
	(0.27)	(0.41)				
Y					0.05***	0.19**
					(0.02)	(0.09)
POP×1000	0.83***	0.67***			0.002**	0.006**
	(0.00)	(0.16)			(1.21^{-5})	(3.7^{-5})
Intercept	180.66***	369.1***	0.51***	0.38***	−4.06	15.41
	(81.9)	(89.91)	(0.06)	(0.06)	(3.5)	(19.36)
R^2	0.44	0.46	0.36	0.22	0.5	0.72
S.E.R.	129.49	126.44	0.089	0.091	0.369	0.274
F stat.	7.3***	8.08***	3.11***	1.72**		
N. obs.	166	125	56	46	166	125

Notes:
Standard errors in parentheses.
All coefficients are estimated using White's heteroscedasticity consistent covariance matrix.
In the last two regressions the value of the McFadden R^2 is reported.
***, **and * denote a 1 percent, 5 percent and 10 percent level of statistical significance.

The positive coefficient on MUNI indicates that more administratively decentralized countries are also characterized by larger national assemblies. This is again consistent with the logic of (vertical) checks and balances, whereby devolving more power to local governments is counterbalanced at the central government level by representatives elected by smaller, that is, more 'local' districts.[4]

As for the country's economic features, a larger public sector is positively correlated with the size of legislatures, which confirms the hypothesis that governments with stronger grips and greater stakes in the economy also have larger legislatures to better control the distribution of the resources. An alternative but more tentative explanation of the positive coefficient on KC is that it reveals a vicious cycle between more redistributive legislation that creates incentives to generate institutions that in turn yield fewer general benefit–cost types of decisions, and so on. The cross-country nature of the sample does not allow one to disentangle what causes what; it is however interesting to note that, by the same logic, countries with more globalized economies tend to have smaller legislatures (holding population size constant), which supplies evidence *a contrario* to the previous argument. The magnitudes of the two coefficients, however, suggest that the limiting effect of globalization seems to counteract only about half of the expansionary effects of a larger public sector, and that in pure percentage terms. Finally, population has the expected positive correlation with the number of parliamentary seats, which is consistent with the idea of an 'optimal' size of electoral districts.

To verify whether these results are robust to changes in the sample, we have estimated the same model on the subset of countries characterized by the highest degree of legislative democracy, that is, those earning a score of 7 on the LIEC scale. The results basically do not change, except for the fact that the controls for the degree of democracy (for example, the covariate MILITARY) lose significance, while the estimates of the other correlations become more precise, notwithstanding the smaller sample (125 countries rather than 166). Both models explain about 50 percent of the variation in the dependent variable and the overall precision of the estimates is quite high, as shown by the *p*-values on the F-statistics.

The estimates concerning the relative sizes of the two houses are the least satisfactory, most likely because of the many nations that have bicameral parliaments (56 observations in the full sample, 46 for which LIEC = 7). Overall, only the degree of legislative democracy is negatively correlated with equality in the sizes of the two chambers, suggesting that more advanced democracies tend to have more specialized legislative chambers. Also the proxy for the degree of administrative decentralization is negatively correlated with equality between the two chambers, possibly because in more decentralized countries the upper chamber assumes the role of the 'house of local jurisdictions', as in the case of the US Senate or of Germany's *Bundesrat*. Parliamentary systems tend to be characterized by more equal parliamentary chamber sizes than presidential ones – where again legislative specialization is pushed to a higher degree. The sub-sample of the most advanced democracies basically confirms the results found in the whole sample. Other covariates, such as the effectiveness of the system of horizontal checks and balances, the electoral system, or population size, never turned out to be statistically significant. The explanatory powers of the models are moderate (explaining between 22 percent and 36 percent of the variation in the regressands), albeit the measures of goodness of fit remain significant at around the 5 percent level.

Finally, the logistic model used to explain the determinants of the adoption of a bicameral legislature reveals that the probability of observing a bicameral parliament is lower in parliamentary systems, especially those of the most advanced democracies, and of countries where more representatives are elected from each district. Conversely, countries characterized by first-past-the-post electoral systems (which are adopted more often in the upper houses, for example, the Italian Senate) are more likely to be characterized by bicameral legislatures, and so are more decentralized countries because of the upper houses' role as chambers representing local jurisdictions. Note that vertical checks and balances often seem to affect the choice of a bicameral legislature and that the measure of decentralization that carries the greater explanatory power here is AUTHOR, the proxy for effective autonomous subnational decision-making power over fiscal variables. Moreover, countries with higher per capita incomes and larger populations are also more likely to have bicameral legislatures. The explanatory power of these models is very high (50 percent of the variation of the dependent variable in the whole sample, 72 percent in the subsample of the most advanced democracies, as indicated by the McFadden R^2), and the estimates are in general also quite precise.

5 PARLIAMENTARY DECISIONS: THE EXAMPLE OF THE BUDGET APPROVAL PROCESS

Once we have analyzed how parliaments are organized, the next step is to consider how they take their decisions. Possibly the most important decisions for which all parliaments across the world are responsible relate to the country's budget balance. Parliaments arose to their current importance by contesting the King's 'power of the purse', and such power is today enshrined in the budget bill. Scholars have thus focused their attention on the rules that govern legislative approval of the budget bill in order to understand, in greater institutional detail, how parliaments (and governments in general) actually take their decisions, and to what extent they are accountable to voters or lobbyists (Persson et al. 1997; Persson and Tabellini 2000).

For this case as well, the 'natural laboratory' of the US states, with their wealth of data and a corresponding ability to hold constant *ceteris paribus* conditions, has been the sample of choice for scholars working at the intersections of economics and political science (Crain and Miller 1990; Poterba 1995). Yet, in this domain interesting results also have been obtained in international samples. Von Hagen (1992) contributed a seminal work on this topic by codifying and describing the budget rules of 12 European Union (EU) member countries in the 1980s.

More work has been done since then. Lagona and Padovano (2007), for example, were able to construct the first time-series, cross-sectional panel of information on the budget rules that characterize the parliaments of 12 European countries over three decades (the 1980s, the 1990s and the early 2000s). In that paper the characteristics of each country's budget procedures are summarized according to: (1) the internal organization of government; (2) the formulation of the budget proposal within the government; (3) the discussion of and rules for approving the budget law in the parliament; (4) the information contained in it; (5) the flexibility granted to bureaus in implementing the budget law; and (6) the stringency of long-term budget documents. Of these six items, three to six are properly 'parliamentarian', while the first two refer more to decisions taken within the executive branch. Each of these six 'stages' is further disaggregated into several rules, up to a total of 30 reported in Table A1 of Lagona and Padovano (2007). These 30 rules come in different variants, corresponding to differences in legislatures' ability to constrain politicians' discretion and profligacy.

The degrees-of-freedom problem endemic to this type of analysis is immediately apparent, both when a researcher wishes to examine the evolution of so many rules across countries and through time, and even more so when this information is used to explain differences in the performances of public finance within a set of countries. Furthermore, the usual procedure for aggregating these rules into an index that sums the numerical values assigned to each rule (von Hagen 1992; de Haan and Sturm 1994; Alesina et al. 1996; Hallerberg et al. 2004) is incorrect methodologically, because it implicitly assumes that the ways in which a budget process constrains fiscal choices can be represented by a linear additive function, wherein all rules have equal weight, that is, they are perfect substitutes in achieving the same degree of fiscal discipline. Many empirical analyses have instead pointed out that certain provisions restrict the choice sets of fiscal decision-makers much more so than others do. Furthermore, the very act of summing the values of the stringency codes into an index assigns to these codes a cardinal value they do not have, as they are based only an ordinal scale. This leads to spurious results once these indices are used in regressions analysis.

Lagona and Padovano (2007) adopt a non-linear principal component analysis of the data that overcomes these methodological problems and also allows one to visualize the evolution of the rules governing budget decision across countries and through time. Figure 10.1 summarizes this information. Two principal components (PRIN1 and PRIN2) explain 78 percent of the original information. As in ordinary principal component analysis, the angle of each rule's vector relative to the axes indicates the principal component best representing that rule; the distance from the origin along the direction of the vector representing each rule denotes increasing degrees of rule stringency.

Figure 10.1 shows that PRIN1 captures most of the rules of stage O (distribution of fiscal power among the different levels of government) and F (flexibility in budget execution). PRIN2, on the other hand, best explains most of the rules of stage N (within-government negotiations on the budget), P (structure of parliamentary processes), I (informativeness of the budget document) and L (long-term planning constraint). With some approximation, PRIN1 can be interpreted as an indicator of how binding are the incentives of the public administration and, more generally, of officials outside the central government in terms of the stringency of the budget process. PRIN2, in contrast, best captures the impact of the binding incentives of the actors within the parliament.

Figure 10.1 also shows that most budget rules are positively correlated with one another, with the exceptions of F6 (no carry-over of unused funds) and, to lesser extents, F5 (change in budget law during execution) and O5 (the number of ministries involved in reconciling the budget's overall balance). Hence, countries with tight budget procedures for, say, the negotiation of the budget proposal within the government (stage N) and the approval of the budget law by the parliament (stage P) tend to allow the possibility of crediting to the next budget any public funds not spent during the prior fiscal year and vice versa. As such, F6 can be interpreted as a sort of hole in the net.

Coming to countries (shaded markers), France, Greece, Luxembourg, the Netherlands, the United Kingdom and, to a lesser extent, Ireland feature the most stringent budget processes in the early 2000s, but with important qualifications. France, Luxembourg, Greece, the Netherlands and the United Kingdom fare better in terms of budget rules captured by PRIN2, specifically those included in L (Greece), F2 (France), O5 (the United Kingdom), F1 (the Netherlands) and P1 (Luxembourg). Ireland, on the other hand, fares better in terms of PRIN1 rules, especially F6. Finally, the evolution of the

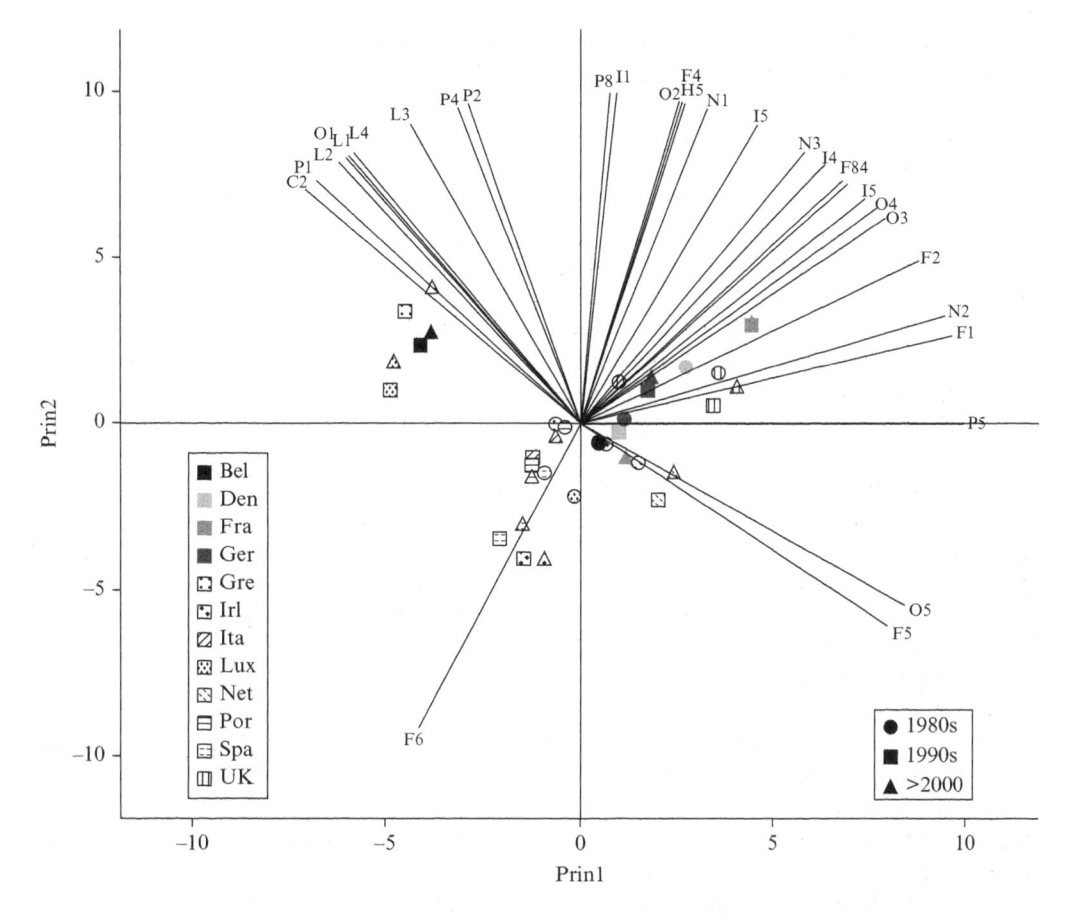

Figure 10.1 Biplot of parliamentary procedures to approve the financial bill, 12 EU countries (average for the 1980s, 1990s and 2000s)

countries' positions through time indicates that when one moves from the 1980s (dots) to the 1990s (squares), a general tendency is evident, coinciding with the Maastricht Treaty, for in-sample countries to tighten their budget procedures. In the 2000s (triangles), this process came to a general standstill, with Italy moderately loosening its budget procedures again. The recent crisis of European sovereign debt suggests that this process has not been carried out far enough, and the recent provisions adopted by the EU Commission should result in an outward movement of the country-dots along the vectors reported in Figure 10.1.

6 HOW AND WHEN PARLIAMENTS DECIDE: THE LEGISLATION CYCLE

A new and promising line of research deals with the timing of parliamentary decisions, that is, with the dynamic aspects of the production of laws, bills and decrees; in a word, of legislation.[5] The special interest group theory of government posits that laws, even when they do not involve financial resources, redistribute property rights. Politicians supply legislation to groups offering the highest political returns. By the same logic, politicians should supply legislation *when* doing so also maximizes their political support. The dynamics of the supply of legislation should thus follow the pattern suggested by the political business cycle theory. Lagona and Padovano (2008) develop a model of governmental and voter behavior in which a legislative cycle is a rational strategy adopted to hold a government coalition together. The model is developed in two steps.

The first step, based on the 'pure presidential model' of Persson et al. (1997), demonstrates that, during a legislative term, voters rationally allow their representatives to appropriate a certain amount of the 'rents from holding office'. Although such redistribution reduces their welfare, voters still re-elect their legislative representative in order to minimize the latter's incentives to appropriate even more wealth. Since all legislators have the same incentives, a representative agent is used. Padovano (1995) goes beyond this oversimplification by considering a plurality of agents, called parties or parliamentary groups, on the government's side. Some of them form a government coalition, while the others comprise the opposition. The presence of more than one parliamentary group in the government coalition increases the groups' incentives to compete among one another in order to maximize the perceived welfare of ordinary citizens. Competition could then be expected to reduce the amount of public expropriation of private wealth to a minimum.

Yet, the model demonstrates that, under certain conditions, the groups' incentives to collude in order to capture a share of the maximally allowed rents are still stronger than the incentives to compete. These conditions basically require that parliamentary groups in the government coalition coordinate on the *timing* of the decisions that secure rents and of those that maximize voters' welfare. Rent-seeking legislation should be concentrated at the beginning of the legislative term, to reserve enough time to punish a potential defector so as to discourage any attempt to break the cartel. Then, as the next election draws near, the groups' incentives to compete and satisfy voters' demands outweigh those of securing access to private rents. At that time all groups concentrate on legislation that maximizes voters' welfare, in order to secure reelection for the next legislature. Collusion is thus a stable equilibrium.

This theory generates several empirical predictions that shed light on the timing of parliamentary decisions and on the types of legislation that parliaments approve. Under the assumption that parliamentary groups choose visible instruments to satisfy voters' demands, such as laws, and less visible ones to appropriate rents, such as administrative decrees, the model generates a *legislative cycle*. The number of laws approved is predicted to be at a minimum when parliamentary groups concentrate on the appropriation of rents; it increases as the legislature draws to its end, when groups switch to maximizing voters' interests and approve laws to that effect. Furthermore, the number of laws approved during the electoral campaign should be enough to induce the voters to prefer the incumbent majority over its challenger. The magnitude of the cycle should then be positively correlated with the number of parliamentary groups/parties that compose the government coalition. Finally, if any conditioning phenomenon, such as a war of attrition within the coalition, makes it impossible to attain the legislative production required to ensure re-election, a change in the governing coalition should take place.

Padovano and Lagona (2008) test these restrictions on data about the supply of

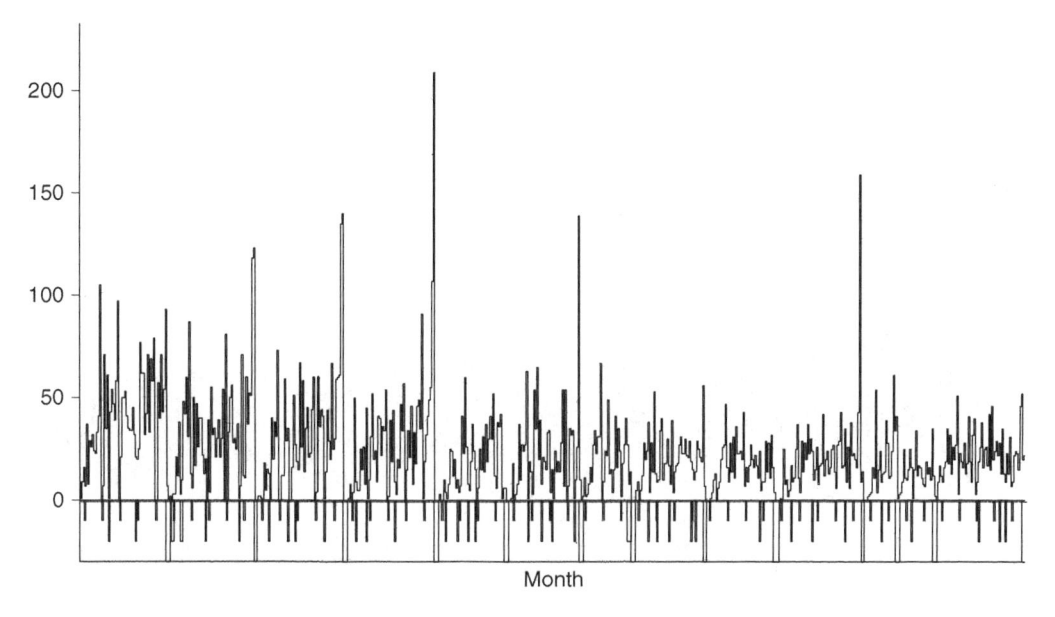

Note: Number of laws approved by the Italian Parliament (May 1948–May 2001); short lines below refer to summer periods (August and September); medium lines refer to months when a change of government occurred; long reference lines denote inter-legislative periods.

Source: Camera dei Deputati.

Figure 10.2 Timing of the approval of laws

legislation by the Italian Parliament during legislatures from I to XIII (1948 to 2001). The empirical analysis provides strong support for the theory. Figure 10.2 describes the timing of the approval laws, while Figure 10.3 illustrates how the empirical model explains the data. The fit of the model is quite high. Interestingly, the model is able to predict the occurrence of a legislative cycle *only* in legislatures that ended at their regular five-year terms and the absence of a cycle when government crises became so severe that no legislation could actually be approved and the parliament had to be dissolved.

Lagona et al. (2011) are able to uncover an opposite cycle in administrative decrees. As they do not require a parliamentary vote to be approved and are therefore less visible, that is, more vulnerable to rent seeking, these decrees tend to be approved at the beginning of the legislature rather than at the end, as for general interest legislation, just as theory predicts. More research in this area in warranted, although the data requirements are still an impeding constraint.

7 PARLIAMENTS IN HISTORY

It is probably fitting to end this chapter with a look at when parliaments started, to have a better understanding of when and why their institutional differences emerged. Because of space constraints, this inquiry can be pursued here at a very 'macro' level only, for

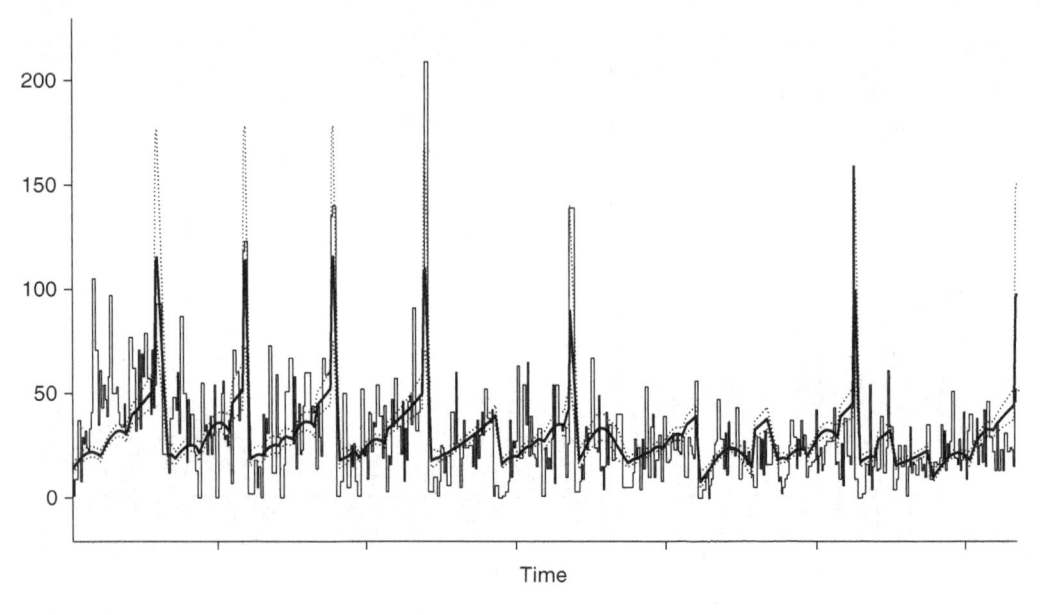

Note: Observed (hairline) and mod3-expected counts (black line) with 95 percent confidence intervals during regular periods; data at either summer months or interlegislative or intergovernment periods are discarded.

Figure 10.3 Fit between the empirical model and actual data

example, that of the fundamental difference between the Westminster and the consensus models of parliament. Yet there is value added in this inquiry, because the origins of the two models are a point that Lijphart (1999) evokes but leaves unspecified. Here we will try to see how and when parliaments appeared, and will follow the evolution of the most interesting parliamentary institutions of the Western world until the bifurcation between the Westminster and the consensus models begins to appear.

7.1 Proto-parliamentary Institutions

Early forms of parliamentary institutions emerged ever since mankind started to organize itself into political societies. Tribal societies, both in the past and in contemporary times, often feature councils of elders, wise men or both alongside the village headman.[6] Political historians find early forms of parliaments in Mesopotamia, where the kings were assisted by councils (Jacobsen 1943; Bailkey 1967); in ancient India, where some form of deliberative assemblies existed, as well as in other ancient Asian societies (Bongard-Levin 1986; Robinson 1997). The scholarly debate focuses on the extent to which these assemblies can be seen as essential to either 'democratic' or 'oligarchic' governments, which are more akin to consensus-oriented political types. Insofar as all citizens could participate in their proceedings, these councils may be considered to be early expressions of direct democracy; yet, as the concept of citizenship was in various ways limited to a subset of the population, they were indeed oligarchic.

It is interesting to see where some outstanding ancient legislative assemblies stand on this continuum. Athens, generally regarded as the cradle of democracy, is placed near the middle but closer to the democratic; hence, the confrontational, model (Bergh and Lyttkens 2011). Every Athenian citizen had the right to participate in the discussions of the city assembly (Εκκλησία), the most important political institution of the city-state. Citizenship requirements, physical presence at the meeting place (the Πνυξ), professional and military duties, however, greatly reduced the share of the total population that could engage actively in political life. Still, several recent studies concur that this share was quite high by the standards of ancient societies: a quorum of 6,000 individuals was required for certain types of decisions (for example, ostracism) over an adult male population, calculated before the Peloponnesian War at around 35,000 individuals (De Sainte Croix 1981; Bergh and Lyttkens 2011).

The Roman Republic marked a step in the evolution towards representative democracy (Lintott 1999). The Roman legislative committees (*Comitia Curiata, Centuriata, PopuliTributa, Plebis*) represented the various categories (family, army, tribe) into which Roman citizens were grouped. The Senate also was an extension of the aristocratic families, at least before the onset of the Roman Empire. Roman legislative assemblies therefore tended to be consensual within, but cross-wisely competitive and confrontational, as the story of the Gracchi brothers shows (Wisemen 1985). Another important innovation of the Roman Republic comprised the far more complex rules and procedures that governed the eligibility, participation, and actual functioning of the Roman legislative and deliberative council, compared to those of the Athenian legislature (Poma 2009). This is a sign that the Romans perceived the costs of participation in active political life and tried to reduce them by making a subset of the population representative of those who were excluded. The crisis of the Roman Republic and the emergence of a dictatorial regime resulted from the difficulties in finding a satisfactory solution to the problem of representation. Another unsolved institutional problem was that of the checks and balances between the various representative bodies of the classes of the population (the *Comitia*) and of the aristocracy (the Senate) – the problem summarized in the maxim *Senatus Populus Que Romanus* (the Senate *and* the People of Rome).

7.2 Middle Ages' Origins of Confrontational Parliaments

In the Middle Ages, the development of parliamentary-type institutions went back to the model of ancient times, where councils of elders surrounded the local chieftains. In a sense, the origins of Westminster-type of parliaments can be traced back to the confrontation between the chieftain-ruler-king and the representatives of the noble subjects (Goldsworthy 1999). Because of its diffusion, Congleton (2011) calls this type of confrontation the 'king-and-council template'.

In Germanic and Scandinavian societies, a *thing* or *ting* (Old Norse and Icelandic *þing*; *ding* in Dutch) was the governing assembly, made up of the freemen of the community. Interestingly, *things* were organized geographically and hierarchically, so that local *things* were represented at the *thing* of a larger area. The *thing* met at regular intervals, legislated, elected chieftains and kings, and took decisions according to the law, which was memorized and recited by the 'law speaker' (the judge). Today, the name of the ancient institution survives in modern ones, like Iceland's Althing, founded in 930 (Moore 2004).

In Anglo-Saxon England, the *Witenagamot* ('meeting of wise men' in Old English) proclaimed the law code of King Ethelbert of Kent circa 600. After the Norman Conquest, William the Conqueror replaced it with a *Curia Regis* ('King's Council'). Membership in the *Curia* largely was restricted to the tenants-in-chief and a few senior ecclesiastics. The tenants-in-chief often struggled with their spiritual counterparts and with the King for power. In 1215, they secured from King John the *Magna Charta*, which established that he could not levy or collect any new taxes without the consent of a council. Members of this council were, however, directly designated by the King. The issue of representation marked a first significant innovation since Roman times when in 1265 Simon de Montfort summoned a parliament of his supporters without royal authorization, which included also two burgesses from each borough. De Montfort's scheme of representation and election was adopted formally by Edward I in the so-called 'Model Parliament' of 1295, where the House of Commons was added to the *Curia Regis*. The English Parliament recognizably assumed its modern, Westminster-type form (Goldsworthy 1999).

The Polish Diet is probably the example closest to the British system; witness its similar evolution in terms of confrontations between the nobles and the King throughout medieval times. According to the Chronicles of Gallus Anonymus, the first legendary Polish ruler, Siemowit, was chosen by a *wiec*, the ancient Polish term for parliament or assembly of the populace. The idea of the *wiec* led in 1182 to the development of the first Polish parliament, the *Sejm*, which basically evolved around the power to elect the King. As the kings derived their legitimacy from election by the *Sejm*, its members traditionally kept strict control over the King's power. From 1374, the king had to receive the *Sejm*'s permission to raise taxes, much in the same way as in England. But the powers of the Polish king were much more limited, as one of the most important customary rules that disciplined his discretionary power read that 'The King can do all good, but no harm'. The powers of the Polish *Sejm* derived also from its roots in the general population: members of the *Sejm* either were representatives of local and regional parliaments or, from 1493, were elected every two years. With the development of the unique Polish Golden Liberty, the *Sejm*'s powers increased. The Polish government consisted of three estates or branches: the King of Poland, the Senate, consisting of Ministers, Palatines, Castellans and Bishops, and the *Sejm* – from circa 170 comprised of nobles acting on behalf of their lands and sent by Land Parliaments. Representatives of selected cities were also included but without any voting powers. Since 1573, at a royal election all peers of the Commonwealth participated in the parliament and therefore became the King's electors.

7.3 France and the Consensus Model

A comparison with the Kingdom of France and with the Catholic Church highlights the institutional advancement of England and Poland in Medieval times, as well as the different forces that led to the evolution towards, first, a Westminster, then to a consensus type of Parliament. The French *États-Generaux* was the assembly of the nobles, clergy and bourgeois summoned by the King of France to discuss situations of crisis, usually of financial nature. Until Louis XIV, the confrontation between the French kings and the *États-Generaux* followed a pattern similar to that of England, because of the King's need to obtain the approval of parliament to raise new taxes and to introduce major deviations (today we would call them 'reforms') from the customary laws. But parliamentary power in France was shorter-lived, because the existing institutions were suppressed as a result of absolutism of the seventeenth and eighteenth centuries. The forces of representation of the emerging class interests, thus compressed, exploded in the French Revolution, when the National Assembly became the lower house of France's bicameral legislature. Consequently, in the French Republics, without the counterbalance of the monarchy, the legislative branch rose to a more prominent position in the institutional framework, facing weaker opposition from the executive branch. Legislators started their political lives with the problem of reaching agreement among themselves, rather than confronting and limiting another governmental branch. This has possibly led to the establishment of a more consensus-oriented type of parliament (Wright 1987).

During the fourteenth and fifteenth centuries, the peculiar context of the Catholic Church witnessed a struggle of the parliaments-kings type, in some ways similar to those taking place in England and Poland (Duffy 2006). The 'Conciliar movement' held that the final authority in spiritual matters resided with the Roman Church as a corporation of Christians, embodied in a general Church council, not with the Pope. In effect, the movement sought – ultimately, in vain – to create an all-Catholic Parliament. The Conciliar movement reached the peak of its importance when the authority of the Pope, between the end of the fourteenth and the beginning of the fifteenth century, was plagued by disputes of legitimacy, and was under the yoke of foreign powers. But the Conciliar Fathers generally failed to reach consensus and, in the Renaissance period, the Pope emerged victorious in this struggle. Still today, the Catholic Church is a theocracy. Not always did the confrontation between the parliament and the king end with the victory of the former.

This brief historical exegesis suggests that the Westminster model tended to emerge when parliaments evolved in a continuous confrontation with the executive power, slowly subtracting from its political power, by establishing more credible and reliable chains of representation of the interests of the citizens than those existing under the absolutist monarchy. The consensus model, instead, tended to arise in situations where parliaments overcame the executive power in an abrupt rather than a continuous fashion, and had not to compete with it for the representation of the citizens' interests within a long-lasting constitutional setting (Goldsworthy 1999; Wright 1987). Many caveats, however, must surround this working hypothesis; it warrants more systematic study and empirical tests.

8   CONCLUSIONS

It is at the same time surprising and reassuring that today public choice is still digging the same mine that it started to quarry at the beginning of its history more than 50 years ago, namely, how democracy works and takes decisions. Rather than showing what has been done, this chapter highlights the considerable amount of scholarly research that remains in order to gain a better understanding of how political institutions (and the institution that is of paramount importance to all others, the parliament) function. More work should be undertaken to generate databases relevant to the production of laws, along with the institutional features and decision-making rules that characterize parliaments around the world. If we consider the great leap forward to be that which propelled the economic growth literature at the end of the 1980s, when cross-country, time-series data started to become available, we can be optimistic about the future of studies of the purposes and effects of the rich diversity of legislative institutions across nations since they first emerged as counterweights to (or rubberstamps for) executive power.

NOTES

1. I would like to thank Jean-Michel Josselin and Emma Galli, as well as the editors of this volume, for helpful comments on a previous version of this chapter.
2. Shugart (1999) does not test this point empirically; we will provide some evidence about it in section 4.
3. Countries thus excluded from the sample are Brunei, Fiji, Guinea, Libya, North Korea, Myanmar, Somalia and the People's Republic of Yemen.
4. Similar results are obtained when the other measures of decentralization are considered. We report the results of the MUNI covariate only because of its slightly larger statistical significance.
5. Shughart and Tollison (1986) is an early example of this line of research.
6. For more details on 'tribal systems', see Chapter 12 by Samson Kimenyi and Olumide Taiwo in this volume.

11 Federal systems
Randall G. Holcombe

1 INTRODUCTION

Public choice has always had a strong interest in federal systems. The Tiebout (1956) model predates the recognition of public choice as a distinct subdiscipline, but Tiebout's model has a clear public choice foundation in which people 'vote with their feet' to support a revealed preference mechanism that can increase the efficiency of public sector resource allocation. In response to Samuelson's (1954, 1955) claim that one can demonstrate in theory the optimal level of public goods production, Tiebout showed that while there may not be an obvious way of finding that optimum theoretically, federal systems of government offer a practical method for doing so, namely intergovernmental competition. Intergovernmental competition is both efficiency enhancing and a way of aggregating individuals' preferences in Tiebout's framework – that is, it is an instrument consistent with the theory of public choice. While federalism was discussed in the public finance literature prior to Tiebout, Tiebout's article laid a clear foundation on which the public choice literature relating to federal systems has developed.

Much of the public choice literature on federal systems builds on Tiebout. Early contributors, such as Barr and Davis (1966), Barlow (1970), Borcherding and Deacon (1972), and Bergstrom and Goodman (1973), looked at the degree to which differences in public sector output across jurisdictions could be accounted for by differences in voter characteristics. One attractive feature of federal systems for public choice research is that differences across jurisdictions can be used in cross-sectional analyses to evaluate the effects of location-specific institutional details, including variations in sociodemographic circumstances and in local constitutional and collective decision-making rules. In those contributions to the literature, governmental efficiency was generated by Tiebout-like competition over tax bases, but citizens' preferences were evaluated following the median voter model developed by Black (1958) and Downs (1957). The public choice assumption was that the characteristics of public sector output in a particular jurisdiction would reflect the demands of the median voter.

One insight of the Tiebout framework is that demographic differences across subnational governmental units may themselves result from a federalist structure, as people sort themselves into jurisdictions that provide a mix of public goods and services preferred by that group, supplied at tax prices consistent with their preferences. Any correlation between demographic characteristics and government characteristics thus is likely to be determined simultaneously, as differences in demographic characteristics can cause differences in the demand for government output, but also as differences in government output across jurisdictions attract people with different demographic characteristics. Thus, the public choice literature on federalism contains a mechanism for preference aggregation that normally is not present in traditional models of public finance.

Typically, the theoretical framework in public choice takes the collective decision-making group as given and examines the way in which individuals' preferences are aggregated into collective decisions. The Tiebout mechanism, whereby people 'vote with their feet', recognizes that one way group preferences can emerge is by people sorting themselves into more homogeneous groups. For example, the constitutional framework laid out by Buchanan and Tullock (1962), Rawls (1971) and Buchanan (1975) does not take into account the possibility of people entering or leaving a decision-making group. Issues facing the European Union in the early twenty-first century, for example, bridge both constitutional economics and federal systems, so the sorting mechanisms that a public choice analysis of federal systems implies should be brought into the domain of constitutional economics.

Another insight is that intergovernmental competition across jurisdictions can enhance the efficiency of government provision in all jurisdictions, perhaps because governments compete for mobile residents, but also because voters can make comparisons across jurisdictions, resulting in 'yardstick competition,' as noted by Besley and Case (1995). Federal systems can generate more efficient resource allocations without anybody moving, if people in one jurisdiction can use outcomes in similar jurisdictions as benchmarks for evaluating their government's performance. Furthermore, as Osborne and Gaebler (1992) point out, federal systems can be laboratories of democracy, a concept articulated by Supreme Court Justice Louis Brandeis,[1] in which different jurisdictions can implement a variety of programs and policies, and the heterogeneous policies across jurisdictions can be compared with one another to see which of them work better.

Federal systems are composed of different levels of government, and the activities undertaken by subnational units vary from one federal system to another. Buchanan's (1965) theory of clubs provides a good efficiency explanation for this, noting that different collective consumption goods will have different optimal-sized sharing groups, so goods that are more efficiently provided at larger scale will be produced by the more centralized level of government, whereas those that can be provided efficiently to smaller sharing groups will be produced at decentralized levels. As Musgrave (1959) and Oates (1972) note, in a federal system where each level of government produces goods and services that best fit that government's scale, government at all levels will be more efficient and social welfare will be higher. One must be cautious about applying this reasoning uncritically, however. Just because an omniscient benevolent dictator could design an efficient federal system of government does not mean that real-world political decision-making will lead to an optimal design.

Riker (1964) observes that political incentives may work against federal systems because higher levels of government may overwhelm lower levels. Central governments have more power, which they can use to turn lower levels into nothing more than their agents. At the same time, lower levels of government may resist cooperating with one another, producing inefficiencies as a result of intergovernmental spillovers. The broad point is that any analysis of federalism that examines only the conditions for efficient federalism will be at best incomplete, because federal systems, like all government policies, are the result of a political decision-making process. The design of federal systems, then, must be understood as a product of politics, and the effects of federalism must also be considered to result from political decision-making. Despite the literature showing the potential efficiencies of federal systems, Weingast (2005) highlights that federalism will produce efficient results only to the extent that the incentives in the political decision-making process pull it in that direction.

The public choice literature on federalism has explored several themes: relationships among governments, the relative efficiency of centralized versus decentralized governments, alternative constitutional frameworks for federal systems, and methodological issues involved in analyzing polycentric systems. Before looking into those themes, the next section considers the creation of federal systems.

2 THE ORIGINS OF FEDERAL SYSTEMS

Federal systems can be created either by one government establishing lower-level governmental units under its jurisdiction, or by a group of governments creating a higher-level national government, making them a federation. The United States offers an example of both types. Local governments in the United States are entirely the creation of the state governments, and local governments have no powers beyond those that are given to them by their states. States have complete control over the creation and dissolution of lower-level governments (counties and cities), their abilities to tax and regulate, and every other local government activity. The federal government, in contrast, was created by the states and, in theory (although not so much in practice), the relationship between the states and the national government is different from the relationship between the states and their local governments. The United States Constitution was written to assign to the federal government limited and enumerated powers, and the Tenth Amendment to the Constitution – a part of the Bill of Rights and the original Constitution – says: 'The powers not delegated to the United States by the Constitution, nor prohibited by it to the States, are reserved to the States respectively, or to the people.' By design, the states of the United States sit above both local governments and the national government in the power structure, although in practice the centralizing tendency that Riker (1964) identified has moved Washington up the hierarchy of power. Using the United States as a template raises a number of interesting issues.

First, one can see that there may be motivations for political decision-makers in a national government to create sub-jurisdictions that result in a federal system, as happened when states chartered local governments within their boundaries, and there may be motivations for political decision-makers to join forces with other governments at the same level to confederate, resulting in a federal system. Second, one can discern the differences in power structures that political incentives produce. The states created local governments with no autonomous powers beyond those granted to them, whereas when the states created a higher-level federal government they limited its powers strictly so as to retain their own autonomy. Third, it is apparent that over time those relationships among governments have changed. Whereas initially the states stood above both the national and local governments in the power structure, that relationship evolved into one in which the national government clearly has substantial power over the states, and the states have virtually no power over the national government.

That evolution began almost as soon as the United States was established. As Holcombe (2002b) argues, the states had considerably more control over the federal government under the nation's original constitution, the Articles of Confederation, than under the Constitution that replaced it in 1789. The reason, it appears, is that powerful political interests – led by Alexander Hamilton, President Washington's first Secretary of the Treasury – wanted a more powerful central government, partly to create a revenue stream to pay off the former colonies' Revolutionary War debts. A major issue in the American Civil War less than a century later was states' rights, and the Union's victory in that bloody conflict clearly established the powers of the federal government as supreme over the states.[2] This raises an issue that is central to the discussion of Riker (1964) and Weingast (2005): how can lower-level governments maintain their autonomy when central governments have the power to take it away? A similar issue is playing out in the European Union (EU) at the beginning of the twenty-first century, as member states debate the degree to which Brussels should have authority to dictate policies to the EU's member states.

3 RELATIONSHIPS AMONG GOVERNMENTS

Relationships among governments can be analyzed in two dimensions: relationships among governments at the same level, and relationships among governments at different levels. Tiebout (1956) clearly falls into the first category, as he looks at intergovernmental competition among jurisdictions without even a suggestion that there need be any central government overseeing the competing local jurisdictions. Local governments compete for residents by offering them the bundles of goods, services, and taxes that correspond with their preferences, and citizens move to the jurisdictions that best fit their preferences.

Buchanan and Goetz (1972) question the effectiveness of Tiebout competition. One issue is that the incentives local government officials have to attract residents are far from clear. Unlike privately owned businesses, which have obvious reasons for attracting paying customers, there is no residual claimant in local government that can profit from luring new citizens. Possibly, the re-election motive of local officials provides an incentive for them to satisfy their current constituents, and policies that satisfy current constituents may also attract new residents with similar preferences. However, it is not clear that current residents would favor policies that would attract future residents, even future residents with preferences identical to theirs. Policies can affect current residents and potential future residents differentially – such as restrictions on development that raise home prices, thereby conferring capital gains on current homeowners while raising the price of entry for those who might move in otherwise. In addition, many factors affect people's locational decisions besides the bundle of goods, services, and taxes offered by local governments, including the availability of jobs, weather, and other amenities. Very likely, the characteristics of local governments will play only a small role in locational decisions.[3] Hence, there are, at least, some unanswered questions.

A significant issue regarding relationships among governments at the same level is intergovernmental spillovers. Internalizing intergovernmental spillovers is a major efficiency motive for having higher-level governments oversee the relationships among lower-level governments, following Musgrave (1959) and Oates (1972), but that leaves open the question of who has an incentive to internalize any externalities. One method of internalizing externalities is through intergovernmental grants that subsidize activities that generate positive spillovers, but Inman (1988) shows that when lower level governments can get grants from higher level governments, there is an incentive to allocate an inefficiently large amount of money to the subsidized spending programs because legislators view central government resources as a common pool resource. At the higher level of government, revenues are raised from taxpayers in every jurisdiction, thus creating the common pool from which subnational governments can draw. Citizens can at most place only a small part of the blame on their own representative for the taxes imposed on them by a legislative majority, because those taxes would be levied with or without their representative's cooperation. Meanwhile, any spending in a legislator's local district is often the direct result of that legislator's efforts. Legislators representing a specific locality view any money they can send to their local jurisdictions as a concentrated benefit for which they can claim credit, but the cost is spread among taxpayers in every jurisdiction.

Incentives at higher-level governments push toward excessive spending. Meanwhile, government decision-makers at lower levels of government rightly view intergovernmental grants as costing their own constituents almost nothing, which again reinforces the same political incentives to overspend. The issue of intergovernmental spillovers and intergovernmental grants shows the importance of looking at the incentives the political system creates for decision-makers, rather than analyzing efficiency issues as if government always makes efficient decisions. There are efficiency incentives for local governments to work together to internalize any intergovernmental spillovers, as Foldvary (1994) outlines, but that leaves open the question of whether the political incentives in a federal system are consistent with efficiency motives.

Revenue-sharing has been a major topic in the literature on federalism, with much scholarship looking at incentives that are generated by different types of intergovernmental grants. Bradford and Oates (1971) note that different grant structures offer different incentives to the recipient governments. Matching grants create an incentive to spend more on the grant activity, for example, whereas categorical grants have no such incentive, merely acting as lump-sum transfers that shift the budget constraint of recipient governments outward. However, Hamilton (1983) establishes that intergovernmental grants tend to stick where they land – there is a 'flypaper effect' – and the incentives created by different types of grants apparently do not have any real effect.

One explanation is fiscal illusion. Another explanation lies in the political decision-making process that generates grants. 'Governments' do not get grants; rather, individuals within particular governmental subunits apply for and may eventually get grant monies for their jurisdictions. If the grant money were siphoned off by the lower level governmental entity and treated as a part of general public revenues, there would be little incentive for individuals within a particular jurisdiction to seek grants in the first place. The issue is not settled: Becker (1996), for example, suggests that studies showing a flypaper effect produce empirical results that are artifacts of their estimating techniques.

The relationships between governments at different tiers raise some interesting public choice issues. It appears that once a federal system is created the central government increasingly tends to exert more power over lower-level governments, so that centralization threatens the federal system. This conjecture appears to be consistent with the history of the United States and of the European Union, although in both cases federalism has been modified but not eliminated. Riker (1964) says that electoral constraints can serve the function of preserving federalism in the face of central government power, because if higher-level governments control lower-level governments excessively, constituents will vote the elected officials of the higher-level governments out of office. Crémer and Palfrey (2002) also note the potential for re-election motives to preserve the balance of power among various levels of government. Przeworski (1991) argues that by limiting the powers of all levels of government, federalism serves as a stabilizing influence because, on the one hand, it allows groups with differing interests to pursue those differences within lower level government and, on the other hand, enables higher-level governments to internalize potential externalities and settle disputes that can arise among lower level jurisdictions.

Despite these stabilizing forces, the federal system in the United States has witnessed political power gravitating toward the national government (Holcombe 2002b). This appears to be the result of the greater revenue-raising power of the national government, because the national government remained small until a federal income tax was enacted in 1913. Growing federal revenue from income taxation not only has increased the size of the national government, but also its exercise of power in other dimensions. For example, although constitutionally it appears that states have the right to set their own highway speed limits and to establish minimum ages for consuming alcoholic beverages legally, the national government effectively has imposed both of those regulations on states by threatening to withhold federal money from them if they do not abide by nationally mandated standards. The national government taxes away money from the citizens of the states, and then returns it to them only if certain conditions are met. The national government imposed a 55 mile per hour speed limit on the states in 1974, which it repealed in 1995, and imposed a legal drinking age of 21 in 1984, which remains in place.

In some cases one can find a ready justification for the concentration of power at the national level. For example, national environmental regulations can mitigate intergovernmental spillovers of public 'bads'. In other cases, such as federal laws that ban the consumption of certain illicit drugs, and require a doctor's prescription for others, there appears to be no clear economic justification for the federal government taking these powers rather than leaving them to the states. Crémer and Palfrey (2002) suggest that at least in some cases mandates by national governments imposed on states are the result of voter demands, possibly due to a majority of voters being able to impose their preferences on a minority.

Another possibility for the centralizing tendencies of federal systems, as suggested by McKenzie and Staaf (1978), is that political leaders in lower-level governments desire centralization as a method of homogenizing their powers and reducing intergovernmental competition. McKenzie and Staaf specifically consider policies under which higher-level governments share revenue with lower level governments, and argue that such sharing reduces intergovernmental differences in tax rates. Greater tax-rate homogeneity means that voters have less incentive to vote with their feet and move to lower-tax jurisdictions, which reduces Tiebout competition. By raising revenue at the central level, taxes are more difficult to escape, and therefore governments are able to tax and spend more. Along these lines, with the growth in online sales, which typically are untaxed by state governments, states are designing a mechanism to coordinate the collection of state sales taxes on Internet purchases.

A similar explanation would apply to regulations imposed by the central government. Although such policies do not enhance the revenues of local governments, they do make regulations more homogeneous, and thus lessen the degree to which local governments are subject to intergovernmental competition. This explanation fits well with Niskanen's (1971, 2001) well-known hypothesis that public-sector bureaucrats want to maximize their discretionary budgets. Regulatory homogeneity imposed at the central level lessens intergovernmental competition, and a system of intergovernmental grants, whereby revenues are raised at the level of the central government but spent at the local level, enhances the budgets of subnational governments and allows budget-maximizing bureaucrats at every level to spend more.

As Weingast (2005) states, federalism must be self-enforcing constitutionally to survive. There must be a balance of forces that prevent a strong central government from usurping all power from lower-level governments, and that prevent lower-level governments from amassing enough power to compromise the efficacy of the central government. It appears that political forces generally favor central governments, partly because they do not face the organizational issues that lower-level governments do in joining forces to increase their power, and partly because at least some incentives facing lower-level governments push toward centralization to reduce intergovernmental competition.

4 FEDERAL SYSTEMS AND EFFICIENCY

Much of the literature on federalism suggests that federal systems are more efficient than centralized systems of government, for many reasons. There may be different optimal sizes of government for the production of different types of goods, as Musgrave (1959) and Buchanan (1965) suggest; Tiebout's (1956) seminal article on intergovernmental competition was intended to demonstrate an efficiency-generating mechanism that Samuelson (1954, 1955) said challenged governmental production of public goods. Hayek (1939) was an early proponent of federalism as a method of checking the power that more centralized governments would be able to wield, anticipating Tiebout's framework. There are two different but related issues here. One is whether there are, in fact, efficiency gains from decentralization (or centralization); the other is the effect of decentralization on the size of government – the Leviathan hypothesis – which will be considered in the following section.

Considering the theoretical framework in which greater efficiency is a primary hypothesis of the federalism literature, there is surprisingly little evidence on the question. Chu (2010) develops a theoretical framework within which centralization reduces conflict and lowers military expenditures, which is an efficiency gain, but this is offset by the Leviathan effect, which Chu assumes unambiguously to be negative. Chu presents no empirical evidence, but does lay out a theoretical framework with empirical implications.

Most empirical studies that examine the relationship between fiscal decentralization and income or growth find that decentralization has a positive effect. Holcombe and Williams (2011) look at a cross-section of US states and use the ratio of local to state and local expenditures as a measure of fiscal centralization. They find that more decentralized states have higher levels of per capita income, supporting the hypothesis that federalism is efficiency-enhancing, and that a greater degree of decentralization therefore is beneficial. Buser (2011) utilizes a panel dataset of 20 Organization for Economic

Co-operation and Development (OECD) nations from 1972 to 2005, and likewise finds that more decentralization leads to higher per capita incomes.

Lowrey (1998) looks directly at the assumptions of the Tiebout model to argue, using public choice reasoning, that intergovernmental competition tends to fail to allocate resources efficiently. The Tiebout model assumes that jurisdictions will be created to satisfy constituent preferences, but Lowrey points out that there are legal barriers to establishing new jurisdictions and therefore that there are limits to what those jurisdictions can offer in terms of the quantities and qualities of public goods. Information problems exist caused by the rational ignorance of voters, which prevent efficient sorting, and there may be unintended consequences, such as the creation of jurisdictions that exclude minorities or limit income redistribution, as Kenny and Reinke (2011) argue. Boettke et al. (2011) address Lowrey's critique explicitly, but one answer is that the competitive mechanism in the Tiebout model clearly oversimplifies reality, in the same way that the model of perfect competition in neoclassical economics oversimplifies actual market conditions. It shows a mechanism that pushes a federal system toward an efficient allocation of resources, and in a more complex world those mechanisms may not work as effectively as the model predicts.

Looking at the efficient allocation of resources, one must consider more than just how efficiently governments operate. In the Tiebout model, people sort themselves into jurisdictions solely based on their preferences for public goods, but in the real world people choose locations based on where the private sector offers the best job opportunities; they also locate to be near family members and on the basis of their preferences for weather, geography, and other amenities. While these other factors may mitigate the operation of the mechanisms in the Tiebout model, they too are important for overall efficiency.

As far as efficiency is concerned, the literature does appear to suggest that more fiscal decentralization leads to higher per capita incomes and more income growth, but this literature is limited in its present form and there clearly is room for additional research. Researchers should be careful to separate arguments for why federal systems could, in theory, be more efficient, such as the claim that federalism can internalize intergovernmental spillovers, and the mechanisms that must exist to actually produce such efficiencies. In fact, the literature has identified many such mechanisms, including Tiebout sorting, benchmark competition, and decentralized governments acting as laboratories of democracy. Arguments that in theory federalism could be more efficient than centralization fall short because they do not identify the ways in which any supposed efficiencies could be realized.

5 FEDERALISM AND LEVIATHAN

Another issue that has featured prominently in the literature is whether federal systems can serve to check the size and growth of government. Brennan and Buchanan (1980, p. 185) argue that 'total government intrusion into the economy should be smaller, *ceteris paribus*, the greater the extent to which taxes and expenditures are decentralized'. Evidence on the issue is mixed. Oates (1985) and Forbes and Zampelli (1989) find no effect of centralization on government size. Stein (1999) suggests that more decentralized revenue structures result in larger governments, whereas Rodden (2003) concludes that decentralization produces smaller governments, and that government is smaller the greater is the share of local government spending raised through own-source revenue rather than intergovernmental grants. Epple and Zelenitz (1981) find that intergovernmental competition limits the revenue-raising ability of local governments, but Epple and Romer (1991) note that because land cannot exit local jurisdictions, local governments can tax land rents effectively. Nelson (1986), Zax (1989), Joulfaian and Marlow (1990), and Crowley and Sobel (2011) all support the Brennan and Buchanan view that greater decentralization limits the size of government.

Crowley and Sobel (2011) look at a detailed data set of municipalities, counties and school districts in the State of Pennsylvania and find that they all tend to levy tax rates well below revenue-maximizing levels. Their paper is unique in that it looks at and finds significant spatial interdependence among the sub-state governments. Spatial interaction is a fundamental consideration in intergovernmental competition, but their paper is the first to model it empirically. They do not draw a strong conclusion from their findings, however. Spatial interdependence could be evidence of competition, which forces competing jurisdictions to offer similar bundles of public goods and services and taxes to remain competitive. The evidence also could indicate intergovernmental collusion as nearby governments offer similar bundles in order to reduce any incentive for residents to move to neighboring jurisdictions.

The Tiebout model suggests that local governments differentiate their offerings of public goods and tax prices to attract residents with preferences similar to those of existing residents, resulting in a sorting of citizens so that local governments more closely correspond to the citizens' desires. Whether spatial interdependence is a sign of more or less competition, it would appear to undermine the sorting mechanism in the Tiebout model. Kenny and Reinke (2011) present evidence that higher-income suburbanites tend to incorporate into their own local jurisdictions to avoid becoming vulnerable to income redistribution policies that might be enacted by their lower-income neighbors. Thus, local governments are created to produce more homogeneous jurisdictions from larger, more heterogeneous ones. Tiebout sorting should produce negative spatial correlation, following this line of reasoning, and a finding of positive spatial correlation would appear to be more an indicator of collusion than of interjurisdictional competition.

As it stands, the empirical literature on the Leviathan hypothesis has not been integrated into the literature on efficiency. It starts with the Brennan and Buchanan framework, in which government tends to be overly large, and decentralization therefore is a way of constraining big government through intergovernmental competition. While the empirical results are somewhat mixed, they do tend to point to the conclusion that decentralization does, in fact, limit governmental size. One possible research project would be to combine the literatures on efficiency and Leviathan to gauge the degree to which smaller governments that appear to result from more decentralization also produce a more efficient allocation of resources.

6 CONSENT AND COERCION

The activities of government might be viewed in two, almost opposite ways. One approach is to see it as a product of politics as exchange. Buchanan and Tullock (1962,

p. 19) note that 'political or collective action under the individualistic view of the state is much the same [as market exchange]. Two or more individuals find it mutually advantageous to join forces to accomplish certain common purposes'. Government is based on consent. Another way of viewing government is that it exists only to force people to do things they would not do voluntarily (Yeager 1985, 2001). If people would contribute voluntarily to the provision of public goods, there would be no reason for forced taxation. If people would abide voluntarily to the regulatory commands of government, there would be no reason for government to place the threat of force behind its regulations.

These two views of government take on an interesting interplay when analyzing the foundations of federal systems. The primary justification for centralization within a federal framework, going back at least to Musgrave (1959), is to internalize intergovernmental spillovers, and to engage in redistributive policies. Regarding spillovers, people have an incentive to free ride on the public goods provided by other jurisdictions, giving governments in every jurisdiction strong incentives to underprovide public goods. Thus, the central government forces everyone to contribute to the public good, internalizing the externality and making everyone better off. The same motivation occurs with respect to income redistribution, as Hochman and Rodgers (1969) argued. People will free-ride on charitable giving by others to less fortunate citizens, and everyone can be better off if government forces the more fortunate to redistribute some of their income to the less fortunate. As the proponents of this type of governmental intervention argue, people are better off because they agree to be coerced.

Boudreaux and Holcombe (1989) note that homeowners' associations, which might be viewed as local governments created by contractual agreement rather than by coercion, tend to assign voting rights in proportion to the dues and assessments that members pay into the association. In homeowners' associations in which every household pays the same dues, voting rights are distributed so that each has one vote. In other homeowners' associations, by contrast, larger (and presumably more valuable) homes have higher assessments (especially in condominium associations) and in those cases voting rights are distributed in proportion to the association's assessments. A possible reason for this is that when people's voting rights are proportional to the amount they pay into the group, the ability of those who pay less to vote to redistribute receipts toward themselves is reduced. Whether this is desirable or not depends on how one evaluates the value of free-riding on redistributional programs versus freedom from coercion. One argument is that redistribution is a legitimate function of the state, and federalism allows people to sort themselves by income and wealth, which prevents the state from abusing this function. The argument on the other side is that some individuals can use the power of the state to take wealth from other citizens in order to transfer it to themselves (which is called robbery if done outside the confines of the state). In that view, federalism helps protect citizens from the coercive power of the state.

In studying governmental coercion, Holcombe (2012) observes that people do not actually agree to granting such powers to the state. Indeed, that is why the government must rely on the threat of force. As such, the argument that they would be better off if they did agree to be coerced is purely hypothetical. Federalism, starting with the Tiebout model, offers a way by which citizens can avoid coercion by moving away from it. Federalism is an institution that in theory bases government more on consensus and, hence, less coercion. It undermines some of the justifications given for having a government in the first place, such as internalizing externalities and redistributing income, which require force to overcome self-interested individual behavior.

7 FEDERALISM: INFORMATION AND INCENTIVES

One way to view the centralization – decentralization trade-off is that centralized systems are top-down systems, wherein decisions are made at higher levels of political authority and then are implemented by those at lower levels, whereas decentralized systems are bottom-up institutions in which decisions are made at the local level, perhaps to be coordinated at a higher level. As Wagner (2007, 2011) explains, this view is overly simplistic in that all choices are made by individuals and all actions are carried out by individuals. Government is often viewed as a unitary actor, but the reality is that government action is much more complex.

Government frequently is depicted as a centralized and planned order, in comparison with market activity, which is decentralized and spontaneous. Whereas every actor in the marketplace does make plans, the aggregate outcome of market activity is unplanned. Wagner styles these two views as comparing the actions of people who are marching in a parade with the throngs of customers at a shopping mall. In both cases there is an orderly movement of people, but in the case of the parade movement is determined by a central plan, and so the overall outcome is the product of that plan. Although the movement of people in a shopping mall is orderly – they are able to avoid collisions and get to the shops they want to visit – there is no central plan, and there is no way to determine ahead of time who will be in which stores at what times.

Wagner argues that government activity at all levels is more like the spontaneous order of the shopping mall than the centrally planned order of the parade. Partly, this conclusion follows from the information available to decision-makers at all levels of government. Decision-makers in a centralized government can make decisions based only on the information they get from the bottom up. Even if one considers those decision-makers to be benevolent despots, they are limited to satisfying the preferences of their own constituents, provided that they can discover what their constituents want from government; that information will be forthcoming only imperfectly, partly because the rational ignorance of constituents means that the constituents themselves may have an unclear idea of their preference orderings, partly because what individuals want for themselves may not be possible in the aggregate, and partly because, along the lines of Hayek (1945), all information cannot be articulated clearly and passed from one person to another. If one considers those decision-makers to be politically motivated, as a public choice approach to the issue suggests one should, the same issues arise, along with one additional complication: decision-makers throughout the hierarchy leading to those in the central government will also have their own interests in mind as they communicate information upward.

A model of a central government as a unitary actor, then, does not convey accurately the ways in which government actually behaves. Information must be passed up the chain of command and, as is inevitable, some relevant data will be lost and some will be distorted. The political motivations of actors higher in the chain of command will alter the information flows to control how those at the top will receive the data those at the bottom are sending. Meanwhile, orders from the top similarly will be altered because of informational incompleteness and because those who receive the orders have their own incentives for behaving differently from the intentions of those who issue them. Thus, there is not as great a distinction between centralized and decentralized systems as there appears at first glance. Individuals at the bottom of the chain of command will therefore have more autonomy than the top-down model of government suggests. Governmental decisions will thus always largely be influenced heavily by the local knowledge available to those at the bottom of the political hierarchy.

The foregoing analysis does not mean that there is no difference between centralized and decentralized systems of governance. For example, when revenues are raised at the central level and redistributed to lower level governments, the responsibility for taxation is more hierarchically diffused. That division of tax-generating labor can produce more revenues in total than would be raised by intergovernmental competition, especially competition over the same tax base. But the tax revenues collected at the central level become a common pool resource that generates political incentives for excessive depletion by reelection-minded politicians. Furthermore, greater centralization of revenue collection dilutes the accountability to local constituents of decision-makers at the national level. Citizens are better able to oversee the activities of subnational governments than of the central government, creating a closer connection between citizen preferences and governmental actions. The point is that a public choice approach to federalism should recognize the informational and incentive problems that plague hierarchical governments. An accurate modeling of political decision-making should take into account that centralized systems are less hierarchical than would be depicted in an organizational flow chart, and also take into account the substantial component of spontaneous and unplanned order that will exist in any type of governmental organization.

8 FEDERAL SYSTEMS IN THE TWENTY-FIRST CENTURY

A public choice analysis of federal systems is very relevant to twenty-first century governments. A key issue is the one Riker (1964) raised about the stability of federal systems. Federal systems divide power among different levels of government and, as Weingast (2005) notes, constitutional mechanisms must be in place that can preserve that balance of power for federal systems to survive. The most interesting issues at the beginning of the twenty-first century focus on the rapidly evolving federalism of the European Union.

The balance of power in Europe has continued to tilt toward giving more authority to the central EU government in Brussels, reducing the fiscal and monetary authority of the individual member states. A significant motivation for forming the EU was to create a large free trade area, but along with the elimination of trade barriers among the members came requirements for more commonality in their individual fiscal and agricultural policies, among others. The adoption of the euro brought with it a common monetary policy for the members of the monetary union. That agreement now appears to be threatened by excessive public debt in several member states. Although the Maastricht Treaty of 1992 required signatories to maintain deficits of no more than 3 percent of gross domestic product (GDP) and total public debts of no more than 60 percent of GDP, those limits were violated widely, so that by 2012 there have been proposals that would impose further restrictions on member states, enforced by the central EU government, in order to stave off the euro's collapse and an erosion of Europe's common market.

A discussion of the details of the issues that face the EU in 2012 go well beyond the scope of this chapter, and easily could fill a chapter (or book!) on its own. For present purposes, note that the fiscal problems that have arisen in a few of the EU member states have resulted in a push toward greater centralization of power. One alternative would have been to allow any EU members with fiscal problems to deal with those issues themselves and make their own tough budgetary decisions. Instead, those member states themselves have asked the central government for fiscal assistance,[4] even while realizing that meeting their requests would result in a transfer of power from the lower level national governments to the central EU government. As Riker (1964) and Weingast (2005) frame the issue, the question is how lower-level governments can prevent higher-level governments from using their newly acquired powers to weaken those of the lower-level governments, but in this case the lower-level governments are asking for exactly that to happen.

One possible reason is that the poorer (and more profligate) states within the EU may see greater centralization as a strategy for securing a redistribution of wealth from the higher-income, more fiscally responsible members. One might view this as rent-seeking, but one of the justifications often given for government is redistribution and – as discussed above – federalism provides a measure of insulation from redistributive policies. Weakening federalism and transferring more fiscal power to the central government may be viewed as a method for overcoming incentives for free-riding on the 'public good' of income redistribution. The purpose is not to take a side on this particular issue, but rather to show how some of the issues associated with federalism discussed above can be applied to contemporary real-world policy matters.

Pressures toward greater centralization in federal systems, raised here with regard to the European Union, were discussed earlier in the US context. In both cases, such pressures primarily have been fiscal in origin. In the United States, the fiscal imperatives for centralization resulted from the greater revenue-raising power of the federal government, beginning with the implementation of income taxation in 1913. In that year, US federal government expenditures accounted for 2.5 percent of GDP; a century later they were nearly 10 times greater. As noted earlier, the US federal government exercises power over the 50 states by offering financial incentives to them. In the European Union, which initially was more decentralized fiscally, the issue is how much control to give the central government in exchange for its fiscally stronger states supporting the fiscally weaker ones. It is interesting to note that proposals to give Brussels powers over the fiscal policies of its member states would go well beyond those the US federal government exercises over its own subnational governments. The states of the United States determine their own budgets and set their own taxing and spending priorities, restricted only to a very limited extent by any federal regulations or oversight. Even programs such as Medicaid, or the 'No Child Left Behind' educational requirements, are enforced on the states only in exchange for their 'voluntary' participation in those programs and acceptance of federal funding.

In the context of fiscal issues pushing toward more centralization, Switzerland offers an interesting case study wherein lower-level governments have substantial autonomy that does not appear to be threatened by higher-level governments. Organized politically much like the United States, Switzerland has a federal government that sits above its cantons (similar to US states). As Feld et al. (2011, pp. 53–4) note, at all levels, Swiss governments enjoy high degrees of fiscal autonomy and make their fiscal decisions relatively independently. The 1990s saw a substantial increase in indebtedness throughout Switzerland's governance hierarchy, but the growth of debt was most pronounced at the federal level, was less pronounced at the canton level, and was essentially non-existent in the aggregate at the local level. Measures to address rising government indebtedness were introduced at the three levels of government, but this has not undermined Swiss federalism, or resulted in a transfer of power from lower-level to higher-level governments. In other words, the pattern observed in the United States and the European Union does not apply to Swiss federalism, and Switzerland's federalist structure may provide insights into how to avoid Riker's (1964) concern about higher-level governments exercising ever-greater power, thus undermining the benefits of federalism.

This section introduces some complex policy issues, and the point of it is not to suggest answers, but rather to show that the theoretical framework laid out in the literature on federalism has direct policy relevance. While that literature contains several strands, an important one addresses the efficiency justifications for federal systems, such as internalizing externalities and producing public goods at the optimal scale. In this context, note that the major policy issues at the beginning of the twenty-first century do not deal with these issues, which have dominated the academic literature on federalism, but rather are related more closely to budgetary matters. Taxation, redistribution, and debt have been the principal concerns, and underlying these issues are Leviathan – government's implacable growth – matters that have been a topic of study in the theoretical and empirical literatures of public choice for decades.[5]

9 CONCLUSION

Federal systems of government have been justified on a number of efficiency grounds. Those justifications fall into two general categories. One is the possibility of gains from having multiple smaller governmental units rather than one large central government. The other is the possibility of gains from having multiple levels of government serving different functions. In the first category, multiple governments allow for intergovernmental competition, which (1) permits people to move to jurisdictions that match their preferences more closely, (2) disciplines inefficient governments by causing them to lose residents, (3) facilitates benchmark competition so that citizens can compare their governments with other jurisdictions regardless of interjurisdictional mobility, (4) promotes individual jurisdictions as 'laboratories of democracy' for experimentation with different policies, and (5) produces more homogeneity within local governments even as it makes governments more heterogeneous, allowing for more efficient targeting of government services. In the second category, multiple levels of government allow for (1) government services to be produced at the optimal scale, (2) intergovernmental spillovers to be internalized through the actions of higher level governments, and (3) a wider scope for governmental redistribution programs.

These justifications treat government as if it was designed and run by an omniscient benevolent dictator. Federal systems may be desirable for the reasons just listed, but the incentives within the political process may stand in the way of realizing these benefits. A realistic assessment of federal systems must take into account the political incentive structure within which they are created, and within which they operate.

Riker (1964) was concerned that the power wielded by the central government could erode a federal system, increasingly pushing it toward centralization, and Riker's concern appears to be descriptive of the evolution of power over the centuries in the United States, and over the decades in the European Union. However, an analysis of both the incentive structure of – and the actual behavior in – federal systems suggests that the push toward centralization is not solely the result of an exercise of power on the part of the central government, but also arises from a willingness within lower-level governments to cede some of their powers. Lower-level governments may benefit from the homogenizing effects of central government regulation and revenue collection, precisely because it lessens the pressures of intergovernmental competition. While there are many differences in the centralizing tendencies in the United States and the European Union, a similarity is found in the move toward more centralized revenue collection schemes, with taxes first collected by the central governments later passed back down to lower levels. This allows lower-level governments to provide their constituents with benefits that can generate political support, paid for from the common pool of national revenues.

This common pool problem leads to an inefficiently large level of government spending, as one can see by looking at the political incentives, and is an example of how taking a public choice approach to federal systems points toward different conclusions than if one were to adopt a model in which government is an omniscient and benevolent dictator. That model depicts a multilayered government as a way of internalizing intergovernmental spillovers and producing public goods at optimal scale, whereas a public choice approach highlights the incentives for inefficient behavior on the part of political decision-makers. To understand government at any level, one must analyze it as the product of a political decision-making process in which the actors behave rationally and self-interestedly.

Government exists only to force people to do things they would not voluntarily choose to do without coercion. To the degree that federal systems allow people to escape governmental coercion by voting with their feet, a mechanism exists for people to mitigate that use of force. When one looks at the justifications for federal systems given in the first paragraph of this conclusion, the ability to escape government coercion is a clear benefit of the first justification because having multiple competing jurisdictions forces governments to be more responsive to the preferences of their citizens. The second justification, however, appears to rest on the coercive powers of government. Internalizing intergovernmental spillovers means overcoming free-riding, requiring the central government to impose its will on lower levels of political authority. Perhaps more significantly, engaging in redistributive activity, which is an increasingly large part of the activities of twenty-first century governments, means forcing those with more income and wealth to transfer some of it to those with less. Federal systems provide means for escaping this coercion by creating jurisdictions that can shelter the wealthy from the political power of the less wealthy.

Whether federalism's ability to lessen government coercion of this type is desirable is a normative question that pits the values of freedom and protection of property rights against the value of economic equality. The empirical evidence, while far from unanimous, does suggest that more decentralized systems tend to tame Leviathan government, resulting in lower taxes and government spending. The empirical evidence also suggests that more decentralized governments generate higher levels of per capita income, which must be viewed as desirable.

In theory, federal systems provide a host of benefits when compared to centralized governments. The political incentives inherent in the structure of government determine how many of these theoretical benefits will be produced in practice.

NOTES

1. In his dissenting opinion in *New State Ice Co. v. Leibmann* U.S. 262 (1932), Justice Louis Brandeis said: 'It is one of the happy incidents of the federal system that a single courageous State may, if its citizens choose, serve as a laboratory; and try novel social and economic experiments without risk to the country.'
2. Obviously, the issue of slavery divided the states, and this statement is not meant to minimize that issue, but rather to note that the Civil War established firmly a hierarchy in which the federal government's powers superseded those of the states.
3. Florida (2002) recognizes these other amenities as important to locational decisions, and argues that government policies are important in creating them.
4. Note that while the initial assistance was in terms of bailout funding to allow those governments to get their fiscal houses in order, many of the countries with fiscal issues were pushing for the issuance of Eurobonds (issued by the EU) to replace individual countries' sovereign debts. This would involve member states ceding even more power to the central government, at the request of those member states.
5. This chapter analyzes federal systems primarily by looking at the political incentives for economic activity, so it is worth mentioning that in the cases of both the United States and the European Union a major reason for their formation was purely political in nature. The United States was formed to unite former British colonies after gaining their independence from Britain, and a major motivation behind the formation of the European Union was to unite countries that had centuries-long histories of warring with each other. That motivation remains a significant one for Europe, so a complete analysis of EU policy would have to weigh the purely economic costs of centralization against the less tangible, but perhaps more significant, goal of a united Europe. The analysis in this chapter, which sticks closely to the economic aspects of federal systems, therefore represents only a partial analysis of the European Union's federal system.

12 Tribal systems
Mwangi S. Kimenyi and Olumide Taiwo

1 INTRODUCTION

A primary tenet of public choice theory is the seemingly simple idea that individuals interacting in the public sector seek to maximize their own utilities just as they do in the private markets. In essence, self-interest is hardwired into all individuals' preference functions and thus the idea that public officials seek to maximize some nebulous public interest in the course of undertaking their public duties is not consistent with the utility maximization assumption. Extending the self-interest assumption to political markets provides powerful insights into the behavior of individuals in their capacities as voters, elected officials or bureaucrats. But if self-interest is hardwired, then it must also be the case that actors in all political systems – including traditional or very primitive systems – are motivated by the same goals. Thus, just as elected politicians in democracies seek to extend their tenures in office, we would also expect the behavior of kings, military dictators or tribal leaders to have similar motivations. The means and strategies for remaining in leadership positions may vary but the reasons for doing so are similar and consistent with self-interest. Likewise, as civil servants in Western democracies seek to maximize the budgets under their control, so would their counterparts in developing countries or those holding similar positions in simple societies. In other words, any differences that we may observe in how individuals behave in different political systems are due only to different institutional constraints, not differences in the utility functions of the actors.

We examine the organization of tribal systems and how such systems deal with collective action problems. Given that most pure tribal systems largely have been replaced by modern systems of governance, our approach is necessarily historical. Our primary aim is to provide a narrative of the organizational aspects of tribal systems with a view to understanding how such societies functioned with respect to the distribution of powers and the roles of their different members, such as tribal chiefs, those in lower positions of authority and ordinary citizens. In addition, we attempt to provide a public choice interpretation of the organization of these societies and their ways of making collective decisions. Scholars have also been interested in understanding how different tribal systems interacted with colonial rulers and whether post-colonial institutions were influenced by the nature of the tribal system in place prior to colonization. We therefore analyze the different indigenous collective choice systems and the effects of colonial rule on them. We extend our analysis to the implications of these systems for transitioning to modern nation-states and discuss some successes and failures of such transitions.

An understanding of what constitutes a tribe and tribal system is crucial to this analysis. Whereas tribes have been viewed as being synonymous with ethnicity, religion, language, customs and homelands, these concepts do not uniquely distinguish a tribe from other social groups. For our purpose, a tribe is a homogeneous band of indigenous people with sovereign rights over a defined territory and governed by a system of widely recognized but unwritten laws. In terms of internal ordering, a tribe is subdivided into clans – subgroups of the tribe who recognize themselves as descendants of specific offspring of the tribal ancestor and typically reside in particular regions of the tribal territory. The clans are further subdivided into lineages – members of the clan who are related genetically to one another. Sometimes, as noted by Dundas (1915, p. 236), a group of tribes is 'so closely related by custom . . . that it is natural to assign a common origin to them'.[1] An ethnic group emerges when tribes are aggregated along lines of descent and customs.[2] However, it is worth noting that while it is appropriate to talk about tribal political systems, there is nothing like an ethnic political system; an ethnic group does not possess any of the internal structures of a tribe. Instead, a group of tribes may constitute what is commonly referred to as ethnic 'nationality'. A tribe is equivalent to an ethnic group only in the case where none of the tribes share anything in common.

2   TRIBAL POLITICAL SYSTEMS

It is impractical to describe tribal organizations around the world in a single framework. In a pioneering study of political organization in primitive societies, Fortes and Evans-Pritchard (1940) documented two distinct forms of tribal organization among eight African tribes. They classified tribal political systems as either segmentary, such as those of the Logoli, Tallensi and Nuer tribes, or centralized, such as those practiced by the Zulu, Ngwato, Bemba, Bayankole and Kede tribes. In segmentary or 'stateless' systems, political authority is dispersed across corporate lineage groups, whereas it is concentrated in the hands of kings and chiefs in centralized political systems. Subsequent to Fortes and Evans-Pritchard's path-breaking study, a large literature on primitive societies from other parts of the world has furnished ethnographic evidence of tribal organizations that differ in many respects from the typology they had advanced. These include the native American Apache, Plains Indian and Pueblo tribes, as well as the native Australian and African Pygmy tribes (Eisenstadt 1959), the Yanomami of Venezuela and Brazil (Helbling 1999), the Kayapo Indians of central Brazil (Helbling 1999; Carneiro 2000), the Mongols, Kalmuks, Turks, Tungus, Manchu, Gilyak and other tribes of the Middle East and Central Asia (Lindholm 1986), the Baito, Sukuma, Oromo, Kikuyu and Buganda of East Africa, the Ibos, Yoruba and Asante of West Africa, and the Barotse of Southern Africa (Samuel and Joshua 2010). Those studies found that in many cases age groups, inter-group alliances, associations, collective ritual groups and sometimes secret societies performed important political functions. Based on evidence that was available at the time of his own study, Eisenstadt (1959) identified a continuum of tribal political organizations ranging from the simplest 'band organizations' to the most complex 'monarchies'. It turns out that political systems of tribal groups that were not included in his study can be conveniently placed into one of the nine categories he developed. However, his analysis also shows that the nine categories can be collapsed into two broader classifications that fit nicely into the scheme of Fortes and Evans-Pritchard (1940), based on distinctions between social and political systems, and the extent to which special political positions and organizational hierarchies have been adopted. For analytical convenience, we restrict our analysis to the two-pronged categorization of tribal systems.[3]

2.1 Rationale for the Existence of Different Political Systems

A primary task in analyzing tribal systems is to explain why a society would opt for a particular type of governance structure. Viewed from today's perspective, tribal systems may appear as grossly inefficient forms of organization. However, we take the view that different political systems exist at one time or other and in different places in response to the benefits and costs of organizing for the provision of collective goods. Thus, we posit that a tribe's adoption of a given governance structure should be consistent with the goal of maximizing social benefits net of the transaction costs of organizing collective action. In essence, we reject references to the idea that tribal or traditional societies are inefficient. Instead, we suggest that different types of tribal political systems reflect efficient organization given the circumstances of time and place. Thus, we could also expect changes in those circumstances to result in a move toward a new, more efficient 'organizational equilibrium'.

A political system is defined primarily by two sets of institutions: those dealing with internal order, and those relating to defense against external threats or plundering of the resources of other polities – war (Fortes and Evans-Pritchard 1940). Although differences may exist in methods, every tribal system exhibits a basic mechanism of internal social control aimed at resolving disputes between its members and regulating the affairs of daily life. Tribal systems are unlikely to differ markedly in that respect. It is rather in the institutions relating to war and defense that we may expect significant differences between tribal systems. In their study, Fortes and Evans-Pritchard (1940) judge that the most noteworthy characteristic distinguishing the centralized system from the segmentary system can be found in the establishment, maintenance and functioning of a permanent organized military force. However, organized armed forces exist primarily for tribal defense and war, implying that our understanding of the choice of political systems is predicated on understanding the demands for defense against external threats and conquest.

It seems to be true that all societies existed as autonomous groups throughout the Paleolithic period, when small bands of people moved from place to place hunting, fishing and gathering; it was not until the Neolithic period that the hunter-gatherers began to settle down into communities. Those settlements, occurring at different places and in different environments, mark the onset of humankind's efforts to adapt to local ecological opportunities and challenges. Although several factors may explain why some settlements chose the centralized system rather than the segmentary system, the most plausible is that the need for organized force arose from the limits imposed by environmental conditions on the mode of livelihood. In contrast to hunters, gatherers and perhaps fixed-cultivation agriculturists, shifting-cultivation agriculturists were likely to have an interest in protecting their existing fields and a desire to expand their territorial ranges when the local soil had been depleted (Helbling 1999). Under such conditions, individuals needed to defend their fallowing fields from confiscation by invaders as well as to appropriate new fertile land from neighboring settlements. Given that an individual farmer is vulnerable to predation, it was cost-effective for the entire settlement to pursue those defensive and expansionary goals collectively. They could do so by pooling their resources to establish an organized armed force for their common defense and the acquisition of new land. This process is best facilitated by a system of central governance.

Ethnographic accounts generally support this perspective from an ecological standpoint. For example, the Bemba tribe (shifting-cultivation agriculturists), the Ngwato and Zulu (who practice rainfall-dependent agriculture along with animal husbandry, and are most likely to be shifting cultivators) have centralized systems. On the other hand, the predominantly pastoralist Nuers and fixed-cultivation agriculturist Tallensi and Logoli tribes have segmentary political systems. The horticulturists, fishers, hunters and gatherers of the Yanomami and Kayapo tribes likewise are segmentary. Hunters and gatherers are unlikely to have the need to protect particular land areas since they typically move from place to place in search of prey. There is also some evidence that settlements supporting fixed cultivation are typically more fertile and well watered compared to those under shifting cultivation, particularly comparing the areas inhabited by the Logoli and the Bemba. Although agriculturists in both settings are likely to demand protection of their crops from invaders, the shifting-cultivators would have additional need for organized military in order to expand their territories as existing landholdings become less productive. Segmentary systems also tend to raise armies of men to fight when the need arises but do not require a permanent force as much as do centralized systems.

Other 'secondary' factors may explain the choice of centralized or segmentary systems aside from the limits imposed by ecological conditions. Lewis (1966), in his study of origin of African kingdoms, identifies two major factors that contribute to centralized governance. The first factor is rooted in secession and the conflicting interest of subgroups within centralized systems. Leaders of emergent factions comprising a centralized tribe may decide to create their own independent states. They would typically defy the tribal supreme leader and organize armies to fight the central force dispatched to quell their dissent. If they successfully defeat the central army, they may subsequently set up a government and develop a centralized system capable of withstanding the reunification efforts of the supreme leader. In many cases, the breakaway factions would have to relocate from the tribal area into entirely new territories. This process has given rise to centralized governance systems among the Toro, Ngoni, Soga, Haya, Nyamwezi and Sukuma tribes of Africa. The second factor that is also related to the first is that tribes that are subject to control by another centralized tribe, including the payment of tribute, may develop their own centralized organization in order to withstand attacks of the monarchy. Lewis suggests that the Nupe and Mossi tribes are likely to have developed through this process.

The causal link between tribal governance and population density remains tenuous. Fortes and Evans-Pritchard (1940) argue that high population density is not a condition for centralized governance. They (1940, p.7) conclude that '[t]here may be some relation between the degree of political development and the size of population, but it would be incorrect to suppose that governmental institutions are found in those societies with greatest density'. Stevenson (1968, p.232) examines seven African societies and finds 'a pronounced general conjunction between state formation and higher population density'. In a later study, Vengroff (1976) is unable to establish a correlation between population density and centralization of governance. Using a different classification of governments, what he finds is that the size of state tends to increase with population density only among societies that have well-developed agricultural systems capable of producing a surplus. However, this conditional correlation is amenable to several interpretations. It could be that high population density creates the need for centralized tribal systems. On the other hand, centralized systems could offer better protection to their members and their means of livelihood. As a result, they are likely to experience lower mortality rates than segmentary tribes that are repeatedly decimated by conflicts. In essence, causality may well go in both directions – population density to centralization and centralization to population growth. Uncertainty about the direction of causality notwithstanding, it is evident that greater population density involves more interactions amongst the people, more exchange, and more collective action problems that demand a central authority. Furthermore, increases in population density are likely to influence the structure of property rights and, hence, the rules governing voluntary exchanges.

In short, we are able to rationalize the existence of different tribal systems using simple principles of economics. Here we see an interaction between property rights, the nature of production, population density and political systems. Systems of production requiring clear definition and protection of property rights call for more structured governmental institutions. Individuals are willing to be taxed and subjected to coercion by a central authority so as to maximize their net gains from production. In addition, greater population density associates with a wider array of collective action failures and more transaction-intensive exchanges. All of these factors increase the demand for central authority.

2.2 Centralized Systems

Centralized tribal systems have two defining characteristics: (1) there is a clear distinction between the political sphere and the lineage and kinship sphere, and (2) political positions are autonomous as leaders are endowed with authority over exclusive jurisdictions (Eisenstadt 1959). Whereas the lineage is the basic unit of social organization, the village is the basic unit of political organization, including the administrative, legislative and judicial functions of government. Depending on its size, a village can be a confluence of lineages or possibly clans of competing and sometimes conflicting interests. The village chief (or head man in some systems) either ascends to the position by inheritance or is selected from among the clan heads. An exception to this rule occurs where clans are coterminous with villages, in which case the corporate kinship and political systems coincide (Gluckman et al. 1949) and the clan head becomes the village chief. In the centralized hierarchy, the village head is the lowest-ranking official in the political system. Although labels may vary slightly, a group of villages constitute a ward and a grouping of wards constitutes a district of the tribal area. Political authority is centralized in the tribal king, the supreme head of the tribe. District chiefs derive authority over their jurisdiction from the king, and they in turn delegate authority to ward chiefs down the hierarchy until it reaches the village level. In most cases, in conformity with natural expectation, the district or regional chiefs who are the immediate subordinates of the king are chosen by the king or members of the king's clan. Generally, at every level of jurisdiction, the chief serves as representative of the central authority, and at the same time as the representative of the people in relation to the central authority.

Centralization of political authority in the king,[4] and by extension the chiefs, does not imply the absence of checks and balances. In making important decisions, all chiefs consult tribal councils composed of the adult members representing the groups located in their jurisdictions. For instance, the village council includes an elder or another adult chosen from each domestic group and is responsible for the collection of taxes, levies and fines, jury duties, law enforcement, intra-village dispute resolution, maintenance of village infrastructure, management of village resources and sustenance of village solidarity. A village chief is simply the head of the council. Misconduct on his part may result in secession by aggrieved subsets of the village; a successful secession is a strong signal to higher authority of rejection of the chief's leadership. As the king is the only tribal leader who does not rise to power by choice, a council of kingmakers (or king's council) is responsible both for selecting the king and acting as counterweights to his authority. Fortes and Evans-Pritchard (1940, p.11), writing generally about central and southern African tribes, observes that:

> The forces that maintain the supremacy of the paramount ruler are opposed by the forces that act as a check on his powers. Institutions such as the regimental organization of the Zulu, the genealogical restriction of succession to kingship or chiefship, the appointment by the king of his kinsmen to regional chiefships, and the mystical sanctions of his office all reinforce the power of central authority. But they are counterbalanced by other institutions, like the king's council, sacerdotal officials who have a decisive voice in the king's investiture, queen mothers' courts, and so forth, which work for the protection of law and custom and the control of centralized power. . . . If a king abuses his power, subordinate chiefs are liable to secede or to lead a revolt against him. If a subordinate chief seems to be getting too powerful and independent, the central authority will be supported by other subordinate chiefs in suppressing him.

Central political systems are organized on the basis of a form of reciprocity – a set of rights and obligations existing between the leaders and the subjects. The king and his advisers employ sanctions to maintain internal social order and organized military forces to defend the tribe against external aggression and advance tribal interests. In exchange for these public goods, subjects pay levies and contribute to welfare of tribal chiefs. Fortes and Evans-Pritchard (1940, p.12) note that 'A chief or a king has the right to exact tax, tribute, and labour service from his subjects; he has the corresponding obligation to dispense justice to them, to ensure their protection from enemies and to safeguard their general welfare by ritual acts and observances'. This reciprocal structure of duties and rights represent the fundamental pillars of government by consent.

Given the structure of central tribal governance, except in instances of misconduct on the part of the chief as a result of which subgroups of the village may secede, the village council is empowered to limit defections from normative behavior. Members of a village group have no incentive for instigating internal conflicts because doing so diminishes village solidarity. Conflicts between members of a lineage are adjudicated by the lineage head, whereas conflicts involving members of different lineages are settled by the village chief in consultation with his council, which acts as the jury. Sometimes evidence in a quarrel may be unclear and judges are unable to reach a conclusion. In that case, they resort to an oath or ordeal, a process whereby parties to the conflict invoke spiritual punishments upon themselves in the event that they misrepresented facts in defense of wrongdoing. The decision to apply a sanction to an offense rests with the chief. Individuals and families who wish to appeal the judgment of the village chief would approach the ward council and, ultimately, appeals of decisions of the district council would be referred to the central tribal council. Inter-tribal disputes are, however, very difficult to settle; they often lead to inter-tribal warfare. When possible, such conflicts are adjudicated by an inter-tribal council comprised of leaders from the tribes involved. Other tribal kings within the ethnic group are involved when necessary.

2.3 Segmentary Systems

Segmentary or 'stateless' systems are notable for their egalitarian principles and lack of distinction between social and political organization. The segmentary lineage functions as both the basic unit of social organization and the basic political unit. There is no administrative territorial unit that functions like centralized systems' villages; rather, territorial units are local communities defined by particular sets of genealogical ties. There are no definite political officers at the community level. Individuals who emerge as community leaders are those who are generous in hosting feasts and in sharing accumulated surplus production with community members. Despite his designation, however, the leader does not have any judicial authority over the community and does not have the backing of an organized force as is the case in centralized tribal systems. The community head can persuade members to act in certain ways, but cannot enforce any rule or coerce them to do anything. When there is a dispute, he can act as a mediator, but cannot enforce any particular settlement. In addition, there is no higher-level tribal political office beyond the community level. In the absence of territorial government, inter-segment relations are the main stabilizing factor and, in particular, are the means of settling conflicts. Describing one of the stable segmentary systems, Carneiro (2000) notes that, among the Kayapo Indian tribe, opposing groups bury each other's dead as a means of creating interdependency that helps bind together the members of the community. Communities or segments resort to self-help or form quick alliances with other segments in order to defend themselves against aggressors.

In the absence of designated political officers, decisions of importance to the segment are made through participation of the entire community and are reached by consensus. Glatzer (2002), writing about the Pashtun segmentary tribal system of Afghanistan, notes that decisions of importance for the whole community are reached at community councils even when influential persons have emerged as community leaders. Describing the decision-making process, he notes that 'according to the tribal ideal of equality, every free and experienced male person of the tribe has the right to attend, to speak and to decide' (ibid., p. 273). Tribal leadership in these societies, often coincident with emergence of charismatic and influential individuals who can convert surplus into prestige, is highly unstable. To remain in positions of tribal leadership, prospective candidates must repeatedly 'convince their followers and adversaries of their superior personal qualities and have to procure and redistribute resources from outside the tribal realm' (ibid., p. 274). Segmentary tribes are also sometimes organized into clans within which political leadership exists, but there is no tribal authority that supersedes clan authority in those cases.

The community council is the jury in the case of intra-community conflict, and cases are resolved purely on the basis of public sentiments generated through public participation. Decisions reached at the community council in segmentary systems are binding and not open to appeal. Subgroups of the community that are dissatisfied with the sanction are likely to break from the community and either establish a new community or join other communities. There are no permanent alliances. Inter-lineage or inter-segment conflict settlements are less efficacious as success depends on existing inter-segment ties. The possibility of a quick resolution of inter-tribal feud is more remote in segmentary systems than in centralized systems and even within tribes inter-group conflicts are generally more likely to result in warfare. In summary, Fortes and Evans-Pritchard (1940) note that lineage segments in segmentary systems are constantly at war with one another.

2.4 Voting and Representation

Decision-making processes in segmentary tribal systems are visibly democratic. However, the absence of direct elections as in today's democracies may lead us wrongly to infer that centralized tribal systems are necessarily dictatorial. To the contrary, citizens express their preferences and act as restraints on the rulers in two ways. First, segments of the tribe can trigger the exit option. In fact, our reading and accounts provide much good evidence of 'voting with the feet', thereby making dictatorial leadership unsustainable. Although the rulers have the right to tax, and thus we can assume that they seek to maximize revenues just as those in modern systems do, excessive extraction from the citizens would be detrimental to the survival of the regime. Ayittey (1988, p. 5) gives an example of the serious consequences flowing from tribal governments imposing excessive controls on economic activities:

> On occasion, there were attempts to control all aspects of commerce. The results were disastrous. In the late 18th century in the kingdom of Dahomey, for example, state regulations and controls were so pervasive that every palm tree, goat and pig was counted and taxed. Each village chief had to report the number of pigs slaughtered, while the butcher's guild had to keep all the skulls of pigs sold in the market. Both reports went to the King, who sent out market inspectors to make periodic checks and to fix prices.
> Food crops were similarly controlled. Products like honey, red and black pepper and ginger were declared royal monopolies and produced in restricted areas under supervision. Dahomey was the most centrally planned economy in West Africa with taxation taking an estimated one-third of the annual production. After some forty years under this system, so many subjects had fled to neighboring territory administered by the French that the Kingdom collapsed under the weight of its own regulation and taxes.

Thus, motivated by the desire to extend their tenures in office, tribal rulers must necessarily take into account the interests of their constituents. Second, citizens are able to exert themselves through 'protest votes', which take the form of referendums on the ruler's performance. A protest vote against a ruler is ultimately a rejection of his authority and a vote for his removal by a superior authority as no ruler is given immunity from prosecution and removal. Although most of the chieftaincies are hereditary, a tribal leader can be dethroned if found to have been wrongly installed or to have earned the disapproval of his subjects, perhaps as a result of crime or misconduct. It is reported among the Buganda of Uganda that local chiefs were appointed by the Kabaka (King) or other high-level traditional authorities and could be abruptly dismissed on account of poor performance. Lewis (1965), writing about tribes of West Africa, notes that indigenous chiefs have always been subject to democratic checks and balances, including the possibility of being overthrown. Citing a specific example, he revealed that during colonial times, 'British Governors complained especially of the Ghanaians, that they were too fond of destooling [overthrowing] their chiefs' (ibid., p. 19). It is reported among the

Ngoni tribe of the Bantu family that villagers are fond of killing their chiefs on account of misrule. In other centralized systems, such as the Yoruba, rulers who abuse their power and authority are exiled and forced to commit suicide (Samuel and Joshua 2010). Tribal leaders are made to swear ritual oaths upon allegation of misdeed. The consequences of misconduct typically range from mysterious sickness to leprosy and death. The most extreme form of protest vote takes place when women strip themselves naked and gather at the residence of the ruler. No ruler remains in office after such an incident. We will show in subsequent sections of this chapter how colonization and post-colonial modern governance systems have subverted these voting rights and have created governments that are not subject to existing checks and balances. We argue that this is the most pressing problem of contemporary governance in Africa and other tribal areas.

3 COLLECTIVE ACTION AND PUBLIC GOODS

Reading from Olson (1965), two problems central to collective action are clearly relevant under tribal systems. The first problem ('free-riding') is that individual interests or preferences may diverge in a large group and this leads to the possibility that not all members will act to achieve a goal that is welfare-improving for the entire group. The second problem, conditional on the first, is the absence of coercion or other special device (selective incentives) to make individuals act in the common interest. Some of the public goods that tribal systems provide – internal order, social protection and dynastic perpetuation, territorial expansion and defense – are basic goods that governments provide in modern states. We discuss next how tribal systems are organized for these functions.

3.1 Internal Order

In all tribal systems, lineage groups serve as the primary units of organization in providing public goods. Joint childrearing and extensive socialization in lineage spheres facilitate the teaching and enforcement of social norms of tribal behavior. Tribal laws and customs are upheld by collective sanctions that are administered in ways that give each domestic group (lineage) strong incentives to control the behavior of its members. Heckathorn (1988, p. 536) provides various accounts of the instrumentality of collective sanctions in tribal societies:

> An explicit system of collective sanctions (CS) exists as a prominent feature of traditional societies wherein kinship governs relations among persons. As Barkun (1968, p. 20) observes, 'Primitive law has long been known to be weak in concepts of individual responsibility. A law-breaking individual transforms his group into a law-breaking group, for in his dealings with others he never stands alone.' For example, according to Karsden (1967, p. 311), among the Jibaros of eastern Ecuador, 'The members of the same family are regarded as, so to speak, organically coherent with each other, so that one part stands for all and all for one . . . . For the deed of one member the rest are held equally responsible.'

Despite the use and perhaps efficacy of these mechanisms at the lineage level, aggregation of lineages at the tribal level leads to the possibility that individuals or lineages may have interests that diverge from the interest of the overall group, and collective sanctions may fail. Heckathorn (1988) shows that normative sanctions may produce ambivalent effects; while the sanctions may provide groups with enhanced incentives to control their members, they also create the potential for groups becoming trapped in the deviant role and attacking the agent administering the sanctions. Centralized and segmentary tribal systems deal with these problems differently.

In centralized systems, the authority of tribal leaders to implement collective moral and penal sanctions against erring members on behalf of the tribe is backed by command of organized force. This is common knowledge to all members of the tribe, and satisfies the condition for a coercive enforcement mechanism. In particular, the threat of coercive sanction is fundamental to sustaining social order. Therefore, group identification, joint production of collective goods, common knowledge of group goals and empowerment of leaders to penalize deviation makes tribal groups analogous to private clubs that serve their members' interests (Buchanan 1965; Kimenyi 1998). On the other hand, segmentary systems have neither special tribal leaders nor organized forces that supply the necessary coercion. Instead, decisions to enforce sanctions are reached by community consensus. The larger the local community, the longer it takes to settle disputes and the more difficult it is to impose and enforce sanctions. When the community council is unable to rally all of its members for the achievement of common goals, lineage segments would splinter and new alliances will arise across groups and communities. Therefore, while the centralized systems solve collective action problems through coercion, segmentary systems do so through the formation of smaller groups and new alliances where preferences are more homogeneous (Olson 1965).

3.2 Social Protection and Dynastic Interests

As a result of dynastic interest in the long-term welfare of the lineage, members engage in joint production and consumption through collective labor supply on family farms. The practice of joint rearing of offspring enables lineages to share the cost of children, who in effect are not public goods only to their parents, but lineage (albeit imperfect) common goods.

The communal system of resource ownership in tribal societies guarantees all members of the tribe a measure of access to productive resources irrespective of whether the political system is centralized or segmentary. Tribes assert ownership over land and forest resources in their territories and distribute the resources among their members. Regarding the relationship between individual members and families on the one hand, and the lineage and tribal group on the other, Nkrumah (1967, p. 203) observes with respect to Africa that 'the basic organization of many African societies in different periods of history manifested a certain communalism . . . in which each saw his well-being in the welfare of the group'. Fortes and Evans-Pritchard (1940, p. 18) confirmed the phenomenon in their study of eight African tribes, writing that 'the welfare and security of his own family or his own clan, such matters are of daily, practical concern to every member of an African society'. Glatzer (2002) observed the same phenomenon among tribal groups in Afghanistan. He points out that 'localized tribes also own common and undivided property: pastures and forests which every member has equal right to use. When a member of a tribe defends the land of his tribe he defends his own security and future of his family' (ibid., p. 273). Children are trained and supported to promote lineage economic and political interests above anything else, thereby shaping individual preferences toward group objectives. Kimenyi (1998, p. 51) observes that '[b]ecause tribes are composed of people who . . . have preferences that are closely related on a variety of matters, decisions that are made by the tribal units are likely to be more representative of individual preferences than would result when many tribes are involved'. Individual compliance with lineage goals is facilitated by the monitoring advantages that arise normally from the intertwining of economic and personal relationships (Pollak 1985; Ostrom 1990). This information advantage lowers the transaction costs of local public good provision.

3.3 Territorial Expansion and Defense

Tribal systems develop regiments of men that are called up in times of war. Usually, the military organization is composed of units of males of the same age, referred to generally as 'age grades'. From early on, boys are brought into camps where they acquire skills in the use of weapons and military tactics. The difference between centralized and segmentary systems is that, in the former, the military is a permanent armed force that remains under the control of the king or chief, whereas in the latter, the term of military service is temporary; the army is called up only during periods of inter-group conflict. The permanence of military organization in centralized systems also implies that it can be used effectively for internal and external deterrence as well as for wars of conquest.

3.4 Voting Rules and Costs

There are two components of the cost associated with voting systems in Buchanan and Tullock's (1962) model. The first component, referred to as the external cost, decreases with the number of people whose agreement is required for collective action. The second component, the decision-time cost, increases along the same axis. The optimal voting rule is one that minimizes the sum of these costs. Following their model, it would seem that tribal voting rules would range from authoritarian rule where the supreme king orders his troops into action, to unanimous consent, where everyone's agreement is required. However, these represent the extremes; the optimal rule will depend on the nature of the issue at hand and the characteristics of the community. Nowhere is a tribal voting rule outrightly authoritarian or outrightly unanimous for two reasons. First, the presence of checks and balances, and the possibilities of voting with the feet and organizing protest votes preclude authoritarian rule in centralized systems. Although the king is supreme, his decisions are subject to opposition and rejection by the king's council and subordinate authorities. Second, cultivation of preferences and banding within segments implies that individuals may not agree with a king's choice but may not oppose the rule. In segmentary systems, the threats to survival of a very small homogeneous group can also be a deterrent to outright rejection of non-unanimous voting rules. This may lead to inconvenient compromise.

In principle, centralization and segmentation are themselves natural solutions to decision-time costs. We argued in a previous section that relative to segmentation, centralization makes it likely that a tribal group will be large. Given the preference-cultivating institutions inherent in tribal systems – the roles of elders, lineage joint production and socialization of children – the decision-time cost function can be approximated by a flat line. That is, the speed with which decisions are made would not essentially differ between a segmentary community and a centralized kingdom. The import therefore is that external costs of decision-making are going to be more important determinants of the size of government. Unanimity is possible only in small homogeneous communities where individual and kinship interests are less likely to conflict. In this setting, the external costs associated with collective decisions are minimized. On the other hand, the external costs associated with centralized decision-making are apt to be high in large commuities, given the necessity of harmonizing a more diverse set of interests. In general therefore, centralized tribal governments are likely to be larger in both size and scope than segmentary tribal governments as a result of this cost. Optimally, a country of 20 million people from a single family of tribes will require a smaller government than a country of similar size with 20 different tribes.

4 ELECTORAL SYSTEMS

Decentralized segmentary tribal systems are inherently democratic though unstable systems, which recognize individual rights to vote and protest. Candidates for leadership positions must possess distinguishing qualities and be able to form alliances across communities. In reference to the Pashtun tribes, Glatzer (2002) outlines the qualities that a leader must demonstrate, which include the abilities to: (1) control tenants, (2) attract many regular guests through lavish hospitality, (3) channel resources from the outside world to followers, (4) demonstrate superior rhetorical qualities and regularly render sound judgments in community councils, and (5) display strength through gallantry in war and conflict. In addition to these qualities, successful candidates must build strong alliances between splintered segments and command the loyalties of low-tiered quasi-political leaders. Individuals and groups compose interest groups once they establish common causes of concern, and garner support across segments. Evidently, the source of interest need not be familial interest; in actual sense familial interests are unlikely to succeed in influencing tribal decisions except when they relate to settlement of feuds between segments.

On the other hand, centralized systems are hybrids of gerontocracy and monarchy based largely on the loyalty of members to the ruling authority. However, members are allowed to vote with their feet and to organize protest votes. Leaders assume their positions either by inheritance or appointment by the supreme leader, the individual around whom tribal life is centered. In most cases, the office of the tribal king or supreme leader is retained by the ruling clan, and the king ascends to his position by right of inheritance. There is no standard process for designating a ruling clan, but in most tribes the clan descends from a tribal hero, or the eldest son of the tribal ancestor. The king is typically succeeded by a very close kinsman, usually his son. If a king has no son, he will be succeeded by his brother's son in patrilineal lineage systems. The king's successor is a sister's son when the system is matrilineal. In other instances, kingship rotates among lineages in the ruling clan. District or regional chiefs typically are appointed by the king and are likely to be members of his clan. At the village level, the chief or headman usually is one of the lineage heads, who customarily advances to the position on the basis of age. It is at the ward level – the level of aggregation between village and district when it exists – that selection of chiefs assumes the form of democracy. However, the common people are not the voters; rather village chiefs simply elect one person from among themselves. A tribe that is in minority in a local territory is overseen by a headman who judges disputes between members of his tribe and joins the territorial chief in adjudicating matters between members of the majority and minority tribes.

A tribal leader is primarily interested in maximizing his sphere of influence. To survive, he must vigorously pursue opportunities to promote the welfare of his group, his only support base. Two strategies are particularly important for extending the leader's tenure. First and foremost, he must expropriate resources from other groups, which he then distributes to his own group. Second, he must develop strong institutions for maintaining internal order. A tribal leader during whose tenure the group plunges into confusion and chaos almost certainly would be dethroned. Interest groups are generally organized along clan or lineage lines. Most of the objectives of family groups have to do with issues of justice or pressure for fairness in resource allocation. Larger groups naturally would like to – and often can – control more resources than smaller groups. Both small and large groups continue to exert pressure on local leaders and higher-level authorities up to the tribal level if need be.

5   TRANSITION TO MODERN STATES: COLONIAL RULE

Tribal societies were generally self-sufficient groups prior to the advent of colonial rule that brought substantial contact with the outside world. Surpluses were redistributed among members of the tribe and there were no serious interest group activities.

At the onset of colonial government, the method of colonial rule employed in most tribal societies depended largely on existing indigenous political structures. In general, centralized political systems were given greater recognition (and more power, at least nominally) by the colonial masters than were segmentary systems. This is partly because centralized political organizations were more visible than those of segmentary organizations. Colonial rulers adopted existing pyramidal political structures, dismantled and suspended the use of organized tribal military forces and replaced the king's authority with colonial authority backed by European (British, French, Belgian or German) guns. The primary effect of colonial intervention was to weaken the authority of the tribal king so that while on the surface maintaining the reciprocal system of rights and obligations between him and his subjects, '[h]e no longer rules in his own right, but as an agent of colonial government' (Fortes and Evans-Pritchard 1940, p. 15). Colonial governors elevated favored, perhaps compliant, individuals and gave them political authority outside of existing indigenous political systems. Inasmuch as the king understandably wanted to maintain his status, this system created tension between the king and the colonial administration at many junctures. Although owing to many idiosyncratic factors, there was a great deal of variation in the extent to which colonial rule weakened the authority of tribal kings, the weakening of their authority also meant a weakening of the mechanisms for organizing collective action (that is, self-governance) in those societies.

Colonial rule in segmentary systems was different but had more deleterious effects. In the absence of a permanent political system, the colonial government built administrative and political systems from scratch by appointing individuals as chiefs over newly formed administrative units. For the first time, the people were subjected to appointed chiefs who exercised authority over their jurisdictions with the backing of organized force. The appointed chiefs were responsible only to distant colonial governments and not to their subjects, as they were unelected; thus the colonizers created from whole cloth governments without popular consent. The indigenous system of collective action – community consensus – was destroyed and replaced by alien, top-down political decision-making backed by colonial force. Unlike in centralized systems, these local chiefs were not restrained by any checks and balances. As a result, they became tyrants and exploited their subjects for personal gain.

In the transition from colonial rule to self-governance, the success or failure of nation-states depended largely on the extent to which tribal systems sustained or rebuilt their indigenous collective choice apparatuses, or adapted the political institutions forced on them by colonial rule to allow ordinary citizens to exercise their natural checks and balances. Unfortunately, in creating the new nation-states of Africa and the Middle East, colonial administrators disrupted established kingdoms, tribal governments and inter-tribal councils. The colonizers, purposefully or out of ignorance, partitioned existing societies into colonies-cum-countries in ways that paid little attention to tribal and geographic heterogeneities. Many tribes were split across externally imposed and not necessarily optimal national boundaries; some countries artificially amalgamated tribes that were age-old enemies under the same central authority. Rebuilding a suitable (and agreed-to) collective choice process was therefore the main task faced by leaders of the newly independent nation-states.

6 TRANSITION TO MODERN STATES: POST-COLONIAL GOVERNMENTS

Colonial authorities handed over the affairs of the new nation-states to charismatic leaders, mostly those who led the struggles against colonial rule. Shortly after independence, those leaders lobbied forcefully for centralized or unitary governments based on arguments that concentrating political power was necessary to maintain social harmony in the presence of diverse tribal groups (Kimenyi 1998). As a result, for example, most post-colonial African states experienced brief periods of apparently peaceful centralized rule. However, instead of fulfilling the objective of unification, those first post-colonial governments descended into chaos. Without the support of colonial forces, political officials appointed by charismatic leaders were an affront to both centralized and segmentary tribal collective choice systems; it constituted a deliberate attempt to usurp the authority of tribal chiefs in the former and did not have a basis grounded in customary practices in the latter. Failing to integrate their native collective choice mechanisms in the emerging nation-states, tribal groups transformed themselves into special interest groups that competed for transfers from the central government. Concentration of power at the center implies that any tribal group that controls the central government also controls the levers of wealth transfer and thus is more able to redistribute resources to its own people at the expense of other groups. This tribally based, interest-group competition is the source of political chaos that engulfed many African states and paved the way for military rule.

Earlier studies of state performance identified ethnic diversity as the cause of state failure. Alesina et al. (1999) suggest that ethnic diversity engenders ethnic division and political competition, which erodes investment in public goods and leads to dismal economic performance. Easterly and Levine (1997) associate ethnic diversity with political instability and Banerjee and Pande (2007) laid the blame for the problem of political corruption on ethnic fractionalization. But new studies demonstrate that ethnic plurality is not the problem in itself; but rather what matters is the degree of compatibility between modern post-colonial governance systems and indigenous collective choice systems. Gennaioli and Rainer (2007) present historical and empirical evidence that demonstrate improved local accountability and public goods provision in centralized tribal areas compared to areas with segmentary pre-colonial political systems in African countries. They attribute their findings to the relatively strong system of checks and balances that is inherent in centralized systems as opposed to the unchecked tyrannical rule of the chiefs created by Europeans in segmentary tribal areas that became part of modern governance. Compared to native states ruled by kings that were brought under indirect rule, Iyer (2010) finds that areas of India where the British exercised direct rule and subverted indigenous collective choice systems during colonial rule have significantly lower levels of public goods – access to schools, health centers and roads – in the post-colonial period. The explanation is that areas subjected to indirect, external political authority experienced less disruption to their native collective choice systems than areas without tribal kings where the British imposed an alien system of governance.

Kimenyi (1998) argues that a federation of autonomous tribal or regional governments with a weak center will facilitate post-colonial tribal self-government by means of indigenous systems of collective action. Olson (1965) argues that efficient collective choice units are essentially small, homogeneous groups. In creating regional tribal governments, two important questions need to be answered: what is the efficient size of a regional tribal government, and how strong should the central government be? In respect of the first question, it follows logically from the foregoing analysis that whereas tribes are efficient units of collective action in centralized tribal systems they are not efficient units in segmentary tribal systems. Even were it feasible to create truly autonomous tribal governments, it is impractical to have as many as 300 regional governments in a country like Nigeria that is home to about the same number of tribes.[5] One potential solution commonly offered is to create ethnic regional governments popularly referred to as 'ethnic nationalities'. The problem here is that whereas tribes are efficient collective choice units in centralized systems, ethnic groups are not.[6] As to the second question, the practicable degree of federalism is constrained by resource endowment. Land had been declared as property of central governments in post-colonial states. As a result, the central government reserves the right to the proceeds of natural resources and controls regional governments through the power of the purse. Therefore, the possibilities of true federalism are quite remote in African countries.

7 IS STRONGMAN LEADERSHIP INEVITABLE?

The foregoing analysis may suggest that collective action problems in nation-states composed of diverse tribal groups are intractable. Given the diversity of preferences among groups and the near-impossibility of true tribal federalism, it is sometimes argued that pluralistic nation-states can prosper only under the leadership of strongmen. In theory, a strongman could provide the coercive, top-down authority required for organizing collective action in the presence of divergent tribal interests. But in practice, strongman governments are comparable to unitary and military governments that are often associated with oppression, ethnic cleansing, conflicts and regional wars. These considerations undermine the strongman argument.

We argue that the strongman idea is not the solution. Instead, a federation of autonomous tribal governments with a weak center is the most suitable political system for a small country that is home to few tribes with indigenous centralized political systems. Kimenyi (1998) has argued extensively in favor of such a system. After many years of infighting, Ethiopia decided in 1994 to embrace that recommendation by creating autonomous tribal governments under a federal system. On the other hand, a government of tribal coalitions would be suitable for a small country where tribal political systems are segmentary. Segmentary tribes lack any sort of strong regional political organization but separate themselves into alliances that constitute efficient units of collective action. The fluidity of alliances and the absence of permanent political structures provide a basis for this form of government.

Neither of the above systems is sufficient for a country with large numbers of tribes. On the one hand, there will be too many tribal or regional governments, for instance as many as 250 in the Democratic Republic of Congo. On the other hand, coalitions are unlikely to succeed when indigenous tribal groups are centralized because the factions would be more powerful than necessary and coalitions would be unsustainable. Repeated failures of coalitions have made the strongman approach more attractive from the viewpoint of foreign observers. Collective action problems are most acute in countries with large numbers of tribes having diverse institutions of indigenous collective choice. Efforts to impose 'one-size-fits-all' political processes are essentially designed to supplant native collective choice mechanisms for at least some groups – and are doomed to fail. A system that seems suitable is one that incorporates collective choice mechanisms at the grassroots level, and requires governance to be both federated and extensively decentralized. The system could require all candidates for national political office to begin electoral contests from the ward up to more aggregated sub-national levels until finally reaching the national level. However, three problems are immediately evident in this grassroots model. First, larger tribal groups will tend to win simple-majority-rule contests and minority tribes will regularly reject the outcomes, leading to wars of attrition. Second, national political positions would still be tribalized – the winner of nationwide contests still identify with particular tribal groups. Third, political parties would tend to be regional parties and no single party would be able to win a simple majority of the votes without committing electoral fraud.

8 AFRICAN KNOWN SUCCESS – BOTSWANA

Botswana has been hailed as a lone star on the African continent and has been classified as a middle-income country by the World Bank. 'There is almost complete agreement that Botswana achieved this spectacular growth performance because it managed to adopt good policies. The basic system of law and contract worked reasonably well' (Acemoglu et al. 2001b, pp. 2–3).

Historical evidence suggests that the country's success mainly can be attributed to its tribal collective choice mechanism. The dominant Tswana ethnic group, a family of eight tribes which constitutes about 80 percent of the country's population, is organized along the centralized political system. Each tribe is headed by a chief who rules his subjects through subordinate kinsmen and hereditary headmen at village and ward levels. General assemblies referred to as *kgotla* at the ward and tribal levels allow adult men of the respective jurisdiction to participate in matters of public interest. 'Matters of importance are discussed at a general meeting of the men in the ward; the opinions they express helping the headman to reach a decision' (Fortes and Evans-Pritchard 1940, p. 60). Although the popular assemblies were said to be common among Bantu tribes, such as the Nguni and Tsonga, they are reported to be especially more actively involved in public affairs among the Tswana.

The second factor that contributes to Botswana's success is the lesser extent to which colonial rule disrupted the tribal collective choice apparatus. British colonial interest in the Bechuanaland (home to the Tswana tribes) was limited to preventing the Germans and the Boers from expanding their hegemony. 'The Tswana tribes were amalgamated into the British empire mostly because of the strategic location of their territory, not because the territory was thought to be particularly valuable or attractive in itself' (Acemoglu et al. 2001b, p. 12). As a result, Botswana did not experience the subversion of native governance that other groups experienced at the hands of the British elsewhere in Africa. The British went further to incorporate traditional governance into the formal state system through the Chieftaincy Act of 1933, which established the House of Chiefs as a 15-member consultative house. The House is made up of eight Chiefs, one from each of the Tswana's tribes, designated as permanent members by right; four sub-chiefs elected from the four former Crown lands; and three specially elected members who need not have any tribal association. All of the members, with the exception of the tribal chiefs, hold their positions temporarily, subject to periodic elections. The Act guarantees the sovereignty of each of the tribes over their own territories. The House also serves as resolution mechanism when conflicts arise between the tribes. However, whereas the House was endowed with consultative powers only, in practice, the House had the authority to summon members of the government before it and, hence, exerts significant influence on the country's governance. Thus, British colonial laws incorporated the traditional system into Botswana's modern system of governance.

9 AFRICAN EMERGING SUCCESS – GHANA

Ghana is the next country that has been widely praised as an emerging stable democracy. The Ghanaians were not as fortunate, as their centralized indigenous collective choice apparatus was not given the Botswana treatment during colonial and much of the post-colonial period. Although multi-party elections began under colonial supervision in 1951, prior to independence in 1957, the country was declared a republic under a post-colonial unitary system of government in 1960. Under the unitary system, only the president, vice president and members of parliament are elected on a national ballot. In administering the country, the president, in consultation with the parliament, appoints executive officers at the regional level who act as his representatives. This governance structure created a situation wherein government influence and citizens' participation were limited to the metropolitan areas while tribal chiefs who were in most cases not aligned with the government controlled the remaining parts of the country. Successive governments, both civilian and military, have passed laws and decrees that sought to erode the influence of the chiefs on matters of resource allocation, inheritance and dispute settlements at local levels, but these attempts were always resisted by the tribal chiefs.

Interest in local participation in governance began with the enactment of the Provisional National Defense Council (PNDC) Law 208 of 1988 that provided the framework for extensive decentralization of government decision-making processes. The comprehensive policy that created local governments was enshrined in the 1992 Constitution of the Republic of Ghana. To complement existing national and regional administration levels, the constitution created District Assemblies, Urban, Zonal, Town and Area Councils, as well as Unit Committees that are localized administrative units. Elections to the local governments are conducted on a non-partisan basis and sponsored by the central government. These officials can be removed from the jurisdiction following a 'protest' vote. Whereas assemblymen are elected by popular vote, district and local executives are either nominated by the president or appointed by him. The president sends nominations for the position of district executives to the district assemblies who would vote to accept or reject. The same procedure applies to all sub-district administrative units. In effect, all regional, district and local executives serve as appointees of the president. They have no immunity from prosecution and can be removed at any time by the president on account of non-performance or abuse of privileges. This structure represents a rebirth of the pre-colonial centralized tribal system in a modern form. In addition to extensive decentralization of governance, the constitution created the National House of Chiefs and houses of chiefs in each region of the country. Each House of Chiefs serves as a consultative body to the government at the level of jurisdiction and is conferred with appellate jurisdiction on matters affecting their constituencies.

The resulting 'hybrid' governance system empowers citizens at the grassroots level to demand accountability from government and, in effect, restored the checks and balances that subjects were able to exercise under pre-colonial tribal systems.

10 CONCLUSION

The central problem of modern governance in tribal societies of Africa and other less developed areas of the globe is the detachment of modern electoral and governance models from the traditional institutions and cultural values of the subjects. Under tribal systems, effective checks and balances ensured that tribal leaders, whether appointed or elected, were accountable to their constituents. Tribal rulers lost their offices when constituents voted with their feet or organized protest votes. The imposition of artificial borders and disruption of tribal collective choice mechanisms during the colonial period supplanted those rights-based tribal economic and political institutions. The drawing of local and national borders diminished the right to vote with their feet; disaffected segments now have little or no room to break away from tyrannical leadership without crossing national, regional or provincial borders. Crossing those borders in modern times is simply an invitation to chaos. Compared to tribal systems, protest votes have lost their potency as the power to oust non-performing or corrupt leaders has been removed from indigenous constituents and transferred to alien institutions that are beyond the citizens' reach or to processes in which they cannot actively participate without travelling to some remote cities. Conflict between the modern government apparatus and the traditional rights-based institutions is the main cause of anarchy in those societies and remains the greatest challenge of modern government.

Modern state-building rests on incorporating elements of tribal systems into modern government. Most importantly, the rights of the people at the grassroots level to force the removal of non-performing or corrupt leaders needs to be restored as traditional principles are being incorporated. Those rights have been well preserved in Botswana, lost but now recovered in Ghana, and may be found again in Kenya. Other countries will need to find ways to recover theirs.

NOTES

1. In his study of the Akamba, Akikuyu and Athekara tribes of eastern Africa, Dundas (1915) concludes that the separation of the tribes from a common origin has probably been of sufficiently long duration to enable each one to develop a distinctive character.
2. Using appropriate nomenclature, we talk of tribes and ethnic groups. Ethnic groups are made up of tribes that emerge from a common ancestral origin. For example, the Yoruba of southwest Nigeria and the Republic of Benin constitute an ethnic group and are thought to have emerged from a common ancestor known as Oduduwa. Within the Yoruba are distinct tribes, such as the Ijebu, Egba-Awori, Oyo, Ekiti, speaking different languages but unified in terms of their systems of government and customs. Similarly, the Akans found in Ghana and Côte d'Ivoire is an ethnic group comprising the Ashanti, Fanti, Akwapim and other tribes who differ in some respects but practice a unifying custom.
3. In this chapter, we shall focus more on Africa. As it is also not possible to discuss all of the institutions in place there now or in the past, the discussion is more of a broad-brush review of the key features of tribal systems in general.
4. In some systems the supreme authority is titled Chief while his subordinates are also chiefs by title, but in effect are sub-chiefs.
5. In fact, tribal groups are persistently demanding their own states from the federal government. The country that started with three regional governments in 1960 already had 36 states by 1996. It is not clear how many states will still be created.
6. Evidence from various parts of the world shows that ethnic groups are not efficient units of governance. Nigeria is only one example. Inter-tribal conflicts, such as 'Operation Wetie' among the Yoruba ethnic group in the late 1950s, the Ife-Modakeke crisis of the early 2000s, also among the Yoruba group, intermittent intra-ethnic crises among the Hausa-Fulani ethnic group, as well as similar within-group conflicts support this point.

PART IV

PUBLIC CHOICE ANALYSES OF THE TOOLS OF GOVERNMENT

13 The politics of elections and congressional oversight
Russell S. Sobel and Adam Pellillo

1 INTRODUCTION

A key insight from economics is that individuals respond to the incentives they face. Public choice postulates that this logic applies not only to individuals in their private actions, but also in their actions as public sector employees or elected representatives. In both the private marketplace and in the public sector, the incentives individuals face are sometimes aligned with actions that are in the best interest of society, leading to efficient and socially beneficial outcomes. In other cases, however, certain incentives can lead individuals to pursue actions that are personally beneficial but socially unproductive and inefficient.

In this chapter, we examine two such cases where existing political incentives distort the behavior of public sector agents. In the first case, we assess how the behavior of decision-makers within public sector agencies is shaped by the process of congressional oversight (which is part of the literature on 'congressional dominance theory'), and in the second we discuss how the behavior of elected officials is shaped by the timing of elections.

2 THE POLITICAL ECONOMY OF OVERSIGHT

2.1 The Structure of Congressional Oversight Committees

Constitutionally, Congress is endowed with the authority to create, monitor and regulate government agencies.[1] Ideally, this would imply that congressional oversight committees and subcommittees would ensure accountability and transparency in the funding and operation of the federal bureaucracy. Yet the structure of congressional oversight also implies that members of Congress are presented with opportunities to influence, perhaps unduly, the management and policy-relevant decisions of the government agencies they oversee. Because oversight committees have the ability to reward or punish agencies through budgetary and other actions discussed below, decision-makers within these organizations have a clear incentive to try to please the individual members of Congress who serve on the committees that sponsor them. By implementing policies that benefit the constituents of congressional oversight committee members, thereby raising their reelection prospects, the agents within government bureaucracies may be able to maintain or increase the resources available to them, advance their own career goals and position themselves for high-paying jobs in the private sector after their public service ends.

As far as the structural organization of Congress is concerned, there are many

Table 13.1 Congressional committee breakdown

US Senate	US House of Representatives
Standing Congressional Committees	
Agriculture, Nutrition, and Forestry	Agriculture
Appropriations	Appropriations
Armed Services	Armed Services
Banking, Housing, and Urban Affairs	Budget
Budget	Education and Labor
Commerce, Science, and Transportation	Energy and Commerce
Energy and Public Works	Financial Services
Finance	Foreign Affairs
Foreign Relations	Homeland Security
Health, Education, Labor, and Pensions	House Administration
Homeland Security and Government Affairs	Judiciary
Judiciary	Natural Resources
Rules and Administration	Oversight and Government Reform
Small Business and Entrepreneurship	Rules
Veterans' Affairs	Science and Technology
	Small Business
	Standards of Official Conduct
	Transportation and Infrastructure
	Veterans' Affairs
	Ways and Means
Joint Congressional Committees	
Joint Committee on Printing	Joint Economic Committee
Joint Committee on Taxing	Joint Congressional Committee on Inaugural
Joint Committee on the Library	Ceremonies
Joint Economic Committee	Joint Committee on Taxation
Special, Select, and Other Congressional Committees	
Impeachment Trial Committee (Porteous)	House Permanent Select Committee on
Indian Affairs	Intelligence
Select Committee on Ethics	House Select Committee on Energy
Select Committee on Intelligence	Independence and Global Warming
Select Committee on Aging	

committees that oversee the activities of government agencies. Committees can be differentiated by the terms 'standing committees', 'subcommittees', 'joint committees', or 'conference committees'. There are also 'select committees' and 'special committees', all of which influence the bureaucratic implementation of public policy. The functions and forms of these committees vary between the US House of Representatives and the Senate; a listing of these committees is given in Table 13.1.

To carry out their responsibilities, members of congressional oversight committees typically draw on reports and analyses by the Congressional Budget Office (CBO), the Congressional Research Service (CRS), and the Government Accountability Office (GAO). Some agencies report to multiple oversight committees, and each committee is in charge of overseeing multiple agencies, a structure that often results in poor levels of inter-committee coordination. In addition, as noted by Vachris (1996), there can be a conflict of goals and incentives between the appropriations and oversight committees.

There are various roles congressional oversight committees are supposed to play in constraining agency behavior in the US government. Among others, these purposes include (1) ensuring that agencies comply with the intentions of Congress, (2) improving the efficiency and efficacy of government operations, (3) evaluating program performance, (4) constraining the authority of those within the agency, (5) investigating waste, abuse and fraud, (6) reviewing and determining budgetary appropriations, (7) ensuring that the public interest is fulfilled, and (8) protecting individual rights and liberties (for example, constraining abuses of authority).[2]

As highlighted in the works of Niskanen (1971, 2001) and others, bureaucrats typically seek to maximize their (discretionary) budgets and enhance their agency's power. Along with budget and power maximization objectives, bureaucrats also tend to seek out 'some balance of expected wealth, ideology, patronage, discretionary power, and ease of management' (Vachris 1996, p. 227). Thus, a fundamental purpose of congressional oversight committees is to check this growth in political power and spending by structuring and/ or limiting appropriations to government agencies. In this sense, congressional oversight committees are a first line of defense against growth in government as well as serving to keep within politically acceptable bounds the bureaucratic authority flowing from the chief executive.

The informational approach (see Krehbiel 1990, 1991) posits that the committee system in Congress is structured so as to allow for deep specialization of knowledge across different policy areas. Within this framework, congressional committees were designed at their onset to allow for a division of labor with respect to the expertise needed to oversee a diverse and ever-growing bureaucracy.[3] In theory, members of the US Congress would be optimally allocated to serve on the committees for which their expertise and knowledge were best suited *ex ante*. However, congressional oversight committee members typically try to self-select onto committee seats that are potentially most rewarding – either electorally or personally (see Shepsle 1978). Legislators typically want committee assignments that offer them the best chances for benefiting their constituents – and their own chances of reelection. Committees that address particular issues that are politically salient or serve as signals that those holding seats on them are working hard to tend to constituents' parochial interests (for example, by securing for them beneficial tax loopholes, regulatory treatment, or subsidies) are particularly attractive to individual members of Congress. According to Johnson (1992, p. 5), for instance, 'legislators from farming states want to be on the House or Senate Agricultural committees where they can protect the government programs so important to their constituents'. Over time, members eventually acquire knowledge and expertise and gain policy influence in particular committees that are important for their re-election (Weingast 1984).[4]

Weingast et al. (1981) illustrate how policies with geographically concentrated benefits and widely dispersed costs are sought out by members of Congress. Weingast and Marshall (1988) describe how the committee system facilitates vote trading (logrolling) among different legislators to secure enactment of policies and programs having the two aforementioned characteristics. Legislators, therefore, have strong incentives to lobby their party's congressional leadership for assignments to seats on committees that allow them to direct taxpayer-financed largesse to their districts or states. In turn, an agency can curry favor with its congressional overseers by altering its output in ways that selectively favor oversight committee members' constituents.

As with most political and economic behavior, the reasons for committee self-selection are likely more complex than can be explained by baseline models – the aims of any particular member of Congress surely are a mixture of electoral incentives, combined with individual preferences for opportunities to influence legislative outcomes in broader policy domains, such as national defense, social welfare or fiscal responsibility. Self-selection can be construed to be self-interested nonetheless; elected representatives seek to maximize their personal objective functions, but these objective functions can include multiple arguments (for example, office-holding motives and career objectives, such as aspirations for higher office, including congressional leadership positions; having influence over policies that comport with their own world views; supplying economic benefits to constituents other than those based on electoral incentives; concerns for reputations and legacies; advancing their own beliefs and ideologies, and so on).[5]

The committee selection or assignment process may be less a function of self-selection based on the preferences of individual members of Congress and more a function of political factors exogenous to him or her (see Frisch and Kelly 2006, p. 21). While legislators may want to self-select onto committees that advance their likelihoods of reelection, they are constrained by structural or informal aspects of congressional organization.[6]

There are some structural and informal congressional institutions that influence how legislators are assigned to different oversight committees and subcommittees. As noted by Shepsle (1975, p. 57), for instance, customary property rights operate in the US Congress:

> nonfreshmen, whenever feasible, may retain committee assignments held in the previous Congress if they wish. If a change is desired, however, a returning member may request a transfer to another (presumably more preferable) committee, in which case he voluntarily yields his property claim on his previously held committee slot; or he may request a dual assignment, in which case he retains his previously held slot and is given an additional assignment as well.[7]

Thus, in addition to self-selection, the seniority system influences committee membership and how political decision-making power is distributed across legislators (see Crain and Tollison 1977; Roberts 1990; Holcombe and Parker 1991). Given congressional specialization, a committee-based division of labor, and a seniority-based system of assigning committee seats, the 'industrial organization' of Congress has been the subject of its own strand of literature (see Weingast and Marshall 1988; Shepsle and Weingast 1994; Crain and Sullivan 1997). This literature emphasizes a 'politics of distribution that was not simple majority-rule voting but rather an on-going game of strategic interaction played in a context of both structural arrangements (committees, jurisdictions) and procedural routines (agenda setting, sequential voting, restrictive rules)' (Shepsle and Weingast 1994, p. 152).

In the rational choice vein of analysis, theories of the industrial organization of Congress lead to predictions that oversight committees systematically politicize government agencies under their scope of authority.

As Crain et al. (1985) discuss, an increase in the number of legislative committees could be associated with greater efficiency in management of government agencies given that legislative specialization might deepen. Yet, on the other hand, a larger number of legislative committees could lead to greater interest group activity since 'more committees allow legislators to mirror interest groups and their concerns better, and hence lead to more rather than less government' (ibid., p. 311).

In this sense, the structure of the congressional oversight system may have significant implications for the growth of government and for the distortion of tax, subsidy, and regulatory policy. Empirically, using data from US states, Crain et al. (1985) report a concave, non-linear relationship between the number of legislative committees and the number of government employees. In other words, as the number of committees per million population increases, the number of state employees per million population increases at a decreasing rate; it then eventually turns negative. This implies that more legislative specialization is likely to be associated with more government. As they conclude (ibid., p. 314), 'what appears to be happening . . . is that more specialized subgroups of legislators are conduits through which laws and programs that increase the size of government pass more easily.'

2.2 Agenda-setting

Oversight committee members typically are granted considerable agenda-setting powers since almost all legislation is forged within policy-relevant committees and subcommittees. Put succinctly, committees shape legislative outcomes. Such committee-based political authority is the result of the industrial organization of Congress (Weingast and Marshall 1988). Committees wield near-monopoly power in terms of influencing the policy process, including the ability to veto the proposals of other, nonmember legislators (Weingast 1984).

According to Munger (1988), the queue for committee decision-making power is structured as follows: the most senior member of the majority party typically becomes the chairperson and his or her policy positions are followed by subcommittee chairs, usually the least senior committee members of the same party affiliation; transfers of legislators from other congressional committees are next in line. Yet in some contexts, subcommittee chairs can exercise more influence than their more senior committee colleagues on the activities of agencies they oversee. For instance, Vachris (1996) argues that subcommittee chairs likely have the most agenda-setting power for antitrust matters. She reports evidence suggesting that Senate Judiciary and House Small Business subcommittee chairmen influence the level and mix of antitrust law enforcement activities (for example, merger enforcement). In alternative specifications, Vachris (1996) finds that the Senate and House Judiciary subcommittees (combined) influence antitrust activities, while in another specification she finds support only for House subcommittee chairs' joint influence on antitrust activities. On the other hand, the Senate Appropriations Subcommittee chair, along with the president, has the most impact on the budget of the Antitrust Division of the US Department of Justice. Thus, in this context, not only do subcommittee chairs shape the activities and budgetary resources available to the Department of Justice's Antitrust Division, that power is split between two different subcommittees. The chairs of congressional oversight committees and subcommittees are 'gatekeepers', endowed with exceptional political authority to determine congressional policy, much more so than rank-and-file representatives and senators (see also Thomas and Grofman 1992).

Other committee members, who possess expertise, experience, or aptitude in particular policy arenas, may also drive legislative outcomes. Such specialization can be construed as accumulated legislative human capital and such legislator-specific knowledge can lead to significant agenda-setting power within the congressional oversight process. Saving's (1997) model illustrates why outcomes that deviate from the preferences of the chamber's median voter may result from the powers of oversight committees and their specialized 'human capital'. Citing empirical studies, Saving (1997) concludes that the human capital advantages of oversight committee members may have a more significant influence on legislative outcomes than mere 'committee power'.

Barriers to entry can also confer significant agenda-setting power given its institutionalization by the congressional committee system.[8] According to Holcombe and Parker (1991, p. 14), 'the [committee] system benefits . . . individual committee members because while they give up non-exclusive access to a large portion of the agenda, they gain exclusive control over a limited part'.

Senior members of Congress typically exercise more decision-making power than freshman and non-senior legislators. Coker and Crain (1994) view the congressional committee system as an institution for generating loyalty to the congressional leadership. As they put it 'the preferences of congressional leaders disproportionately influence the fate of legislation' (ibid., p. 196). Seniority can help allocate committee assignments and while particular committee assignments have become more accessible, junior members of Congress have traditionally had to 'prove themselves on lesser committees before being tapped for service on Appropriations, Finance, or Foreign Relations' (Bullock 1985, p. 792). Legislators seeking promotion to seats on more important committees are required to 'make their bones' by voting in ways consistent with the policy preferences of their party's leadership. They otherwise will be mired on committees overseeing the US Postal Service and agencies of less salience to their electoral aspirations. As estimated by Stewart and Groseclose (1999a, 1999b), committee membership is more valuable in the Senate than in the House and, moreover, seats on the Senate's Finance, Appropriations, and Foreign Relations committees were valued most highly during the 81st and 102nd Congresses. On the other hand, assignment to the committees on Governmental Affairs, Environment and Public Works, and the District of Columbia (a committee created between the 80th and 95th Congresses) was ranked at the bottom. Stewart and Groseclose (1999a) find that the House Ways and Means, Appropriations, and Rules committees were ranked highest in that chamber, while Government Operations, Veterans Affairs, and Small Business (that is, a so-called burden committee) committees were ranked lowest.

The distribution of political power seems to result from the influence of congressional leaders in the committee appointment process or from that of the individual legislators who previously have been appointed to committees and subcommittees. Empirically, Coker and Crain (1994) find that loyalty is positively associated with measures of committee importance; Bullock (1985) finds that seniority is strongly associated with the likelihood of having committee assignment requests granted.

As a testament to the agenda-setting and distributive powers afforded to senior legislators and committee members, Roberts (1990) employs an event study methodology to illustrate how the death in 1983 of Senator Henry 'Scoop' Jackson, the ranking Democrat on the Senate Armed Services Committee from the State of Washington (also referred to by some as the 'Senator from Boeing'[9]), led to significant, state-specific changes in stock market returns. The market values of firms with large manufacturing plants in Washington State (Jackson's constituents) declined after Jackson's death, while those in the state of the next highest ranking member on the Senate Armed Services Committee, Sam Nunn (Georgia), experienced increases in share values.[10] This empirical finding suggests that seniority plays a pivotal role in the allocation of federal spending to constituents. In this sense, the distributive politics framework of Weingast et al. (1981) is embedded in the informal rules and norms regarding seniority and political power in Congress.

The power and influence of oversight committee members are also witnessed in the literature on campaign finance. Munger (1989), for example, finds that contributions by corporate political action committees (PACs) to legislators are significantly influenced by committee assignments. Further, Fleisher (1993) finds that PAC contributions from defense contractors have a positive effect on defense votes in the US House of Representatives. However, the magnitude of this effect is rather small, and those members with weaker ideological stances tend to be more responsive to the impact of PAC contributions from defense contractors.

In sum, there is a significant amount of variation in agenda setting power across committees. As described by Crain and Sullivan (1997, p. 272), 'the degree of monopoly control and policy specialization varies across standing committees in the U.S. Congress. Some committees have wide jurisdictions and attract members with diverse policy preferences. Jurisdictional overlap and resulting turf battles are common aspects of congressional sessions'.

2.3 Congressional Dominance Theory

The 'congressional dominance theory' posits that the members of congressional committees heavily influence the decisions and operations of government agencies (Weingast and Moran 1983; Weingast 1984). Congressional oversight committees are in a position to shape the set of incentives and constraints faced by the managers of government bureaus (for example, through the appointment and appropriations process, along with their powers to craft the language of reauthorization bills and to hold investigative hearings). Congressional dominance theory then predicts that the bureaucratic behavior these incentives and constraints induce would at least in part be consistent with the overarching objectives of the elected representatives who sit on oversight (sub)committees, namely, re-election. In contrast to Niskanen's (1971, 2001) model of bureaucracy, which suggests that agency heads exploit their informational advantage over the legislature in policy-specific areas in order to maximize their bureaus' (discretionary) budgets, the congressional dominance theory says that Congress in general and oversight committee members in particular use their positions of political power to see that bureaus operate in ways that enhance electoral support from constituents.

The influence of oversight committees on the policies and activities of government agencies may not always be visible. Government agency officials independently (and self-interestedly) may change their behavior or internal resource allocations in order to increase (or decrease) the re-election prospects of particular congressional oversight committee members.

The congressional dominance model has not gone unchallenged. Vachris (1996, p. 225), for instance, claims that 'the single principal–agent relationship between Congress and the bureaucracy is not a reflection of institutional reality in the United States'. There are multiple political actors involved in the formation of policy (that is, legislative committees but also interest groups, such as trade unions and corporate lobbies, other public officials in the executive branch, including the president, and even other legislative committees). It is thus uncertain whether the members of a single congressional oversight committee play decisive roles in influencing the activities of government agencies. Further, all agency budget requests must pass muster by the House Committee on Ways and Means and the Senate's Finance Committee. The influence of one congressional oversight committee on bureaucratic behavior may be attenuated by bicameralism and by the structure of the two chambers' committee systems. Then again, Niskanen (2001, p. 267) argues that 'In the American political system . . . the bureau and the specialized committee effectively collude to set the budget agenda, with the executive and the body of the legislature as nearby passive sponsors'. He concludes that 'Barry Weingast was correct to assert the dominance of the legislature in the American political system, but the committees, in effective collusion with the bureaus, are the groups that exercise this power' (Niskanen 2001, p. 267; on multiple-principal, multiple-agent models of bureaucracy, see Chang et al. 2001).

As McCubbins and Schwartz (1984) note, some scholars charge that Congress is *too lax* in influencing the activities of the agencies it oversees. The charge of lax oversight is based on the apparent infrequency of public, full-dress reviews of bureaucratic actions. McCubbins and Schwartz (1984) suggest that there are two forms of congressional oversight: 'police-patrols' (for example, sunset reviews and the commissioning of scientific studies) and 'fire-alarms' (for example, public hearings, congressional investigations, and so on); they then model the choice between these two forms of congressional oversight. A key motivational assumption on the part of McCubbins and Schwartz (1984) is that members of Congress seek to maximize the credit they receive for the benefits delivered to constituents and electorally important special-interest groups. They argue that this motivational assumption implies that legislators will prefer to engage in fire-alarm oversight rather than police-patrol oversight because of the benefits this form of congressional oversight generates. As a poignant example, consider the 2010 Deepwater Horizon disaster in the Gulf of Mexico. In this case, legislators on congressional oversight committees (for example, House Committee on Natural Resources, House Committee on Energy and Commerce, and Senate Committee on Environment & Public Works) quickly called for public hearings and investigations, shifting from weak 'police-patrol' oversight prior to the oil spill to 'fire-alarm' oversight and investigation of the disaster.

A more integrated version of a congressional dominance model would specify that the decision-making processes of government agencies are inextricably linked to oversight committees, but that the relative influence of oversight committees depends on political and institutional circumstances: both likely influence one another to some degree, depending on the particular agency and oversight committee (or subcommittee).

Moe (1987) discusses how the relative influence on government agencies of different political actors (for example, legislative oversight committees, courts, interest groups, presidents, and the government agencies themselves) needs to be better understood.[11] While legislative oversight committees may influence bureaucratic behavior, the activities within the bureaucracies themselves (for example, internal reorganizations or changes in budgetary allocations) must be studied and controlled for when analyzing the relative political influence of legislative oversight committees. Agency decision making may be more of a bureaucratic imperative than a congressional-electoral one, consistent with Moe (1997, p. 466), who concludes that Congress may have difficulty in controlling the bureaucracy and that the bureaucracy may have a large degree of autonomy or insulation from congressional pressure.

2.4 Evidence for Congressional Dominance Theory

Despite the criticisms of the strict congressional dominance theory, there is by now a wealth of empirical evidence supporting the idea that the behavior of public sector agencies is shaped by the structure and membership of oversight committees. Young et al. (2001) find that the audit rate of personal income tax returns by the Internal Revenue Service (IRS) is significantly lower in districts that have representation on IRS oversight committees, such as the House Ways and Means Committee, the House Small Business Committee, and the Senate Finance Committee. Using individual income tax returns from 1992 to 1997 and ordinary least squares regressions, their empirical findings suggest that IRS agents conducted relatively fewer audits in the districts of congressional oversight committee members.

In their study of Federal Emergency Management Agency (FEMA) disaster expenditures, Garrett and Sobel (2003) find that states with congressional representation on committees overseeing FEMA received disproportionally larger disaster-relief funds than their peers after controlling for disaster severity. For each additional member on a House FEMA oversight committee, a state receives around $31 million in additional disaster expenditures relative to what would have been allocated for a similar disaster in another impact area.[12]

Politicization of agency spending by congressional oversight committees has a long history. Anderson and Tollison (1991), for example, document that New Deal spending across states during the Great Depression was influenced by the tenure of representatives and senators in the appropriations process.[13] As they conclude, 'New Deal spending went partly to the needy and partly to those with political clout' (ibid., p. 175). More recently, Alvarez and Saving (1997) find empirical support for the hypothesis that political factors in congressional committees influence the allocation of federal spending across different districts. Specifically, they find that new outlays were allocated to more liberal districts, went to Democratic members, and went to members of 'prestige and constituency committees.' Alvarez and Saving (1997) also find that pork-barreling even affects formulaic spending, since the formulae are composed by particular legislators that benefit from the allocation of funds to their district. They conclude that the 'pork barrel is alive and well, even after many changes to the process of budgeting in recent years'.

Scholars have pointed to political aspects of spending on national security to counter terrorist attacks (Coats et al. 2006) and for national defense in general. Carsey and Rundquist (1999) estimate simultaneous equations to find a reciprocal relationship between per capita defense contract awards and representation on a House defense committee (though they do not find evidence for such a relationship in the Senate). They argue that 'defense committee representation in the House appears tied both to the protection of existing benefits in a state and to the allocation of additional benefits' (ibid., p. 459). Their findings suggest that 'there is a significant relationship between constituency interest and committee representation, but there is also a significant relationship between committee representation and the targeting of distributive benefits' (ibid., p. 462).

Evidence supporting the congressional dominance theory in the setting of trade policies implemented by the International Trade Commission (ITC) is less clear. As reported by De Vault (2002), some studies have found significant results while others have not. Studies generally supporting the theory in this context include Butler (1995), Hansen (1990), and Hansen and Prusa (1996, 1997), while Moore (1992) finds mixed results; others find no influence, including Anderson (1993), De Vault (1993) and Goldstein and Lenway (1989). De Vault (2002) posits three channels through which legislators can influence the policy behavior of the International Trade Commission (ITC): budgetary oversight, legislative oversight, and commissioner appointments. Yet he does not find empirical support for the congressional dominance theory in the context of trade policy. He argues that 'Congress has chosen to influence ITC decisions indirectly through appointments and legislation because this approach produces a given amount of protection at a lower cost than the more direct case-by-case approach' (ibid., p. 20). Statutory language ultimately is more important, De Vault concludes.

3 POLITICAL INFLUENCE AND ELECTIONS

Elections are the primary channel through which citizens can in principle hold elected officials accountable for their actions. Elections therefore clearly shape the behavior of political agents. Indeed, securing re-election is widely accepted in the public choice literature as politicians' main objective. In a world of rationally ignorant voters, politicians must invest considerable effort in delivering readily verifiable benefits to their constituents (while avoiding easily verifiable costs); this incentive is heightened before Election Day. In order to maximize electoral support, political actors may seek to increase expenditures in electorally important states and localities or to implement programs that benefit their constituents narrowly. This process influences not only the behavior of elected officials but also feeds through to the agencies and bureaus they oversee.

The vote motive and its distortionary influence on public policy are less likely to be salient when politicians are 'electorally safe', in a sense. Those politicians who face the prospect of a tightly contested race may feel extra pressure to seek out programs or policies that benefit their constituents directly or associate their names with specific federally funded projects. Thus, in the empirical literature that examines how the behavior of politicians changes around election time, the 'closeness' of the election is often taken into account. For politicians who run for office across multiple geographic areas (such as the president), an additional implication is that they should target their efforts toward the 'battleground' states. After all, there is not much use wasting effort in an area that will vote heavily for the opponent regardless of what is done, or similarly in wasting additional effort in an area already strongly in the incumbent's camp. Thus, even though a state like New York carries a lot of electoral votes, if it always goes for the Democratic Party's presidential candidate, both candidates will find it best to focus their attention on other, more closely contested states. Thus, empirical models attempting to test for the influence of presidential politics generally include a single variable that tries to weight both the number of electoral votes and the expected closeness of the race.[14]

Two of the empirical studies reviewed in the earlier discussion of congressional oversight also attempt to identify election year distortions in the behavior of agencies. Young et al. (2001, p. 217), in their analysis of the political influence on IRS audit rates, conclude that 'in every year of the sample, audit rates were significantly lower in electoral-vote rich states where presidential contests have historically been 'close''.[15] In the analysis of political influences on FEMA disaster policy, Garrett and Sobel (2003) find that states relatively more electorally important to the president have a greater likelihood of being declared a federal disaster area than otherwise. Unlike the case of IRS audits, where the congressional oversight pathway is more indirect, in the case of FEMA disaster policy it is the president who makes the final decision on whether or not a particular weather incident is officially declared to be a disaster (and is therefore eligible for FEMA relief). Additionally, Garrett and Sobel (2003) find that significantly more disasters were declared during election years than in non-election years. In their follow-up study on FEMA, Sobel et al. (2007) find that this spike in disasters in presidential re-election years continues even after FEMA's post-9/11 reorganization.

Figure 13.1 from Sobel et al. (2007) shows the number of official disasters declared by the president, with darker bars indicating re-election years. For each of the four presidents included in their sample, a clear pattern emerges: presidents declare more disasters when they face re-election. Either re-election years coincidentally tend to be times of bad weather or, more likely, the president uses a more lenient standard for declaring disasters when his fate is soon to be decided by the voters.

As the above example illustrates, electoral incentives and the distortions they cause can be manifested in policies that would appear at first glimpse to be immune from political influence. Another case in which political factors have been posited to shape presidential policies is the decision to initiate foreign conflict. Hess and Orphanides (1995) find that foreign conflicts are more likely during recessions and when a president is serving his first term in office than otherwise. Why might this be the case? They construct a model predicting that wars may occur – even if they are potentially avoidable – if the domestic economy is performing poorly. As they write, 'when the president cannot seek reelection or the economy is not in a recession, the probability of war initiation in a year is about 30 percent. By contrast, the probability significantly increases to over 60 percent when both the economy is doing poorly and the president is up for reelection' (ibid., p. 830). This diversionary theory of war implies that conflict may be initiated even if there is not a sensible policy reason for doing so – a significant distortion to policy making caused by electoral incentives. On a strict interpretation of the greater frequency of military conflict as being due to the electoral imperatives of first-term presidents, they estimate that 'well over half of the conflicts initiated or escalated by presidents seeking reelection during economic downturns were potentially avoidable' (ibid., p. 842).

To those inclined to have a more benevolent view of the actions of public sector agents, perhaps even more disturbing than IRS audits, FEMA disaster relief, and the initiation of war being politically manipulated, is the case of how elections influence outcomes in the legal arena. Kubik and Moran (2003), for example, find that there is a gubernatorial election cycle in state executions of convicted murderers. Their empirical results suggest that states have a 25 percent greater probability of executing inmates on

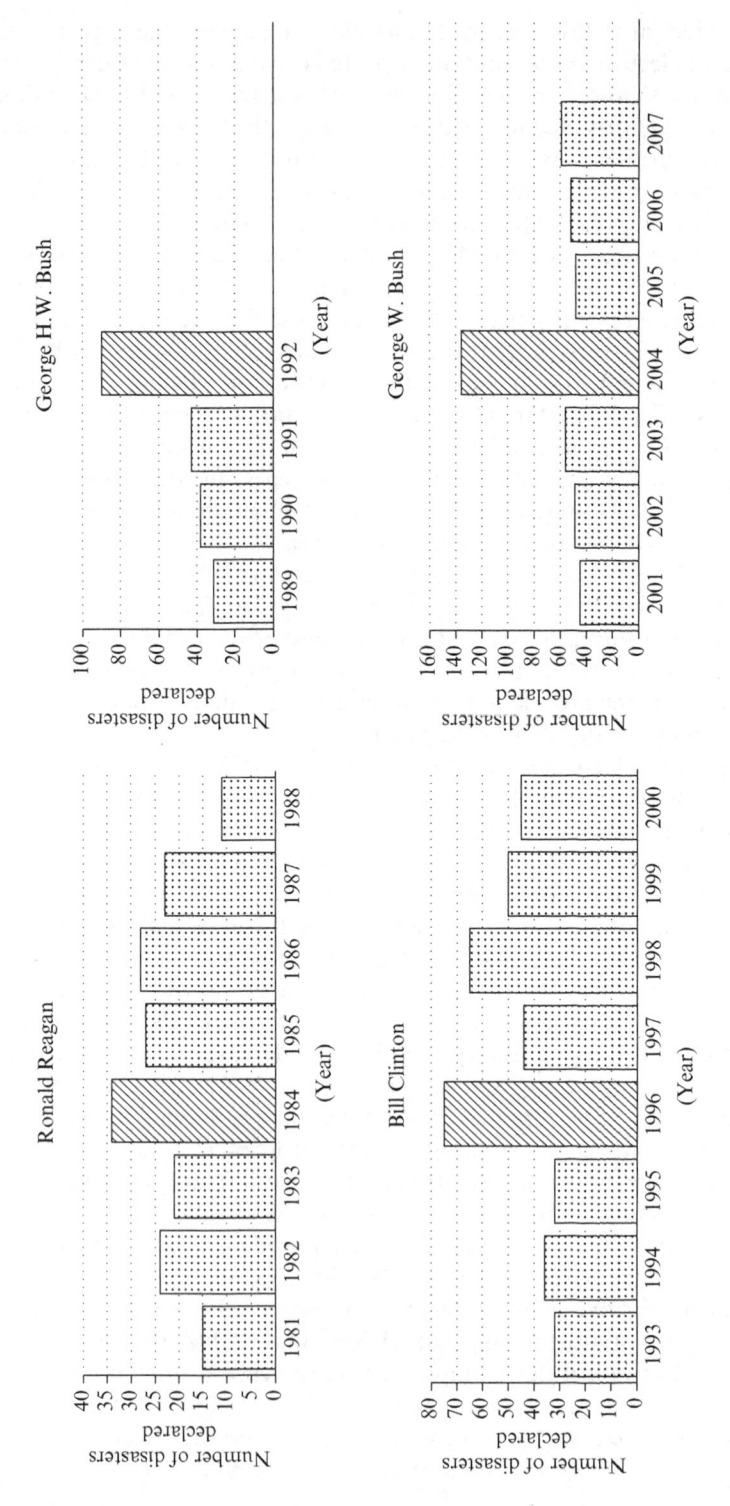

Figure 13.1 Number of disasters declared by President by year (re-election years shown as bars with diagonal lines)

death row during gubernatorial election years than in other years. Similarly, Argys and Mocan (2004), in their analysis of prisoners condemned to death, find that the political affiliation, race, and term status of the governor all influence whether such individuals live or die. Levitt (1997) documents an electoral cycle in police staffing, which is most noticeable during mayoral and gubernatorial election years. As he notes, 'given the importance of crime as a political issue, incumbents will have incentives to increase the police force in advance of elections' (ibid., p. 274).

District attorneys (DAs) have considerable discretion over case outcomes. Not only do DAs decide when there is enough evidence to charge a defendant, they also decide the level of resources to devote to prosecuting the case. The legal system gives considerable leeway to district attorneys to exercise their own personal judgments, from decisions to prosecute to decisions to offer plea bargains. Do elected DAs behave differently during their re-election years? Anecdotally, Mike Nifong, the DA presiding over the infamous Duke lacrosse scandal, did so in the midst of a heated re-election campaign. Ultimately disbarred for his actions, Nifong was found by the North Carolina bar to have engaged in considerable misconduct, including withholding exculpatory DNA evidence (Neff and Blythe 2007).[16]

The empirical literature has indeed found that the behavior of DAs is influenced by elections. Dyke (2007) finds that the probability a defendant will be prosecuted increases during election years. Sobel et al. (2010) examine wrongful convictions in the State of New York. They find that such miscarriages of justice occur disproportionately in years when the prosecuting DA faced re-election, with a noticeable spike in wrongful convictions in the month prior to Election Day.

Even the judges who hear these cases are influenced by the electoral process. In about half of the US states, Supreme Court justices are elected (the others are appointed). Studies of case outcomes clearly suggest that elected judges behave differently and, interestingly, judges who are elected on partisan ballots (ones in which candidates run on political platforms as Democrats or Republicans) tend to be influenced most by political factors (see Helland and Tabarrok 2002, 2006; Sobel and Hall 2007).

Perhaps the most familiar of the documented election-induced behavior is the case of political business cycles.[17] If those with political power can exert sufficient pressure on the fiscal or monetary authorities artificially to expand the economy or reduce unemployment prior to Election Day, then their chances of re-election will likely increase. According to Rogoff (1990, p. 21), 'during election years, governments at all levels often engage in a consumption binge, in which taxes are cut, transfers are raised, and government spending is distorted toward projects with high immediate visibility'. The most notable case of a political business cycle occurred during the Nixon administration (Tufte 1978; Nordhaus 1989), although the empirical results regarding the function and form of politicization of macroeconomic outcomes are mixed overall.

Executive influence on Federal Reserve policies is one mechanism by which politics and elections may intermingle.[18] Grier (1987) identifies cyclical effects in quarterly money growth that correspond with presidential elections, which implies that business cycles may be electorally induced. Patterns of money growth deceleration are observed in the year following an election, while money growth accelerates for the next three years. Williams (1990) confirms that monetary policies (for example, growth in the monetary base and reductions in short-term interest rates) respond to the election cycle and to the approval ratings of the president. Interest rates tend to decline ahead of elections. Such empirical findings question whether monetary policies by the Federal Reserve are immune from political influence.

Yet others have found more ambiguous empirical support for the political business and monetary cycle hypotheses. For instance, McCallum (1978) rejects the political business cycle model for US employment. Heckelman and Whaples (1996) find no political business cycle in gross national product (GNP). Heckelman and Berument (1998) find evidence for political monetary cycles in Japan and inflationary cycles in the United Kingdom, but not for traditional business cycles. In the analysis of Williams (1990), macroeconomic outcomes do not seem to follow from classical political business cycle models.

Most recently – and in contrast to the above findings – Grier (2008) finds an electoral cycle in quarterly real gross domestic product (GDP) growth in the United States. This occurs even when controlling for a variety of covariates (for example, multiple lags of interest rate changes, money growth, inflation, energy prices, lagged output growth, and government spending).

4 CONCLUSION

The political economy of elections and congressional oversight of bureaucratic agencies remains an important topic to be investigated by political scientists and public choice scholars. Congressional oversight committees have vast policy-making powers with respect to foreign policy, health policy, the regulation of the financial services industry and many other policy processes more than is often recognized by casual observers.

In addition, the timing and nature of elections distort the behavior of elected officials and the agencies they oversee. While questions no doubt can be raised about the magnitude of these effects and the channels through which they operate, the empirical public choice literature strongly supports their salience. The most fruitful avenues for future research in this area are likely to be found where government policy supposedly is least influenced by politics and rather is determined by supposedly more objective factors, such as Internal Revenue Service (IRS) audit rates, disaster relief spending, executions of convicted murderers, and wrongful convictions of accused criminals. Moreover, research projects in the field of constitutional political economy may allow a better understanding of how the self-interested behavior of politicians can be constrained.

NOTES

1. As John Stuart Mill (1861, p. 104) wrote, 'the proper office of a representative assembly is to watch and control the government; to throw the light of publicity on its acts; to compel a full exposition and justification of all of them, which any one considers questionable'.
2. See James (2002, pp. 2–3) for a more exhaustive list of the proper functions of Congress in overseeing the operations of the US government.
3. Moran and Weingast (1982) counter this analysis by arguing that the decisions of legislators are seldom based on their own expertise or in-depth study, but are influenced more by their political constituents' resources and knowledge of current affairs.
4. Weingast (1984, pp. 148–9) argues that 'failing to choose policies that maximize political support leaves

a politician electorally vulnerable'; therefore, 'virtually every action they take and every resource they deploy contributes to their reelection'. Further, 'the principle of survival in electoral competition implies that representatives who fail to maximize their chances of reelection are systematically replaced by those who do'.
5. Nonetheless, Faith et al. (1982), for instance, conclude that members of five House of Representatives subcommittees overseeing the Federal Trade Commission (FTC) did indeed use their positions to pursue their narrow electoral and economic interests.
6. According to Crain and Sullivan (1997), there is little empirical support for the hypothesis that the committee system has emerged to assist the re-election efforts of incumbent legislators.
7. Holcombe and Parker (1991) further examine the definition of property rights to legislative committees.
8. Such agenda-setting powers resulting from aptitude or accumulated knowledge and expertise as well as structural barriers to entry are likely to be magnified in congressional committees that deal with matters of foreign intelligence (that is, the Senate Select Committee on Intelligence, the House Permanent Select Committee on Intelligence, the Senate Foreign Relations Committee, the House Foreign Affairs Committee as well as subcommittees like the House Appropriations Subcommittee on Defense), since few other legislators are permitted to oversee or to analyze classified projects or documents – or even to be privy to the precise amounts of budgetary resources appropriated to fund them. This implies that few legislators will have human capital sufficient to understand different intelligence bills and, thus, the influence of legislators sitting on these committees will be much greater. This was famously the case with Congressman Charles Wilson, who helped fund the covert CIA program to support the mujahedeen during the Soviet war in Afghanistan.
9. Interestingly, Roberts (1990) does not find a significant drop in the returns to Boeing's shareholders following Jackson's death. The estimated coefficient was in fact positive (although statistically insignificant). That result can be explained by noting that Senator Nunn was also a major recipient of Boeing's generous political contributions.
10. Yet as noted by Roberts (1990), there can be empirical difficulties when seeking to discern the impact of a single political event on stock market outcomes. As he writes, 'on the day of Jackson's death, news reached the United States that a Soviet pilot had destroyed Korean Airlines (KAL) flight 007 . . . as fate would have it, KAL007 was a Boeing 747'. However, there was some separation between the two events, as Jackson's death did not occur until after the closing of the New York Stock Exchange that day.
11. In the context of the behavior of the Federal Trade Commission (FTC), for instance, Moe (1987, p. 513) argues that 'events essential to any understanding of FTC behavior – most obviously, the historic reorganization carried out by Caspar Weinberger and Miles Kirkpatrick – are simply not part of the story, which consists instead of a thorough rundown on consumerists in Congress and the changing composition of congressional committees'. For a public choice analysis of the FTC, see, for instance, Weingast and Moran (1983); Coate et al. (1990).
12. In a follow-up study, Sobel et al. (2007) find that the reorganization of FEMA under the Department of Homeland Security, created in the wake of 9/11, has changed the dynamics of the political oversight process in a way that has lessened the influence of congressional oversight committee membership on that agency's spending decisions.
13. Work by Wright (1974) also delves into the politicization of New Deal spending, with empirical results supporting the hypothesis that presidential politics (for example, state electoral votes) influenced the allocation of federal expenditures, a finding also shared by Anderson and Tollison (1991). Couch and Shughart (1998) thoroughly investigate the political economy of New Deal spending by analyzing case studies and performing econometric investigations of the political factors associated with the distribution of funds. The political economy of the New Deal is also the topic of Shughart's (2011a) presidential address to the 80th meeting of the Southern Economic Association.
14. In both the public choice and political science literatures, there remains a debate as to the true direction of causality underlying the empirical correlation between voter support and political favors. In essence it is difficult to determine whether politicians simply *ex post* reward 'loyal' voters or instead target resources *ex ante* at 'swing' voters. Here we interpret and summarize the empirical evidence through the lens of the original authors rather than providing a critique of whether these studies adequately address the issue of causation.
15. Disturbingly, Young et al. (2001) discuss the creation of a secret tax collection unit in the IRS, known as the 'Special Services Staff', whose goal is to engage in tax audits that are politically advantageous for particular presidents.
16. The Chairman of the State Bar Disciplinary Hearing Commission specifically pointed to election pressures as a reason for Nifong's actions (Neff and Blythe 2007).
17. The political business cycle was first identified by Nordhaus (1975). We do not engage in a comprehensive discussion of the PBC literature, but instead highlight some of the more prominent findings. The most recent meta-review of the relevant literature can be found in Grier (2008).

18. It may not be the case that the Federal Reserve's monetary policy decision-making processes are influenced directly by political leaders (for example, the president). Decisions to engage in debt monetization (either by increasing the money supply or by purchasing Treasury bills) may be one of the indirect effects through which politics enters into the decisions of the Federal Reserve System's Federal Open Market Committee (FOMC).

14 Judges: why do they matter?
Robert K. Fleck and F. Andrew Hanssen[1]

> Commerce and manufactures can seldom flourish long in any state which does not enjoy a regular administration of justice, in which the people do not feel themselves secure in the possession of their property, in which the faith of contracts is not supported by law, and in which the authority of the state is not supposed to be regularly employed in enforcing the payment of debts from all those who are able to pay. Commerce and manufactures, in short, can seldom flourish in any state in which there is not a certain degree of confidence in the justice of government.
>
> <div align="right">(Adam Smith, <i>Wealth of Nations</i> [1776] 2005, p. 752)</div>

1 INTRODUCTION

It is a truth universally acknowledged that a well-governed country possesses a judicial system that enforces the 'rule of law' and constrains politicians. Careful study of the judiciary is thus essential for understanding the policy-making process. Yet the public choice literature has paid relatively little attention to judges, focusing instead on legislatures, the executive branch, voters, and bureaucracies. Why? Certainly, many judicial decisions involve non-policy questions – is a suspect guilty of murder? But a more important reason for the neglect likely stems from the very nature of the public choice approach. Public choice was born as an attempt to model and measure the effect on public policy of concrete individual objectives, such as the desire to win elections, build budgets, and advance careers. Judges are often assumed to be 'independent' of such objectives. Ergo, public choice theory can have little to say about them. Richard Epstein (1990, p. 827) sums up this view in an article on the courts subtitled, 'The uses and limitations of public choice theory': 'How do judges behave in deciding cases? The question seems to be peculiarly immune to the ordinary techniques of social science analysis. While public choice theory in particular has achieved important breakthroughs in understanding legislative behavior, it has not achieved similar successes in dealing with judicial behavior.'[2] In a similar vein, Judge Richard Posner (1993, p. 2) writes,

> At the heart of economic analysis of law is a mystery that is also an embarrassment: how to explain judicial behavior in economic terms, when almost the whole thrust of the rules governing compensation and other terms and conditions of judicial employment is to divorce judicial action from incentives – to take away the carrots and sticks, the different benefits and costs associated with different behaviors, that determine human action in an economic model.

In this chapter we argue, to the contrary, that public choice theory has much to say about judges. To begin with, judges are not as immune from external influence as many commentators suppose. Some judges run in elections, and even judges who do not run in elections typically have appointers who do. Many judges serve limited terms, and those who serve for life may still seek promotion. And the decisions of even the most politically insulated of judges (such as those on the US Supreme Court) may be undone by the countermoves of actors in other branches of government, who can change laws or rewrite constitutions.

Indeed, the very notion of an independent judiciary raises interesting public choice questions. For example, there is a fundamental time inconsistency problem – although lawmakers may desire *ex ante* to establish an independent court, *ex post* they will want to undo particular court decisions. (This problem may explain why many countries appear to find it very difficult to create independent judiciaries.) Furthermore, if courts can indeed be made independent of other political actors (including voters), who judges the judges? As Epstein (1990, p. 845) writes, independent judges 'may even find it in their interest to do solely what they think is "right" from a legal and moral point of view – at once an appealing and terrifying prospect'.

In sum, establishing a successful judiciary requires 'getting the incentives right' – a central theme in public choice. For this reason, the public choice approach provides a very useful perspective from which to examine the judiciary.

The chapter will proceed as follows. Section 2 reviews three tasks that must be accomplished by a successful judiciary. Section 3 examines the question of judicial independence. Section 4 explores the formal institutional setting in which judges operate. Section 5 addresses the flip side of judicial independence: judicial 'discretion' or 'non-accountability.' Section 6 examines the circumstances under which judicial institutions change.

Although much of our discussion focuses on the institutions of the United States (for the simple reason that those institutions have been the most intensively studied), it is important to recognize that the trade-offs we explore are universal.[3] In most well-governed countries – and in all of the wealthiest countries – an independent judiciary is a primary (perhaps *the* primary) mechanism by which public actors commit to the policies embodied in statutes and constitutions.[4]

2 THE ROLE OF THE COURT IN A DEMOCRATIC SOCIETY

Before entering into detail on the role of the court, we begin by noting that its contribution to successful society is widely acknowledged, and has been demonstrated empirically. Locke, the Founding Fathers of the United States, Hayek (1960), Buchanan (1974), and many others have emphasized the judiciary's importance as a check on other branches of government (see also our chapter's lead-off quotation from Adam Smith). La Porta et al. (2004) examine a cross-section of approximately 60 countries, and find that judicial independence is strongly associated with economic and political freedoms. Feld and Voigt (2003) investigate a cross-section of 57 countries and conclude that gross domestic product (GDP) growth per capita is a positive function of judicial independence.[5]

What do judges do that makes them so important? As we will discuss in this section, an effective judicial system must accomplish three tasks: enforce contracts, define property rights, and accumulate/evaluate information.

2.1 Contract Enforcer

Courts enforce both private contracts and the 'social contract'. Economies become wealthy by allocating resources to the most productive uses, and this requires a reliable system of contracting. It should be emphasized that the need for contract enforcement springs not only – or even primarily – from the threat of fraud or dishonesty. Modern economic systems depend on arrangements in which there are too many contingencies to specify in a formal contract; as a result (as many authors have noted), contracts are necessarily incomplete.[6] Thus, when disagreements arise, an arbiter is required. Judges are a principal means by which contracts are 'completed'.[7]

The same dynamic is present in the social contract. If the (often vague and arcane) terms expressed in statutes and constitutions are to have value, they must be interpreted and enforced. Whether one prefers to view the process in a specifically Lockean framework, or to note simply that in a system of checks and balances, someone must review new laws (and the actions of government broadly) for conformity with constitutional and statutory provisions, the implications for the court are the same: Judges help resolve the fundamental problem articulated by James Madison in *The Federalist* No. 51: 'In framing a government that is to be administered by men over men, the great difficulty lies in this: You must first enable the government to control the governed; and in the next place, oblige it to control itself.'

In evaluating the social contract, it is important to recognize that while some contracts between groups of voters are quite explicit, others are not. For example, a government's promise to pay benefits (such as public pensions) in the future can be easily cast in standard contract terms. Yet other types of contracts are necessarily implicit, or are imprecisely defined. Consider the protection of minorities from 'tyrannies of the majority,' a potential problem in any democratic system.[8] Although laws can formalize certain protections (for example, 'equal protection' clauses), the exact conditions under which a society will need courts to step in to protect minorities from majority-supported rule-making can never be delineated fully *ex ante*.[9] By framing the issue in terms of contract enforcement, it becomes apparent that tyranny of the majority is not only a civil rights concern, but a problem that can stifle economic activity – the prospect of expropriation invariably discourages investment.[10]

2.2 Definer of Property Rights

Courts also function as definers of property rights. This task is especially important in growing economies, because changes in circumstances and technologies require the definition of new rights, which often supersede old rights.[11] Competing claims to these new rights make litigation (the means by which disputes typically are resolved) a frequent occurrence. The manner in which courts assign rights not only affects the allocation of wealth, but – when the costs of trade ('transaction costs' in Coase's famous phrase) are sufficiently high – determines how assets are used.[12] Furthermore, vacillating or arbitrary rights assignments are likely to discourage productive investment, and may inspire attempts to capture rents through litigation rather than through productive activities.

As noted, courts are also assigned the task of overseeing the use of power delegated to other branches of government. This matters not just because courts can stop politicians from abusing power, but because the existence of judicial checks enables the public to delegate more power to politicians than would otherwise be efficient. Fleck and Hanssen (2010) model this formally and apply it to the history of eminent domain in the United States.

2.3 Expertise and Information

The third major task that courts must accomplish is the collection, aggregation, and dissemination of information. When a dispute between contracting parties arises, courts must interpret the dispute in terms of the written contract, similar contracts used elsewhere, previous court decisions, imputed intent, and a range of other factors. When new uses or forms of property arise, courts must reconcile them with existing laws and legal decisions. To do this effectively, judges must engage in costly information-gathering.[13] The judge's information-gathering role is modeled in Maskin and Tirole (2004), who conclude that judicial decision-making (rather than decision-making by a politician) produces the greatest social benefits when the electorate is poorly informed about the disputed issue, and when acquiring decision-relevant information is costly.

Information is aggregated in the process of litigation. Respect for precedent (discussed in more detail below) means that individual court decisions may have broad and lasting effects. This phenomenon is illustrated in the Priest (1977) and Rubin (1977) models of efficient common law. Both scholars propose that inefficient legal standards generate more costs than efficient legal standards, and thus inspire more litigation. Through this process, efficient rules are promoted. As Priest (1977, p.66) writes, 'the common law process will restrain and channel judicial discretion so that the legal rules in force will consist of a larger proportion of efficient rules than the bias or the incapacity of judges might otherwise admit'. Priest suggests that the same mechanism may characterize the development of statutory and constitutional law.

The process described by Priest and Rubin has striking similarities to Hayek's (1945) famous description of the informational role of prices in competitive markets.[14] No single judge, set of litigants, or any other party needs to know which laws are inefficient, nor the best solution to any inefficiency. Disputes are brought in a decentralized fashion, and initially may be decided in different ways by different courts. Litigation declines when an efficient interpretation of a law is established. That interpretation then serves as precedent for other disputes, the number of which decline as the efficient rule is promulgated. However, it should be noted that although appealing, the predictions of the Priest/Rubin model are not easy to test, if for no other reason than that determining whether a given law is efficient is very difficult.[15]

2.4 Summing Up

Scholars have presented evidence that effective court systems are strongly associated with economic and political well-being. Judges enforce contracts, define rights, and collect and analyze information – essential activities in any modern society. Whatever their similarities to other public actors (for example, desires for successful careers or for particular policies), judges are fundamentally different in what they are asked to do. It is important to keep that in mind as we proceed in this chapter.

3 JUDICIAL INDEPENDENCE: WHAT JUDGES DO MAKES INDEPENDENCE IMPORTANT

For judges to be effective enforcers of contracts, definers of property rights, and evaluators of information, they must behave differently – in a fundamental fashion – than other political actors. Put loosely, a good politician is expected to make policy decisions based on 'what voters want' while a good judge is expected to decide cases 'independently' of such concerns. Landes and Posner (1975, p. 875) define an independent judiciary as[16] 'one that does not make decisions on the basis of the sorts of political factors (for example, the electoral strength of the people affected by a decision) that would influence and in most cases control the decision were it to be made by a legislative body'.

For courts to be effective, parties to disputes over rights or contracts must anticipate that court decisions will be grounded in an understanding of the law, not in the political clout of the disputants. New information amassed by courts will not be trusted – nor should it be – if courts can be swayed easily by outside parties. One of the gold standards of the common law is that parties should be judged by what they do rather than who they are. The same point holds with respect to judicial enforcement of the social contract; however, in this case, there is a twist. A major institutional design problem must be resolved in order to create a powerful and independent, yet responsible, judiciary.

3.1 Judicial Independence and the Time Inconsistency Problem

An independent judiciary helps overcome a fundamental time inconsistency problem. To illustrate, imagine a king who sets tax rates. Assume that committing credibly to a *low* tax rate would, by inspiring investment, maximize the king's tax revenue. Also assume that *ex post* – once the investment has been sunk – a *high* tax rate will maximize tax revenue. Although the king may promise a low tax rate *ex ante*, rational investors will invest only if they believe the promise to be credible *ex post*; that is, the king will not impose the high tax rate after the investment has occurred. If the king is unable to commit credibly not to raise tax rates *ex post*, investment will remain low (and tax rates high), despite the fact that the alternative scenario (high investment, low tax rates) would leave *the king and the investors* better off.[17]

An independent court is a mechanism by which a governing party can commit to promises regarding future policy. For example, the king might write the low tax rate into a statute and instruct the court to enforce it. Of course, this simply pushes the problem back a level – now it is the king's commitment to judicial independence that must be made credible. When the court tells the king that he cannot tax at a high rate, what stops the king from removing (or even executing) the judge? Knowing this, the judge decides the case as the king wants. And knowing that, the investors do not invest, and we are back to our low investment/high tax rate outcome. The court cannot serve as a commitment device unless the king can commit to respect the court.

The same dynamic applies in the real world – a court can be independent only if policy-makers and voters can commit not to meddle with judicial decisions after the fact. And committing may be no easier for them than for the king in our story. Formal institutions that limit the number of ways in which judges can be influenced may help. For example, US federal judges serve for life, are paid according to procedures that strictly limit discretionary treatment, and can be removed from the bench only after impeachment and conviction by the Senate for 'high crimes and misdemeanors'. However, these rules remain in force only as long as legislators and voters refrain from altering them. Of course, additional rules can be used to make it difficult to change existing rules – and these additional rules are often written into constitutions. But constitutions can be altered, too, albeit at higher cost. At the limit, formal rules can be ignored completely.

The fact that formal institutions are not the answer (or at least not the whole answer) to the question of what produces effective courts is also suggested by the variation in judicial institutions across equally 'successful' countries. Judges in most of Western Europe (and in the US states) operate with far fewer formal institutional protections than do US federal judges, yet do not appear to be substantially less independent in action.[18] And courts that enjoy enviable formal protections may in fact have little true independence. For example, Ramseyer (1994) concludes that Japanese judicial institutions are on the surface much like those of the United States, but function in a fashion that *limits* judicial independence.[19] Similarly, courts in Russia appear to enjoy extensive formal protections, yet lamentably have proven beholden to politicians.[20] In short, something more than simple protection through formal institutions appears to be at work.

3.2 A Self-enforcing Equilibrium

Salzberger (1993) distinguishes between 'structural independence', which is a product of specific institutional arrangements, and 'substantive independence', which reflects the ability of courts to issue decisions that diverge from the wishes of other political actors. Salzberger's point is that even judges who have weak formal protections may act independently, because judicial independence depends primarily on the willingness of other political actors to respect judicial independence. The same idea is developed in Ferejohn (1998, p. 357), who writes, 'It seems clear, then, that the basic reason constitutional protections for judges have remained strong and stable over the years is that the political branches, or, perhaps, the people themselves, have not really wanted to alter them – at least not badly enough (or for long enough) to incur the substantial costs and political risks associated with such an effort'. The basic idea is that although participants in the political process may gain collectively from altering a particular judicial decision, they gain even more from maintaining an independent judiciary. The polity thus stands as a watchdog, preventing the individual from infringing upon any judge's independence. Judicial independence is incentive-compatible, and thus self-enforcing.

The notion that independent courts are part of a self-enforcing equilibrium helps us understand why establishing them can be so difficult. What is of primary importance is not the institution as defined on paper – there will always be ways to undo or circumvent formal rules.[21] What matters is the unwillingness of the citizen body and its political representatives to allow circumventions. Where does that unwillingness come from? Ferejohn (1998, p. 382) suggests that in the United States, judicial independence is supported by a sufficiently heterogeneous community of interests as to render anti-independence alliances unstable.[22] North and Weingast (1989) propose that in the United Kingdom, judicial independence resulted from centuries of the weakening of royal prerogatives.[23] Neither phenomenon is easily replicated, raising doubts as to whether poorly governed countries can successfully 'import' judicial institutions that have worked well elsewhere.

4 FORMAL INSTITUTIONS: HOW MUCH INDEPENDENCE DO 'INDEPENDENT COURTS' HAVE?

Discussion of the benefits accruing from independent courts tends to mask the reality that even the most insulated judges operate in politically defined settings. The formal rules – which specify how judges are selected, their terms of service, how their salaries are set, and the circumstances under which they can be removed from the bench – are written into law by elected politicians. In addition, judges face the prospect that an outcome they desire (as expressed in a legal decision) may be undone by the other branches of government, or by the voters. An ample body of evidence indicates that judges recognize and respond to the incentives thus created.

4.1 Retention of Office

Most US judges sit on state courts (including county, municipal, and other lower courts), where – unlike life-tenured federal judges – they serve limited terms and face the prospect of being removed from the bench at a term's end.[24] State judges retain office under one of a variety of procedures: re-appointment (usually by a governor), partisan election, non-partisan election, and retention election (in which the judge runs unopposed on a ballot asking simply 'Should Judge X be retained in office?'). In what is perhaps the closest to a traditional public choice approach applied to the study of judges, scholars have looked for evidence that the desire for retention affects judicial decisions. Most studies have focused on comparing appointment and election, or partisan election and other forms of retention.[25] These studies tend to be cross-sectional (cross-state), for the simple reason that judicial selection procedures do not change frequently.[26] The selection procedures are taken as exogenous for the purpose of estimating how the choice between those options affects measures of judicial behavior.[27]

The results of these studies suggest that retention procedures do, at the margin, affect judicial behavior. As compared to appointed judges (or to judges elected on nonpartisan ballots) elected judges have been found to make more partisan decisions (Nagel 1973), send more cases to trial (Elder 1987), dissent less on highly controversial issues (Hall 1987), overturn fewer death sentences (Hall and Brace 1996), give higher tort awards (Tabarrok and Helland 1999), inspire less litigation (Hanssen 1999a), side less with challengers to a regulatory status quo (Hanssen 1999b), impose longer sentences as the date of reelection approaches (Huber and Gordon 2004), and inspire more anti-discrimination claims (Besley and Payne 2005). Shepherd (2009a) concludes that all state judges (appointed as well as elected) face pressure to decide along party lines, but that the effect is stronger for elected judges, and strongest for those running in partisan elections. Hanssen (2000) looks at the indirect effect of selection procedures, concluding that elected judges are less likely to be preempted by officials in the other branches of government.

In short, there is reasonably strong evidence that, as public choice theory would predict, the desires of judges to remain on the bench – and thus the institutional mechanisms that determine retention – affect judicial behavior. It should be noted, however, that linking the effects to broader measures of social welfare has proven challenging. Certainly, no one has presented evidence that economic performance in the US states is nearly as sensitive to differences in judicial institutions as cross-country economic performance appears to be.

4.2 Career Concerns

The view that judicial independence is reduced when politicians have the ability to influence the promotion of judges is longstanding.[28] And, indeed, common law judges do not follow well-defined career paths.[29] Nonetheless, higher court judges do tend to be chosen from lower courts. Does this affect the decisions lower court judges make?

The question is not easy to answer: Not all judges seek promotion, not all decisions have the same effect on a judge's promotion prospects, and, in any case, promotion-seeking decision making may be difficult to distinguish. One of the few scholars to find evidence of promotion seeking behavior on the bench is Cohen (1991, 1992). Cohen (1991) analyzes rulings by federal judges on the constitutionality of the US Sentencing Commission, an issue (Cohen argues) of sufficient interest to the executive branch to have affected promotion prospects, but for which there was no partisan bias. Cohen finds that judges in a position to be promoted were significantly less likely to find the Commission unconstitutional. Cohen (1992) analyzes antitrust decisions and concludes that judges seeking promotion apply harsher penalties (the cases were brought by the promotion-determining executive branch). Coming at the question from a slightly different angle, Salzberger and Fenn (1999) explore whether promotion from the Court of Appeal(s) to the House of Lords in Britain is influenced by whether the judges have decided in favor of or against the government in the past.[30] They conclude that promotion is not affected *unless* judges also tend to reverse lower courts frequently.

4.3 Strategic Behavior: Politicians, Voters, and Judges

The field of constitutional law and economics proposes that the separation of powers serves to create – and also to limit – the discretionary power of the courts (for example, Ferejohn and Weingast 1992a, 1992b; Eskridge 1991). To illustrate, consider the US Supreme Court reviewing a law passed by Congress. Suppose that the Court has an ideal policy point, and so does the House and so does the Senate. The Court recognizes that House and Senate *united* can reverse any Court decision (by changing the law, for example), but that neither *alone* can do so (any proposed law change must be approved by both chambers). The (differing) ideal points of House and Senate then define for the Court a 'contract curve', along which a policy chosen by the Court will not be reversed (because either the House or the Senate will veto a reversal). The theory predicts that a court's freedom of decision will be a function of the number of independent vetoes, and the distance between ideal policy points. Models of this process have come to be known as 'separation of powers' or 'strategic judicial decision-making' models.[31]

The empirical literature has found support for these models. Gely and Spiller (1990) examine two Supreme Court cases and conclude that each shows the Court reacting strategically to changes in political constraints in a plausibly self-interested (that is, policy-interested) manner. Spiller and Gely (1992) conduct an econometric analysis of Supreme Court decisions from 1949 through 1988 involving the National Labor Relations Board, and find further evidence that the Court engages in strategic decision making. Eskridge

(1991) finds the Supreme Court to be more responsive to the policy preferences of the current Congress than to those of the Congress that originally enacted the legislation (contrary to the notion that courts emphasize original intent).[32] In related work, Spiller and Spitzer (1992) conclude that courts prefer to overrule administrative agencies on statutory rather than constitutional grounds, because decisions on statutory grounds attract less scrutiny. Cooter and Ginsburg (1996) test the prediction that courts will be more 'adventurous' in interpreting statutes as the probability of legislative repeal falls, and find consistent differences in judicial behavior across countries.[33]

The separation of powers model also provides a basis for deriving implications about the response of non-judicial actors to the prospect of judicial review. Spiller and Tiller (1997) and Tiller and Spiller (1999) examine how the choice of regulatory instruments provides a means of limiting court discretion. Toma (1991, 1996) provides evidence that congressional budget appropriations are used to signal policy preferences to the Supreme Court. De Figueiredo and Tiller (1996) propose that Congress increases the number of judgeships in order to influence the decisions of the federal judiciary. Applying the model to state courts, Hanssen (2000) concludes that regulatory agencies invest more in preempting judicial review when facing more independently inclined courts (that is, courts whose judges differ in policy preferences from legislators by greater amounts).

A somewhat different take on the issue is developed by Fleck and Hanssen (2012) with reference to tyranny of the majority. Many commentators have suggested that courts – Alexander Hamilton's 'least dangerous branch' – are best positioned to play the role of protectors of tyrannized minorities. Fleck and Hanssen show that, in the presence of a rational and forward-looking majority, a court that decides in favor of a tyrannized minority may actually make that minority worse off. Fleck and Hanssen use the model to analyze some notable court decisions, such as *Serrano v. Priest*, *Kelo v. City of New London*, and recent court rulings on gay marriage.

4.4 Formal Political Institutions Depend on Political Decision-making

The studies discussed to this point take formal judicial institutions as exogenously determined. In reality, formal institutions are legislative creations, passed into law as statutes or as subsequently ratified constitutional amendments. What legislators have created, legislators can undo, and elected officials have sometimes, in reaction to unfavorable judicial decisions, sought to change formal judicial institutions. Perhaps most famously, when faced by a Supreme Court unwilling to sanction a number of his New Deal programs, Franklin Roosevelt proposed increasing the number of sitting justices (his infamous 'court-packing' scheme).

Roosevelt encountered strong opposition from Congress (despite the Democrats holding more than three-quarters of the seats in both houses), and saw his plan blocked (for example, Patterson 1967; Gely and Spiller 1992; Shughart 2004). But other efforts have been more successful. Congress temporarily reduced the size of the US Supreme Court in 1865 to prevent Andrew Johnson from making appointments. In late eighteenth-century Rhode Island, supreme court justices who nullified a legislative act were called before the legislature to explain themselves, and were replaced by the legislature when their terms expired the following year (Carpenter 1918, pp. 17–19). In Delaware, removal of judges by joint address was introduced early in the nineteenth century to supplement

242   *The Elgar companion to public choice*

impeachment, which was judged insufficient to the needs of the legislature to control the courts (Ziskind 1969, p. 139). In Pennsylvania, judges could be removed from office by a two-thirds vote of the legislature affirming that there was a 'reasonable cause', although that cause did not need to be sufficient to justify impeachment (Ziskind 1969, p. 141). Indeed, Pennsylvania's Republicans made the removal of 'obnoxious' judges party policy (Horwitz 1977, p. 253). And the supreme court of Massachusetts was required to render opinions at the command of the governor or the legislature (Hall 1983, p. 348).[34]

4.5   Summing Up

Judges are not – and cannot conceivably be – entirely independent of the world around them. The formal institutions that govern procedures for retention, promotion, compensation, discipline and so forth provide means by which other actors can attempt to influence judicial behavior. At the extreme, formal rules can be altered (or ignored) in order to undo judicial decisions.

That said, judicial institutions are usually designed with the specific goal of insulating judges from these kinds of influences. In thinking about judicial institutions, a useful analogy is the notion of 'high powered' and 'low powered' incentives, often discussed in the context of contracts between firms, or between firms and employees.[35] Policy-makers in the legislative and executive branches face high-powered political incentives – they run in highly partisan elections and campaign in a highly partisan fashion. The institutions in which judges operate serve to mute those incentives, so that it is rare to see even elected judges engaging in aggressive partisanship. In other words, while legislators are expected to function in the shadow of the next election – a potentially important disciplining device (for example, Barro 1973) – judges are expected *not* to do so. Successful legal systems are fundamentally stable, and one seldom finds a sitting judge who claims to be 'working for change' or 'attempting to fix the broken system'.[36]

5   A CONSEQUENCE OF JUDICIAL INDEPENDENCE: JUDICIAL NON-ACCOUNTABILITY

We have heretofore discussed why an effective judiciary requires independence, and why independence is invariably incomplete. However, there is a further issue. A court that is independent, even if only partly so, has discretion, and that discretion may permit judges to deviate from the role society expects them to play.[37] In other words, as well as producing benefits, judicial independence imposes costs. How large those costs are depends on the manner in which judicial discretion is exercised.[38] There have been a number of attempts to understand how judges employ their discretion.

5.1   The Judicial Objective Function

One approach has been to specify a judicial objective function explicitly: what would judges *like* to do? Examples include Higgins and Rubin (1980), Cooter (1983), and Miceli and Coşgel (1994). Typically, a study starts with observed features of judicial behavior (for example, respect for precedent) and develops a model that accounts for those features. However, the basic lack of a constraint makes the modeling exercise difficult – an unconstrained judge can behave as he or she pleases. Posner (1993), who has firsthand experience, compares judges to managers of non-profit enterprises, voters in political elections, and spectators at theatrical performances. While all are useful analogies, none helps us to evaluate the impact of judges in the policy-making process.

A second approach is to investigate the hypothesis that judges act on the basis of individual 'ideology', defined as preferences in policy space.[39] To proxy for a judge's ideology, scholars have used variables such as the party of the appointer (the party of appointed judges is rarely known), previous offices or jobs held, and law school attended. Judicial decisions are then regressed against the proxies (along with other explanatory variables), and the estimated coefficients are interpreted as evidence on the influence of judges' ideology on their decisions. Perhaps best known is the 'attitudinal model,' championed by Segal and Spaeth (1993, 2002).[40] As Segal and Spaeth (1996, p. 973) write 'because in the type of cases that reach the Supreme Court legal factors such as text, intent, and precedent are typically ambiguous, justices are free to make decisions based on their personal policy preferences . . . Even when text, intent, and precedent are clear, they are easily avoided'. The most common version of the attitudinal model places judges on a line running from left to right, and examines whether location on the line is correlated with judicial decisions. Results suggest that liberal judges indeed make more liberal decisions ('pro-worker' decisions, for instance). Segal and Cover (1989, p. 561) find a 0.80 correlation between their measures of ideology and judicial decisions in civil liberties cases.[41] It should be noted that the attitudinal model has focused on the behavior of justices serving on the US Supreme Court. The degree to which ideology can account for decisions of judges in the lower federal courts, much less of state judges who serve limited terms, is less clear.

5.2 Constraining Effect of the Law and Precedent

The attitudinal model has been criticized by scholars who emphasize the constraining effect of 'the law', and especially of precedent.[42] Even judges who presumably have substantial discretion (such as the justices on the US Supreme Court) appear to invest great effort to couch their decisions in terms of existing law, and to acknowledge the controlling effect of precedent even when they seek to dislodge it.[43] That said, *measuring* the degree to which courts follow precedent is very difficult, in large part because cases are most likely to be litigated when the controlling precedent is *not* clear. One effort to do so is Lim (2000), who concludes that justices on the US Supreme Court respect precedent most of the time (particularly when the deciding justices helped create the precedent). If the US Supreme Court – a highly independent court – follows precedent, it is likely that other courts also do.

Why might apparently unconstrained judges follow precedent, rather than deciding as their policy (or other) preferences might dictate? Knight and Epstein (1996, p. 1021) express a view shared by a number of scholars: 'if justices want to establish a legal rule of behavior that will govern the future activity of the members of the society in which their Court exists, they will be constrained to choose from among the set of rules that the members of that society will recognize and accept'. In a similar vein, Easterbrook (1982, p. 817) writes that, 'Each Justice may find it advantageous to follow rules announced by his predecessors, so that successors will follow his rules in turn. *Stare decisis* thus enhances the power of the Justices'.[44] Rasmusen (1994) formalizes the dynamic, modeling judicial decision-making as a repeated game.

5.3 Summing Up

There is a general consensus that independent judges have at least some decision discretion. Indeed, it is difficult to conceive how it could be otherwise – discretion (or non-accountability) is the inevitable consequence of independence. As Seidman (1988, p. 1572) writes,

> It is not possible to have it both ways. It might, of course, be desirable to have an institution that is partially accountable, or accountable in different ways than other branches of government. But there is more to the ambivalent attitude of these defenders of judicial independence than merely suitable moderation. The difficulty they face is that the very attributes that are treated as 'good' are also an 'evil'.

However, even if one believes that judges' personal preferences, and not just 'the law', influence the way the judiciary functions, the more important question is to what degree this distorts the policymaking process. Here the evidence is far from clear. To begin with, identifying 'socially optimal' court decisions is nearly impossible. However, it is not obvious that even possessing discretion, judges are united enough or similar enough to push policy in a particular direction. Judge Benjamin Cardozo (1921, p. 177), who believed that the exercise of discretion by judges was inevitable, wrote as follows:

> The eccentricities of judges balance one another. One judge looks at problems from the point of view of history, another from that of philosophy, another from that of social utility, one is a formalist, another a latitudinarian, one is timorous of change, another dissatisfied with the present; out of the attrition of diverse minds there is beaten something which has a constancy and uniformity and average value greater than its component elements.

6 THE EVOLUTION OF JUDICIAL INSTITUTIONS

Given the tradeoff between independence and accountability, there is no simple answer to the question of how much judicial independence is optimal. Thus, there will inevitably be debate. These debates can lead to changes in judicial institutions – even in countries with good, relatively stable institutions. What can the public choice literature tell us about the nature of these changes?

There have been only a few studies of institutional change in the courts, and they have taken for their starting point Landes and Posner (1975), one of the earliest attempts to apply public choice theory to the courts. Landes and Posner begin by asking how one might reconcile a socially beneficial independent judiciary with public choice accounts of policymaking dominated by interest groups. As they write in their introduction,

> The existence of an independent judiciary seems inconsistent with – in fact profoundly threatening to – a political system in which public policy emerges from the struggle of interest groups

to redistribute the wealth of the society in their favor, the view of the political process that underlies much of the recent economic work, as well as an older political-science literature, on the political system.

(Landes and Posner 1975, p. 876)

Yet, as the authors continue, they explain that 'at a deeper level the independent judiciary is not only consistent with, but essential to, the interest-group theory of government' (ibid., p. 877). Independent courts, because they are free to interpret statutes on the basis of original intent, limit the ability of tomorrow's coalition to alter polices passed into law today. Landes and Posner propose that independent courts thus render interest group legislation more durable, and thereby raise the price that politicians can charge for legislation.[45]

The dynamic described by Landes and Posner has testable implications. Ramseyer (1994) uses that model to explain differences in judicial independence between Japan and the United States, and between Imperial and modern Japan.[46] He notes that Japanese politicians have been much more willing than US politicians to use the institutional structure to punish judges who stray from the policy desires of the ruling party. Ramseyer attributes the difference to the fact that in Japan, a single party ruled for most of the post-Second World War period, while in the United States, parties alternated in power. Long-term rule reduced the value of independent courts as interest group bargain-enforcers (reputation works just fine with a single long-serving party; hence Japanese courts were less independent.

Hanssen (2004a) develops a formal model inspired by the Landes and Posner theory, and tests it on the courts of the American states. The basic logic of the model is that states with more vigorous competition between rival political parties will be more likely to see those parties alternate in power, which will in turn provide state politicians with a stronger incentive to establish very independent courts. The econometric analysis employs a panel that includes political variables and state-level data on judicial institutions. Because the data set encompasses 15 changes in judicial institutions, Hanssen is able to exploit substantial time-series as well as cross-sectional variation in judicial institutions. He finds that the most independence-inducing judicial institutions are associated with more vigorous competition between political parties and larger differences in party platforms, as his model predicts.

It should be emphasized that if judicial institutions are too easy to change, or if they change too frequently, judicial independence will be undermined. Hanssen (2004b) explores the process of institutional change in the US state courts. He identifies three waves of innovations in how judges are selected and retained: partisan judicial elections (mid-nineteenth century), nonpartisan judicial elections (early twentieth century), and the merit plan (mid-twentieth century). Each, he argues, was intended to increase judicial independence. One of these institutions was adopted by some states but not others, and states that chose to change institutions did so *solely* via the method in vogue at that time. Most states changed institutions only once over their history. And states did not revert to earlier institutions after having established a new one. Thus, even efforts to *increase* judicial independence appear to have operated in a very confined fashion, as one would expect given the need to 'commit' to judicial institutions.

7 CONCLUSION

We have argued that public choice theory provides a valuable perspective from which to view the role of the judiciary in a well-governed society. From its beginnings, the public choice school has shown that the incentives facing politicians – for better or worse – influence the way governments function. As the literature we have reviewed in this chapter illustrates, the same logic applies to the judiciary. But although unavoidable incentive problems ensure that judiciaries will never function perfectly, it is unclear how else majority-rule systems can achieve credible commitment to law, avoid tyrannies of the majority, and keep politicians in check.

As we have emphasized, the fact that judicial institutions appear to play a crucial role in well-governed societies does not answer the pressing question of how to improve institutions in poorly governed countries. At a very fundamental level, setting up an effective judiciary presents a problem: the judiciary must be sufficiently independent and powerful enough to serve its purpose (which includes constraining the other branches of government), yet at the same time forebear from using this power to pursue private ends. Looking at well-governed countries shows that, under the right conditions, judicial independence can be part of an incentive-compatible system. Although it may be impossible for poorly governed countries to copy such systems, recent scholarship has done much to illuminate the key issues that need be considered. It has clarified the judiciary's role in 'getting the institutions right' for economic growth, and it has supplied a good start in identifying the mechanisms that get the incentives right for judges.

NOTES

1. Much of this chapter was written while Fleck was a 2010–11 W. Glenn Campbell and Rita Ricardo-Campbell National Fellow and the 2010–11 Arch W. Shaw National Fellow at Stanford University's Hoover Institution. He thanks the Institution for its generous support.
2. The number of studies modeling judges as self-interested actors has increased since Epstein wrote those words, but the view expressed is still held by many scholars. A notable early attempt to treat the court from a public choice perspective is Landes and Posner (1975), who hypothesize that independent courts enforce legislative bargains and, hence, raise the price politicians can charge for legislation. But note that even in their model, the independent court is a passive actor, mechanically applying rules written by legislators.
3. We use the term 'institutions' in the manner of North (1991) to refer to the 'rules of the game,' broadly defined – that is, comprised of both written rules and informal norms.
4. Repressive regimes – by definition – lack courts able to protect individuals from the policies set by rulers. See, for example, Gwartney et al. (1996) and Keefer and Knack (1997) on the benefits of the rule of law. See La Porta et al. (2004) on the link between the rule of law and an independent judiciary.
5. A large literature has investigated the difference between common law and civil law (and other regimes). Civil law relies on professional judges, legal codes, and written records, while common law relies on lay judges, broader legal principles, and oral arguments. We will not review studies on common law versus civil law, but we note that scholars have concluded that common-law countries offer better protection of investor rights (La Porta et al. 1998), enact less aggressive regulation of new entry and of labor markets (Djankov et al. 2002; Botero et al. 2004), and score higher on a variety of measures of security of property rights (La Porta et al. 1999). That said, the exact mechanism through which common law has this effect is unclear. See Glaeser and Shleifer (2002) for additional discussion. See Gennaioli and Shleifer (2007) for a model of the evolution of the common law, and Berkowitz and Clay (2006) for an exploration of civil versus common law institutions in the United States. See Anderson and Parker (2008) on tribal courts in the United States.

6. See, for example, Williamson (1975) on incomplete contracts. See Williamson (2002) for a discussion that extends the notion of contracting to public institutions.
7. Of course, the degree of incompleteness depends in large part on the reliability of courts as gap-fillers. Although private arbitration is widely used in wealthy countries, disputants may always resort to formal litigation as a final option (see, for example, Shavell 1995). And while informal enforcement mechanisms, such as repeat dealings and/or reputation (for example, Klein and Leffler 1981), successfully support many business relationships, they, too, operate in the shadow of the law. That said, in countries where judiciaries clearly lack independence (or are corrupt), private arbitration may become a primary enforcement mechanism; see, for example, McMillan and Woodruff (1999) on Vietnam.
8. Madison ([1788] 1961) stated: 'It is of great importance . . . to guard one part of the society against the injustice of the other part. Different interests necessarily exist in different classes of citizens. If a majority be united by a common interest, the rights of the minority will be insecure.' See our brief discussion of the tyranny of the majority below.
9. See Fleck and Hanssen (2010, 2012).
10. We discuss this in more detail when we turn to the topic of judicial independence. For related work, see, for example, Fernandez and Rodrik (1991), Weingast (1997), Fleck (2000), and Fleck and Hanssen (2006).
11. For example, legal scholars have commented on the apparent willingness of common law courts to define property rights so as to favor new industries and economic growth – see, for example, the cases discussed in Coase (1960) or Freidman (1973), on the development of American law. An interesting recent example is *O'Bannon* v *NCAA*, in which former University of California at Los Angeles (UCLA) basketball player Ed O'Bannon sued the National Collegiate Athletic Association (NCAA) for using his digital avatar in a video game.
12. Also see the seminal study by Calabresi and Melamed (1972), which compares property rules and liability rules.
13. The information required pertains not only to a given dispute, but to the costs and benefits implied for future court cases. A number of scholars, including Glaeser et al. (2001), have expressed skepticism about the conclusion that judges will dedicate the effort necessary to make informed decisions.
14. Also see Ober (2008) on the aggregation of information in democracies, and the consequent effects on innovation.
15. See also Tullock's various analyses and critiques of the common law, among them Tullock (1997, 1980c).
16. For a more detailed review of the literature on judicial independence, see Harnay (2005).
17. For relevant work on time inconsistency problems and the difficulty of overcoming them, see, for example, Kydland and Prescott's (1977, 1980) classic papers and those by North and Weingast (1989), Barzel (1992), Fleck (2000), and Fleck and Hanssen (2006).
18. See, for example, La Porta et al. (2004). Of course, 'independence' is difficult to measure.
19. Ramseyer suggests that had a few key events played out differently, US and Japanese courts might look much more alike today than they currently do (see section 6 for more detail).
20. See, for example, Hay et al. (1996), and Frye and Shleifer (1997). The recent conviction of Mikhail Khodorkovsky provides a vivid illustration of the influence of politics on judicial decisions in Russia – see http://www.nytimes.com/2011/01/01/business/01nocera.html.
21. For example, Congress could vote to make impeaching judges easier, or a president could seek to expand the size of the judiciary, as Franklin Roosevelt attempted to do in his notorious court-packing plan. Or, as Roosevelt also contemplated, term limits for federal judges could be established, retirement ages mandated, or the ability of courts to review specific types of legislation restricted. See Shughart (2004), especially pages 71–2, for a discussion.
22. This raises the interesting possibility that while a heterogeneous citizen body may find agreeing on specific policies difficult, heterogeneity may also strengthen support for an independent judiciary.
23. According to North and Weingast (1989, p.816), the process began with trial by jury in the twelfth century, and culminated with the Glorious Revolution's establishment of judges who 'served subject to good behavior (they could only be removed if convicted for a criminal offense or by action of both houses of Parliament) instead of at the king's pleasure'.
24. It should be noted that federal judges may be removed from office via impeachment, but the standard is high – for treason, bribery, or 'high crimes and misdemeanors,' according to Article II of the US Constitution (this holds for all civil officers, including the presidency). Impeachment of US federal judges is rare; indeed, when the US Senate voted recently to remove a federal judge for bribery, it was only the eighth such ousting in this country's history, and the first in more than two decades (see http://www.nytimes.com/2010/12/09/us/politics/09judge.html). A few states (Massachusetts, New Hampshire, New Jersey, and Rhode Island) grant life tenure to high court justices – see Hanssen (1999a) for more detail.
25. Partisan elections are believed to come closest to creating for judges the incentives faced by other elected office holders. Consistently, Bonneau and Hall (2003) and Bonneau (2007) find that partisan elected judges are more likely to be challenged and defeated than judges running in other types of election.

248 *The Elgar companion to public choice*

26. If they did change frequently, their exogeneity would be suspect.
27. The assumption of exogeneity is seldom examined carefully. Exceptions include Hanssen (2000), which instruments for judicial selection procedures, and Hanssen (2004a, 2004b), which investigate changes in selection procedures over time in a panel data framework.
28. See the discussion in Klarman (1999). Klarman also notes that the prospect of promotion may give judges the incentive to work hard, and concludes that an absolute prohibition on promotion therefore would not be wise.
29. Consider, by contrast, Ramseyer and Rasmusen's (1997) study of Japan's courts, which finds evidence that Japanese judges who decide against the government are more likely to be denied promotion and relegated to less desirable positions.
30. The promotion decision is made by the Lord Chancellor, who is a political appointee and a member of the cabinet.
31. Marks (1988) is often credited as being the first to model judicial behavior in this fashion. See Spiller and Gely (2007) for a review of the literature.
32. Ferejohn and Weingast (1992a) develop a positive theory of statutory interpretation based on interactions between the Supreme Court, the current (enacting) legislature, and future legislatures.
33. Also see the highly influential work by McCubbins, Noll, and Weingast, including their studies of courts (for example, McCubbins et al. 1995) and their models of the political control of agencies and policy (for example, McCubbins et al. 1987, 1989).
34. State legislatures in the early years of this country's history were very aggressive in dealing with judges – see Ziskind (1969) for additional examples.
35. For an overview of the economics literature on incentives within organizations, see Milgrom and Roberts (1992).
36. It is worth noting that another difference between courts and the other branches of government is that courts are typically hierarchical in structure. We will not explore the implications of this difference, because it is not critical to our analysis, but it may be expected to affect judicial behavior, because a rational judge will certainly consider how his or her decisions will influence the decisions made by judges at different levels (or branches) of the judicial system (for example, Songer et al. 1994).
37. Discretion also results from the fact that legislators often enact statutes that require court interpretations in order to function. See Stephenson (2009) for a review of the literature pertaining to the school of legal 'realism'.
38. See Burbank (1999) for a discussion of the tensions that have accompanied attempts to make US courts independent.
39. This approach is similar to the literature that attempts to estimate the effect of ideology (versus constituent interests) on the voting behavior of elected representatives. See, for example, Bender and Lott (1996) for a review and critique of the literature and Poole and Rosenthal (1997) for an overview of their highly influential work.
40. Earlier work in this vein includes Nagel (1961) and Goldman (1975).
41. Segal et al. (1995) update the Segal and Cover data and extend the analysis to include economic issues. See Segal and Spaeth (2002) for further discussion of empirical work based on the attitudinal model.
42. The attitudinal model has also been disputed by supporters of the separation of powers model – see Spiller and Gely (2007).
43. Indeed, scholars of the school of legal formalism argue that although gaps or ambiguities in the law may create the *occasional* opportunity for a judge to express an opinion, judges in fact have little discretion in most cases (for example, Schauer 1988; Tamanaha 2008).
44. See also Eskridge (1991) and Posner (1992, pp. 534–42). The basic presumption is that judges do not like to be overruled, as Higgins and Rubin (1980) and Posner (1993), among others, have proposed. Higgins and Rubin (1980, p. 130) write: 'For reasons not completely understood, judges seem to desire to avoid being reversed.' Higgins and Rubin also explore the possibility that judges who respect precedent are more likely to be promoted, but conclude that it is not supported by the evidence. Knight and Epstein (1996) suggest that respect for precedent makes it more difficult for other actors to undo a court's decision (if that decision is grounded in precedent).
45. See Shughart and Tollison (1998) for a review and analysis of the Landes and Posner model, and of the public choice literature it has inspired.
46. Landes and Posner (1975) conduct a simple empirical 'test' in an appendix to their paper. Anderson et al. (1989) find a positive relationship between the salaries of chief justices in state courts and the willingness of the courts to overturn legislation on the grounds of substantive due process, which they attribute to the legislature's desire for an independent court to enforce interest group bargains.

15 Monetary policy
Rob Roy McGregor

Monetary policy involves actions taken by central banks to affect the level of interest rates and the amounts of money and credit available in an economy. These actions are intended to promote national economic goals such as price stability and sustainable economic growth. Many central banks now operate with a considerable degree of policy-making independence, and many also have inflation targeting mandates. These monetary authorities must nevertheless be mindful of the political context in which they make their policy decisions. This chapter covers important aspects of the political environment that central banks often confront when formulating monetary policy, and addresses both how and why central banks occasionally respond to political pressures.

Moreover, monetary policy decisions are often made by committees that hold regular meetings in which members vote on a one-dimensional issue (the degree of ease or tightness of monetary policy). The availability of data on the decisions of monetary policy committees and the preferences of the committee's individual members provide excellent opportunities to study partisan loyalties and partisan ideologies at the level of individual committee members and the mechanisms by which these committees aggregate preferences to reach a policy decision.

Because the analysis of committee decision-making is of independent interest in the field of public choice, this chapter concludes with a discussion of this intriguing branch of research on monetary policy.

1 ELECTORAL AND PARTISAN INFLUENCES ON MONETARY POLICY

There are several reasons why a central bank's political principals might be interested in influencing monetary policy decisions. First, incumbent politicians typically want to retain office; to the extent that monetary policy can help them achieve this objective, these politicians have an interest in trying to shape central bank decisions. Second, incumbent politicians typically have partisan affiliations, and these political parties have their own constituencies whose interests they need to represent and serve; to the extent that monetary policy can help them satisfy their partisan constituencies, politicians have an interest in trying to shape central bank decisions. Thus, a central bank's political principals have electoral and partisan motives for trying to affect monetary policy decisions. Both motives have been addressed in the literature on the politics of monetary policy.

Empirical studies of the effects of macroeconomic conditions on election outcomes and on the popularity of incumbent governments indicate that the performance of the economy significantly influences voters' decisions (Kramer 1971; Fair 1978; Frey and Schneider 1978a; Hibbs 1987; Chappell 1990). If politicians are interested only in their own electoral advantage and if voters respond only to the conditions prevailing at the time of an election, then opportunistic incumbent governments have an incentive to try to generate favorable economic conditions – high output and employment and low inflation – as elections approach. This idea was given formal expression by Nordhaus (1975) as the theory of the political business cycle. According to this theory, there is a predictable pattern of policy during an incumbent government's term in office. In the early years, the government will implement a restrictive policy to ensure that inflation is brought under control and to prepare the ground for a shift to an expansionary policy in the later years. The subsequent expansionary policy produces rapid output and employment growth with relatively little additional inflation leading into the next election. The inflationary consequences of the pre-election boom are then felt and dealt with after the next election, when the political business cycle pattern repeats itself.

It is also possible for political cycles in policy instruments to exist independently of the ability of policy to affect macroeconomic conditions. Rogoff and Sibert (1988) present a model with rational voters and information asymmetries between the government and the electorate. Attempts by the incumbent government to signal voters about the quality of its performance can generate electoral cycles in policy instruments (for example, taxes, government spending, and money growth) but not necessarily in output and employment. Drazen (2001) incorporates both monetary policy and fiscal policy into a rational opportunistic framework with separate monetary and fiscal authorities. In his analysis, the incumbent government uses fiscal policy to aid its re-election prospects and pressures the monetary authority to accommodate pre-election fiscal expansions and mitigate the effect of those expansions on interest rates. Pre-election increases in money growth then reflect passive accommodation of fiscal pressures rather than an active attempt by the central bank to support the incumbent government's election prospects.

There is some empirical support for the existence of electoral cycles in US macroeconomic policies and outcomes. Grier (1987) finds evidence of an electoral cycle in money growth. Beck (1987) confirms the existence of a cycle in the money supply but finds no cycle in monetary policy instruments; however, this money supply cycle depends on an underlying cycle in fiscal policy. Grier (1989a), on the other hand, does find a significant four-year electoral cycle in the growth of the money supply, even when controlling for the effects of fiscal policy. Haynes and Stone (1989, 1990) present evidence that US real gross national product (GNP), unemployment, and inflation have followed four-year electoral cycles, while Grier (2008) finds an electoral cycle in US output growth.

Following Drazen (2001) and Rogoff and Siebert (1988), it is an open question whether these cycles are deliberate. Conventional wisdom has it that the US Federal Reserve (the Fed) usually wants to avoid becoming the focus of political conflict and so prefers not to take any significant policy actions as an election approaches (Maisel 1973; Woolley 1984). There is evidence that the Fed tends to be more activist after elections than beforehand (Hakes 1988) and that the political monetary cycle arises more from monetary restraint in the early part of a presidential term than from monetary expansion as an election approaches (Beck 1991; Belton and Cebula 1994). Thus, consistent with Drazen (2001) and Rogoff and Siebert (1988), electoral cycles in monetary policies and macroeconomic outcomes may occur even if central bank policy-makers do not actively attempt to support the electoral interests of incumbent politicians.

Research on partisan differences in macroeconomic policies and outcomes has been built on the idea that left-of-center parties and right-of-center parties answer to distinct (often class-based) constituencies with different interests and objectives (Hibbs 1977, 1987). Specifically, left-of-center parties are thought to have a core constituency that is more adversely affected by unemployment and less adversely affected by inflation than the core constituency of right-of-center parties, so left-of-center parties should be more averse to unemployment and more tolerant of inflation than right-of-center parties. As a consequence, left-of-center parties should pursue fiscal and monetary policies that produce a relatively low unemployment/high inflation outcome, while right-of-center parties should pursue fiscal and monetary policies that produce a relatively high unemployment/low inflation outcome. In an empirical analysis of a cross-section of West European and North American countries, Hibbs (1977) provides evidence of the expected partisan differences in unemployment rate outcomes. Cowart (1978) and Minford and Peel (1982) find partisan differences in the monetary policies pursued by left-of-center and right-of-center governments in Europe and the United Kingdom. This pattern also holds for the United States, with Democratic administrations pursuing more expansionary monetary policies than Republican administrations (Beck 1984; Chappell and Keech 1986, 1988; Grier and Neiman 1987; Havrilesky 1987; Haynes and Stone 1989; Hibbs 1987; Alesina and Sachs 1988; Klein 1996).

Political business cycle theory has been criticized for its assumption of voter myopia (which implies that the electorate responds only to conditions prevailing at the time of an election and does not recognize the inflationary consequences of the expansionary policies that temporarily produce these conditions). Politically induced business cycle behavior, however, does not depend on an irrational electorate. In the partisan business cycle models of Alesina (1987), Alesina and Sachs (1988), and Chappell and Keech (1986, 1988), partisan differences and electoral uncertainty combine to create election-related policy surprises that cause fluctuations in real economic outcomes, even with rational forward-looking voters. To be more specific, rational partisan theory predicts that output growth in the first half of right-of-center political regimes should be lower than output growth in the first half of left-of-center political regimes. It also predicts that output growth in the second half of right-of-center and left-of-center regimes should be roughly similar. Systematic differences in macroeconomic policies, though, are expected to characterize the entire terms of right-of-center and left-of-center regimes, with right-of-center regimes pursuing a less expansionary stance than left-of-center regimes. Alesina and Sachs (1988) present supporting evidence based on the behavior of US output and money growth, while Chappell and Keech (1988) present supporting evidence based on the behavior of US unemployment rates and money growth.

Research on electorally motivated political monetary cycles and rational partisan political monetary cycles is based on the assumption that an incumbent government can obtain the monetary policy that it wants from the central bank. For the United States, this means assuming that incumbent politicians directly can influence the Fed's monetary policy decisions in a systematically partisan way. Beck (1982), Havrilesky (1988), Kane (1980), Weintraub (1978), and Woolley (1984) have argued that presidents do, in fact, have substantial influence over the Fed. Havrilesky (1988, 1995) has presented evidence that the Fed occasionally responds to signals of executive branch monetary policy preferences that are reported in the financial press. There is also evidence that the partisan composition of congressional oversight committees can affect monetary policy

(Grier 1991, 1996) and that monetary policy responds to public concerns about inflation and unemployment (Tootell 1999).

In the United States, direct pressure on the central bank is not the only channel of influence available to a president. Since members of the Fed's Board of Governors are presidential appointees, partisan preferences might be reflected in the appointments process. Evidence based on Federal Open Market Committee (FOMC) voting patterns has supported this view: Democratic appointees dissent more frequently in favor of ease, while Republican appointees dissent more frequently in favor of tightness (Puckett 1984; Woolley 1984; Havrilesky and Gildea 1992). The sources of the president's influence on monetary policy – by direct pressure, partisan appointments, or both – have implications for rational partisan business cycle models. Following an election, it might take some time before a new president has an opportunity to appoint a majority of the Federal Reserve Board. Indeed, Waller (1989) and Keech and Morris (1997) argue that the president's ability to influence monetary policy through partisan appointments is limited, and Keech and Morris (1997) go on to document that incumbent presidents have only very rarely had a Board made up exclusively of their own appointees or appointees of fellow partisans. If the principal source of partisan differences in monetary policy is the power to make partisan appointments to the Board, then election surprises might not have significant effects on monetary policy and subsequent macroeconomic performance. Chappell et al. (1993) investigate the channels through which partisan influence from a presidential administration could affect monetary policy decisions. Their evidence suggests that the appointments process is the primary mechanism by which partisan differences in monetary policies arise. There is only weak evidence of direct influence from the current president, although executive branch signaling appears to have been effective without either being continuous or systematically partisan. An extension of this analysis by Chappell et al. (2005) confirms the importance of the power of appointment but finds somewhat stronger evidence of direct influence from the sitting president.

2 THE TIME INCONSISTENCY PROBLEM AND CENTRAL BANK INDEPENDENCE

The time inconsistency problem (Kydland and Prescott 1977) can be applied to explain an inflationary bias that is alleged to plague central banks (Barro and Gordon 1983). Five assumptions underlie the analysis of the time inconsistency problem. First, the central bank chooses policy actions on a period-by-period basis. Second, public expectations of inflation for the upcoming period are determined in advance of the central bank decision, so inflationary expectations are treated as predetermined at the time of the policy decision. Third, the economy can be characterized by an expectations-augmented Phillips curve, which implies that if prices are rising faster than the public expects, then unemployment will temporarily fall below its natural rate. Fourth, the central bank values a reduction of unemployment below its natural rate but also dislikes higher inflation. Finally, the public's expectations are rational.

With inflationary expectations that are predetermined at the time of a policy decision, the central bank sees an opportunity to reduce unemployment via surprise inflation.

Suppose, for example, that expected inflation is zero. The central bank then has an incentive to ease policy and reduce unemployment with surprise inflation because the reduction in unemployment is worth the modest increase in the general level of prices. When expectations are rational, though, the public understands the central bank's objectives and correctly anticipates monetary stimulus, thereby nullifying the real effects of that stimulus. As a consequence, monetary stimulus produces inflation with no reduction in unemployment. At the equilibrium rate of inflation, the marginal output gains from lower unemployment are balanced by the added costs of inflation in the current period. This is suboptimal compared to zero inflation, but zero inflation is not an equilibrium outcome in the absence of credible precommitment.

Critics have argued that the time inconsistency problem does not provide an adequate explanation for the inflation that occurred in the 1970s (DeLong 1997; Mayer 1999) and that time inconsistency issues are not relevant to current central banking practice (Blinder 1997), but these criticisms tend to reflect an overly literal interpretation of the analysis. Time inconsistency analysis does not predict that a central bank will want to generate policy surprises in equilibrium; rather, in an inflationary equilibrium, the central bank's lack of credibility will cause a more restrictive policy to produce a recession, so the central bank will refrain from pursuing a disinflationary policy (Persson and Tabellini 2000).

Chappell and McGregor (2004) draw on detailed records of FOMC deliberations to argue that time inconsistency theory can help explain the excessive monetary expansion that characterized Arthur Burns's tenure as Federal Reserve chairman (1970–78). Evidence from these textual records suggests that the FOMC perceived a Phillips curve tradeoff and political pressures that made it difficult to adopt disinflationary policies. The tendency toward excessively expansionary monetary policy was exacerbated by the short-run planning horizon the committee faced in each of its meetings. In this environment, political pressures for unsustainable employment outcomes and structural changes in the economy that raised the natural rate of unemployment combined to produce higher equilibrium inflation in the 1970s. According to this line of reasoning, the subsequent decline of inflation in the 1980s and 1990s can be attributed to a shift in political preferences to a more inflation-averse stance and a reversal of demographic trends affecting the natural rate of unemployment.

Ireland (1999) offers statistical support for the predictive content of time inconsistency theory. He modifies the Barro–Gordon (1983) model to account for the time series properties of the US unemployment rate and to allow for transitory deviations between the actual and natural rates of unemployment. He then shows that this modified Barro–Gordon model implies that inflation and unemployment should be cointegrated, and his empirical results support this implication. He concludes that since the natural rate of unemployment first rose and then fell over the last four decades of the twentieth century, time inconsistency analysis successfully explains the initial increase and subsequent decrease in inflation over that period.

This suboptimal inflationary equilibrium can be avoided if politicians appoint central bankers who are less concerned with output gains than their political principals (so-called 'conservative' central bankers) and grant them independence in day-to-day policy-making (Rogoff 1985; Waller 1992). Empirical analyses of the relationship between central bank independence and inflation have suggested that countries with more independent central banks tend to experience lower inflation than countries with less independent central banks (Cukierman et al. 1992; Alesina and Summers 1993; Havrilesky and Granato 1993).

A number of industrial countries have moved to grant independence to their central banks, often accompanying this delegation of authority with a mandate that the central bank achieve and maintain price stability and a requirement that the central bank offer public explanations of the reasons underlying its monetary policy decisions. In part, this trend reflects evidence of the link between central bank autonomy and successful control of inflation. Bernhard (2002), however, offers an alternative explanation that stresses the long-run electoral interests of incumbent politicians. The argument is as follows.

Over time, as the structure of industrial economies has changed and as these economies have become more tightly integrated, politicians in these countries have seen their traditional – often class-based – constituencies erode. When the erosion of their traditional constituencies has made it more difficult for incumbent politicians to retain power, these politicians have sought institutional reforms that they believed would assist them in rebuilding their support bases and promoting their goal of remaining in office. Granting independence to the central bank insulates monetary policy from government control and the government from direct responsibility for the central bank's policy decisions. Central bank independence therefore prevents monetary policy from being a source of conflict that might have adverse electoral consequences for incumbent politicians. Central bank independence may also send private sector agents a credible signal of the government's commitment to a policy of low and stable inflation and give them a means of monitoring the achievement of this objective. The opportunities that independent central banks have to explain their decisions, as well as the risks to the outlook on which those decisions are based, in turn give the central bank some leverage over incumbent governments that would prefer not to be seen as attempting to manipulate monetary policy for short-term political gain.

Among the implications of Bernhard's (2002) theoretical analysis are predictions that the central bank will tend to be more independent when party politicians face constituents with a variety of preferences over monetary policy and in systems in which party politicians and coalition partners do not need to be in the majority to influence policy (making them less reluctant to withdraw support to punish the government in a monetary policy dispute). Econometric evidence for 18 industrial democracies is consistent with these predictions (Bernhard 2002).

Despite claims that central bankers have learned from past inflationary mistakes, time inconsistency theory remains highly relevant (Chappell et al. 2005). Part of the decline in US inflation, especially in the 1990s, can be attributed to favorable supply shocks that lowered the equilibrium inflation rate. Records of FOMC deliberations suggest that US monetary policy-makers have remained willing to risk higher inflation. These records also indicate that political pressures for monetary ease, politically attractive short-run inflation-unemployment tradeoffs, and discretionary policy-making remain important features of the monetary policy landscape. Macroeconomic outcomes were certainly more favorable in the 1980s and 1990s than in the 1970s, but this may have been as much the result of favorable economic forces and political circumstances as of better monetary policy-making. Unfavorable economic shocks like those that plagued the 1970s cannot be ruled out going forward, and political pressures for monetary ease could once again intensify. In such a situation, there could be a recurrence of the kind of high inflation equilibrium that characterized the 1970s.

3 CENTRAL BANKS AS BUREAUCRACIES

The analysis of central banks as bureaucracies emphasizes the objectives of the central bank itself rather than those of its political principals. Bureaucracies are often assumed to maximize their budgets or their authority. In the United States, the Fed enjoys a significant degree of policy-making independence; moreover, because the Fed funds its expenses from its substantial earnings on its portfolio of government securities, it also enjoys a degree of budgeting independence that sets it apart from other government bureaucracies. These institutional arrangements may impart an expansionary – and hence inflationary – bias to monetary policy. The Fed regularly turns over to the US Treasury any excess of its revenues over its expenses. This practice, combined with the fact that an open market purchase involves an exchange of an asset that bears no interest (money) for an asset that does bear interest (government securities), gives the Fed an incentive to expand the monetary base and pursue its expense preferences (Toma 1982; Shughart and Tollison 1983). Empirical evidence indicates that the Fed's revenue is positively correlated with its spending (Toma 1982) and that increases in Federal Reserve employment are correlated with expansion of the monetary base (Shughart and Tollison 1983).

Because of its unique budgeting independence, though, the Fed may care more about its authority and prestige than about its budget. The Fed derives its authority and prestige from the importance of its policy-making function, and it enjoys a considerable degree of policy-making independence under current institutional arrangements. These institutional arrangements could be modified by legislative action, however, so the Fed must still be mindful of the political context within which it makes its policy decisions. Concern with protecting its authority, prestige, and independence may explain the Fed's historical caution about what information it releases, how much information it releases, and when it releases information. This caution has been justified on several grounds (Goodfriend 1986). First, market participants may not absorb complete information rationally and efficiently, so limiting the amount of information provided avoids unnecessary market disturbances. Second, prompt release of information might allow major traders to profit from speculation, might make open market operations more costly, and might impair the orderly execution of monetary policy. From this perspective, the practice of limiting information is in society's best interest because it avoids unnecessary disturbances to market expectations and outcomes.

From another perspective, limiting the amount of information provided may also further the central bank's bureaucratic objectives. By providing little information about its policy decisions or the reasons for those decisions, the Fed has encouraged the view that monetary policy decisions should be left to the discretion of central banking professionals who have the necessary expertise for dealing with the complexities of current and prospective economic conditions. Moreover, most US monetary policy decisions are almost always adopted unanimously, so formal dissenting votes are rare; indeed, conscious efforts are made to craft policy directives that will win unanimous support, not just majority support. Those disagreements that do surface in policy deliberations generally do not become public. To the extent that policy decisions reflect policy-maker consensus and internal disagreements can be kept private, the Fed strengthens its bargaining position with its political principals and reduces the likelihood of criticism and interference from those quarters (Woolley 1984; Knott 1986; Havrilesky and Schweitzer 1990; Krause 1994, 1996; Chappell et al. 2005).

Over the years, legislation that would alter the Fed's authority has been introduced in Congress with some regularity, especially during periods of poor economic conditions that prompt legislators to scrutinize the Fed's decisions. The Fed has by and large been successful in resisting efforts to undermine its authority and relative independence from political pressures. Indeed, existing monetary policy institutional arrangements in the United States, including the Fed's historical caution and secrecy, may persist because they suit the purposes of the central bank's political principals.

Havrilesky (1994) has contended that monetary policy responds to political pressures that arise because of rent seeking by interest groups. The argument is as follows. Income redistribution is the 'bread and butter' of politics. When the implementation of redistributive promises generates adverse sectoral effects that threaten to have undesirable electoral consequences, politicians pressure the central bank for monetary relief, and the central bank periodically responds to these pressures. The resulting monetary policy 'surprises' are intended to compensate for the adverse sectoral consequences of redistributive fiscal policies. From this perspective, central bank secrecy is necessary for engineering monetary policies that affect real interest and exchange rates and therefore output and employment. Thus, according to this line of reasoning, existing institutional arrangements are mutually beneficial to the central bank and the executive and legislative branches of the government. Politicians can deflect blame for the consequences of their fiscal policies toward an independent central bank, which may then accommodate these pressures to avoid threats to its bureaucratic autonomy. Havrilesky (1995) has presented evidence that the Fed has been responsive to executive branch monetary policy preferences, especially during periods when it has been under attack by Congress, since the president has the power to veto threatening legislation. It can be argued, then, that the price of the Fed's success in resisting legislative threats is occasional acquiescence to short-run political pressures.

4 COMMITTEE DECISIONS ON MONETARY POLICY

The analysis of committee decision-making is of independent interest in the field of public choice. Monetary policy committees hold regular meetings in which members vote on a one-dimensional issue (the degree of ease or tightness of monetary policy). The availability of data on the decisions made by monetary policy committees and the preferences of the committee's individual members provide an excellent opportunity to study committee decision-making. In the United States, monetary policy directives are adopted by majority vote in regular meetings of the Federal Open Market Committee. Members cast assenting or dissenting votes that are recorded and made available to the public along with the adopted directive. There are also records of FOMC deliberations that can be used to assemble information about members' policy preferences that is much more detailed than the information implicit in the formal voting record. Research has focused on understanding the role of electoral pressures, partisan loyalties, and partisan ideologies at the level of individual committee members and on understanding how committees aggregate individual preferences to arrive at a collective choice.

As noted earlier, analyses of FOMC voting patterns indicate that Democratic appointees to the Board of Governors dissent more frequently in favor of easier monetary policy, while Republican appointees to the Board dissent more frequently in favor of tighter monetary policy (Puckett 1984; Woolley 1984; Havrilesky and Gildea 1992). There is also evidence that the presidents of the district Federal Reserve Banks, who are not political appointees, are much more inclined to dissent in favor of tighter monetary policy than are the politically appointed Board members (Puckett 1984; Woolley 1984; Belden 1989; Gildea 1990; Havrilesky and Schweitzer 1990). Descriptive analyses of monetary policy committee voting records, though, suffer from failure to control for the state of the economy or for the prevailing policy stance when comparing the votes cast by individual members. For example, a committee member who dissents frequently in favor of easier monetary policy during a period when policy is especially restrictive should not necessarily be judged more easy-money oriented than a member who dissents in favor of ease less frequently but during a period when policy is particularly expansionary.

Chappell et al. (1993) develop a method for estimating the parameters of monetary policy reaction functions that can vary across individual members of the FOMC. Specifying differences across committee members as differences in reaction function parameters helps control for the state of the economy and prevailing policy when evaluating members' voting records. In their framework, differences across FOMC members can be interpreted in terms of differences in desired settings of a policy instrument, which are more meaningful indicators of policy preferences than the frequencies of dissenting votes. Their results for the 1960–87 period indicate that there are partisan differences among the governors (with Democratic appointees preferring more expansionary policy than Republican appointees) and that Fed governors tend to favor more expansionary monetary policy than the presidents of the district Federal Reserve Banks. Chappell et al. (2005) confirm these findings for the 1966–96 period.

One intriguing result presented by Chappell et al. (1993) is that both Democratic and Republican governors appear to favor higher interest rates when serving under a president of the opposing party. McGregor (1996) explores this finding in more detail, offering evidence that while Democratic and Republican governors do exhibit preferences in their FOMC voting behavior consistent with their traditional partisan reputations, governors of both parties appear willing to depart from their standard ideologies as elections approach and to vote the political interests of their respective parties. Specifically, governors vote for significantly more expansionary monetary policy in the last two years of administrations of the party of the president who appointed them, but vote for significantly more restrictive policies in the last two years of administrations of the opposing party. Similar conclusions hold when only the last year of the electoral period is examined. Chappell et al. (2005) also confirm these findings for the 1966–96 period.

Chappell et al. (1995) estimate monetary policy reaction functions that describe how individual FOMC members' monetary policy preferences vary according to their professional and career backgrounds, their appointment status as a governor or Reserve Bank president, and their partisan or district Reserve Bank affiliations. Their results provide additional support for the proposition that the governors are more inclined to advocate easier policy than are the district bank presidents. Their evidence also indicates that career experience at the Federal Reserve Board or at federal government agencies is associated with preferences for easier monetary policies. The authors then use their results describing differences in FOMC members' policy preferences to analyse how changes in appointment procedures could affect inflation. These analyses have timely implications for recent legislative efforts to limit the Fed's monetary policy autonomy. These efforts have included some bills that would strip the district Federal Reserve Bank presidents of their FOMC voting rights and other bills that would make the district presidents political appointees and thereby allow them to retain their FOMC voting rights. Proposals like these, if implemented, would strengthen executive branch influence over monetary policy and undermine the Fed's relative independence from political pressures. Chappell et al. (1995) suggest that such changes in the composition of the FOMC could lead to much higher inflation in the long run.

Chappell et al. (2004) study the aggregation of preferences within the FOMC using data on individual members' interest rate policy preferences and the committee's interest rate decisions for the 1970–78 period when Arthur Burns served as chairman. Because FOMC decisions are made by majority vote, the authors take the median voter model (Downs 1957) as a starting point for their analysis. They then extend that model to allow for the possibility that the chairman plays an especially influential role in the decision process, and they formulate alternative models to capture the influence of minority views. Their results confirm that the chairman carries greater weight within the FOMC than rank-and-file members, but their evidence also suggests that other voting members of the committee do influence policy choices. Using similar data for the 1987–96 portion of Alan Greenspan's tenure as Fed chairman, Chappell et al. (2005) find that FOMC members were responsive to the positions advocated by the chairman, even after controlling for macroeconomic conditions; indeed, Greenspan's proposed policy was almost always adopted by the committee.

Data for other monetary policy committees are more limited, but there are now several studies that investigate voting patterns within the Bank of England's Monetary Policy Committee (MPC). These studies have focused on characterizing the monetary policy preferences of the individuals who have served on the MPC, with special attention to differences between its internal members (who are Bank of England insiders) and its external members (who are appointed by the Chancellor of the Exchequer). Gerlach-Kristen (2009) finds that external members dissent more often than internal members and that external members are more responsive than internal members to given changes in inflation relative to target and the output gap. Harris and Spencer (2009) confirm the latter finding. Gerlach-Kristen (2009) and Harris and Spencer (2009) present evidence that internal members tend to favor higher interest rates than external members. Harris and Spencer (2009) also find that internal members are more likely than external members to vote as a bloc and to be on the winning side in interest rate decisions. Besley et al. (2008) suggest that MPC members' reactions to inflation and output gap forecasts appear to be homogeneous – there are no significant differences between members according to their internal/external status, academic background, or experience working in the UK Treasury. There are also data for the monetary policy committee of Sweden's Riksbank that are similar to the data published by the Bank of England for its MPC. At present, there is no research that has attempted to characterize the monetary policy preferences of the individual members of the Riksbank's policy committee.

Both the Bank of England and the Riksbank have limited histories with their current decision-making and data-reporting institutions. In the future, as data for these policy committees accumulate, there will be new and rich opportunities for describing and analysing how different monetary policy committees operate.

5 SUMMARY AND CONCLUSION

While central banks formulate monetary policy with an eye toward promoting price stability and/or sustainable economic growth, their policy decisions are not made in a political vacuum. This chapter has attempted to convey the message that monetary policy cannot be understood fully without an appreciation of how the electoral and partisan motives of a central bank's political principals, the bureaucratic objectives of the central bank itself, and the partisan ideologies and partisan loyalties of individual monetary policy committee members might shape monetary policy decisions. Insights from this perspective suggest, for example, that political pressures to maintain low interest rates as national economies recover from the recent financial crisis will complicate central banks' attempts to avoid unwelcome increases in inflation. Indeed, future histories and analyses of the recent financial crisis and the policy response to that crisis will be interesting new chapters on the politics of monetary policy.

16 Fiscal policy
J. Stephen Ferris[1]

1 INTRODUCTION

Fiscal policy is one of three major policy tools (the others being monetary policy and regulation) used by government to influence the private economy. For some time now, monetary policy – money rules and inflation targeting – has been the focus of policy attention at the aggregate level (Blinder 2006), while regulation/deregulation issues have preoccupied policy analysts at the micro level. However, the events of the last few years, particularly those associated with the 2007–08 financial crisis, have reawakened interest in fiscal policy. In part this is due to the perceived failure of financial regulation to prevent the crisis and the concomitant failure of traditional monetary policy (the hitting of the zero interest rate bound) to moderate the subsequent recession. There are now new fears over the consequences of the huge deficits accumulating to deal with the ongoing recession.

Fiscal policy refers to the government's ability to tax and spend either to influence the economy directly, or to realign the incentives facing private agents and so restructure the economy indirectly. From a public choice perspective, fiscal policy raises a host of collective choice problems associated with how citizens use or abuse the powers of the state to achieve private and collective objectives. From a macro perspective, public choice considerations raise issues associated with endogenizing government within formal macro models.

The reasons why individuals in a community might wish to use government to intervene fiscally in the economy are usually grouped into one of two categories: reasons for government to have a permanent presence in the economy and reasons why temporary government intervention might be desirable. The former are viewed as long run in nature and are usually discussed in terms of the factors that explain the size of government in the economy and/or its growth through time (Borcherding 1985). The reasons for transitory government intervention in the economy relate to perceived gains arising from smoothing the business cycle. The latter are the issues usually dealt with under the heading of fiscal policy.

It is apparent, however, that while it is possible to separate the motives for government spending and taxation conceptually into those directed at long- versus short-run objectives, the actual policies adopted typically combine both. For example, adopting progressivity in income tax rates will help stabilize the business cycle, but at the same time promote the growth of government by lowering the political cost of achieving that size. Similarly, fears that the absence of effective constraints on government spending encourages myopic politicians to adopt excessive debt, can lead to the imposition of constitutional constraints on political behavior, such as the adoption of a balanced budget amendment. These, in turn, restrict government's ability to address instability over the shorter run (Poterba 1997; Hou and Smith 2010). Perhaps more fundamentally, if tax decreases and expenditure increases were equally effective in influencing aggregate demand, one's choice of which policy instrument to use in relation to the business cycle would depend in part upon whether one believed the long-run size of government was too large or too small.[2]

These examples suggest that in many cases the choices made over either the scale or the instruments to be used in intervention will involve elements that interact with the long run and so include more than just the deadweight losses associated with the business cycle. From a public choice perspective, the two sets of considerations become even more interrelated because both sets of decisions are made by the same set of agents.

Even if the theories explaining long- and short-run government policy were strictly separable, the observed measures of taxation and spending used for hypothesis testing combine both in a single time series. Hence, either type of policy cannot be tested independently. This is not something that can be overcome by disaggregation, since each separate element combines both. The result is that tests of any short-run fiscal hypotheses must recognize that the longer-run spending and taxation choices are jointly present in the data and that any actual test will incorporate, at least implicitly, a long-run hypothesis relative to government size. It follows that how the long run is removed from the data becomes an important part of any test of the level or effectiveness of fiscal intervention. From a public choice perspective, both conceptual and data concerns suggest that the two sets of decisions should be tested jointly (Ferris et al. 2008; Winer and Ferris 2008).

Finally, a public choice perspective also means recognizing that fiscal policies reflect collective choices exercised through political institutions and implemented through bureaucratic institutions and bureaucratic processes. Because of this, the characteristics of both the political and the institutional environment will play important roles in the analysis of long- and short-run fiscal choices.

2 PLAN

In the following pages I discuss a subset of these issues, beginning from a basic model designed to illustrate the methodology typically used in fiscal analysis and to provide a point of departure for public choice. I begin by endogenizing the role of government within a traditional macroeconomic model. The model is typical in the sense that it avoids distributional issues, is general equilibrium in nature, and achieves tractability by assuming away various types of transaction and coordination costs. For example, macro models typically assume away the costs of using private markets and that no principal–agent type problems arise within the firm. Under competitive conditions this collapses the distinction between the household and the firm on the private side of the model.[3] For our purposes, the important initial assumption is that the political process lying behind the use of the state to provide government services is competitive and works costlessly so that no principle–agent type problems arise between households, politicians and policy-makers. Beginning this way provides a benchmark against which the stylized theories of government that lead to different predictions for government size and fiscal policy can be compared. It also highlights the macroeconomic significance of the point from which fiscal policy and short-run departures from it are discussed. Throughout, public choice issues associated with the multiple dimensions of fiscal policy are emphasized, together with examples of the hypotheses, tests, and relevant empirical findings. The last section of this chapter deals more explicitly with the measurement issues associated with testing theories of fiscal behavior and the problems posed by combining economic and political data.

3 A TRADITIONAL MACRO MODEL OF GOVERNMENT SIZE AND FISCAL POLICY: THE LONG RUN

I begin by building a simplified closed economy macro model wherein the community comprises two segments: a household sector and a government sector. The household sector consists of a representative agent that maximizes a time separable utility function subject to an aggregate production function from which private consumption, government services, private and government investment can be produced.[4] The household side of the model chooses the level of private consumption goods to produce, c_t, along with its holdings of real money balances, $m_{t+1} \equiv \frac{M_{t+1}}{P_t}$, real holdings of government bonds, $b_{t+1} \equiv \frac{B_{t+1}}{P_t}$, and the level of private investment, $k_{t+1} - (1-\delta)k_t$, that will maximize expected lifetime utility subject to a production technology, given a lump-sum transfer/tax arriving from the government, τ_t, an income tax rate, s_t, and levels of services, g_t, and capital stock, k_t^g, set by the government.[5] Given its knowledge of household behavior, the government then chooses the tax rate, s_t, level of government services, g_t, government investment, k_t^g, and the issues of money and bonds that maximize its objective function.[6] Initially the objective function of the government is assumed to coincide with that of households. This provides a neutral starting position from which alternative theories of the role of government can depart. It also provides a convenient point at which to engage traditional macro analysis, where it is typically assumed that governments maximize household utility and policy is evaluated relative to household preferences.

3.1 The Community Decision Problem

The household is assumed to maximize a continuous concave welfare function of the form,

$$W(c_t, m_t, k_t; s_t, g_t, k_t^g) = \sum_0^\infty \beta^t E_t U(c_t, m_{t+1}; g_t), \qquad (16.1)$$

where $\beta = \frac{1}{1+\rho}$ is the factor discounting future utilities and ρ is the rate of time preference.

Maximization is subject to three constraints on community choice:[7]

(a) the household budget constraint (HBC):

$$k_{t+1} = (1 - s_t)y_t + \tau_t - c_t + (1-\delta)k_t - \frac{M_{t+1} - M_t}{P_t} - \frac{B_{t+1} - R_t B_t}{P_t}, \qquad (16.2)$$

(b) the production function (PF):

$$y_t = f(k_t, k_t^g, z_t), \tag{16.3}$$

where y_t represents aggregate output, and $z_t \sim N(0, \sigma_z^2)$,

(c) the government budget constraint (GBC):

$$k_{t+1}^g = s_t y_t - g_t - \tau_t + (1 - \delta)k_t^g + \frac{M_{t+1} - M_t}{P_t} + \frac{B_{t+1} - R_t B_t}{P_t}. \tag{16.4}$$

The model has one random (exogenous) shock that introduces uncertainty and variability into the model (z_t in the production function), but others could be added to the model and typically are. The maximization problem is subject to initial conditions k_0, k_0^g, M_0, and B_0 and to a set of transversality conditions.[8]

Using a value function, $V(m_t, b_t, k_t, k_t^g)$, to represent the maximized value of $W(.)$ as a function of its current state, the choice problem can be represented as one in dynamic optimization with two sets of decision makers: households and the government.[9] Substituting the production function from (16.3) into the two budget constraints in (16.2) and (16.4), the constrained optimization problem can be represented through the Lagrangian function:[10]

$$L(c_t, m_t, k_t, b_t; s_t, g_t, k_t^g) = U(c_t, m_{t+1}; g_t) + \tfrac{1}{1+\rho} E_t V(m_{t+1}, b_{t+1}, k_{t+1}, k_{t+1}^g)$$

$$+ \mu_{1t}\left((1-s_t)f(k_t, k_t^g, z_t) - c_t + \tau_t + (1-\delta)k_t - k_{t+1} - m_{t+1} + \frac{m_t}{\Pi_t} - b_{t+1} + \frac{R_t b_t}{\Pi_t}\right)$$

$$+ \mu_{2t}\left(s_t f(k_t, k_t^g, z_t) - g_t - \tau_t + (1-\delta)k_t^g - k_{t+1}^g + m_{t+1} - \frac{m_t}{\Pi_t} + b_{t+1} - \frac{R_t b_t}{\Pi_t}\right). \tag{16.5}$$

The first-order conditions for internal household optimization are:

$$L_{c_t} = U_{c_t} - \mu_{1t} = 0, \tag{16.6a}$$

$$L_{m_{t+1}} = U_{m_{t+1}} + \tfrac{1}{1+\rho} E_t V_{m_{t+1}} - \mu_{1t} = 0, \tag{16.6b}$$

$$L_{b_{t+1}} = \tfrac{1}{1+\rho} E_t V_{b_{t+1}} - \mu_{1t} = 0, \text{ and} \tag{16.6c}$$

$$L_{k_{t+1}} = \tfrac{1}{1+\rho} E_t V_{k_{t+1}} - \mu_{1t} = 0. \tag{16.6d}$$

The corresponding first-order conditions for a government determining the policy choices s, g_t and k_t^g to maximize representative household utility are:

$$L_s = -\mu_{1t} f(k_t, k_t^g, z_t) + \mu_{2t} f(k_t, k_t^g, z_t) = 0, \tag{16.7a}$$

$$L_{g_t} = U_{g_t} - \mu_{2t} = 0, \tag{16.7b}$$

$$L_{m_{t+1}} = U_{m_{t+1}} + \tfrac{1}{1+\rho} E_t V_{m_{t+1}} + \mu_{2t} = 0, \tag{16.7c}$$

$$L_{b_{t+1}} = \frac{1}{1+\rho}E_tV_{b_{t+1}} + \mu_{2t} = 0, \text{ and} \qquad (16.7d)$$

$$L_{k^g_{t+1}} = \frac{1}{1+\rho}E_tV_{k^g_{t+1}} - \mu_{2t} = 0. \qquad (16.7e)$$

The envelope conditions for the household (advanced one period) are:

$$E_tV_{m_{t+1}} = E_t\frac{\mu_{1t+1}}{\Pi_{t+1}}, \qquad (16.8a)$$

$$E_tV_{b_{t+1}} = E_t\frac{\mu_{1t+1}R_{t+1}}{\Pi_{t+1}}, \text{ and} \qquad (16.8b)$$

$$E_tV_{k_{t+1}} = E_t\mu_{1t+1}[(1-s_t)f_k(k_{t+1}, k^g_{t+1}) + (1-\delta)] + E_t\mu_{2t+1}[s_tf_k(k_{t+1}, k^g_{t+1})]. \qquad (16.8c)$$

To interpret these conditions, first note that from (16.6a) and (16.7b) the Lagrangian multipliers are found to be $\mu_{1t} = U_{c_t}$ and $\mu_{2t} = U_{g_t}$. Using these in combination with equations (16.7) and (16.8), we find:

$$\frac{1}{1+\rho}E_t\left(\frac{U_{c_{t+1}}R_{t+1}}{\Pi_{t+1}}\right) = U_{c_t}, \qquad (16.9a)$$

$$U_{m_{t+1}} = U_{c_t} - \frac{1}{1+\rho}E_t\frac{U_{c_{t+1}}}{\Pi_{t+1}}, \text{ and} \qquad (16.9b)$$

$$\frac{1}{1+\rho}E_tU_{c_{t+1}}[(1-s_{t+1})f_k(k_{t+1}, k^g_{t+1}, z_t) + (1-\delta)] + \frac{1}{1+\rho}E_tU_{g_{t+1}}[s_{t+1}f_k(k_{t+1}, k^g_{t+1}, z_t)] = U_{c_t}. \qquad (16.9c)$$

The first of these conditions is the household's Euler equation for allocating consumption optimally over time. This is achieved by equating the marginal utility of consumption foregone today with the present value of the expected utility received next period by consuming the gross return realized from saving. The second condition says that the utility generated by holding a real dollar today must equal the utility loss from postponing consumption for one period (and receiving no interest on money holdings.) The third condition states that an optimal investment strategy for the household is to keep accumulating capital as long as the discounted expected utility gain from investment (increasing both expected future private output net of taxes that can be consumed and future taxes that result in more government spending) exceeds the utility foregone today from making that investment.

Turning next to the government's decision problem, we first note that after using the Lagrangian multiplier solutions from (16.6a) and (16.7b) in (16.7a), the optimal tax rate should be set such that the utility gained from additional government spending is just equal to the utility loss from foregone present consumption. That is, s_t is set such that:

$$U_{c_t}f(k_t, k^g_t, z_t) = U_{g_t}f(k_t, k^g_t, z_t), \text{ which implies that } U_{c_t} = U_{g_t}. \qquad (16.10)$$

Deriving the envelope conditions for government and advancing them one period ahead, we find:

$$E_tV_{m_{t+1}} = -E_t\frac{U_{g_{t+1}}}{\Pi_{t+1}}, \qquad (16.11a)$$

$$E_t V_{b_{t+1}} = -E_t \frac{U_{g_{t+1}} R_{t+1}}{\Pi_{t+1}}, \text{ and} \quad (16.11b)$$

$$E_t V_{k_{t+1}^g} = E_t U_{c_{t+1}}[(1-s_{t+1})f_{k^g}(k_t, k_t^g, z_t)] + E_t U_{g_{t+1}}[s_{t+1}f_{k^g}(k_t, k_t^g, z_t) + (1-\delta)]. \quad (16.11c)$$

Substituting these conditions back into (16.7c)–(16.7e),

$$U_{m_{t+1}} + U_{g_t} = \frac{1}{1+\rho} E_t \frac{U_{g_{t+1}}}{\Pi_{t+1}}, \quad (16.12a)$$

$$U_{g_t} = \frac{1}{1+\rho} E_t \frac{U_{g_{t+1}} R_{t+1}}{\Pi_{t+1}}, \text{ and} \quad (16.12b)$$

$$\frac{1}{1+\rho} E_t U_{c_{t+1}}[(1-s_{t+1})f_{k^g}(k_t, k_t^g, z_t)] + \frac{1}{1+\rho} E_t U_{g_{t+1}}[s_{t+1}f_{k^g}(k_t, k_t^g, z_t) + (1-\delta)] = U_{g_t}. \quad (16.12c)$$

Note that the first of these conditions, (16.12a), in conjunction with (16.12b), requires the government to increase the supply of real money balances as long as $U_{m_{t+1}} > 0$. That this is optimal from the household's perspective is discussed following equation (16.22) below. The second is the Euler equation for government and states that government bonds should be issued as long as the utility gain from having more government consumption today exceeds the loss in utility tomorrow when the borrowing must be repaid from foregone future government consumption.[11] The third condition is the optimal investment decision for the government. The government should increase the public capital stock as long as the present value of the expected utility gain from additional private consumption and additional tax revenue (and hence future government output) generated by that investment exceeds the utility cost of foregoing government consumption today.

If we now use the optimal tax rate setting condition from (16.10) that $U_{c_t} = U_{g_t}$, then it can also be seen that the accumulation decisions of the government and the household will be consistent. More specifically, from (16.12c) and (16.9c) the expected returns are equalized when:

$$\frac{1}{1+\rho} E_t U_{c_{t+1}}[(1-s_{t+1})f_k(k_{t+1}, k_{t+1}^g, z_t) + (1-\delta)] + \frac{1}{1+\rho} E_t U_{g_{t+1}}[s_{t+1}f_k(k_{t+1}, k_{t+1}^g, z_t)] =$$

$$\frac{1}{1+\rho} E_t U_{c_{t+1}}[(1-s_{t+1})f_{k^g}(k_t, k_t^g, z_t)] + \frac{1}{1+\rho} E_t U_{g_{t+1}}[s_{t+1}f_{k^g}(k_t, k_t^g, z_t)] + (1-\delta), \quad (16.13)$$

as are the expected utilities from household borrowing and government lending, from (16.12b) and (16.9a):

$$E_t\left(\frac{U_{g_{t+1}} R_{t+1}}{\Pi_{t+1}}\right) = E_t\left(\frac{U_{c_{t+1}} R_{t+1}}{\Pi_{t+1}}\right). \quad (16.14)$$

3.2 Steady State Values

With this background we can solve for steady state values by setting the shock equal to zero, that is, $z_t = 0$, and then imposing the steady state conditions $c_t = c_{t+1} = c^{ss}; g_t = g_{t+1} = g^{ss}$, and so on. Applying this to (16.9a), the household Euler equation gives us:

$$\frac{R^{ss}}{\Pi^{ss}} = (1 + \rho) \text{ or, if } \rho\pi \approx 0, i^{ss} = \rho + \pi^{ss}, \tag{16.15}$$

which represents alternative ways of writing what is called the Fisher equation. Using (16.10) in the steady state version of (16.13), that is, $U_{c^{ss}} = U_{g^{ss}}$, we find that:

$$1 + [f_{k g^{ss}}(k^{ss}, k^{g\,ss}, 0) - \delta] = 1 + [f_{k^{ss}}(k^{ss}, k^{g\,ss}, 0) - \delta], \tag{16.16}$$

and using (16.12b) and (16.12c) together with (16.9a) and (16.9c) and (16.15) we also find that:

$$1 + [f_{k g^{ss}}(k^{ss}, k^{g\,ss}, 0) - \delta] = 1 + [f_{k^{ss}}(k^{ss}, k^{g\,ss}, 0) - \delta] = \frac{R^{ss}}{\Pi^{ss}} = (1 + \rho),$$

so that $f_{k g^{ss}}(k^{ss}, k^{g\,ss}, 0) = f_{k^{ss}}(k^{ss}, k^{g\,ss}, 0) = \delta + \rho.$ \hfill (16.17)

Because we assume that the production function, $f(k_{t+1}, k^g_{t+1}, 0)$, satisfies the Inada conditions, the steady state values of k^{ss} and $k^{g\,ss}$ implied by (16.17) are unique. This, in turn, implies that steady state output is uniquely determined as:

$$y^{ss} = f(k^{ss}, k^{g\,ss}). \tag{16.18}$$

Next, in the steady state, real money holdings must be constant over time. This implies that $m^{ss} = \frac{M_{t+1}}{P_t} = \frac{M_t}{P_{t-1}}$, which in turn means that $\frac{M_{t+1}}{M_t} \equiv \frac{M_t(1 + \theta_t)}{M_t} = \frac{P_{t-1}(1 + \pi_t)}{P_{t-1}}$. That is, in the steady state the rate of growth of the money supply, θ_t, will equal the inflation rate, π_t, so that $\theta^{ss} = \pi^{ss}$. If we assume that money growth enters the model only through lump sum transfers being made by the government, then:

$$\frac{M_{t+j+1} - M_{t+j}}{P_{t+j}} = \theta^{ss} m^{ss} = \tau^{ss}, \text{ for all } j \text{ in the steady state.} \tag{16.19}$$

In this model government bonds have no value other than to reallocate private consumption and government services through time. Hence, the constancy of the stock of government bonds in the steady state requires $b^{ss} = 0$. Using this condition together with (16.19), the government budget constraint collapses to:

$$g^{ss} = sy^{ss} - \delta k^{g\,ss}. \tag{16.20}$$

Using the same information, the household budget constraint reduces to:

$$c^{ss} = (1 - s)y^{ss} - \delta k^{ss}, \tag{16.21}$$

where both g^{ss} and c^{ss} depend upon the tax rate chosen, s.

While it would seem that (16.20), (16.21) and (16.10) are sufficient to define a solution to c^{ss}, g^{ss}, and s^{ss} (and thus result in what is called superneutrality), the marginal utilities in (16.10) are not independent of the level of real money balances, m^{ss}, and hence are not independent of the rate of inflation, θ^{ss}, or the rate of interest i^{ss}.[12] Hence to close the model, we note that in the steady state the demand for money in (16.9a) and (16.9b) must equal the supply of money coming from (16.12a) and (16.12b). In addition, from (16.9a) and (16.9b), we see that:

$$U_{m^{ss}} = \left(\frac{U_{c^{ss}}(R^{ss} - 1)}{(1 + \rho)\Pi^{ss}}\right) = \left(\frac{i^{ss}}{1 + i^{ss}}\right) U_{c^{ss}}. \tag{16.22}$$

The four equations (16.20), (16.21), (16.10) and (16.22) can now be used to solve for the values of c^{ss}, g^{ss}, s^{ss} and m^{ss}.[13] Because c and g are complementary to m^{ss}, (16.22) implies that real money holdings will fall as the steady state money growth rate and money rate of interest rise. Then because real money holdings generate utility and are complementary to the other goods in the model, the optimal rate of inflation will be the one that generates the highest level of real money holdings. This outcome is then consistent with what is called the Friedman rule. This implies that an inflation rate that drives the money rate of interest to zero will be optimal, that is, $\theta^{ss} = -\rho$. In this case $\tau^{ss} = -\theta^{ss}m^{ss}$.

The model above solves for the levels of government activity, g^{ss} and k^{gss}, that are optimal in the sense that these choices maximize household utility subject only to underlying community fundamentals – household tastes and production technology (and an assumed mechanism for collecting taxes). It provides a convenient starting point for the discussion of fiscal policy because to the extent that external random shocks drive the economy temporarily away from this long-run equilibrium, any movement back towards equilibrium will produce an increase in community welfare (should fiscal intervention be implemented at low enough cost).[14] At present, however, there are no reasons in our analysis for policy to be relevant. The absence of externalities and public goods means that the shock present in the model brings about a real change in transformation possibilities to which households will wish to adjust and the model contains no impediments to adjusting optimally. As currently structured, then, the absence of information and flexibility constraints on adjustment imply no departure between private and social costs and, hence, no efficiency loss with readjustment.

It follows that for fiscal policy to become meaningful, the model must contain additional elements (information and transaction costs, frictions, or rigidities in the short run) that mirror constraints on the ability of private agents in the economy to adjust to altered circumstances while not constraining as severely the ability of government to recognize and respond. Typical ways of including frictions into the analysis are to add temporal limits on the information set available to households relative to government and the adoption of Calvo (1983) pricing[15] or costs of adjustment to restrain price flexibility in the short run (in models with price setting). Alternatively, information and other transaction costs can be used to generate reasons for explicit or implicit private contracts. Such obstacles to short-run adjustment, then, lead to a series of temporary equilibria that define a transition process from impact effect back to long-run equilibrium. In such a context, short-run fiscal policy can serve economic efficiency by minimizing the departure from and/or speeding the process of adjustment back to long-run equilibrium.

3.3 Public Choice and Long-run Government Size

Before turning to a description of how fiscal policy can be used to affect short run deviations arising about the steady state, it is worth considering the fiscal features of this long-run equilibrium that have been tested and receive empirical support. To the extent that this departure point is biased, the resulting short run analysis would need to be modified.

The feature of the model that has perhaps received the greatest attention is the hypothesis of Ricardian equivalence and its corollary that government bonds are not net wealth (Barro 1974). In our model, if τ_t is increased with g_t and k_t^g kept constant for all t (representing a reduction in current lump sum taxes), the necessity of meeting the budget constraint means that the government must borrow more today. The transversality condition in the model, then, implies that future taxes (of equivalent present value) must be raised to pay off greater borrowing. Because the government's tax collections are household's tax payments, the formal combining of household and government budget constraints forces the household to recognize that the presently received tax reduction will be matched by a time-value-of-money equivalent increase in the future such that its net wealth is unaffected.[16] It follows that because the consumption possibilities available to the household in the model depend only on the present value of its net income, there is no reason for any consumption choice to be altered.

The limitations of Ricardian equivalence are now well known (Bernheim 1987; Seater 1993) and are reflected in the assumptions built into the formal analysis above. For example, if the households choosing today face a limited rather than an infinite time horizon, then any postponement of taxes today can result in the reallocation of tax liabilities to future generations. It follows that if the utility of future generations is not fully reflected in today's choices (intergenerational altruism) the choices made today will be different than otherwise. Similarly, if reallocating income across time through the government budget constraint can be accomplished at lower (or higher) cost than reallocation through private markets, household wealth will be increased (decreased) and household consumption affected correspondingly.

Early tests by Kormendi (1983) and Aschauer (1985) positioned the Ricardian equivalence proposition with respect to a tax decrease against a Keynesian alternative (where government bonds were viewed as net wealth and household consumption was separable from government spending) and found evidence broadly consistent with Ricardian equivalence. These results initiated a large number of further studies with results that often depended upon the time period chosen for empirical anslysis, the variables included, or both (Feldstein 1982; Haug 1990). Nevertheless, in a survey of the large literature that had grown on Ricardian equivalence, Seater (1993, p. 143) found that, 'despite its nearly certain invalidity as a literal description of the role of public debt in the economy', a 'dispassionate reading of the literature' leads to the conclusion that 'Ricardian equivalence holds as a close approximation'.[17]

The macroeconomic significance of the long-run outcome modeled above is that the addition of exogenous random shocks, either real or nominal, will perturb the endogenous variables symmetrically about that optimum. Hence the case for short-run fiscal policy can be analyzed in the context of foregone utility from symmetric departures from an otherwise efficient long-run equilibrium (as they could not if starting from a position of either a too large or a too small government).[18] However, the assumption that government chooses to maximize a known household utility function is quite problematic from a public choice perspective, both because government services are allocated through political markets that function differently than economic markets and because the agents that make the choices on behalf of the government have no particular reason to maximize household utility at the cost of their own. For this reason, a long list of public choice economists (Buchanan 1949; Tullock 1959; Olson 1965; Caplan 2001, to mention only a few) have argued that utility-maximizing politicians accountable to myopic voters suffering from fiscal illusion or rational ignorance; or who are elected under voting rules that give decision-making power to the median voter (Meltzer and Richard 1981); or are implemented under output-maximizing behavioral incentives within the bureau; or are subject to regulatory capture (Niskanen 1975; Peltzman 1980) result in a government that is too large from the household's perspective. In the context of macro analysis, this implies that the objective function determining choices in the government sector weighs the value of government services and the productivity of government capital more highly than do households. The result would be a steady state where, instead of equations (16.10) and (16.17) holding, we would find a steady state where, from the household's perspective,

$$U_{c^{ss}} > U_{g^{ss}} \text{ and } f_{k^{gss}}(k^{ss},k^{gss},0) < f_{k^{ss}}(k^{ss},k^{gss},0). \tag{16.23}$$

On the other hand, it has been argued that as a monopoly supplier, the government lacks both the incentive and the information needed to respond fully to household demands (Ram 1989) or that governments are run by politicians/bureaucrats with private opportunities for corruption (Giuranno 2009). In either case the level of government service that will be provided is too low.[19] In these cases the objective function modeling governmental choices would place lesser weight on government consumption and investment and the conditions in (16.23) would be reversed. On the margin, then, the household's evaluation of government services would exceed that of private goods while productivity in the government sector would exceed that of the private sector.

Finally, a growing number of public choice economists (Wittman 1989; Breton 1996; Hettich and Winer 1999; Besley et al. 2005), many of whom use probabilistic voting models (Coughlin and Nitzan 1981; Enelow and Hinich 1989; Adams et al. 2005), argue that political competition is the key mechanism that requires politicians and bureaucrats to behave *as if* they maximized household utility. Here, a sufficient level of political competition among political parties is needed to reward those politicians who provide voter-valued services at lower cost and to penalize those who do not. When this is present, the equations in (16.23) will be met with equality.

The household's evaluation of current levels of private versus government consumption and the productivity of private versus government investment is, then, the test for whether government is too large or too small. However, the fact that government services are not marketed makes evaluation of the first of these conditions somewhat problematic (Carr 1989). As a consequence most researchers analyze the effect of a permanent change in government spending on output, wealth, productivity, and/or growth and use these outcomes to assess optimal size. Aschauer (1988) notes, for example, that in general equilibrium a permanent rise in government spending (an injection valued at 1) will withdraw equivalent resources from the private sector, and this will reduce private consumption (whose value in his analysis is represented by γ) and/or private investment (whose value in his analysis is represented by μ). Aschauer then reports estimated values of γ in the range of 0.25 to 0.4 (Aschauer 1985; Kormendi 1983) and an estimate of μ of approximately 0.4 (Ahmed 1986). Because $\mu + \gamma < 1$, he concludes that government is 'too large' with a permanent increase in its size reducing the aggregate value of the pie available to the community and, hence, net wealth.[20] On the other hand, Karras (1996b) examines a wide spectrum of countries and finds that government is overprovided in Africa, underprovided in Asia, and more or less optimally provided in the rest of the world.[21] Moreover, in a series of papers that focus on the productivity of government investment in Europe, Karras (1996a, 1997) finds that the hypothesis of equal marginal products of private and government capital cannot be rejected.[22] Ram (1986) provides one of the few studies concluding that a larger government would produce a positive effect on economic performance and finds a higher level of factor productivity for government than that found in the private sector, at least for the period of the 1960s.

There have been many more empirical studies on the relationship between government size and growth. Most of these concur with Landau (1983) and Barro (1991, 1997), who find increases in the ratio of government consumption to GDP depressing output growth (see also Folster and Henrekson 2001). However, a number of authors have questioned these findings, stressing the 'fragility' of the relationship of most fiscal measures to growth (Easterly and Rebelo 1993) and point to reliability issues coming from simultaneity and selection problems in combination with weak instruments (Agell et al. 2006). Even so, most recent studies tend to confirm the negative impact on growth of government consumption (see Afonso and Furceri 2008; Ghosh Roy 2009; Romero-Avila and Strauch 2009). But while the public consumption-growth relationship may be negative, the relationship between government investment and growth is often found to be positive. Ram's early work (1986, 1989) stressed a positive externality arising (implicitly) from government investment to growth, while Easterly and Rebelo (1993) find a strong positive association arising from the government's provision of transportation and communication capital. Still others point to a strong positive relationship between government provided education expenditures and growth (Landau 1983; Evans and Karras 1994). Expanding dimensionality from size to variability, Romero-Avila and Strauch (2009) investigate the relationship between the size and volatility of most components of government spending/taxes and find that while most components are negatively related to trend growth, public investment is one of the few budgetary line items that have had a positive impact on Europe's economic progress.

Despite a widespread presumption in the public choice literature that government is too large, there seems to me no strong empirical consensus on whether government size overall is too large, too small, or just about right for most countries.[23] While there does seem a consensus that further increases in government consumption would be harmful to growth, there remains sufficient – although not overwhelming – evidence of the positive benefits of government investment to support one's favorite theory of government size. Because of the advantage of having symmetric welfare losses arise from transitory departures from long-run equilibrium, I retain the steady state equilibrium derived in the analysis above as the point of departure for short-run or transition analysis.

4 FISCAL POLICY AND THE SHORT RUN

4.1 Dynamic Stochastic General Equilibrium Modeling

Given stability so that the endogenous variables converge on long-run equilibrium, permanent and transitory changes to the model's fundamentals will set in motion patterns of adjustment in time. This dynamic adjustment process is typically modeled by using first- or, increasingly, second-order approximations to linearize the system about its steady state. The resulting set of linear difference equations is then solved. While a solution that describes the transition process between steady states (comparative dynamics) or back to the old equilibrium (stability analysis) can often be shown to exist, an analytic solution usually is not possible. To make the analysis operational, then, a dynamic stochastic general equilibrium (DSGE) model is constructed by calibrating the linearized model, that is, by applying empirical estimates to the model's key parameters, thus allowing for the simulation of characteristic movements in the specific economy under study. Here the usefulness of the model is judged by how closely the model replicates certain characteristic movements of the economy through time (for example, the humped shaped response of output to external shocks). If successful, the resulting structure can then be used to explore such questions as to the effect on the model's key variables (and ultimately welfare) of changes in government spending, taxes, and deficits (or accumulated debt).

If we modify the real business cycle model developed in section 3 to endogenize labor, the resulting DSGE model has productivity shocks that affect output not only directly but also indirectly by increasing the productivity of labor and, hence, the incentive to work both intra- and inter-temporally. In addition, productivity changes will affect lifetime earnings and therefore both private consumption and labor supply through the resulting wealth effect (Baxter and King 1993). In this context, permanent versus transitory changes in government spending and taxes can produce quite different effects on both aggregate demand and supply (depending on the information structure of the economy and thus the degree to which Ricardian equivalence is expected to hold).

But while DSGE models can be used to describe the effects of alternative policy rules and policy shocks on the time pattern of employment and output, the role of fiscal policy in the short run is not simply to remove the fluctuations produced by external shocks. Some shocks, such as the productivity shock incorporated above, represent changed circumstances to which welfare will be lost if no adjustment is made.[24] Rather, the economic motivation for policy is an improvement in welfare and this requires the existence of private adjustment costs to individuals and private institutions that prevent or slow down readjustments relative to what could be produced by policy. Hence for policy to be relevant in the short run, the dynamics modeled must embody frictions, imperfections, conventions, information and/or other transaction costs that generate one or more externalities whose effects policy can minimize. The need for these types of adjustments to the basic model is suggested by empirical studies that note regularities existing in most economies that cannot be accounted for by flexible price, real business cycle models (Gali and Rabanal 2004; Rotemberg and Woodford 1996). Typical features that are added to the basic model of section 3 include monopolistic competition with Calvo pricing and/or costly price adjustment (Blanchard and Kiyotaki 1987), wage or price contracting (Taylor 1979, 1980), asymmetric information (Lucas 1975), or liquidity constraints (Zeldes 1989) that allow aggregate demand to feature more prominently in both potential shocks and adjustment. These new Keynesian DSGE models are also given additional features, such as price indexation (Christiano et al. 2005), habit formation (Campbell and Cochrane 2000), a financial accelerator (Bernanke et al. 1996), variable capacity constraints (Gilchrist and Williams 2000) and various other strategic complementarities (Cooper and John 1988) to allow the analysis to capture the high degree of persistence observed in the data. It follows that the welfare gains possible from policy in these models will be a function of the types of imperfections built into the analysis.

The difference in approach and emphasis within DSGE modeling can be illustrated by two recent papers. In Uhlig (2010), a DSGE model incorporating real business cycle features is used to evaluate the sizes of government spending and tax multipliers. Applying estimates by Cogan et al. (2009) of the size of the recent US fiscal stimulus package, Uhlig finds spending multipliers that are positive in the short run but become both negative (and largely so) over the long run. The positive multiplier effect in the short run is driven by the negative wealth effect on labor supply (spending is initially funded by government borrowing) and the long-run negative effect on output arises from the higher levels of distortionary taxation needed to pay off higher short-run borrowing. The tax alternative has a smaller short-run effect but remains positive over the long run. Fernandez-Villaverde (2010), on the other hand, introduces financial frictions (arising from asymmetric information between borrowers and lenders) into a new Keynesian DSGE model that incorporates Calvo pricing and habit persistence. The financial friction adds a 'Fischer effect' for firms in the model so that the usual impact on aggregate demand arising from an increase in government spending (with price stickiness) is magnified by the reduction in real firm indebtedness (as the price level increases unexpectedly). This reduces the degree of crowding out in private investment. On the other hand, a reduction in labor taxes lowers inflation, which increases real firm indebtedness and, hence, the premium that firms must pay to borrow. This works to offset the otherwise expansionary effects on output. For this reason spending multipliers become stronger than tax multipliers.

While the usefulness of DSGE modeling to the analysis of fiscal policy in normal times may seem apparent, that empirical estimating technique has been directed primarily at monetary policy, analyzing such issues as alternative money rules and inflation targeting. An August 2010 Econlit search for DSGE models, for example, yielded 426 entries, but this fell to 25 when the search was restricted to fiscal policy (with none arising earlier than 2005). One typical use of DSGE modeling is represented by the work by Mertens and Ravn (2009), who use it to propose frictions to account for the observation that unanticipated tax reductions generate persistent expansionary effects on output, consumption and investment, while anticipated tax cuts produce contractions in output, hours worked and investment at implementation (with expansion only thereafter). In their model the addition of adjustment costs, liquidity constraints and consumption habits were needed to replicate the observed pattern. In a similar vein, Chahrour et al. (2010) use a DSGE model to evaluate the hypothesis that the different sized tax multipliers found empirically by structural vector autoregressions (VARs) versus those using a 'narrative approach' are due to differences in their assumed reduced-form transmission mechanisms rather than to differences in their shock identification schemes. Their model allows them to reject differences in reduced forms and thus conclude that the observed differences in the estimated multipliers result either from different models failing to identify the same tax shocks or from small-sample uncertainty.

In work more applicable to the recent financial crisis, Röger et al. (2010) investigate empirically the role played by fiscal policy across 56 countries during banking crises over the 1970–2008 period. They then use DSGE simulations to provide an interpretation for their key empirical finding that the strong expansionary impact of fiscal policy during the banking crises was not driven by the re-employment of underutilized resources. Their simulations suggest that fiscal multipliers during banking crises are larger because some agents are constrained in their borrowing by the values of their collateral (leading fiscal expansion to have the additional effect of increasing the collateral values of collateral-constrained households and thus relaxing the lending constraints of banks).[25] Erceg and Linde (2010) use a DSGE model to examine the related issue of whether fiscal policy will get a 'free ride' in conditions of a liquidity trap. In a model where the duration of the trap is dependent on the size of the fiscal stimulus, they show that even if the multiplier is initially high for small increases in government spending it may decrease substantially at ever greater spending levels. Hence, it becomes crucial to distinguish between the average and the marginal spending multiplier. Similarly, Christiano et al. (2009) explicitly consider the consequences for the government spending multiplier of the zero interest rate bound. Using a calibrated DSGE model with wage and price frictions, habit formation, variable capacity, and investment costs of adjustment, they show that when the central bank follows a Taylor rule the fiscal multiplier is usually less than one. However, once the zero interest bound is hit (so that expansionary spending does not raise the nominal rate of interest), the multiplier becomes much larger.[26]

Finally, while fiscal and monetary policies are most often discussed separately, it is important to recognize that monetary and fiscal policies necessarily are linked through the government budget constraint. This observation has led to a large literature exploring the implications of having one policy be subservient to the other (see Sargent and Wallace 1987; Leeper 1991). In this context, De Resende and Rebei (2008) use a DSGE model to explore the implications of having fiscal policy dominate monetary policy. In their model with price stickiness and non-zero trend inflation, De Resende and Rebei use a parameter to represent the fraction of government debt that must be backed by current and future budget surpluses versus seigniorage. They then show that variations in this parameter generate significant welfare losses for countries that exhibit a high degree of fiscal dominance – in their sample Mexico and South Korea versus the United States and Canada.[27]

4.2 Empirical Studies of Short-run Fiscal Policy

Much of our knowledge of the effects of fiscal intervention on the economy derives from vector autoregressive analysis (VARs), particularly the work of Blanchard and Perotti (2002) who built a three-variable structural VAR to isolate the effect of exogenous shocks to taxes, T, and government spending, G, on US gross domestic product, GDP, between the first quarter of 1960 and the last quarter of 1997. Because simultaneous contemporary effects arise among the chosen variables, all VAR estimations result in compound lagged coefficients that require additional assumptions for the identification of contemporary effects. Blanchard and Perotti use a policy recognition lag in administrative information on the timing of taxes and transfers to identify the responses of G and T to GDP and so isolate fiscal shocks. Their results suggest that increases in government spending and reductions in taxes both result in relatively small, similarly sized positive multiplier effects on output. In part this is because fiscal shocks impact private investment adversely. Perotti (2005) extended this analysis to the set of Organisation for Economic Co-operation and Development (OECD) countries and found similar results but with a tendency for fiscal multipliers to decline in size after 1980.[28] Studies by such authors as Benassy-Quere and Cimadomo (2006), which extend the investigation to other countries and longer time frames, find expenditure multipliers that are weak and often negative over longer durations.

It is important to recognize that the VAR approach identifies only the effects of fiscal policy shocks – shifts in spending and/or taxes – unrelated to the response of policy to developments within the economy. Thus, if short-run fiscal policy were characterized completely by a feedback rule from cyclical activity in the economy, there would be no exogenous policy shock and VAR methodology would conclude that fiscal policy did not matter. Yet, much of the reason for concern about fiscal policy and its design is precisely because we wish policy to respond endogenously to the state of the economy. Hence, while a fiscal policy shock may not itself cause output to vary much, it need not follow that fiscal policy is unimportant. The way the economy responds to non-policy shocks may depend importantly on the way fiscal policy is structured to respond to the cycle.[29]

An alternative to the VAR method for isolating fiscal policy has been to use political speeches, legislative actions, or both, to identify the timing and duration of tax and spending changes. Ramey and Shapiro (1998) and Edelberg et al. (1999) use this 'narrative approach' to isolate political events and find significant and positive short-run spending effects on US output and consumption. More recently, Romer and Romer (2010) have used a similar approach to separate changes in taxation that arise for reasons related to economic conditions from those that arise for other exogenous reasons. Using only the latter, they find that exogenous tax increases are highly contractionary, producing larger and more significant effects than when all tax increases are included. In a similar vein, Alesina and Ardagna (2009) focus on 'large changes' in fiscal stance to assess the relative effect of government spending versus taxes on output growth and deficits in OECD countries from 1970 to 2007. They find that tax cuts are more likely to increase output growth than spending increases (while spending decreases are more likely than tax increases to reduce deficits).

The range of multiplier sizes found under these two approaches is quite striking and has generated efforts to explain the differences. Tenhofen and Wolff (2007), for example, reconcile the strong multiplier effects under the narrative approach with the weak multiplier effects arising in VARs by arguing that anticipations are missing from the VAR framework. By modeling expectations formation within the VAR framework, Tenhofen and Wolff show that once the model allows for one-period-ahead anticipations, shocks to non-defense government spending can result in significant increases in US consumption (and hence larger multipliers). Others do this by extending the dimensionality of government spending and taxes, as well as the range of potential outputs, to better capture the complexities of different multipliers at work.[30]

4.3 Short-run Fiscal Policy and Public Choice

Public choice adds to the analysis of short term fiscal policy by considering 'the processes through which individual choices are transmitted, combined, and transformed into collective outcomes' (Buchanan [1967] 1987, p. xi). It asks, to what extent the cyclical expenditure and tax policies set by bureaucrats charged with implementing the wishes of political parties depart from the decision-making implied by DSGE analysis or from the objectives embodied in the design of political and bureaucratic institutions. More generally it asks how the mechanisms through which the political process and its institutional framework feed back on policy choices and considers how the incentives or design of bureaucratic decision making can be altered in ways that will improve efficiency and welfare.

The traditional reasons for expecting an independent political effect on policy decisions are based on either opportunistic or partisan reasons for why a political party would wish to influence economic policy.[31] Dealing first with opportunism, Nordhaus (1975) argued that an incumbent political party would use its control over policy to attempt to gain votes by increasing aggregate demand and so output in the period immediately prior to each election. This would work in the presence of information costs if myopic voters associate larger incomes/lower unemployment with more capable politicians. Then, because the benefit of remaining in office is independent of the ideology of the party in power, opportunism predicts higher rates of real output growth and/or lower unemployment rates in the period leading into elections – the appearance of a political business cycle. A consequence of the rational expectations revolution, however, is the recognition that the continued use of pre-election spending will become anticipated such that systematic use would also become ineffective in influencing voters and/or output. A variation of that hypothesis has then evolved, called 'rational opportunism' (Rogoff and Silbert 1988; Rogoff 1990), using short-run asymmetric information with respect to political competence to motivate an equilibrium budget cycle. In this case, knowledge of superior competence leads more able politicians to use higher pre-election spending/promises of lower taxes as a signal. The ability to verify competence and expose cheating *ex post* makes this behavioral strategy feasible over the longer run and thus generates an equilibrium political budget (rather than output) cycle on average.[32]

The second major strand of political influence on fiscal policy argues that the ideology of the political party in power matters (Hibbs 1977). In the case of two contending political parties, the left-of-center party would be expected to spend more when in power than its more conservative rival. Hence, a test for traditional partisanship is a positive sign on the coefficient of a dummy variable representing the time period when the more liberal party is in power. However, because any predictable policy stance will ultimately be recognized by voters, greater government spending from left-wing governments will be adjusted to by voters and become ineffective. For this reason rational partisanship refines the traditional hypothesis by arguing that only so long as the electoral outcome is uncertain will the realization of a more liberal (conservative) political party victory generate an unexpected boost to (contraction in) aggregate output or inflation (Alesina 1987; Alesina et al. 1997). The size of that effect then depends upon: (a) the degree of surprise in the election result; and (b) the passage of time since the election, as the realized outcome will be incorporated in revised expectations.

The two sets of political hypotheses described above have generated a large number of tests, the results of which have been quite mixed.[33] In general, tests for traditional opportunism in output and/or unemployment have been unsuccessful, while tests for rational opportunism and its prediction of a political budget cycle have been only somewhat more successful (Drazen 2001).[34] The relative lack of success in establishing a political business/budget cycle has led to various refinements. For example, Frey and Schneider (1978b) have argued that political parties have multiple objectives besides retaining power so that the pursuit of opportunism comes at the cost of leaving other objectives/promises unfulfilled. This implies that opportunism will be tried only in those cases where elections are close.[35] Abrams and Iossifov (2006), on the other hand, focus on coordination costs. For them an important principal–agent problem arises between politicians and policy makers implying that the implementation of opportunism will be more likely when the decision-making agents share ideologies (measured as belonging to the same political party).[36] On yet another dimension, Shi and Svensson (2006) and Brender and Drazen (2005) find that current cross-sectional evidence of a political budget cycle is explained primarily by the strength of opportunism in lesser versus more developed democracies. This is seen as evidence consistent with the hypothesis that underdeveloped political institutions in newer democracies will have weaker institutional controls on opportunism and hence generate more pronounced budget cycles.[37] Still others have questioned the statistical basis for cross-country studies that find no budget or output cycles by arguing that these studies do not allow for a sufficient degree of heterogeneity among the countries being tested (Bayar and Smeets 2009).

A more serious identification issue arises when the timing of each election is not predetermined. Hence in parliamentary systems, opportunistic behavior suggests not only that pre-election policy may be used to manipulate or signal voters, but also that the election call may be timed to take advantage of favorable economic circumstances. The latter possibility has generated a theoretical and empirical literature in political science under the headings of election timing and cabinet or parliamentary durations (Smith 1996; Kayser 2005; Ferris and Voia 2009). When election timing is endogenous, the direction of causation in any statistical association arising between economic outcomes and election dates becomes complex and more problematic (Ferris and Voia, 2011).

Other dimensions of political decision making processes that can feed back on opportunism and fiscal policy have also been examined. For example, Persson et al. (2004) argue that democracies with proportional versus majority voting rules have less control over spending plans because their governing coalitions are inherently more unstable/fragmentary. Kontopoulos and Perotti (1999) make a similar case for federal versus unitary governments. Both imply a diminished ability to use fiscal tools for opportunism.

When evidence of political influence on fiscal responses is found, the empirical results are more likely to be taken as support for partisan effects than for opportunism. A typical conclusion, quoted here from Alesina (1989, p. 55), is that 'when [opportunistic and partisan] theories are confronted with actual cycles in a number of industrial countries, the pattern of inflation, unemployment, output, and budget deficits indicates that partisan policy making is a fairly widespread phenomenon, with more limited evidence that electoral preoccupations result in major fluctuations'.[38] Not only have partisan effects been found by many authors at the national level (Winer et al. 2008), but partisanship has also been found at state and provincial levels (Besley and Case 2003; Kneebone and McKenzie 2001). Of growing interest is the emergence of a wider political spectrum than a simple left-right measure of partisanship. For example, Brauninger (2005) broadens the partitioning of partisanship from the left–right distinction usually used to test whether program preferences more generally differ systematically across political parties in ways that are sufficient to generate a spending cycle. His results suggest that more subtle dimensions of partisanship play roles in generating predictable party influences on policy and/or output. Similarly, Solé-Ollé and Sorribas-Navarro (2008) rely on coordination cost arguments, such as those advanced by Abrams and Iossifov (2006), to document the presence of partisanship in Spanish intergovernmental transfers. Finally, in an interesting application of DSGE-type analysis to these public choice issues, Blomberg and Hess (2003) modify a real business cycle model to include both partisan and competency effects and generate characteristic variable movements that conformed (better than did the model without these elements) to post-World War II US data.

While opportunism and partisanship have occupied most empirical attention, the relationship between political competition and economic outcomes outlined above has had a long history in public choice and this intersects with the short run by raising the question of whether the degree of political competition matters for the extent and/or design of fiscal policy. That is, not only is political competition needed to align political incentives with household demands in relation to government size, but the degree of political competition may also police political rent seeking in relation to the scaling of policies designed to respond to the business cycle.[39] For example, more vigorous political competition has been found to provide a greater degree of transparency in decision-making, which allows for more informed monitoring of government actions (Alt et al. 2006). This may be one of the underlying factors behind the finding by Besley et al. (2005) that stronger political competition was essential for promoting the enhanced economic performance of the southern US states by offering more salient qualitative choices among policies, policy instruments and governors.[40] Looking more narrowly at government spending, Ferris et al. (2008) find evidence in Canada that political competition is a significant explanatory variable in both long- and short-run dimensions of fiscal policy. In Canada, a closer margin of electoral victory (the measure of greater political competition) is associated not only with a smaller sized government but also with less spending variation about that smaller size (independent of party type).[41] The latter finding is reinforced by other scholars, such as Galli and Padavano (2002), who find that the size of fiscal deficits responds to the degree of government fragmentation (another measure of competition), and Skilling and Zeckhauser (2002), who study differences in debt accumulation between the United States and Japan and conclude that political competition encourages fiscal prudence. Finally, other economists have found a role for political competition in relation to partisanship. Solé-Ollé (2006), for Spain, and Dubois et al. (2007), for France, find that greater political competition reduces the degree of partisanship found in fiscal choices.

4.4 Measurement Issues for Testing Hypotheses on the Role of Politics in Fiscal Policy

The key difficulty in testing hypotheses that relate economic and political variables, such as those discussed above, is that economic variables typically grow through time while political/electoral variables usually do not. Hence one would not expect a stationary or

278 *The Elgar companion to public choice*

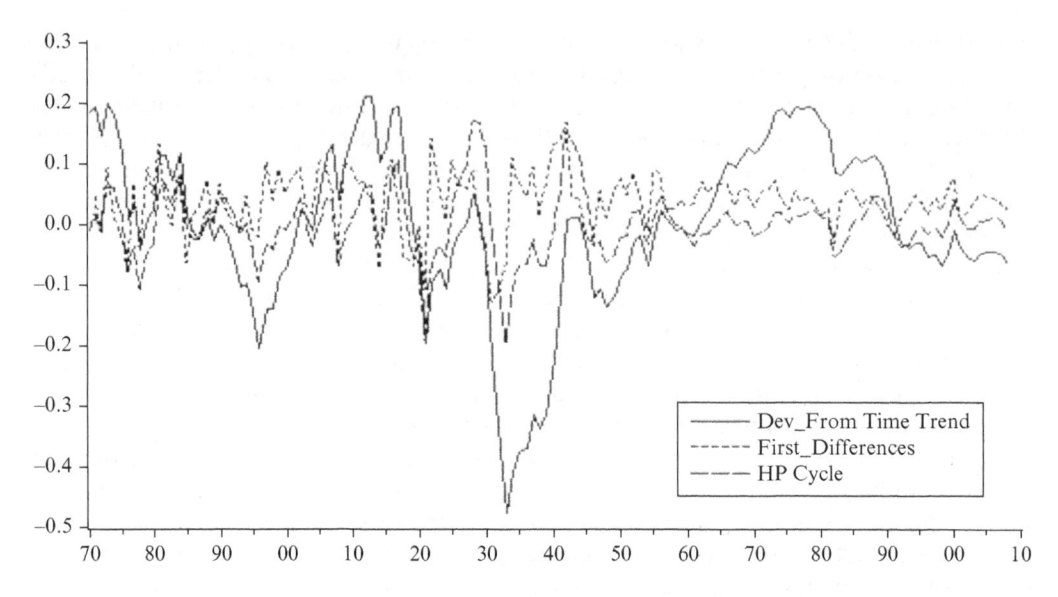

Figure 16.1 Alternative cycles in the log of Canadian real GNP, 1870–2008

I(0) political variable (like partisan party type or an election date) to be able to provide a meaningful economic or statistical explanation for a trending or non-stationary I(1) economic variable (like GDP or government size). In order to apply the test procedures typically used in statistical analysis, political variables would need to be related to other stationary economic measures. The testing of political influence in relation to either short-run fiscal policy and/or economic growth would then seem to present less of a concern because the measures used to describe fiscal policy allow similar stationary variables to be juxtaposed in a meaningful statistical manner.

Hence, if the stationary variables used to measure concepts like fiscal policy and the business cycle were unique and unambiguous, a test of political influence on fiscal policy would be relatively straightforward. However, because fiscal intervention arises in expenditure or taxation as a departure from long-run equilibrium values and because the cycle itself represents a variation in employment, growth or inflation rates relative to their longer-run equilibria, the measures of fiscal intervention and the cycle cannot arise independently of a theory of their long-run magnitudes. It follows that to test hypotheses that relate political variables to either the scale of fiscal intervention or the business cycle, longer-run equilibrium values must be removed from time series data.

In practice non-stationary variables are transformed into stationary variables either by deterministic de-trending, taking a first difference, or by using a filtering technique such as that suggested by Hodrick and Prescott (1997) (HP, hereafter). The separately transformed variables are then tested against each other. Unfortunately, the three techniques do not often generate the same measure of fiscal policy or even imply the same stage of the business cycle. An example of the differences that can arise among the alternate measures is illustrated in Figure 16.1 for the case of the logarithm of Canadian real gross national product (GNP) (between 1870 and 2008).[42] By inspection, it can easily be seen that the resulting cycles are not coincident and that the use of various de-trending techniques can result in quite differently measured relationships. What is worse is that the mechanical use of a de-trending technique can itself sometimes produce spurious cycles in the de-trended data (Harvey and Jaeger 1993), a particular issue when the HP filter is used on time series that are difference stationary (Cogley and Nason 1995). While statistical tests exist to distinguish between trend and difference stationary time series and, hence, point to the appropriate de-trending technique, in many cases the lack of power in the tests means that it is often difficult to distinguish between them.

From a public choice perspective, the important reason why long-run government size has not remained stationary through time is because the factors underlying and so determining it have changed, sometimes systematically and sometimes more dramatically. This is the premise of models built to explain the growth of government and/or its pattern of evolution through time (Borcherding 1985; Kau and Rubin 1981; Ferris and West 1996). It follows that an alternative way to filter the long-run from short-run data series that combine both is explicitly to model the long-run relationship. To the extent that the two sets of considerations are separable and a long-run model can be identified, the subtraction of the long-run estimate from the aggregate measure would result in a short-run series purged of predictable longer-run variations. More accurately, the procedure generates a short-run cycle contingent on the theory utilized to isolate the long run.

The empirical implementation of this approach requires both a theory of government size and cointegration analysis. For example, public choice theory suggests a number of variables that would serve as proxies for the changes in tastes and composition of the electorate underlying the demand for government services and for the changes in technology/organization that have altered the cost of providing government services (and/or collecting taxes). By and large these variables are non-stationary, so that regressing them against government means that the resulting estimates and implied relationships likely will be spurious. However cointegration theory tells us that if a linear combination of these non-stationary variables is stationary, then that set of variables comprises a cointegrating vector and the equation estimate can thus be interpreted as a long-run equilibrium relationship among the variables. The residuals of this equation must (by definition) be stationary and, as such, represent only transitory departures from the long-run equilibrium relationship embodied in the cointegrating equation. It follows that the residuals become a measure of short-run fiscal intervention and random disturbances that can be used both to test theories of fiscal response to the business cycle and to test for the response (or lack thereof) to the I(0) measures of political opportunism, partisanship and/or political competition.[43]

One example of the difference between the residuals generated by a cointegration model of long-run-size government and the residuals arising from the use of an HP filter is illustrated below for case of the log of real per capita government (expenditure) size over the post-World War II period in Canada.[44] As Figure 16.2 shows, the measures are not dissimilar but do contain some significant differences in size and timing. The case for using cointegrated residuals is that, unlike the HP residuals, they are generated with the use of more relevant information than just the internal characteristics of the series itself and thus have a meaning that allows for potentially more insightful interpretations with respect to the short run. Cointegration residuals have then been used together with first differences in an error correction model to represent a more precise description of the systematic process of short-run adjustment about long-run size.

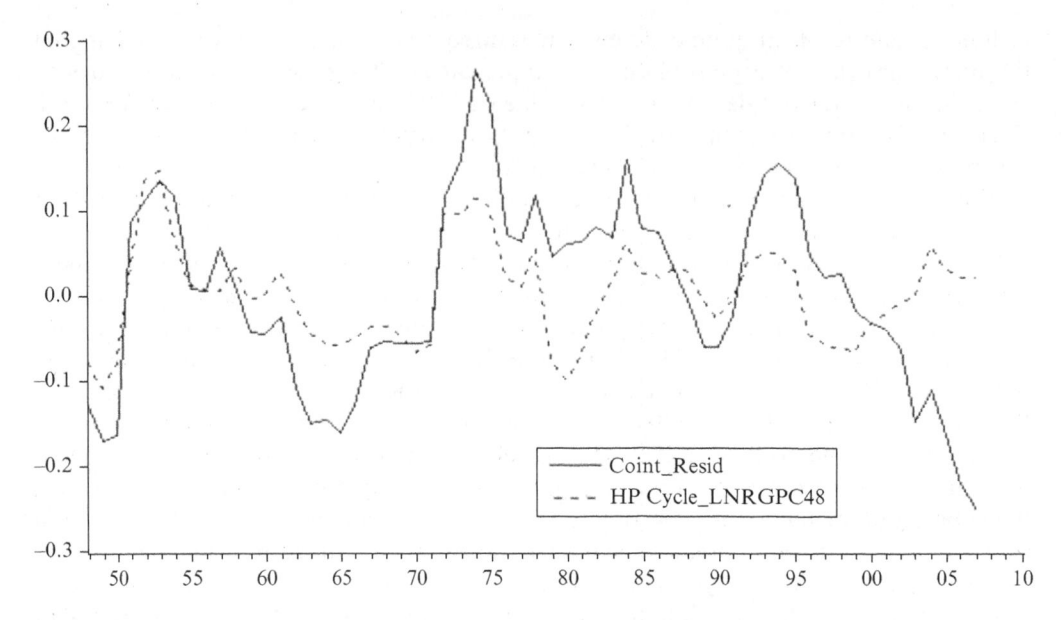

Figure 16.2   Alternative measures of fiscal intervention as a fraction of GDP: Canada, 1948–2008

Finally, a recurring theme of this chapter has been that the short- and long-run reasons for government spending/taxation interrelate conceptually and within the same fiscal measure. This suggests that rather than using a long-run theory to separate the time series into two distinct parts and testing the two theories separately, the two hypotheses should be tested simultaneously on the data. This can be done by combining the separate stages of the Engel-Granger error correction model and estimating the long-run model of government size at the same time the transition process about the long-run equilibrium is estimated.

5   CONCLUSION

In this chapter I have focused on how public choice issues intersect traditional macroeconomic analyses, both in relation to the determination of long-run government size and in relation to the business cycle. By focusing on macroeconomic concerns, however, this approach has been unable to do justice to the growing public choice literature analyzing the consequences for fiscal policy of particular differences in electoral processes and/or political party structures, both among countries and across groups of countries (for example, Angelopoulos et al. 2006; Efthyvoulou 2008; Redzepagic and Llorca 2007). Similarly little attention has been paid to the rapidly growing literature on the significance for policy of differences in the institutional and organizational structure of decision-making within bureaucracies (for example, Besley and Persson 2009). Instead the analysis has been centered on how traditional public choice considerations, such as partisanship, opportunism and political competition, intersect with traditional counter-cyclical macroeconomic policy and the different techniques used within the macro literature to address traditional public choice concerns. The particular object of this chapter has been to highlight the issues involved in measuring the scale and intensity of short-run fiscal intervention and the analytic problems raised by having the long-run policies related to government size and the shorter-run policies related to stabilization combined in a single fiscal measure. As such the analysis reflects the belief that unless greater recognition is made of the issues involved in measuring short-run fiscal intervention it will be difficult to establish any consensus on the scale of actual government intervention that arises at any particular point in time. Without this there will be even less chance of agreeing on the effects (or lack thereof) of different fiscal stimuli on the business cycle.

NOTES

1. I would like to thank Stan Winer for comments that improved the scope and presentation of this chapter.
2. For example, the belief that government is too large means that recessions would be fought more efficiently with tax reductions than with further spending increases.
3. An even more important simplification that has received considerable attention is the assumption that credit markets and the financial intermediaries that bring together savers and investors coordinate costlessly. The recent failure of such financial coordinating mechanisms has made the question of how to incorporate such problems in a tractable way into the analysis perhaps the most important current issue in macroeconomics.
4. To guarantee the existence of a money economy, I assume that the three goods in the utility function – c_t, g_t and m_t – are complements and that the household can become satiated in its holdings of real money balances.
5. The stocks m_t, b_t, k_t and k_t^g use the timing convention where the subscript t will refer to the opening value of the stock in that period. The value of the stock chosen in period t is then denoted by the subscript $t+1$ (which in turn becomes the initial value in period $t+1$), so that the real value of money balances chosen in period t, m_{t+1}, equals the stock of money chosen, M_{t+1} divided by the price level arising in period t, P_t. That is, $m_{t+1} = \frac{M_{t+1}}{P_t}$. The parameter δ represents the depreciation rate and is used to distinguish gross and net investment. Finally, the analysis assumes a separable range of capital projects that fall under the control of government. The microfoundation for this distinction is not specified but can be thought of as arising in the lower costs of internalizing some types of externalities in the investment process by using government (rather than private) means. In practice, these are the assets used to provide internal and external security and projects such as highways.
6. Government bonds, B_t, are the number of one-period claims to $1 issued by the government in period t that pay a nominal rate of return, i_t, in the following period, $t+1$. Hence, the initial nominal value of government bonds outstanding in period t is $(1 + i_t)B_t \equiv R_t B_t$ where R_t is the gross rate of interest and the real value is $\frac{(1+i_t)B_t}{P_t}$.
7. The first constraint (HBC) defines market alternatives limiting household choices in each time period. Combined with the constraint facing governments in the GBC, the two define the aggregate constraint on the community's choices each period. The per capita production function defines the production transformation possibilities facing the community. The production function (PF) is assumed to satisfy standard Inada conditions.
8. The transversality conditions require $\lim_{t \to \infty} e^{-rt} U_c x_t = 0$ for $= m, b, k, k^g$. This implies that households and governments at infinity will not hold assets that could be used to increase present discounted utility.
9. Hence $V(m_t, b_t, k_t, k_t^g) = U(c_t, m_{t+1}; g_t) + \frac{1}{1+\rho} E_t V(m_{t+1}, b_{t+1}, k_{t+1}, k_{t+1}^g)$.
10. The Lagrangian multipliers μ_{1t} and μ_{2t} represent gains in utility that would arise from relaxing slightly the household and government budget constraints. Notice also that (16.5) rewrites the intertemporal price ratios in (16.2) and (16.4) as $\frac{P_t}{P_{t-1}} = \frac{P_{t-1}(1+\pi_t)}{P_{t-1}} = \Pi_t$ to define the gross rate of inflation as one plus the inflation rate, π_t.
11. Substituting (16.12b) into (16.12a) shows that the expected utility gain from reallocating government consumption through time by issuing bonds and creating money must be equalized.
12. The resource constraint for the economy is the sum of the two individual budget constraints which, for the steady state, becomes $sy^{ss} + (1-s)y^{ss} = c^{ss} + \delta k^{ss} + g^{ss} + \delta k^{g\,ss}$ or $y^{ss} = c^{ss} + investment^{ss} + g^{ss}$.
13. In a more general context that distinguishes the services of capital and labor, Chari et al. (1994) solve

for a steady state in which the optimal expected tax rates set on capital and labor differ (with an optimal expected tax rate on capital of zero).
14. On the pitfalls of intervention, see Demsetz (1969).
15. Under Calvo pricing, a fixed random fraction of firms can change their prices each period. Calvo pricing has become popular because it generates average price level persistence easily, while allowing prices to vary across firms in a technically manageable way.
16. A corollary of the hypothesis is that fiscal deficits are stationary. See Bohn (1998), who provides strong evidence of fiscal stability for the United States and Neck and Getzner (2001) for Austria.
17. The theoretical limitations highlighted by the Ricardian equivalence debate provide a much stronger basis for motivating the role of debt finance/tax reduction in relation to short-run policies to address temporary departures from long-run equilibrium (for example, the importance of distribution, liquidity, uncertainty and information asymmetries in transition).
18. Hence, the concern in New Keynesian models, such as Woodford's (2003), that monopoly producers receive a production subsidy to align their outputs with those that would be produced under perfect competition.
19. A literature search in Econlit reveals that very few of the many recent papers on government size take seriously the hypothesis that government may be too small. Those that do typically are concerned with issues of corruption in developing economies (for example, Yavas 1998).
20. This analysis abstracts from further losses that would arise if tax rates were distorting.
21. Recent work on OECD countries by De Witte and Moesen (2010) suggests that only Australia, New Zealand, Norway and the United Kingdom would benefit from larger governments.
22. Unlike earlier work by Kormendi (1983) and Aschauer (1985), Karras (1994) finds that private and government consumption are complements rather than substitutes.
23. The empirical finding that appears most frequently, that an increase in government consumption's share of GDP will decrease the growth rate, need not imply that government consumption services are oversupplied. In the same way that a change in tastes from future to present (private) consumption would reduce growth but raise welfare, the loss of final output need not mean that the new combination of spending is not more highly valued.
24. Hence Woodford's (2001) emphasis on optimal policy defined in terms of government's ability to close the gap between actual and flexible price equilibrium rather than between actual and the stationary state.
25. Note that this reinforces the mechanism used by Fernandez-Villaverde (2010) from the other side of the market.
26. In this case the rise in government spending increases both output and prices. The expectation of inflation then lowers the real interest rate and increases aggregate demand further by raising private spending.
27. It should be noted that DSGE modeling assumes that the behavior of the system out of equilibrium is consistent with the behavior underlying long-run equilibrium. The type of behavior that arises in periods of financial crisis has suggested to some writers that when 'out of the corridor' the behavior of the economic system may be quite different, creating a special role for fiscal policy. On this see Leijonhufvud (2009).
28. As an alternative to specifying identification conditions, Fatás and Mihov (2003) use a Cholesky ordering to identify fiscal shocks and similarly find increases in government expenditures to be expansionary.
29. On the different meanings of fiscal multipliers, see Hansen (1973).
30. See the recent work of Afonso and Sousa (2009) and Afonso and Furceri (2008).
31. See Alesina et al. (1997, particularly pp. 36 and 62) for a convenient summary of opportunistic and partisan political theories and associated empirical tests. Haynes and Stone (1988) suggest that partisan and opportunistic effects may not be separable, where interdependence can be tested with interaction terms. Grier (2008) supplies a careful empirical analysis of political business cycles in the United States.
32. See von Hagen (2010) for the prediction of a projection cycle arising from the institutional incentives of the Stability and Growth Pact of the European Union.
33. See, for example, Serletis and Afxentiou (1998), who argue for the complete absence of any systematic effects in Canada.
34. See Lagona and Padovano (2008), who extend the argument to predict a political legislative cycle.
35. See also Aidt et al. (2009).
36. While this argument is developed for monetary policy, the same argument could be applied to fiscal policy.
37. Fatás and Mihov (2003) produce evidence from a cross-country study of 91 nations that legislative constraints on 'aggressive' discretionary fiscal policy have been successful in reducing the volatility of output and increasing economic growth.
38. However, see Heckelman (2006), who challenges the statistical tests used most often to test for rational partisanship.

39. See Svaleryd and Vlachos (2009), who find evidence of rent-seeking falling with greater electoral competition in Sweden.
40. Similar effects have been found by Padovano and Ricciuti (2009), for Italy, and Rumi (2009), for Argentina.
41. See also Dickson (2009).
42. Note that all three time series are I(0) with ADF statistics of −3.05 for the deviation from time trend, −6.60 for first differences and −8.03 for HP cycle. The critical value of the Mackinnon test statistic at 1 percent is −2.58.
43. Note that the definition of fiscal policy here includes endogenous as well as exogenous responses to the business cycle. As such, it captures a much broader definition of fiscal response than does the measure isolated in SVARs.
44. The model uses the cointegration relationship utilized in Ferris et al. (2008) estimated over the 1948–2008 period.

17 Regulatory policy
Amihai Glazer[1]

Various individuals or groups can benefit from regulation: bureaucrats who seek more power or influence, legislators who can extort rents from regulated firms by threatening even more stringent regulations, regulated firms that want to deter the entry of potential rivals, labor unions that want to require all firms to provide the same working conditions to their members, employees who want to increase demand for the skills required by regulations, or owners of capital who want to increase demand for the types of capital used intensively in complying with regulatory requirements. With such a richness of possible beneficiaries, one might explain any given regulation, perhaps incorrectly, by identifying *ex post* some group that benefits from it.

1 PUBLIC ATTITUDES

Regulation, however, may also appear for other reasons.[2] An important reason might be ideology. The ideology may reflect the utopian or moral views of voters. Alternatively, legislators may have their own ideological preferences. Perhaps surprisingly, regulatory policy, at least concerning the environment, appears to vary little by party. We should recall, for example, that the Clean Air Act of 1970, the most important US legislation up to that time meant to control air pollution, was enacted with the support of the Republican President, Richard Nixon. And it was also under Nixon, rather than under a Democratic president, that the United States established entirely new regulatory agencies, such as the Occupational Safety and Health Administration, the Nuclear Regulatory Commission, the Environmental Protection Agency, the Mine Safety and Health Administration, the National Highway Transport Safety Administration, and the Consumer Product Safety Commission. Also in the United States, partisan differences in support for environmental protection among the general public are often small. For example, from the early 1970s until the mid-1990s, support for greater spending on environmental protection by self-identified Democrats typically was only 10 percent higher than by Republicans. In a study of Canadian policy, McKitrick (2006) finds that air pollution levels generally varied little with the party in power.

One explanation for weak partisan effects can be that all, or most, winning political parties reflect voters' preferences – those of the decisive median voter in the classic Downsian model (Downs 1957). Evidence that the preferences of voters matter is found by comparing the environmental policies of state governors serving terms of office when they face re-election versus terms in which they do not. If elections matter, then governors facing re-election should behave differently than governors in their final terms. Such an effect is found by List and Sturm (2006), suggesting both that elections force officials to reflect the preferences of voters, and that elected officials would prefer to follow some policies that the voters may not.

To shed light on the preferences of voters, Kahn and Matsusaka (1997) study voting on 16 environmental ballot propositions in California. Environmental quality appears as a normal good for people with mean incomes, but some environmental goods are inferior for those with high incomes, at least when supplied collectively. An important price of environmental goods is reduced income in the construction, farming, forestry, and manufacturing industries. Income and price can explain most of the variation in voting; there is little need to introduce preference variables such as political ideology.

2 SPECIAL INTERESTS

2.1 Regulated Industry

Instead of maximizing welfare, or reflecting voters' preferences, regulations may benefit the regulated firms. The seminal work making this argument is Stigler (1971), who contends that politicians want to get elected, but also value receiving bribes, campaign contributions, and the like. Accordingly, politicians set policy to maximize some function of these two arguments. Producers, however, have an advantage over consumers or the general public: firms are better organized, firms are likely better informed about the effects of policy, and any one firm has a greater stake in the outcome than does any one consumer.

Following this line of reasoning, much attention has been paid to how a regulated firm can benefit from regulation, or at least from some features of regulation. For example, regulation may reduce output, either directly or indirectly, by raising costs, thus increasing the market price of final output. If entry is restricted, then these price increases can raise the profits of incumbent firms. For example, compliance with cotton dust standards for textile mills, by reducing output, raised the stock prices of the firms subject to them (see Maloney and McCormick 1982). Furthermore, note that special interests need not be all-powerful to influence legislation; they can instead support a policy that resonates with the public, forging a coalition of 'Baptists and bootleggers': the story is that laws closing liquor stores on Sundays were supported by Baptists, who viewed liquor as immoral, and by bootleggers aiming to suppress their competitors for one day each week (Yandle 1989).

Nevertheless, evidence that special interest groups are not all-powerful comes from the study by Cropper et al. (1992), which examines decisions by the Environmental Protection Agency (EPA) to cancel or continue the registrations of cancer-causing pesticides. The authors find that the EPA indeed balanced risks against benefits in regulating pesticides: increased risks to human health or to the environment raised the likelihood that a particular pesticide was banned by the EPA, and greater benefits from applying the pesticide made black-listing less likely. But special interests did have influence: comments by grower organizations reduced the probability of cancellation, whereas comments by environmental advocacy groups increased it.

2.2 Geographic Variation

Self-interest in the regulatory process can be geographically based. Consider an environmental policy – the so-called non-degradation standard – preventing significant deterioration in air quality in locations where air quality is already good, meeting or exceeding regulatory standards. Northern, urban constituencies supported such legislation, but not because of selfless interest in being 'green'. With poorer air quality, on average, in northern states, such residents benefited from the promulgation and enforcement of the new rules. Although states in the 'rust belt' would incur costs in improving the quality of their air, states in the south and in the west, where air quality was better, were prevented from luring 'smokestack' industries (and jobs) away from the Northeast and Midwest, because they were required to maintain their above-minimum air quality standards (see Pashigian 1985). Bartel and Thomas (1987) argue that regulations promulgated by the Occupational Health and Safety Administration and by the Environmental Protection Agency protect large rust-belt firms from rivalry by smaller, sun-belt firms.

One might think that voters would always favor costless improvements in environmental quality. But note that property values depend on relative, not absolute benefits. So enhanced environmental quality in one location can reduce property values in others, and, indeed, can reduce aggregate property values. Housing prices matter, and may indeed largely motivate local government policy (Fischel 2001). One reason is that housing constitutes a large fraction of household wealth. Data from 1990 surveys in the United States show that median household equity is 11 times larger than the median value of homeowners' liquid assets (Engelhardt and Mayer 1998).

2.3 Workers

Public choice approaches can explain phenomena that are puzzling when political considerations are ignored. Consider the choice of how much labor a firm will hire. Standard profit-maximization equates the ratio of prices of different factors of production to the marginal rate of substitution given by the production function. But a firm that cares about political influence may want to hire more workers than would be justified by cost minimization – workers and their families can exert political pressures to the benefit of the firm. (See, for example, Cassing and Hillman 1986, who show how import restrictions which increase employment in the domestic protected industry induce an increase in the number of voters who would benefit from continued import protection.) Turning to the regulation of prices, the much discussed Averch–Johnson effect argues that a firm can increase its profits when subject to rate of return regulation by using more capital (Averch and Johnson 1962). A firm has an incentive to do so because the new capital is added to the utility's 'rate base', with the regulators approving higher prices to consumers, and so increasing the firm's profits. The political effects just discussed would argue that regulated industries may instead want to hire more labor than called for by cost minimization, or at least not show a bias towards the use of capital. Some evidence is consistent with the last prediction – in a study of the electric power industry, Boyes (1976) does not find support for the Averch–Johnson effect.

Regulation may benefit workers not only by increasing employment, but also by increasing wages. Deregulation of industries provides evidence: following deregulation, prices and earnings premiums fell sharply in trucking, somewhat in airlines, though little in telecommunications and railroads. Furthermore, deregulation causes a decline in the percentage of workers belonging to a union (Peoples 1998).

3 BUREAUCRACY

Regulations are not self-enforcing, but are instead crafted and enforced by the employees of various government bureaus. The bureaucrats typically have incentives that differ from those of the regulated industry, of voters, or of the legislative committees that oversee their activities. One possibility is that regulatory agencies are captured by the industry they are charged with regulating,[3] perhaps through the expectation that a regulated firm will employ or richly reward decision makers in the regulatory agency who cater to the industry's interests (the so-called revolving door between the public and private sectors). But just the opposite may happen – tough regulations may increase demand for former regulators who know what the regulations mean or how to avoid them. Indeed, in a study of the Federal Communications Commission, Jeffrey Cohen (1986) finds that commissioners working for a regulated firm after leaving office are generally less supportive of the industry.

A regulator concerned about his reputation may be led to adopt soft or tough regulations. As Leaver (2009) argues, such a regulator may make decisions that avoid unwarranted publicity. If interest groups act like 'fire alarms'[4] when regulatory 'mistakes' harm them, regulators may take decisions with the aim of keeping interest groups silent and their decisions out of the public eye. But reputational considerations may lead regulators to impose strict regulations: a regulator may signal his intellectual quality by being aggressive. That can occur when the more able a person is the more information he can obtain about the firm that can be used to justify harsher regulation. Firms that want to employ more able individuals may then want to employ former regulators who had been harsh.

A way to examine the influence of voters on regulations is to study whether elected regulators behave differently from appointed ones. Kwoka (2002), who uses a cross-section of 543 electric utilities in the United States, finds that elected commissioners are associated with lower prices. Another study with similar conclusions is Besley and Coate (2003), which uses panel data on regulatory outcomes in the US states, to find that states with elected regulators tend to adopt policies that are more friendly to consumers than to producers.

One interpretation is that regulated firms can capture non-elected regulators. A complementary interpretation, advanced first by Stigler (1971) and then formalized by Peltzman (1976), is that voters-consumers, and not only regulated firms, can influence regulatory bodies.

4 INSTRUMENTS

There are questions that go beyond asking what private activities will be regulated. One can also probe what regulatory instruments will be adopted to achieve a given regulatory goal. Taxes on pollution are imposed rarely; instead, much regulation takes the form of command-and-control standards, where government mandates a particular technology to limit the social cost of a negative externality. We would expect regulated firms to prefer such standards, because they then bear only the cost of abatement, incurring no cost arising from continued emissions. Moreover, consistent with the idea that incumbent firms influence regulation, the required level of pollution abatement has generally been far more stringent for new sources than for existing sources. Such discrimination may worsen pollution by encouraging firms to continue to operate older, dirtier plants. Similar discrimination that advantages incumbent firms is found when regulation takes the form of tradable permits: initial allocation of such permits has been guided by a 'grandfathering' principle, which distributes permits at no charge, based on existing levels of pollution (Keohane et al. 1996).

5 IMPLEMENTATION

Studies of the impact of special interests on the regulatory process commonly encounter endogeneity problems. A special-interest group may organize only if it expects to be effective, perhaps because voters already are predisposed to favor their pet policies. And if policy responds to pressures by special interests, why don't the special interests just lobby for taxpayer-financed cash payments? The influence of special-interest groups may therefore lie not within the content of regulation but within its implementation.

Regulated industries may be able to undermine government regulation when government has difficulty committing to a regulatory policy. Consider the US automobile industry. When in the early 1950s southern Californian politicians became concerned about the damage to health and the environment caused by automobile exhausts, car producers responded by claiming that more research was needed. Predictably, those companies did little and, instead, in 1955 entered into a cross-licensing agreement for sharing patents on emissions control equipment that strongly discouraged any one of them to invest: why spend money when one auto company could free-ride on the investments of the others? However, after California adopted a rule stating that tailpipe-emissions regulations would be implemented if two practical, reasonable cost devices were developed, suppliers of pollution-control equipment to the auto industry undermined their customers' solidarity by developing the necessary technology. The automobile manufacturers then responded by introducing devices of their own.

Later, faced with federal government regulations to reduce emissions even further, increase fuel economy, and improve vehicle safety, manufacturers claimed that meeting those standards was impossible and that, without additional time, they would be forced to cut production and lay off thousands of workers. Illustratively, during a 1992 Vice Presidential debate, Republican candidate Dan Quayle, in voicing his opposition to more stringent corporate average fuel economy (CAFE) standards being pushed by environmentalists, repeated industry claims that 300,000 jobs would be lost (see Glazer and Rothenberg 2001). Industry recalcitrance was especially evident after enactment of the Clean Air Act of 1970, which required firms to produce automobiles with much lower tailpipe emissions. As it set a goal not achievable with 1970 technology, the original requirement for a 90 percent emission reduction by 1975 explicitly was technology-forcing. Had firms expected the standards to be enforced they would have invested so as to comply with them. Alternatively, if firms believed that standards readily would be waived, they would have invested little or nothing. Faced with a unified and resistant industry, the federal government postponed enforcing the standards. Most dramatically, responding to producers' claims that the enforcement of current emission standards would close factories (which, given the limited investment by the auto producers, seemed plausible), Congress weakened requirements or postponed deadlines in 1977 and again in 1988.

In understanding the effectiveness of regulation, we must consider the possibility that firms take actions they are not required to take, but, by meeting some of the desires of the public, legislators, or regulators, they reduce the likelihood that government will impose more stringent regulations. Examples of such self-regulation appear with the release of toxic chemicals; aggregate emissions of 17 of these chemicals fell by 40 percent from 1987 to 1992, though they were not subject to any regulation (see Maxwell et al. 2000).

Similar restraint was shown by banks when setting the prime interest rate they charged (see Glazer and McMillan 1992). During a period when, because of the Iran hostage crisis, the White House did not jawbone banks, the banks increased the prime rate. In particular, in the months after the hostages were taken in November 1979, the White House commented little on increases of the prime interest rate, as the gap between the prime and commercial paper rates (with commercial paper a measure of market interest rates) increased from 1.15 points in October 1979 to about 2.25 points in mid-February. Following the failed rescue mission on 25 April 1980, which dominated public attention, the prime rate was 4.25 percentage points above the commercial paper rate; the week after the prime rate was 6 percentage points above the commercial paper rate, and the week after that almost 7.50 points above. Only on 23 May did the White House publicly complain about high prime rates. The difference between the prime and commercial paper rates then gradually declined, reaching 4.20 percentage points by the end of June. Here, then, is an example where explanations of governmental policy must focus on non-formal regulation, and the preoccupations of government at the time, rather than assume that politicians can immediately and costlessly pursue the policies they prefer.

6 SUMMARY

Regulation can be affected by many different groups. The general public may have ideological preferences, the industries regulated may lobby for regulations that impose low costs on themselves and high costs on competitors, labor unions may want to protect jobs, residents of some area may want to increase property values in that area, the government officials responsible for adopting and enforcing regulations may care about their reputations. These actors may be concerned not only about current regulations, but also about how their actions can affect regulations in the future. Government officials and firms often recognize that policies differ in their credibility, with government favoring credible policies, and regulated firms favoring policies that a future government may not enforce. And firms potentially subject to regulation may take action in one period, such as by reducing prices or increasing employment, which will increase political support for the firms in the future.

NOTES

1. I am indebted to Vikram Abraham for excellent research assistance, and to the editors for valuable suggestions.
2. For a good survey of the politics of environmental policy, see Oates and Portney (2003).
3. For a review of regulatory capture, see Dal Bó (2006).
4. See McCubbins and Schwartz (1984).

18 The public choice perspective on antitrust law
Fred S. McChesney and Katherine M. Larkin-Wong

In the eyes of the world
Being born was my first big mistake.
But in the eyes of my woman I stand
Like a hero, a giant, a man who's as tall as can be.
Any fool can see
That's she's looking through the eyes of love
When she looks at me.[1]

For many years, antitrust was a poor stepson in the house of public choice. Due largely to Chicago School thinking of antitrust in public-interest terms, economists treated normative concepts about antitrust as making positive analysis of antitrust unnecessary. If the government had legislated it, it must be good. And so, iconoclasts urging an evaluation of antitrust in positive, rather than normative, terms were studiously ignored. (Throughout this chapter, 'Chicago School' is used as a metaphor for this approach, but that perspective has many adherents outside Chicago.)

Positive public-choice economics, analyzing antitrust as just another form of economic regulation, has slowly made progress, however. This chapter attempts to capture the major developments in the growing perception that treating antitrust as economic regulation, and thus as susceptible to self-interested manipulation as is any other form of regulation. That attempt to separate positive analysis from the piously normative has distinguished the advances that public choice has brought to one's thinking about antitrust.

1 ANTITRUST STUDIES LEADING TO APPLICATION OF PUBLIC CHOICE THEORY

In understanding the effect public choice scholarship has had on understanding antitrust, one must first be aware of the state of traditional antitrust thinking. When Congress passed the Sherman Act in 1890, there were few economists who supported the policy (McChesney 1995). It was generally thought that cartels had no long-lasting effects because they invariably collapsed, that monopoly arose for efficiency-based reasons, and that in any event the law could do little about whatever anticompetitive practices existed.

Slowly, however, antitrust law became accepted by economists and considered to be one of the great economic pillars of the American democracy. Thinking about antitrust has been the particular province of economists (and economically literate lawyers) at the University of Chicago. Perhaps because of their appreciation of the importance of economic competition, Chicagoans have always taken a rosy normative view of antitrust. By the 1930s, the first notable Chicago School professor interested in antitrust, Henry Simons, called for the expansion of the Federal Trade Commission (FTC) and repeal of the rule of reason in favor of legislation that '[prohibit[ed] . . . the acquisition by any private firm or group of firms of substantial monopoly power, regardless of how reasonably that power may appear to be exercised' (McChesney [1991] 1995, p. 28).[2] Implicit in this call to arms was the view that congressional passage of the Sherman, Clayton and FTC Acts, and their enforcement, was motivated by government actors serving the public interest.

Starting in the 1950s, however, economists slowly began to apply empirical economic methods to their study of antitrust law, although the first studies sought to validate the public-interest view of antitrust. Initially, scholars focused on specific cases or empirical evaluations of certain antitrust doctrines. The results were unfortunate: courts failed to make the determination that would enhance consumer welfare in more than half of the cases surveyed (Rubin 1995a). But why? There was a need to examine the activity of antitrust and its enforcement more systemically.

An important start to this examination came in a seminal article by George Stigler (1966). Stigler was the first to propose a statistical method for antitrust study, one upon which other economists might build. He asked whether the antitrust laws had prevented monopoly and therefore reduced concentration in American industries. His conclusions suggested that the antitrust laws' strengths were not in improving consumer welfare as many had hoped.

Stigler was particularly interested in the effects of antitrust in reducing industrial concentration. He compared (1) the United States with England, which at the time had no antitrust laws; (2) periods before and after the 1950 Celler–Kefauver antimerger amendment to the Clayton Act was passed; and (3) industries that are exempt from the antitrust laws to those that are not. Stigler (1966, p. 236) delivered an unenthusiastic evaluation:

> The substantive findings of this study are meager and undogmatic:
> 1. The Sherman Act appears to have had only a very modest effect in reducing concentration.
> 2. The 1950 Merger Act has had a strongly adverse effect upon horizontal mergers by large companies.
> 3. The Sherman Act has reduced the availability of the most efficient methods of collusion and thereby reduced the amount and effects of collusion.

It should be emphasized, apropos his final conclusion, that Stigler had no evidence of any actual collusion. For him, the 'amount and effects of collusion' could be inferred from the extent of concentration within any industry.

Stigler's article stirred researchers to greater empirical efforts in evaluating antitrust. Posner (1970, p. 365) presented a statistical examination 'of antitrust enforcement by the Department of Justice (DOJ), the FTC, state agencies, and private plaintiffs since the passage of the Sherman Act in 1890'. Posner used his data to test several hypotheses, starting with whether the number of cases filed by the DOJ might increase with growth of the US economy. His data demonstrated that this hypothesis was true until 1940 but that after 1940, despite 'tremendous growth' in the economy, the number of cases filed by the DOJ was stagnant (ibid., pp. 367–8).

These results continued despite a more than doubling in appropriations for the Antitrust Division and a 30 percent increase in the number of attorneys hired by the Division. Nor did Posner's data support the hypothesis that antitrust enforcement activity would decrease during times of economic contraction. Antitrust apparently had a life of its own, independent of macroeconomic events. Why it might function, regardless of economic changes, Posner never asks. Posner was mostly unattentive to any public-choice reasons for his findings, which, by and large, he apparently found puzzling.

Posner also examined restraint-of-trade cases brought by the FTC, finding that the FTC brought more restraint-of-trade cases between 1916 and 1939 than it had in the 31 years since (at the time of Posner's writing). 'There is plainly no reason for supposing that the Commission's level of antimonopoly activity has increased over the years; and this further undermines the hypothesis that antirust activity is determined by overall economic activity' (Posner 1970, p. 370).

Posner's examination of private plaintiff data demonstrated that initially private filings tracked closely the number of filings by the DOJ; it did so until 1945–49, when the number of filings by private plaintiffs began to grow at a rate proportionately larger than that of the DOJ. Posner's explanation was a 'recent rash of procedural rulings highly favorable to antitrust plaintiffs' (1970, p. 374). Finally, Posner examined the number of cases filed by state governments and while noting significant problems with the data set, he found that the number of antitrust cases filed by state governments had also grown significantly since the 1940s (ibid.).

Posner concluded by remarking that he had 'not attempted to account systematically for most of the variations in the quantitative indicia of antitrust enforcement' but he questioned whether politics and the identity of the party in the White House might affect antitrust enforcement (1970, p. 411). Posner reviewed the number of cases brought by Democrat and Republican administrations and found that the difference between the number of enforcement actions initiated when different political parties were in power was negligible (ibid.).

The importance of Posner's study cannot be overstated. He was the first economist to put together a comprehensive data set to examine antitrust enforcement. His data were the basis for a number of follow-on studies. Moreover, Posner was the first economist to question how politics (and thus individual motivations) might affect antitrust enforcement. But his suspicions about the politics behind antitrust were just that – suspicions. He did nothing to explore this dark side of antitrust.

For several years after Posner's study, economists nevertheless continued to search for an economic explanation for the effects of the antitrust laws, without success. Their failure to find one, coupled with the evidence that antitrust had largely failed to solve true problems for competition, resulted in the Chicago School's call for greater economic education of judges and for enforcement agencies to be more attentive in ensuring that the antitrust laws served their public interest intent.

For the Chicago School adherents, then, there was no public-choice consideration of the reasons why antitrust, in their own eyes, had been a bust. Their economic research demonstrated merely that the antitrust laws were not serving their stated public-interest purpose. The evidence demonstrating the consistent failure of antitrust cases to improve the public's economic welfare was attributed to a lack of knowledge or understanding of basic economic principles. Judges and enforcement agencies simply lacked the knowledge of economics that, if applied correctly, would result in an antitrust law that served the public interest. The solution then was simple: the education of judges and agencies to infuse economic principles into antitrust law.

This ignorance-based theory of antitrust 'mistakes' was anomalous. At approximately the same time, Chicago School economists developed a theory of regulatory policy that has been alternatively called the interest group theory of regulation and the economic theory of regulation (Stigler 1971). The economic theory of regulation proceeds from the demonstrated fact that regulation is explained by the benefits it provides to well-organized interest groups and the politicians who represent them, rather than in terms of government officials acting altruistically to benefit the populace at large by correcting market failure.

The Chicago School approach to antitrust thus was incompatible with Chicagoans' own theory of economic regulation. There can be no question that antitrust is a species of economic regulation. The heads of the Antitrust Division of the Justice Department and the Federal Trade Commission are political appointees. When national elections result in change in the political regime in Washington, as in 2008, it is commonplace to read that antitrust enforcement agendas are being revamped. Chicagoans have offered no explanation why they treat antitrust differently from other economic regulation.

2 THE PUBLIC-CHOICE ALTERNATIVE APPROACH

The fundamental tension between altruistic views of antitrust and the fact that it is affected by politics (plus the manifest failure of antitrust cases to achieve any pro-competitive goal) could not last, and it did not. Public choice theorists eventually directed their attention to antitrust laws. The first step was to study systematically whether antitrust enforcement was motivated by a desire to improve competition. The break-through in thinking about antitrust in public-choice terms came with Long et al. (1973).

Long et al. note that if antitrust laws were focused on improving consumer welfare, enforcement agencies could 'use welfare loss models to measure the benefits of bringing particular cases ... [and weigh them] against the associated costs of bringing antitrust actions ... [to] determine their optimal resource allocation strategy' (1973, p. 351). Using the Posner data on cases brought by the Antitrust Division discussed above, they 'compare a benefit-cost model of desirable antitrust activity [defined by economic models of welfare loss] with actual antitrust activity to assess the role of economic factors in the conduct of antitrust policy' (ibid.). They note that certain economic variables (for example, demand inelasticity) would identify industries where gains from collusion or monopolization were greatest, and thus where antitrust would have the greatest pay-off in enhancing competition.

Long et al. begin their analyses by looking at whether the cases brought correlated with aggregate welfare losses and found that 'aggregate benefit measures do a poor job of explaining the distribution of antitrust cases across manufacturing industry groups' (1973, p. 356). They then looked at the cases brought and the various component variables of the welfare-loss models, industry profit rate, sales and concentration. They found that industry sales play an important role in cases being brought by the Antitrust Division while cases were not statistically significantly related to industry concentration. After modifying the equation to examine the relationship between antitrust law enforcement activity and industrial concentration, they found that cases instituted by the Division 'do not increase in proportion to the increase in concentration and, beyond some point, may actually begin to decrease' (ibid., p. 358). Finally, they attempted to allow for variations in the Antitrust Division's prosecutorial costs based on the industry's ability to fight prolonged antitrust battles. To isolate the industry's economic and political power, Long et al. used an industry capitalization variable. The variable did little to explain the Division's case-bringing behaviors.

Those industries were not the ones in which antitrust enforcers had been active, however. The potential for welfare losses in a given industry had little effect on the US Department of Justice's decisions about which enforcement actions to initiate. Because actual measures of cost are not available from the Antitrust Division, they assumed that the cost of filing an antitrust case was equal across all industries. Ultimately, however, they found that 'the potential benefits from antitrust action . . . appear to play a minor role in explaining antitrust activity' (Long et al. 1973, p. 361).

The empirical results of Long-Schramm-Tollison were reinforced in other studies (Siegfried 1975; Asch and Seneca 1976) using different data but asking the same questions and reaching similar conclusions. Lewis-Beck (1979, pp. 177–8), in an underappreciated study using yet another sample, adds to the robustness of the conclusions noted above:

> The foregoing linear regression analyses of the merger and aggregate concentration variables suggest, surprisingly, that antitrust activity is independent of changing levels of economic competition. Notwithstanding legislative intent, the Division's enforcement of the antitrust laws does not appear stimulated by indications of intensified anticompetitive behavior. This finding complements John Siegfried . . . Such results prompt the further question of whether antitrust activity is at all responsive to the economic environment.

Taken together, all of these studies raised an important question: if economic variables are not controlling decisions whether to bring an enforcement action or not, what variables are?

Charlie Weir (1992) adopted a similar perspective in examining the British Monopolies and Merger Commission (since 1999 called the Competition Commission), which is charged with investigating merger bids that have been referred under the Fair Trading Act. Weir examined the variables that most influence the decisions of the Monopolies and Mergers Commission. Weir's goal was to 'identify issues which consistently appear to influence the Commission and so to provide a sort of litmus test which may be of use to firms' (ibid., p. 28).

Summarizing the public-interest framework, Weir suggests that it 'incorporates five main elements which relate to competition: prices and quality; cost reductions; new entry and new techniques, industrial and employment distributions, and foreign trade' (ibid., p. 27). To determine which of these factors consistently affect the decisions of the Commission, Weir collected a sample of 70 Monopolies and Mergers Commission reports published from 1974 to 1990. Based on these reports, Weir constructed a database for regression analysis of whether the bid was allowed or not, as a function of the public-interest independent variables.

Weir's results showed that firms gained little by arguing the positive side of the proposed merger (for example, job creation or greater exports), although some other welfare-related variables did appear to play a role in the Commission's affirmative decisions. Issues that did not appear important to the Commission included: (1) large market shares or horizontal mergers, (2) the more positive aspects of the public interest (greater efficiency, a smaller balance-of-payments deficit, more jobs, and larger investments in research and development). But the most significant contributor to a negative Commission determination occurred when the target firm contested the bid. That is, competition law was useful in helping competitors fend off unwanted takeovers – an issue unrelated to a takeover's competitive effects.

Ultimately, Weir's article shows that the public interest explanation for antitrust/competition actions does not hold up in the United Kingdom, either. If the multiple studies, commencing with that by Long et al. and leading to Weir are correct, the antitrust/competition law authorities do not base case filings on consumer welfare results. The question becomes, what standard do the agencies use?

But a more fundamental question suggests itself. Why do we have antitrust law and enforcement in the first place?

3 THE ORIGINS OF ANTITRUST

To address that question, it is useful to start with an examination of the origins of antitrust. Did antitrust arise to solve anticompetitive problems diminishing consumer welfare? Or does the evidence indicate that other forces drove the rise of antitrust?

The evidence seems unanimous that antitrust cannot be explained by the goal of improving consumer welfare. The seminal research in this respect began with DiLorenzo (1985), who examined the prices and outputs of industries labeled as 'trusts' by Congress in its debate over passage of the Sherman Act. DiLorenzo compared the changes in the trusts' prices and outputs with those of the economy generally leading up to 1890. He found that the trusts had *lowered* prices more and *increased* output more, relative to all industries in the American economy at that time. There was, in short, no economic case for passage of the Sherman Act.

DiLorenzo's conclusions have been seconded in more statistically oriented research. Delorme et al. (1997, p. 317) note that antitrust is 'as susceptible to the influence of special-interest groups as any public policies'. They then examine prices and outputs in the period surrounding passage of the Sherman Act, reaching the same conclusion as did DiLorenzo: prices were falling, output was rising. Their finding 'calls into question any overwhelming need for passage of the Sherman Act based on price or output movements' (ibid., p. 331). Delorme et al. then look at enforcement of the Sherman Act in the decade after 1890, concluding (ibid.) that 'regulation was too broad, penalizing efficient as well as inefficient competitors, or regulation spawned a massive merger movement that decreased the vigor of competition.'

Antitrust is America's gift to the world. With the Sherman Act, the United States became the first country to legislate a national system of competition law and enforcement: 'Economic competition is part of the American creed' (Lewis-Beck 1979, p. 169). But many individual states had their own antitrust statutes before 1890, and the evidence on those state statutes also sheds interesting light on the reasons for antitrust. There are lessons to be learned from America's foray into antitrust regulation even before the Sherman Act.

Boudreaux et al. (1995) examined the interests animating passage of state antitrust statutes, maintaining that by examining the state laws enacted several years before the

Sherman Act and, looking at the interests that most influenced their passage, we learn more about what prompted the Sherman Act itself. They focus on Missouri, a primarily agricultural state, and representative of the states that passed antitrust legislation in the late 1880s.

Boudreaux et al. (1995) hypothesize that, if the public interest explanation for the antitrust laws is correct, then in the 1870s and 1880s economic conditions in Missouri should have been a 'poster child' for the need to pass an antitrust law: the real prices of farm outputs should have been rising (or at least not falling), the volume of farm outputs should have been falling (or not increasing), and the real prices of farm inputs should also have been rising. If the opposite was true, they conclude, 'the cries against monopolization are more plausibly interpreted as rent-seeking attempts of less efficient producers to protect their markets' (ibid., p. 257). Focusing on cattle, hogs, and wheat, they find, in each case, that prices were falling during the late 1880s. Moreover, their results show that farm inputs did not increase in price.

Boudreaux et al. also note that the primary lobbyists for antitrust policies in Missouri were the agrarians. The cattlemen and local retail butchers supported the antitrust laws as a method for breaking up the centralized Chicago meat-packing firms, better known in Missouri as the 'beef trust' which, they claimed, were conspiring to *depress* the price of cattle. Kansas's governor convened in 1888 a conference to write an antitrust act; the conferees sought not to advance consumer protection interests but to 'protect the stock-grower and farmer against the manipulations of such alleged [beef] trust' (1995, p. 265).

The Sherman Act was America's only national antitrust statute from 1890 until Woodrow Wilson's administration. Then, as part of a vigorous political campaign to extend the reach of antitrust, the Clayton Act was passed in 1914 (so, too, was the FTC Act). The Clayton Act brought vertical contracting practices, such as tying and exclusive dealing, ignored beforehand for the most part under the Sherman Act, within the antitrust lens. And for many years, it treated those practices as illegal per se. Even today, they are regarded with suspicion by antitrust enforcers.

Thus, passage of the Clayton Act in 1914 affords yet another opportunity, after passage of state statutes and then the Sherman Act, to examine the possible public-choice rationale behind the new antitrust legislation. Ekelund et al. (1995, p. 272) criticized the public interest explanation for the Clayton Act and hypothesized that 'the business practices proscribed by the law and the establishment of the incipiency doctrine provided the means for *ex ante* wealth transfers among competing social interest groups ... [specifically transfers] that benefitted large incumbent firms and firms in intrastate commerce at the expense of expanding firms'.[3] Analyzing the legislative debate, Ekelund et al. argue that the vertical restraints imposed by the Clayton Act simply handicapped smaller firms by making it more expensive to expand into new markets. Declaring so-called vertical restraints illegal offered gains for established small, rural, independent retailers and manufacturers serving national markets as against new entrants, and that prohibitions on price discrimination protected smaller firms against the discounting policies of their larger competitors resulting in overall higher prices.

Ekelund et al. also examined the US Senate's vote on the Clayton Act. They compared the votes of senators representing agricultural interests against the votes of senators from states where manufacturing was growing, and used states with strong mining interests as a control variable. Their results (1995, p. 286), 'strongly suggest that economic efficiency was not the dominant issue in 1914. Special interests take center stage.' They conclude (ibid., p. 286) that 'the Clayton Act was a means of transferring wealth rather than an attempt to protect or preserve competition in the public interest'.

Ramírez and Eigen-Zucchi (2001) likewise examine passage of the Clayton Act in 1914. Using ordered and multinomial logit analysis, they find that economic interest variables largely explain the Senate votes. Their empirical results support the wealth transfer hypothesis, and show that senators responded to interest groups.

> Senators from states with a high proportion of smaller firms were two times more likely to vote in favor of the Act than senators from states with a high proportion of larger firms. This result holds even after controlling for a large array of political and economic variables. We also found that the agricultural sector at the state level strongly influenced the voting pattern – a large agricultural sector is associated with a higher probability of voting in favor of the Act.
> (Ibid., pp. 158–9)

The studies just discussed are remarkably robust in their conclusions. They demonstrate that the altruistic, consumer-welfare motivated explanations for state antitrust statutes, the Sherman Act and Clayton Act do not hold up to the historical data. Indeed, antitrust legislation seems repeatedly to be the result of pressure from special interests, whose behavior can only be characterized as rent-seeking. The research indicates that attribution of public-interest motivations to the antitrust laws has been misplaced since their enactment. That the studies remain unchallenged, and so uncontroverted, perhaps illustrates the gulf between those who see antitrust as self-evidently beneficial versus the public-choice approach to locating where (with whom?) those benefits lie.

4 HAS ANTITRUST IMPROVED CONSUMER WELFARE?

All antitrust legislation professes the goal of promoting consumer welfare. However, advocates of both public-interest and public-choice approaches agree that antitrust legislation has not had its intended effect of welfare increases. Empirical studies have shown that agency enforcement actions and judicial decisions actually have weakened competitive market forces, reduced efficiency, and, in some cases, caused a lessening rather than a strengthening of competition in various industries. The question, again, is why antitrust law flourishes, in the face of repeated evidence that the public is not well served thereby?

Macroeconomic evidence is summarized by Crandall and Winston (2003, p. 3), who find that 'the current empirical record' that antitrust enhances social welfare 'is weak.' Some of the reasons offered by Crandall and Winston relate to the cumbersome process of antitrust litigation and the fact that antitrust's doctrinal rigidities increasingly are ill-adapted to the quickly evolving, technologically driven economy of today. But Crandall and Winston also point out 'political forces that influence which antitrust cases are initiated, settled or dropped, including situations where firms try to exploit the antitrust process to gain a competitive advantage over their rivals, [and] the power of the market as an effective force for spurring competition and curbing anticompetitive abuses, which leaves antitrust policy with relatively little to do' (ibid., p. 23, internal citations omitted).

Once again, the more modern scholarship illustrates how robust the findings of earlier work were. Studies that have built on the statistical approach Stigler and Posner first utilized further demonstrate how the antitrust laws have failed to serve their consumer welfare purpose. George Bittlingmayer (1985) shows that passage of the Sherman Act and subsequent antitrust cases making price fixing illegal were responsible for the Great Merger Wave, which took place between 1898 and 1902. Merger and price-fixing are obvious alternatives to achieve the same goal. (In one famous case, *Addyston Pipe*, the alleged colluders abandoned their agreement during litigation and simply merged – without challenge from the antitrust enforcers.) Bittlingmayer studied merger activity in the years following the Great Merger Wave and found that 'antitrust policy continued to influence the number of mergers' (1985, p. 117). In short, Bittlingmayer's study demonstrated that, far from discouraging economic concentration (and thus the increased possibility of collusion and monopolization), antitrust policy had often contributed to it.

In another investigation of antitrust's effects, Shughart and Tollison ([1991] 1995) examined how the Sherman and Clayton Acts had affected employment in the United States. Using the data originally compiled by Posner and supplemented later by others, they hypothesized that 'an unexpected increase in antitrust activity can lead to an increase in the general level of unemployment' (p. 169). Their 'most conservative results impl[ied] that on average an unexpected increase of 1 percent in antitrust case activity leads to about a 0.15 percent increase in the overall unemployment rate' (p. 177).

These studies represent a small sample of public choice's contributions to a better understanding of antitrust's practical effects. Despite claims that antitrust laws support consumer welfare, the positive studies of the antitrust laws' impact on markets offer little support for the normative claims. How can this be?

Two possibilities suggest themselves. First, it might be that antitrust is based on a mistaken belief that economists and lawyers can identify problems for competition and fix them. That explanation for antitrust errors rests on the notion that antitrust enforcers are trying to increase consumer welfare, but frequently – being fallible – get it wrong. This is the standard portrayal of antitrust (including that propagated by the Chicago School). And there can be no doubt that many of the truly mistaken cases and enforcement activities in antitrust's past have been corrected.

This approach presupposes that the principles on which antitrust is founded are sound. There is scant evidence that this presupposition is true, and more evidence that it is false. Bittlingmayer (1995) examines what happened when the antitrust laws were suspended. If the economic theory underlying the antitrust laws is correct, suspension of the antitrust laws in the 1930s under the National Industrial Recovery Act (NIRA) should have raised prices and lowered output for cartel members, and lowered output and prices for the firms that supplied the cartels, resulting in higher prices and lower output for buyers from cartelized sectors.

Bittlingmayer examined the effect of NIRA, as well as two major antitrust cases, during the 1930s. He found that stocks moved up sharply after the contemporary antitrust cases and at each point that the NIRA moved through the House or Senate. By contrast, stocks fell after the Supreme Court declared the NIRA unconstitutional, and antitrust enforcement returned. Bittlingmayer then documents further that 'stock-return performance gains . . . [were] apparently not due to cartel gains by some industries at the expense of others' (1995, p. 311), concluding that the suspension of antitrust during the

NIRA's brief existence produced pro-competitive economic benefits. 'The passage of the NIRA was in fact marked by a boom, especially in durable-goods production ... some other factors could have caused the boom but there are few plausible candidates' (ibid., p. 317).

While Bittlingmayer's study considers the effects of antitrust from a macroeconomic perspective, others have looked specifically at the economics underlying specific practices prohibited by the antitrust laws. Asch and Seneca (1976) ask a question that (one would think) economists had already tried to answer: was supposed collusion (as determined from the cases brought) profitable? By comparing stockholders' rates of return, they find that alleged collusion and firm profitability were negatively related. Their suggestion as to why this might occur is telling: 'It may be that, within the range of firm and market structures examined, broadly collusive behavior is the rule ... but that antitrust prosecution centers largely on the *unsuccessful* manifestations of it' (ibid., p. 8, original emphasis). Antitrust enforcement, that is, has been based on erroneous analyses of competitive problems.

There are at least two criticisms of the error-based interpretation of antitrust's failure to fulfill its ostensible purpose of promoting competitive market outcomes. First, as economists ordinarily agree, reliance on error as an explanation for 'unintended' outcomes explains nothing: error can explain anything. Especially with a regulatory regime now well over a hundred years old, the real question is *why* errors have been so pervasive. Moreover, a century after passage of the Sherman Act, there is no reason to believe that antitrust actually has *increased* economic welfare. The best case for antitrust, under this view of antitrust-as-error, is that it has ceased to do as much economic harm as it once did. Reducing the incidence of error overall is hardly a strong claim to justify economic regulation.

Alternatively, the public-choice explanation for antitrust's evident failures stresses that error-based explanations ignore two critical facts. First, antitrust is government regulation, and regulation always produces gains for some and losses for others. And second, there is the fundamental principle of *Homo economicus*: if gains are to be had from regulation, one should expect economic actors to pursue them.

One embellishment on the public-interest interpretation of antitrust's failures has been that the antitrust laws are good laws, but are applied badly because judges and agencies are ill-informed and, sometimes, poorly educated. In the Chicago School model the solution to the antitrust enforcement problem, then, is more education in the principles of economics. In essence, agency practitioners and judges must begin to think more like economists. When they do, the antitrust laws will begin to serve their intended function and promote consumer welfare.

The public choice model suggests different reasons for the problems created by antitrust, and so offers other conclusions as to how to solve them. In that model, the antitrust laws fail to serve their intended purpose because rational, self-interested motives animate the process. Those motives explain not just the behavior of private actors, but also decisions of agency practitioners and judges. In fact, the agencies' failure to prosecute cases based on the likelihood that they will improve consumer welfare can be attributed to their personal interests in satisfying the members of Congress who provide their budgets. Better education is not the answer.

For example, Faith et al. (1982) build on Richard Posner's conclusion that 'FTC investigations are seldom in the public interest and are initiated at the behest of corporations, trade associations, and trade unions whose motivation is at best to shift the costs of their private litigation to the taxpayer and at worse to harass competitors' (pp. 329–30). They present empirical evidence of an 'antitrust pork barrel,' hypothesizing that favorable FTC decisions (defined as dismissals) are non-randomly concentrated on firms headquartered in jurisdictions of members of the House and Senate who serve on key FTC oversight committees.

Faith et al. found that membership on some House and Senate subcommittees had a positive effect on case dismissals for the organizations headquartered within the district. In particular, state representation on the Senate Subcommittee on Antitrust and Monopoly was significantly related to favorable rulings for the period from 1961 to 1969. In the House, the Independent Offices Subcommittee, the Subcommittee on Agriculture and Related Agencies, and the Subcommittee on Monopolies and Commercial Law all wielded substantial power with regard to FTC case decisions. Ultimately, they concluded that from 1961 to 1969, 'where a complaint has been issued, the pork barrel hypothesis [the effect of committee membership on dismissals] can be accepted at better than the 1 percent level of confidence' (Faith et al. 1982, p. 338).

The next question was whether the findings continued into the 1970s after implementation of significant reforms at the FTC. The data showed that after 1970, there was no statistically significant relationship between Senate Membership and FTC decision-making. The results of all five subcommittees in the House when taken together, however, 'tend to bear out the pork barrel hypothesis' (Faith et al. 1982, p. 339). The Subcommittee on Independent Offices and the Subcommittee on Monopolies and Commercial Law continued to have the greatest impact although other committees, including the Subcommittee on the Judiciary and Related Agencies, increased their influence over FTC decision-making. The authors conclude that, 'If anything, the pork barrel relationship . . . became statistically stronger during the reform period of the 1970s' (ibid., p. 342).

Faith et al. demonstrate, with evidence of an antitrust pork barrel, that public interest does not explain antitrust agency case-bringing behavior, but self-interest does. Legislators' interests lie with their constituents. As Faith et al. explain:

> a geographically based system [of democracy] confronts the legislator with a high payoff from representing local interests in the national legislature by trading votes with other legislators to finance numerous local benefits at the expense of taxpayer-consumers in general and with a correspondingly low payoff from voting in terms of cost-benefit analysis, economic efficiency, or the 'national interest'.
>
> (Ibid., p. 330)

Similarly, it is in the interest of regulators to please those members of Congress who sit on oversight and budgetary committees. By ensuring that these overseers have an interest in the agency and believe that the agency is doing the appropriate type of work, the regulators protect their own interests and budgets.

Coate et al. (1990) pursue the notion of antitrust as pork-barrel politics. They used data from FTC agency files to examine the Commission's decision-making when challenging horizontal mergers. They modeled the FTC as responsive to three variables (1) the Department of Justice/FTC merger guidelines, (2) internal agreement or disagreement between the lawyers and the economists and (3) pressure from politicians seeking to block mergers. The FTC has said it relies on the merger guidelines when deciding which mergers to challenge. At the margin, however, attorneys favor antitrust enforcement litigation 'because court challenges increase lawyer's human capital as litigators and raise their subsequent returns in private practice' (ibid., p. 468) or their salary grade in the government. Finally, in keeping with the importance of the antitrust pork barrel, political pressure is included because '[m]erger (or the threat of merger) of a firm in politicians' home districts or states confronts them (and their labor and management constituents) with concentrated expected costs, while the expected benefits are spread among shareholders nationwide' (ibid., p. 469). Moreover, the 'value of the probable loss to the current district is typically greater than the [amorphous and hard to quantify] value of the possible gain to another [district]' (ibid.). Thus, politicians representing a district wherein a constituent faces a (hostile) takeover have greater incentive to put pressure on the agency to challenge the proposed merger or to challenge mergers in general in the hope that the agency will oppose one merger in particular.

To test the effect of these variables empirically, Coate et al. used a probit model with the dependent variable indicating when the Commission voted to file a complaint in a given case. To test the influence of the economists in the Bureau of Economics (BE) against that of the lawyers in the Bureau of Competition (BC), who by hypothesis have stronger individual incentives to proceed against mergers, Coate et al. documented the views of the BC and BE, expressed in internal commission documents, as to the criteria in the merger guidelines on which they relied in recommending action or non-action. Thus, they identified where disagreements occurred; disagreements generally arose when the BE defined the market more broadly than the BC (as the self-interest model of attorney behavior would predict). The effect of politics on a merger was examined both indirectly (through the amount of news coverage generated by the merger) and directly (based on the number of times after the FTC indicated concerns about the merger that FTC commissioners and staff were called before congressional committees to testify about their record of antitrust enforcement).

Coate et al. found that the FTC relies primarily on the variables in the merger guidelines for deciding when to challenge a merger. The study also showed that, when there was a difference between the BE and BC evaluations of a merger, the lawyers in the Bureau of Competition had more influence on the Commission's decision than did BE. Finally, they found that, at the margin, greater political pressure (defined as both more news coverage and congressional attention) prompted the FTC to challenge more mergers.

Coate et al.'s data continue the line of empirical studies suggesting that the public interest model simply does not adequately describe the day-to-day operations of the antitrust agencies. That is, they suggest that much of the FTC's enforcement activity must be explained not only by the factors promulgated in the horizontal merger guidelines, but also as the result of political pressure and self-interest on the part of the lawyers within the antitrust agencies.

Given these results, the question then becomes, why do we still treat antitrust as an exception to the interest-group theory of politics?

5 CONCLUSION

As one economist (McCormick 1996, p. 415) notes, 'Many people have long wondered why it is that economic analysis of antitrust laws and behavior have been immune to the self-interest or public-choice axiom'. Political scientists Wood and Anderson (1993, p. 1) agree. Using data from 1970 to 1989, Wood and Anderson conclude that 'Antitrust Division behavior is strongly affected by the major U.S. political actors, including the president, Congress, and courts.'

How can a policy that has failed so conspicuously for so long, with no social-science evidence in its favor, continue to flourish? How can it do so when, repeatedly, antitrust has been shown to be a political animal? The public-choice answers are self-evident. After well over a century, antitrust has a well-established cadre of politicians, lawyers, economists and consulting firms who prosper thanks to antitrust law and enforcement. (The first-named author confesses to having sometimes benefited thereby.)

Shughart (1995, p. 319), for example, notes that the 'stubborn refusal to reject the naïve public-interest view of antitrust in favor of an alternative public-choice model with substantially greater explanatory power is puzzling'. The issue is not limited to a small group of public-choice economists. Shughart cites studies demonstrating that the private interests of members of the antitrust bureaucracy affect the policy positions they advocate and the cases they choose to prosecute, such that changes in antitrust law in the 1950s – the strengthening of the law on mergers – made 'antitrust expertise a more valuable commodity to the business community and the law firms serving it' (ibid., p. 321). In other words, the policy positions taken by the antitrust agencies improved the worth of their lawyers in private practice. Since 'the ultimate career goal of most members of the FTC's legal staff is a job with a prestigious law firm', such research further supports the idea that self interest motivates the antitrust agencies (ibid.; see also Shughart 1990).

It is a public-choice axiom that, once constituted, concentrated interest groups can be politically powerful, especially when the dispersed opposition is relatively impotent (Olson 1965; McChesney 1991). The forces of personal interest shaping the enforcement of the antitrust law are numerous and well documented. Who has the personal interest to incur the costs of opposing them?

NOTES

1. B. Mann and C. Weil, 'Looking Through the Eyes of Love.' Popularized by Gene Pitney, the song reached number 28 on the Billboard chart in August 1965.
2. All page references to reprinted versions of articles are from McChesney and Shughart (1995).
3. The incipiency doctrine describes the 'view that Section 7 of the Clayton Act was designed to thwart monopoly power "in its incipiency;" ... The "incipiency" doctrine goes back to Congressional discussion of the original Clayton Act' (Fisher, 1987, p. 23).

PART V

PUBLIC CHOICE PERSPECTIVES ON THE RELATIONS BETWEEN GOVERNMENT AND THE GOVERNED

19 Rent seeking
Arye L. Hillman

1 THE CONCEPT OF RENT SEEKING

1.1 Rents and Rent Seeking

The public-choice school was the originator of the view in the modern economics literature that incentives of self-interest apply in all human behavior, including personal behavior of political decision-makers and government bureaucrats, as well as individuals, groups, and corporations seeking favors from government. Rents are akin to favors or gifts; if it is known that political decision-makers and government bureaucrats are prone to exercise discretion in assigning rents, and if the privileged favors that provide the rents are contestable, it is in the self-interest of prospective beneficiaries of the rents to contest the rents. The time, effort, initiative, and resources used in contesting rents are lost to productive contribution to a society's output. A social loss is therefore incurred because of rent seeking. The focus of the rent-seeking literature has been on evaluating the magnitude of the social loss.

The rent-seeking concept was initiated by Gordon Tullock (1967), who observed that contestable rents attract resources. Anne Krueger (1974) used the term 'rent seeking', which has remained the terminology for Tullock's concept. A compendium of papers edited by Buchanan et al. (1980) provided the foundation for further development of the concept of rent seeking and its applications. The literature of the 40 years since Tullock's inaugurating paper has been organized and classified in two volumes edited by Congleton et al. (2008a, 2008b); volume 1 reprints theoretical developments and volume 2 applications. The introduction to the volumes summarizes the literature. Prior collections of papers on rent seeking include Rowley et al. (1988) and Tollison and Congleton (1995).

Politicians are sometimes described as securing 'ego-rents' from political office; that is, they feel good about themselves or obtain expressive utility (Hillman 2010) from their political identity and incumbency in political office – and perhaps, because of the trappings of power and access to emoluments financed by taxpayers, they feel superior to ordinary citizens. In democracies, large sums of money are often spent in contesting political office. The objective of the expenditures may be the ego-rents. However, politicians also derive utility from discretion in creating and assigning rents. The contribution of the rent-seeking literature to political economy is the identification of inefficiency associated with such political discretion.

The inefficiency due to rent seeking can supplement deadweight efficiency losses measured by Harberger (1954) triangles. For example, in the case of monopoly created by government regulation (Peltzman 1976) or protectionist international trade policies (Hillman 1982; Grossman and Helpman 1994), there are deadweight efficiency losses measured by Harberger triangles because of resource misallocation; however, the monopoly profits and protectionist rents are additional sources of efficiency losses when rent seeking takes place to persuade political decision-makers to create and assign the rents.

A government bureaucracy can assign rents (Rowley and Elgin 1988) through interpretations of laws and certification of entitlements. Counter-favors for bureaucrats can be provided in the form of bribes or personal benefits-in-kind. The bribes and benefits become contestable rents that attract resources into rent seeking when the positions of the bureaucrats to whom the bribes and benefits accrue are contestable. In a bureaucratic hierarchy, the lower-level bureaucracy may be obliged to pass parts of bribes received on to superiors; if positions at the levels of the hierarchy are contestable, there is a corresponding hierarchical structure of rent seeking (Hillman and Katz 1987). The bribes reflect corruption but are not in themselves indicators of efficiency losses, which are incurred when resources are attracted to rent seeking. There is therefore a distinction between transfers of income such as through bribes that affect distribution and the social costs of the transfers, which affect efficiency (Tullock 1971c). The social costs arise when the income transfers are contested.

Activities of lobbyists indicate the presence of rent seeking. The lobbyists could have used their time productively rather than in seeking to influence political decisions in favor of the individuals, groups, or corporations that have hired them. Lobbyists are important in facilitating rent seeking because politicians and government officials are understandably reluctant to make themselves open to rent-seeking overtures from all who wish to approach them. Although not necessarily illegal, being open to influence can be politically embarrassing if the information is made public. Lobbyists act as intermediaries who are trusted by politicians. Like politicians and government bureaucrats, lobbyists have an interest in rent-seeking activities remaining surreptitious and so out of the view of voters (Hillman 2009, ch. 2).

Rent seeking, although not necessarily illegal, is unethical in that people seek favors and privileges that allow them to benefit from someone else's productive effort. Ethical people are deterred from engaging in rent seeking.

However, participating in a rent-seeking contest is a rational personal investment (Tullock 1980a). A prisoner's dilemma arises when it is known that persuasion and influence are means of seeking benefit from government. A person or group seeking a favorable political decision will lose out against a competitor in the contest for influence, if it is only the competitor who engages in rent seeking. If undeterred by ethics, in Nash equilibrium all contenders seeking privilege from government engage in rent seeking. Rent seekers can have made the same investments in influence and persuasion, but some person or group can emerge with the rent. Models of rent seeking describe how, in populations that may consist of similar people, unequal outcomes arise in which some individuals benefit from rents and others do not.

With the acknowledgment of rent seeking, two forms of competition are thereby identified. Competition in markets for goods or factors of production is socially beneficial in enhancing efficiency. Competition in the form of rent-seeking contests is a source of social inefficiency (Buchanan 1980).

In a technical context, the theory of rent seeking is part of a broader theory of contests (Konrad 2009). Contests have been studied from the perspective of evoking performance as in sports competition or evoking effort by an employee to benefit an employer. The focus in these cases is on contest design.[1] In these instances, there can be social benefit through the performance or effort evoked in a contest. Rent-seeking contests provide no benefit to society. The socially efficient design for rent-seeking contests provides incentives for the contests not to take place.

The focus in the study of rent seeking is on inefficiency due to unproductive use of resources but issues of fairness and social justice are also present. The assignment of rents through nepotism or favoritism based on friendship and connections is efficient if a rent-seeking contest has been pre-empted in which resources would have been unproductively used. Privilege through nepotism and other forms of favoritism is, however, unfair in not providing equal opportunity to benefit from rents. There is therefore a conflict between efficiency and fairness.

1.2 Cynicism

Rent seeking is open to criticism as being an overly cynical concept because of implications for people's motives. Care therefore needs to be taken when the concept of rent seeking is applied (Hillman 2009, ch. 2). An unqualified application of the concept of rent seeking would interpret all personal favors as investments in rent seeking. Therefore the offer to pay for a cup of coffee or to pay for dinner becomes suspect in terms of attributed intentions. It may be that the only reward sought for paying for coffee or dinner is pleasant company and conversation. However, in the context of political and bureaucratic decisions, asymmetric assignment of benefits raises questions about the determinants of privilege, or about why governments (or political and bureaucratic decision-makers) have decided to treat differently people who, ostensibly, have the same characteristics and merit. Asking why ostensibly equally meritorious or deserving people have been treated differently in politically determined outcomes is not a cynical question.

1.3 Choosing to Acknowledge Rent Seeking

Ideological disposition appears to have had a role in whether economic researchers have been willing to apply the concept of rent seeking in economic analysis (Hillman 1998). The recognition of the incentives for rent seeking is unfavorable to an ideology that is suspicious of markets and is sympathetic to government discretion. For example, the ideology may favor extensive government-enacted redistribution of market-determined incomes. The theory of rent seeking recognizes that discretionary redistribution through government creates rents and that there are incentives for rent seeking if people believe that they can influence whether they will be recipients of the rents. There are further incentives for rent seeking if prospective beneficiaries also believe that they can influence the value of the benefits that will be conferred.

An ideology that views redistribution by government favorably will therefore downplay the importance of, or indeed the existence of, rent seeking. Barriers to acceptance of the rent-seeking concept can also be traced to ideology-related expressive utility (Hillman 2010). Researchers may define their personal identity through expressive voting and rhetoric, and also with reference to the topics that they write about. Expressively 'nice' people may prefer to model benevolent government and redistribution determined according to social-welfare criteria rather than to describe public polices and income redistribution as the outcome of political opportunism and rent seeking. Opportunism and political support are usual requisites of success in politics. While the claim might be that authors who perceive behavior as including rent seeking are overly cynical, those authors who ignore rent seeking when describing political discretion may be either overly naive about political processes, or be ideologically committed to a view of the role of government that is compromised by the recognition of rent seeking.

In introducing rent seeking and further developing the concept, Gordon Tullock and those who joined him did not set out to describe an ideal world. If the world were ideal, politicians and government officials would always act in the public interest and individuals would devote attention only to productive pursuits and not seek privileged, unearned benefits. The emphasis on incentives and self-interest led to the study of rent-seeking behavior in a matter-of-fact way.

Outside of the Virginia School, rent seeking was a topic that attracted attention in Israel beginning in the 1980s, before privatization of the worker cooperative sector of the economy had occurred and when non-market institutions were still prevalent (Hillman 1991). The Bar-Ilan School has paralleled the Virginia School in developing the rent-seeking concept.[2]

A long tradition of benevolent democratic government (see, for example, Congleton 2011 on England) may make rent seeking seem unimportant. Yet rent seeking can emerge in locations least expected when evidence displaces presumption.[3]

1.4 Guilt and Shame

Emotions of shame and guilt are embedded in different forms in a society's culture (Lal 1998). Guilt can inhibit participation in rent seeking. Where shame is present but not guilt, the only inhibition is the likelihood of being discovered. There may, on the other hand, be neither guilt nor shame. As with corruption, guilt is diminished when politicians know that they are not alone in catering to rent-seeking activities but are conforming to a near-norm among their peers. Similarly, in government bureaucracies, it can be a challenge to be the only non-corrupt or non-rent-seeking bureaucrat (Andvig and Moene 1990).

1.5 Outline

Section 2 proceeds to describe measurement of the social cost of rent seeking and inferences from various models. Section 3 describes rent extraction, which is in general associated with rent seeking. Section 4 focuses on low-income societies. The usual setting for rent seeking is the interface between government and the private sector: however, section 5 describes rent seeking within government and, section 6, rent seeking that does not involve government directly. Section 7 returns to models and considers behavior in laboratory and natural experiments. In section 8 rent-seeking models are considered in relation to other political-economy models. Section 9 is concerned with societal resistance to rent seeking. The final section is a brief conclusion.

2 MEASUREMENT AND MODELS

The investigation of rent seeking requires, beyond acknowledgement of the concept, empirical confirmation and measurement.

2.1 Impediments to Measurement

An impediment to measurement of the social cost of rent seeking is that rent-seeking behavior is in general unobserved. Politicians, government officials, and private-sector beneficiaries wish their rent-seeking activities to be surreptitious rather than visible. Indeed, successful rent seekers have incentives to declare that their privileges are due to their personal competence rather than to their success in rent-seeking contests (Hillman 2009, ch. 2). It is therefore rare to observe directly the magnitudes of resources invested in rent seeking. Other impediments to direct measurement are that resources are used by unsuccessful rent seekers whose activities may not be known and that resources used by incumbent beneficiaries in defense of rents may not be observed. Although resources were used in persuasion, rents that were sought may moreover never have been assigned, because political decision makers did not agree to create the rents.

It may be possible to observe the value of the rents that were created and obtained by successful rent seekers. In these instances, the basic question of evaluation of the social cost of rent seeking is whether the value of an observed rent can be used to infer the unobserved value of resources used in contesting the rent. The question can be framed in terms of 'rent dissipation', which is defined as the total value of the resources R used by all rent seekers in contesting a rent relative to the value of the rent V:

$$D \equiv \frac{R}{V}. \tag{19.1}$$

With n contenders for a rent and a contender j making a rent-seeking investment x_j, R in (19.1) is:

$$R = \sum_{j=1}^{n} x_j. \tag{19.2}$$

Rent dissipation is therefore:

$$D \equiv \frac{\sum_{j=1}^{n} x_j}{V}. \tag{19.3}$$

The question regarding social cost concerns the value of D. If $D = 1$, then $V = R$ and rent dissipation is complete, in which case the observed value of V can be used to infer the unobserved value of R.

A value for rent dissipation D can be inferred from a model of a rent-seeking contest by assuming rational optimizing behavior and modeling the decision problem of the contenders for the rent. With risk-neutrality, the objective of contender *i* is to maximize expected utility from participating in a rent-seeking contest, given by:

$$EU_i = \rho_i(x_1, x_2, x_3, \ldots, x_n) V - x_i \qquad (19.4)$$

where $\rho_i(x_1, x_2, x_3, \ldots, x_n)$ is the contest-success function determining how the rent-seeking investments of *n* contenders for the rent translate into the likelihood of contest success for contender *i*. In (19.4), *V* is common to all rent seekers but more generally valuations of the rent may differ (Hillman and Riley 1989; Nti 1999).

Gordon Tullock (1967, p. 232) observed with respect to monopoly that, 'regardless of the measurement problem, it is clear that resources put into monopolization and defense against monopolization would be a function of the size of the prospective transfer', which is indicated in (19.4) by *V*. However, which mathematical function describes the contest-success function? There is no empirical evidence that allows identification of the characteristics of real-life (as opposed to modeled) contest-success functions; unlike auctions that have a formal pre-announced structure and a rule for designating the winner, there are no pre-announced known rules for success in rent-seeking contests. The problem of non-observed rent-seeking investments $(x_1, x_2, x_3, \ldots, x_n)$ is therefore compounded by the absence of information concerning the manner in which political and bureaucratic decision makers respond to influence and persuasion when choosing successful rent seekers.

2.2 Empirical Studies

The response in empirical studies to the absence of data on rent-seeking investments and lack of information on the form of the contest-success function has been to assume complete rent dissipation. With $D = 1$, the value of an observed contested rent *V* becomes a proxy measure for the value of resources *R* unproductively used in rent seeking. In basing conclusions on complete rent dissipation, the empirical studies also assume that all rents are contested rather than assigned by nepotism and other forms of favoritism.

A first place to look for rents is monopoly. Computations of the social cost of monopoly inclusive of rent seeking, by Posner (1975) for the United States and Cowling and Mueller (1978) for the United Kingdom, resulted in social losses above the previously obtained small Harberger measures. The studies of monopoly raise questions such as whether all profits are necessarily indicators of social loss and how to interpret losses, and whether advertising by firms necessarily constitutes rent seeking. When profits attract new entrants, efficient competition is taking place, and advertising can be informative; Littlechild (1981) made the case that Cowling and Mueller (1978) were overly extensive in their identification of monopoly rents and thereby overestimated the social costs of monopoly due to rent seeking.

Government transfers are the primary source of rents. The social cost of contestable transfers in the United States was estimated to be 25 percent of gross domestic product (GDP) (Laband and Sophocleus 1992). For Europe, 18 percent of government revenue was estimated to be subject to rent seeking, equal to 7 percent of gross national product (GNP) (Angelopoulos et al. 2009).

High social costs due to rent seeking have been found for low-income countries. The social loss due to quota rents was estimated to be 15 percent of GNP for Turkey and

7.3 percent for India (Krueger 1974); these are high values of social loss based only on restrictions of international trade. A study of the entire economy of India suggested a social cost of rent seeking of between 35 percent and 50 percent of GNP (Mohammad and Whalley 1984).

Katz and Rosenberg (1989) proposed estimating the social cost of rent seeking on the assumption that all changes in government budgets reflect rent-seeking activities. Changes in government budgets can, of course, be the consequence of demographic change, changes in government, and changes in political priorities, rather than rent seeking. Also, in countries with electoral systems of proportional representation, changes in the government budget can be due to requisites of coalition formation. Budgetary changes therefore need not necessarily indicate prior rent-seeking investments of equal value. However, on the assumption that rent seeking is the only reason for changes in a government's budget, Katz and Rosenberg identified a means of circumventing the impediments to direct measurement of resources used in political persuasion.

2.3 Rent Dissipation in Theoretical Models

The contribution of the theoretical models of rent-seeking contests is to investigate the general validity of the assumption that $D = 1$. The value of D depends on various considerations, including in particular the form of the contest-success function. Two contest-success functions that have been extensively applied were proposed by Tullock (1980b) and in Hillman and Samet (1987).

2.3.1 The Tullock contest-success function

The Tullock contest-success function views investments in rent seeking as purchases of lottery tickets, with the addition of possible scale effects through the number of lottery tickets purchased. The Tullock function is, for rent seeker i:

$$\rho_i(x_1,..,x_n) = \frac{x_i^r}{\sum_{j=1}^{n} x_i^r}, \qquad (19.5)$$

where r is a scale factor for rent-seeking investments. With the Tullock function, complete rent dissipation requires competitive rent seeking, or in practice a sufficiently large number of rent seekers. In the symmetric Nash equilibrium of the Tullock contest, the common rent-seeking investment is:

$$x = \left(\frac{n-1}{n^2}\right) rV. \qquad (19.6)$$

The second-order condition for maximum expected utility requires:

$$r < \left(\frac{n}{n-2}\right). \qquad (19.7)$$

There is positive expected utility from participation in the contest if:

$$r < \left(\frac{n}{n-1}\right). \tag{19.8}$$

If the second-order condition is satisfied, there is an incentive to participate in the contest. When $r = 1$, the Tullock contest is in effect a lottery in which probabilities of success depend on the number of lottery tickets purchased and rent dissipation is:

$$D \equiv \frac{nx}{V} = \left(\frac{n-1}{n}\right). \tag{19.9}$$

For example, with $n = 2$, rent dissipation is 50 percent. As the contest becomes more competitive, as indicated by increasing values of n, rent dissipation increases. For sufficiently large values of n, rent dissipation is all but complete.[4]

2.3.2 The Hillman–Samet all-pay auction

The Hillman–Samet contest-success function describes an all-pay auction; that is, the highest 'bidder' wins the 'prize'. The all-pay auction results from setting $r = \infty$ in the contest-success function (19.5). The all-pay-auction contest-success function has been described as 'discriminating', in the sense that the rule can differentiate among rent seekers and identify the winner precisely; in contrast, the Tullock contest-success function is 'non-discriminating' in only assigning probabilities to being a successful rent seeker (Hillman and Riley 1989). The Hillman–Samet contest-success function provides a justification for the assumption of complete rent dissipation without regard for the number of rent seekers in a contest. In a symmetric Nash equilibrium, with no costs of entry into a contest and risk neutrality of rent seekers:

$$D \equiv \frac{nEx}{V} = 1 \quad \text{for } n \geq 2. \tag{19.10}$$

In (19.10), Ex is the expected value of a rent seeker's investment in quest of the rent V. Two or more risk-neutral contenders for a rent *on average* completely dissipate the rent. The Nash equilibrium all-pay auction involves mixed strategies; it is because of the mixed strategies that the conclusions about complete rent dissipation apply 'on average'.[5] With mixed strategies, contenders in a rent-seeking contest choose the value of their rent-seeking outlays from a distribution that characterizes the mixed-strategy equilibrium. For example, with two rent seekers, the distribution is uniform over the range from zero to the common valuation of the contested rent and the expected value of each contender's rent-seeking outlay is therefore half the value of the rent; thus together the expected value of the two contenders' outlays equals the value of the contested rent V. If there are three contenders, the distribution specifying the mixed-strategy equilibrium changes to place greater weight on smaller 'bids' (because of the smaller probability of any contender winning), and the total value of the bids or outlays of the three contenders remains equal to the value of the contested rent. The shifting of weight in the distribution to lower bids continues as the number of contenders in the contest further increases, with the increase in n always being precisely counterbalanced by the decline in Ex to maintain the total expected investment nEx of rent seekers constant, for a given value of V.[6]

2.3.3 General contest-success functions

Models with more general contest-success functions than the Tullock or Hillman–Samet forms can also predict complete rent dissipation. Quite generally, in any contest in which a rent seeker's probability of winning increases with his or her outlay and decreases with opponents' outlays, competitive risk-neutral rent seekers dissipate the entire rent (Hillman and Katz 1984). Rent dissipation can be shown to be complete when there are only two contenders (as in the all-pay-auction case) under quite general specifications of the contest-success function (Alcalde and Dahm 2010).

2.4 Persisting Rents

Models of rent seeking generally describe the rent sought as a benefit for a point in time. For example, the contested rent is described as an instantaneous monopoly profit or rent from protectionist international trade policies, or an instantaneous benefit received through tax laws or the government budget. Rents tend, however, to persist over time. The recognition of persistence introduces the possibility that a rent may disappear in the future because the government that has created the rent will decide to eliminate it, or a government may decide to open up the rent in the future for re-bidding. When a rent persists over time, rent seekers compete for the present value of the rent, qualified by the possibility of losing the rent at some time in the future. Complete rent dissipation occurs, provided that the conditions are present for complete dissipation if the rent were viewed as available only at a point in time. Whenever a rent is contested or re-contested, rent seekers dissipate the expected value of the rent, making allowance for the possible disappearance or need to re-contest the rent in the future (Aidt and Hillman 2008).

2.5 Collective Aspects of Rent Seeking

The initial models of rent seeking described private benefits sought through the personal efforts of individuals. However, quite often or indeed generally, rent seeking is the collective act of an interest group. The collective rent-seeking effort may be in quest of a common private benefit, as for example, a policy sought, such as a change in the tax laws or changes in government entitlements. The benefit collectively sought can also be a share of a private benefit, for example, a government grant to an industry or geographic region. Group rent-seeking effort may also be undertaken in the quest to secure government spending for the provision of a public good that benefits the group collectively although perhaps differently.[7]

When the benefits are private and shared, different rules can link personal contributions to the collective rent-seeking effort to the sharing of the rent. The incentives associated with different rules determine the extent of free-riding in individuals' choice of effort.[8] The sharing rules based on individual effort require of course that effort be observable; effort-based rules cannot be applied if personal effort is unobservable. Yet moral hazard arises precisely when personal effort is not observed.

The personal contributions of individuals to achieving the collective objective of the rent-seeking group can be proposed as somehow voluntarily and cooperatively coordinated. Incentives appear, however, to be more reasonable for explaining individual behavior than non-incentivized voluntary personal effort.

316 *The Elgar companion to public choice*

In the case of interest groups contesting benefits that are public goods (such as where the government will locate a highway or bridge), rent dissipation is predicted to be low and insensitive to the size of the group when individuals choose personal rent-seeking contributions in Nash equilibria (Ursprung 1990). Rent dissipation increases if members of the group of rent seekers seeking a public good can be additionally incentivized as, for example, by appeal to 'community spirit' or through common ideology (Congleton 1991a). Expressive utility from personal identity defined with reference to ideology can overcome free-riding incentives associated with the public-good benefit. The common objective may be ideological persuasion of others. Hence political campaigns often have dedicated volunteers.[9]

3 RENT EXTRACTION

Rent extraction occurs when political decision makers benefit from the rents that they create. The beneficiaries of rent extraction can also be local levels of government and private individuals.

3.1 Rent Extraction by the Political Rent Creators

We can presume that the rents would not have been created in the first place, were there not benefits for their creators (Appelbaum and Katz 1987). For example, the political benefits extracted in return for rent-creating international-trade policies can be political support in the form of votes or campaign contributions or more direct personal benefits (Hillman 1982; Grossman and Helpman 1994). Rent extraction by political decision-makers also takes place when firms or private individuals pay politicians *not* to implement policies that would reduce private rents, which McChesney (1997) has called 'money for nothing'.

Politically extracted rents are contestable through challenges to the positions of the political decision-makers who are the beneficiaries of the rents. Thus, social costs are incurred when resources are used in political persuasion to create rents; when the rents that have been created are contested by prospective beneficiaries; and also when the government positions of the beneficiaries of rent extraction are contested (Hillman 2009, ch. 2).

The personal benefits to political decision-makers through rent extraction complicate the calculation of the social costs of rent seeking. The resources used in rent seeking provide personal benefits when, for example, politicians are invited to breakfasts and dinners, and special festivities, and are granted use of corporate jets and associated amenities. The resources used in such ways are socially wasted only if the utilities of the politicians who benefit are excluded from the society's measure of total welfare.

3.2 Fiscal Federalism and Rent Extraction

A federal system of government can limit rent creation and rent extraction by lower-level government. In the earlier years of the United States, for example, when state or local governments sought to restrict competition from producers in other localities, the constitutional requirement of free trade among the states, embodied in the 'Commerce Clause', prevented such rent creation and rent extraction (Tullock 1991).

3.3 Political Sensitivity and Rent Extraction by the Private Sector

Rents can be extracted by private-sector firms that take advantage of political sensitivity to unemployment. The rent extraction is associated with moral hazard and the concept of a 'soft budget' (Kornai 1980). Knowing that unemployment is politically costly, firms can choose to hire excess labor. When threats of unemployment arise because of imports or other competition, firms can extract rents through subsidies or protectionist policies that sustain politically desired employment levels while increasing the firms' profits (Hillman et al. 1987).

3.4 Soft Budgets in a Fiscal Federal System

Soft budgets arise in a fiscal federal system when lower levels of government seek to extract revenue from higher-level governments by not undertaking necessary expenditures in anticipation of intergovernmental transfers. The social cost of the rent-seeking behavior is the reduced benefit for the local government's population while waiting for funding from the higher level government (Tullock 1975a).

3.5 Rent Extraction in the Welfare State

With effort at self-reliance not observable, governments deciding on welfare policies in the presence of moral hazard confront the choice between type-1 and type-2 errors. We define a type-1 error as insufficient assistance for people who have made an effort to be self-reliant and have been genuinely unfortunate, and a type-2 error as a policy decision to provide assistance to people who have chosen low effort at self-reliance. When welfare policies are generous, the beneficiaries of type-2 errors are extracting rents. The social cost of rent seeking occurs without a rent-seeking contest. The rents in the form of income transfers are present to be extracted for anyone through choice of low effort at self-reliance (Hillman, 2009, ch. 7.2).

4 POLITICAL INSTITUTIONS AND POLITICAL CULTURE

4.1 The Prevalence of Rent Seeking

The prevalence of rent seeking depends on a society's institutions (Congleton 1980) and political culture (Hillman and Swank 2000). A culture of corruption and rent seeking has been described in low-income countries in south-east Asia (Cassing 2000; Khan and Sundaram 2000) and sub-Saharan Africa (Rowley 2000). Endemic corruption associated with the quest for rents has been described in China in the context of personal enrichment of local government bureaucrats (Kahana and Liu 2010). India is an exception in having democratic institutions with a culture of corruption (Mishra and Gupta 2007).

4.2 Rent Extraction through Corruption

Corruption facilitates rent extraction. Rents can be extracted through the necessity of paying bribes to obtain, for example, a copy of a birth certificate that is in principle available freely or at nominal cost, or rent sharing takes place when a bribe provides a drivers' license to an unqualified driver (who then endangers others).[10] Rent extraction can also take the form of payments to avoid harassment, as in delays in government officials' attending to citizens' requests (Kahana and Nitzan 1999) and through corrupt income-tax officials seeking bribes not to report actual or fabricated tax evasion (Hindriks et al. 1999; Marjit et al. 2000).

4.3 Autocracy and Rent Seeking

Successful rent seeking is in general an easier task in an autocracy than in a democracy. In an autocracy, fewer people need to approve favors and privilege; the ruler alone may decide on the creation and distribution of rents. In a democracy, it may be necessary to persuade multiple political decision-makers to create and dispense rents. The impediments to rent seeking in a democracy have been proposed as explaining why the Industrial Revolution began in England, where parliament composed of decentralized decision-makers was the fiscal authority, and not in more authoritarian Europe (Tullock 1988).

4.4 Persistence of Political Culture

The institutions of communism were accompanied by a culture of rent seeking. In the absence of market allocation, people could rely for personal benefits only on the decisions and favors of others (Hillman 2009, ch. 2). Political liberalization was insufficient to change the political culture and resulted in more rent seeking. In the absence of political liberalization, outsiders without direct access to rent-seeking contests could compete among themselves to become political insiders who could participate directly in contests for rents. Political liberalization ended the privileges of insiders but, with no change taking place from the political culture of rent seeking, the end of insider privilege increased the contestability of rents and the social cost of rent seeking (Hillman and Ursprung 2000). Thus, the transition from socialism replaced communist institutions with the institutions of markets and private property but with the culture of rent seeking sustained, personal benefits were seen to be – and indeed were in fact – primarily obtained not from productive activity but were sought as rents, principally obtainable through privileged privatization of the state's assets (Gelb et al. 1998). Similarly, in numerous cases in Africa and elsewhere, corrupt regimes have been replaced by new corrupt regimes with the maintained political culture of rent seeking and rent extraction.

4.5 Rent Protection

Rent protection is a form of rent seeking that takes the form of a quest to maintain rents already enjoyed. In monarchies and dictatorships, the best investment that might be made is to replace the ruler and thereby obtain the ruler's rents. The ruler expends resources on rent defense, which includes identifying potential threats from those in the population who have the resources required to contest the ruler's position. Because rule is by personal discretion and the ruler views as a threat any individual who has been successful in accumulating personal wealth, people have personal incentives not to be overly successful, so as not to attract the attention of the ruler. The ruler may distribute charity to the people for whom productive incentives have been eliminated.

4.6 Migration to the Welfare State

When people migrate to a western welfare state, cultural priors are maintained if immigrants view the government of the welfare state as the replacement for a charity-giving autocratic ruler left behind (Hillman 2009, ch. 7). In the immigrants' new location, there can be continuation of past behavior of not accumulating personal wealth and being dependent on charity, now through the income transfers from the government of the welfare state (Nannestad 2004).

4.7 Emigration to Escape Rent Extraction

Whereas the welfare state through self-selection attracts unproductive immigrants from low-income countries, productive people also face incentives to emigrate so as to escape the disincentives for personal economic success because of rulers' rent-protection objectives. In an autocratic rent-seeking society, personal proximity to a ruler is more advantageous than personal skills and abilities. The sycophants of a monarch or dictator enjoy rents, while the remainder of the population is the source of the rents through repression and appropriation. If emigration is possible, those people most disadvantaged in being the source of the rents have the greatest incentive to leave. For a usual contest-success function, inhabitants with a comparative advantage in rent seeking remain and the people with a comparative advantage in productive activities leave. Emigration, thus, makes the country poorer. Because the exit of productive people reduces the rents available to be extracted, the population can unravel through emigration incentives, as adverse selection occurs and productive people who had previously remained find themselves confronting even stronger incentives to exit. Low-income countries consequently often are rent-seeking societies that people with a comparative advantage in applying initiative and in productive activity seek to leave (Epstein et al. 1999). The first application of initiative is in planning and implementing departure to a location where personal productive abilities are rewarded.

4.8 Rent Seeking as an Impediment to Innovation

Economic growth is fostered by new ideas applied by innovating entrepreneurs. In a rent-seeking society, new firms are particularly susceptible to impediments to growth when the rent seekers are government officials and ruling elites who seek bribes for circumventing regulations that have been imposed on business activity. Large established firms may on the contrary be favored by government officials and elites because of the rents that such firms can provide; but those enterprises may be moribund and inefficient (Murphy et al. 1993). Under authoritarian regimes, there are often close ties between management positions in large firms and the ruling elites. The close ties facilitate rent seeking. Ideally for the ruling elites, large firms are 'state owned'. Privatization need not, however, change the role of a formerly state-owned firm as a source of privileged rents (Buccola and McCandish 1999).

4.9 Natural Resources and Rent Seeking

Countries with autocratic institutions can be poor notwithstanding substantial natural-resource wealth. In the absence of institutions that protect property rights, including the property rights of the government and the collective rights of citizens, natural-resource wealth is a rent that evokes contestability (Mehlum et al. 2006).[11]

4.10 Foreign Aid

Rent seeking occurs when political elites contest foreign aid that has been provided to help the poor in their countries (Svensson 2000). The evidence is, consistently, that foreign aid has been ineffective overall in promoting economic growth and economic development in poor countries (Doucouliagos and Paldam 2008).

4.11 Unethical Behavior

Rent protection and rent seeking in low-income countries can be part of unethical behavior. Rent protection may entail more than appropriating aid and keeping people poor. In the case of Rwanda, there was genocide when population growth increased the contestability of claims to land, the value of which depended on the price of the principal marketable crop, which was coffee (Verwimp 2003).

4.12 The Historical Record

The contemporary evidence is consistent with the historical record. Gordon Tullock (1988, p. 410) observed that: 'In most of the world, throughout most of history, rent seeking has been a major activity for the more talented and aggressive members of society.' Delorme et al. (2005) confirmed the prevalence of rent seeking in the Roman Empire; Thaize Challier (2010) described rent extraction in Medieval France; and mercantilism has been studied as a rent-seeking society with rent-extracting government (Baysinger et al. 1980; Ekelund and Tollison 1981).

5 RENT SEEKING WITHIN GOVERNMENT

Rent seeking occurs within government in the course of politicians and government bureaucrats seeking to improve their personal career positions. Much of a politician's time can be spent in the activity of seeking to ensure personal political support. Bureaucrats may be engaged in self-promotion and networking activities that increase their prospects for promotion within the administrative hierarchy; much of the activity may revolve around the lunch calendar, and morning and afternoon coffee or tea. In countries with a political culture of corruption, promotion within the bureaucratic hierarchy may require that bribes be paid to superiors (Kahana and Liu 2010). The source of the bribes can be payments received from lower-level bureaucrats who are themselves seeking to further their promotion prospects and subvention obtained from private individuals seeking bureaucratically dispensed favor and privilege. Again, the bribes, although unethical and illegal, are not a source of social loss. The social loss is incurred when the positions to which the bribes accrue are contestable.

6 RENT SEEKING WITHOUT GOVERNMENT

Rent seeking is part of political economy, which studies the relation between government and citizens against the background of political institutions. Rent seeking occurs, however, also in contexts that do not directly involve government.

6.1 Rent Seeking within the Firm

Rent seeking can take place within a firm. Such rent seeking has been described as taking the form of managers' making decisions that increase the value of their own specialized expertise, thereby increasing their incomes while also deterring competition for their positions. Rent seeking by management also takes the form of diversification of the firm's activities, which provide managers with insurance, should any branches of business activity not be profitable; the diversification is beneficial for management but not for shareholders, who would benefit from specialization of the firm according to core competence and who can reduce their exposure to risk by diversifying their personal stock portfolios. Stock markets may internalize such insurance-seeking behavior by management, by reducing market values of diversified firms. When rent seeking takes place within the firm, managers are not necessarily rewarded for their contribution to profits but according to their within-firm rent-seeking competencies. Rent creation and protection within the firm is the basis for a theory that explains unemployment to be the consequence of rent creation by the firm's insiders who exclude outsiders from employment (Lindbeck and Snower 1987). Ownership structure also affects rent seeking within the firm.[12]

6.2 Rent Seeking and Status

Rent seeking occurs in interpersonal relations. Contests for personal status are rent-seeking contests in which the prize is the status achieved. Because status is relative to the achievements of others, the status contest is a prisoners' dilemma in which in the Nash equilibrium resources have been expended by all contenders and no gain in status has been realized. In asymmetric status games in which some people have more wealth than others, there are winners who spend the most in the status contest, with the visible act or consequences of spending conferring status, in particular when it is evident that the spending is intended only for status and not for personal need. Thorstein Veblen (1899) described an example of such contests for status as involving the number of servants lined up in front of the house visibly awaiting the return of the master and mistress. In modern versions of the status game, the spending for status often takes the form of charitable donations that benefit others. When people in need are thereby helped, the expenditures in the contest for status are not socially wasteful; however, if the contests create contestable rents, the contests evoke socially wasteful rent seeking.[13]

6.3 Rent Seeking as Wars of Attrition

Rent seeking occurs when males use resources to compete for a female, or females similarly compete for a male. The rent-seeking contest can take the form of a 'war of attrition' in which the contender with the most resources or the most patience wins the 'prize'. In a war of attrition, as in rent-seeking contests, resources expended are lost to the rent seekers (although the resources may benefit the object of rent seeking). The value of the resources expended by the successful rent seeker is determined by the value of resources invested by the last competitor to leave the field of competition.

6.4 Rent Seeking in Academia

Rent seeking takes place in academia (Brennan and Tollison 1980). There are contests for status, including through publications. Rent seeking can take the form of seeking to please editors and reviewers without regard for the intrinsic merit or value of editorial and reviewer comments (Frey 2005). There is social benefit when a research paper provides a new insight that adds to understanding of a significant phenomenon. However, if papers are written for personal and not social benefit, the characteristics of socially wasteful rent-seeking contests are present.

Rent creation and rent protection take place when groups of researchers define a field as the subject matter of specialized journals that suit the research group and when professional journals are controlled by rent-creating and rent-protecting insiders. Rent seeking takes place in academia internally within university departments and research institutes through contests for leadership positions and for university and departmental resources. The principle of comparative advantage can then apply; academics who take pride in and enjoy research (which may be a rent-seeking activity) may confront other academics whose comparative advantage is not (or is no longer) research but who rather have a comparative advantage in departmental and campus-wide rent seeking.

Academic tenure is a means of rent protection; through tenure, academics who would not be offered their current salary at another university or research institute nonetheless continue to receive their income, which includes as rent the payment above the best alternative offer. However, tenure has an efficiency benefit: inadequately performing tenured faculty are willing to offer positions in their departments to superior or potentially superior academics because of the awareness that the superior performance of the newly hired faculty will not in the future threaten their own positions. The remaining impediment to inferior faculty agreeing to hire superior faculty is envy of the status of superior researchers within the university department or research institute.

6.5 Rent Seeking and the Legal System

The use of resources in contestability in the legal system has attributes of rent seeking. Rent seeking in the form of distributive contests through the legal system would not occur if property rights were perfectly defined and enforced, contracts were completely specified, principles of liability were unambiguously defined, responsibilities and obligations in division of property when couples separate or divorce were predetermined, and legal obligations to pay taxes were specified clearly. The number of lawyers relative to other professions has been proposed as an indicator of the extent of potential for or actual rent seeking in a society. Tax accountants also assist in a distributional quest, facilitated by imprecision and ambiguities, and also inordinate complexity, in the tax laws.[14]

6.6 Rent Seeking and Religion

6.6.1 Rent seeking and personal religious observance
Religious beliefs are a sensitive and personal subject. Nonetheless, an overview of rent seeking requires recognition of the possible relation between rent seeking and time assigned to religious activities. The rent seeking related to religion can occur without the presence of rent-seeking contests. When people believe in an afterlife, because the number of people that can be accommodated is ostensibly unbounded, there is no rent-seeking contest (the rent being the afterlife) when people engage in activities that are intended to provide rewards in the believed world to come. The time spent on religious activities could be used to increase output but the same is true of all time allocated to non-work leisure activities. If the quest for merit is through charitable acts, there are benefits for others, if rents are not created to be contested by beneficiaries. The personal rent-seeking quest has adverse consequences for others if the religion offers as the rent or reward in the world to come a large number of awaiting virgins for those males who kill themselves in the act of maiming and killing non-believers. Religious observance does not entail rent seeking when the intention is spiritual self-improvement, or when the purpose of contemplation and learning is to increase personal awareness of the requisites of ethical behavior; in these circumstances the personal beneficial consequences of ethical awareness also benefit others.

6.6.2 Rent seeking and religious institutions
Rent seeking has been investigated in the context of religious institutions. It has been proposed that within the Catholic Church rent seeking occurs through contests for promoting sainthood (Ferrero 2002). The historical foundations of the enmity of the Church toward non-believers have a rent-seeking interpretation in the objective of the Church to protect its tax base of believers. Islam, in contrast, requires that a special tax be levied on those non-believers who as 'people of the Book' (Jews and Christians) have protected but subservient status; the objective sought by Islam in imposing the tax is not necessarily the revenue but to provide incentives to convert to Islam to avoid the tax.

6.6.3 The medieval Roman Catholic Church and the Protestant Reformation
The medieval Roman Catholic Church and the Protestant Reformation have been placed in a rent-seeking context. Before the Reformation, the Roman Catholic Church had a monopoly on religion in western and central Europe. Protestantism objected to the doctrine that, after the end of life on earth, a person's soul could remain in purgatory between heaven and hell, and that payments to the Church determined the final destination of the soul (Ekelund et al. 1992). The payments to the Church to determine

the direction of exit from purgatory were predicated on price discrimination according to personal wealth of the family of the deceased. The Protestant doctrine of predestination at birth removed the claim of discretionary power of the Church to determine whether the soul is destined for heaven or hell and destroyed the doctrinal foundation of the Church's source of purgatory-based rent extraction. A mechanism of monopoly of the Catholic Church was the role of the priest as necessary intermediary for religious interpretation, and absolution through confession in forgiveness of sins. The preoccupation of the Church with heretics was aimed at preservation of the Church's monopoly on religion and the protection of the rents of the Church. Protestantism ended the monopoly and permitted personal access to reading of the Bible, which with the invention of the printing press enhanced literacy and stimulated economic development.

Against this background, Ekelund et al. (1989) model the Catholic Church as a vertically integrated monopoly supplying 'the conditions of salvation', with prospects for rent extraction enhanced by inelastic demand for afterlife. They also explain usury in terms of rent seeking by the Church, which was both lender and borrower: 'when the church was a lender, it shadow-priced its loans inside the church at market rates (or above), thus extracting rents. When it was a borrower, it enforced the doctrine, thereby extracting rents by reducing its cost of credit on certain loans' (ibid., p. 323).

Rent extraction by the Roman Catholic Church ended where the Protestant Reformation succeeded, and also in England as the consequence of the marital affairs of Henry VIII (who also benefited from appropriation of the assets of the Church in England). Ekelund et al. (2002) describe the Protestant Reformation as occurring where entrepreneurs supported by local rulers sought freedom from the rent extraction of the Church, whereas rent extraction and rent seeking remained embedded in locations in which the Roman Catholic Church maintained its hold.[15]

6.7 Sacrifices as Rent Seeking

Personal rent seeking was ingrained in ancient cultures in the form of sacrifices to the 'gods', from whom rewards or rents were sought by giving up or sacrificing valuable possessions. Different societies or tribes had their own 'gods' to appease and to persuade to grant them favors. Child sacrifice was common in many cultures. If there were many 'gods' who could provide rents, socially wastefully competition occurred in the rent-seeking investments made to influence the different 'gods'. Part of the social cost of the rent seeking was the use of time, effort and resources in the making of idols to worship and to which to offer sacrifices. Rent-seeking investments also took the form of constructing elaborate temples to honor the various 'gods'. Monotheism ended the competitive seeking of favors from the different 'gods'. Abraham's father Terach was a supplier of idols. While his father was away, Abraham destroyed the stock of idols and, when challenged by his father, Abraham replied that the idols had brought about their own demise by fighting among themselves. Terach replied that this was impossible because the idols were inanimate man-made constructions – whereupon the point that Abraham wished to make was made by his father. The consequence of Abraham setting out to sacrifice his son Isaac was the end, in western civilizations for which Judaism is the foundation, of perceived benefit from child sacrifice. Sacrifices continued in other cultures: thus, many centuries after the time of Abraham, when Carthage was besieged by

Rome, children of the elite families were sacrificed to the 'god' Moloch for the purpose of seeking intervention to save the city. The children died and the city was destroyed in a case of ineffective and unethical rent seeking.

7 MODELS AND EXPERIMENTS

7.1 The Diversity of Rent-seeking Models

We return now to the modeling of rent-seeking contests. The first models describing the contesting of rents were motivated by the desire to formulate inclusive measures of the social costs of political discretion. Political economy was basic to the models. In the subsequent development of the theory, rent-seeking models began to take on lives of their own in elaborations and departures from the initial Tullock and Hillman–Samet contest formulations. The early studies recognized the importance for rent dissipation of the specification of the contest-success function; that entry barriers and costs of entry into a contest mattered; and that rent dissipation was affected by whether rent seekers were risk averse and whether rents were valued differently.[16] Thereafter the models were extended to include many different aspects, including asymmetric information, bounded rationality, timing of investments, the reward structure for contributors to group effort and the structure of prizes, whether the rent provides private or collective benefit, whether there is opposition to rent seeking from those from whom the rent would be extracted, whether incumbent beneficiaries of rents have advantages in a contest, whether incumbents can strategically deter or diminish rent seeking by others, whether rent seeking occurs in stages, and whether there are asymmetries in being able to survive a loss in repeated contests. Different permutations of the conditions of rent seeking were considered.[17] It was also recognized that different combinations of circumstances were equivalent (for example, Baik et al. 2006). While there have been debates among economists about the appropriateness of measurement without theory, the theoretical models of rent-seeking contests generally offer the converse of theory without accompanying empirical content. The literature has developed in this way because of the data problems when activities are not observed. Government statistical offices also do not and perhaps cannot provide – or cannot be expected to provide – data for empirical studies of rent seeking.

7.2 Over-dissipation

The different theoretical models provide qualifications to the complete rent-dissipation presumption. Can the value of an observed rent at least be an upper bound on social cost? In sequential bidding in a contest in which the highest bidder wins, participants who enter the contest are caught in a trap because of the ever-present incentive to keep bidding given that past bids are lost. Over-dissipation can result if bidding persists. The incentives to keep bidding (because there is no Nash equilibrium in pure strategies) make it irrational to enter such a contest in the first place, given that someone else has entered. In the simultaneous move game, it is rational to bid and over-dissipation does not occur. Over-dissipation can of course occur if people irrationally base their behavior on subjective rather than the objectively true probabilities of winning (Baharad and Nitzan

2008). Over-dissipation can also occur when the outcome of a rent-seeking game is an 'evolutionary stable equilibrium' (Hehenkamp et al. 2004). Another reason for over-dissipation of the value of a rent is expressive utility from winning a contest (Hillman 2010): however, with expressive utility present as an addition to the monetary gain from winning, the definition of complete dissipation requires amendment so that the value of the rent to be won includes expressive utility from being the winner; with the expressive component of winning recognized, the usual conclusions about rent dissipation apply.

7.3 Experiments on Rent Seeking

The non-observability of real-life rent-seeking activities makes experimental evidence especially valuable. With the rent-seeking models providing multiple theoretical reasons for under-dissipation of contested rents and also suggesting possibilities for over-dissipation, experiments can replicate the assumptions of the models, to allow behavior to be compared with the models' predictions. The experimental evidence is more or less supportive of the predictions of the Nash equilibria of the rent-seeking models. Shogren and Baik (1991) concluded from their experiments that behavior in Tullock contests was consistent with the predictions of the model. Potters et al. (1998) conducted experiments using both the Tullock probabilistic and Hillman–Samet all-pay-auction contest-success functions and found behavior consistent with the predictions of the models after making allowance for some participants in the experiments being confused. Vogt et al. (2002) found convergence in repeated experiments to the equilibrium of the Tullock contest. There are indications of overinvestment in rent seeking relative to predicted Nash equilibria, with overspending declining with risk aversion (Anderson and Freeborn 2010). Again, expressive utility can affect behavior in the experiments. Expressive utility not accounted for in the experiments can result in excess spending relative to the monetary value of rents because of the addition of the expressive benefit from being the winner.

7.4 Natural Experiments

Natural experiments provide evidence on rent seeking. Commenting on a natural experiment involving legislators in a US state legislature, Gordon Tullock expressed wonder at the small sums of money for which one could buy politicians' votes relative to the benefits obtained from the politicians' favorable decisions (Tullock 1989). If resources had been attracted into contesting the politicians' positions based on the bribes received, there had been substantial under-dissipation of rents. Perhaps the politicians did not know the value of the rents that they were providing. Also, perhaps, the politicians were limited in the bribes that they could receive by the realization that one vote would in all likelihood not be decisive in ensuring the policies that were sought.

8 RENT-SEEKING MODELS IN RELATION TO OTHER POLITICAL ECONOMY MODELS

The models of rent seeking are part of a broader political-economy literature. There are models that describe political incumbents as choosing policies to maximize political support from different interest groups while also seeking voter support; in these models, policies are determined by political incumbents trading off the political support of different groups (Peltzman 1976; Hillman 1982; Grossman and Helpman 1994) and the rent-creating behavior of the political decision-maker is explicitly modeled. In contrast, in the rent-seeking models, the political decision-maker is only implicitly present, as the object of persuasion in the creation and assignment of rents.

Another category of political-economy models describes policies determined through political competition. In these models, competing political candidates announce policies to seek political support in the form of campaign contributions from interest groups. The candidates use the campaign contributions in political advertising to persuade voters how to vote. Policies implemented and thereby rent creation and rent assignment are determined endogenously by the policy pronouncement of the winning candidate or party. It is assumed that, if elected, candidates implement their promised policies. The behavior of individual members of interest groups is described as the making of Nash-equilibrium campaign contributions to further the collective objective of improving the election chances of a group's or industry's favored candidate. The individual contributions are made based on the stakes in the outcome of the election, which are defined by the differences in rents associated with implementation of competing candidates' policy pronouncements. In a manner akin to the Tullock contest-success function, the relative values of campaign contributions received by the political candidates determine the candidates' respective probabilities of winning the election and thereby their supporters' probabilities of obtaining rents through sought-after policies (see Hillman and Ursprung 1988; Ursprung 1991).

The models of political-support maximization by incumbents and the models of political competition among candidates for elected office are set in a political-economy context but do not address the question of the value of the social loss due to political discretion in creating and assigning rents.

9 SOCIETAL RESISTANCE TO RENT SEEKING

9.1 Education and Persuasion

It is sometimes proposed that persuasion and education can end a rent-seeking culture (Guttman et al. 1992). Successful rent seekers have also been described as, for reasons of sympathy or empathy, helping out losers (Baik 1994). Particularly when rent-seeking activities are not illegal, convincing people that they should forgo self-interest by not participating in rent seeking or that they should voluntarily share their gains may be difficult. As Friedrich von Hayek (1988) observed, 'educational' ventures or ideologies exhorting people to forgo self-interest have been unsuccessful.

9.2 Taxation

Because rent seeking is socially inefficient, government could be called upon to tax rent-seeking activities (Glazer and Konrad 1999). Yet rent-seeking activities are in general unobservable, with the rent only at times being observed. Because the activities are surreptitious – and also at times ambiguous – and rent seekers may not succeed in their activities, taxation of rent seeking is not readily implementable. Moreover, the proposal that rent seeking be taxed asks governments to tax the activities from which political and bureaucratic decision-makers benefit through rent extraction.

9.3 Countervailing Activities

Resistance to rent seeking can take the form of countervailing activities by those disadvantaged by rent creation (Appelbaum and Katz 1986). In the case of monopoly, buyers can seek to influence political decision-makers to permit competitive markets or to reduce regulated prices. Similarly, domestic buyers, or exporters seeking market access abroad, can seek free trade or reduced protectionist barriers. In such cases, unproductive activity occurs through use of time and resources in the countervailing activities. The efficiency consequences depend on attributes of the contest in which rent seekers are seeking benefits and the countervailing opposition to rent creation and rent assignment that is taking place. Again, rent dissipation depends in particular on the nature of the contest-success function (Ellingsen 1991). An impediment to effective countervailing activity is that the populations that are the source of rents (buyers in the case of monopoly) consist of large numbers of people and so are subject to free-riding incentives (Fabella 1995).

9.4 Voter Dissatisfaction

Resistance to political assignment of rents can take the form of voter dissatisfaction (Peltzman 1976; Hillman 1982; Grossman and Helpman 1994). Because voters in general confront more issues on which to take positions than the number of political candidates, resistance to rent extraction through the political process requires that rent creation and extraction be a salient issue in determining voting decisions. The unobservable nature of rent seeking and voters' rational ignorance limit the discipline that voters can impose on rent seeking and rent extraction through the political process. When political participation in rent seeking and rent extraction are evident, voters can however obtain expressive utility from protest votes against implicated politicians who are seeking reelection.

9.5 Autocracies

Resistance through voting is unavailable in autocracies. However, in behavior that parallels expressive voting, populations can express their opposition to rent seeking and rent extraction by participation in demonstrations that protest political behavior, if participation in demonstrations is not personally dangerous.

9.6 Revolutions and Rent Seeking

Incentives for rent seeking are absent in a market economy in which property rights are protected perfectly and governments are not amenable to influence in assigning benefits or in imposing personal costs. There are also no incentives for rent seeking when an absolute non-contestable hereditary monarch preempts all rent seeking by appropriating all rents. The advantage of the absolute ruler in preventing contestability was the basis for the case by Thomas Hobbes ([1651] 1962) for a 'leviathan' who would own everything and rule absolutely over others. Of course, the leviathan solution for ending rent seeking might not be satisfactory. The leviathan may need to be repressive in engaging in rent defense. A society might prefer to forgo Hobbes's dictator. As previously observed in the context of nepotism and other favoritism, rent seeking can introduce conflict between efficiency and justice. With distributional outcomes of political rent assignment having no necessary ethical merit, the case for societal resistance to rent seeking involves avoidance of injustice as well as avoidance of inefficiency. Although revolutions use resources unproductively in contesting the authority of a leviathan, justice can be on the side of revolutionaries.

10 CONCLUSIONS

The concept of rent seeking enhances understanding of the choice between markets and government discretion. The extent to which rent seeking exists or persists affects the socially desirable size of government (Park et al. 2005). The study of rent seeking also involves the domain of personal ethics and the dilemmas of personal behavior when people confront rent-seeking opportunities and rent seekers. The only way, it would appear, that a society can put an end to the inefficiency and privileged benefits of rent seeking is by ensuring that there are no rents to be sought, which requires limiting political and bureaucratic discretion to create and dispense – and extract – rents. In low-income countries, limiting rent seeking requires curtailing corruption.

NOTES

1. See the papers in Congleton et al. (2008a, part 4, Structure of Contests).
2. Congleton et al. (2008c).
3. For example, the revelation in 2009 that UK parliamentarians of all political parties widely misused locational allowances and concessions suggests norms of behavior consistent with receptiveness to and participation in rent seeking. See http://www.parliament.uk/business/publications/research/key-issues-for-the-new-parliament/the-new-parliament/parliamentary-standards-and-reputation/ (accessed 17 January 2010).
4. Baye et al. (1994) provided a characterization of the Tullock contest for $r > 2$. For a comprehensive collection of papers involving the Tullock contest-success function, see Lockard and Tullock (2001).
5. The absence of Nash equilibrium in pure strategies is evident for the case of the all-pay auction or discriminating contest. In equilibrium, contenders do not make equal bids. If a contender bids V, other contenders bid zero, in which case in equilibrium a contender does not bid V. Nor in equilibrium do all contenders bid zero.
6. See Hillman and Samet (1987). On extensions and further formalizations of the all-pay-auction, see Baye et al. (1996) and Siegel (2009).
7. Guttman (1978) described members of interest groups voluntarily contributing to the quest to obtain benefits through government grants for agricultural research. Other examples of interest groups seeking rents were described by Potters and Sloof (1996).
8. See the papers in Congleton et al. (2008a, part 2, Collective Dimensions).
9. Ursprung (2011) provides an overview of collective rent seeking and explains why the evolutionary process of incentivizing group members is protracted.
10. Shleifer and Vishney (2003) describe these two categories of corruption, which in a rent-seeking context involve rent extraction without and with rent sharing.
11. The contest can be very cruel, as has been documented in the case of 'blood' diamonds in Africa. See Ollson (2007).

12. See the papers in Congleton et al. (2008b, part 5, The Firm).
13. See the papers in Congleton et al. (2008b, part 6, Societal Relations).
14. Gordon Tullock (1975b) observed the link between legal contestability and rent seeking. See also Congleton et al. (2008b, part 3, Political and Legal Institutions).
15. On the Counter-Reformation, see Ekelund et al. (2004).
16. See the papers in Congleton et al. (2008a, part 1, Rents). On risk aversion and the riskiness of rents, and a review of prior literature of the effects of risk aversion on rent dissipation, see Treich (2010).
17. See the papers in Congleton et al. (2008a, part 3, Extensions, and part 4, The Structure of Contests) and Epstein and Nitzan (2007), who study various extensions of the basic rent seeking model.

20 Campaign finance
Thomas Stratmann

1 INTRODUCTION

The role of money in politics has always been a controversial topic and continues to be so. Recent history has seen a rapid increase in campaign contributions and campaign expenditures. In 1996, the race for the White House cost President Bill Clinton and Republican challenger Senator Robert Dole $80 million altogether. Just four years later, candidates George W. Bush and Albert Gore spent $307 million campaigning for the presidency, and in 2004 the expenditures of incumbent Bush and his Democratic opponent, Senator John Kerry, summed to more than $550 million. In the 2008 election, expenditures by Democrat Barack Obama and Republican John McCain exceeded $1.1 billion. The growth in spending is less dramatic, but still worthy of notice, in races for the US Congress. Candidates running for seats in the US Senate and the US House of Representatives spent $283 million in 1989–90, $670 million in 2003–04, and $1.48 billion in 2009–10 on their campaigns.[1] These are nominal figures, but even measured in inflation-adjusted dollars, spending in congressional elections has tripled over the past 20-year period.

As well as noting that spending has increased, it can be seen that patterns of campaign contributions and campaign spending differ sharply between incumbents and challengers. The 407 US House incumbents running for reelection in 2008 collected, on average, $1.4 million in campaign contributions in the 2007–08 election cycle. About 50 percent of those contributions came from individuals and about 43 percent came from political action committees (PACs) and other groups not formally associated with political party organizations.[2] Challengers, in contrast, raised an average of $245,000 with about 63 percent of these contributions coming from individuals and about 10 percent from other, non-party sources.

The preceding numbers refer to direct spending by candidates, but contributions from outside organizations represent another large source of campaign spending. The 2010 congressional elections set a record for this kind of spending in an 'off-year'. Partially fueled by the Supreme Court's ruling in *Citizens United* v. *Federal Election Commission*, in which the Court struck down the restrictions on 'electioneering communications' from corporations and labor unions, expenditures rose from $300 million in 2006 to $477 million in the 2010 congressional races. In 2008, combining presidential and congressional races, expenditures from outside sources totaled $585 million, compared to $448 million in 2004.[3]

In this chapter, I review some of the scholarly literature that explores the causes and consequences of money in politics. First I will focus on contributions that examine how interest groups use contributions and explore whether and how they decide to distribute campaign contributions are consistent with an attempt to shape policy. This is followed by a description of the effects of campaign contributions on policy decisions. Next I will review research on the effects of interest group spending on the outcomes of ballot measures. And finally I will describe some research on the effects of campaign spending in candidate elections.

2 THEORETICAL CONSIDERATIONS

Theory can serve as a useful guide for developing empirical models. The theoretical campaign finance literature is vast, and I will review only briefly some of the works that most closely relate to the empirical findings discussed later. In many theoretical models campaign contributions equal campaign expenditures, and no distinction is made between the two. Many early models posited that campaign contributions and spending do affect voters' and legislators' choices, but were not explicit about the mechanism (see reviews by Morton and Cameron 1992 and Austen-Smith 1987). Later research has attempted to forge those links.

In these latter models of campaign expenditures, advertising is modeled as a way for candidates to transmit information, or signals, to voters. Advertising may serve to increase voter certainty about a candidate's positions or policies (Austen-Smith 1987; Hinich and Munger 1989), inform voters about candidate quality (Coate 2004a; Ortuno-Ortín and Schultz 2005), or signal candidates' qualities or policies (Potters et al. 1997; Prat 2002a, 2002b; Wittman 2007). An important focus of theoretical models is that which makes predictions about voting behavior when some voters are informed and others are uninformed (Grossman and Helpman 1996). Here, it is found that campaign contributions can be used by an incumbent to sway the voting decisions of uninformed voters, or a subset of them (Bombardini and Trebbi 2011).

Some models link contributions to policy outcomes, thereby analyzing the possibility of quid pro quos between candidates and contributors. These models analyze the motives behind contributions. Contributions are given to influence the policy choices of governments (Grossman and Helpman 1994), the platforms of legislators (Grossman and Helpman 1996), or to buy access to politicians (Austen-Smith 1995). If a candidate's ideological position is fixed, some contributors give money in the expectation of policy favors when the candidate is elected (Coate 2004b). On the other hand, when a candidate's position is flexible, contributions can be intended to move a candidate's ideology closer to the contributor's own position (Prat 2002a; Coate 2004a; Ashworth 2006).

Some theoretical models predict that contributors might give money to the candidate whose position is closest to their own, to those who are likely to change their position to the one preferred by the contributor, and to those candidates who have a high probability of winning (Mueller 2003). In these types of models, assumptions about contributor objectives will strongly influence the predictions regarding the allocations they make among candidates running for elected office. Important considerations are whether contributors consider contributions as pure consumption, as investments in policy, as a means of gaining access to the legislator, or as a way of influencing electoral outcomes.

Naturally, the results from testing the predictions of theoretical campaign finance models are quite sensitive to assumptions regarding the objectives of candidates, the rationality of voters, the type of electoral competition, the goals of contributors, and the role of advertising in inducing voters to change their voting behavior. With such a wide range of defensible theoretical positions, empirical work can help researchers determine the assumptions that are most useful and supported by data.[4]

3 FORMATION AND ACTIVITIES OF PACS

A line of empirical research has investigated the industrial organizational characteristics that lead to the formation of political action committees (PACs). Pittman (1988), Zardkoohi (1988), and Grier et al. (1994) examine the factors determining whether an industry establishes a PAC and how much its PAC contributes. They find that industry size, concentration, and the possibility of government regulations help explain variations in both the formation and level of PACs spending. Hart (2001) applies this analysis to firm-level data from the high-technology sector, reporting that larger sales or being regulated by the government increases the probability that a firm forms a PAC. Finally, Apollonio and La Raja (2004) study the determinants of so-called soft money contributions that were outlawed by the 2002 Bipartisan Campaign Reform ('McCain-Feingold') Act.

Bombardini and Trebbi (2011) show that the number of voters represented by an interest group is an important explainer of the patterns of campaign contributions across economic interests. They find a hump-shaped relationship between the voting share of an interest group and its contributions to a legislator. That is, legislators with the least and most industry support in their districts receive the fewest contributions from these industries.

Seeking to explain the growth in campaign expenditures, Lott (2000) hypothesizes that rent seeking is an interest group's primary motive for contributing to political campaigns. Further, he posits that when more rents are available, greater effort will be invested in increasing and gaining access to them. Using data on state government size to represent rent availability, he finds that campaign expenditures are larger in states where governments are larger relative to the private sector.

Empirical work that tests theories about the determinants of the allocation of contributions consistently finds that money flows to incumbents in close races (see, for example, Kau et al. 1982; Jacobson 1985; Poole and Romer 1985; Poole et al. 1987; and Stratmann 1991).[5] Furthermore, the pattern of contributions by labor unions and other special interests, such as the National Rifle Association, serves as anecdotal evidence that groups donate to their friends in Congress. There is also systematic evidence that PACs contribute to the campaigns of candidates whose policy positions are closest to their own (Poole and Romer 1985). That study finds that conservative PACs tend to contribute the most to conservative candidates, and that liberal PACs contribute the most to liberal candidates. Many other studies have supported these findings, and show that interest groups contribute heavily to perceived friends (see, for example, Kau et al. 1982; Grier and Munger 1991; Kroszner and Stratmann 1998).

Snyder (1992) documents that PACs seek to establish long-term investment relationships with legislators by contributing to campaigns early in their careers, and giving frequently. That is, if a PAC contributed to a legislator in the last election cycle, it is likely to contribute to the same legislator in the next election cycle, showing that contributions exhibit a degree of persistence. McCarty and Rothenberg (1996), on the other hand, find that less than 50 percent of the PACs who donated to federal legislators in 1977–78 were still supporting the same legislators in 1985–86, and hypothesize that commitment problems make the establishment of a long-term relationship between contributors and legislators difficult to sustain. In support of this hypothesis, they and Kroszner and Stratmann (2000, 2005) suggest that the problem of long-term commitment can be solved by reputation. They examine the connection between reputations for reliability and corporate campaign contributions. They test whether the effect of high levels of reputation can work ambiguously: while clear and consistent positions reduce uncertainty about a candidate, which could lead to large campaign contributions from favored interests, this clarity could also alienate disfavored interests. Thus, reputation may actually hinder the politician from raising contributions from groups on both sides of an issue. Using data from corporate PAC contributions to members of the US House during the seven election cycles from 1983–84 to 1995–96, they find that the development of a reliable reputation does pay off: the development of a reputation for trustworthiness is rewarded with more generous PAC contributions.

A common finding is that incumbents serving on powerful congressional committees receive more campaign contributions than legislators on less powerful committees (see, for example, Grier and Munger 1991; Romer and Snyder 1994; Milyo 1997). An interesting research design is to examine how patterns of giving change when legislators switch committees. One advantage of this design is that measuring changes in contributions rather than the absolute level of contributions controls for time-invariant factors, such as the makeup of the legislator's constituency, which may be correlated with the level of contributions. Romer and Snyder (1994) examine the effects of changes in a representative's committee and leadership assignments on changes in PAC contributions. In their careful testing they find that committee membership has a large impact on contributions; PACs reallocate their contributions when legislators move off or on a policy-relevant committee and alter their giving with accumulated committee experience, that is, seniority. Their results indicate that PAC giving is related to representatives' committee assignments as well as to the lengths of their committee service.

Examining the allocation of campaign contributions to committee members in the US House of Representatives, Kroszner and Stratmann (1998) consider the contributions of PACs from competing segments of the financial services industry, namely commercial and investment banks, securities firms, and insurance companies. Their theory suggests that the committee system in the US Congress allows for the development of long-run exchange relationships between interest groups and committee members and that the allocation of contributions reflects that relationship. Consistent with their predictions, they find that financial services PACs contribute most to members on the House banking committee, and that each group concentrates its contributions on particular committee members. In addition, they find that contributions to banking committee members fall when their committee service ends, and that members who are not successful in raising large contributions from interested groups often leave the committee.

Instead of focusing on congressional committees when developing hypotheses about the allocation of campaign contributions, other work considers the role of electoral rules in determining how much interest groups will contribute to the election campaigns of incumbents. Stratmann (1992), drawing on Denzau and Munger (1986) with respect to agricultural PACs, posits that the objective of agricultural interest groups is to assemble a congressional majority favoring farm subsidies. This hypothesis has several implications. These PACs may not find it worthwhile to contribute their limited funds to incumbents representing farm districts in, say, North Dakota or Montana, where a large constituency of farmers would lead incumbents naturally to support agricultural subsidies regardless of contributions. Political action committees will do better by contributing to legislators with only a few farmers in their districts, or those who are undecided as to policy. This study documents exactly this pattern of giving: the largest farm contributions flow to the legislators representing the median rural constituency. Strategic giving is further documented by Stratmann (1996), in a study which shows that liberal PACs give most to conservative Democrats.

4 CONTRIBUTIONS AND ELECTIONS

The productivity of campaign spending is an important research question, and answers to this question become even more important when it is observed that incumbency reelection rates are at record highs. One cannot help but wonder whether the fact that incumbents outspend challengers, on average, by a margin of more than three to one contributes to their apparent electoral advantages. The question has particular importance in the context of recent campaign finance reform initiatives. The argument of some advocates, namely that reform would 'level the playing field' between advantaged incumbents and disadvantaged challengers, does not apply if incumbent spending is ineffective in any case.

As might be expected, a dominant question in the empirical literature on campaign expenditures is whether spending affects the identity of the winning candidate. While politicians spend a great deal of their time fund-raising, researchers have found it difficult to establish a quantitatively important connection between spending and a candidate's likelihood of election. Moon (2006) views the apparent ineffectiveness of incumbent campaign spending in congressional elections as one of the major puzzles in the campaign finance literature.

The basic regression equation used to analyze the effects of campaign spending takes the form:

$$incumbent\ vote\ \% = \alpha + \beta\ incumbent\ spending + \gamma\ challenger\ spending$$

$$+ \delta\ candidate\ characteristics + \theta\ constituency\ preferences + \varepsilon \qquad (20.1)$$

With good measures of candidate quality and constituency preferences, the regression equation correctly identifies the marginal impact of campaign spending for both candidates. But good measures of candidate quality and constituency preferences are hard to obtain. A common strategy, starting with Jacobson (1978), is to use incumbents' vote shares in the previous election as a proxy for those missing variables. With this specification, the ordinary least squares (OLS) regressions show that spending by US House incumbents has no effect on vote shares, and some regressions that use this specification have generated point estimates with the wrong (negative) sign on spending (see, for example, Feldman and Jondrow 1984; Ragsdale and Cook 1987; Levitt 1994). The same regressions show that spending by challengers increases their vote shares in US House elections, as would be expected.[6]

There are, however, empirical works on senate elections that have found results more consistent with the hypothesis that campaign spending increases a candidate's vote share. This research shows statistically significant effects of spending by both challengers and incumbents on their respective vote shares (see, for example, Abramowitz 1988; Grier 1989b; Moon 2006). The results are nonetheless similar to those found for House elections, in that the marginal product of challenger campaign spending in Senate races is larger than that of incumbent spending.

These academic works note that an important consideration is that expenditures and vote shares are simultaneously determined. Even if spending influences vote share, the expected vote share may influence spending. Put differently, omitted variables, such as the expected competitiveness of a race, which is correlated with expenditures and vote shares, bias the estimates of the campaign expenditure coefficient. Incumbents who rationally believe that their reelection chances are good will be less concerned (and consequently spend less on their campaigns) than incumbents who face serious challengers. As a consequence, the coefficient on incumbent spending is biased downward.

Not including important candidate characteristics and district partisanship leads to an omitted variable bias. In a heavily Republican district, with a Republican incumbent, donors will likely withhold their contributions, believing that the incumbent will win even without spending much on advertisements. Here, omitting policy-relevant data would lead to underestimation of the coefficient on incumbent spending. The coefficient on incumbent spending will also be biased if variables such as their quality, trustworthiness as a legislator, and similar variables, which are likely to be correlated with spending, are not included in the regression equation. Without good measures of these variables, the effect of candidate spending on votes is underestimated.

Proposals to address the omitted variable problem include two-stage least squares (TSLS) estimation, panel estimation, and the use of better control variables.[7] An example of the latter is work by Abramowitz (1991), who utilizes a measure of elite expectations in his regression model. The elite-expectations measure is meant to control for the possibility that optimistic expectations of winning lead to the combination of low incumbent spending and a large vote share for the incumbent. Abramowitz finds that even controlling for this variable, the coefficient on incumbent spending remains statistically insignificant. In Green and Krasno's (1988) work on this topic, the authors attempt to control for it by including an eight-point scale to measure challenger quality. However, the inclusion of this quality measure does not change the conclusions regarding the ineffectiveness of incumbent spending.

An instrumental variables approach is a feasible option to uncover a causal relation if the instruments are sufficiently correlated with incumbent and challenger spending, but have no direct effect on vote share. Green and Krasno (1988), for example, use lagged spending as the instrument for current incumbent spending. Their instrumental variable estimates show that both incumbent and challenger coefficients have the anticipated signs and are statistically significant. Gerber (1998) instruments for both incumbent and challenger spending using state population and candidate wealth data in analyzing US Senate elections. He reports evidence that Senate incumbent spending and challenger spending are equally productive.[8]

Other work on US Senate elections draws a distinction between spending in contested races and races in which the incumbents' seats are safe. Moon (2006) finds that incumbent spending is actually more productive than challenger spending in contested races. Moon suggests that roughly equal quality of incumbents and challengers explains why the coefficient on incumbent spending is neither negative nor small relative to that of challenger spending: examining races when both candidates have roughly equal quality addresses the omitted variable bias.

Arguing that good instruments are hard to find, Levitt (1994) expressed doubt that previous studies convincingly have established a causal effect. Instead of using a different set of instruments, Levitt suggests examining races where the same candidates meet more than once, referring to such contests as 'repeat-challenger races'. Focusing the analysis in this way, one can control for candidate quality by introducing a candidate-pair indicator variable. The conclusions of Levitt's study are that there is no statistically significant relationship between incumbent campaign spending and incumbent vote shares, and a weak relationship for challengers. In addition, Levitt finds that the point estimates suggest magnitudes for the impact of spending that are practically negligible, even if they were statistically significant.

One potentially important feature of US elections is the different cost of advertising in different areas of the country. In Montana, the cost-per-point for a 30-second, prime-time television spot is less than $100, while the equivalent message would cost more than $1,500 in the Los Angeles area (Stratmann 2009). Such differences mean that the marginal productivity of campaign spending varies geographically. The same media campaign budget buys different numbers of television advertisements in different regions of the country, and differences in costs per point across jurisdictions lead to different amounts of advertising, even though candidates may spend the same total amount.

Instead of examining total spending, Stratmann (2009) analyzes a sample of repeat-challenger races, but employs a measure of television advertising based on total spending relative to the cost of political advertisements in the congressional district, and uses this measure to estimate the impact of advertising on vote shares. Campaign advertising is found to have a qualitatively and quantitatively important effect both for challengers and incumbents. In one of the specifications, a 15 percent increase in incumbent advertising relative to the mean increases the incumbent's vote share by 1.2 percentage points and a 43 percent increase in challenger advertising relative to the mean increases the challenger's vote share by 2.1 percentage points.

One promising approach to a better understanding of campaign advertising involves examining the types of messages candidates send. Abrajano and Morton (2004) analyze the content of television advertisements of candidates and categorize them into 'style' or 'substance', that is, whether candidates' television advertising emphasizes valence issues, or whether they instead send truthful, credible policy messages. Analyzing data from the 2000 US House elections, they find evidence that a candidate's ideology affects this choice. Candidates whose positions are close to that of the median voter generally choose to reveal substance about their records. On the other hand, the farther their policy positions are from the median voter's ideal point, the more likely candidates are to emphasize style issues in their television advertising.

Houser and Stratmann (2008) use a laboratory setting to test Coate's (2004a) prediction that voters' evaluations of candidates are influenced by the sources of the candidate's campaign funds. In their experiment, voters tend to select the high-quality candidate substantially less often when campaigns are financed by special interests. Another important finding is that the incremental increase in the margin of victory due to an additional advertisement is positive but decreasing when campaigns are financed by special interests, in contrast to the positive and roughly constant returns to advertising in publicly financed campaigns. When campaigns are financed privately, voters become concerned about the substantial favor-trading that might be taking place.[9]

A prediction of the Coate (2004a) and Prat (2002a) models is that contributions will have a larger impact on the margin of victory when contributions are limited. The empirical results of Stratmann (2006b) are consistent with this prediction. That study uses the fact that different states have imposed different contribution limits at different times to attempt to measure the impact of contribution limits, and finds that in states with unlimited spending, the marginal product of spending is lower than in states with contribution limits.

If the effect of money is small, one is left to wonder why candidates appear to invest a great deal of effort in raising funds. Perhaps there is so much fund-raising because the cost of raising funds relative to the gain from winning office is low, or because candidates confuse correlation with causation (Levitt 1994). An alternative view is that scholars should develop a different research design to uncover the effects of campaign spending on races for elective office.

5 CONTRIBUTIONS AND VOTING BEHAVIOR AND POLICIES

Many anecdotes suggest that contributions have the potential to influence legislative decisions. For example, in 2008, Representative Rick Renzi of Arizona was charged with conspiracy, wire fraud, and money laundering for an alleged agreement in which he promised to support legislation in exchange for $700,000 acquired in a land deal.[10] In another investigation triggered by a suspicious sale, Representative Randall 'Duke' Cunningham (R-California, 50th District) pled guilty in 2005 to bribery and resigned from office. Cunningham had sold his house to a defense contractor for $1.6 million, at which point the contractor immediately sold the house again at a loss of $700,000. The transaction was said to be payback for Cunningham's earlier having influenced a contract award by the Pentagon in favor of the contractor.[11] Representative William J. Jefferson (D-Louisiana, 2nd District) made headlines in 2005 when federal agents discovered $90,000 in cash hidden in his freezer. Jefferson, who was later convicted of bribery and money laundering, was said to have used his position in Congress to promote products and services in Africa in exchange for which he took cash payments for himself and members of his family.[12]

Such stories suggest that federal legislators have the power to convey significant benefits to individual constituents, and that these individuals are willing to pay for these benefits, as economic theory predicts. Of course, reporting requirements for campaign contributions and restrictions on how contributions can be used necessitate the kinds of subtle maneuvers that make direct exchanges difficult to observe.

These anecdotes notwithstanding, what motivates campaign contributors is an open question. Do contributors to election campaigns expect special favors in return, or do they simply contribute to those candidates most naturally predisposed to their point of view? If the latter, interest groups may simply want to ensure their preferred candidate's election or to demonstrate their appreciation for the incumbent's positions. On the other hand, many theoretical models assume or predict that interest groups buy policy favors with their campaign contributions (see, for example, Grossman and Helpman 1994, 1996, 2001).[13] The evidence is mixed on this point.

The basic problem in studying campaign contributions is the by-now familiar problem of endogeneity and causality. Many works study whether contributions determine the voting behavior of legislators, but a correlation between contributions and voting behavior does not answer the question of whether causality goes from a politician's positions to contributions, or from contributions to a politician's positions. Ordinary least square estimates will overestimate the effect of contributions on the behavior of elected officials if interest groups merely donate to their friends. The same method would underestimate the effect in the case where interest groups focus their donations on potential foes, hoping to turn opponents into friends. Thus, it is not clear whether OLS estimates are biased upwards or downwards.

The main finding is that campaign contributions have not had much of an effect on legislative voting behavior, as summarized by popular voting indexes, such as those produced by the AFL-CIO's Congress on Political Equality (COPE), the liberal Americans for Democratic Action (ADA), and the defense-industry oriented National Security Council (NSC). Bronars and Lott (1997) test whether retiring legislators, who are not threatened by voter retaliation in the next election cycle, change their voting behavior when there is a change in contributions from relevant PACs. Measured as a change in the voting score, they find only modest evidence that changes in contributions influence voting behavior. Further, Ansolabehere et al. (2003) examine the effect of labor and corporate contributions on voting scores assigned by the US Chamber of Commerce, separately using member or district fixed effects or instrumental variables estimation. Regardless of the estimation method, they find no evidence that contributions affect voting in the predicted direction.

An alternative to examining the effect of contributions on voting indexes is to examine the effect of contributions on specific votes in Congress. Since some votes occur repeatedly, one can analyze the link between contributions and votes to examine this subset, and test whether changed contributions are associated with changed voting behavior. Assuming that voter preferences in a district are the same when both votes are taken, observing a change in contributions from special-interest groups between two votes and observing legislators' voting behavior on that issue supports the hypothesis that contributions are behind changes in voting behavior.

An opportunity to study such a situation was presented when Congress considered repealing the Glass–Steagall Act. The House of Representatives voted on this twice, once in 1991, at which time it was defeated, and again in 1998, when it passed. Stratmann (2002) analyzes the voting behavior of legislators over those two votes. Banking interests favored repeal, while the insurance and securities industries opposed it. Stratmann regresses the change in a representative's vote from 1991 to 1998 on the changes in contributions from those three interest groups. The regression results provide evidence of a statistically significant effect of contributions on legislator votes. Stratmann finds that an extra $10,000 in banking contributions increased the likelihood of a House member voting in favor of repeal by approximately eight percentage points. Another result of this research is that contributions had a larger effect on the behavior of junior members of the House than on the behavior of their more senior colleagues. Recent work shows that financial services industries influence legislative voting behavior. Mian et al. (2010) document that legislators receiving campaign contributions from these industries were more likely to vote in favor of the Emergency Economic Stabilization Act of 2008, which was a bill transferring wealth from taxpayers to financial services industries. That that result is causal is supported by their evidence that the voting pattern of retiring legislators does not show sensitivity to campaign contributions.

Stratmann (1998) suggests that the timing of interest group contributions sheds some light on the connection between contributions and legislator behavior. He investigates roll-call votes on agricultural subsidies in the US House of Representatives, significant actions by the House Agriculture Committee, and contributions from agricultural interests. The votes he examined were taken during the first year of the two-year election cycle. The results were suggestive: the number and amounts of agricultural contributions spiked around these events, and few contributions were made when the House was in recess. Stratmann (1998) argues that this pattern of activity can be interpreted as an exchange on a spot market of contributions for votes.

There are many papers that examine the effect of campaign contributions on the voting behavior of legislators. Ansolabehere et al. (2003) provide a survey of articles in the economics and political science literatures estimating the effects of campaign contributions on roll-call votes. Of the nearly 40 articles surveyed, they find that the estimated contribution coefficients are either statistically insignificant or have the wrong sign in roughly 75 percent of the cases. If one were to draw a conclusion about the influence of money in politics based on whether the median estimated contribution coefficient shows a statistically significant effect, one must conclude that it does not.

Developing a meta-analysis of these articles, one considers the signs and significance levels of each of the coefficients that have been reported in the literature. Specifically, using meta-analysis 'it is readily apparent that a set of analyses with small positive t-statistics could be significant in the aggregate even with non-significance in each individual analysis' (Djankov and Murrell 2002, p.749). Stratmann (2005b) conducted a meta-analysis of the papers surveyed in Ansolabehere et al. (2003). Following the methodology suggested in Djankov and Murrell, Stratmann's results suggest that campaign contributions influence legislative voting behavior.

This meta-analysis notwithstanding, the overall conclusion of these voting studies is that Congress as a whole is not for sale, especially so as documented in research that examines whether legislative voting indexes respond to campaign contributions. These voting indexes are often based on votes that have high visibility, and the effect of contributions on policy outcomes is probably smallest on issues with low salience. The effect of contributions on legislative behavior is probably greatest in policy areas with low visibility, low salience, where benefits are concentrated on an industry and where costs are disbursed throughout the electorate, as with agricultural subsidies or some financial services regulation.

A question less explored than the connection between contributions and legislator behavior is whether contributions have an influence on bureaucratic behavior. In Gordon and Hafer (2005), the authors present a model implying that large contributors are less likely to comply with regulations than smaller ones. This conclusion is derived from the assumption that contributions signal a firm's willingness to fight an agency's regulatory intervention. Testing their theory on plant-level data from the Nuclear Regulatory Commission, the authors find support for their hypothesis.

6 CONTRIBUTIONS AND FIRMS' HEALTH

Scholars have started to examine the effect of campaign contributions by corporations on the fortunes of the contributing firms. These works include an interesting study by Jayachandran (2006). Using the unexpected departure of Senator Jim Jeffords from the Republican Party in May 2001, resulting in a shift in the Senate majority, Jayachandran examines the effect of this change on the market value of firms contributing soft money to the Republican and Democratic parties. This event study shows that in the week after Jeffords left the Republican Party, firms lost 0.8 percent of market capitalization for every $250,000 contributed to Republicans. The stock price gain to firms with Democratic contributions is smaller, but not statistically different in magnitude.

Many researchers have taken advantage of the fact that the race for President of the United States is a single election that potentially will impact differentially the fates of myriad private business interests. Using data from prediction markets in the run-up to the Bush/Gore election in 2000, Knight (2007) finds that among a group of 70 'politically sensitive' firms, Republican-favored firms' stocks did particularly well as the prospect of a Bush victory increased. Additionally, using data on the combined hard and soft money contributions of firms, Knight finds that as the probability of a Bush victory increased, firms that had contributed to the Gore campaign lost value, while those who had contributed to Bush's campaign saw their share values increase.

Cooper et al. (2010) study stock-market returns for companies that contribute to political campaigns and find that a firm's future stock returns increase with the number of candidates the firm supports for political office. The authors report that this effect was particularly strong when a firm supported candidates in its own home state, candidates in House races, and Democratic Party candidates. And for the 2000 presidential election, Shon (2010) uses the period of uncertainty associated with the Florida recount to estimate how the prospect of a Bush or Gore presidency affected firm valuations. Shon finds that higher stock returns during the 37-day recount period are associated with increased contributions to the Bush campaign, while contributions to the Gore campaign had the opposite effect.

Lobbying activity has been shown to have important benefits for firms in work by Chen et al. (2010). They separate firms into high-lobbying and low-lobbying groups and analyze the returns to stock portfolios created on the basis of this separation. They find that a portfolio of the highest-intensity lobbying firms generates excess returns of 5.5 percent relative to the baseline of non-lobbying firms. In light of such gains, the authors point out that it is natural to ask why more firms do not engage in intense lobbying. Chen et al. suggest that there is something of a tournament aspect to the returns to lobbying. Only the firms most active in lobbying enjoy these excess returns; a comparable portfolio of firms engaged in moderate lobbying does not see such gains.

But not all researchers are convinced that political activity has the positive effects attributed to it. Ansolabehere et al. (2004) fail to find evidence that the limiting of soft money, due to the passage of the Bipartisan Campaign Reform Act (BCRA), a law designed to curb the ability of firms to give soft money contributions, had a negative impact on firms' stock prices, and Aggarwal et al. (2012) suggest that from the perspective of shareholders, corporations may not be getting anything at all in return for their political contributions. Corporate campaign contributions, in this view, are not investments in future benefits, but, facilitated by poor governance institutions that do not effectively constrain management, instead erode shareholder value. These authors' estimates suggest that an increase in campaign contributions is actually associated with a decrease in excess returns for the firm, specifically a loss of 9.6 basis points for every $10,000 increase in contributions. The authors conclude that campaign contributions do not advance owners' interests, but rather indulge the personal preferences of corporate managers.

While the literature on the effects of lobbying is expanding rapidly, going into greater detail here is beyond the scope of this chapter on campaign finance (see, for example, Ansolabehere et al. 2002; de Figueiredo and Silverman 2006; Richter et al. 2009; Yu and Yu 2011).[14]

7 CAMPAIGN SPENDING ON BALLOT MEASURES

As with candidate elections, spending on ballot initiatives is significant and increasing. In 1992, $117 million was spent in 21 states by groups supporting and opposing various ballot measures; in 1998, interest groups spent close to $400 million in 44 states. Among the states, California is typically the leader in ballot initiative spending. Interest groups spent $522 million between 1992 and 1998 on that state's ballot measures, including $256 million in 1998. Stratmann (2006a) documents that in California between the 2000 primary and the 2004 primary, interest groups spent $494 million on passing or defeating ballot measures (in real March 2004 dollars). Of this total, $344 million was spent in support and $149 million in opposition. In 2008, total spending on ballot propositions exceeded $500 million.

The early literature that examines the effects of campaign spending on ballot initiatives does so by comparing total spending by both sides in order to determine whether the side that spent more also obtained the majority of the vote. Lowenstein (1982), for example, examines ballot measures with 'spending on either the affirmative or the negative side that exceeds $250,000 and that is at least twice as high as the spending on the opposing side'. In this sample, Lowenstein finds that when those supporting the measure were the big spenders, they were successful 67 percent of the time, while when opposing groups spent more, they succeeded in defeating 90 percent of these measures.

Later studies using regression analysis find the same asymmetry. Distinguishing the effects of spending by different groups, Gerber (1998) finds that spending from *opposing* economic groups lowers the probability that a measure will pass, but that spending from citizen groups has no impact on passage rates. This result suggests that economic interest groups can improve a measure's chances of passing by spending nothing on supportive advertising. Other studies reported similar results, such as Bowler and Donovan's (1998), who find that campaign expenditures have little effect on voters' opinions regarding ballot measures. Garrett and Gerber (2001) also find an asymmetry in the effects of spending. They report that total expenditures by supporters have a positive but statistically insignificant effect on ballot measure vote shares, while spending by opponents has a negative and statistically significant effect. The question is then, why would the supporting side spend money when such spending seems to be ineffective or even reduces voter support (Matsusaka 2000b)?

Just as in regressions involving candidate vote shares and spending, the endogeneity of campaign spending on ballot measures is of significant concern. An interest group opposed to a certain ballot measure may observe that there is widespread public opposition to the measure in any case, and, not feeling any real threat, thus may not spend money to help defeat it. If a variable is not included in the regression that captures the public sentiment favoring the status quo, then the effect of negative advertising will be overestimated. The supporting side, on the other hand, may spend large sums to inform voters about the benefits of passing the measure, but if the negative public sentiment is not captured by a variable in the regression, the effect of spending by supporters is underestimated.

Stratmann (2006a) attempts to control for unobserved and observed voter sentiments towards a ballot issue by using geographic area fixed effects and indicators for individual ballot measures. In this design, the unit of observation is the proposition's vote share in 36 of California's counties. Stratmann correlates this vote share to television advertising pertaining to the corresponding ballot measure in the Designated Market Area in which the country is located. A Designated Market Area is a region in which residents can receive the same, or similar, television and radio programs and advertisements. By using the aforementioned controls, this approach captures unobserved voter preferences in a county as well as statewide preferences for or against a particular initiative. Stratmann also divides initiatives into those favored by liberal voters and those favored by conservative voters, and county preferences are allowed to differ for these initiative types. In contrast to previous studies, the estimates from this design show that supporting spending is at least as productive as opposition spending. In particular, having 100 extra supporting television advertisements is estimated to increase a ballot measure's vote share by 1.2 percentage points, and the same number of opposition advertisements decreases this share by 0.6 percentage points. However, these numbers do not imply that advertising has a very large effect on initiative outcomes. To obtain a 1.2 percentage point increase in the fraction of voters favoring passage, the supporting side has to increase its advertising by 23 percent relative to the mean. The opposing side must increase its advertising by 53 percent to obtain a 0.6 percentage point reduction in voter support.

De Figueiredo et al. (2011) suggest instrumental variables as an alternative way of addressing the endogeneity problem. Their instruments are indicators of the extent to which individual ballot measures offer diffuse or concentrated benefits, as well as the magnitude of those benefits. The authors find a statistically significant effect of spending both for and against ballot initiatives after controlling for endogeneity. Using California data, their study estimates that an additional $100,000 in spending favoring a proposition, in 1982 dollars, leads to a 1.45 percentage point increase in an initiative's chance of passage. An additional $100,000 in spending directed against a proposition is associated with a 1.93 percent decrease in the chance of passage.

8 FINAL COMMENT

The analysis of money in politics continues to be an exciting research area. Recent changes in US federal and state laws and regulations promise to lend themselves to scholarly analysis, so that we will obtain a better understanding of this perennially controversial issue. Moreover, recent US Supreme Court decisions that relaxed limits on spending, as, for example, the decision to allow corporations and labor unions to spend unlimited amounts to support or advocate the defeat of a candidate, may allow scholars to draw conclusions about whether money can buy political favors as well as to estimate the extent to which money can enhance the competitiveness of elections.

NOTES

1. Data were obtained from http://www.fec.gov.
2. Calculations made from data available at: http://www.fec.gov/press/press2009/2009Dec29Cong/2009Dec29Cong.shtml (accessed 23 February 2011).
3. See http://www.opensecrets.org/outsidespending/index.php.
4. Some works, however, test theoretical models directly, taking a structural estimation approach. Papers testing formal models of campaign contributions include Bombardini and Trebbi (2011), Gawande and Bandyopadhyay (2000), Goldberg and Maggi (1999), and Snyder (1990).
5. These studies typically do not address whether contributors give more in close races because they hope to influence the outcome, or because participation in the political process is more rewarding when a race is tight, just as sports events seem to draw larger audiences when the teams are more evenly matched.
6. Milyo (2001) suggests that these findings are consistent with the view that incumbents are intertemporal utility-maximizers.
7. One alternative approach is to employ covariance restrictions, as in Erikson and Palfrey (1998).
8. For studies examining the effect of incumbents' war chests on deterring the entry of challengers, see, for example, Epstein and Zemsky (1995), Box-Steffesmeier (1996), and Goodliffe (2001).
9. Stratmann (2006b) finds that the productivity of campaign spending differs depending on whether a state has high or low contribution limits.
10. http://articles.cnn.com/2008-02-22/politics/renzi.indictment_1_renzi-and-sandlin-andrew-beardall-renzi-family?_s=PM:POLITICS (accessed 12 December 2010).
11. http://articles.cnn.com/2005-11-28/politics/cunningham_1_mzm-mitchell-wade-tax-evasion?_s=PM:POLITICS (accessed 12 December 2010).
12. http://articles.cnn.com/2009-08-05/politics/us.rep.trial_1_jefferson-aide-wire-fraud-rep-william-jefferson?_s=PM:POLITICS (accessed 12 December 2010).
13. Only a few studies examine how contributions influence the allocation of time by legislators. One example is the work by Hall and Wayman (1990). This is surely an interesting avenue for future research. Time is a scarce good and there are many political actors competing for a legislator's time.
14. Drazen et al. (2007) study how campaign contribution limits determine lobby formation.

21 Public choice and the law
Paul H. Rubin and Joanna M. Shepherd

It has traditionally been thought that judges, prosecutors and lawyers operated outside the normal domain of interest-group politics. However, more recently, a literature has developed that applies public choice or interest-group reasoning to study the behavior of the various actors within the legal system. In particular, attorneys and judges are both motivated by the same kinds of economic self-interests that have been brought to bear fruitfully in modeling human action more generally. In this chapter we review some of the literature lying at the intersection of public choice and the law.

1 THE ROLE OF LAWYERS

Recent scholarship argues that much of tort law[1] has been shaped by the influence of special interests and rent seeking by the trial lawyers (Epstein 1988; Rubin and Bailey 1994; Zywicki and Stringham 2010). Private businesses and other groups oppose efforts to expand the law's reach and the penalties it imposes on tort-feasors. Thus, the setting is ideal for a public choice analysis of the political forces underlying tort law and its reform. Moreover, the analysis can be particularly rich because the stakes are usually large and the players have many tools available to them for pushing their agendas. The actors on both sides are themselves coalitions of individuals and groups with somewhat differing interests, and so can be studied using tools appropriate to coalition analysis. In addition to the ordinary tactics studied by public choice scholars, such as lobbying and legislative voting, those seeking to expand or to limit tort law can access the courts to effect legal change. As discussed below, efforts to elect legislators, and also judges, favorable to an interest group's cause also are within the realm of possibility. Additionally, issues of federalism are relevant since tort law is a product of both state and federal legal systems, at least in the United States.

We first provide a brief introduction to the law of torts. The level and scope of liability has expanded greatly in the past 50 years. The major change involved moving from contract to tort in product liability claims; we discuss this move and some of the other changes in the law that followed. We then discuss the players in the tort reform game. These are essentially organized groups of attorneys, on the one hand (mainly orchestrated by the American Trial Lawyers Association), and coalitions of business firms and medical doctors, on the other. We also consider the tactics available to these interest groups in supporting or opposing tort reform.

2 TORT LAW[2]

There are several reasons for public choice scholars to study tort reform. The issue is important. For the most recent year for which data is available, 2008, the tort system is estimated to cost $254 billion annually, or 1.79 percent of US gross domestic product (GDP), $838 per capita. (Costs in previous years have been higher: in 2003, for instance, tort costs were 2.23 percent of GDP.) (All data are for 2008, taken from Towers-Perrin 2009.) Of this, previous analysis indicates that administrative costs account for 54 percent and legal fees for about 33 percent of the total (United States Council of Economic Advisers 2004). Additionally, existing law and proposals for reforming it raise important public policy issues. It is agreed by most law and economics scholars who study the tort system that it has serious shortcomings (Landes and Posner 1987, is an exception). Moreover, the actual cost of the system is greater than its money cost. Many other decisions are affected by the change in relative prices caused by the ways of assigning tort liability. For example, tort law leads to higher prices for many products as businesses attempt to self-insure against the cost of potential lawsuits; this will lead rational consumers to economize on them. Some of the products are risk-reducing (for example, medical care and pharmaceuticals); thus it is not clear that tort liability leads to an overall reduction in consumers' exposure to risk. We have shown elsewhere that the current tort system at the margin actually leads to more deaths from design and manufacturing defects (Rubin and Shepherd 2007). Moreover, by undermining contract law, the tort system weakens the rule of law and leads to greater uncertainty for business firms and perhaps reduced investment in product innovation.

Traditionally, tort law governed accidents between 'strangers' – parties with no prior relationship. In the past, tort law generally was a legal backwater, both in terms of practice and in terms of scholarship. Until relatively recently, automobile accidents dominated tort practice, and practitioners were referred to derogatorily as 'ambulance chasers'. Tort law in general did not govern accidents between parties with prior relationships. For the employees of business firms, accidents on the job were covered by workers' compensation, a statutory no-fault system with scheduled benefit payments (Fishback and Kantor 1998). That is, individuals injured at work automatically could collect compensation (a fixed amount that depended on the severity of the injury) with no need to prove fault or negligence. For what is now covered by product liability and approximately so for medical malpractice claims, contractual terms would govern. In practice this meant that there generally was no possibility of recovery for persons injured by product defects;[3] there was liability for malpractice, but it was limited.

The most significant legal change leading to increases in the costs of product liability and medical malpractice claims was simply substituting tort liability for contractual liability. Since about 1960, following a case involving Chrysler,[4] courts generally have been unwilling to enforce contracts between buyers and sellers involving compensation for harms caused by accidents. No matter what terms the parties may want to govern the consequences of an accidental injury, the court will decide and impose its own terms. For example, the parties may want to agree that, should an accident occur, the producer of the product will pay only for lost earnings and medical costs, and will not pay anything for 'pain and suffering'. But if an injury in fact occurs, this voluntary agreement will be null and void. The courts will decide what level and type of damage payment from the manufacturer to the consumer is appropriate. The courts use several related legal concepts to justify the elimination of voluntary contracts. They may rule that the parties have 'unequal bargaining power', so that the agreement is a 'contract of adhesion' and therefore 'unconscionable' or 'against the public interest'. All of these arguments ignore the role of markets and competition in establishing mutually agreeable terms between buyer and seller. (Patients are precluded from promising not to sue for anything other than actual economic damages in return for reductions in physicians' fees for service.) This inefficient outcome may be because in their professional lives lawyers look at contracts as protecting parties or ensuring 'fairness', and do not see market forces at work in freely entered-into bargains.

Following this major regime change, which led courts to abrogate voluntary contractual agreements, numerous subsidiary legal events increased tort-feasors' exposure to risk. These 'innovations' involved both standards for liability and the amounts of damages awarded in the event of an accidental injury. Although most lawyers believe that the change from contract to tort was desirable, economists who study the issue are coming to the conclusion that greater reliance on contract would enhance efficiency (Rubin 1993, 1995b; United States Congressional Budget Office 2003; United States Council of Economic Advisers 2004).

We now discuss some of the areas in which tort law has expanded since its move away from contract.

2.1 Liability Standards

One basic distinction in liability standards is between *strict liability* and *negligence*. Under strict liability, the injurer is liable for any harm, no matter what efforts he has made to prevent it. Under negligence, the injurer is liable only if he did not take the proper amount of care to prevent the accident, where 'proper' is defined by the law's 'reasonable person' standard of precaution. Negligence regimes also differ with respect to the obligations of tort-victims. In a regime of *contributory negligence*, any victim fault in causing the accident (for example, by product misuse) will release the injurer from any liability, even if the injurer also was negligent. In a regime of *comparative negligence* (which is universal in the United States today), if both parties are at fault, the victim is compensated in proportion to the fraction of the accident caused by the injurer's negligence. It is an accepted result in the economic analysis of law that if the standard for determining negligence is based on efficient (cost-justified) levels of care, then any of the negligence rules lead to optimal precautions by both victims and injurers (see, for example, Posner 2007; Shavell 2004). The rules differ only in determining compensation in the event that both parties are at fault.

Tort analysts find it useful to distinguish between *manufacturing defects* and *design defects*. A manufacturing defect occurs when a particular product does not meet its own engineering and performance specifications. If, for example, a new car's brakes fail during normal driving, this is a manufacturing defect. Most analysts agree that strict liability for manufacturing defects is appropriate. Under a strict liability standard, the manufacturer is liable for harm caused by the defect. Such defects are relatively rare and therefore do not impose onerous burdens on business firms, who in any case have incentives to minimize them. There is nothing a consumer can do to avoid these defects (since they occur in the manufacturing process). Manufacturers decide how much to spend on inspection and quality control. The costs of determining that a defect exists are relatively small. A strict liability standard for this class of error thus likely would evolve in a free, unregulated market. Indeed, there is evidence that the original proponents of strict liability for product-related injuries had exactly this class of defects in mind.

Design defects are quite different. Such defects are said to occur when the courts rule that it would have been possible for the manufacturer to configure the product differently and so make it safer. For example, a court may decide that an automobile manufacturer should have put its gas tank in a different location. Design defects apply to all units of some product, not merely to faulty units, so that possibilities for litigation are immense. Product liability expanded greatly when the courts extended strict liability from manufacturing defects to design defects. This extension of tort law requires courts and juries to second-guess product designers and to determine whether a safer alternative was available when the product was still on the drawing board. Such second-guessing is difficult or impossible for non-expert judges and juries, so the litigation of such issues is very expensive. Some of the major problems that scholars have identified in the tort system as it currently operates are due to the extension of something like strict liability to design defects.[5]

Another major class of modern liability cases involves a seller's 'failure to warn.' Originally the law was written so that product warnings would insulate manufacturers from liability. However, the doctrine has been turned around: manufacturers are often found liable for failure to warn, sometimes in circumstances where consumers have misused the product in dangerous and unpredictable ways (see, for example, Viscusi 1991).

2.2 Damage Payments

Damage payments to injured parties have also expanded considerably over time. It is useful to divide damage payments into three classes. Pecuniary damages compensate consumers for actual out-of-pocket expenses. This category of damages comprises about 22 percent of total tort damages (United States Council of Economic Advisers 2004, p. 209). The major categories here are medical expenses and lost wages. Non-pecuniary damages compensate tort victims for other, non-money losses. The most important of these damages are pain-and-suffering damages. This class comprises 24 percent of the total. Payments for hedonic losses, or lost pleasure of life, a relatively new and controversial class of payments in the tort system, are also nonpecuniary payments.[6] As discussed below, punitive damages, over and above the victim's actual economic losses, should be reserved for situations in which an injurer tried to conceal his identity or behavior.

In analyzing damage payments for product liability accidents, we must keep in mind that consumers are themselves paying for whatever compensation they ultimately receive in the form of higher prices for goods and services that might harm them. Damage payments are like insurance: consumers pay premiums as higher prices for products, and receive a payment if injured. Many consumers do find it worthwhile to purchase insurance against tort-related medical costs and lost wages, but it still is appropriate that injurers should also compensate for this class of losses, although some coordination between payments from injurers and payments from direct insurers consistent with the doctrine of 'subrogation' would be useful. (Under subrogation, a person's first party insurer pays the injured party, but then collects from the injurer.)

If given a choice, consumers never buy insurance against pain and suffering. There are sound theoretical explanations for this fact. Essentially, this class of harm does not increase the marginal utility of wealth. Since individuals buy insurance to equalize wealth across states with different marginal utilities of wealth, individuals would not generally purchase insurance for events that do not increase the marginal utility of wealth. This means that consumers would not want insurance for pain and suffering and other non-pecuniary harms. Therefore, insurers who offer such policies would not earn even a normal rate of return (Calfee and Rubin 1992). That is, consumers would not want such insurance even if offered it by their own insurance companies. Since the administrative cost of operating the tort system exceeds that of any other insurance system, consumers would be even more unwilling to pay for promises of compensation for 'pain and suffering' through the tort system than through direct, first-party insurance.

Punitive damages are a more difficult issue. There are some behaviors of firms that ordinary tort damages will not adequately deter. Firms will sometimes invest effort to conceal their culpable behavior. If they succeed, then there is insufficient deterrence. Therefore, a policy of multiplying actual damages by a factor exceeding one can be useful in deterring evasion of responsibility. The multiplier should be the inverse of the probability of detection (Rubin et al. 1997; Polinsky and Shavell 1998).

2.3 Jurisdiction

The United States is a federal system, and most tort law is state law. This creates several issues of interest. First is the issue of whether a particular matter will be litigated in state or federal court. In general, plaintiffs prefer state court and defendants prefer federal court. For class actions, the issue of proper venue is the subject of a major lobbying campaign by proponents of tort reform.[7] A second issue speaks to the particular state in which a case will be tried. Some states and some counties are friendlier to plaintiffs than are others. This depends on matters such as the income and race of residents (who are potential jurors) and whether judges are elected or appointed (Tabarrok and Helland 1999; Helland and Tabarrok 2003). Tort law can serve as a mechanism for transferring wealth from stockholders (who live in all states) and firms (usually headquartered out of state) to the citizens of particular jurisdictions. State judges (and particularly elected judges) therefore have strong incentives to rule in favor of plaintiffs. Cross-state differences in the judicial treatment of tort-feasors and their victims supply arguments for elevating tort-law disputes to the federal level (Rubin et al. 1997).

A related issue is the way in which 'choice of law' issues are handled. This deals with situations in which more than one body of law might govern; for example, a citizen of Colorado harms a citizen of Arizona while both happen to be in Michigan. One contributor to expansion of tort law has been the greater willingness of state courts to hear cases involving their citizens in matters where there might be some ambiguity (O'Hara and Ribstein 2000). Lengthening the already 'long arm' of the law enlarges tort-feasors' liability exposure.

Plaintiffs generally decide where to file cases, and so choose the jurisdiction. The venue of a trial is important for two reasons. First, damages are more likely to be awarded – and to be larger – in some jurisdictions than in others, so plaintiffs naturally want cases heard in those places, and defendants do not. Second, the process of jurisdictional choice by plaintiffs can itself have important implications for the shape of the law as plaintiffs chose friendly jurisdictions and then win favorable precedents that apply to other judicial venues (Fon and Parisi 2003). For students of tort reform, the fact that tort law is formulated at the state level provides rich datasets for testing hypotheses; see, for example, Landes and Posner (1987); Curran (1992); Rubin and Bailey (1994); Rubin et al. (2001); and Helland and Tabarrok (2003).

2.4 Other Issues

There are other important tort issues. One is the role of class actions. A class action is a method of aggregating many small claims. Since litigation is expensive, the litigation system will provide no recourse to plaintiffs whose losses are small. A class action lawsuit can solve this problem by combining these small claims and so taking advantage of economies of scale in litigation. If the underlying law is efficient, then class actions can be an efficient adjunct to the litigation system. However, if the underlying law is itself inefficient, then this form of lawsuit will serve to exacerbate the system's problems. Since there is no actual 'client' in many class action lawsuits, there is little check on the fees charged by attorneys, and so these lawsuits can be very profitable for plaintiffs' and defendants' lawyers alike. A hybrid called 'joined claims' exists in which part of the litigation addresses many similar lawsuits simultaneously, with the remainder reserved for individual claims; this has been used in asbestos litigation (White 2004).

High-profile class-action lawsuits against particular industries have generated considerable incomes for plaintiffs' lawyers. Asbestos has been a big money maker for attorneys; lawyers have made (as of 2004) $41 billion ($21 billion for defendants' lawyers, $20 billion for plaintiffs' lawyers) and are projected ultimately to produce $118 billion in legal fees (White 2004).[8] Tobacco litigation (outsourced to private attorneys by states' attorneys general) has generated $13 billion for plaintiffs' lawyers to be paid out over 25 years (White 2004). As discussed below, this money has significant implications for the political behavior of the parties engaged in the tort reform process.

2.5 The Players

The major players in the tort reform game are lawyers (opposed to tort reform) and businesses and sometimes doctors (in favor). Both sets of parties are well-organized interest groups. Epstein (1988) and Rubin and Bailey (1994) discuss the relative strengths of these groups.[9] The lawyers are in the best position because they merely must oppose any and all forms of tort reform. Moreover, both plaintiffs' and defendants' lawyers favor expansive tort systems; for example, as mentioned above, defense lawyers have earned more from asbestos litigation than have plaintiffs' lawyers.[10] Olson (2003) discusses the common interests of defense and plaintiff lawyers in expansive tort law. (Of course, defense lawyers must be more circumspect in their advocacy since their clients generally favor tort reform.)

A major player on the side of the lawyers is the 'American Association for Justice' (http://www.justice.org/cps/rde/xchg/justice/hs.xsl/default.htm), also known as the American Trial Lawyers Association (ATLA). In many respects this is a standard interest group. It is associated politically with the Democratic Party, and one of its members, John Edwards, was the Democratic nominee for Vice-President during the 2004 election cycle. Members contribute money and sometimes time and other resources to elect the group's favored candidates. Although it allies itself with the Democratic coalition, and pursues its policy agenda in the same ways that other special-interest groups do (for example, lobbying members of Congress and state legislatures, contributing to their election campaigns, and so on), the ATLA also has an additional tool for use in influencing policy: it is able to litigate for favorable precedents. In the litigation process, the ATLA provides various private goods to selected law firms (for example, documents subpoenaed from defendants, information about techniques, data and methods of litigation) as inducements for joining the organization (Rubin and Bailey 1994). A particularly important but insufficiently studied set of the Democratic Party's allies are members of the 'consumer movement', including various 'public interest research groups' (PIRGs) and other associations linked to Ralph Nader.

Various business groups are involved on the side of tort reform. For example, the US Chamber of Commerce and its Institute of Legal Reform (http://www.legalreformnow.com/) are very active. There is also the American Tort Reform Association (http://www.atra.org/).

Business groups are less monolithic and have more difficulty in organizing than the trial attorneys. This is for several reasons. Issues in particular cases are somewhat idiosyncratic: was the gas tank in a particular model in the safest place? There are also standard free-rider problems as in any organization. On many issues different businesses have varying interests. For example, Epstein (1988) points out that machine tool companies have an interest in coordinating workers' compensation programs with tort law; pharmaceutical companies will not care about this issue but will care about whether Food and Drug Administration (FDA) approval is a defense against tort liability, an issue of no interest to the manufacturers of machine tools or of petrochemical companies. However, Epstein's point is somewhat overdrawn. Some policy issues are matters of concern for all businesses. These include the locus of lawsuits (with businesses favoring federal rather than state jurisdiction), procedural rules, such as limits on class actions, and the amount and types of allowable damage payments. These are among the issues that have been at the forefront of battles between the plaintiff bar and manufacturers.

For research purposes it is useful to note that these organizations provide substantial amounts and types of information valuable for students of tort reform and public choice. The ATLA's website provides information from the perspective of plaintiffs' attorneys. The Institute of Legal Reform provides much useful information (http://www.institute-forlegalreform.com/). The ATRA provides lists of 'judicial hellholes' (http://www.atra.org/reports/hellholes/), counties in which tort litigation is particularly harmful to companies, and also state-by-state lists of successful tort reform initiatives. It might appear that this information is biased since it is generated by an interest group playing an active role in the tort reform process. However, if one is studying the effect of tort liability on business decisions, or the role of business political contributions to judicial candidates, then the perception of business organizations is a relevant piece of data, and these reports do supply useful information on business perceptions.

2.6 Tools

The study of tort reform is a fertile field for students of public choice because the players have many tools available for use in supporting or opposing such proposals, and the interplay of these tools is an interesting subject of study. This is best seen by reviewing the history of tort law and tort reform. As discussed above, this body of law has expanded considerably since the 1950s. Rubin et al. (2001) argue that in general lawyers have a comparative advantage in using litigation as a method of promoting legal change. They examined the source of some of these changes (rejection of privity, the doctrine which held that consumers had contracts only with retailers, not manufacturers, and which therefore greatly limited product liability, adoption of strict liability) and found that they indeed arose in the litigation process. That is, in all cases, expansions in tort liability resulted from judicial decisions in states.[11]

Moreover, there is evidence that changes (specifically, the elimination of privity) occurred faster in states with more attorneys per capita (Rubin and Bailey 1994). Rubin and Bailey also describe in detail the process used by ATLA in litigating for the purpose of generating favorable precedents which themselves expanded the scope of tort law. Essentially, lawyers pooled their information through the auspices of the ATLA. This pooling both increased the chances of each lawyer winning a particular case and also helped create precedents favorable to other lawyers working in the same area. In addition, lawyers have the ability to select cases that will be more likely to generate favorable precedents.

Groups favoring tort reform generally responded by utilizing more normal tools of political advocacy. They donated money to political campaigns and lobbied state legislators and members of the US Congress to pass tort reform measures. (For example, Rubin et al. 2001 find that the adoption of workers' compensation and of limits on strict liability were embodied in new laws.) Attorneys then appealed some reforms to courts (often state supreme courts) in an attempt, often successful, to have the reforms declared unconstitutional. (Schwartz et al. 2000 provide a nice discussion of various tactics in the legislation-litigation campaign from the side of tort reform advocates.) More recently, as tort lawyers have become richer, they have also begun to use the lobbying process; this has been less well studied. They have so far used this process mostly defensively to block legislative tort reform initiatives. (For an interesting discussion, see Olson 2003, ch. 9.) For example, a bill introduced in the US Congress to reform class action litigation in various ways (S. 2062, the Class Action Fairness Act) did not pass the Senate. Anecdotal evidence indicates that the failure of this bill was due to the lobbying efforts of lawyers, but the issue has not been carefully studied. When Democrats are in power, tort lawyers have more clout and business reformers less.

On the other hand, proponents of tort reform have been able to use the litigation process to reform some aspects of the issue. Specifically, several Supreme Court decisions have had the effect of limiting awards for punitive damages. A recent case is *State Farm v. Campbell*,[12] in which the Supreme Court indicated that in most circumstances punitive damages cannot be more than nine times larger than actual damages (a 'single digit' multiplier). Groups favoring tort reform have also succeeded in requiring courts to impose stricter scientific standards for qualifying expert witnesses in lawsuits.[13] Additionally, parties on both sides of the tort reform debate invest effort to influence the selection of judges at the state and federal levels. In states where judges are appointed to the bench, as at the federal level, the process of influence is indirect, in that interest groups must sway the decisions of the politicians responsible for naming and confirming appointees.

Because the forces on the side of reform (as well as those opposed to it) have a variety of strategies available to them, the nature of equilibrium is not clear. When one party loses in a particular forum, it can change the locus of combat to another venue. Thus, as described above, the activities of interest groups range from litigation to lobbying to political action aimed at the judicial appointment process. While the groups engaged in the tort reform debate have taken advantage of all tools at hand, it seems plausible that lawyers have a comparative advantage in litigation and businesses in lobbying. Both have entered the political arena on behalf of politicians who will pass laws or appoint judges favorable to their cause; it is not clear where the advantage lies for this method of legal change. The same objectives motivate pro- and anti-tort reformers in states where judges are elected. The lawyers have been doing this for a long time, but recently business has begun contributing to judicial election campaigns and sponsoring political advertisements in the attempt to sway voters' opinions.

2.7 Summary and Possibilities for Future Research

Although the issue is important, the literature relating tort reform and public choice is small; relatively little has been written. This means that research in this area can have a big payoff; it is possible to make a large contribution to understanding and perhaps to policy as well. Moreover, because tort law is mostly state law, there is a good deal of variation available for empirical examination of the issues.

There are many interesting questions to be examined. We have mentioned some in the chapter, but we provide a more complete list here:

1. Both those in favor of tort reform and those opposed to it are coalitions of somewhat disparate individuals and groups. These coalitions could themselves be examined using the tools of public choice. How do they overcome free-rider problems? Are there private (Olson 1965) goods provided to members? Do the particular areas chosen for reform have to do with the coalitional nature of the parties? For example, much litigation on the side of reformers has dealt with damage payments; is this because it is an important issue or because it is a common issue for all potential defendants, and so one on which it is easier to reach agreement?
2. The role of each of these coalitions in the political process could be studied. The trial lawyers seem to be part of the Democratic coalition, and those in favor of tort reform are more likely to be Republicans. The relation between the trial lawyers and members of the 'consumer movement,' including various 'public interest research groups' and other non-profit organizations associated with Ralph Nader is particularly interesting, and has not been carefully examined.
3. Although there has been some analysis of the ATLA and of business groups, we are not aware of any public choice analysis of doctors as agents in the tort reform debate. This could be rectified. Doctors may occupy a middle ground between coalitions and parties, favoring Democrats on some issues, such as increased healthcare

spending, and Republicans on others, including tort reform. This may undermine their effectiveness in the tort reform debate, but this is subject to study.

4. Since many state court judges are elected, it would be possible to study directly contributions and campaign spending by interested parties in judicial elections. Since the rulings of state courts can affect corporations in any state, we would expect a large fraction of contributions to judicial elections to originate out of state, particularly so for jurisdictions known as 'tort hells'. This issue has not been examined in the literature.[14]

5. Some states have passed tort reform laws. The determinants of whether or not a state enacts such legislation and the form the legislation takes could be studied more carefully. Plausible explanatory variables include the number of attorneys in a state and measures of business presence as well as other standard public choice and economic variables. There have been analyses of the determinants of elimination of privity by state (Landes and Posner 1987; Bailey and Rubin 1994) and of the adoption of comparative negligence (Curran 1992) but other legal changes have not been examined closely.

6. Both sides have many potential avenues of influence (litigation, lobbying, contributions to judicial campaigns, and contributions to politicians who will vote for favorable legislation or appoint judges favorable to one side or another). How do agents decide which strategy to use in particular circumstances? For example, are attorneys more likely to contribute to political campaigns in states where judges are appointed?

7. It is possible to study votes in both the House of Representatives and the Senate on tort reform bills. Additionally, in the US Senate, which holds confirmation hearings on federal judges, followed by roll call votes on the recommendation submitted by the Judiciary Committee, could be studied. Campaign contributions from advocacy groups and interested parties (such as the trial lawyers) also merits the attention of public choice scholars.

8. Many legislators at both the federal and the state level are attorneys. Attorneys dealing with tort reform issues as elected representatives raise some obvious conflicts of interest. To what extent do these attorneys represent themselves and to what extent do they represent their constituents? That is, do attorneys who are representatives vote differently than non-attorneys from similar districts?

In sum, there are important and interesting issues relating to tort reform for public choice scholars to examine. There are theoretical tools available for analyzing these issues. There are data available for testing hypotheses. This is a fruitful area for research.

3 THE ROLE OF JUDGES

The judiciary is more insulated from the political process than any other branch of government and, as a result, judges seem less vulnerable than legislators and bureaucrats to the influence of interest group politics. Therefore, scholars of both law and economics and public choice theory have traditionally had a strong preference for more active judicial involvement in law-making. These scholars have maintained that although the law created by legislatures is often inefficient, the common law system has generally led to efficient laws.

However, despite the general preference for litigation over legislation, the judiciary is also susceptible to inappropriate rent-seeking. The courts simply represent another opportunity for interest groups to shape the law.

In this section, we begin with a brief discussion of the efficiency of the common law. Then we discuss the influences on judicial decision-making among both judges with permanent tenure and judges without it.

3.1 The Efficiency of the Common Law

An important premise in law and economics is that the common law, whether consciously or unconsciously, progresses towards efficiency. The earliest version of this hypothesis, alluded to by Coase (1960), and later systematized and extended by Posner (1973) and Ehrlich and Posner (1974), presumed that common law judges balance the tradeoff between general legal standards with high adjudication costs and specific legal rules with low adjudication costs by attempting to minimize social costs. The result of this balancing act is that the judges generally make efficient decisions.

However, many scholars have since attempted to explain the efficiency of the common law without resorting to preferences or utility functions. In the first paper applying an evolutionary model to the common law, Rubin (1977) argued that because inefficient rules impose a loss on one party that is greater than the gain to the other, litigation becomes more likely when rules are inefficient, and so inefficient rules are subject to more selection pressure, and more likely to be overturned. There have been countless extensions and modifications of this evolutionary approach. For example, Priest (1977) argued that inefficient rules generated larger stakes and so were more likely to be litigated, again subjecting them to increased selection pressure. Goodman (1979) argued that efficient precedents were more likely to be upheld in a litigation setting and thus survive than were inefficient precedents. Katz (1988) and Terrebonne (1981) developed models of efficient legal evolution.

Other scholars began critically examining these models and the general notion of legal efficiency (see, for example, Tullock 1997; Aranson 1992; Hadfield 1992; Landes and Posner 1979; Parsons 1983; and Cooter and Kornhauser 1980). However Hirshleifer (1982), building on Rubin's discussion of inefficiency when the stakes in a precedent are asymmetric, provided the most useful and influential criticisms of evolutionary models. He showed that the law could evolve to favor whichever party could most easily organize and mobilize resources for litigation to overturn unfavorable precedents, even if efficient. Hence, interest groups push the development of the common law in social welfare-reducing directions (Bailey and Rubin 1994). Zywicki (2003) provided another important explanation for why the common law may not achieve efficiency goals: as competition among courts for cases has declined, judges and courts have less incentive to provide efficient rules to get the business of disputants.

Thus, the evolutionary models of the common law have themselves evolved to explain why the common law will not always tend towards efficiency. In the next sections, we discuss the roles of self-interest and interest groups on judicial decision-making – two other factors that may prevent the common law from reaching efficiency.

3.2 Influences on Judicial Decision-making

Traditionally, society perceived the role of common law judges as maintaining the rules of an ongoing spontaneous order in which: '[t]he existence of individuals and groups simultaneously observing partially different rules provides the opportunity for the selection of more effective ones' (Hayek 1960, p. 63). The role of judges was simply to clarify the law and provide a neutral interpretation when necessary. The demise of this traditional view has given judges the opportunity to use the bench as a vehicle for pursuing their own personal objectives. In this section, we discuss the self-interested concerns of judges that influence their judicial decision-making and may, ultimately, shape the direction of the common law.

3.2.1 Ideology
First, judges' voting could be influenced by their own fundamental, immutable beliefs about broad social issues, such as the expansion of civil liberties or government regulation of business. Some have argued that judges initially are attracted to the bench because it gives them the opportunity to impose their ideological views on society (Hasen 1997; Young 2001). The attitudinal model developed by Segal and Spaeth (1993) contends that the strength of justices' idiosyncratic conceptions of the 'good society' influences their votes in individual cases. A well-established literature in judicial politics has shown that when judges have preferences over policy outcomes, judicial decisions often reflect their ideology. Thus, trial outcomes tend to reflect the ideological preferences of the judges (see, for example, McCubbins et al. 1989, 1995; Segal and Cover 1989; Gely and Spiller 1990; Spiller and Gely 1992; Segal and Spaeth 1993; Epstein 1995; Segal et al. 1995; de Figuerido and Tiller 1996; Revesz 1997; Segal 1997; Cross and Tiller 1998).

3.2.2 Reputation
Beyond their ideologies, judges could also be influenced by reputation or status concerns. Posner (2007) has suggested that judges are motivated by a desire for power and status. Another federal judge concurs, observing that those judges who issue expansive rulings 'enjoy wide esteem and reputation' (Jacobs 2007, p. 2858). Landes and Posner (1976), Miceli and Coşgel (1994), Whitman (2000), Rasmusen (1994), and Kornhauser (1992a, 1992b) assert that judges are motivated by a desire to avoid having their decisions reversed either by higher courts or by future judges. Smith (2006) and Randazzo (2008) have found empirical evidence of a relationship between judges' reversal aversion and their decision-making. O'Hara (1993) asserts that judges follow the precedents established by colleagues' decisions in other courts in the hope that the precedents established by their own decisions will be accepted as 'good law'.

3.2.3 Career concerns
Others have argued that career concerns influence judicial decision-making. The degree to which this is true will of course depend at least in part on individual-specific circumstances. Specifically, judges without permanent tenure should weigh career concerns more heavily in their decision-making than judges who are sit on the bench for life.

3.2.3.1 Judges without permanent tenure The majority of American state-court judges serve without permanent tenure. In fact, only in three states – Rhode Island, Massachusetts and New Hampshire – do judges enjoy lifetime appointments. Thus, the majority of the judicial business of the United States is handled by judges that must seek reelection or retention.[15]

In contrast to the US states, most foreign countries grant their judges lifetime tenure. However, notable exceptions to these permanent-tenure countries include lower court judges in Japan, who face retention elections after each ten years of service (O'Brien 2006). Likewise, supreme court judges in several Latin American countries must stand for reelection before various legislative bodies. For example, judges in Costa Rica must be reelected every eight years by the Legislative Assembly; judges in El Salvador serve nine-year terms before reelection by the legislature; judges in Guatemala serve five-year terms before being elected by Congress; judges in Honduras serve four-year terms before seeking reappointment by the National Assembly; judges in Panama serve ten-year terms before reappointment is determined by the Legislative Assembly; and judges in Peru serve seven-year terms before facing re-election (Cole 2002).

Judges without permanent tenure have incentives to vote strategically if they believe it will help them get reappointed, re-elected, or otherwise retained (Dubois 1980; Baum 1989; Posner 1993). As a result, such judges may decide cases in ways that benefit specific litigants or establish precedents that are favored by the people responsible for retaining them. This is true whether it is a politician who decides whether to reappoint the judge or the voters in a retention election.

For example, judges seeking reappointment by the governor or legislature may feel pressure to vote in ways that favor the executive or legislative branches. The power over judicial retention held by the governor or legislature offers the political branches of government direct opportunities to sanction judges for unpopular rulings. Judges who consistently vote against the interests of the other branches of government may compromise their chances for reappointment. As a result, in the types of cases in which state governments have a stake, the decision-making of judges seeking reappointment may be influenced by retention concerns.

Brace et al. (1999) find that judges seeking gubernatorial or legislative reappointment are less likely to hear abortion cases in order to avoid controversy on a hot-button social issue. Similarly, Shepherd (2009c) finds that judges facing gubernatorial or legislative reappointment are more likely to vote for litigants representing those branches.

The retention pressures are even stronger for judges seeking reelection, especially as elections have become increasingly competitive and expensive in recent years. Judges seeking reelection have incentives to issue judicial decisions that will help them to attract both votes and campaign contributions. The growing competitiveness of judicial elections likely has increased the pressure on judges to decide cases strategically to help them win support among voters. Moreover, with the costs of winning judicial elections rising dramatically, judges may be compelled to rule in ways that help them to raise campaign funds.

Numerous empirical studies have found a relationship between elections and judicial decision-making. For example, some of the first studies in this area by Hall (1987, 1992) find that judges deviate from expected voting patterns when their terms are nearing an end and electoral pressures intensify. Hanssen (1999a) finds that litigation rates are lower in states where judges are elected and argues that elected judges' strategic voting reduces uncertainty about court decisions so that more cases settle. Besley and Payne (2005) find that states that elect judges have more anti-discrimination claims filed than states that appoint judges; they argue that elected judges have stronger pro-employee preferences, inducing more employees to file claims. Huber and Gordon (2004) find that elected judges impose longer sentences as their re-election approaches, arguing that voters care more about underpunishment than overpunishment of criminals.

Other studies find that the pressure is even greater for judges elected on partisan ballots. Tabarrok and Helland (1999) and Helland and Tabarrok (2002) report that partisan-elected judges are more likely to redistribute wealth in tort cases from out-of-state businesses to in-state plaintiffs, who also are voters. Hall and Brace (1996) supply evidence that partisan-elected judges are less likely to dissent on politically controversial issues. Hanssen (2000) concludes that partisan-elected judges are less likely to vote for challenges to a regulatory status quo. Similarly, Shepherd (2009b) adduces evidence suggesting that the decision-making of judges facing partisan re-elections is aligned with the political preferences of the majority of voters. In contrast, Canes-Wrone and Clark (2009) ascertain that public opinion about abortion policy has a stronger effect on judicial decisions in non-partisan systems than in partisan systems.

Other recent empirical studies have examined the relationship between campaign contributions and judicial decision-making. Shepherd (2009b) reports evidence that contributions from various interest groups are associated with increases in the probability that judges will vote for the litigants whom those interest groups favor. Similarly, Kang and Shepherd (2011) find that judges facing partisan reelections are more likely to decide in favor of business interests as the amount of campaign contributions they have received from those interests increase. Other studies report a correlation between contributions from individual law firms and case outcomes when those law firms appear in court (Ware 1999; Waltenburg and Lopeman 2000; McCall 2003; Cann 2006).

3.2.3.2 Judges with permanent tenure Many judges serve with permanent tenure. For example, although US federal judges are appointed through a process that is often political, they enjoy life tenure once elevated to the bench. Similarly, state supreme court judges in Rhode Island are granted life tenure, and in both Massachusetts and New Hampshire, judges serve until age 70.

Permanent tenure is the norm for judges in most foreign countries. In Great Britain, Scotland, and Northern Ireland, judges are selected by a commission and serve until retirement (Judicial Appointments Commission 2006). In France, Spain and Portugal, aspiring judges are trained in a specialized school, take a competitive examination, and are then selected (and eventually promoted) by a specialized judicial council that is independent of other government branches; judges serve until retirement (World Bank 2001b). In Germany, aspiring judges serve as apprentices to the judiciary, and then are selected through a competitive examination. They serve either for life or for non-renewable specified terms (Landfried 2006) In Italy, a competitive examination after university studies is the primary method of selection, promotion is based primarily on seniority, and judges serve until retirement (Volcansek 2006).

Although judges with permanent tenure need not fear losing their jobs, their judicial decision-making may still be influenced by career concerns. The career concerns take different forms depending on the specific institutional structure of the court. Examples are the powers that governments sometimes wield to control judges' promotions, the ability to grant permanent appointments after probationary appointments, the power over judicial transfers, or the power over judicial salaries and budgets.

Higgins and Rubin (1980), Cohen (1991, 1992), Sisk et al. (1998), Levy (2005), Taha (2004), and Morriss et al. (2005) explain judicial behavior as consistent with the goal of being promoted to a seat on a higher court. In systems that promote judges based on their voting records, a judge has incentives to create a record that is consistent with the ideology of the group responsible for deciding whether that judge is promoted. For example, in the US federal court system, ideological politics play important – sometimes decisive (and divisive) – roles in the appointment and confirmation of judges (Bork 1990, pp. 271–349).

Desires for promotion also influence judges in many foreign courts. In Germany, judges on two of the highest courts are selected by a small group of leading members of political parties; commentators suggest that judges are more likely to be promoted when their records mirror the political orientation of the governmental body choosing them (Landfried 2006). In Australia, the Commonwealth attorney general appoints judges to the High Court and is criticized for making selections based on political patronage rather than merit (Handsley 2006). Likewise, in South Africa, where judges are appointed by the president on the advice of the minister of justice, critics argue that the process pushes through judicial appointees who are loyal to the current government's views (du Bois 2006, n. 118).

The use of probationary appointments is another source of political pressure on judges. For example, in Russia, federal judges are granted life tenure, but only after an initial probationary three-year appointment. After three years, the president chooses whether the judge will be reappointed. Commentators suggest that judges who make decisions consistent with the president's ideology are more likely to be reappointed (International Commission of Jurists 2002).

Another source of political pressure on judges results from the ability of the executive to transfer judges to undesirable courts. If a political appointee determines whether a judge will maintain or improve her geographic location, the judge has an incentive to render decisions that are consistent with the political appointee's ideology. For example, Ramseyer and Rasmusen (2003) have argued that judges in Japan faced strong political pressure from the dominant Liberal Democratic Party (LDP), which wielded influence through its power to reassign judges within the court system. Their empirical analysis suggests that when a judge rendered a decision that was contrary to the interests of the LDP, the Secretariat punished him with a transfer to an unattractive post in an obscure court. As a result, most judges were deterred from ruling against the interests of the LDP. Similarly, in India, the president has employed the power of transfer to exert pressure on judges (Shetreet 1985). Likewise, in Mexico, a ruling against the interest of the government will sometimes result in a federal judge being transferred to another region (Mills 2004).

Government control of judicial salaries and court budgets is another way that political parties can pressure judges. For example, the judicial branch of Venezuela lacks financial autonomy; it has to submit an annual budget to the executive branch, which may reduce or amend the budget. Some commentators argue that executive control over the courts' budget is one of the primary means by which the executive branch pressures the courts, and thus it is a main obstacle to judicial independence (de Temeltas 1996). Similarly, judges in Japan (Ramseyer and Rasmussen 2003), India (Shetreet 1985), and Nigeria (Oko 2005) have reported salary cuts after decisions that were unfavorable to the government. Similary, the utilization by the US Congress of the budget as a signaling device to the judiciary is discussed by Toma (1991, 1996).

3.2.4 Interest group influence on judicial decision-making

As long as the judiciary has the power to shape the law, those who stand to gain or lose from particular rulings have the incentive to influence the judicial selection process. Interest groups have become powerfully active in judicial selection and retention, and, as a result, have influenced both individual case outcomes and the general direction of the common law (see, for example, Shughart and Tollison 1998).

The growing competitiveness and expense of judicial elections, and especially partisan elections, has given wealthy interest groups the opportunity to shape a like-minded judiciary. Between 2000 and 2008, over $200 million was contributed to state Supreme Court campaigns, more than twice the $85 million contributed throughout the 1990s (*Economist* 2009). The average spending in partisan elections alone has risen to over $1.5 million per judicial seat. More costly judicial campaigns have made it extremely difficult for candidates to win elections without substantial funding (Goldberg and Sanchez 2002).

Consequently, wealthy interest groups can often dictate the outcomes of judicial elections by contributing substantial campaign funds to favored candidates. Hence, judges that are sympathetic to the views of interest groups are more likely to win elections. Moreover, once elected, judges have incentives to favor interest groups in their judicial decisions in the hope of obtaining more campaign support in future elections. Thus, the importance of money in judicial elections allows wealthy interest groups to influence the identities of the candidates who are elected to judgeships and how those judges vote after they are elected.

Interest groups can also influence the appointment or reappointment of judges by the governor or legislature. In fact, the appointment process may even allow well-organized interest groups to exert even stronger influences on judicial selection than they wield in electoral politics (Zywicki and Kidd 2010). A judge standing for election must win at least 50 percent of the vote, whereas judges seeking appointment need only be chosen by the governor or legislature. Thus, the appointment process enables interest groups to persuade only a few government officials in a process largely hidden from public view in order to get their preferred judge appointed. As a result, interest group influence is not eliminated. The politics of judicial elections is simply replaced by the politics of appointment.

4 CONCLUSION

Despite the general preference for litigation over legislation, judicial self-interest has been shown to be an important determinant of judicial behavior. Political scientists, economists, and empirically trained legal scholars have made important contributions to the growing body of empirical work that establishes that many of the predictions of the public choice model of judicial behavior hold true in reality.

Moreover, like legislatures, executives, and bureaucrats, the judiciary is also susceptible to inappropriate rent-seeking. The courts simply represent another opportunity for interest groups to shape the law.

NOTES

1. Tort law comprises several parts. Much of it is automobile accident law, which is mostly efficient and of little interest. 'Tort reform' as generally used deals with products liability and medical malpractice law, and that is how we use the term in what follows.
2. This section is based in part on Rubin (2005).
3. The legal doctrine governing was 'privity' which insulated manufacturers from liability because there was no direct relationship between manufacturers and injured customers. Of course, manufacturers could have assumed liability if they had chosen, so the limit was essentially contractual.
4. *Henningsen* v. *Bloomfield Motors*, 32 New Jersey 358, 161 a. 2d 69 (1960).
5. Although products liability is said to be a regime of 'strict liability', the term as used in product liability is not identical to the utilization by economists. For example, a plaintiff must show that some alternative product design was feasible; in pure strict liability, this would not be necessary.
6. This class of damages, based on econometric studies of 'willingness to pay', was actually invented by an economist. The courts have not been friendly to this theory of damages.
7. S. 2062, the Class Action Fairness Act, http://frwebgate.access.gpo.gov/cgi-bin/getdoc.cgi?dbname=109_cong_public_laws&docid=f:publ002.109.
8. Many plaintiffs in asbestos cases are workers who installed asbestos. However, these workers are suing the manufacturers of asbestos, not their own employers, and so the limits in worker's compensation do not bind. This type of lawsuit is an important part of product liability litigation.
9. Insurance companies have more mixed motives. In the short run, they lose from increased liability but in the long run increased liability leads to greater sales of insurance.
10. For completeness, it must be mentioned that some economists (including the authors) have also made money as experts in such litigation.
11. Comparative negligence was a more complicated case, but still consistent with the arguments here.
12. *State Farm Mutual Automobile Insurance Company* v. *Inez Preece Campbell*, 123 Supreme Court 1513 (2003).
13. *Daubert* v. *Merrell Dow Pharmaceuticals, Inc.*, 113 Supreme Court 2786 (1993).
14. Soyong Chong and Paul Rubin are in the process of such an examination.
15. More than 90 percent of cases in the United States are litigated in state courts (ABA).

22 Public choice and the modern welfare state
Roger D. Congleton, with Alberto Batinti, Feler Bose, Youngshin Kim and Rinaldo Pietrantonio

In the 25-year period between 1960 and 1985, social insurance and transfer programs expanded greatly in all Western countries. The fraction of GDP accounted for by government expenditures approximately doubled in much of Europe and grew by 40 percent to 50 percent in most other Organisation for Economic Co-operation and Development (OECD) nations. After 1985, there has been relatively little growth in the scope of the welfare state relative to other parts of the economy.

This chapter summarizes public choice and related research on the political economy of the welfare state. There are essentially two strands of the literature. One stresses the extent to which institutions, voter interests, and ideological shifts account for the period of rapid growth. The other emphasizes the importance of interest groups, who lobby for extensions of the welfare state in order to profit from larger budgets, more generous transfers, or new spending by those receiving the transfers. This chapter suggests that ideas as well as conventional economic interests also played a role in the twentieth century expansion of the welfare state.

1 INTRODUCTION

The welfare state is roughly as old as Western democracy. In much of Europe, various national social insurance programs were adopted at about the same time that broadly elected parliaments began to dominate policy formation. Germany's social security program began in 1889, Sweden's in 1909, and the United Kingdom's in 1911. These early programs usually were adopted by conservative or liberal coalitions and so, initially, could be said to be 'liberal' in their general structure and benefit levels.[1] The social security programs of the United States and Switzerland were adopted somewhat later, in 1935 and 1947, respectively, but also had support from both right-of-center and left-of-center liberals at their inception.

The adoption of national insurance programs was also associated with industrialization and its associated business cycles, which often swamped (bankrupted) the traditional sources of social insurance. In the years before the national income security programs were in place, income insurance had been provided by families, private organizations (such friendly societies, churches, and other private clubs), and by local governments. Congleton (2007a) suggests that an efficient demand-side risk-pooling model can explain many durable features of early national social insurance programs. A 'liberal' welfare state reflects personal demands for income insurance and the economic advantages associated with national provision of income security relative to supply through available private income insurance clubs and firms.

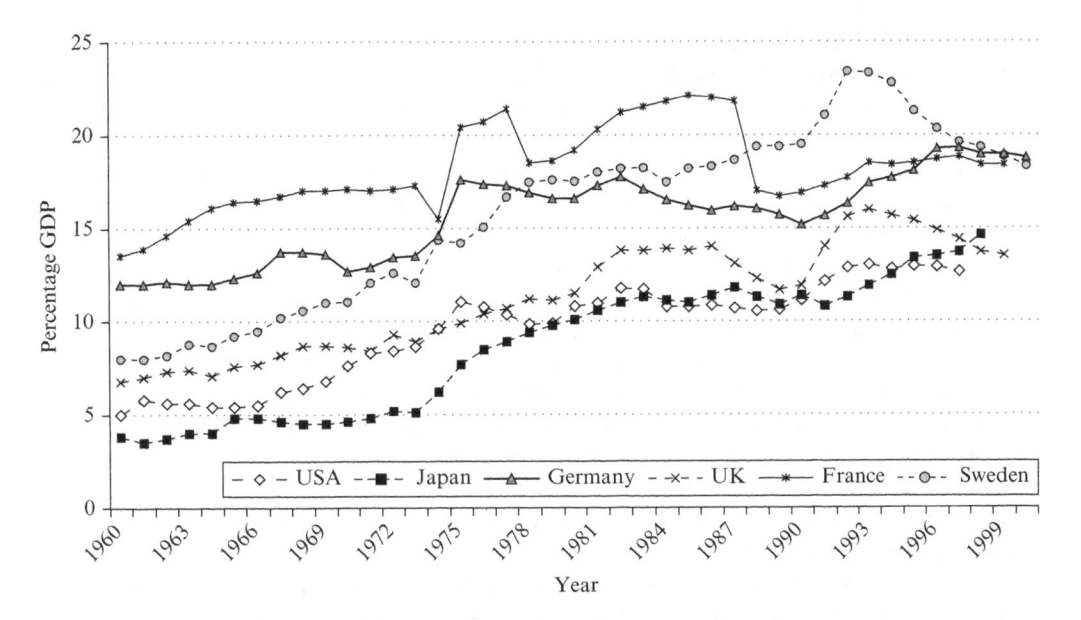

Figure 22.1   Social insurance as a fraction of GDP, 1960–2000

An insurance explanation, rather than transfers, per se, is consistent with the level of funding and conditionality of the benefits provided, especially in the period before World War II. A social insurance rationale for both small and large welfare states is also broadly consistent with empirical evidence developed by Tanzi and Schuknecht (2000), which suggests that only modest changes in the income distributions of OECD countries can be attributed to the size of national social insurance programs during the twentieth century.[2] The main transfers associated with national insurance programs tend to be the implicit subsidies that low income persons receive for their income and health 'insurance policies'.

It should be kept in mind that the early social insurance programs were relatively modest in size and coverage, although they represented significant expansions of central government responsibilities. If the welfare state is a 'nanny' state with a relatively high 'safety net' with very broad coverage, it emerged after World War II. Between 1950 and 1980, social insurance programs increased dramatically. They rose from 4 percent to 13.4 percent of gross domestic product (GDP) in Japan, from 7 percent to 15 percent in the United Kingdom, from 12 percent to 18 percent in Germany, and from 13 percent to 18 percent in France (Figure 22.1). Similar programs in the United States rose from 5 percent of GDP in 1960 to 11 percent in 1980.

The timing of the rapid expansion of those programs after World War II is more difficult to explain than their initial creation during or shortly after times of economic crisis. The modern welfare state evidently reflects more than an increase in the private demand for social insurance. The private demand for insurance tends to increase with income and with perceived risks. Income growth after World War II clearly accounts for part of the expansion in government-provided income insurance, as argued by Hall and Jones (2007). However, unless social insurance is a luxury good, its income elasticity should be closer to one than to three. The doubling and tripling in the sizes of these programs during the 1960s and 1970s relative to GDP requires much greater income elasticity than that associated with private insurance.[3] In the early postwar years, changes in perceived risks are also likely to have played a role. Subjective assessments of income and health risks are likely to have increased during the Great Depression and World War II. In many OECD countries, this increase in demand could be not expressed until after the war was over and democratic governments were re-established. Such increases in perceived risks, thus, would partially explain expansions in many national safety nets during the 1950s.

As peace and prosperity replaced war and sacrifice, however, subjective risk assessments would tend to decrease and thus slow the rate of expansion of social insurance programs. By the late 1960s, one would have expected perceived risks to have stabilized or been reduced by peace and prosperity. This downward trend in risk assessments would have been partly offset to some extent by increases in the average and median age of the electorate, because economic and health risks tend to increase with age. However, the median age of the electorate was falling during the first part of the great expansion of welfare state programs as the 'baby boomer' cohort reached voting age.

Additional factors evidently were important. Congleton and Bose (2010) suggest that the rise of the modern welfare state occurred in large part because of ideological and institutional changes that took place after World War II. In general, ideology shifted in a leftward direction, especially in the period between 1960 and 1980, and political institutions were often modified in a manner that tended to make them more responsive to short term changes in voter preferences by weakening or eliminating second chambers in bicameral legislatures. A summary of their analysis is provided towards the end of this chapter.

The first part of this chapter reviews public choice explanations of the emergence and growth of the major component parts of the welfare state. It begins with an overview of public choice research on public pensions (social security) and follows with a survey of research on the politics of government support for healthcare. It then presents a synopsis of the approach used by Congleton and Bose (2010) to analyze aggregate government expenditures on social insurance and related income-security programs.

It bears keeping in mind that the growth of the welfare state is an important historical phenomenon and an important contemporary policy issue. Public choice theory should be able to account for the broad trajectory of social insurance expenditures if it provides an accurate model of public policy formation. The papers surveyed in this chapter suggest that public choice models of day-to-day politics can provide useful insight into the causes, conditional nature, and average levels of welfare state benefits. With respect to long-term budgetary problems, the proper level of analysis may have to shift from day-to-day politics to quasi-constitutional models. To find a balance between promised benefits and public finances, some of the most durable features of our social insurance programs may have to be revised – if bankruptcy is to be avoided in the long run.

2 GOVERNMENT PROVIDED AND/OR SUBSIDIZED PENSIONS

State pension programs can be considered a form of social insurance analogous to private annuities. In effect, the government uses tax revenues, often earmarked for such purposes, to provide retired and disabled persons with a more or less constant flow of real income as long as they live. Insurance companies sell similar products (annuities) and profit from their large portfolios and knowledge of the distribution of longevity in the communities served. As with private annuities, no equity is accumulated by social security programs that can be passed on to the next generation. Most public pension programs are pay-as-you-go systems, and in contrast to private annuity programs, tend not to be profit centers for national governments. Rather, they are subsidized in various ways. For example, most low-income persons receive a 'discount' on their annuities, even after adjusting for longevity differences between low-income and high-income persons. The subsidies are financed largely by the higher premiums (taxes) paid by high-income persons.

As is true of other social insurance programs, public pension programs are never so generous nor their subsidies so great that public pensions entirely replace private pensions. Rather, the result typically is a mixed system in which public pensions provide a base (which normally varies with income) and private pensions and savings are used to top up that base. Marginal retirement dollars are privately controlled by most taxpayers. Private pensions are themselves often encouraged through a variety of tax preferences, but in this section we focus on the public pension component of social security programs.

As in other areas of public choice, the politics of publicly provided or subsidized pensions begins with an analysis of the economic effects of those programs. How do these affect the welfare of persons receiving the benefits and paying the taxes? And, what effects do the programs have on national savings and labor participation rates? Such effects will shape voters' demands for publicly provided or subsidized pensions, regardless of whether voter interests are narrow or broad. Among the economic analyses of the US social security program, Feldstein's (1974, 1996) research is probably the best known. Feldstein (1974) argued that the substitution effect of a social security program reduces personal savings and its wealth effect induces earlier retirement. Labor participation rates fall rapidly after the age requirements to receive social security are satisfied.

The public choice literature attempts to explain why particular public pension benefit levels are adopted and why they change through time. Many of the purely economic explanations are apolitical in that they take program parameters to be predetermined and use relatively simple mechanistic demographic trends to explain aggregate expenditure levels. By contrast, the public choice literature uses political models – various combinations of electoral, interest group, and social contract theories – to characterize the political demand for social security.

Pioneering theoretical work on the electoral basis of social security was done by Browning (1973, 1975), who used an overlapping-generations model to explain the size of the program. Browning notes that the median voter with respect to social security is a person of approximately median age and income. Such a voter is older than half of the electorate, which – because of voting age restrictions – tends to be older than the population as a whole. Because much of the cost of the program is a sunk cost for the median voter, she supports a much larger benefit level than a young person would, although a smaller program than persons of retirement age would have demanded. As long as rates of return are positive for the median-aged voter, the program will remain in place, even if rates of return for younger persons are negative.

Browning's analysis has been refined in various ways, but remains the main conceptual framework for electoral models of social security programs. For example, Sjoblom's (1985) critique of the Browning model uses his overlapping generation framework to demonstrate that the steady state assumed by Browning may not be credible and so may not be as dynamically sustainable as Browning claims. Sjoblom argues that sustainability may require that the program be constitutionalized in some way. Sjoblom's constitutional conjecture may account for the stability of much of the general architecture of the programs (tax structure, base, and conditionality of benefits), which endures for decades at a time. The Browning model has also been extended by Boadway and Wildasin (1989), who note that initial benefit levels tend to exceed those of the long run steady state.

The median voter approach was not, however, subjected to empirical tests until 1990. Congleton and Shughart (1990) tested the relative explanatory power of median voter, special interest group, and combined models of social security benefit levels using US data. Their median voter model implied that benefit levels reflected the fiscal constraints of the median voter, such as labor income, private pension income, age (life expectancy and remaining work life), real interest rate, growth rate, effective tax base per elderly, the number of retirement benefit recipients, their private pension income, and the size of social security administrative expenditure. Their estimates of that model verified that changes in the median voter's fiscal constraints tended to cause changes in social security retirement benefit levels. Similar models were subsequently developed by Nishimura and Zhang (1995), Zhang (1995), Breyer and Craig (1997), and Tabellini (2000) and tested on international (OECD) datasets.

The main alternative to the electoral explanation of social security benefits are models that focus on the efforts of politically active interest groups. In interest group models, politically active groups representing elderly voters lobby for and obtain these programs as a transfer from younger generations. An early instance of the interest group model of the determination of social security benefits was sketched out by Olson (1965). The number of individual beneficiaries is much smaller than the number of individual contributors who pay the social security taxes while working. However, the former gain more from an expansion in benefits than a single taxpayer pays, which gives retired (and nearly retired) persons a stronger incentive to become involved in the politics of social security benefits than the persons paying the taxes. Olson's analysis was fleshed out by Weaver (1982) in a book-length analysis and has been used in many subsequent papers.

The organization of politically active groups is rarely modeled, but the models implicitly assume that 'formeteurs' or 'political entrepreneurs' create formal organizations of one kind or another that solve the various free-riding and coordination problems of political action.[4] Once organized, formeteurs may encourage single-issue voting, conditional contributions to campaigns, providing elected representatives with information about the breadth of support for such programs, and the writing of books and editorials. Such organizations may also encourage their members and the public at large to vote against candidates proposing public pension cuts and in favor of those proposing pension increases.

In addition to 'outside' interest group models, 'inside' interest group models can also be applied. For example, Niskanen's model of bureaucratic behavior could also be applied to persons working in social security administration(s). Senior social security bureaucrats tend to be an 'inside' interest group insofar as they all have personal stakes in the growth of the social security program. As social security expenditures increase, employment opportunities increase, and senior managers will have somewhat greater discretionary power and non-pecuniary benefits. Persons who think that social security is normatively an important policy area will also tend to be attracted to senior positions in social security programs. Thus, for combinations of narrow and broad self-interests, senior bureaucrats will be inclined to testify and lobby in favor of program expansion.

Congleton and Shughart (1990) develop an interest group model of social security benefit levels that includes both insider and outsider groups and test the model using US data. Their interest group model explained about the same amount of the variation of US social security benefit levels as their pure electoral model. Similar international studies emerged in the late 1990s and early 2000s, as pointed out above.

In addition to the pure electoral and interest group models of public policy formation, there are also models and empirical studies that combine aspects of several models. In such models, social security programs reflect both electoral pressures and the efforts of special interest groups. In an early test of such models, Congleton and Shughart (1990) provide evidence that a combined model does a somewhat better job of explaining the path of US social security benefits than either a pure electoral (median voter) or pure interest group model, although the median voter model somewhat outperforms the pure special interest group model. Kim (2010) updates the Congleton and Shughart (1990) analysis by including later data, using somewhat more sophisticated econometric techniques, and taking account of subsequent changes in social security programs (the Greenspan commission reforms). His results are broadly similar to those in the Congleton–Shughart study. He finds that a combined model does the best job of explaining social security benefits in the United States. In addition, he presents evidence that the reforms proposed by the 1983 Greenspan commission (which can be regarded as quasi-constitutional amendments to the program) affected the growth path of average social security benefits. His results also suggest that interest groups may be becoming more important determinants of benefit levels.

The literature from abroad is largely consistent with the US studies. The results of international research suggest that the growth rate of the economy, real interest rates, inflation, and deadweight cost all have effects on program size and growth. In addition, Galasso and Profeta (2002) suggest that redistributive incentives analogous to those worked out by Usher (1977) and Meltzer and Richard (1981) have affected social security benefit levels. Several studies have found that the ratio of mean-to-median income, the skewness of the income distribution, and average income affect social security expenditures. Galasso and Profeta report that the proportion of elderly is positively related to the size of social security as a share of GDP, but not with respect to benefit levels per retired person. The latter suggests that the constitutionalization of the social security programs (that is their stable age-dependent eligibility criteria) may be more important than the interest group effects of organizations of retired persons.

Overall, the public choice literature on national social security programs implies that the expenditures for public pensions are jointly determined by longer-term considerations and day-to-day politics, given relatively stable fiscal systems and eligibility requirements.

3. RESEARCH ON THE POLITICAL ECONOMY OF SUBSIDIZED MEDICINE

Another major insurance program of the welfare state covers or subsidizes healthcare coverage. As is true of public pension programs, many of these programs are quite old, with roots in the late nineteenth and early twentieth centuries. These programs have historically been smaller than public pension programs, but have gradually become (or are becoming) the largest of the welfare state's programs. The direct subsidization of health insurance coverage, of the costs of medical services, or of both, normally is combined with a variety of direct and indirect healthcare tax preferences and subsidies. However, these are neglected in this section of the chapter in order to focus on government provision of these good and services.

In a manner similar to public pension programs, the nature and growth of these programs reflect day-to-day politics and longer-term quasi-constitutional decisions. In the short run, the extent of public support and breadth of coverage can be varied day to day or year to year. The range of medical procedures supported can also be adjusted at the margin in various ways. Are experimental treatments, dental services, mental health services, health spas, and plastic surgery, for example, to be supported by the government programs and, if so, to what degree? Insurance can be complete, that is medical services paid for entirely by taxpayers, or accessing some or all medical services may require significant copayments. In the long run, basic parameters of the public support for healthcare can be adjusted. The delivery method (subsidy, mandate, or provision) and the financing of the programs can be adjusted. Healthcare, health insurance, or both can be subsidized, health insurance coverage can be mandated, healthcare can be provided directly by state enterprises, and various combinations of these policies may be adopted. Once adopted, however, the general architecture of the healthcare system tends to be stable for decades at a time.

Expenditures on taxpayer supported medicine is a joint consequence of long- and short-run policy choices, demographics, and the technology of healthcare. In most welfare states, the result is a mixed public–private system in which a public base (safety net) can be topped up with purchases of supplemental private insurance or direct private purchase of healthcare services (Besley and Gouveia 1994). The public–private mix and efficacy of healthcare systems vary widely, as indicated by Figure 22.2, which plots the fraction of total healthcare spending by the public sector against average longevity at age 65. There is more variety among healthcare systems in the West than there is among public pension programs.

Economic and political factors affect policy decisions in a manner analogous to those of social security programs. There is a tax price for such programs and the benefits tend to be disproportionately received by relatively old persons (roughly the same persons who receive public pensions). Longevity and average age of the populations served thus have effects on the demand for government subsidies for healthcare insurance and direct provision. Demographic trends in the West tend to increase both healthcare costs and public (median voter) support for government healthcare subsidies, other things being equal. Costs also tend to increase as the range of healthcare services that can be provided increases, which largely reflects technological advance in the diagnosis and treatment of disease.

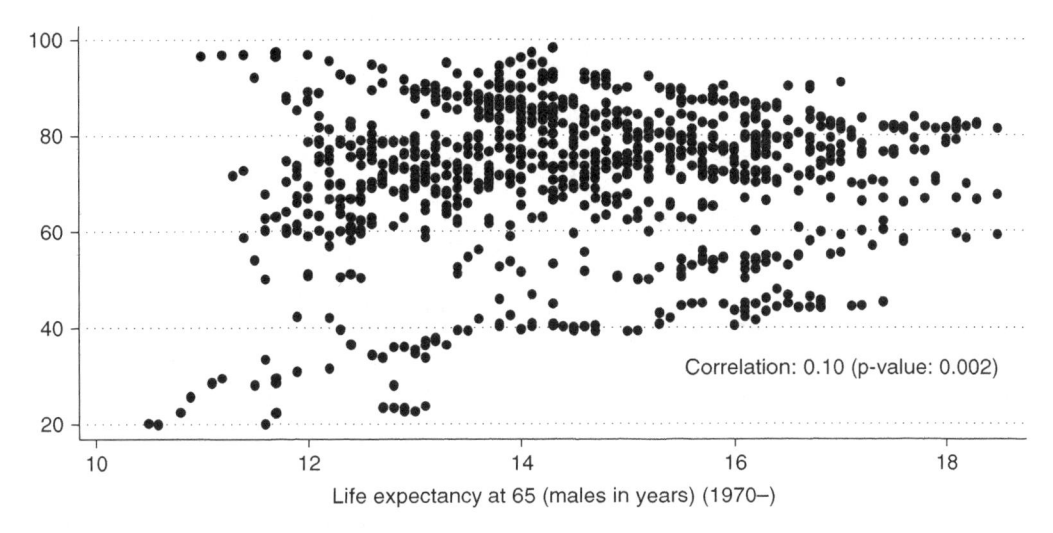

Figure 22.2   Ratio of public to total health expenditure vs. life expectancy at 65

It bears noting that demographic change and technological advance are also partly the consequences of policy choices. Greater longevity may be partly a consequence of public healthcare choices (see Figure 22.2), and technological advance may be partly a consequence of direct and indirect government support for healthcare insurance and medical R&D. System choice also tends to affect healthcare costs, although it is not completely obvious how or why. This section addresses the choice of healthcare system and the next addresses how public policies, especially those subsidizing medical R&D, have affected the cost of medical procedures. As in the case of public pensions, a variety of tax preferences often encourage the provision and purchase of private health insurance, but we focus on the politics of direct public subsidies and production of healthcare services in this and the next section of this chapter.

As in the case of the political economy literature on public pensions, the political economy literature on healthcare begins with models of the private demand for and effects of public healthcare policies, because these determine voter net benefits from such programs. Classic work on the economics of healthcare is that of Arrow (1963) and Pauly (1974). Arrow's analysis suggests that competitive markets tend not to generate Pareto efficient levels of healthcare and medical insurance for a variety of reasons, including externalities (contagious diseases), defects in property rights systems and economies of scale. He also analyzes information problems and barriers to entry that affect markets for healthcare services and health insurance. Pauly (1974) analyzes the consequences of the asymmetric information problems that produce moral hazard. Insured parties will tend to under invest in preventative care when insurance companies cannot perfectly assess or price the risks for specific insurance purchasers. He shows that over, rather than under, insurance is a likely consequence of this type of information asymmetry, although high-risk customers may be underserved. All of these problems imply that the private provision of healthcare is unlikely to be Pareto optimal. Pauly

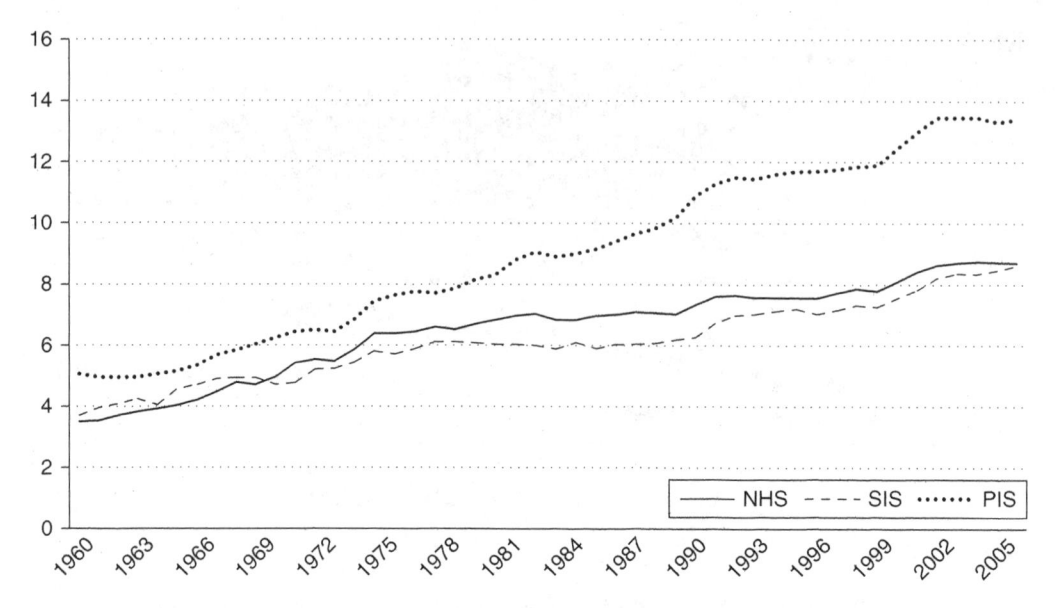

Figure 22.3 Health expenditure as share of GDP, average per subgroup of countries (in percent)

suggests that many of the shortcomings of the healthcare market can be overcome by imposing compulsory limits on the purchase of health insurance, by making information about a person's total insurance purchases available to all insurers, or both.[5] The Arrow and Pauly analyses provide the main analytical frameworks for subsequent work on the politics of public healthcare systems, although their theories were revised, extended, and tested in various ways.

Pauly (1974, 1988) also initiates the public choice analysis of public healthcare provision by analyzing a simple short-run median-voter model of public insurance mandates and subsidies. Congleton and Shughart (1990) test related models by suggesting that the demand for many healthcare programs can be modeled in a manner similar to that of social security, because they tend to benefit retired persons more than working persons. Their estimates of combined US Social Security and Medicare benefit levels were similar to their estimates of social security (public pensions) alone. The early approaches, however, did not model healthcare programs that were not conditioned on age or indirectly targeted at retired persons. Analysis of day-to-day political support for healthcare benefits continued through the 1990s, as with Vogel (1999).

Another important subsequent strand of the public choice literature on healthcare focuses on the long-run quasi-constitutional choice of healthcare systems. Healthcare systems vary substantially among OECD members and the choice of healthcare systems evidently has significant effects on the average quality of healthcare services and, perhaps surprisingly, on their costs. Figure 22.3 illustrates the average cost of the three main healthcare delivery-payment systems. Social insurance systems (SIS) have historically cost less than national healthcare systems (NHS) which, surprisingly, have historically cost less than private insurance systems (PIS) in OECD countries. (Most of the observed systems are mixed systems that include elements of the others, but systems are classified by the largest of their component parts.)

Early analyses of system-level choices concentrated on pure private, pure public, and mixed systems, without accounting for differences in public systems. For example, Breyer (1995) focuses on the manner in which healthcare services may be provided. He assumes that the benefit level of a state-provided health insurance plan is voted on in a referendum and that the social insurance plan is funded by a flat income tax. Voters are distinguished by income and taste over consumption of healthcare. This model is applied to two settings: one in which no greater quantity of healthcare can be consumed than that adopted by the national insurance plan, the other in which additional insurance or healthcare can be bought privately, as is true of most public healthcare systems. In both settings, the level of public insurance is assumed to be driven by the median voter. The political equilibrium in the second case produces a dual private–public regime of healthcare provision, with the tax level depending on the distribution of income and tastes across the population. In the second setting, people with higher than average income and marginal utility of healthcare tend to 'top up' with privately provided healthcare. Gouveia (1997) develops a similar analysis of referendums on healthcare support levels, but includes consideration of different health risks (morbidity). This general line of research continues through Jacob and Lundin (2005) and Pietrantonio (2011).

The Pietrantonio (2011) analyses include an unusually broad range of alternative financing structures and choice of various pure and mixed systems of private, insurance mandates, and public provision. He finds that political equilibria exist for the three major public healthcare systems: ones that are mostly private (PIS), ones that are mostly driven by insurance mandates (SIS), and ones in which healthcare services are largely financed or produced publicly (NHS). His analysis implies that both income and morbidity affect political decisions about which health systems to adopt. Private insurance tends to be adopted in countries where the risk of getting sick is relatively low and the income distribution is relatively unequal, whereas social insurance is adopted where the risk of getting sick is relatively high and the income distribution is relatively more uniform. National health systems tend to be adopted in the intermediate cases.

4 THE POLITICAL ECONOMY OF SUBSIDIZED MEDICAL TECHNOLOGY

National expenditures on healthcare also vary with the range of procedures that are covered by private and public insurance or provided by private and government healthcare centers. The menu of possible procedures is substantially an effect of past technological innovation in healthcare. When healthcare programs were first established they were relatively small, in large part because relatively little true healthcare could be provided by the medical sector. It has long been recognized that technological advances are important determinants of healthcare costs. For example, the importance of technology is noted by Arrow (1963) and Tullock (1995), among many others. Essentially all surveys of the literature on healthcare expenditures note the significance of technological change in explaining healthcare expenditures as, for example, in Besley and Gouveia (1994) and in Folland et al. (2009). Indeed, it can be argued that if public and private insurance have a significant long-run effect on aggregate medical expenditures, it is likely to be through coverage of new procedures, drugs, and devices, and consequent increases in rates of technological innovation in health care.

Not all technological innovations in healthcare increase costs, but many do so by bringing new, more labor- and capital-intensive procedures to the menu of available remedies. Whether cost increasing technologies are more likely than cost reducing ones is not self-evident. However, it seems clear that average medical costs have been rising faster than in other parts of the economy and have been doing so at least partly because technological advances have raised rather than reduced costs; and public and private insurance coverages have been expanded to pay for the new more expensive techniques.

Without advances in the available techniques for treating illnesses, the demand for health insurance would expand more or less at the rate of other insurance, which grows at roughly the same rate as income. But, average health insurance expenditures have increased at a much faster rate than per capita national income. Between 1960 and 2010, healthcare expenditures in the United States tripled as a fraction of GDP, rising from around 5 percent to more than 16 percent.

Technological progress is not, of course, an entirely random event. It is driven to a large extent by research and development (R&D) expenditures. A significant fraction of medical research is paid for directly with tax dollars and much of the rest is subsidized indirectly through tax preferences. Dorsey et al. (2010) reports that out of approximately $100 billion of US expenditures on biomedical research in 2007, $37 billion was financed by federal, state, and local governments (taxes), with the National Institutes of Health (NIH) accounting for about 70 percent of those expenditures. Moreover, without the expansion of insurance coverage, there would be little private research on more elaborate and expensive medical equipment and techniques.[6]

Given the importance of medical innovation for healthcare costs, surprisingly little research has taken place on the political economy of subsidies for medical technologies. This may be partly because the direct expenditure levels are relatively small and difficult to assess directly. They are also somewhat more difficult to model, because of all of the various interconnections between long-run demand, supply, and innovation rates.

As a first approximation, political support for medical R&D can be modeled in a manner similar to that for public pensions and healthcare subsidies. The benefits from medical research tend to be age dependent, because most persons demand sophisticated medical procedures only after they reach retirement age. Moreover, medical innovations take substantial time and so (intergenerational) public support for R&D is less affected by the stability problems noted by Sjoblom (1985). Consequently, informed voters of approximately median age and income are likely to be decisive in determining NIH and other government medical research subsidies.

However, unlike public pensions and medical insurance programs, the typical voter will have very little direct information about the level and allocation of their governments' healthcare R&D expenditures or their ultimate effects. So, there is unusually large scope for interest group interventions of various kinds, including organized groups representing the elderly, the healthcare industry, various non-profit disease lobbies, and academic researchers. A good deal of the allocation of resources takes place in Congress, which assigns budgets to the various specialized disease institutes.

Within the private sector, the probability of successful innovation, expected rate of utilization, and anticipated degree of monopoly power (patents) will be important factors for R&D investments (Weisbrod 1991; Weisbrod and LaMay 1999). Within the public sector, median voter expectations and the efforts of for-profit and non-profit interest groups are likely to be significant determinants of R&D effort. Electoral pressures push research dollars toward investigations of diseases that affect large portions of the population, such as cancer and heart disease. Private dollars, in contrast, will tend to support research in areas where innovations are patentable and few substitutes exist, because these increase anticipated monopoly profits. In neither case will R&D subsidies attempt to minimize the expected losses from disease. Fortunately, such losses tend to be correlated with the size of the beneficiary groups (electoral support) and the absence of readily available substitutes. Consistent with the electoral analysis, the three largest appropriations are to diseases that affect a broad swath of elderly persons. These appropriations account for about half of NIH expenditures: NCI (National Cancer Institute), NIAID (National Institute of Allergy and Infectious Diseases), and NHLBI (National Heart, Lung, and Blood Institute).[7]

This suggests that the electoral support for public subsidies for healthcare R&D can be modeled as a demand for subsidized social insurance. That is to say, new technologies are expected to reduce the risk (losses) from diseases in much the same manner that other insurance does. As is true of the demands for both public pensions and ordinary health insurance, voter support for health-related R&D subsidies is likely to vary with income and age. The success of R&D efforts, in turn, affects the demand for health insurance, per se, as new procedures become available in the future.

Future research is likely to model the mix of R&D subsidies adopted and estimate the extent to which both the level and allocation of those subsidies is electorally or interest-group driven.

5 MODELING A VOTER'S DEMAND FOR SOCIAL INSURANCE

Congleton and Bose (2010) develop a model of the demand for income security that extends the narrowly self-interested voter models used in previous public choice research on the various programs of the welfare state to include effects of ideology and institutions. They argue that voter demand for social insurance is affected by personal risks, income, and insurance costs; and also by a voter's ideological (or other normative) interest in particular insurance programs. Although Meltzer and Richard-like effects are implied by their model, it is not a model of redistribution from one group of voters to another, but rather of the demand for broadly inclusive social insurance programs. Given voter demands, the support levels adopted depend on the political institutions under which policy choices are made. The next few pages provide an overview of their approach and model.

Suppose that an age-dependent random 'shock' strikes people and reduces their ability to work and play. Such shocks include debilitating diseases, accidents of various kinds, technological shocks that affect the value of one's human and physical capital, and business cycles that reduce one's employment opportunities. A tractable model of the effect of such shocks can be created by assuming that all such shocks affect a typical voter's effective work and leisure hours and that only two states of 'endurance' are possible.[8] When 'well' (in the absence of the shock), a typical person (referred to as Alle) has H hours per period to allocate between work, W, and leisure, L. When 'not well' (when affected by the shock), Alle has $S < H$ hours to allocate between work and leisure.

Work produces private good Y, which is desired for its own sake, with $Y_i = \omega W_i$, where ω is the marginal and average product of labor. The probability of being affected by a negative shock is age dependent, with $P = p(A)$ for a person of age A. In addition to economic interests, a person's interest in social insurance is affected by internalized normative theories of various kinds.[9] The norms of greatest interest are ideological and philosophical theories that characterize the ideal level of social insurance – possibly ones associated with theories of 'the good society' or implied by theories of 'social welfare.'

The typical voter, Alle, is assumed to maximize a strictly concave Von-Neumann–Morgenstern utility function defined over private consumption, Y, leisure, L, and the extent to which the actual social insurance, I, departs from his or her ideological ideal, I^{**}, as with $U = u(Y_i, L_i, |I - I_i^{**}|)$. To simplify the analysis, a person's ideology does not affect his or her demand for income and leisure, $U_{YI} = U_{LI} = 0$, although it may affect his or her demand for social insurance.

In the absence of an income insurance program, Alle maximizes:

$$U^{woH} = u(\omega W_i, H - W_i, |I - I_i^{**}|) \qquad (22.1)$$

when well and maximizes:

$$U^{woS} = u(\omega W_i, S - W_i, |I - I_i^{**}|) \qquad (22.2)$$

when she is not well. In either case, her work day (or work week) will satisfy similar first-order conditions:

$$U_Y^T \omega - U_L^T = 0. \qquad (22.3)$$

Alle's workday sets the marginal utility of the income produced by her (or his) work equal to the marginal cost of that work in terms of the reduced utility from leisure.

The implicit function theorem implies that Alle's work day (supply of labor) can be characterized as:

$$W_i^* = w(T, \omega, I, I_i^{**}). \qquad (22.4)$$

In general, Alle's work day varies with her active hours ($T = H$ or S), marginal product (wage rate), current institutions, and vision of the good society. Alle's income falls from $\omega w(H, \omega, I, I_i^{**})$ to $\omega w(S, \omega, I, I_i^{**})$ when affected by the random shock.

Having characterized W_i^* in a setting without social insurance, consider the effects of a government-sponsored program that collects a fraction of the output produced by each taxpayer-resident through an earmarked proportional income tax rate, t, and returns it to 'unwell' residents through conditional insurance demogrants, I. This program provides a 'safety net' (insurance payout) of I units of the private consumption good Y for persons who are less able to work (in state S). Given that program, Alle's net income is $Y^H = (1 - t)\omega_i W^H$ when she is fully able to work, and $Y^S = (1 - t)\omega_i W^S + I$, when she is less able to work.

Naturally, such a program changes Alle's behavior because it changes the net rewards of working when well and when not well. Given the program, Alle now maximizes:

$$U^H = U((1 - t)\omega_i W, H - W, |I - I_i^{**}|) \qquad (22.5)$$

when well and

$$U^S = U((1 - t)\omega_i W + I, S - W, |I - I_i^{**}|) \qquad (22.6)$$

when unwell. Taking the derivative with respect to Alle's work period (W) characterizes the first-order conditions that describe Alle's work day (or work week) during well and unwell periods. These are again similar to each other.

$$U_Y^T(1 - t)\omega_i - U_L^T = 0 \qquad (22.7)$$

Equation 22.7 differs from equation 22.3 in that Alle again equates the marginal utility of net income produced by working (which now includes effects from taxes and the government's income-security guarantee) to the marginal opportunity cost of time spent working.

The implicit function describing Alle's work day is now:

$$W_i^* = w(T, \omega, I, I_i^{**}, t). \qquad (22.8)$$

Equation 22.8 is the same as equation 22.4 if the taxes and benefits equal zero. T again represents the time to be allocated, which is determined by the individual's state of health or work opportunities. (I does not appear because it is determined by the fiscal constraints, the tax rate, risk factors, wage rate, and size of the community.) Partial derivatives of equation 22.8 imply that Alle again works more when she is well than not well, but generally works less when she is covered by a social insurance program than when she is not. Strict concavity of the utility function allows these derivatives to be signed unambiguously.

For most day-to-day purposes, the parameters of a government-sponsored social insurance program are exogenous variables for the individuals who take advantage of them. The exception occurs on Election Day, when the parameters of the program are indirectly controlled by voters. Elected representatives are induced by competitive pressures to pay close attention to the preferences of voters both before and after that day if they want to hold office. On those days, both fiscal constraints and the voter's ideology tend to be important.

The Congleton–Bose characterization of the typical voter's utility function assumes that each voter has a conception of the good society that includes a 'normatively ideal' safety net, which is represented as I_i^{**}. The voter's ideological dissatisfaction with current social insurance levels is, consequently, an increasing function of $|I - I_i^{**}|$, where I is the existing program. Alle's preferred public safety net, I_i^*, as opposed to her normatively ideal one, I_i^{**}, varies with both her own circumstances and ideology, and the fiscal circumstances of the government that sponsors the service.

The actual benefit level, I, is assumed to be determined by a combination of electoral pressures, fiscal realities, and political institutions. If there are N members in the community eligible for the program of interest, $\Sigma p(A_i)$ of them qualify for benefits during a typical work period. For symmetric age-conditioned probability distributions, this can be written as $P^A N$, where P^A is the average probability of being unwell in the community of interest. The tax base is $\Sigma \omega_i W_j^T$, where ($T = H$ or S), depending on whether voter-taxpayer i is in state H or S. For symmetric distributions of age conditioned probabilities and propensities to work, the tax base can be written as $\omega^A W^A N$, where ω^A is the average wage and W^A is the average work period.

The tax revenues are earmarked for the public safety net program(s), so the income guarantee is $I = (t \Sigma \omega_i W_j^T)/P^A N = (t\omega^A W^A N)/P^A N = (t\omega^A W^A)/P^A$. In general, both the average tax base and number of persons drawing benefits varies with the age distribution and nature of relevant health and economic shocks, which are assumed to be fixed for the period of analysis.

A bit of substitution, calculus, and the implicit function theorem imply that a typical voter's preferred government-provided safety net can be characterized as a function of the parameters of his or her (i's) optimization problem:

$$I_i^* = g(\omega_i, A_i, I_i^{**}, P^A, \omega^A, N, S, H). \tag{22.9}$$

The typical voter's demand for social insurance varies with his or her wage rate and age (which determines his or her probability of being affected by the income-reducing shock), the lost hours associated with being 'not well', and his or her ideological welfare norm. For fiscal reasons, it is also affected by the number of taxpayers and the average probability of being subject to the income reducing shock, S, and average wage rates, ω^A. The extended utility function also implies that a voter's preferred government-provided safety net is somewhere between that of a 'rational choice pragmatist', who chooses benefit level I to advance his or her own economic interest, and that of a political idealist, who uses public policies to advance his or her vision of the good society.

Unfortunately, the signs of the partial derivatives of equation 22.9 cannot be determined without making additional assumptions, although conventional economic intuitions and a good deal of evidence suggest that more social insurance tends to be demanded as income and personal risks (age) increase, and as risk aversion and the ideological norm for social insurance increase. For most voters, tradeoffs exist between personal net receipts that are (partly) generated by effects on the size of the tax base similar to those in Meltzer and Richard's (1981) analysis (although in this case the 'transfer' is received only when the person qualifies for it), and also tradeoffs generated by personal ideological goals. Tradeoffs exist as well between a voter's financial self-interest and normative or ideological goals, because very few voters will regard the present benefit level to be normatively ideal.

This voter model can be used to characterize a wide variety of electoral based political equilibria and changes in those equilibria will cause social insurance benefits to change. However, this is not always as straightforward as one might expect, because political institutions affect how changes in voter policy demands affect policy outcomes.

Public choice and the modern welfare state 377

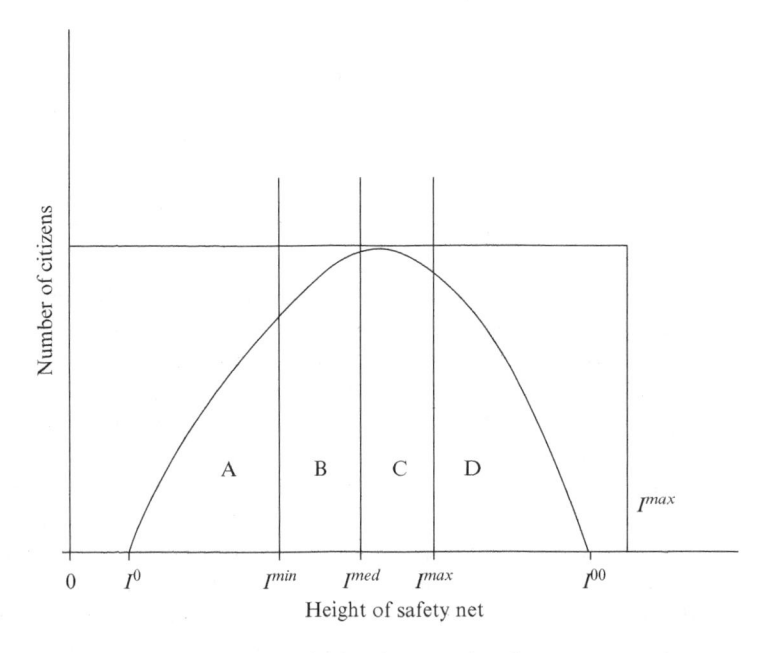

Figure 22.4 Distribution of citizen ideal safety net levels

Under direct democracy, the frequency distribution of voter-preferred income security programs associated with given distribution of utility functions, wages, ages, and norms determines the identity of the median voter (if one exists). Given a one-dimensional policy space, such as occurs above under those fiscal assumptions, choosing a public safety net using majority rule implies that the median voter's ideal program tends to be adopted, I^{med}, and that changes in the program after the median voter's ideal program is adopted reflect changes in her demand for income security. The median voter's demand for the social safety net can be characterized by substituting values for median wage rates and ideology into equation 22.9. The model developed above implies that the median voter's preferred social safety net changes if the median wage rate, age, or social insurance norms change.

The model also implies that if median income is below average income, a risk-neutral median voter's preferred safety net is somewhat *above her ideological ideal*, because she or he tends to be a (subsidized) net beneficiary of the tax-financed insurance program. If there is a widely accepted ideal level of social insurance in the community of interest, I^{**}, the actual policy under direct democracy tends to be a bit more than that ideal level, because of the median voter's subsidized price for social insurance

Under more complex collective decision procedures, the political equilibrium is affected by both the starting point of program negotiations and the particular collective decision-making procedures in place.

As an illustration, consider a series of small increases evaluated by a two-thirds supermajority rule with 0 as the initial point of departure. This procedure yields safety net I^{min} in Figure 22.4, where area A is twice as large as area B. I^{min} is smaller than that preferred by the median voter, because more than a third of the voters oppose further increases. The same voting rule will produce an income security program that is larger than that desired by the median voter if the status quo ante is initially above the median citizen's ideal and incremental reductions are voted on. The policy chosen in that case will be I^{max}, where area D is twice as large as area C.

Note that the same logic implies that shifts in I^{min} and I^{max} tend to produce asymmetric shifts in policy. If the polity of interest is at I^{min}, for example, and I^{min} decreases because of changes in voter income or preferences, *only a minority will favor lowering the social safety net from its previous value* and the safety net program will not be changed. On the other hand, if I^{min} increases, a supermajority would favor increasing I from its previous value. Statistically, such asymmetric policy adjustments will show up as autocorrelation. That is to say, autocorrelation is a predicted consequence of supermajority procedures, rather than an extraneous statistical nuisance if the supermajority voter model describing shifts in I^{min} is essentially correct.

Although no western government explicitly uses supermajority rule to make policy decisions regarding the height of the public safety net, several widely used institutions have similar effects on policy outcomes. For example, systems of government with bicameral legislatures have two veto players. Representatives in each body are selected by somewhat differing electorates, and because of differences in district sizes, voter turnout, and the timing of elections, tend to represent somewhat different interests. If elected representatives cast their legislative votes in a manner consistent with the interests of their respective median voters, these more complex architectures increase the effective size of the majorities required to pass laws.[10]

These supermajority-like effects imply that both income increases and ideological shifts to the left (increases in the ideologically ideal level of the safety net, I^{**}) tend to induce smaller changes in the government-sponsored safety net in countries with bicameral parliaments than in those with unitary ones, and somewhat different final outcomes. Policy adjustments tend to be smaller on average and asymmetric in countries with more veto players, insofar as veto-player interests differ and the effect is analogous to super majority rule.

Congleton and Bose (2010) provide a series of ordinary least squares (OLS) and generalized least squares (GLS) estimates of their ideologically and institutionally augmented model of the size of social insurance programs in OECD countries based on the Huber et al. (2004) dataset. These are consistent with their analysis. Welfare state programs tend to expand with average age, income, and as ideology drifted to the left. They tend to decrease (or increase less) as a nation's political institutions include more veto players.

They conclude that the modern welfare state rose because voter income increased and because ideological norms shifted in directions that favored larger social insurance programs. The growth of social insurance programs in specific countries was also affected by the political institutions under which program reforms were adopted, with less expansion of the welfare state taking place in countries with more veto players. Although their aggregate estimates did not include medical R&D expenditures, similar effects are likely to exist for healthcare R&D subsidies, which have been increasing through time as income and median age increase.

6 ELECTORAL POLITICS, INTEREST GROUPS AND THE MODERN WELFARE STATE

Analysts of democratic politics have long argued that democracies may engage in wholesale redistribution that undermines their viability. Among the first analyses of this possibility, were case studies developed by Aristotle *circa* 330 BCE. The major programs of the welfare state, however, are not pure transfer schemes in the sense of taking money or property from one group and giving it directly to another. Instead, various insurance programs are adopted (and subsidized) that take money from the well to provide healthcare subsidies for the sick and income for the unemployed, elderly, and disabled. The same 'transfers' may be said to exist under both private and public insurance programs, as, for example, a fire insurance program may be said to transfer wealth from persons without fires to those with homes damaged by fires.

Models of social insurance differ from those for unconditional transfers in several respects. First, no altruism, ideological impulse, or conspiracy is necessary to explain the existence of programs that provide benefits to a minority of voters. Second, insurance programs do not necessarily affect average income, although they may affect the variance of income (neglecting moral hazard and adverse selection effects). Third, there are settings in which such insurance can be more efficiently provided by government than in the private sector. Such settings may account for modest social insurance programs based on majority voter interests, who act without fear of revolutionary threat or substantial altruism. That democracies tend to subsidize social insurance, rather than engage in wholesale redistribution, may also reduce problems associated with majority decision making. For example, cycling problems and instability problems tend to be smaller, especially when the fiscal arrangements are quasi-constitutional. However, that does not imply that social insurance programs are without risks for democracies.

The early social-welfare programs were relatively modest in size and remained so until after World War II, as noted above. After World War II, many of these programs expanded rapidly as insurance benefit levels were increased and more persons became eligible for benefits. The path of average benefits rose too quickly after 1945 to be accounted for by demographics and technological advance alone. One possible explanation was that more and more transfers were being adopted and contemporary democracies were on an unsustainable slippery slope to bankruptcy, instability, and constitutional collapse. Another possibility focused on by most of the public choice literature was that electoral support for such programs had increased after the war was over and that the programs were simply reflecting a series of new electoral equilibria. The programs were adjusted at a variety of margins many times during the twentieth century.

However, there was an especially rapid increase in expenditures between 1960 and 1985. To account for such rapid increases in welfare state programs evidently requires a richer model of the politics of social insurance. Such a model was proposed by Congleton and Bose (2010), who suggest that the unusually rapid growth of social insurance programs in that period can be explained by including the effects of ideological norms and the institutions of collective choice. Their analysis of aggregate spending rates did not explicitly account for changes in the mix of expenditures such as the rising importance of healthcare spending, but it did reasonably well at explaining the great expansion between 1960 and 1985 and the subsequent slower expansion rates during the next two decades. A slippery slope theory would have a difficult time explaining the slower growth of that period. Other changes affecting the relative strength of interest groups could also be taken into account. A variety of groups benefit directly from public pension, health insurance, and healthcare R&D programs. The latter include retired persons, members of the various social service bureaucracies, supporting non-governmental organizations (NGOs), and commercial and academic producers of medical and non-medical services for elderly persons.

The normative implications of public choice models of the welfare state are not entirely clear unless one applies relatively simple majoritarian norms such as 'whatever the majority decides is correct'. Many of the early theoretical pieces suggest that social insurance tends to be oversupplied relative to levels that maximize GDP or social welfare. Indeed, Congleton and Bose (2010) note that if pivotal voters have below average income, they tend to demand more than their own normatively 'ideal' level of social insurance.

If the welfare state tends to be larger than it should be, the institutional analysis and empirical results of Congleton and Bose suggest that such a bias can be reduced with institutional reform. Their analytical results imply that the safety nets produced by political institutions with more veto players tend to be less 'democratic' in the sense that they are less connected to the demands of the median or average voter. However, insofar as election-based polities with many veto players tend to provide less social insurance than those with fewer veto players, the welfare states produced by day-to-day politics in such polities may be closer to the mainstream 'normative ideal' (I^{**}) than the median voter's preferred policy would have been.

NOTES

1. The term 'liberal' is used in its older European sense. In 1900 European liberals tended to favor (nearly) universal suffrage, free trade, and modest social safety nets. In contemporary Europe, liberals are the right-of-center defenders of democracy, markets, and civic equality. In the United States, the term liberal refers to the left-of-center defenders of democracy, markets, and civic equality, many of whom would be considered moderate social democrats in Europe. Before World War I, there was not very much difference between European and US usage, although significant differences emerged after that.
2. Private demands for insurance, whether publicly or privately provided, tend to have a small effect on the distribution of national income, because they moderate variations in income due to exogenous economic and health shocks, rather than redistribute income from rich to poor. Unemployment insurance and health insurance tend to shift money to those who are unfortunate, rather than from rich to poor per se. Nonetheless, social insurance reduces the extent to which bad luck reduces personal income and wealth, and thereby also reduces income and wealth variance.
3. See, for example, Mantis and Farmer (1968) or Gruber and Poterba (1994) for estimates of private insurance demand. Both report positive coefficients for income that are consistent with a less-than unitary income elasticity of the demand for insurance.
4. Congleton (2011, p. 28) develops and applies the notion of a fortmeteur: the individuals or groups that found an organization he calls 'formeteurs' and the persons recruited by formeteurs he refers to as 'team members'.
5. Grossman (1972) provides a useful economic model of health in which a person's health is a capital good that depreciates with age. Investments in healthcare can (partly) offset the associated depreciation of health capital. Hall and Jones (2007) analyze the income elasticity of the demand for healthcare.
6. On this point, Weisbrod (1991, pp. 539–40) argues that the introduction of more cost-effective procedures, that is, the shift from retrospective payment systems to prospective payment systems favors the discovery and adoption of drugs that substitute for surgical methods more than the discovery of drugs that are complements to surgery. Baker (1997, 2001) shows how the introduction of HMO practices slowed down the process of adoption of new technologies. Today's research (especially on the part of private

companies) will then be influenced by at least four factors: (i) by the expected supply of rival technologies that will be available at the time of introduction of the new technology; (ii) by the expected institutions and practices that will govern the supply of healthcare (especially the public one) at the time the new technology will be available; (iii) by the influence that the supplier of the new technology will exert in order to introduce it in insurance plans' coverage (both public and private); and (iv) by the rate of diffusion that the particular technology will have in the market.

7. See *National Institutes of Health: Summary of the Presidents FY 2011 Budget*, at: http://bit.ly/ruJwZS. See also the NSF data tables for R&D at http://1.usa.gov/uudO23.
8. The results from a two-state model are very similar to those generated by models with a bounded continuum of shocks on work and leisure opportunities. Very similar results, for example, can be generated from a model that characterizes health states with a uniform probability distribution.
9. Only a few public choice-based studies have explored the effects of norms on voter behavior, although norms and civic duty have long been part of rational-choice explanations of voter turnout. Linbeck (1997a, 1997b) develops a theory of the welfare state that includes a role for norms. See Eichenberger and Oberholzer-Gee (1998) or Congleton (2007b) for applications within a rational choice model of politics. Rational choice models that analyze the economic effects of norms include Congleton (1991b) and Buchanan and Yoon (2000). Early rational choice models of the political effects of ideological theories held by voters were developed by Congleton (1991a) and Hinich and Munger (1994).

    Several electoral turnout studies also stress the importance of norms. Jackman's (1987) study demonstrates that institutional differences and closeness affect turnout at the margin, but suggests that cultural differences are more important determinants of average turnout. (The Swiss and US dummy variables and the unexplained constant term are relatively large in his estimates.) Aldrich (1993) provides an overview of rational choice theories of turnout that take account of civic duty. Plutzer (2002) provides evidence that the propensity to vote is affected by families and peer groups, which are likely mechanisms for the transmission of norms.
10. Such an implicit requirement for supermajorities was first noted by Buchanan and Tullock (1962). More formally, G_{min} is the solution to $\int_{G_{min}}^{+\infty} f(G) = 100 - \varphi$, where $f(G)$ is the distribution of voter ideal points implied by equation 22.15, given the existing distribution of ideologies and wages, and φ is the implied supermajority requirement for the political institutions of interest. Similarly, G_{max} is the solution to $\int_{-\infty}^{G_{max}} f(G) = 100 - \varphi$. Note that $G_{max} = G_{min}$, when $\varphi = 50\%$. Contemporary democracies often differ in the number of veto players and their manner of elections (Congleton and Swedenborg 2006; Tsebelis 2002).

23 Public choice and public education
Lawrence W. Kenny

1 INTRODUCTION

Many economists believe that more vigorous competition makes market players more efficient. Accordingly, greater competition in primary and secondary education also should make that sector perform more efficiently. This chapter examines three types of competition: between public school districts, between public and private schools (aided by vouchers), and between charter schools[1] and traditional public schools. We examine the determinants of the number of school districts, which captures the extent of competition between districts, and factors affecting the adoption of voucher programs and charter schools. The evidence on how each form of competition affects the performance of public schools is then summarized. We do not examine a related literature that attempts to ascertain whether students learn more (1) in private schools than in public schools and (2) in charter schools rather than in traditional public schools.

We also examine the role of the electorate's skills, measured by their educational attainment, on how well government functions. We present evidence on the effects of years spent in school on how well informed they are about their US senators and how that information affects the success of an incumbent senator seeking reelection.

Many argue that we should turn to direct democracy to avoid principal–agent problems in representative government. School spending in a dozen or so states is determined by the results of school tax referendums. We examine evidence on whether the tax rate and school spending level chosen in a referendum are consistent with the preferences of the median voter. In Florida between 1939 and 1968, voters could select any millage tax rate between 0 and 10 mills, where one mill represents a one dollar tax on each thousand dollar value of taxable property.[2] We also compare school spending in Florida during this period with spending in the other 12 referendum states, where voters were given only an up-or-down decision on the school budget. Is spending in the 12 referendum states higher or lower than in Florida as a result of the institutional differences?

Finally we note that the median voter in a special election addressing the public school budget may be a teacher or parent, while the median voter in a general election is likely to be a citizen with broader interests. Do school boards turn to special elections to secure a more favorable median voter? Do referendums proposing higher taxes fare better in special elections than in general elections?

2 THE BENEFITS OF AN EDUCATED ELECTORATE

Nobel-laureate T.W. Schultz (1975) hypothesized that education raises humankind's ability to process information, which enables people to better deal with a dynamic world. He cited evidence from many diverse settings supporting his claim that education does more than provide facts and training in the use of analytical tools (for example, calculus). In the context of the political arena, citizens with more education are hypothesized to face lower costs of acquiring accurate political information amid the claims and counter-claims of political campaigns and consequently become better informed. They are predicted to be better able, for example, to distinguish competent from incompetent candidates and, therefore, to select those who will best represent their interests. Adam Smith ([1776] 2005, p. 642) reached a similar conclusion. He argued that some of the benefits of greater cognitive capacity among the 'common people' included their being 'more disposed to examine, and more capable of seeing through, the interested complaints of faction and sedition, and they are, upon that account, less apt to be misled into any wanton or unnecessary opposition to the measures of government'.

There is a substantial body of complementary evidence supporting this hypothesis. Ramakrishnan and Baldassare (2004, p. 36) reported that in California individuals with a college degree are, relative to those with no more than a high school degree, '70 percent more likely to sign petitions [and] 55 percent more likely to attend meetings on local issues'. Milligan et al. (2004) found that those with at least a high school degree were more likely to follow election campaigns on television or in the newspaper, pay attention to public affairs, participate in political meetings, and discuss political matters.

This greater involvement in politics by the more educated should help to make them better informed. The evidence is consistent with this reasoning. Citizens with more years of schooling have been found to be better informed about where members of Congress place on a left-right, liberal-conservative scale (Powell 1989; Husted et al. 1995). More highly educated voters should be more likely to verify whether an elected official has cast the votes they prefer. Schmidt et al. (1996) found that an incumbent senator's penalty in votes lost for being too liberal or too conservative for the state and party is greater in states where the population exhibits higher levels of educational attainment.[3]

Florida voters between 1939 and 1968 were allowed to vote for the school board's recommended school tax rate or to select any other millage rate between 0 and 10. Holcombe and Kenny (2007) found that in Florida counties where the educational attainments of voters were higher were more likely to rely on their own judgments in setting the school tax rate, voting with greater frequency for higher or lower taxes than the local school board had recommended. It should come as no surprise that in states with more highly educated populations, in which voters are more confident in their political judgments, voters are less likely to impose term limits on governors (Adams and Kenny 1986), or to set limits on educational spending (Husted and Kenny 2007).

Denslow et al. (2010) examined the impact of the surge in property values that took place between 2000 and 2006 on municipal expenditures in Florida. They found that voters' interests in these turbulent years were better represented in cities with more highly educated populations than in cities with less educated populations.[4]

It is clear that education can play an important role in improving the performance of political processes.

3 COMPETITION IN EDUCATION

Nearly one of seven students in primary and secondary schools in 2009 attended institutions not belonging to the traditional public school system. Private schools attracted 10.7 percent of the students. Charter school enrollment has been growing rapidly, and, by 2009, charter schools accounted for 2.8 percent of total K-12 enrollment.[5] Legislator ideology/party affiliation and teachers' unions have played major roles in determining the political fates of voucher and charter school programs.

Republicans and conservatives tend to support vouchers because they believe that more competition will make the provision of education more efficient and that private schools are likely to be more effective in carrying out their educational missions than public schools. Democrats and liberals, on the other hand, tend to oppose vouchers because they have more faith in the public sector and are aligned politically with teachers' unions.

Teachers' unions bargain for (1) higher salaries but no merit pay, (2) job protections, which make it difficult to fire incompetent teachers, (3) smaller class sizes and more in-classroom teachers' aides and (4) work rules that make it more difficult to reassign teachers. The requirements to qualify as a charter school teacher or a private school teacher are less rule-bound than those for traditional public school teachers. Unionized public school teachers may fear the loss of the union's salary premium and job protections if the growth in private and charter schools were to reduce significantly the number of teaching jobs in the public schools. Unions also may oppose vouchers and charter schools because the greater competition for students would make the demand for public school teachers more sensitive to their pay, thereby lowering the union wage premium.

3.1 Number of School Districts

Competition among public school districts is hypothesized to make the public schools more efficient.[6] There is more competition between school districts in metropolitan areas with larger numbers of them. For example, it is easier to evaluate performance when there are five school districts serving rich suburban neighborhoods in a metro area than when there is only one district serving those neighborhoods. If, in the first case, four of the five districts send their graduates to Harvard, Yale, and Princeton, while the graduates of the fifth district end up at Boston Community College, it is clear which district is inefficient. A greater number of school districts facilitates sorting of households on the basis of desired school quality (and willingness to pay for higher quality), which facilitates learning. On the other hand, poorer students may learn less if sorting leaves them with more low-income peers.

3.1.1 Determinants of the number of school districts

A small literature has examined the variation across metropolitan areas in the number of school districts. The number of school districts is determined by the trade-off between (1) providing each household with the preferred level of school characteristics (for example, school quality), implying a large number of districts, and (2) achieving cost savings associated with economies of scale, implying a small number of districts.

A school district attracts families preferring a level of school quality that is relatively

Table 23.1 *Effect of state-wide or county-wide restrictions on the number of school districts in a state*

	1980 Restricted number of districts	1980 Predicted number of districts
State-wide school district Hawaii	1	20
County-wide school district		
Florida	67	567
Louisiana	66	178
Maryland	24	140
Nevada	17	124
Virginia	140	274
West Virginia	55	71

Source: The predicted number of school districts is based on a regression in Kenny and Schmidt (1994).

close to that provided by the school district. Adding another school district to the metropolitan area would allow each district to locate closer to the preferred school qualities of the families attending schools there. This is more beneficial in more heterogeneous metro areas, where there is a wider range of families' preferred school quality levels. Thus there is a greater gain from adding another school district in more heterogeneous metropolitan areas, which should result in more school districts.

Nelson (1990) shows that there were more governments in metro areas with greater variance in income. Fisher and Wassmer (1998) find that income, age, and racial heterogeneity all are significant determinants of the number of school districts. Alesina et al. (2004) produced evidence of trade-offs between economies of scale and racial homogeneity and between economies of scale and income homogeneity; ethnic heterogeneity and religious heterogeneity, on the other hand, had no influence on the number of jurisdictions.

State governments generally assume a greater role in financing primary and secondary education to foster more equality in education spending. This, in turn, leaves rich households unable to sort into a school district providing a stellar education, with correspondingly stellar taxes.[7] Taking advantage of economies of scale becomes relatively more important, and the metro market has fewer but larger school districts. The results in Kenny and Schmidt (1994) support this prediction.

Some state governments impose restrictions on the formation of local governments. The effects are obvious. Nelson (1990) found that an increase in the minimum population needed to start a new local government predictably led to fewer local governments. A number of states have sharply curtailed competition across school districts. In Hawaii, primary and secondary education is provided by one state-wide district. In half a dozen other states, school districts must be county-wide. Table 23.1 reports (a) the actual (restricted) number of school districts and (b) the number of school districts in a state predicted for 1980 by a regression from Kenny and Schmidt (1994) that utilizes data from the 43 non-restricting states for 1950, 1960, 1970, and 1980 to explain the variation across states and over time in the number of school districts in a state.

From Table 23.1 we observe that Hawaii, with one statewide district, had only 5

Table 23.2 *Metropolitan population and number of school districts*

Metropolitan population	Average number of school districts
50,000–100,000	6.5
100,000–400,000	11.1
400,000–700,000	18.9
700,000–1,000,000	29.5
1,000,000+	58.5

Source: The data were taken from Husted and Kenny (2002).

percent of the districts it was predicted to have. The six county-wide states on average had only 35 percent of the predicted number of districts. The most restricted county-wide states were Florida, Nevada, and Maryland, with, respectively, 12, 14, and 17 percent of the districts they would likely have had if not bound by the requirement that school districts span the entire county.

An increase in the number of people living in a metropolitan area could be taken advantage of to make each school district larger. This allocation would allow each jurisdiction to exploit economies of scale, resulting in lower costs. At the other extreme, the metro area can benefit from an increase in the number of jurisdictions, holding typical district size fixed. More districts would allow a more complete sorting of families into districts. Nelson (1990) found that more populous metro areas have both more and larger jurisdictions. The crude relation between metropolitan population and the number of school districts is reported in Table 23.2. A substantial increase in the number of school districts accompanies growth in metro populations. Metropolitan areas with over a million residents have nine times as many school districts (58.5) as the smallest metro areas (6.5).

Between 1939–40 and 1973–74 the number of school districts fell from 117,108 to 16,730, an 86 percent drop. During this period, the number of school districts fell 5.6 percent annually as a number of adjacent school districts merged. In the subsequent 34 years, the consolidation boom fizzled out and the annual decline in the number of districts was only 0.5 percent per year.[8] Kenny and Schmidt (1994) use a panel of state-level data for the academic years 1949–50, 1960–61, 1970–71, and 1980–81 to study the determinants of the number of school districts. They attribute the decline in the number of school districts over these 30 years to the dramatic fall in farm employment, the fall in marginal transportation costs (captured in part by the growth in population density), and the growing involvement of state government in primary and secondary education.

After all of the consolidations that have occurred, are school district consolidations still saving money? Duncombe and Yinger (2007) take issue with studies in the consolidation literature that draw inferences only from cross-sectional data. The use of panel data is preferred because this permits a direct comparison of pre-consolidation costs and post-consolidation costs. Duncombe and Yinger contend that covariates, fixed effects, and a control group are also needed to have a scientifically sound statistical study. They also note that the case studies so common in this literature are of limited value. Duncombe and Yinger (2007) study 12 pairs of districts in upstate New York that consolidated between 1987 and 1995. Their paper does not suffer from the same criticism that the authors leveled at other studies in the literature. Consolidation is found to result in a decline in operating expenses, particularly for mergers of very small districts. Adjustment costs reduce but do not eliminate these cost savings. There is no evidence of economies of scale in capital spending, but there appear to be substantial adjustment costs for capital. On net, costs are estimated to fall by 31 percent when two 300-pupil districts merge and to fall 14 percent when two 1,500-student districts consolidate.

It is important to note that these calculations of the effects of merger do not take into account the loss of consumer surplus associated with having fewer districts to choose from and the additional per pupil transportation costs in larger districts for students and for their parents.

3.1.2 Effects of the number of jurisdictions

The early literature on the effects of competition among school districts (Borland and Howsen 1992, 1993; Zanzig 1997) did not address problems associated with the endogeneity of the number of school districts. This literature has uniformly found that student achievement is higher in metropolitan markets with more school districts. Zanzig (1997) estimated that student test scores rise steadily as the number of school districts in California counties increases from 1 to 3 or 4. Further increases in the number of school districts per county have no additional impact on test scores. Zanzig's results can be interpreted as showing that no more than three or four districts per county are needed to reap the full benefits of competition across public school districts on the efficiency of public schools.

Hoxby (2000) noted that rivers and streams may present barriers to students attempting to get to school. This encourages the formation of additional districts so that students do not have to cross the water. Thus, an increase in the number of streams running through a metropolitan area is expected to result in more school districts. For this reason, Hoxby (2000, 2007) argues that the number of streams can be used as an ideal instrument for the number of school districts, since the number of streams is correlated with the number of school districts but does not directly affect student test scores. She reports that watershed variables have a statistically significant and positive impact on the number of districts. Rothstein (2007), however, attempting to replicate her research, found it very difficult to code Hoxby's key explanatory variables consistently. These coding difficulties have greatly diminished the value of Hoxby's proxies as effective instruments explaining the number of school districts.

Showman (2009) dealt with problems due to the endogeneity of the number of school districts by not including this variable in the regression explaining student achievement. Instead, she uses the metro area population, a dummy variable indicating a state-wide or county-wide restriction on school-district size, and the interaction of these two variables. In the smallest metropolitan areas there is likely to be very little difference between the number of districts that would have been chosen with no restriction and the one district allowed in a single county in such a regulatory setting. Thus, little difference in the performance of unrestricted districts and restricted districts would be expected in very small metro areas. As the metro population rises, there should be an increase in the number of school districts if there are no rules on the formation of school districts. In county-wide states, there is only one school district in a one-county metro area irrespective of the number of people living there. Showman predicted and found that student test scores were lower in state-wide or county-wide states and that this disparity was greatest in the largest metro areas. Thus, Showman's results suggest that inter-school-district competition does make public schools more efficient.

3.2 Vouchers

3.2.1 Determinants of the adoption of a voucher program

School vouchers cover part or all of the tuition charges of participating private schools. This makes private schools a more viable option for a larger number of families. So the competition between private schools and public schools strengthens, which conservatives expect to make the public schools more efficient in order to avoid the loss of public funding that typically is tied to declining enrollment.

Voucher proposals in state-wide referendums have failed miserably. None of the 10 voucher proposals in 1966–2002 identified by Kenny (2005) garnered a majority of votes. School voucher proposals have fared better in state legislatures. Voucher bills passed in one chamber in three states (Arizona, New Hampshire, and Wyoming) and were passed by both chambers and signed by the governor in four other states. The Wisconsin state legislature in 1989 approved vouchers for poor families in the City of Milwaukee. Six years later Ohio passed a voucher program for low-income families in Cleveland and, in 1999, the Ohio Supreme Court ruled that attaching the voucher program to the biennial budget bill violated the state's constitutional single-subject bill requirement. This problem was rectified one month later when the state legislature passed a distinct voucher program.

Florida was the first state to pass a bill authorizing vouchers *state-wide*. The law was passed in 1999, the first year in which Republicans controlled the governor's office and both chambers of the state legislature. Vouchers were bundled with a number of other educational reforms in Florida's *A+ Plan for Education*. Students who were attending a school that had received an 'F' in at least two of the last four years were eligible for a voucher worth more than $4,000. In 2006, the state supreme court ruled that Florida's voucher program was unconstitutional. At that time, 700 students were enrolled in private schools under the Opportunity Scholarship Program. Vouchers were not dead in Florida. Another voucher program, the Florida Tax Credit Scholarship Program, was established in 2001 to encourage private contributions from corporate sponsors to provide scholarships to children from low-income families. Corporations are able to obtain a dollar-for-dollar tax credit for up to 75 percent of their state income tax liability. In 2009, the program was expanded to allow tax credits against the insurance premium tax. In the 2008–09 school year, 24,871 students were enrolled in 1,002 private schools under this program.

Colorado in 2003 passed a voucher bill that provided for vouchers in 11 (of 180) districts with at least eight schools characterized as 'low' or 'unsatisfactory' during the 2001–02 school year. These districts are large urban districts in the Denver, Pueblo, and Colorado Springs metropolitan areas. Vouchers were limited to children eligible for free or reduced-price school lunches. In 2004 the Colorado Supreme Court ruled that Colorado's voucher program was unconstitutional.

Bills granting vouchers to poorer residents of the District of Columbia (DC) have twice been approved by majorities in both chambers of Congress. Immediately after the

Republicans took control of Congress in 1995, amendment 891 to H.R. 2546 passed in the House by a vote margin of 241 yeas to 177 nays. The amendment provided vouchers and a number of other 'reforms' for the DC public schools. The bill was filibustered in the Senate. A cloture vote got a majority (56 votes), but not enough to end the filibuster. In 2003, an amendment (368) to H.R. 2765 that established a voucher worth up to $7,500 was more successful. The amendment passed the House in a very close vote (205 to 203). The final bill was approved by the Senate and signed by President George W. Bush. Congress in March 2009 voted to eliminate funding after the 2009–10 academic year.

What features contribute to the success of voucher proposals? All of the successful voucher programs have been means-tested or school-performance-tested programs that have limited vouchers to students from poor families, to students attending failing schools, or both. In contrast, a *uniform* voucher provides the same benefit to all private school students. Students from rich and poor families receive the same payment for attending private school, and the value of the voucher for households with children already attending a private school is the same as for families sending their children to private school for the first time. The former effect simply transfers wealth to families with children already enrolled in private school. Bearse et al. (2009) calibrated a general equilibrium model of education finance. They found that the bottom 68 percent of the income distribution would be made worse off by switching from the status quo to a uniform voucher system. In contrast, a means-tested voucher would command a majority (bottom 45 percent and top 17 percent) in a referendum pitting it against the status quo. Their model thus explains why means-tested voucher plans have had greater political success than uniform voucher plans.

Voters have less incentive to monitor large school districts than to monitor small school districts, because they are less likely to affect outcomes in large polities. With less parental monitoring and involvement in the schools, inefficiencies are less likely to be discovered. Less parental involvement in the schools allows the teachers' union to be stronger (see Rose and Sonstelie 2010). Also, there may be little effective competition facing districts covering large geographic areas. Due to these effects, very large school districts are expected to be less efficient than small districts. Citizens may be more inclined to allow struggling large school districts to try anything, including vouchers. Three of the five successful voucher programs (Milwaukee, Cleveland, and the District of Columbia) were limited to large, failing school districts.

In Congress there has been greater support for voucher programs confined to the District of Columbia than for a nationwide voucher program. Voucher proposals that would limit vouchers to the District of Columbia garnered a majority in each chamber in 1995 and in 2003. But amendment 57 to the No Child Left Behind Act of 2001 would have provided federal funding for students attending schools across the country considered either to be unsafe or to have been under-performing to enroll in a private school; this amendment was rejected by the US House of Representatives, 155 to 273. A voucher program that is limited to one city (see the 1995 and 2003 votes) provides little threat to teachers' unions in other localities. Thus, there should be less union opposition in the other localities to a one-city voucher program than to a nationwide one. Kenny (2010) reported that Republican House members in states where larger fractions of teachers indicated that they were covered by union contracts were more likely to oppose vouchers in the 2001 nationwide voucher vote. On the other hand, union coverage was unrelated to the votes cast in 2003 on vouchers for DC, presumably because this vote was less threatening to teachers' unions.

It was the most conservative Republican legislators who supported nationwide vouchers in 2001 (Kenny 2010). The DC voucher proposal in 2003 was more acceptable and garnered more Republican votes. The new support tended to come from the more conservative House members in the set of Republicans who had initially opposed vouchers.

Given the sharp divisions separating the two parties on vouchers, Republican control of the state house, state senate, and governor's office is likely to be needed to pass a voucher bill. This was indeed the case in 10 out of 11 instances in which one chamber passed a voucher or in which both chambers voted for vouchers. But voucher proposals were successful only in a minority of Republican-controlled states. Kenny (2005) found that states with the most conservative Republican legislators were more likely to pass a voucher bill than states where Republicans were more moderate. Voucher programs also have been more successful in states that have at least one large city. In such states there is some prospect of having a large failing school district that may benefit from extraordinary measures, such as establishing a voucher program.

3.2.2 Determinants of votes cast for vouchers

Brunner and various co-authors (Brunner et al. 2001; Brunner and Sonstelie 2003; Brunner and Imazeki 2008) have studied votes cast in the 1993 and 2000 California elections on uniform state-wide school voucher proposals. Brunner and Imazeki estimated a simple but very insightful model of the impact of income on support for school vouchers.

In a school market comprised of one district, there is no parental choice. The average quality of a student's classmates is captured by the average income of peer families. Suppose that school vouchers are made available to this market. The richest families will use the voucher to help send their children to private schools. This means that students' peers in private school are high achievers, on average, and, correspondingly, that the private school outperforms the public alternative. High income households experience great gains in peer quality and, thus, should support vouchers. Conversely, for poor households, the exodus of high-quality peers causes a decline in public school quality, leading poor households to oppose vouchers.

Let us now consider what happens to the support for vouchers when there is more choice among school districts. In this semi-Tiebout (1956) equilibrium there is substantial sorting, leaving each jurisdiction relatively homogeneous. High income households sort into districts with high-quality peers for their children and vouchers, thus, offer little gain in peer quality to families in rich districts. But vouchers would allow rich households to send their children to private schools even if they live in poor, low-tax and low-quality school districts. This reduces the demand for living in rich suburbs, leading to lower home prices and capital losses for households in well-heeled neighborhoods. As a result, rich families there oppose vouchers. The children of low-income families already have low-quality peers; vouchers are unlikely to make peer quality much worse. But poor families do benefit from the rise in home prices as better-off families move to poorer communities to take advantage of lower property taxes, while at the same time using vouchers to send their children to private schools with high quality peers.

Brunner and Imazeki's model has stark predictions. In areas with very few school districts, richer families are more likely than poorer families to support vouchers.

Table 23.3 Predicted percentage of 'Yes' votes on California's Proposition 38 in 'No Choice' and 'High Choice' metro areas (percentage)

	Choice among public school districts	
	No choice	High choice
Relative income		
Low income	22.5	29.5
Average income	29.9	28.5
High income	39.2	27.5
Relative fraction college		
Low education	23.4	32.1
Average education	30.7	28.7
High education	41.8	24.6

Source: Brunner and Imazeki (2008).

Conversely, in areas with many school districts, support for vouchers is predicted to fall as average district income rises. The authors tested these predictions by examining the 2000 vote in California on Proposition 38, which would have established a uniform voucher paying each student in private school over $4,000. Since households are sorting within a metro area, the district-level income and education variables are measured relative to their values in the whole metro area.

The predicted percentages of yes votes reported in Table 23.3 are based on regressions in Brunner and Imazeki (2008) that explain the variation across census block groups in terms of support for vouchers.[9] The strong predictions of this model are supported empirically. In areas with no choice among school districts, the richer households are hypothesized to be more supportive of vouchers than the poorer households and, indeed, nearly twice as many high-income households (over 90th percentile) supported vouchers as low income households (below 10th percentile); the difference in the fraction favoring vouchers equals 16.7 percent (= 39.2 − 22.5). Similarly, more educated households were much more likely (by 18.4 percent) to favor vouchers than households with less education.

In contrast, in metro areas with substantial choice in school districts, richer households are expected to be less likely to vote for a voucher program than poorer households. This prediction is also supported empirically. A rise in income is accompanied by an economically small decline (2.0 percent) in votes favoring vouchers. Similarly, more education is associated with a 7.5 percent smaller percentage of votes favoring the voucher proposal.

As noted earlier, public school teachers are staunch opponents of vouchers. Brunner et al. (2001) report less support for vouchers in precincts with larger percentages of the workforce employed in education services (that is, public school teachers and administrators). Gokcekus et al. (2004) find that legislators receiving contributions from teachers' political action committees (PACs) were much less likely to vote for vouchers.

Empirically, there is greater support for vouchers (1) in precincts where larger fractions of voters are registered as Republicans (Brunner et al. 2001), (2) among Republican legislators (Gokcekus et al. 2004), and (3) among conservative voters (Brunner and Sonstelie 2003).

3.2.3 Effects of vouchers on public school productivity

Friedman (1962, ch. 6) was an early proponent of vouchers, arguing that the greater competition between private schools and public schools triggered by vouchers would make public schools more efficient and more responsive to parental wishes. The threat of losing students – and the state funds that come with them – provides public schools with a stronger incentive to do a good job. On the other hand, vouchers may lure to private schools the parents who were the most involved in the public schools, making parental monitoring of public schools less effective, and consequently allowing the public schools to be less efficient.

Private school supply and public school performance are jointly determined. Couch et al. (1993) dealt with this problem by estimating a two-equation recursive procedure, in which income was used to explain private school enrollment but not public school performance. They found that an increase in private school enrollment led to higher public school student test scores, suggesting that competition from private schools had made the public schools more efficient.

A number of studies (Hoxby 1994; Dee 1998; Sander 1998) use the percentage of the population identifying themselves as members of the Catholic Church as an instrument for private school enrollment. This procedure has been criticized. Catholic schools have a much smaller share of the private school market than they had several decades ago. It would be better to have a set of instruments that reflect the fractions of the population affiliated with the various religions, such as Baptists, who also tend to establish private schools.

A voucher program is the policy vehicle for expanding enrollments in private school. A number of scholars have studied the impact of a voucher program on public school performance. Hoxby (2003), Chakrabarti (2008) and Greene and Marsh (2009) utilized data from Milwaukee; Hoxby (2003) and Chakrabarti (2008) took advantage of differences across public schools in the fraction of households eligible for vouchers. All three studies found that the Milwaukee voucher program led to higher test scores for public school students. Still, there is a limit to what can be learned from a voucher plan like Milwaukee's, which confines vouchers to a single city.

Chan and McMillan (2009) and Figlio and Hart (2010) use the variation across public schools in terms of the proximity of private school alternatives at the onset of a voucher program as an identification strategy. Chan and McMillan studied the impact of tuition tax credits in Ontario, Canada. Public schools with more private school students in their catchment area were found to have higher pass rates on standardized tests when the tuition tax credit was established; these gains disappeared when the program was canceled. Figlio and Hart studied the Florida Tax Credit Scholarship Program, which was described earlier. The Florida data contain numerous local educational markets. The authors find that public schools facing more competition from private schools experienced greater growth in test scores.

3.3 Charter Schools

3.3.1 Determinants of charter school supply

Charter schools are free from many public school regulations at the district and state levels. Charter school supporters claim that not being subject to stifling regulations should make charter schools more efficient than traditional public schools. Charter schools receive public funds but are not allowed to charge tuition to bring in additional revenue or to have selective admission standards.

Stoddard and Corcoran (2007) sought to discover the factors that determined whether a state had established a charter school program and, if so, how strong the charter school law was. The authors hypothesize that college graduates would be more likely to support charter schools than those with less education because (1) more educated citizens have a greater demand for educational quality and (2) have a greater propensity to experiment. This hypothesis was strongly supported empirically. States where the population was more highly educated were correctly estimated to be among the first to enact charter school programs and were estimated to be more likely to have a charter school law by 1999. States characterized by more years of educational attainment also enacted stronger charter-schools laws than the laws adopted in states whose citizens had fewer years of schooling, on average.

Dissatisfaction over public school quality is measured as the residual in a regression explaining Scholastic Aptitude Test (SAT) scores.[10] A positive residual means that the schools performed better on that measure than expected, making the schools' students less likely to search for alternative school arrangements, such as charter schools. A larger residual is found to lead to later adoption of a charter school law and to a weaker law.

The strength of the teachers' union is measured by the fraction of instructional employees who are organized. Stoddard and Corcoran (2007) found, as expected, that states in which more teachers belong to unions were less likely to allow charter schools.

Parents with children in private school may support charter schools because they want still more choice and indeed may view charter schools as a cheap substitute for private school. States with more children in private school in 1990, prior to the charter movement taking off, were found to have stronger charter school laws.

We have seen that for vouchers to be successful the governor must be Republican and the Republicans must control the state's house and senate. Ideological influence was measured by the fraction of years in the 1990s in which the governor was a Republican. This variable is not a good measure of whether the Republican Party controlled state government and is not significant.

3.3.2 Effects of competition from charter schools on traditional public school performance

The papers discussed next utilize very large samples of individual level data and rely on 'dummy variables' to hold constant any effects associated with a student that are not captured by the other variables in the regression.[11] Zimmer and Buddin's (2009) research was based on a panel of six districts in California. The authors appear to have five overlapping measures of charter competition in the same regression. This may result in multicollinearity and, thus, less significance for the charter competition variables. Bifulco and Ladd (2006) relied on data from North Carolina and were unable to find any consistent relationship between their measures of competition from charter schools and the test scores of traditional public school students.

Sass (2006), relying on Florida data, found that various measures of charter school competition improved traditional public school math test scores but had no effect on reading test scores. There was strong evidence that competition from charter schools led to higher test scores for traditional public school students when competition was measured as occurring within 2.5 miles from a school. This finding was robust to the use of three alternative measures of the presence of charter schools in the market: a dummy indicating the presence of one or more charter schools, the number of charter schools, and the fraction of students attending charter schools. Much less statistical support was established for the competition hypothesis when the market was defined as within a 5-mile radius or a 10-mile radius of the school.

Booker et al. (2008) used data from Texas for a study of the effects of competition from charter schools on the performance of traditional public schools. Two sets of variables are used in different regressions to capture local charter competition: (1) the number of charter schools 0–5 miles from the public school campus, or the number of charter schools 6–10 miles away, and (2) the number of charter school students either 0–5 miles or 6–10 miles away from the public school campus. All of these local charter school competition variables have the expected positive coefficients for both reading and math scores and are highly statistically significant. The coefficient for competition from a nearby (0–5 miles) charter school is larger than the coefficient for a more distant (6–10 mile) charter school, as expected. Competition from nearby charter schools has a substantial impact on traditional public student test scores.

Competition from local charter schools appears to be best described by charter activity within 2.5 miles (or within 5 miles) of the traditional public school. So it is no surprise that measures of competition at the district level are unrelated to student performance in traditional public schools.[12]

4 REFERENDUMS ON SCHOOL SPENDING

In referendums voters determine school tax rates directly and this has an important influence on public school budgets. Hamilton and Cohen (1974) collected data on the number of school referendums held in each state in the early 1970s. There were 12 states (Arkansas, Delaware, Louisiana, Michigan, Montana, New Jersey, New York, Ohio, Oklahoma, Oregon, Washington, and West Virginia) in which the typical school district held a school budget referendum at least once every three years, while districts in five of these states held essentially one referendum per year. Are referendums panaceas for principal–agent problems in representative government?

Holcombe (1980) utilized election results from school districts in Michigan that held at least two referendums in one month. The outcomes of these two referendums allowed him to calculate the mean and standard deviation of preferred spending levels in the school district, under the assumption of a normal distribution. The one-election sample was added to the statistical analysis after a key assumption was made.[13] Holcombe found that actual spending was 2.4 percent lower on average than that desired by the median voter. Munley (1984) replicated Holcombe's results using New York data and several different distributions of preferred spending levels (for example, normal and log normal), and found the same results.

Romer and Rosenthal (1978, 1979, 1982) showed that the median voter can be induced to vote for greater spending than she prefers to avoid undesirably low spending if the proposal fails. This problem exists because the voters are given only two choices. In contrast, Florida's unrestricted choice referendum, which was described briefly in section 2, allows the voter to select any school tax rate between 0 and 10 mills. The tax rates selected by the voters are ordered and the median tax rate is used to fund the schools. Since the median voter is able, in this unrestricted referendum format, to select his or her preferred tax rate, Florida's unrestricted choice referendum guarantees that the median voter's desired tax rate is selected to fund the schools.

Holcombe and Kenny (2008) tested Romer and Rosenthal's prediction by estimating regressions that explain school expenditures for the 12 restricted choice states listed in Table 24.1 plus Florida for 1947–67. The regressions imply that school spending is 7.0 to 10.6 percent lower in Florida, where spending is at the level preferred by the median voter. School spending is higher in the 12 restricted choice states, presumably because some budget-maximizing school bureaucracies take advantage of lower than desired reversion school budgets to get the median voter to spend more than he/she would prefer.

Shifting gears, it is important to note that the identity of the median voter hinges on the electoral setting. A general election includes federal and state races. In a special election, there are few, if any, races besides the school tax referendum, causing many citizens to stay at home. Those turning out to vote in special elections consist mostly of those with a strong tie to the public schools, namely, parents, teachers and administrators. The median voter in a special election, thus, is expected to be more favorable to schools and their financing than is the median voter in a general election. This is consistent with the mantra of school referendum consultants: 'run a special election – avoid general elections.' Dunne et al. (1997) documented the distribution of referendum dates in Oklahoma. Only 5 percent of school referendum elections were held on a general election date, and only 3 percent took place in the summer, when the school system has more difficulty reaching parents to get their support.

Pecquet et al. (1996) studied school tax elections in Louisiana. They found that the fraction of voters supporting higher school taxes was 2–8 percent lower in general elections, where the median voter is less supportive of primary and secondary education, than in special elections, where the median voter may be a teacher or parent.

5 REDISTRIBUTION THROUGH THE EDUCATION SYSTEM

In Tiebout's world, each metropolitan area is a marketplace of local governments. Households sort into poor school districts with meager budgets providing some learning, average school districts with moderate budgets providing a good education, rich districts with large budgets providing a superior education, and so on for various gradations of school quality or family income.

A very small literature has attempted to explain why some states have not interfered with the substantial inequality in school spending found in Tiebout's municipal marketplace while other states greatly limit the inequality in school spending. Much of this literature has been concerned with estimating the effect of a state Supreme Court ruling that the existing educational finance system is unconstitutional. These court rulings mandate that state government undertake measures that would bring about a sharp fall in the inequality in school spending across the state's school districts. Evans et al. (1997) estimate that these rulings raised state revenues for the state's poorer districts and had no effect on state spending in its richer districts. Card and Payne (2002) find that per pupil state aid and school spending rose less with income after the state supreme court had ruled the state's educational finance system to be unconstitutional. De Bartolome (1997) concludes that about 18 percent of the growth in state aid to schools between 1970 and 1990 was due to an adverse ruling by the state supreme court requiring more equal school aid.

Figlio et al. (2004) explained the differences across states and over time in the inequality across the state's school districts in school spending. We, like our predecessors, find that a Supreme Court ruling that the state's educational finance system is unconstitutional indeed does lead to a reduction in spending inequality. The heterogeneity of the population within a state is measured by the standard deviation in educational attainment in the state. As expected, there is greater variation in school spending in more heterogeneous states.

The ability to sort across school districts also plays a role. We noted earlier that Hawaii has only one school district, and half a dozen other states require county-wide school districts. In these states sorting by desired school quality is very costly if not impossible. In our study the opportunity to sort by desired school quality is measured by the number of school districts per student. Having more districts facilitates more complete sorting, which leads to greater inequality in school expenditures across school districts. That is indeed what we find. Also, there should be more sorting in metropolitan areas than in rural areas. Our finding that there is more inequality in school spending in states in which larger shares of the population live in metro areas is consistent with this reasoning.

Democrats typically represent a state's poorer voters and thus favor more redistribution than do Republicans. As predicted, in our data there is less inequality in school expenditures in states controlled by the Democrats than in states controlled by the Republicans.

The provisions of a state's constitution actually affect the inequality in school spending in the state. Dummy variables for (1) strong language supporting equity ('equal opportunity', 'perfect equality') and (2) moderate language supporting equity ('uniform system of education') have a significantly negative impact on the inequality in school spending. The hypothesis that the state's constitution affects state policies receives additional support when it is noted that the strong language for equity dummy variable has a greater effect on school spending inequality than does the moderate language for equity dummy.

We have examined various factors that explain the variation across states in school spending inequality. We have not considered how to bring about a desired level of inequality in school spending. To reduce the inequality in school spending, the state can (1) give poor school districts larger grants than it gives rich school districts, (2) raise the cost to rich districts of spending more per pupil, or both. The state can place a ceiling on expenditure per pupil. In practice, analyses of school budgets are complicated owing to the diversity of accounting practices across districts and states.

6 CONCLUSION

Voters who are more educated participate at greater rates in the local political process. They are better informed about an incumbent's voting record and exact a greater price, in votes withdrawn, on those who have been too liberal or too conservative for their tastes. Highly educated voters are less likely to rely on school board recommendations and are less likely to place restrictions, such as spending limits and term limits, that undermine their own vote choices. In the turbulent years of Florida's housing bubble of 2004–06, there is evidence that voters' interests were better represented in cities whose residents had more years of schooling, on the average. We can conclude that widespread educational attainment plays a crucial role in making the principals (that is, the voters) more effective in monitoring, rewarding good and punishing bad agents (that is, the elected officials).

The literature on the effect of competition between school districts on student learning has been acrimonious. Hoxby (2000) proposed using the number of rivers and streams flowing through a metropolitan area as an instrument for dealing with the potential endogeneity of the number of districts. Rothstein (2007) noted great difficulties in measuring Hoxby's variable consistently, making replication of her empirical findings problematic. Hoxby's regressions support the hypothesis that an increase in the number of school districts is associated with higher student test scores, but only a few of Rothstein's regressions support the same conclusion. A number of states mandate no more than one school district per county or state. Showman (2009) suggests that test scores are lower in states where school districts must span entire counties and that this disparity in student achievement is largest in the most populous metro areas, which otherwise tend to have more districts, and thus more competition. This represents a creative approach to an important problem.

Some forces affect political support for both vouchers and charter schools. Teachers' unions and liberal legislators oppose both margins of competition for the public schools. Voucher proposals are most successful in states in which the governor is a Republican and the same party controls both legislative chambers. Voucher plans have been enacted in some of the most conservative of these states. Vouchers limited to a large failing school district (as in, Cleveland, Milwaukee, and the District of Columbia) have had more success; vouchers may be viewed as a last-ditch effort when nothing else is working. The programs that have been approved all have limited their benefits to children from poor families or from failing schools. Interesting predictions by Brunner and Imazeki (2008) suggest that (1) in areas with little competition across school districts, rich families are more supportive of vouchers than poor families and (2) in areas with more competition between school districts, rich families are less supportive of vouchers than poor families. There also is some evidence of greater support for charter schools if the public school is performing more poorly than predicted.

There is remarkably consistent evidence that voucher programs lead to improved student achievement. For charter schools the evidence is less consistent. Those studies find that competition from charter schools raised test scores for traditional public school students statistically significantly within 2.5 to 5 miles from the public school campus. Thus, educational competition seems to be geographically localized.

A dozen states have relied on school tax referendums to determine school spending. Holcombe (1980) and Munley (1984) conclude from examining referendum outcomes, in Michigan and New York, respectively, that the level of school spending was very close to that preferred by the median voter. Romer and Rosenthal's (1978, 1979, 1982) studies predicted that a budget-maximizing bureaucracy could induce the median voter to spend more than the preferred level to avoid less-than-desired spending if the budget is rejected. Spending is predicted to be higher in the restricted up-or-down referendum states than in the unrestricted setting in Florida, in which the median voter can select any tax rate within a fairly broad range, including the one he or she prefers. Holcombe and Kenny (2008) found statistical support for this hypothesis.

It also should be recognized that the identity of the median voter in a school-budget referendum hinges on who turns out to vote. A school tax proposal in a special election should attract mostly teachers and parents. Thus, the median voter in the special election would be much more favorable to educational spending than the median voter in a general election. This hypothesis is supported empirically. There is also evidence that most of the school budget referendums were strategically presented to voters in special elections, where turnout tends to be low – and biased toward the special interests of the public schools – than is true of general elections.

NOTES

1. Charter schools are publicly funded elementary or secondary schools that are not subject to some of the regulations that govern traditional public schools. In exchange for facing fewer regulations the charter school agrees to produce certain results that are described in the school's charter. The charter school's students are attending by choice.
2. The millage tax rate is the tax imposed on each $1,000 of taxable property values. To take one example, suppose that the millage tax rate is 6 and that this is being applied to a house with an assessed value of $150,000. The house is valued at 150 mills (150,000/1,000), and the annual property tax bill equals the millage tax rate (6) multiplied by the property value in mills (150), or $900.
3. Estimates of the state party positions were obtained by first estimating a regression for each state explaining its senators' Americans for Democratic Action scores, a measure of how liberal he or she was, for 1960–90 for senators who were subsequently re-elected. The independent variables included the senator's political party affiliation, various measures of the state's and nation's economies, and variables describing the party composition of the state legislature and the US Congress. The estimated values for year and party are taken to be the state-party position that year.
4. The sharp rise in property values over the period far exceeds the growth in income. So there should be little increase in the demand for local government services, implying that the property tax rate should fall. In the least educated communities, very few voters monitor the decisions being made by the jurisdiction's elected officials. With perhaps little input from voters, local officials (1) do not bother to change the millage rate, (2) do not realize how much property tax rates must fall to satisfy the median voter or (3) take advantage of inattentive voters to raise local government spending more than voters desire. On the other hand, in the most educated communities, tax rates are reduced sufficiently to provide the tax revenue desired by the median voter. The authors find that a surge in property values indeed resulted in a smaller rise in property taxes in more educated cities than in less educated cities.
5. The Center for Education Reform, www.edreform.com (accessed 10 October 2011).
6. See Hoxby (2000), for example.
7. Private school of course is another option. But in a voucherless world paying private school tuition does not relieve the taxpayer of the responsibility for paying to support the local public schools. Continuing to pay for public schools makes private schools much more expensive than selecting a public school district that produces the desired school quality, assuming that that option is available.
8. Source: United States Department of Education (2009).
9. The interactions between income and school district choice and between college education and district choice are statistically significant. This means that the effects of income and a college education on support for vouchers are different in metro areas with very few districts than in metro areas with many districts from which to choose.
10. The SAT is a widely used college admissions test in the United States.
11. The dummy variables actually are even more sophisticated. For each student there is a 'dummy variable' for each school the student attended; Mary Smith, for example, has dummy variables for her stays at Lincoln school and at Washington school.

12. See Booker et al. (2008) and Ni (2009).
13. A regression based on the two-election sample and using mean preferred spending to explain the standard deviation of preferred spending levels was estimated. This estimated relationship was used along with the outcome of the district's single election to characterize the distribution of preferred spending levels in the one-election school districts.

24 Public choice and religion
Robert B. Ekelund Jr and Robert D. Tollison

1 INTRODUCTION

The fact that economics is capable of providing important insights into religion and religious behavior is certainly not original. Adam Smith, author of the *Wealth of Nations* (1776 [2005]) and acknowledged founder of economics as a social science, first integrated the study of religious behavior with economics. In a far broader view than that of Marshall and his neoclassical contemporaries – appropriately called political economy – Smith studied the economic problems associated with the provision of religious goods and services. Smith's analysis, while not providing a formal theory of monopoly provision of these products, revolved around incentive failures as characteristic of state-sponsored religious institutions. Modern investigations have greatly expanded the reach of economics in this regard. Beginning with Azzi and Ehrenberg (1975) and following Gary Becker's astute observations on implicit markets and prices (for example, Becker 1981), economists and sociologists developed analyses around market structure (Ekelund et al. 1989), religious participation as cult behavior (Iannaccone 1992), rational behavior (Stark 1997) and comparative statistical studies of the economic impact of *types* of religions (Barro and McCleary 2005). Economic theorists have also focused on religious demands based upon risk preferences (Durkin and Greeley 1991) and on self-insurance (Beard et al. 2011). As such, the economics of religion is one more example of the expansion of the basic paradigm of economics to a new area. Public choice was, of course, such an expansion, as were law and economics, the economic approach to crime, and still other important applications of basic economic methodology to areas outside of the normal purview of neoclassical/orthodox economics.

Public choice approaches to religion incorporate many of these directions but emphasize the formation and development of religious market structure, product innovation and differentiation, and interest-group activity, all within the context of self-interested behavior. The application of the principles of self-interested behavior to religion is based upon the simple conviction that there is no such thing as a 'non-economic' sector of the human universe, which is out of bounds for the work of the economist. There are obviously no guarantees that the economic model will explain behavior very well in these new applications, but there is nothing, short of a closed mind, that prevents a creative economist from trying to expand the domain of the economic model which, in the case of religion, is complementary to many historical and sociological approaches. And the proof of the pudding is clearly in the eating. We will either obtain new and interesting results about religion, or we will not.

The primary vehicle for discussion will be the Catholic Church and its exercise of monopoly power during medieval times. The doctrines of usury and purgatory will provide the principal expository vehicles for discussion, and the latter case of purgatory will be accompanied by a tentative explanation of how various Protestant sects were able to enter the market for religious services in the face of a centuries-old Roman Catholic monopoly.[1]

2 ECONOMICS AND RELIGION

On the eve of the twentieth century the great neoclassical economist Alfred Marshall (1890, p. 1) wrote that 'the two great forming agencies of the world's history have been the religious and the economic'. Like most economists, however, Marshall tended to separate the two spheres, and eschewed opportunities to analyze religious institutions on economic grounds. Several generations have elapsed since Marshall's death, and in the interim the domain of economics has continually expanded. Were he alive today, Marshall might be surprised at the breadth of modern economics, which runs the gamut of human actions – from 'the ordinary business of life' (Marshall's own phrase), to lobbying activities in legislatures, to the form of contemporary music, to the sleep patterns of individuals, to the dynamics of family interactions, and so on. By ranging into the traditional concerns of sociology and other areas of inquiry, modern economics promises to increase our understanding of many interesting and varied aspects of human behavior.

In its expanded form as 'the science of choice', economics models the human decision nexus as a kind of economy, regardless of its specific domain. It matters little whether the problem is perceived as inherently economic or as anthropological, psychological, sociological, political, legal, or religious. For example, public choice theory applies economic principles to the study of political institutions. The basic premise underlying these approaches is that economic elements – opportunity cost, most especially – come into play in all human decisions. Economists therefore have something to contribute to our understanding of such decisions. Whether or not economic elements *dominate* each and every decision is another question, one that cannot be resolved a priori, or in a generalized way. Nevertheless, uncovering the economic elements in a decision nexus and applying economic analysis to the interpretation of the decision-making process should improve our understanding of observed behaviors at the margin.

This study lies outside the ancient tradition that asserts that religious organizations are principally motivated by 'other worldly' interests (for example, salvation). In this older intellectual tradition, the internal workings of religious organizations are treated as 'epiphenomena' or outside the domain of self-interested maximization, primarily because religious belief is defined as a fundamental, faith-based commitment to a system of ideas, norms, and values that lies beyond the calculus of rational choice. We employ the alternative approach that treats religious behavior as the product of rational choice. Spiritual considerations notwithstanding, decisions within religious organizations are made by human beings living in a worldly environment. Economists have long recognized that even actions ostensibly based on non-economic criteria may be satisfying several objectives, non-economic and economic, simultaneously. Here we seek to uncover the purely economic aspects of decisions made by agents who, outwardly at least, were trying to make both economic and non-economic choices.

3 STYLIZED FACTS OF MEDIEVAL LIFE

Imagine a world where religion dominates everyday life as it has, for example, since early temple societies. The priesthood plays an important role in the functioning of the ordinary economy. Ecclesiastical officials enact and enforce laws governing everyday transactions. Kings, princes, and dukes hold at least part of their power by grace of God, mediated by the religious authorities. Polities also arbitrate international disputes, maintain armies, and fight wars to promote their organizational ends. The dominant religious organization (the Christian Church) is immensely rich and controls most of the landed property in society. Most of the revenues of the Church flow from voluntary contributions of the faithful, who receive in return both spiritual and secular services. This thumbnail sketch approximately describes medieval Europe wherein the Roman Catholic Church exerted more power than any single monarch and wielded such authority that historians commonly refer to the West during the Middle Ages as 'Christendom'.

4 THE CHRISTIAN CHURCH IN THE MIDDLE AGES

Christianity thrived as a kind of underground movement, loosely organized, highly decentralized, and persecuted for the first three centuries of its corporate existence. The formal character of the Catholic Church, the single institution that came to embody Christianity in its official capacity, emerged as a result of the Edict of Milan in AD 313.[2] In its early organizational structure, the primary authorities within the Church were bishops, who appointed and supervised priests at the parish level. By the time of Charlemagne, bishops normally were selected by the monarch of the countries in which their dioceses were located. The pope was merely the Bishop of Rome over this early period and did not possess the central authority that has since come to be vested in the Vatican. Secular and ecclesiastic governments actively competed for the right to appoint and oversee clerics and Church administrators between the ninth and twelfth centuries. Despite attempts by some early popes, such as Nicholas I (856–867), to overturn the practice of lay or secular investiture, the papacy was unable to enforce its 'independence' until the twelfth century, when Pope Gregory VII successfully wrested from the secular monarchs the authority to appoint bishops. Following this 'papal revolution' the Roman pope emerged as the supreme judicial and legislative authority in Western Europe.[3] From the twelfth century on, all matters pertaining to the ownership, use, and disposal of Church properties came under his authority. All testamentary cases were adjudicable in Rome, meaning that in the long run, the pope determined the allocation of most property rights in Europe. Henceforth, bishops (who served as heads of regional franchises) were subject to papal approval before assuming their duties, and all monastic orders and new monasteries likewise required the pope's consent.

5 CORPORATE STRUCTURE OF THE MEDIEVAL CHURCH

As the Church increasingly became centralized after the eleventh century, its internal organization began to take on many of the aspects of the modern corporation. The type of contemporary organization that the medieval Church resembled most is the multidivisional or 'M-form' firm. According to Williamson (1975), this kind of firm is characterized by a central office that controls overall financial allocations and conducts strategic, long-range planning, but allows divisional managers (usually regional) a high degree of autonomy in day-to-day operations.[4]

The medieval Catholic Church approximately followed this general pattern, establishing an organizational form that appears to have operated successfully for many centuries in a difficult – and evolving – political and technological environment. The Church assigned operating decisions to essentially self-contained operating divisions, or 'quasi-firms', consisting of monastic orders, dioceses, and other sub-entities. The general office maintained an elite staff, the Curia (papal bureaucracy), that advised the pope in his role as chief executive officer (CEO) and also monitored and audited the behavior of the clergy who were attached to the operating divisions (much in the manner of modern franchise contracts). The general office was the strategic director of Church policy. It planned, evaluated, and controlled Church functions and Church doctrine, without being directly 'absorbed in the affairs of the functional parts' (Ekelund et al., 1996). Finally, the Vatican allocated resources among competing divisions: for example, it could direct funding to special projects or grant tax exemptions to favored units, such as monasteries or specific established 'national' churches.

Unlike General Motors, the medieval Church did not organize its divisions in terms of physically differentiated products. Rather than producing Chevrolets, Pontiacs, and Oldsmobiles, the Church produced services guided by a single theology (with absolute powers of interpretation) that ostensibly were all aimed at the same religious goal – namely, spiritual salvation. Despite the lack of overt physical differentiation, however, the products generated by separate divisions of the Church were distinguishable. Monasteries catered to the spiritual needs of the more intellectually inclined and of higher-income individuals. At the same time, some monks ministered to the poor, and some served as evangelists on the pagan frontiers of Europe. The cathedral chapters served inhabitants of larger urban areas and attracted pilgrims and other travelers who made monetary contributions to the cathedral.

6 POWERS OF THE PAPACY

Since the eleventh century, the pope of the Roman Catholic Church has been elected to a post conferring lifetime tenure and installed according to Catholic dogma as the direct heir to St Peter and the representative of Christ on earth.[5] The doctrine of papal 'infallibility', formalized only in the nineteenth century, is far less sweeping than the term implies, but it does lend an aura of 'supreme' authority to the office. Insofar as there is no official, established mechanism for removing a pope for malfeasance or other cause, the nature of the position might suggest that the pope is less a CEO in the modern sense than an absolute monarch. By the standards of conventional business practice this arrangement would be relatively inefficient because it places the corporate CEO beyond effective accountability to shareholders. But there is reason to believe that the stable security of tenure given to the pope was a reasonable adaptation to medieval circumstances, one that lowered certain transaction costs and provided incentives for efficient papal behavior.

The pope's stable security of office contributed to the efficiency of the medieval Church in several ways. First, it helped to insulate the Holy Office from secular political pressure (for example, having to face re-election). Prior to the Concordat of Worms, secular rulers (for example, Holy Roman Emperors) often appointed and terminated popes at will, for openly political reasons. Restricting the access of temporal rulers to such blatant 'papal patronage' not only served to protect Church assets from governmental confiscation, it also raised the costs of rent-seeking to potential 'replacement' popes and their supporters. Lifetime tenure also reduced potential conflicts of interest on the part of popes, who felt no compulsion to transfer Church wealth to their own account in anticipation of providing for their retirement years. Likewise, lifetime tenure greatly reduced the pope's incentive to take bribes or yield to intimidation by outside forces. Finally, lifetime tenure also meant that the pope had an incentive to promote the long-run over the short-run interests of the Church – the Church itself was a permanent institution that did not have to yield to short-run expediency.[6]

Despite certain advantages, lifetime tenure was not absolute in the Middle Ages. Although tenure was normally quite secure, papal behavior was subject to an informal but effective constraint: the possibility of competition for the position by pretenders who were able to enlist the support of cardinals and bishops discontented with the current regime. In other words, the pope could technically, albeit unofficially, be fired, replaced or subjected to foul play. In the period between AD 1000 and 1450, 20 different 'anti-popes' actively claimed the papal office. Most were elected by rebellious cardinals, and many with the support of various secular rulers. Some of the pretenders were actually more powerful than those who had been elected legitimately. For instance, at the time of the First Crusade, anti-pope Clement III occupied the Church at Rome and commanded the support of most bishops in Germany and Italy. Partly for this reason, Pope Urban II proclaimed the First Crusade from Clermont in southern France. Furthermore, in an era when many officially elected popes held their office for less than a year, several anti-popes maintained power for extended periods. Elected as an anti-pope in 1080, Clement III remained in power until his death in 1100.

The process of competition between popes and anti-popes in the Middle Ages was in many respects analogous to proxy fights that take place today between various shareholder groups of a corporation. Bishops, who held effective property rights in Church assets (with various limits on transferability), might elect an anti-pope to replace an existing pope when they became dissatisfied with the performance of the incumbent. But only when the general clergy (those with grassroots control of Church assets) supported the usurper could the anti-pope hope to succeed in wrestling away control. Failing such support, the pretender had no more prospect of deposing the 'legitimate' pope than dissident stockholders who lack a voting majority have of replacing an unpopular CEO. Thus, even with lifetime tenure as official Church policy, a pope (theoretically at least) could not engage in significant malfeasance without running the risk of encouraging outside challengers.

Ultimately, of course, the tenure of a pope was limited by his mortality. Although elected for life, the average age at election was high, and the typical period of office brief. Among the 63 legitimate popes who held office between AD 1000 and 1400, the average term in office was about six years. Eighteen of the 63 popes served one year or less. During this same interval, two reigning popes resigned, and three were deposed (albeit by political maneuvers of the emperor rather than by internal censure and removal).

In sum, the supply-side of the church was organized along the lines of a modern corporation, and this organization grew up in response to age-old problems of economic organization. The corporate center of the Church in Rome had to resolve massive agency problems in its field operations, devise efficient revenue-sharing schemes, audit local operations, and so on. For example, vertical relations issues had to be addressed such as the formation of agreements between local operatives and Rome so as to avoid problems of double-monopolization. It should also be kept in mind that the Church operated as a not-for-profit entity. This suggests that profits had to be consumed within the Church and that normal expense preference behavior would have been evident in Church operations. It should not be surprising, then, to observe Church investments in facilities and other prerequisites for Church employees.

7 NATURE OF OUTPUT IN THE MULTIDIVISIONAL CHURCH

Given the complex and extensive nature of the medieval Church, it is necessary to distinguish between the institutional Church as a provider of private goods, on the one hand, and as a supplier of public goods, on the other. As a kind of surrogate government, the Church provided a number of social and public goods to medieval society. An entire system of law and courts emerged under Church auspices that supplemented the ramshackle structure of government and legal institutions that existed during the Middle Ages. At a time when governmental social welfare programs were virtually non-existent, the Church maintained an elaborate system of voluntary institutions and practices designed to aid the poor. The Church also organized and supported educational institutions that provided the bulk of human capital investment during the Middle Ages. Long before the emergence of strong nation-states, the Church used its transnational influence to limit armed conflict among petty warlords who dominated the political landscape of Western Europe.

As important as these contributions were, it is not our intention to examine in detail the public-goods aspect of the medieval Church. Our focus is on the Church as a provider of private goods, that is, goods and services that were 'purchased' in something resembling a market context. In this market context, religion is by its nature a service industry. The primary service supplied by the medieval Church to its customers was information about and guidance toward the attainment of eternal salvation. At issue here is neither the veracity of the Church's theological claims, nor its ability to guarantee the end product, but rather the fact that whatever knowledge and information consumers possessed in this regard was provided entirely and exclusively by the Church. An important aspect of this service concerned the afterlife: the idea that the soul continues to exist for all eternity after the death of the body. To a medieval Christian, and to most today, one's existence on earth was a tiny part of 'life' – while the average person might live a mere 40 or 50 years in the earthly realm, the soul's existence in heaven or hell would be forever. Every Christian therefore looked to the Church for advice and guidance on actions required to gain salvation. In this connection, the clergy provided a vital kind of 'brokerage' service for the faithful.

Most people in medieval Christendom accepted the fact that the Church of Rome had a major influence over the disposition of their immortal souls – in other words, whether they went to heaven or hell. This belief is crucial to understanding the medieval Church as an economic organization. By virtue of this fact the Church was the monopoly provider of a pure meta-credence good. The credibility of Church courts, the validity of canon law, the acceptance of the Church as divinely sanctioned arbiter of earthly disputes, and the ultimate trust in the Church's various commercial enterprises, all derived from the credibility of the religious doctrines promulgated by the Church of Rome.

Despite some rather obvious limitations – the customer could not take salvation for a test drive, nor get a sneak preview of heaven (or hell) and return to tell about it – some facts of medieval life make a compelling argument for treatment of the Church's product as a credence good.[7] During medieval times (and earlier) the distinction between the worldly and the spiritual was often blurred. For example, the belief in miracles was very widespread. In the minds of the faithful, miracles constituted credible evidence of divine intervention. Likewise, this intercession of saints in the daily affairs of men was regarded as a way in which God directly effected the 'technology' through which affairs in the physical world were manipulable; interpretations of phenomena without otherwise apparent explanation were regarded as 'evidence' for the efficacy of the divine.

Moreover, as a producer of a credence good, the Church invested heavily in brand name capital. This includes cathedrals, relics, liturgy, saints, icons, and so on. Such investments were designed to enhance the value and believability of the Church's control over the route to heaven and the afterlife. This is not unlike the investment of modern firms in advertising, product warranties, and the like.

Just as today's consumer can evaluate the quality-related claims of an automobile by driving it or by hiring a mechanic to inspect it, a medieval Christian could evaluate claims by a parish priest about the powers of God and the saints by monitoring for 'miracles' and other manifestations of the efficacy of religion. In contrast to ordinary consumer decisions about tangible goods and services made in a modern economy, the evaluation of quality claims in the case of medieval religion involved a process of mutual determination. The basis of acceptable evidence for divine intervention was founded partially on pre-existing theological beliefs.

When economists observe rational individuals voluntarily engaging in some activity or consuming some good, they assume that those individuals expect to achieve net positive utility from their chosen action; or else they would behave otherwise. It also seems self-evident that if said individuals continue to behave in like manner – that is, engage in repeat transactions aimed at consuming the same good – it can be concluded that those persons found their *ex post* gratifications to have met their *ex ante* expectations. If this economic rationale applies to the consumption of ice cream, automobiles, and television programs, it logically should also apply to the consumption of religion. Axiomatically, people engage in religious pursuits because such actions increase their net utility.

There would be no need to belabor this seemingly obvious principle except for the fact that some modern historians and commentators have often insinuated that the Church reduced net social welfare by impeding the advance of science, encouraging superstition, and dissipating surplus productive resources through wasteful expenditures on cathedrals, shrines and so forth. This view overlooks the utility-enhancing nature of religious practice and Church membership. It is as if we were to criticize spending by modern consumers at Disneyland by bemoaning the lost opportunities for utilizing the same funds to repair roads or advance new medical cures. Even granting the dubious anti-clerical assumptions often made by critics of the Church (for example, inhibition of science), Roman Catholicism more likely than not generated huge increases in the utility for many religious consumers, and, in all likelihood, corresponding gains in consumers' surplus.

As an extensive and pervasive monopolist in medieval society, the Church held a major advantage as producer of the credence good of salvation, which included intercession with God. The monopoly status of the Church, coupled with its great temporal power, reinforced the credibility of its claims concerning the quality of its non-testable final product. The Church could convincingly maintain that its temporal position was testament to the veracity of its religious claims. Thus, aspiring entrants to the medieval religious market faced the daunting task of convincing their potential customers that the alternative product they offered was more reliable than that already available from an institution endorsed by an omnipotent God. Obviously, as the Protestant Reformation eventually revealed, this obstacle was not insurmountable. But before losing market share to new entrants, the Church had persistently and successfully erected and maintained 'barriers to entry' for centuries.

8 MARKET STRUCTURE OF THE MEDIEVAL RELIGIOUS INDUSTRY

The medieval Church solidified its monopoly position by defining competing entrants (heretics) as criminals to be either imprisoned or executed. If successful in its 'prosecution', the personal wealth of a dissenting member or a heathen challenger was subject to confiscation by the Church. Often the Church enlisted the authority of secular officials in this regard, and sometimes the spoils were shared. The Church even orchestrated massive military expeditions (the Crusades) in order to prevent the spread of Islam, a competing religion, in some of the earlier 'Holy Wars'. Clearly, the One True Church strove for monopoly power in the theological marketplace, but it also enlisted the aid of secular governments to exclude competitors.

The medieval Church was not an unbridled monopoly. On the local level, the relatively high mobility of peasants in medieval Europe implies a substantial amount of migration across parishes, with the resulting 'Tiebout effects' restraining the ability of priests and other clerics to act as pure monopolists. Conditions among local church parishes provided another kind of restraint on the abuse of monopoly power. Tithes paid by parishioners constituted a small fraction of corporate Church revenue but represented the majority of a local priest's income. In as much as the parish priest had essentially no enforcement power against non-payers (priests were forbidden to withhold sacraments for non-payment), they had to resort to satisfying the parishioners in order to encourage voluntary compliance. Although in theory a priest could sue for unpaid tithes in ecclesiastical court, in practice this remedy rarely was effective.

In sum, the medieval Church was not an unbridled monopoly, not omnipotent, nor did its market power come directly or indirectly from government, as is most often the case with contemporary monopolies. Medieval governments generally were weak, disorganized, and largely unable to provide monopoly rents to special interest groups. The effective monopoly power of the Church came mainly from its distinct position in a rather unique market. Even so, it faced a number of practical constraints. These institutional constraints limited the economic power of the medieval Church somewhat, but the fact remains that the 'owner-operators' of the medieval Church clearly benefitted from a host of effective restrictions on competitive entry. As a result, the Church was able to consolidate its wealth and power over many centuries, reaching its peak during the late Middle Ages.

9 THE DOCTRINE OF USURY

The price of money, like its analogue, the price of goods, was persistently treated by medieval writers as an ethical issue – they perceived justice rather than efficiency as the appropriate goal of economic policy. Ostensibly, this is consistent with a public-interest theory of behavior. The historical record, however, raises doubts about this argument. It shows, for example, that Church officials frequently manipulated the usury doctrine to create or bolster the monopoly power of the Church.

We do not assert that the medieval Church invented the doctrine of usury, or the economic doctrine of just price, for its own economic gains.[8] Rather, in spite of its original (and perhaps lasting) concern for justice, the Church recognized, and acted on, the rent-seeking opportunities of the doctrine at a certain juncture in its history.

The medieval Church established de facto dual credit markets. When the Church was a lender, it priced its loans at market rates (or above), thus extracting rents. But when it was a borrower, it enforced the usury doctrine, thereby extracting rents by reducing its cost of credit on certain loans. At other times it used the doctrine to increase contributions and membership. Through selective enforcement, moreover, the Church could increase the supply of loans for (laic) consumption purposes.

This hypothesis is consistent with the activities of a rent-seeking monopoly, and it accommodates both monetary and non-monetary goals, which were often intertwined in the policies pursued by the medieval Church. The chief monetary goal of the Church was to increase its ability to finance its salvation effort; its main non-monetary goal was to preserve and extend its doctrinal hegemony – that is, to increase the demand for final output and to make it more inelastic. Though fragmentary, Vatican records show a pattern of selective enforcement. When it was in the Church's interest to do so, it enforced the usury prohibition to keep its cost of funds low. When the Church lent money, the usury doctrine by and large was ignored. Moreover, besides the direct use of usury policy to enhance its wealth, the Church made indirect use of it to augment the power of the papal monopoly, including its far-flung bureaucracy. Scholars have tended to over-intellectualize the discussion of the Church and its usury doctrine. By focusing on the application and enforcement of the doctrine, one is better able to see it for what it was – a policy with biblical precedent adapted to the rent-seeking purposes of the Church.

The Church was also involved in the extensive system of price controls that prevailed in medieval towns. Here the modern interest-group theory of regulation offers a clear explanation for these controls and the attendant regulations governing who could sell in the towns and at what prices. These were not 'just' prices; they were 'regulated' prices. For example, there were important price fixing efforts by the guilds and for ordinary commodities on the part of governments at all levels and by the church as well (recall that in medieval times many markets were placed either in or near churches and cathedrals) (DeRoover 1958, p. 428).

10 THE DOCTRINE OF PURGATORY AND PROTESTANT ENTRY

Most medieval church historians agree that the sale of indulgences by the Catholic Church played a prominent role in encouraging competitive entry by competing religions. Indeed, the proximate cause of Martin Luther's successful challenge to the Church's dominant market position is almost universally held to be its record of abuses involving indulgences. In conjunction with this view, part of the explanation for the rise and ultimate success of Protestantism was the attempt by the Catholic Church to extract monopoly rents associated with a plethora of doctrinal innovations, among them the interwoven tenets of purgatory, penance, and indulgences.

As with any monopoly, the aim of the medieval church was to eliminate competition. Output restrictions and price increases were a consequence of such monopoly behavior. As noted above, the medieval Church used various methods to eliminate overall competition in its market, including political and social pressures (for example, shunning through interdict or anathema) against unorthodox rivals, such as Jews and Moslems. It also dealt harshly with heresy, magic, and superstition, which had been practiced from early pre-Christian times, by devising such tools as excommunication, the Crusades, and Inquisitions. But since it was always the prerogative of individuals to 'self-select' among formal and informal belief systems, the Church had to maintain the quality of its product in order to prevent slippage, and it was required to price its services in such a way as to attract new customers. When product price rose and the reputation of the medieval church became tarnished as 'worldly' and venal, the papacy took steps to retain, attract, or regain members. The lowering of relative prices for certain services provided to members of the Church of England provides an example. The Anglican Church was always more independent than its European counterparts. In order to prevent defection (prior to Henry VIII's definitive break), the Church lowered the prices of some services.

The chief price confronted by individual church members over the first millennium was dictated by a certain type of offer of assurances of eternal salvation. Despite the fact that temporal punishments and other forms of penance were administered through the confessional, in which some sins or infractions were more serious than others, individual penitents exercised discrete choice between eternal salvation and eternal damnation. Before the doctrine of purgatory and its accoutrements, the medieval Church did not offer a continuum of choices, certainly none with a halfway house to salvation. The invention and formulation of a package of new doctrines (without or with only suggested biblical precedent) around the eleventh and twelfth centuries fundamentally changed the nature or medieval Church doctrine and the customary offers of earlier ages. Taken together, the invention of purgatory, the distinction between venial and mortal sins, auricular confession, and, most importantly, the granting of indulgences, created a continuum of price-behavior choices by which individuals might attain the main religious product: assurance of eternal salvation. In effect, the choice offered by the medieval Church became continuous. These inventions initially lowered the price of sin, but they also created ever-expanding opportunities for rent extraction from Church members.[9]

In its role as gatekeeper of heaven, the medieval Church engaged in activities akin to those that take place in a system of criminal justice. From this perspective, the theory of deterrence of sin may be set out in a straightforward fashion. Imagine a demand for forgiveness of sin. It is negatively sloped and depicts the maximum demand price believers would be willing to pay for forgiveness. The invention of purgatory, the distinction between venial and mortal sins, and other innovations employed by the medieval Church gave form to such a demand function.

In contrast, the supply curve of forgiveness was dependent on the Church's long-run costs of providing a belief structure. This included the costs of formulating doctrine, providing liturgy, establishing enforcement mechanisms in downstream church 'firms' (for example, 'confession'), administering the sacraments, collecting relics, and so on. An equilibrium price of forgiveness is consistent with this market view.

As in the case of the suppression of crime (Becker 1968; Becker and Stigler 1974), some 'optimum' may be reached. It has been suggested that in regard to sin, the medieval Church merely engaged in a kind of optimal deterrence that involved setting 'efficient' penalties for criminal behavior. The historical record reveals otherwise. The Church did not adhere to a single-price policy of charging the average price for the commission of sins. As a monopolist characterized by a high degree of market power, the medieval Church was able to mold its doctrine and practice into an elaborate scheme of price discrimination. Deterrence, therefore, was not the overriding objective, because it appears that it was subservient to the practice of infra-marginal rent extraction.

Basically, the medieval Church stood in the position of a perfectly discriminating monopoly. The goal was to put all sinners at a point on their demand curves for sin and forgiveness, thereby creating a situation in which maximum monopoly rents could be collected. Optimal deterrence would have required the Church to set different prices for different sins, which, in fact it did not do. Instead, the Church set different prices for different customers, based on their incomes. The medieval Church was a rent extractor, not an agent of optimal deterrence.

On the supply side, the medieval Church was most likely to resist encroachment of new religions, and maintain its incumbent monopoly status, in situations where it could effectively continue to appropriate consumer surplus through price discrimination (Lunt 1962; Ekelund et al. 2002). The conditions necessary for the medieval Church to continue to be successful in its chosen strategy were the following. First, there had to be a large reserve of wealth to tap, which was the case in those societies where feudal institutions supported a landed class. Second, the prevailing wealth distribution had to be relatively stable, in order to repay the Church's 'investment' in information about willingness to pay, and to keep the transaction costs associated with its pricing strategy relatively low. These two conditions usually are met in tradition-bound, authoritarian societies. In other words, the medieval Church was most likely to preserve its incumbent monopoly status in semi-feudal societies that had many low-income people (peasants) who were mild targets of the Church's discriminatory policies, and a strong landed class (nobility) who routinely engaged in rent-seeking activity, whereby they sought to cut their own deals with the established Church.

By contrast, the medieval Church found it difficult to continue its practice of price discrimination in societies which encouraged profit seeking or greater market participation by lower economic classes.[10] Where the power of the monarch was relatively weak and the ownership of property was open to many, profit opportunities presented themselves to an expanding middle class. The distribution of wealth in such societies was constantly changing, making it more difficult for the Church to engage in effective price discrimination. Societies in which political and economic power were decentralized rather than centralized therefore presented problems to the ongoing profitability of the medieval Church.

The main point is that through time, doctrine and practice combined under Church direction to extract as much consumer surplus as possible from Church members through the implementation of second and third degrees of price discrimination. The Church, in short, manipulated both the quality and the full price of its product so as to put members on the margin of defection. In crude terms, the cost and complexity of the price scales for 'assurances of eternal salvation' forced members to self-select out of Roman Catholicism. In one sense the Church's price discrimination strategy put many of its members on the no-rent margin so that any lower priced but similar belief systems would have been attractive substitutes. Protestantism eschewed price discrimination by eliminating the priest as 'middleman'. It featured a return to the lower cost offer that characterized the early Christian Church, which, after the deprecations of the Church monopoly, would have been an appealing alternative to believers. It also repudiated the formalism and much of the complexity of Catholic dogma. These characteristics were shared by all of the reform movements, whether espoused by Luther, Calvin, Zwingli, or others. Calvin's doctrine of predestination – limiting the number of the 'elect' who will attain paradise in contemporary Mormon fashion – quickly was modified to create much more elasticity for those who *might* be worthy. Naturally the behavioral implications of Calvinists are the same as other Protestants because one cannot know from birth whether one is included in the 'elect'.

Protestantism established individual conscience as the Christian's guide and reinstated 'good works' as sufficient to produce 'assurances of eternal salvation'. It therefore provided a lower-cost alternative to Catholicism, and offered to restore lost consumer surplus to many late-medieval Christians, especially the well-heeled. The new religions' diminished emphasis on the institutional Church, with its plethora of rules and regulations, constituted a doctrinal break with established religion, to be sure. But it also offered new economic opportunities in as much as it allowed individuals to recapture lost consumer surplus and to obtain assurances of salvation at less cost than before. While tithing and other monetary payments were part of Protestantism, the good works 'payment' was essentially an 'in-kind' expenditure. Given the state of development of capital markets in these times, the in-kind financing of salvation was surely welcomed by defectors from the Church.

11 PROTESTANT ENTRY: SUCCESSES AND FAILURES

The doctrinal history of the Roman Catholic Church reveals that by the end of the Middle Ages it had evolved a complex pricing scheme that discriminated among its members according to wealth and status, and extracted most of the consumer surplus derived from religion by its parishioners. It seems likely, therefore, that the single most important economic factor in explaining the appeal of Protestantism over Catholicism is the fact that Protestant doctrine offered a more amenable pricing system than the one that had evolved under Catholic doctrine and institutional practice. The 'price' of salvation under the new religious doctrine consisted of payments in kind – the performance of good works – and, by declaring priestly agents unnecessary, eliminated the abuses that had crept into the ecclesiastical bureaucracy. The new religions required no intermediaries between man and God, no confession, no explicit or implicit payments for indulgences, and no half-way houses on the way to salvation (for example, purgatory). The fundamental appeal of Protestantism is that it offered a simple, direct and relatively inexpensive path to eternal life. However, the new religion did not meet with universal success. To understand the ability of the medieval Church to maintain its incumbent monopoly status in some societies, the supply-side elements of the theory must be invoked.

The medieval Church invested resources in acquiring information about the wealth and utility functions of its high-income members and in devising price lists to guide confessors. It can be inferred that it was costly (menu costs) to acquire and to change such lists. In tradition-bound societies where the distribution of wealth was uneven but stable, and wealth-creation opportunities were limited by institutional constraints, the medieval Church could more easily retain its members and still capture large amounts of consumer surplus. In other words, *ceteris paribus*, Protestantism was rejected in rent-seeking societies, and embraced in profit-seeking societies. Catholicism lost its hold on societies characterized by emergent market orders because, ultimately, it was more costly and less profitable to pursue its agenda under such circumstances.

One measure of the economic ossification that enabled the Church to maintain its hegemony is the extent to which restrictive property laws were enforced. Feudal forms of property differ from capitalist forms of property. Some countries practiced primogeniture, and some did not. Primogeniture was confined mostly to Europe, and was practiced mainly among the upper classes who were entrenched within a centralized power system. The law was intended to concentrate wealth in the hands of a few dynastic families, but by disinheriting all younger children, it also caused untold bitterness within the family.

The Church served as a kind of insurer, or employer of last resort, to the landed aristocracy in such cases: younger sons could become retainers through ecclesiastical sinecure, a station that could be relinquished if the eldest son died. Moreover, female children could also find ready 'employment' in the Church nunnery. Prince-bishops, which is what many of the nobility became, were assured that as high church officials they could maintain a lifestyle befitting their dynastic stations. Ecclesiastical careers did not bar anyone from secular family affairs. As long as one did not advance to the subdiaconate (which required a vow of celibacy that could be nullified only by papal dispensation), noble ecclesiastics had little trouble returning to secular life. The medieval Church, in other words, approved of primogeniture precisely because it promoted the kind of stability of wealth distribution that enabled it to price-discriminate successfully among certain members, and it simultaneously provided an incentive to the heads of dynastic families to remain within the system of established religious practice.

As a test of this proposition, Ekelund et al. (2006, pp. 119–34) gathered data on the principal entry points of Protestantism, and the acceptance of the new religion was compared with the conditions most likely to encourage its success or failure. In simplified form, the theory predicts that societies enforcing primogeniture would be most likely to remain Catholic, whereas those societies with more fluid property laws (and hence more opportunities for wealth enhancement by larger strata of society) would find Protestantism more palatable. While these findings may be modified with further study, the results are favorable to the thesis, because the evidence shows that those societies with primogeniture remained Catholic, whereas those with partible inheritance laws embraced Protestantism.[11]

12 CONCLUSION

Public choice, most certainly including interest-group analysis, has been one of the singularly successful applications of rational behavior to political economy. We have argued that this exciting area of economic inquiry applies to the market structure and conduct of religion, specifically in the present chapter, to the evolution of Roman Catholic Christianity.

We have focused attention on the structure and conduct of the Catholic Church's high medieval monopoly and on its status vis-à-vis European society. The organizational vehicle by which the Church achieved upstream power was developed through vertical integration that it achieved over the first millennium. By the end of that time, a monopoly was created over both wholesale (upstream) and retail (downstream) sale of a clearly defined product – a product expounded and refined by the fourth century at the Council of Nicaea. This structure developed alongside a secular political and legal structure which often protected (and sometimes opposed) the Roman Church and its rent seeking. Throughout the high Middle Ages, acting as an effective monopoly, the Church was able to fend off potential entrants while expanding its power and territory by launching the Crusades and adopting other mechanisms. Rent-seeking was a central feature of this emerging monopoly. Manipulations, inventions of the usury doctrine, purgatory, auricular confession and marriage regulations, or both, opened opportunities for rent-seeking to the upstream papacy (which, of course, had to control opportunistic behavior downstream). However, the attempt to 'shear too much wool from their sheep' ultimately lowered the full price of entry to followers and supporters of Martin Luther; thereafter, the marketplace of Christianity once again became competitive as it had been before product definition was solidified at the Council of Nicaea in 325. Public choice, industrial organization, specifically, and economic theory, more generally, helps provide insights into this critical evolution in economic history.

NOTES

1. See Ekelund et al. (1989, 1992, 1996, 2002, 2004, 2006) and Ekelund and Tollison (2011) for background references.
2. The Edict of Milan was a formal act of toleration issued by the co-emperors Constantine and Licinius, each sympathetic to monotheism.
3. We do not mean to imply that the Roman Church establishment in Europe was completely unchallenged. It always faced competition at the fringe from 'heretical' groups, some of them self-described Christians and, of course, from Jews. The Eastern Church, most prominently, was kept at bay by the Roman branch of Christianity. Both were based upon a 'conciliar' and hierarchical structure, but the western and eastern branches were separated to this day by Rome's assertion of papal supremacy over all of Christendom.
4. This hierarchical structure, combined with vertical integration, took centuries to develop in the Roman Catholic Church, being completed about the eleventh century (Ekelund and Tollison 2011).
5. Over the previous millennium popes (bishops of Rome) were elected jointly by the clergy and the people of Rome, a practice which created controls by particular Roman families over appointments to the papacy and to the inevitable political chicanery surrounding such a system.
6. The Concordat at Worms in 1122 CE was aimed at eliminating or reducing the power of 'lay investiture' whereby secular rulers claimed a right to appoint bishops and other clergy in their realms. It was an extension of the many reforms (significantly sponsored by Pope Gregory VII (reign 1073–1085) that included papal celibacy. Papal celibacy had a number of benefits for the church. First, it constrained the transfer of wealth from clerics to their families and, second, it served as a 'credence builder' in the sale of church theology, dogma and practice.
7. Elsewhere, we (Ekelund et al., 2006, pp. 28–29) describe the Church's production of salvation as a *meta-credence* good in that, unlike, for example, an automobile, the consumer has no way of scientifically judging salvation services in advance. The qualities of the service cannot be known no matter the investment of human time or money.
8. We do not, further, suggest that a 'rent-seeking' interpretation of the doctrine is the only way of analyzing usury (see, for example, Glaeser and Scheinkman 1998).
9. Note the contradiction of public interest theory here, that is, a lowering of the price of sin.
10. The argument here is superficially related to Weber's (1958) famous hypothesis about Protestantism and economic growth. The point is, however, that the Protestantism offered a lower cost contract for believers, not a more rigorous, less preferred alternative. The advent of Protestantism came about more rapidly in developing areas because the Catholic Church could not compete effectively in those areas for the reasons outlined above. Protestantism was (controversially) co-linear with economic growth, but for different reasons than those ascribed to Weber.
11. Ours is an *institutional* interpretation of the Protestant split based upon the concentration or dispersion of wealth created by primogeniture (Ekelund et al., 2002, p. 660), as well as by nascent nation states that tired of repatriating wealth to Rome. Naturally there are many dimensions that might be used to explain the split between those countries that became Protestant and those that remained Roman Catholic *at the time*. A reader has suggested that a *geographic* division between Roman/Mediterranean and 'Gothic' countries might explain the split between countries. This distinction, if we understand the suggested basis for the division, does not easily map into the countries and regions becoming Catholic or Protestant. For example, Austria, Bavaria, and parts of the Swiss Confederation remained Catholic. (If these countries or areas were 'Gothic,' they were certainly not Roman/Mediterranean.) Further study of a geographic division may produce interesting results, but the institutions underlying state incentives would also be necessary.

25 Experimental public choice
Laura Razzolini

1 INTRODUCTION

Economics is now considered to be a theoretical, an empirical and an experimental science. While in past years a contribution to the field had to be based on a rigorous theoretical model and then be tested with a sophisticated econometric model, today contributions to economics can be supported by experimental tests, conducted both in the laboratory and in the field. Experimental studies are now regularly reported in the top general-interest journals, and the Nobel memorial prize in economics has been awarded to a number of experimental economists, such as Vernon Smith and Daniel Kahneman, and most recently in 2009 to Elinor Ostrom 'for her analysis of economic governance, especially the commons'. Public choice research has followed this same trend and it has also seen a rapid increase in the use of laboratory experiments as a means to further the field.

In an economic experiment, subjects make real choices with monetary outcomes in a controlled environment. The environment is chosen, characterized and manipulated by the experimenter on the basis of the theory that is tested. At the end of the experiment, subjects are paid in cash amounts that depend on their own decisions and often on the decisions of the other participants with whom they interact. While empirical tests of theories are based on a limited set of observations, such as data obtained from field studies or from surveys, one of the main advantages of experimental research is that the study can be replicated as many times as needed to confirm results and behavior. Another advantage of experiments is that the experimenter can control all those '*ceteris paribus*' factors which the theory usually assumes as fixed. In an experiment such factors can be held constant as treatments are changed.

This chapter surveys research on experiments in public choice: public goods and voluntary provision mechanisms (section 2), externalities, the tragedy of the commons and the Coase theorem (section 3), political economy (section 4), and rent-seeking and lobbying (section 5). A concluding discussion is presented in section 6.

2 EXPERIMENTS ON PUBLIC GOODS AND VOLUNTARY CONTRIBUTION MECHANISMS

Since the days of Adam Smith, it has been well known that self-interested individuals can improve their welfare by trading with one another. An invisible hand operates through the price system so that resources are allocated efficiently. Markets function well only if a good system of governance is in place, so that property rights and legal procedures to enforce those rights are well established. However, as Mueller observes (2003, p. 10), a well-functioning government is in itself a public good, and in the case of public goods, the market may fail to function as an efficient allocative mechanism.

Pure public goods are characterized by the properties of non-exclusion and non-rivalry or jointness in consumption. Non-exclusion implies that once the good has been supplied to one member of society, it is not physically possible to exclude other members from access to it. Jointness in supply implies that the marginal cost of adding one additional user of the good is zero. That is, a public good is non-rival in consumption and adding more users to the good does not reduce the benefits of those already consuming it. Classical examples of a public good are national defense, clean air, and public parks (as long as they are uncongested). The two properties of non-exclusion and non-rivalry lead to the failure of the market system as a means of providing public goods, thus requiring the existence of a government. Non-exclusion leads to free-riding, so that many individuals may consume the public good without contributing to financing its provision; jointness in supply leads to under-provision or no provision at all of the public good. A well-functioning governmental system can in principle overcome these problems and achieve efficiency and Pareto optimality in the provision of a public good.

Experiments have been employed extensively to study the provision of public goods. The theoretical prediction about public goods is quite clear: the Nash equilibrium is to contribute zero and individuals should free ride on each other's contributions. Experiments on public goods ideally can test this prediction and, since the early 1980s, when the first experiments were conducted, a large literature has been created on the topic. The majority of these experimental studies have tried to explain why, contrary to the theoretical prediction, individuals do indeed contribute positive amounts to public goods, both in the laboratory and in the real world (on charitable contributions or donations to public radio and television, see Davis et al. 2006). Experiments have been used to determine clearly the factors that affect contributions and help in reducing the free-rider problem.

The standard public good experiment is framed as an 'investment game' and is conducted with a group of four to five subjects. Each subject is given an endowment of 'tokens' that can be invested in a private account or in a public account. A token invested in the private account yields a higher return to the individual, while a token invested in the public account provides a return to all the members of the group. In this way, the public account investment is non-rival, as all members in the group derive the same benefit from the contribution, which is non-excludable, as everybody enjoys the same benefit whether he/she contributed or not. Let z denote individual j's endowment of tokens, p the private value of tokens, and c the number of tokens contributed to the public account. Then, individual j's payoff is:

$$\pi_j = p(z - c_j) + \frac{a}{N}y, \text{ where } y = \sum_{i=1}^{N} c_i. \tag{25.1}$$

In particular, the marginal individual gain from contributing a token to the public account is $\frac{a}{N}$, where N is the size of the group. The marginal rate of substitution between the public and the private account, also known as the marginal per capita return (MPCR), is:

$$MPCR = -\frac{(\partial \pi_j/\partial y)}{(\partial \pi_j/\partial c_j)} = \frac{a}{pN}. \tag{25.2}$$

When $\frac{1}{N} < MPCR < 1$, each individual is better off by keeping all tokens because the investment in the private account has a higher personal return than the investment in the public account. On the other hand, as in the prisoners' dilemma situation, the socially optimal outcome would be for every individual to contribute all of the tokens to the public account.

In the standard experiments, subjects repeat the investment decisions for several periods and the choices are examined over time and compared to the theoretical zero contribution prediction or to the socially optimal outcome. Comparative statics can easily be performed in the laboratory to check whether by increasing the size of the group N, a lower level of contributions will be realized (as the MPCR is lowered), or whether by increasing the return to the public account a, a greater level of contributions will be realized (as the MPCR is increased). Similarly, experiments can be conducted to check whether there is a difference in contributions between inexperienced and experienced subjects, between male and female subjects, between fixed groups of subjects or randomly varied groups (known partners versus strangers), or when subjects within a group are allowed to communicate ('cheap talk'). In some cases, public good provision has been based on a 'threshold' level (or provision point), in the sense that the group return will be paid out to all subjects only if the total contributions exceed some designated level. That is:

$$\pi_j = p(z - c_j) + A \times \frac{a}{N}\sum_{i=1}^{N}c_i,$$

where $A = 1$ if $\sum_{i=1}^{N} c_i \geq T$, and $A = 0$ otherwise. (25.3)

In this case, theory predicts several non-cooperative equilibria.

These different types of experiments have been conducted to investigate how much and under what circumstances individuals are willing to contribute to public goods, and what institutional factors or mechanisms can increase contributions. It will not be possible to outline all of the studies done on the topic, but I will focus on a few and direct the reader to the comprehensive survey by Ledyard (1995). The earliest papers were by sociologists Marwell and Ames (1979, 1980, 1981). These innovative studies found, surprisingly (only to economists!), little free-riding and contributions unexpectedly (again only to economists!) close to the efficient level. Marwell and Ames (1981), in particular, found that only groups composed of economics students realized a level of contributions close to the zero theoretical prediction: whence came the title of their paper 'Economists free-ride, does anyone else?' Isaac et al. (1984) were the first to use a linear payoff structure for the public goods game, which is now the standard format. They found that experienced subjects contribute less than inexperienced ones, with contributions falling as the number of rounds in the experiment increased.

In general, factors that tend to increase contributions strongly are the possibility of communication among subjects (Andreoni and Petrie 2004), a higher MPCR (Laury et al. 1999), sufficiently large group size (Isaac and Walker 1988), and the existence of a minimal aggregate provision point (Bagnoli and McKee 1991; Bagnoli et al. 1992). More recent studies have focused on behavioral models and have considered factors such as altruism (Andreoni and Miller 2002), impure altruism and 'warm glow' effects

(Andreoni 1988, 1990; Palfrey and Prisbey 1996, 1997; Korenok et al. 2010, 2011), reciprocity (Sugden 1984), inequality aversion (Fehr and Schmidt 1999; Bolton and Ockenfels 2000), reputational concerns (Andreoni 1988; Andreoni and Croson 1998), punishment and sanctions (Fehr and Gächter 2000) or confusion (Andreoni 1995) as additional reasons explaining contributions toward public goods.

In summary, important regularities found in the literature on public goods experiments are:

1. Contributions to the public good start at a relatively high level, usually around 40 percent of the individual endowment.
2. Contributions decrease with repetition, even though they often do not decrease all the way to zero.
3. Individual contributions increase with group size, with the possibility of communication (cheap talk) and of punishment among group members.
4. Contributions increase as the MPCR and the individual endowment are increased.
5. Contributions vary considerably across subjects: some subjects always contribute, some never do and some alternate between contributing and not contributing.

The conclusion we take from this body of experimental work is that subjects do contribute voluntarily to public goods and do so more generously than what the individual self-interested prediction would suggest. Free-riding is not so prevalent and provision of the public good does occur, even though at a lower level than is efficient or Pareto optimal. For this reason, a well-functioning government system should limit itself to eliciting such social behavior.

3 EXPERIMENTS ON NEGATIVE EXTERNALITIES AND THE COASE THEOREM

Since the publication of Hardin's (1968) 'Tragedy of the Commons', economists have realized that 'free' goods, or goods for which property rights are not clearly defined and assigned, create a special challenge, as market forces, which under normal circumstance guarantee an efficient allocation of resources, are absent in this case. Common-pool resources, such as clean air and water, fisheries, forests and wild life, libraries and uncongested roads are goods characterized by the property of non-exclusion, as they are available free of charge to anyone who wishes to use them. These goods are, however, rival in consumption, because one person's use of the common resource reduces the quantity available to others. Hardin supplies a parable that shows how common resources get used more than is desirable from society's point of view, and the outcome is the same as with a negative externality. For instance, in the case of pollution (a 'bad' creating a negative externality), the market economy – if left to its own devices – typically will generate too much pollution because polluters have no incentive to take into account the costs they impose on others. With government intervention, on the other hand, the socially optimal quantity can be achieved by using appropriate (Pigouvian) taxes. In a famous 1960 article, Coase suggested that economies could indeed deal with externalities and reach an efficient solution through bargaining, as long as property rights are properly assigned and transaction costs are sufficiently low. In this case, externalities are internalized by the parties to the transactions.

Ostrom et al. (1994) conducted a series of experiments to test how individuals behave in a common-pool resource environment and how this behavior is affected by the institutional setting. They used the investment game described in the previous section, in which individuals are given an endowment of tokens to either keep or invest in a public account. The return on the public account is determined by the aggregate group investment. For small levels of investment the return exceeds the return on the private account. However, if the aggregate investment exceeds a certain level, the return from the public account becomes less than the individual's private return from not investing. Ostrom et al. used a quadratic return function for the public account as follows:

$$\pi_i = p(z - c_i) + \frac{c_i}{y}(ay - by^2) \text{ where } y = \sum_{i=1}^{N} c_i, \quad (25.4)$$

where, as before, π_i is the payoff for subject i, p is the private return on the number of tokens kept, z is the individual endowment, c_i is person i's investment, y is the sum of the group's investment and a and b are coefficients in the quadratic return function.

Within this framework, Ostrom et al. compared the subjects' behavior to the Nash equilibrium predictions and found that the individual decisions were not consistent with the theory. The individuals' strategy did not show any particular trend. Individuals tended to invest all of their endowment in the public account when the return was greater than the return on the private account. But once the return on the public account fell below that of the private account, individuals moved all their tokens to the private investment. Overinvestment in the public account also tended to increase as the individuals' endowments were increased.

Walker and Gardner (1992) slightly modified the previous experiment by introducing a probability that overinvestment in the public account may lead to the destruction of the common pool resource. Such probability rose as the investment in the public account increased. Subjects' behavior appeared close to the theoretical prediction. Ostrom and Walker (1991) introduced the possibility of communication as an alternative remedy to overinvestment. Even though such communication was allowed over only one period, and was non-binding 'cheap talk,' the subjects immediately realized an improvement in efficiency. With repetition, however, overinvestment returned as the dominant strategy. The gains in efficiency could be sustained only if communication was allowed repeatedly during the experiment.

A different line of experiments has been developed against the backdrop of the 'request game' (Suleiman and Rapoport 1988; Rapoport et al. 1993). In that context, subjects have to decide how many tokens they wish to request from a common 'pot'. The subjects do not know the exact value of the pot; they know only that it has a uniformly distributed value between given lower and upper bounds a and b. An individual's payoff is determined by his request of tokens, by the total requests made by the group and the realized value of the pot. If the total sum of the requests is less than or equal to the realized value, all subjects will receive their request. If the aggregate request is greater than the realized value of the pot, then everyone receives 0 tokens. Therefore, if individual requests are low, it is very likely that all subjects will receive their request. However, as soon as one subject realizes that everyone else will keep their request low, that subject has an incentive to increase his/her request and earn more than the others. This experimental design nicely replicates the 'tragedy of the commons' in the laboratory.

In the simultaneous request game, with n risk-neutral players, the Nash equilibrium strategy for a player is to request the following number of tokens:

$$\frac{a}{n} \quad \text{if} \quad nb < (n+1)a \tag{25.5}$$

$$\frac{b}{n+1} \quad \text{if} \quad nb > (n+1)a. \tag{25.6}$$

In particular, each player's request first decreases and then increases as the range (b–a) of the distribution increases. However, when the game is played over multiple rounds in a sequential fashion as in a laboratory setup, then the solution is much more complex. The first player in the sequence follows the Nash equilibrium pattern, that is, the number of tokens requested first decreases and then increases with ($b - a$), while for the other $n - 1$ players, the predicted request increases as ($b - a$) increases.

This game was created to analyze how uncertainty about the common resource's value, measured by the difference ($b - a$), affects subjects' behavior. When the value of the pot was known with certainty, Suleiman and Rapoport (1988) observed that, in general, subjects requested an equal split of tokens, ($b - a$)/n. As uncertainty on the value of ($b - a$) increased, individuals requested larger amounts above equal sharing. In all treatments, the Nash equilibrium prediction overestimates the actual requests, while the equal share prediction underestimates the actual requests. In addition, when the game was structured as a sequential move game, individuals' requests tended to decline in the order in which they were received, with the last individual requesting the least from the resource.

In general, common-pool resource experiments have replicated the result that individuals tend to over-consume the shared resource. A few experiments, pioneered by Hoffman and Spitzer (1982), have tried to test the validity and applicability of the Coase theorem in solving the problems caused by the presence of (positive or negative) externalities. The set-up represents cleverly the Coase theorem scenario. Two subjects jointly choose some activity. The activity generates positive externalities and positive utility for one subject, but generates negative externalities and disutility for the other. By flipping a coin, one subject is assigned the property rights and is, therefore, the one choosing the activity level and offering side payments. The experiment showed that indeed Coase's theorem works and subjects were able to reach the efficient level of production of the activity, even though side payments were not large enough to fully compensate for the externality generated. By adding a contest to earn the property right on the common activity, Hoffman and Spitzer (1985) observed more aggressive requests for side payments.

A relatively more recent avenue for solving the problems generated by negative externalities has been the use of market-based mechanisms, mostly auctions, in the context of goods for which property rights were not clearly defined or assigned. Since the 1990s, auctions have been used to allocate tradable pollution permits, broadcast spectrum bands and cell phone licenses, timber and even water for irrigation. For instance, in March 2001, an irrigation reduction auction was run in the State of Georgia to deal with a severe drought. Using tobacco settlement money, an auction-like process was run to pay farmers not to irrigate and non-tradable irrigation permits were issued. Several rounds of experiments, both in the laboratory and in the field, were conducted before March 2001 to work out the details of the proposed mechanism and to convince policy makers that the proposed auction would indeed have been a successful method for reducing water consumption. A rich set of experimental work (see Isaac and Holt 1999) has demonstrated that auctions successfully allocate resources, bypass wasteful rent-seeking (see section 5), assign the resources to high-value users and allow these users to discover their own valuations, are fast and fair and, when properly designed, generate high revenue for the government.

In conclusion, this literature confirms the inefficiency associated with common resources: their overuse. Overuse happens when individuals do not take into consideration the negative effects that their own consumption has on the amount of resources left for the use of others. The literature also confirms that shared governance of common resources may be successful in eliminating such inefficiency. Experimental work has provided strong support for the Coase theorem, in that agents do bargain to produce an efficient outcome, provided that an initial assignment of property rights has been established.

4   EXPERIMENTS ON POLITICAL ECONOMY

The majority of laboratory experiments in political science have been conducted by scholars schooled in rational-choice models of human behavior. Palfrey (2006), in *The Handbook of Political Economy*, offers an excellent survey of most experimental work done in the area during the preceding 30 years. He categorizes the published work into four different areas: committee decision-making, elections and candidates competition, information aggregation and committees, and voter turnout and participation games.

Fiorina and Plott (1978) conducted the first experiments on committee decision-making. Subjects were asked to make choices in a two-dimensional policy space, with outcomes determined by majority voting and payoffs depending on the values for each policy as induced in the laboratory. Fiorina and Plott studied the results of these decisions trying to assess who and which committee was indeed able to generate the preferred collective outcome. They also studied how committees' decision-making was sensitive to the particular procedure used in the voting process. Additional work by Plott and Levine (1977), Levine and Plott (1978), and Plott (1991) modified the general structure of this basic experiment by changing committee size, introducing agenda control or agenda-setting, adding or reducing the number of policy options, introducing the possibility of communication or by changing the voting rules.

The main results confirmed by all these experiments were: if the core[1] exists, then the committee will select an outcome within the core; if the core does not exist but the preference profile of the committee's members is close to having a core point, then the committee will select an outcome in the policy space close to that observed when the core existed. Interestingly, experiments on this topic have tested not a behavioral theory of how individuals make choices, but rather the theory of the core which describes the axiomatic properties of social choice.

The second area of experiments in political economy focuses on the existence of a Condorcet winner in competitive elections and on the Median Voter Theorem

(McKelvey and Ordeshook 1990). A Condorcet winner is the candidate who defeats all other candidates in pair-wise simple majority rule elections. The median voter theorem states that in a two-candidate election, the winning candidate will select a platform corresponding to the ideal platform of the median voter, provided that the voters have single peaked preferences[2] on the one-dimensional policy space. In a typical experiment, subjects play the role of candidate and voters, and the common setup is often provided by spatial competition models. The way information is transmitted and shared varies across experiments. When the competition among candidates is modeled as a one-dimensional choice (often as a decision location on a line), and voters are endowed with single-peaked preferences, then the outcome of the election is observed to converge to the Condorcet winner (McKelvey and Ordeshook 1982). This result has been shown to be robust even when information is not complete.

On the other hand, when multiple candidates are competing for a single position, experiments have been modeled as coordination games. In multicandidate elections, many voting Nash equilibria are possible. For instance, in a three-candidate election, in equilibrium each voter should vote only for one of two candidates, because it never pays to vote for a candidate for whom nobody else is voting. This clearly creates a coordination problem. Experimental work has helped identify the mechanisms that appear to facilitate coordination, such as polls, past election results or the outcomes of ballot positions (Forsythe et al. 1993, 1996).

The third area of experiments in political economy deals with the issue of how to aggregate information in committees or juries. In the typical model, a group of individuals must make a decision or choose a policy. The information available to the group is limited in the sense that the outcome from the chosen policy is unknown and depends on the realization of some state of the world. Each member of the group has some personal information about such realization. The problem is how to efficiently and rationally aggregate this imperfect information to reach an equilibrium decision.

The main paper in this area is by Guarnaschelli et al. (2000). In that article, the authors argue that Nash predictions may be misleading because voters in reality are not as sincere as the theory usually assumes, the determination of the Nash equilibrium requires complicated strategic reasoning and multiple applications of Bayes' rule and it involves mixed strategies. Guarnaschelli et al. instead use the prediction from the quantal response equilibrium (QRE) model (McKelvey and Palfrey 1995, 1998), which assumes that individuals behave strategically even though they may be imperfect maximizers so that choices may often not be perfect. The QRE model represents well data from jury models reproduced in experiments and replicated in the field. Guarnaschelli et al. applied, in particular, this model to the voting behavior of juries when its members must vote unanimously about a possible conviction. They designed an experiment isomorphic to the situation faced by a real jury and found that fewer innocent people were convicted if decisions were made by majority rule than by unanimity rule.

The final topic in the area of experiments in political economy is voter turnout. This line of research is based on the voter paradox (Downs 1957), which states that, given the very low probability that one voter will be decisive in a large election, it is rational for individuals not to vote at all, as the costs for voting outweigh the benefits. It is hard to reconcile this theoretical result with the reality of significant turnouts in large elections.

A large body of theoretical, empirical and experimental literature has been published to explain the paradox. In particular, theoretical work by Palfrey and Rosenthal (1983) and experimental research by Schram and Sonnemans (1996) has tried to explain the paradox as rational behavior. Palfrey and Rosenthal (1983) model the turnout problem as a participation game and find many situations in which the decision to participate is actually a Nash equilibrium strategy, so that zero turnout (as the paradox would predict) is not an equilibrium, even for games with high participation costs. Schram and Sonnemans (1996) developed an experiment to study the voting paradox in the laboratory, as it is difficult to analyze this issue using field data. In the experiment, subjects were assigned the role of voters or candidates, valuations for the outcome of the election were induced in the voters and subjects had to choose whether or not to vote. Schram and Sonnemans created two different scenarios for an election in the laboratory and compared the corresponding voter turnout rates under a winner-take-all rule versus proportional representation. They studied a two-party election with varying numbers of voting participants.

The main results can be summarized as: the Nash equilibrium does not predict well actual voter turnout; voting participation is higher in winner-take-all elections; participation is higher in groups of fixed size; participation increases with communication among the individuals and with repetition; and with different group sizes, relative turnout is higher in smaller groups of voters. These results have been confirmed by later experimental studies (Cason and Mui 2001; Grosser and Schram 2006; Levine and Palfrey 2007). In addition, these papers found that turnout may be affected by uncertainty about the size of the group and that turnout increases if subjects are informed about other participants' decisions. In conclusion, much of the recent work on voter turnout shows how experimental analysis is useful to better understand the issue, as traditional theory appears to be a poor predictor of actual voter turnout.

From this short summary of the most relevant experimental work in political economy, a general conclusion emerges that individuals do behave strategically in many different collective decision-making environments, such as committees, juries and political elections. Often surprisingly, many theoretical predictions have been confirmed in the laboratory and whenever the observations in laboratory have departed from the predictions, the results have given rise to the development of alternative theories.

5 EXPERIMENTS ON RENT-SEEKING AND LOBBYING

The term 'rent-seeking' is used to describe competition for government favors and it is also applied to any situation in which individuals spend resources in an attempt to acquire a prize. Examples of rent-seeking behavior include competition for monopoly power, for a political position, or for a government-granted license (for an up-to-date literature compendium on the topic, see Congleton et al. 2008a, 2008b). Contenders engage in lobbying and other costly activities to increase their chances of winning the prize and find it in their best interest to rent seek as long as the cost is less than the expected gain. With a large number of contenders, expenditure in rent-seeking activities may also be large and rent-seeking results in a net cost to society, even if it does produce some social benefits.

The concept of rent-seeking was introduced to the economics profession by Tullock (1967), even though the term 'rent-seeking' was used for the first time by Anne Krueger

(1974). In Tullock's basic model, contenders spend some effort x_i with $i = 1,\ldots, N$, to gain a prize of value V so that the expected private gain from the rent seeking activity is:

$$E\pi = \frac{x_i}{\sum_{j=1,\ldots,N} x_j} V - cx_i, \qquad (25.7)$$

where

$$\frac{x_i}{\sum_{j=1,\ldots,N} x_j},$$

the probability of winning the prize, is an increasing function of the amount of effort spent and cx_i is the total cost of the effort exerted. In this context, the Nash equilibrium amount of effort is given by:

$$x^* = \frac{N-1}{N^2} \frac{V}{c}. \qquad (25.8)$$

The total amount of effort exerted in society is $(N - 1/N)V$ and increases with the number of contenders.

Millner and Pratt (1989) were the first to conduct a laboratory test of the Tullock model and were then followed by the studies of Millner and Pratt (1991), Davis and Reilly (1998), and Potters et al. (1998), among others. In the basic experimental design, subjects were given the opportunity to buy lottery tickets to win a certain prize, with all purchasing information available in all rounds to all subjects. The main conclusions from the experiments were that: (1) subjects spent more than the Nash prediction, confirming over-dissipation of rent; (2) overspending in rent-seeking games increases the less risk adverse individuals are; (3) again subjects learn how to play as they gain experience; and (4) overspending decreases as the number of rounds in the experiments increases. Rent-seeking models and experiments have been used to study political lobbying (Hillman and Samet 1987), and research and development contests (Isaac and Reynolds 1988). Davis and Reilly (1998) designed a rent-seeking experiment to compare the revenue raised in a lottery with revenue raised by an auction in a rent seeking game.

Common to almost all the experiments is that the total expenditure realized in rent-seeking activities by the subjects exceed the theoretical predictions, and the rent was over-dissipated in most treatments.

6 CONCLUSIONS AND SOME COMMENTS

In this chapter we have shown how, over the years, laboratory experiments have expanded our economic knowledge of public choice topics. Because of experiments, we now know much more about why people contribute to public goods, or vote in elections. The majority of the evidence from the laboratory confirms that, contrary to the standard neoclassical assumption, individuals are not that rational, they often are unable to compute the full impact of their actions, they underestimate the true cost and consequences of their actions, and are affected in their decisions by the way choices are framed and by the social context.

A few warnings regarding experiments should be mentioned here. A common criticism is that the typical subject used in experiments is a college undergraduate student, mostly in economics or business, who may not be representative of the real world. Plott (1987), however, has shown that students' responses in the laboratory are not particularly different from the responses that we would get from other subject pools. Recently, Fréchette (2010) has compared the performance of students in the laboratory with that of professionals, or people working in an industry where the game is relevant and can be applied. His conclusions are that, overall, similar results can be found whether professionals or students in laboratory experiments are used as subjects in testing economic models. Experimental economics has also been extended to the field and the majority of the experiments described in this chapter have been replicated, reaching similar conclusions in naturally occurring situations with real persons. After all, the students in the laboratory are not that different from 'real' people; they indeed are real people.

Another criticism is that it may be difficult in the laboratory to control for all of the factors that may affect decisions and choices by subjects. The truth is that it is even more arduous to control for these factors in the naturally occurring world. In the laboratory, the experimenter sets the rules, fixes the institutions, induces preferences with appropriate rewarding schemes, and controls the amount of information and the way information is distributed and revealed to the subjects. All of these factors fall obviously beyond the researcher's control in the real world.

Finally, experimental economics in general, and in its application to public choice in particular, has benefitted from the growing field of behavioral economics, a relatively recent approach to economics built on other social science fields, such as psychology. Standard findings in psychology, suggesting that individuals are not always rational, make mistakes and are sensitive to incentives, have helped to better understand traditional issues in public choice. For instance, it is now well established that individuals are generous and, with the help of conclusions established by behavioral and experimental economists, researchers can now become creative in finding new strategies and ways to increase such generosity. For instance, it has been realized that individual giving to charities is greater if such giving is subsidized (by the government or other entities) with a matching grant rather than with an equivalent rebate (Eckel and Grossman 2008).

In conclusion, this chapter has summarized the different topics in public choice that have been studied in the laboratory and has discussed how the existing theoretical predictions fare when tested in environments that approximate reality.

NOTES

1. The core is a notion of equilibrium developed within cooperative game theory. It identifies the set of outcomes that are stable with respect to coalitional deviations. In particular, an outcome is in the core if there

does not exist some alternative feasible outcome that makes some coalition of individuals better off and that cannot be blocked by the larger group.
2. A peak in an individual's preferences is a point at which all neighboring points are lower. An individual has single-peaked preferences when his/her utility falls as the collective decision moves away from the most preferred outcome in any and all directions.

26 Evolutionary public choice
Uwe Cantner and Michael Wohlgemuth

1 EVOLUTIONARY ECONOMICS – AN INTRODUCTION

In mainstream economics as well as in mainstream public choice the neoclassical paradigm is clearly dominant. Almost all economics of politics nowadays applies the neoclassical model of rational choice to collective decision making (for example, Mueller 1993, p. 511).

One reason for the neoclassical paradigm's dominance over evolutionary approaches may be that the former can be much better described as a clearly defined core of basic assumptions, accepted puzzles and procedures to solve them. The neoclassical concept may be defined in one sentence such as: 'the combined assumptions of maximizing behavior, market equilibrium and stable preferences, used relentlessly and unflinchingly' (Becker 1976, p. 5). Evolutionary approaches are perhaps best defined as 'dynamics first' which implies the more or less relentless rejection of Becker's assumptions. Maximizing representative agents are rejected in favor of boundedly rational individuals who differ in their knowledge, skills, expectations, practices and learning heuristics. The expectations and behavior of some individuals or populations can even be wholly mistaken. Static equilibrium is rejected in favor of process analysis of systems characterized by endogenous change based on the permanent creation of novelty, the competitive selection and the (often path-dependent) learning (learning from own experience) and imitation (learning from others) of potential problem solutions. And with the emergence of novelty, endogenous change and interactive learning, stable preferences become a much more critical assumption that can no longer serve as an adequate starting point in most cases (see Cantner and Hanusch 2002 or Witt 2008 for surveys of evolutionary economics).

Witt (2008, p. 67) underscores the distinction between evolutionary models and the pure neoclassical logic of choice when he states: 'The question in evolutionary economics is therefore not how, under varying conditions, economic resources are optimally allocated in equilibrium given the state of individual preferences, technology, and institutional conditions. The questions are instead why and how knowledge, preferences, technology, and institutions change in historical perspective.' Such questions, obviously, are not limited to the economic realm. Evolutionary economics, by stressing the transformation of social systems from within, driven by individuals' creativity, learning and discovery, is applicable to all aspects of social life, including the political.

However, evolutionary *economists* concentrate mainly on the policy implications derived from their distinctive view of *market* processes (normative conclusions). What is comparatively rare is an evolutionary analysis of political processes (positive analysis). There are some good excuses for evolutionary economists' reluctance to transfer their economic concepts to political phenomena. Even if the overall logic of evolutionary processes can be applied to political competition, fundamental differences between political and economic rivalry, selection, and learning forbid simplistic transfers. But by highlighting these differences and their effects, evolutionary approaches can provide original contributions to a comparative analysis of political institutions, based on issues and criteria that easily escape the narrow confines of the neoclassical economic model (Wohlgemuth 2002a).

Evolutionary political economy is older than public choice theory and even evolutionary biology. In fact, much of Darwin's theory of evolution was inspired by classical political economists such as David Hume and Adam Smith (see Hayek 1979, p. 154). Hence, evolutionary political economy is a historical fact; the question remains if there is an evolutionary *new* political economy that could rival modern public choice. To the extent that evolutionary economics is not merely a metaphorical re-importation from biology, but a general theory of endogenous change based on the generation of variety and competitive selection, of intentional problem-solving conjectures and unintended consequences, it should be applicable to all sorts of interactive processes in society – including politics. Political applications may include the creation of and change in political opinions, the emergence and selection of solutions to political problems, the changing constraints on the knowledge and information available to political actors or the formation, dissemination, and exploitation of new information in the political process. Evolutionary economics can make substantial contributions to political economy on several levels (Witt 2003, p. 78):

(a) What policy-makers do (positive analysis).
(b) What policy-makers could (not) do (the 'art' of policy-making).
(c) What policy-makers ought to do (normative analysis).

So far, evolutionary economics has mostly delivered on levels (b) and (c). Still, as we wish to demonstrate in this chapter, evolutionary approaches to politics can draw on many sources – some of them classical, others quite recent – that promise to be fruitful for the further development of public choice.

2 SCHUMPETER, OR: HOW PUBLIC CHOICE DISCARDED ITS EVOLUTIONARY BEGINNINGS

Joseph Schumpeter is often regarded as a pioneer, if not founder, not only of evolutionary economics but also of public choice theory.[1] Looking back at the development of mainstream public choice and Schumpeter's own views both on democracy and static equilibrium analysis, this seems rather odd.[2] Already Downs (1957, p. 29, fn. 11), in probably the most seminal contribution to public choice theory, states: 'Schumpeter's profound analysis of democracy forms the inspiration and foundation of our whole thesis, and our debt and gratitude to him are great indeed.' In the whole thesis, however, Schumpeter is mentioned only twice with the same quote describing his general approach, which regards the social functions of politics as incidental by-products of the competitive struggle for power and office. Schumpeter's core assertions on irrationality in politics and the vital role of political leadership are neither mentioned nor accepted.[3]

To be sure, Schumpeter and mainstream public choice share the same antagonists: those who assume that people act for the common good once they enter the realm of democratic decision making. Also, public choice scholars would have no problem in endorsing Schumpeter's ([1942] 1987, p. 269) definition of democracy as a method rather than an ideal: 'the democratic method is that institutional arrangement for arriving at political decisions in which individuals acquire the power to decide by means of a competitive struggle for the people's vote'. Very different from a mainstream public choice perspective, however, this 'competitive struggle' is driven by political leaders instead of deference to given voter distributions (ibid., p. 269). By attaching high standards of rationality to political actors, by treating political issues and preferences as given and by modeling political competition as a state in which politicians passively adapt to any given majority will, much of public choice remains ironically close to rationalistic and idealistic traditions which linked democracy to given expressions of a 'volonté générale' (Wohlgemuth 2005). Two major aspects distinguish a Schumpeterian theory of democracy most clearly from the classical doctrine *and* from the modern neoclassical model: (1) political leadership and (2) irrationality in politics.

2.1 Political Leadership

In Downsian spatial voting models (but also Chicago-style efficient political markets, Arrowian social choice, or most of contractarian constitutional economics), collectives act almost exclusively through politicians who take citizens' preferences as *given*. And just as in the neoclassical model of 'perfect' competition, prices and homogeneous goods are given and not created in the competitive process, so are preference distributions and alternatives (the 'issue space') in most economics of politics. In both cases, entrepreneurship and the introduction of 'new combinations' have no room. By strictly adhering to the neoclassical logic of choice, public choice is barred from recognizing the Schumpeterian view that politicians act as entrepreneurs who create and change voters' preferences and opinions, or introduce new political products and forms of organization. Voter preferences, Schumpeter ([1942] 1987, p. 282) writes, 'are not the ultimate data of the process that produces government'. The electorate's choice 'does not flow from its own initiative but is being shaped, and the shaping of it is an essential part of the democratic process'. Hence, the 'psycho-technics of party management and party advertising, slogans and marching tunes, are not mere accessories. They are of the essence of politics. So is the political boss' (ibid., p. 283).

Exactly these essential parts of the democratic process are hardly accepted even as accessories in spatial voting models which are clearly dominated by the view of politicians who take voter preferences as given and imperative. Contrast this again with Schumpeter's view that political leadership has 'only a distant relation, if any, with seeing that the will of the people is carried out.... Precisely in the best instances, the people are presented with results they never thought of and would not have approved in advance' (ibid., p. 278). Exactly these instances of political entrepreneurship and innovation can, by their very nature, not be accounted for in demand-driven equilibrium theories of the economics of politics.

2.2 Irrationality in Politics

If ever there was a common 'hard core' of the entire public choice paradigm, it is the assumption of rational conduct by all actors involved. And if ever there was a 'revolutionary' claim of public choice, it is to break with the notion of 'bifurcated man' who, as soon as he enters the political field, would display standards of behavior that differ from those she uses in market transactions. After all, that's what the economics of politics is all about: the universal application of the basic behavioral assumptions of *Homo economicus* (for example, Buchanan 1972; Downs 1957, pp. 4ff; Mueller 2003, pp. 1–2).

Schumpeter ([1942] 1987, p. 262) in fact denies this. He expects a great deal of utter irrationality as a consequence of human nature and permissive circumstances, for example, when he argues that 'the typical citizen drops to a lower level of mental performance as soon as he enters the political field. He argues and analyzes in a way he would readily recognize as infantile within the sphere of his real interests. He becomes a primitive again'. Lack of mental effort, of rational calculation and of consistent reasoning not only describe Schumpeter's citizen-voter who, as a 'member of an unworkable committee, the committee of the whole nation' (ibid., p. 261), has no impact on the outcomes of collective decision-making. Lower levels of mental performance and pathologies of irrational crowd-behavior even characterize Schumpeter's professional politicians, only in a somewhat milder form (ibid., p. 257).

It is thus obvious that Schumpeter did not subscribe to rationality assumptions as usually applied in modern economic analysis. What is more, he does not apply the *same* rationality assumptions in explaining political and economic phenomena but insists that '(t)here is no such thing as a universal pattern of rationality' (ibid., p. 258, fn. 10). Whereas today's standard economic approach is to deduce different actions only as consequences of different cost–benefit ratios or different objective restraints on action, but never to change the rationality assumptions in the process, Schumpeter does just that.

As argued elsewhere (Kirchgässner 2002; Wohlgemuth 2005; Schnellenbach 2007), there are good reasons why a Schumpeterian argumentation – with its reliance on a crude sociology of the masses and an elitist call for 'leadership' (much in vogue in the 1940s) – has not influenced modern public choice. However, there are also good reasons why Schumpeter's themes, such as 'Human nature in politics' (Schumpeter [1942] 1987, p. 256) as a consequence of bounded rationality in low-stake decision environments and the vital role of political entrepreneurship, should be dealt with in a modern (evolutionary) assessment of the political process.

Many political scientists and some public choice scholars have meanwhile worked on a Schumpeterian agenda of political economy: (1) Non-*Homo economicus* determinants, especially of voter behavior, have been endorsed by scholars who accept bounded rationality, sociological forces and even moral dimensions as relevant for voting behavior under the special conditions of low-cost decisions.[4] (2) Non-adaptive behavior of political competitors has also been recognized by a number of authors who discuss the art of political manipulation, agenda-setting, opinion leadership, decision framing, political innovation and reform and other aspects of supply-side political activity.[5] We now turn to the role of political entrepreneurship in relation to the process of political opinion formation, innovation and reform.

3 OPINION FORMATION, POLITICAL ENTREPRENEURSHIP AND POLITICAL INNOVATION

Discussing the pattern of opinion formation and political innovation we take a dynamic view of the modern political system. We consider this dynamics to be characterized by various political opinions to coexist, the one or the other to dominate, some stability therein, but also changes in political opinions over time.

The issues of 'political innovation' and 'political entrepreneurship' are obviously related to 'bounded rationality'. If all voters were in fact fully informed about all 'given' political alternatives and able to make complete rational use of that knowledge, and if political competition was 'perfect', there would be no room for political leadership. Vote-maximizing parties would simply be passive 'vote takers' in a given 'issue space' in exactly the same way as profit-maximizing firms would be 'price-takers' in a space of 'given goods'.

Cognitive science and experimental psychology have meanwhile substantiated much of what Schumpeter ([1942] 1987, pp. 256, 262) took for granted when he, for example, suspected that the voter's 'power of observation and interpretation of facts, and his ability to draw, clearly and promptly, rational inferences' are very limited, that his 'thinking becomes associative and affective' and would 'tend to yield to extra-rational or irrational prejudice and impulse'. We cannot here discuss the manifold details of the experimental evidence and their often controversial interpretations.[6] But the overall evidence contradicting Bayesian standards of rational behavior and learning is quite impressive.[7]

It has rightly been argued that one has to be careful in drawing inferences from observing anonymous decisions of isolated individuals playing experimental games in which errors are costless (for example, Smith 1985; Wittman 1995). But the peculiarities of *voters'* decisions are very well reproduced by experiments with costless errors, anonymous choice, and a lack of competitive market selection that would yield high-powered incentives to engage in information search and a rational sifting of alternatives. Also 'framing' theories are just another way to express the major element of Schumpeter's ([1942] 1987, p. 263) theory of democracy, which holds that political entrepreneurs 'are able to fashion, and, within very wide limits, even to create the will of the people'. In modern language: if individuals in situations such as those produced by experiments and general elections, are susceptible to anomalies, framing and manipulations of contexts, there will be political (mis-)leaders who know the 'art of manipulation' (Riker 1986) and use it.

This view of voters and of the possibilities for politicians to attract or manipulate them, allows thinking more carefully about the processes of opinion formation, the stability and coexistence of different opinions, as well as the introduction and dissemination of new opinions into a political system.

3.1 Formation, Stability and Coexistence of Political Opinions

Not all political leadership need be manipulative. Much will be simply formative in a rather innocent way. An important case where political 'leadership' and 'framing' in a neutral meaning are active and, in fact, indispensable, is the formation of public opinion. Just as goods (the objects of interactive price-formation) are not simply 'given' in an evolutionary market process, political issues (the objects of interactive opinion-formation) are not given in the political process. Issues have to be discovered or created and then pushed onto the agenda. This activity entails costs and rewards skills since the public's attention is fundamentally scarce and ephemeral; it cannot deal with many issues at a time (Zaller 1992; Witt 1996). As a consequence, in modern, complex political systems, 'attention' becomes a scarce resource that has not yet been well accounted for in neoclassical public choice. The evolution of (objects of) public opinion can be described much in terms of product life cycles. And herein, like competition on open markets, the competition of ideas and opinions is driven by entrepreneurs. We give a few examples:

As Sunstein (1996) shows, many political movements owe attention to their causes – often associated with a surprisingly strong and sudden change in the general public's attitudes – to 'norm entrepreneurs' who deliberately aim at inducing a swing in opinions and values. The emergence of environmental regulation, the expansion of environmental organizations, the use of new instruments in environmental policy and proactive business strategies are explained by Anderson (1997) or Albrecht (2002) as consequences of 'issue entrepreneurship'. Among the most prominent of the 'issue entrepreneurs' in this process are parties, interest groups, intellectuals, judges and the media.[8] Using evolutionary game theory, Arce (2001) shows how 'leading by example' can overcome underprovision and coordination problems inherent in the provision of international public goods. In Kuran's theory of preference falsification and preference change, an important role is attributed to 'activists' with 'extraordinarily great expressive needs' (Kuran 1995, p. 49) who dare formulate dissenting views and introduce new issues even in face of an apparently hostile or indifferent public. In Boulding's (1956) chapter titled the 'Sociology of knowledge', changes in private and public 'images' or *Weltanschauungen* come about 'through the impact on society of unusually creative, charismatic, or prophetic individuals'; as 'bearers of viable mutant images' – they are 'the true entrepreneurs of society' (ibid., pp. 75–6). The political economy of transformation (see Roland 2002) in particular emphasizes the role of political entrepreneurship since during the process of transition 'normal politics' (given actors playing a conventional political game over established issues under fixed constraints) cannot be assumed.[9]

In all of these cases, political entrepreneurs take advantage of the fact that on many issues no strong and articulated opinions (preferences and theories[10]) exist in the first place. The stock of views and knowledge about some issues is devalued over time and new problems arise, which often cannot be assessed by reverting to experience or ideological shortcuts. With the increasing complexity of political activities and environments there are more issues for which there is no public opinion ready at hand, no 'issue space' exists and citizens have no idea where to position themselves. With the expanding range of political and legal issues, activities and alternative public opinions must become ever more selective (Witt 1996).

Hence, an issue's 'career' usually starts with a latent phase, during which only a chosen few are affected by, or intrinsically interested in, a specific political problem, and therefore are aware of and discuss the issue. At that point it cannot yet be assumed that politicians, the media, and not least 'the man in the street' are willing or able to 'take issue'. Some of the latent issues, however, succeed in attracting attention after political entrepreneurs (professional politicians or private agitators) have successfully invested in time, resources and personal contacts.[11]

With a bit of luck and skills these entrepreneurs are successful in seeing that the issue is taken up by larger 'retailers' who are used to dealing with changing opinions in the process of transforming them into political demands and, in the end, into laws and regulations. At this stage, the issue becomes part of 'normal politics': an 'issue space' is created, the media and citizens can take positions, discuss its pros and cons, and expect that others are familiar with the major positions of the contending camps. Often, but not always, the discussion produces a generally accepted point of view, a public opinion that is characterized by a sufficiently large overlap of individuals' viewpoints. Only then does public opinion 'rule' within more or less local communication networks by means of fear of isolation (Noelle-Neumann 1993), preference falsification (Kuran 1995), or various dynamic feedback-mechanisms and network externalities. The latter when working on a global scale with global feedback effects provide for a certain (temporary) stability of the dominant public opinion.[12] With feedback effects working locally – since they are based on social or spatial distances – different public opinions can coexist in a population.[13]

Only after a global or local stability of political opinions has emerged, the time for adherents of the current common understanding has come to transform the issue into the political production of platforms, laws, and regulations. It is at this decision-making and implementation stage, when most of the traditional public choice themes that take issues and interests as 'given' become relevant: bargaining, voting rules, committees, veto-players, coalition-formation, bureaucracy, and so on.

Slembeck (1997, 2003) combines many of the above-mentioned processes of issue- and opinion-formation in a 'cognitive-evolutionary approach to policy-making'.[14] It starts with individuals who hold different 'regulative beliefs', which, by focusing their attention on learned cognitive patterns, lead to selective perceptions and biased interpretations of political information. The rejection of the assumption of given and stable preferences creates room for political learning, persuasion and manipulation. Policy-making can now be analyzed as a path-dependent process of mobilizing attention to different political issues, trials and failures. Cognitive and institutional 'filters' describe the selective environment that constrains the political actors' ability to mobilize political opinion, to transform new problem solutions into policies and implement those policies. Slembeck shows that solutions to political problems are not just out there to be chosen collectively; problems first have to be perceived; discontent has to be given a political voice, an operational definition and a place on the public agenda. As a consequence of limited resources for mobilization, many (perhaps most) individually perceived political problems will never be solved because they do not return 'hits' on the public's radar screen.

3.2 Political Innovation Leading to Reform and Revolution

We turn now to the issue of political innovations and political reforms or even political revolutions. The difference between reform and revolution is a matter of degree: the former we consider being a new political combination whereas the latter requires totally new opinions to be generated or latent opinions (especially when repressed) to be activated, then disseminating into the political system and taking over the majority. For reforming or revolutionary dynamics we first discuss the obstacles political entrepreneurs confront in entering the political scene with new ideas and complete this by briefly analyzing the process of dissemination of the new idea or opinion until it becomes dominant.

Political actors, especially those in government, are in a substantially different position compared to entrepreneurs in an open market setting. In politics, entrepreneurs face many 'barriers to entry'. These become most evident if one models democratic competition not as analogous to an ongoing market process but to a 'franchise-bidding for natural monopoly' scheme.[15] The evolutionary potential of political competition is restricted in two major respects: (1) in one jurisdiction or 'natural' monopoly of government, there is only one set of political problem solutions being tested at a time; hence political evolution is basically limited to learning from consecutive trials and errors (Vanberg 1993b); (2) the forward-pushing and variety-creating entry of political innovators is severely hampered by barriers to the field of policy production.

The first restriction will be discussed below as a major evolutionary argument in favor of *inter*-jurisdictional competition. The second aspect is now discussed briefly. From an evolutionary perspective, the quality of competitive market processes depends much more on the dynamics of entry and exit of alternative suppliers than on the sheer number of existing firms. In some respects, this also holds for political competition. The sheer number of political actors (for example, parties in parliament) does not by itself create evolutionary potential. What is far more important is the ability of an opposition to enter the political arena with alternative views and proposals and to present a credible challenge to the incumbent. The contestability of the political 'market' is rather weak in comparison to typical economic markets. Within the field of party politics, new 'firms' rarely appear and, even among the few established parties, one party can dominate policy production for a considerable time.

One obvious reason relates to differences in award criteria. If a business firm gains, say, 20 percent, or as a newcomer some 4 percent market share, this can often be called a success. By contrast, only with a combined 'market share' of over 50 percent of the seats in parliament can a group of political entrepreneurs enact new policies. Still, a certain amount of protection of incumbents (for example, incumbency periods of several years or representation thresholds for small parties) helps secure governability and the stabilization of citizens' expectations. Also, incumbency protection may enhance political entrepreneurs' propensity to invest in structural reforms, which often create 'payoffs' in terms of economic performance (and votes) only in the long-run, while in the short run – like all investments – requiring sacrifices. In such situations, long-term incumbency periods or plurality voting schemes create a more reliable power base and a longer time-horizon, which may nourish incumbents' hopes of eventually profiting from their investments in political innovations.[16]

Barriers to entry provide opportunities to invest. They ensure this by reducing incentives to oust incompetent cabinets and to reflect changing voter opinions. Hence, there is a fundamental trade-off between (a) institutional conditions that support reliable, consistent and sustainable policies and (b) political rules of the game that would support more political novelties or adaptations to new views and conditions (Wohlgemuth 2000). Trade-offs such as these can be regarded as a special case of the general problem of balancing variability and stability in an effort of finding, as Loasby (2000, p. 307) puts it, 'variation within a stable ambience'.[17]

Still, the case of *political* innovation remains special. Collective decision-making procedures can endure much less variation than market processes, which are able to expose an amazing number of alternatives to ongoing social selection processes without putting the stability of the system at risk. More essentially, innovation is a much more ambivalent notion in the realm of politics than in the realm of economics. Economists tend to agree that the permanent creation of new products and processes is a necessary element of prosperity and progress. In spite of losses of 'old economies', innovation-driven economic development is commonly regarded as a 'positive-sum game'. In evolutionary terms, innovations create the institutional variety and complexity needed to support a society's problem-solving capacity. Similar links between new governments, laws, or regulations and cherished social values, such as progress, development or enhanced problem solving capacity, cannot be taken for granted.

The basic reason is to be found in the fundamental differences between political and economic selection environments. In competitive markets, novelty creates additional variety and thus expands the pool of alternatives which can but do not have to be chosen. In politics most innovations are strict substitutes: the new government, law, and policy takes effect by replacing the old. Whether these novelties are regarded as advantageous by their users cannot be derived from a test of parallel use and voluntary selection. New policies remain subject to monopolistic provision and forced consumption; and because of strong indivisibilities in production and their redistributive intentions or effects, any new political combination (reform) typically produces winners and losers, without, however, providing reassurance that the 'creative destruction' of old policies is of a positive-sum type (Wohlgemuth 2003; Wegner 2008).

Empirical studies of political reforms mostly find that bold political innovations and thus instances of 'heroic' Schumpeterian political entrepreneurship are rare.[18] This observation can be praised as political stability or deplored as political sclerosis. Whatever the normative interpretation is, different degrees of stability or sclerosis, of opportunity or leeway for political change, can be explained by various factors. A first one refers to formal or informal institutions such as the number of 'veto players' as defined by Tsebelis (2002). The more individuals, groups or organizations that are given the formal right or informal power to oppose change, the more likely the status quo is to prevail. In fact, one may also measure the success of charismatic political entrepreneurs by their ability to mobilize *opposition* to change. The number of veto-players in turn depends on the constitutional structure of checks and balances: proportional representation, direct democracy or decentralization (for example, federalism) may increase the number of veto-players – the latter two may, however, also help to encourage political experimentation and the chances of political entrepreneurs to challenge the status quo (see Schnellenbach 2007 and section 4.3 of this chapter).[19]

A second factor of stability is related to the dynamic feedback loops of political opinion formation, as discussed in 3.1. In view of this stability in political opinions the question is how it can be overcome. The basic problem here is 'that agreements are typically harder to change than individual decisions' (Arrow 1974, p. 28). Part of the explanation lies in the fact that commonly held opinions do show a certain kind of stability. The externalities-driven self-enforcing effect exerts powerful pressure to conform so that an overall stability or rigidity of the systems is to be observed. If the prevailing opinion is 'objectively' superior to a new alternative, then that is for the good. If not, then the rigidity of the systems blocks the new opinion from invading, or, as Arrow (1974, p. 28) puts it: 'It may be really true that social agreements ultimately serve as obstacles to the achievement of desired values, even values desired by all or by many.'

Discussing political reform or revolutions thus requires finding an answer as to how these rigidities can be overcome. The mechanisms to be discussed focus on two different enabling factors. The first one hints at events that rather quickly cause an appropriate number of actors to switch from a ruling opinion to a new and alternative opinion – an exogenous shock. The number of changing agents has only to be large enough to reduce the self-enforced benefit of the ruling opinion and to increase the self-enforced benefit of the new one so that the latter is just larger than the former. Whenever a critical level is passed a self-enforcing mechanism for the new opinion sets in; and clear dominance will be observed eventually.[20] In this respect, Boyer and Orlean (1992) refer to a 'general collapse which indirectly destroys the existing structure of conventions. For example, the two World Wars turned out to be social laboratories for the emergence of new conventions and norms' (Boyer and Orlean 1992, p. 170).[21]

The major problem with these approaches to understanding political change lies in the fact that it is not clear how the collective action required to change a ruling opinion comes into effect. A second mechanism, taking this criticism into account, focuses on the social structures and attempts to identify the substructures which permit the invasion of a new opinion more easily. When that happens, again a process of self-enforcement will lead to the dominance of the new opinion. Boyer and Orlean (1992), Ianni and Corradi (2002) as well as Wu and Huberman (2008) look at social structures in the sense of subgroups (socially or geographically) and their connectedness. Interactions between actors are restricted to these subgroups – which in Wu and Huberman (2008) are the core actors or political entrepreneurs.[22] The greater is the degree of localization of a new opinion, the more numerous are the possibilities for its diffusion. Due to the existence of subgroups, the degree of self-enforcement of opinions gets reduced and a new (and, in terms of benefit for the first follower, superior) opinion can much more easily penetrate. Hence a new opinion has to invade only the population locally and then by a self-enforcing dynamics to establish itself. This dynamic, however, is quite slow, implying an equally sluggish, rather 'piecemeal' change or reform.[23]

To summarize, modern evolutionary approaches to public choice both justify and qualify Schumpeter's claim of 'leadership' as a necessary attribute of collective action. If political entrepreneurship were to be limited to heroic acts of charismatic reformers who push through innovative policies against all odds (such as veto-players or public opinion), such 'leadership' would be both rare and potentially dangerous. In addition it would defy attempts to integrate the political entrepreneur into a *general* theory of the political process. We would rather be able to find, applaud, and model the 'political arbitrageur' (Schnellenbach 2007), whose 'alertness' enables him or her to identify opportunities to catch votes by initializing or discovering swings of opinion earlier than his/her rivals.[24] As soon as the assumption of 'given preferences' whose distribution over a 'given issue-space' is known and 'given' to all political actors is (with ample empirical justification) discarded, the 'political entrepreneur' becomes vital. He or she now becomes a necessary explanatory factor for any (evolutionary) theory that tries to explain how issues are created, how scarce attention is being directed to them, how preferences and theories are being changed, how collectives can learn and adapt to news, and so forth.

4 POLITICAL COMPETITION AS A CREATIVE DISCOVERY PROCEDURE

Neoclassical economics and public choice traditionally model the market and politics as a state of equilibrium resulting from a 'procedure for passing from a set of known individual tastes to a pattern of social decision-making' (Arrow 1951, p. 2). This view stands in contrast to Hayek's ([1968] 1978, p. 179) evolutionary understanding of competition as a procedure for the creation, discovery and dissemination of such opinions (preferences and theories), information and abilities 'as, without resort to it, would not be known to anyone, or at least would not be utilized'. Hayek's (1960, pp. 108f) view that democracy is 'above all, a process of forming opinion' and that it is 'in its dynamic, rather than in its static, aspects that the value of democracy proves itself' has invited some scholars close to the public choice enterprise to view political competition also as a 'discovery procedure' and look at its 'dynamic aspects'.[25]

4.1 Democracy as a Discovery Process

These claims rely on three propositions, all of which differ from a neoclassical public choice perspective (Wohlgemuth 2002a, p. 230): (1) political preferences and opinions are based on fallible conjectures and theories; (2) democratic opinion-formation results from an open-ended process of interactive learning and discovery; (3) the important element in this process is not the supremacy, but the contestability of majority opinions. The first two propositions and their use in evolutionary accounts of the political process have already been dealt with above. As we tried to show, the 'immaculate conception of the indifference curve' is a major barrier to an understanding of democracy as an opinion-building process, where 'by far and away the greater number of human preferences are learned, again by means of a mutation-selection process' (Boulding 1970, pp. 118f). It is only under these premises that the meaning of democracy as a knowledge-creating process can be established.

Evolutionary economics regards heterogeneity and variability of products or preferences not as imperfections, but as elementary preconditions of social development. The same is true for an evolutionary economics of democracy. It is not about the most comprehensive, consistent and permanent rule of given majority preferences. It is about the chances of minorities to contest and, perchance, to change majority opinions and policies (Hayek 1960, p. 109). In a straightforward critique of Arrow (1951), Buchanan (1954a, p. 119) argued that the majority principle would be a useful instrument of political control and knowledge-creation, only if cycling did in fact occur: 'It serves to insure that competing alternatives may be experimentally and provisionally adopted, and replaced by new compromise alternatives approved by a majority group of ever changing composition. This is the democratic choice process, whatever may be the consequences for welfare economics.'[26]

The fact that new opinions necessarily emerge in the minds of only a few individuals stresses the importance of entry opportunities for minority views. This entails more than just voting rights. It requires extended spheres of private autonomy and freedom to act, which allow groups and individuals to pursue different aims and to test different practices at the same time, as long as they do not violate the freedom of others to do so as well. No lesser task than the growth of civilization or 'cultural evolution' depends on this, because:

> The conception that the efforts of all should be directed by the opinion of a majority or that society is better according as it conforms more to the standards of the majority is in fact a reversal of the principle by which civilization has grown . . . it is always from a minority acting in ways different from what the majority would prescribe that the majority in the end learns to do better. (Hayek 1960, p. 110)

Hayek has not contributed much more to an evolutionary theory of democracy. But he, like Schumpeter and a few modern public choice scholars, offered important hints as to how evolutionary issues such as the entrepreneurial creation of variety, competitive selection and the endogenous creation and dissemination of knowledge that goes with it, might also be applied to politics.

4.2 Evolutionary Virtues of Political Competition

'Comparative institutional analysis' (Demsetz 1969; Aoki 2001) provides theoretical arguments and empirical findings for the superiority of political competition (democratic, federal, open systems) under the rule of law to 'discover' and propagate 'better' policies and institutions than alternative systems that rely on political monopoly, centralization or isolationism and have weak constitutional safeguards.[27] Static neoclassical public choice theory, by assuming citizens' preferences as given and known, can model both: that democratic failure is a myth (Wittman 1995) in a world near to 'perfect' political competition or that the rational voter is a myth and that 'democracies choose bad policies' (Caplan 2007). Under equally static and heroic assumptions both 'efficient democracy' and even 'efficient rent-seeking' (Becker 1958) can be modeled with the same basic neoclassical methodological tool-kit as 'Leviathan' and 'the anatomy of policy failure' (for example, Mitchell and Simmons 1994).[28]

Evolutionary economists (and Austrian economists, even more so) typically are more inclined towards the 'policy failure' results of their analyses – especially when comparing the political process to the innovative, evolutionary market process (Pelikan 2003; see also section 3 of this chapter). At the same time, an evolutionary analysis of political competition compared to its realistic alternatives (autocracy, centralization, protectionism) provides specific arguments for political competition that are not captured by equilibrium theories which assume anything relevant as being given. In a democracy, rivalry between incumbents and opposition candidates is institutionalized and routinized. This creates stronger incentives for more actors to communicate competing opinions, critique existing policies and propose alternatives. Politicians are more readily pressed to explain and justify their actions in front of the general public. But citizens, too, the inconsequential nature of their individual vote notwithstanding, have more occasions and stronger incentives to participate in opinion-building processes. In addition, the democratic struggle for power forces rival parties and candidates, but also rival interest groups and the media, to broadcast dissent and offer alternatives in order to be successful. Disagreement furnishes the occasion for new information search (Huckfeldt and Sprague 1995); thus, dissenting views tend to sharpen the cognitive component of individually held opinions. Finally, opportunities for open dissent reduce 'fundamental attribution errors' (Kuran

1995, pp. 81ff), which occur when individuals falsely conclude from the lack of open opposition that there must be ample support for the status quo, and adjust their public positions accordingly to minimize the risk of ostracism. Finally, in open societies the dissemination of information and opinions is faster and more encompassing since it can make use of 'weak ties' in communication networks (Granovetter 1973; Wohlgemuth 2002b).

Competition between political opinions and alternatives, like competition as a discovery procedure in general, is justified primarily on the grounds that we do not know in advance what opinions and alternatives exist, nor the conditions under which various policies will be considered to be 'right' or 'acceptable' by those who have to live under them. Thus, very much like Hayek's ([1968] 1978, p. 179) advocacy of the freedom to compete ('if anyone really knew all about what economic theory calls the *data*, competition would indeed be a very wasteful method of securing adjustment to these data') one could state: if anyone knew all about political opinions and opportunities, which most of the economics of politics treats as data ('given preferences, given issue-space'), democracy would be a rather wasteful political institution and a government by elite consent possibly preferable. From an evolutionary-liberal position, our lack of knowledge and hence the high probability of mistaken perceptions and theories does not represent the problem. On the contrary, it provides the main justification for political competition.

4.3 Additional Forms of Political Competition

Evolutionary arguments support even more the idea of supplementing representative democracy with direct democracy and inter-jurisdictional competition. General elections do not *continuously* signal citizens' opinions on *particular* policies. They are capable only of voicing bold aggregate opinions on bundles of promises made by parties and candidates – and thus change the relative political power positions of those political actors only every four or five years. In this direct democracy and inter-jurisdictional competition differ from purely representative democracy. By focusing on specific acts of legislation, referendums and popular initiatives communicate political preferences much more concretely. Even more importantly: they provoke political opinion formation as a result of deliberation focused on concrete alternatives, thus leading to the creation and social use of political skills and knowledge in society.[29]

Inter-jurisdictional competition ('exit') also expresses popular discontent, albeit more indirectly. Compared to voting for representatives, exit entails the individual choice of rules instead of a collective choice of rulers (Wohlgemuth 2008). It is based on individuals' comparative appraisals of the net benefits of combining their mobile resources with various existing political infrastructures in alternative jurisdictions. Using exit, individuals can free themselves (to some extent) from forced consumption of political goods and communicate the results of their comparative institutional analysis via personal decisions. As an ongoing selection mechanism, exit is therefore much more likely to provide political analogues to evolutionary market competition and to the system of relative prices as devices for the discovery and use of local knowledge. Inter-jurisdictional competition constrains the monopoly power of governments and enables citizens actively to choose between concrete sets of political alternatives; it introduces a politically effective form of parallel, rather than of consecutive, innovation and learning from real-life experiences (Vanberg 1993b, p. 15).

Again, neoclassical accounts of inter-jurisdictional competition can produce both: welfare-enhancing effects (following the seminal contribution by Tiebout 1956) or welfare-destroying effects (following the tradition of Musgrave 1959). Whether a 'race to the top' or 'a race to the bottom' is more likely to emerge depends critically on initial assumptions about the political status quo. Starting from the assumption of the state as the ideal provider of public goods, any change triggered by competitive pressures is likely to lead 'downhill'. Starting from a 'Leviathan' model of political misuse of its monopoly, exit and 'yardstick competition' is very likely to make citizens better off.

Compared to these 'pure' theories that treat both political preferences, and the consequences of (given) alternative policies as given and known, evolutionary theories would regard political opinions and political problem-solutions as fallible 'hypotheses'. Under these assumptions, more realistic arguments can be put forward – mostly in favor of open borders, decentralization and inter-jurisdictional variety and mobility. Evolutionary political economy tends to raise different doubts about harmonization and centralization, for example, in the European Union or federal states. Issues such as 'experimentation', 'discovery', 'correction of errors' (or limitation of the scale of errors), 'learning', 'reversibility' are standard currency for evolutionary thinkers. They do not devaluate standard economic issues such as 'efficiency', 'allocation', or 'incentives'. But they add important aspects that deserve attention in positive analysis and normative advice.[30]

5 POLICY IN AN EVOLUTIONARY CONTEXT

Looking at policy-making in an evolutionary context we switch the perspective of analysis. Because of 'the open-ended character of evolutionary processes, their results are not necessarily "good", "best" or "optimal" in any meaningful sense and can even be disastrous' (Schubert 2009, p. 22). Consequently, there may be room for policy intervention to be explored. However, one has to be aware that in an evolutionary context the normative foundations of policy conduct, the objectives of policy-makers and the procedures and means to pursue goals and satisfy norms are not independent of one another.

5.1 Policy with Given Objectives

A first kind of analysis oriented towards the procedural context of policy making assumes that policy-makers' goals are given (Witt 2003, p. 83). Hence, the respective knowledge-creation and opinion formation already has been accomplished. Still, in the evolutionary context politicians are not considered systematically to be better informed than other economic actors. They are also characterized as being subject to bounded rationality and to have differences in their knowledge, skills, expectations, practices and learning behavior. Consequently, a crucial problem policy-makers face is their incomplete knowledge of economic circumstances, patterns and dynamics, the uncertainties involved therein, and based on that their imperfect abilities to cope with the resulting problems (Wegner 2003). Policy-makers are neither perfectly able to design successful policies coping with existing malfunctions of the economic system nor perfectly to anticipate unfavorable paths of development. They face 'model uncertainty' (Schnellenbach 2005), implying that their knowledge of the relationship between means and ends, be that between different economic magnitudes or between policy measures and their economic consequences, is quite restricted.

Hence, the convenient view in more traditional equilibrium approaches where the deviation from the equilibrium serves as an indication for measures that restore the *status quo ante* conditions does not apply in an evolutionary view of the economic system. The various positive and negative feedbacks as well as minor events eventually have major effects, each of which provide for an economic dynamics difficult if at all to understand and consequently to regulate. For chaotic processes set in even very simple contexts, Holyst et al. (1996) as well as Kopel (1997) show the difficulty (i) of identifying the appropriate regulating measures and (ii) of designing the appropriate dose of intervention. Hence, the means–end relationships are neither well understood nor easily regulated in a complex world.

Thus, economic policy cannot work as a simplistic repair shop with obvious deficiencies in the system showing up and adequate measures ready at hand in order to return to its proper functioning. The incompleteness of information and knowledge of boundedly rational politicians allows them to act only in an experimental (Okruch 2003) although conscious way. Therefore, it is not repairing but trial-and-error that characterizes policy interventions. Trial-and-error implies policy learning and the ability to adapt to new information. Metcalfe (1994b, 1995) labels that kind of policy making as adaptive and the politicians as adaptive policy-makers.[31]

5.2 Policy with Given Objectives: Some Procedures

Despite the suggestion that in an evolutionary and complex world policy-makers need to learn about their policies' effectiveness, some more specific policy conclusions can be drawn by looking at the inherently dynamic features of the economic process. Evolutionary dynamics generally are characterized by the appearance of novelty in the sense of new ideas and new products and their subsequent testing and competition in the market for the best solution to satisfy demand. This process is in many cases assumed to improve economic efficiency provided that new ideas emerge and are not preempted. Hence, it is suggested that appropriate policy measures may be undertaken to facilitate that process. Two main aspects are relevant here, the speed, direction and openness of competition and the selection as well as the creation of new ideas to ensure variety generation.

As to competition or selection and the related speed of adjustment, Metcalfe (1994b, 1995) and Moreau (2004) discuss a facilitating function of policy. Here the intended goal is 'to accelerate the market's natural adjustment process and, as a result, avoid some welfare losses in transition periods' (Moreau 2004, p. 855) – exemplified by institutions improving on the matching rate in labor markets. The intervention is here of a more indirect type as market forces are not directed but only enabled. Related to that is a theoretical concept in the sphere of replicator dynamics. In these scenarios, the speed of competition is positively related to the degree of heterogeneity of the competing entities (for example, products) (Metcalfe 1994a). Since competitive selection, by itself, reduces heterogeneity and therefore the dynamics of evolution, novelty and rivalry introduced into the market counteract that tendency and keep the process alive.

More direct interventions (for example, subsidies) are addressed when the openness and direction of the market process are concerned. Here policy-makers may engage in guiding the process (Moreau 2004), as also addressed by the notion of mission-oriented policies (Cantner and Pyka 2001; Ergas 1987). As such a strategy implies targeting specific market outcomes (which the procedure of competition can only 'discover' *ex ante*, see section 4.1, our caveat concerning policy learning raised above comes into play and may cause problems with respect to exploring the required information and exploiting it by an appropriate policy measure. The major dilemma of politicians can also be expressed as one of timing in a 'conflict between exploration and exploitation' (Moreau 2004, p. 865) in the following sense: 'A too short exploration period may lead to erroneous decisions due to inadequate knowledge. But, if this exploration period is too long, once the best policy has been identified unambiguously, the path followed by the system may prevent the implementation of this policy' (ibid., p. 862). In that dilemma any factors working on the extension of the exploration phase appear to be detrimental. Moreau (2004, p. 865) distinguishes internally generated inertias in gathering information from externally created difficulties in encountering the relevant information. As a consequence, the economic system may tend to evolve 'in its own way and goals may finally turn out to be impossible or too costly to reach' (ibid.).

Looking at the evolutionary 'inputs' into the market process (new ideas transformed into new competitive problem solutions), policy measures ought to focus on the generation of variety and thus 'induce learning, because they create incentives to search for a creative response' (Witt 2003, p. 85). This definition of the role of the state shifts the analytic focus from efficiency and clear goal orientation towards creativity and a diffusion orientation whereby it may be the state itself acting creatively (for example, public R&D) or state intervention (for example, taxes, subsidies and prohibitions) prompting private creative activities and responses (Ergas 1987; Cantner and Pyka 2001). As mentioned above, sustaining variety affects the speed of competition and selection. In addition, risks of technological or behavioral lock-in may be minimized 'by maintaining some diversity among the characteristics of market participants and thus in the economic trajectories followed' (Moreau 2004, p. 866).

It would seem that the policy options addressed in this section resemble policy options based on traditional thinking. Keeping up competition, sustaining innovation and new technologies or organizing an appropriate education system, to name only a few, can indeed often[32] be justified by both neoclassical and evolutionary analysis – however, on the basis of a different reasoning.

5.3 The Normative Basis

Turning to normative policy issues in an evolutionary context, 'it is evident that normative reasoning cannot start from some "given" external policy goal' (Schubert 2009, p. 22). The open-ended, non-teleological process of economic evolution therefore 'may complicate normative reasoning' (ibid.). As another complication, one has to take into account that criteria for evaluating the well-functioning of evolutionary processes are not entirely clear and not unequivocal. Based on this rather shaky ground three lines of arguments can be distinguished. A first consideration refers to the fact that the open-endedness of economic evolution does 'not imply that welfare considerations become obsolete' (ibid.). The welfare gains and losses are, however, in an evolutionary framework not as easily identified as in a neoclassical one. The conceptualization of welfare then becomes a major problem as it depends on norms, values, goals and further criteria which themselves are evolving over time. Often, policy measures aiming at the innovativeness of an economy are just assuming that innovations are per se welfare enhancing which is not always necessarily the case (Witt 2003).

The 'evolutionary welfare economist's'[33] awareness of the complexity of both the economic and the political system, the uncertainty and risk involved in both systems, and thus the limited ability to control and steer, by which evolutionary processes are characterized in both markets and politics, severely qualifies the requirement of having a precise and unequivocal measure or criterion of welfare. Economic efficiency in a Pareto sense might be substituted by degrees of effectiveness and optimal risk-adjustment (in terms of portfolio diversification) may have to give way to simple tasks of sensible risk reduction (van den Bergh and Kallies 2009).

With given preferences and given goals and norms these criteria might work well – in the very short run. However, a third consideration denies this conclusion by hinting at the fact that preferences will change (Weizsäcker 1971, 2001, 2005; Witt 2003; Vanberg 2009) over time. As a consequence, intergenerational and intertemporal welfare comparisons become difficult if not impossible. In the long-term, cultural context, evolutionary processes in markets, policies, and belief-systems have to be seen as interdependent and thus developing in a co-evolutionary way. Political and economic environments impose selective pressures upon alternative policies, alternative economic solutions and alternative morals and norms. The changes herein are not totally synchronized; they reveal different speeds and intensities, and they depend on and reinforce each other in often unpredictable ways. Actors herein are boundedly rational, proceeding by trial, error and learning, adapting to the respective selection environments. Hence, political and economic actors experience their environments and adjust to them which, in turn, has a non-negligible influence on the evolution of the selection environment itself. In such a context any evaluation of economic decisions and policies has to remain provisional and fallible, in short: evolving.

6 CONCLUSION

An important element of evolutionary thinking is the concept of the 'empty niche', meaning 'a species that would have a positive population in an ecosystem if it existed. If an empty niche is filled . . . whether by mutation or migration, this changes all the other niches in the system, expanding some and contracting others' (Boulding 1981, p. 14). One may wonder if – whether by mutation within the dominant paradigm or by migration (for example, from neighboring disciplines) – the niche of an evolutionary political economy could be filled or rather re-conquered. Its prospects of winning back a prominent place within the economics profession are far from evident, its population being small and dispersed. But there is room for expansion.

Evolutionary economics, when combined non-dogmatically, for example, with modern market process theory and new institutional economics, should have important contributions to make to modern political economy. There is a strong case for supporting Hayek's (1960, p. 109) claim that democracy should be assessed 'in its dynamic, rather than its static aspects'. And there are no compelling reasons why theories that focus on coordination processes, knowledge creation and dissemination, entrepreneurial action, or evolutionary learning processes should not also be applicable to political systems.

In this chapter, a major focus was on processes of political opinion formation and knowledge creation. It is here that differences between the neoclassical concept of politics as an aggregation of, or adaptation to, given preferences within a given issue space and an evolutionary view of the spontaneous formation and change of opinions, beliefs and, finally, institutions, in a process of communication and learning can be most distinctly shown. These differences in emphasis largely correspond to differences in 'style'. It is easier to apply formal models of a pure logic of choice to a world in which things (including knowledge) are supposed to be 'given'. Evolutionary approaches that stress entrepreneurship, novelty, complexity, error and learning tend to be different in style. Although some of these elements can be illustrated in isolation with highly complex and abstract mathematics, evolutionary public choice that tries to analyze their combined importance for real political processes would almost necessarily tend to be more 'fuzzy', 'verbose' and overly complex.

This creates an evolutionary disadvantage in an academic selection environment in which technique defines content and occasionally trumps substance. But alternative styles and objects of analysis should remain on our agendas if our science is to evolve.

NOTES

1. On Schumpeter as precursor of evolutionary economics, see Fagerberg (2003) or Andersen (2009). On Schumpeter as precursor of public choice: Becker (1958, p. 105), Buchanan and Tullock (1962, p. 335), Kinnear (1999, p. 932), Bernholz (2000, p. 4) or Mueller (2003, p. 2, fn. 1).
2. See Mitchell (1984), Frey (1981), Prisching (1995) or Wohlgemuth (2005) on this irony in the history of ideas.
3. It is even more puzzling to find Wittman (1995, p. 23, fn. 5) pay tribute to Schumpeter in his *Myth of Democratic Failure* – one of the most outspoken denials of Schumpeter's view.
4. Examples are Sears et al. (1980), Kinder and Kiewiet (1981), Frank (1988), Brennan and Lomasky (1989), Kirchgässner and Pommerehne (1993), Brennan and Hamlin (2000), Mueller (2003, ch. 14), and Caplan (2007).
5. See, for example, Frohlich and Oppenheimer (1978), Buchanan and Vanberg (1989), Ostrom (1990), Fernandez and Rodrik (1991), Dunleavy (1991), Harberger (1993), Williamson and Haggard (1994), Ursprung (1994), Schneider et al. (1995), Mintrom (1997), Cowen and Sutter (1997), Wohlgemuth (2000, 2005), Arce (2001), Holcombe (2002a), Albrecht (2002), Wegner (2004), Mukand and Rodrik (2005), Schnellenbach (2007), Hermann-Pillath (2009), and Congleton (2010).
6. See Lau and Sears (1986), Tversky and Kahnemann (1987), Quattrone and Tversky (1988), Frey and Eichenberger (1991), Wahlke (1991), Rosenberg (1991), Brady et al. (1995), Druckmann (2004), and Frohlich and Oppenheimer (2006).
7. Much of the evidence can be explained in terms of Simon's (1957, 1993) model of bounded rationality. Owing to limited cognitive capacities of the mind, individuals rely on rather simple behavioral heuristics and 'rules of thumb' which generally 'satisfice' learned levels of aspiration, instead of engaging in case-by-case optimization based on a comprehensive consultation of data and alternative modes of behavior. More striking evidence of decision anomalies, biases and mistakes may be explained by 'prospect theory' (Kahnemann and Tversky 1984), which claims, among other things, that individuals choose schemata of arranging the outside world which at the moment are most available rather than most 'rational', 'objective' or 'fruitful'. Such conditions can be exploited by others who manipulate individual decisions by

ways of 'framing' the context of a decision and thus producing biased results in the framers' interest. Also the behavioral findings of 'cognitive dissonance' (Festinger 1957; Akerlof and Dickens 1982) have been shown to be relevant for human nature in politics.
8. The role of 'epistemic communities' or 'advocacy networks' that allow political entrepreneurs to reach a 'critical mass' of supporters and spread their political ideas in a somewhat elitist market for agenda-setting in international organizations has been analyzed by Haas (1990) or Zito (2001). The role of political parties as 'going concerns' that might help political entrepreneurs to set an 'entrepreneurial' agenda with longer time-horizons has been discussed by Müller (2002). The role of mass-media has so far been largely ignored by public choice (see Orr 1987 or Udehn 1996 for a critique; Witt 1996 or Besley and Burgess 2001 for rare exceptions). The role of judges in the evolution – especially of common law – has been discussed, for example, by Hayek (1973, pp. 94–123), von Wangenheim (1993), Hathaway (2001), Fon and Parisi (2003) or Eckhardt (2004).
9. For an early evolutionary account of the political economy of transformation, see Murrell (1992), who advocates a gradualist, experimentalist and decentralist approach to transformation. On political transformation as the interaction between 'slow-moving institutions' (culture) and 'fast-mowing institutions' (political and legal acts), see Roland (2004). Pejovich (2006) or Zweynert (2009) provide similar accounts for transformation processes in Russia and Eastern Europe. Hermann-Pillath (for example, 2009) presents an 'evolutionary approach to endogenous political constraints on transition in China'. He claims that without attention to political entrepreneurship, changes in cognitive models, or multi-layered experimentation and competition, the case of China cannot be properly explained. He shows how the emergence of new political entrepreneurs, strategic groups and cognitive models under a regime of endogenous political constraints causes unforeseeable path-dependencies in a system of 'quasi-federalism' (also see Hermann-Pillath 2006). The (economic) success of the Chinese transformation has also been related to its evolutionary, experimental approach by Naughton (1995).
10. As, for example, Vanberg and Buchanan (1989) point out, preferences consist of evaluative and cognitive components. They depend on interests in results (what one wants) and on positive and normative theories about the effects of certain actions (what one expects, believes). Both elements combined determine an opinion: (a) preferences in a narrow sense (interests, tastes) about which the Stigler and Becker (1977) dictum '*de gustibus non est disputandum*' may hold for analytical purposes and (b) theories that inform these preferences (conjectures about the likelihood of alternative actions/policies to accommodate one's interests, worldviews, ideologies, mental models) which are the results of interactive communication and learning; see Wohlgemuth (2002b) for more on this inclusive definition of opinions which drive political behavior and may well change in the process of political interaction. See Denzau and North (1994) on the importance of the cognitive part of preferences analyzed as 'mental models' and 'ideologies'.
11. See Luhmann ([1970] 1975). For similar accounts based on numerous case-studies, see, for example, Zaller (1992), Schneider et al. (1995), and Albrecht (2002).
12. Witt (1996) models the promulgation of public opinion based on critical masses and frequency/intensity effects triggered by mass-media exposure and enclave deliberation (on the latter – and its potential radicalizing impact – see also Sunstein 2001). Also Crespi (1997) and Kuran (1995) model bandwagon effects in the sense of individual benefits in communication networks depending on other individuals who (seem to) think and act in similar ways. See also Boyer and Orlean (1992) for a model on the 'evolution of conventions' as multiple outcomes of coordination games with externalities that can yield some insight into the formation of publicly shared opinions. More dynamic models of information cascades and path-dependencies with Bayesian updating can be found in Bikchandani et al. (1992, 1998). Their models tend to result in one dominant (and possibly Pareto-inferior) convention or opinion prevailing in the whole population.
13. Ianni and Conradi (2002) deal with these local dynamics leading to clustering and neighboring of opinions. Social rank plays a decisive factor in a model by Wu and Huberman (2008) where rank attracts attention and thus affects opinion formation.
14. See Meier and Haury (1990) for a similar theory.
15. Building on a largely neglected idea of Tullock (1965a), the famous paper by Demsetz (1968) and the discussion of Williamson (1976), Wohlgemuth (2000, p. 277) proposes a model of democracy as 'rivalry for incumbency' in which 'based on declarations and promises made by potential producers one (group of) candidate(s) is given the exclusive right provide certain goods and services for a specified period of time and a specified area'.
16. On the 'J-curve' problem of reforms with delayed and unsecure payoffs, see Williamson and Haggard (1994), Fernandez and Rodrik (1991), Roland (2002) or Wegner (2004). Dal Bó and Rossi (2008) isolate the importance of term length and observe that longer terms enhance legislative performance. They suggest that the 'accountability logic' (that would support shorter terms) is overcome by an 'investment logic' (sacrificing short term benefits for long term payoffs). Moe (1990) analyses several ways for incumbents to secure the continuation of their investment in political reforms and/or political rents for their

clients. These include 'self-binding' commitments (intended also to bind incoming new governments) such as constitutionalization, bureaucratization, or co-optation of the opposition and interest groups (that is, logrolling).
17. 'Without variation there is no experience to act as a basis for learning; without a stable framework there is no assurance that any valid connections can be made between actions and outcomes that will have any future relevance. The appropriateness of institutions . . . to the maintenance of this balance is a major determinant of evolutionary pathways' (Loasby 2000, p. 307).
18. One of the greater methodological difficulties is, of course, that of identifying and quantifying 'innovation' (in the economic as well as in the political realm). An easy way is that used by Walker (1969) in his classical study by counting as a political innovation the adoption of any policy that had not been used previously in the observed jurisdiction. A stronger, truly Schumpeterian definition understands 'public entrepreneurs' as individuals who successfully promote 'non-incremental changes of political paradigms' (Schnellenbach 2007) by altering political perceptions and implementing novel policies on a larger scale.
19. A further impediment to bold political innovation or reform relates to a certain 'collective conservatism' (Kuran 1988) of the citizens themselves who are not likely to welcome novelty as such. This can be explained by many factors relating to the political economy of opinion formation, such as the logic of 'preference falsification' (Kuran 1995), the stickiness of shared mental models in self-confirming communication networks (Schnellenbach 2005), status quo bias (Fernandez and Rodrik 1991) or frequency-dependency effects (Witt 1996). The political economy of political reform has provided many econometric or case studies, whose comparative institutional analysis highlights different factors of success (or failure) of more radical political reforms (mostly those which mainstream economists would favor). Williamson and Haggard (1994) discuss the public perception of a crisis, the honeymoon period, a fragmented and demoralized opposition, an embedded team of experts in government, a visionary leader, external pressure or scapegoats, and other conditions for extensive reforms. Kingdon (1995) stresses the emergence of a 'window of opportunity' for which political entrepreneurs get prepared by elaborating on policy proposals that they would push on the agenda 'when the time has come'. The most important factor, according to Schnellenbach (2007), is a widespread opinion amongst relevant social communication networks that the status quo has become unbearable, which would lead to a substantial destabilization of formerly held shared mental models (about how the world works and how it should work).
20. Boyer and Orlean (1992) discuss several factors that allow for overcoming the stability or rigidity of a ruling opinion. They focus on events or exogenous shocks that facilitate a large number of actors to change their minds and to switch to an alternative opinion.
21. As a variant of this exogenous cause, Boyer and Orlean (1992) discuss 'external invasion'. Here a large enough new group of actors with a new opinion enters the competition. A switch in the opinion of the formerly ruling group may occur and the new opinion comes to dominate. Points in case are institutional transformations which 'are more likely to entail processes of complex reconfigurations of institutional elements rather than their immediate replacement' (Stark 1992, p. 22). In this context Thelen (2003) talks of institutional conversion where existing institutional structures are redirected to new purposes. She identifies 'layering' as another mechanism where new arrangements are placed on top of pre-existing ones.
22. In this context, a number of studies suggest the importance of interpretation as a mechanism for opening up the possibility for change. This interpretation of alternative solutions or opinions is due to specific actors. Fligstein (1990) investigates the role of courts and judicial rulings. And Garud and Karnøe (2001) consider the 'mindful deviation' associated with entrepreneurs in the technological context.
23. Stark (1992) and Johnson (2001) underscore the time dimension of institutional transformation and the importance of sequencing and cumulative stages.
24. This definition of entrepreneurship based on 'alertness' and 'arbitrage' refers to Kirzner (1973). In a similar vein, Holcombe's (2002a) theory of political entrepreneurship is Kirznerian rather than Schumpeterian. He focuses on opportunities for political 'profit'. These can be either productive or predatory. Compared to market competition, political institutions of coercive redistribution favor predatory over productive political arbitrage by giving the former substantial leverage and large returns.
25. See Vihanto (1992), diZerega (1989), Wohlgemuth (2003, 2008), and Kerber and Heine (2003), all of whom make explicit reference to Hayek ([1968] 1978).
26. See also Riker (1982, p. 244) for a similar argument.
27. We cannot here try to summarize or evaluate the manifold and often inconclusive empirical findings on the relation between democracy, federalism, or the rule of law and economic or social indicators of 'success'. See Persson and Tabellini (2003), Acemoglu and Johnson (2005) or Jellema and Roland (2011) for recent comprehensive studies. The studies of long phases of institutional change by North (1990, 2005) support the idea that political competition and emulation has been most conducive to political economic progress and growth. Economic historians and economists interested in history have quite naturally adopted a more or less 'evolutionary' perspective when addressing long-term and large-scale develop-

ments. They could not treat institutional change as an outcome of 'rational collective choice' aggregating 'given preferences' in a 'given issue space'. Instead, they had to look at what eighteenth century Scottish historians had regarded as 'the result of human action, but not the execution of any human design' (Ferguson 1767, p.187): as results of entrepreneurship, accidents, path dependencies, belief-formation, learning, yearning and erring in an environment of the unplanned creation of variety under a selective environment of (economic, political, cultural) competition. Contemporary authors include: Jones (1981), Berman (1983), Rosenberg and Birdzell (1986), Mokyr (1990), Donald (1991), Greif (1993), and Volckart (2000).

28. See Mitchell (2001) on Virginia versus Chicago political economy. Witt (1992) makes the point that public choice theorists face the paradoxical situation that their recommendations are pointless if their models suggest that things are the necessary outcomes of rational utility maximization in a world of given preferences. His 'endogenous public choice theorist' can become an 'agent of collective action' only if she views politics and herself as part of interpersonal communication networks with scarce information processing capacity and attention.
29. See Bohnet and Frey (1994), or Feld and Kirchgässner (2000, 2001) with reference to Swiss experiences with popular democracy. See also Matsusaka (Chapter 8 in this volume).
30. On fiscal federalism as a 'laboratory' that allows learning from policy innovations in other states see Oates (1999), on interjurisdictional competition as a creative discovery procedure and learning device see Vihanto (1992), Vanberg (1993a, 1993b), Frey and Eichenberger (1999), Kerber and Heine (2003), Vanberg and Kerber (1994), and Wohlgemuth (2008). On 'yardstick competition' and the pressure for policy imitation or innovation, see Besley and Case (1995) or Rincke (2005). Political and legal scholars close to pragmatism also favor governance structures allowing for political decentralization and experimentalism; see Ostrom (1990), Sabel (1997, 2001), Knight (2001), Okruch (2003), Mukand and Rodrik (2005), and Sabel and Zeitlin (2008). See also Holcombe (Chapter 11 in this volume).
31. For the related issue of policy learning, Freytag and Renaud (2007, p.437) distinguish between active learning and pathological learning.
32. For discussion, along with some examples where policy measures justified as beneficial by neoclassical thinking are seen as detrimental in evolutionary thinking, see Witt (2003).
33. See Witt and Schubert (2010) for some first attempts to develop an alternative branch of welfare economics based on evolutionary thinking.

PART VI

PUBLIC CHOICE PERSPECTIVES ON THE RELATIONS BETWEEN INTERNATIONAL ACTORS

27 International organizations
Roland Vaubel

1 INTRODUCTION

The public choice approach to international organizations and agreements differs from much of the political science literature on international relations because it rejects the unitary actor model. In public choice theory, the actors are individuals (such as voters, politicians, bureaucrats and lobbyists), not countries or states. As individuals, they may be members of collective organizations. Within these organizations, they may take collective decisions according to the rules which they or others have agreed upon.

The actors are guided by interests rather than lofty ideals. Their personal interests lead them to join an organization and participate in its affairs. Moreover, as members, they share the interest of maintaining and expanding the organization. However, these are not interests of the organization but the common interests of its members.

International agreements are not concluded by states but by politicians – members of the participating governments and, in most cases, the majority of parliamentarians. International organizations are established by the same groups of actors but, in addition, they introduce a new class of actors: international bureaucrats. Moreover, the international organization may include a board of supervisors appointed by national politicians to monitor the international bureaucracy, an international court or board of arbitration and an international assembly of parliamentarians controlling both the international bureaucracy and the national politicians taking part in the organization's affairs. The board of supervisors is sometimes called a 'Board of Executive Directors' as in the International Monetary Fund (IMF) and the World Bank, 'General Council', as in the World Trade Organization (WTO), a 'Governing Body' or 'General Conference', as in the International Labor Organization (ILO), or a 'Committee of Representatives' (COREPR), as in the European Union (EU). The members of international courts (including courts of auditors) and arbitration bodies are usually appointed by the participating governments. The members of the international assembly of parliamentarians may be chosen by the national parliaments (as in NATO, the Western European Union until 2010 and the European Community until 1979) or directly by the voters (as in the EC/EU since 1979).

The actors deciding in or about international organizations are influenced by lobbyists representing organized interest groups. I argue that, for more than one reason, these lobbyists are more influential at the international level than at the national, provincial or local level. A public choice analysis of international organizations has to explain which pressure groups have the most influence and which actors are the most responsive to them.

There is a long chain of delegation from the voters in the individual member states to the decision-makers in an international organization. The flow chart of Figure 27.1 visualizes the process. The citizens elect their national parliaments. The national parliaments

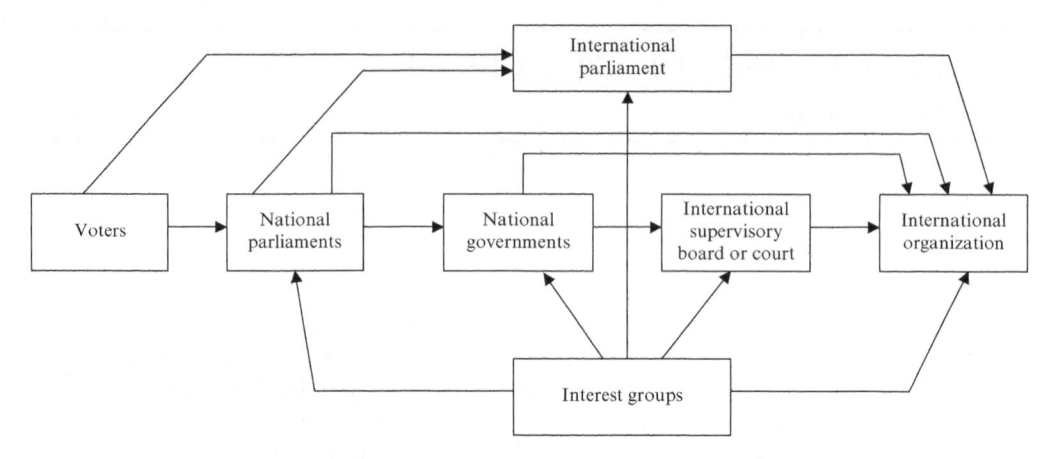

Figure 27.1   Monitoring and influencing international organizations

choose the chief executive unless, as in a presidential system, the latter is also elected by the voters. National executives, in turn, appoint a committee of supervisors (a board or court or both) who are supposed to monitor the staff of the international organization. International parliaments and interest groups add their influence. I shall analyze decision-making at each of these stages step by step.

2   VOTERS

International bureaucrats, the final agents, are farther removed from voters, the ultimate principals, than any other policy-makers. Thus, international organizations suffer from the most severe principal–agent problem. Even a majority of well-informed voters would have little control over the policies adopted by decision-makers in an international organization, and even the decision to join an international organization or agreement is not usually subject to a referendum.[1] Opinion surveys for the European Community confirm that the share of those who do not believe they have much or any influence on political decisions is larger for the European institutions (74 percent) than for the national governments (67 percent).[2] Moreover, in an international organization, the voters' information cost is high and their incentive to be informed is weak.

The high cost of information is, first, due to geographic distance: the seat of the international organization tends to be much farther from the citizen than the national or provincial capital. Second, the international organization uses a language or languages that most citizens do not understand. Third, as political decision-making is centralized at the international level, the scope for comparisons of political performance – so-called 'yardstick competition' – is reduced. Fourth, since parliamentary control tends to be weak or absent, most decisions are taken behind closed doors; neither the minutes nor the voting record are published.[3] Thus, the agents cannot be held accountable by the principals.

Centralization also explains the citizen's weak incentive to collect and exploit information about the international organization. She has less access to international than to

Table 27.1 *Preferred levels of decision-making for the three most important issues in 10 EU member states (percentages based on responses)*

Preferred governmental level	Mass public	Members of national parliaments	Members of European Parliament
Regional	12	7	3
National	45	48	43
European	42	44	54

Source: Schmitt and Thomassen (1999), European Representation Study, table 3.1.

national or local decision-makers, the weight of her vote is lower in international elections, and her share in the benefits of a reform is also reduced.

As the cost of information is higher, and the incentive to be informed is lower, it is rational to be more ignorant about international than national affairs. Opinion polls for the European Union document this ignorance,[4] but there do not seem to be comparable data at the national level. There is evidence, however, that the citizens feel better informed if political decisions are taken at lower levels of government.[5]

Rational ignorance about international organizations would not be a problem if the decisive actors in these organizations shared the preferences of the voters. However, various surveys show that this is not the case. Table 27.1 reports the preferences of voters, national parliamentarians and EU parliamentarians concerning the desired level of decision-making for the three issues that voters consider most important. As can be seen, an international (EU) competency is preferred by a majority (54 percent) of the EU parliamentarians but only by a minority (42 percent) of the voters. Table 27.2 reveals that a larger military role for the European Union is desired by a majority (65 percent) of top Commission officials and EU parliamentarians but only by a minority (46 percent) of voters. Finally, as shown in Table 27.3, less than a minority of voters supports EU membership and believes that their country, on balance, benefits from it, whereas an overwhelming majority of EU and national parliamentarians takes these views.

Democratic control is weakened not only by the long chain of delegation and rational ignorance. Centralization of policies at the international level also undermines the citizens' ability to impose their will because it raises their cost of escaping from undesired policies. The exit option is important because it provides protection against excessive taxation, regulation and redistributive government spending. Political agents are constrained not only by democratic majorities but also by individuals or minorities who leave the jurisdiction if the government does not perform well. International agreements and organizations are equivalent to policy cartels and monopolies, respectively, thus raising the price of government output to the citizens.

The European Union is the only international organization 'harmonizing' tax rates. The 'harmonization' of value-added tax (VAT) rates in 1992 provides a telling example. The Council unanimously set a minimum VAT rate that exceeded the rates prevailing in three of the member states. In this way, it raised the average VAT rate in the EU.

The EU also provides examples of collusive regulation – especially before 1987, when all such regulations required unanimity in the Council.[6] However, the wave of regulations really started after the Single European Act (ratified in 1987) and the Social

Table 27.2 *EU-related opinions of the general public, 50 top Commission officials and 203 members of the European Parliament in nine EU member states (percentage)*

	General public	Top Commission officials and euro-parliamentarians
1. The European Union should strengthen its military power in order to play a larger role in the world:		
Agree strongly	16	31
Agree somewhat	30	34
Disagree somewhat	30	17
Disagree strongly	21	15
Don't know	3	2

Source: European Elite Survey, Centre for the Study of Political Change, University of Siena, May to July 2006 (as published by Roper Center for Public Opinion Research MCMISC 2006-Elite) and Transatlantic Trends 2006, Topline Data, June 2006.

Table 27.3 *EU-related opinions of the general public and top decision-makers among elected politicians, national civil servants and journalists (percentage)*

Issue	General public	National civil servants	Parliamentarians	Media leaders
Support for EU-membership	48	96	92	91
Benefits from EU-membership	43	92	90	86

Notes: Sample size: 3,778 persons in EU-15.

Source: EOS Gallup Europe, The European Union: A View from the Top, Special Study, 1996.

Agreement of the Maastricht Treaty (ratified in 1993) had introduced qualified majority decisions for many kinds of regulations, notably those affecting the labor market.[7] It is important to distinguish between regulations that require unanimous consent versus those subject to majority rule because the resulting political equilibria differ.

If international regulations may be adopted by a majority of the governments, the majority representing the most restrictive governments has an incentive to impose the level of regulation prevailing in the decisive member country on the minority of more liberal countries in order to reduce the latter's competitiveness. This is the so-called 'strategy of raising rivals' costs' (SRRC).[8] It is well known from the theory of industrial organization and the political economy of federalism. Figure 27.2 compares the competitive, the collusive and the SRRC equilibria.

The two axes measure the intensity of regulation in two countries (r_1, r_2). The indifference curves are derived from the utility or loss functions of the two governments. Each government has two objectives: a large domestic capital stock and a small absolute or

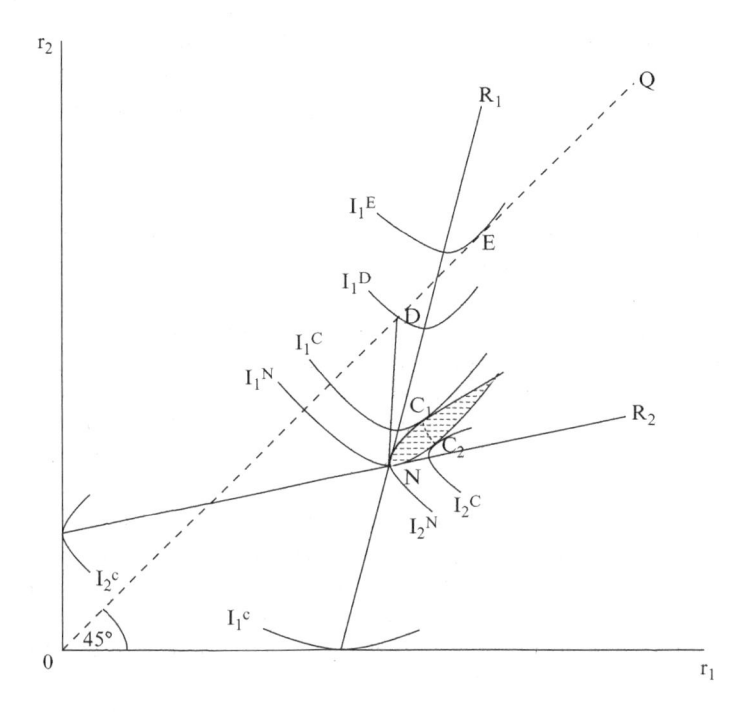

Figure 27.2 Regulatory collusion and raising rivals' costs

squared deviation from the level of regulation that would be ideal in the absence of the capital stock target.[9] A large capital stock and regulations catering to influential interest groups raise the probability that the incumbent politicians will be re-elected. Since capital is mobile, each country's stock depends positively on the other country's level of regulation relative to its own level of regulation. This is why each government wants a high level of regulation in the other country. (Note that the model can also be applied to taxation – with the tax rates on the two axes.)

The points of tangency of the two axes and the indifference curves I_1^o and I_2^o, respectively, indicate the level of regulation that each government would choose if there were no regulation in the other country. Figure 27.2 is drawn in such a way that government 1 prefers more regulation than government 2 does.

Now if, say, government 2 raises its level of regulation, capital will flow from country 2 to country 1 so that government 1 will raise its own regulation (r_1) as well. This is shown by the slope of the reaction curve R_1. Each point on reaction curve R_1 is at the same time the lowest point on the highest attainable indifference curve I_1. The case of r_2 and R_2 is strictly analogous.

The two reaction curves intersect at N, the Nash point. This is the non-cooperative or competitive equilibrium. Even though each government considers a higher level of regulation to be ideal in buying the support of interest groups, they choose the Nash values because each is constrained by the regulatory policy of the other. Each nation is afraid of losing capital to its rival. But competition does not trigger a 'race to the bottom', that is, the origin. The 'race' is to the Nash point.

The graph in Figure 27.2 will now be used to show that both governments can raise their utility by cooperating, that is, colluding. All Pareto-superior combinations are contained in the shaded lens, and the Pareto-optimal combinations are indicated by the contract curve C_1C_2. The precise point the governments pick on the contract curve depends on their bargaining power and skills. Thus, policy collusion not only raises the joint level of regulation but also lowers regulatory risk.

Of course, the collusive solution is Pareto-optimal only from the point of view of the two governments catering to interest groups. The move from N to the contract curve does not indicate a welfare gain for the citizens. On the contrary, as regulation interferes with the freedom of contract, it is likely to hinder Pareto-improving market transactions.

Figure 27.2 may also be used to analyze the strategy of raising rivals' costs. If government 1 commands a majority in the decision making body of the international organization, it can impose a common level of regulation, that is, any point on the diagonal OQ. If it merely imposed its own regulatory level, starting from the non-cooperative Nash point, it would move from N to D. However, government 1 can attain even greater utility by raising regulation to point E, where its highest attainable indifference curve I_1^E is tangent to the diagonal. Thus, government 1 also raises its own level of regulation. The reason is that the common regulation relieves it of the competitive pressure from government 2.

The strategy of raising rivals' costs increases regulation in both countries but much more in country 2 than in country 1. Thus, the competitiveness of country 1 and its capital stock gain at the expense of country 2 even though the overall growth in regulation is likely to reduce the world's capital stock.

If the SRRC solution is compared to collusive regulation, we find that E implies more regulation than C_1C_2 for both countries. This is necessarily true for country 2 and plausible for country 1, but our result for country 1 depends on the shape of the indifference curves.

Majority decisions about common regulations play a significant role in the European Union and in the International Labor Organization. While EU directives are binding on national parliaments, ILO conventions do not enter into force in a member state unless they are ratified by its parliament. Nevertheless, Boockmann and Vaubel (2009) find that a country's level of labor market regulation has a significantly positive effect on the probability that representatives of its government vote for ILO conventions at the committee stage. Moreover, this holds only for ILO conventions that raise the cost of production. Thus, the majority of more restrictive member governments take advantage of the ILO to raise their rivals' costs.

In the European Union, the strategy of raising rivals' costs plays an important role in the regulation of labor, financial and art markets as well as in environmental regulation (Vaubel 2008), but an econometric analysis does not seem feasible due to data problems. Only the final votes are published. Moreover, the suppressed minority frequently votes with the majority in the end because it cannot block the regulation anyway. Open dissent invites retaliation and exclusion. Since no minutes are published and no votes taken at the committee stage, as in the ILO, much of the opposition is hidden and may be inferred only from newspaper reports.

For these reasons, collusion and the strategy of raising rivals' cost cannot be distinguished empirically merely by looking at the voting record. Nor is it helpful to ask whether the international regulation goes beyond any of the previous national regulations,[10] for this is compatible both with collusion and SRRC. However, SRRC is the more likely explanation if the national regulations had been very different because, in that case, the new common regulation implies a much larger increase in costs for the more liberal countries than for the more restrictive ones. Of course, the ability to distinguish between collusion and SRRC is difficult only if the decision may be taken by (a qualified) majority. If unanimity is required, the international regulation cannot be due to SRRC – it can only be collusive.

With regard to public expenditure, there do not seem to be any studies of whether spending by international organizations substitutes for national government expenditure or complements it. It is only within the national states that centralization has been shown to raise the share of government expenditure in GDP.[11] However, staff growth in international organizations has not been associated with a decline of public sector employment in the main member states (Vaubel et al. 2007). The average rate of personnel growth has been 3.2 percent per annum at the international level and 2.1 percent at the national level.

Policy collusion and the strategy of raising rivals' costs imply that increases in taxation and regulation should be positively correlated across countries. The econometric evidence supports this hypothesis.[12] However, the positive correlation alternatively may be due to exit, yardstick competition or common macroeconomic shocks.[13]

To conclude this section, both the 'harmonization' and the centralization of political decision making at the international level give politicians and bureaucrats more power over ordinary citizens.

3 PARLIAMENTARIANS

Since international agreements and organizations weaken voter control, national or international parliamentarians may be supposed to take their place. However, the parliamentarians do not share the preferences of the voters, and voters' powers of control are weak.

Table 27.1 has shown that, relative to the voters, not only euro-parliamentarians but also national parliamentarians are biased towards policy making at the EU level. This is confirmed by the results of referendums. In ten referendums voters have rejected the transfer of power to the EU which their parliament had voted for.[14] But even in those cases in which the voters concurred, the electoral majority was almost always much lower than the parliamentary majority. Table 27.4 presents the evidence.

Moreover, the national parliaments have little control over international organizations. In most countries, international treaties have to be ratified by the national parliaments. But the treaties are negotiated by the governments. The parliamentarians merely have the option of accepting or rejecting the agreement. The governments are the agenda-setters; they possess gate-keeping power. This distinguishes international treaties from ordinary legislation.

The national parliaments have no control over secondary legislation proposed by the international organization. In the European Union, it is true, one-third of the national parliaments may object to legislative proposals on the grounds that they violate the

Table 27.4 A comparison of national referendums and parliamentary votes on issues of EU policy (percentage)

Country	Year	Issue	Yes to referendum	Yes in parliamentary vote
Austria	1994	Accession to EU	66.6	80.0
Finland	1994	Accession to EU	56.9	77.0
Sweden	1994	Accession to EU	52.7	88.0
Malta	2003	Accession to EU	53.6	58.6
Slovenia	2003/04	Accession to EU	89.6	100.0
Hungary	2003	Accession to EU	83.8	100.0
Slovakia	2003	Accession to EU	92.5	92.1
Estonia	2003/04	Accession to EU	66.8	100.0
Spain	2005	EU constitution	76.2	Parl.: 94.2
				Senate: 97.4
Luxembourg	2005	EU constitution	56.5	June: 100.0
				Oct.: 98.2

Source: Haller (2008), tables 1.1, 1.2a and 1.2b.

principle of subsidiarity. However, the Commission is free to reject such complaints provided that it gives some reasons for doing so. The European Union may even adopt measures for which the treaties 'have not provided the necessary powers' if these measures are considered 'necessary ... to attain one of the objectives set out in the Treaties' (Art. 352 Treaty on the Functioning of the European Union, abbreviated TFEU). Thus, the national parliaments have abandoned control over the measures that the Union may take to attain any objectives mentioned in the treaties.[15]

Very few international organizations provide for a parliamentary assembly. If so, the assembly's role tends to be purely consultative. The parliament of the European Union is the only exception but it also lacks the powers of an ordinary parliament. For example, it does not have the right of legislative initiative – this is reserved for the Commission. Nor does it decide on the financial resources of the organization – this is left to the member states. Moreover, the parliament shares with the Council the power of determining significant components of EU expenditure.

The EU parliament's weakness may explain why voters know little about it and why few of them care to take part in its election. For example, shortly after ballots were cast in 2004, people were asked whether the next election would be due in 2006. Only 29 percent realized that this was not the case.[16] Only a minority of citizens votes in the European elections, and the participation rate is continually falling even though the Parliament's competencies have been expanding.[17] In the elections of 2009, turnout was 43 percent, falling short of 30 percent in six member states, while participation in the last national parliamentary election had been 70 percent on average. In most member states, this gap has been widening. Among those who did not intend to participate in the election of 2009, a majority said that their vote would not make any difference (68 percent), that they did not know enough about the European Parliament (60 percent) and that they did not feel sufficiently represented by it (53 percent).[18]

As Tables 27.1 through 27.3 have demonstrated, the EU parliamentarians are not representative of the preferences of the citizens. They are biased in favor of centralization. There seem to be two reasons for this: self-selection and vested interest. Advocates of the international organization are more likely to run for its parliament than its critics. Once elected, they are interested in increasing the power of the organization in which they have influence. To circumvent this bias, the European Constitutional Group (Bernholz et al. 2004) has suggested adding a second chamber, composed of delegates of the national parliaments, which would decide all bills affecting the distribution of power between the international organization and the member states. Vaubel (1999) proposes a chamber with authority to call referendums if competition among governments is threatened. Frey and Stutzer (2006) argue that randomly selected citizens (a board of trustees) should have the right to vote on the international organization's constitution and to recall its executives.

International parliaments tend to be very large. The European Parliament, for example, has 754 members, and they meet – sometimes in Strasbourg, sometimes in Brussels – geographically distant from their constituencies. This and their lack of power may explain why absenteeism has been a serious problem. The most recent comparative analysis showed that, in the second half of the 1990s, 34 percent of the europarliamentarians were absent when votes were taken, compared with less than 10 percent in the Belgian parliament, which also meets in Brussels (Noury and Roland 2002, Table 6). More recent data[19] suggest a higher participation rate (87 percent in 2004–09), but these data are censored: they exclude parliamentarians who were present for less than 100 (out of 5,265) roll call votes. If participation actually has been increasing, as seems likely, this may be due to the expanding powers of the European Parliament or the changing composition of its membership. For parliamentarians from transition countries, life in Brussels and Strasbourg is more attractive than for those from high-income countries. In a cross-section analysis of the Sixth European Parliament (2004–09), Karrer (2010) shows that the participation rate of parliamentarians from Austria, Estonia, Poland, Slovakia and Finland (in this order) is significantly higher than for the rest and that it is significantly lower for parliamentarians from Italy.

These considerations suggest that international agreements and organizations are subject to less parliamentary control than the governments of their member states.

4 THE NATIONAL GOVERNMENTS

Control at the EU center is exercised mainly by the politicians and bureaucrats of the member governments. As Table 27.3 has shown, the preferences of the national bureaucrats are biased towards international 'harmonization' and centralization even more so than are the preferences of national parliamentarians and media leaders. While 48 percent of voters support EU membership, 96 percent of national civil servants do. Ninety-two percent of the national bureaucrats but only 43 percent of voters believe that, on balance, their country benefits from membership. There does not seem to be a survey comparing the preferences of voters and cabinet members with regard to international organizations. However, in the ten referendums listed in note 14, voters not only rebuked the majority of the European Parliament but also that of their own governments.

Quite apart from these biases, control by the national governments is undermined by legal restrictions, high information costs and incentive problems. Control is restricted if the international organization has been given agenda-setting powers. In the European Union, for example, the Council cannot legislate without a prior proposal from the Commission.[20] Moreover, if, on the second reading, Council and Parliament want to amend a Commission proposal against the Commission's wishes, the Council has to decide unanimously rather than by qualified majority, as it could if the Commission assented (Art. 294, section 9, no. 9 TFEU). Since the international organization wants to keep the powers it has acquired, its *'acquis communautaire'*, it will not propose decentralizing measures. Thus, (secondary) legislation is a one-way street towards ever closer union.

The cost of information is high for the national governments, especially for the busy non-expert politicians in the cabinet, and they may deliberately be misled by the international organization. For example, the International Monetary Fund and the International Development Agency (IDA) have been shown to take greater advantage of their ability to borrow when the date of the next quota review or replenishment round approaches (Vaubel 1991, 1996). In this way, they create the impression that an increase in funding is needed urgently. As a former staff member in charge of financing operations at the World Bank once told me, such hurry-up lending has been 'deliberate policy'.

The main incentive problem of national politicians is that they can reap only a small part of the benefits generated by their monitoring efforts (Frey 1984). They have a much weaker incentive to control the spending of an international organization than the outlays of their own governments.

The incentive weakens even more as the international organization attracts more members and their pro-rata national shares of budgetary costs decline. Time series analyses confirm that the number of staff members at the IMF and the real burden of the administrative expenditures of the International Bank for Reconstruction and Development (IBRD) rise significantly as the individual budget shares of the ten largest contributors fall (Vaubel 1991, 1996).

A panel-data analysis for 17 international organizations between 1950 and 2000 reveals that the number of staff members is significantly and negatively correlated with the budget share of the largest contributor (almost always the United States), provided that the latter has a conservative government (Vaubel et al. 2007, table 8). The Reagan administration, in particular, had a noticeably negative impact on staff growth in international organizations: the average rate of increase dropped from 4.6 percent per annum before 1985 to 1.2 percent thereafter (ibid., table 2). The number of staff also is significantly smaller if the international organization has its headquarters in the United States and if its membership contains many industrial (and communist) countries (ibid., table 5, col. 2).

However, US administrations not only monitor the staff sizes of international organizations more closely (if the Republicans are in power) than do other members. They also have a strong and significant influence on the policies of these organizations. He who pays the piper calls the tune. For example, states occupying seats on the United Nations (UN) Security Council and also of particular importance to US diplomacy, participate significantly more often in IMF programs (Dreher et al. 2009a) and receive more aid both from the World Bank (Dreher et al. 2009b) and the UN (Kuziemko and Werker 2006). Loans to these states are less likely to receive satisfactory marks from the independent evaluation office of the World Bank (Dreher et al. 2009c). States that tend to side with the United States in the UN General Assembly are more likely to participate in IMF programs (Thacker 1999) and receive more credit from the IMF (Barro and Lee 2005) and IDA (Barnebeck Andersen et al. 2006); those nations are also required to accept significantly fewer policy conditions from the IMF (Dreher and Jensen 2009). Countries that are significant importers of US products are more likely to receive loans from the IMF (Barro and Lee 2005) and the World Bank (Fleck and Kilby 2006). The same is true for countries receiving humanitarian aid from the United States (Eichengreen et al. 2008). During the international debt crisis of 1982–83, Marc Leland, Assistant Treasury Secretary, quite frankly called the IMF 'a convenient conduit for U.S. influence' (quoted in B. Cohen 1986, p. 229). A more subtle interpretation has been suggested by Anna Schwartz (1988): 'The multilateral agencies . . . seized the opportunity afforded by the debt crisis in the 1980s to enlarge the scope of their involvement in the economies of the problem countries, becoming active participants in the strategy the U.S. had devised.' It is difficult to tell whether the idea and initiative originated from the IMF or from its largest contributor.

As far as the Asian Development Bank is concerned, significantly more aid has been committed to those countries that, since 1987, tended to vote consistently with the Japanese government in the UN assembly (Kilby 2006) and significantly more aid has been given to countries that sided with the United States (Kilby 2011). The United States and Japan contribute the same amount to funding the Bank.

There is also evidence that the IMF's growth forecasts are significantly too sanguine before US presidential elections (Aldenhoff 2007) and biased towards optimism in general (Kenen and Schwartz 1986; Artis 1988; Aldenhoff 2007). This may explain why IMF growth forecasts have been less accurate than those of private and national public institutions (Artis 1988; Vaubel 2009a). International Monetary Fund inflation forecasts have been biased strongly towards optimism when the government of the member state held a seat on the UN Security Council (Dreher et al. 2008).

Most governments lack interest in monitoring the efficiency of the multilateral lending institutions, not only because their contributions are relatively small but also because they expect to be net borrowers. Subsidized loans from these multinational institutions help them to be reelected. Indeed, there is econometric evidence that the member states draw substantially more on their credit lines with the IMF and the IBRD prior to elections (Dreher and Vaubel 2004). The IMF also commits and disburses appreciably more resources immediately after elections (Przeworski and Vreeland 2000; Dreher and Vaubel 2004; Sturm et al. 2005), presumably because the policy conditions agreed in the arrangements can serve as scapegoats for the unpopular measures that often must be taken after the election in order to reverse irresponsible expansionary policies adopted before it.

5   SUPERVISORY BOARDS AND COURTS

The members of the boards supervising international organizations usually are comprised of career civil servants who later return to their countries' ministries or to the central bank. In the cases of the IMF and the World Bank, the supranational bureaucrats collectively are appointed by the Board of Governors, that is, the national ministers responsible for the organization, but they are known to receive detailed instructions from their governments. The executive directors from the United States even receive specific instructions from congressional committees (quoted in B. Cohen 1986, p. 229). Many executive directors represent groups of countries; they for obvious reasons are least likely to be controlled by their own governments. Voters and parliaments know very little about their executive directors. Most documents are kept secret; not even the voting record is published.[21]

Legal restrictions, high information costs and incentive problems limit monitoring by such supervisory boards. As for the first, the staff of the international organization may enjoy agenda-setting power. In the IMF, the executive directors vote on each program proposed by the staff but they cannot amend these proposals or adopt programs on their own (Martin 2006). Staff appointments are removed completely from the Board's discretion (ibid.). Martin concludes that the control exercised by the IMF's Board of Executive Directors is weak and has been declining over time. However, for the International Bank for Reconstruction and Development (IBRD), Kaja and Werker (2009) find a positive and significant impact of board membership on voting power with respect to the distribution of loan commitments.

The supervisors' information cost is high because they are 'kept in the dark' by the staff of the international organization (quoted in B. Cohen 1986, p. 229). The incentive problem relates to salaries. The rate of salary increase that the Board determines for its staff applies to the members of the Board as well (Irwin 1994). Thus, the executive directors have a vested interest in granting generous salary hikes. The same is true for the European Court of Justice. On 24 November 2010, the court determined that the Council's decision to limit the salary increase for EU public servants to 1.85 percent was invalid and that salaries had to rise by 3.7 percent as suggested by the Commission. In this way, the judges raised their own salaries.[22]

Net salaries in these international institutions are much higher than comparable salaries in the member states. In 1986, the last year for which the IMF has published the relevant data, net salaries at the IMF exceeded gross salaries at the Federal Reserve Board in Washington by 64 percent (Vaubel 1991). Irwin (1994) reports that, in the early 1990s, salaries at the World Bank were only 5 percent less than at the IMF. Frey (1985, table 27.3) has shown that net salaries at the OECD exceeded those of comparable German civil servants by 58 percent on average.

The most recent comparison of after-tax salaries relates to the European Commission (Table 27.5). The raw data have been compiled and published by the Commission itself – at the suggestion of the Council with whom the final decision about salary hikes rests. The net salary of a non-expatriate EU official (for example, a Belgian working at the Commission in Brussels) is set equal to 100 to control for differences in the cost of living. I have selected three grades (A4/A5, B4/B5 and C4/C5) for which data from all five reference countries and the European Investment Bank (EIB) are available. The first line (S) refers to unmarried persons, the second (M) to married couples with two children. The overall average for the five reference countries is 58 percent, that is, an average non-expatriate Commission official earns 72 percent more than a comparable national civil servant. Of course, the salary differential is much larger for nationals of low-income countries who are not covered by the Commission's study. In particular,

Table 27.5 Relative net salaries at the European Commission and in the central governments of selected member states

EU grade		Commission		EIB	Germany	UK	France	Denmark	Italy
		Non-expatriate	Expatriate						
A4/A5	S	100	123	147	63	74	81	60	27
(councellor)	M	100	121	149	62	61	80	53	24
B4/B5	S	100	120	151	70	84	59	66	41
(secretary)	M	100	119	158	67	67	53	59	43
C4/C5	S	100	120	147	71	57	57	62	46
(security officer)	M	100	117	154	67	44	50	53	37
Average	S	100	121	148	68	72	66	63	38
	M	100	119	154	65	57	61	55	35
	M + S	100	120	151	67	65	63	59	36

Source: European Commission, Comparative Study of the Remuneration of Officials of the European Institutions, June 2000.

the study, published in 2000, does not include the East European countries that joined in 2004.

The study also shows that salaries are somewhat higher at the European Commission than at the North Atlantic Treaty Organization (NATO) Secretariat or UN agencies in Brussels and, moreover, that salaries at the European Investment Bank are about 50 percent higher than at the Commission (Table 27.5). The reason usually given to justify this wage differential is that the EIB has to be competitive vis-à-vis private banks. However, most members of its management committee, including the chairman, a former politician, do not have any banking experience.

Some international organizations, for example, the IMF, the World Bank and the European Union, have independent evaluation offices, a court of auditors, an anti-corruption agency or a combination of these. There is indeed evidence of a significantly positive correlation between political centralization and corruption (Fisman and Gatti 2002). A recent and well-known case was the United Nations' Iraqi oil for food program. An independent commission of inquiry set up in 2005 and chaired by Paul Volcker revealed serious fraud and corruption in its administration.

In the European Union, two in three respondents believe that fraud against the EU budget is common and only one in five says that EU institutions are effective in fighting it (Eurobarometer, January 2004). In another survey in the same year, 74 percent agreed with the statement that 'clientelism and corruption are problems in the political institutions of the EU in Brussels' (Haller 2008, p. 345). In 1999, the College of Commissioners resigned as a whole because an independent committee of inquiry had found evidence of widespread fraud, corruption, mismanagement and nepotism. In 2003, the director of the European Statistical Office was involved in a corruption scandal and had to resign. In 2002, the Commission's chief accountant was suspended (and later dismissed) after she refused to sign accounts she believed to be unreliable.

The European Court of Auditors (ECA) and the European anti-fraud office (OLAF) may be doing their best but they do not seem to be very successful. OLAF has fewer than 20 investigators. The ECA has refused to clear the Commission's accounts each year since 1994, but spending errors continue to abound.[23] OLAF has estimated the damage from fraud at more than 1.5 billion euros per annum.

There exist 19 international courts of justice; seven of them control an international organization (Alter 2006, table 1). The most important of these is the European Court of Justice (ECJ). Moreover, some international organizations, like the World Trade Organization and the World Bank Group, offer arbitration facilities to its members (the Dispute Settlement Body of WTO and the International Centre for Settlement of Investment Disputes). These arbitration panels do not control their respective organizations but attempt to ensure that members adhere to the organizations' rules.

The role of courts and arbitration bodies is limited by the fact that they can act only if somebody complains. However, their main defect is that they lack the incentive to control the executive and legislative branches of their organizations. Once more, there is a self-selection problem and a vested-interest problem: lawyers who advocate a strong role for the international organization are more willing to join its court and, once appointed, they have a strong personal interest in transferring more competencies to it because, by doing so, they can increase their own power and prestige. The greater the powers of the organization, the larger is the number of interesting and important cases that judges are called upon to decide.[24]

The European Court of Justice (ECJ) is a good example. It is often called a 'motor of integration' – both market integration and political integration (that is, political centralization). It has invented various doctrines (for example, the doctrine of the primacy of EU law and the so-called direct-effects doctrine) for which there is no basis in the European treaties, but which assign more political powers to the European Union. Extensive empirical research reveals that the ECJ systematically favors the Commission, which shares its preferences, against the Council (Jupille 2004, pp. 98ff.). Moreover, even though the balance of weighted 'observations' that individual member governments may submit on cases pending before the court has a significantly positive effect on ECJ decisions, the probability of a ruling in favor of the plaintiff is significantly greater if the Commission is the plaintiff or submits an observation favoring the plaintiff than if the Commission is the defendant or submits an observation favoring the defendant (Carruba, Gabel and Hankla 2008). More simply, the Commission's stance has a stronger marginal effect on the Court's decision than the combined observations of the Council members.

The Court increasingly is criticized for its centralist bias. A court should not propagate a political program – it ought to be an objective and impartial interpreter of the law. How can this bias be curbed?

Self-selection may be limited by requiring judicial experience. In the past, only a minority of the lawyers appointed to the ECJ previously had served in judicial capacities in their home countries.[25] Most of them were professors, civil servants or politicians. Only since 2007 has a slim majority of the judges (14 out of 27) – but not the president of the court – been able to claim prior judicial experience (Vaubel 2009b). To narrow the options further, the judges might have been drawn from the constitutional or highest courts of the member states. This would also improve the integration of EU and national constitutional law. But it still would not have removed the judges' vested interest in transferring powers to the international organization.

The judges of an international court are responsible for two tasks at the same time: (1) of allocating powers between the international organization and the member states and (2) of interpreting the law of the international organization within those powers. The solution, therefore, is to have two courts: one court that has no power beyond adjudicating cases concerning the division of labor between the international organization and the member states (a 'subsidiarity court'), and another that adjudicates all other cases. This is the proposal of the European Constitutional Group (Bernholz et al. 2004). The group proposes that the judges of the EU subsidiarity court ought to be appointed by the highest courts of the member states to which they would return when their terms end.

6 LOBBYISTS

Interest groups are likely to exert more influence in international organizations than at the national level. Theory provides two reasons for this. The first is that, as we have seen, international organizations are farther removed from the attention of voters than national policy-makers. Interest groups try to bring about policy outcomes which, in their absence, the median voter would not prefer. The median voter is the main adversary of organized interest groups. If the median voter knows little about decision making in international organizations, lobbyists have a field day.

The second reason is that, in international organizations, bureaucrats are more influential, and politicians are less influential, than they are in national affairs. Bureaucrats, however, tend to be more responsive to the wishes of lobbyists than politicians because bureaucrats do not need to be re-elected (Crain and McCormick 1984). Politicians, by contrast, may be punished by the electorate if they take their instructions from interest groups rather than the median voter (Peltzman 1976).

These arguments run counter to James Madison's [(1788) 1961) view in *Federalist* no. 10, that political centralization weakens lobbyists' influence by establishing constitutional 'checks and balances' that would block one another. In the US context, commercial and financial interests from New York, cattle farmers from the Midwest and cotton growers from the South would counteract each other at the federal level. Many Americans, especially in the North, still believe this story (for example, Bolick 1993) because it was the federal government that abolished slavery against the economic interests of the South. What Madison did not take into account is that the more encompassing interests would combine at the federal (and international) level, that organized groups with diverse or even partly conflicting interests would strike deals at the expense of the unorganized groups and that both would become more powerful than they had ever been because centralization gives the government more power over the citizens. Nevertheless, since the theoretical arguments run both ways, this is an empirical question. Evidence ought to be brought to bear on it.

There are two major international organizations that grant formal roles to interest groups in their decision making processes: the International Labor Organization (ILO) and the European Union. In the General Conference, the Governing Body and the committees of the ILO, each participating state is represented by four delegates:

two appointed by the government (the Ministry of Labor), one chosen by the national trade union congress and one selected by the national employers' association. Thus, the member governments cannot adopt conventions against the wishes of both interest groups. Conventions are adopted or revised only if one of the two interest groups can obtain from individual governments what it cannot obtain from the other interest group in collective agreements. The voting record shows that, in 1975–95, trade union delegates supported more than 70 percent of the conventions or revisions, whereas the employers' representatives voted for only one half of them (Boockmann 2001). The General Conference requires a two-thirds' majority.

In the European Union, a large number of interest groups is formally represented in the Economic and Social Committee (ECOSOC), which, according to the Treaty, must be consulted on all pertinent legislation. Its members receive compensation from the European Union. The Economic and Social Committee employs a staff of more than 500 (half of them translators), who are also paid by the EU. In addition to the ECOSOC, more than 100 committees run by the Commission include representatives of organized interest groups (Falke 1996, p. 132). The treaties do not provide for this 'comitologie', but the European Court of Justice approved it in 1970.

Interest groups also play formal roles in EU 'anti-dumping' policies. The Commission accepts complaints only from EU producers 'acting on behalf of the industry'.[26] In this way, EU legislators have made sure that all major industries are organized in EU-wide associations. The EU is one of the most frequent users of 'anti-dumping' measures and has frequently been rebuked by the WTO for violating the latter's 'anti-dumping' code.

Another example is the EU's highly protectionist agricultural policy that thus far has prevented a successful conclusion to the Doha Round of international trade negotiations. The large subsidies for domestic farm products and the heavy import levies on imported agricultural products demonstrate the disproportionate influence of the European agricultural lobby. According to the OECD's 2004 survey of agricultural policies, financial support from taxpayers and consumers to EU farmers amounts to 32 percent of the latter's gross receipts compared with 18 percent for the United States.

In 2010, the EU bailout of Greece and Ireland and the European Central Bank's controversial decision to buy government bonds of several highly indebted member states of the euro area revealed the strong influence of the banking lobby. That rescue was reminiscent of how US banks had brought about the IMF quota increase of 1983 in a similar sovereign debt crisis.

According to one analysis, 78 percent of the pages of the EU *Official Journal* cover special-interest legislation (Peirce 1991, table 2). Another study reports that about 72 percent of the EU budget is devoted to catering to organized interest groups (Vaubel 1994). The Commission itself highlights the effectiveness of special-interest groups in shaping its budgetary priorities: in 2005–07 it gave more than 50 million euros to dozens of non-governmental organizations, including the European Trade Union Confederation (4.8 million euros) and the International Lesbian and Gay Association (1.5 million euros).

The Commission supports special-interest groups because bureaucrats and lobbyists have common goals. Both are interested in the centralization of policy, elevating their demands to the European level because it helps them to escape the attention of voters.

The Commission and interest groups form alliances against the median voter, which in the end undermine democratic control.

There appear to be more than 15,000 private lobbyists that attempt to influence the EU's institutions in Brussels. The total number of EU lobbyists, including those from other governmental and non-governmental organizations, has been estimated at 55,000. The lobbyists' main targets are decision-making bodies that are powerful politically, non-elected and small in number, and which take decisions behind closed doors by simple majority votes. In the European Union the Commission and the Court meet these conditions.

A study comparing interest group influence at the European and the national level has concluded that 'the EC system is now more lobbying-oriented than any national European system' (Andersen and Eliasson 1991, p. 178). Madison's prediction does not hold with respect to the European Union, and it probably is a fallacy quite generally.

7 CONCLUSION

In this chapter I have tried to present the ingredients and the structure of a general public choice approach to international organizations. I have given examples from various international organizations and policy fields – most notably from the European Union, the most developed of all international organizations. However, as public choice reasoning focuses on the incentives of individual actors rather than on types of collectively arrived at public policies, much of the conventional literature on specific policies and organizations had to be ignored.

The public choice approach is a positive theory but it also has important normative implications. It shows that international organizations suffer from severe agency problems. These have to be set against the potential benefits of internalizing Pareto-relevant international externalities and of reaping international economies of scale in the production of national public goods. The public choice approach lends support to the view that these benefits are not always worth pursuing.

NOTES

1. An exception is Switzerland. However, these referendums require a popular initiative. In Ireland, a referendum is mandatory if competencies are transferred to the international level, in Denmark only if the transfer is 'significant'. In the European Union, moreover, Treaty revisions have been subject to non-binding referendums in a minority of EU member states. The decision to join the EU has been taken by binding referendums in 12 applicant states and confirmed by a non-binding referendum in six applicant states (beginning in 1972). See Haller (2008, tables 1a, b) and Binzer Hobolt (2009, table 1.1).
2. Eurobarometer 44.1, Nov./Dec. 1995, question 73.
3. As an exception, the Council of the European Community or Union, respectively, has published its voting record since 1993, but this is not true for the Commission or the Court.
4. For example, people were asked the following four questions: 1. Which institution is the main legislative body at the European level? 2. How many member states are there? 3. Where is the seat of the main institutions? 4. Who is the president of the Commission? Only eight percent of the respondents were able to correctly answer all four questions (Eurobarometer 1993).
5. The classic source is Dahl and Tufte (1973, ch. 4, esp. table 4.8).
6. See Vaubel (2008, p. 436).

7. See Vaubel (2008, table 1).
8. For a survey of the literature on the strategy of raising rivals' costs see Boockmann and Vaubel (2009, p. 2).
9. I have provided the formal derivation in Vaubel (2008, pp. 444 ff.). The graph is from joint work with Bernhard Boockmann (see Boockmann and Vaubel 2009).
10. O'Reilly et al. (1996) report that in three of the five cases which they analyze, EU labor regulations go beyond most or all previously existing national regulations.
11. See, for example, Vaubel (1994) and Moesen and Cauwenberge (2000).
12. Heinemann (2007), Pitlik (2007), and Besley and Case (1995, table 4), for example, find that changes in tax rates are positively correlated among neighboring US states.
13. The common shock interpretation does not apply to the analysis of Mark Schneider (1989). He shows that the number of neighboring local communities and the standard deviations of their tax bills and total expenditures have a restraining effect on the number of government workers per capita in US metropolitan areas.
14. In Norway (accession to the EEC in 1972; accession to the EC in 1994), in Switzerland (accession to the European Economic Area (EEA) in 1992), in Denmark (signatory to the Maastricht Treaty in 1992; voting against joining the eurozone in 2000), in Ireland (rejecting the Nice Treaty in 2001), in Sweden (against joining the eurozone in 2003), in France (defeating the EU constitution in 2005), in the Netherlands (also voting against the EU constitution in 2005), and in Ireland (rejecting the Lisbon Treaty in 2008).
15. In a few EU member states, national legislation obliges the government to take instructions from parliament when voting in the Council on Art. 352.
16. Eurobarometer 61, 2004.
17. Website of the European Parliament: www.europarl.europa.eu/parliament/archive/staticDisplay. do?language=EN&id=211.
18. Eurobarometer, Spring 2008.
19. The source is www.votewatch.eu. According to another website (parlorama), the average is 84 percent but these data were incomplete and had to be corrected in response to protests from euro-parliamentarians.
20. The Council (and the Parliament) may, since the Treaty of Maastricht (1993), ask the Commission to draft proposals but the Commission indicated very soon thereafter that it does not feel bound to respond to such requests (Commission Report SEL (95), 731, p. 14).
21. 'The manner in which executive directors and their domestic authorities regularly report to parliament and the public on their participation in the Fund and the Bank is . . . only poorly developed. . . . There is an institutionalized bias against public accountability of executive directors' (Gerster 1993, p. 101ff., 107). See also Irwin (1994).
22. When the Council tried to resist the salary increases proposed by the Commission, civil servants at the Commission first went on strike (as on earlier occasions) and then to court. In 1984, both chambers of parliament in Germany asked the federal government to use its influence in the Council to curb the salary hikes at the Commission. The government rejected this request on the grounds that the Commission's monopoly of legislative initiative was an insurmountable obstacle.
23. In 2007, for example, 11 percent of cohesion spending was found to be erroneous. In 2006, 12 percent of the structure funds had been paid out in error. In 1998, about half the accounts of the Commission's programs were found to be correct.
24. For example, constitutional courts have to adjudicate inter-institutional disputes at the same level of government. As long as competence belongs to the member states, the disputes are decided by national constitutional courts. But once competence is transferred to the European level, the judges of the ECJ are in charge.
25. See, for example, Kuhn (1993, p. 195). In making their choices 'governments have tended not to be overly worried about the judicial qualifications or experience of their nominations' (Nugent 1999, pp. 272ff.).
26. Council Regulation (EC) No. 384/96 on Protection against Dumped Imports, Art. 5, no. 1. According to no. 4, 'the complaint shall be considered to have been made by or on behalf of the Community industry if it is supported by those Community producers whose collective output constitutes more than 50 percent of the total production of the like product'.

28 The political economy of war and peace
Christopher J. Coyne and Adam Pellillo

1 INTRODUCTION

Violent conflict is extraordinarily costly. Causing immense human suffering, loss of life, internal displacement, and destruction of resources, war is effectively 'development in reverse' (Collier et al. 2003). Given its social welfare consequences, the emergence of conflict should be seen as a puzzle to many observers. Yet from a political economy perspective, in order for conflict to occur, one (or more) political actor(s) must expect that the benefits of entering into conflict exceed the costs. Understanding why this calculus would tip in favor of conflict is the central question in the study of the political economy of war and peace.

The tools of public choice economics can be applied to highlight the logic of conflict and political violence. By analyzing the incentives, opportunities, and constraints facing different political actors (for example, government officials, rebels, military officers, insurgents, terrorists, diplomats, and even the occasional firm[1]), we can begin to understand why conflict occurs.[2] This chapter therefore places primary emphasis on the roles of constitutions, governance, legal systems, and bureaucracies because these institutional factors influence the incentives, opportunities, and constraints that political actors face. Consider, for instance, that weak legal institutions may preclude the resolution of disputes through legitimate means or may not allow for the impartial enforcement of contracts. Poor political institutions (or 'bad governance') can hamper the ability of political actors credibly to commit to peace negotiations, providing a rationalist explanation for the emergence of conflict (Fearon 1995). Countries with weak institutions may result in the true social costs of conflict not being internalized in the decision-making calculus of political leaders or may allow for undue influence by foreign financial, military, or logistic support.

While we cannot assess comprehensively all of the proximate causes of conflict in this chapter, our hope is to shed light on some of the institutional and political factors that set the underlying conditions for the emergence of conflict.[3] This political economy perspective differs from other important surveys and analyses of the same topic, which have focused on the ethnic dimensions of conflict (Horowitz 1985), the general causes and consequences of civil war and civil conflict (Sambanis 2002; Collier and Hoeffler 2007; Blattman and Miguel 2010), and more general aspects of defense economics (Sandler and Hartley 2007). Taken together with the current chapter, these surveys should help to illustrate the complexities of conflict while at the same time contributing to our understanding of its underlying causes.

We proceed as follows. The next section briefly assesses the economic approach to conflict. Section 3 discusses the importance of institutions for understanding conflict. After defining the relevant institutions, we explore the variety of channels through which institutions may influence war or peace. Most of the analysis in these sections focuses on intra-state conflict, given that this has become the dominant form of conflict in recent years (see Harbom and Wallensteen 2010). Our focus then shifts to the analysis of inter-state war and peace in section 4. We first consider democratic peace theory in section 4.1, followed by a consideration of the 'capitalist peace' in section 4.2. Section 5 concludes with a discussion of potential avenues for future research and analysis.

2 THE ECONOMIC ANALYSIS OF CONFLICT

2.1 Definitions and Incidence

For our purposes in this chapter, a *conflict* occurs when two (or more) parties resort to violence as a means of dispute resolution.[4] As for the prevalence of different types of conflict and political violence, incidents of intra-state conflict have far exceeded those of inter-state war in the past few decades.[5] As reported by the Uppsala Conflict Data Program (UCDP), there were 36 active armed conflicts in 2009 – none of which were inter-state in nature (Harbom and Wallensteen 2010; see also Collier and Hoeffler 2004; Rocco and Ballo 2008). Five of these conflicts met the intensity threshold (on the basis of more than 1,000 battle-related deaths) to be classified as *civil wars* – Afghanistan, Iraq, Pakistan, Sri Lanka, and Somalia. Since 1960, more than half of all nations have experienced a civil conflict, with 20 percent of countries experiencing at least 10 years of civil war (Blattman and Miguel 2010, p. 4). In sub-Saharan Africa, 29 of 43 countries have experienced civil conflict during the 1980s and 1990s (Miguel et al. 2004). Fortunately, since this time period, civil war has been on the decline, though other forms of social violence (for example, drug-war related violence in Mexico) have been on the rise.[6]

2.2 Economic Approaches to Conflict

The modern economic analysis of conflict for the most part began with Tullock ([1974] 2005, 1980b), Garfinkel (1990), Hirshleifer (1989, 1991, 1996), and Skaperdas (1992). In this section, we discuss some of the formal foundations laid by economists in analyzing a model that includes a choice between production or appropriation.

2.2.1 Choice over production or appropriation: rent-seeking in the context of conflict
One approach to understanding conflict is to model it as a violent competition or contest for resources (be they in the form of rents, tax collections, territory, or even political power). Hirshleifer (1991, 1996) models a choice between two different technologies that can be employed by political actors: a technology of production and a technology of appropriation, conflict, and struggle.[7] 'Struggles' can be construed as rent-seeking, for instance, in the sense of Tullock (1967, 1980b) and Krueger (1974), or as more violent conflicts for access to natural or mineral resources, such as crude oil and diamonds, or as opportunistic attempts to take advantage of weak state capacity.[8]

In conflict models like Hirshleifer's, agents can divide their initial endowments between productive efforts, E_i, or fighting efforts, F_i, in order to maximize steady-state income, I_i.[9] A probabilistic contest-success function, which determines the likelihood that a particular political actor will be victorious in political equilibrium (political actor number 1 here), can be modeled as

$$\frac{P_1}{P_2} = \left(\frac{F_1}{F_2}\right)^m,$$

where the relative price ratio on the left-hand side is referred to as the 'success ratio' and is a function of relative 'fighting efforts,' $\frac{F_1}{F_2}$, along with a 'decisiveness parameter,' m (Tullock 1980b; Hirshleifer 1989).[10] When the decisiveness of conflict is low or the technology favors the agent investing in defensive resources, the stakes are small and peace will be more likely.[11]

These models illustrate the tradeoffs individuals face and how they may choose to allocate their resources in different contexts (for example, when property rights are insecure or institutions impose weak constraints on political rulers). Yet there are limitations to this approach to explaining conflict (see, for instance, Gartzke 1999 and Cramer 2002). As noted by Blattman and Miguel (2010, p.11), 'one drawback of the typical contest model is that insurrection is never fully deterred; arming and fighting always occur in equilibrium. There is typically no decision to fight . . . this prediction of ever-present conflict is unsatisfying since political competition over power and resources is ubiquitous while violent conflict is not'. This highlights the importance of focusing on issues of weak governance, poor constitutional constraints, and other institutional factors that set the contexts for where, when, and how these types of conflict decisions are made.

2.2.2 Greed versus grievance

Successful rebellion or insurrection typically is seen as a function of the resources or time devoted toward these activities (see Grossman 1991). But it is also important to understand why rebellion occurs in the first place. Collier and Hoeffler (2004) discuss how political scientists usually attribute group 'grievances' (along political, social, economic, or ethnic lines, for instance) as the cause of most rebellions, whereas the economics literature (for example, Grossman 1991) usually points to economic incentives (that is, 'greed') and opportunities for appropriating wealth as the proximate cause. In testing the relative impacts of empirical proxies for 'greed' and 'grievance' on the risk of an outbreak of civil war, Collier and Hoeffler (2004) conclude that the 'greed' hypothesis is more strongly associated with the occurrence of civil war than indicators of grievance.

As an example of this economic perspective on rebellion, Miguel, Satyanath, and Sergenti (2004) cite the description of a Liberian warlord provided in Brabazon (2003, p.12): 'Essentially, [Sekou Conneh, a rebel leader] is a businessman, not a soldier or a politician. . . . Occasionally he seems to remember that he should say something politically relevant and will make a short impromptu speech about the struggle for democracy and the freedom of the Liberian people.' There is also evidence from disaggregated conflict studies regarding the role of rebel 'greed.' As reported by Hegre et al. (2009), conflict events in Liberia often took place in areas that were relatively wealthier, which they interpret as providing support for 'opportunity' explanations of conflict.[12]

On the other hand, a greater statistical emphasis on the 'greed' hypothesis of conflict does not necessarily imply that 'grievances' do not matter for conflict or rebellion. In other forms of conflict (for example, terrorism and insurgencies), perceived grievances can motivate individuals to take up arms against the state or their fellow citizens. In fact, there is likely to be an interaction of the two, as was suggested by Jackson (2002) in his analysis of the Lord's Resistance Army in Northern Uganda. In other words, the dichotomy between 'greed' and 'grievance' may be less relevant than the combination of the two forces as propellants of conflict. Further, 'grievances' can turn into 'greed' as the course of conflict between the rebel group and the government proceeds.

The decision to appropriate someone else's assets is also likely to be a function of the constraints imposed by existing institutions. As far as political rulers are concerned, when faced with institutional constraints on appropriation (such as independent judges, legislators, bureaucrats, regulators, and a free media), the probability of theft is quite low. Individual non-state agents (for example, warlords, rebels and insurgents) seeking to appropriate others' property likewise are constrained by existing political and legal institutions (and particularly police and military forces). Thus, as this logic suggests, the relative payoffs to appropriation and production are likely to be functions of the quality of a country's political and legal institutions – what is now commonly referred to as 'good governance'. This line of reasoning points to the conclusion that while rebels may indeed be motivated by 'grievances' against the state, the underlying cause may be the absence of economic opportunities for improving their standards of living, resulting from insufficient protection of property rights, endemic government corruption or weak state capacity.[13] This is the topic of the following sections.

3 INSTITUTIONS AND CONFLICT

In the sections below, we first summarize economic perspectives on conflict and then discuss how institutions emerge, the role of the state, and the structures of political institutions across countries. Along with these factors, we assess how institutional issues, such as credible commitment problems, and the consequences of different structures of institutions, such as low levels of economic development, influence variation in the likelihood of conflict across countries.

3.1 The Rationalist Approach to Conflict

The economic and social consequences of violent conflict are evident and widely known. However, conflict still occurs, suggesting that some political actors gain (or expect to gain) from initiating or prolonging of conflict. According to this view, political agents may view war 'as a costly but worthwhile gamble' (Fearon 1995, p. 383). For instance, rebel groups or insurgents may continue to engage in civil violence as a means of achieving political control, influencing political outcomes or achieving other economic benefits, even though their actions generate significant negative externalities for others. Indeed, as argued by Tullock ([1974] 2005, p. 311), 'gain (or avoidance of loss) is the common reason for undertaking warfare'.

Yet conflict poses an inefficiency puzzle: if there is a dispute between two (or more) agents, and all agents realize that the *ex post* costs of conflict exceed the benefits, then a Coase-style bargain prior to conflict would make both parties strictly better off (see

Powell 2006). Fearon (1995) argues that the '*ex post* inefficiency of war opens up an *ex ante* bargaining range' such that there should exist a set of Pareto-improving agreements that make both sides strictly better off. Yet there are reasons that these bargains do not occur. Fearon points to asymmetric information, commitment problems, and issue indivisibilities (for example, on the basis of religion, ideology, ethnic or regional identity) that preclude compromise between agents as rationalist explanations for the breakdown of negotiations and bargaining.

Additionally, it is likely that one political actor's expectations of the costs and benefits of engaging in conflict are not aligned with another political actor's expectations.[14] But it is also likely to be the case that the expected costs and benefits from the perspective of a political actor are not in line with the overall social costs and benefits. This may be because some political leaders do not internalize the full social costs of conflict, seeing only the benefits of maintaining political power, for instance.[15] However, changes in external financial, military, and logistic support can also distort expectations of relative costs and benefits – particularly over the course of conflict – which can also affect why political actors may see conflict as a 'costly but worthy gamble.'

3.2 What Are Institutions and Why Do They Matter?

Many of the potential covariates of conflict (for example, low levels of economic development, the effects of ethnic fractionalization, dominance, or polarization, and so on) as well as the ability to credibly commit to peace negotiations or communicate with socially distant individuals are likely to be endogenous to a country's institutions. For instance, it has been noted empirically that countries with institutions that protect private property rights are associated with greater levels of economic development (Acemoglu and Johnson 2005). Fearon and Laitin (1996) argue that formal and informal institutions usually preclude conflict between socially distant agents, illustrating why ethnic fractionalization, for instance, is likely to be the result of an endogenous process (see also Easterly 2001; Leeson 2005). It is therefore important to understand the mechanisms by which variation in institutions across countries can be associated with variation in the likelihood of conflict.

But what are institutions and how do they influence the onset or incidence of conflict? *Institutions*, as defined by Nobel Laureate Douglass North (1990, p. 97), are the 'humanly devised constraints that structure political, economic, and social interaction'. Institutions can emerge from a long run evolutionary or spontaneous process or they can be designed or imposed, as in the cases of colonial design of constitutions, country borders, and social institutions, post-World War II Japan and Germany, or more recently in the cases of Afghanistan and Iraq (see Coyne 2008). Formal institutions take into account the codified rules, constitutions, legal and political structures (for example, bureaucracies, judiciaries and legislatures) that govern society.[16] In the context of conflict, institutions can act as constraints on forms of political violence. As expressed by Fearon and Laitin (1996, pp. 717–18), 'a great variety of human transactions and interactions involve the possibility of opportunism – self-interested behavior that has socially harmful consequences. . . . [I]f unchecked by formal or informal institutions, the expectation of such opportunism leads individuals to avoid interactions or to take costly actions to protect themselves . . . making for a "society" of fear, poverty, and disorder.'

This makes highly relevant the choice between conflict and appropriation discussed in the above section.

3.3 The Role of the State and Institutions

One of the most fundamental roles of a legitimate state is the protection of residents from expropriation and violent coercion by others (Buchanan 1975).[17] In general, the state fails to do so when there is a non-state or extra-state actor that engages in violent conflict against the state or its citizens as a means of appropriating resources, achieving political power, or pursuing other ends. In the Weberian sense, when this occurs, the state's monopoly on the legitimate use of force is challenged by another entity.

Yet the government itself can also expropriate the wealth of its citizens or deny them fundamental human rights and civil liberties. Ensuring that political actors do not expropriate private property, for example, or engage in a bellicose foreign (or domestic) policy requires the imposition of political and legal institutional constraints (for example, checks by the judiciary, the legislature, or a free press) on the political elite. Yet endemic corruption, kleptocracy, ethnic favoritism, embezzlement, and nepotism may also spark conflict along both 'greed' and 'grievance' lines.

Unfortunately, first-order institutional arrangements are mostly absent in many countries. Countries with poorly developed political institutions – even those with the trappings of democracies (for example, elections and parliamentary representation) – can experience conflict.[18] Why are the institutional conditions, such as private property rights, accountability and transparency in government, and the freedom of citizens to voice their grievances through peaceful political processes that would lead to cooperation instead of conflict not established?[19] In order to answer this question, we must discuss where institutions come from in the first place.[20]

In contrast to contractarian perspectives on institutional development (for example, Nozick 1974; Buchanan 1975), a more empirically realistic constitutional equilibrium is one based on relative bargaining strength.[21] At the time that legal institutions and political structures are developed, they are not necessarily based on mutually advantageous exchange but on the relative political power of particular political actors. For instance, consider that Acemoglu et al. (2001a) find that the institutions imposed by colonial rulers and settlers hundreds of years ago have influenced variation in economic outcomes across countries in modern times. When those initial institutions were meant to be extractive in nature in order to benefit these political actors (colonists) with relatively greater bargaining strength, they did not adequately constrain the ruling political elite from expropriating citizens' property. Many of the constitutional structures we observe today are moreover a result of colonial planning or exogenous imposition and less so a result of the indigenous development of context-appropriate and mutually agreed upon political, legal, and economic institutions. Consider that many countries (and country borders) in Central Asia, the Middle East, and sub-Saharan Africa were all created by colonizers (see Shughart 2006), many of whom knew little about the political, social, ethnic, and cultural dynamics of these countries.

Olson (2000) illustrated that the development of political, fiscal, and legal institutions can be an indigenous process as well. From a state of anarchy, when political actors are provided with a monopoly of coercion over a particular area, the incentives they face may lead them to transition from 'roving banditry' to 'stationary banditry'. Instead of asset expropriation or confiscatory tax rates, these political actors may slowly lower their tax rates to encourage more production. Over time, they implement the tax revenue-maximizing rate, effectively becoming Leviathans.[22] Through the course of time, stationary bandits would have an incentive to provide public goods (such as security) in order to expand the tax base. In this framework, the development of political, legal, and fiscal institutions does not occur by social contract or voluntary exchanges, which contrasts rather sharply to the contractarian perspectives of Nozick (1974) or Buchanan (1975). Instead, institutions are the result of the demand for the largest tax base as possible by stationary bandits.[23]

In observing political and legal institutions across countries today, many states still do not provide sufficient protection or enforcement of property rights or constraints on executive action. The above suggests that variation in conflict across states may largely be a function of long run historical processes.[24] In this sense, political and legal institutions tend to be inefficient from an economic or social welfare perspective due to the relative bargaining power of political actors (see also Acemoglu 2003). As an example of constitutional constraints in the context of inter-state conflict, consider that with weak constitutional constraints on bellicose foreign or domestic policy decisions, political leaders can initiate conflict with other countries with relative ease. Conversely, with relatively strong constitutional constraints, political leaders face more difficulty in initiating conflict with other countries.[25]

As a more concrete example of these constraints, Choi (2010, p. 442) discusses the role of legislative 'veto' players, arguing that, 'it is reasonable to assume that the president is less likely to start or continue a war if he or she foresees mounting difficulties from legislative veto players capable of restricting, redirecting, and terminating military operations'. Choi's (2010) empirical findings suggest that legislative constraints on executive authority (across all dyads, or pairs of nations) are indeed associated with a lower probability of the onset of a militarized interstate dispute (MID), except for those dyads that are autocratic.[26]

3.4 Weak State Capacity

Huntington (1968, p. 1) argued that 'the most important political distinction among countries concerns not their form of government but their degree of government'. Following Huntington's conjecture, it may be the case that *weak state capacity* is an important determinant of conflict. State capacity can be conceptualized as a function of military power, bureaucratic and administrative quality, and political institutions (see, for instance, Hendrix 2010). Military power, Hendrix (2010, p. 273) argues, is part of the classical Weberian view, which maintains that the state 'claims the monopoly of the legitimate use of force within a given territory'. Strong military power (using military expenditures per capita as a metric) is usually associated with a reduced risk of conflict, as well as shorter conflict durations.[27] As put by de Soysa and Fjelde (2010, p. 288), 'if states have onsets of civil war, then by definition, a state is unable to monopolize the use of force'. Skocpol (1985) argues that state capacity is defined by sovereign integrity, the level of financial resources (for example, tax revenues, official development assistance, military aid, and so forth), the loyalty and skill of officials, the stability of administrative-military control, and the ability to employ resources (for example, public goods provision). As noted by Sobek (2010, p. 267), 'by increasing the value of the status quo, [more capable] states make it more difficult for the prospective rebels to organize . . . [S]trong states also have the ability to deter potential rebels through the threat, or actual use, of physical coercion, which essentially lowers the probability of rebel success'.

As for some of the empirical results regarding the role of state capacity in conflict, Fearon and Laitin (2003) use low income per capita as a proxy for weak state capacity, finding that intrastate conflict typically is associated with weak states. Braithwaite (2010) finds that countries with relatively higher levels of state capacity are better able to resist the possibility of violence spreading from one conflict-torn country to another. Weak state capacity is also likely to be associated with the anti-colonial nationalist movements and ethnic separatist movements that took place after World War II (see Shughart 2006, p. 17).[28]

Thies (2010), however, finds that state capacity is endogenous to civil war (for example, because conflict reduces tax revenues or diminishes overall capacity). Using a simultaneous equation model, he finds that state capacity does not have a significant effect on the likelihood of conflict. Theory supports both directions of causation. Consider that Besley and Persson (2009) develop a model that explains why prior external wars may have led to the development of income tax systems and the building of state capacity. Their empirical specifications highlight that a country's incidence of external conflict up to 1975 has a positive impact (statistically and economically significant) on an array of measures of fiscal capacity, such as share of taxes in GDP and one minus the share of trade taxes in total taxes.

3.5 Political Institutions and Civil Conflict

It is instructive to disaggregate 'political institutions' into different regime types (for example, democracies, autocracies, and military juntas, and so on) in order to understand which particular political regimes are associated with conflict.[29] Elbadawi and Sambanis (2002) find that democracy is associated with a lower incidence of civil war. This is logical considering that consolidated democratic institutions are likely to lead to the avoidance of conflict for a number of reasons. As expressed by Skaperdas (2003, p. 137), 'Modern governance . . . with [its] patchwork of checks and balances, wider representation, professional bureaucracies, and loyalty to nation states has managed . . . to overcome some of the most damaging aspects of appropriation and conflict. Fighting in the battlefield has been supplanted in most cases by fighting in courts and the halls of parliament'. Democratic political regimes typically ensure accountability, transparency, and binding constraints on political actors, as well as the ability for individuals to redress grievances or settle disputes by accessing legal institutions.

Further, facing the electorate periodically induces political rulers to support policies that are preferred by the median voter. This ensures that when political power is vested in the general populace, the likelihood of conflict will be lower.[30] Many of these factors have been identified as reasons for why democracies seldom engage in war with one another (see the section below on the democratic peace hypothesis). On the other hand, the level of economic development in a country has been shown to dominate empirically the level of democracy as a predictor of the onset of conflict (Fearon and Laitin 2003). These findings suggest that the level of development of democratic institutions in a country may be less important than the protections accorded to private property rights (see also Basuchoudhary and Shughart 2010, in the context of transnational terrorism).

Political scientists have suggested that 'anocracies,' or quasi-democratic political regimes, experience a greater incidence of civil wars than their democratic or autocratic peers. As Hegre et al. (2001, p. 33) point out, 'harshly authoritarian states and institutionally consistent democracies experience fewer civil wars than intermediate regimes'. This implies that there is an inverted, U-shaped relationship between the incidence of conflict when distributed along an authoritarian–democratic spectrum, peaking with regimes that allow for dissent and rebellion, but which lack either the military or legal prowess to address it. Hegre et al. (2001, p. 33) argue that anocracies are partly open yet also are partly repressive, resulting in a political equilibrium that 'invites protest, rebellion, and other forms of civil violence.... [S]uch institutional contradictions imply a level of political incoherence, which is linked to civil conflict'. Interestingly, their results suggest no difference in the probability of experiencing a civil war between countries they classify as strong democracies or as harsh autocracies.

3.5.1 Regime uncertainty or instability

Political regime change is often associated with civil war (see Hegre et al. 2001). Cederman et al. (2010) find that changes in political institutions – both democratizations and autocratization – are associated with greater incidence of civil war. However, when a transition to democratic rule creates popular unrest, civil violence tends to materialize more quickly, often taking the form of a coup d'état, than when nations move in the opposite direction. Irregular, unexpected changes in political leadership are also associated with greater risk of civil war onset (Gleditsch and Ruggeri 2010).

Jones and Olken (2009) find that successful assassinations of national leaders can intensify existing moderate-level conflicts, though they can also lead to the end of intense ongoing war. Perhaps most importantly, they put forth evidence that successful assassination of autocrats can induce political regime transitions toward democracy.

3.5.2 Political repression

Is political repression a cause of conflict? State repression could prospectively catalyze the creation (or strengthening) of insurgent groups, rioters, terrorists, and others that oppose the ruling political elite. Yet state political actors could also ruthlessly suppress dissent, preventing any form of conflict from emerging in the first place. As noted by Fielding and Shortland (2010), pressure by security forces can disorganize insurgent groups and deter future protests or riots, yet a crackdown can likewise lead to the escalation of conflict, resulting from the repression of civil rights, and the interference with ordinary daily life, which produce a civilian backlash against the state. As noted by Shughart (2006), when state capacity is sufficiently strong to deter any form of conventional war – that is, the state has well-equipped militaries, for instance, that preclude intra-state war from emerging – then terrorism may become the strategy of choice for those seeking political change by violent means.

Rocco and Ballo (2008, p. 348) define a repressive action as one that is 'aimed at weakening opposition in order to reinforce the government's position'. Repression effectively reduces the opposition's political and/or economic rights, but its effects may also spill over to innocent bystanders. Provocation is 'a repressive action that reduces the opposition's status quo utility to the point of making the risks and the costs of a war worthwhile, since the war gives it an opportunity to overthrow the ruler and stop the repression' (ibid., p. 355). The probability of provocation is greater if 'the rent a ruler can extract from his status is high and if the regular army is sufficiently effective'. They list a series of civil wars in Africa that were triggered by government provocation, citing examples such as Algeria (in 1992, an anti-Islamist took control of the government, outlawing the dominant Islamist group, FIS, and reversing the electoral outcome), Rwanda (the Rwandan army's massacre of civilian Tutsis), and Sudan (the imposition of Islamic Shar'ia law).

Empirically, it appears that anocracies – the semi-democratic political regimes discussed above – also face a relatively high probability of political repression (see Regan and Henderson 2002). This is peculiar considering that conventional wisdom would suggest that autocratic governments should be even *more* repressive. Regan and Henderson (2002, p. 133) argue that the inverted U-shape relationship they estimate between regime type and political repression is observed because 'demands in a highly autocratic society will in effect be muted by fear of retribution, while demands in a highly democratic society will be channeled politically'.

As Fearon (2004) finds, wars that originate in coups d'état or revolutions usually are of short duration because the 'technology' for acquiring state power hinges on rapid defections from within the state's military or security apparatus. Conversely, insurgencies may last much longer, as each insurgency's success or failure depends upon either a military victory or a negotiated settlement.

Leaders may engage in conflict because they are seeking to maintain or consolidate their power. As Rocco and Ballo (2008, p. 348) argue, non-democratic government leaders will seek to reduce their risk of facing a coup d'état or political revolution by either bargaining with the coup's leaders (see Azam and Mesnard 2003; Azam 2006) or repressing the insurrection. Repression may be intensified to such a degree that it provokes a rebellion/revolt or even civil war.

Why would a political leader seek to foment unrest to such a degree that a civil war is provoked? Rocco and Ballo (2008, p. 354) construct a model where the incumbent government receives a rent from being in power yet faces the risk of being overthrown by another group. Without political power, there is no rent for rulers. To secure political power, therefore, the rulers in government may repress their citizens. Yet too much repression can foment revolt, leading to civil conflict. However, this may not necessarily be a bad thing from the perspective of the government if the probability of victory is greater than the probability of remaining in power peacefully. The government's probability of victory is a function of the relative effectiveness of the government and rebel armies.[31] Ultimately, Rocco and Ballo's (2008, p. 360) model suggests that 'war is more likely when the government suffers from high political risk, when the rent from power is high and when the regular army is quite effective . . . [G]overnment beliefs about the probability of an accidental revolt and the possibility of foreign intervention affect the costs and benefits of provoking a civil war'.

3.6 Credible Commitment Problems

A credible commitment problem occurs when a political actor has an incentive to renege on previous peace negotiations, statements, or agreements; contracting is therefore incomplete in equilibrium. The incentives that lead to time inconsistency of negotiations or bargaining can be structural in nature (for example, due to political imperatives or optimal military strategies) or can be the result of behavioral aspects and specific leader characteristics (for example, impulsiveness or time-inconsistent preferences).

With respect to the former, if a chief executive's prior agreement to end a conflict or not to initiate one is not enforced by the judiciary, legislature, media, or other third parties (such as supranational entities like the UN or other peace brokers and diplomats), then a commitment to peace negotiations may be less credible. Political rulers may signal a willingness to commit to a peace agreement, but then realizing the gains from reneging on that agreement (for example, preemptive military actions that shock one's adversary or marshal domestic political support), they may very well do so. The inability of political actors to credibly commit to peace negotiations may explain why contracts cannot be enforced between disparate, self-interested agents.

Credible commitments to negotiations or ceasefires truly matter for the emergence of a stable peace. As Leventoğlu and Slantchev (2007) discuss, most conflicts end with negotiated settlements. When commitments are non-credible, agreements are *not* binding. When this is the case, actors cannot be certain of the time consistency of prior negotiations, statements, or agreements, which influences their expectations of a peaceful negotiation in the future. Under such expectations, agents involved in conflict may not be willing or able to strike peaceful terms.

Sometimes a commitment problem can arise when two parties do not have recourse to a third party that is willing to enforce a peace treaty or other agreement. Credible commitment problems can also block the resolution of disputes between government agents and rebel groups. Empirically, policy-makers' lack of credibility has been identified as a factor promoting insurgency (see Keefer 2008). The credible commitment problem has also been shown to be one of the causes of failed peace negotiations and the renewal of conflict.[32] This being so, military victory by one side or the other may lead to a more stable peace after a conflict has ended (see Flores and Nooruddin 2009). Further, as Derouen and Bercovitch (2008) find, conflict often resumes when civil wars end with negotiated settlements. Given that neither side may be able to commit to a peaceable resolution of a conflict, the actors involved may have incentive to renew it.

Azam and Mesnard (2003) model a conflict between a government and an excluded group. Given the specific form of conflict technology, the excluded group is able to overthrow the government if it invests resources sufficient to overcome the government's expenditures on defense. To pacify the excluded group, the government offers a social contract that promises a wealth transfer to the group sufficient to mute the rebels' opposition. Yet in the absence of a credible commitment mechanism, the government would be forced to promise a larger transfer than otherwise in order to pacify the group, because the expected value of the promised transfer would be lower if there is a nonzero probability that the government will renege. This illustrates why the level of credible commitment may be a significant explanatory factor in the observance of conflict. The absence of a credible commitment may help explain the inefficiency puzzle of war, that is, why Pareto-improving agreements are not reached in the context of conflict, either beforehand or after it has started.

What are potential solutions to the credible commitment problem? Given that poor contract enforcement is a hallmark of weak political and legal institutions, a Pareto-improving political transformation would be to implement *ex ante* binding constitutional constraints on political actors to ensure the time consistency of policy. As Rocco and Ballo (2008, p. 364) argue, 'a self-enforcing set of constitutional rules providing credible guarantees to the minorities would reduce both the opportunities for rent and political risk'. As emphasized by Sobek (2010, p. 268), 'highly capable states may be more able to win civil wars or more able to credibly commit to negotiated solutions.'

3.7 Asymmetric Information

Asymmetric information has been identified as one of the potential contributors to conflict (Fearon 1995). Initial differences in information sets may influence bilateral estimates of the costs and benefits associated with entering into conflict or the expectations of probabilities assigned to victory, incurring physical harm, and the like (see Tullock [1974] 2005, for example). This may be due to a misunderstanding of military capabilities (for example, due to deliberate misrepresentation, ineffective intelligence gathering or lack of understanding of a political actor's intent).[33] Differences in local circumstances and local knowledge can also affect the duration and termination of conflict. For instance, mountainous or cavernous terrain (for example, Afghanistan), dense forests (for example, Colombia, the Democratic Republic of Congo) and urban hideouts (for example, Iraq) can provide safe havens for insurgents; counterinsurgency efforts may be stymied by the absence of critical local information that may be learned only after boots already are on the ground. Asymmetric information may also lead to conflict because of linguistic fractionalization or misunderstanding of other's culture, conventions, intentions, and norms.

However, asymmetric information cannot explain why civil conflicts continue or subsequently are resumed after one side has been defeated (Fearon 2004; Powell 2006; Blattman and Miguel 2010). Ostensibly, after the initiation of conflict, political actors can update their beliefs regarding their probability of victory after observing relative military strengths and weaknesses. The revelation of such information should open up a range of bargaining alternatives to conflict, though this may take a number of iterations of 'updating,' particularly when relative military strengths and weaknesses are in a state of flux due to external intervention, more troop deployments, or developments of new military technologies.

3.8 Low Levels of Economic Development

Low levels of income per person, negative income shocks, and slow economic growth have been identified as robust correlates of conflict, especially civil war (Collier and Hoeffler 1998, 2004; Sambanis 2002; Fearon and Laitin 2003; Blattman and Miguel 2010).[34] However, the relationship between conflict and low per capita incomes can move in both directions. As Blattman and Miguel (2010, p. 4) argue, 'conflicts devastate life, health, and living standards'; thus it may well be the case that conflict is both induced by low incomes but conflict can also lead to lower rates of economic growth in the long run. The plausible endogeneity of economic growth and civil war has been noted by Sambanis (2004). Both hypotheses about causality are logically valid, especially considering that conflict can affect physical and human capital accumulation adversely. In order to isolate the effects of economic factors on the likelihood of conflict onset, Miguel et al. (2004) investigate the impact of negative economic shocks on the likelihood of civil conflict by exploiting rainfall shocks as an instrument for changes in economic growth. They find that reductions in annual economic growth increase the likelihood of civil conflict the following year.

Economic freedom is also associated with a lower likelihood of the onset of civil war (de Soysa and Fjelde 2010). Using the Index of Economic Freedom from the Fraser Institute, de Soysa and Fjelde find that this relationship is robust even when controlling for measures of government type (for example, democracy, autocracy) and other common covariates (for example, ethnic fractionalization). In contrast to the results of Fearon and Laitin (2003) and Collier and Hoeffler (2004), they find that, holding all else constant, per capita income is not statistically significant (in either logged or lagged specifications).

3.9 Institutions and Ethnic Tensions

Empirical results regarding the role of ethnic tensions in conflicts have been mixed, possibly because of different functional forms and definitions of ethnic tension (that is 'fractionalization', 'polarization', 'dominance', 'ethno nationalism').[35] In theory, causality between ethnic tensions and formal institutions may move in both directions. Historical ethnic tensions may have influenced the development of political, legal, and fiscal constitutions, while formal institutions such as these may not have been sufficiently developed to coordinate behavior between disparate groups along more productive equilibria. In this sense, social fragmentation (for example, ethnolinguistic,[36] religious, or regional fractionalization) may be endogenous to a society's institutions (see Easterly 2001; Leeson 2005). As described by Shughart (2006, p.8), the creation of artificial nation-states at the Paris Peace Conference led to 'some close-knit groups [being] divided by new, unwanted national borders; others were marginalized politically under governments controlled by irreconcilably different ethnic or religious factions'. According to Elbadawi and Sambanis (2000), along with economic dependence on natural resources and poverty, failed political institutions are associated with a greater risk of civil war in African nations. They argue that 'deep political and economic development failures – not tribalism or ethnic hatred – are the root causes of Africa's problems' (2000, p.245). As noted by Fearon and Laitin (2003, p.88), civil wars 'have structural roots, in the combination of a simple, robust military technology and decolonization, which created an international system numerically dominated by fragile states with limited administrative control of their peripheries'.[37]

Take, for instance, the policies of Europe's African colonizers: colonial policies of indirect rule led to the division of indigenous peoples into privileged ruling groups and unprivileged 'ruled' groups (see, for instance, Shughart 2006; Mizuno and Okazawa 2009, p.409). This likely had significant effects on postcolonial development in Africa, as 'accountability of the government, democratic competition, property rights protection, prevention of corruption, and rule of law were lacking in many African countries [after independence], which made politics in African countries favorable only for narrow elite groups' (Mizuno and Okazawa 2009, p. 409). The competition for resources that may occur between different ethnic groups may be the result of poor political and legal institutions.[38] As Wood (2003) notes, while this does not always occur, political elites and political entrepreneurs have the ability to polarize societies along ethnic lines.[39] Thus, a synthesis of these factors may be informative – weak political and legal institutions can endogenize the nefarious aspects of ethnic fractionalization (for example, political power in the hands of one dominant ethnic group), and such poorly channeled ethnic fractionalization can lead to conflict.

3.9.1 Issue indivisibilities
Conflict may be due to 'issue indivisibilities' among political actors. When particular issues, such as religion and ideology, are contested, there may be little room for peaceful compromise or dispute resolution (Fearon 1995). Bargaining may break down or not even begin.[40] With such beliefs and preferences, political agents may be obstinate at the bargaining table.[41] This is especially true when multiple actors are involved in a conflict and must necessarily agree to settle their dispute (see Cunningham 2006).

Peter Bernholz (2006, p. 224) discusses how ideologies with 'supreme values' – that is, values that include an aim or bundle of aims that is strictly (or lexicographically) preferred to all others – can underpin terrorist activities.[42] This observation is consistent with Rapoport's (1984) thesis that 'doctrine is the ultimate source of terror.' As summarized by Shughart (2006, p. 8), terrorism has occurred over time in waves of (1) ethnic separatism and national liberation (for example, Algeria, Cyprus, and Israel), (2) international-level ethno-national movements and left-wing terrorism (for example, the Palestine Liberation Organization [PLO], the Euskadi ta Askatasuna [ETA], and Maoist or Marxist-inspired ideological groups, such as the Red Brigades and the Baader–Meinhof 'gang'), and (3) an Islamic movement to restore Caliphate hegemony and Shar'ia law through violence. The latter certainly is a matter of 'issue indivisibilities' that prevent bargaining solutions from being reached. However, under particular circumstances (for example, historical experiences or grievances, political disenfranchisement, ethnic favoritism) these 'issue indivisibilities' can be manifested in violent conflict. Group-based hatred can also lead to conflict in certain contexts (see Halperin 2008 for a discussion of the role of group-based hatred in the Israeli-Palestinian conflict).

4 THE POLITICAL ECONOMY OF COOPERATION

In the sections below, we will consider how two different institutional arrangements – one political and another economic – have contributed to the emergence and consolidation of peace *across* countries. This differs from the above analysis, which has focused mainly on the institutional factors that influence the onset of intra-state and extra-state conflict. First, we will discuss the democratic peace hypothesis, which sheds light on the politico-institutional determinants of cooperation across countries, and secondly we will assess the capitalist peace hypothesis, which says that the 'payoffs' from trade and exchange lead to the emergence of norms and conventions that likewise preclude conflict.

4.1 The Democratic Peace Theory

4.1.1 Background and theory

In the broadest sense, the democratic peace theory holds that democracies rarely engage in violent conflict with one another because of shared norms and the existence of political institutions that constrain the likelihood of conflict (see Russet 1993; Rosato 2011).[43] The theory does not predict that democracies will never engage in violent conflict, but rather that they are less likely to do so against other democratic nations.[44]

The democratic peace theory is supported by two main propositions (see Gelpi and Griesdorf 2001; Rosato 2011). The first is that because of the development of informal institutions, such as social norms which foster liberal principles of respect, tolerance, and discourse, there is less to gain from resorting to violence (see Russett 1993; Dixon 1994; Weart 1998). To the extent that nations share such democratic values, they are less likely to engage in violent conflict because they recognize mutual benefits from committing to peaceful dispute resolution. Doyle (1983a, 1983b) and Russett (1993) extend the logic of norms to explain why democracies may be more likely to wage war against non-democracies. In the absence of shared norms, democracies cannot be confident that non-democracies will engage in peaceful dispute resolution.

A second proposition focuses on the nature of democratic political institutions. As discussed above, a key aspect of effective democratic politics is the existence of mechanisms that allow voters to monitor elected officials and to hold them accountable for their actions. Wherever such institutions exist, re-election-minded public officials generally will respond to the preferences of their constituents. In the context of international conflict, this point of view holds that public officials will resort to military force internationally only when domestic support for declaring war is adequate (see Russett 1993; Owen 1997; Schultz 1998).

Several different sub-channels operate within the broader democratic political-institutional environment that shape decisions on war versus peace between democracies.[45] One sub-channel flows though the idea discussed above that democratic leaders are constrained by the preferences of the voting public. When this logic is expanded to international relations between democracies, it implies that both sides face constraints which make conflict less likely because of the aforementioned interests of groups having stakes in maintaining peace.

A related sub-channel is that public officials undertake conflicts only when they think they can win since losing will harm their chances for reelection.[46] If two democracies know this, they will tend to have an incentive to reach some kind of peaceful settlement. Since democratic leaders will engage in war only when the relevant constituent groups are supportive, a commitment to war serves as a credible signal that they are serious about conflict. This credible commitment to conflict again raises the benefit of reaching some kind of settlement.

Finally, a third sub-channel is that the democratic process slows the mobilization of resources, thereby making war less likely. The underlying logic is that leaders must satisfy a variety of constituents and follow established procedural rules in order to engage in war. This limits the possibility of immediate resource mobilization, slowing the war process and making conflict less likely. Proponents of the democratic peace theory note that these mechanisms are either absent or weak in non-democracies, which may provide insight into why non-democracies are more likely to engage in conflict with other states.

4.1.2 Evidence for and against the democratic peace theory

The earliest empirical tests of the democratic peace hypothesis were carried out by Babst (1964, 1972), who reported support for the theory. Small and Singer (1976), however, responded to Babst, concluding that the evidence pointed in the opposite direction. This exchange can be seen as the origin of an academic controversy that continues to this day.[47]

Since the 1980s, a large number of empirical studies have built on this early literature. The most common design of these studies employs a dyadic approach that focuses on pairs of nations – for example, the United States and France, or Germany and China.[48] The empirical results are rather inconclusive. Many studies find support for the democratic peace hypothesis, even when militarized inter-state disputes are small scale in nature (Rummel 1979, 1983, 1985; Maoz and Abdolali 1989; Bremer 1992; Maoz and Russett 1992, 1993; Gleditsch 1995; Russett 1995; Rousseau et al. 1996; Raknerud and Hegre 1997; Oneal and Russett 1997, 1999; Beck et al. 1998; Bennett and Stam 2000; Danilovic and Clare 2007).

Mousseau (2000, 2003) also finds support for the democratic peace hypothesis operating through the channel of contracting, and the associated norms, which arise through markets. Specifically, he argues that economic development fosters values and preferences which support democratic peace and democratic consolidation. Mousseau's studies are especially interesting because they highlight how the origins of democratic norms and values are grounded in the market norms of contract – trust, interaction for mutual gain and equality before the law. As the intensity of contracting increases in a society *pari passu* with expansions in the extent of the market, so too do the associated values and norms. Mousseau's finding that contract intensity may be the actual cause of democracy and peace, calls into question the primacy of democracy in promoting peace. As we will discuss in further detail in the following section, these findings imply that democracy, by itself, may not be enough to ensure sustainable peace.

Building on this work, a more recent strand of literature focuses on how the level of economic development and the maturity of democratic institutions influence the likelihood of war between nations. Mousseau et al. (2003) find that, if at least one of the two democratic countries involved in war has a low level of development, democracy per se does not prevent conflict. Specifically, Mousseau (2005) reports that democracy is a statistically significant determinant of peace only when both nations in a dyad have reached a level of development that exceeds the global median. He also finds that it is the poorest democracies that are likely to engage in conflict with other democracies. Similarly, Mansfield and Snyder (2005) accept the democratic peace thesis for mature or consolidated democracies, but reject it for immature democracies. Their argument is that immature democracies do not have well-developed checks and balances that constrain elected officials. In the absence of effective constraints, elected officials can use conflict as a means of rallying popular support. Mandelbaum (2007) emphasizes that liberty manifested in a limited and constrained government, in contrast to mob rule, is central to international peace. His logic is that popularly elected government officials, absent effective checks on their behaviors, can generate perverse outcomes, including conflict.

The empirical evidence supporting the democratic peace hypothesis has been called into question on two fronts. The first line of criticism is focused on the definition of democracy. Critics of the democratic peace theory contend that its supporters define democracy narrowly, thereby excluding examples that cut against the theory's predictions (see, for example, Layne 2001; Rosato 2003, 2011). For instance, Ray (1993) points out that the following could be counted as wars between democracies under a broader definition: the American Revolution, the French Revolutionary Wars, the War of 1812, the Belgian Revolution, the American Civil War, the Spanish American War, World War I, World War II, the Israeli War of Independence, and the Yugoslav Wars. The disagreement over what constitutes a democracy led Rosato (2003, p. 600) to conclude 'the farther back we go in history the harder it is to find a consensus among both scholars and policymakers on what states qualify as democracies. Depending on whose criteria we use, there may have been no democratic wars prior to 1945, or there may have been several'.

The second line of criticism is focused on the robustness of previous empirical findings supporting the theory. For example, Oneal et al. (1996) re-estimate the model of Maoz and Russett (1993) and find that it is not robust to the inclusion of a variable that captures economic interdependence between countries derived from bilateral trade flows. Oneal and Ray (1997) propose an alternative measure of democracy, which relies on the governance score from the Polity III index, of the less democratic state in each dyad. Using this new measure, they supply support for the democratic peace hypothesis. Specifically, their results suggest that as the less democratic state in each dyad becomes more democratic, the likelihood of interstate conflict falls.

Rosato (2003) scrutinizes the fundamental claim that democracy causes peace, given the main consensus in the literature that *joint* democracy – that is, two countries in a dyad are both democratic – is associated with peace. He contends that if democracy actually is the cause of peace then a *monadic* effect should exist. He tests the democratic peace theory along these lines and does not find support for the central claims of the theory.[49] This is likely consistent with a series of studies contending that it is the similarity between the *form* of political institutions of states, and not democracy per se, that is a main driver of peace. For example, Raknerud and Hegre (1997) find that there is actually an 'autocratic peace effect,' whereby two non-democratic states are less likely to engage in war. Werner (2000) further buttresses the 'political similarity' hypothesis, noting that the 'democratic peace' is the result of comparing a restricted subset of similarly governed states.

In addition to the literature on political similarity, a series of studies consider alternative, non-democratic explanations for peace. The authors of these studies hold that joint democracy is one of only several potential explanations for peace and that the findings of previous studies supporting that hypothesis may be spurious. Farber and Gowa (1995) emphasize the importance of alliances formed during the Cold War as contributors to peace. Rauchhaus (2009) suggests that when there is a nuclear symmetry across states (that is, two countries both have nuclear arsenals), peaceful stability emerges. However, when there is asymmetry across states (that is, one state has a nuclear weapon but another does not), then the likelihood of an interstate dispute rises. Another line of research, which we will discuss in more detail in the next section, emphasizes the relative importance of economic factors. Other scholars, such as Gibler (2007), highlight the role of stable borders. After controlling for the absence of territorial disputes, he finds that the absence of democracy is irrelevant in explaining the onset of conflict.

Yet another line of criticism has been leveled at the two main theoretical channels – norms and political institutions – through which the democratic peace supposedly operates. For example, Reiter and Stam (2002) point to cases where democratic states have used military force to advance their narrow interests as instances that stand in contrast to the liberal democratic norms associated with respect, tolerance and peace. In terms of political institutions, Chiozza and Goemans (2004) find that losing a war significantly reduces the tenure of autocrats, but does not materially impact the tenure of democratically elected leaders. Weeks (2008) concludes that non-democratic leaders are as accountable for war as their democratic counterparts, which runs counter to the claim that democratic political institutions impose a unique set of checks and balances that limit the likelihood of conflict between states.

Critics have also raised questions regarding the effectiveness of specific groups and constituents in limiting the initiation of violent conflict. The issue is that just as there can be groups opposed to conflict, groups favoring it can influence policy. For example, Snyder (1991) discusses how logrolling among pro-war coalitions contributed to US involvement in the Korean and Vietnam Wars. Studies by Desch (2002) and Downes (2009) report that democracies are neither more nor less likely to wage war than non-democracies. These empirical results cut against the prediction that democracies will enter wars only when they expect to win and that this serves as a signal of credible commitment which contributes to the peaceful resolution of disputes.

In sum, the democratic peace hypothesis is one of the most widely accepted claims regarding international relations among politicians, practitioners, and academics. Despite this general acceptance, there is ongoing debate regarding the accuracy of the theory's central claims.

4.2 The Capitalist Peace Theory

4.2.1 Background and theory

In contrast to the democratic peace theory, the capitalist peace theory holds that economic ties between countries are the primary cause of peaceable international relations.[50] At its core, the capitalist peace theory predicts that interstate trade and other economic connections between nations raise the cost of interstate conflict as the result of the benefits flowing from repeated interactions. Close economic ties reduce uncertainty about future relations, providing an incentive to resolve potential conflicts without resorting to violence.

Gartzke (2007, p. 171) identifies three channels through which capitalism can contribute to peace. First, countries with similar policy goals have little to gain by trying to change the policies of their trading partners forcibly. Second, the dynamism of capitalist economies allows both parties to benefit, through trade, from differences in resource endowments and comparative advantages. Third, if the relevant parties can foresee the potential future gains from peace, or potential future losses from conflict, they will have stronger incentives to work toward negotiating peaceful resolutions to any disagreement. Dorussen and Ward (2010) highlight how economic traders become mediators in potential conflict situations because they have such large stakes in the continuation of peace.

As with the democratic peace theory, the central claim of the capitalist peace theory is not that capitalism will eradicate conflict completely, but rather that conflict is less likely between countries that are integrated economically.

While some scholars see democratic peace and capitalist peace as competing explanations for the avoidance of conflict, the two are more accurately viewed as being related. Scholars such as F.A. Hayek ([1944] 1976) and Milton Friedman (1962) argue that economic freedom is a precondition for political freedom. More recently, Lawson and Clark (2010) have tested the Friedman-Hayek hypothesis and find that it holds up reasonably well. Likewise, as discussed in the previous subsection, Mousseau (2000, 2002, 2003, 2005, 2009) argues that democracy is a descendent of contract-intensive economies, further highlighting the connection between economic freedom and democracy. Scholars such as Hegre (2003) and Weede (2004, 2006) have underscored the importance of economic development, which results from economic freedom, to the emergence of effective democratic institutions.[51] Weede (2011) views democracy as one channel through which capitalism can promote peace. Given this interconnection between political and economic institutions, a central question in the literature is whether trade and economic interconnectedness is more or less important than democracy for peace.

4.2.2 Evidence for and against the capitalist peace theory

Numerous empirical studies support the claim of an inverse relationship between dyadic trade and conflict (see Gartzke and Li 2003; Oneal 2003; Oneal et al. 2004; Dorussen 2006; Xiang et al. 2007).[52] The empirical approach of Souva and Prins (2006) posits that in addition to trade, foreign investment also has a positive effect on peace. Gartzke (2005, 2007, 2009) puts forth evidence that economic freedom and financial market openness reduce the likelihood of war. Furthermore, after controlling for financial market openness, Gartzke (2007, 2009) concludes that democracy has little or no independent effect on peace. McDonald (2009) employs alternative measures of economic freedom and finds that free markets have a stronger effect on peace than political freedom does. Boehmer and Nordstrom (2008) support the conjecture that strong trade relations between states are the most important determinant of joint participation in international organizations (see also Dourussen and Ward 2008, 2010). The underlying idea is that membership in multilateral organizations further strengthens economic ties and thus contributes to the capitalist peace.

While empirical evidence supporting the capitalist peace theory exists, there has not been a firm consensus in the literature to date. Barbieri (2002) provides an empirical analysis of the relationship between trade and conflict from 1870 to 1992. He fails to find support for the capitalist peace theory. Goenner (2004) remarks that empirical studies on this relationship can suffer from omitted variable bias.[53] Likewise, Kim and Rousseau (2005) question previous results regarding the primacy of trade over democracy for peace. Using data from international disputes during 1960–88, they find no statistical evidence of the pacifying effect of trade. Like Goenner (2004), they argue that earlier models were misspecified, resulting in spurious results.

Another question motivating recent research on the capitalist peace theory is whether, and how, the composition of trade matters. The motivating question underlying this strand of research is whether the negative relationship between trade and conflict holds across all goods or only for certain tradables. In its strong form, the capitalist peace thesis holds that trade promotes peace in general. However, a weaker form of the thesis may be valid in which trade in 'strategic goods' may reduce the peace-related benefits of international exchange and, hence, actually increase the potential for conflict.

One of the earliest studies to bring attention to the issue of the heterogeneity of trade was Hirschman's (1945) analysis of how the German National Socialists used trade to strengthen their domestic political power. Specifically, he highlights how German policy focused on exporting finished manufactured goods to Eastern Europe to make these countries more dependent on German industry. According to Hirschman (1945), the creation of this trade dependence allowed the Nazis to pursue their foreign policy objectives aggressively.

Likewise, some researchers emphasize that when war increases the relative price of exports, exporting countries may become more hostile toward importing countries. Polachek (1980) identifies this mechanism at work in the case of oil exporters and oil importers. Li and Reuveny (2011) build on Polachek and specify the conditions under which one member of a dyad is likely to engage in conflict against its pair. The likelihood of conflict depends on the number of alternative buyers and sellers, as well as on the sensitivity of each party's supply and demand to conflict. Dorussen and Ward (2011) raise some issues with the models of Polachek and Li and Rueveny. They point out that these models neglect the possibility of a third party intervening to avoid conflict. This is not unreasonable given the widespread benefits of trade that extend beyond dyads. Further, Dorussen and Ward point out that even if conflict can generate better terms of trade for one country, it is unclear that this necessarily would lead to war. It is possible that greater hostility by one country would not be met with greater hostility by the other.

In general, a central issue with empirical studies attempting to address the importance of strategic goods is defining what goods comprise that category. One approach has been to identify tradable goods that are more likely to lead to war. For example, Dorussen (2006) contends that goods whose production is concentrated in few hands – for example, energy, minerals and mining – are more likely to lead to conflict than are production processes relying heavily on foreign capital. Goenner (2010) employs the Herfindahl–Hirschman Index, a measure of industrial concentration, as a means of identifying strategic goods. In doing so, he categorizes the production of energy, non-ferrous metals and nuclear materials as tradables that plausibly increase the likelihood of war.

Large-N statistical analyses of heterogeneous trade are relatively new and only a handful of studies exist to date. Gasiorowski and Polachek (1982) analyze US–Warsaw Pact trade and conflict data during détente (the easing of US–Soviet hostilities). Increases in East–West trade, they conclude, led to a significant decline in US–Warsaw Pact tensions. Disaggregating trade, they find trade in manufactured goods to be especially pacifying. Polachek and McDonald (1992) support this hypothesis in empirical specifications using manufactured goods. Dorussen (2006) argues that the relationship is stronger for manufactured goods, except for chemical and metals industries, and weaker for commodities that are easier to take by force. Li and Rueveny (2011) also surmise that trade in energy contributes to the increased likelihood of conflict.[54]

As noted earlier, scholarly research has focused recently on the relationships between trade, intergovernmental organizations and peace. To reiterate, the underlying logic is that in addition to the direct benefits of dyadic trade, there are also spillover benefits for other countries. The flow of trade between two countries influences indirectly the flow of trade between other trading partners that are outside that dyad. Dorussen and Ward (2008, 2010, 2011) have incorporated both network effects and heterogeneous trade into their empirical studies and find that conflict is less likely when countries are part of the global network of trade. Interestingly, they also find that heterogeneity in the goods traded does not matter as much after controlling for membership in trade networks.

In sum, there is some, but by no means complete, consensus of an inverse relationship between international trade and international conflict. Proponents of the capitalist peace theory agree that the composition of trade also matters. However, there is disagreement regarding exactly what goods contribute either to peace or conflict. At least in the short-term the focus of research on the capitalist peace theory will most likely continue to revolve around issues of alternative model specifications and trade data aggregation. The other area of continuing research will be on understanding and quantifying not just the direct benefits of trade on peace, but also the indirect effects as well. Finally, one remaining research question is whether political or economic factors dominate.

5 CONCLUSION

In this chapter, we have assessed the political economy of war and peace, focusing on how different institutions influence conflict and contribute to the emergence and consolidation of intra-state and inter-state peace. Regarding future research in this area, scholars can benefit from the gathering of new data on these topics. Regan et al. (2009), for instance, have developed a detailed dataset on country-level institutions and elections between 1972 and 2005. Given the interplay of institutions and political leaders (see Jones and Olken 2009, for instance), scholars can also take advantage of the data on political leaders contained in Goemans et al. (2009).

Institutional change typically is an internal phenomenon, thus understanding the incentives of the political elite within particular countries and contexts are crucial. After all, as Olson (2000, p. 3) noted, 'historical outcomes surely depend not only on the incentives and self-interest of those with power but also on their morals and temperaments'. Along with empirical assessments of conflict, there needs to be a greater analytical understanding of how institutions influence conflict and cooperation directly and indirectly, by disaggregating them into specific constraints (and incentives). Historical, behavioral, and micro study-based analyses of conflict will also contribute to our understanding of the causes and consequences of inter-state and intra-state conflict.

NOTES

1. Guidolin and La Ferrara (2007), for instance, find that the death of Jonas Savimbi, the UNITA rebel group leader in Angola, led to a decline in stock market returns among mining companies holding concessions in that country. They conclude that moderate levels of civil conflict can actually be financially beneficial for a handful of firms whose profitability is determined by the prolonging of conflict. This illustrates that some investors or companies may turn a blind eye to conflict given its profitability.
2. As described by Acemoglu (2003, p. 621), under a theory of social conflict, 'societies choose different policies, some of which are disastrous for their citizens, because those decisions are made by politicians or politically powerful social groups that are interested in maximizing their own payoffs, not aggregate output or social welfare.' Tullock ([1974] 2005, p. 312) argued that 'it is clear that . . . an extremely bloody

and destructive war and, looked at from the standpoint of the entire citizenry of the two countries, [is] undesirable. Looked at from the standpoint of the dictator, however, it has a positive discounted value.'
3. We are cognizant that there are multiple factors not discussed in this chapter that are central to understanding war or peace. For instance, we exclude analysis of the role of foreign intervention (for example, military, financial, and material support), the trade in small-arms, post-conflict economic reconstruction, the role of geography (for example, terrain, natural resources, commodities, such as diamonds or cocaine, that fund rebel groups) that influence the onset, duration, and recurrence of conflict, as well as the industrial organization of terrorist, insurgent, and rebel groups, and the influence of ideology or behavioral factors on the decision-making of political actors. Our exclusion of these factors is not intended to downplay the importance of them for understanding conflict and peace. Instead, our central focus is on the institutions and political elements that influence the costs and benefits associated with these various factors. For instance, adverse geography and rough terrain can challenge the ability of states to establish monopolies on the legitimate use of force (see Acemoglu et al. 2009). Likewise, natural resource rents could induce agents to choose to appropriate others' property rather than to engage in productive behavior.
4. Conflict is defined and operationalized in different ways in the literature, depending on the objectives of the researcher. The Uppsala Conflict Data Program's (UCDP) definitions can be found at http://www2.pcr.uu.se/research/UCDP/data_and_publications/definitions_all.htm. An *intra-state war* is defined by the Correlates of War Project as a war that is fought within state borders between a government and a non-government entity (a civil war). Intra-state wars are associated with at least 1,000 combat-related deaths in one year (Small and Singer 1982). An inter-state war is defined as a war between two states with at least 1,000 battle-related fatalities in total in a given year. Conflict can also be extra-state in nature, where a conflict is between a state and a non-state entity outside of the state's own territory (for instance, the conflict between Israel and the Hezbollah militia). Another conflict dataset by the Uppsala Conflict Data Program and the Centre for the Study of Civil War at the International Peace Research Institute (UCDP/PRIO) similarly differentiates conflict along different dimensions (for example, intra-state or inter-state). The UCDP/PRIO definition of armed conflict is construed to be those forms of political violence that are associated with at least 25 deaths in one year. Specifically, conflict is defined as 'a contested incompatibility that concerns government and/or territory where the use of armed force between two parties, of which at least one is the government of a state, results in at least 25 battle-related deaths (Gleditsch et al. 2002).
5. An unbundling of 'conflict' illustrates the variety of forms of political violence that have been observed over time: interstate wars, civil wars, terrorism, coups d'état, state-sanctioned violence and political repression, genocides, rebellions, social unrest and riots, insurgencies, guerilla warfare, covert operations, violence related to social fractionalization (for example, along ethnic, linguistic and religious lines), military and diplomatic interventions, and drug-trade related violence (and more). After conflict and political instability often come efforts to reconstruct the economy (both indigenously and externally), demobilize, disarm, and reintegrate former combatants, consolidate or fundamentally reform political institutions, provide healthcare and basic services to citizens, refugees, and internally displaced persons, prevent the outbreak of further conflict, and move towards a more stable and peaceful society.
6. These forms of civil violence are not classified as 'civil conflict' or 'civil war' by the UCDP, however.
7. This choice over production or predation is by no means abstract. Grossman and Kim (1996) note that the Vikings and the Mongols were *almost entirely* predatory in their economic activities. See also Olson (2000).
8. Neary (1997) compares the properties of rent-seeking models and economic models of conflict, illustrating how both models describe the allocation of resources in pursuit of a fixed prize. Conflict models typically involve a higher level of expenditures on 'predatory' or 'appropriative' activities than do rent-seeking models, which is expected given the relative welfare costs of the two activities.
9. In some instances, this is referred to as a split between 'guns' and 'butter', subject to a particular resource constraint (see Garfinkel and Skaperdas 2000).
10. The probabilistic contest success function was first put forth by Tullock (1980b). According to Garfinkel and Skaperdas (2000), the most commonly employed functional form of this contest success function in the literature is $p(F_1, F_2) = \frac{F_1}{F_1 + F_2}$ where p is the probability of success or is the proportionate share of the 'prize' won by a game's player.
11. Similarly, Grossman and Kim (1996, p. 57) develop a model of interaction between 'predator' and 'prey', where, given initial endowments, the predator 'allocates its resources to either the production of consumables, or to offensive weapons that the predator uses to appropriate the prey's property, or to both'. The 'prey' agent can dedicate endowment resources to defensive fortifications or productive capital. Predators solve a similar problem, but instead of defensive fortifications they invest in offensive weapons. As put by Hirshleifer (1991), when an individual's endowment is relatively small, the dominant strategy will be to shift resources toward predatory activities. This may explain why civil conflict and civil war typically occur in countries with low levels of economic growth and development.

12. The literature on terrorism, by contrast, suggests that the leaders of such groups tend to be young and highly educated (see Pape 2005; Shughart 2011b), thereby lending support to the 'grievance' hypothesis.
13. As argued by Sobek (2010, p. 267), 'states have the ability to address the demands of their citizens in ways that reduce the incentive for political violence, which limits the ability of rebels to overcome the problems with collective actions . . . strong states can [also] simply deter resistance through their ability to physically coerce dissenters'. Thies (2010, p. 322) argues that 'the incentive to rebel is a product of the probability of victory and the state's capacity to defend itself' and this is largely a function of its ability to extract tax revenues. Basuchoudhary and Shughart (2010) emphasize the role that economic liberty plays in reducing terrorism in societies characterized by ethnic tensions.
14. Consider, for instance, the legal literature on the decision to settle or litigate. Two (or more) parties will end up in court if the parties have different expectations of the costs and benefits of doing so (see Landes 1971; Gould 1973; Shavell 1982). Analogously, in the context of conflict, two (or more) parties may end up in conflict based on differing expectations.
15. Nevertheless, bargaining does occur between political actors. Peace treaties are often brokered and negotiations can occur after rounds of conflict (or even prior to the onset of conflict). Consider Lee's (1988) 'paid-rider' framework, where the state offers sanctuary to a terrorist organization so long as the group does not strike domestic civilian or government infrastructure or buildings. This bargaining equilibrium has been realized in some contexts, like Germany's provision of refuge to the Red Army Faction (Baader-Meinhof Gang) in the 1960s (Shughart 2006), France's offer of sanctuary to Arab and Basque terrorists (Lee 1988), or, perhaps more poignantly, Afghanistan's preferential treatment of al Qaeda in the 1990s and early 2000s.
16. Informal institutions, which are not considered in detail herein, similarly govern political, economic, and social interactions but are not codified in any formal or legal sense. These informal institutions include such things as norms, conventions, social capital and religious practices (see Williamson 2000).
17. In the United States, for instance, as noted by Tullock ([1974] 2005, p. 16), 'the police and the courts stand ready to use violence against anyone who attempts to take your property'. It is not the case that such legal institutions actually lead to the application of violence, yet moreover it is the credibility of the threat of using violence that motivates action.
18. As discussed below, these types of political institutions (that is, anocracies) experience a disproportionate number of conflicts, which suggests that it may not be democracy per se that inhibits conflict, but other institutional factors such as overall state capacity.
19. As argued by Shughart (2006, p. 8), terrorism, for instance, is largely a function of 'cartographic and constitutional failure'.
20. As put by Olson (2000, p. 1), 'In a Hobbesian anarchy, where there is no restraint on individuals' incentives to take things from one another, or in a kleptocracy, where those in power seize most assets for themselves, there is not much production or many gains from social cooperation through specialization and trade.' Buchanan (1975) argued from a contractarian perspective, that individuals would see it as mutually advantageous to impose binding constraints on their own behavior in order to shift efforts from appropriation in the natural state of anarchy to production in a constitutional form of government. Similarly adopting a contractarian view of the state, Nozick (1974) held that we should expect to see a single political entity emerge from a natural state of anarchy with a monopoly on the legitimate use of force owing to the benefits of specialization, division of labor, and economies of scale. While the dynamics described in the contractarian perspective could lead to first-order constitutional systems and classically liberal political and legal institutions if implemented in practice, casual empiricism suggests that this has not occurred in many countries.
21. See Holcombe's (1994, ch. 2) economic theory of rights. Bargaining power, he claims, can be a result of economic resources or military prowess.
22. In other words, 'the stationary bandit, because of his monopoly on crime and taxation, has an encompassing interest in his domain that makes him limit his predations because he bears a substantial share of the social losses resulting from these predations' (Olson 2000, p. 9).
23. As argued by Olson (2000, p. 25), 'To reach the maximum income attainable at a given tax rate, a society must enforce contracts (including those involving long-term loans) impartially, but the full gains are again reaped only in the long run'. All of this also suggests that leader time horizons and time preferences also matter for the onset of conflicts. Olson wrote (2000, p. 26) 'at the limit, when an autocrat has no reason to consider the future output of a society, his incentives are those of a roving bandit, which is, in effect, what he becomes'.
24. This line of reasoning also suggests that both historical and current institutions can be somewhat endogenous to political actors, which makes the institutional analysis of conflict more complex. As noted by Weingast (1997), the rule of law must be self-enforcing, as political leaders can reduce the efficacy of political and legal institutions through their actions.
25. As we discuss below in the section on democratic peace theory, mass public opinion (or other 'citizen constraints') can also influence whether war is declared.

26. Other institutional examples stem from the economic analysis of terrorism. Basuchoudhary and Shughart (2010) find that institutions that promote economic liberty are actually more effective at precluding terrorism in societies characterized by ethnic tensions than political institutions that afford protections to individual civil rights.
27. Regardless of the state's relative military capacity or strength, however, the tactical advantages of insurgents can lead to protracted civil conflicts. Consider historical examples of the Palestine Liberation Organization (PLO), the Viet Cong, the Irish Republican Army (IRA), Spain's Euskadi ta Askatasuna (ETA) or more recent examples of insurgents in Afghanistan and Iraq, where relatively strong states with superior military capacity (that is, superior technology and better trained soldiers) have not been able to fully counter insurgencies, perhaps because of terrain issues or asymmetric tactics. As summarized by Shughart (2006, p. 21), 'relatively small groups of urban guerillas, though overmanned and outgunned by regular armies on the ground, can demoralize great empires by waging campaigns of carefully planned attacks on targets inevitably left pregnable by the larger, but less flexible forces arrayed against them'. On the other hand, the relative strength of the state in these circumstances may have prevented terrorist or insurgent momentum from snowballing into full rebellions and intra-state wars.
28. Note that we do not consider in this section whether a strong, overarching state is preferred from a social welfare perspective. Weak states are associated with conflict, yet this may be because the legitimacy of the state is questionable or because the political elite seek to impose its will on groups within its country that would prefer autonomy or independence. Allowing for full autonomy of different ethnic or political groups may be optimal from the perspective of overall social welfare. Though, of course, this is unlikely to be compatible with the incentives of government officials in central governments, particularly when tax bases and the revenues from resource sales are at stake.
29. While a detailed discussion of the characteristics of these different political institutions is beyond the scope of this survey, a consideration of some of the relevant literature's empirical findings shed light on the relationship between institutional quality and the incentives for conflict versus cooperation.
30. Yet, then again, elections sometimes can actually lead to conflict. Consider the 1991 legislative elections in Algeria, for instance. The Islamic Salvation Front (FIS) was voted into power yet the Algerian government responded by negating the electoral outcome, which subsequently contributed to a devastating civil war that resulted in the deaths of more than 120,000 individuals (Wantchekon 1999, p. 246). This does not necessarily undermine the argument presented above, but does offer an example of why elections must be compatible with the incentives and constraints faced by status quo political actors. Ethnic fractionalization can also drive electoral results, leading to the view that elections can be nothing more than an 'ethnic census' (Horowitz 1985; Kimenyi and Romero 2008, p. 8). The main findings of Coyne (2008) and Basuchoudhary and Shughart (2010) suggest that 'democracy' is oversold as a solution to intrastate conflict.
31. See Tullock ([1974] 2005), who specifies more fully the probabilities associated with rebellions, coups, and other forms of political violence.
32. This is because one episode of conflict reveals information about the relative military strengths of the parties involved. We discuss this in more detail in the subsequent sub-section on asymmetric information.
33. Political actors may also have strategic incentives to misrepresent their intentions or hoard private information about their military capabilities. For instance, as discussed by Blattman and Miguel (2010, p. 16), 'field generals have incentives to mislead civilian leaders about the capability of their military forces if they hope to keep the fighting going for longer than citizens would like (to keep military budgets at high levels, for instance)'.
34. As discussed above, a society's level of economic development is a function of its political institutions (see Acemoglu et al. 2001a; Acemoglu and Johnson 2005).
35. See, for instance, Elbadawi and Sambanis (2000, 2002); Fearon and Laitin (2003); Collier and Hoeffler (2004); Sambanis (2004); Montalvo and Reynal-Querol (2005); Cederman and Giardin (2007); and de Soysa and Fjelde (2010). Empirical results suggest, for instance, that conflicts involving ethnic polarization, that is, the 'sons-of-the-soil' wars, tend to last relatively longer (see Fearon 2004).
36. Many scholars define 'ethno-linguistic fractionalization' (ELF) as one measure of ethnic tensions in a society in accordance with the following Herfindahl–Hirschman index, widely adopted in the industrial organization literature as a measure of the size distribution of firms in a properly defined 'market': $ELF = 1 - \sum_{i-1}^{n} s_i^2$ where s_i is the share of ethnolinguistic group i of all n groups in a society.
37. For a detailed analysis of how colonization led to weak state capacity and fragile states, see Shughart (2006).
38. See, for instance, Posner (2004).
39. This can occur, for instance, through sheer political power or political disenfranchisement or even through the usage of propaganda (for example, the role of Radio Télévision Libre des Mille Collines in the Rwandan genocide, where Yanagizawa-Drott (2009) estimates that nearly 45,000 Tutsi deaths can be accounted for due to this source of propaganda). See also Kirk (1983) and Glaeser (2005).

40. As noted by Cowen (2004, p. 2), 'Almost everyone wants peace on his or her terms, but for many sets of preferences the offer curves do not intersect . . . [S]ometimes the compensating variation will be infinite (or undefined) because the parties do not like the idea of paying cash for certain values, or do not like the idea of trading those values through a more complicated form of barter'.
41. Usher (2011) makes the argument that economists have no theory for locating bargains on the contract curve in the Edgeworth-Bowley box.
42. Bernholz (2006) argues that terrorism based on such incompatible ideologies typically leads to fundamental social conflict. However, he also notes that such ideologies are not necessarily sufficient for terrorist activities to occur. Many individuals hold beliefs that are lexicographically preferred to other sets of values or aims (for example, Jews, Christians, Muslims, Hindus and Sikhs), but we still observe peaceful coexistence among many members of these disparate groups.
43. The democratic peace theory can be traced back to Immanuel Kant ([1795] 1983), who identified liberal constitutional republics as supplying one necessary condition for the emergence of 'perpetual peace'. In modern times, the democratic peace theory has played a central role in US foreign policy (see Bennett and Ikenberry 2006) and is one of the theories of conflict most accepted by academics. Levy (1989, p. 270), for instance, writes that the democratic peace theory 'comes as close as anything we have to an empirical law in international relations'.
44. We should also note that there is a related literature exploring why democracies are less likely, as compared to other forms of government, to engage in conflict with any other governmental type. Discussions of the literature related to this claim can be found in Oneal and Ray (1997) and Oneal and Russet (1999).
45. See Bueno de Mesquita and Lalman (1992); Russett (1993); Schultz (1998); Bueno de Mesquita et al. (1999, 2004); and Bueno de Mesquita (2006).
46. However, an alternative viewpoint is that public officials may enter into conflict as a means of diverting the public's attention away from particular domestic issues. Diversionary war theory holds that when political leaders face opposition at home (for example, because of economic downturns, unemployment, or political/military crises), they may resort to violence as a means of evading responsibility for those events. Hess and Orphanides (2001) argue that incumbent leaders may start prospectively avoidable conflicts in order to divert the electorate's attention away from a poorly performing economy. Such violence can be interstate or intrastate in nature, although the evidence is sparse for the former type of conflict. Tir and Jasinski (2008) is one example of empirical support for the diversionary use of force against ethnic minorities.
47. Rummel (1979, 1983, 1985) is another earlier contributor to the democratic peace debate. His empirical results support the theory's central prediction.
48. For a discussion of some of the problems with this standard approach, see Ward et al. (2007) and Maoz (2009). There is also a smaller literature arguing that democracies are more peaceful in general – whether they interact with other democracies or non-democracies (see Benoit 1996; Boehmer 2008; Rummel 1995; Souva and Prins 2006). In general, the evidence for this position is weaker than that relating to dyadic peace between democracies.
49. See Rosato (2005) for a response to some of the criticisms of this approach.
50. The notion of the capitalist peace has a long history that can be traced back to Montesquieu, Adam Smith, Thomas Paine, Frederic Bastiat, John Stuart Mill, and Richard Cobden (Gartzke 2007).
51. It should be noted that an ongoing debate questions the relationship between democracy and economic growth (see Knack and Keefer 1995; de Haan 1996; Hall and Jones 1999; Barro 1997; Tavares and Wacziarg 2001).
52. See Barbieri et al. (2009) for a discussion of the limits of existing trade data.
53. Applying Bayesian averaging, he tests several alternatives and finds that trade interdependence does not explain peace, but that joint democracy does.
54. Dorussen and Ward (2011) point to some of the limits of these studies, including differences in definitions of conflict, the level of aggregation in trade data, and model specification. Ideally, dyadic trade flows at the commodity level would be analyzed to identify the specific goods that contribute to peace or conflict (Polachek 1992). However, because of data limitations, each of the existing empirical studies approaches the problem idiosyncratically, making it difficult to compare the findings across studies (Dorussen and Ward 2011).

29 Collective action and (counter)terrorism
Daniel G. Arce M.

1 INTRODUCTION

Terrorism is a form of asymmetric conflict where violence is used against civilians and passive military personnel in order to influence a target audience beyond that of the immediate victims for political, religious or ideological purposes. Given that terrorism and responses to terrorism are political acts calculated to have maximum effect, both phenomena fall under the rubric of public choice. For example, transnational counterterror activity involves the voluntary actions of one or more countries and as such counterterrorism can exhibit classic Olsonian collective action problems (Olson 1965), depending on the direction of the externality produced by each target nation's action. It is also the case that modern terrorist organizations themselves are highly decentralized, employing cell structures or attempting to inspire affiliates or start-ups to act in support of their cause. Hence, terror organizations themselves face collective action problems and also classic agency problems in the sense of Mitnick (1975). In particular, when terrorist organizers face an adverse selection problem (for example, in recruiting conventional versus suicide operatives), the screening process reveals why poverty may not ultimately be a driver of terrorism. Finally, given all the attention and effort paid to (counter)terror activities, the general lack of political resolution – on the part of terrorists and the governments they target – begs the question as to how these behaviors constitute the actions of rational individuals.

It is the purpose of this chapter to examine terrorism and counterterrorism through the lens of public choice, paying particularly close attention to issues related to collective action. The chapter is broken up into three sections. The first deals with collective action issues faced by target governments. The second addresses the rationality of counterterror strategies and the actions of terrorists themselves. This is followed by an examination of collective action issues within terror organizations.

2 THE FUNDAMENTAL EXTERNALITIES OF TRANSNATIONAL COUNTERTERRORISM

Terrorism is regarded as a transnational phenomenon whenever two or more countries are involved; for example, if the perpetrators and victims come from different countries, if the victims themselves are citizens of more than one country, or if more than one country is involved in the process (for example, a terrorist travels internationally to execute the operation). Once terrorism assumes a transnational character a collective action problem appears owing to the potential externalities associated with counterterror activities. For example, proactive/pre-emptive actions are akin to the voluntary provision of a public good. Examples of proactive activities include destroying training camps, compromising a cell, and freezing assets. Successful proactive exercises produce a benefit that is both non-exclusive and non-rival, as it reduces a terrorist group's ability to strike against any of its potential targets. Hence, we should expect pre-emptive strategies to be underprovided, and to exhibit other classic Olsonian properties such as the degree of underprovision being increasing in the number of countries involved; and asymmetry in preemptive capacity or targeting status to imply that one or a few select countries pick up the preemptive burden (akin to Olson's 1965 exploitation hypothesis whereby a disproportionate share of the common good is provided by the larger members of the group that acts collectively).

By contrast, defensive (deterrent) actions often create public 'bads,' in the sense of Hardin's (1968) 'tragedy of the commons'. Examples of defensive counterterror policies include the hardening of targets, such as screening passengers boarding commercial airlines by requiring them to pass through metal detectors, or requiring them to submit to body scans and biometric methods of personal identification. A negative transnational externality is created because once a target becomes more difficult to attack terrorists may substitute an alternative target nation or attack a nation's citizens on foreign soil. For example, the vast majority of US victims of terrorism are attacked beyond their homeland's borders. The ramifications echo the tragedy of the commons, insofar as target nations overspend on defensive policies and the small may be exploited by the large, given that nations with insufficient deterrent capacity become magnets for terror activity, such as has been the case for Southeast Asia and al Qaeda's activities following America's 'Operation Enduring Freedom' in Afghanistan.

What is distinct about the treatment of these externalities and their associated collective action problems is that within a counterterrorism framework both the free-rider problem and the tragedy of the commons can occur *simultaneously* (Arce and Sandler 2005). To wit, consider a two-country model of counterterrorism-as-collective action. Preemptive action produces a public benefit, B, at a private cost, c. Defensive policies produce a private benefit, b, and create a public cost, C. These benefits and costs need not be symmetric but for the ease of exposition I assume that they are. The result is the counterterror policy scenario given in Figure 29.1, first introduced by Arce and Sandler (2005), with a status quo (inaction) baseline outcome of (0,0).

In accordance with the classical assumptions of collective action, the following relationships hold: $2B > c > B > 0$ and $2C > b > C > 0$. The 2 × 2 game in bold in the north-west corner of Figure 29.1 involves pre-emption and the status quo. It constitutes a voluntary provision of public goods game, where the status quo is dominant and free-riding is endemic because (proactive, proactive) Pareto-dominates (status quo, status quo). The 2 × 2 game in bold in the south-east corner of Figure 29.1 is a tragedy-of-the-commons game, where the (defensive, defensive) outcome is Pareto-dominated by (status quo, status quo). As two distinct versions of the familiar prisoners' dilemma are embedded in Figure 29.1, it is denoted as PD-squared (PD^2). A strategic form is appropriate because counterterror policy decisions are often made under conditions of imperfect information.

Several novel policy implications stem from this scenario. First, the cooperative solution to the defensive game – the Benthamite-utilitarian outcome that maximizes the sum of the players' payoffs – is (status quo, status quo). Yet this solution to the commons problem is the undesirable free-riding outcome for the 2 × 2 proaction game. In other

Country 2

		Proaction	Status quo	Defensive
Country 1	Proaction	$2B - c, 2B - c$	$B - c, B$	$B - c - C, B + b - C$
	Status quo	$B, B - c$	$0, 0$	$-C, b - C$
	Defensive	$B + b - C, B - c - C$	$b - C, -C$	$b - 2C, b - 2C$

Figure 29.1 Transnational counterterror collective action as PD^2

words, for the collective action problem involving defensive counterterror policies, action is dominant and inaction (or reduced action) is desirable. By contrast, in the proaction game inaction is dominant and action is desirable. More to the point, however, is that defensive policies are again dominant in the 3 × 3 version of the game and lead to the worst possible outcome (in the utilitarian sense). Hence, successful collective action requires that countries relinquish their right individually to determine their respective defensive counterterror postures, which are courses of action those in power are unlikely to adopt.

The fundamental externalities that arise from counterterror policies have been (re)discovered time and again in different guises and policy scenarios. Several extensions are of note. For example, if the countries can implement both proactive and defensive policies, then Figure 29.1 becomes a 4 × 4 game (not illustrated) appended by the strategy 'both'. Under the classic assumptions on b, B, c and C stated above, defensive actions remain the dominant policy outcome. What can mitigate the dominance of defensive policies is the existence of a nation that is the primary target of terrorism (for example, the United States). In this case, additional benefits accrue to the primary target from proaction. For example, suppose that when player 1 is proactive this produces an additional benefit of b_1 for player 1 in Figure 29.1 (not illustrated). This b_1 can either be thought of in terms of a selective private incentive or as an asymmetry due to player 1 experiencing a disproportionate number of attacks. In either case, Olson's (1965) classic conjectures hold. For b_1 large enough, country 1 has an extra incentive unilaterally to act to produce this additional benefit; consequently, this country is 'exploited' by country 2, which continues to deter. The equilibrium is in the northeast corner of Figure 29.1, where PD^2 is transformed in such a way that other nations are privileged by the target status of country 1. That is, the target country unilaterally is proactive while the remaining countries pursue defensive policies.

Two notable studies increase our understanding of counterterror externalities by extending the scenario captured by Figure 29.1 to allow for continuous action. First, Sandler and Siqueira (2006) consider separate proaction and deterrence games. In a continuous context, deterrence strategies are strategic complements in that deterrence creates an incentive for a similar action on the part of other countries who do not want to become softer targets. Once again, in a simultaneous move context this leads to overdeterrence relative to the Pareto optimum. Yet in a Stackelberg (leader–follower) framework the leader internalizes the negative externality of over-deterrence and there is a second mover advantage (for the follower). Furthermore, the Stackelberg outcome is Pareto superior to the Nash outcome. By contrast, in a continuous context proactive strategies are strategic substitutes in that countries can free-ride on the proactive operations of other countries. Proaction therefore creates an incentive for an offsetting or opposite reaction. In a Stackelberg framework the leader shifts the burden of the positive externality of proaction onto the follower. That is, there is a first-mover advantage. Yet the Stackelberg outcome is Pareto-inferior to the Nash outcome.

In Sandler and Siqueira (2006) pre-emption and deterrence are not considered simultaneously. In Arce and Sandler (2005) and Sandler and Siqueira (2006) only the actions of target countries are considered and terrorists themselves go unmodeled. Instead, terrorists are passively assumed to produce the externalities under study. By contrast, Cadigan and Schmitt (2010) produce similar externalities in a three-player model with two target nations and endogenous terrorist actions. Here, the target nations face a proaction dilemma where they can influence the probability of success of a terrorist attack. Defensive counterterror strategies produce a negative externality when the terrorist's budget is limited such that it can afford only to attack one of the targets. Hence, the commons aspect of defensive policy arises endogenously as a function of the terrorist's characteristics. In a novel test of these fundamental externalities Cadigan and Schmitt perform three-player experiments of this interaction in a laboratory setting. Their experimental findings confirm overspending on own protection (defensive policy) and free-riding on the preemptive efforts of others. A noteworthy result that goes unexplained is that terrorists under-attack relative to what their budgets otherwise would allow.

3 (COUNTER)TERRORISM AND RATIONAL ACTION?

By the tenth anniversary of the events of 11 September 2001 untold billions were spent in the name of homeland security and transportation safety. Furthermore, enormous additional costs have been created in terms of forfeited civil liberties and unintended consequences of policy actions. What has been achieved for all the expenditure and effort? For example, Sandler et al. (2009) find benefit–cost ratios ranging from US$0.09 to $0.35 for homeland security. Moreover, the direct fatalities associated with 9/11 were approximately 3,000 lives lost. Yet given that after 9/11 US citizens substituted the far more dangerous practice of driving on American highways for airline travel, an unintended consequence of the terrorist attacks on the World Trade Center and the Pentagon is estimated to be as many as an additional 2,300 automobile accident fatalities (Blalock et al. 2009). In the same way, it is increasingly apparent that terrorism is a similarly inefficient way to achieve political goals. If this is the case, then why are some individuals willing to die for the cause in suicide attacks? In this section I explore the rationality of (counter)terror actions.

3.1 Returns to Counterterror Policy

The 9- to 35-cent overall return per dollar spent as calculated in Sandler et al. (2009) is derived from a careful study of the benefits of counterterrorist policies measured in terms of avoiding the reduction in economic growth and lives lost caused by transnational terrorism. Forfeited growth is calculated using the widely cited Blomberg et al. (2004) methodology in which the existence of a terrorist event for a given year causes a 0.048 percent decrease in gross domestic product (GDP) per capita. The value of lives lost is calculated by using studies of terrorist events to create a composite distribution of deaths and injuries. Deaths are valued at $2 million each, consistent with the compensation of the families of 9/11 victims. Injuries are predicted using the composite model's estimated percentages of fractured skulls, traumas, respiratory problems, and other non-fatal injuries. The incidences of post-traumatic stress disorder (PTSD) and severe depression among terrorism's victims is also taken into account. Injuries and psychological disorders are then transformed into fractional deaths by applying the concept of disability adjusted life years (DALYs), commensurate with the global distribution of weights assigned to mental and physical impairments reported in Lopez et al. (2006).

Prior to addressing the rationality of policies with such low benefit–cost ratios it is useful to keep several points in mind. First, the Blomberg et al. (2004) growth equation is a 'ping' model that is expressed in terms of the incidence of terrorism for a given year, but not the discrete number of events for that year. This is in keeping with the literature on the influence of conflict on growth. Yet while the incidence of civil war for a given year may be consistent with 'ping' data, this approach does not capture the effects of multiple terrorist events within a given year. For example, the events of 9/11 would be counted as one 'ping' for the year 2001. Second, no indirect casualties – such as the highway fatalities identified in Blalock et al. (2009) – are included in Sandler et al. (2009); neither is the psychological trauma experienced by terrorism's victims or by third parties. For example, millions watched the events of 9/11 on live television and a substantial number of *Madrideños* witnessed the aftermath of the 3/11 train station bombings in that city. Third, there is some evidence that counterterror strategy has been more effective than governments have admitted publicly.

As of this writing it is certainly true that no mass-casualty event has taken place on US soil since 9/11. Our awareness of the foiled plot to detonate liquid explosives on transatlantic flights originating from Heathrow Airport on 9 August 2006 is the exception, rather than the rule. For example, Gordon Woo (2006) cites an internal Lloyds of London study estimating that between 9/11 and the Heathrow interdiction more than 50 planned 9/11-style attacks were blocked successfully. These planned attacks reportedly targeted North America, Western Europe, and/or Singapore. The point is that any study examining the benefit–cost ratio of counterterror policy will be sensitive to the alternative hypothetical scenarios considered. For example, the proper counterfactual for computing the cost of the war in Iraq is not the number of troops there, but how many aircraft carriers, sorties, inspectors, and so on would be needed in that region to enforce so-called no-fly zones, to ferret out weapons of mass destruction (WMD), if any, and to ensure compliance with other multinational policy mandates. In this way, Sandler et al. (2011) are judicious in formulating their counterfactuals and consider an alternative approach when evaluating the effect of Interpol's stolen and lost travel documents database, known as MIND/FIND. Specifically, in addition to positing the number or character of attacks avoided they also find that only 0.29 percent of the 'hits' on stolen and lost travel documents at US ports of entry would need to be terrorism-related in order to justify Interpol's total cost of creating MIND/FIND for *all* of its member nations.

Caveats aside, the small benefit–cost ratios are not surprising given that, on average, about 2,000 fatalities occur in any given year as a result of transnational terrorism, whereas more than 42,000 people die annually in automobile accidents in the United States. Approximately 40 percent of these fatalities are alcohol-related, yet far more is spent on homeland security than on preventing fatal highway accidents caused by drunk drivers. From an economist's perspective, the pattern of expenditures and relatively low benefit–cost ratios for investments in homeland security demand a rational explanation. In some sense, the over-deterrence outcome predicted by Arce and Sandler (2005) and experimentally verified by Cadigan and Schmitt (2010) points to the conclusion that the observed, huge investment in homeland security may not be cost–benefit justified. Another way to look at this is that governments facing a determined terrorist threat suffer from 'double defense' non-convexities in their cost structures (Bernhardt and Polborn 2010). That is, a particular terrorist group needs only to be incapacitated once; if it cannot attack again then by definition there is inefficient duplication in terms of the counterterror actions that did not produce the incapacitation.

There is a public choice aspect to this over-expenditure as well. Siqueira and Sandler (2007) add voter behavior to the issue of counterterror strategies. When voters realize that pre-emptive strategies may induce reprisals by terrorists (backlash) they favor governments that are even more likely to free-ride on the preemptive efforts of other target nations. As defensive efforts are less likely to produce reprisals/backlash, deterrence is again preferred. In addition, Gassebner et al. (2008, 2010) find evidence of a 'one strike, you're out' phenomenon when it comes to a government's ability to survive terrorist attacks. Specifically, incumbent governments experience a 13.8 percent greater likelihood of a cabinet change when elections are called in the wake of a terrorist event. An example is the outcome of the (scheduled) Spanish elections that immediately followed the 3/11 Madrid train station bombings. Terrorists understand this as well; after bombing the Brighton hotel where Margaret Thatcher was staying in the 1980s, and failing to kill her, the IRA issued a statement. It read: 'Today you have been lucky. But you have to be lucky every time. We only have to be lucky once' (King 2008). There are many ways to lose office due to terrorism, and politicians' behaviors will reflect the downside risk they face in all of its forms.

If downside political risk is a major determinant of counterterror policy then it is likely that target governments have preferences that reflect loss aversion. Consider, for example, the idea of terrorism-as-deterrence, a concept advanced by Kydd and Walter (2006), in which terrorists act as defenders/deterrers to prevent undesirable behavior on the part of a target government.[1] For example, al Qaeda often presents its objectives in terms of deterring US aggression (Abrahms 2006a). Although they do not consider the particular case of terrorism-as-deterrence, Carlson and Dacey (2006a, 2006b) do consider loss aversion on the part of the 'challenger' in a general model of deterrence. When translated to the situation of target-nation-as-victim against terrorist-as-defender, a loss-averse target nation will aggressively engage in countermeasures (that is, overspend) in order to avert the outcome the terrorist (defender) seeks to achieve. That is, when faced with a determined terrorist organization where planned mass-casualty attacks are almost a sure thing, loss aversion induces extreme risk aversion over losses. Such an attitude is captured by testimony written in the Joint House-Senate Intelligence Inquiry into 11 September 2001: 'terrorists need to be successful only once to kill Americans and demonstrate the inherent vulnerabilities they face' (United States Congress 2002). Finally, it may be the case that the incumbent government is signaling something to its constituency by over-spending on counterterror measures.

3.2 What Should the Public (and Terrorists) Understand about Policy?

When the government conducts specific counterterror policies, what should its constituency – and perhaps terrorists themselves – understand about these policies? For example, when the Department of Homeland Security (DHS) raises the terror alert threat advisory level from yellow (elevated) to orange (high), is this like free advertising for terrorist groups that seek to disrupt routine daily activities? When considering such a change does DHS recognize that it produces loss of life – even in the absence of a terror event – because some citizens will substitute automobile travel for air travel? One study that addresses these types of issues is Basuchoudhary and Razzolini (2006), who consider the observable properties of security checks and profiling. For example, it makes no sense to profile terrorists purely on the existence of a given attribute (for example, passport country of origin), as terrorists could easily circumvent such profiling. Indeed, it is for this reason that a Brazilian passport is so valuable on the open market – Brazil is so multi-ethnic that almost anyone could pass as Brazilian! At the same time, there is no denying that certain attributes make it easier for terrorist organizations to recruit, train and indoctrinate operatives. That is, effective terrorism requires effective screening of operatives.[2] Hence, Basuchoudhary and Razzolini (2006) find that the likelihood of a security check should be inversely proportional to the difficulty in recruiting and training an operative with the given attribute(s). This suggests that some profiling will (probabilistically) occur and should not be considered to be a violation of civil liberties per se. At the same time, just as the optimal level of greenhouse gas abatement is not 100 percent, the optimal level of screening will allow some terrorists to get through.

Rational randomness is also a theme that stems from a resurgence of interest in Colonel Blotto games. The basic structure of a Colonel Blotto game is given in Figure 29.2. In its purest form an attacker and defender engage in conflicts over N battlefields. This scenario is naturally extended to be between a target government (defender) and its attacker adversary (terrorists), who are engaged in conflict over N targets. The defender has budget B^D and the attacker's budget is B^A. Their respective valuations of each target are v_i^D and v_i^A. The fundamental asymmetry between target nation and terrorist can be captured by assuming that $B^D > B^A$. The target government allocates defensive resources $d_i(B^D, v_i^D)$ to target i and the attacker allocates resources $a_j(B^A, v_j^A)$ to the same target.

When resources are allocated discretely, the optimal (mixed) strategies balance the payoff at each target so that a contestant wins by a little at as many targets as possible, and loses substantially at only a few targets (Borel [1921] 1953). This characteristic

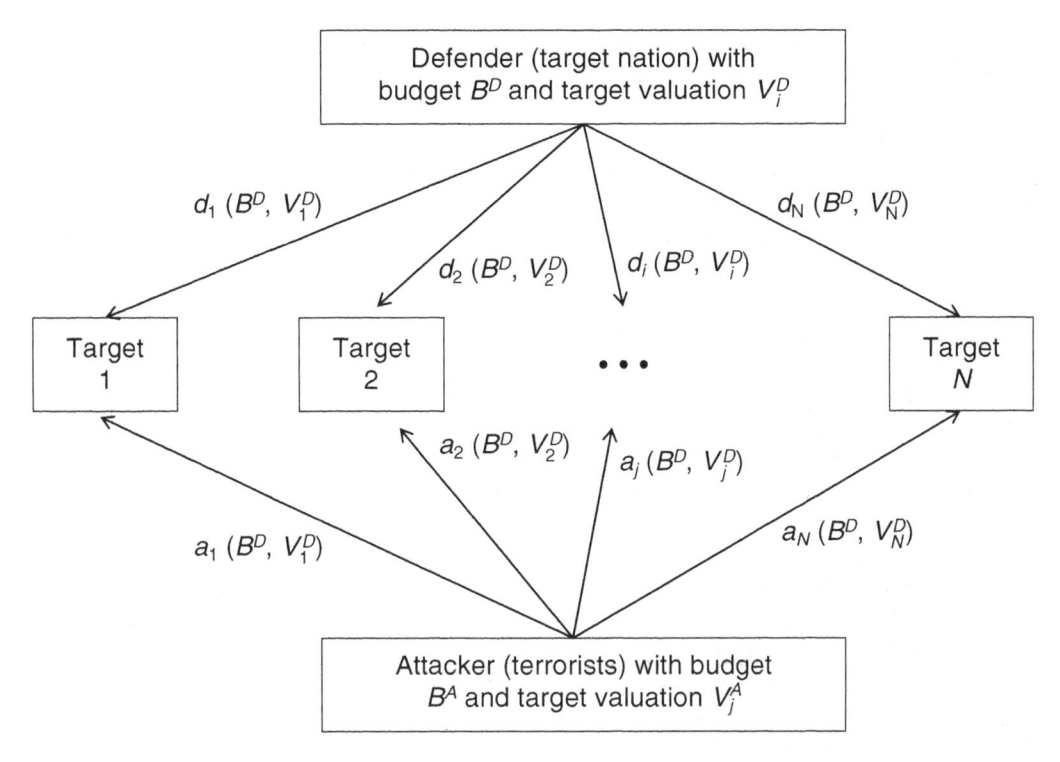

Figure 29.2 Colonel Blotto game

holds for the minimax solution in a zero-sum context or the Nash equilibrium when the game is not zero-sum (Dresher 1961). A general solution for the case of continuous resource allocation is provided by Roberson (2006). The characteristic that the solution to Blotto games exhibits that is important for public consumption is Dresher's (1961) 'no soft-spot' principle. That is, the target government distributes defensive resources in a pecking order in which high-value or highly vulnerable assets are protected with more resources first, *leaving some targets unprotected.* In equilibrium the government defends only those high-valued targets that the attacker finds desirable to attack with all of its resources. As a consequence, low valued targets go undefended. The attacker therefore (randomly) attacks only one of those targets that the defender chooses to defend. Hence, just as Basuchoudhary and Razzolini (2006) establish a pattern of probabilistic profiling that corresponds to a mixed strategy, terrorists similarly mix over their targets, thereby creating an aura of uncertainty and randomness. As a consequence, the public should expect some targets to remain vulnerable to attack.

There are also variations on the Blotto game in which the government may find it advantageous to reveal its strategy to terrorists. For example, Bier et al. (2007) consider a two-target version where the defender does not know the attacker's valuations. The defender's strategies are probabilities of successful defense (at rising marginal cost) and the attacker observes the defender's allocation of resources to counter-measures. The result is a pure strategy equilibrium where one target may be left undefended if the defender's valuation is sufficiently small. Bernhardt and Polborn (2010) similarly consider a two-target game and show that if the value defenders assign to them differs sufficiently, it may be advantageous for the defender to reveal its strategy to the attacker.

3.3 On the Rationality of Terrorism

In a series of papers, Abrahms (2006a, 2006b, 2012) raises the issue of whether terrorism is an efficient means for achieving political goals. Until this point the success of terrorism was widely accepted and based upon several high-profile examples related to post-colonial independence. In particular, the independence of Israel followed the 1946 bombing of the King David Hotel by the Zionist organization Irgun. The hotel served as the headquarters for British authorities in Palestine and TransJordan. In the same way, the independence of Algeria is often attributed to terrorist actions against the colonial French from 1954 to 1962, and suicide bombings precipitated the withdrawal of US and French troops from Lebanon during 1983.

Yet when examining the record of terrorists as a whole relative to their stated demands and goals, Abrahms finds that terrorist groups are successful only 7 percent of the time. Note that Abrahms is concerned with total success relative to these demands. When one considers that 90 percent of all terrorist groups have a lifespan of less than one year, and of those that survive for at least a year most last for less than a decade (Rapoport 1992), then such a lack of success is to be expected. New terrorist groups survive at a rate that approximates that of new business ventures. Furthermore, Abrahms (2006b) identifies a self-defeating component of terrorism in which large-scale attacks undermine support because of the collateral damage they produce and their potential for miscommunicating the degree to which the supporting population can be appeased through limited concessions. Of those terrorist campaigns that are successful, the common denominator is the use of passive military personnel as targets rather than civilians. Yet the success rate of terrorism pales in comparison to that of economic sanctions, which have a success rate of 34 percent (Pape 1997) and are widely regarded as an ineffective form of coercion.

The disparity between the level of violence and what it achieves has caused researchers to divide terrorist goals into process and outcome categories. The exceedingly short lifespan of terrorist groups (Rapoport 1992; Blomberg et al. 2010) implies that they need to think in terms of survival first, and survival is a process goal. A major determinant of survival is terrorists' ability to amass resources from period to period. One of the ways that they do this is by provoking an overreaction by target governments that will increase both the stock of recruits and sympathies within the population terrorists seek to represent (Faria and Arce 2005; Kydd and Walter 2006). This phenomenon is known in the theoretical literature as 'backlash'. As mentioned above, Siqueira and Sandler (2007) find that the potential for backlash exacerbates the underprovision of proactive policies because governments realize that their constituencies have sufficient foresight to understand that proactive countermeasures may provoke future terrorism. Arce and Sandler (2010) derive the way in which counterterror policy should reflect the potential for backlash. In addition, militant terrorists use 'spectaculars' (mass casualty attacks) to provoke target governments into an overreaction, thereby satisfying process goals. At the same time, politically motivated terrorists realize that backlash can to some extent be mitigated by (tentative) political concessions that appease the audience(s) that both militant terrorists and target governments seek to influence. This leads to the novel insight that terrorist spectaculars are a pooling phenomenon that occurs when the government has incomplete information about whether the terrorist group that conducts the spectacular is doing so for process or outcome goals. The upshot is that in equilibrium terrorism occurs but it rarely achieves outcome goals to the full extent that they are articulated by terrorist groups. Moreover, counterterror intelligence should recognize the potential for backlash in order to better inform policy.

3.4 On the Rationality of Suicide Operatives

The modern roots of suicide terrorism stem from the 1983 suicide bombings of US and French barracks in Beirut. The attacks are credited with leading to the withdrawal of peacekeeping troops from Lebanon. From the perspective of terrorist organizers, suicide operations are a rational tactic for influencing a target audience by instilling fear, particularly since suicide attacks are, on average, more deadly than conventional attacks. Moreover, no longstanding terrorist organization uses suicide as its exclusive modus operandi. Yet the question remains as to the rationality of the suicide operative.

In her extraordinary survey of 12 books on suicide terrorism, Crenshaw (2007, p. 160) remarks that there is no longer the need to introduce an analysis of suicide attacks by explaining to the uninitiated that such tactics are not rooted in psychopathology on the part of the operative. Similarly, Iannaccone (2006, p. 4) notes that the most effective soldiers are not those with nothing to live for, but those with something to die for. To paraphrase, status and honor are important motivators, as are a shared sense of moral conviction. Above all, it is critical that operatives build strong mutual bonds of trust and affection. The most salient benefits include fame, honor, recognition, the perceived value of the suicidal act, rewards to family and friends, anticipated personal rewards in this life or next, and harm and humiliation imposed on enemies. In general, the stream of expected benefits starts well before the suicidal act and extends well beyond its conclusion. Socially constructed benefits weigh heavily in the suicide operative's calculations, as do the subjective probabilities attached to the anticipated outcomes (Iannaccone 2006, pp. 14–16).

In a celebrated paper, Wintrobe (2006) identifies the motivation of extremist followers of an organization as arising from preferences for solidarity with a group. Hence, solidarity functions as a selective private incentive for the suicide operative that also serves as a means to align the operative's preferences with those of leadership. This alignment also makes the operative less susceptible to deterrence actions. The key insight is that if an indivisibility exists between leaderships' intermediate and ultimate goals then there are enormous potential gains for the group that can be facilitated by those members who sacrifice themselves for the cause. Solidarity is the means by which organizers ensure the commitment of suicide operatives.

Other studies as well focus on the public and club goods properties of terrorist organizations that employ suicide tactics (for example, Iannaccone and Berman 2006; Berman 2009); however, the role of target governments in providing an environment ripe for suicide tactics is highly understudied. One exception is McBride and Richardson (2012), who recognize that, in addition to possessing a threshold level of group capital that can be used as a commitment device, suicide operatives must also have sufficient individual capital to be able to carry out the complexities of a suicide mission. As a consequence, target governments can reduce the number of suicide bombings by achieving (1) an increase in the market returns to individual human capital at all levels; (2) a decrease in the returns to group participation; (3) an increase in the screening costs for identifying suicide operatives; and (4) an increase in the training costs of suicide operatives. What they find is that most counterterror tactics (attrition, direct action, and civic action) cannot simultaneously satisfy these conditions.[3] For example, if screening costs are high and are also positively related to group size, then civic action to raise the market returns to individual capital will reduce the optimal group size, thereby having the unintended consequence of facilitating the identification of potential suicide operatives from those group members who remain. Alternatively, infiltrating terrorist groups may alter the group's screening process in such a way that suicide operatives can be better identified because recruiters exert more resources in identifying candidates. Finally, banning religious attire may reduce the opportunity cost associated with affiliating with a terrorist organization, thereby enabling its members to 'hide in plain sight', being indistinguishable visibly from society at large.

4 ORGANIZING TERROR

Terrorism falls under the category of asymmetric conflict because terrorists lack the resources to engage well-armed target governments directly. Yet at the same time terrorist operations are often highly decentralized whereas counterterror activities are highly centralized (at the level of homeland security) and this difference can create an asymmetry in terrorists' favor if they can overcome the moral hazard and adverse selection problems associated with decentralization. Decentralization insulates the principal (terrorist leadership) from the adverse effects of a foiled plot.

Terrorist organizations often use a cell or network structure to securely organize operational activities. In a theoretical study of the mathematical structure of terrorist cells, Farley (2003) suggests that terrorist organizations can be modeled as an *ordered set*: a network with a built-in hierarchy. Furthermore a 'fishbone' lattice having a single leader with no one reporting to more than one other person and being immediately connected to at most two other operatives is particularly robust to the loss of members.

Brams et al. (2006) alternatively characterize the 19-member network of 9/11 hijackers and the 62-member 9/11 hijacker network neighborhood as *directed graphs*: graphs where the direction of the connections between nodes matter. They then use the connections between the graphs to characterize who each individual can influence. These influence sets are then organized hierarchically. Those at the top can be identified as the true threats to world order. Finally, Enders and Su (2007) recognize that cell structure may be endogenous given that target governments have incentives to disrupt the cells. This then creates a trade-off between security (infiltration risk) and the flow of information in terrorist cells (density). Hence, terrorists will substitute out of high density networks as infiltration risk increases and vice versa. When networks become less dense, leadership must substitute away from logistically complex tasks to logistically simpler ones.

A network or cell structure necessarily implies that those group members operating at the end nodes are implementing policies conceived by those at the top. Furthermore, 'middlemen' abound. For example, Bapat (2006) and Byman and Kreps (2010) examine the state-sponsorship of transnational terrorism – for example, the Taliban and al Qaeda or Iran and Hezbollah – and the way in which substitution of monetary incentives for shared ideological convictions can result in a loss of the sponsoring state's control. Hence, both sponsoring states and counterterror officials have an incentive to manipulate information in order to maintain control or increase suspicions.

More directly, Shapiro (2007) and Shapiro and Siegel (2009) examine the tradeoff between the political impact of terrorism and counterterror policy when middlemen control the flow of funding between planners and operatives and can skim off some of these funds, thereby affecting an operation's success. Shapiro and Siegel's motivation comes from translations of internal al Qaeda documents purporting to require operatives to provide detailed receipts for reimbursement as well as requests to tone down violent activities in areas where local authorities have become particularly sensitive to operatives' activities. The presence of middlemen – who are generally less ideologically motivated than leadership – exacerbates the agency problem within a terrorist organization. At the same time, the presence of middlemen often provides an additional link that strengthens the security of the organization by insulating leadership from the funding issues that must be resolved in order to support terrorist cells logistically. One implication of their findings is that counterterror policies of freezing terrorists' assets may excuse middlemen for not delivering funds to their ultimate destination or, alternatively, facilitate an operation's success, thereby unintentionally lowering the tensions between middlemen and leadership.

An entirely different question is that of screening and training terrorist operatives, especially when it comes to suicide operatives. Within the adverse selection paradigm this is known as the problem of adverse claims (Mitnick 1975) as it pertains to operative loyalty and the human capital required to carry out a terrorist operation successfully. Arce and Siqueira (2010) address this issue by recognizing that suicide operatives cannot accept contracts (specifying a mission's degree of violence and probability of success) in which the monetary component of the contract is contingent upon observing the mission's outcome. By contrast, conventional operatives can accept a state-contingent contract. Hence, Arce and Siqueria are able to provide a theory of terrorist organizations in which both suicide and conventional attacks are employed. The screening process for mission assignment is therefore based upon contracts that differentiate operative types in terms of whether they possess social (intrinsic) preferences for the organization's mission or the likelihood of success of that mission. The presence of social preferences is a contribution to the economic roots of terrorism because intrinsic motivation, rather than poverty, can explain suicide missions. Hence, neither psychopathology nor poverty is necessary to produce suicide operatives.

5 CONCLUSION

This chapter has examined the phenomena of terrorism and counterterrorism through the lens of public choice, particularly as it pertains to collective action. For example, whereas many collective action problems are modeled either as the free-rider problem when it comes to the voluntary provision of public goods or as a commons' problem, transnational counterterror policy exhibits both problems simultaneously. This is because proactive counterterror policy has a public goods component and defensive counterterror policy (hardening targets) can produce a negative bi-directional externality. Hence, inefficiency can be more pronounced than in separate and distinct collective action settings. At the same time, key insights from Olson (1965), such as exploitation, selective incentives, and selective disincentives can be used to more efficiently tailor counterterror policy.

The decentralized nature of terrorist organizations that employ cell and network structures create agency problems for terrorist organizers and planners. These agency problems can stem from moral hazard on the part of financial middlemen who direct funds to operatives, adverse selection problems in screening and training conventional and suicide operatives, or both. This particular literature is rapidly developing as the agency theoretic structure of terrorist organizations is becoming better understood. Yet the connection between this literature and that of the endogenous network structure of terrorist organizations remains an open question.

Finally, the issue of low benefit–cost ratios for homeland security is surely going to be raised as we mark upcoming anniversaries of the events of 11 September 2001. Public choice is the proper contextual backdrop for examining why aggregate counterterror measures have a benefit–cost ratio that is relatively low, and whether new measures of benefits and costs need to be introduced. In the same way, the distinct lack of success of the vast majority of terrorist campaigns raises the issue of whether a more efficient non-violent outlet for terrorist organizations can be found or if violence is, indeed, instrumental.

NOTES

1. Interestingly enough, both Aumann (2005) and Schelling (2005) focus on the issue of deterrence in the post-9/11 world as part of their Nobel lectures. See Arce and Sandler (2009) for a full theoretical exploration of terrorism-as-deterrence.
2. On this point, see Arce and Siqueira (2010).
3. The exception is covert action. These tactics are described in the US Army/Marine Corps Counterinsurgency Manual (United States Department of the Army 2007).

References

Abrahms, Max (2006a), 'Al Qaeda's scorecard: a progress report on Al Qaeda's objectives', *Studies in Conflict & Terrorism*, **25**, 509–29.
Abrahms, Max (2006b), 'Why terrorism does not work', *International Security*, **31**, 42–78.
Abrahms, Max (2012), 'The political effectiveness of terrorism revisited', *Comparative Political Studies*, **45**, forthcoming.
Abrajano, Marisa A. and Rebecca B. Morton (2004), 'All style and no substance? The strategic calculus of campaign advertising', Working Paper, New York University.
Abramowitz, Alan I. (1988), 'Explaining Senate election outcomes', *American Political Science Review*, **82**, 385–403.
Abramowitz, Alan I. (1991), 'Incumbency, campaign spending, and the decline of competition in U.S. House elections', *Journal of Politics*, **53**, 34–56.
Abrams, Burton A. and Plamen Iossifov (2006), 'Does the Fed contribute to a political business cycle?', *Public Choice*, **129**, 249–62.
Abrams, Sam, Torben Iversen and David Soskice (forthcoming), 'Informal social networks and rational voting', *British Journal of Political Science*.
Acemoglu, Daron (2003), 'Why not a political coase theorem? Social conflict, commitment, and politics', *Journal of Comparative Economics*, **31**, 620–52.
Acemoglu, Daron (2006), 'A simple model of inefficient institutions', *Scandinavian Journal of Economics*, **108**, 515–46.
Acemoglu, Daron and Simon Johnson (2005), 'Unbundling institutions', *Journal of Political Economy*, **113**, 1369–401.
Acemoglu, Daron and James A. Robinson (2001), 'A theory of political transitions', *American Economic Review*, **91**, 938–63.
Acemoglu, Daron and James A. Robinson (2006), *Economic Origins of Dictatorship and Democracy*, Cambridge: Cambridge University Press.
Acemoglu Daron, Simon Johnson and James A. Robinson (2001a), 'The colonial origins of comparative development: an empirical investigation', *American Economic Review*, **91**, 1369–401.
Acemoglu Daron, Simon Johnson and James A. Robinson (2001b), 'An African success story: Botswana', http://www.colby.edu/economics/faculty/jmlong/ec479/AJR.pdf (accessed 10 February 2011).
Acemoglu, Daron, James A. Robinson, and Rafael J. Santos-Villagran (2009), 'The monopoly of violence: evidence from Colombia', National Bureau of Economic Research, NBER Working Paper Series, No. 15578, Cambridge, MA.
Adams, James D. and Lawrence W. Kenny (1986), 'Optimal tenure of elected public officials', *Journal of Law and Economics*, **29**, 303–28.
Adams, James F., Samuel Merrill III and Bernard Grofman (2005), *A Unified Theory of Party Competition*, New York: Cambridge University Press.
Afonso, António and Davide Furceri (2008), 'Government size, composition, volatility, and economic growth', European Central Bank Working Paper Series No. 849, Frankfurt am Main.
Afonso, António and Ricardo M. Sousa (2009), 'The macroeconomic effects of fiscal policy', European Central Bank Working Paper Series No. 991, Frankfurt am Main.
Agell, Jonas, Henry Ohlsson and Peter Skogman Thoursie (2006), 'Growth effects of government expenditure and taxation in rich countries: a comment', *European Economic Review*, **50**, 211–18.
Aggarwal, Rajesh K., Felix Meschke and Tracy Yue Wang (2012), 'Corporate political donations: investment or agency', working paper, University of Minnesota' available at: http://papers.ssrn.com/abstract=972670 (accessed 20 May 2012).
Ahmed, Shaghil (1986), 'Temporary and permanent government spending in an open economy: some evidence for the United Kingdom', *Journal of Monetary Economics*, **17**, 197–224.

Aidt, Toke S. and Arye L. Hillman (2008), 'Enduring rents', *European Journal of Political Economy*, **24**, 445–53.
Aidt, Toke S., Francisco José Veiga and Linda Gonçalves Veiga (2009), 'Election results and opportunistic policies: A new test of the rational political business cycle model', University of Cambridge Working Paper No. 0934
Akerlof, George A. (1983), 'Loyalty filters', *American Economic Review*, **73**, 54–63.
Akerlof, George A. and William T. Dickens (1982), 'The economic consequences of cognitive dissonance', *American Economic Review*, **72**, 307–19.
Albrecht, Johan (2002), 'Environmental issue entrepreneurship: a Schumpeterian perspective', *Futures*, **34**, 649–61.
Alcalde, José and Matthias Dahm (2010), 'Rent seeking and rent dissipation: a neutrality result', *Journal of Public Economics*, **94**, 1–7.
Aldenhoff, Frank-Oliver (2007), 'Are economic forecasts of the International Monetary Fund politically biased? A public choice analysis', *Review of International Organizations*, **2**, 239–60.
Aldrich, John (1993), 'Rational choice and turnout', *American Journal of Political Science*, **37**, 246–78.
Aldrich, John (1995), *Why Parties? The Origin and Transformation of Party Politics in America*, Chicago, IL: University of Chicago Press.
Aldrich, John. (2004), 'William H. Riker', in Charles K. Rowley and Friedrich Schneider (eds), *The Encyclopedia of Public Choice*, vol. 1, Boston: Kluwer Academic, pp. 321–4.
Alesina, Alberto (1987), 'Macroeconomic policy in a two party system as a repeated game', *Quarterly Journal of Economics*, **102**, 651–78.
Alesina, Alberto (1989), 'Politics and business cycles in industrial democracies', *Economic Policy: A European Forum*, **8**, 55–98.
Alesina, Alberto and Silvia Ardagna (2009), 'Large changes in fiscal policy: taxes versus spending', paper prepared for *Tax Policy and the Economy 2009*. Revised October 2009.
Alesina, Alberto and Jeffrey D. Sachs (1988), 'Political parties and the business cycle in the United States, 1948–1984', *Journal of Money, Credit, and Banking*, **20**, 63–82.
Alesina, Alberto and Lawrence H. Summers (1993), 'Central bank independence and macroeconomic performance: some comparative evidence', *Journal of Money, Credit, and Banking*, **25**, 151–62.
Alesina, Alberto, Reza Baqir and Caroline Hoxby (2004), 'Political jurisdiction in heterogeneous communities', *Journal of Political Economy*, **112**, 348–96.
Alesina, Alberto, Reza Baqir and William Easterly (1999), 'Public goods and ethnic division', The World Bank Policy Research Working Paper 2018.
Alesina, Alberto, Ricardo Hausmann, Rudolf Hommes and Ernesto Stein (1996), 'Budget institutions and fiscal performance in Latin America', *Journal of Development Economics*, **59**, 233–53.
Alesina, Alberto, Nouriel Roubini and Gerald D. Cohen (1997), *Political Business Cycles and the Macroeconomy*. Cambridge, MA: MIT Press.
Alt, James E., David Dreyer Lassen and Shanna Rose (2006), 'The causes of fiscal transparency: evidence from the U.S. states', *IMF Staff Papers*, **53**, 30–57.
Alter, Karen J. (2006), 'Delegation to international courts and the limits of recontracting political power', in Darren Hawkins, David A. Lake, Daniel Nielson and Michael J. Tierney (eds), *Delegation and Agency in International Organizations*, Cambridge: Cambridge University Press, pp. 312–38.
Alvarez, Michael R. and Jason L. Saving (1997), 'Congressional committees and the political economy of federal outlays', *Public Choice*, **92**, 55–73.
American Political Science Association (APSA) (1903), 'Constitution of the American Political Science Association', *Proceedings of the American Political Science Association*, **1**, 6–17.
Andersen, Esben S. (2009), *Schumpeter's Evolutionary Economics*, London: Anthem Press.
Andersen, Svein S. and Kjell A. Eliasson (1991), 'European Community lobbying', *European Journal of Political Research*, **20**, 173–87.
Anderson, Alison (1997), *Media, Culture and the Environment*, London: Routledge.
Anderson, Gary M. (1993), 'Agency discretion or statutory direction: decision making at the U.S. International Trade Commission', *Journal of Law and Economics*, **36**, 915–35.

Anderson, Gary M. and Robert D. Tollison (1991), 'Congressional influence and patterns of New Deal spending, 1933–1939', *Journal of Law and Economics*, **34**, 161–75.
Anderson, Gary M., William F. Shughart II and Robert D. Tollison (1989), 'On the incentives of judges to enforce legislative wealth transfers', *Journal of Law and Economics*, **32**, 215–28.
Anderson, Lisa R. and Beth A. Freeborn (2010), 'Varying the intensity of competition in a multiple prize rent seeking game', *Public Choice*, **143**, 237–54.
Anderson, Terry L. and Dominic P. Parker (2008), 'Sovereignty, credible commitments, and economic prosperity on American Indian reservations', *Journal of Law and Economics*, **51**, 641–66.
Andreoni, James (1988), 'Why free ride? Strategies and learning in public goods experiments', *Journal of Public Economics*, **37**, 291–304.
Andreoni, James (1990), 'Impure altruism and donations to public goods: a theory of warm-glow giving', *Economic Journal*, **100**, 464–77.
Andreoni, James (1995), 'Cooperation in public-goods experiments kindness or confusion?', *American Economic Review*, **85**, 891–904.
Andreoni, James and Rachel Croson (1998), 'Partners versus strangers: random rematching in public goods experiments', in Charles R. Plott and Vernon L. Smith (eds), *Handbook of Experimental Economics Results*, vol. 1, Amsterdam: North-Holland, pp. 776–83.
Andreoni, James and John H. Miller (2002), 'Giving according to GARP: an experimental test of the rationality of altruism', *Econometrica*, **70**, 737–53.
Andreoni, James and Ragan Petrie (2004), 'Public goods experiments without confidentiality', *Journal of Public Economics*, **88**, 1605–23.
Andvig, Jens Chr. and Karl Ove Moene (1990), 'How corruption may corrupt', *Journal of Economic Behavior & Organization*, **13**, 63–76.
Angelopoulos, Konstantinos, Apostolis Philippopoulos and Vanghelis Vassilatos (2006), 'Rent-seeking competition from state coffers: a calibrated DSGE model of the euro area', CESifo Working Paper No. 1644.
Angelopoulos, Konstantinos, Apostolis Philippopoulos and Vanghelis Vassilatos (2009), 'The social cost of rent seeking in Europe', *European Journal of Political Economy*, **25**, 280–99.
Ansolabehere, Stephen, John M. de Figueiredo and James M. Snyder Jr (2003), 'Why is there so little money in U.S. politics?', *Journal of Economic Perspectives*, **17**, 105–30.
Ansolabehere, Stephen, James M. Snyder Jr and Micky Tripathi (2002), 'Are PAC contributions and lobbying linked? New evidence from the 1995 lobby disclosure act', *Business and Politics*, **4**, 131–55.
Ansolabehere, Stephen, James M. Snyder Jr and Michiko Ueda (2004), 'Did firms profit from soft money?', *Election Law Journal: Rules, Politics, and Policy*, **3**, 193–8.
Aoki, Masahiko (2001), *Toward a Comparative Institutional Analysis*, Boston, MA: MIT Press.
Apollonio, Dorie E. and Raymond J. La Raja (2004), 'Who gave soft money? The effect of interest group resources on political contributions', *Journal of Politics*, **66**, 1134–54.
Appelbaum, Elie and Eliakim Katz (1986), 'Transfer seeking and avoidance: On the full social cost of rent seeking', *Public Choice*, **48**, 175–81, reprinted in Roger D. Congleton, Arye L. Hillman and Kai A. Konrad (eds) (2008), *Forty Years of Research on Rent Seeking 1 – The Theory of Rent Seeking*, Heidelberg: Springer, pp. 391–7.
Appelbaum, Elie and Eliakim Katz (1987), 'Seeking rents by setting rents: the political economy of rent seeking', *Economic Journal*, **97**, 685–99, reprinted in Roger D. Congleton, Arye L. Hillman and Kai A. Konrad (eds) (2008), *Forty Years of Research on Rent Seeking 1 – The Theory of Rent Seeking*, Heidelberg: Springer, pp. 555–69.
Aranson, Peter (1992), 'The common law as central economic planning', *Constitutional Political Economy*, **3**, 289–317.
Aranson, Peter H. and Peter C. Ordeshook (1981), 'Regulation, redistribution, and public choice', *Public Choice*, **37**, 69–100.
Arce M., Daniel G. (2001), 'Leadership and the aggregation of international collective action', *Oxford Economic Papers*, **53**, 114–37.
Arce M., Daniel G. and Todd Sandler (2005), 'Counterterrorism: a game-theoretic approach', *Journal of Conflict Resolution*, **49**, 183–200.

Arce M., Daniel G. and Todd Sandler (2009), 'Deterrence: credibility and proportionality', *Economics and Politics*, **31**, 384–408.
Arce M., Daniel G. and Todd Sandler (2010), 'Terrorist spectaculars: backlash attacks and the focus of intelligence', *Journal of Conflict Resolution*, **54**, 354–73.
Arce M., Daniel G. and K. Siqueira (2010), 'Motivating operatives for suicide missions and conventional terrorist attacks', Working Paper, University of Texas at Dallas.
Argys, Laura M. and H. Naci Mocan (2004), 'Who shall live and who shall die? An analysis of prisoners on death row in the United States', *Journal of Legal Studies*, **33**, 255–82.
Aristotle ([n.d.] 1996), *Aristotle: the Politics and the Constitution of Athens*, revised student edition by Stephen Everson (ed), Cambridge and New York: Cambridge University Press.
Aristotle ([n.d.] 2005), *Politics*, trans. Benjamin Jowett, Stillwell, KS: Digireads.com Publishing.
Aron, Janine (2000), 'Growth and institutions: a review of the evidence', *World Bank Research Observer*, **15**, 99–135.
Arrow, Kenneth J. (1950), 'A difficulty in the concept of social welfare', *Journal of Political Economy*, **58**, 328–46.
Arrow, Kenneth J. (1951), *Social Choice and Individual Values*, New York: Wiley & Sons.
Arrow, Kenneth J. (1963), 'Uncertainty and the welfare economics of medical care', *American Economic Review*, **53**, 941–73.
Arrow, Kenneth J. (1974), *The Limits of Organization*, New York: W.W. Norton.
Artis, Michael J. (1988), *How Accurate is the World Economic Outlook?* Staff Studies for the World Economic Outlook, Washington, DC: International Monetary Fund.
Asch, Peter and Joseph J. Seneca (1976), 'Is collusion profitable?', *Review of Economics and Statistics*, **58**, 1–12
Aschauer, David A. (1985), 'Fiscal policy and aggregate demand', *American Economic Review*, **75**, 17–27.
Aschauer, David A. (1988), 'The equilibrium approach to fiscal policy', *Journal of Money Credit and Banking*, **20**, 41–62.
Ashworth, Scott (2006), 'Campaign finance and voter welfare with entrenched incumbents', *American Political Science Review*, **100**, 55–68.
Aumann, Robert J. (2005), 'War and peace', Nobel Memorial Lecture, 8 December, http://nobelprize.org/nobel_prizes/economics/laureates/2005/aumann-lecture.html, reprinted as Aumann, Robert J. (2006), *PNAS*, **103**, 17075–8.
Austen-Smith, David (1987), 'Interest groups, campaign contributions and probabilistic voting', *Public Choice*, **54**, 123–39.
Austen-Smith, David (1995), 'Campaign contributions and access', *American Political Science Review*, **89**, 566–81.
Averch, Harvey and Leland L. Johnson (1962), 'Behavior of the firm under regulatory constraint', *American Economic Review*, **52**, 1052–69.
Ayittey, George B.N. (1988), 'Restoring Africa's free market tradition', The Heritage Foundation, http://www.policyarchive.org/handle/10207/bitstreams/11336.pdf (accessed 10 February 2011).
Azam, Jean-Paul (2006), 'The paradox of power reconsidered: a theory of political regimes in Africa', *Journal of African Economies*, **15**, 26–58.
Azam, Jean-Paul and Alice Mesnard (2003), 'Civil war and the social contract', *Public Choice*, **115**, 455–75.
Azzi, Corey and Ronald Ehrenberg (1975), 'Household allocation of time and religiosity: replication and extension', *Journal of Political Economy*, **85**, 415–23.
Babst, Dean V. (1964), 'Elective governments: a force for peace', *The Wisconsin Sociologist*, **2**, 9–14.
Babst, Dean V. (1972), 'A force for peace', *Industrial Research*, **14**, 55–8.
Bagnoli, Mark and Michael McKee (1991), 'Voluntary contribution games: efficient private provision of public goods', *Economic Inquiry*, **29**, 351–66.
Bagnoli, Mark, Shaul Ben-David and Michael McKee (1992), 'Voluntary provision of public goods: the multiple unit case', *Journal of Public Economics*, **47**, 85–106.
Baharad, Eyal and Shmuel Nitzan (2008), 'Contest efforts in light of behavioral considerations', *Economic Journal*, **118**, 2047–59.

Baik, Kyung Hwan (1994), 'Winner-help-loser group formation in rent-seeking contests', *Economics and Politics*, **6**, 147–62.
Baik, Kyung Hwan, Bouwe R. Dijkstra, Sanghack Lee and Shi Young Lee (2006), 'The equivalence of rent-seeking outcomes for competitive-share and strategic groups', *European Journal of Political Economy*, **22**, 337–42, reprinted in Roger D. Congleton, Arye L. Hillman and Kai A. Konrad (eds) (2008), *Forty Years of Research on Rent Seeking 1 – The Theory of Rent Seeking*, Heidelberg: Springer, pp. 323–28.
Bailey, Martin and Rubin, Paul (1994), 'A positive theory of legal change', *International Review of Law and Economics*, **14**, 467–77.
Bailkey, Nels (1967), 'Early Mesopotamian constitutional development', *American History Review*, **72**, 1211–36.
Baker, Laurence C. (1997), 'The effect of HMOs on fee-for-service health care expenditures: evidence from Medicare', *Journal of Health Economics*, **16**, 453–81.
Baker, Laurence C. (2001), 'Managed care and technology adoption in health care: evidence from magnetic resonance imaging', *Journal of Health Economics*, **20**, 395–421.
Banerjee, Abhijit and Rohini Pande (2007), 'Parochial politics: ethnic preferences and politician corruption', *CEPR Discussion Paper*, no. DP6381.
Bapat, Navin A. (2006), 'State bargaining with transnational terrorist groups', *International Studies Quarterly*, **50**, 215–29.
Barbieri, Katherine (2002), *The Liberal Illusion. Does Trade Promote Peace?* Ann Arbor, MI: University of Michigan Press.
Barbieri, Katherine, Omar M.G. Keshk and Brian M. Pollins (2009), 'Trading data: evaluating our assumptions and coding rules', *Conflict Management and Peace Science*, **26**, 471–91.
Barkun, Michael (1968), *Law without Sanctions: Order in Primitive Societies and the World Community*. New Haven, CT: Yale University Press.
Barlow, Robin (1970), 'Efficiency aspects of local school finance', *Journal of Political Economy*, **78**, 1028–40.
Barnebeck Andersen, Thomas, Henrik Hansen and Thomas Markussen (2006), 'U.S. politics and World Bank lending', *Journal of Development Studies*, **42**, 772–94.
Baron, David P. (1993), 'Government formation and endogenous Parties', *American Political Science Review*, **87**, 34–47.
Baron, David P. (2000), 'Legislative organization with informational committees', *American Journal of Political Science*, **44**, 485–505.
Barr, James L. and Otto A. Davis (1966), 'An elementary political and economic theory of the expenditures of local governments', *Southern Economic Journal*, **33**, 149–65.
Barro, Robert J. (1973), 'The control of politicians: an economic model', *Public Choice*, **14**, 19–42.
Barro, Robert J. (1974), 'Are government bonds net wealth?', *Journal of Political Economy*, **82**, 1181–206.
Barro, Robert J. (1991), 'Economic growth in a cross-section of countries', *Quarterly Journal of Economics*, **106**, 407–43.
Barro, Robert J. (1997), *Determinants of Economic Growth: A Cross-Country Empirical Study*, Cambridge, MA: MIT Press.
Barro, Robert J. and David B. Gordon (1983), 'A positive theory of monetary policy in a natural rate model', *Journal of Political Economy*, **91**, 589–610.
Barro, Robert J. and Jong-Wha Lee (2005), 'IMF programs: who is chosen and what are the effects?', *Journal of Monetary Economics*, **52**, 1245–69.
Barro, Robert J. and Rachel M. McCleary (2005), 'Which countries have state religions?', *Quarterly Journal of Economics*, **120**, 1331–70.
Bartel, Ann P. and Lacy Glenn Thomas (1987), 'Predation through regulation: The wage and profit effects of the Occupational Safety and Health Administration and the Environmental Protection Agency', *Journal of Law and Economics*, **30**, 239–64.
Barzel, Yoram (1992), 'Confiscation by the ruler: the rise and fall of Jewish lending in the middle ages', *Journal of Law and Economics*, **35**, 1–13.
Barzel, Yoram (2001), *A Theory of the State: Economic Rights, Legal Rights, and the Scope of the State*, Cambridge: Cambridge University Press.

Basuchoudhary, Atin and Laura Razzolini (2006), 'Hiding in plain sight – using signals to detect terrorists', *Public Choice*, **128**, 245–55.
Basuchoudhary, Atin and William F. Shughart II (2010), 'On ethnic conflict and the origins of transnational terrorism', *Defence and Peace Economics*, **21**, 65–87.
Battacharya, Sourav (2008), 'Preference monotonicity and information aggregation in elections', Working Paper, University of Pittsburgh.
Baum, Lawrence (1989), 'State supreme courts: activism and accountability', in Carl E. Van Horn (ed.), *The State of the States*, Washington, DC: CQ Press, pp. 103–30.
Baumol, William J. (1952), 'Book review of *Social Choice and Individual Values*' by Kenneth J. Arrow, *Econometrica*, **20**, 110–11.
Baxter, Marianne and Robert G. King (1993), 'Fiscal policy in general equilibrium', *American Economic Review*, **83**, 315–34.
Bayar, Ali and Bram Smeets (2009), 'Economic and political determinants of budgets in the European Union: A dynamic random coefficient approach', CESifo Working Paper No. 2546.
Baye, Michael R., Dan Kovenock and Casper G. de Vries (1994), 'The solution to the Tullock rent-seeking game when R>2: mixed strategy and mean dissipation rates', *Public Choice*, **81**, 363–80.
Baye, Michael R., Dan Kovenock and Casper G. de Vries (1996), 'The all-pay auction with complete information', *Economic Theory*, **8**, 362–80, reprinted in Roger D. Congleton, Arye L. Hillman and Kai A. Konrad (eds) (2008), *Forty Years of Research on Rent Seeking 1 – The Theory of Rent Seeking*, Heidelberg: Springer, pp. 209–23.
Baysinger, Barry, Robert B. Ekelund Jr and Robert D. Tollison (1980), 'Mercantilism as a rent-seeking society', in James M. Buchanan, Robert D. Tollison and Gordon Tullock (eds), *Towards a Theory of the Rent-Seeking Society*, College Station: Texas A&M University Press, pp. 97–112, reprinted in Roger D. Congleton, Arye L. Hillman and Kai A. Konrad (eds) (2008), *Forty Years of Research on Rent Seeking 2 – Applications: Rent Seeking in Practice*, Heidelberg: Springer, pp. 475–508.
Beard, Charles A. ([1913] 1968), *An Economic Interpretation of the Constitution of the United States*, New York: Macmillan.
Beard, T. Randolph, Robert B. Ekelund, Jr, George S. Ford and Robert D. Tollison (2011), 'Self-protection, insurance and religious choice', manuscript, Auburn University.
Bearse, Peter, Buly A. Cardak, Gerhard Glomm, and B. Ravikumar (2009), 'Why do education vouchers fail?', Center for Applied Economics and Policy Research, Working Paper no. 014-2009.
Beck, Nathaniel (1982), 'Presidential influence on the Federal Reserve in the 1970s', *American Journal of Political Science*, **26**, 415–45.
Beck, Nathaniel (1984), 'Domestic political sources of American monetary policy: 1955–1982', *Journal of Politics*, **46**, 786–817.
Beck, Nathaniel (1987), 'Elections and the Fed: is there a political monetary cycle?', *American Journal of Political Science*, **31**, 194–216.
Beck, Nathaniel (1991), 'The Fed and the political business cycle', *Contemporary Policy Issues*, **9**, 25–38.
Beck, Nathaniel, Jonathan N. Katz and Richard Tucker (1998), 'Taking time seriously: time-series-cross-section analysis with a binary dependent variable', *American Journal of Political Science*, **42**, 1260–88.
Becker, Elizabeth (1996), 'The illusion of fiscal illusion: unsticking the flypaper effect', *Public Choice*, **86**, 85–102.
Becker, Gary S. (1958), 'Competition and Democracy', *Journal of Law and Economics*, **1**, 105–9.
Becker, Gary S. (1968), 'Crime and punishment: an economic approach', *Journal of Political Economy*, **76**, 169–217.
Becker, Gary S. (1976), *The Economic Approach to Human Behavior*, Chicago, IL: University of Chicago Press.
Becker, Gary S. (1981), *A Treatise on the Family*, Cambridge, MA: Harvard University Press.
Becker, Gary S. and George J. Stigler (1974), 'Law enforcement, malfeasance, and compensation for enforcers', *Journal of Legal Studies*, **1**, 1–18.

Belden, Susan (1989), 'Policy preferences of FOMC members as revealed by dissenting votes', *Journal of Money, Credit, and Banking*, **21**, 432–41.
Belton, Willie J., Jr and Richard J. Cebula (1994), 'Does the Federal Reserve create political monetary cycles?', *Journal of Macroeconomics*, **16**, 461–77.
Benassy-Quere, Agnès and Jacopo Cimadomo (2006), 'Changing patterns of domestic and cross-border fiscal policy multipliers in Europe and the US', CEPII Research Centre Working Paper 06-24.
Bender, Bruce and John R. Lott, Jr (1996), 'Legislative voting and shirking: a critical review of the literature', *Public Choice*, **87**, 67–100.
Bennett, Andrew and G. John Ikenberry (2006), 'The *Review*'s evolving relevance for U.S. foreign policy 1906–2006', *American Political Science Review*, **100**, 651–8.
Bennett, D. Scott and Allan C. Stam (2000), 'Research design and estimator choices in the analysis of interstate dyads: when decisions matter', *Journal of Conflict Resolution*, **44**, 653–85.
Benoit, Kenneth (1996), 'Democracies really are more pacific (in general): reexamining regime type and war involvement', *Journal of Conflict Resolution*, **40**, 636–57.
Benson, Bruce L. (1983), 'Logrolling and high demand committee review', *Public Choice*, **41**, 427–34.
Bentley, Arthur F. (1907), *The Process of Government*, Chicago, IL: University of Chicago Press.
Bergh, Andreas and Carl Hampus Lyttkens (2011), 'Between Burkina Faso and Brazil? Measuring institutional quality in Ancient Athens', University of Lund, Department of Economics Working Paper n. 10/2011.
Bergman, Torbjörn (2004), 'Sweden: democratic reforms and partisan decline in an emerging separation-of-powers system', *Scandinavian Political Studies*, **27**, 203–25.
Bergstrom, Theodore C. and Robert P Goodman (1973), 'Private demand for public goods', *American Economic Review*, **63**, 280–96.
Berkowitz, Daniel and Karen Clay (2006), 'The effect of judicial independence on courts: evidence from the American states', *Journal of Legal Studies*, **35**, 399–440.
Berman, Eli (2009), *Radical, Religious and Violent: The New Economics of Terrorism*, Cambridge, MA: MIT Press.
Berman, Harold (1983), *Law and Revolution: The Formation of the Western Legal Tradition*, Cambridge: Harvard University Press.
Bernanke, Ben, Mark Gertler and Simon Gilchrist (1996), 'The financial accelerator and the flight to quality', *Review of Economics and Statistics*, **78**, 1–15.
Bernhard, William (2002), *Banking on Reform: Political Parties and Central Bank Independence in the Industrial Democracies*, Ann Arbor, MI: University of Michigan Press.
Bernhardt, Dan and Mattias K. Polborn (2010), 'Non-convexities and the gains from concealing defenses from committed terrorists', *Economics Letters*, **107**, 52–4.
Bernheim, B. Douglas (1987), 'Ricardian equivalence: an evaluation of the theory and evidence', in Stanley Fisher (ed), *NBER Macro Annual*, vol. 2, Cambridge, MA: MIT Press, pp. 263–304.
Bernholz, Peter (2000), 'Democracy and capitalism: are they compatible in the long-run?', *Journal of Evolutionary Economics*, **10**, 3–16.
Bernholz, Peter (2006), 'International political system, supreme values, and terrorism', *Public Choice*, **128**, 221–31.
Bernholz, Peter, Friedrich Schneider, Roland Vaubel and Frank Vibert (2004), 'An alternative constitutional treaty for the European Union', *Public Choice*, **91**, 451–68.
Berry, Christopher R. (2009), 'Direct democracy and redistribution', Working Paper, University of Chicago Harris School.
Besley, Timothy (2005), 'Political selection', *The Journal of Economic Perspectives*, **19**, 43–60.
Besley, Timothy (2006), *Principled Agents? The Political Economy of Good Government*, Oxford: Oxford University Press.
Besley, Timothy and Robin Burgess (2001), 'Political agency, government responsiveness and the role of the media', *European Economic Review*, **45**, 629–40.
Besley, Timothy and Anne Case (1995), 'Incumbent behavior: vote seeking, tax setting, and yardstick competition', *American Economic Review*, **85**, 25–45.

Besley, Timothy and Anne Case (2003), 'Political institutions and policy choices: evidence from the United States', *Journal of Economic Literature*, **41**, 7–73.
Besley, Timothy and Stephen Coate (2003), 'Elected versus appointed regulators: theory and evidence', *Journal of the European Economic Association*, **1**, 1176–206.
Besley, Timothy and Stephen Coate (2008), 'Issue unbundling via citizens' initiatives', *Quarterly Journal of Political Science*, **3**, 379–97.
Besley, Timothy and Miguel Gouveia (1994), 'Alternative systems of health care provision', *Economic Policy*, **9**, 199–258.
Besley, Timothy and Abigail Payne (2005), 'Implementation of anti-discrimination policy: does judicial discretion matter" *CEPR Discussion Paper*, no. 5211.
Besley, Timothy J. and Torsten Persson (2009), 'The origins of state capacity: property rights, taxation, and politics', *American Economic Review*, **99**, 1218–44.
Besley, Timothy, Neil Meads and Paolo Surico (2008), 'Insiders versus outsiders in monetary policymaking', *American Economic Review: Papers and Proceedings*, **98**, 218–23.
Besley, Timothy J., Torsten Persson and Daniel M. Sturm (2005), 'Political competition and economic performance: theory and evidence from the United States', National Bureau of Economic Research, NBER Working Paper Series, No. 11484, Cambridge, MA.
Bier, Vicki, Santiago Oliveros and Larry Samuelson (2007), 'Choosing what to protect: strategic defensive allocation against an unknown attacker', *Journal of Public Economic Theory*, **9**, 563–87.
Bifulco, Robert and Helen F. Ladd (2006), 'The impacts of charter schools on student achievement: evidence from North Carolina', *Education Finance and Policy*, **1**, 50–90.
Bikhchandani, Sushil, David Hirshleifer and Ivo Welch (1992), 'A theory of fads, fashion, custom, and cultural change as informational cascades', *Journal of Political Economy*, **100**, 992–1026.
Bikhchandani, Sushil, David Hirshleifer and Ivo Welch (1998), 'Learning from the behavior of others: conformity, fads, and informational cascades', *Journal of Economic Perspectives*, **12**, 151–70.
Binmore, Ken (1994), *Game Theory and the Social Contract, Vol. 1 – Playing Fair*, Cambridge, MA: MIT Press.
Binzer Hobolt, Sara (2009), *Europe in Question: Referendums on European Integration*, Oxford: Oxford University Press.
Bittlingmayer, George (1985), 'Did antitrust policy cause the great merger wave?', *Journal of Law and Economics*, **28**, 78–118.
Bittlingmayer, George (1995), 'Output and stock prices when antitrust is suspended: the effects of the NIRA', in Fred S. McChesney and William F. Shughart II (eds), *The Causes and Consequences of Antitrust: The Public-Choice Perspective*, Chicago, IL: University of Chicago' IL Press, pp. 287–318.
Black, Duncan. (1948a), 'On the rationale of group decision making', *Journal of Political Economy*, **56**, 23–34.
Black, Duncan (1948b), 'The decisions of a committee using a special majority', *Econometrica*, **16**, 245–61.
Black, Duncan (1948c), 'The elasticity of committee decision with an altering size of majority', *Econometrica*, **16**, 261–72.
Black, Duncan (with R.A. Newing) (1951), *Committee Decisions with Complementary Valuation*, Glasgow: William Hodge.
Black, Duncan (1958), *The Theory of Committees and Elections*, Cambridge: Cambridge University Press.
Black, Duncan (1972), 'Arrow's work and the normative theory of committees', unpublished manuscript.
Blalock, Garrick, Vrinda Kadiyali and Daniel H. Simon (2009), 'Driving fatalities after 9/11: a hidden cost of terrorism', *Applied Economics*, **41**, 1717–29.
Blanchard, Olivier J. and Nobuhiro Kiyotaki (1987), 'Monopolistic competition and the effects of aggregate demand', *American Economic Review*, **77**, 647–66.
Blanchard, Olivier J. and Roberto Perotti (2002), 'An empirical characterization of the dynamic

effects of government spending and taxation on output', *Quarterly Journal of Economics*, **117**, 1329–68.
Blattman, Christopher and Edward Miguel (2010), 'Civil war', *Journal of Economic Literature*, **48**, 3–57.
Blinder, Alan S. (1997), 'What central bankers could learn from academics – and vice versa', *Journal of Economic Perspectives*, **11**, 3–19.
Blinder, Alan S. (2006), 'The case against the case against discretionary fiscal policy', in Richard W. Kopcke, Geoffrey M.B. Tootell and Robert K. Triest (eds), *The Macroeconomics of Fiscal Policy*, Cambridge, MA: MIT Press, pp. 225–62.
Blomberg, S. Brock and Gregory D. Hess (2003), 'Is the political business cycle for real?', *Journal of Public Economics*, **87**, 1091–121.
Blomberg, S. Brock, Rozlyn C. Engel and Reid Sawyer (2010), 'On the duration and sustainability of transnational terrorist organizations', *Journal of Conflict Resolution*, **54**, 303–30.
Blomberg, S. Brock, Gregory D. Hess and Athanasios Orphanides (2004), 'The macroeconomic consequences of terrorism', *Journal of Monetary Economics*, **51**, 1007–32.
Blume, Lorenz, Jens Muller and Stefan Voigt (2009), 'The economic effects of direct democracy – a first global assessment', *Public Choice*, **140**, 431–61.
Boadway, Robin W. and David E. Wildasin (1989), 'A median voter model of social security', *International Economic Review*, **30**, 307–28.
Boehmer, Charles R. (2008), 'A reassessment of democratic pacifism at the monadic level of analysis', *Conflict Management and Peace Science*, **25**, 81–94.
Boehmer, Charles R. and Timothy Nordstrom (2008), 'Intergovernmental organization memberships: examining political community and the attributes of political organizations', *International Interactions*, **34**, 282–309.
Boehmke, Frederick J. (2005), *The Indirect Effect of Direct Legislation: How Institutions Shape Interest Group Systems*, Columbus, OH: Ohio State University Press.
Boesche, Roger (1996), *Theories of Tyranny, from Plato to Arendt*, University Park, PA: Pennsylvania State University Press.
Boettke, Peter J., Christopher J. Coyne and Peter T. Leeson (2011), 'Quasimarket failure', *Public Choice*, **149**, 209–24.
Bohn, Henning (1998), 'The behavior of US public debt and deficits', *Quarterly Journal of Economics*, **113**, 949–63.
Bohnet, Iris and Bruno S. Frey (1994), 'Direct-democratic rules: the role of discussion', *Kyklos*, **47**, 341–54.
Boix, Carles (2003), *Democracy in Redistribution*, Cambridge: Cambridge University Press.
Boix, Carles and Alicia Adsera (2008), 'Constitutions and democratic breakdowns', in José Maria Maravall and Ignacio Sanchez-Cuenca (eds), *Controlling Governments*, Cambridge: Cambridge University Press, pp. 247–301.
Boix, Carles and Milan Svolik (2010), 'The foundations of limited authoritarian government: institutions and power-sharing in dictatorships', http://ssrn.com/abstract=1352065 (accessed 1 October 2010).
Bolick, Clint (1993), *Grassroots Tyranny: The Limits of Federalism*, Washington, DC: Cato Institute.
Bolton, Gary E. and Axel Ockenfels (2000), 'ERC: A theory of equity, reciprocity and competition', *American Economic Review*, **90**, 166–93.
Bombardini, Matilde and Francesco Trebbi (2011), 'Votes or money? Theory and evidence from the US Congress', *Journal of Public Economics*, **95**, 577–611.
Bongard-Levin, Grigorji M. (1986), *A Complex Study of Ancient India. A Multi-Disciplinary Approach*, Delhi: Ajanta Publications.
Bonneau, Chris W. (2007), 'The effects of campaigns in state supreme court elections', *Political Research Quarterly*, **60**, 489–99.
Bonneau, Chris W. and Melinda Gann Hall (2003), 'Predicting challengers in state supreme court elections: context and the politics of institutional design', *Political Research Quarterly*, **56**, 337–49.
Boockmann, Bernhard (2001), 'The ratification of ILO conventions: a hazard rate analysis', *Economics and Politics*, **13**, 281–309.

Boockmann, Bernhard and Roland Vaubel (2009), 'The theory of raising rivals' costs and evidence from the International Labour Organization', *The World Economy*, 32, 862–87.
Booker, Kevin, Scott M. Gilpatric, Timothy Gronberg and Dennis Jansen (2008), 'The effect of charter schools on traditional public school students in Texas: are children who stay behind left behind?', *Journal of Urban Economics*, 64, 123–45.
Borcherding, Thomas E. (1985), 'The causes of government expenditure growth: a survey of U.S. evidence', *Journal of Public Economics*, 28, 359–82.
Borcherding, Thomas E. and Robert T. Deacon (1972), 'The demand for the services of non-federal governments', *American Economic Review*, 62, 891–901.
Borda, Jean-Charles de (1781), 'Mémoire sur les élections au scrutin', *Histoire de l'Académie Royale des Sciences*, Paris.
Borel, Emile ([1921] 1953), 'La théorie du jeu les équations intégrales à noyau symétrique', *Comptes Rendus de l'Académie*, 173, 1304–8, translated by Savage, Leonard J. (1953), 'The theory of play and integral equations with skew symmetric kernels', *Econometrica*, 21, 97–100.
Bork, Robert H. (1990), *The Tempting of America*, New York: Simon and Schuster.
Borland, Melvin V. and Roy M. Howsen (1992), 'Student academic achievement and the degree of market concentration in education', *Economics of Education Review*, 11, 31–9.
Borland, Melvin V. and Roy M. Howsen (1993), 'On the determination of the critical level of market concentration in education', *Economics of Education Review*, 12, 166–9.
Botero, Juan, Simeon Djankov, Rafael La Porta and Florencio C. Lopez-De-Silanes (2004), 'The regulation of labor', *Quarterly Journal of Economics*, 119, 1339–82.
Boudreaux, Donald J. and Randall G. Holcombe (1989), 'Government by contract', *Public Finance Quarterly*, 17, 264–80.
Boudreaux, Donald J., Thomas J. DiLorenzo and Steven Parker (1995), 'Antitrust before the Sherman Act', in Fred S. McChesney and William F. Shughart II (eds), *The Causes and Consequences of Antitrust: The Public-Choice Perspective*, Chicago, IL: University of Chicago Press, pp. 255–70.
Boulding, Kenneth E. (1956), *The Image*, Ann Arbor, MI: University of Michigan Press.
Boulding, Kenneth E. (1970), *Economics as a Science*, New York: McGraw-Hill.
Boulding, Kenneth E. (1981), *Evolutionary Economics*, Beverly Hills, CA and London: Sage.
Bowen, Howard R. (1943), 'The interpretation of voting in the allocation of economic resources', *Quarterly Journal of Economics*, 58, 27–48.
Bowler, Shaun and Todd Donovan (1998), *Demanding Choices: Opinion, Voting, and Direct Democracy*, Ann Arbor, MI: The University of Michigan Press.
Bowler, Shaun and Todd Donovan (2004), 'Measuring the effect of direct democracy on state policy: not all initiatives are created equal', *State Politics and Policy Quarterly*, 4, 345–63.
Box-Steffesmeier, Janet M. (1996), 'A dynamic analysis of the role of war chests in campaign strategy', *American Journal of Political Science*, 40, 352–72.
Boyer, Roland and André Orlean (1992), 'How do conventions evolve?', *Journal of Evolutionary Economics*, 2, 165–77.
Boyes, William J. (1976), 'An empirical examination of the Averch-Johnson effect', *Economic Inquiry*, 14, 25–35.
Brabazon, James (2003), 'Taylor's nemesis', *BBC Focus on Africa*, October–December, 10–3.
Brace, Paul, Melinda Gann Hall and Laura Langer (1999), 'Judicial choice and the politics of abortion: institutions, context, and the autonomy of courts', *Albany Law Review*, 62, 1265–303.
Bradford, David F. and Wallace E. Oates (1971), 'The analysis of revenue sharing in a new approach to collective fiscal decisions', *Quarterly Journal of Economics*, 85, 416–39.
Brady, Gordon L., J.R. Clark, and William L. Davis (1995), 'The political economy of dissonance', *Public Choice*, 82, 37–51.
Braithwaite, Alex (2010), 'Resisting infection: how state capacity conditions conflict contagion', *Journal of Peace Research*, 47, 311–19.
Brams, Steven J., Hande Mutlu and Shawn Ling Ramirez (2006), 'Influence in terrorist networks: from undirected to directed graphs', *Studies in Conflict and Terrorism*, 29, 703–18.
Brauninger, Thomas (2005), 'A partisan model of government expenditure', *Public Choice*, 125, 409–29.

Bremer, Stuart A. (1992), 'Dangerous dyads: conditions affecting the likelihood of interstate war 1816–1965', *Journal of Conflict Resolution*, **36**, 309–41.
Brender, Adi and Allan Drazen (2005), 'Political budget cycles in new versus established democracies', *Journal of Monetary Economics*, **52**, 1271–95.
Brennan, H. Geoffrey (2008a), 'Homo economicus and homo politicus: an introduction', *Public Choice*, **137**, 429–38.
Brennan, H. Geoffrey (2008b), 'Psychological dimensions in voter choice', *Public Choice*, **137**, 475–89.
Brennan, H. Geoffrey (2008c). 'Crime and punishment: an expressive voting view', *European Journal of Law and Economics*, **20**, 235–52.
Brennan, Geoffrey and James M. Buchanan (1980), *The Power To Tax: Analytical Foundations of a Fiscal Constitution*, Cambridge: Cambridge University Press.
Brennan, H. Geoffrey and James M. Buchanan (1984), 'Voter choice: evaluating political alternatives', *American Behavioral Scientist*, **28**, 185–201.
Brennan, H. Geoffrey and James M. Buchanan (1985), *The Reason of Rules: Constitutional Political Economy*, Cambridge: Cambridge University Press.
Brennan, H. Geoffrey and Giuseppe Eusepi (2011), 'Buchanan, Hobbes and contractarianism: the supply of rules?', in Miguel Puchades-Navarro (ed.), *Constitutional Economics and Public Institutions. Essays in Honour of Jose Casas-Pardo*, Cheltenham, UK and Northampton, MA, USA: Edward Elgar, forthcoming.
Brennan, H. Geoffrey and Alan Hamlin (1995), 'Constitutional political economy: the political philosophy of *homo economicus*?', *The Journal of Political Philosophy*, **3**, 280–303.
Brennan, H. Geoffrey and Alan Hamlin (1998), 'Expressive voting and electoral equilibrium', *Public Choice*, **95**, 149–75.
Brennan, H. Geoffrey and Alan Hamlin (2000), *Democratic Devices and Desires*, Cambridge: Cambridge University Press.
Brennan, H. Geoffrey and Alan Hamlin (2002), 'Expressive constitutionalism', *Constitutional Political Economy*, **13**, 299–311.
Brennan, H. Geoffrey and Alan Hamlin (2004), 'An introduction to the status quo', *Constitutional Political Economy*, **15**, 127–32.
Brennan, H. Geoffrey and Alan Hamlin (2008), 'Revisionist public choice theory', *New Political Economy*, **13**, 77–88.
Brennan, H. Geoffrey and Alan Hamlin (2009), 'Positive constraints on normative political theory', in Geoffrey Brennan and Giuseppe Eusepi (ed.), *The Economics of Ethics and the Ethics of Economics: Values, Markets and the State*, Cheltenham, UK and Northampton, MA, USA: Edward Elgar, pp. 106–28.
Brennan, Geoffrey and Loren E. Lomasky (1989), 'Large numbers, small costs: the uneasy foundation of democratic rule', in Geoffrey Brennan and Loren E. Lomasky (eds), *Politics and Process – New Essays in Democratic Thought*, Cambridge: Cambridge University Press, pp. 42–59.
Brennan, H. Geoffrey and Loren Lomasky (1993), *Democracy and Decision: The Pure Theory of Electoral Preference*, Cambridge: Cambridge University Press.
Brennan, H. Geoffrey and Philip Pettit (2004), *The Economy of Esteem: An Essay on Civil and Political Society*, Oxford: Oxford University Press.
Brennan, H. Geoffrey and Robert D. Tollison (1980), 'Rent seeking in academia', in James M. Buchanan, Robert D. Tollison and Gordon Tullock (eds), *Toward a Theory of the Rent-Seeking Society*, College Station: Texas A&M Press, pp. 344–56.
Breton, Albert (1996), *Competitive Governments: An Economic Theory of Politics and Public Finance*, New York: Cambridge University Press.
Breyer, Friedrich (1995), 'The political economy of rationing in social health insurance', *Journal of Population Economics*, **8**, 137–48.
Breyer, Friedrich and Ben Craig (1997), 'Voting on social security: evidence from OECD countries', *European Journal of Political Economy*, **13**, 705–24.
Bronars, Stephen G. and John R. Lott (1997), 'Do campaign donations alter how a politician votes? Or, do donors support candidates who value the same things that they do?', *Journal of Law and Economics*, **40**, 317–50.

Bronfenbrenner, Martin (1952), 'Book review of *Social Choice and Individual Values*' by Kenneth J. Arrow, *The Journal of Business*, **25**, 134–5.
Brooker, Paul (2009), *Autocratic Regimes*, 2nd edn, New York: Palgrave Macmillan.
Brown, T. Malcom (1952), 'Book review of *Social Choice and Individual Values*' by Kenneth J. Arrow, *The Canadian Journal of Economics and Political Science*, **18**, 400–403.
Browning, Edgar K. (1973), 'Social insurance and intergenerational transfers', *Journal of Law and Economics*, **16**, 215–37.
Browning, Edgar K. (1975), 'Why the social insurance budget is too large in a democracy', *Economic Inquiry*, **13**, 373–88.
Brunner, Eric and Jennifer Imazeki (2008), 'Tiebout choice and universal school vouchers', *Journal of Urban Economics*, **63**, 253–79.
Brunner, Eric and Jon Sonstelie (2003), ' Homeowners, property values, and the political economy of the school voucher', *Journal of Urban Economics*, **54**, 239–57.
Brunner, Eric, Jon Sonstelie and Mark Thayer (2001), 'Capitalization and the voucher: an analysis of precinct returns from California's Proposition 174', *Journal of Urban Economics*, **50**, 517–36.
Buccola, Steven T. and James E. McCandish (1999), 'Rent seeking and rent dissipation in state enterprises', *Review of Agricultural Economics*, **21**, 358–73 reprinted in Roger D. Congleton, Arye L. Hillman and Kai A. Konrad (eds) (2008), *Forty Years of Research on Rent Seeking 2 – Applications: Rent Seeking in Practice*, Heidelberg: Springer, pp. 593–608.
Buchanan, J.M. (1949), 'The pure theory of government finance: a suggested approach', *Journal of Political Economy*, **57**, 496–505.
Buchanan, James M. (1954a), 'Social choice, democracy, and free markets', *Journal of Political Economy*, **62**, 114–23.
Buchanan, James M. (1954b), 'Individual choice in voting and the market', *Journal of Political Economy*, **62**, 334–43.
Buchanan, James M. ([1967] 1967), *Public Finance in Democratic Process*, Chapel Hill, NC: University of North Carolina Press.
Buchanan, James M. (1959), 'Positive economics, welfare economics, and political economy', *Journal of Law and Economics*, **2**, 124–38.
Buchanan, James M. (1965), 'An economic theory of clubs', *Economica*, **32**, 1–14.
Buchanan, James M. ([1969] 2000), 'Is economics a science of choice?', in Erich Streissler (ed.), *Roads to Freedom: Essays in Honour of Friedrich A. von Hayek*, London: Routledge & Kegan Paul, 1969, pp. 47–64, reprinted in Geoffrey Brennan, Hartmut Kliemt and Robert D. Tollison (eds), *The Collected Works of James M. Buchanan*, vol. 12, *Economic Inquiry and Its Logic*, Indianapolis, IN: Liberty Fund, pp. 3–21.
Buchanan, James M. (1972), 'Toward analysis of closed behavioral systems', in James M. Buchanan and Robert D. Tollison (eds), *Theory of Public Choice*, Ann Arbor, MI: University of Michigan Press, pp. 11–23.
Buchanan, James M. (1974), 'Good economics – bad law', *Virginia Law Review*, **60**, 483–92.
Buchanan, James M. (1975), *The Limits of Liberty: Between Anarchy and Leviathan*, Chicago, IL: University of Chicago Press.
Buchanan, James M. ([1979] 1984), 'Politics without romance: a sketch of positive public choice theory and its normative implications', Inaugural Lecture, Institute for Advanced Studies, Vienna, Austria, IHS-Journal, *Zeitschrift des Instituts für Höhere Studien*, Wien 3 (1979), pp. B1–B11, reprinted in James M. Buchanan and Robert D. Tollison (eds), *The Theory of Public Choice – II*, Ann Arbor, MI: University of Michigan Press, pp. 11–22.
Buchanan, James M. ([1979] 1999), 'Politics without romance: a sketch of positive public choice theory and its normative implications', from 'Inaugural Lecture', Institute for Advanced Studies, Vienna, Austria, HIS Journal, *Zeitschrift des Instituts für Höhere Studien*, 3 Wien, 1979: B1–B11, reprinted in Geoffrey Brennan, Hartmut Kliemt and Robert D. Tollison (eds), *The Collected Works of James M. Buchanan*, vol. 1, *The Logical Foundations of Constitutional Liberty*, Indianapolis: Liberty Fund, pp. 45–59.
Buchanan, James M. (1980), 'Rent seeking and profit seeking', in James M. Buchanan, Robert D. Tollison and Gordon Tullock (eds), *Toward a Theory of the Rent Seeking Society*, College Station, TX: Texas A&M University Press, pp. 3–15, reprinted in Roger D. Congleton, Arye

L. Hillman and Kai A. Konrad (eds) (2008), *Forty Years of Research on Rent Seeking 1 – The Theory of Rent Seeking*, Heidelberg: Springer, pp. 55–67.

Buchanan, James M. (1987), 'Constitutional economics', in John Eatwell, Murray Milgate and Peter Newman (eds), *The New Palgrave: A Dictionary of Economics*, Basingstoke: Palgrave Macmillan, pp. 585–8.

Buchanan, James M. (1990), 'The domain of constitutional economics', *Constitutional Political Economy*, **1**, 1–18.

Buchanan, James M. (2004), 'The status of the status quo', *Constitutional Political Economy*, **15**, 133–44.

Buchanan, James M. and Charles J. Goetz (1972), 'Efficiency limits of fiscal mobility: an assessment of the Tiebout model', *Journal of Public Economics*, **1**, 25–43.

Buchanan, James M. and Gordon Tullock (1962), *The Calculus of Consent: Logical Foundations of Constitutional Democracy*, Ann Arbor, MI: University of Michigan Press.

Buchanan, James M. and Viktor Vanberg (1989), 'A theory of leadership and deference in constitutional construction', *Public Choice*, **61**, 15–27.

Buchanan, James M. and Yong J. Yoon (2000), 'A Smithean perspective on increasing returns', *Journal of the History of Economic Thought*, **22**, 43–8.

Buchanan, James M., Robert D. Tollison and Gordon Tullock (eds) (1980), *Toward a Theory of the Rent Seeking Society*, College Station, TX: Texas A&M University Press.

Bueno de Mesquita, Bruce (2006), 'Game theory, political economy, and the evolving study of war and peace', *American Political Science Review*, **100**, 637–42.

Bueno de Mesquita, Bruce and David Lalman (1992), *War and Reason: Domestic and International Imperatives*, New Haven, CT: Yale University Press.

Bueno de Mesquita, Bruce and Kenneth Shepsle (2001), 'William Harrison Riker: 1920–1993', *Biographical Memoirs*, National Academy of Sciences, **79**, 3–22.

Bueno de Mesquita, Bruce, Michael T. Koch and Randolph M. Siverson (2004), 'Testing competing institutional explanations of the democratic peace: the case of dispute duration', *Conflict Management and Peace Science*, **21**, 255–67.

Bueno de Mesquita, Bruce, James D. Morrow, Randolph M. Siverson and Alastair Smith (1999), 'An institutional explanation of the democratic peace', *American Political Science Review*, **93**, 791–807.

Bueno de Mesquita, Bruce, James D. Morrow, Randolph M. Siverson and Alastair Smith (2000), 'Political institutions, political survival, and political success', in Bruce Bueno de Mesquita and Hilton L. Root (eds), *Governing for Prosperity*, New Haven: Yale University Press, pp. 59–84.

Bueno de Mesquita, Bruce, James D. Morrow, Randolph M. Siverson and Alastair Smith (2001), 'Political competition and economic growth', *Journal of Democracy*, **12**, 58–72.

Bueno de Mesquita, Bruce, Alastair Smith, Randolph M. Siverson and James D. Morrow (2003), *The Logic of Political Survival*, Cambridge, MA: MIT Press.

Bullock, Charles S. III (1985), 'U.S. Senate committee assignments: preferences, motivations, and success', *American Journal of Political Science*, **29**, 789–808.

Burbank, Stephen B. (1999), 'The architecture of judicial independence', *Southern California Law Review*, **72**, 315–52.

Burke, Edmund ([1790] 1960), 'Reflections on the revolution in France', in Walter J. Bate (ed.), *Edmund Burke Selected Works*, New York: Modern Library, pp. 343–423.

Buser, Whitney (2011), 'The impact of fiscal decentralization on economic performance in high-income OECD nations: an institutional approach', *Public Choice*, **149**, 31–48.

Butler, David A. (1995), *Does 'Independent' Mean 'Free from Influence?': Escape Clause Decision-Making at the United States International Trade Commission*, New York: Garland Publications.

Byman, Daniel and Sarah E. Kreps (2010), 'Agents of destruction? Applying principal–agent analysis to state-sponsored terrorism', *International Studies Perspectives*, **11**, 1–18.

Cadigan, John and Pamela M. Schmitt (2010), 'Strategic entrzy deterrence and terrorism: theory and experimental evidence', *Public Choice*, **143**, 3–22.

Calabresi, Guido and A. Douglas Melamed (1972), 'Property rules, liability rules, and inalienability: one view of the cathedral', *Harvard Law Review*, **85**, 1089–128.

Calcagno, Peter T. and Christopher Westley (2008), 'An institutional analysis of voter turnout:

the role of primary type and the expressive and instrumental voting hypotheses', *Constitutional Political Economy*, **19**, 94–110.
Calfee, John E. and Paul H. Rubin (1992), 'Some implications of damage payments for nonpecuniary losses', *The Journal of Legal Studies*, **21**, 371–411.
Calvo, Guillermo A. (1983), 'Staggered prices in a utility maximizing framework', *Journal of Monetary Economics*, **12**, 983–98.
Camobreco, John F. (1998), 'Preferences, fiscal policies, and the initiative process', *Journal of Politics*, **60**, 819–29.
Campbell, John Y. and John H. Cochrane (2000), 'Explaining the poor performance of consumption-based asset pricing models', *Journal of Finance*, **55**, 2863–78.
Canes-Wrone, Brandice and Tom S. Clark (2009), 'Judicial independence and nonpartisan elections', *Wisconsin Law Review*, **2009**, 21–65.
Cann, Damon (2006), 'Justice for sale? Campaign contributions and judicial decision making', *State Politics and Policy Quarterly*, **7**, 281–97.
Cantner, Uwe and Horst Hanusch (2002), 'Evolutionary economics, its basic concepts and methods. A tribute to Mark Perlman, editor of the *Journal of Evolutionary Economics* 1991–96', in Hank Lim, Ungsuh K. Park and Geoffrey C. Harcourt (eds), *Editing Economics – Essays in Honour of Mark Perlman*, London and New York: Routledge, pp. 182–207.
Cantner, Uwe and Andreas Pyka (2001), 'Classifying technology policy from an evolutionary perspective, *Research Policy*, **30**, 759–75.
Caplan, Bryan (2001), 'Has Leviathan been bound? A theory of imperfectly constrained government with evidence from the states', *Southern Economic Journal*, **67**, 825–47.
Caplan, Bryan (2007), *The Myth of the Rational Voter. Why Democracies Choose Bad Policies*, Princeton, NJ: Princeton University Press.
Card, David and Abigail A. Payne (2002), 'School finance reform, the distribution of school spending, and the distribution of student test scores', *Journal of Public Economics*, **83**, 49–82.
Cardozo, Benjamin N. (1921), *The Nature of the Judicial Process*, New Haven, CT: Yale University Press.
Carlson, Lisa J. and Raymond Dacey (2006a), 'Sequential analysis of deterrence games with a declining status quo', *Conflict Management and Peace Science*, **23**, 181–98.
Carlson, Lisa J. and Raymond Dacey (2006b), 'Confusion of loss aversion and risk attitude in international relations and peace science', *Peace Economics, Peace Science and Public Policy*, **12**(2), art. 1.
Carlsson, Hans and Eric van Damme (1993), 'Global games and equilibrium selection', *Econometrica*, **61**, 989–1018.
Carneiro, Robert L. (2000), 'The transition from quantity to quality: a neglected causal mechanism in accounting for social evolution', *Proceedings of the National Academy of Sciences*, **97**, 12926–31.
Carpenter, William S. (1918), *Judicial Tenure in the United States*, New Haven, CT: Yale University Press.
Carr, Jack L. (1989), 'Government size and economic growth: a new framework and some evidence from cross-section and time series data: comment', *American Economic Review*, **79**, 267–71.
Carroll, Lewis (1884), *The Principles of Parliamentary Representation*, London: Harrison and Sons.
Carruba, Clifford J., Mathew Gabel and Charles Hankla (2008), 'Judicial behavior under political constraints: evidence from the European Court of Justice', *American Political Science Review*, **102**, 435–52.
Carsey, Thomas M. and Barry Rundquist (1999), 'The reciprocal relationship between state defense interest and committee representation in Congress', *Public Choice*, **99**, 455–63.
Cason, Timothy N. and Vai-Lam Mui (2005), 'Uncertainty and resistance to reform in laboratory participation games', *European Journal of Political Economy*, **21**, 708–37.
Cassinelli, C.W. (1960), 'Totalitarianism, ideology, and propaganda', *The Journal of Politics*, **22**, 68–95.
Cassing, James H. (2000), 'Economic policy and political culture in Indonesia', *European Journal of Political Economy*, **16**, 159–71.

Cassing, James H. and Arye L. Hillman (1986), 'Shifting comparative advantage and senescent industry collapse', *American Economic Review*, **76**, 516–23.
Cederman, Lars-Erik and Luc Girardin (2007), 'Beyond fractionalization: mapping ethnicity onto nationalist insurgencies', *American Political Science Review*, **101**, 173–85.
Cederman, Lars-Erik, Simon Hug and Lutz F. Krebs (2010), 'Democratization and civil war: empirical evidence', *Journal of Peace Research*, **47**, 377–94.
Chahrour, Ryan, Stephanie Schmitt-Grohé and Martín Uribe (2010), 'A model based evaluation of the debate on the size of the tax multiplier', National Bureau of Economic Research, NBER Working Paper Series, No. 16169, Cambridge, MA.
Chakrabarti, Rajashri (2008), 'Can increasing private school participation and monetary loss in a voucher program affect public school performance? Evidence from Milwaukee', *Journal of Public Economics*, **92**, 1371–93.
Chan, P.C. Winnie and Robert McMillan (2009), 'School choice and public school performance: evidence from Ontario's tuition tax credit', Working Paper, University of Toronto.
Chang, Kelly H., Rui J.P. de Figueiredo, Jr and Barry R. Weingast (2001), 'Rational choice theories of bureaucratic performance and control', in William F. Shughart II and Laura Razzolini (eds), *The Elgar Companion to Public Choice*, Cheltenham, UK and Northampton, MA, USA: Edward Elgar, pp. 271–92.
Chappell, Henry W. Jr (1990), 'Economic performance, voting, and political support: a unified approach', *Review of Economics and Statistics*, **72**, 313–20.
Chappell, Henry W. Jr and William R. Keech (1986), 'Party differences in macroeconomic policies and outcomes', *American Economic Review: Papers and Proceedings*, **76**, 71–4.
Chappell, Henry W. Jr and William R. Keech (1988), 'The unemployment rate consequences of partisan monetary policies', *Southern Economic Journal*, **55**, 107–22.
Chappell, Henry W. Jr and Rob Roy McGregor (2004), 'Did time inconsistency contribute to the Great Inflation? Evidence from the FOMC transcripts', *Economics and Politics*, **16**, 233–51.
Chappell, Henry W. Jr, Thomas M. Havrilesky and Rob Roy McGregor (1993), 'Partisan monetary policies: presidential influence through the power of appointment', *Quarterly Journal of Economics*, **108**, 185–218.
Chappell, Henry W. Jr, Thomas M. Havrilesky and Rob Roy McGregor (1995), 'Policymakers, institutions, and central bank decisions', *Journal of Economics and Business*, **47**, 113–36.
Chappell, Henry W. Jr, Rob Roy McGregor and Todd Vermilyea (2004), 'Majority rule, consensus building, and the power of the chairman: Arthur Burns and the FOMC', *Journal of Money, Credit, and Banking*, **36**, 407–22.
Chappell, Henry W. Jr, Rob Roy McGregor and Todd Vermilyea (2005), *Committee Decisions on Monetary Policy: Evidence from Historical Records of the Federal Open Market Committee*, Cambridge, MA: The MIT Press.
Chari, V.V., Lawrence J. Christiano and Patrick J. Kehoe (1994), 'Optimal fiscal policy in a business cycle model', *Journal of Political Economy*, **102**, 617–52.
Chehabi, Houchang E. and Juan J. Linz (1998), 'A theory of Sultanism 1: a type of nondemocratic rule', in Houchang E. Chehabi and Juan J. Linz (eds), *Sultanistic Regimes*, Baltimore, MD: Johns Hopkins University Press, pp. 3–25.
Cheibub, José Antonio (2002), 'Presidentialism and democratic performance', in Andrew Reynolds (ed.), *The Architecture of Democracy*, New York: Oxford University Press, pp. 104–40.
Cheibub, José Antonio (2007), *Presidentialism, Parliamentarism, and Democracy*, Cambridge: Cambridge University Press.
Cheibub, José Antonio and Fernando Limongi (2002), 'Democratic institutions and regime survival: parliamentary and presidential democracies reconsidered', *Annual Review of Political Science*, **5**, 151–79.
Chen, Hui, David C. Parsley and Ya-wen Yang (2010), 'Corporate lobbying and financial performance', working paper.
Childers, Matthew and Mike Binder (2010), 'Engaged by initiatives? How the introduction and use of citizen initiatives increase voter turnout', working paper, UCSD.
Chiozza, Giacomo and Henk E. Goemans (2004), 'International conflict and the tenure of leaders: is war still *ex post* inefficient?', *American Journal of Political Science*, **48**, 604–19.

Choi, Seung-Whan (2010), 'Legislative constraints: a path to peace?', *Journal of Conflict Resolution*, **54**, 438–70.
Christiano, Lawrence J., Martin Eichenbaum and Charles L. Evans (2005), 'Nominal rigidities and the dynamic effects of a shock to monetary policy', *Journal of Political Economy*, **113**, 1–45.
Christiano, Lawrence J., Martin Eichenbaum and Sergio Rebelo (2009), 'When is the government spending multiplier large', National Bureau of Economic Research, NBER Working Paper Series, No. 15394, Cambridge, MA.
Christiano, Thomas (2004), 'Is normative rational choice theory self-defeating?', *Ethics*, **115**, 122–41.
Chu, Angus C. (2010), 'Nation states vs. united empire: effects of political competition on economic growth', *Public Choice*, **145**, 181–95.
Clark, William Roberts, Matt Golder and Sona Nadenichek Golder (2009), *Principles of Comparative Politics*, Washington, DC: CQ Press.
Coase, Ronald H. (1960), 'The problem of social cost', *Journal of Law and Economics*, **3**, 1–44.
Coase, Ronald H. (1981), 'Duncan Black: a biographical sketch', in Gordon Tullock (ed), *Towards a Science of Politics*, Blacksburg, WV: Center for Study of Public Choice.
Coate, Malcolm B., Richard S. Higgins and Fred S. McChesney (1990), 'Bureaucracy and politics in FTC merger challenges', *Journal of Law and Economics*, **33**, 463–82.
Coate, Stephen (2004a), 'Pareto improving campaign finance policy', *American Economic Review*, **94**, 628–55.
Coate, Stephen (2004b), 'Political competition with campaign contributions and informative advertising', *Journal of the European Economic Association*, **2**, 772–804.
Coats, R. Morris, Gökhan Karahan and Robert D. Tollison (2006), 'Terrorism and pork-barrel spending', *Public Choice*, **128**, 275–87.
Cogan, John, Tobias Cwik, John B. Taylor and Volker Wieland (2009), 'New Keynesian versus old Keynesian multipliers', Stanford Institute for Economic Policy Research Discussion Paper No. 08-30.
Cogley, Timothy and James M. Nason (1995), 'Effects of the Hodrick-Prescott filter on trend and difference stationary time series: implications for business cycle research', *Journal of Economic Dynamics and Control*, **19**, 253–78.
Cohen, Benjamin J. (1986), *In Whose Interest? International Banking and American Foreign Policy*, New Haven, CT and London: Yale University Press.
Cohen, Jeffrey E. (1986), 'The dynamics of the "revolving door" on the FCC', *American Journal of Political Science*, **30**, 689–708.
Cohen, Mark A. (1991), 'Explaining judicial behavior or what's "unconstitutional" about the Sentencing Commission?', *Journal of Law, Economics, and Organization*, **7**, 183–99.
Cohen, Mark A. (1992), 'The motives of judges: empirical evidence from antitrust sentencing', *International Review of Law and Economics*, **12**, 13–30.
Coker, David C. and W. Mark Crain (1994), 'Legislative committees as loyalty-generating institutions', *Public Choice*, **81**, 195–221.
Cole, Laurie (2002), 'Access to justice and independence of the judiciary in the Americas', *The Summit of the Americas Follow-Up Series*, no. 1.
Collier, David (1979a), 'The bureaucratic-authoritarian model: synthesis and priorities for future research', in David Collier (ed.), *New Authoritarianism in Latin America*, Princeton, NJ: Princeton University Press, pp. 363–98
Collier, David (1979b), 'Overview of the bureaucratic-authoritarian model' in David Collier (ed.), *New Authoritarianism in Latin America*, Princeton, NJ: Princeton University Press, pp. 19–32.
Collier, David and Robert Adcock (1999), 'Democracy and dichotomies: a pragmatic approach to choices about concepts', *American Review of Political Science*, **2**, 537–65.
Collier, David and Steven Levitsky (1997), 'Democracy with adjectives: conceptual innovation in comparative research', *World Politics*, **49**, 430–51.
Collier, Paul and Anke Hoeffler (1998), 'On the economic causes of civil war', *Oxford Economic Papers*, **50**, 563–73.
Collier, Paul and Anke Hoeffler (2004), 'Greed and grievance in civil war', *Oxford Economic Papers*, **56**, 563–595.

Collier, Paul and Anke Hoeffler (2007), 'Civil war', in Todd Sandler and Keith Hartley (eds), *Handbook of Defense Economics, vol. 2: Defense in a Globalized World*, Amsterdam and Oxford: North-Holland (Elsevier), pp. 711–39.
Collier, Paul, Lani Elliott, Håvard Hegre, Anke Hoeffler, Marta Reynal-Querol and Nicholas Sambanis (2003), *Breaking the Conflict Trap: Civil War and Development Policy*, World Bank Policy Research Report, Washington, DC: Oxford University Press.
Commager, Henry Steele (1978), *The Empire of Reason: How Europe Imagined and America Realized the Enlightenment*, London: Weidenfeld & Nicolson.
Condorcet, Jean-Antoine-Nicolas de Caritat, Marquis de (1785), *Essai sur l'application de l'analyse à la probabilité des décisions rendues à la pluralité des voix*, Paris.
Congleton, Roger D. (1980), 'Competitive process, competitive waste, and institutions', in James M. Buchanan, Robert D. Tollison and Gordon Tullock (eds), *Toward a Theory of the Rent Seeking Society*, College Station, TX: Texas A&M University Press, pp. 153–79, reprinted in Roger D. Congleton, Arye L. Hillman and Kai A. Konrad (eds) (2008), *Forty Years of Research on Rent Seeking 1 – The Theory of Rent Seeking*, Heidelberg: Springer, pp. 69–95.
Congleton, Roger D. (1991a), 'Ideological conviction and persuasion in the rent-seeking society', *Journal of Public Economics*, **44**, 65–86, reprinted in Roger D. Congleton, Arye L. Hillman and Kai A. Konrad (eds) (2008), *Forty Years of Research on Rent Seeking 2 – Applications: Rent Seeking in Practice*, Heidelberg: Springer, pp. 769–90.
Congleton, Roger D. (1991b), 'The economic role of a work ethic', *Journal of Economic Behavior and Organization*, **15**, 365–85.
Congleton, Roger D. (2007a), 'On the feasibility of a liberal welfare state: agency and exit costs in income security clubs', *Constitutional Political Economy*, **18**, 145–59.
Congleton, Roger D. (2007b), 'The moral voter hypothesis: economic and normative aspects of public policy formation within democracies', *Journal of Public Finance and Public Choice*, **25**, 3–30.
Congleton, Roger D. (2010), 'On the evolution of organizational government', George Mason University Working Paper in Economics, No. 10-26, available at: http://ssrn.com/abstract=1661529 (accessed 12 January 2010).
Congleton, Roger D. (2011), *Perfecting Parliament. Constitutional Reform, Liberalism and the Rise of the Western Democracy*, Cambridge: Cambridge University Press.
Congleton, Roger D. and Feler Bose (2010), 'The rise of the modern welfare state: ideology, institutions, and income security', *Public Choice*, **144**, 535–55.
Congleton, Roger D. and William F. Shughart II (1990), 'The growth of social security: electoral push or political pull?', *Economic Inquiry*, **28**, 109–32.
Congleton, Roger D. and Birgitta Swedenborg (eds) (2006), *Democratic Constitutional Design and Public Policy, Analysis and Evidence*, Cambridge, MA: MIT Press.
Congleton, Roger D., Arye L. Hillman and Kai A. Konrad (eds) (2008a), *Forty Years of Research on Rent Seeking 1 – The Theory of Rent Seeking*, Heidelberg: Springer.
Congleton, Roger D., Arye L. Hillman and Kai A. Konrad (eds) (2008b), *Forty Years of Research on Rent Seeking 2 – Applications: Rent Seeking in Practice*, Heidelberg: Springer.
Congleton, Roger D., Arye L. Hillman and Kai A. Konrad (2008c), 'Forty years of research on rent seeking: an overview', in Roger D. Congleton, Arye L. Hillman and Kai A. Konrad (eds), *Forty Years of Research on Rent Seeking*, vols 1 and 2, Heidelberg: Springer, pp. 1–42.
Conover, Pamela J. and Stanley Feldman (1981), 'The origins and meaning of liberal/conservative self-identification', *American Journal of Political Science*, **25**, 617–45.
Converse, Philip E. (1964), 'The nature of belief systems in mass publics', in David E. Apter (ed.), *Ideology and Discontent*, New York: Free Press, pp. 206–61.
Cooper, Michael J., Huseyin Gulen and Alexei V. Ovtchinnikov (2010), 'Corporate political contributions and stock returns', *Journal of Finance*, **65**, 687–724.
Cooper, Russell and Andrew John (1988), 'Coordinating coordination failures in Keynesian models', *Quarterly Journal of Economics*, **103**, 441–63.
Cooter, Robert D. (1983), 'The objectives of private and public judges', *Public Choice*, **41**, 107–32.
Cooter, Robert D. (2000), *The Strategic Constitution*, Princeton, NJ: Princeton University Press.

Cooter, Robert D. and Tom Ginsburg (1996), 'Comparative judicial discretion: an empirical test of economic models', *International Review of Law and Economics*, **16**, 295–313.

Cooter, Robert and Lewis Kornhauser (1980), 'Can litigation improve the law without the help of judges?', *Journal of Legal Studies*, **9**, 139–63.

Couch, Jim F. and William F. Shughart II (1998), *The Political Economy of the New Deal*, Cheltenham, UK and Northampton, MA, USA: Edward Elgar.

Couch, Jim F., William F. Shughart II and Al L. Williams (1993), 'Private school enrollment and public school performance', *Public Choice*, **76**, 301–12.

Coughlin, Peter J. and Shmuel Nitzan (1981), 'Electoral outcomes with probabilistic voting and Nash social welfare maxima', *Journal of Public Economics*, **15**, 113–21.

Cowart, Andrew T. (1978), 'The economic policies of European governments, part I: monetary policy', *British Journal of Political Science*, **8**, 285–311.

Cowen, Tyler (2004), 'A road map to Middle Eastern peace? A public choice perspective', *Public Choice*, **118**, 1–10.

Cowen, Tyler and Daniel Sutter (1997), 'Politics and the pursuit of fame', *Public Choice*, **93**, 19–35.

Cowling, Keith and Dennis C. Mueller (1978), 'The social cost of monopoly power', *Economic Journal*, **88**, 727–48, reprinted in Roger D. Congleton, Arye L. Hillman and Kai A. Konrad (eds) (2008), *Forty Years of Research on Rent Seeking 2 – Applications: Rent Seeking in Practice*, Heidelberg: Springer, pp. 67–88.

Coyne, Christopher J. (2008), *After War: The Political Economy of Exporting Democracy*, Stanford, CA: Stanford University Press.

Crain, W. Mark (1990), 'Legislative committees: a filtering theory', in W. Mark Crain and Robert D. Tollison (eds), *Predicting Politics: Essays in Empirical Public Choice*, Ann Arbor, MI: University of Michigan Press, pp. 149–66.

Crain, Mark W. and Robert E. McCormick (1984), 'Regulators as an interest group', in James M. Buchanan and Robert D. Tollison (eds), *The Theory of Public Choice II*, Ann Arbor, MI: University of Michigan Press, pp. 287–304.

Crain, W. Mark and James C. Miller, III (1990), 'Budget process and spending growth', *William and Mary Law Review*, **31**, 1021–46.

Crain, W. Mark and John T. Sullivan (1997), 'Committee characteristics and re-election margins: an empirical investigation of the US House', *Public Choice*, **93**, 271–85.

Crain, W. Mark and Robert D. Tollison (1977), 'The influence of representation on public policy', *Journal of Legal Studies*, **6**, 355–61.

Crain, Mark W. and Robert D. Tollison (eds) (1990), *Predicting Politics*, Ann Arbor, MI: University of Michigan Press.

Crain, Mark W., Robert D. Tollison and Thomas H. Deaton (1991), 'The price of influence in an interest-group economy', *Rationality and Society*, **15**, 437–49.

Crain, W. Mark, Robert D. Tollison, Brian L. Goff and Diek Carlson (1985), 'Legislator specialization and the size of government', *Public Choice*, **46**, 311–15.

Cramer, Christopher (2002), '*Homo economicus* goes to war: methodological individualism, rational choice and the political economy of war', *World Development*, **30**, 1845–64.

Crandall, Robert W. and Clifford Winston (2003), 'Does antitrust policy improve consumer welfare? Assessing the evidence' *The Journal of Economic Perspectives*, **17**, 3–26.

Crawford, Vincent and Joel Sobel (1982), 'Strategic information transmission', *Econometrica*, **50**, 1431–51.

Crémer, Jacques and Thomas R. Palfrey (2002), 'Federal mandates by popular demand', *Journal of Political Economy*, **108**, 905–27.

Crenshaw, Martha (2007), 'Explaining suicide terrorism: a review essay', *Security Studies*, **16**, 133–62.

Crespi, Irving (1997), *The Public Opinion Process: How the People Speak*, Mahwah, NJ: Lawrence Erlbaum Associates.

Crombez, Christophe (2000), 'Institutional reform and codecision in the European Union', *Constitutional Political Economy*, **11**, 41–57.

Cropper, Maureen, William N. Evans, Stephen J. Berardi, Maria M. Ducla-Soares and Paul R.

Portney (1992), 'The determination of pesticide regulation: a statistical analysis of EPA decision making', *Journal of Political Economy*, **100**, 175–97.
Cross, Frank and Emerson H. Tiller (1998), 'Judicial partisanship and obedience to legal doctrine: whistle-blowing on the Federal Court of Appeals', *Yale Law Journal*, **107**, 2155–76.
Crowley, George R. and Russell S. Sobel (2011), 'Does fiscal decentralization constrain Leviathan? New evidence from local property tax competition', *Public Choice*, **149**, 5–30.
Cukierman, Alex, Steven B. Webb and Bilin Neyapti (1992), 'Measuring the independence of central banks and its effect on policy outcomes', *World Bank Economic Review*, **6**, 353–98.
Cunningham, David E. (2006), 'Veto players and civil war duration', *American Journal of Political Science*, **50**, 875–92.
Curran, Christopher (1992), 'The spread of the comparative negligence rule in the United States', *International Review of Law and Economics*, **12**, 317–32.
Currie, Gregory (1984), 'Individualism and global supervenience', *British Journal for the Philosophy of Science*, **35**, 345–58.
Dahl, Robert A. (1996), 'The future of democratic theory', unpublished manuscript, Instituto Juan March de Estudios e Investigaciones, Madrid.
Dahl, Robert A. and Edward R. Tufte (1973), *Size and Democracy*, Stanford, CA: Stanford University Press.
Dal Bó, Ernesto (2006), 'Regulatory capture: a review', *Oxford Review of Economic Policy*, **22**, 203–25.
Dal Bó, Ernesto and Martin Rossi (2008), 'Term length and political performance', National Bureau of Economic Research, NBER Working Paper Series, no. 14511.
Dalton, Russell J. (2008), 'Direct democracy and good governance: does it matter?', in Shaun Bowler and Amihai Glazer (eds), *Direct Democracy's Impact on American Political Institutions*, New York: Palgrave MacMillan, pp. 149–67.
Danilovic, Vesna and J. Clare (2007), 'The Kantian liberal peace (revisited)', *American Journal of Political Science*, **51**, 397–414.
Davis, Douglas D. and Robert J. Reilly (1998), 'Do too many cooks always spoil the stew? An experimental analysis of rent-seeking and the role of a strategic buyer', *Public Choice*, **95**, 89–115.
Davis, Douglas D., Laura Razzolini, Robert Reilly and Bart Wilson (2006), 'Raising revenues for charity: auctions versus lotteries' in Douglas D. Davis and R. Mark Isaac (eds), *Research in Experimental Economics*, vol. 11, *Experiments Investigating Fundraising and Charitable Contributors*, New York: JAI Press.
De Bartolome, Charles A.M. (1997), 'What determines state aid to school districts? A positive model of foundation aid as redistribution', *Journal of Policy Analysis and Management*, **16**, 32–47.
De Figueiredo, John M. and Brian S. Silverman (2006), 'Academic earmarks and the returns to lobbying', *Journal of Law and Economics*, **49**, 597–626.
De Figueiredo, John M. and Emerson H. Tiller (1996), 'Congressional control of the courts: a theoretical and empirical analysis of expansion of the federal judiciary', *Journal of Law and Economics*, **39**, 435–62.
De Figueiredo, John M., Ho Ji Chang and Thad Kousser (2009), 'Financing direct democracy: revisiting the research on campaign spending and citizen initiatives', working paper, UCLA.
De Figueiredo, John M., Ho Ji Chang and Thad Kousser (2011), 'Financing direct democracy: revisiting the research on campaign spending and citizen initiatives', *Journal of Law, Economics and Organization*, forthcoming (first published online 23 June 2011).
De Haan, Jakob. (1996), 'New evidence on the relationship between democracy and economic growth', *Public Choice*, **86**, 175–98.
De Haan, Jakob and Jan-Egbert Sturm (1994), 'Political and institutional determinants of fiscal policy in the European community', *Public Choice*, **80**, 157–72.
De Resende, Carlos A. Jr and Nooman Rebei (2008), 'The welfare implication of fiscal dominance', Ottawa, Bank of Canada Working Paper 08-28.
De Sainte Croix, Geoffrey Ernest Maurice (1981), *The Class Struggle in the Ancient Greek World*, Ithaca, NY: Cornell University Press.

De Soysa, Indra and Hanne Fjelde (2010), 'Is the hidden hand an iron fist? Capitalism and civil peace, 1970–2005', *Journal of Peace Research*, **47**, 287–98.
De Temeltas, Josefina Calca (1996), 'Commentary: comparative constitutional approaches to the rule of law and judicial independence', *Saint Louis University Law Journal*, **40**, 997–9.
De Vault, James M. (1993), 'Economics and the International Trade Commission', *Southern Economic Journal*, **60**, 463–78.
De Vault, James M. (2002), 'Congressional dominance and the International Trade Commission', *Public Choice*, **110**, 1–22.
De Witte, Kristof and Wim Moesen (2010), 'Sizing the government', *Public Choice*, **145**, 39–55.
Dee, Thomas S. (1998), 'Competition and the quality of public schools', *Economics of Education Review*, **17**, 419–27.
DeLong, J. Bradford (1997), 'America's peacetime inflation: the 1970s', in Christina D. Romer and David H. Romer (eds), *Reducing Inflation: Motivation and Strategy*, Chicago, IL: University of Chicago Press, pp. 247–80.
Delorme, Charles D., Jr, Stacey Isom and David R. Kamershen (2005), 'Rent seeking and taxation in the Ancient Roman Empire', *Applied Economics*, **37**, 705–11, reprinted in Roger D. Congleton, Arye L. Hillman and Kai A. Konrad (eds) (2008), *Forty Years of Research on Rent Seeking 2 – Applications: Rent Seeking in Practice*, Heidelberg: Springer, pp. 559–65.
Delorme, Charles D., Jr, Frame W. Scott and Kamerschen David R. (1997), 'Empirical evidence on a special-interest-group perspective to antitrust', *Public Choice*, **92**, 317–35.
Demsetz, Harold (1968), 'Why regulate utilities?', *Journal of Law and Economics*, **11**, 55–65.
Demsetz, Harold (1969), 'Information and efficiency: another viewpoint', *Journal of Law and Economics*, **12**, 1–22.
Denslow, David A., James Dewey and Lawrence W. Kenny (2010), 'Are more educated electorates more effective in making governments more responsive to voter wishes?', working paper, University of Florida.
Denzau, Arthur T. and Robert J. Mackay (1983), 'Gatekeeping and monopoly power of committees: an analysis of sincere and sophisticated behavior', *American Journal of Political Science*, **4**, 740–61.
Denzau, Arthur T. and Michael C. Munger (1986). 'Legislators and interest groups: how unorganized interests get represented', *American Political Science Review*, **80**, 86–106.
Denzau, Arthur T. and Douglass C. North (1994), 'Shared mental models: ideologies and institutions', *Kyklos*, **47**, 3–31.
DeRoover, Raymond (1958), 'The concept of the just price: theory and economic policy', *Journal of Economic History*, **18**, 418–34.
Derouen, Karl R., Jr and Jacob Bercovitch (2008), 'Enduring internal rivalries: a new framework for the study of civil war', *Journal of Peace Research*, **45**, 55–74.
Desch, Michael C. (2002), 'Democracy and victory: why regime type hardly matters', *International Security*, **27**, 5–47.
Dewey, John (1920), *Reconstruction in Philosophy*, New York: Henry Holt & Co.
Diamond, Martin (1959), 'Book review of *An Economic Theory of Democracy*' by Anthony Downs, *The Journal of Political Economy*, **67**, 208–11.
Dickson, Vaughan (2009), 'Seat-vote curves, loyalty effects and the provincial distribution of Canadian government spending', *Public Choice*, **139**, 317–33.
Diermeier, Daniel and Keith Krehbiel (2003), 'Institutionalism as a methodology', *Journal of Theoretical Politics*, **15**, 123–44.
Diermeier, Daniel and Antonio Merlo (2000), 'Government turnover in parliamentary democracies', *Journal of Economic Theory*, **94**, 46–79.
Diermeier, Daniel, Hülya Eraslan and Antonio Merlo (2002), 'Coalition governments and comparative constitutional design', *European Economic Review*, **46**, 893–907.
DiLorenzo, Thomas D. (1985). 'The origins of antitrust: an interest-group perspective', *International Review of Law and Economics*, **5**, 73–90.
Dixon, William J. (1994), 'Democracy and the peaceful settlement of international conflict', *American Political Science Review*, **88**, 14–32.
DiZerega, Gus (1989), 'Democracy as a spontaneous order', *Critical Review*, **3**, 206–40.

Djankov, Simeon and Peter Murrell (2002), 'Enterprise restructuring in transition: A quantitative survey', *Journal of Economic Literature*, **40**, 739–92.
Djankov, Simeon, Rafael La Porta, Florencio Lopez-de-Silanes and Andrei Shleifer (2002), 'The regulation of entry', *Quarterly Journal of Economics*, **117**, 1–37.
Donald, Merlin (1991), *Origins of the Modern Mind: Three Stages in the Evolution of Culture and Cognition*, Cambridge: Harvard University Press.
Dorn, David, Justina V. Fischer, Gebhard Kirchgassner and Alfonso Sousa-Poza (2008), 'Direct democracy and life satisfaction revisited: new evidence for Switzerland', *Journal of Happiness Studies*, **9**, 227–55.
Dorsey, E. Ray, Jason de Roulet, Joel P. Thompson, Jason I. Reminick, Ashley Thai, Zachary White-Stellato, Christopher A. Beck, Benjamin P. George and Hamilton Moses III (2010), 'Funding of US biomedical research, 2003–2008', *Journal of the American Medical Association*, **303**, 137–43.
Dorussen, Han (2006), 'Heterogeneous trade interests and conflict', *Journal of Conflict Resolution*, **50**, 87–107.
Dorussen, Han and Hugh Ward (2008), 'International organizations and the Kantian peace: a network perspective', *Journal of Conflict Resolution*, **52**, 189–212.
Dorussen, Han and Hugh Ward (2010), 'Trade networks and the Kantian peace', *Journal of Peace Research*, **47**, 29–42.
Dorussen, Han and Hugh Ward (2011), 'Disaggregated trade flows and international conflict', in Christopher J. Coyne and Rachel L. Mathers (eds), *The Handbook on the Political Economy of War*, Cheltenham, UK and Northampton, MA, USA: Edward Elgar, pp. 515–33.
Doucouliagos, Hristos and Martin Paldam (2008), 'Aid effectiveness on growth: a meta study', *European Journal of Political Economy*, **24**, 1–24.
Dow, Jay and Michael Munger (1990), 'Public choice in political science: we don't teach it, but we publish it', *PS: Political Science and Politics*, **23**, 604–9.
Downes, Alexander B. (2009), 'How smart and tough are democracies? Reassessing theories of democratic victory in war', *International Security*, **33**, 9–51.
Downs, Anthony (1957), *An Economic Theory of Democracy*, New York: Harper & Row.
Downs, Anthony (1967), *Inside Bureaucracy*, Boston, MA: Little, Brown.
Downs, Anthony (1959), 'Book review: of *The Theory of Committees and Elections*' by Duncan Black, *Journal of Political Economy*, **67**, 211–12.
Downs, Anthony (1964), 'Book review of *The Calculus of Consent*' by James M. Buchanan and Gordon Tullock, *Journal of Political Economy*, **72**, 87–8.
Doyle, Michael W. (1983a), 'Kant, liberal legacies, and foreign affairs', *Philosophy and Public Affairs*, **12**, 205–35.
Doyle, Michael W. (1983b), 'Kant, liberal legacies, and foreign affairs, part 2', *Philosophy and Public Affairs*, **12**, 323–53.
Drazen, Allan (2001), 'The political business cycle after 25 years', in Ben S. Bernanke and Kenneth Rogoff (eds), *NBER Macroeconomics Annual 2000*, Cambridge, MA: MIT Press, pp. 75–117.
Drazen, Allan, Nuno Limão and Thomas Stratmann (2007), 'Political contribution caps and lobby formation: theory and evidence', *Journal of Public Economics*, **91**, 723–54.
Dreher, Axel and Nathan Jensen (2007), 'Independent actor or agent? An empirical analysis of the impact of U.S. interests on International Monetary Fund conditions', *Journal of Law and Economics*, **50**, 105–24.
Dreher, Axel, and Roland Vaubel (2004), 'Do IMF and IBRD cause moral hazard and political business cycles? Evidence from panel data', *Open Economies Review*, **15**, 5–22.
Dreher, Axel, Stephan Klasen, James R. Vreeland and Eric D. Werker (2009c), *The costs of favoritism: is politically driven aid less effective?* Centre for European Governance and Economic Development, Research Discussion Paper 97, Universität Göttingen.
Dreher, Axel, Silvia Marchesi and James R. Vreeland (2008), 'The political economy of IMF forecasts', *Public Choice*, **137**, 145–71.
Dreher, Axel, Jan-Egbert Sturm and James R. Vreeland (2009a), 'Global horse trading: IMF loans for votes in the UN Security Council', *European Economic Review*, **53**, 742–57.
Dreher, Axel, Jan-Egbert Sturm and James R. Vreeland (2009b), 'Development aid and

international politics: does membership of the UN Security Council influence World Bank decisions?', *Journal of Development Economics*, **88**, 1–18.

Dresher, Melvin (1961), *The Mathematics of Games of Strategy: Theory and Applications*, Englewood Cliffs, NJ: RAND.

Drinkwater, Stephen and Colin Jennings (2007), 'Who are the expressive voters?', *Public Choice*, **132**, 179–89.

Druckmann, James N. (2004), 'Political preference formation: competition, deliberation and the (ir)relevance of framing effects', *American Political Science Review*, **98**, 671–86.

Du Bois, François (2006), 'Judicial selection in post-apartheid South Africa', in Kate Malleson and Peter H. Russell (eds), *Appointing Judges in an Age of Judicial Power*, Toronto: University of Toronto Press, pp. 280–312.

Dubois, Eric, Matthieu Leprince and Sonia Paty (2007), 'The effects of politics on local tax setting: evidence from France', *Urban Studies*, **44**, 1603–18.

Dubois, Phillip (1980), *From Ballot to Bench: Judicial Elections and the Quest for Accountability*, Austin, TX: University of Texas Press.

Duffy, Eamon (2006), *Saints and Sinners, A History of the Popes*, 3rd edn, New Haven, CT: Yale University Press.

Duggan, John and Thomas Schwartz (2000), 'Strategic manipulability without resoluteness or shared beliefs: Gibbard-Satterthwaite generalized', *Social Choice and Welfare*, **17**, 85–93.

Duncombe, William and John Yinger (2007), 'Does school district consolidation cut costs?', *Education Finance and Policy*, **2**, 341–75.

Dundas, Charles (1915), 'The organization and laws of some Bantu tribes in East Africa', *Journal of the Royal Anthropological Institute of Great Britain and Ireland*, **45**, 234–306.

Dunleavy, Patrick (1991), *Democracy, Bureaucracy and Public Choice: Economic Explanations in Political Science*, New York: Prentice-Hall.

Dunne, Stephanie W., Robert Reed and James Wilbanks (1997), 'Endogenizing the median voter: public choice goes to school', *Public Choice*, **93**, 99–118.

Durkin, John and Andrew Greeley (1991), 'A model of religious choice under uncertainty', *Rationality and Society*, **3**, 178–96.

Dyck, Joshua (2009), 'Initiated distrust: direct democracy and trust in government', *American Politics Research*, **37**, 539–68.

Dyck, Joshua and Edward L. Lascher (2009), 'Direct democracy and political efficacy reconsidered', *Political Behavior*, **31**, 401–27.

Dyke, Andrew (2007), 'Electoral cycles in the administration of criminal justice', *Public Choice*, **133**, 417–37.

Easterbrook, Frank H. (1982), 'Ways of criticizing the court', *Harvard Law Review*, **95**, 802–32.

Easterly, William (2001), 'Can institutions resolve ethnic conflict?', *Economic Development and Cultural Change*, **49**, 687–706.

Easterly, William and Ross Levine (1997), 'Africa's growth tragedy: policies and ethnic divisions', *Quarterly Journal of Economics*, **112**, 1203–50.

Easterly, William and Sergio Rebelo (1993), 'Fiscal policy and economic growth: An empirical analysis', *Journal of Monetary Economics*, **32**, 417–58.

Eckel, Catherine C. and Philip J. Grossman (2008), 'Subsidizing charitable contributions: a natural field experiment comparing matching and rebate subsidies', *Experimental Economics*, **11**, 234–52.

Eckhardt, Martina (2004), 'Evolutionary approaches to legal change', *Thünen-Series of Applied Economic Theory*, Working Paper 47, University of Rostock.

Economist, The (11 June 2009), 'Not for sale', available at: http://www.economist.com/node/13832427?story_id=13832427 (accessed 20 August 2010).

Edelberg, Wendy, Martin S. Eichenbaum and Jonas D.M. Fisher (1999), 'Understanding the effects of a shock to government purchases', *Review of Economic Dynamics*, **2**, 166–206.

Efthyvoulou, Georgios (2008), 'Political cycles in a small open economy and the effect of economic integration', Birkbeck Working Papers in Economics and Finance 0808, London: Birkbeck College

Ehrlich, Issac and Richard Posner (1974), 'An economic analysis of legal rulemaking', *Journal of Legal Studies*, **3**, 257–86.
Eichenberger, Reiner and Felix Oberholzer-Gee (1998), 'Rational moralists: the role of fairness in democratic economic politics', *Public Choice*, **94**, 191–210.
Eichengreen, Barry, Poonam Gupta and Ashoka Mody (2008), 'Sudden stops and IMF-supported programs', in Sebastian Edwards and Márcio G.P. Garcia (eds), *Financial Markets Volatility and Performance in Emerging Markets*, National Bureau of Economic Research, NBER: University of Chicago Press, pp. 219–66.
Eisenstadt, Shmuel N. (1959), 'Primitive political systems: a preliminary comparative analysis', *American Anthropologist*, New Series, **61**, 200–20.
Ekelund, Robert B., Jr and Robert D. Tollison (1981), *Mercantilism as a Rent-Seeking Society*, College Station, TX: Texas A&M University Press.
Ekelund, Robert B. Jr and Robert D. Tollison (2011), *Economic Origins of Roman Christianity*, Chicago, IL: University of Chicago Press.
Ekelund, Robert B., Jr, Robert F. Hébert and Robert D. Tollison (1989), 'An economic model of the medieval church: usury as a form of rent seeking', *The Journal of Law, Economics and Organization*, **5**, 307–31.
Ekelund, Robert B., Jr, Robert F. Hébert and Robert D. Tollison (1992), 'The economics of sin and redemption: purgatory as a market-pull innovation?', *Journal of Economic Behavior and Organization*, **19**, 1–15.
Ekelund, Robert B., Jr, Robert F. Hébert and Robert D. Tollison (2002), 'An economic analysis of the Protestant Reformation', *Journal of Political Economy*, **110**, 646–71.
Ekelund, Robert B., Jr, Robert F. Hébert and Robert D. Tollison (2004), 'The economics of the counter-reformation: incumbent firm reaction to market entry', *Economic Inquiry*, **42**, 690–705.
Ekelund, Robert B., Jr, Robert F. Hébert and Robert D. Tollison (2006), *The Marketplace of Christianity*, Cambridge: MIT Press.
Ekelund, Robert B., Jr, Robert F. Hébert, Robert D. Tollison, Gary M. Anderson and Audrey B. Davidson (1996), *Sacred Trust: The Medieval Church as an Economic Firm*, New York: Oxford University Press.
Ekelund, Robert B., Jr, Michael J. McDonald and Robert D. Tollison (1995), 'Business restraints and the Clayton Act of 1914: public- or private-interest legislation?', in Fred S. McChesney and William F. Shughart II (eds), *The Causes and Consequences of Antitrust: The Public-Choice Perspective*, Chicago, IL: University of Chicago Press, pp. 271–86.
Elbadawi, Ibrahim and Nicholas Sambanis (2000), 'Why are there so many civil wars in Africa? Understanding and preventing violent conflict', *Journal of African Economics*, **9**, 244–69.
Elbadawi, Ibrahim and Nicholas Sambanis (2002), 'How much war will we see? Explaining the prevalence of civil war', *Journal of Conflict Resolution*, **46**, 307–34.
Elder, Harold W. (1987), 'Property rights structures and criminal courts: an analysis of state criminal courts', *International Review of Law and Economics*, **7**, 21–32.
Elgie, Robert (ed.) (1999), *Semi-Presidentialism in Europe*, Oxford: Oxford University Press.
Ellingsen, Tore (1991), 'Strategic buyers and the social cost of monopoly', *American Economic Review*, **81**, 648–57, reprinted in Roger D. Congleton, Arye L. Hillman and Kai A. Konrad (eds) (2008), *Forty Years of Research on Rent Seeking 1 – The Theory of Rent Seeking*, Heidelberg: Springer, pp. 399–408.
Enders, Walter and Xuejuan Su (2007), 'Rational terrorists and optimal network structure', *Journal of Conflict Resolution*, **51**, 33–57.
Enelow, James M. and Melvich J. Hinich (1989), 'A general probabilistic spatial theory of elections', *Public Choice*, **61**, 101–13.
Engelhardt, Gary V. and Christopher J. Mayer (1998), 'Intergovernmental transfers, borrowing constraints, and savings behavior: evidence from the housing market', *Journal of Urban Economics*, **44**, 135–57.
Epple, Dennis and Thomas Romer (1991), 'Mobility and redistribution', *Journal of Political Economy*, **99**, 828–58.
Epple Dennis and Allan Zelenitz (1981), 'The implications of competition among jurisdictions: does Tiebout need politics?', *Journal of Political Economy*, **89**, 1197–217.

Epstein, David (1997), 'An informational rationale for committee gatekeeping power', *Public Choice*, **91**, 271–99.
Epstein, David and Peter Zemsky (1995), 'Money talks: deterring quality challengers in congressional elections', *American Political Science Review*, **89**, 295–308.
Epstein, Gil S. and Shmuel Nitzan (2007), *Endogenous Public Policy and Contests*, Heidelberg: Springer.
Epstein, Gil S., Arye L. Hillman and Heinrich W. Ursprung (1999), 'The king never emigrates', *Review of Development Economics*, **3**, 107–21, reprinted in Roger D. Congleton, Arye L. Hillman and Kai A. Konrad (eds) (2008), *Forty Years of Research on Rent Seeking 2 – Applications: Rent seeking in Practice*, Heidelberg: Springer, pp. 265–79.
Epstein, Lee (1995), *Contemplating Courts*, Washington, DC: CQ Press.
Epstein, Richard A. (1988), 'The political economy of product liability reform', *American Economic Review*, **78**, 311–15.
Epstein, Richard A. (1990), 'The independence of judges: the uses and limitations of public choice theory', *Brigham Young University Law Review*, **1990**, 827–55.
Erceg, Chistopher J. and Jesper Linde (2010), 'Is there a fiscal free lunch in the liquidity trap?', CEPR Discussion Papers, 7624.
Ergas Henry (1987), 'The importance of technology policy', in Partha Dasgupta and Paul Stoneman (eds), *Economic Policy and Technological Performance*, Cambridge: Cambridge University Press, pp. 51–96.
Erikson, Robert S. and Thomas R. Palfrey (1998), 'Campaign spending and incumbency: an alternative simultaneous equations approach', *Journal of Politics*, **60**, 355–73.
Erikson, Robert S., Gerald C. Wright and John P. McIver (1993), *Statehouse Democracy: Public Opinion and Policy in the American States*, Cambridge: Cambridge University Press.
Escribà-Folch, Abel (2009), 'Do authoritarian institutions mobilize economic cooperation?', *Constitutional Political Economy*, **20**, 71–93.
Escribà-Folch, Abel and Joseph Wright (2010), 'Dealing with tyranny: international sanctions and the survival of authoritarian rulers', *International Studies Quarterly*, **54**, 335–59.
Eskridge, William N. Jr (1988), 'Politics without romance: implications of public choice theory for statutory interpretation', *Virginia Law Review*, **74**, 275–338.
Eskridge, William N. Jr (1991), 'Overriding Supreme Court statutory interpretation decisions', *Yale Law Journal*, **101**, 331–455.
Evans, Paul and Georgios Karras (1994), 'Are government activities productive? Evidence from a panel of U.S. States', *The Review of Economics and Statistics*, **76**, 1–11.
Evans, Peter B. (1989), 'Predatory, developmental, and other apparatuses: a comparative political economy perspective on the third world state', *Sociological Forum*, **4**, 561–87.
Evans, Peter B. (1995), *Embedded Autonomy: States and Industrial Transformation*, Princeton, NJ: Princeton University Press.
Evans, William N., Sheila E. Murray and Robert M. Schwab (1997), *Journal of Policy Analysis and Management*, **16**, 10–31.
Fabella, Raul V. (1995), 'The social cost of rent seeking under countervailing opposition to distortionary transfers', *Journal of Public Economics*, **57**, 235–47.
Fagen, Richard R. (1963), 'Book review of *The Theory of Political Coalitions* by William H. Riker', *The American Political Science Review*, **57**, 446–7.
Fagerberg, Jan E. (2003), 'Schumpeter and the revival of evolutionary economics: an appraisal of the literature', *Journal of Evolutionary Economics*, **13**, 125–59.
Fair, Ray C. (1978), 'The effect of economic events on votes for president', *Review of Economics and Statistics*, **60**, 159–73.
Faith, Roger L., Donald R. Leavens and Robert D. Tollison (1982), 'Antitrust pork barrel', *Journal of Law and Economics*, **25**, 329–42.
Falke, Josef (1996), 'Comitology and other committees: a preliminary empirical assessment', in Robin H. Pedler and Günther F. Schäfer (eds), *Shaping European Law and Policy. The Role of Committees and Comitology in the Political Process*, Maastricht: European Institute of Public Administration, pp. 96ff.
Farber, Henry S. and Joanne Gowa (1995), 'Polities and peace', *International Security*, **20**, 123–46.

Faria, João Ricardo and Daniel G. Arce M. (2005), 'Terror support and recruitment', *Defence and Peace Economics*, **16**, 263–73.
Farina, Francesco (2005), 'Constitutional economics I', in Jürgen G. Backhaus (ed.), *The Elgar Companion to Law and Economics*, Cheltenham, UK and Northampton, MA, USA: Edward Elgar, pp. 184–222.
Farley, Jonathan David (2003), 'Breaking al Qaeda cells: a mathematical analysis of counterterrorism operations', *Studies in Conflict and Terrorism*, **26**, 399–411.
Farrant, Andrew (1996), 'The socialist "calculation" debate: Lange versus Mises and Hayek', *Economic Notes*, **71**, 1–4, available at: http://www.libertarian.co.uk/lapubs/econn/econn071.pdf (accessed 19 May 2012).
Farris, Charles D. (1958), 'Book review of *An Economic Theory of Democracy*' by Anthony Downs, *The Journal of Politics*, **20**, 571–3.
Fatás, Anotonio and Ilian Mihov (2003), 'The case for restricting discretionary fiscal policy', *Quarterly Journal of Economics*, **118**, 1419–47.
Fearon, James D. (1995), 'Rationalist explanations for war', *International Organization*, **49**, 379–414.
Fearon, James D. (2004), 'Why do some civil wars last so much longer than others?', *Journal of Peace Research*, **41**, 275–301.
Fearon, James D. and David D. Laitin (1996), 'Explaining interethnic cooperation', *American Political Science Review*, **90**, 715–35.
Fearon, James D. and David D. Laitin (2003), 'Ethnicity, insurgency, and civil war', *American Political Science Review*, **97**, 75–90.
Fehr, Ernst and Simon Gächter (2000), 'Cooperation and punishment in public goods experiments', *American Economic Review*, **90**, 980–94.
Fehr, Ernst and Klaus M. Schmidt (1999), 'A theory of fairness, competition, and cooperation', *Quarterly Journal of Economics*, **114**, 817–68.
Feld, Lars P. and Gebhard Kirchgässner (2000), 'Direct democracy, political culture, and the outcome of economic policy: a report on the Swiss experience', *European Journal of Political Economy*, **16**, 287–306.
Feld, Lars P. and Gebhard Kirchgässner (2001), 'The political economy of direct legislation: direct democracy and local decision-making', *Economic Policy*, **16**, 329–67.
Feld, Lars P. and John G. Matsusaka (2003), 'Budget referendums and government spending: evidence from Swiss cantons', *Journal of Public Economics*, **87**, 2703–24.
Feld, Lars P. and Stefan Voigt (2003), 'Economic growth and judicial independence: cross-country evidence using a new set of indicators', *European Journal of Political Economy*, **19**, 497–527.
Feld, Lars P., Gebhard Kirchgässner and Christolph A. Schaltegger (2011), 'Municipal debt in Switzerland: new empirical results', *Public Choice*, **149**, 49–64.
Feld, Lars P, Christoph Schaltegger and Jan Schnellenbach (2008), 'On government centralization and fiscal referendums', *European Economic Review*, **52**, 611–45.
Feldman, Paul and James Jondrow (1984), 'Congressional elections and local federal spending', *American Journal of Political Science*, **28**, 147–63.
Feldstein, Martin (1974), 'Social security, induced retirement, and aggregate capital accumulation', *Journal of Political Economy*, **82**, 905–26.
Feldstein, Martin (1982), 'Government deficits and aggregate demand', *Journal of Monetary Economics*, **9**, 1–20.
Feldstein, Martin (1996), 'Social security and saving: new time series evidence', *National Tax Journal*, **49**, 151–64.
Fenno, Richard F., Jr (1973), *Congressmen in Committees*, Boston, MA: Little, Brown.
Ferejohn, John A. (1974), *Pork Barrel Politics: Rivers and Harbors Legislation*, Stanford, CA: Stanford University Press.
Ferejohn, John A. (1998), 'Independent judges, dependent judiciary: explaining judicial independence', *Southern California Law Review*, **72**, 352–84.
Ferejohn, John A. and Barry A. Weingast (1992a), 'A positive theory of statutory interpretation', *International Review of Law and Economics*, **12**, 263–79.

Ferejohn, John A. and Barry A. Weingast (1992b), 'Limitation of statutes: strategic statutory interpretation', *Georgetown Law Journal*, **80**, 565–82.
Ferguson, Adam (1767), *An Essay on the History of Civil Society*, Edinburgh: A. Millar.
Fernandez, Raquel and Dani Rodrik (1991), 'Resistance to reform: status quo bias in the presence of individual-specific uncertainty', *American Economic Review*, **81**, 1146–55.
Fernandez-Villaverde, Jesus (2010), 'Fiscal Policy in a Model with Financial Frictions', *American Economic Review*, **100**, 35–40.
Ferree, Karen and Smitha Singh (1999), 'Institutional change and economic performance in Africa, 1970–1995', mimeo.
Ferrero, Mario (2002), 'Competing for sainthood and the millennial church', *Kyklos*, **55**, 335–60.
Ferris, J. Stephen and Marcel C. Voia (2009), 'What determines the length of a typical Canadian parliamentary government?', *Canadian Journal of Political Science*, **4**, 881–910.
Ferris, J. Stephen and Marcel C. Voia (2011), 'Does the expectation or realization of a Federal election precipitate Canadian output growth?', *Canadian Journal of Economics*, **44**, 107–32.
Ferris, J. Stephen and Edwin G. West (1996), 'Testing theories of real government size: U.S. experience, 1959–1989', *Southern Economic Journal*, **62**, 537–53.
Ferris, J. Stephen, Soo-Bin Park and Stanley L. Winer (2008), 'Studying the role of political competition in the evolution of government size over long horizons', *Public Choice*, **137**, 369–401.
Festinger, Leon (1957), *A Theory of Cognitive Dissonance*, Palo Alto, CA: Stanford University Press.
Fielding, David and Anja Shortland (2010), 'An eye for an eye, a tooth for a tooth': political violence and counter-insurgency in Egypt', *Journal of Peace Research*, **47**, 433–48.
Figlio, David N. and Cassandra M.D. Hart (2010), 'Competitive Effects of means-tested school vouchers', National Bureau of Economic Research, NBER Working Paper Series, no. 16056.
Figlio, David N., Thomas A. Husted, and Lawrence W. Kenny (2004), 'Political economy of the inequality in school spending', *Journal of Urban Economics*, **55**, 338–49.
Finer, Samuel E. (1997), *The History of Government*, vols 1, 2 and 3, Oxford: Oxford University Press.
Fiorina, Morris P. (1982), 'Legislative choice of regulatory forms: legal process or administrative process?', *Public Choice*, **39**, 33–66.
Fiorina, Morris P. and Charles R. Plott (1978), 'Committee decisions under majority rule: an experimental study', *American Political Science Review*, **72**, 575–98.
Fiorino, Nadia and Roberto Ricciuti (2007), 'Legislature size and government spending in Italian regions: forecasting the effects of a reform', *Public Choice*, **131**, 117–25.
Fischel, William A. (2001), *The Homevoter Hypothesis: How Home Values Influence Local Government Taxation, School Finance, and Land-Use Policies*, Cambridge, MA: Harvard University Press.
Fishback, Price V. and Shawn Everett Kantor (1998), 'The adoption of workers' compensation in the United States, 1900–1930', *Journal of Law and Economics*, **41**, 305–41.
Fisher, Franklin M. (1987), 'Horizontal mergers: triage and treatment', *The Journal of Economic Perspectives*, **1**, 23–40.
Fisher, Ronald C. and Robert W. Wassmer (1998), 'Economic influences on the structure of local government in U.S. metropolitan areas', *Journal of Urban Economics*, **43**, 444–71.
Fisman, Raymond and Roberta Gatti (2002), 'Decentralization and corruption: Evidence across countries', *Journal of Public Economics*, **83**, 325–45.
Fleck, Robert K. (2000), 'When should market-supporting institutions be established?', *Journal of Law, Economics, and Organization*, **16**, 129–54.
Fleck, Robert K. and F. Andrew Hanssen (2006), 'The origins of democracy: a model with application to Ancient Greece', *Journal of Law and Economics*, **49**, 115–46.
Fleck, Robert K. and F. Andrew Hanssen (2010), 'Repeated adjustment of delegated powers and the history of eminent domain', *International Review of Law and Economics*, **30**, 99–112.
Fleck, Robert K. and F. Andrew Hanssen (2010), 'Judicial review as a constraint on tyranny of the majority', *Journal of Law, Economics, and Organization*, first published online 21 November, doi:10.1093/jleo/ews034.
Fleck, Robert K. and Christopher Kilby (2006), 'World Bank independence: a model and statistical analysis of U.S. influence', *Review of Development Economics*, **10**, 224–40.

Fleisher, Richard (1993), 'PAC contributions and congressional voting on national defense', *Legislative Studies Quarterly*, **18**, 391–409.
Fligstein, Neil (1990), *The Transformation of Corporate Control*, Cambridge, MA: Harvard University Press.
Flores, Thomas Edward and Irfan Nooruddin (2009), 'Democracy under the gun: understanding postconflict economic recovery', *Journal of Conflict Resolution*, **53**, 3–29.
Florida, Richard (2002), *The Rise of the Creative Class: And How It's Transforming Work, Leisure, Community, and Everyday Life*, New York: Perseus Book Group.
Foldvary, Fred (1994), *Public Goods and Private Communities: The Market Provision of Social Services*, Aldershot, UK and Brookfield, VT, USA: Edward Elgar.
Folland, Sherman, Allen C. Goodman and Miron Stano (2009), *The Economics of Health and Health Care*, 6th edn, New York: Prentice-Hall.
Folster, Stefan and Magnus Henrekson (2001), 'Growth effects of government expenditure and taxation in rich countries', *European Economic Review*, **45**, 1501–19.
Fon, Vincy and Francesco Parisi (2003), 'Litigation and the evolution of legal remedies: a dynamic model', *Public Choice*, **116**, 419–33.
Forbes, Kevin F. and Ernest M. Zampelli (1989), 'Is Leviathan a mythical beast?', *American Economic Review*, **79**, 568–77.
Forsythe, Robert, Roger B. Myerson, Thomas A. Rietz and Robert J. Weber (1993), 'An experiment on coordination in multi-candidate elections: the importance of polls and election histories', *Social Choice and Welfare*, **10**, 223–47.
Forsythe, Robert, Roger B. Myerson, Thomas A. Rietz and Robert J. Weber (1996), 'An experimental study of voting rules and polls in three-candidate elections', *International Journal of Game Theory*, **25**, 355–83.
Fortes, Meyer and Edward E. Evans-Pritchard (1940), 'Introduction', in Fortes, Meyer and Edward E. Evans-Pritchard (eds), *African Political Systems*, London: Oxford University Press.
Frank, Robert H. (1988), *Passions within Reason*, New York: Norton.
Fréchette, Guillaume R. (2010), 'Laboratory experiments: professionals versus students', in Guillaume R. Fréchette and Andrew Shotter (eds), *The Methods of Modern Experimental Economics*, Oxford: Oxford University Press, forthcoming.
Frey, Bruno S. (1981), 'Schumpeter, political economist', in Helmut Frisch (ed.), *Schumpeterian Economics*, New York: Praeger, pp. 126–42.
Frey, Bruno S. (1984), 'The public choice view of international political economy', *International Organization*, **38**, 199–223.
Frey, Bruno S. (1985), *Internationale Politische Ökonomie*, München: Vahlen.
Frey, Bruno S. (2005), 'Publishing as prostitution: choosing between one's own ideas and academic success', *Public Choice*, **116**, 205–23, reprinted in Roger D. Congleton, Arye L. Hillman and Kai A. Konrad (eds) (2008), *Forty Years of Research on Rent Seeking 2 – Applications: Rent Seeking in Practice*, Heidelberg: Springer, pp. 749–67.
Frey, Bruno S. and Reiner Eichenberger (1991), 'Anomalies in political economy', *Public Choice*, **68**, 71–89.
Frey, Bruno S. and Reiner Eichenberger (1999), *The New Democratic Federalism for Europe: Functional, Overlapping and Competing Jurisdictions*, Cheltenham, UK and Northampton, MA, USA: Edward Elgar.
Frey, Bruno S. and Friedrich Schneider (1978a), 'An empirical study of politico-economic interaction in the United States', *Review of Economics and Statistics*, **60**, 174–83.
Frey, Bruno S. and Friedrich Schneider (1978b), 'A politico-economic model of the United Kingdom', *The Economic Journal*, **88**, 243–253.
Frey, Bruno S. and Alois Stutzer (2000), 'Happiness, economy and institutions', *Economic Journal*, **110**, 918–38.
Frey, Bruno S. and Alois Stutzer (2006), 'Strengthening the citizens' role in international organizations', *Review of International Organizations*, **1**, 27–44.
Freytag, Andreas and Simon Renaud (2007), 'From short-term to long-term orientation – political economy of the policy reform process', *Journal of Evolutionary Economics*, **17**, 433–49.
Friedman, Lawrence M. (1973), *A History of American Law*, New York: Simon & Schuster.

Friedman, Milton (1962), *Capitalism and Freedom*, Chicago, IL: University of Chicago Press.
Friedrich, Carl J. and Zbigniew Brzezinski (1965), *Totalitarian Dictatorship and Autocracy*, 2nd edn, Cambridge, MA: Harvard University Press.
Frisch, Scott A. and Sean Q. Kelly (2006), *Committee Assignment Politics in the U.S. House of Representatives*, Norman: University of Oklahoma Press.
Frohlich, Norman and Joe A. Oppenheimer (1978), *Modern Political Economy*, Englewood Cliffs: Prentice-Hall.
Frohlich, Norman and Joe A. Oppenheimer (2006), 'Skating on thin ice: cracks in the public choice foundation', *Journal of Theoretical Politics*, **18**, 235–66.
Frye, Timothy and Andrei Shleifer (1997), 'Invisible hand and the grabbing hand', *American Economic Review, Papers and Proceedings*, **87**, 354–8.
Galasso, Vincenzo and Paola Profeta (2002), 'The political economy of social security: a survey', *European Journal of Political Economy*, **18**, 1–29.
Gali, Jordi and Pau Rabanal (2004), 'Technological shocks and aggregate fluctuations: How well does the real business cycle model fit postwar U.S. data?', in Mark Gertler and Kenneth Rogoff (eds), *NBER Macroeconomics Annual 2004*, Cambridge, MA: MIT Press, pp. 225–88.
Galli, Emma and Fabio Padovano (2002), 'A comparative test of alternative theories of Italian public deficits (1950–1998)', *Public Choice*, **113**, 37–58.
Galli, Emma and Fabio Padovano (2003), 'Corporatism, policies and growth', *Economics of Governance*, **4**, 245–60.
Gandhi, Jennifer (2008), *Political Institutions under Dictatorship*, Cambridge and New York: Cambridge University Press.
Gandhi, Jennifer and Adam Przeworski (2007), 'Authoritarian institutions and the survival of autocrats', *Comparative Political Studies*, **40**, 1279–301.
Garfinkel, Michelle R. (1990), 'Arming as a strategic investment in a cooperative equilibrium', *American Economic Review*, **80**, 50–68.
Garfinkel, Michelle R. and Stergios Skaperdas (2000), 'Conflict without misperceptions or incomplete information: how the future matters', *Journal of Conflict Resolution*, **44**, 793–807.
Garrett, Elizabeth (2010), 'Direct democracy', in Daniel A. Farber and Anne Joseph O'Connell (eds), *Research Handbook on Public Choice and Public Law*, Cheltenham, UK and Northampton, MA, USA: Edward Elgar, pp. 137–72.
Garrett, Elizabeth and Elisabeth R. Gerber (2001), 'Money in the initiative and referendum process: evidence of its effects and prospects for reform', in M. Dane Waters (ed.) *The Battle Over Citizen Lawmaking*, Durham, NC: Carolina Academic Press, pp. 76–82.
Garrett, Thomas A. and Russel S. Sobel (2003), 'The political economy of FEMA disaster payments', *Economic Inquiry*, **41**, 496–509.
Gartzke, Erik (1999), 'War is in the error term', *International Organization*, **53**, 567–87.
Gartzke, Erik (2005), 'Freedom and peace', in James D. Gwartney and Robert A. Lawson (eds), *Economic Freedom in the World*, Vancouver, BC: Fraser Institute, pp. 29–44.
Gartzke, Erik (2007), 'The capitalist peace', *American Journal of Political Science*, **51**, 166–91.
Gartzke, Erik (2009), 'Production, prosperity, preferences, and peace', in Peter Graeff and Guideo Mehlkhop (eds), *Capitalism, Democracy and the Prevention of War and Poverty*, London: Routledge, pp. 31–60.
Gartzke, Erik and Q. Li (2003), 'Measure for measure: concept operationalization and the trade interdependence-conflict debate', *Journal of Peace Research*, **40**, 553–71.
Garud, Raghu and Peter Karnøe (eds) (2001), *Path Dependence and Creation*, Mahwah, NJ: Lawrence Erlbaum Associates.
Gasiorowski, Mark and Solomon W. Polachek (1982), 'Conflict and interdependence: east-west trade and linkages in the era of détente', *Journal of Conflict Resolution*, **26**, 709–29.
Gassebner, Martin, Richard Jong-A-Pin and Jochen O. Mireau (2008), 'Terrorism and electoral accountability: one strike, you're out!', *Economics Letters*, **100**, 125–9.
Gassebner, Martin, Richard Jong-A-Pin and Jochen O. Mireau (2010), 'Terrorism and cabinet duration', *International Economic Review*, forthcoming.
Gawande, Kishore and Usree Bandyopadhyay (2000), 'Is protection for sale? Evidence on the

Grossman-Helpman theory of endogenous protection', *Review of Economics and Statistics*, **89**, 139–52.

Geddes, Barbara (1994), *Politician's Dilemma: Building State Capacity in Latin America*, Berkeley, CA and London: University of California Press.

Geddes, Barbara (1999), 'What do we know about democratization after twenty years?', *American Review of Political Science*, **2**, 115–44.

Gelb, Alan, Arye L. Hillman and Heinrich W. Ursprung (1998), 'Rents as distractions: why the exit from transition is prolonged', in Nicolas C. Baltas, George Demopoulos and Joseph Hassid (eds), *Economic Interdependence and Cooperation in Europe*, Heidelberg: Springer, pp. 21–38.

Gelpi, Christopher F. and Michael Griesdorf (2001), 'Winners or losers? Democracies in international crisis, 1918–94', *American Political Science Review*, **95**, 633–47.

Gely, Rafael and Pablo T. Spiller (1990), 'A rational choice theory of Supreme Court statutory decisions with applications to the *State Farm* and *Grove City* cases', *Journal of Law, Economics, and Organization*, **6**, 263–300.

Gely, Rafael and Pablo T. Spiller (1992), 'The political economy of Supreme Court constitutional decisions: the case of Roosevelt's court-packing plan', *International Review of Law and Economics*, **12**, 45–67.

Gennaioli, Nicola and Ilia Rainer (2007), 'The modern impact of precolonial centralization in Africa', *Journal of Economic Growth*, **12**, 185–234.

Gennaioli, Nicola and Andrei Shleifer (2007), 'The evolution of common law', *Journal of Political Economy*, **115**, 43–68.

Gerber, Alan (1998), 'Estimating the effect of campaign spending on Senate election outcomes using instrumental variables', *American Political Science Review*, **92**, 401–11.

Gerber, Elisabeth R. (1996), 'Legislative response to the threat of popular initiatives', *American Journal of Political Science*, **40**, 99–128.

Gerber, Elisabeth R. (1999), *The Populist Paradox: Interest Group Influence and the Promise of Direct Legislation*, Princeton, NJ: Princeton University Press.

Gerber, Elisabeth R. and Arthur Lupia (1995), 'Campaign competition and policy responsiveness in direct legislation elections', *Political Behavior*, **17**, 287–306.

Gerber, Elisabeth R., Arthur Lupia, Mathew D. McCubbins and D. Roderick Kiewiet (2001), *Stealing the Initiative: How State Government Responds to Direct Democracy*, Upper Saddle River, NJ: Prentice-Hall.

Gerlach-Kristen, Petra (2009), 'Outsiders at the bank of England's MPC', *Journal of Money, Credit, and Banking*, **41**, 1099–115.

Gerster, Richard (1993), 'Accountability of executive directors in Bretton Woods institutions', *Journal of World Trade*, **27**, 88–116.

Ghosh Roy, Atrayee (2009), 'Evidence on economic growth and government size', *Applied Economics*, **41**, 607–14.

Gibbard, Allan (1973), 'Manipulation of voting schemes: a general result', *Econometrica*, **41**, 587–602.

Gibler, Douglas M. (2007), 'Bordering on peace: democracy, territorial issues, and conflict', *International Studies Quarterly*, **51**, 509–32.

Gilbert, Michael D. (2009), 'How much does the law matter? Theory and evidence from single subject adjudication', working paper, University of Virginia School of Law, available at: http://works.bepress.com/michael_d_gilbert/9/ (accessed 17 February 2011).

Gilchrist, Simon G. and John C. Williams (2000), 'Putty clay and investment: a business cycle analysis', *Journal of Political Economy*, **108**, 928–60.

Gildea, John A. (1990), 'Explaining FOMC members' votes', in Thomas Mayer (ed.), *The Political Economy of American Monetary Policy*, New York: Cambridge University Press, pp. 211–27.

Gilligan, Thomas W. and Keith Krehbiel (1987), 'Collective decision-making and standing committees: an informational rationale for restrictive amendment procedures', *Journal of Law, Economics and Organization*, **3**, 287–335.

Gilligan, Thomas W. and Keith Krehbiel (1989), 'Asymmetric information and legislative rules with a heterogeneous committee', *American Journal of Political Science*, **33**, 459–90.

Ginsburg, Tom and Zachary Elkins (2010), 'Public choice and constitutional design', in Daniel A.

Farber and Anne Joseph O'Connell (eds), *Research Handbook in Public Choice and Public Law*, Cheltenham, UK and Northampton, MA, USA: Edward Elgar, pp. 261–82.

Giuranno, Michele G. (2009), 'Regional income disparity and the size of the public sector', *Journal of Public Economic Theory*, **11**, 697–719.

Glaeser, Edward L. (2005), 'The political economy of hatred', *Quarterly Journal of Economics*, **120**, 45–86.

Glaeser, Edward L. and José Scheinkman (1998), 'Neither a borrower nor a lender be: an economic analysis of interest restrictions and usury laws', *Journal of Law and Economics*, **41**, 1–36.

Glaeser, Edward L. and Andrei Shleifer (2002), 'Legal origins', *Quarterly Journal of Economics*, **117**, 1193–229.

Glaeser, Edward, Simon Johnson and Andrei Shleifer (2001), 'Coase versus the Coasians', *Quarterly Journal of Economics*, **116**, 853–99.

Glatzer, Bernt (2002), 'The Pashtun tribal system', in George Pfeffer and Deepak K. Behera (eds), *Concept of Tribal Society*, Contemporary Society: Tribal Studies, vol. 5, New Delhi: Concept, pp. 265–82.

Glazer, Amihai and Kai Konrad (1999), 'Taxation of rent-seeking activities', *Journal of Public Economics*, **72**, 6–72.

Glazer, Amihai and Henry McMillan (1992), 'Pricing by the firm under regulatory threat', *Quarterly Journal of Economics*, **107**, 1089–99.

Glazer, Amihai and Lawrence Rothenberg (2001), *Why Government Succeeds and Why It Fails*, Cambridge, MA: Harvard University Press.

Gleditsch, Kristian Skrede and Andrea Ruggeri (2010), 'Political opportunity structures, democracy, and civil war', *Journal of Peace Research*, **47**, 299–310.

Gleditsch, Nils Petter (1995), 'Geography, democracy, and peace', *International Interactions*, **20**, 297–323.

Gleditsch, Nils Petter, Peter Wallensteen, Mikael Eriksson, Margareta Sollenberg and Harvard Strand (2002), 'Armed conflict 1946–2001: a new dataset', *Journal of Peace Research*, **39**, 615–37.

Gluckman, Max, J. Clyde Mitchell and John A. Barnes (1949), 'The village headman in British Central Africa', *Africa: Journal of the International African Institute*, **19**, 89–106.

Goemans, Henk E., Kristian Skrede Gleditsch, and Giacomo Chiozza (2009), 'Introducing archigos: a dataset of political leaders', *Journal of Peace Research*, **46**, 269–83.

Goenner, Cullen F. (2004), 'Uncertainty of the liberal peace', *Journal of Peace Research*, **41**, 589–605.

Goenner, Cullen F. (2010), 'From toys to warships: interdependence and the effects of disaggregated trade on militarized disputes', *Journal of Peace Research*, **47**, 547–59.

Gokcekus, Edward, Joshua J. Phillips and Edward Tower (2004), 'School choice: money, race, and congressional voting on vouchers', *Public Choice*, **119**, 241–54.

Goldberg, Deborah and Samantha Sanchez (2002), *The New Politics of Judicial Elections*, Washington, DC: Justice at Stake Campaign.

Goldberg, Pinelopi K. and Giovanni Maggi (1999), 'Protection for sale: an empirical investigation', *American Economic Review*, **89**, 1135–55.

Goldman, Alan H. (1999), 'Why citizens should vote: a causal responsibility approach', *Social Philosophy and Policy*, **16**, 201–17.

Goldman, Sheldon (1975), 'Voting behavior on the United States Court of Appeals revisited', *American Political Science Review*, **69**, 491–506.

Goldstein, Judith and Stefanie A. Lenway (1989), 'Interests or institutions: an inquiry into congressional–ITC relations', *International Studies Quarterly*, **33**, 303–27.

Goldsworthy, Jeffrey (1999), *The Sovereignty of Parliament: History and Philosophy*, Oxford: Oxford University Press.

Golembiewski, Robert T. (1966), 'Book review of *The Logic of Collective Action*' by Mancur Olson, *American Sociological Review*, **31**, 117–18.

Goodfriend, Marvin (1986), 'Monetary mystique: secrecy and central banking', *Journal of Monetary Economics*, **17**, 63–92.

Goodin, Robert E. and Kevin W.S. Roberts (1975), 'The ethical voter', *American Political Science Review*, **69**, 926–8.
Goodliffe, Jay (2001), 'The effect of war chests on challenger entry in U.S. House elections', *American Journal of Political Science*, **45**, 830–44.
Goodman, John (1979), 'An economic theory of the evolution of the common law', *Journal of Legal Studies*, **7**, 393–406.
Goodman, Leo A. (1953), 'Book review of *Social Choice and Individual Values*' by Kenneth J. Arrow, *American Sociological Association*, **18**, 116–17.
Gordon, Sanford C. and Catherine Hafer (2005), 'Flexing muscle: corporate political expenditures as signals to the bureaucracy', *American Political Science Review*, **99**, 245–61.
Gould, John P. (1973), 'The economics of legal conflicts', *The Journal of Legal Studies*, **2**, 279–300.
Gouveia, Miguel (1997), 'Majority rule and the public provision of a private good', *Public Choice*, **93**, 221–44.
Grafen, Alan (1990), 'Biological signals as handicaps', *Journal of Theoretical Biology*, **144**, 517–46.
Granovetter, Mark (1973), 'The strength of weak ties', *American Journal of Sociology*, **78**, 1360–80.
Gray, Clive and Malcolm McPherson (2001), 'The leadership factor in African policy reform and growth', *Economic Development and Cultural Change*, **49**, 707–40.
Green, Donald P. and Jonathan S. Krasno (1988), 'Salvation for the spendthrift incumbent: reestimating the effects of campaign spending in House elections', *American Journal of Political Science*, **32**, 884–907.
Green, Donald P. and Ian Shapiro (1996), *Pathologies of Rational Choice: A Critique of Applications in Political Science*, New Haven, CT: Yale University Press.
Greene, Jay P. and Ryan H. Marsh (2009), *The effect of Milwaukee's parental choice program on student achievement in Milwaukee public schools*, SCDP comprehensive longitudinal evaluation of the Milwaukee Parental Choice Program, Report no. 11.
Greene, Kenneth V. and Phillip J. Nelson (2002), 'If extremists vote how do they express themselves? An empirical test of an expressive theory of voting', *Public Choice*, **113**, 425–36.
Greif, Avner (1993), 'Contract enforceability and economic institutions in early trade: the Maghribi traders' coalition', *American Economic Review*, **83**, 525–48.
Grier, Kevin B. (1987), 'Presidential elections and Federal Reserve policy: an empirical test', *Southern Economic Journal*, **54**, 475–86.
Grier, Kevin B. (1989a), 'On the existence of a political monetary cycle', *American Journal of Political Science*, **33**, 376–89.
Grier, Kevin B. (1989b), 'Campaign spending and Senate elections, 1978–84', *Public Choice*, **63**, 201–20.
Grier, Kevin B. (1991), 'Congressional influence on US monetary policy: an empirical test', *Journal of Monetary Economics*, **28**, 201–20.
Grier, Kevin B. (1996), 'Congressional oversight committee influence on US monetary policy revisited', *Journal of Monetary Economics*, **38**, 571–79.
Grier, Kevin B. (2008), 'US presidential elections and real GDP growth, 1961–2004', *Public Choice*, **135**, 337–52.
Grier, Kevin B. and Michael C. Munger (1991). 'Committee assignments, constituent preferences, and campaign contributions', *Economic Inquiry*, **29**, 24–43.
Grier, Kevin B. and Howard E. Neiman (1987), 'Deficits, politics, and money growth', *Economic Inquiry*, **25**, 201–14.
Grier, Kevin B., Michael C. Munger and Brian E. Roberts (1994), 'The determinants of industrial political activity, 1978–1986', *American Political Science Review*, **88**, 911–26.
Grofman, Bernard (1981), 'The theory of committees and elections: the legacy of Duncan Black', in Gordon Tullock (ed.), *Toward a Science of Politics*, Blacksburg, WV: Center for Study of Public Choice, pp. 11–57.
Grofman, Bernard (1987), 'Black, Duncan', in John Eatwell, Murray Milgate and Peter Newman (eds), *The New Palgrave: A Dictionary of Economics*, London: Macmillan, pp. 250–51.
Groseclose, Tim (1994), 'The committee outlier debate: a review and a reexamination of some of the evidence', *Public Choice*, **80**, 265–73.

Grosser, Jens and Arthur Schram (2006), 'Neighborhood information exchange and voter participation: an experimental study', *American Political Science Review*, **100**, 235–48.

Grossman, Gene M. and Elhanan Helpman (1994), 'Protection for sale', *American Economic Review*, **84**, 833–50, reprinted in Roger D. Congleton, Arye L. Hillman and Kai A. Konrad (eds) (2008), *Forty Years of Research on Rent Seeking 2 – Applications: Rent seeking in Practice*, Heidelberg: Springer, pp. 131–48.

Grossman, Gene M. and Elhanen Helpman (1996), 'Electoral competition and special interest politics', *Review of Economic Studies*, **63**, 265–86.

Grossman, Gene M. and Elhanen Helpman (2001), *Special Interest Politics*, Cambridge, MA: MIT Press.

Grossman, Herschel I. (1991), 'A general equilibrium model of insurrections', *American Economic Review*, **81**, 912–21.

Grossman, Herschel I. and Minseong Kim (1996), 'Predation and production', in Michelle R. Garfinkel and Stergios Skaperdas (eds), *The Political Economy of Conflict and Appropriation*, Cambridge: Cambridge University Press, pp. 57–72.

Grossman, Michael (1972), *The Demand for Health: A Theoretical and Empirical Investigation*, New York: Columbia University Press.

Gruber, Jonathan and James Poterba (1994), 'Tax incentives and the decision to purchase health insurance: evidence from the self-employed', *Quarterly Journal of Economics*, **109**, 701–33.

Guidolin, Massimo and Eliana La Ferrara (2007), 'Diamonds are forever, wars are not: is conflict bad for private firms?', *American Economic Review*, **97**, 1978–93.

Gunnell, John (2006), 'The founding of the American Political Science Association', *American Political Science Review*, **100**, 479–86.

Guttman, Joel M. (1978), 'Interest groups and the demand for agricultural research', *Journal of Political Economy*, **86**, 467–84.

Guttman, Joel M., Shmuel Nitzan and Uriel Spiegel (1992), 'Rent seeking and social investment in taste change', *Economics and Politics*, **4**, 31–42.

Guarnaschelli, Serena, Richard D. McKelvey and Thomas R. Palfrey (2000), 'An experimental study of jury decision rules', *American Political Science Review*, **94**, 407–23.

Gwartney, James D., Robert Lawson and Walter Block (1996), *Economic Freedom of the World, 1975–1995*, Vancouver: Fraser Institute.

Haas, Ernst B. (1990), *When Knowledge is Power: Three Models of Change in International Organizations*, Berkeley, CA: University of California Press.

Haas, Jonathan (1982), *The Evolution of the Prehistoric State*, New York: Columbia University Press.

Haber, Stephen (2006), 'Authoritarian government', in Barry R. Weingast and Donald A. Wittman (eds), *The Oxford Handbook of Political Economy*, Oxford and New York: Oxford University Press, pp. 693–707.

Haber, Stephen, Armando Razo and Noel Maurer (2003), *The Politics of Property Rights: Political Instability, Credible Commitments, and Economic Growth in Mexico, 1876–1929*, Cambridge, UK and New York: Cambridge University Press.

Hadfield, Gillian (1992), 'Biases in the evolution of legal rules', *Georgetown Law Journal*, **80**, 583–616.

Hajnal, Zoltan L., Elisabeth R. Gerber and Hugh Louch (2002), 'Minorities and direct legislation: evidence from California ballot propositions', *Journal of Politics*, **64**, 154–77.

Hakes, David R. (1988), 'Monetary policy and presidential elections: a nonpartisan political cycle', *Public Choice*, **57**, 175–82.

Hall, Kermit L. (1983), 'The judiciary on trial: state constitutional reform and the rise of an elected judiciary, 1846–1860', *The Historian*, **45**, 337–54.

Hall, Melinda Gann (1987), 'Constituent influence in state supreme courts: conceptual notes and a case study', *Journal of Politics*, **49**, 1117–24.

Hall, Melinda Gann (1992), 'Electoral politics and strategic voting in state supreme courts', *Journal of Politics*, **54**, 427–46.

Hall, Melinda Gann and Paul R. Brace (1996), 'Justices' response to case facts: an interactive model', *American Politics Quarterly*, **24**, 236–61.

Hall, Richard L. and Frank W. Wayman (1990), 'Buying time: moneyed interests and the mobilization of bias in congressional committees', *American Political Science Review*, **84**, 797–820.
Hall, Robert E. and Charles I. Jones (1999), 'Why do some countries produce so much more output per worker than others?', *Quarterly Journal of Economics*, **114**, 83–116.
Hall, Robert E. and Charles I. Jones (2007), 'The value of life and the rise in health spending', *Quarterly Journal of Economics*, **122**, 39–72.
Haller, Max (2008), *European Integration as an Elite Process*, New York and London: Routledge.
Hallerberg, Mark, Rolf Strauch and Jürgen von Hagen (2004), 'The design of fiscal rules and forms of governance in European Union countries', European Central Bank Working Paper Series no. 419.
Halperin, Eran (2008), 'Group-based hatred in intractable conflict', *Journal of Conflict Resolution*, **52**, 713–36.
Hamilton, Alexander, James Madison and Jon Jay ([1787–88] 2008), *The Federalist Papers: Oxford World's Classics*, Lawrence Goldman (ed.), Oxford: Oxford University Press.
Hamilton, Bruce W. (1983), 'The flypaper effect and other anomalies', *Journal of Public Economics*, **22**, 347–61.
Hamilton, Howard D. and Sylvan H. Cohen (1974), *Policy Making by Plebiscite: School Referenda*, Lexington, MA: Lexington Books.
Hamlin, Alan and Colin Jennings (2007), 'Leadership and conflict', *Journal of Economic Behavior and Organization*, **64**, 49–68.
Hamlin, Alan and Colin Jennings (2009), 'Expressive political behavior: foundations, scope and implications', Working Paper 08-19, Department of Economics, University of Strathclyde, *British Journal of Political Science*, forthcoming.
Hamlin, Alan and Colin Jennings (2011), 'Expressive political behaviour: foundations, scope and implications', *British Journal of Political Science*, in press.
Handsley, Elizabeth (2006), '"The judicial whisper goes around": appointment of judicial officers in Australia', in Kate Malleson and Peter H. Russell (eds), *Appointing Judges in an Age of Judicial Power*, Toronto: University of Toronto Press, pp.122–44.
Hansen, Christian B. (1973), 'On the effects of fiscal and monetary policy: a taxonomic approach', *American Economic Review*, **63**, 546–71.
Hansen, Wendy L. (1990), 'The International Trade Commission and the politics of protectionism', *American Political Science Review*, **84**, 21–46.
Hansen, Wendy L. and Thomas J. Prusa (1996), 'Cumulation and ITC decision-making: the sum of the parts is greater than the whole', *Economic Inquiry*, **34**, 746–69.
Hansen, Wendy L. and Thomas J. Prusa (1997), 'The economics and politics of trade policy: an empirical analysis of ITC decision making', *Review of International Economics*, **5**, 230–45.
Hanssen, F. Andrew (1999a), 'The effect of judicial institutions on uncertainty and the rate of litigation: the election versus appointment of state judges', *Journal of Legal Studies*, **28**, 205–32.
Hanssen, F. Andrew (1999b), 'Appointed courts, elected courts, and public utility regulation: judicial independence and the energy crisis', *Business and Politics*, **1**, 179–201.
Hanssen, F. Andrew (2000), 'Independent courts and administrative agencies: an empirical analysis of the states', *Journal of Law, Economics, and Organization*, **16**, 534–71.
Hanssen, F. Andrew (2004a), 'Is there a politically optimal level of judicial independence?', *American Economic Review*, **94**, 712–29.
Hanssen, F. Andrew (2004b), 'Learning about judicial independence: institutional change in the state courts', *Journal of Legal Studies*, **33**, 431–74.
Harberger, Arnold C. (1954), 'Monopoly and resource allocation', *American Economic Review*, **44**, 77–87.
Harberger, Arnold C. (1993), 'Secrets of success: a handful of heroes', *American Economic Review Papers and Proceedings*, **83**, 343–50.
Harbom, Lotta. and Peter Wallensteen (2010), 'Armed conflicts, 1946–2009', *Journal of Peace Research*, **47**, 501–9.
Hardin, Garret (1968), 'The tragedy of the commons', *Science*, **162**, 1243–48.
Hardin, Russell (1989), 'Why a constitution?', in Bernard Grofman and Donald Wittman (eds), *The Federalist Papers and the New Institutionalism*, New York: Agathon Press, pp.100–20.

Hardin, Russell (1990), 'Contractarianism: wistful thinking', *Constitutional Political Economy*, **1**, 35–52.
Hardin, Russell (1997), 'Economic theories of the state', in Dennis C. Mueller (ed.), *Perspectives on Public Choice: A Handbook*, New York: Cambridge University Press, pp. 21–34.
Hardin, Russell (2003), *Liberalism, Constitutionalism, and Democracy*, Oxford: Oxford University Press.
Harnay, Sophie (2005), 'Judicial Independence', in Jürgen G. Backhaus (ed.), *The Elgar Companion to Law and Economics*, Cheltenham, UK and Northampton, MA, USA: Edward Elgar, pp. 407–23.
Harris, Mark N. and Christopher Spencer (2009), 'The policy choices and reaction functions of Bank of England MPC members', *Southern Economic Journal*, **76**, 482–99.
Harsanyi, John C. (1965), 'Book review of *The Theory of Committees and Elections*' by Duncan Black, *Econometrica*, **33**, 651–3.
Hart, David M. (2001), 'Why do some firms give? Why do some firms give a lot? High-tech PACs, 1977–1996', *Journal of Politics*, **63**, 1230–49.
Hasen, Richard L. (1997), '"High court wrongly elected": a public choice model of judging and its implications for the Voting Rights Act', *North Carolina Law Review*, **75**, 1305–67.
Hathaway, Oona A. (2001), 'Path dependence in the law: the course and pattern of legal change in a common law system', *Iowa Law Review*, **86**, 601–61.
Haug, Alfred A. (1990), 'Ricardian equivalence, rational expectations, and the permanent income hypothesis', *Journal of Money Credit and Banking*, **22**, 305–26.
Harvey, Andrew C. and A. Jaeger (1993), 'Detrending, stylized facts and the business cycle', *Journal of Applied Econometrics*, **8**, 231–47.
Havrilesky, Thomas M. (1987), 'A partisanship theory of monetary and fiscal policy regimes', *Journal of Money, Credit, and Banking*, **19**, 308–25.
Havrilesky, Thomas M. (1988), 'Monetary policy signaling from the administration to the Federal Reserve', *Journal of Money, Credit, and Banking*, **20**, 83–101.
Havrilesky, Thomas M. (1994), 'The political economy of monetary policy', *European Journal of Political Economy*, **10**, 111–34.
Havrilesky, Thomas M. (1995), *The Pressures on American Monetary Policy*, 2nd edn, Norwell, MA: Kluwer Academic.
Havrilesky, Thomas M. and John Gildea (1992), 'Reliable and unreliable partisan appointees to the Board of Governors', *Public Choice*, **73**, 397–417.
Havrilesky, Thomas M. and James Granato (1993), 'Determinants of inflationary performance: corporatist structures vs. central bank autonomy', *Public Choice*, **76**, 249–61.
Havrilesky, Thomas M. and Robert Schweitzer (1990), 'A theory of FOMC dissent voting with evidence from the time series', in Thomas Mayer (ed.), *The Political Economy of American Monetary Policy*, New York: Cambridge University Press, pp. 197–210.
Hay, Jonathan R., Andrei Shleifer and Robert W. Vishny (1996), 'Toward a theory of legal reform', *European Economic Review*, **40**, 559–67.
Hayek, Friedrich A. (1939), 'The economic conditions of interstate federalism', *New Commonwealth Quarterly*, **5**, 131–49.
Hayek, Friedrich A. von ([1944] 1976), *The Road to Serfdom*, Chicago, IL: University of Chicago Press.
Hayek, Friedrich A. von (1945), 'The use of knowledge in society', *American Economic Review*, **35**, 519–30.
Hayek, Friedrich A. von (1960), *The Constitution of Liberty*, Chicago, IL: University of Chicago Press.
Hayek, Friedrich A. von ([1968] 1978), 'Competition as a discovery procedure', in Friedrich A. von Hayek, *New Studies in Philosophy, Politics, Economics and the History of Ideas*, London: Routledge, pp. 179–90.
Hayek, Friedrich A. von (1973), *Law, Legislation, and Liberty, vol. I: Rules and Order*, Chicago, IL: University of Chicago Press.
Hayek, Friedrich A. von (1979), *Law, Legislation, and Liberty, vol. III: The Political Order of a Free People*, Chicago, IL: University of Chicago Press.

Hayek, Friedrich A. von (1988), *The Fatal Conceit: The Errors of Socialism*, London: Routledge.
Haynes, Stephen E. and Joe A. Stone (1988), 'Does the political business cycle dominate U.S. unemployment and inflation? Some new evidence', in Thomas D. Willet (ed.), *Political Business Cycles: The Political Economy of Money, Inflation and Unemployment*, Durham, NC: Duke University Press, pp. 276–93.
Haynes, Stephen E. and Joe A. Stone (1989), 'An integrated test for electoral cycles in the US economy', *Review of Economics and Statistics*, **71**, 426–34.
Haynes, Stephen E. and Joe A. Stone (1990), 'Political models of the business cycle should be revived', *Economic Inquiry*, **28**, 442–65.
Heckathorn, Douglas D. (1988), 'Collective sanctions and the creation of prisoner's dilemma norms', *American Journal of Sociology*, **94**, 535–62.
Heckelman, Jac C. (2006), 'Another look at the evidence for rational partisan cycles', *Public Choice*, **126**, 257–74.
Heckelman, Jac C. and Hakan Berument (1998), 'Political business cycles and endogenous elections', *Southern Economic Journal*, **64**, 987–1000.
Heckelman, Jac C. and Robert Whaples (1996), 'Political business cycles before the Great Depression', *Economics Letters*, **51**, 247–51.
Hegre, Håvard (2003), 'Disentangling democracy and development as determinants of armed conflict', World Bank, mimeo.
Hegre, Håvard, Tanja Ellingsen, Scott Gates and Nils Petter Gleditsch (2001), 'Toward a democratic civil peace? Democracy, political change, and civil war, 1816–1992', *American Political Science Review*, **95**, 33–48.
Hegre, Håvard, Gudrun Østby and Clionadh Raleigh (2009), 'Poverty and civil war events: a disaggregated study of Liberia', *Journal of Conflict Resolution*, **53**, 598–623.
Hehenkamp, Burkhard, Wolfgang Leininger and Alex Possajennikov (2004), 'Evolutionary equilibrium in Tullock contests: spite and overdissipation', *European Journal of Political Economy*, **20**, 1045–57, reprinted in Roger D. Congleton, Arye L. Hillman and Kai A. Konrad (eds) (2008), *Forty Years of Research on Rent Seeking 1 – The Theory of Rent Seeking*, Heidelberg: Springer, pp. 473–85.
Heinemann, Friedrich (2007), 'The drivers of deregulation in the era of globalization', in Peter Bernholz and Roland Vaubel (eds), *Political Competition and Economic Regulation*, New York, London: Routledge, pp. 245–66.
Helbling, Jürg (1999), 'The dynamics of war and alliance among the Yanomami', in Georg Elwert, Stephan Feuchtwang and Dieter Neubert (eds), *Dynamics of Violence*, Berlin: Duncker & Humblot, pp. 103–20.
Helland, Eric and Alexander Tabarrok (2002), 'The effect of electoral institutions on tort awards', *American Law and Economics Review*, **4**, 341–70.
Helland, Eric and Alex Tabarrok (2003), 'Race, poverty, and American tort awards: evidence from three data sets', *Journal of Legal Studies*, **32**, 27–58.
Helland, Eric and Alexander Tabarrok (2006), *Judge and Jury: American Tort Law on Trial*, Oakland, CA: Independent Institute.
Hendrix, Cullen S. (2010), 'Measuring state capacity: theoretical and empirical implications for the study of civil conflict', *Journal of Peace Research*, **47**, 273–85.
Henisz, Witold J. (2000), 'The institutional environment for economic growth', *Economics and Politics*, **12**, 1–31.
Herrmann-Pillath, Carsten (2006), 'Cultural species and institutional change in China', *Journal of Economic Issues*, **40**, 539–74.
Hermann-Pillath, Carsten (2009), 'An evolutionary approach to endogenous political constraints on transition in China', in Thomas Heberer and Gunter Schubert (eds), *Regime Legitimacy in Contemporary China: Institutional Change and Stability*, Abingdon: Routledge, pp. 129–52.
Hess, Gregory D. and Athanasios Orphanides (1995), 'War politics: an economic, rational-voter framework', *American Economic Review*, **85**, 828–46.
Hess, Gregory and Athanasios Orphanides (2001), 'War and democracy', *Journal of Political Economy*, **109**, 776–810.

Hettich, Walter and Stanley L. Winer (1999), *Democratic Choice and Taxation: A Theoretical and Empirical Analysis*, New York: Cambridge University Press.

Hibbs, Douglas A. Jr (1977), 'Political parties and macroeconomic policy', *American Political Science Review*, **71**, 1467–87.

Hibbs, Douglas A. Jr (1987), *The American Political Economy*, Cambridge, MA: Harvard University Press.

Higgins, Richard S. and Paul H. Rubin (1980), 'Judicial discretion', *Journal of Legal Studies*, **9**, 129–38.

Hillman, Arye L. (1982), 'Declining industries and political-support protectionist motives', *American Economic Review*, **72**, 1180–87, reprinted in Roger D. Congleton, Arye L. Hillman and Kai A. Konrad (eds) (2008), *Forty Years of Research on Rent Seeking 2 – Applications: Rent Seeking in Practice*, Heidelberg: Springer, pp. 105–12.

Hillman, Arye L. (1991), 'Liberalization dilemmas', in Arye L. Hillman (ed), *Markets and Politicians: Politicized Economic Choice*, Boston, MA and Dordrecht: Kluwer Academic, pp. 189–207.

Hillman, Arye L. (1998), 'Political economy and political correctness', *Public Choice*, **96**, 219–39, reprinted in Roger D. Congleton, Arye L. Hillman and Kai A. Konrad (eds) (2008), *Forty Years of Research on Rent Seeking 2 – Applications: Rent Seeking in Practice*, Heidelberg: Springer, pp. 791–811.

Hillman, Arye L. (2009), *Public Finance and Public Policy: Responsibilities and Limitations of Government*, 2nd edn, New York: Cambridge University Press.

Hillman, Arye L. (2010), 'Expressive behavior in economics and politics', *European Journal of Political Economy*, **26**, 403–18.

Hillman, Arye L. and Eliakim Katz (1984), 'Risk-averse rent seekers and the social cost of monopoly power', *Economic Journal*, **94**, 104–10, reprinted in Roger D. Congleton, Arye L. Hillman and Kai A. Konrad (eds) (2008), *Forty Years of Research on Rent Seeking 1 – The Theory of Rent Seeking*, Heidelberg: Springer, pp. 97–103.

Hillman, Arye L. and Eliakim Katz (1987), 'Hierarchical structure and the social costs of bribes and transfers', *Journal of Public Economics*, **34**, 129–42, reprinted in Roger D. Congleton, Arye L. Hillman and Kai A. Konrad (eds) (2008), *Forty Years of Research on Rent Seeking 1 – The Theory of Rent Seeking*, Heidelberg: Springer, pp. 523–36.

Hillman, Arye L. and John G. Riley (1989), 'Politically contestable rents and transfers', *Economics and Politics*, **1**, 17–40, reprinted in Roger D. Congleton, Arye L. Hillman and Kai A. Konrad (eds) (2008), *Forty Years of Research on Rent Seeking 1 – The Theory of Rent Seeking*, Heidelberg: Springer, pp. 185–207.

Hillman, Arye L. and Dov Samet (1987), 'Dissipation of contestable rents by small numbers of contenders', *Public Choice*, **54**, 63–82, reprinted in Roger D. Congleton, Arye L. Hillman and Kai A. Konrad (eds) (2008), *Forty Years of Research on Rent Seeking 1 – The Theory of Rent Seeking*, Heidelberg: Springer, pp. 165–84.

Hillman, Arye L. and Otto Swank (2000), 'Why political culture should be in the lexicon of economics', *European Journal of Political Economy*, **16**, 1–4.

Hillman, Arye L. and Heinrich W. Ursprung (1988), 'Domestic politics, foreign interests, and international trade policy', *American Economic Review*, **78**, 729–45, reprinted in Roger D. Congleton, Arye L. Hillman and Kai A. Konrad (eds) (2008), *Forty Years of Research on Rent Seeking 2 – Applications: Rent Seeking in Practice*, Heidelberg: Springer, pp. 113–29.

Hillman, Arye L. and Heinrich W. Ursprung (2000), 'Political culture and economic decline', *European Journal of Political Economy*, **16**, 189–213, reprinted in Roger D. Congleton, Arye L. Hillman and Kai A. Konrad (eds) (2008), *Forty Years of Research on Rent Seeking 2 – Applications: Rent Seeking in Practice*, Heidelberg: Springer, pp. 219–43.

Hillman, Arye L., Eliakim Katz and Jacob Rosenberg (1987), 'Workers as insurance: Anticipated government intervention and factor demand', *Oxford Economic Papers*, **39**, 813–20, reprinted in Roger D. Congleton, Arye L. Hillman and Kai A. Konrad (eds) (2008), *Forty Years of Research on Rent Seeking 2 – Applications: Rent Seeking in Practice*, Heidelberg: Springer, pp. 585–92.

Hindmoor, Andrew (2006), *Rational Choice*, London: Palgrave Macmillan.

Hindriks, Jean, Michael Keen and Abhinay Muthoo (1999), 'Corruption, extortion, and evasion',

Journal of Public Economics, **74**, 395–430, reprinted in George T. Abed and Sanjeev Gupta (eds) (2003), *Governance, Corruption, and Economic Performance*, Washington, DC: International Monetary Fund, pp. 396–436.

Hinich, Melvin J. and Michael C. Munger (1989), 'Political investment, voter perceptions, and candidate strategy: an equilibrium spatial analysis', in Peter C. Ordeshook (ed.), *Models of Strategic Choice in Politics*, Ann Arbor, MI: University of Michigan Press, pp. 49–68.

Hinich, Melvin J. and Michael C. Munger (1994), *Ideology and the Theory of Political Choice*, Ann Arbor, MI: University of Michigan Press.

Hinich, Melvin J. and Michael C. Munger (forthcoming), *Choosing in Groups: Analytical Politics II*, New York: Cambridge University Press.

Hirschman, Albert O. (1945), *National Power and the Structure of Foreign Trade*, Berkeley, CA: University of California Press.

Hirschman, Albert O. (1970), *Exit, Voice, and Loyalty: Responses to Decline in Firms, Organizations, and States*, Cambridge, MA: Harvard University Press.

Hirshleifer, Jack (1982), 'Evolutionary models in economics and law', *Research in Law and Economics*, **4**, 1–60.

Hirshleifer, Jack (1989), 'Conflict and rent-seeking success functions: ratio vs. difference models of relative success', *Public Choice*, **63**, 101–12.

Hirshleifer, Jack (1991), 'The technology of conflict as an economic activity', *American Economic Review*, **81**, 130–34.

Hirshleifer, Jack (1996), 'Anarchy and its breakdown', in Michelle R. Garfinkel and Stergios Skaperdas (eds), *The Political Economy of Conflict and Appropriation*, Cambridge: Cambridge University Press, pp. 15–40.

Hite, Katherine and Paola Cesarini (ed., Foreword by Nancy G. Bermeo) (2004), *Authoritarian Legacies and Democracy in Latin America and Southern Europe*, Notre Dame, IN: University of Notre Dame Press.

Hobbes, Thomas ([1651] 1939), *Leviathan: or the Matter, Form, and Power of a Commonwealth Ecclesiastical and Civil*, in Edwin A. Burtt (ed.) (1939), *The English Philosophers from Bacon to Mill*, New York: Modern Library, pp. 129–234.

Hobbes, Thomas ([1651] 1962), *Leviathan*, New York: Collier Books.

Hochman, Harold M. and James D. Rodgers (1969), 'Pareto optimal redistribution', *American Economic Review*, **59**, 542–57.

Hodrick, Robert J. and Edward C. Prescott (1997), 'Postwar U.S. business cycles: an empirical investigation', *Journal of Money, Credit, and Banking*, **29**, 1–16.

Hoffman, Elizabeth and Matthew L. Spitzer (1982), 'The Coase theorem: some experimental tests', *Journal of Law and Economics*, **25**, 73–98.

Hoffman, Elizabeth and Matthew L. Spitzer (1985), 'Entitlements, rights, and fairness: an experimental examination of subjects' concepts of distributive justice', *Journal of Legal Studies*, **14**, 259–97.

Holcombe, Randall G. (1980), 'An empirical test of the median voter model', *Economic Inquiry*, **18**, 260–74.

Holcombe, Randall G. (1994), *The Economic Foundations of Government*, New York: New York University Press.

Holcombe, Randall G. (2002a), 'Political entrepreneurship and the democratic allocation of economic resources', *Review of Austrian Economics*, **15**, 143–59.

Holcombe, Randall G. (2002b), *From Liberty to Democracy: The Transformation of American Government*, Ann Arbor, MI: University of Michigan Press.

Holcombe, Randall G. (2012), 'Consent or coercion? A critical analysis of the constitutional contract', in Alain Marciano (ed.), *Constitutional Mythologies*, Dordrecht: Springer, pp. 9–23.

Holcombe, Randall G. and Lawrence W. Kenny (2007), 'Evidence on voter preferences from unrestricted choice referendums', *Public Choice*, **131**, 197–15.

Holcombe, Randall G. and Lawrence W. Kenny (2008), 'Does restricting choice in referenda enable governments to spend more', *Public Choice*, **136**, 87–101.

Holcombe Randall G. and Glenn R. Parker (1991), 'Committees in legislatures: a property rights perspective', *Public Choice*, **70**, 11–20.

Holcombe, Randall G. and DeEdgra W. Williams (2011), 'The cartelization of local governments', *Public Choice*, **149**, 65–74.
Holmer, Freeman (1959), 'Book review of *The Theory of Committees and Elections*' by Duncan Black, *The Western Political Quarterly*, **12**, 587–8.
Holyst Janusz A., Tilo Hagel, Günter Haag and Wolfgang Weidlich (1996), 'How to control a chaotic economy?', *Journal of Evolutionary Economics*, **6**, 31–42.
Hornblower, Simon (1992), 'Creation and development of democratic institutions in Ancient Greece', in John Dunn (ed.), *Democracy: The Unfinished Journey, 508 BC to AD 1993*, Oxford: Oxford University Press, pp. 1–16.
Horowitz, Donald L. (1985), *Ethnic Groups in Conflict*, Berkeley, CA: University of California Press.
Horwitz, Morton J. (1977), *The Transformation in the Conception of Property in American Law, 1780–1860*, Cambridge, MA: Harvard University Press.
Hotelling, Harold (1929), 'Stability in competition', *Economic Journal*, **39**, 41–57.
Hou, Yilin and Daniel L. Smith (2010), 'Do state balanced budget requirements matter? Testing two explanatory frameworks', *Public Choice*, **145**, 57–79.
Houser, Daniel and Thomas Stratmann (2008), 'Selling favors in the lab: experiments on campaign finance reform', *Public Choice*, **136**, 215–39.
Hoxby, Caroline (1994), 'Do private schools provide competition for public schools?', National Bureau of Economic Research, NBER Working Paper Series, no. 4978.
Hoxby, Caroline (2000), 'Does competition among public schools benefit students and taxpayers?', *American Economic Review*, **90**, 1209–38.
Hoxby, Caroline (2003), 'School choice and school competition: evidence from the United States', *Swedish Economic Policy Review*, **10**, 9–65.
Hoxby, Caroline (2007), 'Does competition among public schools benefit students and taxpayers? Reply', *American Economic Review*, **97**, 2038–55.
Huber, Evelyne, Charles Ragin, John D. Stephens (assembled the initial version, which was updated by), David Brady, Jason Beckfield and John D. Stephens (2004), *Comparative Welfare States Data Set*, Chapel Hill, NC: University of North Carolina Press.
Huber, Gregory A. and Sanford C. Gordon (2004), 'Accountability and coercion: is justice blind when it runs for office?', *American Journal of Political Science*, **48**, 247–63.
Huckfeldt, Robert and John Sprague (1995), *Citizens, Politics, and Social Communication – Information and Influence in an Election Campaign*, Cambridge: Cambridge University Press.
Huntington, Samuel P. (1968), *Political Order in Changing Societies*, New Haven, CT: Yale University Press.
Huntington, Samuel P. (1991), *The Third Wave: Democratization in the Late Twentieth Century*, Norman, OK: University of Oklahoma Press.
Husted, Thomas A. and Lawrence W. Kenny (2002), 'The legacy of *Serrano*: the impact of mandated equal spending on private school enrollment', *Southern Economic Journal*, **68**, 566–83.
Husted, Thomas A. and Lawrence W. Kenny (2007), 'Explanations for states adopting limits on educational spending', *Public Finance Review*, **35**, 586–605.
Husted, Thomas A., Lawrence W. Kenny and Rebecca B. Morton (1995), 'Constituent errors in assessing their senators', *Public Choice*, **83**, 251–71.
Iannaccone, Lawrence R. (1992), 'Sacrifice and stigma: reducing free-riding in cults, communes, and other collectives', *Journal of Political Economy*, **100**, 271–92.
Iannaccone, Lawrence R. (2006), 'The market for martyrs', *Interdisciplinary Journal of Research on Religion*, **2**, art. 4, 4–16.
Iannaccone, Lawrence R. and Eli Berman (2006), 'Religious extremism: the good, the bad, and the deadly', *Public Choice*, **128**, 109–29.
Ianni Antonella and Valentina Corradi (2002), 'The dynamics of public opinion under majority rules', *Review of Economic Design*, **7**, 257–77.
Inman, Robert P. (1988), 'Federal assistance and local services in the United States: the evolution of a new federalist fiscal order', in Harvey S. Rosen (ed.), *Fiscal Federalism: Quantitative Studies*, Chicago, IL: University of Chicago Press, pp. 33–78.
International Commission of Jurists (2002), 'Russian federation – attacks on Justice 2002 – Russia', available at: http://bit.ly/u9Gsrx (accessed 7 October 2010).

Ireland, Peter N. (1999), 'Does the time-consistency problem explain the behavior of inflation in the United States?', *Journal of Monetary Economics*, **44**, 279–91.
Irwin, Michael H.K. (1994), 'Banking on poverty: an insider's look at the World Bank', in Kevin Danaher (ed.), *50 Years is Enough: The Case against the World Bank and the International Monetary Fund*, Boston, MA: Global Exchange, pp. 152–60.
Isaac, R. Mark and Charles A. Holt (eds) (1999), *Research in Experimental Economics*, vol. 7, Stamford, CT: JAI Press.
Isaac, R. Mark and Stanley S. Reynolds (1988), 'Appropriability and market structure in a stochastic invention model', *Quarterly Journal of Economics*, **4**, 647–72.
Isaac, R. Mark and James M. Walker (1988), 'Group size effects in public goods provision: the voluntary contributions mechanism', *Quarterly Journal of Economics*, **103**, 179–99.
Isaac, R. Mark, James M. Walker and Susan H. Thomas (1984), 'Divergent evidence on free riding: an experimental examination of possible explanations', *Public Choice*, **43**, 113–49.
Iyer, Lakshmi (2010), 'Direct versus indirect colonial rule in India: long-term consequences', *Review of Economics and Statistics*, **92**, 693–713.
Jackman, Robert W. (1987), 'Political institutions and voter turnout in the industrialized democracies', *American Political Science Review*, **81**, 405–24.
Jackson, Paul (2002), 'March of the Lord's Resistance Army: greed or grievance in northern Uganda?', *Small Wars and Insurgencies*, **13**, 29–52.
Jacob, Johanna and Douglas Lundin (2005), 'A median voter model of health insurance with ex post moral hazard', *Journal of Health Economics*, **24**, 407–26.
Jacobs, Dennis (2007), 'The secret life of judges', *Fordham Law Review*, **25**, 2855–63.
Jacobsen, Thorkild (1943), 'Primitive democracy in Ancient Mesopotamia', *Journal of Near Eastern Studies*, **2**, 159–72.
Jacobson, Gary C. (1978), 'The effects of campaign spending on congressional elections', *American Political Science Review*, **72**, 469–91.
Jacobson, Gary C. (1985), 'Money and votes reconsidered: congressional elections 1972–1982', *Public Choice*, **47**, 7–62.
James, Martin O. (2002), *Congressional Oversight*, New York: Nova Science.
Jayachandran, Seema (2006), 'The Jeffords effect', *Journal of Law and Economics*, **49**, 397–425.
Jellema, Jon and Gérard Roland (2011), 'Institutional clusters and economic performance', *Journal of Economic Behavior and Organization*, **79**, 108–32.
Johnson, Cathy Marie (1992), *The Dynamics of Conflict between Bureaucrats and Legislators*, New York: M.E. Sharpe.
Johnson, Juliet (2001), 'Path contingency in postcommunist transformations', *Comparative Politics*, **33**, 253–74.
Jones, Benjamin F. and Benjamin A. Olken (2009), 'Hit or miss? The effect of assassinations on institutions and war', *American Economic Journal: Macroeconomics*, **1**, 55–87.
Jones, Eric L. (1981), *The European Miracle: Environments, Economies and Geopolitics in the History of Europe and Asia*, Cambridge: Cambridge University Press.
Joulfaian, David and Michael L. Marlow (1990), 'Government size and decentralization: evidence from disaggregated data', *Southern Economic Journal*, **56**, 1094–102.
Judicial Appointments Commission (2006), 'JAC launches new system for judicial appointments', available at: http://www.judicialappointments.gov.uk/about-jac/155.htm (accessed 20 December 2010).
Jupille, Joseph H. (2004), *Procedural Politics: Issues, Interests and Institutional Choice in the European Union*, Cambridge: Cambridge University Press.
Kahana, Nava and Shmuel Nitzan (1999), 'Uncertain preassigned non-contestable and contestable rents', *European Economic Review*, **43**, 1705–21, reprinted in Roger D. Congleton, Arye L. Hillman and Kai A. Konrad (eds) (2008), *Forty Years of Research on Rent Seeking 1 – The Theory of Rent Seeking*, Heidelberg: Springer, pp. 455–71.
Kahana, Nava and Liu Qijun (2010), 'Endemic corruption', *European Journal of Political Economy*, **26**, 82–8.
Kahn, Matthew E. and John G. Matsusaka (1997), 'Demand for environmental goods: evidence from voting patterns on California initiatives', *Journal of Law and Economics*, **40**, 137–73.

Kahnemann, Daniel and Amos Tversky (1984), 'Choices, values, and frames', *American Psychologist*, **39**, 341–50.
Kaja, Ashwin and Eric D. Werker (2009), *Corporate Misgovernance at the World Bank*, Harvard Business School BGIE Unit Working Paper, 09-108.
Kane, Edward J. (1980), 'Politics and Fed policymaking: the more things change the more they remain the same', *Journal of Monetary Economics*, **6**, 199–211.
Kang, David C. (2002), *Crony Capitalism: Corruption and Development in South Korea and the Philippines*, Cambridge and New York: Cambridge University Press.
Kang, Michael S. and Joanna M. Shepherd (2011), 'The partisan price of justice: an empirical analysis of campaign contributions and judicial decisions', *New York University Law Review*, **86**, 69–130.
Kant, Immanuel ([1795] 1983), *Perpetual Peace and Other Essays*, Indianapolis, IN: Hackett.
Kanthak, Kristin (2004), 'Exclusive committee assignments and party pressure in the U.S. House of Representatives', *Public Choice*, **121**, 391–412.
Karras, Georgios (1994), 'Government spending and private consumption: some international evidence', *Journal of Money Credit and Banking*, **26**, 9–22.
Karras, Georgios (1996a), 'Is government investment underprovided in Europe: evidence from a panel of fifteen countries', *Economia Internazionale*, **50**, 223–35.
Karras, Georgios (1996b), 'The optimal government size: further international evidence on the productivity of government services', *Economic Inquiry*, **34**, 193–203.
Karras, Georgios (1997), 'On the optimal government size in Europe: theory and empirical evidence', *Manchester School of Economic and Social Studies*, **65**, 280–94.
Karrer, Inga (2010), '*Explaining the Attendance of the Members of the European Parliament from a Public Choice Perspective*', Bachelor's thesis, Universität Mannheim.
Karsden, Rafael (1967), 'Blood revenge and war among the Jibaro Indians of Eastern Ecuador', in Paul Bohannan (ed.), *Law and Warfare: Studies in the Anthropology of Conflict*, Garden City, NY: American Museum of Natural History Press, pp. 303–26.
Katz, Avery (1988), 'Judicial decisionmaking and litigation expenditure', *International Review of Law and Economics*, **8**, 127–43.
Katz, Eliakim and Jacob Rosenberg (1989), 'Rent seeking for budgetary allocation: preliminary results for 20 countries', *Public Choice*, **60**, 133–44.
Kau, James B., Donald Keenan and Paul H. Rubin (1982), 'A general equilibrium model of congressional voting', *Quarterly Journal of Economics*, **97**, 271–93.
Kau, James B. and Paul H. Rubin (1981), 'The size of government', *Public Choice*, **37**, 261–74.
Kayser, Mark A. (2005), 'Who surfs, who manipulates? The determinants of opportunistic election timing and electorally motivated economic intervention', *American Political Science Review*, **99**, 17–27.
Keech, William R. and Irwin L. Morris (1997), 'Appointments, presidential power, and the Federal Reserve', *Journal of Macroeconomics*, **19**, 253–67.
Keefer, Philip (2008), 'Insurgency and credible commitment in autocracies and democracies', *World Bank Economic Review*, **22**, 33–61.
Keefer, Phillip and Stephen Knack (1997), 'Why don't poor countries catch up? A cross-national test of an institutional explanation', *Economic Inquiry*, **35**, 590–602.
Kelman, Mark (1988), 'On democracy-bashing: a skeptical look at the theoretical and "empirical" practice of the public choice movement', *Virginia Law Review*, **74**, 199–273.
Kenen, Peter B. and Stephen B. Schwartz (1986), *The Assessment of Macroeconomic Forecasts in the International Monetary Fund's World Economic Outlook*, Working Papers in International Economics, no. G-86-40, Princeton University.
Kenny, Lawrence W. (2005), 'The public choice of educational choice', *Public Choice*, **124**, 205–22.
Kenny, Lawrence W. (2010), 'The appeal of vouchers for failing large city school districts: voting in Congress on two very different voucher proposals', *Journal of School Choice*, **4**, 5–22.
Kenny, Lawrence W. and Adam Reinke (2011), 'The role of income in the formation of new cities', *Public Choice*, **149**, 75–88.
Kenny, Lawrence W. and Amy B. Schmidt (1994), 'The decline in the number of school districts in the U.S.: 1950–1980', *Public Choice*, **79**, 1–18.

Keohane, Nathaniel O., Richard L. Revesz and Robert N. Stavins (1996), 'The positive political economy of instrument choice in environmental policy', available at SSRN: http://ssrn.com/abstract=5096 (accessed 20 May 2012).

Kerber, Wolfgang and Klaus Heine (2003), 'Institutional evolution, regulatory competition and path dependence', in Pavel Pelikan and Gerhard Wegner (eds), *The Evolutionary Analysis of Economic Policy*, Cheltenham, UK and Northampton, MA, USA: Edward Elgar, pp. 191–222.

Kessler, Anke S. (2005), 'Representative versus direct democracy: the role of information asymmetries', *Public Choice*, **122**, 9–38.

Khan, Mushtaq H. and Jomo K. Sundaram (2000), *Rents, Rent Seeking and Economic Development: Theory and Evidence in Asia*, Cambridge: Cambridge University Press.

Kiewiet, D. Roderick and Kristin Szakaly (1996), 'Constitutional limitations on borrowing: an analysis of state bonded indebtedness', *Journal of Law, Economics, and Organization*, **12**, 62–97.

Kilby, Christopher (2006), 'Donor influence in multilateral development banks: the case of the Asian development bank', *Review of International Organizations*, **1**, 173–95.

Kilby, Christopher (2011), 'Informal influence at the Asian Development Bank', *Review of International Organizations*, **6**, 223–57.

Kim, Hyung Min and David L. Rousseau (2005), 'The classical liberals were half right (or half wrong): new tests of the "Liberal Peace", 1960–88', *Journal of Peace Research*, **42**, 523–43.

Kim, Youngshin (2010), Growth of social security: dynamic effects of public choice', unpublished PhD dissertation, George Mason University, Fairfax, VA.

Kimenyi, Mwangi S. (1998), 'Harmonizing ethnic claims in Africa: a proposal for ethnic-based federalism', *Cato Journal*, **18**, 43–63.

Kimenyi, Mwangi S. and Roxana Gutierrez Romero (2008), 'Identity, grievances, and economic determinants of voting in the 2007 Kenyan elections', University of Connecticut, Department of Economics Working Paper Series, no. 200838.

Kinder, Donald R. and Roderick Kiewiet (1981), 'Sociotropic voting: the American case', *British Journal of Political Science*, **11**, 129–61.

King, Paul (2008), 'Editorial: The mechanics of terrorism', *NATO Review*, April, p. 1, available at: http://www.nato.int/docu/review/2008/04/EN/index.htm (accessed 1 October 2011).

Kingdon, John W. (1995), *Agendas, Alternatives and Public Policies*, New York: Harper Collins.

Kinnear, Douglas (1999), 'Public choice theory', in Phillip O'Hara (ed.), *Encyclopedia of Political Economy*, London: Routledge, pp. 931–33.

Kirchgässner, Gebhard (2002), 'On the role of heroes in political and economic processes', *Kyklos*, **56**, 179–96.

Kirchgässner, Gebhard and Werner W. Pommerehne (1993), 'Low-cost decisions as a challenge to public choice', *Public Choice*, **77**, 107–15.

Kirk, Richard M. (1983), 'Political terrorism and the size of government: a positive institutional analysis of violent political activity', *Public Choice*, **40**, 41–52.

Kirzner, Israel (1973), *Competition and Entrepreneurship*, Chicago, IL: University of Chicago Press.

Kitschelt, Herbert and Steven Wilkinson (eds) (2007), *Patrons, Clients, and Policies: Patterns of Democratic Accountability and Political Competition*, Cambridge, UK and New York: Cambridge University Press.

Kitto, Humphrey D.F. (1957), *The Greeks*, Harmondsworth: Penguin Books.

Klarman, Daniel (1999), 'Commentary: nonpromotion and judicial independence', *Southern California Law Review*, **72**, 455–63.

Kliemt, Hartmut (1986), 'The veil of insignificance', *European Journal of Political Economy*, **2**, 333–44.

Klein, Benjamin and Keith B. Leffler (1981), 'The role of market forces in assuring contractual performance', *Journal of Political Economy*, **89**, 615–41.

Klein, Michael W. (1996), 'Timing is all: elections and the duration of United States business cycles', *Journal of Money, Credit, and Banking*, **28**, 84–101.

Knack, Steven and Philip Keefer (1995), 'Institutions and economic performance: cross-country tests using alternative measures', *Economics and Politics*, **7**, 207–27.

Kneebone, Ronald D. and Kenneth J. McKenzie (2001), 'Electoral and partisan cycles in fiscal policy: an examination of Canadian provinces', *International Tax and Public Finance*, **8**, 753–74.
Knight, Brian (2007), 'Are policy platforms capitalized into equity prices? Evidence from the Bush/Gore 2000 presidential election', *Journal of Public Economics*, **91**, 389–409.
Knight, Jack (2001), 'A pragmatist approach to the proper scope of government', *Journal of Institutional and Theoretical Economics*, **157**, 28–48.
Knight, Jack and Lee Epstein (1996), 'The norm of *stare decisis*', *American Journal of Political Science*, **40**, 1018–35.
Knott, Jack H. (1986), 'The Fed chairman as a political executive', *Administration and Society*, **18**, 197–231.
Konrad, Kai A. (2009), *Strategy and Dynamics in Contests*, Oxford: Oxford University Press.
Kontopoulos, Yanos and Roberto Perotti (1999), 'Government fragmentation and fiscal policy outcomes: evidence from OECD countries', in James M. Poterba and Jurgen von Hagen (eds), *Fiscal Institutions and Fiscal Performance*, Chicago, IL: University of Chicago Press, pp. 81–102.
Kopel, Michael (1997), 'Improving the performance of an economic system: controlling chaos', *Journal of Evolutionary Economics*, **7**, 269–89.
Korenok, Oleg, Edward L. Millner and Laura Razzolini (2012a), 'Are dictators averse to inequality?', *Journal of Economic Behavior and Organization*, **82**, 543–7.
Korenok, Oleg, Edward L. Millner and Laura Razzolini (2012b), 'Impure altruism in dictators' giving', *Journal of Public Economics*, forthcoming.
Kormendi, Roger C. (1983), 'Government debt, government spending and private sector behavior', *American Economic Review*, **73**, 994–1010.
Kornai, Jànos (1980), 'Hard and soft budget constraint', *Acta Oeconomica*, **25**, 231–46, reprinted in Roger D. Congleton, Arye L. Hillman and Kai A. Konrad (eds) (2008), *Forty Years of Research on Rent Seeking 2 – Applications: Rent Seeking in Practice*, Heidelberg: Springer, pp. 569–83.
Kornhauser, Lewis A. (1992a), 'Modeling collegial courts I: path dependence', *International Review of Law and Economics*, **12**, 169–85.
Kornhauser, Lewis A. (1992b), 'Modeling collegial courts II: legal doctrine', *Journal of Law, Economics and Organization*, **8**, 441–70.
Kort, Fred (1959), 'Book review of *The Theory of Committees and Elections*' by Duncan Black, *The Journal of Politics*, **21**, 325–7.
Kramer, Gerald H. (1971), 'Short-term fluctuations in US voting behavior, 1896–1964', *American Political Science Review*, **65**, 131–43.
Krause, George A. (1994), 'Federal Reserve policy decision making: political and bureaucratic influences', *American Journal of Political Science*, **38**, 124–44.
Krause, George A. (1996), 'Agent heterogeneity and consensual decision making on the Federal Open Market Committee', *Public Choice*, **88**, 83–101.
Krehbiel, Keith (1990), 'Are congressional committees composed of preference outliers?', *American Political Science Review*, **84**, 149–63.
Krehbiel, Keith (1991), *Information and Legislative Organization*, Ann Arbor, MI: University of Michigan Press.
Krehbiel, Keith (2004), 'Legislative organization', *Journal of Economic Perspectives*, **18**, 113–228.
Kroszner, Randall S. and Thomas Stratmann (1998), 'Interest group competition and the organization of Congress: theory and evidence from financial services political action committees', *American Economic Review*, **88**, 1163–87.
Kroszner, Randall S. and Thomas Stratmann (2000), 'Congressional committees as reputation-building mechanisms: repeat PAC giving and seniority on the House Banking Committee', *Business and Politics*, **2**, 35–52.
Kroszner, Randall S. and Thomas Stratmann (2005), 'Corporate campaign contributions, repeat giving, and the rewards to legislator reputation', *Journal of Law and Economics*, **48**, 41–71.
Krueger, Anne O. (1974), 'The political economy of the rent-seeking society', *American Economic Review*, **64**, 291–303, reprinted in Roger D. Congleton, Arye L. Hillman and Kai A. Konrad (eds) (2008), *Forty Years of Research on Rent Seeking 2 – Applications: Rent Seeking in Practice*, Heidelberg: Springer, pp. 151–63.

Kubik, Jeffrey D. and John R. Moran (2003), 'Lethal elections: gubernatorial politics and the timing of executions', *Journal of Law and Economics*, **46**, 1–26.
Kuhn, Britta (1993), *Sozialraum Europa: Zentralisierung oder Dezentralisierung der Sozialpolitik?*, Idstein-Wörsdorf: Schulz-Kirchner.
Kuran, Timor (1988), 'The tenacious past: theories of personal and collective conservatism', *Journal of Economic Behavior and Organization*, **10**, 143–71.
Kuran, Timor (1995), *Private Truths, Public Lies: The Social Consequences of Preference Falsification*, Cambridge: Harvard University Press.
Kuziemko, Ilyana and Eric D. Werker (2006), 'How much is a seat on the Security Council worth? Foreign aid and bribery at the United Nations, *Journal of Political Economy*, **114**, 905–30.
Kwoka, John E., Jr (2002), 'Governance alternatives and pricing in the US electric power industry', *Journal of Law, Economics and Organization*, **18**, 278–94.
Kydd, Andrew H. and Barbara F. Walter (2006), 'The strategies of terrorism', *International Security*, **31**, 49–80.
Kydland, Finn E. and Edward C. Prescott (1977), 'Rules rather than discretion: the inconsistency of optimal plans', *Journal of Political Economy*, **85**, 473–91.
Kydland, Finn E. and Edward C. Prescott (1980), 'Dynamic optimal taxation, rational expectations and optimal control', *Journal of Economic Dynamics and Control*, **2**, 79–91.
La Porta, Rafael, Florencio Lopez-de-Silanes, Cristian Pop-Eleches and Andrei Shleifer (2004), 'Judicial checks and balances', *Journal of Political Economy*, **112**, 445–70.
La Porta, Rafael, Florencio Lopez-de-Silanes, Andrei Shleifer and Robert W. Vishny (1998), 'Law and finance', *Journal of Political Economy*, **106**, 1113–55.
La Porta, Rafael, Florencio Lopez-de-Silanes, Andrei Shleifer and Robert W. Vishny (1999), 'The quality of government', *Journal of Law, Economics, and Organization*, **15**, 222–79.
Laband, David N. (1988), 'Transactions costs and production in a legislative setting', *Public Choice*, **57**, 183–6.
Laband, David N. and John P. Sophocleus (1992), 'An estimate of resource expenditure on transfer activity in the United States', *Quarterly Journal of Economics*, **107**, 959–83.
Laband, David N., Ram Pandit, John P. Sophocleus and Anne M. Laband (2009), 'Patriotism, pigskins, and politics: an empirical examination of expressive behavior and voting', *Public Choice*, **138**, 97–108.
Laffont, Jean-Jacques and David Martimort (2000), 'Mechanism design with collusion and correlation', *Econometrica*, **68**, 309–42.
Lagona, Francesco and Fabio Padovano (2007), 'A non-linear principal component analysis of the relationship between budget rules and fiscal performance in the European Union', *Public Choice*, **130**, 401–36.
Lagona, Francesco and Fabio Padovano (2008), 'The political legislation cycle', *Public Choice*, **134**, 201–29.
Lagona, Francesco, Antonello Maruotti and Fabio Padovano (2011), 'Opposing cycles in legislative production', *CREI Working Papers*, no. 32.
Lal, Deepak (1998), *Unintended Consequences: The Impact of Factor Endowments, Culture, and Politics on Long-Run Economic Performance*, Cambridge, MA: MIT Press.
Landau, Daniel L. (1983), 'Government expenditure and economic growth: a cross-country study', *Southern Economic Journal*, **49**, 783–92.
Landes, William M. (1971), 'An economic analysis of the courts', *Journal of Law and Economics*, **14**, 61–107.
Landes, William M. and Richard A. Posner (1975), 'The independent judiciary in an interest group perspective', *Journal of Law and Economics*, **18**, 875–901.
Landes, William M. and Richard A. Posner (1976), 'Legal precedent: a theoretical and empirical analysis', *Journal of Law and Economics*, **19**, 249–307.
Landes, William M. and Richard A. Posner (1979), 'Adjudication as a private good', *Journal of Legal Studies*, **8**, 235–84.
Landes, William M. and Richard A. Posner (1987), *The Economic Structure of Tort Law*, Cambridge, MA: Harvard University Press.

Landfried, Christine (2006), 'The selection process of constitutional court judges in Germany', in Kate Malleson and Peter H. Russell (eds), *Appointing Judges in an Age of Judicial Power*, Toronto: University of Toronto Press, p. 196–210.

Lascher, Edward L. Jr, Michael G. Hagen and Steven A. Rochlin (1996), 'Gun behind the door? Ballot initiatives, state policies, and public opinion', *Journal of Politics*, **58**, 760–75.

Latham, Earl (1967), 'Book review of *The Logic of Collective Action*' by Mancur Olson, *Political Science Quarterly*, **82**, 145–8.

Lau, Richard R. and David Sears (1986) (eds), *Political Cognition*, Hillsdale, NJ: Lawrence Erlbaum Associates.

Laury, Susan K., James M. Walker and Arlington W. Williams (1999), 'The voluntary provision of a pure public good with diminishing marginal returns', *Public Choice*, **99**, 139–60.

Laver, Michael and Kenneth A. Shepsle (1996), *Making and Breaking Governments: Cabinets and Legislatures in Parliamentary Democracies*, Cambridge: Cambridge University Press.

Lawson, Robert A. and J.R. Clark (2010), 'Examining the Hayek-Friedman hypothesis on economic and political freedom', *Journal of Economic Behavior and Organization*, **74**, 230–9.

Lax, Jeffrey R. and Justin H. Phillips (2010), 'Explaining democratic performance in the states', working paper, Columbia University.

Layne, Christopher (2001), 'Shell games, shallow gains, and the democratic peace', *International History Review*, **23**, 799–813.

Leaver, Clare (2009), 'Bureaucratic minimal squawk behavior: theory and evidence', *American Economic Review*, **99**, 572–607.

Ledyard, John O. (1995), 'Public goods: a survey of experimental research', in John H. Kagel and Alvin E. Roth (eds), *The Handbook of Experimental Economics*, Princeton, NJ: Princeton University Press, pp. 111–94.

Lee, Dwight R. (1988), 'Free riding and paid riding in the fight against terrorism', *American Economic Review*, **78**, 22–6.

Lee, Stephen J. (2000), *European Dictatorships, 1918–1945*, 2nd edn, London and New York: Routledge.

Leeper, Eric M. (1991), 'Equilibria under "active" and "passive" monetary and fiscal policy, *Journal of Monetary Economics*, **27**, 129–47.

Leeson, Peter T. (2005), 'Endogenizing fractionalization', *Journal of Institutional Economics*, **1**, 75–98.

Leijonhufvud, Axel (2009), 'Out of the corridor: Keynes and the crisis', *Cambridge Journal of Economics*, **33**, 741–57.

Leventoğlu, Bahar and Branislav L. Slantchev (2007), 'The armed peace: a punctuated equilibrium theory of war', *American Journal of Political Science*, **51**, 755–71.

Levine, David K. and Thomas R. Palfrey (2007), 'The paradox of voter participation: a laboratory study', *American Political Science Review*, **101**, 143–58.

Levine, Michael E. and Charles R. Plott (1978), 'A model of agenda influence on committee decisions', *American Economic Review*, **68**, 146–60.

Levitt, Steven D. (1994), 'Using repeat challengers to estimate the effects of campaign spending on election outcomes in the U.S. House', *Journal of Political Economy*, **102**, 777–98.

Levitt, Steven D. (1997), 'Using electoral cycles in police hiring to estimate the effect of police on crime', *American Economic Review*, **87**, 270–90.

Levmore, Saul (1992), 'Bicameralism: when are two decisions better than one?', *International Review of Law and Economics*, **12**, 145–62.

Levy, Gilat (2005), 'Careerist judges', *Rand Journal of Economics*, **36**, 275–97.

Levy, Jack S. (1989), 'The causes of war: a review of theories and evidence', in Philip E. Tetlock, Jo L. Husbands, Robert Jervis, Paul C. Stern and Charles Tilly (eds), *Behavior, Society and Nuclear War*, vol. 1, New York: Oxford University Press, pp. 209–333.

Levy Jr, Marion J. (1966), 'Book review of *The Logic of Collective Action*' by Mancur Olson, *The American Journal of Sociology*, **72**, 218.

Lewin, Lewin (1991), *Self-Interest and Public Interest in Western Democracies*, trans. Donald Lavery, London: Oxford University Press.

Lewis, Arthur M. (1965), *Politics in West Africa*, Oxford: Oxford University Press.

Lewis, Herbert S. (1966), 'The origins of African kingdoms', *Cahiers d'études africaines*, **6**, 402–7.
Lewis, John D. (1967), 'Book review of *The Logic of Collective Action*' by Mancur Olson, *Annals of the American Academy of Political and Social Sciences*, **369**, 210–11.
Lewis-Beck, Michael S. (1979), 'Maintaining economic competition: the causes and consequences of antitrust', *Journal of Politics*, **41**, 169–91.
Li, Quan and Rafael Reuveny (2011), 'Trading for peace? Disaggregated bilateral trade and interstate military conflict initiation', *Journal of Peace Research*, forthcoming.
Lichbach, Mark I. (1995), *The Rebel's Dilemma*, Ann Arbor, MI: University of Michigan Press.
Lijphart, Arend (1999), *Patterns of Democracy: Government Forms and Performance in Thirty-Six Countries*, New Haven, CT: Yale University Press.
Lim, Youngsik (2000), 'An empirical analysis of Supreme Court Justices' decision making', *Journal of Legal Studies*, **29**, 721–52.
Lindahl, Erik (1919), *Die Gerechtigkeit der Besteuerung*, Lund: Gleerupska.
Lindbeck, Assar (1997a), 'The interaction between norms and economic incentives: incentives and social norms in household behavior', *American Economic Review Papers and Proceedings*, **87**, 370–77.
Lindbeck, Assar (1997b), 'The Swedish experiment', *Journal of Economic Literature*, **35**, 1273–319.
Lindbeck, Assar and Dennis Snower (1987), 'Efficiency wages versus insiders and outsiders', *European Economic Review*, **31**, 407–16, reprinted in Roger D. Congleton, Arye L. Hillman and Kai A. Konrad (eds) (2008), *Forty Years of Research on Rent Seeking 2 – Applications: Rent Seeking in Practice*, Heidelberg: Springer, pp. 657–66.
Lindholm, Charles (1986), 'Kinship structure and political authority: the Middle East and Central Asia', *Comparative Studies in Society and History*, **28**, 334–55.
Lintott, Andrew (1999), *The Constitution of the Roman Republic*, New York: Oxford University Press.
Linz, Juan J. (1975), 'Totalitarian and authoritarian regimes', in Fred I. Greenstein and Nelson W. Polsby (eds), *Handbook of Political Science*, Reading, MA: Addison-Wesley.
Linz, Juan J. (1994), 'Presidential or parliamentary democracy: does it make a difference?', in Juan José Linz and Arturo Valenzuela (eds), *The Failure of Presidential Democracy*, vol. 2, Baltimore, MD: Johns Hopkins University Press, pp. 3–87.
Linz, Juan J. (2000), *Totalitarian and Authoritarian Regimes*, Boulder, CO: Lynne Rienner.
Lipset, Seymour M. (1959), 'Some social prerequisites for democracy: economic development and political legitimacy', *American Political Science Review*, **53**, 69–105.
List, Christian and Philip Pettit (2006), 'Group agency and supervenience', *The Southern Journal of Philosophy*, **44**, 85–105.
List, John A and Daniel M Sturm (2006), 'How elections matter: theory and evidence from environmental policy', *Quarterly Journal of Economics*, **121**, 1249–81.
Littlechild, Stephen (1981), 'Misleading calculations of the social cost of monopoly power', *Economic Journal*, **91**, 348–63, reprinted in Roger D. Congleton, Arye L. Hillman and Kai A. Konrad (eds) (2008), *Forty Years of Research on Rent Seeking 2 – Applications: Rent Seeking in Practice*, Heidelberg: Springer, pp. 89–104.
Loasby, Brian J. (2000), 'Market institutions and economic evolution', *Journal of Evolutionary Economics*, **10**, 297–309.
Lockard, Alan and Gordon Tullock (eds) (2001), *Efficient Rent-seeking: Chronicle of an Intellectual Quagmire*, Dordrecht: Kluwer Academic.
Locke, John ([1689/1764] 2010), *Two Treatises of Government*, Thomas Hollis (ed), London: A. Millar et al., 1764. Liberty Fund, Online Library of Liberty, available at: http://oll.libertyfund.org/title/222 (accessed 27 February 2011).
Locke, John ([1690] 1939), *Second Treatise on Government*, in Edwin A. Burtt (ed.), *The English Philosophers from Bacon to Mill*, New York: Modern Library, pp. 403–503.
Long, William F., Richard Schramm and Robert D. Tollison (1973), 'The economic determinants of antitrust activity', *Journal of Law and Economics*, **16**, 351–64.
Lopez, Alan D., Colin D. Mathers, Majid Ezzati, Dean T. Jamison and Christopher J.L. Murray (2006), *Global Burden of Disease and Risk Factors*, Washington, DC: World Bank.

Lott, John R. Jr (2000), 'A simple explanation for why campaign expenditures are increasing: the government is getting bigger', *Journal of Law and Economics*, **43**, 359–93.
Lowenstein, Daniel H. (1982), 'Campaign spending and ballot propositions: recent experience, public choice theory and the First Amendment', *UCLA Law Review*, **29**, 505–641.
Lowenstein, Daniel H. (1983), 'California initiatives and the single-subject rule', *UCLA Law Review*, **30**, 936–74.
Lowrey, David (1998), 'Consumer sovereignty and quasi-market failure', *Journal of Public Administration Research and Theory*, **8**, 137–72.
Lucas, Robert. E. (1975), 'An equilibrium model of the business cycle', *Journal of Political Economy*, **83**, 1113–44.
Luhmann, Niklas ([1970] 1975), 'Öffentliche Meinung', in Niklas Luhman, *Politische Planung: Aufsätze zur Soziologie von Politik und Verwaltung*, Opladen: Westdeutscher Verlag, pp. 9–34.
Lunt, William E. (1962), *Financial Relations of the Papacy with England, 1327–1534*, Cambridge, MA: Mediaeval Academy of America.
Lupia, Arthur (1994), 'Shortcuts versus encyclopedias: information and voting behavior in California insurance reform elections', *American Political Science Review*, **88**, 63–76.
Lupia, Arthur (2001), 'Dumber than chimps? An assessment of direct democracy voters', in Larry J. Sabato, Howard R. Ernst and Bruce A. Larson (eds), *Dangerous Democracy? The Battle over Ballot Initiatives in America*, Lanham, MD: Rowman & Littlefield, pp. 66–70.
Lupia, Arthur and John G. Matsusaka (2004), 'Direct democracy: new approaches to old questions', *Annual Review of Political Science*, **7**, 463–82.
Lupia, Arthur and Mathew D. McCubbins (1998), *The Democratic Dilemma: Can Citizens Learn What They Need to Know?*, New York: Cambridge University Press.
Lupia, Arthur, Yanna Krupnikov, Adam Seth Levine, Spencer Piston and Alexander von Hagen-Jamar (2010), 'Why state constitutions differ in their treatment of same-sex marriage', *Journal of Politics*, **72**, 1222–35.
Macey, Jonathan R. (1988), 'Transaction costs and the normative elements of the public choice model: an application to constitutional theory', *Virginia Law Review*, **74**, 471–518.
Machiavelli, Niccolò ([1515] 1984), *The Prince*, Oxford: Oxford University Press.
Mackie, Gerald (2008), 'An examination of the expressive theory of voting' unpublished paper, University of California, San Diego.
Madison, James, Alexander Hamilton and John Jay ([1788] 1961), *The Federalist Papers*, ed. Clinton L. Rossiter, New York: New American Library.
Maisel, Sherman J. (1973), *Managing the Dollar*, New York: W.W. Norton.
Maloney, Michael T. and Robert E. McCormick (1982), 'A positive theory of environmental quality regulation', *Journal of Law and Economics*, **25**, 99–123.
Mandelbaum, Michael (2007), *Democracy's Good Name. The Rise and Risks of the World's Most Popular Form of Government*, New York: Public Affairs Press.
Mansfield, Edward D. and Jack Snyder (2005), *Electing to Fight. Why Emerging Democracies Go to War*, Cambridge, MA: MIT Press.
Mantis, George and Richard N. Farmer (1968), 'Demand for life insurance', *Journal of Risk and Insurance*, **35**, 247–56.
Manweller, Mathew (2004), *The People versus the Courts: Initiative Elites, Judicial Review and Direct Democracy in the American Legal System*, Bethesda, MD: Academica Press.
Maoz, Zeev (2009), 'The effects of strategic and economic interdependence on international conflict across levels of analysis', *American Journal of Political Science*, **53**, 223–40.
Maoz, Zeev and Nasrin Abdolali (1989), 'Regime types and international conflict, 1816–1976', *Journal of Conflict Resolution*, **33**, 3–35.
Maoz, Zeev and Bruce Russett (1992), 'Alliance, contiguity, wealth, and political stability: is the lack of conflict among democracies a statistical artifact?', *International Interactions*, **17**, 245–67.
Maoz, Zeev and Bruce Russett (1993), 'Normative and structural causes of democratic peace, 1946–1986', *American Political Science Review*, **87**, 624–38.
Marjit, Sugata, Vivekananda Mukherjee, Arijit Mukherjee (2000), 'Harassment, corruption and tax policy', *European Journal of Political Economy*, **6**, 75–94.

Marks, Brian A. (1988), 'A model of judicial influence on congressional policy-making: *Grove City College v. Bell*', Working Paper in Political Science P-88-7, Hoover Institution.
Marshall, Alfred (1890), *Principles of Economics*, London: Macmillan.
Marshall, Monty G. and Keith Jaggers (2000), *Polity IV Project: Political Regime Characteristics and Transitions, 1800–1999*, INSCR Program, Center for International Development and Conflict Management.
Martin, Lisa L. (2006), 'Distribution, information and delegation to international organizations: the case of IMF conditionality', in Darren G. Hawkins, David A. Lake, Daniel L. Nielson and Michael J. Tierney (eds), *Delegation and Agency in International Organizations*, Cambridge: Cambridge University Press, pp. 140–64.
Marwell, Gerald and Ruth E. Ames (1979), 'Experiments on the provision of public goods. I. Resources, interest, group size, and the free-rider problem', *American Journal of Sociology*, **84**, 1335–60.
Marwell, Gerald and Ruth E. Ames (1980), 'Experiments on the provision of public goods. II. Provision points, stakes, experience, and the free-rider problem', *American Journal of Sociology*, **85**, 926–37.
Marwell, Gerald and Ruth E. Ames (1981), 'Economists free ride, does anyone else? Experiments on the provision of public goods, IV', *Journal of Public Economics*, **15**, 295–310.
Maskin, Eric and Jean Tirole (2004), 'The politician and the judge: accountability in government', *American Economic Review*, **94**, 1034–54.
Matsusaka, John G. (1992), 'Economics of direct legislation', *Quarterly Journal of Economics*, **107**, 541–71.
Matsusaka, John G. (1995), 'Fiscal effects of the voter initiative: evidence from the last 30 years', *Journal of Political Economy*, **103**, 587–623.
Matsusaka, John G. (2000a), 'Fiscal effects of the voter initiative in the first half of the 20th century', *Journal of Law and Economics*, **43**, 619–48.
Matsusaka, John G. (2000b), 'Elisabeth R. Gerber, *The Populist Paradox: Interest Group Influence and the Promise of Direct Legislation*' (book review), *Public Choice*, **104**, 394–7.
Matsusaka, John G. (2001), 'Problems with a methodology used to evaluate the voter initiative', *Journal of Politics*, **63**, 1250–56.
Matsusaka, John G. (2004), *For the Many or the Few: The Initiative, Public Policy, and American Democracy*, Chicago, IL: University of Chicago Press.
Matsusaka, John G. (2005a), 'The eclipse of legislatures: direct democracy in the 21st century', *Public Choice*, **124**, 157–77.
Matsusaka, John G. (2005b), 'Direct democracy works', *Journal of Economic Perspectives*, **19**, 185–206.
Matsusaka, John G. (2006), 'Direct democracy and electoral reform', in Michael P. McDonald and John Samples (eds), *The Marketplace of Democracy: Electoral Competition and American Politics*, Washington, DC: Brookings Institution Press, pp. 151–70.
Matsusaka, John G. (2007), 'Direct democracy and social issues', working paper, USC Marshall School of Business.
Matsusaka, John G. (2008), 'Direct democracy and the executive branch', in Shaun Bowler and Amihai Glazer (eds), *Direct Democracy's Impact on American Political Institutions*, New York: Palgrave MacMillan, pp. 115–35.
Matsusaka, John G. (2009), 'Direct democracy and public employees', *American Economic Review*, **99**, 2227–46.
Matsusaka, John G. (2010), 'Popular control of public policy: a quantitative approach', *Quarterly Journal of Political Science*, **5**, 133–67.
Matsusaka, John G. and Richard L. Hasen (2010), 'Aggressive enforcement of the single subject rule', *Election Law Journal*, **9**, 399–419.
Matsusaka, John G. and Nolan M. McCarty (2001), 'Political resource allocation: benefits and costs of voter initiatives', *Journal of Law, Economics, and Organization*, **17**, 413–48.
Maxwell, John W., Thomas P. Lyon and Steven C. Hackett (2000), 'Self-regulation and social welfare: the political economy of corporate environmentalism', *Journal of Law and Economics*, **43**, 583–617.

Mayer, Thomas (1999), *Monetary Policy and the Great Inflation in the United States: The Federal Reserve and the Failure of Macroeconomic Policy, 1965–79*, Cheltenham, UK and Northampton, MA, USA: Edward Elgar.

Mayhew, David R. (1966), *Party Loyalty among Congressmen*, Cambridge: Harvard University Press.

Mays, William (1961), 'Book review of *The Theory of Committees and Elections*' by Duncan Black, *Philosophy*, **36**, 248–9.

McBride, Michael and Gary Richardson (2012), 'Stopping suicide attacks: optimal strategies and unintended consequences', *Defence and Peace Economics*, **23**, 413–29.

McCall, Madhavi (2003), 'The Politics of judicial elections: the influence of campaign contributions on the voting patterns of Texas supreme court justices, 1994–1997', *Politics and Policy*, **31**, 314–43.

McCallum, Bennett T. (1978), 'The political business cycle: an empirical test', *Southern Economic Journal*, **44**, 504–15.

McCarty, Nolan and Lawrence S. Rothenberg (1996), 'Commitment and the campaign contribution contract', *American Journal of Political Science*, **40**, 872–904.

McChesney, Fred S. (1991), 'Rent extraction and interest-group organization in a Coasean model of regulation', *Journal of Legal Studies*, **20**, 73–90.

McChesney, Fred S. ([1991] 1995), 'Be true to your school: Chicago's contradictory views of antitrust and regulation', *Cato Journal*, **10**, 775–98, reprinted (and updated) in Fred S. McChesney and William F. Shughart II (eds), *The Causes and Consequences of Antitrust: The Public-Choice Perspective*, Chicago, IL: University of Chicago Press, pp. 323–40.

McChesney, Fred S. (1995), 'In search of the public-interest model of antitrust', in Fred S. McChesney and William F. Shughart II (eds), *The Causes and Consequences of Antitrust: The Public-Choice Perspective*, Chicago, IL: University of Chicago Press, pp. 25–32.

McChesney, Fred S. (1997), *Money for Nothing: Politicians, Rent Extraction, and Political Extortion*, Cambridge, MA: Harvard University Press.

McChesney Fred S. and William F. Shughart II (eds) (1995), *The Causes and Consequences of Antitrust: The Public-Choice Perspective*, Chicago, IL: University of Chicago Press

McCormick, Robert E. (1996), 'Book Review of *The Causes and Consequences of Antitrust: The Public-Choice Perspective*', *Public Choice*, **87**, 414–16.

McCormick, Robert E. and Robert D. Tollison (1981), *Politicians, Legislation, and the Economy: An Inquiry into the Interest-Group Theory of Government*, Boston, MA: Martinus Nijhoff.

McCormick, Robert E. and Chad S. Turner (2000), 'On legislatures and legislative wage efficiency', in William F. Shughart II and Laura Razzolini (eds), *The Elgar Companion to Public Choice*, Cheltenham, UK and Northampton, MA, USA: Edward Elgar, pp. 240–57.

McCubbins, Mathew D., Roger Noll and Barry L. Weingast (1987), 'Administrative procedures as instruments of political control', *Journal of Law, Economics, and Organization*, **3**, 243–77.

McCubbins, Mathew D., Roger Noll and Barry L. Weingast (1989), 'Structure and process, politics and policy: administrative arrangements and the political control of agencies', *Virginia Law Review*, **75**, 431–82.

McCubbins, Mathew D., Roger Noll and Barry R. Weingast (1995), 'Politics and courts: a positive theory of judicial doctrine and the rule of law', *Southern California Law Review*, **68**, 1631–83.

McDonald, Patrick (2009), *The Invisible Hand of Peace: Capitalism, the War Machine and International Relations Theory*, Cambridge: Cambridge University Press.

McGregor, Rob Roy (1996), 'FOMC voting behavior and electoral cycles: partisan ideology and partisan loyalty', *Economics and Politics*, **8**, 17–32.

McGuire, Robert A. (1988), 'Constitution making: a rational choice model of the Federal Convention of 1787', *American Journal of Political Science*, **32**, 483–522.

McGuire, Martin C. and Mancur Olson (1996), 'The economics of autocracy and majority rule: the invisible hand and the use of force', *Journal of Economic Literature*, **34**, 72–96.

McKelvey, Richard D. (1976), 'Intransitivities in multidimensional voting models and some implications for agenda control', *Journal of Economic Theory*, **18**, 1–22.

McKelvey, Richard D. and Peter C. Ordeshook (1982), 'Two-candidate elections without majority rule equilibria: an experimental study', *Simulation and Games*, **13**, 311–35.

McKelvey, Richard D. and Peter C. Ordeshook (1990), 'A decade of experimental research on spatial models of elections and committees', in James M. Enlow and Melvin J. Hinich (eds), *Readings in the Spatial Theory of Voting*, Cambridge, England: Cambridge University Press, pp. 99–144.
McKelvey, Richard D. and Thomas R. Palfrey (1995), 'Quantal response equilibria in normal form games', *Games and Economics Behavior*, **7**, 6–38.
McKelvey, Richard D. and Thomas R. Palfrey (1998), 'Quantal response equilibrium for extensive form games', *Experimental Economics*, **1**, 9–41.
McKenzie, Richard B. (ed.) (1984), *Constitutional Economics: Containing the Economic Powers of Government*, Lexington, MA: Lexington Books.
McKenzie, Richard B. and Robert J. Staaf (1978), 'Revenue sharing and monopoly government', *Public Choice*, **33**, 93–7.
McKitrick, Ross (2006), 'The politics of pollution: party regimes and air quality in Canada', *Canadian Journal of Economics*, **39**, 604–20.
McLean, Ian (1990), 'The Borda and Condorcet principles: three medieval applications', *Social Choice and Welfare*, **7**, 99–108.
McMillan, John and Christopher Woodruff (1999), 'Dispute resolution without courts in Vietnam', *Journal of Law, Economics, and Organization*, **15**, 637–58.
McNollgast (1995), 'Politics and the courts: a positive theory of judicial doctrine and the rule of law', *Southern California Law Review*, **68**, 1631–83.
Meade, James E. (1963), 'Book review of *The Calculus of Consent*' by James M. Buchanan and Gordon Tullock, *The Economic Journal*, **73**, 101–4.
Mehlum, Halvor, Karl Moene and Ragnar Torvik (2006), 'Institutions and the resource curse', *Economic Journal*, **116**, 1–20, reprinted in Roger D. Congleton, Arye L. Hillman and Kai A. Konrad (eds) (2008), *Forty Years of Research on Rent Seeking 2 – Applications: Rent Seeking in Practice*, Heidelberg: Springer, pp. 245–64.
Meier, Alfred and Susanne Haury (1990), 'A cognitive-evolutionary theory of economic policy', in Kurt Dopfer and Karl-Friedrich Raible (eds), *The Evolution of Economic Systems: Essays in Honour of Ota Sik*, London: Macmillan.
Meier, Kenneth J. and Kevin B. Smith (1994), 'Say it ain't so, Moe: institutional design, policy effectiveness, and drug policy, *Journal of Public Administration Research and Theory*, **4**, 429–42.
Meltzer, Allan H. and Scott F. Richard (1981), 'A rational theory of the size of government', *Journal of Political Economy*, **89**, 914–27.
Mertens, Karel and Morten O. Ravn (2009), 'Understanding the aggregate effects of anticipated and unanticipated tax policy shocks', *CEPR Discussion Papers*, no. 7505.
Metcalfe, J. Stanley (1994a), 'Competition, Fisher's principle and increasing returns in the selection process', *Journal of Evolutionary Economics*, **4**, 327–46.
Metcalfe, J. Stanley (1994b), 'Evolutionary economics and technology policy', *Economic Journal*, **104**, 931–44.
Metcalfe, J. Stanley (1995), 'Technology systems and technology policy in an evolutionary framework', *Cambridge Journal of Economics*, **19**, 25–46.
Mian, Atif, Amir Sufi and Francesco Trebbi (2010), 'The political economy of the US mortgage default crisis', *American Economic Review*, **100**, 1967–98.
Miceli, Thomas J. and Metin M. Coşgel (1994), 'Reputation and judicial decision-making', *Journal of Economic Behavior and Organization*, **23**, 31–51.
Miguel, Edward, Shanker Satyanath and Ernest Sergenti (2004), 'Economic shocks and civil conflict: an instrumental variables approach', *Journal of Political Economy*, **112**, 725–53.
Milgrom, Paul and John Roberts (1992), *Economics, Organization, and Management*, Englewood Cliffs, NJ: Prentice-Hall.
Mill, John Stuart (1861), *Considerations on Representative Government*, London: Savill and Edwards.
Miller, Kenneth P. (2009), *Direct Democracy and the Courts*, New York: Cambridge University Press.
Milligan, Kevin, Enrique Moretti and Philip Oreopoulos (2004), 'Does education improve

citizenship? Evidence from the United States and the United Kingdom', *Journal of Public Economics*, **88**, 1667–95.

Millner, Edward L. and Michael D. Pratt (1989), 'An experimental investigation of efficient rent-seeking', *Public Choice*, **62**, 139–51.

Millner, Edward L. and Michael D. Pratt (1991), 'Risk aversion and rent-seeking: An extension and some experimental evidence', *Public Choice*, **69**, 81–92.

Mills, Jon (2004), 'Principles for constitutions and institutions in promoting the rule of law', *Florida Journal of International Law*, **16**, 115–31.

Milyo, Jeffrey (1997), 'The electoral and financial effects of changes in committee power: GRH, TRA86, and money committees in the U.S. House', *Journal of Law and Economics*, **40**, 93–112.

Milyo, Jeffrey (2001), 'What do candidates maximize (and why should anyone care)?', *Public Choice*, **109**, 119–39.

Minford, Patrick and David Peel (1982), 'The political theory of the business cycle', *European Economic Review*, **17**, 253–70.

Mintrom, Michael (1997), 'Policy entrepreneurs and the diffusion of innovation', *American Journal of Political Science*, **41**, 738–70.

Mises, Ludwig (1944), *Bureaucracy*, New Haven: Yale University Press.

Mishra, Santap Sanhari and Rahul Gupta (2007), 'Corruption and its treatment: an Indian perspective', in Rahul Gupta and Santap Sanhari Mishra (eds), *Corruption: The Causes and Combating Strategies*, Hyderabad: ICFAI University Press, pp. 278–93.

Mitchell, William C. (1974), 'Book review of *Bureaucracy and Representative Government*' by William A. Niskanen, *The American Political Science Review*, **68**, 1775–7.

Mitchell, William C. (1984), 'Schumpeter and public choice, part I: precursor of public choice?', *Public Choice*, **42**, 73–88.

Mitchell, William C. (1988), 'Virginia, Rochester, and Bloomington: twenty-five years of public choice and political science', *Public Choice*, **56**, 110–19.

Mitchell, William C. (2001), 'The old and new public choice: Chicago versus Virginia', in William F. Shughart II and Laura Razzolini (eds), *The Elgar Companion to Public Choice*, Cheltenham, UK and Northampton, MA, USA: Edward Elgar, pp. 3–32.

Mitchell, William and Michael C. Munger (1991), 'Economic models of interest groups: an introductory survey', *American Journal of Political Science*, **35**, 512–46.

Mitchell, William C. and Randy T. Simmons (1994), *Beyond Politics: Markets, Welfare, and the Failure of Bureaucracy*, Boulder, CO: Westview Press for the Independent Institute Book.

Mitnick, Barry M. (1975), 'The theory of agency: the policing 'paradox' and regulatory behavior', *Public Choice*, **24**, 27–42.

Mizuno, Nobuhiro and Ryosuke Okazawa (2009), 'Colonial experience and postcolonial underdevelopment in Africa', *Public Choice*, **141**, 405–19.

Moe, Terry. M. (1987), 'An assessment of the positive theory of congressional dominance', *Legislative Studies Quarterly*, **12**, 472–520.

Moe, Terry M. (1990), 'Political institutions – the neglected side of the story', *Journal of Law, Economics, and Organization*, **6**, 213–53.

Moe, Terry M. (1997), 'The positive theory of public bureaucracy', in Dennis C. Mueller (ed), *Perspectives on Public Choice: A Handbook*, Cambridge and New York: Cambridge University Press, pp. 455–80.

Moe, Terry M. and Michael Caldwell (1994), 'The institutional foundations of democratic government: a comparison of presidential and parliamentary systems', *Journal of Institutional and Theoretical Economics*, **150**, 171–95.

Moesen, Wim and Philippe van Cauwenberge (2000), 'The status of the budget constraint, federalism and the relative size of government', *Public Choice*, **104**, 207–24.

Mohammad, Sharif and John Whalley (1984), 'Rent seeking in India: its costs and policy significance', *Kyklos*, **37**, 387–413.

Mokyr, Joel (1990), *The Level of Riches*, Oxford: Oxford University Press.

Montalvo, José G. and Marta Reynal-Querol (2005), 'Ethnic polarization, potential conflict, and civil wars', *American Economic Review*, **95**, 796–816.

Moon, Woojin (2006), 'The paradox of less efficient incumbent spending: theory and tests', *British Journal of Political Science*, **36**, 705–21.
Moore, Cristopher J. (2004), *In Other Words*, New York: Walker.
Moore, Michael O. (1992), 'Rules or politics? An empirical analysis of ITC anti-dumping decisions', *Economic Inquiry*, **30**, 449–66.
Moran, Mark J. and Barry R. Weingast (1982), 'Congress as the source of regulatory decisions: the case of the Federal Trade Commission', *American Economic Review*, **72**, 109–13.
Moreau, François (2004), 'The role of the state in evolutionary economics', *Cambridge Journal of Economics*, **28**, 847–74.
Morriss, Andrew, Michael Heise and Gregory C. Sisk (2005), 'Signaling and precedent in federal district court opinions', *Supreme Court Economic Review*, **13**, 63–97.
Morton, Rebecca and Charles Cameron (1992), 'Elections and the theory of campaign contributions: a survey and critical analysis', *Economics and Politics*, **4**, 79–108.
Moulin, Herve (1983). *The Strategy of Social Choice*. Amsterdam: North Holland.
Moulin, Herve and H. Peyton Young (1987), 'Condorcet, M.', in John Eatwell, Murray Milgate and Peter Newman (eds), *The New Palgrave: A Dictionary of Economics*. London: Macmillan, pp. 566–7.
Mousseau, Michael (2000), 'Market prosperity, democratic consolidation, and democratic peace', *Journal of Conflict Resolution*, **44**, 472–507.
Mousseau, Michael (2002), 'An economic limitation to the zone of democratic peace and cooperation', *International Interactions*, **28**, 137–64.
Mousseau, Michael (2003), 'The nexus of market society, liberal preferences, and democratic peace: interdisciplinary theory and evidence', *International Studies Quarterly*, **47**, 483–510.
Mousseau, Michael (2005), 'Comparing new theory with prior beliefs: market civilization and the liberal peace', *Conflict Management and Peace Science*, **22**, 63–77.
Mousseau, Michael (2009), 'The social market roots of the democratic peace', *International Security*, **33**, 52–86.
Mousseau, Michael, Håvard Hegre and John R. O'Neal (2003), 'How the wealth of nations conditions the liberal peace', *European Journal of International Relations*, **9**, 277–314.
Mueller, Dennis C. (1967), 'The firm decision process: an econometric investigation', *Quarterly Journal of Economics*, **81**, 58–87.
Mueller, Dennis C. (1993), 'The future of public choice', in Dennis C. Mueller, *The Public Choice Approach to Politics*, Aldershot, UK and Brookfield, VT, USA: Edward Elgar, pp. 510–14.
Mueller, Dennis C. (2003), *Public Choice III*, Cambridge: Cambridge University Press.
Mueller, Dennis C. (2008), 'Constitutions, economic approach to', in Steven N. Durlauf and Lawrence E. Blume (eds), *The New Palgrave Dictionary of Economics*, Basingstoke: Palgrave Macmillan.
Mueller, Dennis C. (2009), *Reason, Religion, and Democracy*, Cambridge: Cambridge University Press.
Mukand, Sharun W. and Dani Rodrik (2005), 'In search of the holy grail: policy convergence, experimentation, and economic performance', *American Economic Review*, **95**, 374–83.
Müller, Wolfgang C. (2002), 'Parties and the institutional framework', in Kurt R. Luther and Ferdinand Müller-Rommel (eds), *Political Parties in the New Europe*, Oxford: Oxford University Press, pp. 249–93.
Munck, Gerardo and Jay Verkuilen (2002), 'Conceptualizing and measuring democracy: evaluating alternative indices', *Comparative Political Studies*, **35**, 5–34.
Munger, Michael C. (1988), 'Allocation of desirable committee assignments: extended queues versus committee expansion', *American Journal of Political Science*, **32**, 317–44.
Munger, Michael C. (1989), 'A simple test of the thesis that committee jurisdictions shape corporate PAC contributions', *Public Choice*, **62**, 181–6.
Munley, Vincent G. (1984), 'Has the median voter found a ballot box that he can control?', *Economic Inquiry*, **22**, 323–36.
Murphy, Kevin M., Andrei Shleifer and Robert W. Vishny (1993), 'Why is rent seeking so costly to growth?', *American Economic Review*, **83**, 409–14, reprinted in Roger D. Congleton, Arye

L. Hillman and Kai A. Konrad (eds) (2008), *Forty Years of Research on Rent Seeking 2 – Applications: Rent Seeking in Practice*, Heidelberg: Springer, pp. 213–18.
Murrell, Peter (1992), 'Evolutionary and radical approaches to economic reform', *Economics of Planning*, **25**, 79–95.
Musgrave, Richard A. (1959), *The Theory of Public Finance*, New York: McGraw-Hill.
Myerson, Roger B. (2008), 'The autocrat's credibility problem and foundations of the constitutional state', *American Political Science Review*, **102**, 125–39.
Nagel, Stuart S. (1961), 'Political party affiliation and judges' decisions', *American Political Science Review*, **55**, 843–50.
Nagel, Stuart S. (1973), *Comparing Elected and Appointed Judicial Systems*, Beverly Hills, CA: Sage Publications.
Nannestad, Peter (2004), 'Immigration as a challenge to the Danish welfare state?', *European Journal of Political Economy*, **20**, 755–67, reprinted in Roger D. Congleton, Arye L. Hillman and Kai A. Konrad (eds) (2008), *Forty Years of Research on Rent Seeking 2 – Applications: Rent Seeking in Practice*, Heidelberg: Springer, pp. 281–93.
Napolitano, Giulio and Michele Abrescia (2010), *Analisi Economica del Diritto Pubblico*, Bologna: Il Mulino.
Naughton, Barry (1995), *Growing Out of the Plan*, Cambridge: Cambridge University Press.
Neary, Hugh M. (1997), 'A comparison of rent-seeking models and economic models of conflict', *Public Choice*, **93**, 373–88.
Neck, Reinhard and Michael Getzner (2001), 'Politico-economic determinants of public debt growth: a case study for Austria', *Public Choice*, **109**, 243–68.
Neff, Joseph and Anne Blythe (2007), 'Panel disbars Duke lacrosse prosecutor', *Raleigh News & Observer*, 16 June.
Nelson, Michael A. (1986), 'An empirical analysis of state and local tax structure in the context of the Leviathan model of government', *Public Choice*, **49**, 283–94.
Nelson, Michael A. (1990), 'Decentralization of the subnational public sector: an empirical analysis of the determinants of local government structure in metropolitan areas in the U.S.', *Southern Economic Journal*, **57**, 443–57.
Ni, Yongmei (2009), 'The impact of charter schools on the efficiency of traditional public schools: evidence from Michigan', *Economics of Education Review*, **28**, 571–84.
Nishimura, Kazuo and Junsen Zhang (1995), 'Sustainable plans of social security with endogenous fertility', *Oxford Economics Papers*, **47**, 182–94.
Niskanen. William A. (1971), *Bureaucracy and Representative Government*, Chicago, IL: Aldine-Atherton.
Niskanen, Wiliam A. (1975), 'Bureaucrats and politicians', *Journal of Law and Economics*, **18**, 617–44.
Niskanen, William A. (1994), *Bureaucracy and Public Economics*, Aldershot, UK and Brookfield, VT, USA: Edward Elgar.
Niskanen, William A. (2001), 'Bureaucracy', in William F. Shughart II and Laura Razzolini (eds), *The Elgar Companion to Public Choice*, Cheltenham, UK and Northampton, MA, USA: Edward Elgar, pp. 258–70.
Nkrumah, Kwame (1967), 'African socialism revisited', in *Africa: National and Social Revolution: Collection of Papers read at the Cairo Seminar*, Prague: Peace and Socialism, pp. 200–208.
Noelle-Neumann, Elisabeth (1993), *The Spiral of Silence: Public Opinion – Our Social Skin*, Chicago, IL: University of Chicago Press.
Nordhaus, William (1975), 'The political business cycle', *Review of Economic Studies*, **42**, 169–90.
Nordhaus, William D. (1989), 'Alternative approaches to the political business cycle', *Brookings Papers on Economic Activity*, **2**, 1–68.
North, Douglass C. (1981), *Structure and Change in Economic History*, New York: Norton.
North, Douglass C. (1990), *Institutions, Institutional Change, and Economic Performance*, Cambridge: Cambridge University Press.
North, Douglass C. (1991), 'Institutions', *Journal of Economic Perspectives*, **5**, 97–112.
North, Douglass C. (2005), *Understanding the Process of Economic Change*, Princeton, NJ: Princeton University Press.

North, Douglass C. and Barry R. Weingast (1989), 'Constitutions and commitment: the evolution of institutions governing public choice in seventh-century England', *Journal of Economic History*, **49**, 803–32.
Noury, Abdul G. and Gérard Roland (2002), 'More power to the European parliament?', *Economic Policy*, **17**, 279–319.
Nozick, Robert (1974), *Anarchy, State, and Utopia*, New York: Basic Books.
Nti, Kofi O. (1999), 'Rent seeking with asymmetric valuations', *Public Choice*, **98**, 415–30, reprinted in Roger D. Congleton, Arye L. Hillman and Kai A. Konrad (eds) (2008), *Forty Years of Research on Rent Seeking 1 – The Theory of Rent Seeking*, Heidelberg: Springer, pp. 149–64.
Nugent, Neill (1999), *The Government and Politics of the European Union*, Houndmills: Macmillan.
O'Brien, David M. (2006), 'The politics of judicial selection and appointments in Japan and ten south and southeast Asian countries', in Kate Malleson and Peter H. Russell (eds), *Appointing Judges in an Age of Judicial Power*, Toronto: University of Toronto Press, pp. 355–74.
O'Donnell, Guillermo A. (1973), *Modernization and Bureaucratic-Authoritarianism; Studies in South American Politics*, Berkeley, CA: Institute of International Studies, University of California.
O'Donnell, Guillermo A. (1999), *Counterpoints: Selected Essays on Authoritarianism and Democratization*, Notre Dame, IN: University of Notre Dame Press.
O'Donnell, Guillermo A., Philippe C. Schmitter and Laurence Whitehead (1986), *Transitions from Authoritarian Rule: Latin America*, Baltimore, MD: Johns Hopkins University Press.
O'Donnell, Guillermo A., J. Vargas Cullel and Osvaldo M. Iazzetta (2004), *The Quality of Democracy: Theory and Applications*, Notre Dame, IN: University of Notre Dame Press.
O'Driscoll, Gerald (1980), 'Justice, efficiency, and economic analysis of law', *Journal of Legal Studies*, **9**, 355–66.
O'Hara, Erin A. (1993), 'Social constraint or implicit collusion? Toward a game theoretic analysis of stare decisis', *Seton Hall Law Review*, **24**, 736–78.
O'Hara, Erin A. and Larry E. Ribstein (2000), 'From politics to efficiency in choice of law', *University of Chicago Law Review*, **67**, 1151–232.
O'Reilly, Jacqueline, Bernd Reissert and Volker Eichener (1996), 'European regulation of social standards: social security, working time, workplace participation, occupational health and safety', in Günter Schmid, Jacqueline O'Reilly and Klaus Schömann (eds), *International Handbook of Labour Market Policy and Evaluation*, Cheltenham, UK and Northampton, MA, USA: Edward Elgar, pp. 868–98.
Oates, Wallace E. (1972), *Fiscal Federalism*, New York: Harcourt Brace Jovanovich.
Oates, Wallace E. (1985), 'Searching for Leviathan: an empirical study', *American Economic Review*, **75**, 748–57.
Oates, Wallace E. (1999), 'An essay on fiscal federalism', *Journal of Economic Literature*, **37**, 133–45.
Oates, Wallace E. and Paul R. Portney (2003), 'The political economy of environmental policy', in Karl-Göran Mäler and Jeffrey R. Vincent (eds), *Handbook of Environmental Economics*, vol. 1, Amsterdam: North Holland, pp. 325–54.
Ober, Josiah (2008), *Democracy and Knowledge: Innovation and Learning in Classical Athens*, Princeton, NJ: Princeton University Press.
Oko, Okechukwu (2005), 'Seeking justice in transitional societies: an analysis of the problems and failures of the judiciary in Nigeria', *Brooklyn Journal of International Law*, **31**, 9–82
Okruch, Stefan (2003), 'Knowledge and economic policy: a plea for political experimentalism', in Pavel Pelikan and Gerhard Wegner (eds), *The Evolutionary Analysis of Economic Policy*, Cheltenham, UK and Northampton, MA, USA: Edward Elgar, pp. 67–95.
Ollson, Ola (2007), 'Conflict diamonds', *Journal of Development Economics*, **82**, 267–86.
Olson, Mancur (1962), 'Book review of *The Calculus of Consent*' by James M. Buchanan and Gordon Tullock, *The American Economic Review*, **52**, 1217–18.
Olson, Mancur (1965), *The Logic of Collective Action: Public Goods and the Theory of Groups*, Cambridge, MA: Harvard University Press.
Olson, Mancur (1993), 'Dictatorship, democracy and development', *American Political Science Review*, **87**, 567–76.

Olson, Mancur (2000), *Power and Prosperity: Outgrowing Communist and Capitalist Dictatorships*, New York: Basic Books.
Olson, Walter (2003), *The Rule of Lawyers: How the New Litigation Elite Threatens America's Rule of Law*, New York: St. Martin's Press.
Oneal, John R. (2003), 'Measuring interdependence and its pacific benefits', *Journal of Peace Research*, **40**, 721–5.
Oneal, John R. and J.L. Ray (1997), 'New tests of the democratic peace: controlling for economic interdependence, 1950–85', *Political Research Quarterly*, **50**, 751–75.
Oneal, John R. and Bruce M. Russett (1997), 'The classical liberals were right: democracy, interdependence, and conflict, 1950–1985', *International Studies Quarterly*, **41**, 267–93.
Oneal, John R. and Bruce M. Russett (1999), 'The Kantian peace: the pacific benefits of democracy, interdependence, and international organizations, 1885–1992', *World Politics*, **52**, 1–37.
Oneal, John R., Frances H. Oneal, Zeev Maoz and Bruce M. Russett (1996), 'The liberal peace: interdependence, democracy, and international conflict, 1950–85', *Journal of Peace Research*, **33**, 11–28.
Oneal, John R., Bruce M. Russett and Michael L. Berbaum (2004), 'Causes of peace: democracy, interdependence, and international organizations, 1885–1992', *International Studies Quarterly*, **47**, 371–93.
Ordeshook, Peter C. (1992), 'Constitutional stability', *Constitutional Political Economy*, **3**, 137–75.
Orr, Daniel (1987), 'Notes on the mass media as an economic institution', *Public Choice*, **53**, 79–95.
Ortuño-Ortín, Ignacio and Christian Schultz (2005), 'Public funding of political parties', *Journal of Public Economic Theory*, **7**, 781–91.
Osborne, David and Ted Gaebler (1992), *Reinventing Government: How the Entrepreneurial Spirit is Transforming the Public Sector*, Reading, MA: Addison-Wesley.
Ostrom, Elinor (1990), *Governing the Commons. The Evolution of Institutions for Collective Action*, Cambridge: Cambridge University Press.
Ostrom, Elinor and James K. Walker (1991), 'Communication in a commons: cooperation without external enforcement', in Thomas R. Palfrey (ed.), *Laboratory Research in Political Economy*, Ann Arbor, MI: University of Michigan Press, pp. 287–322.
Ostrom, Elinor, Roy Gardner and James Walker (1994), *Rules, Games, and Common Pool Resources*, Ann Arbor, MI: University of Michigan Press.
Owen, John M. (1997), *Liberal Peace, Liberal War: American Politics and International Security*, Ithaca, NY: Cornell University Press.
Padovano, Fabio (1995), *A Positive Theory of Political Collusion and Government Growth*, Ph.D. dissertation, George Mason University.
Padovano, Fabio and Francesco Lagona (2008), 'The political legislation cycle', *Public Choice*, **134**, 201–29.
Padovano, Fabio and Roberto Ricciuti (2009), 'Political competition and economic performance: evidence from the Italian regions', *Public Choice*, **138**, 263–77.
Pagden, Anthony (2008), *Worlds at War: The 2,500 Year Struggle Between East and West*, New York: Random House.
Palfrey, Thomas R. (2006), 'Laboratory experiments in political economy', in Barry R. Weingast and Donald Wittman (eds), *The Handbook of Political Economy*, Oxford: Oxford University Press, pp. 941–63.
Palfrey, Thomas R. and Jeffrey E. Prisbey (1996), 'Altruism, reputation and noise in linear public goods experiments', *Journal of Public Economics*, **61**, 409–27.
Palfrey, Thomas R. and Jeffrey E. Prisbey (1997), 'Anomalous behavior in public goods experiments: how much and why?', *American Economic Review*, **87**, 829–46.
Palfrey, Thomas R. and Howard Rosenthal (1983), 'A strategic calculus of voting', *Public Choice*, **41**, 7–53.
Pape, Robert A. (1997), 'Why economic sanctions do not work', *International Security*, **22**, 90–136.
Pape, Robert A. (2005), *Dying to Win: The Strategic Logic of Suicide Terrorism*, New York: Random House.
Park, Hyun, Apostolis Philippopoulos and Vanghelis Vassilatos (2005), 'Choosing the size of the

public sector under rent seeking from state coffers', *European Journal of Political Economy*, **21**, 830–50.
Parker, Glenn R. and Suzanne L. Parker (1998), 'The economic organization of legislatures and how it affects congressional voting', *Public Choice*, **95**, 117–29.
Parkinson, Cyril N. (1957), *Parkinson's Law*, New York: Ballantine Books.
Parsons, Wes (1983), 'The inefficient common law', *Yale Law Journal*, **92**, 863–87.
Pashigian, Peter (1985), 'Environmental regulation: whose self-interests are being protected?', *Economic Inquiry*, **23**, 551–84.
Patterson, James T. (1967), *Congressional Conservatism and the New Deal: The Growth of the Conservative Coalition in Congress, 1933–1939*, Lexington, KY: University of Kentucky Press.
Pauly, Mark V. (1974), 'Overinsurance and public provision of insurance: the roles of moral hazard and adverse selection', *Quarterly Journal of Economics*, **88**, 44–62.
Pauly, Mark V. (1988), 'Positive political economy of Medicare, past and future', in Mark V. Pauly and William L. Kissick (eds) and Laura E. Roper (associate ed.), *Lessons from the First Twenty Years of Medicare: Research Implications for Public and Private Sector Policy*, Philadelphia, PA: University of Pennsylvania Press, pp. 49–72.
Pecquet, Gary M., R. Morris Coats and Steven T. Yen (1996), 'Special versus general elections and composition of the voters: evidence from Louisiana school tax elections', *Public Finance Quarterly*, **24**, 131–47.
Peirce, William S. (1991), 'Unanimous decisions in a redistributive context: the council of ministers of the European Union', in Roland Vaubel and Thomas D. Willett (eds), *The Political Economy of International Organizations: A Public Choice Approach*, Boulder, CO: Westview Press, pp. 267–85.
Pejovich, Svetozar (2006), 'The effects of the interaction of formal and informal institutions on social stability and economic development', in Kartik C. Roy and Jörn Sideras (eds), *Institutions, Globalisation and Empowerment*, Cheltenham, UK and Northampton, MA, USA: Edward Elgar, pp. 56–74.
Pelikan, Pavel (2003), 'Why economics policies need comprehensive evolutionary analysis', in Pavel Pelikan and Gerhard Wegner (eds), *The Evolutionary Analysis of Economic Policy*, Cheltenham, UK and Northampton, MA, USA: Edward Elgar, pp. 15–45.
Peltzman, Sam (1976), 'Toward a more general theory of regulation', *Journal of Law and Economics*, **19**, 211–40.
Peltzman, Sam (1980), 'The growth of government' *Journal of Law and Economics*, **23**, 209–87.
Pennock, Roland (1958), 'Book review of *An Economic Theory of Democracy*' by Anthony Downs, *The American Political Science Review*, **52**, 539–41.
Peoples, James (1998), 'Deregulation and the labor market', *Journal of Economic Perspectives*, **12**, 111–30.
Perotti, Roberto (2005), 'Estimating the effects of fiscal policy in OECD countries', CEPR Discussion Paper, no. 4842.
Persson, Torsten and Guido Tabellini (2000), *Political Economics: Explaining Economic Policy*, Cambridge, MA: The MIT Press.
Persson, Torsten and Guido Tabellini (2003), *The Economic Effects of Constitutions*, Cambridge: MIT Press.
Persson, Torsten, Gérard Roland and Guido Tabellini (1997), 'Separation of powers and political accountability', *Quarterly Journal of Economics*, **112**, 1163–202.
Persson, Torsten, Gérard Roland and Guido Tabellini (2004), 'How do electoral rules shape party structures, government coalitions and economic policies?', *CEPR Discussion Paper*, no. 4226, London: Centre for Economic Policy Research, available at: http://www.cepr.org/pubs/dps/DP4226.asp (accessed 20 May 2012).
Pietrantonio, Rinaldo (2011), 'Different schemes for healthcare expenditure: a political economy study on OECD countries', unpublished PhD dissertation (draft), George Mason University, Fairfax, VA.
Pincus, Steven C.A. (2009), *1688: The First Modern Revolution*, New Haven, CT: Yale University Press.

Pitlik, Hans (2007), 'A race to liberalization? Diffusion of economic policy reform among OECD-economies', *Public Choice*, **132**, 159–78.
Pittman, Russell W. (1988), 'Rent-seeking and market structure: comment', *Public Choice*, **58**, 173–85.
Plato ([n.d.] 1945), *The Republic of Plato*, trans. Francis MacDonald Cornford, London and New York: Oxford University Press.
Plott, Charles R. (1987), 'Dimensions of parallelism: some policy applications of experimental methods', in Alvin E. Roth (ed), *Laboratory Experimentation in Economics: Six Points of View*, New York: Cambridge University Press, pp. 193–229.
Plott, Charles R. (1991), 'A comparative analysis of direct democracy, two-candidate elections and three-candidate elections in an experimental environment', in Thomas R. Palfrey (ed), *Contemporary Laboratory Research in Political Economy*, Ann Arbor, MI: University of Michigan Press, pp. 11–31.
Plott, Charles R. and Michael E. Levine (1977), 'Agenda influence and its implications', *Virginia Law Review*, **63**, 561–604.
Plutzer, Eric (2002), 'Becoming a habitual voter: inertia, resources, and growth in young adulthood', *American Political Science Review*, **96**, 41–56.
Polachek, Solomon W. (1980), 'Conflict and trade', *Journal of Conflict Resolution*, **24**, 55–78.
Polachek, Solomon W. (1992), 'Conflict and trade: an economics approach to political international interactions', *Peace Economics, Peace Science and Public Policy*, **5**(2), art. 3, reprinted in Walter Isard and Charles Anderton (eds) (1999), *Economics of Arms Reduction and the Peace Process*, Amsterdam: Elsevier Science, pp. 89–120.
Polachek, Solomon W. and Judith A. McDonald (1992), 'Strategic trade and the incentive for cooperation', in Manas Chatterji and Linda Rennie Forcey (eds), *Disarmament, Economic Conversion, and Management of Peace*, Westport, CT: Praeger, pp. 273–84.
Polinsky, A. Mitchell and Steven Shavell (1998), 'Punitive damages: an economic analysis', *Harvard Law Review*, **111**, 869–962.
Pollak, Robert A. (1985), 'A transaction cost approach to families and households', *Journal of Economic Literature*, **23**, 581–608.
Poma, Gabriella (2009), *Le Istituzioni Politiche del Mondo Romano*, Bologna: Il Mulino.
Poole, Keith T. and Thomas Romer (1985), 'Patterns of political action committee contributions to the 1980 campaigns for the U.S. House of Representatives', *Public Choice*, **47**, 63–112.
Poole, Keith T. and Howard Rosenthal (1997), *Congress: A Political-Economic History of Roll Call Voting*, New York: Oxford University Press.
Poole, Keith T., Thomas Romer and Howard Rosenthal (1987), 'The revealed preferences of political action committees', *American Economic Review*, **77**, 298–302.
Posner, Daniel N. (2004), 'The political salience of cultural difference: why Chewas and Tumbukas are allies in Zambia and adversaries in Malawi', *American Political Science Review*, **98**, 529–45.
Posner, Richard A. (1970), 'A statistical study of antitrust enforcement, *Journal of Law and Economics*, **13**, 365–419.
Posner, Richard A. (1973), *Economic Analysis of Law*, Boston, MA: Little Brown.
Posner, Richard A. (1975), 'The social costs of monopoly and regulation', *Journal of Political Economy*, **83**, 807–27, reprinted in Roger D. Congleton, Arye L. Hillman and Kai A. Konrad (eds) (2008), *Forty Years of Research on Rent Seeking 2 – Applications: Rent Seeking in Practice*, Heidelberg: Springer, pp. 45–65.
Posner, Richard A. (1992), *Economic Analysis of Law*, 4th edn, Boston: Little, Brown.
Posner, Richard A. (1993), 'What do judges and justices maximize? (The same thing everybody else does)', *Supreme Court Economic Review*, **3**, 1–41.
Posner, Richard A. (2007), *Economic Analysis of Law*, 7th edn, New York: Aspen Law and Business.
Powell, Robert (2006), 'War as a commitment problem', *International Organization*, **60**, 169–203.
Poterba, James M. (1995), 'State responses to fiscal crises: the effects of budgetary institutions and politics', *Journal of Political Economy*, **102**, 799–821.
Poterba, James M. (1997), 'Do budget rules work?', National Bureau of Economic Research, NBER Working Paper Series, no. 5550, Cambridge, MA.

Potters, Jan and Randolph Sloof (1996), 'Interest groups: a survey of empirical models that try to assess their influence', *European Journal of Political Economy*, **12**, 403–42.
Potters, Jan, Randolph Sloof and Frans van Winden (1997), 'Campaign expenditures, contributions, and direct endorsements: the strategic use of information and money to influence voter behavior', *European Journal of Political Economy*, **13**, 1–31.
Potters, Jan, Caspar G. de Vries and Frans van Winden (1998), 'An experimental investigation of rational rent seeking', *European Journal of Political Economy*, **14**, 783–800, reprinted in Roger D. Congleton, Arye L. Hillman and Kai A. Konrad (eds) (2008), *Forty Years of Research on Rent Seeking 1 – The Theory of Rent Seeking*, Heidelberg: Springer, pp. 663–80.
Powell, Lynda W. (1989), 'Analyzing misinformation: perceptions of congressional candidates' ideologies', *American Journal of Political Science*, **33**, 272–93.
Prat, Andrea (2002a), 'Campaign advertising and voter welfare', *Review of Economic Studies*, **69**, 999–1018.
Prat, Andrea (2002b), 'Campaign spending with office-seeking politicians, rational voters, and multiple lobbies', *Journal of Economic Theory*, **103**, 162–89.
Priest, George L. (1977), 'The common law process and the selection of efficient rules', *Journal of Legal Studies*, **6**, 65–82.
Prisching, Manfred (1995), 'The limited rationality of democracy: Schumpeter as the founder of irrational choice theory', *Critical Review*, **9**, 301–24.
Przeworski, Adam (1991), *Democracy and the Market*, Cambridge: Cambridge University Press.
Przeworski, Adam and Fernando Limongi (1993), 'Political regimes and economic growth', *Journal of Economic Perspectives*, **7**, 51–69.
Przeworski, Adam and James R. Vreeland (2000), 'The effect of IMF programs on economic growth', *Journal of Development Economics*, **62**, 385–421.
Przeworski, Adam, Michael E. Alvarez, José A. Cheibub and Fernando Limongi (2000), *Democracy and Development: Political Institutions and Material Well-Being in the World, 1950–1990*, Cambridge and New York: Cambridge University Press.
Puckett, Richard H. (1984), 'Federal Open Market Committee structure and decisions', *Journal of Monetary Economics*, **14**, 97–104.
Quattrone, George A. and Amos Tversky (1988), 'Contrasting rational and psychological analysis of political choice', *American Political Science Review*, **82**, 719–36.
Ragsdale, Lyn and Timothy E. Cook (1987), 'Representatives' actions and challengers' reactions: limits to candidate connections in the House', *American Journal of Political Science*, **31**, 45–81.
Raknerud, Arvid and H. Hegre (1997), 'The hazard of war: reassessing the evidence for the democratic peace', *Journal of Peace Research*, **34**, 385–404.
Ram, Rati (1986), 'Government size and economic growth: a new framework and some evidence from cross-section and time series data', *American Economic Review*, **76**, 191–203.
Ram, Rati (1989), 'Government size and economic growth: A new framework and some evidence from cross-section and time series data: Reply', *American Economic Review*, **79**, 281–4.
Ramakrishnan, S. Karthick and Mark Baldassare (2004), *The Ties that Bind: Changing Demographics and Civic Engagement in California*, San Francisco, CA: Public Policy Institute of California.
Ramey, Valerie A. and Matthew D. Shapiro (1998), 'Costly capital reallocation and the effects of government spending', *Carnegie Rochester Conference on Public Policy*, **48**, 145–94.
Ramírez, Carlos D. and Christian Eigen-Zucchi (2001), 'Understanding the Clayton Act of 1914: an analysis of the interest group hypothesis', *Public Choice*, **106**, 157–81.
Ramseyer, J. Mark (1994), 'The puzzling (in)dependence of courts: a comparative approach', *Journal of Legal Studies*, **23**, 721–47.
Ramseyer, J. Mark and Eric B. Rasmusen (1997), 'Judicial independence in a civil law regime: the evidence from Japan', *Journal of Law, Economics, and Organization*, **13**, 259–86.
Ramseyer, J. Mark and Eric B. Rasmusen (2003), *Measuring Judicial Independence: The Political Economy of Judging in Japan*, Chicago, IL: University of Chicago Press.
Randazzo, Kirk A. (2008), 'Strategic anticipation and the hierarchy of justice in the U.S. district courts', *American Politics Research*, **36**, 669–93.

Rapoport, David C. (1984), 'Fear and trembling: terrorism in three religious traditions', *American Political Science Review*, **78**, 658–77.
Rapoport, David C. (1992), 'Terrorism', in Mary Hawkesworth and Maurice Kogan (eds), *Routledge Encyclopedia of Government and Politics*, vol. 2, London: Routledge, pp. 1061–79.
Rapoport, Amnon, David V. Budescu and Ramzi Suleiman (1993), 'Sequential requests from randomly distributed shared resources', *Journal of Mathematical Psychology*, **37**, 241–65.
Rasmusen, Eric B. (1994), 'Judicial legitimacy as a repeated game', *Journal of Law, Economics, and Organization*, **10**, 63–83.
Rauchhaus, Robert (2009), 'Evaluating the nuclear peace hypothesis: a quantitative approach', *Journal of Conflict Resolution*, **53**, 258–77.
Rawls, John (1971), *A Theory of Justice*, Cambridge, MA: Harvard University Press.
Ray, James L. (1993), 'Wars between democracies: rare, or nonexistent?', *International Interactions*, **18**, 251–76.
Razo, Armando (2008), *Social Foundations of Limited Dictatorship*, Stanford, CA: Stanford University Press.
Razo, Armando (2010), 'Social structures, informal institutions, and governance in dictatorships', unpublished manuscript, Bloomington, IN: Indiana University.
Regan, Patrick M., Richard W. Frank and David H. Clark (2009), 'New datasets on political institutions and elections, 1972–2005', *Conflict Management and Peace Science*, **26**, 286–304.
Regan, Patrick M. and Errol A. Henderson (2002), 'Democracy, threats, and political repression in developing countries: are democracies internally less violent?', *Third World Quarterly*, **23**, 119–36.
Redzepagic, Srdjan and Matthieu Llorca (2007), 'Does politics matter in the conduct of fiscal policy? Political determinants of the fiscal sustainability: evidence from seven individual central and eastern European countries', *Panoeconomicus*, **54**, 489–500.
Reiter, Dan and Allan C. Stam (2002), *Democracies at War*, Princeton, NJ: Princeton University Press.
Revesz, Richard (1997), 'Environmental regulation, ideology, and the D.C. circuit', *Virginia Law Review*, **83**, 1717–72.
Richter, Brian K., Krislert Samphantharak and Jeffrey F. Timmons (2009), 'Lobbying and taxes', *American Journal of Political Science*, **53**, 893–909.
Riker, William H. (1957), 'Events and situations', *Journal of Philosophy*, **54**, 57–70.
Riker, William H. (1958a), 'The paradox of voting and congressional rules for voting on amendments', *American Political Science Review*, **52**, 349–66.
Riker, William H. (1958b), 'Causes of events', *Journal of Philosophy*, **56**, 281–92.
Riker, William H. (1962a), *The Theory of Political Coalitions*, New Haven, CT: Yale University Press.
Riker, William H. (1962b), 'Book review of *The Calculus of Consent*' by James M. Buchanan and Gordon Tullock, *Midwest Journal of Political Science*, **6**, 408–11.
Riker, William H. (1964), *Federalism: Origins, Operations, and Significance*, Boston, MA: Little, Brown.
Riker, William H. (1980), 'Implications from the disequilibrium of majority rule for the study of institutions', *American Political Science Review*, **74**, 432–46.
Riker, William H. (1982), *Liberalism against Populism: A Confrontation between the Theory of Democracy and the Theory of Social Choice*, San Francisco, CA: Freeman.
Riker, William H. (1986), *The Art of Political Manipulation*, New Haven, CT: Yale University Press.
Riker, William H. (1990), 'Heresthetic and rhetoric in the spatial model', in James M. Enelow and Melvin Hinich (eds), *Advances in the Spatial Theory of Voting*, New York: Cambridge University Press, pp. 46–65.
Rincke, Johannes (2005), 'Yardstick competition and policy innovation', Discussion Paper 05-11, Mannheim: Centre for European Economic Research.
Roberson, Brian (2006), 'The Colonel Blotto game', *Economic Theory*, **29**, 1–24.
Roberts, Brian E. (1990), 'A dead senator tells no lies: seniority and the distribution of federal benefits', *American Journal of Political Science*, **34**, 31–58.

Robinson, Eric W. (1997), *The First Democracies: Early Popular Government Outside Athens*, Stuttgart: Franz Steiner Verlag.
Robinson, James (1963), 'Book review of *The Theory of Political Coalitions*' by William H. Riker, *The Journal of Conflict Resolution*, 7, 763–8.
Rocco, Lorenzo and Zié Ballo (2008), 'Provoking a civil war', *Public Choice*, 134, 347–66.
Rodden, Jonathan (2003), 'Reviving Leviathan: fiscal federalism and the growth of government', *International Organization*, 57, 695–729.
Roe v. Wade (1973), 410 U.S. 113, available at: http://caselaw.lp.findlaw.com/scripts/getcase.pl?court=US&vol=410&invol=113; (accessed 25 April 2012).
Röger, Werner, Istvan P. Szekely and Alessandro Turrini (2010), 'Banking crises, output loss and fiscal policy', *CEPR* Discussion Papers, no. 7815.
Rogoff, Kenneth (1985), 'The optimal degree of commitment to an intermediate monetary target', *Quarterly Journal of Economics*, 100, 1169–89.
Rogoff, Kenneth (1990), 'Equilibrium political budget cycles', *American Economic Review*, 80, 21–36.
Rogoff, Kenneth and Anne Sibert (1988), 'Elections and macroeconomic policy cycles', *Review of Economic Studies*, 55, 1–16.
Roland, Gérard (2002), 'The political economy of transition', *Journal of Economic Perspectives*, 16, 29–50.
Roland, Gérard (2004), 'Understanding institutional change: fast-moving and slow-moving institutions', *Studies in Comparative International Development*, 38, 109–31.
Romer, Christina D. and David H. Romer (2010), 'The macroeconomic effects of tax changes: estimates based on a new measure of fiscal shocks', *American Economic Review*, 100, 763–801.
Romer, Thomas and Howard Rosenthal (1978), 'Political resource allocation, controlled agendas, and the status quo', *Public Choice*, 33, 27–43.
Romer, Thomas and Howard Rosenthal (1979), 'Bureaucrats versus voters: on the political economy of resource allocation by direct democracy', *Quarterly Journal of Economics*, 93, 563–87.
Romer, Thomas and Howard Rosenthal (1982), 'Median voters or budget maximizers: evidence from school expenditures referenda', *Economic Inquiry*, 26, 556–78.
Romer, Thomas and James M. Snyder Jr (1994), 'An empirical investigation of the dynamics of PAC contributions', *American Journal of Political Science*, 38, 745–69.
Romero-Avila, Diego and Rolf Strauch (2009), 'Public finances and long-term growth in Europe: evidence from a panel data analysis', *European Journal of Political Economy*, 24, 172–91.
Root, Hilton L. (1989), 'Tying the King's hands: credible commitments and royal fiscal policy during the old regime', *Rationality and Society*, 1, 240–48.
Rosato, Sebastian (2003), 'The flawed logic of democratic peace theory', *American Political Science Review*, 97, 585–602.
Rosato, Sebastian (2005), 'Explaining the democratic peace', *American Political Science Review*, 99, 467–72.
Rosato, Sebastian (2011), 'On the democratic conflict', in Christopher J. Coyne and Rachel L. Mathers (eds), *The Handbook on the Political Economy of War*, Cheltenham, UK and Northampton, MA, USA: Edward Elgar, pp. 281–314.
Rose, Heather and Jon Sonstelie (2010), 'School board politics, school district size and the bargaining power of teachers', *Journal of Urban Economics*, 67, 438–50.
Rosenberg, Nathan and L.E. Birdzell Jr (1986), *How the West Grew Rich: The Economic Transformation of the Industrial World*, New York: Basic Books.
Rosenberg, Shawn W. (1991), 'Rationality, markets, and political analysis: a social psychological critique of neoclassical political economy', in Kristen R. Monroe (ed), *The Economic Approach to Politics: A Critical Reassessment of the Theory of Rational Action*, New York: HarperCollins, pp. 386–404.
Rotemberg, Julio J. and Michael Woodford (1996), 'Real business-cycle model and the forecastable movements in hours, output and consumption', *American Economic Review*, 86, 71–89.
Rothstein, Jesse (2007), 'Does competition among public schools benefit students and taxpayers? Comment', *American Economic Review*, 97, 2026–37.

Rousseau, David L., Christopher Gelpi, Dan Reiter and Paul K. Huth (1996), 'Assessing the dyadic nature of the democratic peace, 1918–88', *American Political Science Review*, **90**, 512–33.

Rousseau, Jean-Jacques ([1762] 2010), *The Social Contract or Principles of Political Right*, trans. G.D.H. Cole, public domain, available at: http://www.constitution.org/jjr/socon.htm (accessed 27 February 2011).

Roux, Georges (1980), *Ancient Iraq*, 2nd edn, Harmondsworth: Penguin Books.

Rowley, Charles K. (1987), 'Borda, Jean-Charles de (1733–1799)', in John Eatwell, Murray Milgate and Peter Newman (eds), *The New Palgrave: A Dictionary of Economics*, London: Macmillan, pp. 262–3.

Rowley, Charles K. (1991), 'Duncan Black: pioneer and discoverer of public choice', *Journal of Public Finance and Public Choice*, **2**, 83–7.

Rowley, Charles K. (2000), 'Political culture and economic performance in sub-Saharan Africa', *European Journal of Political Economy*, **16**, 133–58.

Rowley, Charles K. and Robert Elgin (1988), 'Government and its bureaucracy: a bilateral bargaining versus principal–agent approach', in Charles K. Rowley, Robert D. Tollison and Gordon Tullock (eds), *The Political Economy of Rent Seeking*, Boston, MA: Kluwer Academic, pp. 267–90.

Rowley, Charles K., Robert D. Tollison and Gordon Tullock (eds) (1988), *The Political Economy of Rent-Seeking*, Boston, MA: Kluwer Academic.

Rubin, Paul H. (1977), 'Why is the common law efficient?', *Journal of Legal Studies*, **6**, 51–63.

Rubin, Paul H. (1993), *Tort Reform by Contract*, Washington, DC: American Enterprise Institute.

Rubin, Paul H. (1995a), 'What do economists think about antitrust? A random walk down Pennsylvania Avenue', in Fred S. McChesney and William F. Shughart II (eds), *The Causes and Consequences of Antitrust: The Public-Choice Perspective*, Chicago, IL: University of Chicago Press, pp. 33–61.

Rubin, Paul H. (1995b), 'Fundamental reform of tort law', *Regulation*, **4**, 26–33.

Rubin, Paul H. (2002), *Darwinian Politics: The Evolutionary Origin of Freedom*, New Brunswick, NJ: Rutgers University Press.

Rubin, Paul H. (2005), 'Micro and macro legal efficiency: supply and demand', *Supreme Court Economic Review*, **13**, 19–34.

Rubin, Paul H. and Martin J. Bailey (1994), 'The role of lawyers in changing the law', *The Journal of Legal Studies*, **23**, 807–31.

Rubin, Paul H., John Calfee and Mark Grady (1997), 'BMW v. Gore: mitigating the punitive economics of punitive damages', *Supreme Court Economic Review*, **5**, 179–216.

Rubin, Paul H., Christopher Curran and John F. Curran (2001), 'Litigation versus legislation: forum shopping by rent seekers', *Public Choice*, **107**, 295–310.

Rubin, Paul H. and Joanna M. Shepherd (2007), 'Tort reform and accidental deaths', *Journal of Law and Economics*, **50**, 221–38.

Rumi, Cecilia (2009), 'Political alternation and the fiscal deficit', *Economic Letters*, **102**, 138–40.

Rummel, Rudolph J. (1979), *Understanding Conflict and War, vol. 4: War, Power, Peace*, Beverly Hills, CA: Sage.

Rummel, Rudolph J. (1983), 'Libertarianism and international violence', *Journal of Conflict Resolution*, **27**, 27–71.

Rummel, Rudolph J. (1985), 'Libertarian propositions on violence within and between nations: a test against published research results', *Journal of Conflict Resolution*, **29**, 419–55.

Rummel, Rudolph J. (1995), 'Democracies *are* less warlike than other regimes', *European Journal of International Relations*, **1**, 457–79.

Russett, Bruce (1993), *Grasping the Democratic Peace: Principles for a Post-Cold War World*, Princeton, NJ: Princeton University Press.

Russet, Bruce (1995), 'And yet it moves (Bruce Russett on the Democratic Peace)', *International Security*, **19**, 164–77.

Sabel, Charles F. (1997), 'Design, deliberation, and democracy: on the new pragmatism of firms and public institutions', in Karl-Heinz Ladeur (ed.), *Liberal Institutions, Economic Constitutional Rights, and the Role of Organizations*, Baden-Baden: Nomos, pp. 101–49.

Sabel, Charles F. (2001), 'A quiet revolution of democratic governance: towards democratic experimentalism', in OECD (ed.), *Governance in the 21st Century*, Paris, pp. 121–48.
Sabel, Charles F. and Jonathan Zeitlin (2008), 'Learning from difference: the new architecture of experimentalist governance in the EU', *European Law Journal*, **14**, 271–327.
Salzberger, Eli M. (1993), 'A positive analysis of the doctrine of separation of powers, or: why do we have an independent judiciary?', *International Review of Law and Economics*, **13**, 349–79.
Salzberger, Eli M. and Paul Fenn (1999), 'Judicial independence: some evidence from the English Court of Appeal', *Journal of Law and Economics*, **42**, 831–47.
Sambanis, Nicholas (2002), 'A review of recent advances and future directions in the quantitative literature on civil war', *Defense and Peace Economics*, **13**, 215–43.
Sambanis, Nicholas (2004), 'What is civil war? Conceptual and empirical complexities of an operational definition', *Journal of Conflict Resolution*, **48**, 814–58.
Samuel, Oni and Segun Joshua (2010), 'Resurgence of traditional institutions of governance: imperative for state-building in Africa', *Slovenská politologická revue*, **3**, 2–15.
Samuelson, Paul A. (1954), 'The pure theory of public expenditure', *Review of Economics and Statistics*, **36**, 387–9.
Samuelson, Paul A. (1955), 'Diagrammatic exposition of a theory of public expenditure', *Review of Economics and Statistics*, **37**, 350–56.
Sander, William (1998), 'Private schools and public school achievement', *Journal of Human Resources*, **34**, 697–709.
Sandler, Todd, Daniel G. Arce M. and Walter Enders (2009), 'Transnational terrorism', in Bjørn Lomborg (ed.), *Global Crises, Global Solutions*, 2nd edn, Cambridge: Cambridge University Press, pp. 516–62.
Sandler, Todd, Daniel G. Arce M. and Walter Enders (2011), 'An evaluation of Interpol's cooperative-based counterterrorism linkages', *Journal of Law and Economics*, **54**, 79–110.
Sandler, Todd and Keith Hartley (eds) (2007), *Handbook of Defense Economics, vol. 2: Defense in a Globalized World*. Amsterdam and Oxford: North-Holland (Elsevier).
Sandler, Todd and Kevin Siqueira (2006), 'Global terrorism: deterrence versus preemption', *Canadian Journal of Economics*, **39**, 1370–87.
Sargent, Thomas J. and Neil Wallace (1987), 'Some unpleasant monetarist arithmetic', *Quarterly Review*, **531**, Federal Reserve Bank of Minneapolis.
Sass, Tim R. (2006), 'Charter schools and student achievement in Florida', *Education Finance and Policy*, **1**, 91–122.
Satterthwaite, Mark (1975), 'Strategy-proofness and Arrow's conditions: existence and correspondence theorems for voting procedures and social welfare functions', *Journal of Economic Theory*, **10**, 187–218.
Saving, Jason L. (1997), 'Human capital, committee power, and legislative outcomes', *Public Choice*, **92**, 301–16.
Schauer, Fred (1988), 'Formalism', *Yale Law Journal*, **97**, 509–48.
Schelling, Thomas C. (1960), *The Strategy of Conflict*, Oxford: Oxford University Press.
Schelling. Thomas C. (2005), 'An astonishing sixty years: the legacy of Hiroshima', Nobel Memorial Lecture delivered 8 December 2005, available at: http://nobelprize.org/nobel_prizes/economics/laureates/2005/schelling-lecture.html, reprinted as Schelling, Thomas C. (2006), *PNAS*, **103**, 6089–93.
Schlozman, Daniel and Ian Yohai (2008), 'How initiatives don't always make citizens: ballot initiatives in the American states', *Political Behavior*, **30**, 469–89.
Schmidt, Amy B., Lawrence W. Kenny and Rebecca B. Morton (1996), 'Evidence on electoral accountability in the U.S. Senate: are unfaithful agents really punished?', *Economic Inquiry*, **34**, 545–67.
Schmitt, Hermann and Jacques Thomassen (eds) 1999, *Political Representation and Legitimacy in the European Union*, Oxford: Oxford University Press.
Schneider, Mark (1989), 'Intercity competition and the size of the local public work force', *Public Choice*, **63**, 253–65.
Schneider, Mark, Paul Teske and Michael Mintrom (1995), *Political Entrepreneurs; Agents for Change in American Government*, Princeton, NJ: Princeton University Press.

Schnellenbach, Jan (2005), 'Model uncertainty and the rationality of economic policy: an evolutionary approach', *Journal of Evolutionary Economics*, **15**, 101–16.
Schnellenbach, Jan (2007), 'Public entrepreneurship and the economics of reform', *Journal of Institutional Economics*, **3**, 183–202.
Schofield, Norman (1997), 'Multiparty electoral politics', in Dennis C. Mueller (ed), *Perspectives on Public Choice*, Cambridge: Cambridge University Press, pp. 271–95.
Schram, Arthur and Joep Sonnemans (1996), 'Voter turnout as a participation game: an experimental investigation', *International Journal of Game Theory*, **25**, 385–406.
Schubert, Christian (2009), 'Darwinism in economics and the evolutionary theory of policymaking', Papers on Economics & Evolution, no. 0910, Max Planck Institute of Economics, Jena.
Schuessler, Alexander A. (2000a), 'Expressive voting', *Rationality and Society*, **12**, 87–119.
Schuessler, Alexander A. (2000b), *A Logic of Expressive Choice*, Princeton, NJ: Princeton University Press.
Schultz, Kenneth A. (1998), 'Domestic opposition and signaling in international crises', *American Political Science Review*, **92**, 829–44.
Schultz, Theodore W. (1975), 'The value of the ability to deal with disequilibria', *Journal of Economic Literature*, **13**, 827–46.
Schumpeter, Joseph A. ([1942] 1987), *Capitalism, Socialism, and Democracy*, 6th edn, London: Unwin.
Schwartz, Anna J. (1988), 'International debts: what's fact and what's fiction', *Economic Inquiry*, **27**, 1–19.
Schwartz, Victor E., Mark A. Behrens and Leah Lorber (2000), 'Tort reform past, present and future: solving old problems and dealing with "new style" litigation', *William Mitchell Law Review*, **27**, 237–69.
Sears, David O., Richard R. Lau, Tom R. Tyler and Harris M. Allen Jr (1980), 'Self-interest vs. symbolic politics in policy attitudes and presidential voting', *American Political Science Review*, **74**, 670–84.
Seater, John J. (1993), 'Ricardian equivalence', *Journal of Economic Literature*, **31**, 142–90.
Segal, Jeffrey A. (1997), 'Separation-of-powers games in the positive theory of Congress and the courts', *American Political Science Review*, **91**, 28–44.
Segal, Jeffrey A. and Albert D. Cover (1989), 'Ideological values and the votes of U.S. Supreme Court justices', *American Political Science Review*, **83**, 557–65.
Segal, Jeffrey A., Lee Epstein, Charles M. Cameron and Harold J. Spaeth (1995), 'Ideological values and the votes of U.S. Supreme Court justices revisited', *Journal of Politics*, **57**, 812–23.
Segal, Jeffrey and Harold J. Spaeth (1993), *The Supreme Court and the Attitudinal Model*, Cambridge and New York: Cambridge University Press.
Segal, Jeffrey and Harold J. Spaeth (1996), 'The influence of *stare decisis* on the votes of United States Supreme Court Justices', *American Journal of Political Science*, **40**, 971–1003.
Segal, Jeffrey and Harold Spaeth (2002), *The Supreme Court and the Attitudinal Model Revisited*, Cambridge and New York: Cambridge University Press.
Seidman, Louis Michael (1988), 'Ambivalence and accountability', *Southern California Law Review*, **61**, 1571–600.
Serletis, Apostolos and Panos C. Afxentiou (1998), 'Electoral and partisan cycle regularities in Canada', *Canadian Journal of Economics*, **31**, 28–46.
Shapiro, Ian (2003), *The State of Democratic Theory*, Princeton, NJ: Princeton University Press.
Shapiro, Jacob N. (2007), 'Terrorist organizations' vulnerabilities and inefficiencies: a rational choice perspective', in Jeanne K. Giraldo and Harold A. Trinkunas (eds), *Terrorism Financing and State Responses: A Comparative Perspective*, Stanford, CA: Stanford University Press, pp. 56–71.
Shapiro, Jacob N. and David A. Siegel (2009), 'Underfunding in terrorist organizations', in Nasrullah Memon, Jonathan D. Farley, David L. Hicks and Torben Rosenorn (eds), *Mathematical Methods in Counterterrorism*, Wien: Springer, pp. 349–82.

Shapley, Lloyd S. and Martin Shubik (1954), 'A method for evaluating the distribution of power in a committee system', *American Political Science Review*, **48**, 787–92.
Shavell, Steven (1982), 'Suit, settlement, and trial: a theoretical analysis under alternative methods for the allocation of legal costs', *Journal of Legal Studies*, **11**, 55–81.
Shavell, Steven (1995), 'Alternative dispute resolution: an economic analysis', *Journal of Legal Studies*, **24**, 1–28.
Shavell, Steven (2004), *Foundations of Economic Analysis of Law*, Boston, MA: Harvard University Press.
Shepherd, Joanna M. (2009a), 'The influence of retention politics on judges' voting', *Journal of Legal Studies*, **38**, 169–206.
Shepherd, Joanna M. (2009b), 'Money, politics, and impartial justice', *Duke Law Journal*, **58**, 623–85.
Shepherd, Joanna M. (2009c), 'Are appointed judges strategic too?', *Duke Law Journal*, **58**, 1589–626.
Shepsle, Kenneth A. (1975), 'Congressional committee assignments: an optimization model with institutional constraints', *Public Choice*, **22**, 55–78.
Shepsle, Kenneth A. (1978), *The Giant Jigsaw Puzzle: Democratic Committee Assignments in the Modern House*, Chicago, IL: University of Chicago Press.
Shepsle, Kenneth A. (1979), 'Institutional arrangements and equilibrium in multidimensional voting models', *American Journal of Political Science*, **23**, 27–59.
Shepsle, Kenneth (2006), 'Rational choice institutionalism', in R.A.W. Rhodes, Sarah A. Binder and Bert A. Rockman (eds), *The Oxford Handbook of Political Institutions*, Oxford and New York: Oxford University Press., pp. 23–38.
Shepsle, Kenneth A. and Barry R. Weingast (1994), 'Positive theories of congressional institutions', *Legislative Studies Quarterly*, **19**, 149–79.
Shetreet, Shimon (1985), 'Judicial independence: new conceptual dimensions and contemporary challenges', in Shimon Shetreet and Jules Deschênes (eds), *Judicial Independence: The Contemporary Debate*, Dordrecht: Martinus Nijhoff, pp. 590–681.
Shi, Min and Jakob Svensson (2006), 'Political budget cycles: do they differ across countries and why?', *Journal of Public Economics*, **90**, 1367–89.
Shin, Don Chull (1994), 'On the third wave of democratization: a synthesis and evaluation of recent theory and research', *World Politics*, **47**, 135–70.
Shleifer, Andrei and Robert W. Vishney, 2003, 'Corruption', *Quarterly Journal of Economics*, **108**, 599–617.
Shogren, Jason F. and Kyung Hwan Baik (1991), 'Reexamining efficient rent seeking in laboratory markets', *Public Choice*, **69**, 69–79, reprinted in Roger D. Congleton, Arye L. Hillman and Kai A. Konrad (eds) (2008), *Forty Years of Research on Rent Seeking 1 – The Theory of Rent Seeking*, Heidelberg: Springer, pp. 651–61.
Shon, John (2010), 'Do stock returns vary with campaign contributions? Bush vs. Gore: the Florida recount', *Economics and Politics*, **22**, 257–81.
Showman, Katie (2009), 'Evidence on the effects of inter-school-district competition: comparisons of state-limited school district states with other states', Florida State University working paper.
Shugart, Matthew S. (1999), 'Presidentialism, parliamentarism and the provision of collective goods in less-developed countries', *Constitutional Political Economy*, **10**, 53–88.
Shughart, William F. II (1990), *Antitrust Policy and Interest-Group Politics*, New York: Quorum.
Shughart, William F. II (1995), 'Retrospect and prospect', in Fred S. McChesney and William F. Shughart II (eds), *The Causes and Consequences of Antitrust: The Public-Choice Perspective*, Chicago, IL: University of Chicago Press, pp. 319–22.
Shughart, William F. II (2004), 'Bending before the storm: the U.S. Supreme Court in economic crisis, 1935–1937', *Independent Review*, **9**, 55–83.
Shughart, William F. II (2006), 'An analytical history of terrorism, 1945–2000', *Public Choice*, **128**, 7–39.
Shughart, William F. II (2011a), 'The New Deal and modern memory', *Southern Economic Journal*, **77**, 515–42.
Shughart, William F. II (2011b), 'Terrorism in rational choice perspective', in Christopher J. Coyne

and Rachel L. Mathers (eds), *The Handbook on the Political Economy of War*, Cheltenham, UK and Northampton, MA, USA: Edward Elgar, pp. 126–53.

Shughart, William F. II and Robert D. Tollison (1983), 'Preliminary evidence on the use of inputs by the Federal Reserve System', *American Economic Review*, **73**, 291–304.

Shughart, William F. II, and Robert D. Tollison (1986), 'The political economy of legislation and the growth of government', *Research in Law and Economics*, **9**, 111–27.

Shughart, William F. II and Robert D. Tollison ([1991], 1995), 'The employment consequences of the Sherman and Clayton Acts', *Journal of Institutional and Theoretical Economics*, **147**, 38–52, reprinted in Fred S. McChesney and William F. Shughart II (eds), *The Causes and Consequences of Antitrust: The Public-Choice Perspective*, Chicago, IL: University of Chicago Press, pp. 165–78.

Shughart, William F. II and Robert D. Tollison (1998), 'Interest groups and the courts', *George Mason Law Review*, **6**, 953–69.

Shughart, William F. II and Robert D. Tollison (2005), 'The unfinished business of public choice', *Public Choice*, **124**, 237–47.

Siegel, Ron (2009), 'All-pay contests', *Econometrica*, **77**, 71–92.

Siegfried, John J. (1975), 'The determinants of antitrust activity', *Journal of Law and Economics*, **17**, 559–74.

Simon, Herbert A. (1957), *Models of Man*, New York: Wiley.

Simon, Herbert A. (1993), 'Rational processes in social affairs', in Herbert A. Simon *Reason in Human Affairs*, Stanford, CA: Stanford University Press, pp. 75–107.

Siqueira, Kevin and Todd Sandler (2007), 'Terrorist backlash, terrorism mitigation and policy delegation', *Journal of Public Economics*, **91**, 1800–15.

Sisk, Gregory, Michael Heise and Andrew Morriss (1998), 'Charting the influences on the judicial mind: an empirical study of judicial reasoning', *New York University Law Review*, **73**, 1377–500.

Sjoblom, Kriss (1985), 'Voting for social security', *Public Choice*, **45**, 225–40.

Skaperdas, Stergios (1992), 'Cooperation, conflict, and power in the absence of property rights', *American Economic Review*, **82**, 720–39.

Skaperdas, Stergios (2003), 'Restraining the genuine *homo economicus*: why the economy cannot be divorced from its governance', *Economics and Politics*, **15**, 135–62.

Skilling, David and Richard J. Zeckhauser (2002), 'Political competition and debt trajectories in Japan and the OECD', *Japan and the World Economy*, **14**, 121–35.

Skocpol, Theda (1985), 'Bringing the state back in: strategies of analysis in current research', in Peter B. Evans, Dietrich Rueschemeyer and Theda Skocpol (eds), *Bringing the State Back In*, Cambridge: Cambridge University Press, pp. 3–37.

Slembeck, Tilman (1997), 'The formation of economic policy: a cognitive-evolutionary approach to policy-making', *Constitutional Political Economy*, **8**, 225–54.

Slembeck, Tilman (2003), 'Ideologies, beliefs, and economic advice – a cognitive-evolutionary view on economic policy-making', in Pavel Pelikan and Gerhard Wegner (eds), *The Evolutionary Analysis of Economic Policy*, Cheltenham, UK and Northampton, MA, USA: Edward Elgar, pp. 128–61.

Small, Melvin and J. David Singer (1976), 'The war proneness of democratic regimes, 1816–1965', *The Jerusalem Journal of International Relations*, **1**, 50–69.

Small, Melvin and J. David Singer (1982), *Resort to Arms: International and Civil War, 1816–1980*, Beverly Hills, CA: Sage.

Smith, Adam ([1776] 2005), *An Inquiry into the Nature and Causes of the Wealth of Nations*, Hazleton, PA: Pennsylvania State University Electronic Classics Series.

Smith, Alastair (1996), 'Endogenous election timing in majoritarian parliamentary systems', *Economics and Politics*, **8**, 85–110.

Smith, Daniel A. and Caroline J. Tolbert (2004), *Educated by Initiative: The Effects of Direct Democracy on Citizens and Political Organizations in the American States*, Ann Arbor, MI: University of Michigan Press.

Smith, Janet K. (1982), 'Production of licensing legislation: an economic analysis of interstate differences', *Journal of Legal Studies*, **11**, 117–37.

Smith, Joseph L. (2006), 'Patterns and consequences of judicial reversals: theoretical considerations and data from a district court', *Justice System Journal*, **27**, 29–43.
Smith, Mark (2002), 'Ballot initiatives and the democratic citizen', *Journal of Politics*, **64**, 892–903.
Smith, Vernon L. (1985), 'Experimental economics: reply', *American Economic Review*, **75**, 265–72.
Smithies, Arthur (1941), 'Optimum location in spatial competition', *Journal of Political Economy*, **49**, 423–39.
Snyder, Jack L. (1991), *Myths of Empire: Domestic Politics and International Ambition*, Ithaca, NY: Cornell University Press.
Snyder, James M. Jr (1990), 'Campaign contributions as investments: the U.S. House of Representatives, 1980–1986', *Journal of Political Economy*, **98**, 1195–227.
Snyder, James M., Jr (1992), 'Long-term investing in politicians: or, give early, give often', *Journal of Law and Economics*, **35**, 15–43.
Sobek, David (2010), 'Masters of their domains: the role of state capacity in civil wars', *Journal of Peace Research*, **47**, 267–71.
Sobel, Russell S., Christopher J. Coyne and Peter T. Leeson (2007), 'The political economy of FEMA: did reorganization matter?', *Journal of Public Finance and Public Choice*, **17**, 49–65.
Sobel, Russell S. and Joshua C. Hall (2007), 'The effect of judicial selection purchases on judicial quality: the role of partisan politics', *Cato Journal*, **27**, 69–82.
Sobel, Russell S., Matt E. Ryan and Joshua C. Hall (2010), 'Electoral pressures and the legal system: friends or foes?', in Edward J. Lopez (ed., Foreword by Robert D. Tollison), *The Pursuit of Justice: Law and Economics of Legal Institutions*, New York and Oakland, CA: Palgrave/Macmillan and The Independent Institute, pp. 37–50.
Sobel, Russell S. and Adam Pellillo (2012), 'The politics of elections and congressional oversight', in Michael Reksulak, Laura Razzolini and William F. Shughart II (eds), *The Elgar Companion to Public Choice*, 2nd edn, Cheltenham, UK and Northampton, MA, USA: Edward Elgar, this volume, ch. 14.
Solé-Ollé, Albert (2006), 'The effects of party competition on budget outcomes: empirical evidence from local governments in Spain', *Public Choice*, **126**, 145–76.
Solé-Ollé, Albert and Pilar Sorribas-Navarro (2008), 'The effects of partisan alignment on the allocation of intergovernmental transfers: differences-in-differences estimates for Spain', *Journal of Public Economics*, **92**, 2302–19.
Songer, Donald R., Jeffrey A. Segal and Charles M. Cameron (1994), 'The hierarchy of justice: testing a principal–agent model of Supreme Court-Circuit Court interactions', *American Journal of Political Science*, **38**, 673–96.
Sorensen, Aage B. and Seymour Spillerman (1993), *Social Theory and Social Policy: Essays in Honor of James Coleman*, Westport, CT: Greenwood.
Souva, Mark and Brandon Prins (2006), 'The liberal peace revisited: the role of democracy, dependence, and development in militarized interstate dispute initiation, 1950–1999', *International Interactions*, **32**, 183–200.
Spence, A. Michael (1973), 'Job market signaling', *Quarterly Journal of Economics*, **87**, 355–74.
Spence, A. Michael (2002), 'Signaling in retrospect and the informational structure of markets', *American Economic Review*, **92**, 434–59.
Spiller, Pablo T. and Rafael Gely (1992), 'Congressional control or judicial independence: the determinants of U.S. Supreme Court labor-relations decisions, 1949–1988', *RAND Journal of Economics*, **23**, 463–92.
Spiller, Pablo T. and Rafael Gely (2007), 'Strategic judicial decision making', working paper, forthcoming in Keith E. Whittington, E. Daniel Kelemen and Gregory A. Caldeira (eds), *Oxford Handbook of Law and Politics*, Oxford: Oxford University Press.
Spiller, Pablo T. and Matthew T. Spitzer (1992), 'Judicial choice of legal doctrine', *Journal of Law, Economics, and Organization*, **8**, 8–46.
Spiller, Pablo T. and Emerson H. Tiller (1997), 'Decision costs and the strategic design of administrative process and judicial review', *Journal of Legal Studies*, **26**, 347–70.
Stark, David (1992), 'Path dependence and privatization strategies in east central Europe', *East European Politics and Societies*, **6**, 17–54.
Stark, Rodney (1997), *The Rise of Christianity: How the Obscure, Marginal Jesus Movement*

Became the Dominant Religious Force in the Western World in a Few Centuries, San Francisco, CA: HarperCollins.
Stein, Ernesto (1999), 'Fiscal decentralization and government size in Latin America', *Journal of Applied Economics*, **2**, 357–91.
Stephenson, Matthew C. (2009), 'Legal realism for economists', *Journal of Economic Perspectives*, **23**, 191–211.
Steunenberg, Bernard (1994), 'Decision making under different institutional arrangements: legislation by the European community', *Journal of Theoretical and Institutional Economics*, **150**, 642–69.
Stevenson, Robert (1968), *Population and Political Systems in Tropical Africa*, New York: Columbia University Press.
Stewart, Charles III and Tim Groseclose (1999a), 'The value of committee seats in the House, 1947–91', *American Journal of Political Science*, **42**, 453–74.
Stewart, Charles III and T. Groseclose (1999b), 'The value of committee seats in the United States Senate, 1947–91', *American Journal of Political Science*, **43**, 963–73.
Stigler, George J. (1966), 'The economic effects of the antitrust laws', *Journal of Law and Economics*, **9**, 225–58.
Stigler, George J. (1971), 'The theory of economic regulation', *Bell Journal of Economics and Management Science*, **2**, 3–21.
Stigler, George J. (1979), 'The size of legislatures', *Journal of Legal Studies*, **5**, 17–34.
Stigler, George J. and Gary S. Becker (1977), 'De gustibus non est disputandum', *American Economic Review*, **67**, 76–90.
Stoddard, Christiana and Sean P. Corcoran (2007), 'The political economy of school choice: support for charter schools across states and school districts', *Journal of Urban Economics*, **62**, 27–54.
Stokes, Donald E. (1963), '*Spatial* models of party competition', *American Political Science Review*, **57**, 368–77.
Stratmann, Thomas (1991), 'What do campaign contributions buy? Deciphering causal effects of money and votes', *Southern Economic Journal*, **57**, 606–20.
Stratmann, Thomas (1992), 'Are contributors rational? Untangling strategies of political action committees', *Journal of Political Economy*, **100**, 647–64.
Stratmann, Thomas (1995), 'Logrolling in the U.S. Congress', *Economic Inquiry*, **3**, 441–56.
Stratmann, Thomas (1996), 'How reelection constituencies matter: evidence from political action committees' contributions and congressional voting', *Journal of Law and Economics*, **39**, 605–35.
Stratmann, Thomas (1998), 'The market for congressional votes: is timing of contributions everything?', *Journal of Law and Economics*, **41**, 85–114.
Stratmann, Thomas (2002), 'Can special interests buy congressional votes? Evidence from financial services legislation', *Journal of Law and Economics*, **45**, 345–74.
Stratmann, Thomas (2005a), 'The effectiveness of money in ballot measure campaigns', *Southern California Law Review*, **78**, 1041–64.
Stratmann, Thomas (2005b), 'Some talk: money in politics. A (partial) review of the literature', *Public Choice*, **124**, 135–56.
Stratmann, Thomas (2006a), 'Is spending more potent for or against a proposition? Evidence from ballot measures', *American Journal of Political Science*, **50**, 788–801.
Stratmann, Thomas (2006b), 'Contribution limits and the effectiveness of campaign spending', *Public Choice*, **129**, 461–74.
Stratmann, Thomas (2009), 'How prices matter in politics: the returns to campaign advertising', *Public Choice*, **140**, 357–77.
Stringham, Edward (2001), 'Kaldor-Hicks efficiency and the problem of central planning', *Quarterly Journal of Austrian Economics*, **4**, 41–50.
Sturm, Jan-Egbert, Helge Berger and Jakob De Haan (2005), 'Which variables explain decisions on IMF credit? An extreme bounds analysis', *Economics & Politics*, **17**, 177–213.
Sugden, Robert (1984), 'Reciprocity: the supply of public goods through voluntary contributions', *Economic Journal*, **94**, 772–87.

Suleiman, Ramzi and Amnon Rapoport (1988), 'Environmental and social uncertainty in single trial resource dilemmas', *Acta Psychologica*, **68**, 99–112.
Sunstein, Cass R. (1996), 'Social norms and social roles', *Columbia Law Review*, **96**, 903–40.
Sunstein, Cass R. (2001), *Designing Democracy: What Constitutions Do*, Oxford: Oxford University Press.
Svaleryd, Helena and Jonas Vlachos (2009), 'Political rents in a non-corrupt democracy', *Journal of Public Economics*, **93**, 355–72.
Svensson, Jacob (2000), 'Foreign aid and rent seeking', *Journal of International Economics*, **51**, 437–61, reprinted in Roger D. Congleton, Arye L. Hillman and Kai A. Konrad (eds) (2008), *Forty Years of Research on Rent Seeking 2 – Applications: Rent Seeking in Practice*, Heidelberg: Springer, pp. 165–89.
Tabarrok, Alexander and Eric Helland (1999), 'Court politics: the political economy of tort awards', *Journal of Law and Economics*, **42**, 157–88.
Tabellini, Guido (2000), 'A positive theory of social security', *Scandinavian Journal of Economics*, **102**, 523–45.
Taha, Amed E. (2004), 'Publish or paris? Evidence of how judges allocate their time', *American Law and Economics Review*, **6**, 1–27.
Tamanaha, Brian Z. (2008), 'The bogus tale about the legal formalists', St John's Legal Studies Research Paper no. 08-0130.
Tanzi, Vito and Ludger Schuknecht (2000), *Public Spending in the 20th Century: A Global Perspective*, New York: Cambridge University Press.
Tavares, Jose and Romain Wacziarg (2001), 'How democracy affects growth', *European Economic Review*, **45**, 1341–78.
Taylor, John B. (1979), 'Staggered wage setting in a macro model', *American Economic Review*, **69**, 108–13.
Taylor, John B. (1980), 'Aggregate dynamics and staggered contracts', *Journal of Political Economy*, **88**, 1–24.
Tenhofen, Jorn and Guntran B. Wolff (2007), 'Does the anticipation of government spending matter? Evidence from an expectations augmented VAR', Deutsche Bundesbank Research Centre, Discussion Paper Series 1, 2007–14, Frankfurt am Main.
Terrebonne, R. Peter (1981), 'A strictly evolutionary model of common law', *Journal of Legal Studies*, **10**, 397–408.
Thacker, Strom C. (1999), 'The high politics of IMF lending', *World Politics*, **52**, 38–75.
Thaize Challier, M.-Christine (2010), 'Socio-political conflict, social distance, and rent extraction in historical perspective', *European Journal of Political Economy*, **26**, 51–67.
Thelen, Kathleen (2003), 'How institutions evolve: insights from comparative historical analysis', in James Mahoney and Dietrich Rueschemeyer (eds), *Comparative Historical Analysis in the Social Sciences*, Cambridge: Cambridge University Press, pp. 208–40.
Thomas, Scott J. and Bernard Grofman (1992), 'Determinants of legislative success in House committees', *Public Choice*, **74**, 233–43.
Tiebout, Charles M. (1956), 'A pure theory of local government expenditures', *Journal of Political Economy*, **64**, 416–24.
Thies, Cameron (2010), 'Of rulers, rebels, and revenue: state capacity, civil war onset, and primary commodities', *Journal of Peace Research*, **47**, 321–32.
Tiller, Emerson H. and Pablo T. Spiller (1999), 'Strategic instruments: legal structure and political games in administrative law', *Journal of Law, Economics, and Organization*, **15**, 349–77.
Tir, Jaroslav and Michael Jasinski (2008), 'Domestic-level diversionary theory of war: targeting ethnic minorities', *Journal of Conflict Resolution*, **52**, 641–64.
Todd, Allan (2002), *The European Dictatorships: Hitler, Stalin, Mussolini*, Cambridge: Cambridge University Press.
Tollison, Robert D. (1982), 'Rent seeking: a survey', *Kyklos*, **35**, 575–602.
Tollison, Robert D. and Roger D. Congleton (1995), *The Economic Analysis of Rent Seeking*, Aldershot, UK and Brookfield, VT, USA: Edward Elgar.
Toma, Eugenia F. (1991), 'Congressional influence and the Supreme Court: the budget as a signaling device', *Journal of Legal Studies*, **20**, 131–46.

Toma, Eugenia F. (1996), 'A contractual model of the voting behavior of the Supreme Court: the role of the Chief Justice', *International Review of Law and Economics*, **16**, 433–47.
Toma, Mark (1982), 'Inflationary bias of the Federal Reserve System: a bureaucratic perspective', *Journal of Monetary Economics*, **10**, 163–90.
Tootell, Geoffrey M.B. (1999), 'Whose monetary policy is it anyway?', *Journal of Monetary Economics*, **43**, 217–35.
Towers Perrin (2009), '2009 update of U.S. tort costs', available at: http://bit.ly/tsJWlT (accessed 1 August 2011).
Trechsel, Alexander and Uwe Serdült (1999), *Kaleidoskop Volksrechte: Die Institutionen der Direkten Demokratie in den Schweizerischen Kantonen 1970–1996*, Basel–München–Genf: Verlag Helbing and Lichtenhahn.
Treich, Nicolas (2010), 'Risk-aversion and prudence in rent-seeking games', *Public Choice*, **145**, 339–49.
Tridimas, George (2010), 'A political economy perspective on direct democracy in ancient Athens', mimeo, University of Ulster.
Tsebelis, George (2002), *Veto Players: How Political Institutions Work*, Princeton, NJ: Princeton University Press.
Tsebelis, George and Jeannette Money (1997), *Bicameralism*, Cambridge: Cambridge University Press.
Tuck, Richard (2008), *Free Riding*, Cambridge, MA: Harvard University Press.
Tufte, Edward R. (1978), *Political Control of the Economy*, Princeton, NJ: Princeton University Press.
Tullock, Gordon (1959), 'Problems of majority voting', *Journal of Political Economy*, **67**, 571–9.
Tullock, Gordon (1965a), 'Entry barriers in politics', *American Economic Review*, **55**, 458–66.
Tullock, Gordon (1965b), *The Politics of Bureaucracy*, Washington, DC: Public Affairs Press.
Tullock, Gordon (1967), 'The welfare costs of tariffs, monopolies, and theft', *Western Economic Journal*, **5**, 224–32, reprinted in Roger D. Congleton, Arye L. Hillman and Kai A. Konrad (eds) (2008), *Forty Years of Research on Rent Seeking 1 – The Theory of Rent Seeking*, Heidelberg: Springer, pp. 45–53.
Tullock, Gordon (1971a), 'The charity of the uncharitable', *Western Economic Journal*, **9**, 379–92.
Tullock, Gordon (1971b), 'The paradox of revolution, *Public Choice*, **11**, 89–99.
Tullock, Gordon (1971c), 'The cost of transfers', *Kyklos*, **24**, 629–43, reprinted in James M. Buchanan, Robert D. Tollison and Gordon Tullock (eds), *Toward a Theory of the Rent Seeking Society*, College Station: Texas A&M University Press, pp. 269–82.
Tullock, Gordon (1972), 'Book review of *Bureaucracy and Representative Government*' by William A. Niskanen, *Public Choice*, **12**, 119–24.
Tullock, Gordon ([1974] 2005), 'International conflict: two parties', in Gordon Tullock, *The Social Dilemma: The Economics of War and Revolution*, Blacksburg, WV: Center for Study of Public Choice, pp. 87–106. Reprinted in Charles K. Rowley (ed), *The Selected Works of Gordon Tullock*, vol. 8, *The Social Dilemma: Of Autocracy, Revolution, Coup d'Etat, and War*, Indianapolis, IN: Liberty Fund, pp. 311–33.
Tullock, Gordon (1975a), 'Competing for aid', *Public Choice*, **21**, 41–52, reprinted in Charles K. Rowley, Robert D. Tollison and Gordon Tullock (eds), *The Political Economy of Rent Seeking*, Boston and Dordrecht: Kluwer Academic, pp. 299–311.
Tullock, Gordon (1975b), 'On the efficient organization of trials', *Kyklos*, **28**, 745–62, reprinted in Roger D. Congleton, Arye L. Hillman and Kai A. Konrad (eds) (2008), *Forty Years of Research on Rent Seeking 2 – Applications: Rent Seeking in Practice*, Heidelberg: Springer, pp. 361–78.
Tullock, Gordon (1980a), 'Rent seeking as a negative sum game', in James M. Buchanan, Robert D. Tollison and Gordon Tullock (eds), *Toward a Theory of the Rent Seeking Society*, College Station, TX: Texas A&M University Press, pp. 16–36.
Tullock, Gordon (1980b), 'Efficient rent seeking', in James M. Buchanan, Robert D. Tollison and Gordon Tullock (eds), *Towards a Theory of the Rent-Seeking Society*, College Station, TX: Texas A&M University Press, pp. 97–112, reprinted in Roger D. Congleton, Arye L. Hillman and Kai A. Konrad (eds) (2008), *Forty Years of Research on Rent Seeking 1 – The Theory of Rent Seeking*, Heidelberg: Springer, pp. 105–20.

Tullock, Gordon (1980c), *Trials on Trial: The Pure Theory of Legal Procedure*, New York: Columbia University Press.
Tullock, Gordon (1988), 'Why did the Industrial Revolution occur in England?', in Charles K. Rowley, Robert D. Tollison and Gordon Tullock (eds), *The Political Economy of Rent Seeking*, Boston and Dordrecht: Kluwer Academic, pp. 409–19.
Tullock, Gordon (1989), *The Economics of Special Privilege and Rent Seeking*, Boston and Dordrecht: Kluwer Academic.
Tullock, Gordon (1987), *Autocracy*, Dordrecht: M. Nijhoff.
Tullock, Gordon (1991), 'Accidental freedom', in Arye L. Hillman (ed), *Markets and Politicians: Politicized Economic Choice*, Boston and Dordrecht: Kluwer Academic, pp. 93–112.
Tullock, Gordon (1995), 'The cost of medical progress', *American Economic Review Papers and Proceedings*, **85**, 77–80.
Tullock, Gordon (1997), *The Case Against the Common Law*, The Blackstone Commentaries Series, vol. 1, ed. Amanda J. Owens, The Locke Institute, Durham, NC: Carolina Academic Press.
Tversky, Amos and Daniel Kahnemann (1987), 'Rational choice and the framing of decisions', in Robin M. Hogarth and Melvin W. Reder (eds), *Rational Choice*, Chicago, IL: University of Chicago Press, pp. 67–94.
Udehn, Lars (1996), *The Limits of Public Choice – a Sociological Critique of the Economic Theory of Politics*, London: Routledge.
Uhlig, Harald (2010), 'Understanding the impact of fiscal policy: some fiscal calculus', *American Economic Review*, **100**, 30–34.
United States Congress (2002), 'Joint inquiry into intelligence community activities before and after the terrorist attacks of September 11, 2001', Washington, DC: Senate Report No. 107-351, House Report No. 107-792.
United States Congressional Budget Office (2003), *The Economics of U.S. Tort Liability: A Primer*, Washington, DC: USGPO.
United States Council of Economic Advisers (2004), *Economic Report of the President*, Washington, DC: USGPO.
United States Department of the Army (2007), *The US Army/Marine Corps Counterinsurgency Field Manual*, Chicago, IL: University of Chicago Press.
United States Department of Education (2009), *Digest of Education Statistics*, Washington, DC: USGPO.
Ursprung, Heinrich W. (1990), 'Public goods, rent dissipation, and candidate competition', *Economics and Politics*, **2**, 115–32, reprinted in Roger D. Congleton, Arye L. Hillman and Kai A. Konrad (eds) (2008), *Forty Years of Research on Rent Seeking 1 – The Theory of Rent Seeking*, Heidelberg: Springer, pp. 329–46.
Ursprung, Heinrich W. (1991), 'Economic policies and political competition', in Arye L. Hillman (ed.), *Markets and Politicians: Politicized Economic Choice*, Boston, MA and Dordrecht: Kluwer Academic, pp. 1–25.
Ursprung, Heinrich W. (2011), 'The evolution of sharing rules in rent-seeking contests: incentives crowd out cooperation', *Public Choice*, forthcoming (first published online 9 March 2011).
Ursprung, Tobias (1994), 'The use and effect of political propaganda in democracies', *Public Choice*, **78**, 259–82.
Usher, Dan (1977), 'The welfare economics of the socialization of commodities', *Journal of Public Economics*, **8**, 151–68.
Usher, Dan (2011), 'Bargaining unexplained', Public Choice, forthcoming (first published online 26 January 2011).
Vachris, Michelle A. (1996), 'Federal antitrust enforcement: a principal–agent perspective', *Public Choice*, **88**, 223–38.
Van den Bergh, Jeroen C.J.M. and Giorgos Kallies (2009), 'Evolutionary policy', Papers on Economics & Evolution, no. 0902, Max Planck Institute of Economics, Jena.
Van den Hauwe, Ludwig (2005), 'Constitutional economics II', in Jürgen G. Backhaus (ed.), *The Elgar Companion to Law and Economics*, Cheltenham, UK and Northampton, MA, USA: Edward Elgar, pp. 223–38.

Vanberg, Viktor J. (1993a), 'Rational choice, rule-following and institutions: an evolutionary perspective', in Uskali Mäki, Bo Gustafsson and Christian Knudsen (eds), *Rationality, Institutions and Economic Methodology*, London.: Routledge, pp. 171–200.
Vanberg, Viktor J. (1993b), 'Constitutionally constrained and safeguarded competition in markets and politics with a reference to a European constitution', *Journal des Economistes et des Etudes Humaines*, **4**, 3–27.
Vanberg, Viktor J. (1994), *Rules and Choice in Economics*, London and New York: Routledge.
Vanberg, Viktor J. (2009), 'Evolving preferences and policy advice in democratic society', Papers on Economics and Evolution, no. 0919, Max Planck Institute of Economics, Jena.
Vanberg, Viktor and James M. Buchanan (1989), 'Interests and theories in constitutional choice', *Journal of Theoretical Politics*, **1**, 49–63.
Vanberg, Viktor and Wolfgang Kerber (1994), 'Institutional competition among jurisdictions: an evolutionary approach', *Constitutional Political Economy*, **5**, 193–219.
Vaubel, Roland (1991), 'The political economy of the International Monetary Fund: a public choice approach', in Roland Vaubel and Thomas D. Willett (eds), *The Political Economy of International Organizations: A Public Choice Approach*, Boulder, CO: Westview Press, pp. 204–44.
Vaubel, Roland (1994), 'The political economy of centralization and the European Community', *Public Choice*, **81**, 151–90.
Vaubel, Roland (1996), 'Bureaucracy at the IMF and the World Bank: a comparison of the evidence', *The World Economy*, **19**, 195–210.
Vaubel, Roland (1999), 'Enforcing competition among governments: theory and application to the European Union', *Constitutional Political Economy*, **10**, 327–38.
Vaubel, Roland (2008), 'The political economy of labor market regulation by the European Union', *Review of International Organizations*, **3**, 435–65.
Vaubel, Roland (2009a), 'Lessons from the financial crisis: The international dimension', *Economic Affairs*, **29**, 22–6.
Vaubel, Roland (2009b), 'Constitutional courts as promoters of political centralization: lessons for the European Court of Justice', *European Journal of Law and Economics*, **28**, 203–22.
Vaubel, Roland, Axel Dreher and Ugurlu Soylu (2007), 'Staff growth in international organizations: a principal–agent problem? An empirical analysis', *Public Choice*, **133**, 275–95.
Veblen, Thorstein ([1899] 1934). *The Theory of the Leisure Class*, New York: Modern Library.
Vengroff, Richard (1976), 'Density and state formation in Africa', *African Studies Review*, **19**, 67–74.
Verwimp, Philip (2003), 'The political economy of coffee, dictatorship, and genocide', *European Journal of Political Economy*, **19**, 161–81, reprinted in Roger D. Congleton, Arye L. Hillman and Kai A. Konrad (eds) (2008), *Forty Years of Research on Rent Seeking 2 – Applications: Rent Seeking in Practice*, Heidelberg: Springer, pp. 191–211.
Vihanto, Martti (1992), 'Competition between local governments as a discovery procedure', *Journal of Institutional and Theoretical Economics*, **148**, 411–36.
Viscusi, W. Kip (1991), 'The dimensions of the product liability crisis', *The Journal of Legal Studies*, **20**, 147–77.
Vogel, Ronald J. (1999), *Medicare: Issues in Political Economy*, Ann Arbor, MI: University of Michigan Press.
Vogt, Carsten, Joachim Weimann and Chun-Lei Yang (2002), 'Efficient rent seeking in experiment, *Public Choice*, **110**, 67–78, reprinted in Roger D. Congleton, Arye L. Hillman and Kai A. Konrad (eds) (2008), *Forty Years of Research on Rent Seeking 1 – The Theory of Rent Seeking*, Heidelberg: Springer, pp. 681–95.
Voigt, Stefan (1997), 'Positive constitutional economics: a survey', *Public Choice*, **90**, 11–53.
Voigt, Stefan (1999), *Explaining Constitutional Change*, Cheltenham, UK and Northampton, MA, USA: Edward Elgar.
Voigt, Stefan (2004), 'Constitutional political economy', in Charles K. Rowley and Friedrich Schneider (eds), *The Encyclopedia of Public Choice*, New York: Springer, pp. 436–40.
Volcansek, Mary L. (2006), 'Judicial selection in Italy: a civil service model with partisan results', in Kate Malleson and Peter H. Russell (eds), *Appointing Judges in an Age of Judicial Power*, Toronto: University of Toronto Press, pp. 159–75.

Volckart, Oliver (2000), 'The open constitution and its enemies: competition, rent seeking and the rise of the modern state', *Journal of Economic Behavior and Organization*, **42**, 1–17.
Von Hagen, Jürgen (1992), 'Budgeting procedures and fiscal performance in the European communities', *European Commission Economic Papers*, no. 96.
Von Hagen, Jürgen (2010), 'Sticking to fiscal plans: the role of institutions', *Public Choice*, **144**, 487–503.
Von Neumann, John and Oskar Morgenstern (1944), *The Theory of Games and Economic Behavior*, Princeton, NJ: Princeton University Press.
Wade, Robert (1990), *Governing the Market: Economic Theory and the Role of Government in East Asian Industrialization*, Princeton, NJ: Princeton University Press.
Wärneryd, Karl (1990), 'Conventions: an evolutionary approach', *Constitutional Political Economy*, **1**, 83–107.
Wagner, Richard E. (2007), *Fiscal Sociology and the Theory of Public Finance*, Cheltenham, UK and Northampton, MA, USA: Edward Elgar.
Wagner, Richard E. (2011), 'Municipal corporations, economic calculation, and political pricing: exploring a political antinomy', *Public Choice*, **149**, 151–65.
Wahlke, John C. (1991), 'Rational choice theory, voting behavior and democracy', in Albert Somit and Rudolf Wildenmann (eds), *Hierarchy and Democracy*, Baden-Baden: Nomos, pp. 165–87.
Walker, Jack L. (1969), 'The diffusion of innovation among the American states', *American Political Science Review*, **63**, 880–99.
Walker, James M. and Roy Gardner (1992), 'Probabilistic destruction of a common-pool resource: experimental evidence', *Economic Journal*, **102**, 1149–61.
Waltenburg, Eric N. and Charles S. Lopeman (2000), 'Tort decisions and campaign dollars', *Southeastern Political Review*, **28**, 241–63.
Waller, Christopher J. (1989), 'Macroeconomic policy games and central bank politics', *Journal of Money, Credit, and Banking*, **21**, 422–31.
Waller, Christopher J. (1992), 'The choice of a conservative central banker in a multi-sector economy', *American Economic Review*, **82**, 1006–12.
Wangenheim, Georg von (1993), 'The evolution of judge-made law', *International Review of Law and Economics*, **13**, 381–411.
Wantchekon, Leonard (1999), 'On the nature of first democratic elections', *Journal of Conflict Resolution*, **43**, 245–58.
Ward, Michael D., Randolph M. Siverson and Xun Cao (2007), 'Disputes, democracies, and dependencies: a reexamination of the Kantian peace', *American Journal of Political Science*, **51**, 583–601.
Ware, Stephen J. (1999), 'Money, politics, and judicial decisions: a case study of arbitration Law in Alabama', *Journal of Law and Politics*, **15**, 645–86.
Waters, M. Dane (2003), *Initiative and Referendum Almanac*, Durham, NC: Carolina Academic Press.
Weart, Spencer R. (1998), *Never at War: Why Democracies Will Not Fight One Another*, New Haven, CT: Yale University Press.
Weaver, Carolyn L. (1982), *The Crisis in Social Security: Economic and Political Origins*, Durham, NC: Duke University Press.
Weber, Max (1947), *The Theory of Social and Economic Organization*, New York: Free Press.
Weber, Max (1958), *The Protestant Ethic and The Spirit of Capitalism*, New York: Scribner's.
Weede, Erich (2004), 'The diffusion of prosperity and peace by globalization', *The Independent Review*, **9**, 165–86.
Weede, Erich (2006), 'Economic freedom and development', *CATO Journal*, **26**, 511–24.
Weede, Erich (2011), 'The capitalist peace', in Christopher J. Coyne and Rachel L. Mathers (eds), *The Handbook on the Political Economy of War*, Cheltenham, UK and Northampton, MA, USA: Edward Elgar, pp. 269–80.
Weeks, Jessica L. (2008), 'Autocratic audience costs: regime type and signaling resolve', *International Organization*, **62**, 35–64.
Wegner, Gerhard (2003), 'Evolutionary markets and the design of institutional policy', in Pavel

Pelikan and Gerhard Wegner (eds), *The Evolutionary Analysis of Economic Policy*, Cheltenham, UK and Northampton, MA, USA: Edward Elgar, pp. 46–66.

Wegner, Gerhard (2004), 'Political learning: the neglected precondition of constitutional reform', *Constitutional Political Economy*, **15**, 339–58.

Wegner, Gerhard (2008), *Political Failure by Agreement. Learning Liberalism and the Welfare State*, Cheltenham, UK and Northampton, MA, USA: Edward Elgar.

Weingast, Barry R. (1984), 'The congressional-bureaucratic system: a principal–agent perspective (with applications to the SEC)', *Public Choice*, **44**, 147–91.

Weingast, Barry R. (1995), 'The economic role of political institutions: market-preserving federalism and economic development', *Journal of Law, Economics, and Organization*, **11**, 1–31.

Weingast, Barry R. (1997), 'The political foundations of democracy and the rule of law', *American Political Science Review*, **91**, 245–63.

Weingast, Barry R. (2005), 'The performance and stability of federalism: an institutional perspective', in Claude Ménard and Mary M. Shirley (eds), *Handbook of New Institutional Economics*, Dordrecht: Springer, pp. 149–72.

Weingast, Barry R. and William J. Marshall (1988), 'The industrial organization of Congress; or, why legislatures, like firms, are not organized as markets', *Journal of Political Economy*, **96**, 132–63.

Weingast, Barry R. and Mark J. Moran (1983), 'Bureaucratic discretion or congressional control? Regulatory policymaking by the Federal Trade Commission', *Journal of Political Economy*, **91**, 765–800.

Weingast, Barry R., Kenneth A. Shepsle and Christopher Johnsen (1981), 'The political economy of benefits and costs', *Journal of Political Economy*, **89**, 642–64.

Weintraub, Ronald E. (1978), 'Congressional supervision of monetary policy', *Journal of Monetary Economics*, **4**, 341–62.

Weir, Charlie (1992), 'Monopolies and Mergers Commission, merger reports and the public interest: a probit analysis', *Applied Economics*, **24**, 27–34.

Weisbrod, Burton A. (1991), 'The health care quadrilemma: an essay on technological change, insurance, quality of care, and cost containment', *Journal of Economic Literature*, **29**, 523–52.

Weisbrod, Burton A. and Craig L. LaMay (1999), 'Mixed signals: public policy and the future of health care R&D', *Health Affairs*, **18**, 112–25.

Weizsäcker, Carl Christian von (1971), 'Notes on endogenous change of tastes', *Journal of Economic Theory*, **3**, 345–72.

Weizsäcker, Carl Christian von (2001), 'Welfare economics bei endogenen präferenzen: Thünen vorlesung, 2001', *Perspektiven der Wirtschaftspolitik*, **3**, 425–46.

Weizsäcker, Carl Christian von (2005), 'The welfare economics of adaptive preferences', Working Paper Series of the Max Planck Institute for Research on Collective Goods 2005-11, Max Planck Institute for Research on Collective Goods, Bonn.

Werner, Suzanne (2000), 'The effect of political similarity on the onset of militarized disputes, 1816–1985', *Political Science Quarterly*, **53**, 343–74.

White, Michelle (2004), 'Asbestos and the future of mass torts', *Journal of Economic Perspectives*, **18**, 183–204.

Whitman, Douglas G. (2000), 'Evolution of the common law and the emergence of compromise', *Journal of Legal Studies*, **29**, 753–81.

Wicksell, Knut ([1896] 1967), *A New Principle of Just Taxation*, Finanztheoretische Untersuchungen. Jena, reprinted in Richard A. Musgrave and Alan T. Peacock (eds), *Classics in the Theory of Public Finance*, New York: St. Martin's Press, pp. 72–118.

Williams, John T. (1990), 'The political manipulation of macroeconomic policy', *American Political Science Review*, **84**, 767–95.

Williamson, John and Stephan Haggard (1994), 'The political conditions for economic reform', in John Williamson (ed.), *The Political Economy of Policy Reform*, Washington: Institute for International Economics, pp. 527–96.

Williamson, Oliver E. (1975), *Markets and Hierarchies: Analysis and Antitrust Implications*, New York: Free Press.

Williamson, Oliver E. (1976), 'Franchise bidding for natural monopolies – in general and with respect to CATV', *Bell Journal of Economics*, **7**, 73–104.
Williamson, Oliver E. (2000), 'The new institutional economics: taking stock, looking ahead', *Journal of Economic Literature*, **38**, 595–613.
Williamson, Oliver E. (2002), 'Theory of the firm as governance structure: from choice to contract', *Journal of Economic Perspectives*, **16**, 171–95.
Wilson, Woodrow (2005), 'Socialism and democracy', in Ronald J. Pestritto (ed.), *Woodrow Wilson: The Essential Political Writings*, Lanham, MD: Lexington Books, pp. 77–80.
Winer, Stanley L. and J. Stephen Ferris (2008), 'Searching for Keynesianism', *European Journal of Political Economy*, **24**, 294–316.
Winer, Stanley L., Michael W. Tofias, Bernard Grofman and John H. Aldrich (2008), 'Trending economic factors and the structure of Congress in the growth of government: 1930–2002', *Public Choice*, **135**, 415–48.
Wintrobe, Ronald (1998), *The Political Economy of Dictatorship*, Cambridge and New York: Cambridge University Press.
Wintrobe, Ronald (2001), 'How to understand, and deal with dictatorship: an economist's view', *Economics of Governance*, **2**, 35–58.
Wintrobe, Ronald (2006), 'Extremism, suicide terror and authoritarianism', *Public Choice*, **128**, 159–95.
Wisemen, Timothy Peter (1985), 'Competition and co-operation', in Timothy Peter Wiseman (ed.), *Roman Political Life 90 B.C.–A.D. 69*, Exeter: Exeter University Press, pp. 3–20.
Witt, Ulrich (1992), 'The endogenous public choice theorist', *Public Choice*, **73**, 117–29.
Witt, Ulrich (1996), 'The political economy of mass media societies', Papers on Economics & Evolution, no. 9601, Max Planck Institute of Economics, Jena.
Witt, Ulrich (2003), 'Economic policy making in evolutionary perspective', *Journal of Evolutionary Economics*, **13**, 77–94.
Witt, Ulrich (2008), 'Evolutionary economics', in Steven N. Durlauf and Lawrence E. Blume (eds), *The New Palgrave Dictionary of Economics*, 2nd edn, vol. 3, pp. 67–73.
Witt, Ulrich and Christian Schubert (2010), 'Extending the informational basis of welfare economics: the case of preference dynamics', Papers on Economics & Evolution, no. 2010-05, Max Planck Institute of Economics, Jena.
Wittman, Donald (1989), 'Why democracies produce efficient results', *Journal of Political Economy*, **97**, 1395–424.
Wittman, Donald A. (1995), *The Myth of Democratic Failure: Why Political Institutions are Efficient*, Chicago, IL: University of Chicago Press.
Wittman, Donald (2007), 'Candidate quality, pressure group endorsements, and the nature of political advertising', *European Journal of Political Economy*, **23**, 360–78.
Wohlgemuth, Michael (2000), 'Political entrepreneurship and bidding for political monopoly', *Journal of Evolutionary Economics*, **10**, 273–95.
Wohlgemuth, Michael (2002a), 'Evolutionary approaches to politics', *Kyklos*, **55**, 223–46.
Wohlgemuth, Michael (2002b), 'Democracy and opinion falsification: towards a new Austrian political economy', *Constitutional Political Economy*, **13**, 223–46.
Wohlgemuth, Michael (2003), 'Democracy as an evolutionary method', in Pavel Pelikan and Gerhard Wegner (eds), *The Evolutionary Analysis of Economic Policy*, Cheltenham, UK and Northampton, MA, USA: Edward Elgar, pp. 96–127.
Wohlgemuth, Michael (2005), 'Schumpeterian political economy and Downsian public choice: alternative economic theories of democracy', in Alain Marciano and Jean-Michel Josselin (eds), *Law and the State: A Political Economy Approach*, Cheltenham, UK and Northampton, MA, USA: Edward Elgar, pp. 21–57.
Wohlgemuth, Michael (2008), 'Learning through institutional competition', in Andreas Bergh and Rolf Höijer (eds), *Institutional Competition*, Cheltenham, UK and Northampton, MA, USA: Edward Elgar, pp. 67–89.
Wolfson, Sandy, Delia Wakelin and Matthew Lewis (2005), 'Football supporters' predictions of their role in home advantage', *Journal of Sports Sciences*, **23**, 365–74.
Woo, Gordon (2006), 'Small world constraints on terrorism planning. Risk management

solutions', presented at the Conference on Mathematical Methods of Counterterrorism, 28 September, Washington, DC.
Wood, B. Dan and James E. Anderson (1993), 'The politics of U.S. antitrust regulation', *American Journal of Political Science*, **37**, 1–39.
Wood, Elisabeth J. (2003), 'Civil wars: what we don't know', *Global Governance*, **9**, 247–60.
Woodford, Michael (2001), 'Fiscal requirements for price stability', *Journal of Money Credit and Banking*, **33**, 669–728.
Woodford, Michael (2003), *Interest and Prices: The Foundations of Monetary Policy*, Princeton, NJ: Princeton University Press.
Woolley, John T. (1984), *Monetary Politics: The Federal Reserve and the Politics of Monetary Policy*, New York: Cambridge University Press.
Wootton, David (1990), 'Leveller democracy and the puritan revolution', in J.H. Burns (ed.), *The Cambridge History of Political Thought, 1450–1700*, Cambridge: Cambridge University Press, pp. 412–42.
World Bank (2001a), *World Development Report 2002: Building Institutions for Markets*, Oxford and New York: published for the World Bank by Oxford University Press.
World Bank (2001b), 'Governing the justice system: Spain's judicial council', available at: http://www1.worldbank.org/prem/PREMNotes/premnote54.pdf (accessed 11 July 2011).
Wright, Gavin (1974), 'The political economy of New Deal spending: an econometric analysis', *Review of Economics and Statistics*, **56**, 30–38.
Wright, Gordon (1987), *France in Modern Times*, New York: Norton.
Wright, Joseph (2008), 'Do authoritarian institutions constrain? How legislatures affect economic growth and investment', *American Journal of Political Science*, **52**, 322–43.
Wu, Fang and Bernardo A. Huberman (2008), 'How public opinion forms', in Christos Papadimitriou and Shuzhong Zhang (eds), *Internet and Network Economics*, Berlin-Heidelberg: Springer, pp. 334–41.
Xiang, Jun, Xiaohong Xu and George Keteku (2007), 'Power: the missing link in the trade conflict relationship', *Journal of Conflict Resolution*, **51**, 646–63.
Yanagizawa-Drott, David (2009), 'Propaganda and conflict: theory and evidence from the Rwandan genocide', working paper.
Yandle, Bruce (1989), 'Bootleggers and baptists in the market for regulation', in Jason F. Shogren (ed.), *The Political Economy of Government Regulation*, Heidelberg: Springer, pp. 29–54.
Yavas, Abdullah (1998), 'Does too much government investment retard the economic development of a country', *Journal of Economic Studies*, **25**, 296–308.
Yeager, Leland B. (1985), 'Rights, contract, and utility in policy espousal', *Cato Journal*, **5**, 259–94.
Yeager, Leland B. (2001), *Ethics as a Social Science*, Cheltenham, UK and Northampton, MA, USA: Edward Elgar.
Young, Marilyn, Michael Reksulak and William F. Shughart II (2001), 'The political economy of the IRS', *Economics and Politics*, **13**, 201–20.
Young, Robert (2001), 'Reflections of a survivor of state judicial election warfare', *Civil Justice Report*, **2**, New York: Manhattan Institute for Policy Research.
Yu, Frank and Xiaoyun Yu (2011), 'Corporate lobbying and fraud detection', *Journal of Financial and Quantitative Analysis*, forthcoming (first published online 6 June 2011).
Zaller, John R. (1992), *The Nature and Origins of Mass Opinion*, Cambridge: Cambridge University Press.
Zanzig, Blair R. (1997), 'Measuring the impact of competition in local government education markets on the cognitive achievement of students', *Economics of Education Review*, **16**, 431–41.
Zardkoohi, Asghar (1988), 'Market structure and campaign contributions: does concentration matter? A reply', *Public Choice*, **58**, 187–91.
Zax, Jeffrey S. (1989), 'Is there a Leviathan in your neighborhood?', *American Economic Review*, **79**, 560–7.
Zeldes, Stephen P. (1989), 'Consumption and liquidity constraints: An empirical investigation', *Journal of Political Economy*, **97**, 305–46.
Zhang, Jie (1995), 'Social security and endogenous growth', *Journal of Public Economics*, **58**, 185–213.

Zimmer, Ron, and Richard Buddin (2009), 'Is charter school competition in California improving the performance on traditional public schools?', *Public Administration Review*, **69**, 831–45.

Ziskind, Martha Andes (1969), 'Judicial tenure in the American Constitution: English and American precedents', *The Supreme Court Review*, **1969**, 135–54.

Zito, Anthony R. (2001), 'Epistemic communities, collective entrepreneurship and European integration', *Journal of European Public Policy*, **8**, 585–603.

Zweynert, Joachim (2009), 'Interests versus culture in the theory of institutional change?', *Journal of Institutional Economics*, **5**, 339–60.

Zywicki, Todd J. (2003), 'The rise and fall of efficiency in the common law: a supply-side analysis', *Northwestern Law Review*, **97**, 1551–63.

Zywicki, Todd J. and Jeremy Kidd (2010), 'Public choice and tort reform', George Mason University School of Law working paper.

Zywicki, Todd J. and Edward Peter Stringham (2010), 'Common law and economic efficiency', in Francesco Parisi and Richard A. Posner (eds), *Encyclopedia of Law and Economics*, Cheltenham, UK and Northampton, MA, USA: Edward Elgar, forthcoming, available at: http://papers.ssrn.com/sol3/papers.cfm?abstract_id=1673968 (accessed 20 May 2012).

Index

Abrahms, M. 502
Abrajano, M.A. 337
Abramowitz, A.I. 336
Abrams, B.A. 276, 277
Abrescia, M. 163
abstention 21–2, 119–20, 121
abstract science of economic behavior 112
academia and rent seeking 322
Acemoglu, D.
   autocracy 91–2
   Botswana 211
   colonial institutions 474
   dictatorship and democracy 5, 61–3, 70, 94
agency problems
   direct democracy 129–30
   international organizations 452
agenda-setting function of committees 149, 221–3
Aggarwal, R.K. 342
Akerlof, G.A. 150
Albrecht, J. 432
Aldrich, J. 52
Alesina, A. 209, 251, 385
   fiscal policy 274, 276
Alvarez, M.R. 225
American Association for Justice 350–51
American Trial Lawyers Association (ATLA) 351
Ames, R.E. 417
Ancient Greece 48, 66–9
Anderson, A. 432
Anderson, G.M. 225
Anderson, J.E. 303
anocracies 477, 478
Ansolabehere, S. 339, 340, 342
antitrust law 291–303
Apollonio, D.E. 333
Arce, D.G.
   counterterror policy 495, 497, 499, 502, 505
   political leadership 432
Ardagna, S. 274
Argys, L.M. 229
Aristotle 41, 85
Arrow, K.J. 14, 15, 16–18, 49, 437
   economics of healthcare 369, 370, 371
   impossibility theorem 15, 17, 18, 49
   and stability of political opinion 17, 435–6
Asch, P. 300

Aschauer, D.A. 268, 269
asymmetric information
   and conflict 480
   direct democracy 130–31
Athens, ancient 67–9, 175
ATLA (American Trial Lawyers Association) 351
attitudinal model, judges 243
auctions 420–21
autocracies 83–106
   economic approaches 88–91
   institutional theories 97–103
   institutions 91–7
   political science theories 84–8
   and rent seeking 318, 328
Averch–Johnson effect 286
Ayittey, G.B.N. 202
Azam, J.-P. 479
Azzi, C. 400

Babst, D.V. 484
Baik, K.H. 326
Bailey, M.J. 350, 352
Baldassare, M. 383
Ballo, Z. 478, 480
ballot measures, campaign spending 342–3
Banerjee, A. 209
Bank of England Monetary Policy Committee 258
Bapat, N.A. 504
Barbieri, K. 487
Barkun, M. 203
Baron, D.P. 150
Barro, R.J. 270
Bartel, A.P. 286
Basuchoudhary, A. 500, 501
Battacharya, S. 130
Baumol, W.J. 17
Bearse, P. 389
Beck, N. 250, 251
Becker, E. 183
Becker, G.S. 400, 428
   neoclassical paradigm 427
behaviorism 40
Benassy-Quere, A. 274
benefit–cost ratio, counterterror policies 498–500
benevolent governments 99

584 *Index*

Bercovitch, J. 479
Bernhard, W. 254
Bernhardt, D. 501–2
Bernholz, P. 482
Berry, C.R. 135
Berument, H. 230
Besley, T. 371
   bundling of issues 131
   conflict and state capacity 476
   judicial behavior 239, 358
   political competition and economic performance 277
   regulatory policy 287
   yardstick competition 180
bicameral legislatures 29, 162–3, 168–9
Bifulco, R. 393
Bittlingmayer, G. 299–300
Black, D. 12, 13, 14–16, 17, 49
Blanchard, O.J. 273–4
Blattman, C. 471, 480
Blomberg, S.B. 277
Boadway, R.W. 366
Boehmer, C.R. 487
Boehmke, F.J. 141
Boettke, P.J. 186
Boix, C. 67, 70, 94–5, 97, 103
Bombardini, M. 333
Boockmann, B. 456
Booker, K. 394
Borda, Jean-Charles de 12–13
Bose, F. 364, 373–8, 379, 380
Botswana 211
Boudreaux, D.J. 188, 296–7
Boulding, K.E. 432, 437, 443
Bowler, S. 136, 140, 342
Boyer, R. 436
Boyes, W.J. 286
Brabazon, J. 471
Brace, P. 239, 357, 358
Bradford, D.F. 183
Braithwaite, A. 476
Brams, S.J. 504
Brandeis, Louis 180
Brauninger, T. 277
Brender, A. 276
Brennan, H.G. 72, 78, 79, 112, 113, 186
Breyer, F. 371
Bronars, S.G. 339
Bronfenbrenner, M. 17
Brown, T.M. 18
Browning, E.K. 365
Brunner, E. 390–91, 397
Buchanan, J.M. 4, 18, 25–31, 31–2, 123, 275, 475
   bicameralism 162

   constitutional political economy 72, 75, 78–9, 80
   constitutions 41–2, 50, 51, 59, 71
   costs of voting 205
   direct democracy 128
   evolutionary democracy 437
   federal systems 180, 182, 185, 186, 187
   logic versus science of electoral behavior 112
   political behavior and public choice theory 45, 46
   politics as exchange 187–8
   pre- and post-constitutional decision-making 143–4
   rent-seeking 307
   vote trading 146
Buchanan's paradox 50
Buddin, R. 393
budget approval process 169–71
budget-constrained bureau 36
budgets and bureaucrats 36
Bueno de Mesquita, B. 96, 97, 98
Bullock, C.S. 222
bundling and direct democracy 131
bureaucracies 34–7
   and autocracies 104
   and bribery 308
   central banks 255–6
   and regulatory policy 287
Buser, W. 185–6
Byman, D. 504

Cadigan, J. 497, 499
Calcagno, P.T. 120
Caldwell, M. 154, 166
California, ballot initiative spending 342, 343
campaign finance 331–44
Canes-Wrone, B. 358
capital punishment, influence of US election cycle 227–9
capitalist peace theory 486–9
Card, D. 396
Cardozo, Benjamin N. 244
career concerns, effect on judicial decision-making 240, 356–60
Carlson, L.J. 499
Carneiro, R.L. 201
Carsey, T.M. 225–6
Case, A. 180
Catholic Church, medieval 323–4, 402–13
central banks
   as bureaucracies 255–6
   influences on monetary policy 249–52
   and time inconsistency problem 252–5
centralization in federal systems 191

centralized tribal systems 196, 197–201, 204, 206–7
Chahrour, R. 272
Chakrabarti, R. 392
Chan, P.C.W. 392
Chappell, H.W. 251, 252, 253, 257–8
charter schools 392–4
Chehabi, H.E. 87
Chen, H. 341
Chicago School and antitrust 291–4
China 65–6
Chiozza, G. 486
Choi, S.-W. 475
Christian Church, medieval 323–4, 402–13
Christiano, L.J. 273
Chu, A.C. 185
Cimadomo, J. 274
civil conflict and political institutions 476–8
Clark, J.R. 487
Clark, T.S. 358
Clark, W.R. 98
class actions, tort law 350
Clayton Act 297–8
Cleisthenes 68, 70
Coase, R.H. 17
  Coase theorem 418–19, 420
  efficiency of common law 355
  information problem 48
Coate, M.B. 301–2
Coate, S. 131, 287, 337–8
coercion as basis of government 188–9
Cohen, J.E. 287
Cohen, M.A. 240
Cohen, S.H. 394
Coker, D.C. 151, 222
Coleman, James 46
collective action
  and (counter)terrorism 494–506
  problems 51–2
  rent seeking 315–16
  tribal systems 203–6
collective choice 4
  Botswana 211
Collier, P. 471, 481
Colonel Blotto games 500–502
colonial rule, effect on tribal systems 207–8
Commager, H.S. 69
committee preference outlier hypothesis 148–9
committees 147–51, 163
  and campaign finance 334
  congressional oversight 217–26
  monetary policy decisions 256–9
common law efficiency 355
common-pool resource experiments 418–20
community decision problem 262–5

companies, *see* firms
competence of voters 139–40, 382–3
competition
  in education 384–94
  political 437–40
Competition Commission, UK 295–6
Conciliar movement 177
Condorcet, J.-A.-N. de Caritat, Marquis de 12–13, 49
Condorcet's paradox 13, 14, 20, 48
Condorcet winners 421–2
conflict 469–89
  economic analysis 470–72
  and institutions 472–82
Confucius 65–6
Congleton, R.D. 5, 175, 307
  democratization 63
  welfare state 362, 364, 366, 367, 370, 373–8, 379–80
Congress, US, campaign finance and voting behavior 339–40
congressional dominance 163, 223–6
congressional oversight committees 217–21
congressional (presidential) systems 154, 166
Conover, P.J. 45
Corradi, V. 436
consensus model of parliament 155–6, 176–7
consent as basis of government 187–8
Constitutional Political Economy (journal) 51
constitutional political economy (CPE) 72–82
constitutional scope 50–51
constitutionalism 72–3
constitutions 41–3, 59–60
contest-success functions 313–15
contract enforcement role of courts 235
contractualism 74
conventions and constitutions 59–60
Converse, P.E. 45
Cooper, M.J. 341
Cooter, R.D. 162, 241
Corcoran, S.P. 393
corruption and rent extraction 318
Coşgel, M.M. 356
costs
  of collective action 26–7
  of decision-making 59
  of expressive voting 113–14
  of information, international organizations 452–3, 460, 462
  of repression and loyalty in dictatorships 90
  of voting in tribal systems 205–6
Couch, J.F. 392
Council of Five Hundred 68
counterterrorism 494–504

courts
  and direct democracy 141
  independence 239–42
  international courts of justice 464–5
  role of 234–6
Cover, A.D. 243
Cowart, A.T. 251
Cowling, K. 312
Crain, W.M. 151, 220–21, 222, 223
Crandall, R.W. 298
Crawford, V. 140
credibility dilemma, autocrats 103
credible commitment, peace negotiations 479–80
Crémer, J. 184
Crenshaw, M. 503
Cropper, M. 285
Crowley, G.R. 187
Cunningham, Randall 'Duke' 338
Curia Regis 176
Cusanus, N. 48
cynicism and rent seeking 309

Dacey, R. 499
Dahl, R.A. 85
Dalton, R.J. 135, 141
damage payments 348–9
Davis, D.D. 424
De Bartolome, C.A.M. 396
De Figueiredo, J.M. 139, 241, 343
De Resende, C.A. 273
de Soysa, I. 475, 481
De Vault, J.M. 226
decision-making costs 59
Declaration of the Rights of Man (France) 50–51
defense, tribal systems 205
deference, norm of 148
Delorme, C.D. 296, 320
demand-constrained bureau 36
democracy
  and civil war 476–7
  development of 61–4
  as a discovery process 437–8
democratic coherence problem 48–50
democratic peace theory 483–6
democratization and autocratic survival 87–8
Denslow, D.A. 383
Denzau, A.T. 149, 334
Derouen, K.R. 479
Desch, M.C. 486
Dewey, J. 44
Diamond, M. 22
dictatorships, *see* autocracies
Diermeier, D. 84

DiLorenzo, T.D. 296
direct democracy 127–42; *see also* referendums
discipline, role of committees 150–51
Djankov, S. 340
Dodgson, C. ('Lewis Carroll') 14
Donovan, T. 136, 140, 342
Dorsey, E.R. 372
Dorussen, H. 486, 488, 489
Dow, J. 151
Downes, A.B. 486
Downs, A. 18–23, 146
  bureaucracy 35
  challenged by William H. Riker 24
  on *Calculus of Consent* 31
  on Duncan Black 15
  on Joseph Schumpeter 428
  voter rationality 45
Doyle, M.W. 483
Drazen, A. 250, 276
Dresher, M. 501
Drinkwater, S. 120
DSGE (dynamic stochastic general equilibrium) model 271–3
Dubois, E. 277
Duncombe, W. 386
Dundas, C. 196
Dunne, S.W. 395
Dyke, A. 229
dynamic stochastic general equilibrium (DSGE) model 271–3
dynastic interests, tribal systems 204–5

Easterbrook, F.H. 243–4
Easterly, W. 209, 270
economic development and conflict 480–81
economics and religion 401
Edelberg, W. 274
education 382–98
efficiency and federal systems 185–6
ego-rents, politicians 307
Ehrenberg, R. 400
Ehrlich, I. 355
Eigen-Zucchi, C. 298
Eisenstadt, S.N. 196
Ekelund, R.B. 297–8, 324, 413
Elbadawi, I. 476, 481
Elder, H.W. 239
elections
  and campaign finance 335–8
  and judicial decision-making 229, 357–8
  and monetary policy 249–50
  and political behavior 226–31
  and terrorism 499
electoral choice 112–13
electoral systems, tribal systems 206–7

employees and regulatory policy 286
Enders, W. 504
enforcement mechanisms, autocracies 101–2
Enlightenment 69
Environmental Protection Agency (EPA) 285
environmental regulation 284–5, 285–6, 287–8
Epple, D. 187
Epstein, L. 243
Epstein, R.A. 233, 234, 350, 351
equality as the state of nature 58
Erceg, C.J. 273
Escribà-Folch, A. 95
Eskridge, W.N. 240–41
États-Generaux 176
ethnic diversity and post-colonial state failure 209
ethnic tensions and conflict 481
European Commission, salaries 462–3
European Court of Justice 464–5
European Parliament 458–9
European Union 190–91, 453–4, 456
  and interest groups 466–7
  and national governments 457–8, 459–60
Eusepi, G. 78, 79
Evans 395
Evans-Pritchard, E.E. 196, 197, 198, 200, 202, 204, 207, 211
evolutionary public choice 427–44
executions, influence of US election cycle 227–9
executive, role in direct democracy 141
exit (inter-jurisdictional competition) 439–40
experimental public choice 415–25
expressive rationality 80–81
expressive voting 111–25

Fagen, R.R. 25
Faith, R.L. 300–301
Farley, J.D. 504
Farris, C.D. 23
Fearon, J.D. 472, 473, 476, 478, 481
Federal Emergency Management Agency (FEMA) 225, 227
federal legislation, US 145–6
Federal Open Market Committee 256–8
Federal Reserve 229–30, 251–2, 255–6
federal systems 179–94
  and efficiency 185–6
  EU 190–91
  information and incentives 189–90
  and Leviathan hypothesis 186–7
  origins 181–2
  Switzerland 191–2
  US 191
  see also fiscal federalism

Feld, L.P. 136, 142, 192, 234
Feldman, S. 45
Feldstein, M. 365
FEMA (Federal Emergency Management Agency) 225, 227
Fenn, P. 240
Fenno, R.F. 144
Ferejohn, J.A. 147, 238
Fernandez-Villaverde, J. 272
Ferree, K. 161
Ferris, J.S. 277
Fielding, D. 477
Figlio, D.N. 392, 396
Finer, S.E. 64, 65, 66, 68, 69
Fiorina, M.P. 421
Fiorino, N. 164
firms
  and campaign contributions 341–2
  and regulatory policy 285
  rent seeking 321
fiscal federalism
  and income 185–6
  and rent extraction 316–17
fiscal policy 260–81
  long-run macro model 262–70
  short-run 271–80
Fisher, R.C. 385
Fjelde, H. 475, 481
Fleck, R.K. 236, 241
Fleisher, R. 223
Florida
  referendum on school spending 395
  school vouchers 388
Foldvary, F. 183
Folland, S. 371
Forbes, K.F. 186
foreign aid and rent seeking 320
foreign conflict initiation, influence of election cycle 227
Fortes, M. 196, 197, 198, 200, 202, 204, 207, 211
France 50–51, 176–7
fraud, EU institutions 463–4
Frey, B.S. 136, 276, 459
Friedman, M. 392, 487
functional and institutional theory 40

Gaebler, T. 180
Galasso, V. 367
Galli, E. 277
Gandhi, J. 92, 93, 94, 96
Gardner, R. 419
Garrett, E. 343
Garrett, T.A. 225, 227
Gartzke, E. 486, 487

Gasiorowski, M. 488
Gassebner, M. 499
gatekeeper function of committees 149
Geddes, B. 87, 95
Gely, R. 240
Gennaioli, N. 209
Gerber, A. 336, 342
Gerber, E.R.
   campaign finance 343
   direct democracy 129, 130, 134, 135, 139, 142
Gerlach-Kristen, P. 258
Ghana 211–12
Gibler, D.M. 485
Gilbert, M.D. 141
Gilligan, T.W. 150
Glatzer, B. 201, 204, 206
Goemans, H.E. 486, 489
Goenner, C.F. 487, 488
Goetz, C.J. 182
Gokcekus, E. 391
Golembiewski, R.T. 34
Goodman, J. 355
Goodman, L.A. 18
Gordon, S.C. 239, 340–41, 358
Gouveia, M. 371
governability dilemma, autocrats 103–4
government
   by coercion 188–9
   by consent 187–8
   intergovernmental relationships 182–5
   performance, effect of direct democracy 135
   and rent seeking 320–21
Grafen, A. 122
Great Britain, *see* United Kingdom
Great Merger Wave 299
Greece, ancient 48, 66–9
greed as cause of conflict 471–2
Green, D.P. 45, 336
Greene, K.V. 120
Grier, K.B. 229, 230, 250, 333
grievance as cause of conflict 471–2
Groseclose, T. 222
Guarnaschelli, S. 422
guilt and rent seeking 310
Gunnell, J. 44

Haber, S. 96–7
Hafer, C. 340–41
Hajnal, Z.L. 139
Hall, M.G. 239, 357, 358
Hall, R.E. 363
Hamilton, A. 182
Hamilton, B.W. 183
Hamilton, H.D. 394

Hamlin, A. 111, 119
Han Empire 66
Hanssen, F.A. 236
   judicial behavior 239, 241, 357–8
   judicial institutions 245
Harberger triangles 307
Hardin, G. 418
Harris, M.N. 258
Harsanyi, J.C. 16
Hart, C.M.D. 392
Hart, D.M. 333
Hasen, R.L. 141
Havrilesky, T.M. 251, 256
Hayek, F.A. von 327, 487
   competition 439
   evolutionary democracy 437, 438, 444
   federalism 185
   information role of prices 236
   knowledge problem 47
   role of judges 356
Haynes, S.E. 250
healthcare 368–73
Heckathorn, D.D. 203, 204
Heckelman, J.C. 230
Hegre, H. 471, 477, 485, 487
Helland, E. 239, 358
Henderson, E.A. 478
Hendrix, C.S. 475
Hess, G.D. 227, 277
Hibbs, D.A. 251
Hillman, A.L. 118, 119
Hillman–Samet all-pay auction 314
Hirshleifer, J. 355, 470
Hirschman, A.O. 150, 488
Hitler, Adolf 85
Hobbes, Thomas 57–8, 61, 328–9
Hochman, H.M. 188
Hodrick, R.J. 278
Hoeffler, A. 471, 481
Hoffman, E. 420
Holcombe, R.G.
   coercion 188
   congressional committees 222
   federal systems 181, 185
   school spending 383, 394, 395, 397, 398
Holmer, F. 16
Holyst, J.A. 441
homeowners associations, voting rights 188
Homo economicus 43–6, 75
homogeneity of society and costs of decision-making 28–9
Hornblower, S. 67, 68
Hotelling, H. 17, 21
Houser, D. 337–8
Hoxby, C. 387, 392, 397

Huber, G.A. 239, 358
Huberman, B.A. 436
Huntington, S.P. 475

Iannaccone, L.R. 503
Ianni, A. 436
identification and expressive voting 119–20
identity and expressive voting 118–19, 124–5
ideology
　influence on fiscal policy 275
　influence on judicial decision-making 243, 356
Imazeki, J. 390–91, 397
IMF (International Monetary Fund) 462
impossibility theorem (Arrow) 17, 49
incentives and federalism 182–3, 189–90
income
　and conflict 480–81
　effect of fiscal decentralization 185–6
independence
　Federal Reserve 255–6
　judiciary 237–44
individual choice 4
individual rationality 75–6
individualism 73–4
industry regulation 285
information
　autocracies and democracies 104–5
　and direct democracy 139–40
　and federalism 189–90
　role of courts 236
　role of legislative committees 149–51
information costs and international organizations 452–3, 460, 462
information problems 47–8
　direct democracy 130–31
initiatives 127
Inman, R.P. 183
innovation
　political 433–6
　and rent seeking 319–20
instability 49–50
institutional theories of autocracy 97–13
institutions 41
　and autocracies 91–7
　and conflict 472–82
inter-jurisdictional competition 439–40
interest groups 51–2, 366–7
　and direct democracy 141
　influence on judicial decision-making 360
intergovernmental relationships 182–3
International Labor Organization (ILO) 456, 465–6
international organizations 451–67

investment games 416–17
Iossifov, P. 276
Ireland, P.N. 253
irrationality in politics 430
Isaac, R.M. 417
issue indivisibilities and conflict 482
Iyer, L. 209

Jackson, Henry 'Scoop' 222–3
Jackson, P. 472
Jaggers, K. 87
Jayachandran, S. 341
Jefferson, W.J. 338
Jennings, C. 111, 119, 120
Johnson, C.M. 219
Jones, B.F. 477
Jones, C.I. 363
Joulfaian, D. 187
judiciary 233–46, 354–60
　independence 237–42
　influences on 229, 239–40, 356–60
　institutional change 244–5
　roles 234–6
jury problem 12

Kahn, M.E. 140, 285
Kaja, A. 462
Kane, E.J. 251
Kang, M.S. 358
Karras, G. 270
Karrer, I. 459
Karsden, R. 203
Katz, A. 355
Katz, E. 313
Keech, W.R. 251, 252
Kenny, L.W.
　federalism 186, 187
　school districts 385, 386
　school spending 383, 395, 398
　school vouchers 389–90
Kim, H.M. 487
Kim, Y. 367
Kimenyi, M.S. 205, 209, 210
king-and-council template 175
Knight, B. 341
Knight, J. 243
knowledge function of committees 149–50
knowledge problem 47–8
Kontopoulos, Y. 276
Kopel, M. 441
Kormendi, R.C. 268
Kornhauser, L.A. 356
Kort, F. 16
Krasno, J.S. 336
Krehbiel, K. 84, 148, 150

Kreps, S.E. 504
Kroszner, R.S. 334
Krueger, A.O. 52, 307, 424
Kubik, J.D. 227
Kuran, T. 432, 438
Kurosawa, Akira 60
Kwoka, J.E. 287
Kydd, A.H. 499

La Porta, R. 234
La Raja, R.J. 333
Laband, D.N. 121
Ladd, H.F. 393
Lagona, F. 169, 170, 172–3, 173
Laitin, D.D. 473, 476, 481
Landau, D.L. 270
Landes, W.M.
　judicial independence 237, 244–5
　judicial motivation 356
Latham, E. 33–4
law 345–61
　as constraint on judges' behavior 243–4
　legal system and rent seeking 322–3
　see also judiciary
Lawson, R.A. 487
leaders' motivations and characters 85–6
Leaver, C. 287
Lee, S.J. 85
legalism, China 66
legislation cycle 171–3
legislative committees, *see* committees
Legislative Index of Electoral Competition (LIEC) 161
legislative organization theories 146–51
legislatures 143–51; *see also* parliaments
Leland, Marc 461
Leventoğlu, B. 479
Leviathan hypothesis 185, 186–7
Levine, M.E. 421
Levine, R. 209
Levitt, S.D. 229, 337
Levmore, S. 162
Levy, M.J. 34
Lewin, L. 43
Lewis, A.M. 202
Lewis, H.S. 198
Lewis, J.D. 34
Lewis-Beck, M.S. 295
Li, Q. 488
liability standards 347–8
LIEC (Legislative Index of Electoral Competition) 161
Lijphart, A. 162, 174
Lim, Y. 243
Limongi, F. 88

Lindahl, E. 123
Linde, J. 273
Linz, J.J. 86, 87, 154
Lipset, S.M. 61
List, J.A. 284
Littlechild, S. 312
Loasby, B.J. 434
lobbying
　international organizations 465–7
　and rent seeking 308
　and tort reform 352
Locke, J. 39, 58–9
logic of choice 112–13
logrolling 29
Lomasky, L.E. 113
Long, W.F. 294–5
long-run fiscal policy 262–70
Lott, J.R. 333, 339
Lowenstein, D.H. 139, 141, 342
Lowrey, D. 186
loyalty costs 90
Lull, Ramon 48, 49
Lupia, A. 130, 135, 140

Mackay, R.J. 149
Mackie, G. 116–17, 118
Madison, James 68, 235, 465
Magna Carta 176
majority representation and direct democracy 137–9
Mandelbaum, M. 484
manipulation of voting 49
Mansfield, E.D. 484
Manweller, M. 141
Maoz, Z. 485
marginal approach to CPE 78–9
Marlow, M.L. 187
Marshall, A. 401
Marshall, M.G. 87
Marshall, W.J. 149, 219
Martin, L.L. 462
Marwell, G. 417
Maskin, E. 236
Matsusaka, J.G.
　direct democracy 129, 130, 131, 135, 136, 137, 138, 140, 141, 142
　voter preferences on environmental goods 285
Mayhew, D.R. 146
Mays, W. 16
McBride, M. 503
McCallum, B.T. 230
McCarty, N.
　direct democracy 129, 130, 131
　political action committees 333–4

McChesney, F.S.
  antitrust 292
  rent extraction 316
McCormick, R.E.
  antitrust 303
  legislature size 162–3, 164
McCubbins, M.D. 140, 224
McDonald, J.A. 488
McDonald, P. 487
McGregor, R.R. 253, 257
McKenzie, R.B. 184
McKitrick, R. 284
McLean, I. 48
McMillan, R. 392
Meade, J.E. 30
median voter theorem 15, 365, 422
medical technology, state funding 371–3
medieval, *see* Middle Ages
Mertens, K. 272
Mesnard, A. 479
Mesopotamia 64–5
Metcalfe, J.S. 441
methodological individualism 4, 73–4
Mian, A. 340
Miceli, T.J. 356
Middle Ages
  Church 323–4, 402–13
  parliaments 175–6
migration and rent seeking behavior 319
Miguel, E. 471, 480, 481
Miller, K.P. 141
Milligan, K. 383
Millner, E.L. 424
Minford, P. 251
minimal winning coalitions 24
Mises, L. 45, 48
Missouri, antitrust law 297
Mitchell, W.C. 37, 123
Mocan, H.N. 229
Moe, T.M.
  congressional oversight 224–5
  legislatures in presidential systems 154, 166
monarchy 58
monetary policy 249–59
Monetary Policy Committee, Bank of England 258
money, influence on votes 139
Monopolies and Mergers Commission (UK) 295–6
Moon, W. 335, 337
Moran, J.R. 227
Moreau, F. 441, 442
Morris, I.L. 252
Morton, R.B. 337
motivational symmetry 75, 80

motivations
  for dictators 85–6, 89–90
  individuals 19, 75–6, 80–81
  of legislators 144
  for political contributions 332
  politicians 19
  voters 19, 111–25
Mousseau, M. 484, 487
Mueller, D.C. 312, 415
Munger, M.C. 123, 151, 221, 223, 334
Munley, V.G. 394, 397
Murrell, P. 340
Musgrave, R.A. 180, 182, 185
Mussolini, Benito 85
Myerson, R.B. 92, 94

Nagel, S.S. 239
Napolitano, G. 163
narrative approach to fiscal policy analysis 274
National Industrial Recovery Act (NIRA) 299–300
national insurance programs 362–4
natural experiments on rent seeking 326
natural resources and rent seeking 320
negative externalities 418–21
negligence 347
Nelson, M.A. 187, 385, 386
Nelson, P.J. 120
new institutional economics and autocracy 88
Nicolas of Cusa 48
Nifong, Mike 229
Niskanen, W.A. 34–7, 45
  budget-maximizing bureaus 185, 219, 223, 224
  information problem 48
Nkrumah, K. 204
Nordhaus, W. 250, 275
Nordstrom, T. 487
norm of deference 148
normative individualism 74
normative motivations 81
North, D.C. 63, 238, 473

O'Driscoll, G. 47
O'Hara, E.A. 356
Oates, W.E. 180, 182, 183, 186
Olken, B.A. 477
Olson, M. 11, 31–4, 45, 489
  collective action 51–2, 203, 209
  collective action and terrorism 494, 495, 496, 506
  interest group model of social security benefits 366
  state as stationary bandit 60–61, 88, 99–100, 474–5

Olson, W. 350
Oneal, J.R. 485
opinion formation 431–6
optimal voting rule 59
organizational design, autocratic institutions 96–7
organizations
    international 451–67
    terrorist 504–5
Orlean, A. 436
Orphanides, A. 227
Osborne, D. 180
Ostrom, E. 415, 419
over-dissipation of rents 325–6

PACs (political action committees) 333
Padovano, F. 169, 170, 172, 172–3, 277
Pagden, A. 68
Palfrey, T.R. 184, 421, 423
Pande, R. 209
Parker, G.R. 222
Parkinson, C.N. 35
parliamentarians and international organizations 457–9
parliaments 153–78
    bicameralism 162–3, 168–9
    budget approval process 169–71
    characteristics 156–61
    committees 163
    determinants of characteristics 164–9
    history of 173–7
    legislation cycle 171–3
    size 164, 166–8
    types of 153–6
    see also legislatures
partisanship
    and fiscal policy 276–7
    and monetary policy 249–52
Pauly, M.V. 369–70
Payne, A. 239, 358, 396
peace 482–9
Pecquet, G.M. 395
Peel, D. 251
Peltzman, S. 287
Pennock, R. 22–3
pensions 364–7
Perotti, R. 273–4, 274, 276
persisting rents 315
personal status and rent seeking 321–2
Persson, T. 172, 276, 476
Pietrantonio, R. 371
Pincus, S. 63
Pittman, R.W. 333
Plato 85
Plott, C.R. 421, 425

plurality vote rule 12
Polachek, S.W. 488
Poland 176
Polborn, M.K. 501–2
policy
    economic, and autocracies 99–103
    effects of direct democracy 133–7
    in evolutionary context 440–43
politaea 41
political action committees (PACs) 333
political business cycles 229, 250–51
political competition 437–40
political economy
    of cooperation 482–9
    of dictatorships 99–103
    experiments 421–3
    models and rent seeking 326–7
    of oversight 217–26
political entrepreneurship 431–6
political ideology, *see* ideology
political influence
    and elections 226–30
    on fiscal policy 275–80
political innovation 433–6
political institutions
    and civil conflict 476–8
    and rent seeking 317–20
political philosophy 40
political reform and innovation 433–6
political repression and conflict 477–8
political science 39–40
    and autocracy 84–8
    and public choice 41–53
politicians 429
    behavioral changes at election time 226–7
    campaign finance and voting behavior 338–41
    rent seeking 307
politics
    as choice 74
    as exchange 74, 187–8
popes, Roman Catholic 403–5
population density and tribal governance 198–9
pork barrel politics and antitrust 301–2
Posner, R.A.
    antitrust 292–3, 300–301
    costs of monopoly 312
    judicial behavior 233, 243, 355, 356
    judicial independence 237, 244–5
post-colonial governments 208–9
post-constitutional stage of decision-making 143–4
Potters, J. 326, 424
Pratt, M.D. 424

pre-constitutional stage of decision-making 143–4
predictive science of choice 112–13
preference outlier hypothesis 148–9
Prescott, E.C. 278
presidential systems 154, 166
price discrimination, medieval Church 410–11
Priest, G.L. 236, 355
principal–agent problems, *see* agency problems
Prins, B. 487
prisoners' dilemma game and CPE 79–80
private sector rent extraction 317
Profeta, P. 367
Progressives 44
property rights definition, role of courts 235–6
Protestantism 323–4, 411–13
Przeworski, A. 63, 88, 92, 93, 94, 99, 184
public choice, origins and development 12–38
public goods experiments 415–18
purgatory doctrine, medieval Church 409–11

quantal response equilibrium (QRE) model 422

Rainer, I. 209
Raknerud, A. 485
Ram, R. 270
Ramakrishnan, S.K. 383
Ramey, V.A. 274
Ramirez, C.D. 298
Ramseyer, J.M. 238, 245, 359
Randazzo, K.A. 356
Rapoport, A. 419–20
Rapoport, D.C. 482
Rasmusen, E.B. 244, 356, 359
rational choice 19, 40, 43–6
    and bureaucracy 35
rational ignorance about international organizations 453
rational opportunism 275
rational partisanship 251, 275
rational voter abstention 21–2
rationality 75
    and conflict 472–3
    and counterterrorism 497–502
    and politics 430
    and terrorism 502–4
Rauchhaus, R. 485
Ravn, M.O. 272
Rawls, J. 59, 76, 180
Ray, J.L. 485
Razo, A. 100, 102, 103
Razzolini, L. 500, 501
re-election motivation, committees 147–9
Rebei, N. 273

Rebelo, S. 270
referendums 127–8
    on school spending 394–5, 397–8
reform, political 433–6
Regan, P.M. 478, 489
regime instability and civil war 477
regulatory policy 284–9
    and federal system 184–5
    and international organizations 453–7
Reilly, R.J. 424
Reinke, A. 186, 187
Reiter, D. 486
relational perspective, dictatorships 99–103
religion 400–413
    and economics 401
    medieval Church 402–13
    and rent seeking 323–4
rent dissipation 311, 313–15, 325–6
rent extraction 316–17
rent protection 318–19
rent seeking 52–3, 307–29
    academia and 322
    autocracies and 100–101, 318, 328
    collective action 315–16
    and conflict 470–71
    cynicism and 309
    experiments 326, 423–4
    firms 321
    foreign aid and 320
    government and 320–21
    guilt and 310
    innovation and 319–20
    legal system and 322–3
    lobbying and 308
    migration and 319
    models 311–16, 325–7
    natural experiments on 326
    natural resources and 320
    personal status and 321–2
    political economy models and 326–7
    political institutions and rent 317–20
    politicians 307
    religion and 323–4
    and revolutions 328–9
    sacrifices as 324–5
    societal resistance to 327–9
    status and 321–2
    taxation and 327–8
    tenure, academic, and 322
    unethical behavior and 320
    voter dissatisfaction about 328
    wars of attrition and 322
rent-seeking coalitions, ancient Athens 68
Renzi, R. 338
representation, tribal systems 202–3

repression
  and civil war 477–8
  costs, dictatorships 90
reputation
  and campaign finance 334
  and judicial decision-making 356
resource ownership, tribal systems 204–5
retention of office, effect on judicial behavior 239–40
Reuveny, R. 488
revenue-sharing and federalism 183
revolutions
  and political innovation 433–6
  and rent seeking 328–9
Ricardian equivalence 268
Ricciuti, R. 164
Richardson, G. 503
Riker, W.H. 23–5
  on *Calculus of Consent* 31
  democratic coherence problem 49, 50
  federal systems 180, 181, 182, 183–4, 190, 191, 192, 193
Roberson, B. 501
Roberts, B.E. 222
Roberts, K.W.S. 111
Robinson, J. 25
Robinson, J.A.
  autocracy 91–2
  dictatorship and democracy 5, 61–3, 70, 94
Rocco, L. 478, 480
Rodden, J. 186–7
Rodgers, J.D. 188
Roe v. Wade 50
Röger, W. 273
Rogoff, K. 229, 250
Roman Catholic Church, medieval 323–4, 402–13
Roman Republic 175
Romer, C.D. 274
Romer, D.H. 274
Romer, T.
  agency problems in direct democracy 129
  agenda-setting power of committees 149
  local governments 187
  political action committees 334
  school spending 394, 397–8
Romero-Avila, D. 270
Roosevelt, Franklin 241
Rosato, S. 485
Rosenberg, J. 313
Rosenthal, H.
  agency problems 129
  committees as agenda setters 149
  school spending referenda 394, 397–8
  voter turnout 423

Rothenberg, L.S. 333–4
Rothstein, J. 387, 397
Rousseau, D.L. 487
Rousseau, J.-J. 39
Roux, G. 65
Rowley, C.K. 13, 52, 307
Rubin, P.H. 350, 352, 355, 359
Rundquist, B. 225–6
Russett, B. 483, 485

Sachs, J.D. 251
sacrifices as rent seeking 324–5
salaries, international organizations 462–3
Salzberger, E.M. 238, 240
Sambanis, N. 476, 481
Samuelson, P.A. 117, 179, 185
Sandler, T. 495, 497, 498, 499, 502
Sass, T.R. 393
Satyanath, S. 471
Saving, J.L. 222, 225
Schelling, T.C. 25
Schmidt, A.B. 383, 385, 386
Schmitt, P.M. 497, 499
Schneider, F. 276
Schofield, N. 154
schools, US 382–98
  charter schools 392–4
  referendums on school spending 394–5
  school districts 384–8
  spending inequality 395–6
  vouchers 388–92
Schram, A. 423
Schubert, C. 440, 442
Schuessler, A.A. 118, 119
Schuknecht, L. 363
Schultz, T.W. 382–3
Schumpeter, J.A. 428–30, 431
Schwartz, A.J. 461
Schwartz, T. 224
science of electoral behavior 112
Seater, J.J. 268
security dilemma, autocrats 103–4
Segal, J.A. 243, 356
segmentary tribal systems 196, 197–9, 201–2
  collective action 204
  effect of colonial rule 208
  electoral systems 206–7
Seidman, L.M. 244
selective incentives and collective action 33
Selectorate Theory 96, 97, 98
self-interest 19, 195
semi-presidential systems 154–5
Seneca, J.J. 300
separation of powers 240–41
Serdült, U. 142

Sergenti, E. 471
Seven Samurai (film, Kurosawa) 60
Shapiro, I. 45
Shapiro, J.N. 505
Shapiro, M.D. 274
Shapley, Lloyd 23
Shepherd, J.M. 239, 357, 358
Shepsle, K.A. 104, 147, 149, 220
Sherman Act 296–7
Shi, M. 276
Shogren, J.F. 326
Shon, J. 341
short-run fiscal policy 271–80
Shortland, A. 477
Showman, K. 387–8, 397
Shubik, Martin 23
Shugart, M.S. 154
Shughart, W.F. II 151
  antitrust 299, 303
  conflict 477, 481, 482
  welfare state 366, 367, 370
Sibert, A. 250
Siegel, D.A. 505
signaling 121–2
Simons, Henry 291–2
Singer, J.D. 484
Singh, S. 161
single-peaked preferences 21, 15
Siqueira, K. 497, 499, 502, 505
Sjem (Polish parliament) 176
Sjoblom, K. 366, 372
Skaperdas, S. 476
Skilling, D. 277
Skocpol, T. 475
Slantchev, B.L. 479
Slembeck, T. 433
Small, M. 484
Smith, Adam 120
  benefits of educated electorate 383
  judicial system 233
  religious behavior and economics 400
Smith, J.L. 356
Smithies, A. 21
Snyder, Jack 484, 486
Snyder, James 333, 334
Sobek, D. 476, 480
Sobel, J. 140
Sobel, R.S. 187, 225, 227, 229
social contracts
  and development of the state 57–9
  enforcement role of courts 235
social insurance demand, modeling 373–8
social protection, tribal systems 204–5
socialism (Wilson) 44
socialist calculation debate 46–7

soft budgets in fiscal federal system 317
Solé-Ollé, A. 277
Solon 67
Sonnemans, J. 423
Sonsteli, J. 390
Sorribas-Navarro, P. 277
Souva, M. 487
Spaeth, H.J. 243, 356
Sparta 67
spatial competition 18, 21
Spence, A.M. 122, 150
Spencer, C. 258
Spiller, P.T. 240, 241
spillovers, intergovernmental 182–3
Spitzer, M.L. 241, 420
SRRC (strategy of raising rivals' costs) 454–7
Staaf, R.J. 184
Stalin, Josef 85–6
Stam, A.C. 486
state capacity as determinant of conflict 475–6
state pensions 364–7
stateless tribal systems, *see* segmentary tribal systems
states, origins of 57–71
stationary bandits
  autocrats 99–100
  states 60–61
status and rent seeking 321–2
Stevenson, R. 198
Stewart, C. 222
Stigler, G.J. 164
  antitrust 292
  regulation 285, 287
Stoddard, C. 393
Stokes, D.E. 45
Stone, J.A. 250
strategy of raising rivals' costs (SRRC) 454–7
Stratmann, T. 139, 334, 335, 337, 337–8, 338, 339–40, 342, 343
Strauch, R. 270
Stringham, E. 48
strongman leadership, tribal systems 210
Sturm, D.M. 284
Stutzer, A. 136, 459
Su, X. 504
succession in autocracies 89
suicide terrorists 503–4
Suleiman, R. 419–20
Sullivan, J.T. 223
sultanistic regimes 86
Sumer 64–5
Sunstein, C.R. 432
supervisory boards, international organizations 461–4
Svensson, J. 276

Svolik, M. 94–5, 97, 103
Switzerland 191–2

Tabarrok, A. 239, 358
Tanzi, V. 363
taxation
  and federal system 184, 185–6
  and rent seeking 327–8
  see also fiscal federalism; fiscal policy
Tenhofen, J. 274
tenure
  academic, and rent seeking 322
  judges, influence on decision-making 357–60
  Roman Catholic popes 403–4
Terrebonne, R.P. 355
terrorism 494–506
Thaize Challier, M.-C. 320
Thies, C. 476
thing (medieval parliament) 175
Thomas, L.G. 286
Tiebout, C.M. 179, 182, 185
Tiebout model 179, 186, 187
Tiller, E.H. 241
time inconsistency
  and central bank independence 252–5
  and judicial independence 237–8
Tirole, J. 236
Todd, A. 85–6
Tollison, R.D. 151
  antitrust 299
  legislature size 162–3, 164
  New Deal spending 225
  rent-seeking 52, 307
Toma, E.F. 241, 360
tort law 346–54
total approach to CPE 79
totalitarianism 86
Trebbi, F. 333
Trechsel, A. 142
tribal systems 195–213
  centralized 196, 197–201, 204, 206–7
  collective action and public goods 203–6
  defense 205
  dynastic interests in 204–5
  effect of colonial rule 207–8
  electoral systems 206–7
  political systems 196–203
  post-colonial governments 208–12
  resource ownership 204–5
  segmentary 196, 197–9, 201–2
  social protection 204–5
  strongman leadership 210
  voting and representation 202–3, 205–6
Tsebelis, G. 162, 435

Tullock, G. 18, 25–31, 31–2, 34, 35, 180, 371
  autocracies 83, 89
  bicameralism 162
  on *Bureaucracy and Representative Government* 37
  constitutions 42, 59, 71, 72
  costs of voting 205
  direct democracy 128
  political behavior and public choice theory 45
  politics as exchange 187–8
  pre- and post-constitutional decision-making 143–4
  rent-seeking 52, 307, 310, 312, 320, 326, 423–4
  vote trading 146
  warfare 472
Tullock contest-success function 313–14

Uhlig, H. 272
unanimity rule 59
uncertainty and political behavior 20–21
unethical behavior and rent seeking 320
United Kingdom 62, 63
  Monopolies and Mergers Commission 295–6
United States
  antitrust law 296–8
  attempts to change judicial institutions 241–2
  congressional oversight committees 217–30
  Constitution 50–51, 60, 69, 70–71, 181
  direct democracy 132–42
  education 382–98
  Federal Reserve 229–30, 251–2, 255–6
  federal system 181–2, 184, 191
  influence on international organizations 460–61
  legislatures 144–51
  monetary policy decision-making 251–2, 256–8
  rise of democracy 69–70, 70–71
  tort law 346–54
universalism, norm of 148
unstructured institutions 104
usury and the medieval Church 408–9
utility income of voters 19

Vachris, M.A. 219, 221, 224
Vaubel, R. 456, 459
Veblen, T. 321
vector autoregressive analysis (VAR), short-run fiscal policy 273–4
veil of insignificance 75, 76–7, 80–81
Vengroff, R. 198

veto power of president 30
Vogel, R.J. 370
Vogt, C. 326
Voigt, S. 70, 234
voluntary contributions to public goods 415–18
Von Hagen, J. 169
vote-trading in legislative process 146–7
voter paradox 18, 77, 422–3; *see also* Condorcet's paradox
voter turnout experiments 422–3
voters
   abstention 21–2, 119–20, 121
   competence 139–40, 382–3
   and counterterror policies 499
   demand for social insurance 373–8
   and direct democracy 139–41
   dissatisfaction about rent seeking 328
   expressive voting 113–25
   and international organizations 452–7
voting and representation, tribal systems 202–3, 205–6
vouchers for education 388–92, 397

Wagner, R.E. 189
Walker, J.K. 419
Walker, J.M. 419
Waller, C.J. 252
Walter, B.F. 499
war and peace 469–89
   election cycle influence on initiation of conflict 227
Ward, H. 486, 488, 489
wars of attrition and rent seeking 322
Wassmer, R.W. 385
Waters, M.D. 142
Weaver, C.L. 366
Weber, M. 86
Weede, E. 487
Weeks, J.L. 486
Weingast, B.R. 63, 149, 223
   committees 163, 219

   federalism 180–81, 182, 185, 190, 191
   judicial independence 238
Weintraub, R.E. 251
Weir, C. 295–6
welfare state 362–80
   and rent extraction 317
Werker, E.D. 462
Werner, S. 485
Westley, C. 120
Westminster parliamentary system 155
Whaples, R. 230
Whitman, D.G. 356
Wicksell, K. 59
Wildasin, D.E. 366
Williams, D.W. 185
Williams, J.T. 229, 230
Williamson, O.E. 403
Wilson, Woodrow 44
Winston, C. 298
Wintrobe, R. 83, 85, 89–91, 503
Witt, U. 427
Wohlgemuth, M. 437
Wolff, G.B. 274
Woo, G. 498
Wood, B.D. 303
Wood, E.J. 482
Woolley, J.T. 251
workers and regulatory policy 286
Wright, J. 95
Wu, F. 436

Yinger, J. 386
Young, M. 225, 227

Zampelli, E.M. 186
Zanzig, B.R. 387
Zardkoohi, A. 333
Zax, J.S. 187
Zeckhauser, R.J. 277
Zelenitz, A. 187
Zimmer, R. 393
Zywicki, T.J. 355